VIETNAM
CAMBODIA AND LAOS
HANDBOOK

FIRST EDITION

MICHAEL BUCKLEY

MOON
PUBLICATIONS INC.

VIETNAM, CAMBODIA AND LAOS HANDBOOK
FIRST EDITION

Published by
 Moon Publications, Inc.
 P.O. Box 3040
 Chico, California 95927-3040, USA

Printed by
 Colorcraft Ltd., Hong Kong
 Printed in China

© Text and photographs copyright Michael Buckley, 1996.
 All rights reserved.
© Illustrations and maps copyright Moon Publications, Inc., 1996.
 All rights reserved.

Some photographs and illustrations are used by permission
and are the property of the original copyright owners.

ISBN: 1-56691-029-3
ISSN: 1082-5142

Editors: Kevin Jeys, Emily Kendrick, Taran March
Copy Editors: Sharon Brown, Asha Johnson
Proofreaders: Nicole Revere, Matt Orendorff, Deana Corbitt Sheilds, Diana DeStafeno
Production & Design: Carey Wilson
Cartographers: Bob Race, Brian Bardwell, Jason Sadler
Index: Nicole Revere

Front cover photo: reconditioned sailing junk at Halong Bay, Vietnam, by Michael Buckley
All photos by Michael Buckley unless otherwise noted.

Distributed in the USA and Canada by Publishers Group West
Printed in China.

Please send all comments,
corrections, additions,
amendments, and critiques to:

**VIETNAM, CAMBODIA
AND LAOS HANDBOOK
MOON PUBLICATIONS, INC.
P.O. BOX 3040
CHICO, CA 95927-3040, USA
e-mail: travel@moon.com**

Printing History
1st edition — September 1996

CONTENTS

MAPS

(continues on next page)

MAPS
(continued)

MAP SYMBOLS

— — — INTERNATIONAL BORDER	★ RUINS, ATTRACTIONS	
—··—··· PROVINCE BORDER	● ACCOMMODATIONS	▲ WAT
——— MAIN ROAD	■ SIGHT, POINT OF NOTE	
——— OTHER ROAD	○ CITY	⌂ TEMPLE, PAGODA
— — — CART PATH, ROUGH ROAD (MAY BE PAVED IN PART)	○ TOWN, VILLAGE	✝ CHURCH, CATHEDRAL
—·—·— PATH, TRAIL	▲ MOUNTAIN	
——⊐⊏— BORDER CROSSING	⑨ NUMBERED ROAD	⬟ STUPA
▒▒▒▒ BOAT ROUTE, FERRY ROUTE	✈ INTERNATIONAL AIRPORT	WATER
+++++ RAILROAD	✈ SMALL AIRPORT, AIRSTRIP	♒ WATERFALL
——— BRIDGE		

CHARTS AND SPECIAL TOPICS

INDOCHINA

VIETNAM

CAMBODIA

(continues on next page)

CHARTS AND SPECIAL TOPICS
(continued)

ABBREVIATIONS

4WD—four-wheel drive

air-con—air-conditioning

ARVN—Army of the Republic of Vietnam, until 1975

ASEAN—Association of Southeast Asian Nations

ATM—automatic teller machine

B.E.—Buddhist Era

Bldg.—building

BLDP—Buddhist Liberal Democratic Party

Blvd.—boulevard

CPP—Cambodian People's Party

cyclo—from French cyclo-pousse, or bicycle-powered trishaw

DMZ—Demilitarized Zone

EFEO—École Française d'Extrême Orient (French School of the Far East)

EMS—express mail service

ext.—extension

FCCC—Foreign Correspondents Club of Cambodia

FUNCINPEC—United Front for an Independent, Neutral, Peaceful, and Cooperative Cambodia, from a French acronym

GH—guesthouse

GPO—general post office

IDD—international direct dialing

kph—kilometers per hour

KS—Khach San (Vietnamese for hotel)

lambro—after the brand name Lambro 550cc, a three-wheel van

Lao PDR—Lao People's Democratic Republic

LPRP—Lao People's Revolutionary Party

moto—motorcycle-taxi

MP—Member of Parliament

NGO—nongovernmental organization

NLF—National Liberation Front

NVA—North Vietnamese Army, until 1975

R&R—Rest & Recreation

RAC—Royal Air Cambodge

RCAF—Royal Cambodian Armed Forces

SRV—Socialist Republic of Vietnam

UBND—Uy Ban Nhan Dan, or People's Committee

UNCHR—United Nations Center for Human Rights

UNDF—United Nations Development Programme

UNESCO—United Nations Educational, Scientific, and Cultural Organization

UNHCR—United Nations High Commissioner for Refugees

UNTAC—United Nations Transitional Authority of Cambodia, 1992-93

VASCO—Vietnam Air Service Company

VVAF—Vietnam Veterans of America Foundation

WHO—World Health Organization

IS THIS BOOK OUT OF DATE?

What's true today is likely to change tomorrow in volatile Vietnam, Cambodia, and Laos. Regulations chop and change, new borders open up, new regions are flung open. In Vientiane, new wiring is being installed for telephone systems, so the numbers may change; in Phnom Penh, street names are undergoing alterations. Elsewhere, some hotels were closed for renovations and will most likely triple their prices upon reopening. And a military museum may alter its captioning and shift exhibits around to suit "politically correct" times.

A guidebook is a two-way process, and your input is essential. Can you help keep this book up to date? If you notice any details that have changed or are inaccurate, drop a line. If you notice a guesthouse or restaurant has closed down, or a new one has opened up, I'd like to hear about it. Marking this information on a map is especially useful—feel free to photocopy maps from this book, mark them up (add new sites, and cross off travel facilities that may have closed down), and send them along. Business cards (called "card visit") from hotels and restaurants are very useful—you can note prices and conditions on the cards and mail those along with corrected maps. Brochures and rate cards from hotels are also useful.

I believe a guidebook must do much more than present the facts. It must also make sense of them. I'm keen on evaluating destinations, ranking the sights, and rating them fairly for travelers. If you thought a place was not fairly covered—or was overrated—write and say why. And if there's a worthwhile destination I've overlooked, I'd love to hear about it. I welcome suggestions, comments, ideas, beefs, bones of contention, travel tips, and hairy travel tales—the hairier, the better. Contributors will be acknowledged in the next edition. Thanks for your help.

Drop a postcard or letter to:

> Michael Buckley
> *Vietnam, Cambodia and Laos Handbook*
> c/o Moon Publications
> P.O. Box 3040
> Chico, CA 95927-3040, USA
> or e-mail: travel@moon.com

STOP PRESS

The Vietnamese government has been enforcing name changes on hotels, restaurants, and businesses. Vietnamese businesses must bear only a Vietnamese name, while joint-venture and foreign-owned businesses can retain an English name. These changes may cause some identification problems with listings in this book. A hotel featured here as Hoan Kiem Hotel may have a sign saying Khach San Hoan Kiem; a restaurant listed as Cha Ca Restaurant might now appear as Nha Hang Cha Ca; other businesses may change names entirely. Some business owners have chosen to post a large Vietnamese sign with a smaller English subtitle. It's difficult to say whether and where the name-change regulations will be strictly enforced though businesses in Saigon should be least affected. Happy trails!

ACKNOWLEDGMENTS

This is a lengthy book, and with it goes a long list of thank-yous to those who have contributed directly or indirectly. A guidebook depends on the network that supports it.

Special thanks to Bill Newlin for getting this project underway over a beer in Hong Kong, and for smoothing the path. Patrick Morris, cyclist extraordinaire, provided gritty details on road conditions in Vietnam, minutiae along the way, and a host of missing links—the kind of information that comes from long hours in the saddle. Patrick contributed a section on the Central Highlands by motorcycle. Scott Harrison and D'Arcy Richardson wrote pages of detailed notes on everything from what kind of spice was being used in Hoi An to exactly how many people you can fit in a bus loaded with logs to window height. Good one D'Arcy! Scott provided some excellent photographs.

My gratitude to culinary anthropologists Jeff Alford and Naomi Duguid for their article on Vietnamese food, Nancy Yildiz for tips on shopping in Vietnam and weaving in Laos, Toni Shapiro for her article on Khmer dance, Hans Kemp for his piece on classic Saigon cars, and Gary McFarlane for his tale on strolling through minefields in Cambodia, and his bicycle touring odyssey through Central Asia and Indochina.

Guides, experts, and those whose brains I've picked include the following. In Hanoi and Saigon, Rocky Dang showed me the snake village and the firecracker village, and organized great trips to Cuc Phuong and Mai Chau. In the quest for the best artworks, eclairs, and croissants in Hanoi, there is no finer guide. Thanks also to Hoang Van Cuong, Nguyen The Vy, and Nguyen Cuong. Fredy Champagne provided a host of details on touring in Vietnam, and special information on touring for veterans. Pete Cherches provided copious notes. In Phnom Penh, staff at *Phnom Penh Post* were most helpful— Kathleen Hayes, Alan Pierce, and Richard McDonough, and Bill Irwin for last-minute input. In Vientiane, my thanks to Elsie Webber; for supplementary material on Laos, thanks to Phil Schlesinger and Mike McBeth.

In Bangkok, Kevin Miller coordinated logistics and assisted in the way of supplementary Indochinese digestive material—and helped sort out the fish at Lake Tonle Sap. Thanks to the Artasia crew, too. In Hong Kong, Daryl Bending, Lisa Humphries, and Barbara Bale provided valuable information on the China connection and all sorts of other peculiarities.

Fellow travelers make a big difference: on my last trip to Vietnam, Stuart Washington seemed to pop up everywhere in a 333-induced daze, on the trail from Laos to the Mekong Delta to the highlands of Sapa and back again, providing doses of black humor. Others along the trail: Brendan Baker, Philippe Hamal, Herman Hilbers, Carola Bisschop, Alice Daunt, Micaela Small, Ilya Gutlin, spaced-out archaeologist Dennis Griffin, and the much-traveled Martin Saunders, who hails from the UK but whose real home is Southeast Asia—from where he contributed valuable material on Laos.

In Vancouver, I'd like to thank Jack Joyce of ITM for assistance with maps and expert advice, Peter Sevcik and Irene Holman, Tony McCurdy of Wanderlust Books, Dwight Elliott of the Travel Bug, Anne Smith for industrious clipping, and Carolyn Carvajal for help with video, maps, and fine art touches. Tom Quinn assisted in fine-tuning background material on belief systems. For assistance with language sections: Patsie Lamarre (for French and Captain Haddock suggestions), Alison Norman (Lao language), My Van Truong and Ngo Van Nham (Vietnamese), and Sokhanar Oun (Cambodian).

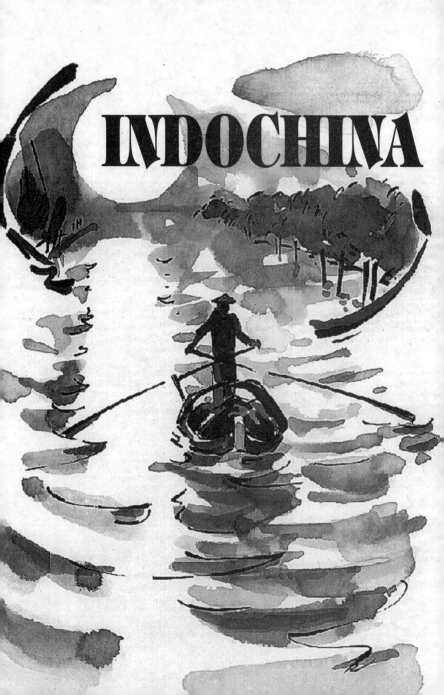

INDOCHINA

GRAND ADVENTURE

After a long history of fighting off foreign invaders, Indochina is looking forward to a new invasion from abroad—camera-toting tourists. The 1990s mark a major turning point for travel to Indochina. With the normalization of relations between Laos, Thailand, Cambodia, Vietnam, and China, the region is more accessible than ever before. For the first time in over 25 years, it's possible to ride a bicycle around Angkor Wat, motorcycle through hilltribe areas of North Vietnam, or cruise on a cargo boat through the Mekong Delta. Throughout the region, authorities are busy turning battlefields into marketplaces. In Vietnam they're turning battlefields into tourist attractions. The war has become a kind of theme park—christened "Cong World" by one Western reporter—where you can scramble through Vietcong tunnels or visit war museums.

Until 1993 individual travel in Vietnam was not officially recognized, and travelers were hamstrung by complicated permits. The system was scrapped in early 1993, and areas such as the Central Highlands and the mountains north of Hanoi were opened for the first time. For cash-strapped Vietnam, tourism is seen as a quick way to earn vital foreign exchange. The normalization of relations between Vietnam and China in 1991 means two new border crossings, and a promise of reestablished rail links. With the 1994 lifting of the US trade embargo, American travel agents and banks can operate freely, and direct air links are planned.

Cambodia, previously a war zone off limits to all but the foolish and/or well-heeled, is now freely accessible because of the UN peacekeeping operation in 1992. That year all travel permits in Cambodia were rescinded. You can now go where you want, although not many venture far because of Khmer Rouge guerrillas, bandits, and landmines.

Laos remains a stumbling block for individual travelers. It has adopted a small-scale tourism model similar to Bhutan's, with the emphasis on high-paying tour groups. With the new Friendship Bridge spanning the Mekong between Thailand and Laos, this situation may change. Laos recently opened to foreigners some border crossings into Thailand, Vietnam, and China.

In the 1990s there has been a substantial increase in the amount of direct air traffic coming into Indochina as the three nations are welcomed back into the world community. Air links

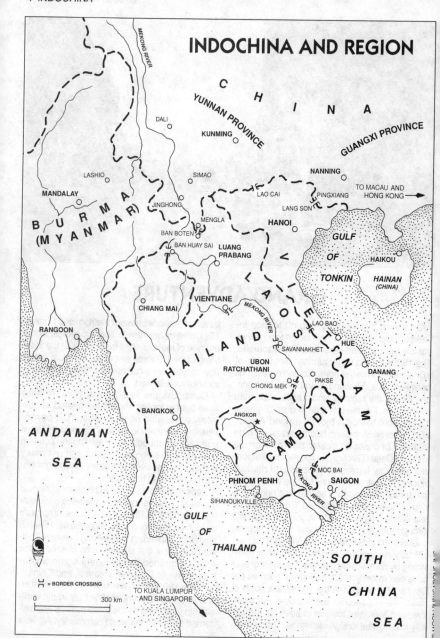

INDOCHINA AND REGION

C H I N A

YUNNAN PROVINCE

GUANGXI PROVINCE

DALI

KUNMING

LASHIO

SIMAO

NANNING

MANDALAY

LAO CAI

PINGXIANG

TO MACAU AND
HONG KONG

JINGHONG

LANG SON

BURMA
(MYANMAR)

MENGLA

HANOI

GULF

BAN BOTEN

OF

BAN HUAY SAI

TONKIN

LUANG
PRABANG

HAIKOU

HAINAN
(CHINA)

RANGOON

L
A
O
S

V
I
E
T
N
A
M

VIENTIANE

CHIANG MAI

MEKONG RIVER

LAO BAO

HUE

T
H
A
I
L
A
N
D

SAVANNAKHET

UBON
RATCHATHANI

PAKSE

DANANG

CHONG MEK

ANDAMAN

ANGKOR ★

SEA

C
A
M
B
O
D
I
A

BANGKOK

MOC BAI

SAIGON

PHNOM PENH

MEKONG
RIVER

SIHANOUKVILLE

GULF

MEKONG RIVER

OF

SOUTH

⊐⊏ = BORDER CROSSING

THAILAND

CHINA

0   300 km

TO KUALA LUMPUR
AND SINGAPORE

SEA

have been established regionally to Bangkok, Hong Kong, Singapore, Kuala Lumpur, Seoul, and Osaka, and internationally to Paris, Frankfurt, and Sydney. The air network is rapidly expanding, particularly into Vietnam.

What is Indochina? On maps, the Indochinese Peninsula encompasses all the lands between China and India and those greatly influenced by these two nations—Thailand, Burma, Malaysia, Singapore, Vietnam, Cambodia, and Laos. But most often Indochina refers to Vietnam, Laos, and Cambodia. The word has colonial connotations, identified with the French Union de l'Indochine, which lasted from 1889 to 1951. In this period French Indochina printed its own stamps and paper bills. Vietnam, Cambodia, and Laos share a common colonial history, subjugated by the French in the latter half of the 19th century for purposes of trade and profit. Revolutionary movements to shake off the French began with the founding of the Indochinese Communist Party in Hong Kong in 1930. The term Indochina *(dong duong)* is also used by the Vietnamese—Ho Chi Minh dreamed of unification of not only North and South Vietnam but also the entire Indochinese area.

In fact, this is taking place, though not in the way Ho Chi Minh envisioned. It's proceeding due to capitalist, not socialist, economics. Since the mid-1980s all three countries have become converts to private enterprise. Other Southeast Asian nations like the look of the new Indochina. They're eager to integrate all three countries into ASEAN, the six-member Association of Southeast Asian Nations. In July 1995 Vietnam joined ASEAN; Cambodia and Laos are set to follow. This could result in a coherent block of nations lying between China and India.

New trading routes have spurred new economic growth. It may soon be possible to motor all the way from Singapore to Beijing on a trans-Asian highway. One of the newly opened link roads is Route 9, which enables transport of goods from Thailand via Laos to Vietnam in a matter of a day or so. During the American Vietnam War this same route was a feeder for the Ho Chi Minh Trail. Because of activity on the trail all three countries were dragged into the war, with intense fighting from 1960 to 1975. With that war over, the fanatical Khmer Rouge openly began to attack Vietnamese towns, fur-

ther fueling the traditional enmity between Khmers and Vietnamese. This led to a decade of warfare between the Khmer Rouge and the Vietnamese. After the 1978 Vietnamese invasion of Cambodia, the Chinese stepped into the fray and attacked northern Vietnam. Vietnamese withdrawal from Cambodia in 1989 led to rapprochement and reconciliation. A dramatic turn of events in 1993 placed an elected government in power in Cambodia, although armed conflict with the Khmer Rouge continues.

The American Vietnam War is a blip in the time line of Indochina. More lasting is the impact of the French. The French left behind opera houses and churches, tennis courts and villas, Renaults and Citroëns, and, a great boon to today's traveler, the know-how for baking baguettes and croissants and frying up beefsteak. In numerous Vietnamese cafés you can find *café filtre,* Vietnamese coffee filtered onto a thick base of sweetened condensed milk. The French beret still perches on the heads of those in the colder regions of Vietnam.

Unfortunately, the locals also inherited French runaround bureaucratic skills. Officials in Laos will stonewall you, in Vietnam they'll hold you for ransom if you don't have the correct stamps, and in Cambodia soldiers ask for handouts to supplement their meager salaries.

Visiting newly opened Indochina is a grand adventure. You're the center of attention in Vietnam; in Cambodia the warmth and spontaneity of the people is positively infectious; in Laos the approach is more reserved and dignified. So go! I hope this book will inspire and inform. *Bon courage et bonne chance!*

INDOCHINA HIGHLIGHTS

Local authorities in Indochina are prone to overrating their tourist attractions. In Vietnam cultural attractions promoted with much fanfare—though they might have once been splendid—are often casualties of the Vietnam War. Hué was reduced to rubble in fierce fighting between the Vietnamese and Americans in 1968; and B-52 bombing destroyed most of the Cham site of My Son. Cambodia's Angkor Wat, by contrast, is truly phenomenal: one of the few sites that not only lives up to the hype but exceeds all expectations. In Laos the fabled Plain of Jars is a dud, though the flight up in a light Chinese aircraft does wonders for your heart rate.

This book adopts an opinionated approach by giving regional highlight "menus" and providing critical evaluation of sites. The opinions are those of the author, tempered by interviews with numerous travelers on what they found impressive—and what they didn't. The author's opinions draw on extensive travels to many parts of Asia. A number of bike, boat, and walking tours have been introduced to cover smaller nooks and crannies; strings of minor sights are occasionally joined into cohesive theme tours. Except for Angkor in Cambodia, Indochina lacks outstanding historical and cultural attractions. This, however, has not prevented travelers from having a fine time. It's all a matter of expectations. Shift your focus to meeting people, visiting markets, stopping in small villages, exploring streetlife, eating tasty Vietnamese food.

This man, now in his seventies, survived the war against the French and the Americans.

How you travel has a lot to do with what you see and experience. Touring on your own is a great way to meet people. Touring is easy around the main cities and sites—you can explore by rented bicycle or motorcycle, by cyclo, or on foot. Hanoi and Siem Reap are leisurely places to cycle. Boat touring is another excellent way of getting around scenic sites like Hué, Halong Bay, Nha Trang, or Luang Prabang. Small towns like Hoi An or Luang Prabang are easily covered on foot.

Indochina's scenic wonders hold its greatest touring potential: in Vietnam, the coastline with its pristine beaches, the limestone outcrops of Halong Bay, and the vast ricefields of the Mekong Delta; in Laos, the rugged scenery along the Mekong; in Cambodia, old-growth forest around Angkor and luminous-green ricefields and tall sugar palms in the countryside. The weather often comes into play here: thick fog can restrict visibility in Halong Bay; coastal typhoons mean you won't be able to swim at Nha Trang.

More than anything else, it's the people you meet that make Indochina a real experience. Indochina is home to a great diversity of people—artists and intellectuals, farmers and duck herders, hardy hilltribers, French-educated city folk. You might find yourself regaled with tales from a Vietnam War veteran, listening to lines recited by an eccentric poet in Dalat, or sharing a bottle of lizard wine in the Central Highlands.

Historical/Cultural

Angkor in Cambodia is a wonder of the Eastern world, with 70 ruins in a forested zone of 200 square km. Angkor is the top archaeological site of Southeast Asia, and was declared a World Heritage Site in 1992. Angkorologists puzzle over the mysteries of these magnificent ruins. The most impressive sites are Angkor Wat and Angkor Thom. The former royal cities of Phnom Penh and Luang Prabang also possess a glut of temples. The best museums in Indochina are the National Museum in Phnom Penh, featuring Khmer statuary, and the Cham Museum in Danang, with Cham statuary. The port town of Hoi An in central Vietnam is a kind of outdoor museum, with well-preserved Chinese and Vietnamese wooden buildings from the 19th century.

HOW LONG?

Ideally, you need six weeks to three months to see Indochina. It's easiest to plan the trip in five chunks: northern Vietnam, central Vietnam, southern Vietnam, Cambodia, and Laos. Each segment is worth seven days to a month. For shorter trips you might consider eliminating sections. It's better to see fewer areas thoroughly than to rush through and come away with superficial impressions. Thus, on a shorter trip you might cover northern Vietnam and Cambodia only. You don't have to see all of Vietnam—you could easily spend a month in the north alone. You should go by your interests, and aim for a variety of experiences.

A planned route is a good base for travel. Draft a rough route on paper and figure out which stops you'll make along the way. Actual travel time can eat into your itinerary—you can lose two days on a train traveling from Saigon to Hanoi. And you could consume an entire week chasing visas in a place like Bangkok or Hong Kong. Always build in extra time for transportation delays, bad weather, and other problems.

Colonial Architecture

The French presence is strongest in Hanoi, the former capital of Indochina. In colonial times the size of Hanoi's public buildings—such as its Opera House—caused critics in France to protest its *folie des grandeurs*. Slow-paced Hanoi exudes the charm of an Asia from a bygone era. Saigon, Phnom Penh, and Vientiane showcase former French administrative buildings and renovated villas, and the hill resort of Dalat boasts several thousand Provençal cottages.

Vietnam War Relics

A tour of the Demilitarized Zone (DMZ) is well worth it; a day-trip from Hué covers a dozen sites including Vinh Moc Tunnels and the former American base at Khe Sanh. A fascinating day-trip from Saigon takes in Cu Chi Tunnels, where the Vietcong lived underground. There are war museums scattered around the country, notably the War Crimes Museum in Saigon and the Army Museum in Hanoi. The Military Museum in Dien Bien Phu contains relics from the Vietnamese struggle with the French.

Landscapes

Karst scenery in northern Vietnam is a standout. Karst is eroded limestone that forms into bizarre caves, pinnacles, and outcrops. You can cruise by boat among the karst islets at Halong Bay. Other scenic zones in Vietnam accessible by boat are offshore islands near Nha Trang and the lush tropical Mekong Delta. A boat trip on the Mekong from Ban Huay Sai to Luang Prabang in Laos takes in karst scenery, stands of giant bamboo, and old-growth forest. There are very few national parks in Indochina, though on the advice of international conservationists a network is being established.

Hilltribe Groups

Numerous hilltribe groups live in mountain border areas of Indochina, maintaining their own customs, dress, and language. In the far northwest of Vietnam at Lai Chau, Dien Bien Phu, and Sapa live Hmong, Tai, Zao, and Tay. Travelers on a small group tour can stay in local villages to learn about the culture and tradition of these fascinating people. In Laos the hard-to-reach northern provinces of Phong Saly, Udomxai, and Luang Nam Tha have the greatest diversity of hilltribes. The best place to see hilltribers is at weekly markets that draw villagers from outlying areas.

Food and Markets

The largest cities have the widest selection of restaurants: Vientiane, Phnom Penh, Saigon, Hanoi. Coastal Vietnamese towns like Bai Chay, Hoi An, and Nha Trang serve fresh seafood. Southern Vietnam offers a cornucopia of tropical fruit, with succulent varieties like mangosteen, spiny soursop, and dragon fruit. Market foodstalls are great places to eat fresh food and observe local bustle. In the Mekong Delta are floating markets. The French imparted a café culture in Vietnam. Small convivial places abound in the towns, while large cities offer bistros and bakeries.

Festivals and Events

New Year festivals are the best—Tet (Vietnam, usually February), Pimai (Laos, usually mid-April), and Chaul Chhnam (Cambodia, mid-April). Laos has preserved traditions that have

Baguettes are baked every morning all over Indochina.

long disappeared in other parts of Asia. Festivals are being revived in Cambodia with the return of King Norodom Sihanouk, and the Vietnamese are reinventing traditional culture for the purpose of attracting tourism.

Performing Arts

The outstanding attractions are Cambodian dance, with occasional shows in Phnom Penh, and water puppetry performances in Hanoi.

Rest and Recreation

Some of the best spots in Indochina are simply places for relaxing—beach resorts, the old fishing village of Hoi An, the easygoing ancient capital of Luang Prabang. The French, who were heavily into rest and recreation, set up breezy seaside centers like Vung Tau and cool hill resorts like Dalat and Sapa.

Vietnam boasts a 3,200-km coastline, with some 125 large and small beaches—plenty for the beach potato to contemplate. Some beaches offer swimming and snorkeling facilities. In Nha Trang there's windsurfing and diving; at China Beach, bodysurfing and boardsurfing (BYOB). It's not the Côte d'Azur—not yet, anyway.

Adventure Travel

You can go caving (bring your own gear) or trekking to hilltribe villages in northern Vietnam. Other adventure travel like canoeing, kayaking, whitewater rafting, and elephant trekking will most certainly take off in Indochina.

Until rental equipment becomes readily available, it's a case of bring-it-yourself and do-it-yourself, or fall in with a tour. Sea Canoe Thailand and Mountain Travel Sobek, for example, have started offering kayak touring in Halong Bay in Vietnam.

GETTING READY

INFORMATION SOURCES

Networking

Good information is the key to a great trip. Your best sources of information are staging points like Bangkok, Hong Kong, or Singapore; you'll find the latest material, brochures, and maps there. You'll find a dearth of bookstores and travel information in Vietnam, Laos, or Cambodia. Tourist offices are set up strictly for groups; if they exist at all, they are useless for individual travelers. Few tourist offices exist in Cambodia and none at all in Laos (use tour agents instead). Government tourist offices in Vietnam are a joke—you get blank stares from staff manning desks without a shred of paper on them, except perhaps for glossy brochures on Thailand.

Traveler Cafés: Your best source of current information is other travelers, preferably those coming from the opposite direction. A lot of emphasis in this book has been placed on the traveler network, the web of contacts that operates through traveler cafés in Vietnam. For Cambodia and Laos, which are less traveled, the grapevine exists but not so much through cafés. Legendary Indochina watering holes include Tintin Pub in Hanoi, Saigon's Apocalypse Now bar, the Foreign Correspondents' Club in Phnom Penh, and Vientiane's Mixai Café.

Maps

Since quality maps are in short supply in Indochina, you should take along whatever you can get your hands on. International Travel Maps publishes a series of excellent maps on the region. The series includes a *Vietnam Travel Map* (with Hanoi and Saigon submaps), *Hanoi City Map, Saigon City Map, Cambodia Travel Map, Laos Travel Map, Southeast Asia Travel Map, Thailand Travel Map,* and *China Travel Map.* In the works is a map of the Mekong Delta, and a regional map of Indochina; there's also a softcover *Vietnam Road Atlas* underway. For more details, contact International Travel Maps, 345 West Broadway, Vancouver, BC V5Y 1P8, Canada, fax (604) 879-4521.

German cartographic publishing house Nelles produces a map of Vietnam, Laos, and Cambodia. Singapore-based Periplus Travel Maps has a highly accurate Cambodia map with invaluable submaps of Phnom Penh and Angkor. Periplus also issues maps of Vietnam (with town and city submaps), Bangkok, Singapore, and other parts of Asia.

Town and regional maps are extremely difficult to find in Indochina. Some topographic maps are sold by surreptitious vendors in the streets of Hanoi and Saigon. In Vietnam I was often reduced to making my own maps, or photographing crude maps on hotel walls or park entrances—some are redrawn for your edification in this book.

Media

Vietnam, Cambodia, and Laos are changing fast. To keep pace you could subscribe to *Indochina Digest,* a four-page newsletter with short news articles on business and current affairs. The newsletter is published weekly by the humanitarian aid and information group, Vietnam Veterans of America Foundation, 2001 South St. NW, Suite 470, Washington, DC 20009, USA, fax (202) 483-9314. From Hong Kong comes *Business News Indochina,* a 16-page extended newsletter that is an essential source for economic perspectives. Published monthly, it's available from BNI, G.P.O. Box 9794, Hong Kong, fax (852) 2856-1184. A subscription to either newsletter is expensive—BNI costs $395 for 12 issues.

Of the many publications that cover the Asian beat, outstanding is Hong-Kong-based business publication *Asia, Inc.* magazine, which carries biting journalism. *Business Traveller* and the *Far Eastern Economic Review* are good sources, too. In Bangkok, a good news source is a four-page supplement called Inside Indochina, appearing in the *Bangkok Post* on Tuesday. The *Phnom Penh Post,* covering Cambodia, is an excellent newspaper printed in Bangkok and available from Asia Books.

Satellite TV reception is available in major cities in Indochina. Hong Kong-based StarTV, mostly owned by Rupert Murdoch's News Corporation, beams out four channels in English on the AsiaSat satellite. Any place with a satellite dish can receive them. StarTV includes BBC World Service news coverage. Limited CNN Global News programming is available via satellite in Indochina.

Guides

Guides are invaluable in territory where little English or French is spoken. They can do a lot more than show you the sights—they can point you to better restaurants, smooth over problems with police, and handle language prob-

IMPROVISING

Indochina is a developing tourist region and often facilities are poor or nonexistent. So you have to be resourceful and improvise. Here are a few tips:

√ Language problems? Find a local English speaker. They get to practice their English, you get a guide. It's a fair trade-off.

√ Lost? It's useful to ask hotel staff for a "Card Visit" bearing the name and address of your hotel so you can show it to a cyclo or moto driver when returning to the hotel.

√ No map of town? Check the biggest hotel in town. Sometimes there's a map on the wall. You may not be able to get a copy, but you can probably glean enough details for orientation purposes.

√ No taxis? Take a cyclo for short distances, or a motorcycle-taxi for longer distances. In places like Phnom Penh flag down the nearest motorcyclist.

√ No bicycle rentals? Ask the hotel staff if you can borrow a personal bicycle. An offer of $2 will be appreciated.

√ No motorcycle rentals? Hail the nearest moto driver. Tell him to take a walk, and you'll bring the machine back in the evening. Offer $5. If you prefer to just be a passenger, hire the moto and driver by the day—the driver will act as your guide.

√ Can't decide if you want to spend the day touring by bicycle or by boat? Take the bike with you on the boat. The boatman won't bat an eyelid, as bicycles go everywhere with the locals.

√ No bank in sight? Find the nearest jeweler's shop. Jewelers sell gold and trade in cash US dollars. Changing $200 or $300 will not faze them.

√ No hotel in town? Go to a restaurant, stay late, make friends—they have a floor. . . . Or make the sleeping gesture (palms together under tilted head) and ask local kids where you can find a house to stay the night. They'll generally direct you to a suitable place.

√ No hot shower in your hotel? Ask for a thermos of hot water (supplied in hotels in Vietnam), soak a thin towel, and apply it. This sushi-bar toweling technique will wipe off the grime and refresh you.

√ No restaurants? Find the markets, which always have foodstalls. Market food is fresh, tasty, and cheap.

√ Can't find the bus station? Go to the markets. The buses generally leave close by, and cyclos and other forms of transport are clustered around the bus station.

√ Problems with police or officialdom? Try greasing palms with packs of fancy foreign cigarettes or small cash advances. If the situation is not clear, offer only cigarettes, which cannot be misconstrued as bribes. If you hand over a pack of cigarettes, the other party may just pocket it—then you press your case.

√ Can't afford a long phone call back home? Send a fax. Most post offices and many hotels offer fax services. Payment is usually by the page, and you can cram a lot of writing onto a page. Phone lines in Indochina are erratic—at least with a fax the other party doesn't have to personally answer the line. Supply the other party with a hotel or post office fax number so s/he can fax back. This is far preferable to sorting through a load of letters at poste restante.

√ The last bus already left for the place you want to go, or you missed the cursed crack-of-dawn express departure? Stand out on the main highway and flag down a long-distance bus that's passing through. Hitching is another possibility, and could well be more comfortable than a bus.

lems. Official guides are expensive, charging around $10-15 a day, and expecting to travel by car. Moto drivers can act as unofficial guides, charging $2 a day on top of a $5 moto charge.

MONEY

Most visitors to Indochina carry traveler's checks and some US cash. Credit cards are of very limited use, though they're accepted by larger hotels, restaurants, and shops in major cities. There may be markups of four percent or higher on purchases involving credit cards. Cash advances on credit cards are possible, but commissions are high. Most traveler's checks are accepted—keep to larger banks when changing, and avoid hotel desks or shops. Independent moneychangers operating in Phnom Penh and Vientiane offer reasonable rates.

Cash US dollars are the most convenient way of settling bills. However, there is no insurance against theft. What you can do is convert traveler's checks to US cash at banks in major cities as needed. In Indochina commission rates vary one to two percent for converting traveler's checks to US cash, so a $100 check nets $98-99. In Kunming the Bank of China rate is 1.25% per check on traveler's checks to US cash. In Bangkok it's around 1.5%. For easier calculations and better value, carry US denomination traveler's checks.

Dollars

Unless you plan to carry around a shoebox full of Vietnamese dong, use cash US dollars to settle larger bills. Local currency is better for settling smaller bills. In Vietnam, dollar prices for foreigners are often quoted in hotels, at train stations and ferry terminals, and for planes. You can mix dollars and the local currency for bill payment. Thai baht is also accepted in Laos and Cambodia. In Cambodia you can pay big with dollars, baht, and riels. Restaurants in places like Saigon often give you menu prices in dollars; Phnom Penh menus list three currencies. While other cash currencies like the Deutschmark, the French franc, and the British pound are negotiable in Indochina, they are not widely recognized, and may be rejected even in the larger cities.

All prices quoted in this book are in US dollars. US dollars are used as actual currency in all three countries, it's easier to think in US dollars when trading, and the local currencies are subject to rapid inflation and fluctuation, whereas the US dollar is not. Once out of the country, local currency is only suitable for wallpaper, so you don't want to get stuck with it (it's hard to change back into dollars). It's extremely useful to carry a calculator: makes conversion from local currency to dollars much easier, and saves confusion.

Banks and hotels often refuse to accept worn or creased bills, or those with writing or markings on them. You would do well to only accept the same from banks, hotels, or offices. Sophisticated places have bill-checking machines to detect fake US bills. Another problem is change. If you proffer a $100 bill, the other party may have no change. Maintain a good supply of smaller-denomination US bills ($5, $1) for situations like these. An example here is crossing borders: when you cross you may be stuck for a while without local currency, or be stranded with a poor exchange rate. You can still use $1 or $5 bills for taxis.

There is no blackmarket for dong, kip, or riel. Changing with locals is, however, a matter of convenience, especially if there

CONVERSION RATES

APPROXIMATE RATES FOR ONE US DOLLAR:

Vietnam	11,000 dong
Cambodia	2400 riel
Laos	920 kip
Thailand	25 baht
Hong Kong	7.7 HK dollar
China	8.3 renminbi
Myanmar/Burma	5.6 kyat
Malaysia	2.5 ringgit
Singapore	1.4 Singapore dollar

Rates vary slightly for traveler's checks and cash. Rates may be higher for large US bills. Some banks offer commission-free conversions but a slightly lower rate, while others may offer a better rate but a one percent or higher commission for converting traveler's checks.

one piastre bill issued by Banque de L'Indochine

are no banks around, or if they're closed. Try a hotel or jewelry shop for changing US cash. Never change on the streets or in a crowd. Deal one on one, and inside a shop. Negotiate rates with a hand calculator. Always count out dong, riel, or kip bills carefully before handing over your US dollars. Check that bills have not been folded, causing you to count them twice, and that lower denomination bills have not been substituted in the stack. If Vietnamese dong is all in low bills it can take a long time to count, so insist on higher denominations. Unofficial exchange is useful for one other transaction: changing local currencies back into dollars when leaving the country. Most banks will only change a small amount.

Forgeries

In June 1994 a New York teller came across $100,000 in fake $100 bills from Macau. These near-perfect bills were created with intaglio printing, a process by which ink from incised lines etched into a metal plate leaves a raised impression on paper and makes them feel like the real thing. The bills were traced to North Korea, and then to Iran, where a US congressional task force says the bills were printed using US equipment and American-trained engravers and printers. Another series of excellent forgeries has been traced to Montreal. The images are sharp and the ink is perfect—no clerk in the US could spot such a bill as counterfeit in commercial transactions. The Montreal bills apparently were shifted through Asia and South America. In Cambodia,

fake US bills have surfaced in Phnom Penh. In early 1995 police in the Cambodian border town of Poipet arrested four Thais with $1.5 million in counterfeit bills stashed inside a suitcase.

The US has begun issuing tamper-resistant bills, starting with the $100 note. The new design includes a double portrait of Benjamin Franklin, bears a translucent watermark, and features inks that change color when viewed from different angles. This doesn't mean, however, that old bills will be recalled—that would be an international disaster.

A veteran Hong Kong moneychanger offered the following advice for spotting fake $100 bills:

- Check the spelling. How many *P*s, for instance, are there in "Independence"?

- Look at Ben's face. If Franklin looks like he's got the mumps, it's a fake. Fake bills fail in skin detail. There may also be blemishes in the field surrounding Franklin, which should be solid green.

- Look at the printing in the corners on the front. The details around the 100 should be distinct. Fake bills tend to fade at the corners.

- Check the trees on the back of the $100 for distinct leaves. On bogus bills the leaves blend together.

ATMs

Automatic teller machines (ATMs) in Bangkok, Hong Kong, Singapore, Kuala Lumpur, and

Manila offer withdrawals in local currency. Visa's PLUS electronic banking network and MasterCard's Cirrus system are rapidly filling the world with ATMs operated by plastic cards; American Express operates its own worldwide system of machines, spitting out cash and traveler's checks. Vietnam may be next; in 1995 40 ATMs were installed at hotels and airports in Hanoi and Saigon under a pilot scheme launched by the Bank of Vietnam and MasterCard.

You can use your credit card, with a secret four-digit personal identification number (PIN) encoded in the card's magnetic strip. These withdrawals are treated as cash advances with interest accruing from the date of withdrawal unless there is money in your credit card account back home. Each transaction may be billed $2-4 at the home bank, so a smaller number of large transactions is more economical. The service fee is offset by the fact that the exchange rate is more favorable through ATMs. Credit cards and ATMs employ close to wholesale exchange rate (the one quoted in newspapers).

You can also tap into an ATM using a regular bank card with a four digit PIN, as long as the ATM bears the appropriate PLUS or Cirrus symbol. The amount will be withdrawn from your regular account, so no interest accrues. Inquire at your home bank branch about this possibility, and about daily limits and bank fees for each transaction. Also ask for a list of ATM locations in Asia where your card can be put to work.

Costs

Your major expenses in Indochina are accommodations, food, and transportation. Adjust to the fact that a dollar is a lot of money in Indochina—it may represent a day's salary to a local. Sit down with another traveler and figure out prices for items you'll most likely need. Newcomers to Vietnam are often savaged by rip-off street vendors; in Laos, by contrast, vendors tend to be honest. On a budget, two can survive on $20-25 a day in the larger cities, while one person can live on about $15-20 a day.

Hotels are overpriced in Indochina. You can get far better accommodation for the same price in Thailand or Indonesia. Some good deals, however, are still available. In the budget area, family-run guesthouses are inexpensive, clean, offer good security, and, best of all, you get to

know the family. Renovated French hotels have lots of character, with spiral staircases, art deco ornaments, vintage French plumbing and fixtures, and bidets in the large bathrooms. Don't always judge a hotel by its lobby: some of the best deals in Indochina are run-down colonial villas that look luxurious from a distance, but rent rooms for $10-20 a night.

Basic guesthouse rooms, when available, cost $5 and up. Budget accommodations are around $10-20, with air-con, hot water, and phone; moderate lodgings are $20-50 with all of the previous, plus color TV and fridge. In the luxury/business class, standard rooms run $50-100, deluxe rooms $100-200. These are jammed with such creature comforts as satellite TV. There are only a handful of super luxury hotels in Indochina: the Sofitel Metropole in Hanoi, Saigon's Floating Hotel, the Saigon Omni, the Sofitel Cambodiana in Phnom Penh, and the Belvedere in Vientiane. Top-end accommodations are $200 and up a night, $200-500 for a suite.

Dining out is inexpensive except in fancy hotels in cities like Hanoi or Saigon. Restaurant pricing is not an exact science; there are too many variables. However, street and market food costs mostly under $2 a head per meal; a budget meal in a basic restaurant will run under $5 per person; a moderately priced restaurant charges $5-10 a head; and an upscale restaurant in a large city will want $10 and up for a meal.

VISAS

To paraphrase Lao Tzu, "The journey of a thousand miles begins with a single visa." Start the long march by making sure your paperwork is in good order. Visas and other red tape can tie you in knots—work well in advance to save yourself the angst.

When applying for the relevant visa for entering Vietnam, Cambodia, and Laos, your passport must be valid for at least six months. The Lao visa consumes a whole page. A Vietnamese or Cambodian visa is sometimes issued as a paper folder, sometimes stamped in the passport. It depends what regulations are in force at the time, which depends on who has the power to authorize visas.

If given a choice, a paper visa allows more latitude—it means you can separate passport and visa, which is to your advantage when dealing with police or hotel staff. And it means you can apply for several visas at once. When exiting the country you'll have to surrender a paper visa, so Vietnamese border officials will stamp your exit point in your passport to make it clear you've left. A photocopy of the visa is your only souvenir.

Carry a stash of passport photos on your person, as some applications require three or four photos. Also carry copious copies of the initial pages of your passport in case you apply for a paper visa. If applying for a visa in person, dress as formally as possible. Visa-issuing offices keep short hours: visit early in the morning, and don't count on the embassy dispensing visas—staff may direct you to another location for that. Bring small US bills—$5 bills are good—as most visa fees are in US cash only, no local currency accepted. Sometimes it helps to bring a big fat novel so it looks like you mean business, like you'll hang around all day if necessary. Patience and persistence are your greatest assets when applying for visas and other paperwork. If you don't get what you're after, keep trying.

All embassies are not created equal. You can get a Vietnamese visa yourself in Bangkok, but in Vientiane in Laos you'll have to go through an agent, and the visa will cost two or three times as much. A Lao tourist visa, only available through an agent, may cost $100 in Bangkok, while it's $20 direct from the embassy in Phnom Penh. Some embassies readily hand out visas; others refuse to deal with individuals and tell you to go through agents, who add to the fee. Visa regulations change like the phases of the moon. Apart from the information given here, refer to the visa sections under "Immigration and Customs" in the On the Road sections of the Vietnam, Cambodia, and Laos chapters.

Red tape is costly in Indochina: $100 for a Lao visa, $20 for a Cambodian visa, $48 for a Vietnamese visa, plus $50 in extra Vietnamese red tape costs (visa extension, land border exit point) all add up to over $200 in rubber stamps. That's a lot of money for some colored ink. The high cost of visas is attributed by embassy staff to fax and telex communications with the motherland, even though embassies send out a long list of applicants for clearance on a single fax or telex. You'll pay a premium for a multiple-entry visa, a business visa, or a visa with longer validity.

Visa Tips

In Bangkok and Hong Kong travel agents all use the same handful of "visa brokers" well-connected with embassy officials. Some are better connected than others (a lot of under-the-table activity here). Embassy staff play games with agents—a visa may be delayed if staff has not received a telex or fax of confirmation from the motherland. Travel agents in Bangkok or Hong Kong can advise on ways to get several visas issued at the same time. You can initiate the paperwork before you arrive in a place like Bangkok or Hong Kong by contacting a reputable agency by fax and arranging a deposit on a visa. If a paper visa is possible, send photocopies of initial passport pages ahead; the agency will fill out the forms for you. You can either have the completed paper visa posted to you, or have it waiting for you for pickup.

Visa issue is a major source of fundraising for embassies. If you want the visa faster, you'll have to pay a premium. A Vietnamese visa issued in four days in Hong Kong for $50 can be obtained in one day for $100. In Bangkok, a regular Vietnamese visa is $48; if you want the visa back in less than five working days, add $20. In Hanoi I was informed a 60-day Chinese visa would cost $50 and would be ready in five working days. Since a weekend was coming up, that meant a full week. But, said the Chinese official with a grin, if I paid another $50 I could pick it up that afternoon. After bargaining, I arranged to pick it up in two days. The embassy's sliding scale of fees appeared to run thus: $50 for same-day issue, $40 for next-day issue, $30 for two-day pickup.

Document Duplication

It would be nice to have a document dispenser strapped to your waist in Indochina—punch in a code and out comes the document requested. Here you're constantly asked for all kinds of documents: hotel staff in Vietnam not only want to see your passport, they also want to check visa validity, entry/exit form, and may even demand to see a customs declaration or health documents. Once you reach Laos, Cambodia, or Vietnam, head for the nearest photocopier and copy your visa and initial passport pages onto one piece of paper, double-sided if necessary. Make a bunch of copies. With these handy you won't have to keep surrendering your original passport to all the clowns who ask for it—hotel staff, motorbike renters, railway ticket clerks. Not to mention policemen bent on extra income—or bent policemen. You might have to leave your passport when renting a motorcycle and carry the photocopies to satisfy police elsewhere. In this case get a receipt for the passport and a written explanation in Vietnamese of why you're not carrying the original documents.

Thai Visa

Inexpensive Thai visas are readily available from embassies abroad or within Indochina at Vientiane, Phnom Penh, Saigon, and Hanoi. Validity varies from one to six months. If using Thailand as a base, with frequent comings and goings, consider a multiple-entry visa; these can be valid for a six-month period from the date of issue. You can arrive in Thailand without a visa—you get 30 days on arrival in Bangkok or at a Lao land border like Nong Khai or Chong Mek. Overstays beyond 30 days are charged $4 a day, payable on departure.

Vietnamese Visa

The Vietnamese visa starts running from the date you specify on your application. You cannot arrive before the specified date; if you arrive after it, you lose time on the visa. A Vietnamese visa costs $25-150 depending on type and place of issue. Abroad the visa can take three weeks or longer to obtain, within Asia most likely within seven working days. There are numerous Vietnamese embassies around the globe. Within the Asian sphere there are embassies in Bangkok, Hong Kong, Singapore, Kuala Lumpur, Beijing, Tokyo, Jakarta, Rangoon, Manila, Phnom Penh, and Vientiane.

Vietnamese embassies are of the hit-and-miss variety—sometimes everything is fine; other times you encounter obstacles. Obtaining an ordinary one-month visa in Beijing can be tricky, and you can experience delays in Phnom Penh. In Hong Kong, on the other hand, a three-month multiple-entry visa is $150, and six-month visas are available. The Vietnamese visa is normally valid

road border crossing between Vietnam and Cambodia

for arrival by air via Saigon or Hanoi, where immigration will make you fill in another set of forms and demand photos. If you enter or exit Vietnam overland, you must add the name of that border to your initial visa, usually in a city close to the particular border, for an extra $15-20. In Bangkok, you might request the addition of Lao Bao or Moc Bai entry points to your initial visa, though success with these is not guaranteed. In Hong Kong or Beijing, you can request addition of the Lang Son or Lao Cai entry points to your initial visa. Officials at these land borders sometimes reduce your one-month visa to seven days. Check the expiry date of the visa after you're stamped in—you may have to head for an extension sooner than you think. Vietnamese visa extensions cost $15-25 depending on the time period requested. Extensions are erratic—Hué is good for extensions, Hanoi is bad.

In late 1995, the Vietnamese Immigration Department announced that visa extensions would no longer be issued within Vietnam for those on one-month tourist visas. This new regulation appears to be directed at backpackers and foreign workers, as other kinds of visas are not affected. Extensions are still granted to those traveling on business, journalist, or diplomatic visas, and to overseas Vietnamese. Tour groups are unaffected since they rarely spend more than a month in Vietnam. To get around these regulations, consider trying to get a longer initial visa. Another choice might be a multiple-entry Vietnamese visa where you can exit into, say, Cambodia, then re-enter Vietnam. The same situation might apply to exiting into southern China.

Cambodian Visa

Cambodian visas and paperwork are easy to deal with, but there are few embassies abroad. You can obtain a visa in Bangkok, Vientiane, Hanoi, or Saigon in a day or two for around $20. Through an agent, it's perhaps $15 more. Validity varies—usually two weeks. On arrival by air in Phnom Penh, you can obtain a one-month visa on the spot for $20. Extensions for one, two, or three months are easy to get in Phnom Penh; go through hotel staff. Land border crossing stamps are not required for Cambodia. Cambodia permits a marine border crossing in the Gulf of Thailand, although Thailand does not officially recognize the crossing. It's possible to cross from Thailand by boat (no Thai exit stamp) into Cambodia via Koh Kong (Cambodian entry stamp).

Lao Visa

Lao visas cater to group tours; individuals are frowned upon. Thus a Bangkok agent may pass you off as a "tour" of one or two people with a one-night hotel package in Vientiane. The package will cost you $100, even though the visa fee stamped in your passport is $12. A 15-day tourist visa is available in Bangkok in four working days; if you want a longer visa try to obtain a 30-day business visa through an agent. The Lao visa runs from a fixed, specified date; you have one month to get there from the date of issue. If you plan on entering Laos by an odd land border, tell the travel agent—this point may be added to the initial visa. Overstays on the tourist visa are charged $4 a day when exiting Vientiane. Tourist visa extensions are also possible. You can try other consulates in Asia— Hanoi, Saigon, Danang, Kunming, Beijing, Ran-

goon—for Lao tourist visas, but they're more likely to dispense transit visas valid for seven to 10 days. The transit visa is issued within two days, costs $15-20, but is nonextendable and only valid within a 30-km radius of Vientiane.

Chinese Visa

Chinese visas are easy to obtain; allow one to five working days. Cost depends on nationality. In Bangkok, it's $22 for an Australian, $40 for a Canadian, and $100 for a Brazilian. A Chinese visa is generally issued for one or two months, allowing three months to get there. Extensions within China are easy, and there is little restriction on your movements. Health documents may be scrutinized on entry. In Asia, there are Chinese embassies in Bangkok, Hong Kong, Singapore, Delhi, Islamabad, Hanoi, Phnom Penh, and Vientiane.

Burmese Visa

You can now obtain a four-week tourist visa for Burma (Myanmar) and move around the country independently. The visa allows three months to reach the country from the date of issue. A business visa will allow you to travel up to six months. There are Burmese embassies or consulates in Bangkok, Singapore, Kuala Lumpur, Hanoi, Vientiane, and Kunming; visas cost about $20. On arrival at Rangoon Airport those not on arranged tours must change $300 into Foreign Exchange Certificates—Burmese tourist monopoly money—at the state's inflated exchange rates.

PACKING

A notebook computer with negotiation software for Vietnam? A flak jacket for Cambodia? An armful of novels for those long languid trips down the Mekong in Laos? There's no end to the amount of stuff you can cram into your bags to cover all needs—but most of it is dead weight. It's far more enjoyable to travel light and not worry about your stuff, meanwhile leaving space for purchases en route. Travelers can become fixated with their stuff and spend hours in needless aggravation over what to take. Get that part over quickly and shift your attention to other, more important matters, like plotting your route, determining what to see, learning languages, reading up on the areas you'll visit. Knowledge is the most important thing to carry with you.

One greatly overlooked consideration in travel gear is communication. This is the whole point of the trip: you want to maximize communication with those you meet along the way. Bring language phrasebooks. Take photos of family, friends, your neighborhood, city postcards, and so on. They're always great talking points and help answer the question you'll be asked everywhere, "Where are you from?"

Gifts are good communicators: postcards, balloons, cosmetics, pens. Gifts need not be big or expensive—they're a way of saying thank you, not a redistribution of wealth. Due to the repressive nature of life in Indochina, foreign magazines are hard to obtain: even if available, they're well beyond the budget of most locals. So don't toss away that in-flight magazine. Fashion magazines and news magazines are greatly appreciated for the pictures, and the English or French language content. An overwhelming percentage of Indochinese males smoke. Foreign-

LIGHTEN YOUR LOAD

There are many reasons why you should cut baggage weight and bulk. The most obvious is that if you have less to carry, you enjoy greater mobility—you can walk straight onto a plane with hand luggage, and you don't have to stash gear on the roof of a bus. Bags out of sight are prone to petty pilfering or outright loss. Carrying only hand luggage is very liberating. And if the worst should happen—if it should all disappear—you have less to lose. The biggest decision you'll have to make is what size bags to take. Packs themselves can be quite heavy, especially those with elaborate internal frame systems, padded hip belts, and webbing.

Before leaving home assemble all your baggage on the floor, and separate items into essential, optional, and dubious categories. Discard the dubious, reconsider the optional, and cut the essential in half. Then double the amount of money you'll take. You need to leave some space in your bags for purchases along the way. And leave space for money to make the purchases: if you change $200 in Vietnam, you may have a stack of dong the size of a shoebox. You have to carry that somewhere. Well before you set off, pack all your gear exactly as you would on the road. Wear the same shoes you'll use on the road and walk a dozen blocks with your gear—or, better yet, hike up the nearest mountain. See how you feel. If you stagger around like a drunk, cut the gear down until manageable. Remember that in a tropical climate you'll develop big sweat patches wherever a heavy bag presses on your clothing. If you want to find out where the real weight lies, use a postal scale to weigh your gear.

There are several ways to cut corners on baggage weight and bulk. Clothing is one of the biggest offenders. Bring only items with multiple uses. A sarong, or two-meter length of dress material, easily purchased in Asia, can be used as scarf, sheet, dress, or beach towel. Avoid heavy items like towels, which will just turn to soggy mildew in your pack. Instead take a sport towel, a thin synthetic sponge strip the size of a scarf that will dry quickly and can be put to many uses. Cut clothing to a bare minimum and prepare to wash what you do bring frequently, using hotel laundry services. That's preferable to carrying it around all the time. You can always purchase extra clothing or have it tailor-made along the way if need be.

Miniaturizing toiletry supplies is an excellent way of saving weight and bulk. Secure tiny plastic bottles from a camping store and decant shampoo, powders, and potions into them. Eliminate heavy glass bottles and repackage their contents in smaller plastic containers.

If carrying drugs, be sure to transfer the identifying labels. Saw the end of your toothbrush—you don't need the full length, and the smaller brush will fit more easily into a toiletry bag. You don't really need a hefty bar of soap; pick up a few miniature airline washroom soap packets to fill in for the times when your hotel doesn't supply soap. Males should consider whether they really need to shave—not shaving will cut down on gear. Women travelers should consider leaving perfume and cosmetics at home.

When traveling, use the post office to mail out souvenirs, purchases, and excess gear. It's expensive to post gear out, but think about the advantages: you won't have to carry the stuff, and the chances of it getting stolen are greatly reduced.

brand cigarettes and lighters are excellent gifts, and low-key bribes for those in uniform. Foreign-brand cigarettes can be purchased within Indochina, or you can pick up a duty-free carton en route.

Packs and Carry Bags

If you're traveling independently, avoid a suitcase or a large backpack with a frame. It's better to divide your load into two smaller softpacks: an oversize day-pack for camera gear and valuables (this bag never leaves your sight), and a medium duffel bag or travel bag for the main load of clothing and other items. Ideally, these bags should be airline carry-on size, measuring about 50 by 40 by 25 cm, or 52 liters in volume. In theory, carry-on weight is five kilos, but airlines rarely check. If the check-in clerk is fussy, you can compress a soft duffel bag to a smaller size with webbing straps. Some travel bags can be used as foam-padded backpacks or carried suitcase-style with a handle. The carrying capacity can also expand. Most likely, with two smaller bags, you could take the lot onto an aircraft as carry-on—depending on freight weight for that flight, and the mood of the check-in clerk.

In Indochina the two-bag system enables easy maneuvering on buses, trains, and planes. You can fit gear into overhead racks on buses or trains, and store it under the seat in minibuses. On motorcycle-taxis place the main load over the gas tank or on the rear rack, or wedge it between handlebars and seat. The system also works well for leaving one bag behind in a hotel when off on two- or three-day trips. Lockable zips keep out prying fingers. Inside, nylon stuffsacks separate and serve as waterproofing; Ziploc bags are excellent for this function too. A garbage bag is good for protecting the entire pack from rain or dust.

Clothing

For hot climates cotton clothing or a cotton/polyester mix is best. Dress loosely—tight-fitting nylon or polyester clothing will wreak havoc with your body's ventilation system. Choose clothing that is lightweight, washes quickly, and dries fast. Jeans are heavy, bulky, hot, and take a long time to dry. You really only need two sets of clothing—one to wear, and one to wash. Dark-er clothing doesn't show dirt, but lighter colors deflect heat and are less likely to attract mosquitoes. Long-sleeved shirts protect against mosquito bites. Also take modesty into account, especially with women's clothing. You can buy clothing en route in Indochina, but ready-made sizes often do not fit larger-framed Westerners. This problem is solved by custom-ordering clothes in a place like Saigon or Phnom Penh. All you have to do is hand over a shirt or skirt, and the tailor will copy it. Shoes, however, are more difficult to find—make sure yours will last the distance.

Be prepared for adverse weather conditions. Carry a hat and sunglasses with UV block to counter harmful rays. You need a pair of sturdy lightweight walking shoes; make sure they're not too tight, as your feet can swell in a hot climate. Although you can wear sandals in southern Vietnam, shoes are advisable to protect against cuts and scrapes when riding a bicycle or walking over sharp limestone rocks. The Viet-

It can get cold in northern Vietnam and the higher elevation areas of Laos.

namese coast is prone to lashing winds and rain—waterproof yourself with a light jacket and hood. If your trip coincides with the monsoon season, take more substantial gear for wet weather.

If you start out in tropical Thailand, you tend to overlook the fact you can freeze your ass off in the highlands of Laos, or in Vietnam's Central Highlands and the far north. If you're planning to visit highland areas, pack a pile sweater. Layering of T-shirt, shirt, pile sweater, and rain jacket should ward off the cold. In Hanoi you can purchase a Chinese parka for the north and then resell it to another traveler.

Mosquito Net

The mosquito net presents a dilemma: should you rely on the quality of mosquito nets in hotels in Indochina? Generally they're okay. But for the odd time when you're without a net, is it worth carrying one? Depends where you go. If you're planning on any remote-area travel, you should definitely carry a net to avoid malaria. This includes visits to hilltribe villages where you may stay overnight, or roughing it on overnight boat trips. You can buy mosquito netting and army surplus nets quite cheaply in markets in Saigon or Phnom Penh.

There are several kinds of mesh used in mosquito nets. At all costs avoid no-see-um netting, as the mesh is so fine air does not circulate, and you'll boil in a humid tropical climate. There are a number of compact lightweight mosquito nets on the market. In England you can buy the Micronet, made by Lifesystems; another quality net is produced by Safariquip. In the US, Long Road Travel Supplies makes the Savanna, a net that suspends from the ceiling and covers a twin-size bed. It weighs half a kilogram. The mesh used in this product, however, does not allow the maximum air circulation needed in the tropics. The net sells for around $55. Contact Long Road, 111 Avenida Drive, Berkeley, CA 94708, tel. (800) 359-6040, fax (510) 540-0652.

The best netting on the market is white nylon fire-retardant mesh made in Thailand. This knitted mesh will keep mosquitoes out, but is large enough to allow good air circulation. This mesh is used in nets made by Coghlan's and Thai Occidental. Coghlan's manufactures a net that weighs in at 200 grams and sells for $15. This cheap one-person net features grommet holes for suspension from walls, and is available in Canada and the US. Thai Occidental makes a well-designed net called the Spider that sells for around $50. This net is ideal if spending a lengthy period in malaria-exposed areas. The half-kilogram net can be deployed indoors over a twin bed, or outdoors suspended from a line stretched between two trees. You can order a standard Spider or one sprayed with permethrin. Order from Thai Occidental, 5334 Yonge St., Toronto, Canada, tel. (416) 496-2490. Orders can be shipped overnight to the US, or within three days anywhere in the world.

Other Sleeping Gear

A sleeping bag may be useful in northern Vietnam or Laos for trekking or roughing it in villages, but is otherwise unnecessary in Indochina. Hot climates require breezy beds; a sheet sleeping bag or sarong will do fine, or take a whole bed along in the form of a hammock, available for a few dollars in Vietnam or Cambodia. Locals string up hammocks on overnight boat trips in Indochina; hammocks are even deployed on trains in Vietnam.

Useful Gadgets

A flashlight is essential because blackouts are common. Actually, two flashlights would be a good idea. Carry a miniature pocket flashlight for finding your way down unlit alleys, or locating your hotel room or the washroom in a blackout. Maglites are good. For exploring caves or dark pagodas you need a larger model with a strong beam; some are waterproof and can be attached to your head for hands-free operation. Flashlight battery life is short, so bring plenty of backup batteries. Remove or invert batteries when the unit is not in use to avoid burnout. Avoid lithium batteries as they cannot be replaced in Indochina.

You will constantly need purified drinking water in Indochina. Locally produced mineral water is sold in cheap plastic bottles that break easily, so take along a tough plastic water bottle with a leakproof seal for carrying water on daytrips or train trips. For remote areas where you must rely on river water, consider taking a small filter, particularly an inexpensive compact model with an iodine filter. Otherwise, use iodine tablets. These are sold under the label Potable

Aqua in Europe and the US, or Coghlan's in Canada. The maker produces another bottle called Neutralizer, with tablets to remove the unpleasant iodine taste in the water. You can use Gatorade crystals to achieve the same effect; these also supply potassium and sodium.

Take a Swiss Army pocketknife with blade, scissors, tweezers, and can opener, or buy a cheap Chinese copy in Vietnam. Heavy-duty duct tape is invaluable for emergency repairs to equipment—you can carry a smaller amount by rerolling the tape. A pocket compass is very useful for city orientation and map use. A wristwatch with built-in alarm is good for those bus departures at the break of dawn. A small solar-powered calculator is useful when dealing with confusing currency exchange rates. Newshounds might consider a palm-size shortwave radio to pick up the BBC, VOA, Radio France International (RFI), and Radio Australia.

Electrical Devices

The best advice on electrical devices is not to bring them or rely on them. If you must tote them along, be sure to use backup power in the form of rechargeable nickel-cadmium or nickel metal-hydride battery packs. For sensitive equipment use a voltage regulator or surge protector—blackouts are common. Wiring in most Indochina hotels dates back to the French era and would never pass Western safety inspections. Power circuits are often overloaded. Power runs the gamut from 220 volts in urban areas to 110 volts in towns and the countryside; it's best to bring switchable 220/110-volt devices. Plugs in use range from dual Continental round prongs to American flat parallel prongs—there's no standardization. Batteries are available, but alkaline batteries are expensive and AAAs are hard to find.

Toiletries

Items like soap, toothpaste, shampoo, deodorant, and cosmetics are available in the major cities of Indochina, although local brands are of poor quality and Western brands are expensive. Carry a minimal amount to save on weight. Carry back-up supplies of toilet paper. Speaking of backups, many sewage systems in Vietnam cannot cope with toilet paper—if there's a bin provided, place used paper in that, not the toilet.

Tampons and sanitary pads are unavailable in rural areas. Pack items like nail clippers and a nailbrush, which serves double duty for quick cleaning of clothing.

Medical Kit

This is one area where you should not skimp. Bring a large medical kit, perhaps shared between several people. Medicines are in short supply and of dubious quality in Indochina; best to bring your own. See "Health" later in this chapter for full details.

Photography and Film

Color print film is widely available in Indochina, but outside the major cities slide film is hard to find, particularly Kodachrome 200 ISO. Not much black-and-white film is available anywhere. Take along a supply of batteries for your camera—you may find them on the road, or you may not. You can purchase film in Hong Kong or Bangkok, strip off the cardboard packaging to reduce bulk, and put the film canisters into Ziploc bags. Do your best to keep film cool and dry; the greatest damage is done by humidity. Always pass film around X-ray scanners at airports. Do not mail film from Indochina—you may never see it again. A bonded courier service is more reliable, though not cheap.

Documents and Printed Matter

Your most valuable documents are your passport and stamped or paper visas. Take along a dozen photocopies of initial passport pages for visa applications and other uses. Bring a stack of passport photos—20 is about right. Be fussy about your passport photo and dress formally: remember, the person issuing the visa will most likely never see you, just the photo. Keep some passport photos in your wallet. An International Health Certificate is only required in China. An International Driver's License is good identification. An important personal document is medical insurance, and a card showing your blood type and any other important medical information. Assemble all document numbers, addresses, and phone and fax numbers on single pages and then use reduction double-sided photocopies to compress the material. Pack documents in a thin Ziploc bag to protect them from rain.

Cheap dictionaries and phrasebooks are available at markets in Cambodia and Vietnam for a dollar or so. Books are heavy—swap reading material with travelers along the way.

Baggage Security

The three things I'd really hate to go missing are documents, money, and camera gear, especially exposed film. The rest is dispensable—inconvenient if lost, but replaceable. Travelers tend to carry a lot of cash in Vietnam, Cambodia, and Laos because banking is inefficient. It's impossible to insure cash, so wear a moneybelt or neck pouch, and sew inner pockets on pants or vest. Make it hard for a would-be thief to figure out where you keep your stash of cash. Keep large denomination US bills in a spot you must practically disrobe to reach; stick smaller US bills in a more accessible spot, like a button-down shirt pocket; and carry local currency in yet a third location. Some hotels have safes: you can place your valuables in an envelope, signing along the sealed part of the envelope; hotel staff will then tape it and put it in the safe. This is okay for a night out in a larger city, but don't leave a credit card in a hotel safe—somebody might decide to use it while you're out. Keep your passport tucked away on your person; show photocopies on demand rather than the original document.

Budget hotels in Vietnam often offer rooms with two metal rings on the door, through which you loop the hotel padlock. Bring a small brass padlock or combination lock with a long reach on it, because some rings are wide on door closures. It's better to use your own padlock than one supplied by the hotel—the hotel key can be picked up by anyone, and sometimes the keys fit other locks as well. It depends how you feel about the hotel. Definition of a secure hotel: one where you have no second thoughts about leaving your camera behind in the room. If the hotel is family-run, grandma will make sure no one gets to your stuff.

When on the move keep your luggage in sight—on trains, on buses, on minibuses. Do not store anything on the roof if at all possible. If on a train, padlock luggage to the overhead rack—there are some compact retractable cable locks that can be purchased for this purpose. You will most likely want to leave your main luggage behind at a hotel when heading off for a three-day trip to the Mekong Delta or Halong Bay. For this reason it's good to have zippered luggage: a small padlock secures two zips together and prevents petty theft. But beware: if you padlock through the *top* rings of the zippers, they can still be easily separated and the contents rifled. What you want to do is padlock through the *bottom* rings of joining zippers. Some packmakers now use zips that fold over one another, with brackets for padlocks.

When storing luggage, add a few labels, both inside and out, with your passport number on them. Tell the hotel staffer you'd like him or her to check the passport number before returning the gear. Another reason for using passport ID is that if the hotel gives you a receipt for the luggage and you lose it, you have a backup method of retrieving the gear. Checked baggage headed for aircraft should also be labeled.

GETTING THERE

Air Links

There are two air approaches to Indochina—direct, or via a gateway city like Bangkok, Hong Kong, or Singapore. There are direct flights into Vietnam from Australia, France, the Netherlands, and Germany. Vietnam Airlines operates joint services with Cathay Pacific, Malaysian Airlines, Korean Air, Singapore Airlines, and China Airlines—to name a few—on international routes. Air links are planned direct to Vietnam from Canada, the US, and the UK. For the present, direct flights are expensive, but weighed against this is the cost of staying elsewhere for a week collecting visas.

Flights routed into Phnom Penh or Vientiane will most likely transit in Bangkok. However, the direct flight network is expanding in Cambodia and Laos. Royal Air Cambodge has direct flights into Phnom Penh from Bangkok, Hong Kong, Singapore, Kuala Lumpur, and Saigon, and is establishing links to Kunming, Guangzhou, and Paris. Lao Aviation operates direct flights into Bangkok, Chiang Mai, Rangoon, and Kunming, and is planning to expand links to China's Yunnan Province.

Bangkok, Hong Kong, and Singapore are the transport hubs of Asia, with frequent discount flights from Europe, North America, and Australia. In the November-February peak season, book well in advance, three months or more. There are aerial bottlenecks all over Asia at Tet, the Lunar New Year. Stay out of Asian airspace at this time.

Bargain connecting flights in Asia include: Hanoi-Vientiane $90, Saigon-Phnom Penh $50, Bangkok-Phnom Penh $125, Kunming-Bangkok $160, Saigon-Bangkok $150. For those keen on tracking baggage labels, some relevant air codes are: Bangkok, BKK; Hong Kong, HKG; Singapore, SIN; Kunming, KMG; Guangzhou, CAN; Hanoi, HAN; Danang, DAD; Hué, HUI; Saigon, SGN; Phnom Penh, PNH; Vientiane, VTE; Luang Prabang, LPQ.

Many travelers to Indochina stop first in Bangkok or Hong Kong because of these cities' frequent air connections, visa services, travel agents, and good information sources. You can complete all your trip preparations in either city, including last-minute purchases. Other possible stops include Singapore, Kuala Lumpur, and Manila. For Canadian, US, Australian, New Zealand, and European passport holders, these cities do not require visas for stays of 14 days or less. Some are even more generous: Malaysia offers a two-month stay on arrival for UK or US passport holders; Hong Kong offers a month or longer.

Bangkok is the primary gateway for Vietnam, Cambodia, and Laos. The most frequent air connections to Vietnam are through Bangkok, although an increasing number of travelers from East Asia and the US visit Indochina via Hong Kong or the Philippines. Flights from the US west coast to Hong Kong and Manila may be $100 cheaper than flights to Bangkok, though this is offset by the fact it's cheaper to stay in Bangkok. Hong Kong handles southern China and northern Vietnam, and is particularly good for connections into Hanoi.

Australians may arrive first in Singapore, though hotels are very expensive and so are flights to Vietnam. Kuala Lumpur is trying to become a more suitable southern gateway by offering much better value for flights into Vietnam. Kunming in Yunnan Province offers frequent air connections to Bangkok, Chiang Mai, Hong Kong, Guangzhou, Singapore, and Vientiane. Inter-Asia flights only allow 20 kg of baggage on flights in economy class (30 kg business class, and 40 kg first class). Anything over these limits may be surcharged.

VIA BANGKOK

Bangkok is like the futuristic Los Angeles in the science fiction movie *Blade Runner*—a city seemingly out of control, clogged with traffic crawling beneath a skyline of towering apartment blocks and banks. The Big Mango is a paradox. Delve below the ugly exterior and you'll find homely neighborhoods with superb restaurants tucked down side alleys, and enough sights to keep you busy for weeks. Transport-wise, Bangkok is a disaster—try and get around on the Chao Phraya River if you can.

Airport Arrival

For a stay of up to 30 days no visa is required. You're stamped in at the airport; for overstays there's a charge of $4 a day. Bangkok's Don Muang Airport is 25 km north of the city center—a ride in can take one to two hours. Your options include taking a metered taxi, which should cost no more than 200 baht to reach town (make sure the driver turns the meter on); or a train to Bangkok's Hualampong Station for about 25 baht. To reach the railway station, walk over an overhead bridge through the Amari Airport Hotel and down to a platform. Air-con buses also run past the airport into town, but the going is very slow.

Accommodations

There are several budget areas in Bangkok. The largest is the Banglamphu/Khao San Road area, a rabbit warren of guesthouses and small hotels. Prices here range from $10-20 for a basic room to $20-40 for one with air-conditioning. Other guesthouses are found near the National Library, and at Soi Kasemsan 1 near Siam Square. Midrange hotels catering to families, group tours, and business travelers are located on side streets off Sukhumvit Road. Moderate accommodations here run $35-100 for a room; luxury hotel rooms are $100 and up. Small business hotels clustered on Sukhumvit sois 7, 9, and 11 charge $30-50 a night. There is fierce competition among luxury hotels in Bangkok, which means walk-in customers can often negotiate 10-50% off list prices. Discounts are also provided in the off-season or for longer stays.

Travel Agents

There are many along Khao San Road in Bangkok's premier backpacker budget zone. A more upmarket strip of travel agents and airlines is located along Silom Road. There are a few travel agents at the corner of Wireless (Wittayu) Road and Ploenchit, near the Vietnamese Embassy. Travel agents in the Indochina trade include:

Diethelm, 140/1 Wireless Rd., tel. 255-9150, fax 256-0248

East-West, 46/1 Sukhumvit Soi 3, tel. 253-0681

Exotissimo, 21/17 Sukhumvit Soi 4, tel. 253-5240, fax 254-7683; Silom branch at 755 Silom Rd., tel. 235-9196

Marvel Holidays, 279 Khao San Rd., tel. 282-9339, fax 281-3216

MK Ways, 57/1 Wireless Rd., tel. 254-4765, fax 254-5583;

Sathorn branch at 18/4 Sathorn Tai Soi 3, tel. 212-2532

Siamwing, 173/1 Surawong Rd., tel. 253-4757, fax 236-6808

SMI Travel, 580 Ploenchit, tel. 252-5435, fax 251-1785

Thai Indochina Supply Co., 79 Pan Rd., 4F, Silom, tel. 234-1555

Thavee Travel, 65 Sukhumvit Soi 3, tel. 252-0097, fax 253-8789

Transindo, Thasos Bldg./10F, 1675 Chan Rd., tel. 287-3241, fax 258-3235

Vista Travel, 244 Khao San Rd., tel. 280-0348

Tickets

A number of agents offer ticket and visa package deals. A $220 package includes a Vietnamese visa, and Bangkok-Saigon and Hanoi-Vientiane flights. Other flights in the region include Bangkok-Saigon $150, Bangkok-Hanoi $160, Bangkok-Kunming $160, Bangkok-Phnom Penh $125, Bangkok-Vientiane $100, all prices one-way.

Visas

You can apply directly for a one-month visa at the Vietnamese Embassy, 83/1 Wireless Rd., tel. 251-5837, a few doors down from the American Embassy. Visa cost is $48 and it takes five working days to obtain. The Lao Embassy is located at 520, 502/1-3 Soi Ramkhamhaeng 39, Bangkapi, tel. 353-6667. This embassy usually only deals with invitation letter applications directly. The Cambodian Embassy is on Rajadamri Rd. at the intersection of Sarasin Rd. near Lumpini Park—visas issued within a few days. The Chinese Embassy, at 57 Rajadapisek Rd., tel. 245-7036, issues a one-month visa within four working days for $12-100 depending on nationality. A one-day or same-day visa costs more.

Supplies

It's easy to obtain US cash dollars in Bangkok. Banks deduct a 1.5% commission when changing traveler's checks to cash. There are ATMs everywhere; use your four-digit code to access machines bearing a Visa Plus or MasterCard Cirrus symbol. There's no need to convert Thai baht back to dollars on leaving Thailand if you're heading for Cambodia or Laos, as you can continue to use baht there. Bangkok medical services are good. Drugstores are not as well-stocked as in Hong Kong and you should be careful with storage conditions for drugs (also check expiration dates). Mefloquine (Lariam) for malaria is not available through drugstores. There are many Western-style department stores in Bangkok for last-minute supplies. For film, check expiration dates and make sure the film has been stored in air-conditioned premises. Quality processing for print and E6 slide films is readily available in Bangkok.

Resources

Bangkok offers plenty of English-language material on Indochina—books, magazines, maps, phrasebooks. You can find books on the Indochina region that may be out of print in the West. In the Silom area, try Asia Books on the third floor of Thaniya Plaza, or DK Book House in the basement of the CCT Building at 109 Surawong. At 29 Sathorn Tai Road is Librarie Française, with books in English, French, and Italian. In the Siam Square area is DK Book House on Soi 6 and Bangkok Books at 302 Soi 4. Along Sukhumvit is a DK Book House near the corner of Soi 8, and branches of Asia Books at 221 Sukhumvit, the Landmark Plaza, Times Square building, and the Skydome in the World Trade Center. Khao San Road is the big trading center for secondhand books. The bi-weekly *Phnom Penh Post* is available at Asia Books. The *Bangkok Post* carries an Indochina Supplement in the Tuesday issue. For longer stays in Bangkok, check out Moon's *Bangkok Handbook* by Michael Buckley.

VIA HONG KONG

Like perishable foodstuffs, all the information that follows has a precise expiration date—1 July 1997. On this date Hong Kong will cease to be a British colony, and will begin a new life as a Special Administrative Region of China. Supposedly, the economic, social, and legal status quo will remain for another 50 years, but few believe China will keep its promises. The Chinese have reneged on international agreements many times before. The squabble between Britain and China over transitional arrangements has left Hong Kong with no guarantee of a free press, or of an independent and fair high court—and with no idea of exactly who or what will administer the territory after the July 1997 handover.

Hong Kong is attached to mainland China, but has over 200 outlying islands; Hong Kong Island, Lantau, Lamma, and Cheng Chau are the largest. Ferry trips across Hong Kong Harbor to Lantau or Cheng Chau are relaxing escapes from the hustle and bustle of business centers like Hong Kong Central and Kowloon.

Airport Arrival

On entry at Hong Kong's Kai Tak Airport, no visa is required for stays of a month or longer. The exchange rate is US$1=HK$7.75; prices in this section are quoted in US dollars, not Hong Kong dollars. The Bank of China has circulated new BOC Hong Kong dollar notes in five denominations, which will account for five to nine percent of the annual issue of banknotes in the colony. When you change money at the airport counter, be sure to get some coins—useful for buses and phone calls. Before you leave the airport, pick up a free tourist map and other literature.

There's an efficient airport bus service with fares under $3; exact change required in Hong Kong coins. Bus A1 to Tsimshatsui on the Kowloon side takes 15 minutes; A2 to Central and Wanchai on the Hong Kong side is 20 minutes; A3 to Causeway Bay on Hong Kong side 20 minutes. All buses depart Kai Tak Airport every 15 minutes 0700-2330. There's a taxi rank opposite the airport bus stop at Kai Tak: a taxi to Tsimshatsui costs around $4; to Hong Kong Island (north side) about $9.

Accommodations

Budget accommodations are scarce in Hong Kong. You'll find budget rooms largely in Chungking and Mirador Mansions, two rather daunting tower blocks on either side of the Holiday Inn Golden Mile, at the bottom end of Nathan Road in Kowloon. Also try the Victoria Hostel on Hankow Road (parallel to Nathan Road, behind Hyatt Regency), with dormitory beds from $7 a night and rooms from $20. A good room is about $35 and up in Kowloon. The YMCA on Salisbury Road is not cheap, but does offer some dormitory accommodations. The YHA on Mount Davis, Hong Kong side, is for members only and is not cheap either—usual YHA rules apply, including curfew. In larger hotels rates start at about $65 for a twin room in low season. Hong Kong travel agencies offer discounted rooms in the large hotels, sometimes up to 50% off rack rate, although rooms can be fully booked during busy months. Luxury hotel rooms start at around $140 a night.

Travel Agents

Many travel agents offer visas, ticketing, tours, and information for Vietnam and China. Laos and Cambodia are handled more from within Indochina, or Bangkok. Regulations concerning overland travel into Vietnam wax and wane with the phases of the moon—always inquire about current conditions.

A highly recommended travel agency is **Phoenix Services Agency**, Room B, 6F, Milton Mansions, 96 Nathan Rd., Kowloon, Hong Kong, tel. 2722-7378, fax 2369-8884—an experienced agent for travel in China and Vietnam with pleasant staff and friendly service. Phoenix can arrange custom tours to Vietnam, Trans-Mongolian train tickets, and other international travel.

Hong Kong agents dealing with Vietnam and China include **Friendship Travel**, Room 604, 6F, Mohan's Bldg., 14-16 Hankow Rd., Kowloon, tel. 2312-1888, fax 2366-1623; **Gathering Travel**, Room 2203, 22F, Wu Sang House, 655 Nathan Rd., Mongkok, tel. 2397-3923, fax 2381-5523; **Lee Wah Travel,** Room 905 Bank Center, 936 Nathan Rd., Kowloon, tel. 2770-3288, fax 2780-6331, with another office on the Hong Kong side at Room 1102 United Overseas Bank Bldg., 54 Des Voeux Rd., Central, tel. 2847-3368, fax 2523-6577. Also try **Mekong Travel,** 1210 Hollywood Plaza, 610 Nathan Rd., Kowloon, tel. 2782-1956, fax 2782-0095; and **Star Tours & Travel,** 8F Wah Ying Cheong Kin Bldg., 236 Nathan Rd., Jordan, Kowloon, tel. 2367-6663, fax 2369-6173.

Tickets

Sample ticket prices from Hong Kong include Hong Kong-Saigon-Hong Kong $565; Hong Kong-Hanoi-Hong Kong $516; Hong Kong-Hanoi/Saigon-Hong Kong $540; Hong Kong-Saigon-Bangkok-Hong Kong $492; Hong Kong-Saigon $270 one-way; Hong Kong-Hanoi $270 one-way; Hong Kong-Kunming $200 one-way. You may be able to strike better deals by packaging a roundtrip flight and Vietnamese visa for $450 or less—fixed dates, may be valid for two weeks only. A cheaper way of getting in and out of Vietnam from Hong Kong is via Canton. Get a Chinese visa for $30, take an overnight $15 boat to Guangzhou, and fly to Hanoi for $130. The total cost one-way to Hanoi is $175. Some agents offer inexpensive Hong Kong-Guangzhou-Hanoi-Hong Kong packages. Cheaper yet, travel overland from Hong Kong to Nanning, then fly Nanning-Hanoi for $70. Or just keep going by land to Hanoi.

Visas

The Chinese Embassy is located in the China Resources Building in Wanchai. You can approach the embassy yourself, but travelers often go through agents for convenience. One-month Chinese visas are easy to obtain, and usually available within two days. Cost depends on nationality: around $25-40 for a two- to three-month visa, $35 for double-entry, and $50-90 for a three-month multiple entry.

The Consulate General of Vietnam is located on the 15th floor of Great Smart Tower, 230 Wanchai Rd., Wanchai, tel. 2591-4510, fax 2591-4524. However, you must go through a travel agent. A one-month visa costs $55 and takes four to seven working days to obtain. A visa with a Lao Cai or Lang Son land-entry stamp costs $60-90; allow five to 10 working days for processing. Sometimes the embassy issues both Lao Cai and Lang Son on the same visa, sometimes only one, at other times neither.

Supplies

You can change money on just about every street corner in Hong Kong. American cash dollars are widely available from banks and moneychangers, and ATMs abound. Hong Kong medical facilities are very good and pharmacies are well-stocked—try those attached to large department stores. Hong Kong is synonymous with shopping. Be wary of "deals" on electronic goods, as the goods may be of dubious quality and often unreturnable. Numerous photo shops sell film, where you can get slight discounts on volume.

Resources

Hong Kong offers English-language bookstores selling books, magazines, maps, and phrasebooks, all often printed in Hong Kong. In Kowloon, try **Swindon's** at 13 Lock Rd., **Peace Books** at 35 Kimberley Rd., and **Times Books** at 96 Nathan Rd. In Hong Kong Central there's the **South China Morning Post Bookshop** at the Star Ferry pier, and a specialized travel bookstore, **Wanderlust Books,** at 30 Hollywood Rd. Useful magazines on sale in Hong Kong are: *Asia, Inc., Business Traveller,* and the *Far Eastern Economic Review.* For longer stays in Hong Kong, consult Moon's *Hong Kong Handbook* by Kerry Moran.

GETTING AROUND

Transport in Indochina is an eclectic mix of French museum pieces, recycled US and Russian vehicles, sparkling Japanese imports, and hybrids thrown together from spare parts. In Vietnam brand-new Toyotas share the road with old French Citroëns and Renaults, speeding trucks, and throngs of motorcycles and bicycles. In Cambodia, decrepit Dodge buses jostle oxcarts; in the hilltribe areas of the northeast elephants may be the only way of getting around. In Laos, modifications on three-wheelers include the jumbo and the sidecar-taxi.

Market freight moves with passengers, meaning you may end up with a flock of geese on your lap. Drivers are something else again—the Vietnamese are among Asia's most reckless. Traffic mishaps are common sights along Vietnam's main roads. Driving at night is very dangerous because hardly anyone uses reflectors or lights of any kind. Infrastructure is weak in Indochina: journeys in Indochina were actually faster in the 1920s than they are today. Much was destroyed during the wars. Because of weak infrastructure, boat travel is a lifeline for passengers and goods in remote parts of Laos and the Mekong Delta region of Vietnam. Boat transport offers intriguing views of territory inaccessible by road.

Vehicle and transport terms used in this book include:

Planes

Antonov-24: A 50-seat Russian turbo-prop from the 1960s, still in use on domestic runs in Laos and Cambodia. In the 1980s Eastern European nations dumped these crates as fast as they could on the communist Far East nations and upgraded to American- and European-manufactured planes like the ATR-72. This is what the Vietnamese are now doing. Meanwhile, for domestic flights, the Vietnamese still use the Tupolev-134, a Russian jet originally designed for bombing runs. The white haze that fogs the interior is normal—it's the air-conditioning.

Trains

Reunification Express: Name of a number of express trains on the line from Hanoi to Saigon, which was originally built by the French as part of the Trans-Indochina Railway. The line, called the Transindochinois, was constructed between 1899 and 1936. The trains crawl along at a top speed of 40 kph, and the full trip takes at least 38 hours. Most trains are diesel, hauling vintage cars from the French era and more recent models from Eastern Europe and India.

In Cambodia trains are regularly blown up by Khmer Rouge soldiers, the passengers shot or robbed. Laos doesn't have a railway.

Boats

Cargo Boat: A largish wooden craft, usually overloaded with goods. Sometimes single deck, sometimes double deck. The cargo boat takes passengers on longer runs—passengers string up hammocks overnight, and there's usually a small cooking area and onboard toilet. Travel can be slow. Cargo boats are found in Vietnam's Mekong Delta, on the Phnom Penh-Angkor river route in Cambodia, and along the Mekong in Laos.

Fast Boat: A long sleek motorboat in Cambodia that can carry 50 seated passengers in

basket boats in Nha Trang, Vietnam

daylight hours if no problems are encountered. On stretches of the Mekong in Laos, longtail boats of Thai origin serve as fast boats. Crash helmets are supplied for the ride.

Fishing Boat: Modified as a touring vessel at Halong Bay and Nha Trang in Vietnam. To get out to a fishing boat, locals use a *thung chai,* or "basket boat."

Junk: A fishing and transport vessel of Chinese origin, with a covered deck and high masts with cotton lugsails braced by bamboo battens. To discourage rot and mildew the sails are dipped in a liquid from a beetroot-like plant. This process gives the sail its dark red-tan color. Converted junks can be rented to cruise Halong Bay.

Sampan: A small covered family boat used by fisherfolk and rented or adapted for river cruises like those along the Perfume River in Hué. Similar small wooden craft are deployed to navigate scenic spots in Luang Prabang in Laos; Tam Coc Caves and the Mekong Delta in Vietnam; and Lake Tonle Sap in Cambodia.

Four-Wheel Vehicles
Gazelle: A brand of Russian Army jeep rented in northern Vietnam. The roomy Gazelle can accept four passengers and luggage. In the south, reconditioned US Army jeeps, painted yellow, are favored by Vietnamese police. Jeeps with elongated midsections are sometimes used on rough dirt roads as public transportation.

Mekong 4WD: A copy of a Toyota Land Cruiser, assembled in Vietnam with Japanese

and South Korean assistance. Expensive chauffeured Mekong 4WDs are available for rent.

Renault Van: A French relic, with distinctive red or yellow snout, employed in Central Vietnam for short runs. There is a comprehensive network of Toyota minibuses in Vietnam doing things that Toyotas were never designed to do, like carrying 30 passengers.

Share-taxi: In Cambodia, Toyotas used for long-distance passenger runs with expenses split by six or so passengers. In Vietnam, share-taxis are sometimes stretched Citroëns, or even old Fords, bearing record-breaking numbers of passengers.

Metered Taxi: Found in larger cities like Hanoi, Saigon, and Vientiane. Toyotas are the popular choice for metered taxis. Lesser and cheaper breeds of unmetered taxi and rental cars are Russian or French.

Songtao: Means two row-seats, a term applied in Laos and Thailand to pickup trucks with open backs modified for passenger use. A much larger version in Laos is a closed Isuzu truck with rows of seats in the back.

Motorcycle-Engine Vehicles
Moto: Abbreviation for Japanese or Russian motorcycle-taxis. These are flagged down at major intersections or markets. The driver takes you as a pillion passenger. Some drivers will take two pillion passengers, but this is dangerous. Some drivers earn a living from motos. In Vietnam motorcycle-taxis are called *xe môtô*

om or *Honda om* (Honda cuddle)—"Honda" the generic term for any kind of motorcycle. In Cambodia it's *moto dup,* with a similar meaning. Motos fill in those crucial 10-km gaps between highway bus stop and hotel, or airport and town. The most important part of a moto is the driver. Before you board, take quick stock of his sanity and physical condition. Moto drivers in Vietnam have an alarming habit of using hand gestures when showing you around, leaving only one hand available to control the handlebars.

Moto Buggy: Variant of a moto, with a chariot at the back, hauled by a motorcycle engine. In Vietnam called *xe Honda loi.*

Sidecar-Taxi: In Luang Prabang and Pakse in Laos you'll find this variant of a motorcycle-taxi, with an open sidecar. The vehicle can carry three passengers—two in the sidecar, one sitting behind the driver, plus freight. Sidecar-taxis have no power on hills.

Cargo Moto: A flatbed motorcycle designed to carry lots of freight, but occasionally accepting human cargo. The driver sits at the back behind a two-wheel metal cart. In Vietnam, the vehicle is called *xich lo may.*

Lambro: Species of three-wheeler similar to Thailand's *tuk-tuks,* with a motorcycle engine installed. In Vietnam, the popular model is a Lambro 550cc, called *xe lam.* In Laos, some smaller three-wheelers accept up to four passengers; the larger stretched versions taking six to eight passengers are called jumbos. Lambros and jumbos are shuttle vehicles, generally ranging 10 to 15 km to cover gaps untraveled by buses. They can carry incredible quantities of freight—sometimes the load is so great the front upends.

Human-Powered Vehicles
Cyclo: The three-wheel bicycle-taxi found in Vietnam, Cambodia, and Laos. The term comes from the French *cyclo-pousse* meaning bicycle-push. The cyclo was introduced to Hanoi in the 1930s to replace the rickshaw, a passenger cart with a human runner up front. In other parts of Asia, the driver of this three-wheeler is up front or at the side; in Indochina, the driver is at the back. The cyclo passenger seat is supported by two wheels up front, and the driver sits on a saddle over the back wheel. You get a grandstand view, and, if you're out at night, a bumper car ride, since cyclos have no lights or reflectors. The slow pace of these trishaws is perfect for touring. Cyclos can carry two passengers plus luggage, or half a dozen schoolchildren. Cyclos are also used as delivery vehicles, moving loads of furniture, chickens, or pigs in baskets.

Deluxe Cyclo: Plush, color-coded cyclos attached to major hotels in places like Hanoi, Haiphong, and Saigon have padded seats, front suspension, and sunroof. These luxury cyclos are used by the Vietnamese for special occasions, and at any time by VIPS (foreigners qualify).

Cyclos navigate the streets near a busy market in Phnom Penh, Cambodia.

Bicycle Buggy: Variant of a cyclo with a detachable bicycle and the driver up front hauling a two-wheel wooden chariot. On a flat road this contraption can carry four passengers. Found in the Mekong Delta and in upcountry Cambodia.

Bicycle-Taxi: Just the bare bicycle, with a wooden and metal rack on the back. The passenger sits on the rack, women sitting sidesaddle. A wood section on the top frame accepts child passengers. Found in the Mekong Delta and also in parts of Central Vietnam, this vehicle is called *xedap om* (bicycle cuddle) in Vietnamese and *cong dup* in Cambodia.

Industrial Bicycle: A reinforced-frame bicycle adapted for pushing freight. Old French bicycles were used to ferry supplies into the war zone at Dien Bien Phu, and the bicycle was used extensively during wartime on the Ho Chi Minh Trail. An industrial bike can be loaded with 200 kg of supplies. In villages, these bikes move great quantities of pottery and other goods.

YOUR OWN TRANSPORT

Your own transport gives you the freedom to stop where you please, with full control over your itinerary. Another attraction is the greater degree of comfort—you're not squished into a tiny space. Local buses and minibuses are abominably crowded; you have to fight your way on and defend your seat.

Motorcycling

You can easily purchase motorcycles in Saigon or Hanoi and resell them after use. Cheaper models are the Russian Minsk 125cc and 175cc. Insurance is a problem in Vietnam: if you lose a rental bike, you pay the full value. This could mean $2000 for a new Honda Dream 100cc. Rentals are often Honda scooters, like the Honda Cub 50cc, 70cc, or 90cc. In Laos there's very little access to roads outside Vientiane Prefecture by motorcycle, though this may change. In Cambodia motorcycles are commonly rented in the Angkor area. Elsewhere use of long-distance rental motorcycles is dangerous—bandits are partial to motorbikes and will shoot the driver right off the bike to get it.

Bicycling

You can buy Taiwanese, Chinese, Thai, or Vietnamese bicycles in the capital cities or large urban centers. You can bring a bicycle into Laos, Cambodia, or Vietnam. There are pseudo-mountain bikes for sale in Vientiane and Saigon—these are imported Chinese- or Taiwanese-made models. You can also buy 10-speeds and pseudo-mountain bikes in Bangkok, Hong Kong, or Kunming. These cost anywhere from $100 for low-end models with fake Shimano gears to $260 for higher-end models with real gears. The bikes are serviceable, but shoddily built. However, some American companies are now making mountain bikes in China under joint-venture agreements. *Vietnam News* reports that a Vietnamese company is manufacturing bicycles with frames made of rattan reinforced with steel rods. These cheap bikes are not built to last.

Bicycle rentals are available in the major cities, particularly in Vietnam. Gearless Chinese-manufactured brands like Phoenix and Forever are the sturdiest. Thai- or Vietnamese-made bikes are not so reliable.

If bringing in your own bike by air, twist the handlebars to align with the frame, remove the pedals, pad vulnerable points with foam or bubblewrap, and place the entire bike in a large plastic sleeve. Most airlines will allow transport of the bike like this—it goes as one piece of luggage. For the second piece, take the largest duffel bag still within airline regulation size for checked baggage (around 90 by 38 by 36cm or 130 liters in volume). That still leaves you one carry-on piece, which you should also maximize. To save on logistical headaches, try to fly straight into Vietnam with a bike.

Overland bikers are searching for ways to get from Hong Kong overland through China into Vietnam, then continue through Laos to Thailand. A Swedish traveler bought a Chinese mountain bike for $100 in Hainan, fitted it with improvised racks made of bamboo, cycled down along the Chinese coast, crossed the Lang Son/Huu Nghi border into Vietnam, rode all the way down to Saigon, and continued on toward Phnom Penh. The entire trip took about 10 weeks. The bike lasted the distance, though some repairs were required en route.

Traffic operates on a different set of rhythms in Asia—you might find yourself riding through uncontrolled intersections, with vehicles cutting you off. Keep moving, be aware of what's around you at all times, and stay out of the way of trucks.

Renting Vehicles

No self-drive cars are available as yet, but you can readily commandeer all forms of chauffeured transport. In Saigon you can rent French classics like the Citroën Traction 15, a vintage gangster model with long black snout and running boards. Vehicles with driver can be rented by the hour, the day, the week, or longer. Foreigners often hire minivans for long-distance travel. Motos and cyclos are ideal vehicles for touring around town, and they're a lot cheaper than car rentals. If you put together a small group you can split expenses on fishing boats to tour scenic areas, or even rent yachts with bunks for overnight trips.

Kayaking

A little-explored alternative to landlubbing is a foldup kayak. There are skeins of rivers and canals throughout the region, and certainly your own transport will get you right off the track and into the unknown—and probably into lots of trouble as well (physical trouble, as in rapids, and bureaucratic trouble). You can transport a folding kayak to your starting point by plane—it goes as one piece of baggage. Then it's a matter of where to launch. Kayaking has been tried with success in the Mekong Delta—an Australian couple kayaked through the Delta to the Cambodian border. Other possibilities include the Halong Bay area north of Hanoi, where many islands are scattered through the region. Sea Canoe Thailand, an operator based in Phuket, Thailand, as well as Mountain Travel Sobek in the US, have started kayak touring in Halong Bay.

Hiking

Never underestimate a good pair of feet, as they can take you a long way. Pounding the pavement is probably the best way to get to know a place. You see more, you do more, you're more involved, you meet people more easily.

TOURS

This book was written with independent travel in mind. Often you'll find yourself teaming with others to split expenses for a hired minibus, jeep, taxi, or boat for day-trips or longer forays. Impromptu small groups are easy to arrange through traveler cafés in Vietnam, but more difficult in Laos or Cambodia. You can switch to small group touring with three or four people, or latch onto a group tour and stay on when the tour ends. Some travelers, for example, meet up with a bicycle tour operator in Saigon, ride to Hué, then continue on their own.

In a sense, organized groups are forerunners for individual travelers, so monitor group tour itineraries for new ideas. Operators arrange tours of the Vietnamese coast in cruise ships, trips by converted junk from Saigon to Phnom Penh, bicycle and motorcycle tours, elephant safaris, hiking and eco-touring, and special tours for war veterans. Refer to the On the Road section of Vietnam for more details.

Indochina Specialist Agencies

In Vietnam, tours originating abroad may come under the control and guidance of Vietnam Tourism and Saigon Tourist, though private operators within Vietnam are providing competition. The following is a sampling of operators specializing in travel to Indochina. Some can assist with obtaining visas.

North America: Adventure travel outfits like **Bolder Adventures, InnerAsia Expeditions, Overseas Adventure Travel, Mountain Travel Sobek, Abercrombie & Kent,** and **Top Guides** offer Indochina itineraries. On the US East Coast, try **Mekong Travel,** 151 First Ave., Suite 172, New York, NY, tel. (212) 420-1586. On the West Coast is **South Sea Tour & Travel,** 210 Post St., Suite 910, San Francisco, CA, tel. (415) 397-4644; and **Asian Pacific Adventures,** 826 South Sierra Bonita Ave., Los Angeles, CA, tel. (213) 935-3156.

Europe: In the UK, **Indochina Travel,** 598 Chiswick High Rd., London W45RT, tel. 995-3883; and **Regent Holidays,** 15 John St., Bristol, tel. 921-1711. In France, several agencies in Paris: **La Maison de l'Indochine,** 36 Rue des Bourdonnais, tel. 284360; and **Voyageurs au Vietnam,** 55 Rue Sainte-Anne, tel. 861688. In Geneva, Switzerland, **Artou,** at 8 Rue de Rive, tel. 218408; and **Exotissimo,** 8 Avenue du Mal, tel. 812166. In Germany, **Indoculture Tours,** Bismarkplatz 1 D-7000 Stuttgart 1, tel. 617057.

Australia/New Zealand: In Sydney, **Orbitours,** 7F, Dymocks Bldg., 428 George St., tel. 221-7322; and **Tour East,** 99 Walker St., 12F, North Sydney, tel. 956-9303. In Melbourne, **Vietnam Ventures,** 92 Victoria St., Richmond, tel. 428-0385. In Auckland, try **Destinations,** Premier Bldg., 41 Durham St., tel. 390464.

Asia: Refer to the operators mentioned under Bangkok and Hong Kong. In Manila, **Vietnam Tours** in Corinthian Plaza Bldg., Paseo de Roxas, Makati, tel. 810-4391. In Tokyo, **Rainbow Tours/Saigon Tourist,** 7F, Crystal Bldg., 1-2 Kanda Awajicho, Chiyoda-ku, tel. 253-5855. In Singapore, **Tour East,** 70 Anson Rd., Apex Tower, tel. 220-2200; and **Vietnam Tourism,** 101 Upper Cross St., #02-44, People's Park Center, tel. 532-3130.

Inter-Asia Routes

New border openings in the region mean lots of new routes. In late 1994 a six-member team of drivers in two Volvo station wagons tackled a 10,000-km overland route from Singapore via Malaysia, Thailand, Laos, Vietnam, and China to Beijing. They drove over the Friendship Bridge from Thailand into Laos, dipped down to the Lao Bao crossing into Vietnam, and carried on over the Lang Son border into China. Apart from potholed roads, the team encountered a few bureaucratic obstacles. The first Beijing ministry they approached for permission wanted a fee of $400,000; team organizers secured the necessary permission through Xinhua News Agency for $12,000.

. A major limitation in Indochina is the weather. You really have to organize your trip around it. The monsoons will not only make it difficult for you to see, they'll make certain areas inaccessible. Flooding and typhoons can shut down transportation in Vietnam. With three different climate zones in the region there is no one optimum time to visit Indochina. A bad time in Laos could be a good time in the Delta.

Bangkok-based Routes: It's possible to travel overland from Bangkok to Hong Kong. The route proceeds from the Laotian border town of Lao Bao to central Vietnam, then north to Kunming or Nanning, and east to Hong Kong. A variant is to fly from Bangkok to Phnom Penh, or go by sea from Thailand to Cambodia, then take a side trip to Angkor and continue overland to Saigon, from where you can make your way overland north to China. For a Bangkok loop route, fly into Saigon, make your way north to Hanoi, fly to Vientiane, and carry on overland to Bangkok. For a longer trip in Laos, fly from Vientiane to Luang Prabang, take a boat along the Mekong to Ban Huay Sai, and the exit to Thailand. A variant of the Bangkok loop route involves continuing north from Hanoi to Kunming in China, then flying back to Bangkok.

The China Connection: If you have a multiple-entry Chinese visa, and a Vietnamese visa with Lang Son (Huu Nghi) and Lao Cai stamps on it, you can leave from Hong Kong to travel overland through China, enter Vietnam at Lang Son, go down to Hanoi, loop back up to Sapa and Lao Cai, and carry on across the Chinese border to Kunming. Or start from Hong Kong, head overland through China to Hanoi, cross to central Vietnam, turn west to the Lao Bao crossing into Laos, and proceed to Vientiane. From there you travel by boat and road to the far northwest, crossing the Ban Boten border into China to reach Jinghong and Kunming.

The Golden Quadrangle: Exciting new routes are opening up in the "Golden Quadrangle," an area jointly promoted by China, Laos, Burma, and Thailand. Already land crossings are used by local tourists in these areas—Chinese tourists from Kunming and Jinghong cross into Burma and Laos. It may take a while for foreigners to follow in their footsteps, but who knows? A Thai company is constructing a road from Chiang Rai in Thailand via Chiang Tung in Burma to Chiang Rung in China. Boat travel may also be possible along stretches of the Mekong from China to Laos.

Burma has opened land and air routes into northern Thailand, and eased up on visa restrictions and individual travel. Previously forbidden areas like Lashio on the Burma Road are now open, although no visits are permitted to sensitive border areas where the government is battling drug traffickers and insurgents. It's possible to fly from Chiang Mai to Mandalay; there's also a border crossing from northern Thailand at Mae Sai to Tachilek. In the future it may be possible to cross from Burma to Yunnan, making a Rangoon-Kunming-Hanoi overland route possible.

Extended Overland Routes

For the ride of your life, crossing through Vietnam provides a novel if time-consuming way to get to Nepal. This is the Vietnam-Tibet-Nepal route. Start out in southern Vietnam (or Cambodia), travel north of Hanoi, and head through the Lao Cai border to Kunming. Travelers in the past have approached Kunming from Hong Kong or Beijing, but going through Vietnam puts you right in the southwest of China. From here there are several options. You could try an overland route by proceeding through Dali, Lijiang, and Markam to Lhasa. This is a wild and rugged route with an ascent to the Tibetan Plateau and takes a few weeks to cover. One snag on this route: Chinese police are prone to turning travelers back at the town of Zhongdian, north of Lijiang.

An alternative route involves making your way overland to Chengdu and flying to Lhasa. This may require booking a short tour to Tibet and staying on. Or you can head from Chengdu via the Aba Grasslands through Zoige and Songpan to Xiahe and Lanzhou. From Lanzhou you can go overland to Golmud via Lake Kokonor, then travel south over the high passes to Lhasa. Travelers on this route have been charged $200 for a truck ride from government-operated and arranged sources. From Lhasa you can overland or fly to Kathmandu, Nepal. From Kathmandu, carry on to Delhi, then cross the Amritsar border to Pakistan, and keep going to Quetta, Tehran, and Istanbul. Phew!

Karakoram Route: After visiting Vietnam, make your way to Kunming, then cut a huge arc through southwestern and western China to Kashgar before heading down the Karakoram Highway into Gilgit and Islamabad in Pakistan (you'll need a Pakistan visa before being allowed into Pakistan). From there you can overland to India via the Amritsar border into Delhi. In the reverse direction, the problem would be where to secure a Vietnamese visa.

Asia to Europe Overland: The opening of the Vietnamese-Chinese border has provided a "missing link" in Asian overland travel. The major hurdle in the fine sport of border crossing is obtaining visas and paperwork. To make visa issue easier, carry some glowing recommendations on official-looking letterhead.

The world's longest railway journey just got longer—now, you can ride the rails all the way from Saigon to Moscow and beyond. From Thailand, proceed by air or boat to Cambodia, then travel overland to Saigon and Hanoi and cross overland to Beijing. From Beijing take the Trans-Mongolian train through Outer Mongolia and Russia to Europe. Visa issue is complicated. Mongolian visas issued on the spot in Vientiane in Laos give you three months to get there; Mongolian visa issue in Hanoi is also reportedly easy. You can pick up a two-month Chinese visa in Hanoi. You can obtain Russian and Mongolian transit visas in Beijing with a confirmed rail ticket. You can most likely extend the Mongolian visa for two weeks in Ulan Bator, and extend the Russian visa for a like period of time in Moscow.

Coming from Europe, the only visa for Russia apart from a transit visa is a business visa or personal invitation visa. These can be arranged through a contact in Russia, or through a travel agent in Scandinavia or the Baltic States. A one-month Russian business visa costs $60; a three-month multiple entry runs $90; a Uzbeki visa is $130. You can obtain a Mongolian visa in Ulan Ude.

In 1992 a completely new trans-Asian rail route opened, running from Beijing to Xian and then on via Urumqi to Alma Ata in Kazakhstan. From here you can travel via Tashkent to Samarkand and Bukhara in Uzbekistan, and eventually Moscow. The visa situation is tricky—Uzbekistan requires a separate visa. For details, consult *Central Asia* by Giles Whittell (Cadogan, 1993) and *Silk Route by Rail* (Trailblazer Publications, 1993).

You can travel all the way from Australia to Europe via the Vietnam route. Island-hop from Australia through Indonesia to Malaysia, travel up through Thailand, cross over to Cambodia, move on to Saigon and into Hanoi and China. From Beijing take the Trans-Mongolian train all the way to Europe. Coming from the other direction, you can obtain a Vietnamese visa in Beijing or Hong Kong

HEALTH

Health care is either poor or nonexistent in most parts of Indochina. Western-run nongovernmental organizations (NGOs) arrange transport of medical equipment considered obsolete in the West but state of the art in Vietnam. An American dentist visiting a dental school in Saigon found 1950s techniques practiced with 1940s equipment, and tattered pages of photocopied medical journals used as reference material. In southern Laos blunt razor blades may be used for incisions in eye surgery if nothing else is available. In Hanoi the tendons of rat's tails may serve as sutures. Quality drugs and supplies are in extremely short supply.

In hospitals around Indochina injection-happy doctors tend to be aggressive in their treatment, forging ahead without proper testing data. Often they will pump foreign patients with antibiotics in search of a quick solution. Food poisoning can be a problem in hospitals. In major cities inquire through embassy staff about facilities with international standards or Western doctors in residence, as well as places for dental treatment. Clinics attached to embassies may be the best in town. In Vientiane are the Australian and Swedish clinics; in Hanoi, the best facility is the Swedish Embassy clinic. In 1995 Vietnam's Minister of Health signed a decree allowing for the first time foreign investors to open hospitals, clinics, medical consultancies, and medical-technical services. Four US firms have submitted joint-venture proposals with Vietnamese hospitals—two in Saigon, two in Hanoi.

Medicines and drugs are available at pharmacies in Indochina, but are of questionable quality. Drugs readily deteriorate if not stored in a cool, dry place. Consult expiry dates and check for signs of tampering. Beware of drugs from East European nations, and be on the lookout for fake medication—the World Health Organization (WHO) reports that in some third-world countries fake drugs contain only a placebo or aspirin. Buy from air-conditioned premises if you can, as the shelf life of drugs like antibiotics is greatly decreased in hot and humid conditions. You can easily obtain reliable medicine in Hong Kong, Singapore, and Bangkok without a prescription. Certain antimalarial drugs, however, are not sold in Bangkok.

This section is not intended to alarm travelers but to make them aware of the potential risks of traveling in Indochina. The real hazards apply to visits to remote areas, or extended stays in rural areas. You need to remain alert for symptoms of ailments, and know when it's time to get out. Advice on drugs and potions in the following sections may not apply to pregnant women, children, and those with certain medical conditions or allergies. Specialist advice should be sought from a family doctor prior to departure.

MEDICAL INSURANCE

Make sure you carry comprehensive medical insurance, including emergency evacuation coverage. Under some private coverage schemes you pay up front for evacuation by whatever aircraft happens to be around—hopefully not a Russian one—and the insurance company reimburses you later. Helicopter charter services like New Zealand-run Lao Westcoast Helicopter in Vientiane, and VASCO, operating out of Saigon and Hanoi, can assist in emergencies. Evacuation in Indochina is largely a matter of rocketing off to Singapore, Hong Kong, or Bangkok, where there are excellent health care facilities.

Carriers
Medical carriers like AEA International and International SOS will cover the cost of evacuation by private jet and postevacuation expenses up to $10,000. The cost of coverage under these comprehensive schemes is around $140-180 a month. Case scenario: a motorcycle accident near Hué, with your leg fractured in three places. A private jet flies in from Singapore with a medical team on board, landing at Danang. You're picked up by ambulance and flown to a hospital in Singapore within 24 hours of the accident. Doctors calculate possible loss of the leg through infection if you'd arrived any later.

International SOS is a 24-hour worldwide private company with regional head offices in Geneva, Singapore, and Philadelphia in the US, with numerous branches and associated organizations. In the US contact International SOS, P.O. Box 11568, Philadelphia, PA, tel. (215) 244-1500; in the UK SOS, P.O. Box 304, London SW148AL, tel. 44-171-392-1666; in Geneva SOS at Rue Sautter 11, 1205 Geneva, tel. 41-22-789-0826. In Singapore contact SOS at Robinson Rd., P.O. Box 108, Singapore 9021, tel. 65-221-3981. In Vietnam, International SOS is at 151 Vo Thi Sau, Q3, Saigon, tel. 84-8-242-866; in Hanoi SOS is in the Boss Hotel, 60 Nguyen Du, Suite 208, tel. 84-4-226228, fax 84-4-269166. In Cambodia, in association with SOS, is IMC Clinic, at 83 Issarak Blvd., Phnom Penh, mobile tel. 015-912765; international standards.

AEA International is a Singapore-based organization that will evacuate you to Singapore. There are branches in Hong Kong, India, Japan, Vietnam, and Thailand. In Singapore contact AEA at 331 N. Bridge Rd., 17F Odeon Towers, Singapore 0718, tel. 65-3382311, fax 65-3387611. In Hanoi contact AEA at 4 Tran Hung Dao St., tel. 84-4-213555, fax 84-4-213523; in Saigon OSCAT/AEA at 65 Nguyen Du St., Q1, tel. 84-8-298520, fax 84-8-298551; in Vung Tau OSCAT/AEA at 1 Duong Than Thai St., Vung Tau, tel. 84-64-58776, fax 84-64-58779. The US

MEDICAL KIT

Camping and outdoor stores sell prepackaged medical kits you can customize to your needs. These come in compact versions with sterile gauze squares, adhesive tape, bandages in assorted shapes and sizes (including knuckle and fingertip bandages), antibacterial towelettes, needle, razor blade, and safety pins. Take along a small Swiss Army knife with scissors and tweezers. For travel in Indochina choose a kit that is comprehensive yet compact. A couple of people traveling together can share a medical kit. Following are some medical kit tips:

- Treating simple cuts, bites, and scratches is very important in a tropical climate as these are slow to heal and easily infected. Bring an extra supply of Band-Aids, antiseptic cream, and some sort of calamine lotion or antihistamine to reduce itching from bites or sunburn. To assist in cleanup take Q-Tips, dental floss, and a bar of antibacterial soap. To promote cleanliness and dryness in areas like the feet and groin you should carry antifungal cream or talcum powder.

- Take a bottle of iodine tablets to purify water. Iodine tablets are cheap, require little space, and are extremely effective.

- A variety of "blockers" is essential—15-factor sunscreen, lipscreen, mosquito repellent, earplugs (essential to reduce noise in hotels or on transport), condoms (just in case).

- Stock your own drugs—antimalarials, pain and headache medications (codeine is good), anti-

histamines and decongestants (cough and cold medication), medicines for stomach problems (including oral rehydration salts), and antiworm tablets. A two-week supply of antibiotics would be useful. Carry these drugs but hope you never have to use them. Don't use unless really necessary, and at all costs avoid drug "cocktails" (using several drugs at the same time). Antibiotics lose their effectiveness if used every time a minor problem occurs.

- Because of the poor health care in Indochina, it's highly recommended you carry sterile needles and syringes as anti-AIDS and anti-hepatitis protection. These needles can be used for blood samples or any injections you might require. Kits can be purchased ready-made, sealed, and labeled so you won't look like a junkie to customs officers.

- Eye irritation is a potential problem due to dust; you might want to take along eyedrops. Dental care is abysmal in Indochina: depending on the state of your dental work, consider carrying a few items to deal with problems. A tiny tube of benzocaine gel will deal with toothache. There are travel-size dental repair kits on the market that address the calamity of lost fillings.

- If you're dependent on specific brands of medicine that may not be available in Indochina, take a supply with you. This extends to birth control pills, and to items you may well overlook. You'll make an absolute fool of yourself trying to mime contact lens solution to a shopkeeper in Hanoi who's never heard of such a thing.

address is AEA International, 6449 Tauler Court, Columbia, MD 21045, tel./fax (301) 596-7436.

INFORMATION AND INOCULATIONS

For current information on who's winning in the battle against mosquitoes, and other viruses and bugs, contact the Centers for Disease Control and Prevention in Atlanta, Georgia, in the US, which monitors outbreaks of disease around the globe. Its Traveler's Hotline, tel. (404) 332-4565, provides information by voice recording or automated fax transmission. In England contact the Medical Advisory Service for Travellers (MASTA) at the London School of Hygiene and Tropical Medicine, tel. 071-631-4408. British Airways Travel Clinics also supply information. Highly recommended medical guides are Dirk Schroeder's *Staying Healthy in Asia, Africa, and Latin America* (Moon Publications, 1993) and Richard Dawood's *Travellers' Health* (Oxford University Press, 1994). For pocket-size guides, try Stephen Bezruchka's *The Pocket Doctor* (The Mountaineers, 1992) and the *Collins Gem Holiday Health* booklet (HarperCollins, 1995).

Get an armful of inoculations before you leave home; try a travel clinic, which also supplies information. Consult your family doctor about the trip. Have your teeth checked before departure. Recall all those items you're dependent on: if you wear glasses or contact lenses, take an extra set along, and carry your prescription for new lenses. Bring a good medical kit. Prepare a personal medical card to carry in your wallet. Print or type all the details on a small card, then laminate it. Include identification, with passport number, blood type, preexisting medical conditions, special medications, medical insurance details, and a name of a relative or friend to contact in an emergency.

Why go to this trouble? It's essential to have this information at your fingertips in an emergency, and it may alert others to problems. For example, some blood types like O-negative are rare in Asia, which presents a potential problem for O-negative travelers with a sudden need for blood.

You don't have to show any vaccination certificates in Indochina, but it's highly recommended you get jabs or boosters against typhoid and polio/tetanus, and consider shots for hepatitis A. On the road these inoculations can be obtained at the Red Cross in Bangkok, at clinics in Hong Kong or in Singapore, and at the Swedish Clinic in Hanoi. If entering China, you'll most likely be asked to show a health certificate. Officials even scrutinize the document for a cholera vaccination, which is practically useless. To satisfy their whims, you should get that section stamped in big letters, "Cholera not medically indicated."

Coming Home

Then there's coming home. Some bugs in the system may lie dormant for six months or longer before multiplying. If you have any reason to suspect a condition or problem, get blood and/or stool tests, and inform your doctor where you've been traveling. What might be mistaken for flu could well be malaria, and a doctor in the West should be alerted to this possibility.

ACCLIMATION ILLNESSES

Sun Exposure and Prickly Heat

Adjusting to the tropics can take two to six weeks. Problems that can occur if you're not acclimated include heatstroke, sunburn, and prickly heat. Take it easy on arrival to allow yourself time to adapt to the new environment. Avoid strenuous activity, wear a hat, apply sunscreen, and drink plenty of fluids.

Your body deals with excess heat by turning into a kind of air-conditioning unit. Sweat glands are activated, beginning in the forehead and spreading down to the soles of the feet; skin ducts secrete fluid that is mostly water and about 1% salt. Cooling is accomplished by the evaporation of sweat, and is quicker if helped by convection—the air movement of a breeze or fan. Sweating is the best avenue for heat loss, but sweating too much without fluid replacement is a problem. Sweating on a very hot day, you can lose a liter of water an hour, and, if working hard, you may lose up to four liters an hour. The body isn't very good at signaling when it's lost too much water; you can lose quite a lot before you begin to get thirsty. If you don't restore water and electrolytes, your blood pressure will begin to fall, and you'll feel dizzy. In a worst-case scenario, the body's heat system shuts down, leading to brain-damaging heatstroke if not countered immediately by cooling the body in water and restoring fluids and salts.

In tropical areas there's a firm correlation between clothing and health. Wear loose, light clothing—cotton is best because it breathes and will not shrink. If you wear tight synthetic clothing, particularly socks and underwear, you may fall victim to prickly heat (an itch and a heat rash) or fungal infections—particularly between the toes and in the groin. Humidity, increased perspiration, and heat favor the growth of fungi and bacteria on the skin; to counter these, stay clean, dry between the folds of the skin, and apply a light dusting of talcum powder.

If the rot persists, switch to very loose clothing. For foot problems, wear sandals for a few days. Women afflicted with groin or vaginal infections should don cotton underwear and a skirt; males with groin infections should wear loose cotton boxer-style shorts. Apply talc to affected areas to keep them dry and free of sweat. Another remedy is soap with an antibacterial agent, or antifungal cream. Infection of the urinary tract and bladder (cystitis) in women is associated with sexual activity; this infection is much more frequent in the tropics, probably because of dehydration. If symptoms are pain and more frequent urination, drinking plenty of water should alleviate the problem. If there is no sign of improvement, antibiotics may be required.

Dire Rear

Stomach problems are common on the road. The greatest risk with diarrhea is dehydration: you have to drink plenty of clear fluids, water, unsweetened juices, or clear soups. Do not drink alcohol or milk, and avoid fruit, green vegetables, and spicy or fatty foods, as these items tend to aggravate diarrhea. Pack something for the runs—Imodium or Pepto-Bismol for minor cases, and an antibiotic for more memorable instances. Most cases of the runs resolve in a few days. If symptoms persist, with diarrhea and blood or mucus in the stool, this indicates a more serious illness, such as amoebic or bacillary dysentery. In such a case get a stool test to identify the bug.

Influenza and Respiratory Problems

Coughs, colds, and sore throats are common problems when traveling in Indochina, often related to road dust and overkill air-conditioning. Carry your own cough and cold medicines. There are virulent strains of flu running around Asia, and you may come down with a bad case. Do not treat cold symptoms lightly—you might acquire a strain of Asian flu that could lay you flat for a week, accompanied by fever and stomach problems. What at first appears to be flu may actually be more serious, perhaps the onset of typhoid or malaria. Initial symptoms can be very similar.

Tuberculosis: The "white plague" is threatening to make the comeback of the century. Vaccines, antibiotics, and improved hygiene nearly erased TB from industrialized nations; however, the disease now appears to be resistant to most of the drugs previously used to treat it. Tuberculosis thrives in crowded and dirty living conditions where both ventilation and the people are poor. The airborne bacteria are readily transmitted through coughing, sneezing, or spitting by people in an infectious stage of TB. Vietnam and Cambodia are among the hot spots for infection. TB is the number one killer in the 15-to-45-year age group in Cambodia, according to French-based Médecins Sans Frontières (Doctors Without Borders).

TAINTED FOOD AND WATER

Constantly monitor the quality of your food and water in Indochina. Boil it, peel it, cook it, filter it—or forget about it. Insanitary conditions, with cockroaches and rats running around kitchens, can be dangerous. Observe basic sanitary hygiene. Keep your hands clean when eating, though know restaurant face towels, if not clean, can lead to eye infections.

Stick to drinking purified bottled water, even when brushing your teeth. When buying bottled water ensure the seal is intact. Carry your own plastic water bottle when traveling. In many places in Indochina you'll be offered water with ice in it. Don't drink it! In Vietnam, if you buy a bottled or canned soft drink or beer, you can often ask for a small ice-bucket—keep the drink on ice near your table just like champagne. Beer is cheap and goes through a fermenting process that renders it

Chopping up a block of ice in a market shack in Siem Reap, Cambodia. One good reason to avoid ice in these parts.

safe to drink, though don't drink too much—you can get terrific tropical hangovers. Other relatively safe drinks are tea and coffee, assuming the water used has been sufficiently boiled.

French colonial-type ceramic filters for purifying water have been spotted in first-class railway waiting rooms in Vietnam. Chinese thermoses are ubiquitous in hotel rooms in the north. This water is generally piping hot and thus a good source of drinking water. However, the problem is how to transfer it—hot water can melt plastic. One solution is to uncork the thermos and leave it to cool off overnight; your drinking water is ready the next morning. In areas where there is no bottled water you need to use iodine tablets or a personal filter.

Ensure all food is thoroughly cooked. The baguettes sold fresh daily throughout Indochina are generally safe because they're baked at extremely high temperatures—high enough to fry

any bugs within. Dairy products should be avoided, although yogurt is good for your stomach as a natural antibacterial agent. Hazards to the stomach increase with salads, ice cream, unpasteurized milk, raw or undercooked eggs, and undercooked meat or seafood, particularly shellfish, crabs, and prawns if not boiled for at least 10 minutes. The latter may be infected with parasites or their larvae; in Laos, raw or undercooked fish may carry tiny worms that cause liver flukes. An American pamphlet tenders this advice for Laos: "Avoid cold buffets, custards, and any frozen desserts," which shouldn't be that difficult in Vientiane (I never saw any custards on my trip).

Cholera
Cholera is an acute intestinal infection caused by contaminated food or water. Symptoms include an abrupt onset of watery diarrhea, vomiting, dehydration, and muscle cramps. The available vaccine for cholera is only 50% effective in reducing the illness and has a brief validity period. People with severe cases respond well to simple fluid and electrolyte-replacement therapy (oral rehydration). Cholera outbreaks have been reported in Indochina, Burma, and China. Outbreaks occur mainly in rural areas where locals have little access to clean drinking water.

Typhoid
Typhoid fever is a bacterial infection transmitted through tainted food or water, or directly between people. Symptoms include fever, headache, loss of appetite, constipation or diarrhea, and fatigue. Typhoid fever can be treated directly with antibiotics. A vaccine is good protection against typhoid.

MOSQUITO-BORNE DISEASES

Malaria
Malaria is prevalent in certain parts of Indochina. The major cities—Vientiane, Phnom Penh, Saigon, Danang, Hanoi—present no risk, apparently because of water pollution. Malaria-carrying mosquitoes are fussy about the water where they lay their eggs, and the water in these

urban centers is too polluted for their taste. Coastal and urban areas of Vietnam are considered low-risk, as are the deltas. In remote areas of the countryside in Vietnam, Laos, and Cambodia, the risk is very real, particularly around Angkor Wat, Luang Prabang, and the jungle border zones of Vietnam.

Of the hundreds of varieties of mosquitoes in Indochina only a handful carry malaria. Of the *Anopheles* mosquitoes males are vegetarian, feeding entirely on plant juices. The female mosquito, who bites to obtain protein sustenance for her eggs, can fly around carrying more than twice her own weight in blood. Malaria is caused by protozoa that infect red blood cells. If her human victim is infected, the mosquito ingests malarial parasites along with her quota of blood. Some of the ingested parasites are hardy enough to survive the mosquito's oral digestive juices, and are passed on alive to the mosquito's next victim.

Four kinds of malaria parasite can inhabit humans. Malaria parasites can be identified by blood tests. *Falciparum,* the deadliest type, accounting for 95% of all malarial deaths, thrives in the hottest climates and is now resistant to chloroquine. *Vivax,* more widespread, causes fevers and anemia. The two other types of malaria—*ovale* and *malariae*—are less common. A victim can actually suffer from several malarias at once. Once the malaria parasite is in the bloodstream it's carried to the liver, where it reproduces. At some later indeterminate time (anywhere from days to years), the parasite reenters the bloodstream, producing chills and headache and diarrhea, followed by high fever and nausea. In serious cases delirium and coma follow. The malaria parasite is devious—it attacks, withdraws, and attacks again, sometimes with devastating results.

There is currently no guaranteed effective remedy against malaria. Every time a promising new drug appears, mosquitoes quickly mutate and develop resistance. This situation is ongoing and researchers wait for reported cases of foreigners with malaria from different areas before deciding how resistant the mosquitoes have become. Antimalarial drugs should be taken two weeks before entering a malarial zone, and for four weeks after leaving. Antimalarials do not prevent infection. Instead, they suppress multiplication of the parasite in the liver. If you stop taking the malarial tablets too soon, you increase the odds of developing full-blown malaria. Due to side effects, long-term use of antimalarials is not recommended.

Mefloquine (Lariam) is the drug currently recommended for Indochina. The adult dosage is 250 mg (one tablet) once a week. Side effects include dizziness and gastrointestinal disturbances, symptoms that tend to be mild and temporary. Infants and pregnant women should not take mefloquine.

Chloroquine is no longer effective in parts of Southeast Asia, and Fansidar is deemed too dangerous because of side effects. In mefloquine-resistant areas such as Thailand and the Philippines, the antibiotic doxycycline is recommended. This drug, however, may increase chances of sunburn. The drug proguanil (Paludrine), used simulataneously with chloroquine, is an alternative to mefloquine or doxycycline. Halofantrine (Halfan) is reserved for self-treatment of malaria after symptoms become apparent.

In the 1950s WHO declared war on malaria with weapons ranging from DDT to mosquito-killing fungi. It was believed malaria could be eradicated within a few decades, but mosquitoes have proved far more resilient than ever imagined, and the outlook for malaria control is grimmer than ever. Now WHO's strategy is to get back to fundamentals: the best protection against malaria is to ensure you're not bitten in the first place. Especially around dusk and dawn, cover up with long-sleeved shirt, scarf, and long pants tucked into socks, and use a repellent. Mosquitoes will often swarm over one person but virtually avoid another, behavior apparently linked to scents. Biting mosquitoes seem to be turned on by sweat, lactic acid, and the scent of bananas, perfume, and cologne, among other things. If you smell "bad," mosquitoes won't want to bite you—use some kind of mosquito repellent for exposed flesh. In Vientiane a soap called Mos-Bar is marketed for similar effects. A good natural repellent is oil of citronella. Pay special attention to areas like the legs and ankles as mosquitoes favor ground-level meals. Tucking pants into socks is also effective.

The active ingredient in most insect repellents is DEET (diethyl meta-toluamide), which operates on the stealth principle, emitting a vapor that keeps insects from sensing your presence. DEET wards off mosquitoes, fleas, ticks, chiggers, and other insects. But it can be toxic, so do not apply concentrations greater than 35% and avoid contact with eyes and mouth. DEET-based products can damage synthetic fibers, painted surfaces, and plastics, so avoid getting any on eyeglasses or plastic wristwatches. Since it's highly flammable, keep it away from fire sources. An insecticide called permethrin is also highly effective, licensed for use with clothing and netting.

In air-conditioned hotels, the risk of mosquito bites is extremely low—after all, the windows are closed. Thus, in four-star hotels mosquito nets will probably not be provided. In other accommodations always deploy a net around your bed at night. Check hotel room cupboards if you don't see a net installed, or ask staff to provide one. Keep the flammable nets well away from fire sources like candles or mosquito coils. Consider carrying your own net if visiting rural areas, areas without hotels, or on long train or bus trips. Mosquito netting is sold by the meter in markets in Phnom Penh and Saigon. Avoid no-see-um netting: the mesh is too fine to allow air to circulate. It's a good idea to impregnate a net with insecticide to take care of any holes.

Dengue Fever

Dengue fever, carried by *Aedes albopictus,* or tiger mosquitoes, is a low-incidence threat in urban areas. It may also affect larger rural towns. Dengue can take two forms—dengue hemorrhagic fever and the less severe classical dengue fever. The tiger mosquito is more active during the day, especially at dawn and dusk. Dengue fever is a bit of a mystery. If a person has symptoms, it's a matter of resting up, restoring fluids, and waiting till the fever passes. No vaccine is available. Symptoms include fever, headache, severe joint and muscle pains, and rash. Cases of dengue fever have been detected throughout Indochina, but the risk of infection is small for travelers except during periods of epidemic transmission, usually during the rainy season. In 1995 an epidemic hit the northwest of

Cambodia, around Battambang, resulting in the deaths of hundreds of children. Adult fatalities from dengue fever are rare.

Japanese Encephalitis

This viral disease (JE) is spread by mosquitoes, particularly in rice-growing and pig-farming areas. It's commonly spread from pigs to humans by *Culex* mosquitoes. Risk is seasonal. In subtropical regions, JE is associated with the rainy season. Only certain mosquito species are capable of transmitting the disease, and they bite mostly at dusk and dawn. Mild symptoms are flu-like at the onset, with headache and fever. More serious complications include swelling of the brain (encephalitis), which can be fatal. The chance a traveler in Asia will contract JE is very small. There's a vaccine available for JE through travelers clinics, but it's really only recommended for those who intend to make extensive visits to rural areas during transmission season. You should avoid mosquito bites at all times in these areas; use a repellent and net at night.

NOXIOUS CREATURES

Worms

Intestinal worms are common in rural areas. The larvae are often present on unwashed vegetables or undercooked meat. Intestinal worms are awful to contemplate, but not of great medical concern since drugs to kill them are highly effective. If you think you've picked up a worm or two, a simple stool examination on your return home will identify the culprits, and elimination is accomplished with antiworm tablets. Also be careful of infestation by the larvae of hookworms, contracted by walking barefoot on moist soil or on beaches in infected areas.

Laos presents some special worm hazards. Avoid eating raw or undercooked fish, as the fish may carry tiny worms that cause liver flukes, or opisthorchiasis. Particularly avoid eating *paddek,* chunks of fermented freshwater fish, and *nam paddek,* a sauce from fermented fish. The risk is higher in rural areas. Around Khong Island in the Mekong in southern Laos it's possible to contract liver flukes from swimming. In the same area are blood flukes, which can cause schisto-somiasis (bilharzia)—an infection that develops after the larvae of a flatworm have penetrated the skin. Water treated with chlorine or iodine is virtually safe, and salt water poses no risk. The medication to treat both blood and liver flukes is praziquantel (Biltricide). Schistosomiasis may also be present in parts of Vietnam.

Insects

Most are of the bothersome kind—bedbugs, lice, mites, and scabies. In cheaper accommo-dations bedbugs can be a problem: consider carrying anti-flea powder to dust bedding. Spe-cial shampoos can counter lice, and infected clothing should be washed in very hot water. When scratched, insect bites are easily infected in a tropical climate, and such wounds heal slowly. Avoid scratching bites, and use calamine lotion or antihistamine tablets to reduce itching. If bites become infected, treat with antibiotic cream. If heading into wet jungle areas, use sturdy footwear and tuck pants into socks to counter leeches.

Venomous Creatures

There is a low-incidence risk from venomous snakes, spiders, scorpions, centipedes, and sea creatures. Poisonous snakes such as co-bras and kraits exist in Indochina, but only attack when provoked—and hardly ever if you keep still. However, the Hanuman snake, found near Siem Reap in Cambodia, is a tree snake that drops onto its victims. If bitten, clean the wound, and take yourself—and the snake, if possible—to the nearest medical facility with antivenin. Scorpions have been sighted in Cambodia in Sihanoukville—check inside your shoes in the morning, and keep your bed away from the wall. Venomous species may lurk in the water: among them are sea snakes and the stonefish, which spikes the foot that steps on it.

Plague Carriers

Vietnam is listed as a plague-infected country. Plague is spread by fleas from rats infected with the disease-causing organism. A vaccine for prevention and treatment is available but is nor-mally only recommended for those contemplat-ing extended stays in rural areas, or people bent on fondling wild rodents.

Rabies

Avoid being licked, scratched, or bitten by a rabid mammal. Dogs are the greatest offend-ers, though monkeys also pose a risk. Rabies is a deadly disease that attacks the brain, and unless treated it can kill within two months. If bit-ten by a rabid animal, clean the wound thor-oughly with soap and water, then seek prompt medical attention. Vaccination against rabies is recommended only for veterinarians and animal handlers, travelers planning extended visits to areas known for rabies risk, and spelunkers risking rabies from cave bats. Pre-exposure vaccination (a series of shots) does not nullify the need for postexposure vaccine, though it re-duces the number of injections.

HUMAN HAZARDS

Hepatitis

Hepatitis is a viral infection of the liver, primari-ly spread through contaminated food and water, dirty needles, or sexual contact via body fluids like blood, saliva, or urine.

Hepatitis A (infectious hepatitis) is transmit-ted by the fecal-oral route, through direct per-son-to-person contact, from contaminated water or shellfish, or from fruit or uncooked vegetables contaminated through handling. Hepatitis A damages liver cells. They swell up, stop functioning, and cannot dispose of the body's toxic waste material, especially bile. When bile builds up in the blood it causes jaun-dice, a condition that turns the skin and eyes yellow and darkens the urine. Other symptoms include fever, fatigue, loss of appetite, nausea, aches and pains, and light stools. Havrix, a new hepatitis A vaccine that provides immu-nity expected to last five to 10 years, is now being introduced in the West. The vaccine con-tains hepatitis A virus produced in cell culture and rendered harmless by treatment with for-malin. Two doses at least six months apart are required.

Hepatitis B (serum hepatitis) is transmitted through tainted blood, needles, or sexual con-tact. A high percentage of prostitutes carry this virus. Hepatitis B differs from hepatitis A in that it may lead to chronic liver disease or cancer. You can be immunized against hepatitis B.

Other strains of hepatitis are mysterious, and are still in the process of being identified by researchers. They're often lumped under the label "non-A, non-B" because they don't react in blood tests for types A or B. They appear to be more closely aligned with hepatitis B in regard to modes of transmission. There is no known vaccine or treatment for these strains.

AIDS and STDs

Acquired immunodeficiency syndrome (AIDS) is linked to human immunodeficiency virus (HIV), although researchers are hazy on how the virus operates. The HIV virus has been detected in Indochina, and cases are spreading rapidly in Vietnam due to widespread prostitution. As of mid-1995, 2600 people tested HIV-positive in Vietnam; 131 developed AIDS and 55 died. WHO estimates over 570,000 Vietnamese will be infected with HIV by 1998, and 15,000 will die as a result. In Cambodia prostitution was rampant during the 1992 UN occupation of the country. The government records 740 cases of HIV infection, while WHO estimates 6,000. Some experts believe the figure could be 10 times higher. In Laos, of 16,600 people tested, there were 42 HIV-positive cases. Laos fears its inadequate health care system may not be able to cope with the problem.

DO NOT TOUCH

កុំប៉ះពាល់

Under UN auspices, a vigorous campaign is underway in all three countries to combat AIDS. The Australian government is funding 23 AIDS projects in Southeast Asia, including Vietnam and Cambodia, with the main emphasis on education.

Travelers are at risk for AIDS if they have sexual intercourse with an infected person, use contaminated or unsterilized syringes or needles for any injections or skin-piercing procedures, or encounter infected blood products. Prostitutes are a major risk: they have multiple sex partners and often associate with intravenous drug users.

Condoms and spermicides decrease, but do not entirely eliminate, the risk of HIV transmission. While Western nations have virtually eliminated the risk of infection of transfusion-associated HIV, in poorer nations like Vietnam, Cambodia, and Laos the resources for testing blood products for HIV are limited. Western-run organizations like the International Red Cross in Phnom Penh screen blood for the AIDS virus and hepatitis. For any medical procedures insist on the use of a sterile disposable needle, prepackaged in a sealed container. It might be worth carrying a few in your medical kit.

STDs: Since AIDS hit the scene, it seems other sexually transmitted diseases (STDs) have faded from public consciousness. Risks still exist from infected partners of genital herpes, chlamydia, gonorrhea, and syphilis. Again, the use of condoms lessens the chances of transmission, but does not provide absolute protection.

Mines and War Materiel

One of the greatest risks to life and limb in remote areas of Vietnam, Cambodia, and Laos is landmines and unexploded ordnance. In Vietnam and Laos landmines are mostly left over from the Vietnam War; the risk is real only in places like the DMZ. Cambodia has well over three million mines, and more are placed each day by both the Khmer Rouge and government forces. Never approach or touch live war materiel. See the Cambodia section for minefield etiquette.

Military Menaces

Insurgency exists in Laos and Cambodia. The risk is very low in Laos from disgruntled Hmong tribesmen, but quite high in Cambodia from the genocidal Khmer Rouge. The Khmer Rouge kidnapped and killed a handful of foreigners in 1994-95; banditry involving demobilized soldiers and police is also widespread in Cambodia. Government soldiers may demand handouts from travelers. The police in Vietnam are after the same, but are more refined in their approach—perhaps charging big-noses for "insurance" to visit a site, or fining a minibus driver for not possessing "a license to drive foreigners."

Drugs

Marijuana is widely available in Indochina. The use of soft drugs is tolerated or ignored in Cambodia and Laos, where they're sold in the markets for less than the price of tobacco. Marijuana is sold in Vientiane, Phnom Penh, and Siem Reap as a cooking condiment. In Saigon cyclo drivers somtimes sell marijuana to travelers and then inform the police, who are always keen on extra income. Opium smoking is prevalent among the Hmong hilltribe people of Indochina, though it is officially outlawed in Vietnam. On the hard drug front Vietnam is following the lead of Thailand and Malaysia, exacting harsh penalties. In June 1995 a Hong Kong-born British citizen was executed in Vietnam for drug trafficking; he was intercepted two years earlier at Saigon airport with five kilos of heroin.

VIETNAM

What do you expect from a country that had a thousand years of mandarin rule, followed by a hundred years of the French civil service, followed by the Communist Party?"

—FRUSTRATED FOREIGN INVESTOR,
QUOTED IN *THE ECONOMIST*

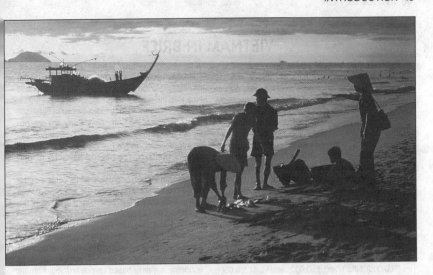

INTRODUCTION

In early 1994, the Clinton administration lifted the US trade embargo against Vietnam, bringing the war to an official close, and enabling Vietnam to get on with rebuilding its shattered economy. A year later, the US flag was flying over the US liaison office in Hanoi—the first time the American flag has flown over a US government building in the north since 1955. The war is history now, relegated to museums. Among the more unusual tourist attractions in Vietnam today are the relics of war—captured weaponry at the War Crimes Museum in Saigon, preserved tactical tunnels at Cu Chi and Vinh Moc, fragments of downed B-52s at the Army Museum in Hanoi. Mementos of the war bolster national unity and provide a sense of legitimacy to the rule of the Communist Party. For their part, the Vietnamese bear no animosity toward Americans. In fact, Americans visiting the area say this is the friendliest place in Southeast Asia.

Though it's the Vietnam War that lingers with those who know Vietnam through film, television, and personal experience, it's the French presence that strikes those who actually visit. There are stately French-built mansions and tree-shaded boulevards in Hanoi, art galleries in Hanoi and Saigon selling works heavily influenced by French styles, cafés serving French bread and drip filter coffee in Saigon, French villas dotting the hills of Dalat. The origin of some customs are French, but the interpretation is pure Vietnamese: one visitor spotted a black Citroën Traction, straight out of 1930s France except for the roof, which was covered in white geese. The Vietnamese still move at bicycle pace. On the streets, schoolgirls in graceful white *ao dais* cycle by; and women with conical hats sit on top of loads of produce, being wheeled around in bicycle-powered contraptions.

Equally important as the rapprochement with the US is the reopening of the door to China, closed after bitter border warfare in 1979. Though animosity between the Vietnamese and Chinese harks back several thousand years, in late 1991 Hanoi and Beijing agreed to put all that behind them, opening several trading frontiers. Renewed trade has boosted the economy in the north; smuggled goods account for an even larger trade. Two border crossings to China also opened to foreigners. In 1994 the Viet-

VIETNAM IN BRIEF

The Land: Vietnam shares borders with Cambodia, Laos, and China, and features 3,200 km of coastline facing the South China Sea. With an area of 332,000 square km, Vietnam's topography varies from coastal plains to mountain ranges.

Climate: Vietnam has a tropical monsoon climate, with dry and wet seasons. Conditions vary from north to south and with elevation changes.

People: With a population of 72 million, Vietnam is the most densely populated country in Southeast Asia. There's a vigorous campaign to limit children to one or two per family. A variety of ethnic groups inhabit the Central Highlands and northern mountain regions. Population distribution is roughly 80% rural and 20% urban. The largest cities in the north are Hanoi (Greater Hanoi district 2.5 million, urban Hanoi around one million) and Haiphong (Greater Haiphong district 1.5 million, urban area about 500,000); in the center, Danang (500,000), Nha Trang (250,000), and Hué (250,000); in the south, Saigon (Ho Chi Minh district four million, urban Saigon perhaps two million).

Language: Vietnamese is a tonal language that uses a Roman alphabet together with tone markers. Chinese, French, English, and Russian are also spoken. There are over 55 minority languages. The literacy rate is 88%.

Religion: Officially there is none. Percentages on religious beliefs are impossible to come by since the government suppresses religion and does not permit proselytizing. It is believed an estimated 60% of the population adhere to some form of Buddhism, with strong Confucian and Taoist influences. Catholics account for perhaps eight percent of the population; in the Mekong Delta, the Cao Dai and Hoa Hao faiths are strong.

Government: Vietnam is a Socialist Republic under the rule of the Communist Party, the only political party permitted. Its General Secretary is the country's leader, and its Politburo the most powerful government body. The National Assembly rubber-stamps Party decisions.

National Flag: A bright yellow star centered on a blood-red background. The red is symbolic of lives lost in Vietnam's movement toward unification; the star represents a brighter future. The flag is based on the 1954 North Vietnam flag.

Economy: After switching to a market-based economy, Vietnam managed to overcome rampant inflation—the legacy of years of warfare. Vietnam's economy is mainly based on rice farming. Primary agricultural exports are rice, rubber, coffee, and tea. Major industries include chemical fertilizer, cement, textiles, steel, sawn logs, and paper. Vietnam also exports electricity, crude oil, and coal. Seaports are Saigon, Danang, and Haiphong. Per capita annual income is $220. The unit of currency is the dong (US$1=11,000 dong).

Festivals: The most important festival is Tet, determined by the lunar calendar but usually falling in February. Before the onset of Tet, transportation is booked solid. Most businesses close for a five-day period.

namese opened a land crossing with Laos, making it possible to travel by land from Thailand all the way to Hong Kong. After a long period of isolation, Vietnam is open again—to China, to Laos, to Cambodia, to the West. The tiny nation that defeated the French and the Americans—and gave the Chinese a bloody nose—is open for business.

Tourists are welcome in Vietnam, a sign of a return to normalcy after the years of insanity called "war." The Vietnamese bear no grudge against the French or Americans—they're eager to put the past behind them and forge ahead. After being out in the cold for so long, the Vietnamese are keen to rejoin the international community. An international marathon in Saigon and international surfing competition in Danang are efforts in that direction.

Now is the time to go to Vietnam. It's safe, it's inexpensive, it's new, it's exciting. The welcome mat is out, the doors are open, the people are friendly. See for yourself. *Chào Viêtnam!*

THE LAND

GEOGRAPHY

Encompassing 332,000 square km, Vietnam is roughly the size of Italy or Japan. The S-shaped peninsula of Vietnam faces the South China Sea, which the Vietnamese, none too keen on China's presence in the area, call the Eastern Sea. To the north and west, Vietnam is bordered by China, Laos, and Cambodia. The majority of the population is concentrated in two fertile delta areas where rice is intensively cultivated: the Red River Delta in the north, and the Mekong Delta in the south. In between lies a long, narrow coastal plain. The Vietnamese describe their country as a bamboo pole supporting a basket of rice at either end. From north to south, Vietnam stretches about 1,800 km, with its width varying from as little as 60 km in the center to as much as 600 km along the northern border with China.

In terms of geography, history, and culture, Vietnam falls into three divisions—the north, called Bac Bo by the Vietnamese; the center, Trung Bo; and the south, or Nam Bo.

The North: The Red River, descending from China's Yunnan Province, courses through north Vietnam before emptying into the Gulf of Tonkin. It joins several other tributaries near Hanoi, creating a skein of rivers that feed the 15,000-square-km Red River Delta. The Red River is unruly. Dikes built to contain it require constant raising to keep pace with river sedimentation. Flanking the delta is a region of spectacular karst topography with grottoes, caves, and sheer cliffs formed from porous limestone. Sugarloaf peaks rise dramatically from valley floors, similar to parts of southern China or the south of Thailand. Wind and water act on the limestone most dramatically at the islets comprising Halong Bay. Vietnam shares an 1,150-km mountainous border with China to the north. Located in the northwest, the Hoang Lien Son range near the Chinese border features Vietnam's highest peak—Mount Fansipan, elevation 3,134 meters.

The Center: The main features of this area include the coast and highlands. The palm-fringed tropical coastline with white-sand beaches sup-

ports fishing villages. The soil here is dry, rocky, or saline, so the area is not conducive to farming. The Central Highlands, however, do contain plateau areas such as the Pleiku Plateau and Dac Lac Plateau, with rich volcanic soil ideal for growing tea and coffee. Stretching 1,200 km along the western flank of Vietnam is the Truong Son Range in the Central Highlands, which forms Vietnam's border. Vietnam shares a 1,650-km northwestern border with Laos, and a 930-km western border with Cambodia. Parts of the Cambodian border are a subject of dispute between the two nations.

The South: The prominent feature here is the 50,000-square-km Mekong Delta, an alluvial fan formed by branches of the Mekong River. The Mekong courses down from China through Laos and Cambodia into Vietnam and empties into the South China Sea. The Vietnamese call it Cuu Long, or River of the Nine Dragons—a reference to the number of Mekong tributaries, which is actually seven. The Mekong does not pose a great flood threat: when the Mekong swells in monsoon season, it backs up into Tonle Sap Lake in Cambodia. Irrigation in the delta is achieved through an ancient system of canals. Another feature of the delta is swamp and marshland areas—the Plain of Reeds near the Cambodian border, and U-Minh Mangrove Forest, near Camau at the tip of the peninsula.

Coastal Ecology, Offshore Islands

Vietnam has a 3,200 km of coastline, stretching from the Gulf of Tonkin to the Gulf of Thailand. The coastal and marine environment harbors rich biodiversity and resources. Marine habitats remain under severe threat due to unregulated practices like dynamite fishing, overfishing, and coral mining.

Numerous islands lie off the coast. These, together with the Con Dao archipelago, are recognized as Vietnam's. However, other island groups are contested. Phu Quoc Island is claimed by Cambodia. Cambodia and Thailand both claim islands in the Gulf of Thailand; China asserts sovereignty over the Paracels. Spratly Islands are contested in whole or part by China, the Philippines, Malaysia, Brunei, Indonesia, and Taiwan.

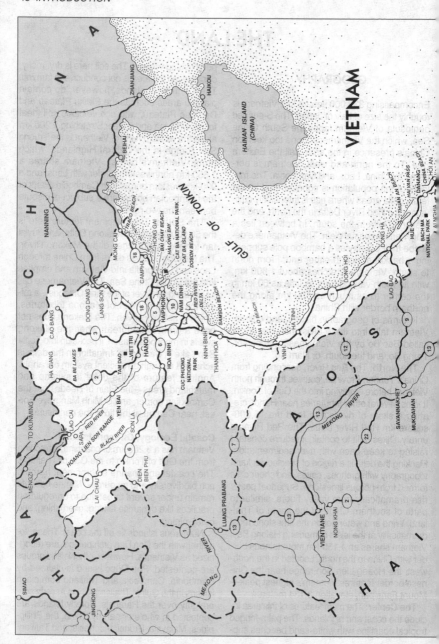

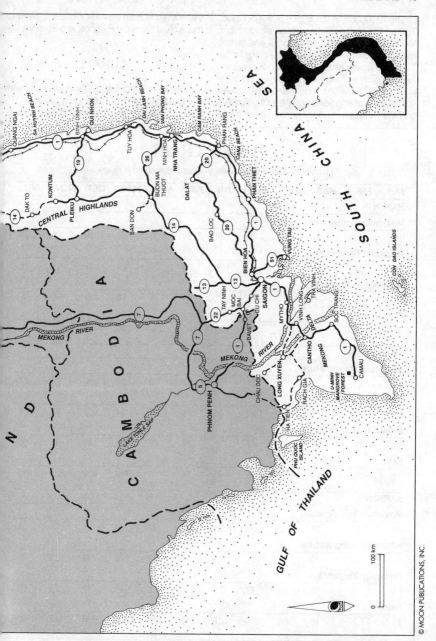

© MOON PUBLICATIONS, INC.

The flashpoint of the region is the Spratlys. Taiwan has built a meteorological station there, Vietnam plans to build lighthouses and fishing harbors, and China is surveying the place for oil. Territorial waters around these islands may be a lucrative source of undersea oil, fish, and other resources. Both Vietnam and China have issued statements claiming sovereignty over the Spratlys and the Paracels, and there have been naval skirmishes in both areas. Official Vietnamese maps must show the Paracels and Spratlys.

CLIMATE

Vietnam has a tropical monsoon climate, with wet and dry seasons. The country straddles different climatic zones—tropical in the north, sub-

CLIMATE CHART

All temperatures in degrees Celsius. Rainfall measured in millimeters.

	JAN.	FEB.	MAR.	APRIL	MAY	JUNE	JULY	AUG.	SEPT.	OCT.	NOV.	DEC.
HANOI												
Maximum Temperature												
	21	21	23	28	32	33	33	32	31	29	26	22
Minimum Temperature												
	14	14	17	20	23	26	26	26	24	22	18	15
Humidity Percentage												
	68	70	76	75	69	71	72	75	73	69	68	67
Rain												
	20	30	40	80	200	240	320	340	260	100	50	25
DANANG												
Maximum Temperature												
	26	27	29	31	33	33	33	22	32	30	29	27
Minimum Temperature												
	17	18	19	22	24	25	25	25	24	22	20	18
Humidity Percentage												
	86	86	86	85	81	77	78	77	84	85	86	86
Rain												
	95	30	10	15	45	40	95	115	440	530	225	210
SAIGON												
Maximum Temperature												
	32	33	34	35	33	32	31	31	31	31	31	31
Minimum Temperature												
	21	22	23	24	24	24	24	24	23	23	23	22
Humidity Percentage												
	61	56	58	60	71	78	80	78	80	80	75	68
Rain												
	15	5	10	50	220	330	310	270	340	260	120	60

tropical in the south. Because of climactic fluctuations, there's no best time to visit the country as a whole, although Nov.-April is the dry season in the north, Central Highlands, and south. Among the best times to visit some major cities: Hanoi, Oct.-Jan.; Hué and Danang, Feb.-April; Saigon, Dalat, and the Mekong Delta, Dec.-March.

Avoid peak monsoon periods as mountain roads may be impassable, and flooding may impede progress on the plains. Stifling heat and humidity strike in summer (June-Aug. in the north and center, March-May in the south). If conditions are not conducive to travel in one part of the country, consider going elsewhere.

The North

There are two distinct seasons in the north—a cold dry winter from November to April, and a hot rainy summer from May to October. Seasonal changes are similar to those in the south of China. In winter, the average temperature is 22° C, dipping to around 16° C in January, the coldest month. It can be chilly in Hanoi around this time, and freezing in the mountains at higher elevations. There is fine rain or continuous drizzle along the north-central coast in February and March falling up to 100 km inland, encompassing Hanoi. Called *crachin* by the Vietnamese, this phenomenon is often accompanied by fog and mist. From May to October the weather is hot and humid with heavy rainfall. Peak times are July and August, when the temperature soars to 33° C. The occasional devastating typhoon or tropical storm may strike at this time.

Central Highlands

Weather patterns in the highlands resemble those in the north more than the south. The highlands experience cooler temperatures, with conditions depending on altitude. At 1,475 me-

ters, Dalat is the coolest place; the annual average temperature is 19° C, rainfall around 2000 mm. Dalat's dry season lasts from December to March. Pleiku, elevation 780 meters, has an annual average temperature of 22° C, and rainfall of almost 2,500 mm a year. Other parts of the Central Highlands get up to 3,300 mm of rainfall per year. The rainy season is April to September, peaking June to August. The dry season is November to April.

Central Coast

Conditions are erratic in the center, which has a transitional climate between that of north and south. Around Hué and Danang, it rains almost without interruption from September to December; flooding can be a problem. Avoid these areas in September and October, which see the most rainfall. Hué is one of the wettest places in Vietnam, with an annual average rainfall approaching 3,000 mm. The best time to visit Hué and Danang is February to April, when rain is less frequent. Temperatures can reach 35° C in June on the coast, and typhoons can be a problem between July and November. Nha Trang is farther south, so it's drier; typhoons may strike here October to December.

The South

With a subtropical climate similar to Thailand's, southern Vietnam stays evenly hot throughout the year and sees the greatest number of sunny days. The thermometer hovers around 27° C. The dry season runs from November to April; lower humidity from December to February makes this the best time to visit. The hottest months are March and April, with stifling heat and unpleasantly high temperatures reaching 35° C. The rainy season runs from May to October and is characterized by midafternoon storms.

FLORA AND FAUNA

Originally, Vietnam was covered in dense forest. Much of the forest cover has been stripped—a process that has accelerated since 1945. From 1945 to 1975, intense warfare and extensive use of defoliants decimated the forest cover and its wildlife residents. The American War against Vietnam marked the first time that military technology was employed to destroy the environment of an entire country. During this strategy of "ecocide," it is estimated the Americans dropped over 85 million liters of defoliants, affecting a quarter of South Vietnam, stripping bare an estimated 10,000 km of land. The most devastated areas were the Ho Chi Minh Trail, the riverbanks in the Mekong Delta, along the Demilitarized Zone, and around US bases and airfields. The north was riddled with craters and shattered by seven million tons of bombs. In the Mekong Delta, more than half the mangrove swamps were destroyed by chemical poisoning and napalm.

Since 1975, population growth and rampant use of resources for rebuilding and firewood has further reduced woodland areas. Forest cover is now estimated at less than 20% of the total land area, down from over 40% in the early 1940s. Reforestation projects cannot keep pace with losses from cultivation and logging operations. Further loss of forest lands may lead to catastrophic soil erosion, mud slides, flooding, and changing climate patterns. These changes, combined with heavy monsoons, may prove an ecological disaster much worse than war.

An attempt to shore up further loss of woodlands through the creation of national parks has proved to be a half-hearted solution. National parks and forest reserves in Vietnam are poorly managed and too small to sustain breeding populations of endangered species. The two largest parks are in the north—Cuc Phuong and Cat Ba National Parks. Ethnic minority groups live within both park boundaries and often hunt wild animals. Other smaller national parks include Ba Be Lakes in the north, Cat Tien Reserve and Bach Ma National Park in the center, and Con Dao Islands in the south. There is a sprinkling of forest preserves, including U-Minh

Mangrove Forest in the south, the former French hill stations of Tam Dao and Bavi in the north, and Bach Ma in the center. Cuc Phuong was the first national park, established in 1962 with the help of the World Wildlife Fund (WWF). The WWF maintains an office in Hanoi and is advising on the creation of more nature reserves.

With wide variation in elevation and climate zones, Vietnam's flora is diverse. At higher elevations in the mountainous northwest are rhododendrons, orchids, needle trees, and rare dwarf bamboos; on the central coast in extremely dry areas you can find cactus plants and pines; in the humid south are zones with tropical fruit trees; and in the far south are mangrove swamps.

Many species of wildlife face decline and probable extinction in Vietnam in the near future, due to loss of forest habitat, widespread hunting and poaching, and an illegal traffic in wildlife. Tigers, for example, are sought for their skins, and other body parts used in Chinese traditional medicine. The government does very little to prevent this kind of traffic.

At present Vietnam's wildlife is diverse, and includes species extinct in other parts of Asia. In the early 1990s a small herd of one of the rarest large mammals in the world—the Javan rhinoceros—was discovered in Vietnam. The one-horn rhino, believed to have been wiped out during the war, was discovered in the swamps and thickets of Cat Tien Reserve, to the southwest of Dalat. The Javan rhino can weigh up to 1,500 kg and is the rarest of the five existing species. Only 50 other individuals survive in a reserve in Java. More than 50 species of mammals live in Vietnam. Among the larger species are the Indian elephant, Himalayan black bear, rhinoceros, clouded leopard, tiger, wild buffalo, antelope, deer, wild boar, and tapir. There is a variety of simian species, including the world's last Delacourt langurs.

Two species of crocodile inhabit Vietnam, estuarine and Siamese, as well as two species of python, reticulated and Indian. These reptiles are found in the U-Minh Mangrove Forest, a huge mangrove swamp at the southern tip of

FIND OF THE CENTURY

In 1992, in the dense rainforests of northern Vietnam, British biologist John MacKinnon stumbled across the skull of a goat-like creature mounted on a post in a hunter's house. It took him only a moment to realize he was looking at an animal unknown to modern science. Subsequent analysis of the specimen's DNA showed this was not only an unknown species but in fact a new genus, now called *Pseudoryx*. The creature has been christened *Pseudoryx nghetinhensis*, meaning false oryx of Nghe Tinh, the former name of the province where it was found. The common name is Vu Quang ox, or *sao la*. David Hulse, head of the World Wildlife Fund, hailed the find as "the biological equivalent of discovering a new planet."

Vu Quang ox

The *Pseudoryx* skulls were discovered in Vu Quang forest reserve, near the Laotian border to the northwest of Vinh. Although it bears superficial similarities to the Arabian oryx of the antelope family, genetic analysis revealed the creature is more closely related to the ox. The world's newest creature may actually be one of the oldest: the Vu Quang ox most likely separated from its closest cattle-like relatives five to 10 million years ago. The creature is thought to be similar to a long-extinct species that once lived in India. Only three other new genuses of large land mammal have been documented this century.

The Vu Quang ox has large eyes, straight sharp horns, and a brownish head patterned with white patches. It developed a narrow concave hoof for negotiating steep, slippery mountain terrain. The ox weighs about 100 kg when fully grown. In June 1994, a live specimen of the Vu Quang ox caused a sensation when it was displayed at a forestry institute in Hanoi. In July of 1994 villagers captured a second specimen in the Vu Quang forest reserve. However, in October, the Vietnamese press reported both captive oxen had died of respiratory and digestive ailments; their keepers knew little of the animal's diet and habitat.

Two new species of primitive deer-like creatures have also been found in north Vietnam. A Vietnamese biologist on the track of the Vu Quang ox found instead the skull of what is believed to be a new species—the slow-running deer, or *Quang khem*. Another variety now named the giant muntjac was discovered; a live specimen is held by a Laotian military group. The giant muntjac is twice as heavy as the common muntjac; the deer-like creature's large canine teeth were probably used in fights between males before it evolved elaborate antlers.

Vu Quang forest reserve may hold other life-forms unknown to science, from fish to plants. This region is so remote even local Tai and Hoa tribes rarely venture into it. The World Wildlife Fund proposes the area be set aside as a nature reserve. So far the Vietnamese government has expanded the reserve from 16,000 to 60,000 hectares and shut down logging in the park. Vu Quang reserve abuts the 365,000-hectare Nakai Nam Theum National Conservation Area in Laos. There are proposals to link the two, creating a large jointly managed reserve.

giant muntjac

BOB RACE / 2

the peninsula. Poisonous snakes include the king cobra, krait, and pit viper.

Very little marine life is protected, though there's a small marine reserve at Cat Ba National Park in the north harboring dolphins and hawksbill turtles, and another at Con Dao Islands National Park.

The prospect for birds is brighter. Many largely escaped the ravages of the Vietnam War by simply relocating. Over 600 species are found in Vietnam. Unusual birds include the white-winged wood duck, the osprey, and the crested Argus pheasant, associated with the legendary phoenix. The eastern saurus crane, regarded as a symbol of longevity and good luck, made an auspicious return to the Mekong Delta. The cranes completely disappeared during the Vietnam War years, but returned in the late 1980s from breeding grounds in Cambodia. A preserve in the Mekong Delta has been established to protect them. Several other bird sanctuaries are scattered around the Mekong Delta, particularly in the U-Minh Mangrove Forest zone.

HISTORY

Excavations show the Red River Delta, the cradle of Vietnamese culture, was inhabited as far back as 5000 BC; stone implements have been discovered in limestone cave dwellings. The Vietnamese people trace their origins to a tribal group known as the Lac Viet, or Dongson culture. The group may have been of Mongolian origin, migrating from southern China and settling in the north of Vietnam at the beginning of the Bronze Age. Large bronze drums unearthed in the Dongson area indicate sophisticated knowledge of mining and casting. The bronze drum was the symbol of the Au Lac Kingdom, which probably reached its zenith in the 3rd century BC, when Co Loa near Hanoi became its citadel.

Chinese Rule

The Red River Delta's early history is dominated by China, which regarded the place as an unruly province. The Han dynasty annexed north Vietnam in the 2nd century BC and named it Annam, or "pacified south." The Chinese rigorously imposed their own model on the Vietnamese. They introduced ancestor worship and Confucianism, established schools to spread Chinese script, and levied high taxes to support a system of mandarin rule. The north remained part of China for close to a thousand years, but the Chinese failed to assimilate the Vietnamese. Chinese rule was repeatedly challenged. Vietnamese rebels have acquired legendary status, women warriors figuring prominently among them. Around 40 AD, the Trung sisters organized nobles to drive out the Chinese. Their rebellion was crushed two years later, and the sisters committed suicide by throwing themselves into a river.

More successful was the rebel Ngo Quyen, a military genius who took on the soldiers of the Chinese Tang dynasty in 939 AD at the battle of Bach Dang River. A flotilla of armed Chinese junks was attempting to reinforce the Chinese garrison in Hanoi. Ngo Quyen laid iron-tipped bamboo stakes in the riverbed: Chinese vessels were impaled on the stakes at low tide, and ambushed by a Vietnamese army. This decisive engagement laid the foundation for an independent state in the north. A new emperor, Dinh Bo Linh, ascended the throne in 967 AD. To remain independent, the Vietnamese paid tribute to the Chinese, a system typical of Chinese relations with other parts of Southeast Asia.

Other Kingdoms

In the south, other kingdoms flourished. In the Mekong Delta area, the Indianized Funan culture ruled from the 1st to 6th centuries AD. Funan's wealth was based on maritime trade; its largest port city was Oc-Eo. Oc-Eo's trade links reached as far as Rome, Persia, India, Burma, and China. Archaeologists have unearthed artifacts from the site that include Roman coins, Indian rings, and Burmese jade. The Funan kingdom mysteriously collapsed, usurped by the pre-Khmer Chenla Empire in the 7th century AD.

Along the coast, another great maritime empire, the Kingdom of Champa, was taking shape. The original capital of Champa was close to Danang. The empire reached its zenith in the 10th and 11th centuries AD. After the Angkor dynasty was established, it absorbed the Chenla Empire; the Cham and Khmers then engaged in several centuries of warfare. The war ended when the Khmers were attacked from the west by the Thais, and the Cham were attacked from the north by the Viets.

VIETNAMESE DYNASTIES

From the 10th century onward, Vietnam was ruled by a series of imperial dynasties, with administrative structures copied from the Chinese. The emperor ruled through the Mandate of Heaven, mediating between the heavens and the earth. Nine ranks of mandarins controlled the armed forces, justice, finance, and public works. The system was elitist and totalitarian, and often did not endear itself to the people, who were at times heavily taxed or coerced into labor projects.

Ly Dynasty (1010-1225)
The Ly dynasty period consolidated Vietnamese independence in the north. The Kingdom of Dai Viet, as it became known, became a formidable military power, invincible from attacks by the Chinese, Cham, and Khmer. Buddhism flourished; the nation's first university (the Temple of Literature in Hanoi) was founded; and embankments for flood control were built along the Red River.

Tran Dynasty (1225-1400)
By the year 1225 three kingdoms occupied the territory of present-day Vietnam. The Dai Viet Kingdom, centered in Hanoi, occupied the north; the Kingdom of Champa, centered in Vijaya, occupied the central coast; and the Khmer Empire, at Angkor, covered the south of Vietnam as well as present-day Cambodia. In the late 13th century, Mongol emperor Kublai Khan invaded Vietnam three times in an attempt to drive south to control the spice routes of Indonesia. Setting aside their differences, the Viet and Chams joined forces to repulse the Mongols. Thus, the Vietnamese were one of only two nations—the other was Egypt—to defeat the Mongols. Military hero Tran Hung Dao repeated a successful tactic by embedding steel-tipped bamboo stakes in the Bach Dang River to sink the Mongol fleet. The last great battle took place in 1287 in the

---

VIETNAMESE DYNASTIES

Ngo dynasty; 939-965; Co Loa (Vinh Phuc)

Dinh dynasty; 968-980; Hoa Lu (Ninh Binh)

Early Le dynasty; 980-1009; Hoa Lu

Ly dynasty; 1010-1225; Thang Long (Hanoi)

Tran dynasty; 1225-1400; Thang Long

Ho dynasty; 1400-1407; Dong Do (Hanoi)

Post Tran dynasty; 1407-1413

Later Le dynasty; 1427-1524; Dong Kinh (Hanoi)+

Mac dynasty; 1527-1592

Northern Trinh; 1539-1787; Hanoi*

Southern Nguyen; 1558-1778; Hué*

Quang Trung; 1787-1792

Tay Son dynasty; 1788-1802; Hué, Saigon, Hanoi**

Nguyen dynasty; 1802-1945; Hué

Under Chinese rule 1414-1427

+Nominal rule until 1788

*By the mid-17th century, Vietnam was divided into feuding clans in the north and south

**The Tay Son brothers ruled from Hué and Saigon Citadels in the south, and Hanoi Citadel in the north

---

Red River valley, where the Vietnamese routed Mongol troops.

Spurred by this victory, the Viet themselves became expansionists, turning on the Chams. The conflict between these two kingdoms dragged on for several centuries. Having exhausted their resources in the campaign against the Cham, the Vietnamese were victimized by the Ming dynasty Chinese, who reestablished direct rule in the early 15th century. The Chinese suppressed Vietnamese culture and language, and plundered Vietnam's resources—precious stones, elephant tusks, rare woods, and spices—for export to China.

Later Le Dynasty (1427-1524)
The harsh rule of the Ming dynasty sparked another great revolt in 1418, led by wealthy

CARVING UP VIETNAM

0   500 km

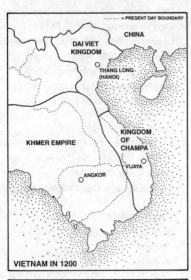

...... = PRESENT DAY BOUNDARY

CHINA

DAI VIET KINGDOM

THANG LONG (HANOI)

KHMER EMPIRE

KINGDOM OF CHAMPA

ANGKOR

VIJAYA

VIETNAM IN 1200

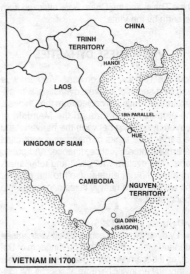

CHINA

TRINH TERRITORY

HANOI

LAOS

18th PARALLEL

KINGDOM OF SIAM

HUE

CAMBODIA

NGUYEN TERRITORY

GIA DINH (SAIGON)

VIETNAM IN 1700

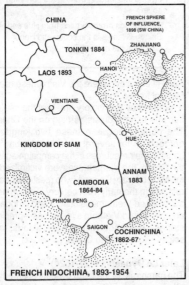

CHINA

FRENCH SPHERE OF INFLUENCE, 1898 (SW CHINA)

TONKIN 1884

ZHANJIANG

LAOS 1893

HANOI

VIENTIANE

HUE

KINGDOM OF SIAM

ANNAM 1883

CAMBODIA 1864-84

PHNOM PENG

SAIGON

COCHINCHINA 1862-67

FRENCH INDOCHINA, 1893-1954

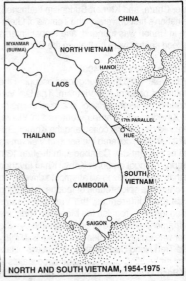

MYANMAR (BURMA)

CHINA

NORTH VIETNAM

HANOI

LAOS

17th PARALLEL

HUE

THAILAND

SOUTH VIETNAM

CAMBODIA

SAIGON

NORTH AND SOUTH VIETNAM, 1954-1975

landowner Le Loi, whose forces finally defeated the Chinese in 1426. Two years later, China recognized Vietnam's independence. Le Loi declared himself Emperor Le Thai To, and established his new capital at Hanoi. The Later Le dynasty is viewed as a golden age in Vietnamese history, as Vietnam tried to break away from Chinese civilization. The Vietnamese language gained favor with scholars, although Chinese remained the language of the elite.

In this period the Vietnamese began expanding south, crushing the Kingdom of Champa in 1471. In the mid-15th century Angkor fell to the Thais, and the Khmer capital was reestablished at Phnom Penh. The Khmers asked the Vietnamese for help against the Thais—the Vietnamese agreed in return for the right to settle the area of Saigon.

Trinh and Nguyen Dynasties

As Vietnamese settlers moved south from the capital of Hanoi, the ruling Le dynasty lost control. In 1620, the Nguyen family broke from the empire and established their own dynasty, ruling from Hué. By the mid-17th century Vietnam was divided into north and south at the 18th Parallel, controlled by two clans, the Trinh and the Nguyen. Feuding between them continued into the 18th century. The southern Nguyen clan extended Vietnamese control through the Mekong Delta, administered from the citadel at Gia Dinh (Saigon). By the early 18th century, the Viet controlled the territory from the Chinese frontier to the Gulf of Thailand.

During the period of the Trinh and Nguyen dynasties, the first contacts were made with Western traders. In the early 16th century Portuguese sailors set up a trading colony at Faifo (Hoi An). In the early 17th century the Dutch were allowed to establish trading posts in the north. Interest in trading with Vietnam dropped off by the late 17th century, but foreign missionaries remained. Among them were Franciscan missionaries from the Philippines and Jesuits expelled from Japan. The first French to visit Vietnam were missionaries who dabbled in politics. In fact, both the Trinh and the Nguyen clans negotiated military supplies through missionaries—the Portuguese and French supporting the south, the Dutch supporting the north.

Tay Son Rebellion

In 1765 three brothers from a merchant family—dubbed the Tay Son rebels—precipitated a popular revolt against corrupt landlords and mandarins in central Vietnam. The Tay Son revolt quickly spread south, crushing the Nguyen clan in Saigon in 1783. The royal family was executed, with the exception of Prince Nguyen Anh, who fled to the French mission in Ha Tien. In the north, the Tay Son overpowered the Trinh clan, bringing the entire country under the aegis of the Tay Son brothers by 1787.

ROUGH JUSTICE

After assuming power in 1802, new emperor Gia Long ordered his soldiers to exhume the body of the last of the Tay Son brothers and urinate upon it in front of the deceased's wife and son. Mother and child were subsequently torn apart by elephants.

Such rough justice was common in Vietnam's past. Trampling by elephants was the fate of adulterous women under the mandarin system. Thieves were beheaded with a sword, as were foreign missionaries who incurred the wrath of the emperor. The emperor's word was final, as he ruled with the Mandate of Heaven.

This legal system was bolstered by Confucian ethics—the mandarins kowtowed to the emperor, and ordinary folk prostrated themselves to the mandarins. The despotism, corruption, and flaunted wealth of some of the Nguyen dynasty emperors and mandarins did not endear them to the average Vietnamese, who railed against social injustices.

When the French maintained royal rule as a convenience, ordinary Vietnamese resented the mandarins even more, considering them collaborators with the French. As part of their "civilizing mission," the French introduced the Napoleonic code, claiming they'd eliminated backward forms of justice. However, dissidents in the French colonial era could be sentenced to 10 years, life imprisonment, or even death for simply distributing anti-French leaflets. The French imported the guillotine to behead political offenders in public, and established notorious penal colonies like Poulo Condore in the South China Sea.

Quang Trung, the brother who ruled in the north, decisively stopped yet another Chinese advance in 1788, routing a 200,000-strong army near Hanoi. This feat is one of the most celebrated in Vietnamese history, adding Quang Trung's name to the roster of heroes. Quang Trung introduced land reform, a fairer system of taxation, and a new system of education. After this promising start, he died in 1792, leaving the north in great confusion.

Nguyen Dynasty

Meanwhile, the exiled Prince Nguyen Anh was befriended by Pierre Pigneau de Béhaine, an 18th-century Jesuit missionary who dreamed of building a French empire in Asia. Pigneau de Béhaine negotiated a treaty on Nguyen Anh's behalf with Louis XVI in 1787 for military assistance. Louis XVI soon changed his mind, but the undaunted Pigneau de Béhaine recruited a force of 400 French deserters in India and sailed back to Vietnam in 1789 on two ships loaded with weapons. Nguyen Anh built up the French-trained army of mercenaries, pushing back the Tay Son rebels in 1799 and finally defeating them in 1801. A year later, after subduing the far north, Nguyen Anh proclaimed himself Emperor Gia Long, ruling from Hué. This was the first time a single court controlled Vietnam from north to south. This called for a change of name: a combination of the names Annam (north) and Viet Thuong (south) resulted in the new Viet Nam.

Gia Long ushered in the era of the last Vietnamese dynasty, the Nguyen dynasty (1802-1945), with its capital in Hué. Gia Long embarked on a series of ambitious projects. He built the Mandarin Road connecting Hanoi to Saigon, and star-shaped citadels in provincial capitals along the designs of French military architect Vauban. The Nguyen dynasty headquartered itself in Hué's Royal City, off-limits to most mortals—only mandarins, princesses, and scholars resided there. In return for their military assistance, French merchants were allowed commercial concessions, and thus gained a foothold in Vietnam.

FRENCH COLONIAL ERA

Emperor Minh Mang, Gia Long's successor, reversed the policies of his father, drawing trade concessions to foreigners and issuing an imperial edict in 1825 outlawing Christian proselytizing. Christianity interfered with Confucian ethics maintained by the court as a system of ruling the peasants. The Vatican was opposed to ancestor worship (one of the cornerstones of Confucianism) and the polygamy the emperor practiced. Both of Minh Mang's successors—Thieu Tri and Tu Duc—were anti-Christian. Emperor Tu Duc ordered the execution of 25 European priests, 300 Vietnamese priests, and thousands of Vietnamese Catholics from 1848 to 1860.

The French used these attacks as a pretext for unleashing a military campaign against Vietnam. They attacked Danang twice, in 1847 and 1858. After the second attack, 14 battleships from France and the Spanish Philippines rode monsoon winds south toward Saigon. Upon reaching Saigon in 1859, the French used explosives to breach the walls of Gia Dinh Citadel and captured it. Counterattacks by the Vietnamese using elephants proved futile. In 1862

Hué Cathedral features a blend of Oriental and French architecture.

the French signed a treaty with Emperor Tu Duc to take over three southern provinces, to be known as the colony of Cochinchina. Several ports were opened to French and Spanish commerce, and missionaries were promised the freedom to disseminate their faith throughout the country. By 1867, the Mekong Delta area was added to Cochinchina. In 1873, French forces started making inroads into Tonkin with an attack on Hanoi citadel; in 1883 they attacked Hué citadel in central Vietnam. By 1887 the French controlled the entire peninsula, encompassing the colony of Cochinchina and the protectorates of Tonkin, Annam, and Cambodia. The protectorate of Laos was added in 1893.

The French governed Cochinchina directly as a colony. In Annam and Tonkin protectorates they found it expedient to allow emperors of the Nguyen dynasty to remain as puppets. Although the administrative mandarin system remained in place in Tonkin and Annam, real power was held by the French Senior Resident, supposedly only a technical adviser to the mandarins. The Senior Resident was an assistant to the governor-general located in each protectorate.

Exploiting Indochina

Governor-general Paul Bert, in his short tenure in Hanoi in the mid-1880s, set about organizing France's *mission civilisatrice* (civilizing mission) in the new colonies. The French justified their rule of Indochina by claiming, as Francis Garnier phrased it, that France was bringing "into light and liberty the races and peoples still enslaved

THE HIGH LIFE

The French have a reputation as poor colonizers—repressive, racist, self-interested. In Vietnam they imported their lifestyle lock, stock, and barrel. Here the French lifestyle could be maintained at lavish levels; a bevy of domestic servants was cheap. Upon arrival in Haiphong or Saigon, the French began assembling domestics—cook, amah (nanny), coachman, laundry boy, rickshaw driver, gardener, errand boy, and assorted other coolies. In the days before electric fans, the French even employed human fan wavers. Since the French favored white—wearing everything from white drill suits to white cork hats—there was plenty of work for the laundry boy. Hitting domestics was common; whipping and beating plantation employees was standard.

Liberated from domestic worries, French settlers and civil servants tended to business affairs and the pursuit of leisure. After a short work day with a long siesta, the evening was free for socializing at cafés, restaurants, or the theater. For the more decadent, perhaps a visit to a casino, brothel, or opium den. By the 1920s, Indochina was the most profitable of all French overseas possessions. As it became richer from trade, further refinements arrived. In the major cities, the French set up exclusive clubs like the Cercle Sportif, with a pool, tennis courts, and dining area. Journalist Howard Sochurek describes the scene in 1950:

In the private homes, the French traditions were carried on. If you went to dinner, it was always formal. You dressed in a white jacket and black trousers. The generals and the top military of course observed this very strictly. So if you attended a dinner thrown by de Lattre it was usually in a chandeliered governor's house, with many, many servants, great long tables, the finest of cutlery and glassware. It was like something out of the past. The women were some of the most exotic in the world, mixtures of French and Vietnamese. Fantastic creatures. They would all come dressed to the hilt, driving up in their Citroëns. Nobody worked very hard. All the finest imports were available—caviar, French wines and champagnes. A fantastically easy and gracious way of life, because of the tremendous number of servants and the wealth they got out of the rubber plantations and the trading of rice and the other businesses. In 1950, they still had all that.

by ignorance and despotism." However, it's dubious whether the French created much more than a new version of slavery. Education of the Vietnamese was a half-hearted affair—proper education could create potential revolutionaries, and later, it did. Instituting the French penal code largely meant turning Indochina into a police state. A network of French security forces ruthlessly snuffed out any protest. Only in Cochinchina did a select few Vietnamese have the right to vote.

Paul Doumer, who became governor-general of Indochina in 1897, single-handedly put the French possessions on a profitable basis during his five years in power—building roads, bridges, lighthouses, and railways, and raising revenues through a system of taxes and customs duties. His most lucrative endeavor was the creation of state monopolies on salt, alcohol, and opium. Insidiously, Doumer built an opium refinery in Saigon that concocted a new faster-burning blend to encourage consumption. Vietnamese addiction rose sharply, and opium sales accounted for one third of the colonial administration's income. Doumer assisted in the creation of powerful financial interests, headed by the Banque de l'Indochine, which issued its own Indochinese currency. Such advances put the colonies on a semi-autonomous basis. By the end of Doumer's term in 1902, Hanoi was the capital of the French Indochinese Union.

The French were also keen on exploiting the mineral and lumber resources in the remote provinces of Yunnan and Guangxi in southern China—a French zone of interest after 1898. Tonkin, much closer to the rugged mountainous southwest of China than the treaty ports of Shanghai or Canton, was the key to ferreting away this wealth. By 1900 several parts of Yunnan were opened to French trade, and by 1910 a French-engineered railroad connected Kunming with Hanoi and Haiphong.

By the 1920s, near-slave labor had transformed the jungles of Indochina with bridges, highways, harbors, and canals. Vietnam supplied raw materials to fuel French industrialization. Rice was exported despite starvation of local people. Rubber was the second biggest export of the 1920s. At one Michelin Tire Company plantation, 12,000 of 45,000 indentured workers died from malaria, dysentery, or malnutrition between 1917 and 1944. Small wonder then the Vietnamese would flee at the approach of plantation recruiters. Many Vietnamese perished working in substandard conditions on tea or coffee plantations, or in coal or tin mines. Appropriation of land for mines or other uses caused a breakdown in the land ownership system among the peasantry, and the system of taxes caused minor uprisings.

Meanwhile, the Nguyen dynasty lumbered along, with a rapid turnover of emperors as each fell out of favor with the French. The polygamous Emperor Tu Duc left behind a large imperial family, opening the way for power struggles. The dissident Emperor Ham Nghi resisted the French, and was captured and exiled to Algeria. The French handpicked his successor, Dong Khanh. Another dissident, Emperor Duy Tan, staged a revolt against French rule in 1916; for his pains, he was also exiled. In 1925 his grandson Bao Dai became emperor. Schooled in France, Bao Dai retained a fondness for a decadent French lifestyle. He assumed the throne in 1932, and remained emperor during the Japanese occupation from 1940 to 1945. Although the French attempted to revive Bao Dai's reign, he was essentially out of the picture after 1945.

The Vietminh

Communism in Vietnam is dominated by the personality of Ho Chi Minh, who left Vietnam in 1911 and spent a lengthy period in Western Europe, where he became a founding member of the French Communist Party in 1920. Ho studied revolutionary strategy in Moscow, and moved on to China and Thailand before returning to Vietnam. In 1930 Ho Chi Minh and his comrades formed the Indochinese Communist Party in Hong Kong.

In 1940 Japan invaded Vietnam. At first the Japanese cooperated with the pro-German Vichy French, but assumed direct control of Vietnam six months before WW II ended. In 1941 Ho Chi Minh slipped back into Vietnam for the first time in almost 30 years, founding the Vietminh (the League for the Independence of Vietnam) as a nationalist movement to fight the Japanese. In 1942, Ho stepped back across the Chinese border, and was imprisoned by the Nationalist Chinese for a year. He got out by making a deal to provide information on the Japanese.

When Japan surrendered in August 1945, the Allies agreed that Britain would occupy south Vietnam and the Nationalist Chinese would take over the north. The country was in complete chaos. Before the Chinese arrived, the Vietminh marched down to liberate Hanoi. On 2 September 1945, Ho Chi Minh proclaimed the Democratic Republic of Vietnam. This statement was not officially recognized internationally. Nevertheless, the last emperor of Vietnam, Bao Dai, complied with Ho Chi Minh's demands to abdicate, and left for exile in France. In negotiations with the French, Ho Chi Minh agreed to the return of 25,000 French colonial troops in the north for a period of five years rather than face occupation by the Nationalist Chinese. To justify his decision to angry comrades, Ho evoked ancient fears of the Chinese invader: "The last time the Chinese came, they stayed a thousand years. The French are foreigners. They are weak. Colonialism is dying. The white man is finished in Asia. As for me, I prefer to sniff French shit for five years than eat Chinese shit for the rest of my life."

Meanwhile the south quickly fell again into French hands. British troops—mainly Gurkhas—helped a small force of French paratroopers freed from prison gain control. Incredibly, the British also enlisted the help of defeated Japanese troops to fight Vietnamese insurgents. Some 35,000 French reinforcements arrived in October 1945, marching off through the Mekong delta and into the highlands to gain control of the south. They were constantly harassed by guerrillas as the retreating Vietminh burned villages and destroyed bridges. The French could take Vietnamese territory, but could not hold it. Nevertheless, by early 1945, French General Jacques Leclerc claimed victory in the south.

In the north, the arrangement of a "free" Vietnamese state within the French Union (as the French empire was now called) was doomed to failure. In November 1946, in a dispute over the collection of customs duties, the Vietminh clashed with the French in Haiphong. The French responded by bombing Haiphong, with great loss of civilian life. By December Hanoi too was a battleground, with buildings aflame and tanks rumbling through the streets. The Vietminh fled to the hills of the north, and the First Indochina War was under way.

Ho Chi Minh's regime was soon recognized by the Soviet Union and the new government of Mao Zedong in China. Chinese communists began to supply arms and logistical assistance to the Vietminh across the border. In 1950 the Vietminh attacked a French force at Cao Bang near the Chinese border. The French garrison was wiped out, and the Vietminh made off with a great stock of weapons. The weary French were increasingly funded by a US obsessed with communist expansion. By 1954, the US was paying for 80% of France's Indochina military expenditure.

From an obscure, poorly armed force, the Vietminh quickly grew into a formidable military threat. Their commitment to the cause of an independent Vietnam was absolute. As Ho Chi Minh warned a French official, "You can kill 10 of my men for every one I kill of yours, but even at those odds, I will win and you will lose." This proved remarkably prophetic in the ensuing battles against the French and Americans—the north Vietnamese suffered heavy losses, but their motivation remained strong. Realizing their losses would be catastrophic in conventional battles, the Vietminh adopted guerrilla tactics. Ho Chi Minh outlined this approach in an interview in 1946 when he compared the French to an elephant, and the Vietnamese to a tiger: "When the elephant is strong and rested near his base we will retreat. And if the tiger ever pauses, the elephant will impale him on his mighty tusks. But the tiger will not pause and the elephant will die of exhaustion and loss of blood." It remained for brilliant military strategist General Vo Nguyen Giap to implement this approach.

Dien Bien Phu

In 1954, the French sought to block Vietminh expansion into Laos by dropping six battalions of paratroopers into Dien Bien Phu, near the Laos border. The French garrison could receive supplies only by air and required 200 tons of supplies a day. Vietminh General Vo Nguyen Giap hauled heavy artillery onto the surrounding peaks, a feat the French had considered impossible. The Vietminh artillery could fire on the airfield, effectively cutting off the French garrison. After 55 days of intense bombardment, on 7

May 1954, 10,000 starving French troops surrended to the Vietminh.

Partition

The next morning nine delegations met in Geneva to discuss settlements in Indochina and Korea. In Vietnam, the solution presented proved little more than a ceasefire. Zhou Enlai, representing the Chinese delegation, infuriated Vietminh negotiator Pham Van Dong by proposing a partition of Vietnam. Zhou Enlai had China's interests in mind—it suited China to have a weaker, divided Vietnam at its doorstep.

The Geneva Accords of 22 July 1954 divided Vietnam in two at the 17th parallel. In the north the communists ruled under Ho Chi Minh; the south fell under the rule of Catholic leader Ngo Dinh Diem. Diem returned from self-imposed exile at Maryknoll Seminary in New Jersey in July 1954 to become Prime Minister of South Vietnam. Diem had previously served under Emperor Bao Dai; the US backed his rise to power.

The Geneva Accord called for withdrawal of French troops from the north and Vietminh troops from the south; free elections would be held in 1956 to reunify Vietnam. Civilians and soldiers had nine months to move freely between the two areas. An estimated 850,000, mostly Catholic Vietnamese, left the north for the south, while about 80,000 people journeyed north. Ho Chi Minh and other communist leaders launched a land reform campaign in the north—thousands of real and purported landlords were tried before kangaroo courts and shot, their families left to starve. Diem staged a rigged election in 1955 to oust Bao Dai and justify his rule of the south. When Diem and the US realized Ho Chi Minh would prevail in any honest election, the South Vietnamese announced they had no intention of honoring the Accords.

AMERICAN INTERVENTION

Trouble in the South

Vietnam became the linchpin in the US attempt to stop communist expansion in Southeast Asia. The late 1940s and early 1950s were the time of the Cold War, when the Soviet Union and the United States squared off across the globe. After the communist takeover of China in 1949 and the

start of the Korean War in 1950, anticommunist hysteria reached fever-pitch in the United States. Ho Chi Minh was identified as part of the communist conspiracy, cleverly manipulated by Moscow. In 1954 President Dwight Eisenhower expounded the "domino theory": if Vietnam succumbed to communism, other Asian nations would fall like dominoes, until even Australia was threatened. American strategy was to build up the South Vietnamese army so it could prevent invasion from the north across the 17th parallel. To this end, from 1956 on, American advisers were sent to the south to train the Army of the Republic of Vietnam (ARVN).

Meanwhile, resistance to Diem developed under remnants of the Vietminh who'd drifted south. They became known as Vietcong, short for Viet Nam Cong San (Vietnamese Communist), at first a derogatory term to describe all the South Vietnamese groups opposed to President Diem in the 1960s. The name was coined by Diem's publicists, who wished to avoid the heroic associations Vietminh conferred. In the north, the Vietcong was christened the National Liberation Front (NLF) by Ho Chi Minh in 1960, a clear indication the north was backing an open war in the south. The Vietminh, now fully communist-dominated, metamorphosed into the North Vietnamese Army (NVA), which operated either with Vietcong or in separate NVA units. Although the NLF (Vietcong) claimed to be independent of the NVA, the north provided direction and funding.

The Demise of Diem

In the early '60s President Ngo Dinh Diem's totalitarian regime was running into problems in the south. The Vietcong were making progress in rural villages, carrying out propaganda work and targeting village officials for selective assassination. By 1961 the Vietcong claimed to control large swaths of the countryside. Diem and his brother Nhu, head of the feared security forces, employed a Strategic Hamlets Program to try to win back control. The idea, employed by the US in the Philippines during the Spanish-American War and the British in Malayasia in the '50s, was to put farmers into fortified villages surrounded by ditches, barbed wire, and spiked bamboo. This would supposedly cut them off from the Vietcong. The Vietnamese resented being uprooted and forced to move into what seemed to be concentration camps. When the Vietcong attacked, the farmers often opened the gates and let them in.

US President John Kennedy came under increasing pressure to boost support for Diem. In 1961, the number of US advisers in Vietnam stood at 700; within two years it was up to 16,000. Increasingly, American "advisers" went into combat and on bombing missions. US advisers believed South Vietnamese troops were not disciplined enough to defeat the Vietcong. In a 1963 engagement near Mytho, a small Vietcong force inflicted heavy casualties on a larger ARVN force.

In 1963, Diem's Catholic regime increased its vicious repression of Buddhists in the south. In May 1963 Buddhists were refused permission to display Buddhist flags or meet on the anniversary of Buddha's birthday. Nine people were killed as government troops fired on a protest march. The world was shocked by televised images of a protesting monk who set himself on fire. When Diem began exploring negotiations with Hanoi, the US backed a coup that overthrew the government and assassinated Diem and Ngu.

The elimination of Diem did nothing to stop the political rot in South Vietnam: a series of bungling military juntas succeeded one another. Generals Ky and Thieu held the reins from 1965 on.

The American War

Although it's called the Vietnam War by the Western media, the Vietnamese have seen so many wars they refer to this one as the American War. In June 1964, President Johnson ordered an attack on the North by US bombers because of "renewed hostile actions against United States ships on the high seas in the Gulf of Tonkin." He was referring to an unsuccessful action by three North Vietnamese patrol boats that fired on the USS *Maddox*, deployed "to test the effectiveness of radar installations in the north." US bombers attacked ports and oil storage installations in North Vietnam. After the attack, US Congress approved the Gulf of Tonkin Resolution giving the president the power to "take all necessary measures to repel any armed attacks against the forces of the US and further aggression."

Thus, simmering since 1954, the Second Indochina War at last broke out. American involvement escalated rapidly. Some 3,500 Marines landed in Danang in March 1965, ostensibly to protect the airfield. By the end of 1965 there were nearly 200,000 US soldiers in Vietnam; by the end of 1966 there were double that number; by the beginning of 1968 some 520,000 American troops occupied the country. The Americans tried to set up a series of firebases as a barrier along the 17th parallel, but the NVA bypassed the block, pouring troops and supplies down the Ho Chi Minh Trail through the mountains of Laos and Cambodia.

The US invited Allied nations to rally round the flag. Australia, New Zealand, South Korea, and Thailand sent token forces; by the end of 1967 there were 8,300 Australian troops and 4,500 Korean troops in Vietnam. Meanwhile, in the north, Hanoi was receiving armaments and advice from the Russians and Chinese. Heavy arms from China were transported to North Vietnam along a railway line from Nanning built in the 1950s.

US helicopter in the Central Highlands

PHOTO COURTESY OF UPI

Apocalypse Now

Although they had far superior firepower, the Americans—like the French before them—were frustrated by their failure to lure the North Vietnamese into conventional battle. Guerrillas would strike and then disappear into the local community or a vast tunnel network. The Vietcong maintained political control of many vil-

THE HO CHI MINH TRAIL

The Ho Chi Minh Trail was never a single trail. It was, instead, a network of jungle paths, sometimes up to a dozen branches, running along the spine of the Truong Son mountain range heading through the jungles of Laos and Cambodia. The trail network was the major reason the war spilled over into Laos and Cambodia. And it was the key to North Vietnam's success.

The Vietcong could survive on between 15 to 60 tons of supplies a day coming down the trail. In 1959, when the trail was first used, the journey took up to six months. Later in the war, the journey required six weeks; toward the end of the war supplies could move in little more than a week on an improved crushed stone surface. By then, the Ho Chi Minh Trail comprised some 15,000 km of camouflaged roadway.

The trail was built and maintained by 300,000 full-time workers and many other part-time peasants. Perils along the trail were many. During the rainy season, streams would turn into rapids, and floods would wash away the trails. In the dense forests, marchers were so weighed down by rain-sodden packs they couldn't stand upright. Flimsy meter-wide bridges with bamboo planks and rope handrails were strung over crossings, then easily dismantled to avoid detection. Malaria and amoebic dysentery were a constant threat. It is believed 10% of those who set out in the early days died from disease.

There were several modes of travel on the trail. In the beginning, most traveled on foot, wearing Ho Chi Minh sandals made from worn truck tires. This footwear left soldiers susceptible to snakebite and leeches, so they carried antivenin. Troops carried cooked rice rations in a linen tube hung around the body. Pack animals were sometimes used on the trail, as well as industrial-strength bicycles. The bicycles were copied or adapted from French models, and were first used to ferry supplies at Dien Bien Phu. Reinforced cargo bicycles, maneuvered with extended handlebars, could carry 200 kilos of rice. In the last stages of trail use, 10,000 Chinese and Russian trucks were deployed, each carrying up to six tons of supplies.

American forces, using high-tech weaponry to destroy bridges, roads, and railways, were unable to prevent thousands of enemy soldiers from advancing on bicycles. When they encountered a downed bridge, the North Vietnamese simply formed a human chain and manhandled their bikes across the span. A modern army would have been immobilized, with its trucks and tanks unable to continue till the bridge was restored.

Attacks on the Ho Chi Minh Trail by US bombers had limited success. A B-52 bomber could drop a hundred 350-kg bombs in 30 seconds, clearing a 1.5-km swath through the jungle, but the effort was not worth the result. It's estimated the raids stopped only one in every hundred North Vietnamese. Trucks moved along the trail by night. In an effort to stop them, the Americans dropped hundreds of battery-powered sensors resembling plants. The Vietnamese fooled these acoustic sensors by using tape recordings of trucks; "sniffer" sensors intended to detect humans were easily deceived by leaking bags of buffalo urine hung from trees. Vietnamese engineers built submerged pontoon bridges about 30 cm underwater to avoid aerial detection, and the trail was well camouflaged. By 1970, the trail was defended by antiaircraft guns. In 1971, when American General Creighton Abrams tried to cut the trail west of the DMZ using ARVN troops in helicopters, half his troops were killed or wounded and Abrams was forced to retreat.

Although several touring agencies claim to show travelers the trail, it's dubious whether the trail still exists. Much of its length has been reclaimed by the jungle, though a section between Khe Sanh and Aluoi via Dakrong Bridge was paved with Cuban assistance in the mid-1970s. Trekking in remote areas is dangerous due to the massive amount of unexploded ordnance. Minor trails are still maintained and active, used for smuggling goods from Laos and Cambodia into Vietnam. The bounty travels on the backs of porters, just as before. As one Hanoi official put it: "The Vietnamese have a very long tradition of guerrilla warfare. They are good at carrying things on their backs."

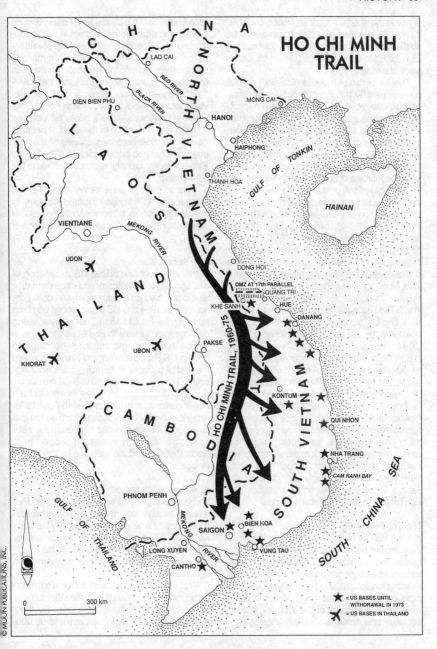

HO CHI MINH TRAIL

CHINA

LAO CAI

RED RIVER

BLACK RIVER

DIEN BIEN PHU

MONG CAI

NORTH VIETNAM

HANOI

HAIPHONG

GULF OF TONKIN

THANH HOA

HAINAN

LAOS

VIENTIANE

MEKONG RIVER

UDON

DONG HOI

DMZ AT 17th PARALLEL

QUANG TRI

KHE SANH

HUE

DANANG

THAILAND

PAKSE

HO CHI MINH TRAIL, 1960–75

UBON

KHORAT

KONTUM

QUI NHON

CAMBODIA

NHA TRANG

CAM RANH BAY

SOUTH VIETNAM

GULF

OF

THAILAND

PHNOM PENH

MEKONG

SAIGON

BIEN HOA

SOUTH CHINA SEA

LONG XUYEN

RIVER

VUNG TAU

CANTHO

0   300 km

★ = US BASES UNTIL
    WITHDRAWAL IN 1973

✈ = US BASES IN THAILAND

© MOON PUBLICATIONS, INC.

lages in the south. American troops could not distinguish between guerrillas and villagers. US soldiers on patrol often treated any Vietnamese as a threat to be liquidated. Civilian casualties were alarmingly high.

The American use of chemical warfare was condemned by the international community. Among chemical devices used were napalm, Agent Orange, and Agent Blue. The Americans also launched sustained bombing raids. During the years of the Rolling Thunder air campaign of 1965-68, well over seven million tons of bombs were dropped over Vietnam and Laos—twice the tonnage of bombs dropped during all of WW II. Against this onslaught, the Vietcong and the NVA countered with a degree of organization and dedication unparalleled in human history. Theirs was a 50-year struggle, one that had achieved only partial success in 1954. Only their degree of dedication could have withstood the exceedingly high casualty rates sustained: few of those within the Vietcong ranks in 1964 were alive when the war ended.

Exactly who was winning the war was difficult to tell. The first significant engagement between NVA and US troops occurred at Khe Sanh in late 1967. By January 1968, a force of 6,000 US Marines and ARVN forces were holed up at Khe Sanh near the Lao border, surrounded by an estimated 40,000 NVA troops. The US military feared another Dien Bien Phu, though unlike the French, the Americans had far superior air support. The battle became merely a testing ground, assuming an importance it hardly deserved. Neither side could claim victory at Khe Sanh. The Americans held their ground, but abandoned the base a few months later, calling it strategically unimportant. Though NVA losses were very heavy, the north later claimed Khe Sanh a victory, as it served as a major diversion for the 1968 Tet Offensive.

The Tet Offensive

In 1968 Ho Chi Minh was ailing, and the North Vietnamese believed it would be his last Tet celebration. So instead of observing the traditional cease-fire period for the Lunar New Year, Vietcong forces unleashed over 100 separate attacks on targets across South Vietnam on 31 January. The audacity of the Vietcong attacks astounded the Americans. In Hué, Vietcong and NVA troops held the citadel for 24 days. Groups of Vietcong attacked key targets in Saigon, including Tan Son Nhat air base, the presidential palace, and the radio station. Commandos blasted their way into the American Embassy in an attack that lasted six hours. Later that day— 1 February—the American public watched television footage of South Vietnamese Police Chief General Loan walk up to a captured Vietcong suspect and shoot him in the head. It became one of the most notorious images of the war, one that changed public opinion in the United States. Clearly, brutality was not confined to the communists.

Vietcong losses were heavy in the Tet Offensive, and NVA troops infiltrated the south in increasing numbers to replace Vietcong units. In September 1969, Ho Chi Minh died at the age of 79.

The Secret War

There was never an official US declaration of war against North Vietnam, and little information was dispensed on exactly what was going on. As early as 1964, the US began secret bombing raids on the Ho Chi Minh Trail in Laos, using old American planes with Royal Lao markings. In March 1969, two months after he came to power, US President Richard Nixon approved the first of a series of bombing raids on Cambodia. Total secrecy applied to B-52 cross-border raids directed at what was thought to be a major communist headquarters. In April 1970, American and ARVN troops pushed 30 km into Cambodia. No communist headquarters were found; the raid only increased support from North Vietnam and the Vietcong for the Khmer Rouge.

American Withdrawal

Vietnam was the first fully televised war. Pictures of napalm victims and summary execution stunned the world. News of the My Lai Massacre in 1968 sent out greater shock waves. There were large demonstrations in the West, particularly in Western Europe, against American involvement.

President Richard Nixon advocated "Vietnamization," which called for South Vietnamese troops to fight the war on their own. By 1972 American troop strength was down to 95,000,

An American official punches a Vietnamese trying to board an evacuation airplane in Nha Trang.

the bulk of them support troops. The Americans concentrated on supplying heavy weapons to the South Vietnamese. Meanwhile, peace talks dragged on in Paris throughout 1972. In response to a North Vietnamese offensive across the 17th parallel, Nixon ordered the bombing of Haiphong and Hanoi by 200 B-52s during the 1972 Christmas season. There was great devastation on the ground, and heavy bomber losses too, as the Vietnamese wielded Russian-supplied surface-to-air missiles. Both the Russians and the Chinese, though not speaking with each other, supplied North Vietnam with sophisticated weapons. The North Vietnamese also depended on shipments of Chinese rice to feed their population.

On 27 January 1973 a ceasefire was finally agreed upon in Paris. By the end of March the last US combat forces had left Vietnam, and America's messy misadventures in Indochina came to an end. South Vietnamese President Nguyen Van Thieu retained a well-equipped army of a million men, but morale was low.

The Fall of Saigon

As with the Geneva Accord, the peace did not hold. Negotiations between north and south went nowhere. In January 1974 Thieu announced the war had resumed, and his army attacked communist positions. On 10 March 1975 the NVA launched a major offensive, routing southern troops. Saigon fell on 30 April 1975, the last US personnel departing by helicopter from the roof of the US Embassy. After nearly 30 years of warfare, Vietnam was unified, independent, and communist. The two halves of Vietnam formally unified as the Socialist Republic of Vietnam (SRV) on 2 July 1976.

AFTER UNIFICATION

Pariah State

The fruits of victory were bitter. At least three million Vietnamese were killed between 1954 and 1975. In 1995 Hanoi officials released statistics accounting for 1.1 million communist soldiers dead, and two million Vietnamese civilians killed. Vietnam was left with an appalling legacy of bomb craters and unexploded ordnance. Lives were devastated. The infrastructure lay in ruins, making the rebuilding of roads, railways, schools, and hospitals a high priority. The new government hoped for Western aid; Nixon had promised three billion dollars in war reparations, but no money was forthcoming. Instead the US imposed an economic embargo on Vietnam, pressuring other Western nations to adhere to it.

The North Vietnamese rounded up southerners who'd played active roles in the war and threw them into re-education camps. Even so, they showed remarkable restraint toward their former enemies—most inmates survived their sentences. Upon release, they were given menial jobs. Austerity and repression reigned.

MISSING IN ACTION

The first office opened by the US in Vietnam after the war was the MIA Office in Hanoi. Clearing up the MIA issue was a US precondition for lifting its economic embargo against Vietnam. The Vietnamese never really understood why the Americans were so concerned over the fate of some 2,000 MIAs when there were 300,000 Vietnamese unaccounted for. It all seemed rather arrogant, but for the Americans, MIA investigation was a face-saving procedure. Some 200 "live sightings" were investigated in 1992-93, but no Americans were ever found. From 1993 to 1994 teams of investigators were flown into Vietnam to search for remains.

The exact number of MIAs is debatable. Because of covert operations in Laos and Cambodia, some MIAs were falsely reported by the US as missing in action in Vietnam.

The Vietnamese have a far greater MIA problem, with an estimated 300,000 missing. Nguyen Manh Dau, chairman of the Policy Department of the Ministry of Defense, has appealed to the Americans for help. "Only the American side knows where many of our soldiers died," says Dau. One recent find of 85 sets of remains were unearthed thanks to documents supplied by the Vietnam Veterans of America. American veterans groups have asked members to send in photos and other material that might assist in the search for burial sites of Vietnamese soldiers. Search parties in Vietnam have been thwarted by unexploded bombs and mines and difficult terrain.

In December 1978 Vietnamese troops invaded Cambodia to depose the genocidal Khmer Rouge regime. The Khmer Rouge had attacked Vietnamese border towns and targeted ethnic Vietnamese for liquidation. Vietnamese troops remained in Cambodia 10 years. For putting an end to the atrocities of the Khmer Rouge, the Vietnamese received no thanks. Instead, the Chinese attacked north Vietnam in February 1979 as punishment for attacking their Cambodian ally, and both Western and Eastern nations imposed an economic embargo. Vietnam was treated as an outcast by the international community, denied bank loans that would have enabled it to rebuild its economy. The only country Vietnam could turn to for help was the Soviet Union. In the 1980s Soviet experts arrived in force and immediately began work on Soviet naval bases. But the kind of aid coming from the Soviet bloc proved inappropriate to the country's rural needs.

Exodus of the Boat People

In 1978, the government launched an assault on capitalist activity in Saigon, particularly targeting the wealthy Chinese business community in Cholon. When China engaged Vietnam in a vicious border-war in the north, a quarter of Vietnam's ethnic Chinese fled the country—the first of the "boat people." Most of the exodus was from Saigon. An estimated 675,000 people departed Vietnam by mid-1979, about 70% of them ethnic Chinese. Some crossed the northern border into China, but most left in boats, hoping to reach Hong Kong, Malaysia, or Thailand. An estimated 30% died at sea—from drowning, dehydration, or pirates. Up to a third of the boats fell victim to pirates—

remembering the fallen at a war memorial service

SOUL SEARCHING

The Vietnam War created a high level of public distrust of generals and presidents in the United States. American Presidents Lyndon Johnson and Richard Nixon, along with the top military command in Vietnam, repeatedly lied to Congress and concealed from the people what was occurring in Indochina. For the US, the aftermath of the war would lead to years of soul searching. Senior State Department figure George Ball called the war "the greatest single error made by America in its history." In 1995, on the 20th anniversary of the end of the war, Robert McNamara in his book *In Retrospect* revealed that he and the other top brass who got Americans into Vietnam "were wrong, terribly wrong." McNamara served in the Kennedy and Johnson administrations, and was the architect of the US buildup in Vietnam in the 1960s.

McNamara repudiated America's once-cherished "domino theory," which held that Communism had to be stopped in Vietnam or it would spread throughout the region. McNamara writes: "We totally underestimated the nationalist aspect of Ho Chi Minh's movement. We saw him first as a Communist, and only second as a Vietnamese nationalist."

McNamara's confessions sparked off angry recriminations among veterans—why did McNamara wait 25 years to reveal his opposition to the war? How could he sit back and watch 1.1 million Americans serve in Vietnam, resulting in 58,000 deaths? Vietnamese General Vo Nguyen Giap described McNamara's revelations as "honest, courageous."

---

mostly Thai—in the South China Sea. Boats were plundered, women raped, passengers murdered.

Despite the risks of the journey, many refugees continued to leave. In early 1989 the international community slammed the door on Vietnamese refugees after an international conference on Indochinese refugees in Geneva determined less than 10% fled political persecution. As refugees escaping economic hardship for a better life in the West, the later boat people were not eligible for refugee status under international law, and faced repatriation. Meanwhile they were held in grossly overcrowded camps in Southeast Asia.

In 1992 the British and Vietnamese agreed to repatriate 55,700 boat people living in camps in Hong Kong. Despite protests from the UN, some Vietnamese refugees were forcibly repatriated from these camps. In 1995, 22,000 boat people still lived in detention in Hong Kong. Other nations, such as Germany, have also entered into agreements with Hanoi on the repatriation of illegal immigrants.

Doi Moi

War in Cambodia and against the Chinese was a drain on the nation's already limited resources. The economic embargo took its toll. Due to failed farm-collectivization experiments, there was a drastic food shortage, and famine struck parts of the country. By 1985 inflation was running at 700%, and radical economic reform was required if Vietnam were to survive. In 1986 Nguyen Van Linh was appointed Secretary General of the Communist Party, and the Vietnamese leadership announced a policy of *doi moi*, or "new thinking," roughly along the lines of Soviet *perestroika*. Hard-liners were replaced in 1986 and 1987 as the party embraced capitalist market principles.

Taking over as Secretary General in 1991, party chief Do Muoi vowed to continue the reforms begun by Linh. After decades of international isolation, Vietnam began to establish diplomatic relations with other nations. The climate was more favorable after the withdrawal of Vietnamese troops from Cambodia in 1989 and the signing of the Cambodian Peace Agreement in late 1991. Vietnam began repairing its strained relations with China. In 1993, French President François Mitterrand visited Hanoi, the first Western head of state to visit the capital since 1954. Also in 1993 Premier Vo Van Kiet visited Japan, South Korea, Australia, and Western Europe to establish trade links, and General Secretary Do Muoi traveled to Thailand and Singapore for trade talks. In July 1995 Vietnam became the seventh member of ASEAN, another major step in ending its isolation.

Lifting the Embargo

In time for Tet 1994, US President Bill Clinton finally brought hostilities to a close by announcing the lifting of the Vietnamese trade embargo. By 1995 another major legal hurdle was resolved concerning the settlement of property claims and frozen assets. Consequently, full diplomatic relations were established between Hanoi and Washington. Attending the opening of the US Embassy in Hanoi in August 1995 was US Secretary of State Warren Christopher. Vietnam was included in the list of the world's most promising emerging markets for US business, announced by the US Department of Commerce in mid-1995.

GOVERNMENT

There is only one political party in the Socialist Republic of Vietnam—the Vietnamese Communist Party. The VCP was founded by Ho Chi Minh in 1930, and has ruled a unified Vietnam since 1975. A new constitution approved in 1992 reinforced the party's authority by stating the VCP will continue to be the only political player in the nation. How long the VCP can maintain its Marxist-Leninist charade in the wake of economic reforms is questionable.

Although the party boasts 2.1 million members, real power is held by the 13-member Politburo. Members of the Politburo include the Communist Party General Secretary (the top position), the President (second in command), and the Premier. The Politburo is elected by the Central Committee, whose 100-plus members meet several times a year. The National Assembly is Vietnam's highest legislative authority, with about 500 deputies elected for five-year terms. In effect, the National Assembly rubber-stamps Politburo decisions and party-initiated legislation at its twice-yearly meetings. Party Congresses, at which major policy changes are discussed and ratified, are held intermittently; recent ones were in 1986 and 1991.

Corruption is a major problem. Former party chief Nguyen Van Linh warned the party daily newspaper, *Nhan Dan*, in 1993 that "the evils of bureaucratism, corruption and bribery . . . have reached a serious level without any sign of abating . . . not a small number of people including leading cadres . . . misappropriate public funds, accept bribes and seek personal gain in an illegal manner." Linh continued, "Their filthy deeds cause the people to doubt the party's leadership, breed internal disunity and erode the masses' confidence in the party."

If there is a lack of confidence, no one is allowed to show it. Dissent is simply not permitted. The government continues to prohibit an independent press and independent organizations. In 1991 three Vietnamese were arrested for advocating a multiparty system: they received sentences of six to 13 years. Others have been given harsh sentences after convictions for "activities aiming to overthrow the government." One offender was sentenced to 20 years for publishing a newsletter critical of the Vietnamese government. In 1993 a new press law went into effect prohibiting the publication of works hostile to socialism in Vietnam, or "falsifying history."

Administration

Vietnam is divided into 50 provinces. The number of provinces has fluctuated slightly, and provincial boundaries keep changing. In addition, there are three independent municipalities—Greater Hanoi, Greater Haiphong, and Greater Saigon. Everything in the SRV is controlled from Hanoi—the provinces are merely administrative cells with little independent political authority. The provincial capital is usually the largest city. Apart from widespread corruption, a great obstacle to efficient administration is an elaborate stonewalling system the Vietnamese appear to have inherited from French bureaucrats. The burgeoning bureaucracy and poorly developed legal system have stymied efforts of foreign investors—over 100 steps are required to conclude a joint-venture contract.

ECONOMY

One of the world's poorest countries, Vietnam has an annual per capita income of around $220. Left with a shattered infrastructure and economy in 1975, and isolated for almost 20 years by the international community, Vietnam has lots of catching up to do to compete with Southeast Asian neighbors like Thailand. Due to its central geographic position in Southeast Asia and its ready access to seaports, Vietnam is poised to assume an important role in the near future.

Since 1986 and the dawn of *doi moi* (new thinking), Vietnam has pursued capitalist market reforms and made remarkable economic progress. While happily patting capitalist traders on the back with one hand, the government slaps the face of those who contest Marxist doctrine with the other.

Rapprochement with the US has meant a tremendous boost for Vietnam's economy. In July 1993, the US stopped blocking interna-tional loans to Vietnam; within a month, the International Monetary Fund, the World Bank, and the Asian Development Bank all pledged new funds. The economic growth rate reached an all-time high of 8.8% in 1994, but inflation also crept up that year to 14%.

Economic facts and figures are difficult to pin down because of the "shadow economy." The per capita annual income figure of $220 does not explain how 90% of the families in Saigon own at least one motorbike. Experts say the real income figure is more likely higher in urban areas because many people are involved in the black-market or receive money from overseas relatives. Rampant smuggling, especially of Chinese goods, could mean the country's foreign purchases per annum are some $500 million higher than official figures. There is heavy smuggling of Chinese goods in the north, especially electronics, compact discs, and toys. Cars and other consumer goods are smuggled into Vietnam from

THE RHYTHM OF RICE

Vietnam produces about 24 million tons of rice a year. It's the world's third largest ex-porter of rice after Thailand and the United States. In Vietnam, rice is the staple, eaten three times a day. The scale of production—with whole villages working together to slosh through boggy crops—gives rice growing a near-mythic quality, and there are indeed many legends associated with rice.

An estimated 8,000 strains of rice are cultivat-ed around the world, several thousand in Viet-nam alone. Rice planting in Vietnam gets under way twice a year, in February and July, after rains fill up the paddies. Farmers plough with the help of reluctant water buffalo, churning the mud to a gooey consistency. Rice seedlings are cultivat-ed in patches of standing water that serve as nurseries, protected from birds by scarecrows and children. In 30 to 50 days the seedlings are transplanted to the fields, a task that requires hours of patient stooping in knee-deep muddy water. Within three to four months, the crop is ready for harvest. Farmers reap the crop by hand, cutting the stems close to the ground. The stubble is burned, and the best seeds are saved for the next cycle.

The harvested rice, still in its brown husks, is dried in the sun and threshed in pedal-driven de-vices. It may also be left along the shoulder of a roadway to dry, where it may be run over by cars and trucks. Only when the harvested rice is safe-ly stored can the festivals begin.

In the north, an unusual rice festival among mi-nority groups involves a competition between un-married women. The task is to cook a pot of rice, suspended from a pole attached to the woman's back by a sash. Each woman must quickly chew a stick of sugarcane to produce fiber for the fire, then balance the pot of rice over the fire. To make the task more difficult, each woman is also given an infant to hold, and must contain a frog within a 1.5-meter diameter circle around the fire. The win-ner is the one who makes the best-tasting rice in the shortest time, keeps the frog contained, and sufficiently soothes the terrified infant.

rice harvesting,
northern Vietnam

Thailand and Singapore by way of Cambodia and Laos to avoid 150% import duties.

Vietnam's main trading partners are neighboring countries—Hong Kong, Taiwan, Singapore, South Korea, and Japan. Australia, Malaysia, and France also have large investments, and US investment is rising. Vietnam is a new member of the Association of Southeast Asian Nations (ASEAN), comprising Brunei, Indonesia, Malaysia, Thailand, Singapore, and the Philippines. ASEAN membership will undoubtedly boost Vietnam's economy.

Major Economic Pursuits

During the 1990s foreign investment has flooded into Vietnam. Acronyms are springing up everywhere—Huda (the initial letters from Hué and Danish forming a beer brand name), Vietsovpetro (a Russian-Vietnamese petroleum venture), Artex (an arts and crafts export company). Import/export is often abbreviated to "imex," so Donimexco stands for Dong Nai Import Export Company.

Agriculture: Vietnam is mainly an agrarian nation. An estimated 70% of the labor force works in agriculture. The largest crops are rice, rubber, coffee, and tea. Crops can be adversely affected by recurrent flooding and typhoons: a million tons of rice were lost this way in 1994.

Still, Vietnam exported 2.2 million tons of rice that year. To boost confidence, the National Assembly voted in 1993 to grant farmers long-term land-use rights.

Fishing: Vietnam's fishing fleet harvests over one million tons of seafood annually: exports are worth over $500 million. After rice, fish is the most important staple in Vietnam, and it's a major source of protein.

Industry: Major industries includes chemical fertilizer, cement, textiles, steel, sawn logs, and paper. Light industry has a bright future. The combination of an educated, highly skilled workforce and low wages is attractive to foreign investors. Vietnam could become one of Asia's leading producers of computer software.

Energy: Coal and oil are among Vietnam's top exports. The country may harbor large oil and gas reserves; one study estimates they may be equivalent to those of oil-rich Brunei. Vietsovpetro produced 6.7 million tons of oil from two major fields in 1994. Since Vietnam lacks pipelines and refineries, oil is shipped to other countries for refining. Foreign oil companies are actively exploring for offshore oil—Australia's Broken Hill Proprietary Co. announced the discovery of commercial quantities of oil in its Dai Hung field, and Mitsubishi Oil Co. also struck black gold offshore.

THE PEOPLE

Population figures in Vietnam are hard to come by because the last census was conducted in 1989, and the next census won't occur until the end of the century. It is estimated the population currently stands at about 72 million.

Viet

The Viet or Kinh form the majority group, an estimated 85% of the population. The Viet are of Mongolian origin and probably migrated from southern China to settle the Red River Valley, living in limestone caves. Mixing with Malayo-Polynesian, Muong, and Tai tribes is believed to have created the Viet ethnic hybrid. The Viet are concentrated in the two great rice-producing areas, the Red River and Mekong Deltas, as well as on the coastal plains and in the major cities. More than half the population live in the lowland provinces of the Red River and Mekong Deltas.

There are two ongoing national demographic campaigns. The first encourages population shifts to less populated areas through the creation of new economic zones. As part of a family planning campaign, the Viet are encouraged by the government to have no more than two children, similar to the one-child limit in China. Subtle penalties and incentives are part of the package. Minorities are not subject to these regulations. According to *Vietnam News,* the childbirth rate of six children per woman in 1960 had fallen to fewer than four by 1993; officials want to cut annual population growth from the present 2.1% to 1.7% by the year 2000.

Almost 80% of the Viet live outside the urban centers. Rural life is spartan in all respects—lodging, facilities, meals, transportation. Farmfolk follow the simple rhythm of rice growing: sowing, harvesting, and celebrating festivals. Their diet consists of rice, supplemented by fresh vegetables and fish. Men and women wear loose-fitting cotton tops and dark pants; both sexes don conical hats to ward off the sun and rain. Due to a lack of electricity, most people retire early at night. To relax, men smoke cigarettes or a pipe, while women chew betel nut, a mild stimulant that stains the mouth bright red. It also stains the teeth—first brown, then, over a long period of time, black. In former times, Vietnamese women in the north used to blacken

BETEL NUT CHEWERS

If you see an old Vietnamese woman in the countryside with a row of black teeth, gums stained red, and lips dyed a shade of scarlet, chances are she's a devoted betel chewer. Hang around a bit longer and you'll probably see the addiction at work: after several minutes of chewing and sucking on the bitter-tasting nut, patrons spit out gobs of bright red betel juice.

The practice of chewing betel dates back to the dawn of recorded history in Asia. It was long the habit of royalty, and emperors put their finest craftsmen to work creating elaborate silver or lacquered betel boxes. These are still made as gifts.

The reddish-brown acorn-sized betel nut is the fruit of the areca palm tree. Betel nut is served in slices rolled up in a leaf dabbed with pulverized lime to cut the acidity. Betel nut is a mild stimulant, producing a sense of euphoria similar to alcohol, and leaves the chewer feeling slightly anesthetized. Although chewed in the belief it freshens the mouth and strengthens the teeth, betel nut chewing has been linked to oral cancer, gum disease, and the spread of tuberculosis. Many longtime enthusiasts lose teeth.

Prolonged chewing of betel nut stains the teeth first brown and later black.

THE LOST KINGDOM OF CHAMPA

One of the oldest ethnic groups in Indochina is the Cham. Records of the Kingdom of Champa stretch back to the first century AD. The people are described as having dark skin, deep-set eyes, turned-up noses, and frizzy hair; they dressed in sarongs, like the Malays. The origin of the Cham is lost in time; they're most likely seafarers who arrived by boat from the Indonesian archipelago. The Cham speak a Malay-Polynesian language; stelae from the Cham dynasties were inscribed in both Sanskrit and in similar-looking Cham script. The Indianized culture of Champa was almost completely extinguished by Viet conquest.

At the peak of their prosperity in the 10th and 11th centuries, the Cham controlled an area from north of Hué to the Mekong Delta, carving out a kingdom situated between the Khmer and the Viet. Their economy was based on agriculture, ocean fishing, and maritime trading. Their principal exports appear to have been slaves (prisoners of war) and sandalwood; the latter was in great demand for temple building throughout Southeast Asia. The Cham themselves did not indulge in extensive temple building. They constructed brick-and-sandstone towers for Hindu worship, with the main sites at My Son and Tra Kieu (now largely destroyed). Crumbling Cham towers are today scattered along the central coast of Vietnam; the best extant examples are in Nha Trang and Phan Rang.

In Danang is a Cham Museum with a fine collection of Cham sculpture, reflecting contacts with Java and later Cambodia. A recurring image in Hindu Cham art is that of Uroja, the mother figure who gave birth to Champa. Uroja means "breast" in the Cham language, and was represented in sculpture by breast or nipple motifs. The Cham were also ardent worshippers of Hindu lingas and yonis.

The civilization made a great impression on Marco Polo with its advanced use of agriculture and irrigation and encouragement of the arts and sciences. He visited in the year 1285, seven years after Kublai Khan attacked the kingdom and exacted a yearly tribute of elephants and aloe wood from the aging Cham king. Polo reported:

In this kingdom no girl may marry without the King having seen her first. If he likes her, he marries her himself. Those who prove agreeable to him he retains for some time, and when they are dismissed, he furnishes them with a sum of money, in order that they may be able to obtain, according to their rank in life, advantageous matches. The King had 326 children and at least 150 of his sons were well trained in the arts of war. The kingdom abounds in elephants. There are also many forests of ebony of a fine black which is worked into various handsome articles of furniture. Every year the King sends elephants and sweet-scented wood as a tribute to the Great Khan.

---

their front teeth with a kind of lacquer, as a display of white teeth was considered shocking. The practice was discontinued under the French.

Urban Viet live in cities that are quite small by Southeast Asian standards. Space is at a premium, with families living in cramped apartments where two or three generations share a single roof—sometimes even the same room. Running water is a luxury. Most families share plumbing facilities or use communal water pumps. Shopping for fresh produce is a daily ritual, although refrigerators are finding their way into more urban homes. A private television set may turn into a local theater as neighbors crowd around to watch a popular program. The main form of private transport is the bicycle, with motorcycles making their mark in places like Saigon and Hanoi. At night, cafés are popular hangouts for the young, the old, and the lovestruck.

The most developed urban centers are prim and proper Hanoi, and her brash sister Saigon. Clothing is indicative of lifestyles here: while men in Hanoi are decked out in old army gear and baggy pants, in Saigon they wear jeans and western fashion, a legacy of American influence.

In the 16th century, the Dominican friar Gabriel de San Antonio visited the Cham and returned with a more macabre account. He found the civilization brilliant, but unbalanced; similar to the Aztecs, they sacrificed humans. On certain days, San Antonio reported, the Cham sacrificed hundreds of people. The gall of the dead was collected and sent to the Cham king, who bathed in it to gain immortality.

Apart from this bloodletting, the Kingdom of Champa was weakened by battles with both the Khmer and the Viet. In 1471, the Viet raided and captured the Cham capital of Vijaya. An estimated 60,000 Cham troops were killed, and an equal number captured and carted off into slavery. The Kingdom of Champa was reduced to a tiny area centered on Nha Trang, which lingered for another 250 years. In 1720 the last remnants of the Kingdom of Champa were surrounded by powerful Viet forces. The king and his subjects fled south to the Mekong Delta, at that time controlled by Khmers. Although the Cham had in the past battled the Khmer, they preferred Khmer rule to the Viet's because of a shared Indic tradition. By 1820 the Mekong Delta, too, had fallen under the control of the Viet. While some Cham remained, other groups moved farther up the Mekong to settle east of Phnom Penh in the province of Kompong Cham and along the shores of the Tonle Sap.

For hundreds of years the Cham were devout Hindus; Islam was introduced in the 18th and 19th centuries, most likely by traders from India and Indonesia. In contrast to the Cham in Vietnam, who remained only partly Islamicized, the Cham in Cambodia widely adopted Sunni Islam customs and maintained links with other Muslim communities in Thailand and Malaysia. The Cambodian Cham— numbering perhaps 400,000—prospered, settling in 200 towns and villages. Cambodia served as a haven for the Cham for the next couple of centuries. But during the Pol Pot era, the Cham were branded "recent immigrants" and marked for expulsion or death. Up to two-thirds of the Cham community was wiped out in the post-1975 era—Cham were killed, starved to death, or driven out of the country. A small group fled to Laos, where they now prosper in Vientiane. Today there are an estimated 80,000 Cham descendants in Vietnam, 165,000 Cham in Cambodia, and 250 in Laos. Other small communities exist in Thailand, Malaysia, and southern China.

Cham Tower

BOB RACE

Hoa and Viet-Kieu

Although a minority, the ethnic Chinese, or Hoa, have wielded such power in the past they are now considered mainstream. Over a million Hoa inhabit Vietnam, most living in the south. They're mostly traders, merchants, and middlemen. The Hoa have successfully retained their own school system, religion, language, and customs. Traders from different parts of China—Canton, Fuzhou, Chaozhou, Hainan— form strong community centers to support their members. Before 1975, ethnic Chinese controlled most of the commerce in the south, with a large contingent in Saigon. After years of persecution following reunification, there are signs the Hoa are resuming this role in Saigon. After

1975, the boat people fleeing Vietnam were largely Hoa.

Viet-Kieu represent the estimated 2.5 million overseas Vietnamese. Roughly half that number have settled in the United States. The biggest Viet-Kieu communities reside in California. Other countries containing large populations of Viet-Kieu are France (250,000), Canada (120,000), Australia (110,000), and Germany (95,000). Vietnamese communities are also scattered in Eastern European countries, Western Europe, China, and Thailand. Viet-Kieu are an important source of foreign exchange for the Vietnamese government. Several hundred thousand visit relatives every year; others are lured back to help finance new ventures.

Amerasians

As living reminders of US involvement in the war, Amerasians faced ostracism or discrimination by Vietnamese society, and were forced onto the streets to make ends meet by begging or petty crime. For more than a decade, Amerasians fathered by US soldiers were ignored by the governments of both Vietnam and the United States. Most of the estimated 40,000 Amerasians lived around Saigon. In 1989, the US finally took responsibility for those of obvious white or black parentage, permitting them to emigrate to the US under the UN Orderly Departure Program.

MONTAGNARDS

There are over 50 minority groups in Vietnam, ranging in size from several hundred to over a million people. Minority groups account for six to eight million people, and are mainly concentrated in the mountainous western part of the country, where they occupy two-thirds of the border areas. Most minorities are found in equal or greater numbers on either side of the border in southern China, Cambodia, Laos, northern Thailand, and Burma. The French collectively called them *montagnards,* or mountain people.

The Vietnamese, Chinese, French, and British designate the same group of people by different names. The Zao, for example (pronounced "zao" in the north of Vietnam and "dao" in the south), are equivalent to the Yao in Laos or Thailand, also known as the Man or Mien. The Vietnamese government defines the minority groups by linguistic families, although this division is not precise—other factors include geographical location and traditional dress.

Under French rule, most minorities were forced into unpaid labor and subjected to heavy taxes. This led to a number of minority revolts against the French. The French attempted to exploit differences between minorities and the Viet; deploying Tai and Nung as local militia and border guards. In the Central Highlands a number of ethnic groups worked with the Americans, which led to reprisals by the Viet majority after 1975.

Between 1945 and 1975 the North Vietnamese tried to gain the cooperation of ethnic groups by granting them constitutional rights similar to those of the Viet majority. In the north and northwest the government established two autonomous regions with their own administrative bodies. After 1975, however, the autonomous regions were abolished. The Vietnamese have since pursued a policy of paternalism, trying to bring the Montagnards into the fold by settling nomadic groups and foisting majority values on them.

Northern Montagnards

The largest concentration of Montagnards is in the far north of Vietnam. In some parts of the north, particularly the northwest, ethnic groups actually outnumber the Viet. Most ethnic clans in the north descended from China. A large number practice beliefs based on animism and ancestor worship.

Hmong-Zao Group: The Hmong (420,000) and Zao (40,000) are found in the mountains bordering China and Laos. They arrived in Vietnam from China in the 19th century.

The **Hmong** (also known as the Miao or Meo) are closely related to the tribes living across the border in Laos. Their preference for living at higher elevations—above 1,500 meters—allows them the isolation to pursue their ancient ways. The Hmong are found particularly in mountain areas around Dien Bien Phu, Lai Chau, and Sapa. They live in simple wooden houses, and practice slash-and-burn cultivation, growing dry rice and maize. They grow hemp as their primary textile material, and cultivate opium poppies. They also raise chickens, ducks, pot-bellied pigs, goats, and buffalo. The Hmong are among the poorest of the nation's minority groups, with little access to modern education or health care—they have no written language. Hmong men often wear black pajama outfits and carry flintlock rifles. Hmong women wear elaborately embroidered dresses—either black, white, red, green, or flowered according to their clan—and large heavy earrings, bracelets, and necklaces.

The **Zao** (also known as Dao, Yao, Man, or Mien) share the same linguistic family and similar origins as the Hmong. They mostly inhabit Lao Cai and Ha Giang provinces, near the Chinese border. Several subgroups abound, including the Red Zao. Red Zao women wear spectacular red turbans with braided or beaded sections, pompoms, or coins dangling off them, and silver neck pieces. On market day, Red Zao men wear black turbans and dark-blue jackets with an embroidered patch on the back.

Tai-Kadai Group: Communities from the Tai language group arrived from China as early as the 4th century. In the northeast are the Nung, estimated at 700,000, and Tay, 1.2 million; in the northwest other Tai groups number perhaps 800,000.

The **Nung** live near the Chinese border in Cao Bang and Lang Son provinces. They're strongly influenced by Chinese traditions and are mostly Buddhist. The Nung share the same language, culture, and customs as the **Tay** and often live together in the same villages. Tay groups are more widespread in the north and northwest, and are well integrated into mainstream Vietnamese culture. They've adopted Vietnamese dress, and, due to intermarriage, may live in villages of mixed ethnic groups. Other Tay groups wear traditional clothes reflecting their southern Chinese origins—black pants, Chinese-style cotton tunics, and plaid woolen head-scarves. A subgroup closely related to the Tay is the Giay, numbering possibly 30,000. They live in villages built close to the Tay or Nung.

The **Tai** live between the Red and Black River Valleys in the northwest. Tai is also spelt Thai, which invites confusion when speaking of natives of Thailand, with whom they have little in common. The Tai are valley-dwelling farmers who've mastered wet rice cultivation methods, often producing two harvests a year. The Tai compete directly with the Viet, and some cultural assimilation occurs. Tai villages are composed of 20 to 50 families living in raised wooden longhouses. Tai groups are identified by the colors of their dress—black, white, or red. Black Tai women, for instance, wear black sarongs and bright, tight-fitting blouses with rows of silver or metal buttons down the front. The hair is coiled in a topknot and covered with a black turban bearing multicolored embroidery; after marriage, Black Tai women wear a silver hairpin.

Muong: The Muong live mainly around Hoa Binh and Thanh Hoa provinces, to the west and south of Hanoi. This group of 900,000 are cousins of the ancient Viet, and speak a similar dialect. Many Muong have been assimilated into Vietnamese society, but in remote regions they still live in longhouses on stilts and hunt with blowpipes. The Muong cultivate rice, sugarcane, tea, and coffee; silk production is also common in villages. Muong men largely wear city-bought clothing; Muong women still wear traditional garb of long black skirts, pastel blouses, and conical hats.

Tibeto-Burman Groups: Border zones in the far north contain some tiny groups from the Tibeto-Burman language family, such as Phula, Hani, Lahu, Sila, and Cong. These obscure groups are isolated and rarely encountered by visitors.

Central and Southern Montagnards

Ethnic groups in the center and south are mostly descended from people who lived in the area before the Viet pushed south from the north.

Malayo-Polynesian Group: In the Central Highlands, from the Malayo-Polynesian linguistic family, are the Jarai (or Giarai), numbering about 240,000; Ede (or Rhade), about 190,000; and Raglai, 70,000. All are of Malay and Indonesian origins. These groups are mostly matriarchal, although increasing Vietnamization since 1975 is changing this. **Jarai** villages comprise 50 or more longhouses with matriarchal families. The people cultivate fruit trees, rice, and beans; they also hunt, fish, and raise livestock. Women take the initiative in choosing a marriage partner. The **Ede** build traditional longhouses and affix a pair of wooden breasts to the top, symbolizing the power of women. In Ede traditional society, the woman's family selects a husband for the daughter, and property is inherited only by daughters. Most Ede have been converted to Catholic or Protestant religions, but retain traces of animism in the worship of spirits of the forest, stream, or hill.

The matriarchal **Cham,** who reside in the coastal provinces south of Qui Nhon (particularly around Phan Thiet) and in the Mekong Delta province of Chau Doc, also belong to the Malayo-Polynesian group. There are an estimated 80,000 Cham, divided into two groups—the Hindu Cham, found mainly in central Vietnam, and the Muslim Cham of southern Vietnam and the Mekong Delta. Although the two groups co-exist, there is no intermarriage. The

Cham derive from an Indianized culture that once ruled a kingdom in coastal and south Vietnam until eclipsed by the Viet.

Mon-Khmer Group: In the Kontum and Buon Ma Thuot areas of the Central Highlands groups from the Mon-Khmer language family include the Bahnar (150,000), Sedoun (100,000), and Mnong (65,000). The same groups also live on the Cambodian side of border. The **Sedoun** are a warlike people who almost annihilated the Bahnar in the 19th century. **Bahnar** tribespeople were sacrificed to spirits or sold into slavery in Thailand. Remaining Bahnar are concentrated in Gia Lai and Kontum provinces. They practice animism mixed with elements of Catholicism, and engage in settled and shifting cultivation. The **Mnong** are a matriarchal group living near Buon Ma Thuot. They speak a language similar to Cambodian, have no script, and live in houses flat to the ground. The Mnong are famed as elephant hunters; elephant spirit worship is a part of their animist practices.

Other members of the Mon-Khmer language group include the Bru Van-Kieu, found in the former DMZ area and Khe Sanh, and Stieng, in Song Be Province. In the Dalat area are the Lat and Koho tribespeople.

The **Khmer** (ethnic Cambodian) form a large contingent in the Mekong Delta, estimated at about 700,000. Some are descendants of the original Khmer Empire inhabitants displaced by the advancing Viet. Other groups are refugees from Pol Pot's reign of terror. The Khmer, practicing Theravada Buddhists, are strong in Chau Doc Province, up by the Cambodian border. They're easily distinguished from the Viet by their dark rounded faces and *kramas* (checkered scarves).

RELIGION

In Vietnam, communism is allegedly the mass faith, and those in power closely monitor religious groups. Karl Marx believed religion to be the opiate of the masses, employed by repressive regimes to divert the attention of the people from their true enemies. Therefore, in a true communist society, religion does not exist. A modified version of this: religious practices that do not harm political rule can be tolerated. This is the case in Vietnam.

During the Vietnam War, dissident Buddhists mounted a campaign against the Catholic regime of Diem, who often accused Buddhists of maintaining communist ties. But when the communists came to power they began repressing both Buddhism and Catholicism by putting them under the control of state organizations—the Buddhist Church of Vietnam, and the Council of Union of Vietnamese Catholics. Schools, hospitals, and other institutions run by religious organizations were taken over after 1975, land owned by religious groups was confiscated, many religious leaders were sent to re-education camps, and proselytizing was severely restricted.

Since the late 1980s the official stance has softened, with more freedom allowed to Catholics, Buddhists, and other groups. There has been a resurgence of worship in pagodas and churches throughout the country. Problems still exist, however. According to the Puebla Institute, a human-rights organization based in Washington, DC, 131 Vietnamese religious prisoners were held in Vietnam in 1994—72 Buddhists, 35 evangelical Protestants, and 24 Catholics.

BUDDHISM

An estimated 60% of the population follow some sort of Buddhist beliefs, though considerably watered down from their original strength, or mixed with other faiths. Both major schools of Buddhism are represented in Vietnam: in the north and the center Mahayana Buddhism predominates (due to Chinese influence), while in the south pockets of Theravada Buddhism prevail due to Indian and Cambodian influence.

Communism and Buddhism don't see eye to eye. Communists have historically replaced Buddhist teachings with communist ideology, weakening the power of the monasteries and eliminating Buddhist privileges, isolating and

THE MARKET ECONOMY SHRINE

On peak days, the tiny shrine of **Den Ba Chua Kho** attracts up to a thousand visitors. Nicknamed "the market economy shrine," it lies to the east of Hanoi in Ha Bac Province. A government ban on superstitious practices has not prevented a flourishing trade at the shrine. Pilgrims once visited it only in the spring, but since the early 1990s the turnout has been year round. Suppliants bring trays of offerings to a dozen different altars in the temple, filled with the smoke of joss sticks. Among the offerings are beer, cigarettes, fruit, flowers, paper gold ingots, and bundles of imitation American $100 bills.

The 11th-century shrine was built in honor of Ba Chua Kho, a queen involved in heroic battles against the Chinese during the Ly dynasty. It's believed the queen acknowledges the wishes of suppticants, wielding the power to multiply their symbolic offerings into affluence. Thus, wishes for material possessions such as real estate or a new motorcycle can be granted.

Unfortunately, the queen hails from the pre-French era, and cannot read today's romanized Vietnamese script. So suppliants must rely on interpreters available on-site to translate their messages into Chinese characters, which the good queen can then read. Payment to cover the interpreter's service fee and a basic worship materials package makes this a very costly place to worship, but visitors don't seem to care—they're elated to reach the shrine in person. Another curious industry here is the hiring of porters to visit Den Ba Chua Kho by those physically unable to reach it—most likely because they're too busy making money elsewhere.

discrediting the monastic leadership. Such is the case in Vietnam. The communist government declared the Buddhist Church of Vietnam, set up in 1981, as the only legal Buddhist authority. Dissident monks and émigré communities in France, Australia, and the US support the banned Unified Buddhist Church of Vietnam (UBCV), which was the main Buddhist organization in former South Vietnam and the largest of 22 Buddhist groups in Vietnam.

The UBCV is militantly opposed to state control of Buddhism. The organization was the driving force behind a sit-down demonstration in Hué in May 1993 in support of religious freedom—the largest demonstration in Vietnam since 1975. Thich Tri Tuu, the abbot of Thien Mu pagoda, was later sentenced to four years in prison for his part in the demonstration. In late 1994 the Supreme Patriarch of the UBCV, Thich Huyen Quang, who'd been under house arrest since 1982, was taken into custody in Quang Ngai province. A month later, the second-highest leader of the UBCV, Thich Quang Do, was detained for committing "provocative acts." He was later sentenced to five years in jail for "undermining the policy of solidarity," a national security crime in Vietnam's criminal code.

Buddhist Beliefs

Buddhism focuses on suffering—its causes and eradication. It is based on the teachings of Siddhartha Gautama, born around 560 BC in what is now Nepal. The essence of Buddha's teachings is the Eightfold Path, also known as the Middle Path because it steers a course between materialists and ascetics. The Path consists of right understanding, right thought, right speech, right action, right livelihood, right effort, right mindfulness, and right concentration.

The ultimate goal of Buddhism is cessation of suffering, or attainment of nirvana—enlightenment, ultimate truth, gaining of wisdom. Mahayana Buddhists work toward the enlightenment (and salvation from suffering) of all beings, while Theravada (Hinayana) Buddhists believe in the personal quest for enlightenment. Only those who dedicate themselves fully to the Path can attain enlightenment. For most adherents, the likelihood of attaining nirvana is remote because it requires such intense dedication.

A more humble pursuit involves redressing the balance of karma. Karma is cause and effect: good deeds have good effects; bad deeds have bad effects. Many Buddhists believe they may have inherited bad karma from previous existences, a situation that must be corrected by doing good deeds in the present life.

Mahayana Buddhism was most likely introduced from China in the 2nd century AD. It received royal patronage after the 9th century, and by the 12th century was promoted to the state religion. After a lengthy period of stagnation, Mahayana Buddhism underwent a major revival in the 1920s. In addition to faith in Buddha, Mahayana Buddhists believe in a vast array of bodhisattvas, or enlightened beings. Mahayana Buddhism is concentrated in the north and center of Vietnam: the most important sect is the Thien (Zen) meditation sect. Zen master Thich Nhat Hanh introduces the sect in *Vietnam, Lotus in a Sea of Fire*:

Thien (Zen) differs from orthodox religions in that it is not conditioned by any set of beliefs. In other words, Thien is an attitude or a method for arriving at knowledge and action. For Thien the techniques of right eating and drinking, of right breathing and right concentration and meditation, are far more vital than mere beliefs. A person who practices Zen meditation does not have to rely on beliefs in hell, nirvana, rebirth, or causality; he has only to rely on the reality of his body, his psychology, biology, and his own past experiences of the instructions of Zen Masters who have preceded him. His aim is to attain, to penetrate, to see; once he has attained sartori (insight) his action will conform by itself to reality.

Theravada Buddhism is concentrated in the south of Vietnam, in the Mekong Delta, where adherents are found in small numbers, mostly in Khmer communities. Theravada Buddhism was most likely introduced by Indian seafarers and later reinforced by Cambodian settlers. Theravada Buddhists claim to adhere to the original teachings of Buddha.

THE GODDESS OF MERCY

A very popular deity in Vietnamese Buddhism is Quan Am, modeled on the Chinese bodhisattva Guanyin, or Goddess of Mercy. Quan Am is a female form of Avalokitesvara, the masculine Hindu bodhisattva who personifies the virtue of compassion. At some point around a thousand years ago, Avalokitesvara underwent a transformation in China, emerging as Guanyin. The Vietnamese version of this quasi-folk legend is that Avalokitesvara made the great sacrifice of renouncing his chance at nirvana, choosing instead to return to Earth as Quan Am. The Vietnamese believe this transformation took place in the grotto shrine of the Perfume Pagoda near Hanoi.

Quan Am is usually sculpted as a standing all-white female figure holding a vase of holy water, and sometimes a willow branch for sprinkling the water of compassion onto mankind. In another version she holds her adopted son in one arm and stands on a lotus blossom. Quan Am looks remarkably like the Virgin Mary, or Madonna and Child, a similarity Western missionaries probably used to their advantage.

According to Chinese legend, Quan Am was unfairly thrown out on the streets by her husband, and took refuge in a monastery disguised as a monk. A woman unjustly accused Quan Am of fathering her son and then abandoning the child. Quan Am accepted the blame and took responsibility for the care of the child. She found herself once more on the streets, this time as a "father" with a "son." Only years later, when she was close to death, did she reveal her true female identity. The Emperor of China, hearing her story, made Quan Am the guardian spirit of mother and child. Quan Am is believed to have the power to bestow male offspring on believers, which explains her popularity. Childless couples and those without a son make offerings to her image.

Quan Am statue outside a Dalat temple

Pagodas

Active places of Mahayana Buddhist worship in Vietnam are called pagodas, or *chua*. The Vietnamese pagoda is usually a single-story structure with a bell tower, sacred pond, and yard at the front; a main building consisting of a front hall, central hall, and altar hall; and at the back living quarters for the monks or nuns, and perhaps some gardens. A multitiered Chinese-style pagoda sometimes stands in the grounds, generally housing sacred relics.

A Vietnamese pagoda is a community center of sorts. At festival time, pagodas are thronged with devotees and beggars and ablaze with incense. The grounds take on a carnival-like atmosphere. With its eclectic mix of Buddhism, Taoism, and Confucianism, the Vietnamese pagoda often functions in the area of wish-fulfillment—monks tell fortunes, sell talismans, advise on house construction location. Some pagodas are famed for statues of deities that can grant special wishes, such as pregnancy to infertile women. Another important function monks perform is to recite incantations at funerals. The pagoda becomes a repository for small funerary jars, each containing the ashes of the deceased with a photo and nameplate.

Iconography

Pagoda wall motifs often feature dragons, a divine and benevolent symbol formerly associated with the emperor. Dragons may be wrapped around columns, with forms ingeniously collaged from beer-bottle shards. Occasionally in a pagoda courtyard you'll find a dragon screen made of glazed tiles to deflect evil spirits. The dragon symbolizes power and is one of the four sacred animals of Chinese and Vietnamese mythology. The others are the phoenix, representing peace; the turtle, symbolizing long life; and the unicorn, representative of wisdom. These animals appear in paintings or statuary as temple guardians and bearers of good luck. Other common pagoda motifs include the Taoist yin-yang symbol—a circle split by an S-line—which symbolizes the fusion of opposites; and the reverse swastika, symbolizing the heart of Buddha, or long life. Actually, the swastika is based on this symbol, not the reverse. Common statuary in pagodas includes the following.

Buddhas: Mahayana Buddhists believe in a series of Buddhas, among them Amitabha, Buddha of the Past; Sakyamuni, the historical Buddha of this age; and Maitreya, Buddha of the Future. Some Buddha sculptures are massive efforts in sandalwood or bronze, weighing up to several tons. Another figure, the Laughing Buddha, usually represents a historic wandering Chinese monk, but is sometimes associated with the Maitreya Buddha.

Avalokitesvara: Mahayana adherents believe in a vast array of bodhisattvas, or enlightened beings. Avalokitesvara is the bodhisattva of compassion, usually represented with a forest of arms and multiple heads. The latter are supposed to have burst from the original head as a result of contemplating the suffering of human beings. At some point Avalokitesvara meta-

morphosed into a female form—in Vietnamese, this popular deity is known as Quan Am.

Chinese Folk Deities: Chinese-style pagodas are sometimes dedicated to Thien Hau, goddess of the sea and protector of sailors and fisherfolk. Another common figure in Chinese pagodas is Quan Cong, a deified Chinese general from the Three Kingdoms period (3rd century AD). Statuary depict Quan Cong as red-faced with a long beard, sometimes astride a red horse, and flanked by companions General Chau Xuong and mandarin Quan Binh. Temple guardian statuary may take the form of Chinese warriors.

BUDDHIST HYBRIDS

In Vietnam Confucian, Taoist, and animist beliefs are inextricably entwined with Buddhism. In fact, the Vietnamese refer to their faith as *Tam Giao,* the Triple Religion. In the Mekong Delta are exotic homegrown hybrids like Cao Daism and Hoa Hao Buddhism. Adherents of the sects do not believe in a superior being. Confucianism and Taoism are often referred to as Chinese folk religions.

Confucianism

Confucianism is a code of ethics derived from the teachings of Chinese philosopher Confucius (551-479 BC). Confucianism was introduced to Vietnam by the Chinese to bolster their rule. Confucius promoted respect for authority and family elders and enshrined the concept of imperial rule through the Mandate of Heaven. The teachings emphasize the Three Bonds: loyalty of minister to emperor, son to father, and wife to husband. When the Vietnamese established their own dynastic line, Confucianism conveniently continued under the mandarins and the royal court. Confucius himself is often worshipped as a temple deity, such as at the Temple of Literature in Hanoi.

Ancestor Worship

Ancestor worship long predates Confucianism as an animist cult, but Confucianism reinforced and enhanced the practice. Ancestor worship hinges on the belief that the soul lives on after death and protects descendants, so descendants must pay homage to the spirit of the deceased and keep them informed of important changes. Pagodas often feature a section where memorial tablets and photos of the deceased are displayed, and many Vietnamese maintain an in-house family memorial altar where incense sticks are regularly lit.

Taoism

Taoism was introduced from China around the same time as Confucianism. It derives from the works of Chinese philosopher Lao Tzu (6th-5th centuries BC), and is based on the *I Ching* or The Book of Changes. Taoism is similar to Confucianism but provides a spiritual dimension that Confucianism lacks. Taoist belief hinges on the concept of harmony, maintaining the balance between the contradictory forces of *yin* (female) and *yang* (male). The fusion of yin and yang in temporary harmony can provide people and things with a sense of direction. This fundamental law applies to just about anything—the family, the nation, or nature itself. Upsetting the yin-yang harmony leads to illness or tragedy. Taoist beliefs incorporate magic, alchemy, exorcism, faith healing, the search for immortality, and faith in spirits and ghosts. Because it functions in combination with Buddhism and Confucianism, it is not possible to give a figure for the number of adherents in Vietnam.

Cao Daism

Cao Daism is a hodgepodge of Buddhism, Confucianism, Taoism, and Catholicism, with a bit of Islam thrown in. The founder of Cao Daism was Ngo Van Chieu, a civil servant who experienced visions in the mid-1920s that led him to declare his existence as the first Cao Dai Pope. The all-knowing Divine Eye, symbol of Cao Dai or Supreme Spirit, occupies the central temple altar. In 1943 Ngo Van Chieu died and was succeeded by Pham Cong

Tac, who was deported to the Comoros Islands by the French. He returned to Vietnam in 1946. When Ngo Dinh Diem came to power in the south in 1954, violent resistance from the Cao Dai and Hoa Hao sects was crushed, and Pham Cong Tac fled to Cambodia. Although Cao Dai lands were confiscated and the leadership disbanded after 1975, the temples were returned in 1985. The faith is now making a comeback, with an estimated 1,000 churches in the south and two million followers. The sect is particularly strong in the Mekong Delta. Cao Dai headquarters are at Tay Ninh, 96 km northwest of Saigon.

Hoa Hao Buddhism

This militant sect was founded in the village of Hoa Hao in Chau Doc Province in the Mekong Delta, led by the faith healer Huynh Phu So. The breakaway Buddhist movement gained 1.5 million adherents; the faith emphasizes simplicity of worship and places little stress on ritual or temple building. Hoa Hao followers were

---

WAR AND BUDDHISM

Zen master Thich Nhat Hanh played a major role in nonviolent opposition to the war in Vietnam. Thich Nhat Hanh was born in central Vietnam in 1926 and ordained a monk in 1942 at the age of sixteen. In 1964, along with a group of university professors and students, Thich Nhat Hanh founded the School of Youth for Social Service, an organization based entirely on Gandhian principles. Thousands of Buddhist monks, nuns, and laypeople were shot or imprisoned for their work, which involved the creation of projects to help war victims. Teams of young people journeyed to the countryside to build schools and health clinics or rebuild bombed villages.

In 1969, at the request of the Unified Buddhist Church of Vietnam, Thich Nhat Hanh set up the Buddhist Peace Delegation to the Paris Peace Talks. After the signing of the Paris Accords in 1973, he was refused permission to return to Vietnam and settled in a small community southwest of Paris. He is recognized today as one of the greatest exponents of Theravadan and Zen teachings. He is a prolific speaker and writer, and a tireless campaigner in a number of causes: assisting Vietnamese boat people; working with refugees in camps in Thailand, Malaysia, and Hong Kong; and applying the balm of Buddha's teachings to the psychologically damaged veterans of the Vietnam War. Handwritten copies of Thich Nhat Hanh's books continue to circulate illegally in Vietnam. Among his best-known meditation manuals are *Peace Is Every Step* and *The Miracle of Mindfulness.*

anti-French; when the Japanese invaded Vietnam, they were supported by Hoa Hao militia. In 1947 Huynh Phu So was killed by the Vietminh for refusing to ally himself with the communists—as a result, Hoa Hao Buddhists became anticommunist. The tide turned in 1956 when a Hoa Hao leader was publicly guillotined by the Diem regime. Then elements of the Hoa Hao army sided with the Vietcong. After 1975 the Hoa Hao army was disbanded. Today the stronghold of Hoa Hao Buddhism is Chau Doc near the Cambodian border.

CATHOLICISM

Roman Catholic missionaries from France, Spain, and Portugal introduced Christianity to Vietnam in the 16th century. In the early 17th century, Portuguese Jesuits founded missions in Hanoi, Hoi An, and Danang. The mandarins perceived the Roman Catholic religion as a threat to their Confucian order of society. In the early 18th century a decree forbidding Christianity was enforced in the north; in the south, foreign missionaries were told to leave. Persecution of Catholics and Catholic missionaries led to the eventual conquest of the entire country by the French—though this seems to have been but a pretext for plundering the country's resources.

However, some resources—building materials for cathedrals were brought in piece by piece. Gothic-style cathedral spires can be seen in Saigon, Dalat, Hué, and Hanoi. There are also Montagnard churches in places like Dalat and Kontum; Montagnards mix Christian and animist beliefs.

Under the French, the church wielded considerable power: the Catholic church was once the country's biggest landowner. After 1954, Catholics moved south to the protection of the Diem regime. Because of strong Catholic support for the US presence in southern Vietnam, the church was the target of a backlash after 1975. Foreign nuns and priests were expelled, seminaries and schools closed, church lands confiscated, and proselytizing forbidden.

About six million people—representing some eight percent of the population—are thought to be Catholic; Vietnam has the second largest Catholic contingent in Southeast Asia, after the Philippines. The bulk of funding for the churches comes from Catholics in the US and France. Although communication with the Vatican is restricted, in 1994 the Archbishop of Hanoi, Pham Dinh Tung, was allowed to go to Rome to be invested by Pope John Paul II in the Vatican's 120-member college of cardinals.

The Pope views Vietnam as a fruitful frontier, but Vietnam and the Vatican have been at loggerheads over religious freedom. The Vietnamese government insists on its right to veto all church appointments. In early 1995 Archbishop Paul Nguyen Van Binh, leader of the community in Saigon, died, and the Vatican's initial nomination was Bishop Nguyen Thuan, a nephew of former South Vietnamese president Diem. This nomination was rejected. The Vietnamese government is suspicious of the Vatican. Hanoi is concerned that elements of the Catholic community can be manipulated by external forces to act against the regime.

OTHER FAITHS

Minorities in Vietnam adhere to a great number of beliefs. In addition to those already mentioned are the following:

Protestantism: About 300,000 Protestants live in Vietnam. The largest contingent is formed of Montagnards from the Central Highlands, who were converted by French and Portuguese missionaries. The religion was introduced in 1911. Churches are called Good News Churches (Tin Lanh).

Hinduism: In central Vietnam, descendants of the Cham follow Hindu and Brahman beliefs, worshipping the holy trinity of Shiva, the Destroyer; Vishnu, the Preserver; and Brahma, the Creator. A tiny Tamil community once existed in Saigon—a Hindu temple remains there, patronized by local Vietnamese and those of Indian origin.

Islam: In the 18th and 19th centuries, Cham descendants on the south coast and Mekong Delta converted to Islam. Muslim Cham or Cham Bani are easily distinguished by the preferred headgear of men—a crimson fez with a long golden tassel, or white Muslim prayer cap. In the Phan Rang area, men wear white turbans with red tassels. The largest Cham mosque stands in Chau Doc in the Mekong Delta.

Animism: Although superstitious practices are banned by the communist government, spirit worship is well entrenched among hilltribe groups. Animists believe powerful spirits residing in forests, rocks, streams, wind, and rain, must be appeased by gifts of food, flowers, and incense. Spirits can also live in animals. The Mnong tribespeople of the Central Highlands, famed as elephant catchers, practice elephant spirit worship.

THE ARTS

Vietnam's artistic roots lie in Chinese culture; the Chinese dominated the area for a thousand years. Vietnamese art forms are not as distinct as other cultures in Southeast Asia, as the Vietnamese drew heavily on Chinese prototypes. While the Vietnamese arts of poetry and water puppetry date back to the 13th century, such distinct elements of Vietnamese culture as painting and the use of romanized script derive from 1920s French influence.

LANGUAGE AND LITERATURE

Written Vietnamese uses a Roman script with tonal markers called *quoc ngu*. The language was developed by 17th-century French Jesuit missionary Alexandre de Rhodes. The first *quoc ngu* dictionary was published in 1651, but the script was used by only the Catholic church at first, and later by the colonial administration. The study of *quoc ngu* became compulsory in secondary schools in 1906, and a new curriculum entirely in *quoc ngu* was established several years later. Not until 1920 was *quoc ngu* adopted as the national script, with the first major literary volume in *quoc ngu* published in 1925.

The Vietnamese language is variously thought to have derived from Austro-Asiatic or Sino-Tibetan languages. Due to Chinese influence, Chinese ideograms *(chu nho)* were used by scholars for formal and official documents until the 20th century. In a breakaway move, the Vietnamese devised their own characters in the 13th century. This system, called *chu nom*, used Chinese characters to render phonetic Vietnamese in popular stories, tales, and poetry. Vietnam has a well-developed heritage of poetry. Originally, folk literature—fables, legends, songs—was an oral tradition, and works were recited by itinerant storytellers. Folk tales in verse glorified the deeds of Vietnamese heroes, or explained such phenomena as the origin of the watermelon, or how the water buffalo acquired wrinkled skin and horns.

A classic Vietnamese work is *Kim Van Kieu* by poet Nguyen Du (1765-1820). The verse epic relates the bittersweet love of Thuy Kieu, Princess of the Moon, for the poet Kim Trong. Thuy Kieu forsakes her lover and prostitutes herself to obtain money for her father's release from prison. The theme of the separation of the young lovers and saving the family name holds universal appeal. Carving out a special niche is 18th-century poetess Ho Xuan Huong, whose works ridicule pompous officials, praise free love, and advocate equality for women. Her trademark is poetry with both literary and pornographic levels of meaning.

Chu nom was first expressed only in verse—the French introduced the concept of prose. In the French colonial era prose came to the fore: by the 1930s, the Chinese literary tradition had been replaced by romanized Vietnamese script due to French preference for *quoc ngu*. This lead to a literary renaissance in Vietnam, with the rise of novels, short stories, and essays. Although the essays and fiery anticolonial rhetoric of Ho Chi Minh propelled the communists to power, communist authorities have since clamped down on writers. A number of poets, authors, and journalists have been imprisoned by the present regime. Others have been reduced to writing "politically correct" material. A safer area than politics is the realm of love and personal relations.

PERFORMING ARTS

Music and Dance

Traditional instruments figure prominently in festivals, and as accompaniment to water puppetry and drama. Originally music played an important part in religious ceremonies, with orchestras and dance troupes sponsored by royalty.

Unique to Vietnam is the monochord *(dan bau),* which has a single brass string stretched across a trapezoidal wooden resonance chamber one meter long, 12 cm wide, and 15 cm deep. At one end is a bamboo rod with its own small sound box in the shape of a tiny gourd; at the other is a conventional peg. The instrument produces a surprising range of haunting sound, and can mimic the specific tones of the Vietnamese language. Hence it's popular as accompaniment to romantic songs on film and in the theater.

Other unusual stringed instruments include the 16-string zither *(dan tranh)* and two-string vertical violin *(dan co).* Among the wind instruments, the oldest is the bamboo flute. Extremely difficult to master is the double trumpet *(ken doi),* composed of two bamboo pipes fused together, each pierced with seven holes. A popular percussion instrument is the bamboo xylophone *(to rung);* a variation is the stone xylophone *(dan da).*

Dance in Vietnam remains essentially a folk tradition, specific to villages and ethnic groups; performances most often take place during festivals. Occasionally, a special dance performance is staged at a tourist venue as a "cultural show." You might see the Conical Hat Dance from Hué, or the Dance of the Princesses from Hanoi, a Montagnard courtship dance, or a sensuous Cham dance. In Hué, imperial song and dance routines have been resurrected for the benefit of tourists.

Drama

Today's Vietnamese theater presents three types of performances: *cheo, cai luong,* and *tuong.* All three have been employed for propaganda purposes. *Cheo* is the oldest form of theater, a mix of mime, dance, song, and poetry. *Cheo* became a form of peasant protest against feudal masters, and later against the French—the Vietnamese version of the Blues.

Cai luong, or renovated theater, is of fairly recent origin, deriving from the days of the Nguyen dynasty and featuring spoken drama with short acts. *Cai luong* performances evolved

(continues on page 90)

POLITICALLY INCORRECT

Vietnam clamps down on writers who dare to speak out against the official state line. Some writers, however, have acquired an international reputation, which emboldens them. Since publishing is entirely a government operation in Vietnam, getting a "politically incorrect" manuscript published is quite a feat.

The Sorrow of War, by Bao Ninh, was published privately in 1991 by a group of Hanoi writers (read: underground publishing). It is the work of a North Vietnamese soldier who recalls his war experience and postwar trauma. Ninh went to war in 1965 at the age of 18. Of the 500 men who went with him, only 10 returned home after the fall of Saigon. Of those, six more committed suicide between 1976 and 1987. Bao Ninh overturns the official version of soldiers returning from the glorious front lines healthy in body and spirit. Ninh returns to a Hanoi that is a dilapidated capital, its citizens uninterested in victory parades.

The Sorrow of War was picked up by Secker and Warburg and published in London in 1993. It has been translated into English, Swedish, and Norwegian. Bao Ninh is delighted by the international reception and by royalties that buy him more time to write.

Duong Thu Huong's 1988 novel, *Paradise of the Blind,* portrays the communist system as exploitative and corrupt. Huong is a former anti-American resistance fighter who was expelled from the Communist Party in 1990 for advocating democracy; she was imprisoned for seven months in 1991. On a private visit to France in 1994, the dissident writer was presented with the order of Chevalier des Arts et des Lettres, the country's highest literary award. The French Culture Minister cited her as a writer of the first order who characterized the role of Vietnamese women in the fight for liberty and independence. The award was vigorously protested by the Vietnamese government: it seems liberty and independence are good values as long as they don't get out of hand. Huong's *Novel Without a Name,* published by William Morrow (New York, 1995), tells the story of a 28-year-old captain in the NVA during the war.

GOOD MORNING, APOCALYPSE

In 1992 ex-Marine Dan Thomas found himself standing in the old American Embassy compound in Saigon in full battle gear. Across the street, black smoke rose from burning tires as Vietcong troops drew nearer. Tanks flying the yellow-and-red striped flag of South Vietnam raced by. Wrong year? Bad dream? No, Dan had been sitting at Kim Café when he was recruited as an extra for a film—in effect, to play himself. The South Korean film company paid extras $30 a day, plus a $5 bonus for anyone willing to submit to a military crew cut.

These days it's easy to find American extras in Saigon. But before the days of individual travel, the Vietnamese had to settle for Russians or visiting Swedes to play the American parts. Today there's a famous bar in Saigon named after the movie *Apocalypse Now*, with a poster of the movie on the wall. Sometimes the Vietnamese tend to confuse their movies: one T-shirt sighted in Hanoi featured the logo "Good Morning, Apocalypse" emblazoned on the front, while on the back, printed in large letters, was "Vietnam Now!"

While the Vietnamese have produced films about the war era, most are of the boring propaganda documentary genre. The Vietnamese have hardly any film industry, only a few competent technicians, and no laboratory capable of processing high-quality film. However, the Vietnamese have gained experience with moviemaking during co-production of French movies. Since deregulation in 1992, private film production companies have appeared in Vietnam, mainly producing Kung Fu flicks or melodramatic romances in imitation of those from Hong Kong.

Hollywood Combat Formulas

American television coverage and postwar movies have had an incredible effect on the way we view Vietnam—all war, all combat, faceless Vietcong. The Americans filmed in the Philippines or Thailand: since America didn't win the war, standard heroic combat formulas had to be tinkered with. *The Green Berets,* a John Wayne film made in 1968, is the first and only Hollywood movie about Vietnam to suggest any degree of American military success. Heroic movies are also preoccupied with the issue of finding and rescuing MIAs. Sylvester Stallone took on Vietnam single handedly in *Rambo: First Blood II* (1985) and won, only to find he'd been duped by Uncle Sam. Rambo went to Vietnam in search of MIAs; ironically, he ended up a box office hero in Asia, an icon to many Asian kids. Also in the comic book action genre are three *Missing in Action* movies (1984-87) starring Chuck Norris. *Hamburger Hill* (1987) delivers a brutal documentary-style movie about the 1969 battle in which the Americans suffered heavy losses.

Some of the combat movies tackle the moral quagmire in which the Americans found themselves in Vietnam. *Casualties of War* (1989) is based on a true story about the kidnap, rape, and murder of a Vietnamese woman by US soldiers. In *Platoon* (1986) the plot pits American against American. *Gardens of Stone* (1987) mostly derives its drama from boot camp in the States. The first half of *Full Metal Jacket* also takes place in boot camp; the second half is set in Hué during the 1968 Tet Offensive. These movies present the grunt's-eye view of combat—harrowing accounts of the war's horror told from the perspective of naive recruits who had no idea what they were getting into or why. A sequence in *Forrest Gump* is the final word on this theme of startled innocence. The lead character, though immersed in the carnage and horror of the Vietnam War, emerges completely unscathed—because he's too stupid to know what's happening.

Shaking up the formulas, other Hollywood flicks examine the turmoil of returning American vets and the scars and side effects of the war: *The Deer Hunter* (1978), *Coming Home* (1978), *Jacob's Ladder* (1990), *Born on the Fourth of July* (1990). Two classics that broke out of the Hollywood mold are *Apocalypse Now* (1979) and *Good Morning, Vietnam* (1987).

Most of the Hollywood films are banned in Vietnam, although some—such as *Born on the Fourth of July*—have been screened. Others find their way into video stores on the blackmarket, either smuggled in or brought in by third parties. *Rambo* and *Good Morning, Vietnam* lead the way. With the lifting of the embargo, the national cinematographic service in southern Vietnam will import and distribute films by Paramount, MGM, and Universal Studios through an agreement with United International Pictures. It remains to be seen whether any American-made war movies about Vietnam will be allowed to play in theaters in Vietnam.

(continues on next page)

GOOD MORNING, APOCALYPSE

(continued)

The French Are Back

The French have had enough time to come to terms with Vietnam and offer a frank and perceptive view of their colonial past with a spate of movies—*Indochine* (1991), *l'Amant* (1992), and *Dien Bien Phu* (1992). These go for the human element; the Vietnamese are portrayed with real depth and real speaking parts. The French films also enjoy the advantage of location filming in Vietnam. French movies come up with interesting subject matter: a French-Algerian co-production called *Poussières de Vie* (Dust of Life), released in 1994, tackles the story of Son, born from a liaison between an American soldier and a Vietnamese woman, who is sent to re-education camp in Vietnam in 1975.

SELECT FILMOGRAPHY

French Colonial Era Classics

Indochine: Directed by Régis Wargnier, this movie is set in 1930s Vietnam. The plot involves a love triangle, with an undercurrent of Vietnamese resistance to French rule. Eliane, played by Catherine Deneuve, runs a large rubber plantation in the south. She has adopted an Annamite princess, Camille (Linh Dan Pham), after the death of the girl's parents in a plane crash. Both women fall in love with Jean-Baptiste (Vincent Pérez), a French naval officer. The movie shows French high life contrasted with the brutal lot of Vietnamese peasants pressed into plantation service. In the middle are the elite Vietnamese ruling group, the mandarins. Times are changing for the mandarins. Tanh, Camille's intended husband, was educated in Paris, where he acquired new ideals; now he refuses to respect the shrine of his ancestors. Camille, the "Red Princess," makes a break with her adopted mother.

With its Hollywood-like glossy treatment, *Indochine* has been responsible for a boost in French tourism to Vietnam. People come looking for the exact pinnacle of limestone in Halong Bay, the exact building of Hué Citadel seen in the movie. Viewers began to realize Vietnam is not all bomb-scarred landscapes—it has power and poetry too. Halong Bay, Tam Coc Caves, the mountain landscapes of the north, the citadel and tombs of Hué, and the Hotel Continental in Saigon all figure in the movie.

L'Amant (The Lover): This 1992 release is based on the novella of the same name by Marguerite Duras. Set in the Saigon of the 1930s, it concerns a steamy affair between a French schoolgirl and the elegant son of a wealthy Chinese family. The tale of the forbidden liaison was filmed on location in Saigon and Cholon in French and English versions. It stars English actress Jane March and American actor Tony Leung, and is directed by Jean-Jacques Annaud. The movie is based on a true story. It sparked a controversy in France over whether the lead actor and actress actually enjoyed on-screen sex.

Dien Bien Phu: Released in 1992, this film is an RIP on celluloid—the French finally coming to terms with their great defeat at the hands of the Vietminh in 1954. Director Pierre Schoendoerffer was there as a combat photographer.

Traps: The decay of French colonial rule in Vietnam is well portrayed in *Traps,* an Australian movie made in 1993. This movie presents a refreshingly non-Hollywood perspective. The setting is 1950s Vietnam, with a journalist and his photographer wife arriving on assignment to report on colonial life. They become guests of a French rubber plantation owner and his defiant daughter. The central theme, of characters desperately trying to find themselves, echoes the attempts of a new Vietnam trying to find a new voice. The movie was filmed on location in Vung Tau and other parts of the south; the Vietnamese did not attempt to modify the script. Director Pauline Chan was born and raised in Vietnam; she left at the age of 15.

American War Classics

Apocalypse Now: Francis Ford Coppola's 1979 release was very loosely based on Joseph Conrad's novella *Heart of Darkness,* set in the Belgian Congo. Coppola's crazy colonel Kurtz is modeled on Conrad's character of the same name, and also on CIA agent Anthony Posepny (Tony Poe), who operated out of northern Laos and offered tribal recruits one US dollar for every set of communist ears they brought back. In *Apocalypse Now,* renegade

CIA man Kurtz (Marlon Brando) lives in an Angkor-style temple deep in Cambodia; another agent (played by Martin Sheen) is dispatched from Vietnam to find him and terminate his command. This hallucinatory movie was one of the first postwar American films on Vietnam, and one of the few to delve into America's "dirty war" in Cambodia.

Francis Ford Coppola took a lot of risks making this movie, dodging all the Hollywood formulas in favor of a blunt and brutal approach. There is no attempt at heroic portrayal; the movie shows the war as a kind of madness. *Apocalypse Now* went way over schedule and budget. Later a movie was made about the movie, titled **Hearts of Darkness** (1991), with on-set footage shot by Coppola's wife Eleanor during filming in the Philippines, as well as more recent interviews with the director, cast, and crew. This is a fascinating glimpse into the madness and magic behind the scenes as the movie—like the Vietnam War—spiraled out of control and turned into a filmmaker's nightmare.

Good Morning, Vietnam: A comedy about Vietnam? They said it couldn't be done. In this movie, it was not only done—it was brilliantly done. The movie stars the maniacal Robin Williams, ad libbing his way through the script about disc jockey Adrian Cronauer, who defied both musical and military decorum on Saigon's Armed Forces Radio in 1965. The loud call "Go-o-o-o-o-o-o-od Morning, Vietnam!" was coined in real life by disc jockey Jean Leroy, working for the American Forces Vietnam Network. The movie also stars Tung Thanh Tran and Forest Whitaker. Directed by Barry Levinson, this 1987 movie breaks ground, showing the manipulation of truth by the American military and presenting a more sympathetic, human view of the Vietnamese. For these reasons, the movie has gained acceptance in Vietnam itself. The Vietnamese find it funny, too. The soundtrack on audiocassette turns up on cruise boats in places like Nha Trang.

The Oliver Stone Trilogy: Epic wars demand epic movies, and director Oliver Stone set out to capture three different dimensions in three movies. Stone is himself a Vietnam vet, and *Platoon* (1986), starring Tom Berenger, Willem Dafoe, and Charlie Sheen, is easily the most gripping and realistic of the combat movies to come out of the United States. *Born on the Fourth of July* (1990) captures the anguish of a high school football star (Tom Cruise) who is drafted, sent to Vietnam, and comes home in a wheelchair. Based on the true experience of veteran Ron Kovic, but liberally fictionalized.

The third movie, *Heaven and Earth* (1993), captures a dimension not explored in any other American movie—the Vietnamese viewpoint. This film is based on Le Ly Hayslip's true story, adapting events from her two books, *Child of War, Woman of Peace* and *When Heaven and Earth Changed Places.* The story is narrated by Le Ly Hayslip—played by Hiep Thi Le—with Haing S. Ngor as her father, Joan Chen as her mother, and Tommy Lee Jones as her American husband. This powerful drama unfolds in Ky La, a village close to Danang, and captures the upheavals in village life. Neither the North Vietnamese, the South Vietnamese, nor the Americans appear in a good light as they bully, abuse, and coerce the villagers. Le Ly Hayslip is caught in the middle—between North and South, Americans and Vietnamese, greed and compassion, capitalism and communism, war and peace, Father Heaven and Mother Earth. Le Ly Hayslip's faith in Buddhism, the middle way, is the key to her survival.

Ironically, Le Ly Hayslip's books have yet to be translated into Vietnamese and published in Vietnam; permission is being delayed by Culture Ministry objections to the portrayal of the North Vietnamese.

Operation Dumbo Drop: This 1995 Walt Disney movie provides a different take on the war—an amiable war saga for children. The Vietnam War is relatively bloodless in this adventure-comedy focusing on one good American deed. The action is inspired by a "true" story as told to Disney by US Major James Morris. In 1968, NVA troops shot a Montagnard village's only elephant to punish villagers working with the Americans. A US special forces band lands the tricky assignment of delivering a full-size elephant to the village in time for an important ceremony. The special forces group travels to Ban Don to purchase another elephant; the rest of the movie is pure Disney fiction involving transport of the pachyderm by plane, flatbed truck, and boat, with narrow escapes, airborne antics, elephant rampages, and lots of slipping around in elephant plop. Finally, the weary elephant arrives. The movie, shot in Thailand, is directed by Simon Wincer and stars Danny Glover, Ray Liotta, and Dinh Thien Le.

(continues on next page)

GOOD MORNING, APOCALYPSE
(continued)

Vietnamese Classics

The Girl on the River: This 1987 movie, made by Vietnam's leading director, Dang Nhat Minh, is set during the Vietnam War, in the south. A flotilla of boats anchored on the banks of a river serves as a brothel for ARVN soldiers. The heroine of the movie is a prostitute who rescues an injured Vietcong leader on the run. She saves his life and they fall in love. Before he leaves, they promise to reunite after the war. However, with reunification of the country, the man becomes a high official who denies he ever met her. His wife, a journalist, finds out about the heroine and writes an article about her, which her husband tries to have censored.

Wild Reed: A 1993 film, with government assistance accounting for half the $60,000 budget. This movie by Vuong Tuan Duc is one of the first in Vietnam to address the tragedy of Vietnam's estimated 300,000 MIAs. It shows the anguish of a North Vietnamese officer who returns to his hometown with a Vietnamese MIA search team in 1976 to discover his wife has remarried, believing him dead.

into a nationwide protest against the French, and colonial censors banned performances of certain plays. In the 1920s, a new form of drama, *kich noi,* was introduced. After 1954, *kich noi* was used to disseminate communist doctrine to large audiences.

Tuong drama arrived from China in the 14th century. Performances follow strict rules of facial expression, stylized gestures, and accented speech; performers wear elaborate costumes and paint their faces in different colors. The story is usually an epic taken from Vietnamese legends and myths, or a historical plot portraying the lives of national heroes. The imperial Nguyen court brought tuong to its peak in Hué in the 19th century, making the most of the Confucian concepts embodied in *tuong,* stressing absolute authority of the monarch. In the 20th century, *tuong* moved to the stage and became dissociated from court intrigues, centering instead on everyday life, with characters depicting people's joys and sorrows. Modern versions of *tuong* feature aspects of the life of Ho Chi Minh and other communist leaders. *Tuong* has fallen out of favor as a popular entertainment form: the last bastion of *tuong* is the city of Qui Nhon, where the Dao Tan Troupe resides.

Water Puppetry

The most original theatrical form in Vietnam is water puppetry, or *roi nuoc.* Like much original Vietnamese culture, water puppetry derives

water puppets, Hanoi

from the Red River Delta area, centered around Hanoi. This unique and exuberant form of puppetry employs the surface of the water as a stage and focuses on themes such as herding ducks, plowing with water buffalo, harvesting rice, sampan fishing, and naval battles.

Water puppetry was a folk art form long before it became a theatrical one. Performances are believed to date back to the 12th century. Temporary theaters were constructed in the village pond and performances marked the beginning or end of the rice-planting cycle. Offering prayers for good crops and good rainfall was essential. The water itself became part of the festive ritual, with washing of Buddha statues, boat racing, and swimming contests. Water puppetry uses a fair dose of satire, perhaps as a way for country folk to let off steam. Traveling puppetry guilds were later able to tour with shows, and water puppetry became part of court entertainment during the Ly and Tran dynasties. Guilds exist today in a number of northern provinces; the best place to see water puppetry is in Hanoi.

In contrast to puppets controlled above by strings, water puppets are manipulated from below, so the means of manipulation remains completely concealed. A dozen puppeteers stand waist-deep in water behind a pagoda set, meant to resemble an ancient village communal house. The puppeteers hide behind a bamboo screen in a manipulation room about four to five meters long and three to four meters wide. Invisible to the audience, the puppeteers maneuver the puppets with bamboo or wooden poles ingeniously rigged to pulleys and strings. To the audience, the life-like puppets skipping across the water appear nothing short of magical. Sometimes a series of six or more puppets may be operated from a single base, requiring three or four puppeteers.

Skits presented in water puppet theater are short—sometimes only two or three minutes—and the entire performance lasts about an hour. Themes include satirical digs at village life, folk stories, mythology, and historical events. A light and sound show is provided by aquatic fireworks and festive, rhythmic sound effects. Sound may involve traditional instruments and snippets of *tuong* or *cheo* opera. Skits are introduced and narrated by Chu Teu, a clownish water puppet whose outward appearance is that of a strong and dignified young ploughman—albeit one wearing a loincloth and sporting pigtails. Chu Teu's role is master of ceremonies—he opens the show, introduces the program, acts as an intermediary between audience and puppet characters, and makes fun of everyone and everything. Water provides natural amplification, and produces reflections that enhance the theatrical effect. Water puppets are made of lacquered wood. The handcarved puppets are a folk art in themselves: characters include fishermen, duck-tenders, wrestlers, emperors, and national heroes, as well as frogs, fish, turtles, phoenixes, and aquatic dragons.

FINE ARTS

Architecture

Heavy Chinese influence is apparent in the architecture of pagodas and palaces, such as those at the imperial citadel in Hué. Very little is left of original Vietnamese architecture after years of neglect and warfare. Many older structures were made of wood, which has a limited lifespan. Other older structures were knocked down to make way for French buildings. Surviving examples of urban architecture with Vietnamese elements are the long narrow "tube houses" in the old quarter sectors of Hoi An and Hanoi. In Hoi An semidetached two-story mansions constructed with columns of wood sit on marble bases. Structures are held in place with large wooden nails; on the roof are "Yin and Yang" tiles, so named for the way they lock together. Merchant houses feature a shop front, family living quarters with a courtyard, and a rear storage section.

Sculpture

Sculpture lives in the past in Vietnam. Vietnamese art first flourished with the emergence of the Dongson culture in the Red River Delta near Thanh Hoa. This culture produced magnificent bronze sculptures with clear elements of Chinese style. The most renowned are huge bronze kettle drums over a meter in height and width, with geometric and naturalist decoration on the drum head. The exact function of the drums is not known. Possibly they were used for summoning rain, or buried with important deceased

THE ALLURING *AO DAI*

One of the first things the visitor notices on a trip to Vietnam is schoolgirls riding bicycles three or four abreast, the panels of their long *ao dai* dresses billowing behind them like orchid petals. Or, on a Boeing run by Vietnam Airlines, stewardesses in beautiful sky-blue or pink *ao dais*. Anthony Grey described the *ao dai* in his novel *Saigon* as "demure and provocative . . . women seemed not to walk but to float gently beneath the tamarinds on the evening breeze." The *ao dai* covers everything, but its gossamer-thin fabric hides almost nothing. It's very practical, maintaining modesty but allowing ventilation and freedom of movement. It does not crush, and dries quickly after washing.

traditional ao dai

Ao dai means long gown, and is pronounced "ow yai" in the south and "ow zai" in the north. It's a close-fitting knee-length gown, split to the waist and worn over flowing white or black satin pants. The gown features a high collar and tight sleeves. The *ao dai* is adapted from a Chinese dress, called the *cheong sam,* originally worn by both sexes. Pants and buttoned coats were worn by men and women during the latter years of the Nguyen dynasty. In traditional society, design and color indicated the status of the wearer: yellow fabric was reserved for the emperor, purple for high-ranking mandarins, blue for court officials. The emperor alone could use gold brocade and the five-claw dragon design. Emperor Minh Mang imposed the wearing of pants on the entire female population of Vietnam.

The *ao dai* is of recent design. In the early 1930s Cat Tuong, a Vietnamese writer who dabbled in fashion design, modified the *cheong sam.* The new design tightened the bodice and moved the opening from the front to the shoulder and side seam. Cat Tuong also employed a greater range of colors and motifs for the *ao dai.* In the 1950s, two tailors in Saigon incorporated raglan sleeves into the design, with seams running diagonally from the collar to the underarm. As the *ao dai* evolved it became less popular as dress for men.

Between 1975 and the late 1980s, in a period of severe austerity, the *ao dai* fell from grace, and Vietnamese women switched to Western-style blouses and pants. Since 1990, however, the *ao dai* has made a bold comeback as the national dress. It is the dress seen in tourist advertising, and is worn by hotel receptionists and office workers, particularly in the south. Spectacular *ao dais* with handpainted designs on the bodice are worn for holidays—especially at Tet—and for weddings.

Although *ao dais* in standard sizes are mass-produced for work and school uniforms, Vietnamese women prefer custom-made versions. At a Saigon tailor shop, a team of specialized cutters, sewers, and fitters can mold an ensemble in several hours. The resulting *ao dai* fits the woman's figure perfectly.

persons. The tradition of sculpting in bronze survived, and in pagodas and temples the visitor will see elaborate sculptures in the shape of prominent deities and real and mythical animals. Sculpting of large statues in sandalwood is another medium seen in pagodas.

The former Kingdom of Champa, which flourished in coastal Vietnam in the 10th and 11th centuries, was remarkable for its sandstone sculpture. The artistic style draws on Indian influences, as the Cham culture itself existed outside the Vietnamese mainstream. The Kingdom of Champa was overrun by the Viet in the 15th century and virtually extinguished. The finest display of Cham sculpture is in a museum in Danang; examples of Dongson and Cham art and sculpture can be seen in museums in Saigon and Hanoi.

Painting

With the exception of mural painting, folk art, and portraits on silk, painting was not a highly developed art form in Vietnam. Vietnamese painting is largely of modern origin, derived from French tutelage. In 1925 the French established the Ecole des Beaux-Arts de L'Indochine in Hanoi, training a generation of painters from across Indochina. The training was largely European; a major part of the syllabus involved the work of French Expressionists. French influence explains why Vietnamese art appeals so widely to the Western eye—it's a unique mix of European and Asian styles.

From 1945 to 1987, Vietnamese painting entered a phase of social realism. Visiting an exhibition in 1945, Ho Chi Minh was bored by the flowers and women; he said the works did not show the realities of daily life. The following year the paintings exhibited were titled "National Unity" and "General Insurrection" and featured revolutionaries and peasants. Thus a school of social realism was launched, featuring "politically correct" art that dominated the artistic arena for the next 40 years. Individual art was suppressed in favor of art that served the revolutionary cause.

In the early 1950s Bui Xuan Phai, considered the master of contemporary painting, started a campaign with other painters for more freedom of expression. The movement was severely repressed. Phai lost his teaching job at the Hanoi Fine Arts School, and had trouble obtaining supplies. Often he resorted to painting on newsprint. Phai was not allowed to hold an exhibition until 1984, two years before his death. He never earned more than a few hundred dollars from his art, yet today a single Phai painting can fetch $25,000.

In modern Vietnam social realism has been completely abandoned. Movement began in 1986 with the advent of doi moi. Individual styles once forbidden—abstract and even surrealist art—are now common. You can find nudes, permitted since 1990; one Hanoi artist caused a sensation with a 1994 exhibition featuring male nudes. Another sensational exhibition in 1994 was called "As Seen From Both Sides," which culled works from Vietnamese and American painters involved in the Vietnam War. The exhibition toured 14 American cities before arriving in Vietnam for shows in Hanoi and Ho Chi Minh City in 1994.

Since 1989, Vietnamese art has gained momentum on the international market. Prices for original artworks have soared, making it possible for younger artists to live off the proceeds of their work. Paintings are sold in European countries such as France and Sweden, and the Asian art centers of Hong Kong and Singapore. A Vietnamese painter's dream is an exhibition in Paris.

Folk Art

There is a vibrant tradition of village folk art in Vietnam. Villages in the Red River Delta, for example, specialize in the production of ceramics, silk weaving, woodblock printing, and the carving of furniture with mother-of-pearl inlay. These craft skills are largely of Chinese origin.

In the 15th century Emperor Le Than Ton sent an envoy to the Chinese court to investigate the art of lacquerware. Resin from the lacquer tree is milked and applied in repeated coats to wood, leather, metal, or porcelain. After lacquer application, the piece can be decorated, painted, or inlaid with mother-of-pearl. The art of mother-of-pearl inlay has been practiced for over a thousand years, and is one of the more original folk arts in Vietnam. Pieces of mollusk shell are glued to recessed wood for trays, screens, and bowls. Pictures are also created on wood this way. Vietnamese pottery shows distinct Chinese influence in both design and execution.

Among the types produced are celadon and blue and white porcelain.

Handicraft shops in Vietnam sell items with mythical animals or landscapes embroidered on silk or velvet. Another very different source of folk art comes from Montagnard groups: these hilltribers excel at weaving, embroidery, and basketry.

CUSTOMS AND CONDUCT

The Vietnamese are among the warmest, friendliest, and most hospitable people in Asia. Avoiding offense is mostly a matter of common sense.

Temple Manners
Pagodas are sacred places, so when visiting, dress properly (no shorts, sandals, dirty jeans, or T-shirts). Determine if shoes must be removed, and ask permission if taking photos. Treat all Buddha images and statues with respect. Making a small donation to the pagoda's contribution box would be appreciated.

Terms of Address
Vietnamese names consist of three elements. The name Nguyen Van Tan breaks down as Nguyen (family name) Van (middle) and Tan (given name). The order is thus inverted from the Western, but titles are still applied to the third name. So if the title like General or Mr. is applied, it becomes Mr. Tan. In the Vietnamese White Pages for Saigon or Hanoi, residential listings are by given name followed by family name and middle name—thus, *Tan* Nguyen Van. The reason for this is that half the population goes under the family name of Nguyen: the Nguyen emperors allowed people to take their family name. Other common family names are Tran, Le, Phan, and Ngo. Vietnamese women do not change their names after marriage. When addressing people, you need to use the given name, and take into account age, sex, status, and other factors. It's worth taking the time to find out how to use the system. For more details, see the Vietnamese language section at the back of this book.

Lien Xo!
Lien Xo! means "Russian" and is chanted by children in Vietnam upon encountering any Caucasian. This becomes quite annoying if you stay in Vietnam long enough. It's a derogatory term because the Vietnamese didn't like the penny-pinching Russians. Hanoi and Moscow were closely aligned in those days, but since the collapse of the Soviet Union there are very few Russians left in Vietnam. To correct this impression, repeat your nationality in Vietnamese.

Dress
Caucasians in shorts remind the old folks of the colonial French—which is not a good idea. Although rural men wear shorts or rolled-up pants when slushing through rice paddies, it is not culturally acceptable for women to wear shorts. Exposure of skin by women is frowned upon, so dress modestly, even in the hot and humid south.

Entry to pagodas and places like Ho Chi Minh's Mausoleum may be refused to foreigners in shorts. Travelers should be aware that Ho Chi Minh has acquired a sacred status in Vietnam—images and statues of the leader are treated with great respect.

Body Language
In most situations, observe how a Vietnamese person of your sex and age behaves, and do as he or she does. A simple example is using a toothpick after dining. Most Vietnamese cover their mouths with the left hand, and use the toothpick with the right.

Do not use a crooked single finger to beckon someone—in Vietnam this gesture is used for summoning animals. Instead, turn the palm of the hand downward, slightly cupped, while wriggling four fingers. The okay symbol (thumb and forefinger pressed into a circle) is understood in Vietnam. It can also mean "zero," as in money. Crossed fingers is a bad gesture. It refers to a prostitute.

A useful gesture in Vietnam is "screwing-in-the-lightbulb," which consists of an upturned palm with fingers held as if grasping a bowl. The hand is then rotated back and forth near the ear in the rhythm used when installing a lightbulb. This can mean "I don't know," "I don't understand," or "the price is too high." The double gesture—two hands at once to both ears, plus a grimace—really drives the point home.

Avoid touching a Vietnamese. Back-slapping a guide or patting a child on the head may not be welcome. The head is sacred to Buddhists. While members of the opposite sex refrain from touching each other in public, it's common to see two young men walking hand-in-hand. Avoid pointing your feet at anyone—this is considered rude, as the foot is the lowliest part of the body.

Saving Face, Losing Face

It is considered bad form to display anger in Vietnam—smile instead. Stay calm, or you will lose face. In many situations, "face" is important. Do not shout when bargaining.

An important cultural note: A smile on a Vietnamese face does not necessarily indicate amusement—it can also convey anger, fear, embarrassment, disagreement. Thus, as you pick up your mangled bicycle from a head-on collision with another cyclist, the other party may smile or even manage a nervous laugh.

Gifts

Anything foreign will do just fine, thank you—foreign cigarettes for men, foreign cosmetics for women, and so on. Items do not have to be expensive. Baseball caps with foreign logos are all the rage, as are T-shirts with foreign slogans

on them (not too risqué). Foreign magazines are greatly appreciated; women prefer fashion magazines. For children, pens and balloons are ideal. Many Vietnamese men smoke—foreign brands such as 555 or Salem are much appreciated, and you can break open a pack to hand out individual cigarettes.

Taboo Shots

Do not photograph bridges, military installations, or strategic infrastructure. Do not photograph military parades or official functions. Photojournalists require special visas to visit Vietnam and may require special permission to photograph sensitive events or subjects.

Dealing with Police

Most Vietnamese are terrified of the police with good reason. If you show no fear, the police may be taken aback. In the early postwar years of travel in Vietnam, you needed permits to visit any place outside Saigon or Hanoi. The police had a field day holding passports of foreigners, asking for and receiving $100 fines for being in a place without a permit. The 1993 abolition of permits was intended to curb these corrupt practices. Now that this game is up, police are discovering other ways of extracting money. A group of foreigners in a jeep east of Pleiku were fined $7 each for touring the "wrong village"—the total fine came to $50. Vietnamese drivers are sometimes fined $10 or so for not possessing a "license to drive foreigners

the Hanoi Boys

around," or carrying irregular insurance. Others have been told by a policeman on an ancient Russian motorcycle that their brand-new Toyotas are "not roadworthy."

Police often count on the fact that foreigners are pressed for time. So one tactic is to sit it out with a fat book and see what gives. Police must go to a higher authority to hold you overnight; if you're stubborn, they may give up. Keep smiling and ask, "What's the problem? I don't understand what the problem is here." Do not produce original documents, as this gives police the leverage they need for fines—if you give them $50, they return your passport. Show only photocopies and insist the originals are elsewhere. Sometimes a five-dollar bill will expedite the case to a favorable conclusion. Packs of foreign cigarettes have a similar effect. If you must pay a fine, remember that all fines are negotiable—so bargain.

ON THE ROAD

Vietnam opened to Western tourism in the 1980s. The early days of travel were harrowing, with snarls of frustrating red tape. For a long time, individual travelers were neither recognized nor allowed. Now they are, and travel permits are not required except in a handful of sensitive areas.

Vietnam's fledgling tourist industry appears to be taking off. From a paltry 60,000 visitors in 1989, arrivals rocketed to 670,000 in 1993, according to the Vietnam National Tourism Administration. There were over a million arrivals in 1994: Vietnam hopes to attract several million visitors annually by the end of the century. Although a complete breakdown of figures was not released, 125,000 of the 1993 arrivals were Vietnamese from overseas—half of them from the United States. Most certainly, Asian visitors from Taiwan, Singapore, Hong Kong, and China account for a large percentage of visitors.

VIETNAM HIGHLIGHTS

Vietnamese tourist authorities are fond of grafting pretty women in colorful *ao dai* dress onto the landscape to brighten up brochures. For instance,

a row of soot-gray mandarin statues in Hué may feature the addition of a young woman with a bright yellow *ao dai.* This may be because Hué's major attraction—the Royal Citadel—was levelled during the Vietnam War. A similar fate befell a number of key sites around the country, although the enterprising Vietnamese have created new attractions out of the debris of war with tours to the DMZ and visits to tactical tunnels and army museums. What remains in the way of architecture is mostly French—the grand public buildings in Hanoi and Saigon, the villas at the former hill station of Dalat.

The ethnic minorities of the northwest are fascinating—an array of groups without the accompanying commercial hoopla found in Thailand. Among the natural wonders are the karst scenery of the mountainous north, Halong Bay's grottoes, and the Mekong Delta waterways lined with lush tropical vegetation. Pristine beaches are a major draw, and fishing villages dot the coastline, along with semi-developed resorts like China Beach and Nha Trang.

Many visitors say the highlight of their trip to Vietnam is not the sights but the experiences. The Vietnamese are friendly and hospitable.

CHANGING THE RULES

In September 1995 the Vietnamese Immigration Department announced that no more tourist visa extensions would be issued. Those traveling on business, journalist, or diplomatic visas are not affected by the changes. Overseas Vietnamese are restricted to a maximum extension of six months.

The regulations appeared to be directed at foreigners working in Vietnam on tourist visas, and at backpackers who "stay too long, spend too little, wander beyond the approved tourist zones, and have a detrimental effect on Vietnamese society," according to a source in Hanoi. If the government could have its way, all visitors would arrive on tightly controlled high-paying package tours. In a bid to cater to higher-class tourists, Hanoi has ordered state-run guesthouses upgraded to hotels, and will not issue any new permits for private guesthouses, the natural choice for low-budget travelers. The government is also moving against unlicensed and uninsured private tour operators. The main beneficiary of all this? The state, of course. Most foreign-invested projects in new hotels and resort developments are joint ventures with local government bodies.

After 30 years of warfare, the older folk have some tales to tell. Over half of Vietnam's current population were born after 1975, however, and have no experience of the wars that molded the older generation. Gourmet food is resurgent in Vietnam, with superb Viet-French and Chinese cuisine in Saigon and Hanoi. The food quality varies. Hué offers above-average fare; Dalat and Hoi An are good. On the coast, there's seafood at Nha Trang and at Halong Bay.

The weather in Vietnam can play havoc with travel plans—typhoons at beaches, thick fog at Halong Bay, flooding in the Mekong Delta. Because of the varied climate zones, no season is best. If you want to cover the entire country, consider devoting half your time to the north, the other half to the center and south. You can travel the entire country via a series of stepping stones—Hanoi, Hué, Danang, Nha Trang, Dalat, Saigon are the most common. It's also eminently possible to concentrate on one region alone—spend all your time in the north, south, or center—and return for the others some other time. Vietnam is the kind of place you'll want to return to.

Hanoi and the North

The north was the last area of Vietnam to open up to tourism, and holds the greatest potential. There's spectacular karst scenery with sugarloaf peaks at Halong Bay and Tam Coc Caves. The landscape is evocative of parts of Thailand, the Philippines, or the south of China. Hanoi is a common base for exploring the north. Often visitors enjoy touring from Hanoi to the Chinese border, crossing over into China from either of the two open borders.

Hanoi offers most of the cultural and historical highlights in the north. It has the best-preserved French architecture in Indochina and a charming ambience with numerous cafés and art galleries. You can walk or bicycle around the lively Old Quarter, or out to Ho Chi Minh Mausoleum and the Army Museum. At night you can visit a water puppet theater—a fantastic and unique art form.

The top day-trips from Hanoi are the Perfume Pagoda trip or the Tam Coc Caves and Bich Dong tour. To the southwest, limited hiking is available at Cuc Phuong National Park, which, like other national parks in Vietnam, is a reserve in name only. Also in this area, Mai Chau offers fine scenery and markets and a look at various ethnic groups. Several Hanoi tour operators provide hiking trips to the southwest of two to four days, staying at minority villages en route. These are available for Cuc Phuong National Park, Hoa Binh, and Mai Chau.

In the Gulf of Tonkin ugly, gray Haiphong is the gateway to the fascinating regions of Cat Ba Island and Halong Bay, where you can commandeer a converted fishing boat or a modified red-sailed junk for a leisurely cruise among hundreds of karst islands, cliffs, and outcrops. This area was once the domain of pirates, with hideaway caves and inlets. Allow one to three days for the entire trip from Hanoi, longer if returning via Cat Ba Island. Sunbathing, swimming, snorkeling, and caving are the order of the day. Limestone outcrops provide excellent caving. Halong Bay has deep grottoes to explore, and near Cat Ba National Park lie Trung Trang Caves.

Minority groups abound in the rugged and mountainous northwest near the Tonkinese Alps. There are lots of opportunities to get off the track and organize your own treks to villages, best arranged in a 4WD vehicle. Stopping points along the northwest route include Dien Bien Phu, Lai Chau, and the old French hill resort of Sapa, located near the Chinese border. Ethnic groups are best seen at markets, where women dress in full costume and men occasionally do too. Because of poor roads, trips to the northwest are time-consuming—allow a minimum of three days when traveling from Hanoi. You can carry on from Hanoi through the Lao Cai border into China. A rail spur leads all the way from Hanoi to Kunming.

The best place to experience Tet (Lunar New Year) is in the more traditional north. Villagers take time out from hard toil to get into the Tet spirit with special festivities. Firecracker competitions are held in several villages close to Hanoi.

Hué and the Center

Vietnam's central region is not universally popular. Some like it, some prefer to skip it. The center has beaches, but few historical sites. Most find it's on the way or in the way, so they check it out anyway. Gateway to the center is the Hué-Danang-Hoi An triangle, which holds the main historic and cultural interest. A land-border crossing into Laos is possible about 150 km due northwest of Hué at Lao Bao.

Hué, the former imperial capital, is the educational and cultural heart of central Vietnam. Dowdy tombs and the Royal Citadel—the main attractions—are somewhat overrated, if not completely destroyed. When it's not pouring, Hué is pleasant enough, offering quiet boating on the Perfume River and cycling along back roads.

The top day-trip from Hué is the DMZ tour to Vinh Moc Tunnels and Khe Sanh base—all highly educational, but don't believe any hype about trekking along the Ho Chi Minh Trail. Any portion of the fabled trail not reclaimed by the jungle would be dangerous ground because of the massive amount of unexploded ordnance lying around. Also, consider that the trail was chosen because it was inconspicuous. The scenery is on the boring side.

Danang is a nasty port city, but host to the Cham Museum, which features a fine collection of artifacts from the fascinating Cham civilization. Within easy reach of Danang are China Beach (swimming) and the Marble Mountains.

Hoi An, a well-preserved maritime trading town, is a favorite among travelers. It's one of the very few places in Vietnam where you can find traditional architecture. There's good food for a change, and it's an excellent place to stroll around.

Central Vietnam has a long coastline with numerous white-sand beaches and fishing villages. Typhoons can lash the coast toward the

AN EARLY AMERICAN TOURIST

In December 1973 travel writer Paul Theroux dropped by to ride what trains he could in South Vietnam. Theroux describes an encounter with the Director of Vietnam Tourism in Saigon in his travel narrative The Great Railway Bazaar. The director advises Theroux that the train he is planning to take is the worst in the world. He should instead go to a beach like Vung Tau. Or to the Central Highlands so he can say he slept in a bunker at Pleiku. Or to Hué, described in the Lovely Hué brochure as a "scenic beauty" (the booklet had not been updated—it failed to mention Hué was obliterated five years previously). Posters were printed showing pretty Vietnamese girls in places like Danang and Hué with a slogan "Follow Me!" The director was hoping to attract many tourists from Japan and America who had heard so much about the country. There were two main selling points—the beaches and the war. An estimated 70,000 people had been killed since the ceasefire went into effect in 1972: when Theroux brought up the question of getting shot, the director told him there was nothing to worry about—tourists would visit only noncombat areas. While riding the train from Saigon to Bien Hoa, the station master mentioned to Theroux at one point that this was usually where the Vietcong fired on the train. Theroux joked, "Perhaps we should close the windows then."

latter part of the year. Nha Trang is an established beach resort, meaning it has a few umbrellas and seaside cafés and five km of white sand and coconut palms. You have to put up with aggressive cyclos and Mafia types around Nha Trang. But, it has some fine Cham towers and there are excellent day-trips to offshore islands by fishing boat. There is limited diving and windsurfing equipment available. Future developments for the foreign beach-potato will focus on China Beach near Danang, where occasional surf comes up. Other coastal spots include Cua Dai Beach near Hoi An, and Thuan An Beach near Hué. Pristine spots—still fishing villages—include Lang Co Lagoon north of Danang and Dai Lanh Beach north of Nha Trang.

If you want to get off the track, the Central Highlands is the place to go. Some prefer the solitude and open spaces here, compared to the more crowded coastal cities. The highlands has forest cover and deep waterfalls. Don't expect any wonders in the way of ethnic groups in the highlands—most have parted from their traditional ways and are increasingly becoming Vietnamized. Half-hearted—and expensive—elephant rides are available at Ban Don near Buon Ma Thuot.

Dalat is the former French hill resort set in pinewoods, with many villas. The Vietnamese rave on about this place, but it's quite ordinary. The pinewoods around Dalat are great for motorcycling and hiking.

Saigon and the South

The south is blessed with the most consistently balmy weather in Vietnam, which gives you a chance to put your camera to good use. Not to mention your beach towel—the humidity will make you sweat like a pig. What the south lacks in real attractions, it more than compensates for in energy level and cultural exchange. Most travelers use Saigon as a base for exploring the south. It's possible to go by land from Saigon to Phnom Penh if your paperwork is in order.

Saigon is the powerhouse of the south—noisy, raucous, rough and ready. It has the worst traffic in Vietnam, with bicycles now being replaced by motorcycles; it also has more than its share of beggars and prostitutes, con men and drug addicts, shysters and hustlers. Down-

town you can find faded colonial grandeur and the stark War Crimes Museum; over in Cholon stand peaceful pagodas. Saigon has great cuisine, with a selection of restaurants to suit all, and excellent shopping. It's also the only place in the country with anything resembling nightlife. Clubs range from disco joints to karaoke bars; quieter nightlife is found at open-air cafés, or on boat cruises on the Saigon River.

A good day-trip from Saigon is the Cao Dai Temple and Cu Chi Tunnels tour, which will delight seekers of the bizarre. Another option is a one-day trip to the Mekong Delta, particularly to the town of Mytho. Further afield is Vung Tau, a mundane beach resort rife with prostitutes; a better bet is Long Hai Beach, with pristine coastline close by.

The Mekong Delta is a region of waterways, deep-green ricefields, fruit orchards, floating markets, and more coconuts than you'd ever want to contemplate. A visit to this tropical wonderland is highly recommended. The towns of Mytho, Cantho, and Vinh Long are easily accessible from Saigon, and make great bases for exploring surrounding areas by small boat. This is a fertile region; markets present exotic species of fruit. Getting right into the delta may require a week or longer—you can strike out for Ha Tien or Chau Doc at the extremities. Throw in some river trips if you can—that's the real way to see this region. Some travelers motorcycle around; you can often load motorcycles onto boats.

HAZARDS

War Materiel

Unexploded ordnance poses a big problem in Vietnam. If you venture into the former DMZ, follow your guide and do not stray from marked paths, do not touch or disturb any shells or mines you may come across, and do not climb inside bomb craters. Since 1975, thousands of Vietnamese have been killed or maimed by leftover ordnance while cultivating the fields. Xinhua news agency reported in January 1995 that Chinese soldiers removed 700,000 landmines from the Sino-Vietnamese border during a 500-day campaign to demilitarize the frontier. The mines were presumably laid after the 1979 border war with Vietnam. Makes you wonder how many mines are still left up that way.

Drugs

Vietnam is soft on drug use when compared to Malaysia or Thailand, which can both bestow a death penalty or life imprisonment for offenses. However, in 1993, a Hong Kong man convicted of importing five kilograms of heroin was the first to be handed a death penalty in Vietnam. There has been the odd case of a foreigner being set up in Vietnam—sold drugs by a cyclo driver and then arrested. This appears to be a fundraising venture. Some drugs are used medicinally in Vietnam—among these are marijuana, which is also used as a cooking spice. Hilltribes, especially the Hmong, grow opium poppies in the far northwest. Opium cultivation was outlawed in 1954, although cultivation for personal and medicinal use was permitted. In 1984 all cultivation and possession of opium became illegal.

Crime

Although physical attacks are uncommon in Vietnam, theft directed at foreigners is increasing in Saigon and other big cities. Pickpockets are more common, and beggars more aggressive. Thieves will more likely be interested in your whole backpack or suitcase rather than something from within. Keep your bags in sight, or lock them up. Avoid blackmarket moneychanging—rates are no different from those in banks. Never change money on the street.

Women Travelers

Karaoke has unfortunately altered Vietnamese males' perceptions of Western women. The only ones they've seen are the karaoke TV kind cavorting in bikinis or rolling around on beds in skimpy lingerie to the strains of Bob Marley or Boney M hits. Karaoke seems to be a synonym for sex among the Vietnamese; high-class bars offer private rooms with karaoke "hostesses." Women should be aware that certain cheap hotels, especially in the south, serve as short-time brothels patronized by Vietnamese men who drink in the lobby. Sexual harassment of Western women is rare in Vietnam, but it's best to be careful.

SPORTS AND RECREATION

Adventure tourism is in its infancy in Vietnam, but things are shaping up, and there's great potential for trekking, diving, windsurfing, whitewater rafting, ocean and river kayaking, and other pursuits. Until rental equipment becomes readily available, it's a case of bring-it-yourself and do-it-yourself, or fall in with a tour.

Beaches: Resort areas are located at Nha Trang Beach (with offshore islands), China Beach in Danang, and Bai Chay near Halong Bay. Along the coast are pristine beaches like Cana, Dai Lanh, Lang Co Lagoon, and Canh Duong. Sun worshippers should bear in mind that typhoons strike the beaches. This makes them windy—bad news for swimmers, good news for surfers. Pacific coast beaches have quick dropoffs, which means undertow problems. On the Gulf of Thailand near Cambodia are stretches of sand near Ha Tien, and at Phu Quoc Island offshore.

Marine Sports: You can get your hands on snorkeling equipment at Nha Trang, but quality is spotty. There's limited diving equipment for rent too—diving is best at offshore islands. Many islands dot the coast to the north of Nha Trang. China Beach hosted an international surf meet in October 1993.

Boating: Fishing vessels can be hired for island day-trips. Onboard seafood is often included with the package. Kayaking is a possibility in the Mekong Delta and at Halong Bay, but you have to bring your own equipment.

Caving: Vietnam's north is a spelunkers paradise, featuring thousands of caves in limestone formations. The Halong Bay area is good for grottoes and several very deep caves. There are also huge caves at Trung Trang near Cat Ba National Park. The most spectacular caves are probably those at Phong Nha, about 45 km northwest of Dong Hoi. The main cave here is eight km long.

Bicycling: Vietnam moves at bicycle pace; the bicycle is as yet the main form of private transport. Bicycle hire is available in major cities.

Hanoi and Hué are pleasant to cycle around. Bikes in Vietnam are used mostly for practical purposes and not for sport. During the Vietnam War cargo bicycles carted supplies. In 1994 the Back to Dien Bien Phu Bicycle Race commemorated these hardships with a race from Hanoi to Dien Bien Phu. In the rougher Central Highlands, a mountain bike is ideal. Bikes are easily ferried around on boats or other vehicles.

Hiking: In the mountains of the northwest you can hike into valleys, staying in minority villages overnight. Good areas to visit are Mai Chau, Dien Bien Phu, Lai Chau, and Sapa. You can hire a jeep to reach a trailhead, and porters can carry supplies if needed. From Sapa, you can organize a trek to the summit of Mt. Fansipan, which at 3,143 meters is Vietnam's highest peak.

Running: The Vietnam International Marathon is held alternately in Saigon and Hanoi every January. The first marathon was run in 1990. About 1,500 runners participate. The world's largest, strangest, and silliest running club—the **Hash House Harriers**—welcomes visitors to its chapters in Saigon and Hanoi. Find out when the weekly run is scheduled and show up at the trailhead in your shorts—there's a beery gathering of hares and hounds after the run.

Golf: After being banished for years under communist rule as bourgeois decadence, golf has made a comeback as "a good sport for health and the spirit." In February 1994 an 18-hole course was opened at Dalat Pine Lake Golf Course; the site actually dates back to the 1920s under the French. Two other 18-hole courses are located at Song Be Golf Resort, 20 km north of Saigon; and King's Island Golf Resort, 45 km west of Hanoi. There are Malaysian, Singaporean, Hong Kong, and Australian joint-venture plans to develop other courses near Hanoi, Saigon, and Vung Tau, complete with hotels, villas, and resort facilities.

FESTIVALS AND HOLIDAYS

Public holidays and certain festivals are known as Red Flag Days, when national flags fly from many residences and offices.

National Holidays

Jan. 1: New Year's Day
Jan./Feb.: Tet
Feb. 3: Anniversary of 1930 founding of Communist Party
April 30: Liberation Day, commemorating 1975 fall of Saigon
May 1: International Worker's Day (May Day)
May 19: Anniversary of the birth of Ho Chi Minh
Sept. 2: National Day, commemorating 1945 independence proclamation by Ho Chi Minh

Lunar Calendar Festivals

On lunar festival days, many Vietnamese flock to pagodas. The lunar calendar is divided into 12 months of 29 or 30 days, making a year of about 355 days. Every four years an extra month—a leap month—is added to keep the lunar calendar in sync with the solar calendar. Due to this juggling of months, lunar calendar dates are moveable. Festivals usually take place at the time of the full moon.

The Vietnamese 12-year cycle follows the Chinese zodiac, with years corresponding to rat, buffalo, tiger, cat, dragon, snake, horse, goat, monkey, rooster, dog, and pig. So 1996 is the Year of the Rat, 1997 the Year of the Buffalo, 1998 the Year of the Tiger. According to astrologers, a child's future can be predicted based on the hour, month, and year of birth; the shape and character of the zodiac animal in the year of birth also affects the person's fate. The animal years are further influenced by one of the five elements—metal, water, wood, fire, or earth.

In addition to the following national festivals, there are many regional village and minority celebrations, especially in the north.

January/February: Tet, or Lunar New Year, takes place in late January or early February. In a "leap year" it can take place in early March. The country comes to a standstill at Tet for five days of holidays.

March: On the 6th day of the second lunar month is **Hai Ba Trung Day,** commemorating the Trung sisters who led a revolt against the Chinese around 40 AD.

May: The birth, death, and enlightenment of Buddha is celebrated on the 8th day of the fourth lunar month.

August: On the 15th day of the seventh lunar month is **Trung Nguyen,** Wandering Souls Day. The dead, hungry and naked, return to their

fireworks for sale, near Hanoi

THE SPIRIT OF TET

Tet is Christmas, New Year, and the Fourth of July all rolled into one—not to mention everyone's birthday. Individual birthdays are not celebrated in Vietnam—everyone is simply a year older at Tet. Tet Eve is celebrated with fireworks; four or five days of festivities follow. Just before Tet roads are bottlenecked, but once Tet starts the roads are quiet. Most businesses close and railways shut down for four days, but a few buses operate. There's lots of activity at the pagodas and temples, and special water-puppet shows for children. Tet is best in the north, where festivities are more traditional. Other traditional sites include Hué and Hoi An.

Coming from the word *Tiet,* meaning festival, Tet marks the first days of the Lunar New Year and the start of spring. It's a time to pay debts, forgive others, correct one's faults, and start the new year with a clean slate. In common with the Western Christmas celebration, the Vietnamese buy a tree, exchange greeting cards, wish each other Happy New Year *(chuc mung nam moi!),* and eat themselves silly. Women buy peach or apricot branches and bunches of flowers several days before Tet. It's auspicious if the branches bloom on the first morning of Tet: apricot and peach blossoms are reputed to keep demons out of the homes at this time. Some families buy an entire apricot tree and display it like a Christmas tree, decorated with greeting cards from well-wishers. Another popular choice in the south is a fruit tree with miniature oranges. It can stand up to several meters tall, bearing more than a hundred oranges.

To drive evil spirits away you have to make a lot of noise. That's where firecrackers come in. Massive strings of fireworks, the longer the better, are attached to the front of a residence and ignited. Strings are measured in meters; a four-meter string is quite respectable. The louder the fireworks, the better. In 1995 the government placed a ban on the manufacture of fireworks due to the deaths of 71 revelers and injuries to 765 others during Tet in 1994. The ban did not, however, seem to make a lot of difference in the level of noise during 1995 Tet—not even in Hanoi.

Countdown to Tet

The countdown to Tet begins up to a month before the festival starts. Two weeks before Tet there is a noticeable increase in the number of shoppers. People buy clothes and presents for family and friends, and stock up on food for guests over the five-day holiday. Public and private buildings may get a new coat of paint. Stalls are set up to sell New Year greeting cards, candied fruit, decorations, and firecrackers. Exactly a week before Tet, in a simple household ceremony, offerings of fresh fruit, cooked food, and paper models are made to the Ong Tao, the Spirit of the Hearth. Ong Tao must leave the hearth to report household events from the old year to the Jade Emperor. The departure of the Spirit leaves the home unprotected for a week, until New Year comes. Houses are decorated in red and gold. Bright woodcut prints announcing the upcoming year and its featured zodiac animal adorn the walls, and people take down the print from the previous year. Everyone must wear new clothes, so clothes vendors are out in force. Families begin choosing Tet trees. Office parties are held, and Tet bonuses distributed.

Two days before Tet, people are busy cleaning their houses and decorating their Tet trees, and rushing about doing last-minute shopping. Traditionally, no cooking, cleaning, sewing, digging, or drawing of water is done during the Tet festival—everything must be arranged in advance. Some families still make traditional *banh chung,* a cake of sticky rice filled with bean paste and pork, symbolizing the earth.

On Tet Eve, everything closes early as families head home to celebrate the first dinner of Tet. Huge balloons appear on the streets, eagerly bought by homeward-bound shoppers. Elaborate offerings of chicken and glutinous rice are made to ancestors as everyone awaits the magic hour of midnight. Catholics attend pre-midnight mass. Just before midnight, fireworks are set off. Families and friends meet to exchange greetings. Just after midnight, Buddhists go to their favorite pagoda to pray for a good year. Many families eat a simple meal after midnight, perhaps with some rice wine or champagne.

The first person to cross the home threshold after midnight must be a person of good character or misfortune can follow for the entire year. Not leaving anything to chance, some folks discreetly arrange their first visitor ahead of time. Elders present packets of lucky money to children. By 0200 the fireworks have died down—only to resume with ferocity at dawn. The sidewalks are littered with scraps of red firecracker paper, and the air is heavy with the odor of fireworks.

The first day of Tet, people dress in their finest new clothes and visit relatives. Village festivities may include singing competitions, cockfighting, and Chinese chess competitions with real people as the pieces. Gambling is popular. Parks are full of holiday celebrants.

The second day of Tet involves visits to special guests and close friends. Young people looking for partners stroll to the nearest lake to make a wish that the person of their dreams will appear before them.

The third day of Tet is reserved for visits to teachers, friends, and business associates. Visitors are served candied fruit, *banh chung,* spring rolls, sausage, and drinks. Negative talk is taboo. The attitude of the first days of the New Year sets the tone for the remainder of the year. When leaving the house, elaborate wishes are exchanged, "I hope that your business may prosper and that money may flow into your house like water."

On the fourth day of Tet, people are supposed to return to work, but seldom do. In the city, people go back to their offices to wish co-workers happy New Year. It is not until the sixth day of Tet that people get serious about work again, and Vietnam returns to normal.

---

relatives to eat and take a look around. If not treated with respect, ghosts can wreak havoc. Offerings are made in Buddhist homes and temples, feasts are placed on tables for the ghosts.

September: The 15th day of the eighth lunar month marks **Trung Thu,** the Midautumn Festival. Of Chinese origin, the festival is celebrated with the baking of mooncakes and lantern parades.

November: On the 28th day of the ninth lunar month is a celebration of the birthday of Confucius.

ACCOMMODATIONS

There are more hotel rooms in the city of Bangkok than in the entire country of Vietnam. Accommodations in Vietnam are consistently higher-priced and of lower quality than their Thai counterparts. Costs for moderate hotels in Vietnam are roughly double the rates in Thailand. Vietnam is woefully short of hotels to meet the influx of tourists, particularly in Hanoi. Many hotels are run-down, and horror stories abound. One American tourist checked into a $175 per night room in Saigon to discover a windowless chamber. She was informed by the management that a room with a view would cost $200. Only after she started to gather up her bags did the manager relent and give her a suite with windows.

Among the air-conditioned nightmares of Vietnam you might find some of the following: The Mosquito Pond Hotel, The Rusted French Villa, The Taxi-Girl Hotel, Khach San Boom Boom, The Rat and Roach Inn, Grand Hôtel Ordinaire, The Hanoi Hilton, The Rat Bat Guesthouse, and The Boney M Karaoke Hotel. That gives you some idea of what's out there. Most towns or

cities in Vietnam feature some kind of rudimentary accommodations, whether government guesthouse or Russian blockhouse. Socialist architecture has a happy knack of making things look gloomy and decrepit even before the building is completed. You might luck out and get an ancient French hotel with vintage Gallic plumbing and fixtures still in place, though not necessarily functioning properly. Some places offer cavernous bidets and bathtubs. Take care in bathrooms—the wiring in budget hotels is very dangerous, more dangerous when water is present.

Most accommodations, including guesthouses, provide mosquito nets. The net is sometimes tucked into hideaway boxes above the bed, spread with the help of wooden arms. Another type of net is hung off four poles mounted at the corners of the bed; yet another is a squarish net suspended over the bed, attached by strings to nails mounted on the walls. Check the cupboards if you don't see a net in place, or ask the staff to provide one.

advertisement for a Pleiku budget hotel

Budget/Moderate

For a $5 basic fan room in the central Vietnam town of Quang Ngai you get: "1 double bed, 1 table, chairs, 1 bathroom, 1 pair of plastic slippers, sweet-scented soap for bathing, 1 neon light system and ceiling fan, and 1 thermos with enough hot water for making tea." And, hopefully, 1 mosquito net and 1 roll of toilet paper. The thermos, a Chinese habit, is very useful—it provides purified water, and in a pinch, can be used to soak down hot towels in lieu of a hot shower. Basic rooms go for $5-10, and may share bathrooms. "Room for Rent" is another way of saying "hotel" without attracting government taxes. Family-run places are homey—look for them. A step up are budget rooms with air-conditioning or hot water, or both. Prices are usually in the $10-20 range—government guesthouses are often in this category.

From here, prices spiral into the moderate $20-50 zone depending on the number of creature comforts, gadgets, circuitry, and appliances added. With air-conditioning and phone, $20; add a color TV and fridge, $30. In this price range you might find a renovated French hotel with lots of character; a good value.

Luxury/Super Luxury

Business or luxury-class hotels charge $50-100 for standard rooms and $100-200 for deluxe rooms. Major hotels extract 10% government tax and 5-10% service charge on top of listed prices. Hotels accept Visa, MasterCard, Diners Club, American Express, and JCB cards, but levy a surcharge of up to four percent for credit cards. High-end hotels provide in-house movies, minibar, IDD, room safe, satellite TV, and individual air-conditioning control; facilities include health club, business center, and restaurants.

There are only a handful of hotels in Vietnam that approach international first-class standards—the Metropole in Hanoi, and the Century Hotel and Floating Hotel in Saigon. These hotels charge considerably more—easily $200-300 for top-end accommodations, and $200-500 for a suite.

Mystery Hotels

Sometimes you run into a brick wall in Vietnam. Yes, you've struck a hotel for Vietnamese only, Asians only, even Taiwanese only. The reason for rejecting you could be one of the following: the staff have never had a foreigner stay there before and are afraid of the police; the place is deemed not comfortable for foreigners and the owner does not have a "foreigner-dealing license"; the military reserves the hotel for high-profile guests (you'll know you've found the latter if you get a gun shoved in your face). Or the hotel may be a "short-time" joint with taxi girls lounging around the lobby; these places don't want to lose money renting rooms overnight. "Taxi girl" is a euphemism for a loose woman: the term comes from "taxi dancers" who are metered for time spent with customers on the dance floors of seedy nightclubs. Often hotel and nightclub are under one roof—this species is called a Karaoke TV (KTV) Hotel. Most of these are aimed at businessmen from Hong Kong, Singapore, and Taiwan, with karaoke hostesses "entertaining" in private rooms. These hotels will wave you away.

Other Options

You may arrive in a place without a hotel. Here you have to improvise. Stay in a village with a family—make the mime for sleeping and a kid will direct you to a possible place to sleep. Restaurants and noodlehouses are another possibility. In one case, in the Mekong Delta, we were not only welcomed through the front door—we slept on it. I and two fellow travelers were provided with old doors as beds. Traveling in north Vietnam, we were once given impromptu beds in a village schoolhouse, under the gaze of a stucco Ho Chi Minh, at a cost of 25 cents each.

Hotel Check-In

Hotels dispense forms that ask for date of arrival, visa number, visa validity, entry/exit card number, what you ate for breakfast, and other idiotic questions. The best thing to do is make photocopies of one of these completed forms and just pass them out along the way. There used to be a procedure in Vietnam in the early days of individual travel whereby all travelers carried permits listing places they wanted to visit. Hotels would demand passport, paper visa, and travel permit (often three separate documents), which

were then ferried off to the local police to be registered, recorded, stamped, sealed, signed, and delivered back to the hotel. You can bet a bit of money changed hands along the way. Travel permits are long gone, but for some reason the registration procedure persists—maybe money still changes hands. The policy seems to vary. Some hotels do not ask for a passport; others don't bother with "registration" if you pay up front; still others adamantly insist on retaining your passport. In one place in the Delta, the front desk even insisted on seeing the customs form.

More than one traveler has rushed out of a hotel in a bleary-eyed daze at the crack of dawn to catch an express bus, and left behind a passport at the front desk. You may well need your original passport for other transactions, such as banking or motorcycle rentals. Therefore, if the hotel insists on keeping the passport for "registration," try to retrieve it the same night or the next morning, or try to leave them only a photocopy. You can argue that your passport is a valuable document that belongs to your government (which is true) and cannot be left in the care of a hotel.

FOOD AND DRINK

In Vietnam in the 1970s and 1980s, a thousand years of Chinese and French-influenced culinary tradition went down the drain as austerity set in and restaurants came to be regarded as bourgeois indulgence. Some of the best chefs fled the country. The Vietnamese emulated the Soviet example of giving restaurants numbers, after the street address—thus avoiding all bourgeois pretension. So the restaurant at 202 Hué St. in Hanoi is known as Restaurant 202. Thang Loi Hotel in Hanoi has a Restaurant A and a Restaurant B.

Happily, there has been a remarkable return of gourmet Vietnamese food in the 1990s. Key ingredients are now in much better supply. You can eat well; a good variety of Vietnamese, French, and Chinese cuisine exists in Saigon, Hanoi, Hué, and Hoi An. Seafood is found along the coast at Nha Trang, Vung Tau, and Bai Chay. Foreigners generally find the list of exotic and endangered on some menus to be be-

yond the pale—dishes here include pangolin, python, gecko, and bat. Vegetarian food is widely available—especially in marketplaces—because Mahayana Buddhist monks in Vietnam are largely vegetarian.

You'll find cheaper food in markets or at streetstalls—a hearty meal with soups and other courses for under $2. Cafés are also a source of less expensive meals; they may really be restaurants, masquerading as cafés to avoid taxes. Budget restaurants can cost up to $5 a head; moderate restaurants, with a plusher setting, perhaps $5-10 a head; classy restaurants or those in some first-class hotels in major cities may cost $10 and up per person—a lot of money in Vietnam when you consider the daily wage is around $1. Western-style food will mean Western bills. It's tastier and less expensive to keep to Vietnamese fare. So dig in—*Chuc an ngon!* (Good appetite!)

(continues on page110)

VIETNAMESE CUISINE
by Naomi Duguid and Jeffrey Alford

Bread, yogurt, processed cheese, coffee, beer, and fruit: if worst comes to worst in Vietnam you can survive on these familiar foods—at least in the cities. But you'll be missing out on one of the world's finest cuisines. Granted, finding what you want to eat here is not always as straightforward as it is in Thailand or Malaysia; street foods and night markets are not nearly as elaborate or abundant, and restaurants can be confusing if you aren't familiar with Vietnamese food. But with a few helpful hints, finding great food needn't be a problem.

Regional Variations
Although a wide variety of foods are found all across the country, Vietnamese cuisine can be divided into three distinctive regional cuisines: southern, central, and northern. If you've eaten at Vietnamese restaurants outside Vietnam, you'll most likely have eaten southern-style food, with its wide variety of fresh herbs and complex tropical flavors. Food from the center tends to have more chile heat than that of the other regions; shrimp paste is also used extensively. As you move north, the food has more of a Chinese feel, with greater use of preserved vegetables, tree fungus, and dried mushrooms, and fewer fresh herbs and greens. There are more stir fries, and black pepper is used instead of chiles. People from the north will tell you southern food is flamboyant and unsubtle, while those from the south say northern food lacks taste and freshness. We find it all delicious.

Flexible Flavors
The final tastes in almost any Vietnamese meal, whether a simple market soup or an elaborate feast, are determined by choices made by you—the person eating. A table salad *(xalach dia)* of assorted fresh herbs, salad greens, and sprouts, and vinegared vegetables, comes as an accompaniment to almost every meal, and there are always condiments on hand. One of the most pleasurable aspects of eating Vietnamese food is the act of sampling, altering, and enhancing your food as you eat.

Vietnamese soups exemplify the freshness, complex flavors, and flexible do-it-yourself aspect of Vietnamese cuisine. Large bowls of *pho* (hot soup) are a favorite breakfast in Vietnam, and can also be found in stalls and restaurants later in the day. The soups are hearty and delicious. The Vietnamese are famous for their soup broths—filled with noodles, bean sprouts, sprigs of fresh herbs, and lean pieces of chicken, pork, or beef. You can garnish your soup with more fresh herbs or sprouts from the table salad, or with any of the many little sauces and condiments that may be set out.

Vietnamese dipping and flavoring sauces are varied and wonderful. The most common of these is known as *nuoc mam* or *nuoc cham.* It's a pale blend of salty, pungent fish sauce diluted with fresh lime juice and sometimes vinegar, spiced with garlic and chopped chiles, and sweetened with a touch of sugar. You can drizzle it over your rice, use it as a dip for spring rolls or grilled meats, or add a spoonful to your soup. Other dipping sauces include *nuoc leo,* a peanut sauce from the Hué region now widely found throughout the country; *tuong ot,* a red hot chile sauce similar to the Thai *sriracha;* and *mam tom,* a pungent shrimp sauce also from central Vietnam. One of our favorite condiments is a simple combination often served at soup stalls and restaurants: a pile of black pepper and a pile of salt placed side-by-side on a small dish and served with a wedge of lime. You squeeze a little lime juice into the dish and blend some salt and pepper with it to make a paste into which you dip bits of meat from your soup.

Roll Your Own
The other do-it-yourself element in many Vietnamese meals comes with roll-your-own rice-paper rolls. For example, grilled chunks of lemongrass beef *(thit bo nuong),* grilled meatballs *(nem nuong),* or freshly steamed shrimp *(tom)* all come served with a salad plate together with a stack of moist rice papers *(banh trang)* or fresh rice wrappers *(banh uot).* You lay a wrapper on your open palm, put in a piece or two of meat, several strips of pickled radish, perhaps some herbs, sprouts, or rice vermicelli, then tuck over the ends and roll it up. You now have your own unique fresh spring roll that can be dipped in *nuoc cham* or *nuoc leo,* or eaten simply on its own.

Street and Market Foods
Travelers in Vietnam sometimes complain about not getting enough to eat and always being hungry. Vietnamese food is relatively low in fats and oils; visitors accustomed to a diet high in dairy and

meat, and who may not be accustomed to eating large quantities of carbohydrates, frequently find themselves hungry, simply because they're not eating enough food to maintain their normal caloric intake. One way of avoiding this "starving feeling" is to start the day with a big breakfast, and then snack on bread and sandwiches available from street vendors frequently throughout the day. You'll also find, especially in the south, stalls selling fresh fruit: depending on the place and season, slices of fresh papaya, pineapple, or ripe jackfruit.

For breakfast, head to any neighborhood market. Generally, in the center of the market you'll find many vendors side by side, all selling hearty soups and other hot foods such as rice with curries (cari). Market food is at its best, and offers the greatest selection in the morning before the day gets hot. If you're looking for something special—say, bun bo Hué—simply ask someone. If it can be found nearby or in the market, people will tell you where to go. Vendors tend to specialize in one or two dishes; most streetstalls and even restaurants are not set up to prepare a range of different dishes.

While breakfast in the south and north is generally soup, in rural areas it can be xoi—sticky rice steamed in a leaf wrapper. Often peanuts or mung beans are steamed with the rice. Xoi is not only healthy and delicious but also makes a great portable breakfast.

Some stalls in large markets are signposted Com Chay, which means vegetarian. Here you can find a variety of tasty and creative dishes, centered around tofu or mushrooms.

To keep up your fluid intake—essential in the heat—bottled water is available in the cities. In hotels and guesthouses, a thermos of boiled water is usually provided. In the south, look for freshly pressed sugarcane juice available from vendors on the main streets in the afternoon and evening. Vietnamese beer is good; try Saigon Beer or 333. Vietnam grows its own tea in the region around Dalat. Tea is consumed morning to night; it's served before or after but never during a meal. For another caffeine hit, try Vietnamese coffee black and hot or iced with condensed milk, gafe suda—our favorite. The coffee is made in individual slow-drip filters and can be very strong.

In the late afternoon and evening, the least expensive and most entertaining food option is to go out for street food. Check out the main streets or small side streets in the center of town; there are always vendors, usually with a single specialty. You'll see a small wooden stand with a few stools and several tables set out on the sidewalk. In Hanoi and the north generally, there are fewer streetstalls, but you can still find small restaurants open to the street, doing a roaring trade selling soups and stir fries.

Restaurant Specialties

In addition to trying street food, you'll want to experience restaurant food. If you're in the southern part of the country and looking for a treat, head for a Bo Bay Mon or "Beef Seven Ways" restaurant. You can order just one or two dishes or go for the entire feast. Beef dishes include beef fondue (bo nhung dam), grilled beef-stuffed leaves (bo la lot), beef pâté steamed in banana leaves (cha dum), and beef rice soup (chao thit bo). Another restaurant specialty, often eaten for lunch in the south, is banh xeo, a kind of crepe filled with finely chopped vegetables and meat. In central Vietnam this is called banh khoai and looks like a cross between an omelette and a crepe. In the northern cities you'll find restaurants that have their menus posted outside, French-style, making them easy to spot for lunch or supper. Confirm prices before ordering.

We find that one of the best ways to make the most of your trip is to come with a good Vietnamese cookbook. Not only is a cookbook an excellent source of names of dishes and ingredients, it can also provide valuable insights into culture and daily life. We particularly recommend Binh Duong and Marsha Kiesel's Simple Art of Vietnamese Cooking and Bach Ngo and Gloria Zimmerman's The Classic Cuisine of Vietnam. Nicole Routhier's The Foods of Vietnam is also very good.

Common Street and Market Foods

Pho bo Hanoi (Hanoi soup) is a substantial beef and rice-noodle soup, available in streetstalls for breakfast and in some specialty restaurants all over the country.

Bun bo Hué (beef noodle soup Hué-style) is a substantial, meaty, meal-in-one noodle soup flavored with shrimp paste and a little chile heat. Found in streetstalls in Hué and nearby towns in the center.

Hu tieu (Saigon soup) consists of noodles with chicken and/or pork and vegetables, either bathed in broth or served with broth on the side in a separate bowl. A satisfying meal-in-one available in some restaurants, as well as at markets and streetstalls in the south.

Pho ga (Hanoi chicken soup) and **mien ga** (chicken soup with cellophane noodles) are comforting

(continues on next page)

VIETNAMESE CUISINE
(continued)

and sustaining meals-in-one. Hanoi soup is available in restaurants in Saigon and in markets and street-stalls in the north, while *mien ga* is found in the south and the center.

Bo vien (beef balls) are small, slightly chewy beef meatballs served floating in a clear aromatic broth, sometimes with added rice noodles and fresh herbs. Most easily found in Saigon and Nha Trang, though available all over. Sold by street vendors, at stalls and markets, and in restaurants.

Nem nuong (grilled meatballs) are small pork meatballs, lightly spiced and grilled. Sold in street-stalls, markets, and restaurants; try eating them in bread.

Cha gio (fried spring rolls) are made of rice papers wrapped around finely chopped pork, assorted vegetables, and cellophane noodles, then deep fried; served with a plate of fresh greens and dipping sauce. These snack foods are sold in markets and streetstalls all over the country.

SNACKS

The low caloric value of Vietnamese food leaves the traveler with a growling stomach, so you may well find yourself prowling around in search of snacks. Cafés are the ideal place to find snacks, and with the dearth of nightlife in Vietnam, cafés also function as gathering places.

The Sandwich Bar
Banh mi (sandwiches) are made to order from delicious French-style baguettes and usually include pickled strips of white radish and carrot. You can choose a selection of pâtés and cured meats. You may want to avoid mayonnaise as a health precaution. Baguettes made from rice flour are sold in streetstalls from Haiphong to the Mekong Delta from midmorning until after sunset; when there's a choice, go for the vendor who heats the bread on a grill before assembling the sandwich. You'll see a small charcoal brazier by the side of the stall or under the sandwich cart. Don't buy bread in the afternoon—by then it's really only useful as a hard-edged weapon.

To go with your bread, pâté or cheese? The pâté is homemade, the consistency of Spam, and wrapped in banana-leaf—as long as it's not too old, it's okay. Spam-pâté is usually made from pork. Cheese is usually processed in boxed segments; try either the Laughing Cow variety (La Vache Qui Rit or Vache Jolie) or the sterner nonlaughing cow (Nouvelle Vache).

Floating market vendors congregate on the Mekong Delta.

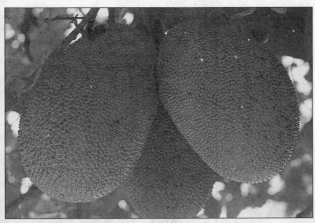

Jackfruit can grow to monstrous proportions.

Palatable but poor quality. There's a cake shop in Hanoi that makes cheese close to feta in taste. Another topping is jam—a French transplant. Varieties include papaya and pineapple.

Which came first—the duck or the egg? In Hanoi you can have both at once. The duck egg is incubated to a critical moment and then boiled, which results in a soft crunchy duck emerging from the egg. Not for the faint-hearted, this dish is called *trung vit lon*—but get some coaching lessons on the correct tones as this collection of words can also refer to something quite rude.

Exotic Fruit

Vietnam offers a profusion of tropical fruit, especially in the Mekong Delta. These exotic specimens will tickle your taste buds, quench your thirst, or at the very least arouse your curiosity. Among the rarer and more exotic are dragon fruit *(thanh long)*, found in the Nha Trang area, and water coconut *(dua nuoc)*, from the Mekong Delta. Juice bars in the south turn out concoctions with crushed ice and sweetened condensed milk and other murky mixtures. Fruit is also used to make a variety of jams and jellies. You can also get exotic items like custard apple ice cream in Saigon. Fruit is seasonal, and offerings vary from north to south.

Durian *(sau rieng)* is a round greenish fruit studded with sharp spikes. It's the size of a football, can weigh up to 14 kg, and is only available in the summer in the south. Broken open with a sharp knife, it reveals white pod-like sections that have the texture of a very ripe French Camembert, which is why the fruit is nicknamed "the cheese that grows on trees." Despite its awful smell, durian has an exotic taste, described by 19th-century naturalist Alfred Russel Wallace thus: "A rich butter-like custard highly flavoured with almonds gives the best general idea of it, but intermingled with it come wafts of flavour that call to mind cream-cheese, onion-sauce, brown sherry, and other incongruities." In Asia, the smooth and highly nutritious flesh of the durian is reputed to be an aphrodisiac.

Also in the football-size league is the jackfruit *(mit)*, a cousin of the durian. Jackfruit is bright yellow and very sweet and crisp with a sweet fragrance. The large hard seeds can be steamed, shelled, and eaten. Jackfruit can grow to monstrous proportions, with some specimens weighing in at 40 kilograms. As the fruit ripens, the skin turns from green to brown, and is covered with blunt spines. The tender fruit is either eaten raw or cooked in various sweet and savory dishes.

Rambutan *(chom chom)* has hairy reddish spines surrounding a translucent fruit which tastes like lychee. Similar tasting, but with a smooth exterior skin, is the smaller longan *(trai nhan)*. Mangosteen *(mang cut)* has a leathery maroon husk with soft, delicious white flesh inside. The taste reminds Westerners alternately of cream, lemonade, and fragrant apple. When eating this fruit, avoid the large seed in the center, which can be bitter if bitten. Also watch out for mangosteen juice, which stains.

COMMON FOOD WORDS

Some food words in Vietnamese derive from French—*gato* (from gateau, or cake), *gafe* (coffee), *phomai* (from fromage, or cheese), *biftek* (beefsteak), *ômlet* (omelette), and *xocola* (chocolate).

bun—noodles
pho—soup
cuon—salad or lettuce
goi cuon—fresh spring rolls
gao—uncooked rice
gao nep—sweet glutinous rice
com—cooked rice
ot—chiles
gung—ginger
nuoc—sauce, liquid
nuoc mam—fish sauce
thit—meat, often meaning pork
thit heo—pork
thit bo—beef
bo—beef
ga—chicken
cha—pâté
tom—shrimp
muc—squid
nuong—grilled

Some fruit is used in salads or for other purposes. A fresh young coconut is often cut in half, and the flesh scooped out with a spoon—ice cream and candied fruit can then be served in the shell along with the coconut flesh. Starfruit (*trai khe*) is used in salads and juices; you'll know the cool, watery fruit inside is ripe when the waxy skin turns from green to deep yellow. Starfruit is also known as the star apple, or carambola.

A bit more familiar in taste for Westerners is the pomelo *(buoi)*, a relative of the grapefruit, and tasting similar, though it has a huge husky exterior. Watch out for the translucent segment skin, which can be very bitter. Uglifruit *(cam sanh)* is a grapefruit-tangerine hybrid, with dark-green or mottled skin. It is often used for orange juice that is guzzled in Saigon. The persimmon *(hong)* looks like a tomato but has a stretched bright orange glossy skin. Inside, the fruit offers a smooth firm flesh.

The Java apple *(man)*, also known as rose apple, is bright red, pale pink, or greenish, and has a sweet and sour acquired taste. The tiny Vietnamese apple is extremely sour—a bite will bring tears to your eyes, though it doesn't appear to have much effect on the locals who happily munch away. Locals in the south also feed on tamarind, a bean-like fruit with a brittle skin, and pods that will make you pucker like you've never puckered before. The flesh is used to flavor curries, and also used for cleaning brass.

Quite unlike any apple you've seen before—or are likely to see again—is the custard apple *(mang cau)*, a round fruit with a scaly, bumpy green exterior. It looks like something from the Twilight Zone. Inside lies a white heart with black button-like seeds. Custard apple is excellent in fruit juices with a dash of orange juice. Pureed custard apple, watered down and pepped up with a little lime or orange juice, makes an exotic milkshake. In the same fruit family, with a similar taste but an entirely different appearance, is the spiny soursop *(mang cau xiem)*, a longish fruit with a thin skin that has rows of dark-green curved spines. The white pulp offers a delicious sour-sweet flavor.

Most exotic of all is dragon fruit *(thanh long)*, so named because it grows on a creeping cactus-like plant said to resemble a green dragon. The fruit is oval-shaped, about the size of a small pineapple, magenta in color, with a smooth skin sprouting green petals. Inside, the pulpy and translucent white flesh is scattered with thousands of black crunchy seeds—the succulent flesh is an excellent thirst-quencher. The fruit is grown mostly in arid parts of Binh Dinh Province around Qui Nhon, and is in great demand, with exports to Hong Kong, Taiwan, and China. Dragon fruit is in season from May to September.

DRINK

Drinks are cheap if you stick to Vietnamese fare. An imported Coke could cost 75 cents; a whole young coconut will cost you 10 or 20 cents. Vendors cut the top off a young coconut and provide a straw. After you drink a young coconut, give it back to the waiter and he'll hack it open for you and provide a spoon to scrape out the flesh. Some vendors serve coconut milk with the fleshy bits floating in it. Coconut milk is safe to drink while still fresh in the shell; it may be a different story if transferred to a glass with ice

(top) buffalo heading out to rice terraces for morning ploughing;
(bottom) the road going to Sapa, in the far north

(top) Cao Dai service, Tay Ninh;
(bottom) souvenir masks painted on woven baskets, Hanoi

added. Fresh fruit juice is another thirst-quencher, but untreated water may be added, or suspect ice. Bottled water is widely available and of decent quality—make sure it's sealed when you purchase it.

Mainstream drinks are tea and coffee. Often, upon entering a house you may be offered green tea—a Chinese-derived habit. In cafés, you can also order black tea with lemon. Most Vietnamese prefer to drink tea, but in the cities you can easily find coffee. The coffee plant was introduced to Vietnam in the 19th century under the French—the most sought-after beans are Robusta, grown in Dak Lak province, and Arabica, grown in Lam Dong. Filter kits are provided to the caffeine-addicted in cafés. The waiter brings an individual filter cup containing a few teaspoonfuls of coffee grains; this sits over the regular cup and you wait about 10 or 15 minutes for piping-hot water to filter through. The Vietnamese add butter to their coffee to counter the bitter flavor, and some Hanoi cafés serve yolk-cream coffee—egg yolk mixed

with sugar and butter. A large dollop of sweetened condensed milk is an ingredient in *gafe suda,* or iced coffee.

Imported wine is expensive in Vietnam, so try the local wines. Dalat mulberry wine looks and tastes like port. The local firewater is rice wine. You may find some imported Eastern Bloc bottles of champagne on the dusty shelves of a café—good for bathing in, but not much else. Beers are cheap and safe to drink. Brasseries et Glacières d'Indochine (BGI) is a company that brewed in French colonial times, and is back again, this time with local partner Tien Giang. BGI has breweries in Saigon, Mytho, and Danang. Huda, from Hué, is a joint-venture Danish beer; Vinagen is Canadian; Halida is a joint venture with Carlsberg; Tiger Beer comes from Singapore. Popular local brands include 333 and Saigon Export. On the streets, the locals make their own brew, called *bia hoi,* literally meaning "fresh beer." It's siphoned from a curbside keg and costs a pittance.

SHOPPING

Shopping is low-key in Vietnam. Saigon and Hanoi are not in the same league as Bangkok or Hong Kong. But with Vietnam's long tradition of handicrafts and its ready workforce, the potential is certainly there. Vietnamese handicraft specialties include lacquerware vases, boxes, trays, and wall panels, mother-of-pearl inlay, ceramics,

embroidery, and traditional clothing. Modern Vietnamese painting combines styles from East and West in a unique and pleasing hybrid. The widest selection of galleries and handicraft shops can be found in Hanoi, Hué, Hoi An, and Saigon. For examples of some crafts see "Fine Arts" in the Indochina chapter above.

GREAT BUYS AND TIPS
by Nancy Yildiz

The booming free-market economy in Vietnam has provided a wealth of tourist souvenirs and practical items for sale, such as cards, ceramics, T-shirts, lacquerware, paintings, stamps, and stone carvings. Many items are overpriced, so it's essential to comparison shop and bargain hard. Start by browsing through the government fixed-price stores in Saigon and Hanoi to get an idea of price range and quality. You can gain a wealth of information by chatting with the sales clerks.

One of the great buys is greeting cards with traditional Vietnamese designs handpainted on silk, selling from 10 to 50 cents each. You can special order brass or rubber stamps bearing Happy Birthday, Merry Christmas, or Thank You messages so you'll be prepared for all occasions. Cards are usually cheaper in the streetstalls, but stores offer a wider selection.

Printed T-shirts are sold everywhere with various logos such as Saigon, Hanoi, or a waving Ho Chi Minh. Wearing these in Cambodia can get you in a lot of trouble; the locals detest the Vietnamese. The Vietnamese community in the US may also take offense. Prices vary from $1 to $3 depending on whether they're 100% cotton or a cotton-synthetic mix. For a wide range of hand-embroidered T-shirts with rural scenes, sailboats, and so on, try the shops in Hanoi along Hang Gai and Ly Quoc Su Streets. The shirts come in all colors and sizes and make great gifts for under $3 each.

For knickknack collectors, there are handmade figurines of fishermen, cyclos, water buffalo, or silver cigarette cases and snuff boxes. Try the stores along Dong Khoi Street in Saigon and Hang Khay Street in Hanoi (south side of Hoan Kiem Lake). Be aware that the silver content varies from 20% to 92%, and that prices vary accordingly. Cheaper items ($2-5) are usually made of nickel-silver alloys, not sterling silver.

In the small souvenir line, avoid buying items made of ivory or tortoiseshell; these materials derive from endangered species. For stamp collectors, stalls near the GPO in Hanoi and Saigon sell an excellent range of modern stamps—for less than $20 you can start your own collection. Old coins and banknotes are also available but the prices are steadily climbing; unless you know what you're doing, you could get ripped off.

For Art Lovers

Galleries selling both traditional and modern paintings and woodblock prints abound in every major city. But it can be a headache determining the "right" price to pay when you're not sure whether the paintings are mass-produced or one-of-a-kind, and when little is known about the artists. Starting price is often 10 to 15 times higher than actual worth. Therefore, take time to shop and ask lots of questions.

For around $3 to $12, you can pick up mass-produced prints or silk paintings of traditional market scenes, landscapes, or portraits. Browse through the art section in government fixed-price tourist stores. Once you get a feel for the prices and what you like, try your hand at bargaining in the numerous souvenir shops or art galleries.

For more expensive paintings, $30 to $300 and up, including reproductions, original oils and watercolors, and woodblock prints, shop in the numerous art galleries, including the Vietnamese Art Association in Hanoi and the Ho Chi Minh Association of Fine Arts in Saigon. Ask for background information on the artist, and don't be surprised to find the same artist's work at different prices in more than one gallery. It's a time for hard bargaining; most paintings are overpriced. If you're really hooked on paintings and want to meet the artists, you'll have a better chance in Hué or Hoi An. Both have good galleries and more reasonable prices.

Hoi An, a quaint town near Danang, also offers a good selection of old and reproduction ceramics at reasonable prices. However, upon leaving Vietnam, tourists have reported that Customs may confiscate items which appear to be old. The export of Buddha images and items of "high cultural value" is forbidden.

IMMIGRATION AND CUSTOMS

VISAS

Visa Types

In September 1995 the Vietnamese government announced that one-month tourist visas would no longer be renewed within Vietnam. This change of policy does not apply to those on business, journalist, or diplomatic visas, or to overseas Vietnamese. Because of the change, if you are planning to stay longer than a month in Vietnam, you might look into the issue of a longer-term visa from, say, Hong Kong, or issue of a multiple-entry visa. The other alternative for staying longer in Vietnam is to exit from Saigon to Phnom Penh and pick up a new visa there for another month.

Vietnamese visas are complicated. You generally must use the visa within three months from the time of application. Unlike most visas that are stamped when you actually arrive, the Vietnamese visa specifies a fixed starting date when issued. You cannot arrive before this date; if you arrive later, you lose time on your visa. Visas are usually valid for a period of one month; extensions of two to four weeks are possible once in Vietnam. Individual visa applications are faxed to a "sponsoring agency" in Vietnam, which turns out to be Vietnam Tourism or some other government organ. This information is encoded at the top of your visa, next to the handwritten visa number. It might read 4567/DLHP, which means it was issued by Dulich Haiphong (Haiphong Tourism). This can be bothersome. In one case, when a traveler with a DLHP visa applied for an extension in Hanoi, he was told to go to Haiphong.

Visas are usually valid for air arrival, specifying two points for entry or exit—Hanoi (Noi Bai Airport) and Thanh Pho Ho Chi Minh (Tan Son Nhat Airport in Saigon). To cross a land border into or out of Vietnam, you need a special stamp on your visa. Once in Vietnam, there's little restriction on your movements. Only a few sensitive border regions and ethnic areas currently require internal travel permits.

The Vietnamese visa may be either stamped directly in your passport or issued on paper. If it's

available, a paper visa is preferable. For a paper visa, you don't have to submit an original passport—just a photocopy of initial passport pages. You can rack up quite a paperwork bill heading through Vietnam. Consider this: the initial visa may cost $50 or more; two land border points along the way will cost $50; and an extension costs $20. You're looking at $120 in stamps and chops.

The **tourist visa** is usually single entry, and valid one month. Single-entry and transit visas cost $25 (extensions $10); a multiple-entry visa costs $40-100 (extensions $16). These are basic prices—a visa costs double or triple that when obtained through a travel agent. On visa applications be vague about things like your profession or contacts in Vietnam. Statements like "dedicated missionary" or "expose photojournalist" will cause indefinite delays.

Valid three to six months, the **business visa** may allow for multiple entry. Business visas cost $45-160 and up; extensions may cost over $100. For this visa you must present an invitation letter from a Vietnamese company recognized by the Vietnamese government as a bona fide business with international trading capabilities. Some business-class hotels in Saigon can broker business visas, as can some travel agents in Hong Kong or Bangkok.

Visiting diplomats, journalists, or those visiting family in Vietnam require **special visas.** Start paperwork well in advance: the process could take several months to finalize. Journalists are expected to be escorted by an assigned Vietnamese guide, an expensive venture.

Visa Issue

Allow two to four weeks for processing of the visa from your home base; turnaround time is faster if a courier service is involved. The relevant embassy must fax Hanoi for approval, and this takes time. Your visa can be arranged through an agent or visa-handling service. Costs vary from $25 to $120 for a visa via an agent; fast visas can cost up to $170; business visas or multiple entries can be more than $200. In Paris, two travelers got a visa valid for a five-month stay, and a specified entry date; visas are readily obtainable in London. In Hamburg, applications can be made through Saigon Tourist, Hamburger Str. 132, 200 Hamburg 176; in Paris, through Vietnam Tourism, 4 Rue Cherubini, 75002 Paris. In North America numerous agents can arrange Vietnamese visas through embassies in Ottawa (Canada), Los Angeles (US), or Mexico City. When fully operational, the Vietnamese embassy in Washington will process visas. There are hundreds of Vietnamese-run travel agencies in the US, particularly on the West Coast, usually charging around $75 for a standard visa. In Australia, visas are processed through the Vietnamese embassy in Canberra.

There are a number of points in Asia where you can obtain Vietnamese visas through agents in three to four days—Singapore ($100); Vientiane ($120); Phnom Penh ($70). In Tokyo, you can arrange a visa through Saigon Tourist; in Singapore, try Vietnam Tourism at 101 Upper Cross St. #02-44 People's Park Centre, or the agency Tour East, 70 Anson Rd., Apex Tower, Singapore 0207. In Beijing, a one-month Vietnamese visa takes a week to get, costs $60, and is good for land crossing into Vietnam. The easiest places to obtain visas are in Bangkok or Hong Kong, only a four- to five-day turnaround time. Regulations in Hong Kong and Bangkok chop and change. Sometimes paper visas are issued, sometimes the visa is stamped in the passport; sometimes it takes three days to obtain, sometimes five; sometimes border point stamps are available, sometimes not.

In Hong Kong, a standard visa through an agent costs $55 and takes an average of four working days to obtain; for $65 you can get a visa with land border crossing points. For $100 you can receive your Vietnamese visa in 24 hours; for $150 you can secure a multiple-entry three-month visa. Delays are sometimes deliberately created by the embassy maintaining a fax has not arrived when in fact it has—in order to powertrip and show the agent why it's necessary to "pay dues." For an additional fee you can get Lao Cai or Huu Nghi border points added to your visa in Hong Kong. For more information on Hong Kong and Bangkok agents, see the general introduction to this book.

In Bangkok, a visa costs $48 (1200 baht), and takes four to seven working days; you can

go through an agent or apply to the embassy yourself. For a visa to return in under four working days, add $20. The embassy must fax the sponsor agency in Vietnam—your visa can be delayed if the fax is not returned or if the embassy claims it hasn't been received. One traveler pre-ordered a visa from a Bangkok agent, who forgot to get it. The agent made amends by obtaining the visa the same day.

Visa on Arrival: With prior arrangement through an agent and at least a one-week notice, a Vietnamese visa can be issued at Tan Son Nhat Airport, Saigon. You must show officials at the airport a letter of sponsorship indicating your visa is waiting. Some hardy souls have arrived at Tan Son Nhat Airport without a valid Vietnamese visa. Experiences with this vary. On a group tour, some travelers were immediately granted visas, and thus proceeded on their merry way. For individuals the story is a bit different: one lone traveler, after reciting a sob story about meeting friends, was fined $80 on arrival, placed under house arrest at expensive Tan Son Nhat Transit Hotel for several days, then bingo, received a 20-day visa. It wound up costing him a packet, after the fine, hotel bills, and eventual visa. Moral of the story: better to wait four days in Bangkok or elsewhere and get your paperwork in order there.

Land-Border Stamps

The Vietnamese visa is only valid for arrival *by air* in Saigon or Hanoi. If you arrive or exit at a land border, you must have the name of that border point stamped onto your visa. Certain border points may only be stamped in by certain offices. If you're crossing from Phnom Penh to Saigon, get the border point added to your visa in Phnom Penh—it may not be issued in Bangkok. Traveling in the opposite direction, you get the stamp in Saigon. If coming from Hong Kong, you can get land-border stamps added at the same time as your visa. If moving into China from Hanoi, you must get border stamps in Hanoi. For the Lao Bao border into Laos, the best place to pick up a stamp is Danang; from the opposite side, you can get a stamp in Savannakhet.

If you don't have the relevant border stamp, you'll have to negotiate with border guards who are fond of US dollars. The maximum number of entry/exit stamps appears to be four. That means if you automatically get two on your visa from air arrivals, you have two more up your sleeve. You could cross Moc Bai from Cambodia and exit Lao Cai into China, for example. Land-border stamps cost around $15-20 extra each.

There are two **Chinese border** crossings in the north—the Lao Cai-Hekou border (border stamp is Lao Cai) on the Hanoi to Kunming route, and the Dong Dang border (border stamp is Huu Nghi Quan) on the Hanoi-Lang Son-Nanning route. Travelers who don't have the appropriate stamps for entry or exit have been allowed to proceed after a good five-hour argument and a $20-30 payout. More than one traveler has confused the two northern land borders with China and turned up at the wrong one, which means the stamp is invalid. The port of entry performs registration, and border officials may decide you only have transit authority, meaning they can reduce a one-month Vietnamese visa to seven days. If this happens, you need to hightail it to Hanoi to extend the visa.

In Hong Kong, the Vietnamese consulate sometimes stamps both China border entry points on the visa, sometimes only one, and sometimes none at all. If you have a multiple-entry Chinese visa and the relevant Vietnamese land-border stamps, it's possible to overland from Hong Kong through Nanning to Hanoi, then exit back up through Lao Cai to Kunming. From Kunming you can carry on through China westward, or fly to Bangkok.

To cross the **Lao border** go to Lao Bao, west of Dong Ha. From Lao Bao you can proceed to Savannakhet, and on to Vientiane or over the Mekong to Thailand. One traveler crossed from Vietnam at Lao Bao, decided he didn't like Laos, and came back to the border, convincing the guard to let him back in as though he'd never exited. The best place to get a Lao Bao stamp is at the immigration police in Danang if exiting Vietnam, or the Vietnamese Consulate in Savannakhet if entering Vietnam. You might also try to get a Lao Bao entry stamp added to an initial visa issued in Bangkok. Travelers have also managed to pick up Lao visas at the Lao Consulate in Danang, and Vietnamese visas in Savannakhet; though if you have a chance, you should try and get these ahead of time to avoid being stuck if the visa breezes change direction.

On the Saigon-Phnom Penh route, the **Cambodian border** point is Moc Bai/Bavet. One traveler reported that after he received his Vietnamese paper visa in Bangkok, he duly went to the Vietnamese consulate in Phnom Penh to get the Moc Bai stamp added. The consulate took his visa, destroyed it, and stamped a new visa with new entry date straight in the passport as the traveler stared in starry wonder. This cost $10; they asked for $15. From Saigon, travelers report agents will handle a Cambodian visa, Vietnamese exit stamp, and even a Vietnamese reentry stamp, all within a day.

ARRIVAL AND DEPARTURE PAPERWORK

Registration

When you enter the country, officials at the port of arrival will stamp your visa, then register you. In Saigon and Hanoi you must fill out laborious forms at the airport that look like a visa application all over again. You even need a passport photo for the form. At land borders, officials simply record the information in a logbook.

Entry/Exit Card

The seemingly unimportant entry/exit card you hurriedly fill out upon arrival can come back to haunt you. First, don't lose it! It can be important if you plan on leaving through land borders or obtaining a visa extension. Not having this piece of paper upon exit can create major hassles.

If you apply for a visa extension, officials often look at the box on this card listing where you plan to stay. If you put down someone's residence, chances are the visa may not be renewed. If you're applying in Danang and put down a hotel in Saigon, you're sometimes required to return to Saigon to receive the extension. Several travelers who wrote the name of an actual hotel in Saigon were told to go there and get their "license number" before applying for an extension. Solution to all this rigmarole? Write "unknown" in the appropriate box and there seems to be no problem.

Customs Declaration

The tricky box here requires specifying currencies, precious metals, and credit cards. If you put specific amounts of currency in that box, a customs officer may ask to see the color of your money; if there's a discrepancy, the officer may confiscate the difference—this has happened at land borders. A vague "travelers checks, credit card" may suffice. Technically, you don't have to declare amounts of money under $3000. Customs officers are touchy about the import of blank or recorded video tapes: some foreigners have had these seized upon entry. There is no restriction on the number of rolls of film you may bring in.

PAPERWORK WITHIN VIETNAM

The Vietnamese love red tape. There's so much paperwork you could wear the stuff. Make sure yours is in good shape. The more chops and seals and stamps you accumulate, the better you'll look. An automatic document dispenser would be nice. Carry a few extra passport photos in your wallet—you never know when you'll need them. You need documents for hotel registration, to change money, to rent bicycles, motorcycles, or cars.

Where possible, do not hand over originals in Vietnam. Carry copies of absolutely everything, and use the copies in day-to-day transactions. Hotels will repeatedly ask for your passport, paper visa, entry card, and so on. Some even insist on seeing your customs form. Get all the material together and copy it onto double-sided pages; hand those out to hotel staff. You can also photocopy a typical hotel registration form instead of filling it in each time; just hand over a photocopy of the completed form.

In some cases you may be parted from your original documents. If, for example, you leave your passport for an extension in Hanoi, it could take three days. During this time, you may wish to travel to Halong Bay. In this case, you have to get a note from a travel agent, in English and Vietnamese, saying the agent is holding the passport for the purpose of extension. Carry photocopies of the initial pages of the passport with you. Be aware you'll have great trouble cashing traveler's checks without an original passport.

Bureaucratic games in Vietnam are legendary. The Hanoi Boys stand out in this department.

Some Hanoi officials have issued exit stamps for Lao Cai and taken away the entry/exit card, claiming it would not be needed at the border. This is *not* true—not having the card will cause a long day at the immigration office at the border. You may have to get down on your knees, find a phrasebook for Vietnamese, and chant, "two, four, six, eight—time to renegotiate!"

Visa Extensions

New government regulations announced in September 1995 stated that no extensions would be granted for one-month tourist visas. So the following section may be wishful reading—but some travelers (on business, journalist, and diplomatic visas) are allowed extensions. And who knows what can be achieved under the table? Or if extensions will again be allowed?

In the past, visa extensions for tourist visas, usually for two to four weeks, cost $15-25 and were issued on the spot or the same day. An exception was Hanoi, where extensions could take three days or longer. Applying for visa extensions was erratic—sometimes it worked, sometimes not, depending on where you applied. It also depended on the particular chief at the office. Most places you could apply directly for the extension yourself. In Saigon or Hanoi, because of the volume of applications, it was best to go through an agent.

A sampling around the country: Saigon, two days, $20-25; Hué, five minutes, $20; Vung Tau, two hours, $20; Danang, one day, $15; Nha Trang, one day, $20-25; Hanoi, minimum three working days, sometimes five, $15-25. Travelers reported trouble in Hanoi. After asking for a one-month extension, they were only given 10, 14, or 20 days; these extensions should have been cheaper, say $10-15 for a two-week extension. Some travelers were refused extensions altogether and told to leave the country within two days—they had to scramble for a flight to Vientiane.

The maximum number of extensions appeared to be two. Some travelers were able to extend their initial visa for a total stay of three months. A second extension was more expensive—around $35. You were generally not permitted to apply for an extension unless you were within a week of expiry of the visa. If planning to stay longer, insist on a one-month extension the first time—or go elsewhere. Two extensions of two weeks each were okay, but that cost you $30; it was better to get one extension of one month for $20. Sometimes the visa was stamped, "No more extensions." Extension of business visas is possible—an extension will most likely cost over $100 through an agent.

Border Stamps

Land-Border Exit: If you wish to exit Vietnam by land, you need the relevant border point added to your Vietnamese visa. This stamp costs $10 and up and is best arranged through a travel agent. You must be close to the border in question. If you want to cross into Cambodia, the land-border stamp is issued in Saigon. If you want to cross into China, the stamp is normally issued in Hanoi, and you must get your Chinese visa first. It may be possible to arrange a visa extension and a land-border exit stamp through the same travel agent, and get all the paperwork done at the same time.

Re-entry Stamp: If you wish to return to Vietnam after crossing over to a neighboring country, you need either a new visa or a re-entry stamp on your existing visa. A re-entry stamp effectively turns a single-entry Vietnamese visa into a multiple-entry one. In Saigon, a re-entry visa can be arranged through an agent at the same time as you apply for a Cambodian visa.

Internal Travel Permits

Before 1993, you needed permits to go *anywhere*. The old permits listed 12 places on a page, and then you needed another permit. In early 1993, the whole system was scrapped and the previously off-limits Central Highlands plus the area north of Hanoi were flung open without permit. Very few places now require permits: minority areas like Lat village near Dalat, a few villages near the Lao border out of Buon Ma Thuot, and Kontum or Khe Sanh. Certain water routes in the Mekong Delta may be sensitive. Permits usually cost around $5 per person.

VIETNAMESE EMBASSIES

Within Asia

Some of the following embassies, such as those in Hong Kong, Cambodia, and Laos, cannot be approached directly except for diplomatic visas or business visas with invitation. Vietnamese embassies are best approached through travel agents. An exception is in Thailand, where you can apply for the visa yourself. But this will take just as long, if not longer, than having an agent procure the visa.

Cambodia: Monivong Blvd. (Achar Mean) at 436 St., Phnom Penh, tel. 25481

China: 32 Guanghua Lu, Jianguomenwai, Beijing, tel. 532-1125

Hong Kong: 15F Great Smart Tower, 230 Wan Chai Rd., Wan Chai, tel. 2591-4510 (Consulate General)

Indonesia: 25 Jalan Teuku Umar, Jakarta, tel. 310-0358

Japan: 50-11 Motoyoyogi-Cho, Shibuya-ku, Tokyo 151, tel. 466-3312

Laos: That Luang Rd., Vientiane, tel. 413400 (also a consulate in Savannakhet)

Malaysia: 4 Pesiaran Stonor, Kuala Lumpur, tel. 484036

Myanmar (Burma): 30 Komin Kochin, Yangon, tel. 50361

North Korea: 7 Munxu St., Pyongyang

Philippines: 54 Victor Cruz, Malate, Manila, tel. 500364

Singapore: 10 Leedon Park, Singapore 1026, tel. 468-3747

South Korea: 33-1 Han Nam Dong, Yong-ku, Seoul, tel. 794-3570

Thailand: 83/1 Wireless Rd., Bangkok, tel. 251-7201

Other Embassies Abroad

Australia: 6 Timbarra Crescent, O'Malley, Canberra, ACT, tel. 866058

Belgium: Ave. de la Floride 130, 1180 Brussels, tel. 374-9370

Canada: 695 Davidson Drive, Gloucester, Ottawa, tel. 744-0698

France: 62 Rue Boileau, 75016 Paris, tel. 4524-5063

Germany: Konstantinstrasse 37, 5200 Bonn, tel. 357-0201

India: 17 Kautilya Marg Chanakyapury, Delhi, tel. 301-7714

Italy: Piazza Barberini 12, 00187 Rome, tel. 475-5286

Mexico: Calle Sierra Ventana 255, 11000 Mexico DF, tel. 540-1612

Mongolia: Enkhe-taivan, Oudamjni 47, Ulan Bator, tel. 50465

Russia: Bolshaya Pirogovskaya Ul.13, Moscow, tel. 245-0925

Sweden: Orby Slottsvag 26, 125 36 Alvsjo, Stockholm, tel. 861214

United Kingdom: 12-14 Victoria Rd., London W8 5RD, tel. 937-1912

USA: 1233 Twentieth St. NW, Suite 501, Washington, DC 20036, tel. 861-0737 (liaison office)

Vietnam also maintains embassies or consulates in Eastern Europe (Bulgaria, Hungary, Romania, Czech and Slovak Republics, and Poland), the Middle East (Egypt, South Yemen, and Iraq), Africa (Algeria, Angola, Libya, Madagascar, Mozambique, and Ethiopia), and Central America (Nicaragua).

TOURISM AGENTS

Official tourism agencies in Vietnam are expensive—Vietnam Tourism and Saigon Tourist routinely charge double or more the price of other agencies. With daily tariffs of $80 and up per person, the tours cater to the well-heeled, offer the best accommodations, and feature some unimaginative itineraries. Vietnam Tourism has a monopoly on anything to do with foreigners that smells like big bucks, from cruise ships and motorcycle rallies to Central Highlands elephant safaris. Government tourist offices in the provinces are not in the least interested in individual travelers, or in shelling out free maps and travel literature. Their raison d'etre is to make money, not squander it on handouts.

Far preferable to the official agencies are the services of joint-venture or private agents and transport companies, which can charge a more modest $40 a day per person. Lists of local agents in Hanoi and Saigon are given in the Services and Information chapters for those sections. At any of these places you can hire a guide. Guides can smooth over problems with police, point you to better restaurants, and save

you from being ripped off. If you want a cheaper guide, hire a moto or cyclo driver. They can usually speak a little English, and might charge a bit extra on top of the hourly vehicle rental rate. So a moto driver acting as an unofficial guide might charge $2 a day extra for guide services on top of a $5 daily moto charge. Tourism office guides want $10-20 a day and expect to travel in a hired car.

As an individual traveler you may find yourself in search of a group in order to cut costs. Part of the attraction here is the comfort zone—Vietnamese public transport is crowded, crammed, and excruciatingly slow. With a bit of extra effort you can launch your own expeditions by assembling a small group. This gives you a strong hand in designing and steering the tour—a lot more fun. By advertising in traveler cafés, for example, you can put together a group in your own jeep or 4WD vehicle. To visit Halong Bay, you can easily assemble a group at Bai Chay and rent a fishing boat or sailing junk for the day. Motorcycling is best done with a companion in case of accident—team up with other riders by advertising. Bringing your own bicycle into Vietnam is easy, but finding roads without heavy traffic is difficult. For more information, see "Getting Around" later in this chapter.

Traveler Cafés

Apart from a strong hit of coffee, traveler cafés in Vietnam are an excellent source of current information, and the owners can often fix you up with cheap guides, half- or one-day tours, motorcycle and bicycle rentals, or long-distance minibuses. You can also post notices to join up with other travelers for rented jeeps or minibuses for custom tours. There's even coordination along the superhighway: you can hop on a minibus from Saigon's Kim Café to Nha Trang, hook up with another minibus from Vinagen Café in Nha Trang, and move along the coast to Hanoi's Darling Café.

North: In Hanoi, the major cafés are Darling Café, 4 Hang Quat; Darling Café Hanoi, 33 Hang Quat; Queen Café, at 65 Hang Bac; and the Green Bamboo, 42 Nha Chung Street.

Center: In Hué, Café #3 Le Loi organizes boat rentals and DMZ tours. In Hoi An, there are many cafés—try the ones numbered 20, 22, 24, and 26 on Nguyen Hue Street, or Café des Amis by the waterfront. In Danang, Café

Lien, opposite Marble Mountain Hotel, is the spot. In Nha Trang, Vinagen Café (Five Brothers) has bulletin boards for rides; in Dalat, Stop 'N Go Café is the rendezvous point; no tours, but keeps traveler logbooks.

South: In Saigon, Pham Ngu Lao street has a large concentration of traveler cafés—the Khao San Road of Saigon. Here you'll find Sinh Café, Kim Café, 333 Bar, Long Phi Café, and Saigon Café.

MONEY, MEASUREMENTS, AND COMMUNICATIONS

MONEY

An editorial in *The Asian Wall Street Journal* suggested the first thing Vietnam has to do if it's serious about joining the world economy is change the name of its currency. The word is the brunt of numerous jokes such as the businessman who wakes up in the morning and says, "I feel like a million dong!" Actually, there is such a thing as a 1,000,000-dong note, which is worth $100. You'll occasionally see it displayed in the window of a jeweler's—it's much larger than regular bills, and there's no Ho Chi Minh on it. There's also a large 500,000-dong note.

The exchange rate hovers at around 11,000 dong to the dollar. The dong comes in denominations of 100, 200, 500, 1000, 2000, 5000, 10,000, 20,000, and 50,000. You'll see only 100 and 200 dong notes upcountry in small towns. Even smaller denominations than this are circulated. One of the peculiar sights at a bank in Vietnam is a Mercedes unloading sacks of dong, with tellers presiding over mountains of dong that must be counted by hand; more sophisticated banks use dong-counting machines. There must be very few bank robbers in the country—too much hard work lugging the stuff around.

To lighten your load of dong, it's best to seek out the newer bills in circulation—10,000 dong (red), 20,000 dong (blue), and 50,000 dong (green) notes. While the larger bills reduce your wad, the next problem is convincing locals in smaller towns that this is legal tender, and getting change. They're still using 100-dong notes in some parts of Vietnam. You will most likely pay big expenses like hotels or train tickets in US dollars.

Be careful using the 20,000-dong bill—it looks very similar to the 5000-dong bill, with the same coloration. You can tell the difference at a glance

because Ho Chi Minh's smile is more radiant on the 20,000-dong bill. The 20,000 dong features a kind of blue halo around Uncle Ho. Blackmarket shysters sometimes try and substitute 5000-dong bills for 20,000-dong notes. Bargaining in Vietnamese is quite easy because you can read off the number printed on the bill you wish to use. On the 10,000-dong bill, for example, is written *muoi nghin dong*.

Dong cannot be taken out of Vietnam, but nobody wants to change your dong back into dollars. So as you get nearer to departing Vietnamese shores, scale back your accumulation of dong.

American Dollars

A fistful of dollars, or a fistful of dong? Due to logistical problems, larger transactions in Vietnam are usually conducted in US cash dollars. You're not expected to drop one and a half million dong on the counter for an airline ticket. The US dollar is almost legal tender in Vietnam, although the government has moved to tighten the monetary system and curb everyday use of dollars. The government is trying to stop the unauthorized use of dollars by Vietnamese companies and shops. Airlines, telecommunications and shipping firms, and foreign companies are allowed to deal in US dollars. Other cash currencies are not accepted so readily by some places, like hotels. German marks, which are more stable than US dollars, have been knocked back, and so have French francs and British pounds. This may be due to unfamiliarity, but it's also got a lot to do with the status of the US dollar.

Be aware that there are fake US bills circulating in Asia—blackmarket dealers may traffic in them. Some $100-bill forgeries are state of the art. Study any bills you receive from any source carefully; see "Money" under "Getting Ready" in the Indochina chapter for tips on spotting fake bills. Some Vietnamese banks maintain detection equipment that will search for flaws in US bills.

Banking

Vietnam's Bank of Foreign Trade (Vietcombank) will handle most transactions—there is at least one Vietcombank in every major city. Foreign-run banks operate in Hanoi and Saigon, including Hong Kong Bank, Bangkok Bank, Banque National de Paris, Credit Lyonnais, Deutsche Bank, Britain's Standard Chartered Bank, Internationale Nederlanden Bank, and ANZ Bank. In 1995 Citibank upgraded its Hanoi office to a full branch, becoming the first American bank to operate in Vietnam since 1975. The Bank of America opened a branch in Hanoi shortly after. These banks cash traveler's checks and handle money transfers from abroad. Vietcombank and foreign banks offer cash advances on credit cards, usually with a high commission of four percent or more. Credit cards are starting to come into use in Saigon and Hanoi but not elsewhere. Saigon has double the number of establishments accepting credit cards than Hanoi. Accepted in Saigon are American Express, Visa, MasterCard, Diners Club, and JCB cards.

In 1995, 40 **ATMs** (automatic teller machines) were installed at hotels and airports in Hanoi and Saigon under a pilot scheme launched by the Bank of Vietnam and MasterCard. The ATMs accessible in Thailand and Hong Kong operate on the secret 4-digit number encoded in the card's magnetic strip. If coming from the US you may have to arrange to alter a 6-digit code to a 4-digit. Money drawn on ATMs is treated as a cash advance, with interest running immediately.

Costs

Gouging foreigners is a national sport in Vietnam. This infuriating practice is based entirely on racial and economic criteria: if you have a big nose, you pay through it. The practice will make your blood boil because it applies to just about everything. Somebody charging you triple for a coffee or a baguette can precipitate a major argument that will put you in a foul mood for the rest of the day. I was charged 50% above local price to send an airmail letter to Canada. One foreigner, married to a Vietnamese and living in Vietnam, is consistently charged more than his wife to place a phone call to the same place in the United States. One reason for this behavior may be that for many years under the French, the Vietnamese were treated little better than dogs. And still, today, foreigners can afford to eat in restaurants that are beyond the reach of locals and can afford privileges that the average Vietnamese cannot—such as the use of taxis or chauffeured cars.

Viet-Kieu, or overseas Vietnamese, hit middle ground—they're charged higher than locals, but not as high as foreigners. If they speak fluent Vietnamese, they can probably get local prices; if not, prices are higher. The government leads the way. On Vietnam's official airline there are three prices: one for locals, another for overseas Vietnamese, a third (much higher) for foreigners. So if a foreigner and a Vietnamese friend sit down for lunch, what price is charged? Here the locals are confounded, because regardless of who pays, the Vietnamese person will scrutinize the bill. So hiring a Vietnamese guide can more than pay off by saving you from rip-offs. The same applies when shopping—the guide becomes your negotiator. A hard-nosed negotiator is a real asset on a trip through Vietnam.

Junks ply the waters of Halong Bay on the 10,000-dong note.

To avoid misunderstandings, *always* establish the price of an item beforehand and write it down. If you're in a small restaurant or at a streetstall with no menu or pricing, write up your order and have it itemized in dong, so in effect you receive the bill before you begin to eat. The same applies to a cyclo ride; some travelers even pay up front for cyclos to avoid confusion. Tipping is not expected, and bargaining the norm for services like cyclos.

The traveler is most vulnerable to rip-offs within the first few days of arriving in Vietnam. For this purpose, hustlers will casually inquire how long you've been in the country—so don't let on. To avoid rip-offs, it's a good idea to assemble your own list of common purchases—get assistance from other travelers for the current rates. Find out the cost of a sandwich, a beer, bottled water, a cyclo ride across town, bicycle parking rates, and so on. Bear in mind that when it comes to signs in Vietnam, you're literate. You can read the bulletin boards listing prices for long-distance buses and other services. Find them. Read them. Point to them when negotiating your fare.

You won't be quoted Vietnamese prices. The magic formula for deciding foreigner prices for items such as airline tickets, train sleepers, and hotels seems to be to multiply the Vietnamese price by 2.5. So foreigners pay between two and three times more than Vietnamese. A Vietnamese price for a hotel room may be 30,000 dong ($2.80), but for a foreigner it might be $7. In some cases, the foreigner price is much more; for entry to the Perfume Pagoda near Hanoi, foreigners pay five times the local price.

MEASUREMENTS AND COMMUNICATIONS

Maps

Buy as much map material as you can outside Vietnam. The most accurate, up-to-date map of Vietnam is produced by International Travel Maps in combination with the Cartographic Mapping Institute of Hanoi (CMI). It provides topographic features, the names of provinces and provincial capitals, and realistic road and route detail; submaps offer details of Central Saigon and Central Hanoi. In the ITM/CMI series are also separate maps of Hanoi (single-sided) and Saigon (double-sided). Projected maps in this series include maps of the Mekong Delta, Dalat area, Hué, and so on. Another map on the market is Periplus Editions' Vietnam Travel Map, which is less detailed as a country map, but carries a number of city submaps.

Within Vietnam useful city maps are available, but supply is erratic—sometimes a good map of Hué may be on sale only in Saigon. Pick up maps where you find them, as you might not see them again. Reading Vietnamese maps presents few problems except perhaps for deciphering the keys.

Books

Because of government monitoring of printed material, it's difficult to find reading material in English or French in Vietnam. What is available may be pirated or photocopied to get around government import restrictions. A single bookstore in Bangkok will probably stock more reading material on Vietnam than you'll find in the entire city of Saigon. The material will be more intelligible, too. Government-run bookstores in Vietnam sell boring tomes of pure propaganda, written in garbled English.

Media

In a half-hearted attempt to modernize Vietnam TV (VTV), the Vietnamese culture ministry has replaced irrigation documentaries and folk-dance contests with spicier pirated videos from Hong Kong and the United States. Satellite TV has not made great inroads into Vietnam. Dish distribution is tightly controlled—only major hotels and embassies have been permitted to install dishes that can pick up Hong Kong-based StarTV, which includes BBC programs. On radio, Voice of Vietnam broadcasts in a dozen foreign languages, although broadcasts are brief. On shortwave radio you can pick up the BBC, Radio Australia, and Voice of America.

Press laws in Vietnam prohibit criticism of official government policy. Newspapers or magazines that do not comply are shut down by the Ministry of Culture for a few weeks or longer. Publishers may also be ordered to recall a particular issue. The Casting and Metallurgy Association was asked to recall a 1995 issue of *Knowledge and Technology* because only five of

24 stories concerned metals and engineering—the rest concerned crime, cannibalism, a man with 105 wives, and the secrets of embalming. Obviously, these were stories with no mettle.

Foreign magazines are often full of saucy articles and criticism of just about everything and are sold in Vietnam in upper-crust hotel lobbies. But they're priced so high that the average Vietnamese is not likely to lay hands on them. Among the foreign magazines on sale are *Newsweek, Time,* and *Paris Match.* You can also buy the *International Herald Tribune, Sydney Morning Herald, Le Monde,* and day-old copies of the *Bangkok Post.*

There are several weekly English-language newspapers produced in Vietnam, including *Saigon Times* and *Vietnam Investment Review. Vietnam News* is issued weekdays, as is the French *Le Courier du Vietnam.* Hotel newsstands and gift shops in Saigon and Hanoi also carry *Vietnam Today,* a business magazine published in Singapore, and *Destination: Vietnam,* a California-based travel publication. Both are distributed in Vietnam by Xunhasaba, the state corporation for import and export of books and periodicals, and in the US by Global Directions, 58 Genebern Way, San Francisco, CA 94112. Global Directions also publishes *Destination: Vietnam,* the bi-monthly glossy magazine highlighting traveler features, tips, and lists of restaurants and sights. *Business News Indochina,* a journal published monthly in Hong Kong, is available in Vietnam also. From a Swiss group comes *Vietnam Economic Times,* available in the US from Vietnam Resource Group, 955 Lenfant Plaza North SW, Suite 4000, Washington, DC 20024.

Post Office and Courier

Post offices in Vietnam offer regular and express mail service, parcel service, telex, telegram, fax, and possibly courier services. Poste restante is available in major Vietnamese cities—letters all go into one big box at the main post office. Incoming mail is not guaranteed in Vietnam. Some mail arrives minus stamps; some mail arrives very late; some mail never arrives. At one point in the 1980s, the government stopped all magazines and photos arriving by post. Outgoing mail takes about two weeks to reach the West by air. For letters and packages, it's advisable to pay a small extra fee for registration of items, and make sure stamps are cancelled in front of you. Do not fully package materials as you'll have to open up for "customs" inspection prior to mailing. If you're heading to Bangkok, Hong Kong, or Singapore, save your bundle and mail from there—the service is more efficient, faster, safer, and cheaper.

Vietnamese postal rates are high by Asian standards, and impossibly high by local standards. An airmail postcard to Hong Kong or Sydney costs 41 cents; to Paris 43 cents; to New York, 50 cents. With an income of perhaps $1 a day, few Vietnamese can afford to send postcards or letters. If you want to correspond,

The post office in Dalat is in a converted French villa.

supply your Vietnamese correspondent with stamps. Regular mail items are accepted up to two kilograms. Cheaper rates are offered for small parcels or printed matter; books can be sent as printed matter up to five kilograms. For overseas parcels, the maximum weight is five kilograms unless a postal service agreement exists with the destination country, when it can rise to 10 kg or more.

For greater security and speed, a courier such as DHL, UPS, or TNT is preferable, though rates are exorbitant. Courier services operate from the larger cities, including Hanoi, Haiphong, Danang, Qui Nhon, Nha Trang, and Saigon. In Hanoi and Saigon, DHL operates from the central post office.

Fax and Phone

There are bilingual phone directories for both Saigon and Hanoi: you can help yourself to detailed information on fax rates, IDD phone rates, and EMS postal rates. Within Vietnam, calling is erratic, and a private telephone is a complete luxury. From Vietnam, IDD dialing is not cheap— the first three minutes to the USA, the UK, or France direct dial cost $13.80; for a person-to-person call it's $17.62. To Australia the first three minutes cost $12 direct dial, and $15.15 person-to-person; to Hong Kong or Bangkok the rates are $11.40 direct, and $14.35 person-to-person. For operator-assisted international calls, dial 110; for direct dialing, the prefix is 00, plus country code followed by the number. For domestic calls, dial 101 to place operator-assisted calls. Dial 01 for direct domestic dialling, plus country code and number. The Vietnam country code is 84. Some area codes: Hanoi 4, Saigon 8, Haiphong 31, Danang 51, Hué 54, Qui Nhon 56, Nha Trang 58, Dalat 63, Vung Tau 64.

A cheaper and more convenient communication mode is the fax, mostly paid by the page. Fax rates for selected destinations: to Hong Kong, Malaysia, Thailand and Singapore, $5.70 first page and $4.42 second; to Australia, Laos, Russia, and China, $6 first page and $4.72 second; to the USA, Canada, Europe, and New Zealand, $6.90 first page and $5.73 second. Consider faxing instead of telephoning—you can cram a lot of material onto one page. Beware of hotels that don't list fax rates. Some are prone to charging double or even triple the rate charged by the post office in the interest of fundraising. Receiving a fax incurs charges in hotels but is usually inexpensive.

A bewildering number of foreign companies— French, Japanese, Australian, Malaysian, Korean, and American—supply new telecommunications equipment to Vietnam. With fewer than 10 lines per 1,000 people, the Vietnamese have a long way to go. Vietnam will be plugged into a modern telecom network when it's linked by submarine cable to Hong Kong and Thailand. The cable will utilize fiber-optics technology and connect Vietnam to other cable systems in the region.

One thing coming down the phone line that has the Vietnamese government very worried is the anarchic Internet. The bulletin boards of Varenet (Vietnam Academic, Research and Education Network) have been bombarded with criticism of the Hanoi government by disgruntled expatriate Vietnamese in the United States. Varenet launched a quasi-commercial Internet service in 1994 called Netnam, but the government is nervous. Cut off from events in Vietnam, exiled dissidents have tended to fade away; the Internet may allow their voices to be heard again, cheaply and instantaneously.

Time Zone

Vietnam is all on one time zone: Greenwich mean time +7 hours; Eastern standard time +12; Pacific standard time +15. Figures may vary with daylight saving time. When in Hanoi or Saigon, time in London is -7 hours; Paris -6; New York/Toronto -12; San Francisco/Vancouver -15; Sydney +3 hours.

Metric and Electric

Vietnam follows the metric system. The Vietnamese words for gram, kilogram, ton, kilometer, and liter sound almost the same as in English, though rendered with tones. Currents in Vietnam are 220V/50 cycles in urban areas, and 110V/50 cycles in rural areas. There's rarely enough electricity to go around—service is erratic, with blackouts or power surges common. Wiring is often improvised, sometimes with exposed wires hanging around bathrooms. Sockets may be two-prong, with American-style flat pins (220V, mostly in the south), or Russian- and European-style round pins (mostly in the north). Don't even think about using a hair dryer.

SERVICES AND INFORMATION

Tourist Information

Current information about Vietnam is difficult to find, especially outside Vietnam. Vietnam Tourism and Saigon Tourist have only a few offices abroad. You can apply through these offices for visas. Vietnam Tourism maintains offices in Indiana, at P.O. Box 53316, Indianapolis, IN 46253, USA, tel. (317) 388-0788, fax (317) 298-3454 (mostly deals with group tours, no individuals); in Paris at 4 rue Cherubini 75002, Paris, tel. 42-868637, fax 42-604332; and Singapore at 101 Upper Cross St. #02-44, People's Park Centre, Singapore 0105. Saigon Tourist staffs offices in Hamburg at Hamburger Str. 132, 200 Hamburg 76, fax 4940-296705; and Tokyo at 7F Crystal Bldg. 1-2, Kanda Awajicho, Chiyoda-Ku, Tokyo 101, fax 813-3253-5757.

Traveler Network

Vietnam is changing fast, and guidebook listings often cannot keep pace. New hotels are going up, new restaurants opening, new regions opening to travelers. Keep your ears and eyes open. The best way of getting up-to-the-minute information is to frequent traveler cafés. Here you can meet travelers coming from the opposite direction, their brains bulging with fresh data. Traveler cafés serve mediocre food, but over the bowls of noodles backpackers gather to swap tales. Sauce and source: Most of the cafés maintain traveler logbooks with comments about destinations.

Business Services

Major hotels in Hanoi and Saigon offer business centers, providing translation, telecommunications, and secretarial services. There are also independent operators. Software can easily handle combinations of Vietnamese and English text. Computers are slowly creeping into Vietnam, though a high percentage of software is pirated, a throwback to the days of the US embargo. If bringing in electrical devices, it's best to run them off rechargeable batteries; bring a recharge unit that can be plugged into the wall. This way you don't have to worry about

a sudden surge of electricity zapping a laptop computer. Power surges are common, so use a surge protector with sensitive equipment.

Film and Photocopy

Konica and Fuji dominate the Vietnamese film market. Since the lifting of the embargo, Kodak has joined the fray, setting up a mini-lab in Saigon and several shops in Hanoi. Photocopy machines are widely available in Vietnam; copies are inexpensive.

Business Hours

Business is most often conducted from 0700 or 0800 to 1600 or 1700, closing at midday for one or two hours. Market hours are 0730-1700 daily; post offices, 0730-1800 and often till 2200; embassies and consulates, 0800-1100 and 1400-1630 Mon.-Fri.; banks and airlines, 0800-1130 and 1300-1630, half-day Saturday, closed Sunday. Some foreign banks and airlines keep Western hours, from, say, 0900 to 1530. Museums are generally open 0800-1130 and 1300-1630 Tuesday to Sunday.

Health Care

See "Health" in the Indochina chapter for a complete rundown on health hazards in Indochina. Vietnamese health care is woefully substandard. Equipment and skills date to the 1930s, or perhaps even the Dark Ages. However, conditions are improving. One big obstacle to updating Vietnam's health care system has been the block on foreign input. In early 1995, the Minister of Health signed a decree allowing foreign investors to open hospitals, clinics, medical consultancies, and medical-technical services in Vietnam. The proposed joint-venture facilities would serve the country's growing expatriate population. Four US firms have submitted joint-venture proposals for Vietnamese hospitals—two in Saigon, two in Hanoi. Until these ventures make progress, in the event of an emergency, you are best advised to evacuate to Singapore, Bangkok, or Hong Kong. Evacuation insurance is advisable.

ANTI-AIDS CAMPAIGN

In every large city billboards carry AIDS awareness slogans hinting at the consequences of an unregulated sex industry. The SIDA posters (using the French acronym for AIDS) are displayed because the World Health Organization (WHO) will not provide funding unless public awareness posters are in place. Recently, the government has been converting slogans to read AIDS since the French acronym is identical to that of the Swedish International Development Agency (SIDA), a health-care group active in Vietnam.

Pasteur Institutes in Saigon, Nha Trang, and Dalat were set up as medical research outfits. Among founder Alexandre Yersin's first projects was isolation of a plague bacillus; he was later involved in research on the prevention of malaria and set about planting quinine trees in Vietnam. Now the Pasteur Institutes play a role in researching a modern scourge—they've conducted research on AIDS since 1991. In 1995 2,300 HIV-positive cases were recorded in Vietnam. The number of confirmed AIDS cases rose to 130; most deaths due to AIDS-related illness have occurred in Saigon. WHO estimates Vietnam may have 400,000 HIV cases by the year 2000.

Vietnam's National Committee on AIDS prevention has initiated a program to integrate an AIDS-prevention program into the training curriculum for the national political system, medical colleges, and schools nationwide. The Australian government will pilot a project with the Vietnam Youth Project in Vietnam using *Streetwise Comics,* Australian publications that help street kids understand HIV and AIDS problems. The project will train Vietnamese staff to produce a series of bilingual mini-comics on AIDS prevention.

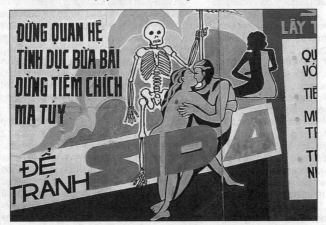

This poster warns: "To avoid AIDS, don't engage indiscriminately in sex, don't use drugs."

GETTING THERE

BY AIR

Over 23 airlines from as many countries schedule flights to Vietnam and maintain representative offices there. The national carrier, Vietnam Airlines, has offices in over 20 countries. More connections are on the way. A number of aviation agreements have been signed to open new routes to Europe, Australia, Japan, and the United States. There will also be more frequent flights in the region from Vietnam to Bangkok, Vientiane, Phnom Penh, and Hong Kong.

There are two flight paths into Vietnam: direct, or via a staging point such as Bangkok, Hong Kong, or Singapore, with frequent connections to Saigon or Hanoi. It's generally cheaper at present to approach Vietnam from Bangkok or Hong Kong. For more information, see "Getting There" in the Indochina chapter. Carriers flying into Vietnam include Cathay Pacific, Malaysian Airlines, Korean Air, Singapore Airlines, China Airlines, Air France, Thai International, Lufthansa, KLM, Philippine Airlines, and Japan Airlines. Vietnam Airlines often arranges joint service with these airlines, taking over the final leg from, say, Bangkok or Hong Kong.

The majority of flights into Vietnam are routed through Saigon. With some carriers it's possible to arrive in Hanoi and depart from Saigon, or vice versa. A third international airport is open at Danang, but thus far flights to Danang have been routed through Saigon or Hanoi. The only international flight that bypasses Saigon and Hanoi is a RegionAir direct flight from Singapore to Vung Tau twice weekly. This caters to those in the oil and gas industry, and also to businesspeople and tourists.

Customs

On entry each person is allowed 200 cigarettes or 50 cigars, one liter of spirits, and one liter of wine. On exit, your entry/exit card and customs form are collected, with a cursory check only. Buddha images, antiques, or items "of high cultural value" may not be exported unless accompanied by a Customs Export permit. Dong export is not permitted, but neither is conversion back to dollars. Spend it all before you depart, or find an incoming traveler to change with. Departure tax is $8.

Inter-Asia Flights

Flights from Bangkok to Saigon, and Hong Kong to Hanoi take less than two hours. The airline hubs of Bangkok and Hong Kong dominate the Vietnam trade. Cheaper flights into Saigon (prices quoted are one-way) are from Bangkok ($150), Phnom Penh ($50), Kuala Lumpur ($150), Canton (Guangzhou; $140). Cheaper flights into Hanoi (one-way) are from Vientiane ($90), Bangkok ($160), Nanning ($80), Canton ($125).

On inter-Asia flights luggage is restricted to 20 kg on economy class and 30 kg for business class—anything above those weights may be subject to a surcharge. This means if you fly in from North America to Hong Kong with a 70-kg luggage allowance, and you stop for several days in Hong Kong, your allowance will plummet to 20 kg for the Hong Kong-Hanoi leg. But if your flight is booked as one ticket with a transit in Hong Kong, the original baggage weight is allowed.

Bangkok and Hong Kong agents offer roundtrip packages with visa. Bangkok agents may offer a Bangkok to Saigon entry flight and a Hanoi to Vientiane exit flight, plus Vietnamese visa, all for $240. A package from Hong Kong to Saigon and return from Hanoi to Hong Kong can be obtained for $450 including visa; the regular airfare is $540 roundtrip. Flying into Hanoi from Canton rather than Hong Kong represents a big savings—the flight is only $125, but you have to add in the costs of a Chinese visa and boat to Canton, an extra $40 or so. A flight from Hong Kong to Hanoi or Saigon one-way is around $260.

Kunming is becoming an interesting staging point. Hong Kong-Kunming is $195 one-way, and Kunming-Bangkok is $160 one-way. You cover the Hanoi-Kunming stretch by land—have the Lao Cai border point added to your Vietnamese visa. This is not a problem from Hong Kong or Hanoi, but would be a problem if starting from Bangkok.

FLYING GHOSTS

In the mid-1980s the Vietnamese government issued a series of stamps showing historic aircraft—a German Fokker Triplane from 1917, a Soviet Yakolev II from 1946. Cynics wondered if these planes weren't part of Vietnam's newest fleet. Indeed, in the embargo days, Vietnam's fleet was mostly composed of aging Russian Tupolev-134 jets and Ilyushin-18 turboprops that groaned and creaked when aloft. For hair-raising flights, nothing beat the Yakolev-40 light aircraft. In Vietnamese, Vietnam Airlines is rendered Hang Khong Vietnam, which foreigners quickly dubbed "Hang On Vietnam." Ex-fighter pilots specialized in vertical takeoffs and landings learned from wartime days. Exit doors—if you could find them—were marked in Russian.

Vietnam Airlines was forced to use Russian aircraft because the embargo prevented leasing planes with American technology or parts. In 1992 Vietnam Airlines found a way around the restrictions by chartering instead of leasing planes, and by agreeing not to fly under its own name. This resulted in the acquisition of two Boeing 767s and a Boeing 737 painted completely white—somewhat disconcerting to passengers like myself boarding in Bangkok. After our flying ghost took off, we were relieved to hear a French accent emanating from the cockpit—hopefully the pilot. The in-flight service was uniquely Vietnamese: a hostess dressed in a dreamy *ao dai* trundled down the aisle to deliver a single fruit to each passenger. I gazed at the fruit in wonder: I'd never seen this species before. Here I was on an unmarked plane with an unknown fruit. A new species at 7,000 meters! Puzzled, I turned to my Vietnamese neighbor, and she gave me sign-language instruction on how to dissect the fruit and which parts to eat. And so I devoured the unknown species (which, by the way, was delicious).

In mid-1992, Vietnam Airlines purchased two 80-seat ATR-72s from France. The ATR-72 is a turbo-prop made by Avions de Transport (ATR), a joint venture between France's Aerospatiale and Italy's Alenia Spa. With the lifting of the embargo, Vietnam Airlines is retiring its old Russian crates—the Tupolev jets—to boost the airline's safety reputation. There are maintenance concerns with the Tupolevs, which have to be flown to Moscow for checks. The airline's fleet now includes Airbus A-320s leased from Air France, an assortment of leased Boeings, and a handful of ATR-72s. Vietnam Airlines plans to more than double its fleet by the year 2000.

After getting the cold shoulder from the US for so long, Vietnamese airline officials are suddenly being treated like royalty. Delta was the first airline to host a visit to the US by Vietnamese executives. Nguyen Hong Nhi of Vietnam Airlines was wined and dined, given a tour of Disney World, and photographed next to a Wookie, the furry copilot in *Star Wars*. It was a bizarre experience for Nhi, a former air force general who shot down eight American aircraft in his MiG-21, but he said he had "a lovely time" in the States.

Fares from Singapore to Vietnam are pricey. On Vietnam Airlines, a one-way fare Hanoi to Singapore is $310; on Singapore Airlines, a one-way fare Saigon to Singapore is $237. It's a better value to take a Vietnam Airlines flight from Saigon to Kuala Lumpur for $150 one-way. Other flights come into Saigon from Seoul, Taipei, Manila, and Osaka; and into Hanoi from Seoul, Beijing, and Kaohsiung.

Other International Flights

Student travel organizations (you often don't have to be a student) and bucket shops in large cities are the best sources of cheap fares. Shop around until you find the right deal. Cheaper fares may necessitate restrictions such as one-month advance purchase, nonrefundable tickets, or a three-month limit on use of return fare. Always find out how long the agency you're dealing with has been in business before buying a ticket.

From Europe: Bucket shops in London, Amsterdam, Antwerp, and Paris offer competitive flights into Hong Kong or Bangkok. From Paris, Air France operates expensive direct routes into Hanoi and Saigon; Lufthansa has direct flights from Frankfurt to Saigon. Vietnam Airlines operates Boeing 767 flights on the Paris-Berlin-Dubai-Saigon-Hanoi route.

From Australia: There are flights from Sydney and Melbourne to Saigon, with onward connections to Hanoi. You can enter Hanoi and depart from Saigon. Roundtrip three-month excursion fares on joint Qantas-Vietnam Airlines flights are competitive.

From Canada: Korean Airlines flies Vancouver to Seoul, where you transfer to a Saigon flight. More expensive are flights from Vancouver into Saigon via Singapore on Singapore Airlines, or into Hanoi on Cathay Pacific via Hong Kong. From Toronto or Montreal, flight paths are eastward via Bangkok.

From the US: Since the lifting of the trade embargo, US airlines are scrambling for direct routes into Vietnam—first off the mark are United, Continental, and Northwest Orient. Delta Airlines has an arrangement to fly to an intermediate point where passengers transfer to Vietnam Airlines for the last leg. By the time you have this book in your hands, direct flights from the US should be possible. Korean Airlines flies Los Angeles-Seoul-Saigon, and EVA Airlines offers same-day connections from San Francisco or Los Angeles via Taipei to Saigon.

BY SEA

Western cruise liners and smaller vessels dock at coastal ports. A popular cruise route runs from Hong Kong with four or five stops along the coast of Vietnam before continuing to Bangkok, Singapore, or Manila. See "Cruising" under "Tours," below. Commercial ports open to cruise ships include Halong Bay, Haiphong, Danang, Qui Nhon, Nha Trang, Vung Tau, and Saigon. Smaller ports open include Thanh Hoa in the north, and Mytho, Cantho, and Vinh Thai on the Mekong River. Pilotage is compulsory for all vessels entering or leaving Vietnamese ports, and paperwork must be in order for entry.

BY LAND

There are many land border crossings from Vietnam into neighboring nations, but only four at present are open to foreigners. In the north are two crossings to China, at Lao Cai and Huu Nghi (Dong Dang), accomplished by train, bus, minibus, jeep, or a combination of these. In the center is the Lao Bao road crossing to Laos; you can rent vehicles along this stretch. In the south is the Moc Bai crossing to Cambodia—you can travel the route by taxi, minibus, bus, or moto. Long-distance cyclists have crossed all four borders.

You must possess a pre-issued border stamp to enter or exit by a land border. When crossing, be wary of customs and immigration officials working far from the reach of authorities in Saigon or Hanoi. They may be looking for extra income. One traveler reports a customs official counting his money to see if it matched the currency declaration. Later the traveler noticed some of the bills were missing.

GETTING AROUND

BY AIR

Vietnam Airlines, the national carrier, operates about 15 domestic routes. Vietnam Airlines is a third-world carrier, so expect third-world safety standards and service. Conditions are much improved on international runs where appearances must be maintained. The smaller Pacific Airlines, a joint-stock airline with state-owned corporations as shareholders, operates on the Saigon to Hanoi route, and also flies to Taiwan. It's not certain how long Pacific Airlines will remain in business. It has only a few jets at its disposal and is beset by financial problems. Vietnam Air Service Company (VASCO) oper-

ates light planes and helicopters on a charter basis. It flies helicopters from Hanoi to Haiphong, Cat Ba, and Halong Bay, and operates light planes from Saigon to Cantho, and Saigon to Con Dao Islands. There are plans to expand the helicopter service to other parts of the country.

Vietnam Airlines issues its own time table booklet with domestic and international flights; you can track it down in Saigon or Hanoi. There are frequent flights between the cities of Hanoi, Saigon, Hué, and Nha Trang. The time table will inform you which Russian crates are still flying around. While Boeings and Airbuses are used on the Hanoi-Saigon route, lesser breeds like Tupolev-134s (TU3) are used on more obscure

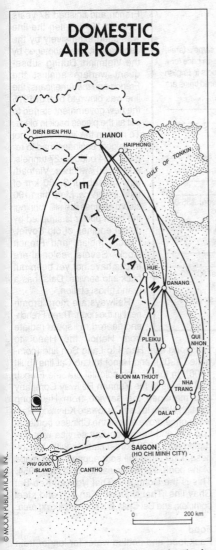

DOMESTIC AIR ROUTES

DIEN BIEN PHU

HANOI

HAIPHONG

GULF OF TONKIN

V
I
E
T
N
A
M

HUE

DANANG

PLEIKU

QUI NHON

BUON MA THUOT

NHA TRANG

DALAT

SAIGON (HO CHI MINH CITY)

PHU QUOC ISLAND

CANTHO

0   200 km

© MOON PUBLICATIONS, INC.

employed. Not recommended for those with heart problems. Baggage is limited to 20 kg per person on domestic flights.

Vietnam Airlines charges double to triple local price for foreigners, and you usually pay in dollars. Supposedly the increased tariff covers insurance; a Vietnamese family may settle for 250,000 dong for injury, whereas a foreigner might sue for $250,000. Fares are based on distance; a two-hour flight from Hanoi to Saigon covering 1,138 km costs $160 one-way, while a one-hour flight from Hanoi to Danang covering 606 km costs $80 one-way. There is no discount for roundtrip fares, which double the price of one-way fares. Sample fares are as follows. From Hanoi to Danang, $80; to Hué, $80; to Nha Trang, $130; to Saigon, $160. From Saigon to Dalat, $25; to Nha Trang, $45; to Danang, $85; to Hué, $85; to Haiphong, $150; to Hanoi, $160.

Domestic flights can save a long haul by bus or train. The Hué to Hanoi flight is popular here, because there's not a whole lot to miss on the road route. Saigon to Buon Ma Thuot takes only 50 minutes in a 34-seat Yakolev and costs $45; by road, the route is a much cheaper dogleg 18 hours by bus. A similar situation exists for Danang to Pleiku—a $30 flight can save a lot of time. If there's flooding in a particular region, you might consider flying over it.

Support systems for Vietnam Airlines are poor. Computer bookings are often botched; if a plane appears to be booked out, try standby. You can sometimes arrange to ride a Vietnam Airlines bus or minibus from its downtown office to the airport or vice versa. With the exception of Saigon's Tan Son Nhat Airport, airport facilities are dismal. Arrive well in advance for a domestic flight or you may find the clerks have sold your seat to another passenger. Before you board, make sure you keep your film to one side. At Saigon's Tan Son Nhat Airport are two sets of X-ray machines to pass through before you board a domestic flight. Frequent X-rays can fog film.

BY TRAIN

Trains are good places to mingle. On the neutral ground of trains, people speak more freely. That's if you can hear them. Trains are noisy—

domestic flights. The Tupolev has a tainted safety reputation, and the crew are not renowned for service, either. The Tupolev is a 70-seat Russian jet being phased out in favor of 80-seat French ATR-72s. On some trips like the Saigon to Dalat run, a 34-seat Yakolev-40 (YAK40) is

TRAIN FARES

By applying the logic absorbed from the following sample fares, you can arrive at rough calculations for the foreign price for a particular train. Some stations hand out photocopied sheets in English with price calculations and brief time tables. Odd-numbered trains are southbound; even-numbered trains are northbound.

HANOI TO SAIGON, 1,726 KM

S3/CM5 trains; 38/42 hours; soft seat $64; hard sleeper $90-98-107; soft sleeper $115

S7 train; 46 hours; hard seat $48; soft seat $56; hard sleeper $82-91-99; soft sleeper $108

HUÉ TO SAIGON, 1,038 KM

S3/CM5 train; 24/26 hours; soft seat $40; hard sleeper $55-60-65; soft sleeper $76

S7 train; 28 hours; hard seat $29; soft seat $35; hard sleeper $50-55-60; soft sleeper $66

HANOI TO HUÉ, 688 KM

S3/CM5 trains; 14/16 hours; soft seat $26; hard sleeper $37-40-44; soft sleeper $51

S7 train; 18 hours; hard seat $20; soft seat $23; hard sleeper $33-37-40; soft sleeper $44

engines roaring, carriages swaying around, loudspeakers screeching in the cars—so a set of earplugs is a good idea if you're trying to sleep. Trains are more expensive than buses and don't necessarily get you there any faster. However, you do have legroom, and you can recline in soft seat class or even sleep overnight. Also, there's less chance of an accident. Comfort allows you to enjoy the scenery; the railway passes some spectacular stretches on parts of the coast, particularly between Hué and Danang.

The most common trains used by travelers are the Reunification (Thong Nhat) Expresses running between Saigon and Hanoi. Not really expresses, these rarely make it over 40 kph, but they sure beat local trains, which can crawl along at 15 kph. Express trains are often forced to share the track with slower trains, some traveling in the opposite direction. Time tables for expresses are posted at most stations and can be viewed in hotel lobbies.

The Reunification Express runs along an old meter-gauge line begun in 1899 under the French and finished 37 years later. In 1942, when the line was used extensively by the Japanese, it was sabotaged by the Vietminh. During subsequent warfare against the French and the Americans, the line was blown to bits. In 1975 the new government started to put all the pieces back in place. To reopen the line from Hanoi to Saigon, engineers had to repair 1,334 bridges, 27 tunnels, and 1,300 switches. Vietnam now has about 3,000 km of track in service. More than 100 steam engines are still running; the main power is supplied by diesel engines of old Soviet, Czech, Indian, and French stock. Several colonial-era tracks have not yet been put back into service. Dalat has a grand ghost station.

Railways are more prominent in the north. Three French-engineered rail spurs radiate from Hanoi: the Hanoi to Haiphong line, Hanoi to Lang Son line (completed 1902), and Hanoi to Lao Cai line (built 1906). In the French colonial era, the French had shares in the Yunnan Railway Company and managed the service from Haiphong through Hanoi to Lao Cai toward Kunming. Railways once drove across the Chinese border at Lao Cai and Lang Son, but service was disrupted after 1979 border clashes with the Chinese. One other rail spur appearing on maps of the north is an industrial line built after 1954. This is the Dong Anh-Thai Nguyen-Kep-Bai Chay line. Thai Nguyen is an iron and steel complex, and Bai Chay is a coal-producing area.

Food

Pack food and bottled water for longer train trips. Train meals are free with your overpriced foreign ticket. They're delivered to your seat and vary from the adequate (bread and pâté) to the highly suspect (box with rice, stale vegetables, egg, and meat). Foreigners are often given a complimentary Coke to offset the fact they've paid more than double for their rail ticket. Attendants rove up and down the cars dispensing beer from ice buckets, tea from kettles. Newspapers and other items are also available at an extra cost. The dining car serves food to order, but the fare is not a great improvement over what you get at your seat. It's best to buy fresh food from stations along the route and hang it in plastic bags in your car. Smoking is permitted in all classes at all times, creating a stale cigarette smell. No ashtrays are provided.

Classes
In socialist Vietnam there are no classes—it's just that some seats are softer than others. Prices vary according to softness of bunk, degree of privacy, and height above the floor. If you're going to pay double or triple local price, you deserve more. Use the first-class waiting rooms at stations even if you've got a hard seat ticket. These waiting rooms have comfortable couches to snooze on, tea service, TV, fridge, toilet, even a shower cubicle. On trains, there are two types of seats, hard *(ngoi cung)* and soft *(ngoi em)*, and usually two types of sleeper, hard sleeper *(nam cung)* and soft sleeper *(nam em)*.

Hard seats are facing high-backed benches made of wooden slats, with about 80 places in each crowded hard seat car. On long runs, passengers sleep bolt upright, or on the floor, or string hammocks between seats. Sleep is often interrupted by screeching static on speakers placed at both ends of each car. You can stow luggage on overhead racks or under seats; it's a good idea to padlock your possessions to a piece of metal.

Soft seats resemble aircraft-style seats, but think Russian aircraft after a combat mission. Seats may be broken at the reclining angle, or have broken armrests. About 64 seats to a car, arranged in pairs on either side of the aisle. This class is less crowded, seats are numbered, and there is greater legroom. Soft seat is a good budget alternative to a hard sleeper and sometimes more comfortable. If your train trip is daytime only, soft seat is preferable to hard sleeper, and cheaper.

A **hard sleeper** features six bunks in three tiers to each compartment. There are about seven compartments to each hard-sleeper car, so 42 bunks to the car. This sleeper really is

hard—no mattress is provided. The bunk is just hard wood with a straw mat on it, although you can try asking for a blanket. You can close the compartment door at night. Pricing varies slightly for the three levels of bunks—the top is cheapest, the middle medium-priced, the lowest the most expensive. During the day passengers may sit on the lower bunks, which have access to a window table.

A **soft sleeper** consists of four bunks in each enclosed compartment, with six compartments to a car, or 24 beds. Each bunk is supplied with a mattress and pillow; there's a mirror on the compartment door and decent lighting. This class would be the equivalent of a hard sleeper on Chinese trains. A soft sleeper is expensive, about double the price of a soft seat. To get around the expense, some travelers buy hard class tickets, then negotiate with the conductor to upgrade to soft class once on the train (payment in cash).

A **deluxe sleeper** consists of two bunks to an enclosed compartment with thicker and softer mattresses. This class is rare. It's only found on top trains, and presumably only used by the top brass.

Pricing
A Reunification Express train is typically composed of seven to 12 cars, including a dining car and a goods car for mail and heavy items like bicycles and motorcycles. Staff may occupy half a sleeping car, sometimes shared with the goods car. The top trains are S3/S4 and CM5/CM6, offering soft seats, hard sleepers, and soft sleepers. These trains stop only at major cities, and take between 38 hours (S3/S4) and 42 hours (CM5/CM6) to cover the 1,726 km on the Hanoi-Saigon route. With hard seat cars are S7/S8 and S9/S10, typically composed of nine passenger cars: three hard seat, two soft seat, three hard sleeper, and one soft sleeper. These trains stop at more stations along the Hanoi to Saigon route and take 46 hours to cover the entire distance.

On Hanoi to Haiphong trains there are only hard seats or soft seats available; from Hanoi to Lao Cai, hard seats, soft seats, and hard sleepers; from Hanoi to Dong Dang, hard seats.

Prices vary slightly for each kind of train—it depends on comfort, speed, distance, and the size of your nose. Foreigners pay two to three times more than Vietnamese and usually pay in dollars rounded out to the nearest figure. The markup is higher for the soft classes. Foreign prices are not usually posted at railway stations. If you're keen on calculations, you can use the posted Vietnamese prices as a rough gauge. On average, if you multiply the Vietnamese price by 2.5 you'll arrive at a dong price that roughly converts to the price a foreigner is expected to pay. Because of this pricing system, it's much cheaper to travel by bus than train—in theory there is no foreign markup on buses—but buses are nowhere near as comfortable.

Consider travelling by soft seat—it's only marginally more expensive than hard seat, but a lot cheaper than a hard sleeper. For day-trips, the soft seat is preferable to other classes; for overnight trips, you'll still get some sleep on a soft seat since you can recline.

As a high-paying foreigner, you'll be sold a ticket through a separate wicket dealing in US dollars. You need to show your passport. To avoid disappointment, book several days in advance for sleepers—a three-day advance booking is a good idea. Travel agents can arrange your ticket for a small surcharge. Tickets can be booked by phone in major cities.

BY ROAD

Rental Vehicles
You can assemble your own small group and hire a car and driver from numerous travel agencies and government tourism offices. Self-drive vehicle rentals are not available as yet, except for motorcycles. Vehicles ranging from a car to a minibus, or even full-size bus, can be used for touring around a city or further afield. Calculation of costs depends on the type of vehicle, time, distance, number of passengers, and several other variables. Russian cars are cheaper, Japanese cars more expensive. In the south you can rent museum pieces—old Peugeot 203s or Citröen Tractions. Vehicles are mostly priced per 100 km, but you can arrange hire by half or full day. Cars usually work out to $25-40 a day. An example here is driving from Hué to Danang. It's only 108 km, and there's great scenery along the route. A hired car allows you

to dawdle, and once you get to Danang, you could use the car to visit Hoi An, 35 km further on. Another shared route that works well by hired car is the run from Saigon to the Cambodian border. Buses along the route are often stopped by police looking for smugglers, but share-taxis or rental cars go through quickly. If you hire a vehicle over a period of three or four days, you pay a small surcharge to cover the driver's extra time and lodging.

4WD Vehicles
On the rugged roads of the north and Central Highlands, 4WD vehicles are the only way to go. These vehicles are higher-priced than regular cars, but essential on rough roads. Modern vehicles include Toyota Land Cruisers and Japanese jeeps. A close relative of the Land Cruiser is a Mekong 4WD, assembled in Vietnam as part of a Japanese joint venture. Other joint ventures are under way with Japanese, French, American, and German companies for trucks, cars, and motorcycles to be produced in Vietnam. The incentive here is that Vietnam's import tax on new cars is 200% while the tax on cars assembled in Vietnam is 40%.

To visit the mountainous north, you can rent a Russian Army jeep in Hanoi. The Gazelle is a roomy Russian model with two bucket seats in the front, room for three passengers in the back, and a luggage section with space for jerry cans right up the back. That's a total of five people. You can negotiate the number of days you need the vehicle and assemble a rough schedule, but allow flexibility for additional days and extra places to visit. Then work out a fixed price. Pay half up front, half on completion of the trip. In the south, although you don't really need a jeep to tour, reconditioned US Army jeeps are a status symbol. Many are still running in pristine condition.

Traveler Minibuses
Local long-distance transport can be exasperatingly slow—breakdowns due to overloading, stop and drop, moving of cargo, stampeding ducks and pigs. It can take five hours to cover a mere 100 km. Thus many travelers eye the tourist vans plying the coast. If you want to spend more time at the actual destination rather than getting there, consider minibuses. These are organized by traveler cafés, and are popular

along the Saigon to Hué section. Think of it—you can get up at 0900 instead of 0500 and still arrive at the same time, with your legs not writhing from cramps. The disadvantage of minibuses is that you're insulated from the locals—you only get to talk to other travelers. When you do encounter locals, it's not under the best of circumstances. Imagine an air-conditioned tour bus descending on a small village, and 15 people streaming out, all armed to the teeth with cameras and video equipment. Another disadvantage is being forced to move at the same pace as the group. To solve these problems, you can use the traveler minibuses as straight transport from A to B, then go your own way, perhaps picking up another minibus later.

Public Bus and Minibus

Using regular local buses, you can travel all the way from Hanoi to Saigon for a mere $20, though you might arrive with a few loose screws and a jangled spine. Buses are dirt cheap, but also uncomfortable. You're often wedged into a tiny space surrounded by curious locals, heaving children, and squawking chickens. Buy a small foam pad for bus rides, available cheaply from markets, with colorful covers. You can use the pad as a buttsaver, pillow, or backrest.

Avoid buses that stop and drop every kilometer or so. Try and track down express buses. Unfortunately, a classier bus may come equipped with a video machine; pray there's no karaoke device attached. Even these buses offer limited legroom. Space is at a premium on local buses. All buses transport goods—sacks of rice, cut wood, chicken feed, sugar, batteries strewn along the floor, bananas, bicycles, chickens stacked all over the roof. A crawler with a seat-high load may only be able to do 30 kph—if it doesn't break down. There may be other complications. On one bus, our driver noticed smoke rising, opened a hatch inside the bus to have a closer look, and a huge flame shot up. Obviously the bus had overheated a bit. Eventually the fire was doused, and after some minor surgery the bus was on its way again.

Faster but not necessarily safer are Toyota minibuses. There's a comprehensive network of these, but they're uncomfortable, with passengers stuffed in tightly. You'll also notice the distinctive red or yellow snout of the Renault van—there are many of these in central Vietnam, used for short range runs.

You can't complain about the prices on these forms of transport—about 60 cents for 100 km. That compares with roughly 75 cents/100 km for a minibus, and about $4/100 km for a soft seat on a train. A bus from Saigon to Dalat covers 310 km in six to seven hours for $1.80; by minibus it's marginally more, perhaps $2.20. Technically there's no foreign surcharge on buses, but you'll be charged above the Vietnamese price.

One way to gain more legroom is to purchase several seats. Sometimes the driver will even size you up and *ask* you to buy several seats. This is because it's possible you'll require the space of two Vietnamese. This especially applies to minibuses, where they *really* pack them in. Sometimes in a bus or minibus, two Westerners will purchase a row of three seats. Another problem is what to do with your bags. If the underseat space is filled with produce, you may end up with your luggage on your lap; it's not a good idea to put it on the rooftop. Riding local buses or minibuses for longer than 10 hours is not recommended if you value your sanity. Everybody reaches the limits of patience on bus rides. Two Western women, after enduring children vomiting on them, elbows in the ribs, and sundry other insults, drew the line at a passenger who boarded with an unidentified animal moving around inside a burlap bag. "That," shouted one of them hysterically, "is *not* sharing my seat!"

Share-Taxis

In bus depots, often located near markets, you'll spot smaller vehicles that may be used for short-run destinations. You can find old elongated Citröens used as share-taxis. These classic vehicles bear record-breaking figures on the odometer (if it's not shot) and carry record-breaking numbers of passengers. Jeeps are sometimes used on dirt roads as share-taxis; there are also jeeps with elongated backs.

Motorcycle Rental

Motorcycle rental is available in Saigon, Dalat, Nha Trang, Hué, Danang, Hoi An, and Hanoi. Greater numbers of travelers frequent these cities; thus the cottage industry of motorcycle

MOTORCYCLE TOURING

You're free to go where you please on your own motorcycle. However, you need good riding skills to handle the road-warrior mentality in Vietnam, and you need mechanical know-how. Your motorcycle will most certainly not be brand-new, and older models tend to break down or lose parts due to vibration on rough roads. Motorcycles can easily be transported on trains and larger boats, and have also been sighted on the tops of buses.

Highway 1, the main route from Hanoi to Saigon, is not exactly the Indochina Expressway. Sometimes it's but a single lane, or dirt. Motorcycles must share the road with trucks, cars, bicycles, and the occasional oxcarts, as well as large patches of rice or other crops drying in the sun. The Vietnamese must rank among Asia's most aggressive drivers. Their reckless attitude toward speed leads to many accidents, often fatal for motorcyclists because of the lack of helmets. There is nothing in the way of insurance—a common reaction at the scene of an accident is for the rider or driver to recover and take off as fast as possible. If the police arrive, damage compensation is paid on the spot.

Foreigners without Vietnamese licenses do not usually encounter problems with police, although it would be nice to at least have an International Driver's License. Police occasionally may try and make pocket money by saying your papers are not in order. If police attempt to flag you down, smile, wave back, and keep on going. If stopped, you suddenly do not understand *anything*. Just keep smiling.

Now for the good news: Gasoline is cheap in Vietnam. Unheard of for a Marxist country, Vietnam produces its own gasoline. It's a bit over a dollar a US gallon for unleaded gas, probably enough to carry you 100 km on a motorcycle. Countdown kilometer stones (French-style, every kilometer) allow you to track your progress. There are two options for acquiring a motorcycle for touring: rent long-term from an agency, or buy a used motorcycle and resell it after touring.

Long-Term Rental

Two Australian travelers made it all the way from Saigon to Hanoi and beyond on Honda 90cc bikes. They rented them in Saigon for $3.50 a day each, with the proviso they would send the bikes back by train at the end of the tour. It cost $30 each to ship the bikes. The owner held their paper visas as security—these were mailed on to a friend in Hanoi,

who also handled putting the bikes back on a train. The leisurely tour consumed a month with many stops, perhaps 10 days of actual motorcycling. The riders traveled with shouldered backpacks, the weight resting over the rear rack. They said the best part of the ride was the coastal strip from Saigon to Hué. The biggest problems along the route were 1) trucks; 2) more trucks; 3) holes in the road, big ones in the south, fewer but deeper ones in the north; 4) riders making sudden U-turns (they collected three bicycles this way); and 5) rain.

From Hanoi, a number of Westerners have rented 125cc and 175cc Russian motorcycles to head northwest to Sapa via Dien Bien Phu. From Sapa, you can aim for the railway at Lao Cai, then load yourself and your bike onto a train bound for Hanoi. Some ride the full loop, though this is exhausting because of bad road conditions. On a larger bike you can stow one small bag over the gas tank at the front, and place another small bag sideways at the back.

Buying a Motorcycle

Japanese imports are very expensive. In Saigon, Honda 50cc, 90cc, and 125cc motorcycles sell in the $1300-1600 range. Honda cubs are imported from Japan; the Honda Dream 100 is imported from Thailand and Indonesia. Top of the line is a gleaming Honda Dream II, which can cost $2500 new. Apart from Hondas, Suzuki, Yamaha, and Kawasaki hold a small share of the market. Big-engined bikes are forbidden for import to Vietnam; the ones around before the rules came down are sold for high profits. Travelers often settle for Russian motorcycles, which are fairly hardy beasts, and have a good spare parts pool. You can buy a used Minsk 175cc in Hanoi or Saigon for $250-350, or new for $500-600. You can probably sell the bike for $100 less than you paid for it. Bikes like the Minsk 125cc and 175cc are easily sold, but others, like a Czech-made Jawa 350cc, present problems because spare parts are hard to find.

You need papers of some nature to resell the bike. Foreigners are not supposed to possess ownership papers, but this is bypassed by registering under a Vietnamese friend's name. You can have your plates made up in Saigon at Ben Thanh market. Regular plates are white with black lettering; police and government plates are green with white lettering; army plates are red with white lettering. The NN prefix indicates a plate for a foreign businessperson; NG on a white plate with red lettering indicates a diplomat. Green (government) plates would be nice, because police are less likely to bother you.

Three on one bike? An enterprising Englishman bought a 750cc Ural with a sidecar in Saigon for $800. He was on his way to Hanoi, where he was counting on selling the Russian bike for $700. The Ural was hard to maneuver on rough roads, so he took it easy. To cut costs, he picked up travelers en route for a small charge—one passenger in the sidecar, a second sitting behind the driver.

rental. The owner will want to keep your passport, paper visa, credit card, or plane ticket as security for a newer Japanese bike. Before renting consider what may happen if there's an accident or the bike is stolen. Also consider your riding skills. Reckless drivers abound in Vietnam, and if you have an accident, medical facilities are very poor.

The most common motorcycle in Vietnam is a Honda. A rental will likely be a scooter such as the Honda 50cc, 70cc, or 90cc. Top of the line for rentals is a Honda Dream 100cc, a nightmare if it gets stolen, because it will set you back a few thousand dollars. The renter is generally responsible for theft or damage to the bike. Apparently the legal limit for riding a bike without a Vietnamese license is 70cc, but nobody takes much notice, and licenseless foreigners rent higher-powered Russian and Czech bikes. Helmets are not mandatory in Vietnam. You can buy one for $10-35; they are more commonly worn in the north than in the south.

A place like Saigon requires skilled riding. There are estimated to be over a million motorcycles in the city, vastly outnumbering cars. Accidents between motorcycles are common.

Motos

Motorcycle-taxis are known in Vietnamese as *xe môtô om* or *honda om* (Honda cuddle)—"Honda" being generic for any kind of motorcycle. They're excellent for touring around a town, or covering short-haul destinations. As a backpacker you develop a kind of symbiotic relationship with motos, as they fill in those crucial 10-km gaps between highway and hotel, or airport and town. An express bus, for example, may drop you 10 km outside Nha Trang. A moto can take you and your pack straight to a hotel. You can hire a moto like a taxi for a one-way trip, or by the hour, or by the half or full day. As a touring vehicle, motos are great. The driver takes care of all the traffic and mechanical problems, leaving you to focus on the scenery. In effect, the moto driver is your guide. The charge should be around $5-7 for a full day of touring.

Motos can also be used for touring up to 40 or 50 km out of town. If carrying luggage, two

Moto drivers can repair a Russian motorcycle if trouble occurs on the road.

bags are better; you can strap a small backpack sideways on a motorcycle. Moto operators deal a lot with market freight. They often have rear side racks to carry loads, and rubber rack-straps to hold them in place. Once you get over the sight of a huge pig slung across the back of a motorcycle, you realize a backpack is not a problem. Balance is. So it's wise to adapt your luggage to suit. A big backpack will make for an unstable load on a moto, especially if you're still wearing it. Better to have two smaller packs—you can throw one up front on the gas tank, or strap it to sidesaddle racks at the back, or wear a day pack. On a Honda 70cc scooter, a smaller pack will fit nicely, wedged down vertically between handlebars and seat. The driver's knees hold it in place.

Lambros

A lambro is a species of three-wheeler similar to a Thai *tuk-tuk,* with a motorcycle engine installed. In Vietnam, they're called *xe lam.* The maker's brand is Lambretta 550, abbreviated here to lambro. They're usually overloaded for the 550cc engine capacity. You'll see the vehicle stuffed with a dozen passengers plus market goods. They're used as shuttle vehicles on fixed routes, generally traveling up to 10 or 15 km to cover holes in the bus system. You often find them around markets. Lambros are unstable, and when impossibly overcrowded can keel over or the front can flip up.

Cyclos

Cyclos, or bicycle trishaws, were introduced in Hanoi in the early 1930s, replacing rickshaws. Cyclos are a leisurely way to take in the sights and you can turn them into touring vehicles by hiring one by the hour or the half day. Cyclo drivers often make good guides, charging around $3 for the day. Cyclos are great for short hauls.

Fares are negotiable, usually 2000 dong a kilometer, or 80 cents an hour. Negotiate for cyclo prices by holding up the relevant number of digits on your hand; make sure it's dong not dollars you're talking about. Foreigners can get into nasty arguments with cyclo drivers over disputed fares. To save argument, some travelers prefer to pay up front.

When you first arrive in Vietnam cyclos seem quaint; by the time you leave you may never want to ride in one again. Unfortunately, cyclo drivers can be very aggressive, and think that foreigners cannot walk from point A to point B unassisted. If the foreigner has luggage and is still walking, s/he must be absolutely crazy. Cyclo drivers will relentlessly pursue you along the streets of Saigon, Nha Trang, or Danang. Even if you're sitting in a goddamn cyclo, another driver will pull up and ask you if you want a cyclo! If you're riding a rented bicycle, a cyclo driver will sidle up and ask if you're tired, demanding to transport you *and* the bicycle back to your hotel.

In cities like Saigon, Hanoi, and Haiphong, major hotels maintain a small fleet of luxury cyclos with padded seats, plush armrests, front suspension, sunroof, even headlights. The suspension-model cyclos are used for VIPs or by family members for marriage negotiation visits; fares on these models don't run much higher than for regular ratty cyclos. You can squeeze two passengers into one cyclo, or take one cyclo for each passenger and travel in a convoy.

In the Mekong Delta there are variants on bicycle-taxis. You can find a bicycle-buggy, consisting of a detachable bicycle and a driver up front hauling a two-wheel wooden chariot behind. On a flat road, this contraption can haul four passengers. A bare bicycle is often used to ferry chickens and ducks around markets; passengers sit on a wooden and metal rack over the back wheel, and an extra child can be carried up front on the top frame. These are called *xedap om* (bicycle cuddle). Foreigners rarely use them.

Bicycles

The bicycle is the prime mode of personal transport in Vietnam, though mopeds and motorbikes are starting to catch up in Saigon. There are an estimated 20 million bicycles in Vietnam, roughly one bike for every three people—a per-head ratio similar to China. Sturdy Chinese-made bicycles are flooding the market in Vietnam, with lesser breeds arriving from Thailand. Vietnam also makes its own bicycles in French-built factories. Over 100,000 bikes are produced annually. The Huu Nghi (Friendship) model costs $20, and the Doan (Corporate) model costs up to $35. You get what you pay for; the bikes have a habit of falling apart quickly. A smuggled Chinese bicycle sells for $60 and up.

Bicycles in Vietnam are used not only as the "family car" but also as freight vehicles. In rural areas you'll see bike riders performing impos-

BICYCLE TOURING

Foreigners have explored large swaths of Vietnam by bicycle. Some have even traversed the length of China before taking on Vietnam as an afterthought, then carried on through Laos into Thailand. You can cycle through land borders in Vietnam. A mountain bike or hybrid is preferable for touring.

The best bike routes are those away from heavy traffic. Unfortunately, Highway 1 is becoming very busy with truck traffic. It's therefore unpleasant for cycling, although bicycles have found parts of the coast agreeable. Between Buon Ma Thuot and Pleiku in the Central Highlands is a great road for cycling. However, there are no places to stay. The Mekong Delta has good routes. There are small towns with hotels, and you can transport the bike on local ferries for the best of both worlds. Cycling can be sweaty work in the delta. Another route involving ferry hops is Hanoi to Halong Bay and beyond on the coast road. Cat Ba Island has little traffic. It's a bit hilly, but a great place to ride.

Cyclists should note that prevailing winds blow northeast in summer and southwest in winter. To avoid head winds, you should head north in summer (July), south in winter (January). Typhoon season is October to December for the central and north coast. Cycling in the north is more difficult because accommodations, bottled water, and food variety are not as common as in the south. It's unpleasant to be reduced to drinking jugs of bitter tea or consuming bowls of *pho*.

Bicycles can easily be transported on trains and boats, or the tops of buses. Domestic flights are trickier because of a 20-kg weight restriction. A bicycle counts as a 50-kg weight on trains—say $1.50 from Hué to Hanoi. However, foreigners are often charged $5 for "foreign bikes," even though they're lighter than local bikes. An English couple figured since they were paying so much extra for their rail ticket they didn't have to follow regulations, so they just wheeled their bikes straight onto hard seat class. On buses or boats, the cost should be about no more than a third of a regular passenger fare.

sible balancing acts—transporting a score of live geese or a load of fish traps that totally obscures them. Heavy loads are transported on industrial bicycles that are not ridden but pushed. These are ingeniously decked out with heavy-duty panniers; when the full load of pottery or whatever is in place, the bike can be steered by means of a handlebar extension. When the industrial bike has no load, it can be ridden.

Bike Rental: You can rent a bike in places where travelers gather—Saigon, Nha Trang, Hué, Hanoi—for about a dollar a day. Bike-repair stands abound on street corners and repairs are very cheap. Before cycling off on a rental, check the tires, make sure the wheels spin freely, and determine that at least one brake works. Also check the saddle height; your leg should be almost fully extended from the saddle position to the pedal at its lowest point to maximize leg power. Pay attention to one-way streets downtown: be especially careful when cycling near schools in the morning, or in market areas.

In busy areas like markets, always park in designated bike parking areas, which have attendants who require a token fee. This is to prevent your rental bike from being either towed officially or stolen unofficially. Bike parking spots may have thousands of bikes that all look like yours. Mark your vehicle! Put a brightly colored wrapper on the back rack or wherever, or tie some cloth onto the handlebars. If you're in a busy area and there's no bike parking in sight, try to find a bicycle-repair place and lock your bike close to the owner. When you return, pay the bike repairman a small fee for watching the bike.

Because they lack gears, rented bikes are not suitable for long-distance forays, although you can easily cover 10 km in an hour by bike, making a destination within 20 km feasible as long as the going is flat. Bike-repair stands are easy to find and very cheap.

Buying a Bike: In Saigon, a Phoenix 10-speed from Shanghai costs $100 with rack, water-bottle cage, and fenders (mudguards). For $130 you can purchase a Taiwan-made 10-speed or even an 18-gear pseudo–mountain bike. About $190 will secure a Federal 12-speed with real Shimano shifters and a tube made in Indonesia. Sometimes you can get your hands on used Western bikes sold by ship hands visiting Saigon. A Japanese bike with Shimano equipment costs around $260.

AROUND TOWN

The public bus system in Vietnamese cities is useless—slow, crowded, and cumbersome. And you have to figure out where the bus lines travel. Foreigners can easily afford better transport. Options include rented bicycle or motorcycle, cyclo (bicycle trishaw) or moto (motorcycle-taxi), or rented car. Do not underestimate the power of

HEROES OF THE BOULEVARDS

Vietnamese city streets are invariably emblazoned with the same 20 or so names—a miniglossary of Vietnamese revolutionary heroes and heroines. This system gets confusing—you become hazy about whether the Army Hotel was on Pham Ngu Lao Street in Hanoi, or in Saigon. And that place called Number 3 Hotel—was that on Le Loi Boulevard in Hanoi or Hué? Hotels are often named after the street or town. You'll see a Dien Bien Hotel in Dien Bien Phu town and on Dien Bien Phu St. in Haiphong.

Streets in Vietnam once bore French names—governors-general, administrators, admirals, literary figures, and so forth. In Saigon there was Rue Paul Bert, Rue Amiral Courbat, Rue d'Espagne, Quai de Belgique, Place Pigneau de Béhaine, Boulevard Bonnard, and streets named after Kipling and Rousseau. After the French left in 1954, naturally all the names in North and South Vietnam were changed. After reunification in 1975, there were further name changes, especially in the south. A few French names remain in the medical hero line—Pasteur, Curie, Calmette, and Yersin. Hotels previously known by French names—the Hotel Majestic and Hotel Continental in Saigon—underwent name changes after 1975, but are now reverting to the original names because it's easier on tourists. This process of name changing is ongoing. You may find that different maps do not agree on street or hotel names.

Even the name of Vietnam's greatest revolutionary hero hasn't stuck. After 1975, Saigon was changed to Ho Chi Minh City. The tongue-twister never caught on, and most still call it Saigon. In any case, Ho Chi Minh City refers to Greater Saigon, which is the size of a province. The inner city is known all round as Saigon.

In historical order, here are some sources of names for the byways and boulevards of Vietnamese cities:

Hai Ba Trung: Named after the famous Trung sisters, who temporarily ousted the Chinese around 40 AD.

Ly Thuong Kiet: Military commander who led campaigns against the Chinese and Cham in the 12th century.

Tran Hung Dao: Vietnamese general who defeated a Mongol fleet dispatched by Kublai Khan in the 13th century.

Le Loi: Vietnamese leader who ended several decades of Chinese Ming rule in 1427.

Trung Trac: Nguyen Trung Trac was executed by the French in 1868. The resistance leader turned himself in to protect his relatives, held hostage by the French in Rach Gia.

Le Qui Don: 18th-century encyclopedist and historian.

Nguyen Hue: Named after one of the brothers of the 18th-century Tay Son rebellion, who later became Emperor Quang Trung.

Duy Tan: Emperor who lent support to an armed uprising against the French in 1916.

Phan Boi Chau: Nationalist in the early 1900s, imprisoned by the French.

Nguyen Thai Hoc: Communist leader guillotined by the French in 1930.

Tran Phu: First Secretary General of the Communist Party of Indochina, killed by the French in 1931.

Nguyen Thi Minh Khai: The first Communist Party Secretary for Saigon; she was executed by the French in 1941.

Hoang Van Thu: Leader of the Vietnamese Communist Party, executed by the French in 1944.

Dien Bien Phu: Famous battle site where the Vietminh defeated the French in 1954.

30 Thang 4 Street: Commemorates the fall of Saigon on 30 April 1975. Individual towns often have a "fall" date posted on a major artery—in Dalat, for example, there's a boulevard called Duong 3 Thang 4, which refers to the 3 April 1975 liberation of the town.

walking—Vietnamese towns like Hoi An are easily covered on foot. A number of walking, bicycle, and boat tour suggestions have been included in this book because these are ideal ways of taking in the surroundings. Bicycle rentals are cheap—perhaps one or two dollars a day. Chinese models are better. Use designated bicycle parking spots for security. If you don't want to ride yourself, you can hire a cyclo.

In a place like Saigon a rented motorcycle requires skilled riding and can be a liability because you're not supplied with a helmet. If nervous about riding, the solution is simple: hire a moto driver, so you become a passenger. In Danang a rented motorcycle is great, allowing you to get out of town to nearby sights. Motorcycles are rented for $5-10 a day depending on quality.

Cyclos and motos can be hired by the hour or day; always negotiate rates before setting out. A cyclo ride is a relaxing way of getting around; you can hire one for as little as $2 a day. More luxurious and expensive models with sunroofs and other gadgets are available outside ritzy hotels. Motos, good for longer-distance touring or anything involving hills, charge roughly $7 a day. Occasionally, you might hop on a lambro (short for Lambretta, or small three-wheel vehicle), which shuttles along fixed routes.

Travel agencies in most towns can arrange car hire by the half or full day, or travel by minibus or larger vehicle. Taxis do not cruise the streets, but may be available from ranks near the train station or local market. In Saigon and Hanoi are metered taxis, though these are expensive, charging $2 on boarding and 70 cents a kilometer.

In Hué and Hoi An, you can rent a local boat to tour the area. You pay by the hour, or arrange a half-day rate. Prices range from $3 for a few hours up to $15 for a half day for the entire boat, holding six passengers and up.

OTHER MODES OF TRAVEL

Hitching

Some travelers have had great success hitchhiking. The concept is alien to most Vietnamese, but the idea of chatting in English or French must be appealing to bored drivers. Getting around by hitching can be much faster than by bus, and a good deal more comfortable. Minor payment expected.

Hiking

The best way to see rural villages and minority areas in Vietnam is to start walking, preferably with a guide. Your guide can arrange for overnight stays in villages, which means you can keep on walking. A fit hiker could cover 20 km a day in this fashion. Longer hikes can also be undertaken in national parks. The best places for this kind of walking are in the north. For more information, see the following sections in "Around the North" in this chapter: "In the Southwest" and "Cuc Phuong National Park" under "Near Hanoi"; "Cat Ba Island" under "Gulf of Tonkin"; and "Sapa" under "The Tonkinese Alps."

Boat Transport

Around Hué or Hoi An you can rent a sampan to cruise along the town's river; at the Perfume Pagoda or Tam Coc Caves a small boat is the only way to get around. In Halong Bay and at Nha Trang you can club together with others to rent a fishing vessel to tour offshore islands. At Halong you can also sleep overnight on vessels fitted with bunks. Some refitted junks are also available for hire—essentially yachts with maroon cotton panels for sails.

Because of a lack of bridges, you'll often use ferry crossings in Vietnam. Waterways are a lifeline for goods and passenger transport in some areas. The waterways of the Mekong Delta are best toured by large wooden craft, leaving from points like Cantho or Chau Doc. Ferries run to the delta from Saigon. You can sleep overnight using a hammock on one of these vessels. They're usually overloaded with goods and have no safety equipment. Out of Haiphong, much larger rusting hulks are used as ferries to ports along the northern coast.

Kayaking has been tried with success in the Mekong Delta. An Australian couple brought in fold-up kayaks by plane and paddled up to the Cambodian border. Their tour lasted a couple of weeks; they had a few brushes with police, but nothing serious. The kayakers stayed with families and on sampans, sometimes mooring alongside, sometimes lifting the kayaks aboard a boat. They packed the kayaks onto a regular

a heap of basketware on the roof of a cargo boat

ferry to return to Saigon. The Halong Bay area north of Hanoi holds great potential for kayaking, with many islands scattered through the region. Sea Canoe Thailand, a sea kayak operator from Phuket, Thailand, has been permitted to conduct short trips in this area, as well as Mountain Travel Sobek, an American tour operator.

TOURS

International adventure travel operators stage trips some individuals may find difficult due to logistics, equipment, or permission requirements. Weighed against this are the cost ($100-150 and up per person per day) and the slow group pace. You might find yourself chafing at the restrictions. For more information on doing it yourself, see "Getting Around" earlier in the chapter. Regardless of whether or not you join a tour, you can garner plenty of ideas from the following short sampling of adventure travel operators.

Tours for Veterans
Going back to Vietnam can be a healing experience. A return can alleviate what psychotherapists have identified as post-traumatic stress disorder—loosely characterized by a set of symptoms including depression and withdrawal, drug and alcohol dependence, and inability to hold a job. The ability to walk around rural Vietnam without worrying about snipers or booby traps must certainly offer a new perspective.

An early returnee, Patrick Campbell, summed up the experience: "Before I came over here, I thought of Vietnam the way I left it: helicopters and shooting and ducking and dodging. I thought that way until three or four days after I got back [to Vietnam]. By then I could see that it wasn't like that anymore." Patrick was involved in building a medical clinic in Vung Tau in 1988. The project was under the auspices of Vietnam Veterans Restoration Project (VVRP), which has since completed six additional projects in Vietnam—building clinics and supplying medical and alternative energy technology. In 1994 VVRP worked to set up a facility near Saigon to house Vietnamese amputees being fitted for artificial limbs. The limbs are provided free by another American NGO, Vietnam Assistance for the Handicapped. For more information on the work of VVRP, contact Steve Stratford, P.O. Box 369, Garberville, CA 95542, tel. (707) 923-3357. The founder of VVRP, Fredy Champagne, organizes tours to Vietnam for vets, and is involved with bicycle and motorcycle tours. Contact him at Vietnam Friends, P.O. Box 69, Garberville, CA 95542, tel./fax (707) 923-3658.

Agencies in Vietnam have been set up by Vietnamese veterans to assist tours to former battlefields, as well as arrange meetings with former field commanders and officers from ARVN, Vietcong, and NVA units. One problem disabled veterans face in Vietnam is a complete lack of wheelchair access in the country. Tour companies don't have any wheelchair-lift equipped vans, and the wheelchair-bound must be carried up and down stairs by a porter. There has been little attempt to make restaurants or hotels accessible.

Ecotouring and Hiking

A few outfits are delving into the rainforests. **Top Guides** organizes tours in north Vietnam led by wildlife biologists from Vietnam and Malaysia. The route goes through Tai villages and into thick jungle; you stay in longhouses or camp out. The group studies the habitat of local species including the endangered langur monkey. Contact Top Guides, 1825 San Lorenzo Ave., Berkeley, CA 94707, tel. (800) 867-6777.

Some tour organizers and traveler cafés have started hiking tours to visit mountain areas and minority groups in the north. Darling Café offers a two-day hike in Sapa, and one-day hikes in Lai Chau or Phung Tho. Overnight tours stay in villages. The café also offers four-day hikes around Mai Chau. If you're joining a tour like this, a sleeping bag is an asset; it gets cold in the mountains. Some US operators are offering short hiking tours in the northwest to visit minority groups. Contact: **The Global Spectrum,** 1901 Pennsylvania Ave. NW, Washington, DC 20006, tel. (800) 419-4446; **All Adventure Travel,** 5589 Rapahoe #208, Boulder, CO 80303, tel. (800) 537-4025; **Asian Pacific Adventures,**

VIETNAM ROUTE STRATEGIES

Most travelers start or end trips to Vietnam from Hanoi or Saigon. Because of weak infrastructure and horribly overcrowded buses and minibuses, many opt for rented vehicles, throwing together their own small groups, or joining traveler minibuses. For adequate leg space, travel by train is a viable option.

Vietnam is a skinny country: a glance at the map will show the main route runs from Saigon to Hanoi or the reverse. Many fly into Hanoi, work their way toward Saigon, and fly out of Saigon (or the reverse). A good route taking in the Central Highlands is Hanoi-Hué-Danang-Quang Ngai-Pleiku-Buon Ma Thuot-Nha Trang-Dalat-Saigon or the reverse. Or you could spend all your time looping around the north, or around the south. Some travelers start in the south, explore the Mekong Delta, proceed up to Nha Trang, and turn back to Saigon. Others arrive in Hanoi from Hong Kong, loop around the northwest and north, and fly from Hanoi on to Bangkok.

The opening of land border crossings to Cambodia, Laos, and China has created new overland routes through Vietnam. The land routes are: into Cambodia, Saigon-Moc Bai-Phnom Penh; into Laos, Dong Ha-Lao Bao-Savannakhet; and into China, Hanoi-Lang Son-Nanning or Hanoi-Lao Cai-Kunming. You can travel from Bangkok through Laos to the Lao Bao border, proceed into Vietnam near Khe Sanh, continue from here to Hanoi, cross to Nanning, and carry on overland to Hong Kong. Another viable route is to enter Vietnam from China,

proceed south to Saigon, take the road to Phnom Penh, and then, after a side trip to Angkor, plane-hop from Phnom Penh to Bangkok. In the other direction, starting in Saigon, you could go overland to Lao Cai, head for Kunming, and fly from Kunming to either Bangkok or Hong Kong.

In Vietnam you have to base your trip on the weather. A monsoon will not only make it difficult for you to see the sights, it will also render certain areas completely inaccessible due to roads of mud. Visiting in the dry season, I had to completely change plans when typhoons and flooding hit central Vietnam. With several different climate zones, there is no best time to visit. Keep in mind that certain parts of Vietnam—especially in the north—can dip to freezing at night around December.

The onset of Tet, the Lunar New Year, creates special traffic hazards—commuters wheeling around on motorcycles or bicycles with entire peach trees or miniature orange trees strapped to the sides. Airline seats are booked solid and roads are jammed as every Tan Thanh and his dog try to get home for the sacred family dinner. But once those dinners get underway, consider this: the highways are empty for five days. Everybody stays home at Tet. The hitch is that the railways, bus companies, and other transport companies shut down or scale back operations. Attractions are open for the holidays—if you've arranged your own transport you'll have the place to yourself. Lunar New Year is celebrated over much of Southeast Asia in different guises; air transport in the entire region is chockablock.

826 South Sierra Bonita Ave., Los Angeles, CA 90036, tel. (213) 935-3156; **InnerAsia Expeditions,** 2627 Lombard St., San Francisco, CA 94123, tel. (800) 777-8183; and **Overseas Adventure Travel,** 349 Broadway, Cambridge, MA 02139, tel. (800) 221-0814.

In the future, specialized tours—such as those for birdwatchers—will no doubt be offered. Birdlife abounds in Vietnam's handful of national parks and reserves in both north Vietnam and the Mekong Delta region. Some have been established with the help of the World Wildlife Fund (WWF). Wildlife enthusiasts should keep an eye on research projects run by nonprofit research organizations like Earthwatch in the United States. Projects are classed as study tours; you pay your own way to assist a research project, but the tours are tax-deductible in the United States.

Bicycling

In the spirit of cultural exchange and exploration, San Francisco-based **VeloAsia Cycling Adventures** offers innovative small-group trips at reasonable prices. Director of this nonprofit project, Patrick Morris, supports environmentally friendly, nonimpact tourism. These fun tours aim for a complete experience, focusing on sightseeing and fine dining at destinations along the route, alternate activities like swimming and hiking, and cultural spiels from local guides. Vietnamese language lessons are also arranged. Among the several itineraries offered are the Saigon-to-Hanoi route, an exploratory tour to Sapa in northwest Vietnam, and a wild trip to the rainforests of the Central Highlands by mountain bike with jeep support. Contact VeloAsia, 1271 43rd Ave., San Francisco, CA 94122, tel./fax (415) 664-6779.

Several other outfits offer bicycle touring. **Cycle Vietnam** organizes trips from Hanoi to Saigon, featuring 1,000 km of cycling, the remainder by tour-bus. Its annual biking adventure may attract up to 50 bicyclists, though not all riding in one pack. Contact Cycle Vietnam, P.O. Box 4481, Portland, OR 97208, tel. (800) 661-1458, fax (503) 331-1458.

Motorcycling

Cycle Vietnam also offers fully supported 20-day small-group tours on Honda 100cc motor-cycles from Saigon to Hanoi, for $3200; land-only package. Make sure you possess evacuation insurance if touring by motorcycle.

In October 1992 a group of French riders took on La Route Mandarine between Saigon and Hanoi. The group of 17 participants rode big-engined bikes—some flown in—accompanied by a press entourage. Eleven bikes were 1957 Harley-Davidson Sportsters, once used as the police escort for South Vietnamese President Nguyen Van Thieu, rebuilt and restored for the trip. The group rode as a convoy with biking police at the front and rear; the pack was followed by mechanics, interpreters, organizers, and security police in vans, as well as an ambulance. Along the route, the group donated books, medical supplies, and equipment to local schools and hospitals. After leaving Saigon, they headed up to Nha Trang. South of Danang, there was an accident with a truck, and four bikes went down. The leader, Daniel Roussel, suffered serious injury and was airlifted to Singapore. Farther north the group encountered an early monsoon; about 160 km short of Hanoi, the riders had to cancel the last leg due to washed-out roads and ferry crossings.

Luxury Train Trips

The **Vietnamerican Trading Co.** offers a **Vietnam By Rail** itinerary. Travelers ride in an antique French sleeping car and dining/lounge car, with a staff of eight, on the Saigon-to-Hanoi run. The special car is tacked onto the regular Reunification Express trains. On the two-week journey, stops are made at Saigon, Nha Trang, Danang, Hué, and Hanoi. For details, contact Vietnamerican, 420 Downing St., Denver, CO 80218, USA, tel. (303) 744-6200, fax (303) 744-6590. The private cars used on this tour can be chartered by groups of 12 to 40 persons for customized trips.

Kayaking

A company based in Phuket, Thailand, called **Sea Canoe Thailand,** conducts sea kayaking expeditions at Halong Bay and Cat Ba Island. In Vietnam the company operates under a joint-venture name—Sea Canoe Vietnam. Tours are scheduled in May-June and September-October. The operator uses inflatable rubber kayaks; groups are escorted by a junk to prevent hassles

various Hmong Montagnards (Highland people) from northwest Vietnam

(top) a floating market in the Mekong Delta;
(bottom) going to market, Saigon

with boat people in the area. All-inclusive tours with hotels, cultural shows, sea kayaking instruction, guides, and gear are expensive; however, there are four-day sea kayak tours from the Halong Bay piers for $700 per person. For more details, contact Sea Canoe Thailand, P.O. Box 130, Phuket 83000, Thailand, tel./fax 66-76-214-249. These tours can also be booked through agents in the US, such as Maluku Adventures, P.O. Box 7625, Menlo Park, CA 94026, tel. (415) 854-1321, (415) 364-9945.

An American operator, **Mountain Travel Sobek,** has recently announced kayak tours in Halong Bay. Also expensive, MTS tours cost $2690 excluding airfare for a 14-day tour, plus a $300 surcharge for small groups. For more information, contact Mountain Travel Sobek at 6420 Fairmount Ave., El Cerrito, CA 94530, USA, tel. (510) 527-8100, fax (510) 525-7710.

Sailing on a Junk

The French joint-venture organization **Voiles Vietnam** offers cruising on the *Song Saigon,* billed as the largest traditionally built junk in Asia. The luxury 26-meter vessel features five cabins and carries 10 passengers; for day-trips, the vessel can carry larger groups. November to April offers the Mekong Delta itinerary, with some trips up to Phnom Penh from Mytho on the Mekong. From May to September the junk is in the Nha Trang area, cruising offshore islands; it offers snorkeling, windsurfing, and diving equipment, with a dive instructor onboard. Trips can be customized; regular itineraries range from two to six days at $200 per person per day. Contact Voiles Vietnam, 17 Pham Ngoc Thach, Q3, Saigon, tel. (848) 231589, fax (848) 231591.

Cruising

Western cruise liners have been docking at Halong Bay, Haiphong, Hué, Danang, Qui Nhon, Nha Trang, Vung Tau, and Saigon since 1992. Among the available boats are the *Caledonian Star* via Lindblad Tours; the *Europa,*

Hapag Lloyd; *Ocean Pearl,* Pearl Cruises and Croisières Paquet; *Song of Flower,* Seven Seas Cruise Line; *Golden Odyssey,* Royal Cruise Line; and *Sea Goddess,* Cunard Line. These vessels hold 100 to 800 passengers each. Smaller vessels allow for greater maneuverability and the freedom to explore areas and call on ports not accessible to larger ships. A popular cruise route travels from Hong Kong, stopping four or five times along the coast of Vietnam before continuing to Bangkok, Singapore, or Manila. Onshore and inshore touring falls under the auspices of Vietnam Tourism. At Halong Bay, for example, passengers must transfer to motorboats or junks to tour the karst islets.

Seven Seas Cruise Line started itineraries to Vietnam in 1993, offering 10-night cruises from Hong Kong to Singapore on the 125-meter *Song of Flower.* The 170-passenger vessel passes through the Gulf of Tonkin and Halong Bay and docks in Hong Gai, Danang, Nha Trang, and Saigon. A second itinerary runs from Hong Kong to Saigon, with stops at Hainan Island, Hong Gai, Haiphong, Qui Nhon, and Nha Trang. The tariff for a 10-day cruise ranges $6000 to $9000 per person, based on double occupancy, including airfare, pre- and postcruise hotel nights, and shore excursions. The *Song of Flower* offers a full range of onboard facilities, including casino, video and book library, health club, jacuzzi, and sauna—in effect a five-star floating hotel. Onboard lectures were delivered by none other than Bob Haldeman, former White House Chief of Staff under President Richard Nixon. For more details, contact Radisson Seven Seas Cruise Line, 600 Corporate Dr., Suite 410, Fort Lauderdale, FL 33334, tel. (800) 333-3333, fax (305) 772-3763.

Some other addresses for Vietnam cruises: Cunard Line, 555 Fifth Ave., New York, NY 10017, tel. (800) 221-4770; and Pearl Cruises, 6301 Northwest 5th Way #4000, Fort Lauderdale, FL 33309, tel. (305) 772-8600.

SCOTT HARRISON

HANOI

PROUD AND PRUDISH

To visit Hanoi is to steep yourself in history, tradition, and legend in a capital that has been inhabited continuously for almost a millennium. Hanoi's present architecture is mainly from the 19th and 20th centuries, and the stately French-built section of town is largely intact. Hanoi is cleaner, leafier, and quieter than other big cities in Vietnam; in a single word, the primary difference is "cooler." There's cooler weather, more drizzle, less traffic, less hype; the streets seem quieter, with few large billboards. There's a cooler mentality here, too—prouder, more prudish. Hanoi is a magnet for intellectuals and artists, while Saigon seems to attract entrepreneurs and hustlers.

Hanoi streetlife is fascinating. In the morning, you can see tai chi practitioners, martial arts exponents, and joggers along Hoan Kiem Lake. Bicyclists wearing berets ride past with baguettes tucked into their baskets. Strolling through the old French sector, you can find a street occupied by outdoor barbers clipping their customers in front of mirrors hung off building walls. On Trang Tien Street there's a beautician at work: a woman with a flashlight mounted on her head, cleaning a customer's ears. At street corners in the Old Quarter, men with green pith helmets chat over steaming bowls of noodles. Further along the street, women sell fresh-cut flowers from the backs of bicycles.

The City Rises

Although the banks of the Red River have been inhabited for thousands of years, Hanoi traces its founding to 1010—the year Emperor Le Thai To moved his capital from Hoa Lu to this site. He named the town Thang Long, or Soaring Dragon, after an auspicious dream about a dragon arising from the city.

Originally, Hanoi was laid out in a pattern dictated by Chinese geomancy. At its center was a walled royal city with a cosmic mountain; ceremonial rites and recreational functions took place in this zone. The One Pillar Pagoda was constructed in 1049; the Temple of Literature, located to the south, was the first educational institution in Vietnam, established in 1070. East of the citadel and north of Hoan Kiem Lake was the artisan and commercial area, now the Old Quarter. On the other side of the lake, east and south, was the quarter for visiting residents; later this became the French zone. To the far south of the city lay a region of cemeteries, sickness, and death, where a leper colony and abattoir were relegated.

In the 12th century palaces built by Ly dynasty emperors sprouted along the Red River and around West Lake; the city was protected from Red River flooding by construction of a massive dike. Though flooding was contained, the Vietnamese could not keep out the Mongols. In the late 13th century the Mongols sacked the city, and for the next hundred-odd years the city's fortunes fluctuated. In 1428 Vietnamese leader Le Loi ousted the Chinese from the area and renamed the city Dong Kinh (Eastern Capital), later corrupted by the French to "Tonkin."

From the 16th century on, the city fell into a period of decline, culminating in the shifting of the imperial court to Hué. In 1805 Emperor Gia Long, ruling from Hué, ordered the ancient citadel of Thang Long destroyed, replacing it with a smaller citadel constructed in the style of French military architect Sébastien de Vauban. In 1831, Emperor Tu Duc renamed the city Hanoi, or City on the Bend of the River. This strategic bend attracted the French, investigating the Red River as an alternate trade route to the Mekong for shipping goods from China. In 1873 Francis Garnier was sent to reconnoiter the area. After negotiations with Emperor Tu Duc failed, Garnier attacked and destroyed Hanoi Citadel. Upon seeing what a small French force could accomplish, Tu Duc acceded to French demands. Many old structures in Hanoi were razed to make way for new French buildings. From 1882 on, Hanoi and Haiphong were the focal points of French exploitation of the north, and Hanoi was made capital of the new protectorate of Tonkin.

In 1902, after a merger of French protectorates and colonies, Hanoi was selected as the capital of the French Indochinese Union. It was a convenient base for exploring China

routes, the climate mild in comparison to Saigon's. French colonial rule came to an end in 1954; after the departure of the French, Ho Chi Minh set about expanding Hanoi's industrial base. The city's factories were targeted by US bombers from 1966 to 1972; oddly enough, central Hanoi survived the US blitzkrieg. Portions of the city hit by B-52 bombing lay mainly to the south of Hanoi. The Old Quarter and Hoan Kiem District were not bombed, although Long Bien Bridge was a constant target. Between 1965 and 1973 up to three-quarters of the inner city population was evacuated.

Cessation of hostilities led to rapid migration back to the capital. Today Hanoi is one of three independent municipalities in Vietnam, covering an area of 2,139 square km. The inner city is distributed in four districts; Greater Hanoi comprises 11 peripheral districts. The present population is estimated at 3.1 million.

Hanoi at the Crossroads

Hanoi today is a city on the brink of transformation. With the opening of Vietnam to tourism and joint-venture projects, developers envision a Hanoi studded with high-rise buildings. Land prices in Hanoi are skyrocketing. Bids are in for 20- and 30-story office towers and apartment blocks in Central Hanoi. The Hanoi People's Committee wish list includes 5,000 hotel rooms for businesspeople around West Lake, a region where present structures discharge waste straight into the water. Motorcycles and mopeds are challenging bicycles as the primary mode of private transportation. Electronic goods, previously hard to come by, are now flooding in from China, arriving either legally or illegally.

Construction of high-rise office and apartment buildings and an increase in the number of hotel rooms will inevitably place more stress on road and sewage systems, power supply, and other facilities. Hanoi could become another nightmarish Asian metropolis of towering concrete monoliths and interminable traffic jams. Or, if managed properly, it could remain a low-rise city with high-density population, retaining its charming character.

In 1994 the authorities evicted tenants from 150 French villas in three major streets in central Hanoi with the intention of renovating the properties and renting them at inflated prices to those

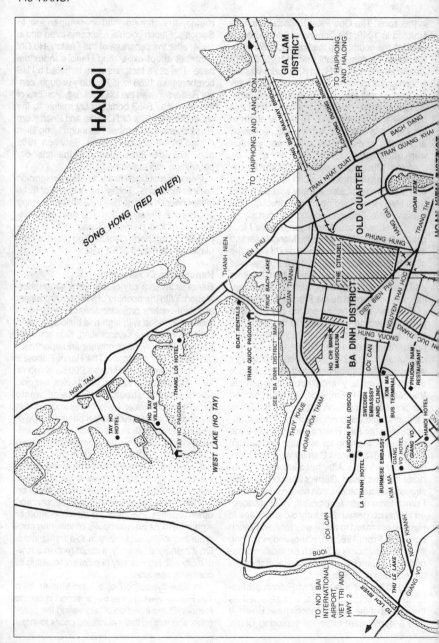

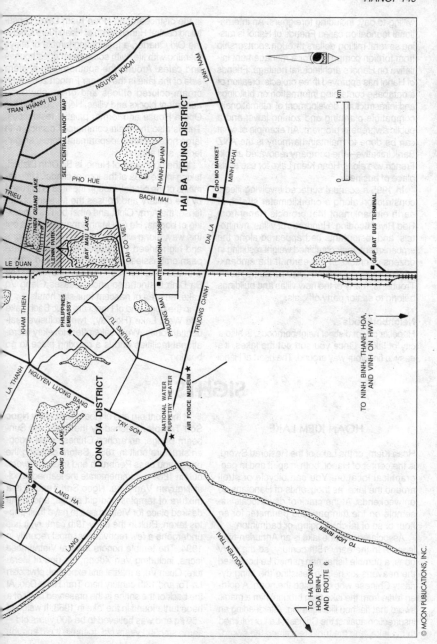

© MOON PUBLICATIONS, INC.

willing to pay, including foreigners. An international foundation called Friends of Hanoi is raising several million dollars through sponsorship from foreign companies for a management initiative on Hanoi's architectural heritage. Friends of Hanoi has approved three projects: creation of a database containing information on buildings and infrastructure; development of internationally compatible planning and zoning laws; and a public awareness program. An example of what can be done to maintain harmony is the ANZ Bank initiative—the company renovated an old French villa along Hoan Kiem Lake for use as its place of business.

In 1995 a scandal surfaced involving illegal construction along a one-kilometer stretch of earth embankment that protects Hanoi from Red River flooding. Hundreds of villas, minihotels, and restaurants had appeared along the embankment, their combined weight resulting in dozens of cracks in the earth. If the embankment collapses, the flood could consume Hanoi. Trouble is, many of the new villas and buildings belong to senior party officials.

Neighborhoods

Hanoi, a city of distinct neighborhoods, is also a city of lakes. Once you sort out the lakes, it's easy to find your way around. The heart of Hanoi is the district around Hoan Kiem Lake, constituting central Hanoi. North of Hoan Kiem Lake is the Old Quarter, a fascinating jumble of alleys teeming with life, with some great guesthouses and cafés. Around the southern and eastern side of the lake is the former French zone, with cream-colored offices and green-shuttered apartment blocks and villas. Here you'll find the Opera House and former palatial residences. This is also the main commercial district, with large hotels, banks, department stores, art galleries, and shops.

In the northwest of Hanoi is Ba Dinh District, taking in the area of the former citadel. Little remains of the citadel, though the area is still used by the military and houses the Ministry of Defense, the Army Club, and other bodies. Speaking of bodies, Ho Chi Minh's mausoleum is out this way, along with the Ho Chi Minh Museum, and high-priced villas used by Eastern European embassies. The area is leafy and green, with wide boulevards—ideal for bicycling. The Ba Dinh District also encompasses Giang Vo Lake, an area of nascent four-star hotels.

In the north end of Hanoi are Truc Bach Lake and West Lake (Ho Tay), two exclusive residential zones. West Lake offers low-key recreational facilities and is a relaxing place to go boating.

SIGHTS

HOAN KIEM LAKE

Hoan Kiem, or the Lake of the Restored Sword, is the center of Hanoi, both in spirit and in geographical location. You can bicycle or stroll around the lake, as thousands of Hanoians do on weekends. At the crack of dawn locals assemble on the thin parkland perimeter for an hour or so of tai chi, jogging, or badminton.

Associated with the lake is an Arthurian-type legend. In the early 15th century, so the story goes, a humble fisherman named Le Loi asked the heavens for help in resisting the Ming dynasty Chinese who occupied the north. A golden turtle from the lake then brought him a magic sword that flashed like lightning. After leading an insurrection against the Chinese, Le Loi returned to the lake, and the turtle reclaimed the sword.

At the northern end of Hoan Kiem is tiny **Ngoc Son Temple,** reached by the bright red Sunbeam Bridge, an arched Chinese-style wooden structure built in 1855. Before crossing the bridge you pass Penbrush and Inkslab towers, built in 1864 to commemorate the learned scholar Nguyen Van Sieu. Ngoc Son Temple is a mixture of temples and gift shops, and is the desired place for Vietnamese to have their photos taken. Built in the early 19th century, it has undergone a few renovations, most recently in 1994. The temple honors several Vietnamese icons, including Van Xuong, the god of literature; Quan Vu, a martial arts exponent; physician La To; and 13th-century hero Tran Hung Dao. At the back of the shrine is the preserved body of a huge turtle found in the lake in 1968. It weighed 250 kg and was believed to be 400 years old—some say 500 years old, to make it old enough o serve as the turtle of legend. On an islet at the south end of the lake is a dilapidated three-tiered tower, built in honor of the valiant turtle. Turtles are occasionally still sighted in the lake. On the west bank, next to the ANZ Bank, is a small temple with a statue of Le Loi.

There are several other pagodas in the vicinity of the lake. Popular with locals is **Bada Pago-da**, or Heavenly Mistress of the Stone, to the west of Hoan Kiem on Nha Tho Street. The pagoda was built in the 15th century after the discovery of a stone statue of a woman. The statue, imbued with magic powers, disappeared, and was replaced with a wooden replica. The pagoda bears bonsai trees, oriental vases, and an impressive array of Buddha statuary.

OLD QUARTER

A stroll through Hanoi's happily chaotic Old Quarter will quickly lay to rest the conception

---

WATER PUPPETRY

Without a doubt, one of the top attractions in Hanoi is water puppetry. This exuberant and magical art form is intended for children but will delight adults as well. Unique to Vietnam, it's seen regularly only in the north. The exact origins of water puppetry are uncertain, but it's known the Red River Delta area nurtured and preserved this traditional theater over many centuries. Water puppetry was a village festival art before it became a theatrical one. Temporary theaters were constructed in village ponds, and performances marked such auspicious occasions as the beginning or end of the agricultural cycle.

For performances, a dozen puppeteers stand waist-deep in water behind a pagoda set; invisible to the audience they manipulate puppets with a series of bamboo poles, pulleys, and strings. The puppets are made of lacquered wood and appear remarkably lifelike when skipping across the water. What goes on under the water is a closely guarded secret—some puppeteers have to swim under other puppeteers. Water plays a key part in the show—the surface is seething during a naval battle, or romantically calm when a group of fairies drifts across. Underwater fireworks bring flashing dragons to life and furnish a haze of smoke for mythical settings. Puppeteers and percussionists provide explosive sound effects—rhythmic music and zany sound effects maintain the tempo.

Repertoire

The traditional water puppetry repertoire includes up to 100 short skits. A 75-minute performance usually presents 15 to 20 short pieces, derived from fables, local legends, historic events, or adapted from popular theater. Such mythical animals as the phoenix, lion-dog, unicorn, and dragon are often shown in aquatic dances. Satirical takes at rural life are common. You'll most likely see the story of the magic sword, a mixture of myth and history similar to the Arthurian legend of Excalibur.

Venues

There are several locations for viewing water puppetry shows in Hanoi. Show duration is usually around 75 minutes. In town is **Kim Dong Water Puppetry Theater,** 57 Dinh Tien Hoang St., tel. 260553, with performances nightly in the high season. Kim Dong Theater is a large 300-seat venue at the northeast side of Hoan Kiem Lake. Shows start at 2000 and cost $2 per seat, $4 for a front seat with a water puppetry audiocassette thrown in. There's a $1 charge for a still camera, $5 for a video camera. Thang Long water puppetry troupe runs the show; the theater provides a live traditional music ensemble of five who sing, play instruments, and provide acoustic effects.

The **National Water Puppetry Theater,** at 32 Truong Chinh St., tel. 244545, stages shows at 1930 on Tuesday, Thursday, Saturday, and Sunday. The theater is located at the southern edge of town; take a minibus from Darling Café, Queen Café, or another traveler café at 1900 hours. You can also bicycle out there—about six km out. Entry is $2 for foreigners, still camera free, video camera $10. The national troupe is Vietnam's best, and has toured Japan, Australia, and Europe; it was set up in 1956 by Ho Chi Minh himself.

Water puppetry shows are also staged at **Song Ngoc Theater** east of Lenin Park off Le Dai Hanh Street. Inquire through hotels or traveler cafés for show times. On the seventh day of the third lunar month, usually in April, there's a water puppetry festival at Thay Pagoda, 40 km west of Hanoi.

OLD QUARTER WALKING TOUR

Although the following tour covers some of the more colorful streets in the Old Quarter, really you can dive in anywhere and wander at will. A good starting point is the fountain above Hoan Kiem Lake. From here you can proceed in a long counterclockwise arc through the area. Heading north up Dinh Liet Street you encounter wool clothing—scarves from China, handmade sweaters, yarn products. There are more clothing and cosmetics outlets down the first side alley. To the left are Russian watch shops; to the right, running along Gia Ngu Street, is a busy food market worth a detour.

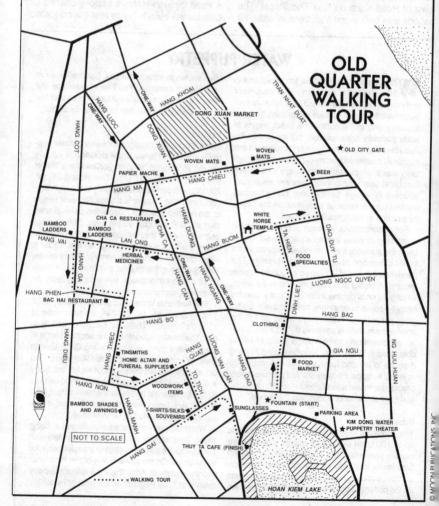

OLD QUARTER WALKING TOUR

NOT TO SCALE

●●●●●● = WALKING TOUR

Proceeding north you cross Hang Bac, one of the oldest streets in Hanoi. It was once known for its silversmiths, brought to the capital to cast silver bars and coins in a silver ingot factory. Some jewelers remain at this crossroads, though farther east along Hang Bac the main trade is in marble (for etching tombstones), wood (coffinmakers), and tourism (cafés, motorcycle rental outlets). Onward, upward, northward along Ta Hien Street, with small stalls selling luxury food items, and some specialty restaurants. Luxury goods are smuggled in from China, Cambodia, or Thailand—the labels may be the real thing or fakes. Follow this street to Hang Buom.

White Horse Temple

A little way west on Hang Buom is White Horse Temple (Bach Ma), one of the oldest in Hanoi and the most sacred in the Old Quarter. When Emperor Le Thai To set about building his capital, he went to a temple to consult the local land oracle. A white horse emerged from the temple and galloped west; the emperor decided to build his citadel walls along the hoof prints and declared the white horse the city guardian. The present White Horse Temple was reconstructed in the 18th and 19th centuries and used as a center of Taoist worship.

Go east along Hang Buom and turn north up Dao Duy Tu past some shops entirely stocked with beer (some smuggled in from China). Here you'll find an old brick city gate, Quan Chuong, built in the mid-18th century. This was one of the original 16 city gates, once closed at night with massive wooden doors. Noodle stalls now operate from inside the structure. Parts of a former city rampart and dike still stand along Tran Nhat Duat Street. On to the next street, Hang Chieu. *Chieu* means "mats"—you'll find all kinds of woven products.

Dong Xuan Market

Walking along Sugar Street (Hang Duong), just before you reach Sweet Potato Street (Hang Khoai), you'll run across Dong Xuan Market, Hanoi's oldest and newest and biggest. It's both a thousand years old and brand-new. How so? Well, it burnt to the ground in 1994, with a fearful loss of merchandise. Today the covered market is under reconstruction. Intriguing at Dong Xuan is the plant and animal area, with a section for pets—hamsters, budgies, cats. There's also a rather grisly collection of lizards, pythons, macaques, and pangolins destined for restaurant tables or traditional medicines. The area outside the market to the east side features spice, rice, and dried-fish stalls.

Walk back to Hang Ma Street. "Ma" denotes paper offerings to the spirits of deceased relatives. Paper money, houses, cars, and fridges are burned to assist spirits in the afterlife. The street also offers other colorful paper products—gift wrapping, wedding decorations, lanterns, papier-mâché masks.

You can smell the next street before you see it—the odors of ginger, musk, powders, and potions. This is the street of herbal medicines, called Lan Ong, featuring a variety of roots, leaves, bark, and dried herbs. If you continue west you'll cross a street called Hang Dong. Originally this street specialized in copperware; now the trade is in collapsible metal door shutters used nights on Hanoi shop fronts.

Continuing west you'll reach Hang Vai, the street of the bamboo ladders. Bamboo is often used for construction scaffolding in Asia in place of metal—it's light, strong, and durable. Buildings in this portion of the Old Quarter are obscured behind stacks of bamboo poles and ladders, the latter still made by hand.

Make your way down Hang Ga and turn left on Hang Phen. One of the Old Quarter's specialized restaurant lies along here—halfway along the street at number 7 on your right is a restaurant devoted solely to veal dishes. Uncle Hai's serves steak; cow brains, stomach, tongue, and liver; and fetal calves.

The next stop is Hang Thiec. *Thiec* means "tin-smiths." This area once produced metal products, candlesticks, oil lamps, opium boxes, and mirrors. Today sheet-metal workers on Hang Thiec bang away with a deafening din, producing metal storage boxes and plumbing supplies. Another side street in the area, Hang Manh, specializes in the manufacture of bamboo shades and awnings.

Red Banners and Ray-Bans

Hang Quat is the most colorful street in the whole quarter, with a riot of bright red banners and flags and eye-catching displays of objects for the home altar—most intended for religious use and funerals. For a funeral, relatives and friends in white headbands form a procession, bearing red banners and garlands of flowers.

Leading off Hang Quat at the east side is tiny To Tich, a wood turner's street offering musical instruments and other wooden goods. Hang Gai features silk and cotton items, with embroidery and souvenir shops; the western end leads to Hang Bong. *Bong*

(continues on next page)

OLD QUARTER WALKING TOUR
(continued)

means "cotton"—here you'll find knocked-off Tintin-in-Halong T-shirts and other pirated logos. T-shirts can be custom-made.

On the street leading back to Hoan Kiem Lake vendors sell eyeglasses, mostly sunglasses, so you might call it Ray-Ban Street. Ray-Bans here sell for $4, so Ray-Ban Copy Street might be more accurate. And to go with Ray-Bans, of course, mafioso. You'll find them around the corner on a side street,

sitting at cafés—all wearing fake Ray-Bans. Shiny new Honda Dream motorcycles are parked nearby.

The ideal place to finish your walking tour is at Thuy Ta Café by the side of Hoan Kiem Lake. The place has a derelict air, service is slow, and drinks are overpriced, but the views are great. You can get ice cream or coffee and go upstairs to an open balcony overlooking the lake—an oasis of calm in the heart of Hanoi.

---

that the city is gray, dull, reserved, and austere. In the anarchic jumble of the Old Quarter thrives a lively commerce in trade and handicrafts. The place is full of character—and characters. You might come across a woman trundling down a street with a shoulder pole of dual baskets bearing porcelain, or an old woman who reveals blackened teeth when she smiles, or a group of men crouched over bamboo bongs at tiny sidewalk stools. The quarter is a medieval maze of alleys with shops, homes, and cafés. It's best to tackle the area on foot, allowing time to stop and poke around. Unfortunately, the sidewalks are often blocked by parked motorcycles, the narrow roads filled with bicycles and motorbikes. Exercise care when walking.

The Old Quarter is known as the Quarter of the 36 Streets. The derivation of the name is not

clear. East of the former citadel was the artisan and merchant quarter; in the 15th century, workshop villages clustered around this area to satisfy the royal court's need for quality products. Houses and shops stood side by side in this royal city, in a cooperative system like that of imperial Beijing or medieval Florence. Guilds worked together to transport merchandise from outlying villages, often along the Red River. Guild names were applied to streets—Silk Street, Paper Street, Basket Street. Each guild maintained its own pagoda and patron deity; most of these "community centers" have since been turned over to other uses such as schools. Many street signs in this district begin with Pho Hang. "Pho" means "alley," "hang" means "shop" or "merchandise," and "bac" means "silversmiths," so Pho Hang Bac refers to the alley with the shops of silversmiths.

narrow shophouses in the Old Quarter

There may at one time have been 36 guild locations in the Old Quarter, but the number is more likely abstract or just plain lucky. In Asia, nine is an auspicious number; taken in the four compass directions, it multiplies to 36. In any case there are double that number of streets in the area now, and only a fraction of the activity revolves around handicrafts. Most streets are now concerned with trades—retail shops, tailors, repair shops. Trades have changed with the times—you'll find entire streets given over to the sale of Russian watches, smuggled cigarettes, bootleg whiskey, motorcycle parts, shoes, pillows, Korean-made luggage, and Chinese thermos flasks. Increasingly, parts of the Old Quarter are dedicated to minihotels and restaurants for tourists.

One thing that hasn't changed much in the Old Quarter is the size of its shophouses. Shops were taxed according to the width of their market frontage, so crafty old Hanoians built narrow shop fronts with long narrow homes behind them containing living space and storage. These red-tiled three- or four-story structures are called "tube houses," as they're only three meters wide at the front, but up to 60 meters deep. The local government is formulating plans to preserve the Old Quarter from demolition or alteration, as developers have their beady eyes on this sector, dreaming of high-rise buildings. The Old Quarter is in surprisingly good condition, with few changes to the original layout; it has been recognized by UNESCO as an important heritage site.

FRENCHTOWN

Hanoi is home to the best-preserved colonial architecture in Indochina. From 1902 to 1953 Hanoi was the capital of the French Indochinese Union, and the grandiose public buildings and exquisite villas here attest to the fact.

When North Vietnam became a French protectorate in 1883, the French settled to the south and east of Hoan Kiem Lake, razing Vietnamese housing except for some key pagodas and creating a ville Française, or Frenchtown, of several square kilometers. By 1884 the first avenues appeared, shaded with tamarind and banyan trees and lined with green-shuttered apartment blocks flung up by contract workers from France; in 1885 the first hotel appeared.

One of the oldest structures in Frenchtown is **St. Joseph's Cathedral,** built in 1886, located on Nha Chung Street to the southwest of the lake. The somber Gothic exterior with its square towers is now grimy and gray; to see the interior, illuminated by stained-glass windows, attend services in the early morning or late afternoon.

At the west side of Hoan Kiem Lake is the **ANZ Bank.** The bank moved into a turn-of-the-century villa reduced to a warehouse, eventually restoring it to its former elegance. The results are quite stunning.

From here stroll along Trang Thi Street, heading east to Trang Tien. This street, known in the French era as Rue Paul Bert, was one of the most elegant shopping thoroughfares in Hanoi. On the southeast corner of the intersection of Hang Bai and Trang Tien streets is a department store that used to be Godard's under the French.

At 15 Ngo Quyen is the **Hotel Metropole,** which opened under the same name in 1911. In its heyday the Metropole was the center of French social life, frequented by visiting celebrities and senior French officers and their wives or consorts. The building was showing its age when the French group Accor decided to pour $9 million into renovations in 1990. Architects were careful to preserve the character of the hotel, maintaining the original hardwood floors and shuttered windows in the rooms, as well as the vintage 1920s plumbing. Today the Metropole is once again the hub of foreign business and highbrow social life in the capital.

Opposite the Metropole is the **Government Reception Hall,** formerly the offices of the Governor-Resident of Tonkin. The 19th-century palace is a grand specimen of *belle époque* architecture, its ornate and spacious rooms used for state functions, official receptions, and VIP guests.

A Night at the Opera

Looming at the end of Trang Tien is the block-wide **Opera House,** a flamboyant structure built in 1911 in neo-classical style as an exact, though smaller, replica of the Paris Opera. The lavish 900-seat Hanoi Opera was the focal point for socializing during the French era, patrons flocking to see productions of Victor Hugo or Molière. The Opera House exterior, with its elaborate wrought-iron work and shutters, is little changed except for the addition of a large air raid siren on the rooftop. If you want to see the interior, attend an evening cultural performance. Tickets are reasonable, and you can check out the acoustics as well as the furniture.

Other Edifices

In the vicinity of the Opera House are several other buildings. The Revolutionary Museum was previously the neo-classical Museum of Indochinese Mines. The History Museum was built in 1926 and was formerly a museum and archaeological research institute under the auspices of the Ecole Française d'Extrême-Orient. It's an unusual structure with mixed Oriental and French features.

To the north of Hanoi is a curious piece of French and Vietnamese engineering. In 1902 Governor-General Paul Doumer cut the ribbon for a bridge named in his honor; the bridge, now called Long Bien Railway Bridge, spans 1.6 km across the Red River. At the time of the Vietnam War this was the only bridge across the river and was thus a prime target for US bombers. As fast as American bombs knocked out the spans, however, the Vietnamese repaired them; the bridge therefore became a hodgepodge of different styles. You can view the work up close by traveling across Long Bien Railway Bridge—it carries train and bicycle traffic, as well as hand-cart-pushers and pedestrians. Chuong Dueng Bridge, farther south, was built in 1985.

BA DINH SQUARE

From Ba Dinh Square Ho Chi Minh addressed half a million Vietnamese with his Declaration of Independence speech in 1945. Today the square is a shrine and pilgrimage site. Legions of schoolchildren and droves of visitors from all over Vietnam converge on Ho Chi Minh's mausoleum, museum, and house. A Ho Chi Minh Arch was completed to mark the 50th anniversary of the independence declaration. In the same area are the former Presidential Palace and the One Pillar Pagoda. If your timing is right, you can visit all the sites in one go—start early in the morning, visit the mausoleum and Ho's house, then see the One Pillar Pagoda and Ho Chi Minh Museum. Monday and Friday are bad days to visit since the mausoleum and museum are both closed.

The Mausoleum

Getting into the mausoleum is not always easy: plan to arrive early, and be sure to bring your passport. Posted hours for the mausoleum are: Tuesday, Wednesday, Thursday, Saturday, and Sunday 0730-1100. However, these hours seem to vary slightly in summer and winter—0800-1000 is more reliable. Ho Chi Minh's body is apparently taken off for upkeep in September-October. Visitors entering the mausoleum area must be respectful. Leave outside weapons, explosives, fire, radioactive materials, toxic products, cameras. Inside there's no talking, touching the walls, hands in pockets, smoking, sunglasses, or immodest clothing. The latter includes shorts, sleeveless tops, and hats.

When the mausoleum is open for visits, the surrounding boulevards are barricaded and guarded. There are car and bike parking areas to the west of Ho Chi Minh Museum off Ngoc Ha Street. Foreigners follow a different route through the Ho Chi Minh memorial complex than Vietnamese visitors, in effect jumping the queue. Officially, as a foreigner, you're supposed to register by showing your passport at an office at 5 Ngoc Ha Street, south of the Ho Chi Minh museum, then proceed to a baggage and camera deposit east of the museum. In practice, however, you can eliminate the first step, and, after depositing your bags, roll up to the street corner on Hung Vuong Boulevard where it intersects Chua Mot Cot Street east of the Ho Chi Minh Museum. Guards will check your passport, wait for a group to assemble, then lead you through the mausoleum and on to Ho Chi Minh's house.

Ho Chi Minh was embalmed using the same secret techniques applied to the body of Lenin. In his last years, Ho was quite frail, suffering from tuberculosis and recurrent malaria. As Ho lay dying, the chief Soviet embalmer, Dr. Sergei Debov, flew to Hanoi with two transport planes of air-conditioners and other equipment. Using special chemicals, the embalming team required a full year to complete their work, and the body

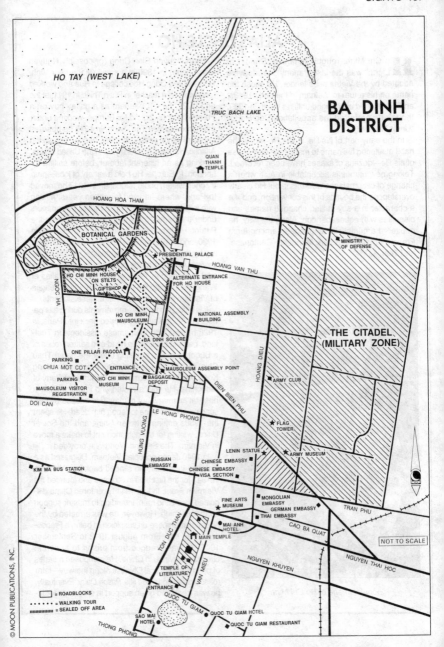

BA DINH DISTRICT

HO TAY (WEST LAKE)

TRUC BACH LAKE

QUAN THANH TEMPLE

HOANG HOA THAM

BOTANICAL GARDENS

MINISTRY OF DEFENSE

PRESIDENTIAL PALACE

HO CHI MINH HOUSE ON STILTS

GIFTSHOP

HOANG VAN THU

ALTERNATE ENTRANCE FOR HO HOUSE

NGOC HA

HO CHI MINH MAUSOLEUM

NATIONAL ASSEMBLY BUILDING

THE CITADEL (MILITARY ZONE)

BA DINH SQUARE

ONE PILLAR PAGODA CHUA MOT COT

PARKING

ENTRANCE

PARKING

HO CHI MINH MUSEUM

MAUSOLEUM VISITOR REGISTRATION

MAUSOLEUM ASSEMBLY POINT

BAGGAGE DEPOSIT

HOANG DIEU

ARMY CLUB

DOI CAN

LE HONG PHONG

DIEN BIEN PHU

FLAG TOWER

HUNG VUONG

LENIN STATUE

ARMY MUSEUM

KIM MA BUS STATION

RUSSIAN EMBASSY

CHINESE EMBASSY

CHINESE EMBASSY VISA SECTION

FINE ARTS MUSEUM

MONGOLIAN EMBASSY

GERMAN EMBASSY

THAI EMBASSY

TRAN PHU

TON DUC THANG

MAI ANH HOTEL

CAO BA QUAT

NOT TO SCALE

MAIN TEMPLE

NGUYEN THAI HOC

TEMPLE OF LITERATURE

VAN MIEU

NGUYEN KHUYEN

ENTRANCE

QUOC TU GIAM

SAO MAI HOTEL

QUOC TU GIAM HOTEL

THONG PHONG

QUOC TU GIAM RESTAURANT

□ = ROADBLOCKS

••••• = WALKING TOUR

||||||||| = SEALED OFF AREA

© MOON PUBLICATIONS, INC.

ALIAS UNCLE HO

Ho Chi Minh, roughly meaning "Bringer of Light," was the last of many pseudonyms adopted by the Vietnamese leader. He chose the name on his return to Vietnam in the early 1940s, and it remained unchanged until his death in 1969, though he preferred the appellation Boc Ho, or "Uncle Ho."

In the early part of his life, Uncle Ho was in the habit of altering his name to mark each new phase of his life—dozens of aliases have been recorded. Taking new names is acceptable in Asia when a change of circumstance warrants it, but Ho clearly overstepped the bounds of this convention, and like a character in a spy thriller, changed names and disguises with equal abandon. Along the way, he mastered a number of languages—among them French, English, Russian, Mandarin, Cantonese, and Thai.

popular image of Ho Chi Minh

Born Nguyen Sinh Cung (or possibly Nguyen Van Thanh) in 1890 in a small village near Vinh, Ho attended Quoc Hoc college in Hué and worked for a while as a teacher in Phan Thiet. In 1911, at the age of 21, he left Vietnam as a galley boy on a French freighter bound for Europe, working under the name Nguyen Tat Thanh. In 1913 he boarded another French vessel, this time headed across the Atlantic. He spent almost a year in the United States, working as an itinerant laborer, before sailing for London. In Europe, Ho held a variety of jobs—pastry chef, waiter, photo retoucher. In 1917 he moved to Paris, where he lived for seven years, mixing with leftists and contributing to radical newspapers under the name Nguyen Ai Quoc, or Nguyen the Patriot. He joined the French Communist Party in 1920, and in 1924 he left Paris for Moscow for training by the Communist International, which he received under the name of Comrade Linh. He was sent to Canton in 1925, where, under the alias of Wang, he founded the Revolutionary Youth League of Vietnam and mobilized Vietnamese students.

It is difficult to track his movements during this period: in 1927 he secretly slipped back into Paris; in 1928 he was with Vietnamese dissidents in Thailand, bearing the shaven head and saffron robes of a Buddhist monk, traveling under the name Thau Chin. In 1929 he assembled rival factions in Hong Kong and in 1930 formed the Communist Party of Indochina. He was arrested and imprisoned in a hospital infirmary, but managed to escape by persuading an employee to report him dead. He spent the 1930s drifting between China and the Soviet Union, waiting for the right moment to make a move in Vietnam. The Second World War provided it.

In 1940 Japan occupied Vietnam. Disguised as a Chinese journalist, Ho slipped back into Vietnam in 1941 for the first time in 30 years and founded the Vietminh Front. In late 1941 he entered China disguised as a blind man, intending to muster support for the Vietminh. However, he was arrested by the Nationalist Chinese on suspicion of being a Franco-Japanese spy. From August 1942 to September 1943 Ho was dragged from prison to prison in Guangxi Province in China. He composed a series of poems in classical Chinese along the way—later reassembled under the title *Prison Dairy*. Eventually, he was freed and given support in exchange for intelligence on the Japanese. In August 1945, as Japan was about to surrender, Ho led the August Revolution that took control of much of the country. On 2 September 1945 Ho proclaimed the Democratic Republic of Vietnam, reading the Declaration of Independence near the present site of his mausoleum. In the south, the British ruthlessly suppressed the Vietminh, and with the return of the French to Vietnam, the Vietminh fled Hanoi and took up armed resistance—a struggle that would last for the next 30 years.

Ho never married, although evidence suggests he had several liaisons. Supposedly he was wedded to the revolution: Ho spent a good deal of his time promoting a unified Vietnam as one happy family. Thus he cultivated the image of "Uncle Ho"—he preferred the informal name to the more formal "President." His personal charm, humility, simplicity, and sincerity enabled him to converse easily with farmers, monks, or politicians. In *A Vietcong Memoir,* Truong Nhu Trang describes a meeting with Uncle Ho:

I was immediately struck by Ho Chi Minh's appearance. Unlike the others, who were dressed in Western-style clothes, Ho wore a frayed, high-collared Chinese jacket. On his feet he had rubber sandals. In contrast to the tense-looking younger men around him, he gave off an air of fragility, almost sickliness. But these impressions only contributed to the imperturbable dignity that enveloped him as through it were something tangible. . . . He exuded a combination of inner strength and personal generosity that struck me with something like a physical blow. He looked directly at me, and at the others, with a magnetic expression of intensity and warmth.

is apparently sent back to Moscow for regular checkups. Dr. Debov is also responsible for pickling other communist luminaries: he is the director of the Scientific and Research Center for Biological Structures in Moscow, which cares for the body of Vladimir Lenin. Due to a falling out with the Russians, Mao Zedong was embalmed without Soviet help. The Chinese had to lean on the Vietnamese for information on the secret embalming process.

Ho Chi Minh's Mausoleum is closely modeled on Lenin's in Moscow's Red Square. Lenin's Mausoleum, built in 1930, was based on a cubist design—the cube was envisaged, like a pyramid, as a symbol of eternity. Mao Zedong occupies a similar squarish structure in Tiananmen Square, Beijing.

All this is quite odd when you consider communism stresses cremation as a land saver, and none of the three leaders wanted to be on public display. Lenin asked to be buried next to his mother, and Ho Chi Minh and Mao Zedong both requested cremation.

Ba Dinh Square is sometimes used for large parades; to the north and south of the mausoleum are review stands. The mausoleum is guarded by an elite military regiment. At the front of the building, on the hour every hour there is a ceremonial changing of the guard, with a pair of goose-stepping Vietnamese soldiers relieving their cohorts. The white-gloved goose-stepping sentinels are modeled on those at Lenin's Mausoleum in Red Square, where the ritual was suspended by Boris Yeltsin in 1993.

Ho's air-conditioned mausoleum consists of granite and marble quarried from the Marble Mountains near Danang. It was built 1973-75. Inside, Ho's glass sarcophagus is guarded by four unblinking soldiers, one at each corner of the bier. Your escort propels you through the chilly vault, making sure you don't pause, talk, sneeze, or put your hands in your pockets. No time to dawdle here—just a few seconds to take in marble-faced Ho, with eerie lighting on his head and hands.

House on Stilts

After exiting the Mausoleum, a guide will take you through to Ho Chi Minh's House on Stilts. If you want to come back at another time, you can visit the area from a gate just south of the large wrought-iron gates of the Presidential Palace. Again, you must be escorted by a guide, and may have to wait till a small group assembles. The house is open 0730-1100 and 1330-1630. Constructed in 1958, it was modeled on the house Ho lived in while fighting the French from a hideout near the Chinese border. The house sits next to a pond stocked with carp; Ho was fond of jogging in a leafy area nearby lined with mango trees.

The wooden house has been preserved as it was during Ho Chi Minh's working life. The house is raised on wooden pillars, with the lower section open. Upstairs are two rooms—a bedroom, and a winter workroom with desk, telephone, and books. The portable typewriter here is said to be the one Ho used to type his Declaration of Independence. Ho used the open downstairs section for working in summer and for holding meetings. There are 10 chairs here for the 10 members of the politburo, and three telephones. A sobering thought—Ho Chi Minh ran the whole Vietnam War from here. Nearby is a concrete bunker under a hill, a bomb shelter 10 meters deep with room for 10 people. A hanging 105mm shell acted as a gong for an air-raid alarm. Behind the bomb shelter is the hut where Ho died in 1969.

If you entered the House on Stilts area from the mausoleum, you'll be escorted back to the One Pillar Pagoda after a stop at a gift shop. You can then visit Ho Chi Minh Museum.

Presidential Palace

When the north achieved independence in 1954, Ho Chi Minh declined to move into the Presidential Palace, saying the building belonged to the people. Formerly the Palace of the Governor-general of Indochina, it was built between 1900 and 1908 in Edwardian style. The gardens surrounding the mansion once contained botanical specimens from around the world. There are frangipani, banyan, mango, and other trees in this area, and at the back of the palace is a French trellis draped with bougainvillea. Now air-conditioned, the palace is used for official functions and as a party guesthouse. The building itself and a large zone around it are off limits—the area is a working compound for high officials. Other mustard-colored colonial buildings in the area include the former servants' quarters, and an electrical power station used during the time of the Governor-general of Indochina. Between 1954 and 1958, Ho Chi Minh lived in the gardener's quarters. One of the buildings is now a souvenir shop. A new white building near the palace was constructed in 1993 to house VIP guests.

Ho Chi Minh Museum

In contrast to the often dowdy exhibits in Ho Chi Minh museums in other parts of the country, the museum in Hanoi offers lavish and striking displays on the life and times of Uncle Ho. Most are captioned in Vietnamese and English. If you need further explanation, consult gung-Ho patriotic guides available at the ground-level reception area for a donation.

The museum is open 0800-1100 and 1330-1600 daily except Monday and Friday. For-

changing of the guard at Ho Chi Minh Mausoleum

eigners enter from the east side; Vietnamese enter from the north. No photography is allowed within the museum, and bags must be deposited on entry. Museum exhibits are on the top floor. The ground and first floors contain cloakrooms, meeting rooms, an auditorium, library and research facility, bookstore, several gift shops, and a small café.

The museum opened in 1990 to commemorate the centenary of Ho's birth. The concrete building was designed by a Soviet architect and has fluted sides to resemble a lotus, the Buddhist symbol of purity. In the front foyer is a larger-than-life-size statue of Ho Chi Minh backed by another Buddhist sacred symbol, the banyan tree. Upstairs in the main display area, the lotus-petal motif is echoed in the design of several exhibits. Still, the museum manages to veer away from the propagandist tone that haunts others of its kind around Vietnam. The thought-provoking displays make you wonder what motivated Ho Chi Minh and other Vietnamese revolutionaries to take on what seemed at the time a hopeless cause.

The top-floor museum exhibits are arranged chronologically, from Ho's birth in 1890 to his death in 1969, with a small section on the 1975 reunification of north and south. The arrangement can be quite confusing. There are several layers to the display: the personal life of Ho Chi Minh (photos, personal possessions); document display stands with newspaper clippings, letters, and so on, often in French or Russian; and displays depicting events in Vietnam and other parts of the world at specific dates. This all comes with a kind of revolutionary packaging of offbeat sculptural enhancement in metal, stone, and wood—no expense has been spared here.

Proceeding clockwise, exhibits are arrayed around four corner displays based on key events in Ho's life.

North Corner/1890: Birth of Ho Chi Minh. The display shows a model of Chua Village, near Vinh, where Ho was born. Side exhibits portray world events and artistic and revolutionary movements from 1890 to 1920, with pictures of Chaplin, Picasso, Lautrec, Rousseau, and Einstein. The impact of Marx and Lenin, and the October Revolution of 1917, are also depicted.

East Corner/1930: Founding of the Communist Party of Indochina by Ho Chi Minh in Hong Kong. Ho fled Hong Kong in 1933 with the help of a British lawyer. A section devoted to world events from 1930 to 1945 concerns the struggle against fascism, with paintings including Picasso's *Guernica* and works by Dali, Max Ernst, Matisse, Miro, and Chagall. Another side section here highlights the struggle between socialism and capitalism—between the US (symbolized by a plaster cast of a Ford with Ohio plates coming out of a wall, and a portrait of Dizzy Gillespie) and the USSR (with a picture of the Kremlin). Another wall shows pictures from the Nuremberg Trials.

South Corner/1945: Declaration of Independence by Ho Chi Minh, and beginning of resistance to the French. The Vietnamese declaration was modeled on both the French and the American declarations. Side panels feature the world revolutionary movement in Africa, South America, and Asia in the 1950s. A video salon shows the struggle for independence and social progress in Vietnam.

West Corner/1969: Death of Ho Chi Minh, with his alarm clock stopped at 9:47 a.m., 2 September. Here are pictures of the funeral with gifts received at the time from provincial groups in Vietnam, and from Russia, China, Cuba, Chile, Mongolia, Laos, India, and other countries. The display is laid out in the shape of sacred lotus petals. Around it is a small section on the American War, with military hardware and part of a US plane downed while attacking Hanoi. This section also contains a cigarette case, comb, and thermos made from recycled aluminum US plane parts, and a watch donated by the US Communist Party. The exhibit concludes with the 1975 reunification of Vietnam, the dream that Ho did not live to see realized. The last document case here emphasizes re-establishing diplomatic relations as a unified Vietnam—receiving foreign heads of state and the like.

After visiting the museum, check out the tacky Ho Chi Minh souvenir trinkets at the gift shops. Patrons can buy busts of Ho or framed pictures for the home altar, copies of Ho's poetry, Uncle Ho postcards, stamps, posters, Ho hats and badges, but no Uncle Ho T-shirts. Ho souvenirs are also sold by sidewalk vendors in front of the museum.

THE BOULEVARD BICYCLE TOUR

There are very few Asian capitals where you can cycle along and have the entire road to yourself. Hanoi is one of them. The Ba Dinh District, with its wide boulevards, leafy parks, and light traffic, is perfect for cycling. Before setting out on this tour, you might like to drop in and see Uncle Ho at the Mausoleum in the morning, but perhaps come back another time for the Ho Chi Minh Museum, which is a real time-chewer. There are roadblocks around the mausoleum in the morning, but these disappear around 1100 or 1130, after which you can cycle past the front of the mausoleum. Only bicycles are allowed outside the mausoleum along Hung Vuong Boulevard—no cyclos or motorcycles.

Start the tour on the west side of Ho Chi Minh Museum, near the bicycle parking area. Ride north on Ngoc Ha Street toward **Bach Thao Park,** which used to be a botanical garden under the French and is now parkland. You can cycle through the park and carry on to **Quan Thanh Temple.** Inside this Taoist temple is a black bronze statue of General Tran Vo and a large bronze bell, both from the 17th century. The temple is known for its private school of *gong fu,* originating from a monastery in China. In the late afternoon, students dressed in black practice in the courtyard. There's an art gallery on the temple grounds.

Silk Lake and Shrimpcake

North of the temple a causeway cuts between two lakes. To your left is Ho Tay. To your right is **Ho Truc Bach,** or White Silk Lake. In the 18th century, a palace stood at this lakeside; concubines disloyal to the emperor were imprisoned here and forced to weave fine white silk.

A very different kind of prisoner landed here in 1967—US Air Force Major John Sidney McCain. A small concrete **USAF plaque** shows a pilot parachuting down into the lake. The plaque reads: "On October 26, 1967 at Truc Bach Lake, the soldiers and people of Hanoi captured US Air Force major John Sney Macan, pilot of the A4B1 plane shot down over Yen Phu Power Plant—one of ten aircraft shot down the same day." The plaque is dedicated to the antiaircraft gunners who protected Hanoi during this period; there were gun emplacements around neighboring West Lake. The small relief statue is the only one of an American left in Vietnam. John Sidney McCain, the pilot of the A-4 Skyhawk, survived his in-

juries and over five years of prison life. He was elected to the US Senate from Arizona and has returned to Hanoi on missions related to American MIAs. After the embargo was lifted in 1994, Senator McCain said, "I feel that we are finally putting the war behind us, as we have put every war behind us. A nation must do that, and I am grateful to have survived to see it when so many of my friends didn't."

On a small promontory known as Goldfish Islet stands **Tran Quoc Temple,** one of the oldest temples in Hanoi. Originally reserved for high-ranking court monks, this temple contains some unique statuary. The temple was removed to this location in the 17th century after Red River floodwaters started to eat away its foundations.

The causeway between the two lakes is host to a number of restaurants. Good fare can be found at **Banh Tom Restaurant**—you can sit inside a circular building, or outside under rooftop umbrellas and the branches of a huge tree. The specialty here is West Lake shrimpcake, shrimps cooked in batter. You can also order soup, fish, eel, snail, or rabbit. The snails come from West Lake. If you just want a drink, try the open-air Olympic Café facing West Lake, near the boat rentals. In this area you can hire a pedalboat or sculling boat; for longer forays across West Lake, try a speedboat or dragon boat. If you're feeling energetic, you could make a detour of a few hours out to Tay Ho Pagoda. The pagoda can also be reached by speedboat from the Olympic Café area.

Ten-Ton Buddha

Chances of getting lost along the next stretch are quite good, but persevere and keep asking for directions—you'll get there. If you loop around the back of Truc Bach Lake, you'll come to **Ngu Xa Temple,** which holds the largest bronze Buddha statue in Vietnam—10 tons of it. The 3.5-meter-high Buddha is cast in meditation pose. Ngu Xa is a bronze-working neighborhood where locals craft small Buddhas and other bronze objects.

Cycling southward you'll eventually reach Phan Dinh Phung Boulevard, an exclusive area with numerous finely restored French villas, and Cua Bac Church, a classic French church. Turning south on Hung Vuong Boulevard you'll have the entire roadway to yourself—only bicycles are allowed south of the Presidential Palace. When visiting hours for the

(continues on page 164)

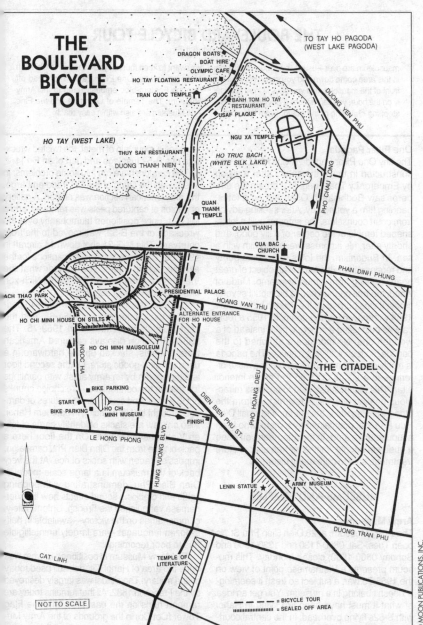

THE BOULEVARD BICYCLE TOUR

TO TAY HO PAGODA
(WEST LAKE PAGODA)

DRAGON BOATS
BOAT HIRE
OLYMPIC CAFE
HO TAY FLOATING RESTAURANT
TRAN QUOC TEMPLE
BANH TOM HO TAY RESTAURANT
USAF PLAQUE
NGU XA TEMPLE

DUONG YEN PHU

HO TAY (WEST LAKE)

THUY SAN RESTAURANT
DUONG THANH NIEN

HO TRUC BACH
(WHITE SILK LAKE)

QUAN THANH TEMPLE

QUAN THANH

PHO CHAU LONG

CUA BAC CHURCH

PHAN DINH PHUNG

ACH THAO PARK

PRESIDENTIAL PALACE

HOANG VAN THU

HO CHI MINH HOUSE ON STILTS
ALTERNATE ENTRANCE
FOR HO HOUSE

HO CHI MINH MAUSOLEUM

NGOC HA

THE CITADEL

PHO HOANG DIEU

BIKE PARKING

START
BIKE PARKING
HO CHI MINH MUSEUM
FINISH

DIEN BIEN PHU ST.

LE HONG PHONG

HUNG VUONG BLVD.

LENIN STATUE

ARMY MUSEUM

DUONG TRAN PHU

CAT LINH

TEMPLE OF LITERATURE

NOT TO SCALE

= BICYCLE TOUR
= SEALED OFF AREA

© MOON PUBLICATIONS, INC.

THE BOULEVARD BICYCLE TOUR
(continued)

mausoleum are over—usually by 1130—roadblocks in this area come down and you can cycle past the front of the mausoleum. If you pass in front precisely on the hour, you can witness a Soviet-style goose-stepping changing of the guard. From this point, if you want to keep touring, you can visit Ho Chi Minh Museum and the One Pillar Pagoda, or head off through Eastern-bloc embassy-land to the Army Museum. The Temple of Literature and the Fine Arts Museum are also within easy reach.

One Pillar Pagoda

The tiny One Pillar Pagoda (Chua Mot Cot) was constructed in the 11th century after a vision by Emperor Ly Thai Tong. In a dream the emperor saw Bodhisattva Quan Am on a lotus, handing him a young boy. After seeking advice from court counselors, the emperor built a lotus-shaped temple at the center of a lily pond, and shortly after, his empress presented him with a son. In Buddhism, the lotus represents purity and regeneration—the lotus is an object of great beauty arising from a muddy swamp. Made of wood, the frail pagoda had to be rebuilt several times; it was burned by the French before their 1954 withdrawal from Vietnam. In 1955 a replica was built using a concrete pillar instead of a wooden one. No monks are attached to the pagoda, so technically it's a shrine. The pagoda is highly revered, and childless couples make offerings to a statue of Quan Am on an interior altar. This place is also said to possess miraculous healing powers. A few meters from the One Pillar Pagoda is the entrance to small Dien Huu Pagoda, maintained by a monk who is an acupuncture expert. In the afternoon you'll see a queue of people waiting for free acupuncture treatment, said to cure many disorders.

MUSEUMS AND TEMPLES

Army Museum

The Army Museum, at 28 Dien Bien Phu St., is open Tues.-Sat. 0800-1130 and 1330-1600 and Sunday 0800-1500; closed Monday. This museum presents a Vietnamese point of view on the 1965-75 war, a subject so fresh it seemingly doesn't belong in a museum. You get an idea of what it must have been like living in Hanoi with B-52s flying overhead. In the central court-yard lies a mountain of metal, the twisted wreckage of a B-52 fuselage and part of an F-111.

The curators have run into some problems: in 1994, with the lifting of the US trade embargo, the anti-American section was altered. A gallery of photos of captured pilots was removed, and a MiG-21, once positioned triumphantly over the wreckage of the B-52, was moved to the front courtyard. This MiG-21 shot down 14 aircraft in 1967-68. There are few English captions for the exhibits, which makes you wonder what the Vietnamese references to Presidents Nich-xon and Gion-xon are all about.

The front salon focuses on the 1930-45 period, the back salon covers 1954-68, and the central salon concentrates on 1969-75. The 1954-68 section displays captured American fliers' helmets, stacked up like hardware in a used sporting-goods store. On the second floor is a gallery run by an army artist, with paintings for sale. In the central salon are choice chunks of US aircraft and some horrific pictures of damage wrought by US bombing in southern Hanoi. Also on view are stacks of identity cards of fallen Vietnamese soldiers. On the floor here a pack-bicycle from the Dien Bien Phu campaign, impossibly laden with sacks of rice. At the very back of the museum is a large scale-model of Dien Bien Phu, demonstrating with popping lights and crackling sound effects how the Vietnamese vanquished the French. Unfortunately, commentaries on the victory—available in half-a-dozen languages—are largely unintelligible due to poor recordings.

The Army Museum is positioned in what was once the area of Hanoi Citadel, still used today by the military. The citadel was largely destroyed by the French in 1882. All that remains today are rampart ruins on the east side, and the Flag Tower (Cot Co) in the grounds of the Army Museum. The hexagonal Flag Tower was built in 1812 and is a symbol of Hanoi, featured on maps and other items. In its day the tower was used for signaling outlying stations with lights. You can scramble to the top of the 60-meter-high turret for a fine view of the area.

Opposite the Army Museum is a park with the biggest *lien xo* in Vietnam—Vladimir Lenin. Although Lenin statues have toppled in Russia and many Eastern European countries, a few remain in far-flung places like Mongolia or Vietnam. As elsewhere in the communist world, Hanoians joke about this particular pose of Lenin. They point out that Lenin has his hands over his pockets—a dig at the cheapskate reputation of Russians in Vietnam.

Fine Arts Museum

Located at 38 Cao Ba Quat, the Fine Arts Museum is open 0800-1200 and 1300-1600 daily except Monday; entry is $1. The museum is housed in a colonial building that served as the Ministry of Information under the French, and contains three floors of sculpture, ceramics, and painting. On the top floor is an ethnology section with minority costumes, some Cham pieces, bronze drums (circa 1000 BC), stone lintels, and a fine 16th-century Quan Am statue with a forest of arms. On the second floor are paintings, ceramics, lacquerware, water puppets, folk art items, and an excellent display of 11th to 18th century Buddha statues.

The ground floor is devoted to painting. For almost 40 years Vietnamese painting was of the Social-Realism school, or "politically correct" art, featuring revolutionary fighters and happy peasants. Some examples can be found in the Fine Arts Museum, although such works are only a minor part of the collection. In modern Vietnam the style has been abandoned. At the Fine Arts Museum you'll find French-influenced work and modern and abstract themes. A shop sells sculpture and painting. Another wing of the Fine Arts Museum contains a sculpture salon, with antique wooden furniture on display upstairs.

Other Museums

In the vicinity of the Opera House is a glut of museums. The museums are usually open Tues.-Sun. 0800-1130 and 1330-1600. The

Revolutionary Museum at 25 Tong Dan St. tells the story of Vietnam's 1150-year struggle against the Chinese, French, Japanese, and Americans through gruesome displays of executions and torture devices. If you've seen the Ho Chi Minh Museum and the Army Museum, visiting this museum is overkill. The **History Museum,** down the street at 1 Pham Ngu Lao, covers Vietnam's Neolithic history, the arrival of Buddhism, and the unwelcome onset of the Chinese. The emphasis is on archaeology, with items culled from temples, citadels, and other sites throughout Vietnam, as well as other parts of Asia. The museum exhibits are difficult to decipher without a translator. For those interested in aerial warfare, the **Air Force Museum,** on Truong Chinh St. on the southern outskirts of Hanoi, showcases a variety of Russian planes, helicopters, and antiaircraft guns. During the war Truong Chinh St. was known as Chien Thang B-52.

Temple of Literature

Van Mieu, or the Temple of Literature, is Hanoi's best-preserved ancient site. The temple is long and narrow, and faces south, so you must go all the way to the southern entrance on Quoc Tu Giam Street. It's open daily from dawn to dusk.

Van Mieu is Vietnam's oldest institution of higher education, dating from the 11th century. Dedicated to Confucius, the temple served as a national university for more than 700 years, educating mandarins (high court officials). Confucianism managed to break the Buddhist monopoly on education at the time. Students at Van Mieu used an ideographic writing called *cho nho* based on Chinese characters. In 1802 Emperor Gia Long transferred the seat of learning to Hué. The system of recruiting civil servants ended in the north in 1915, and in Hué in 1919.

The Temple of Literature is divided into five walled courtyards with adjoining doors and porticos. Entering at Van Mieu Gate in the south, the path leads through gardens to bare courtyards where wooden hostels for teachers and students once stood. From here, gates enter into a garden with a collection of 82 stone stelae supported on massive tortoise pedestals. From the 15th to late 18th centuries, in the Le dynasty, triennial exams were held here—successful candidates had their names, birthdates, and deeds engraved on stone stelae. Van Mieu thus became a kind of shrine to honor scholars.

Continuing north you cross a paved courtyard and come to the House of Ceremonies, the main temple where sacrifices were offered to Confucius on the second and 10th lunar months. Two dragons adorn the rooftop, with a lunar disc between them. The temple is built on wooden pillars and is lacquered in bright red, with Chinese and Vietnamese motifs and features. Around the interior altar are incense burners mounted on cranes—symbols of longevity—and tortoises, as well as bonsai plants in Chinese pots. This section underwent major renovations in the 1920s, 1950s, and 1990s. The temple is still used by the University of Hanoi for Vietnamese literature lectures.

The northern part of the temple lies in ruins. It was originally the National Academy, an important seat of learning, but was destroyed by bombing in 1954.

At Tet, Van Mieu is the site of traditional celebrations, including "live" games of Chinese chess. In a practice that dates back to the 15th century, young people dressed in red or yellow outfits hold sticks indicating the piece they represent, and are moved on instructions of the players. The games take place in an open courtyard at Van Mieu.

Quan Su Pagoda

Important as a Buddhist educational institution is Quan Su (Ambassador) Pagoda, at 73 Quan Su Street. The temple was founded in the 17th century as a haven for visiting Buddhist scholars from as far afield as Cambodia and Laos. The present pagoda was constructed between 1936 and 1942 and is a major center for Buddhist instruction in Vietnam. Monks come from all over Vietnam to study here. Quan Su is headquarters of the North Vietnam Buddhist Association.

West Lake and Tay Ho Pagoda

Named after a lake in Hangzhou, China, of similar shape, West Lake covers an area of five square km and has a circumference of about 12 km. The lake was once the site of palaces for

emperors and lords, but all were destroyed during feudal wars. Today top party officials maintain luxurious villas on the quiet shores, and nouveau riche Vietnamese are moving in, too. Greedy joint-venture developers envisage an area bristling with hotels. Commercial uses of the lake range from fishing to flower growing. Fish-breeding cages are laid in the lake, yielding up to 600 tons of fish in a good season. Egrets, cranes, and wading birds visit as well. On the east side of the lake are large flower villages where roses and peach trees are grown.

For visitors, West Lake is associated with quiet recreation. You can bicycle around the shores of the lake or take a cruise. A good place to aim for is Tay Ho Pagoda, which can be reached by bike, or by boat from the Olympic Café area on the southeast side of the lake.

Boat Rentals: For a relaxing paddle in a small area designated by red flags, you can rent a sculling boat, pedalboat, or rowboat for under $1.50 an hour. To go further afield, you can rent a speedboat for $6-10 an hour—it takes about 15 minutes from here to Tay Ho Pagoda, one-way. Mock-imperial dragon boats cost $20 an hour for up to 15 passengers, or $40/hr for 16-40 passengers. For reservations, contact Olympic Café, tel. 257105. There's an extra charge for onboard food service or if you want to dress like a mandarin (for some reason, French tourists love to dress as mandarins and sit on dragon boats).

Tay Ho Pagoda: Tay Ho Pagoda is considered a popular lucky site of the wish-fulfilling variety. There is a large wall mosaic here—the lower section depicts the realm of the sea, the middle band shows the earth, and the top band depicts the sky. Offerings placed at the various shrines include candied lotus seed, sticky rice in red conical packets, eggs, miniature bottles of apricot brandy or vodka, cake, fruit, and roses. Muttering, sometimes crying, supplicants burn paper money at lakeside urns. On the alley leading to the pagoda are eateries that serve up aquatic snails from the lake, eaten with noodles and garnish. They also sell shrimpcakes—small shrimp fried in batter and sometimes mixed with sweet potato.

ACCOMMODATIONS

In 1990 there were only a handful of accommodations accepting foreigners in Hanoi. Now there are over 20 major hotels and 80 smaller hotels and guesthouses for foreign guests. There is still a chronic shortage of accommodations, however, and very little for budget travelers. The better hotels are often full, and some hotels in the moderate range—such as the Boss Hotel—are permanently occupied by businesses. If you don't reserve ahead, try to time your arrival for midday checkout to increase your chances of securing a good room. It's best to find a place to drop your luggage, then head off to search for a hotel. Peak tourist season—June to August—is especially difficult: you're also competing with vacationing Vietnamese at this time.

The room shortage has meant Hanoi hoteliers can jack up their prices to unreasonable levels. One alternative to this racket is to find a minihotel, usually family-run. Minihotels are going up as Hanoi residents discover they can profit by converting an old building or part of their home into lodgings. Prices range from $20 to $80 a room, depending on whether the place has air-conditioning, a minibar, and satellite TV. In the Old Quarter, narrow three- and four-story buildings sometimes have only two rooms to each floor—one at the front, one at the back. As part of a growing awareness of the city's architectural heritage, police have been instructed to ensure that housing development in this area is architecturally appropriate. This means new accommodations are supplied by renovating existing structures—which favors the rise of more minis.

Some important considerations for staying in Hanoi: hot water in winter, air-con in summer, secure luggage storage if going out of town, and advance reservation if returning from a trip out of town. Luxury hotels charge a 10% government tax and 5-10% for service; be wary of a six percent surcharge for use of a credit card. Room prices may include breakfast.

The largest hotel operator in Hanoi is Hanoi Tourism, which owns seven hotels, including the Bong Sen and Hoa Binh, and has a share in the Sofitel Metropole. There are a number of hotel projects underway, including the 300-room SAS Park Hotel, the 394-room Lien West Lake Resort, and the Horizon Hotel.

OLD QUARTER

In this zone, north of Hoan Kiem Lake, minihotels and guesthouses have lots of character. These are two- or three-story structures; some may be five stories high. Smaller places can be like living in someone's house, with the gates locked between 2300 and 0500. Guesthouse owners sometimes run small restaurants and rent bicycles.

Guesthouse/Budget
Traveler cafés offer some rudimentary accommodations with shared bath facilities. **Queen Café,** at 65 Hang Bac, has 10 rooms for $5-8; rooms are cramped with paper-thin walls and shared hot shower facilities. **Darling Café Hanoi,** at 33 Hang Quat, offers six doubles at $10 each. Nearby **Tourist Café,** at 6 To Tich, has a few rooms with bath for $8-12. **Ta Hien Guesthouse,** at 22 Ta Hien St., tel. 255888, has 11 rooms for $10 (fan), $12 (phone), and $15 (air-con)—recommended. **46 LNQ Guesthouse,** 46 Luong Ngoc Quyen, tel. 256948, has nine rooms for $12-20 and its own small restaurant. Opposite is **Nha Khach 55,** at 55 Luong Ngoc Quyen, tel. 268539—half a dozen soulless and windowless rooms for $10 and up. **My Kinh Hotel,** 72 Hang Buom, tel. 255726, has 22 rooms for $10-20-30. At the edge of the Old Quarter is **Dong Do Guesthouse,** 27 Tong Duy Tan St., tel. 233275, with rooms for $15-50.

Especen Minihotels
Especen, a private organization with French, Australian, and American partners, runs 10 minihotels—some around the lake, some tucked into the Old Quarter. The minis range from five to 16 rooms, with a total of 80 rooms available. Prices range from $10 to $15 with shared bathroom, and $20-40 with air-con and bath included, and are a good value. The front doors are closed

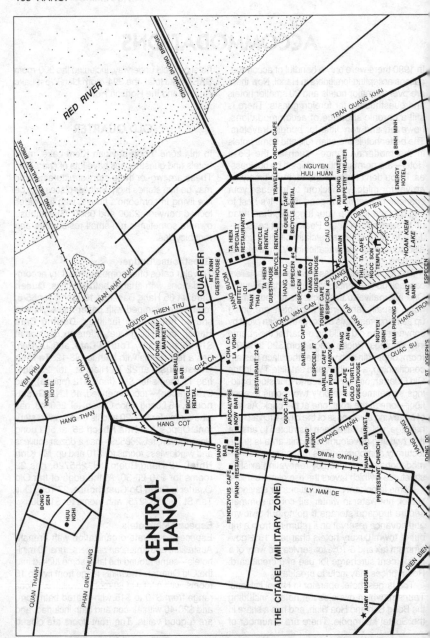

N KHANH DU

HISTORY MUSEUM

REVOLUTIONARY MUSEUM

OPERA HOUSE

GMD/ARMY HOTEL

MINIBUSES TO NORTHEAST

LE THANH TONG

TONG DAN

CAFE DE PARIS

ITALIAN EMBASSY

CLUB OPERA

BICYCLE RENTAL

NATIONAL BANK

HANOI TOURISM

PHAN CHU TRINH

LO DUC

HOA MA

POST OFFICE

GOVERNMENT GUESTHOUSE

FORMER TONKIN GOVERNOR'S OFFICES

IDD/TELECOM

METROPOLE

LOTUS RESTAURANT

BODEGA CAFE

TRANG TIEN

TRANG TIEN

DAN CHU HOTEL

SMILING PUB

LE BISTROT

HOAN KIEM HOTEL

NGO QUYEN

LE TRACH

BAC NAM

BODEGA I

BODEGA

HAI BA TRUNG

HOA BINH

HUU

LE VAN

HANG BAI

HANG KHAY

SOPHIA GUESTHOUSE

AIR FRANCE BICYCLE RENTAL

MOTORCYCLE SHOPS

HOAN KIEM DISTRICT

VIETNAM TOURISM

IMMIGRATION POLICE

BA TRIEU

FRENCH EMBASSY

RESTAURANT 202

ESPECEN #6

PHU GIA

LE THAI TO

NHA CHUNG

TOURISTS' MEETING CAFE

NGO DU

LOTUS GUESTHOUSE

GREEN BAMBOO CAFE-BAR

NGUYEN THAI HOC

VIETNAM AIRLINES (INTERNATIONAL BOOKINGS)

LY THUONG KIET

LAO VISA SECTION

VIETNAM AIRLINES (DOMESTIC)

NGUYEN DU

CANADIAN EMBASSY

19 DECEMBER MARKET

TRAN HUNG DAO

CAMBODIAN EMBASSY

BOSS HOTEL

THIEN QUANG LAKE

LENIN PARK

A LITTLE ITALIAN

QUAN SU PAGODA

QUAN SU

TRAN BINH TRONG

VIP CLUB

HOAN KIEM GUESTHOUSE

INDOCHINE

DONG LOI

ROSE HOTEL

SAIGON HOTEL

AUSTRALIAN EMBASSY

PHAN BOI CHAU

CAPITAL HOTEL

LAOTIAN EMBASSY

CIRCUS ARENA

LE DUAN

HANOI RAILWAY STATION

30-4 HOTEL

BLUE

250 m

0

© MOON PUBLICATIONS, INC.

around 2300—you have to ring the front bell after that. Especen's head office is at 79E Hang Trong St., to the west side of Hoan Kiem Lake, tel. 266856, fax 269612. In the Old Quarter are the following hotels. **Especen #4,** at 16 Trung Yen St., tel. 261512, combines three Old Quarter buildings for a total of 16 rooms—$8-10 with shared bath, and a few rooms for $20 with hot water, air-con, and fridge (triples possible). **Especen #5,** at 10A Dinh Liet St., tel. 253069, has five rooms for $10-12 with outside bath. **Especen #7,** at 23 Hang Quat St., tel. 251301, has five rooms for $25-30. **Especen #3,** at 5 To Tich, tel. 260879, features 14 rooms in the $8-25 range.

Moderate Minis

Phung Hung, 2 Duong Thanh St., tel. 265556, is a minihotel run by the Hanoi Tourism Service Company (TOSERCO) with rooms for $20-30. **Gold Turtle** (Kim Quy), 38 Hang Hom St., tel. 243944, fax 260082, has five rooms for $30 each. **Quoc Hoa,** 10 Bat Dat St., tel. 232528, fax 267424, is a family-run minihotel with rooms for $25-32 and superior rooms for $45-65. **Trang An Hotel,** 58 Hang Gai, tel. 261135, fax 258511, is a narrow five-story structure with 10 rooms in the $45-75 range with air-con and TV.

HOAN KIEM DISTRICT

Budget

Lotus GH, 42V Ly Thuong Kiet, has a few rooms for $6-12. A dorm setup costs $4 a bed. The small guesthouse is run by a doctor and his family. The entire block here is numbered 42—with 42A, 42B, 42C, and so on—which means 42V is toward the west end. **Trang Tien Hotel,** 35 Trang Tien, tel. 256341, fax 251416, offers 14 rooms for $8-10 with outside bath, and 32 rooms for $20-40 with bath and air-con. **Bodega I,** 57 Trang Tien, tel. 267784, fax 267787, rents 18 rooms for $25-30. On the ground floor is a café; the next floor is a restaurant; the top floor is the hotel. Three blocks along 41 Hang Bai St. is **Bodega II,** with six rooms for $15-20. **Sophia GH,** 6 Hang Bai St., tel. 253069, has dilapidated rooms for $20—you might be able to reduce the price by bargaining.

Green Bamboo, 42 Nha Chung St., tel./fax 264949, consists of a handful of rooms for $12 d

or $15 t including bath with hot water. **Guesthouse 8,** at 8 Nha Chung, tel. 268500, has rooms for $8 and up. **Guest House Culture** (Nha Khach Van Hoa), 22A Hai Ba Trung, tel. 253044, features doubles for $10-15 and triples as low as $10. The guesthouse is one block south of Hoan Kiem Lake, set off the street through a passageway; bicycle rentals available. West of Hoan Kiem are **Especen #1,** at 76 Hang Trong, tel. 266856, with rooms for $20-30; **Especen #2,** 59 Hang Trong St., tel. 251346; and **Especen #9** at 9A Phan Chu Trinh.

Moderate/Luxury

To the west side of the lake are the following hotels. **Phu Gia,** 136 Hang Trong St., tel. 255493, fax 259207, has 50 rooms for $25-30-50 in an older-style four-story hotel. The front rooms include views over Hoan Kiem Lake. **Nam Phuong,** 16 Bao Khanh St., Hoan Kiem, tel. 258030, fax 258964, is a cheap and clean minihotel located one block from Hoan Kiem Lake. Rooms are $20-35 d with air-con and hot water. **Thien Trang,** 24 Nha Chung St., tel. 269823, is a reasonably priced minihotel; bicycle rentals available.

To the south side of the lake lie the following hotels. **Bac Nam Hotel,** 20 Ngo Quyen, tel. 267877, fax 268998, is a private hotel with 19 rooms for $25-40-50 and two suites for $70. **Hoan Kiem Hotel,** 25 Tran Hung Dao, tel. 254204, has rooms for $40-55. **Hoa Binh Hotel** (Peace), 27 Ly Thuong Kiet, tel. 253315, fax 269818, offers 120 air-con rooms for $18-50-73 s, $22-43-55 d, and suites for $92. This hotel has been in business since 1923 and features real French ambience—lobby with revolving doors, original mirrors and staircases, top-floor bar. It underwent major renovation in 1993 and is very popular with French group tours. The hotel also operates a 16-room villa. **Dan Chu** (Souvenir Hotel), 29 Trang Tien, tel. 254937, fax 266786, is a renovated French hotel with 41 rooms for $60-100 standard and $90-110 suite.

Facing Thien Quang Lake is the **Boss Hotel** at 60 Nguyen Du St., tel. 265859, fax 257634. This business hotel consists of 25 rooms but usually only half are available; rates $60-70 d. Businesses like SOS International and Pacific Airlines operate from here; the place is run by Oscan Enterprises, a tour operator. The hotel is small, modern, and includes business center and VIP lounge.

To the east side of Hoan Kiem are the following hotels. **Binh Minh Hotel,** 27 Le Thai To, tel. 266441, fax 266442, has good rooms for $30-40. **Energy Hotel** (Nan Luong), 30 Le Thai To, tel. 253167, fax 259226, is run by the Ministry of Energy. Rooms cost $30-55. **Government Guesthouse,** 2 Le Thach St., tel. 255801, fax 259227, has 44 rooms for $45-75, featuring French decor in spacious rooms. This building is located in the back wing of what was once an office and residence complex of the Governor of Tonkin. The front wing, on Ngo Quyen, opposite the Metropole Hotel, is reserved for VIPs and diplomats.

Popular with foreign businesspeople, Army Guesthouse and Army Hotel, run by the Ministry of Defense, have a total of 84 rooms between them. The **Army Guesthouse** (a.k.a. Guesthouse of the Ministry of Defense, or GMD-33A), at 33A Pham Ngu Lao, tel. 265540, fax 265539, has 40 doubles for $44-70 and three suites for $80-100. Facilities include a business center. At the opposite end of the compound is the **Army Hotel,** 33C Pham Ngu Lao, tel. 252896, fax 259276, with 49 rooms $41-62. Rooms feature air-con, satellite TV, and fridge. Between the two hotels is a VIP wing—an old colonial mansion reserved for state guests.

Super Luxury

Pullman Sofitel Metropole, 15 Ngo Quyen St., tel. 266919, fax 266920, has 109 rooms, with rates $160-210 for rooms and $220-360 for suites. Add $25 for double occupancy. As the only luxury-class hotel in Hanoi, the Metropole is heavily booked. Reservations at least one month in advance are advised. The Metropole is the grande dame of Hanoi hotels. It first opened in 1911, and underwent extensive renovations in the early 1990s as part of a joint-venture with

the French group Accor. Added creature comforts include individually controlled air-conditioning, satellite TV, in-house video, and room safes. The Metropole is a Hanoi meeting point—visitors and travelers come for afternoon tea, to read international newspapers kept at the bar, use the pool, or sample the superb French cuisine. The hotel also features office space, with Singapore Airlines, Malaysia Airlines, and a helicopter service onsite. The Metropole has contracted for a $34-million 135-room expansion with new office space.

OTHER AREA ACCOMMODATIONS

Truc Bach Lake

A little north of the Old Quarter is the Truc Bach Lake area, with a few moderately priced places. **Especen #8,** at 42 Chau Long St. to the east side of the lake, tel. 236890, has 15 rooms. Southeast of the lakes, **Hong Ha Hotel** (Red River Hotel), at 78 Yen Phu, tel. 254911, offers

---

HANOI HILTON BECOMES A HOTEL

In the spring of 1973, *New York Times* reporter Malcolm Browne flew into Hanoi from Vientiane to visit the "Hanoi Hilton," the infamous prison where US airmen were held and interrogated. Foreign press correspondents had been invited in for a day to witness the release of the last group of American POWs. The correspondents strolled through the Hanoi Hilton, but were not allowed to talk to the stony faced prisoners, standing at attention in their purple-and-pink-striped prison garb. Browne records that "simply being in the enemy's capital and politely shaking their hands with smiling officials wearing green pith helmets was the strangest experience of all."

The Hanoi Hilton, where downed American airmen were interned and tortured, is known to the Vietnamese as Hoa Lo. It was a former French prison in downtown Hanoi, where the French interned and tortured Vietnamese activists. Until 1994 the building was used as a Vietnamese prison. At the end of 1994, workers began knocking down the walls of Hoa Lo to make way for a 22-story hotel and office complex, a Singapore joint-venture project called Hanoi Towers. The $60-million tower will include 204 hotel apartments, office space, shops, and a convention center, and is scheduled for completion in 1997. Building on the site was delayed because of a campaign to save the historic building—under the French many north Vietnamese leaders were held in this prison. A compromise was reached: a monument will honor the memory of Vietnamese nationalists imprisoned at Hoa Lo.

doubles for $20-35, as well as a few lower-priced rooms. **Bong Sen** (Lotus), 34 Hang Bun St., tel. 254017, fax 233232, has 26 rooms with air-con, TV, and fridge for $43-50-60. **Huu Nghi** (Friendship), 23 Quan Thanh, tel. 253182, fax 259272, features 38 air-con rooms for $35-60.

Railway Station Area
Budget/Moderate: 30-4 Hotel, 115 Tran Hung Dao St., tel. 260807, fax 252611, is right opposite the station; the place has 24 rooms for $6-8 and five rooms for $30 each. **Nat Phuong,** 39 Le Duan, tel. 2503765, is a minihotel with five rooms for $15 s or $25-30 d. **Anh Duong GH,** at 33 Le Duan, tel. 265220, is a six-room guesthouse with rooms for $15-20-50. **Hoan Kiem GH,** 76 Hai Ba Trung, tel. 268944, has $20 doubles. Do not confuse this place with the pricier Hoan Kiem Hotel.

Moderate/Luxury: Capital Hotel (Thu Do), 109 Tran Hung Dao St., tel. 261266, fax 261121, offers 27 rooms for $50-70. The front desk rents bicycles. **Dong Loi,** at 94 Ly Thuong Kiet St. on the corner of Le Duan, tel. 255721, fax 267999, has 30 rooms for $50 single or double, and two suites for $72 each. Operated by TOSERCO and built in the 1930s, this place has character—spiral staircase, molded ceilings, and art nouveau light fixtures. **Rose Hotel** (Hoa Hong), 20 Phan Boi Chau, tel. 254438, fax 254437, offers 21 elegant rooms in the $40-60 range. **Saigon Hotel,** 80 Ly Thuong Kiet St., tel. 268499, fax 266631, has 44 rooms for $80-105 (for double occupancy add $15); suites for $150. The hotel features a business center, rooftop terrace bar, and satellite TV. It's a joint venture between Saigon Tourist and the National Railway Company, with a Hanoi Taxi rank out front.

Farther north, just east of the railway tracks, are several hotels. **Blue II Hotel,** 6 Dinh Ngang, tel. 233541, fax 236393, is a four-story minihotel with eight rooms for $40-80 with air-con, StarTV, fridge, and phone. Nearby is **Alpo Minihotel,** at 9 Nguyen Thai Hoc, tel. 232770, fax 232770, with eight rooms on five floors for $35-40 s or $70-80 d.

Ba Dinh District
Budget/Moderate: Just west of the railway tracks is **Quoc Tu Giam Hotel,** 27 Quoc Tu Giam, tel. 257106, fax 257691, with several rooms for $15, 16 air-con rooms for $30, and two suites for $45 each. Also in this area are **Mai Anh Hotel,** 109A Nguyen Thai Hoc, tel. 232702, with rooms for $20-40; and **Sao Mai Hotel,** 17 Thong Phong Alley, tel. 255827, with doubles for $20 and up. **Dong Loi Mini,** 70 Nguyen Khuyen St., tel. 259173, offers $20 doubles. **Trang An GH,** 46 Hang Chao St., tel. 232837, has doubles for $15 and up—the family here is helpful.

Farther west of the Army Museum is **La Thanh Hotel,** at 218 Doi Can St., tel. 257057. This rambling 100-room place has standard rooms for $20 (some lower than that), and superior rooms with TV and fridge for $30-40. The hotel is four km from town—the front desk can rent you a bicycle or a car with driver.

Giang Vo Lake
Budget/Moderate: Still in the Ba Dinh District, but over three km from town, is a cluster of highrise hotels around Giang Vo Lake. The cheap hotel of the area, patronized by Vietnamese, is **Giang Vo Hotel,** A1 Giang Vo, tel. 256598, with several hundred rooms in five-story apartment blocks. Rooms range from $10 to $20 and up. **Dong Do Hotel,** Giang Vo St., tel. 351382, fax 334228, has 20 single rooms for $45 (add $10 for doubles), and four rooms for $60-90. On the top floor is the Sunset Bar. **Orient** (Phuong Dong), 23 Lang Ha St., tel. 345397, fax 246396, farther out from Giang Vo Lake to the southwest, rents rooms for $50-90.

Luxury/Super Luxury: Hanoi Heritage Hotel, 80 Giang Vo St., tel. 344727, fax 351458, has 41 rooms. Most are $85-95 s, while some deluxe rooms run $110 s; add $15 for double occupancy. This is a Singapore joint-venture hotel, favored by foreign businesspeople for its atmosphere. The hotel features a restaurant with Asian cuisine, and the Club Bleu nightclub with karaoke booths.

Super luxury **Hanoi Hotel,** D8 Giang Vo St., tel. 252240, fax 259209, is a 10-story hotel with 76 rooms—rates vary $120-160 standard, and $200-400 suite. Rooms include minibar and satellite TV. This Hong Kong joint venture involved the renovation of a 10-year-old building at a cost of $6 million. Hanoi Hotel encompasses a business center, tennis court, nightclub, and a large Chinese restaurant.

Lenin Park Area

Staying in the southern end of Hanoi is not recommended—it's the junkyard of the city—but the Lenin Park area is not too bad. East of Lenin Park are two moderate hotels: **Viet Long**, 116A Tue Tinh St., tel. 226499; and **Especen #6**, at 30 Mai Hac De St., tel. 265697. Way down south toward Giap Bat Bus Terminal is the **Queen Hotel**, 189 Giai Phong St., tel. 291237, with rooms for $30-45.

West Lake

West Lake is an exclusive villa zone about five km north of the city center. You need transport to commute. In the future this zone will see a lot of hotel building; some minihotels are also going up in the area, with much lower prices. **Thang Loi Hotel**, Yen Phu St., tel. 268211, fax 252800, has 175 rooms for $57-63 s and $74-81 d, with

suites $90-120. The main wing, built as a gift from Cuba in 1975, is an uninspiring concrete blockhouse; nearby are some traditional bamboo bungalows. The hotel occupies a landscaped site on a peninsula jutting into West Lake, with swimming pool and tennis courts. There's a nightly disco from 2000 to midnight; Sunday is the big night out.

Tay Ho Hotel, Nghi Tam St., tel. 232380, fax 232390, has 118 air-con rooms and 27 suites, with satellite TV and business center. Rooms cost $55 s, $70 d. **Ho Tay Villas**, tel. 258241, has 68 rooms in the $40-55 range. It was once the Communist Party Guesthouse but is now open to those who can afford the rates. If there's a conference in progress, the place may be booked. Another hotel out on West Lake peninsula is **Quang Ba Trade Union GH**, tel. 263834, fax 263825, with 85 rooms and three villas.

FOOD

RESTAURANTS

There are many places to eat in Hanoi, but not much variation in the menus. Vegetarians visiting Hanoi often complain they're the same half-dozen dishes over and over again. French-style cooking caters mainly to foreigners (read: expensive). Most Hanoi restaurants serve a palatable but unimaginative mix of Vietnamese, Chinese, and European cuisine. You won't find the variety of food available in Saigon, but with some persistence, culinary experiences are still to be had. Poke around and you'll find good, cheap, tasty Vietnamese food. Arrive early for dinner, as many Hanoi restaurants get underway at 1800 and close by 2100. A few Western-oriented restaurants stay open to 2200 or 2300. A good test of restaurants is to see how many cyclos are out front—if there are a lot waiting, it must be good.

An interesting feature of Hanoi restaurants is that they're often family-run and operate from converted two-story dwellings with the family living in the same quarters. This gives a place a real homey feel—true of Restaurant 22, Bittet Loi, and Restaurant 202. Naming a restaurant after the street number is a Russian idea—no pretentious bourgeois address.

Snakes and snails and puppy dog tails are sometimes featured on specialty restaurant menus—so avoid or seek out as befits your state of mind or palate. Hot dog means something quite different in Hanoi—dog meat is a delicacy, believed to enhance stamina in men. There is a string of shacks along the lower east side of West Lake that specialize in dog, eaten at certain times of the month. In the Old Quarter, at 7 Hang Phen, is Bac Hai, a restaurant solely devoted to the parts of the cow. Aquatic snails from West Lake are eaten particularly at Tay Ho Pagoda, along with West Lake shrimpcakes. Snakes from the village of Le Mat sometimes pop up on the menu.

Old Quarter

In this area are lots of small eateries and pubs, intimate places located in converted houses. **Cha Ca La Vong**, at 14 Cha Ca, has no sign and no menu, and the chefs only prepare one dish. At the table you'll get a charcoal brazier and a boneless river fish in a fry pan, usually enough for two people. You sprinkle herbs, shallots, and peanuts on the fish, add the mix to cold noodles, spice it with chili sauce, and Bob's your uncle. Tasty! Costs about $5 a head. This place can be crowded. Down the street, **Restau-**

rant 22 at 22 Hang Can St. (2nd and 3rd floors), tel. 267160, serves Viet-French food. Quality varies with the chef—from good to mediocre.

Along Ta Hien are a number of specialty restaurants serving rabbit, goat, snake, and turtle. These places are busy at night—especially numbers 11, 13, 17, and 19 Ta Hien. **Bittet Loi** (Loi's Beefsteak), 51 Hang Buom St., tel. 251211, is open daily from 1600. It's a small place, packed at night. Serves beefsteak, prawn, pigeon, and crab. Good service—you can see dishes being prepared in Loi's kitchen. Excellent for steak and fries smothered in a scrumptious garlic sauce.

Piano Restaurant, 50 Hang Vai St., tel. 232423, serves French-style dishes in an old mansion with live piano music at night. Sounds good until you experience erratic service and see the small portions. Seafood is pricey and. Better value is nearby **Hoang Nam Restaurant** at 46 Hang Vai St., tel. 23243, a small place serving Hanoi dishes. Around the corner is the **Piano Bar and Restaurant** at 93 Phung Hung, serving Vietnamese and Western food; live music at night.

Nguyen Sinh, 17 Ly Quoc Su, tel. 265234, is situated down an alley. Downstairs is a deli with cold cuts, pâté, pickles, and juice—good for breakfast. There are two small dining rooms upstairs a the back; on the menu is stuffed eel, mushroon rabbit, stir-fried goat, squid, and steamed fish Mixed reviews; service can be slow.

Street Treats

Many Hanoi streets feature impromptu food stalls. To the southwest fringe of the Old Quar ter, near the railway tracks, is some unique street food, with both indoor seating and street side seating at tiny wooden stools. The stalls are mostly clustered around Tong Duy Tan Street Cam Chi Street offers stir-fried food and noodles for about 50 cents a dish. You can buy from any of the stalls and take the fare to anothe stall to sit down. Cam Chi means "Forbidden Way"—the street once led to a gate to Hano Citadel.

The western extension of Tong Duy Tan Street becomes Ga Tan. This avenue specializes in medicinal chicken or beef soup for around 60 cents a serving. You get soup, bread and chicken pieces. In the soup are lotus seeds spinach, dates, ginger, and herbs—a booster for those cold winter days. On really cold days patrons purchase a shot glass of whiskey.

Farther south, nearer the railway station, is Nam Ngu Street which is full of noodle stalls. You can get yellow noodles, white noodles, flat noodles, clear noodles, thin vermicelli, and soups. Indochine Restaurant is also on this street.

Hoan Kiem District

Restaurants in this zone are moderate to high-priced. Western food comes with a Western price tag, and seafood is also pricey. Pizza can cost $4-8 depending on size; a dish of crab might run $7.

Indochine, 16 Nam Ngu, tel. 246097, is located in an alley near Saigon Hotel. The restaurant occupies a renovated historic building and serves Vietnamese cuisine with particular

---

BEETLE ESSENCE

If you ask for it, your server at Cha Ca Restaurant at 14 Cha Ca Street will bring you a special flavoring. It's a liquid made from the scent gland of an insect known as *ca cuoúg*—a member of the Coleoptera (or beetle) order. The highly prized secretion has a fruity aroma. At Cha Ca, it is dispensed with an eyedropper from a glass vial, and you're charged by the drop. The beetle is found only in the summer in the north, and the gland from one beetle produces only three or four drops. One hundred beetles must be harvested to produce a small vial of the liquid, which explains the 2000-dong-a-drop price tag.

At number 17 Cha Ca St. is Tuyet Nhung restaurant, which bases its business around beetle liquid. Sometimes it's mixed with fish sauce or chili sauce—as a dip for fish, chicken, pork, or beef dishes, or as a condiment in bowls of noodles. The small restaurant keeps frozen specimens of the insect in jars, and sells vials of the liquid. An artificial liquid is produced in Thailand, called Maengdana. But for gourmets there's a big difference between real and artificial—something akin to the difference between fresh and canned fruit.

noodlehouse serving special beetle sauce

section. Dishes are overpriced and portions small. **Lotus Restaurant,** 16 Ngo Quyen (on the 4th floor above the art galleries, opposite the Metropole), tel. 267618, is a large salon with a garden terrace. It serves Vietnamese food including Hanoi specialties. Prices are double those of other restaurants in the area, but the place is often booked. East of the Opera House is an upscale restaurant called **Au Palmier** on Dac Thai Than Street.

Le Beaulieu is the Metropole's top restaurant—for reservations call 266919, ext. 8028. This high-class restaurant serves French and Asian cuisine and features the best wine selection in Vietnam.

Other Areas

Ba Dinh District: Quoc Tu Giam, close to the hotel of the same name, on the street of the same name, enjoys a good reputation. It serves crab, eel, snail, and other specialty dishes. **Phuong Nam** on Giang Vo St. is popular with Vietnam Tourism guides.

East of Lenin Park: Restaurant 202, at 202A Hué St., tel. 259487, offers excellent Vietnamese, French, and Chinese cuisine at reasonable prices. Can be expensive for seafood; often packed in the evening. In the same area, east of Lenin Park, is **Viet Phuong,** at 4 Mai Hac De St., with a delicious array of roast rabbit, eel soup, steamed crab, meat-stuffed tomatoes, and pork rolls. There are cheap foodstalls on the southern end of Mai Hac De Street.

West Lake: There are a number of floating restaurants on the strip between West Lake and Truc Bach Lake, but the food is generally under par and overpriced. The best of the bunch is the nonfloating **Banh Tom Ho Tay,** a circular restaurant with a rooftop terrace. It's a pleasant place with good fare—eat outside under umbrellas, or inside if the weather is cold. The specialty of the house is West Lake shrimpcake.

CAFES AND BAKERIES

French habits linger in Hanoi, with cafés serving baguettes, drip-filter coffee, and even croissants and creme caramel. Doyen of the pastry shops is **Café 252** (a.k.a. Café Kinh Do), at

care given to presentation. Two chefs—one from Hanoi, the other from Saigon—ensure a mouthwatering selection of dishes from north, south, and central Vietnam. Open for lunch from 1030, and dinner from 1700. **Le Bistrot,** 34 Tran Hung Dao, tel. 266136, caters to the expat crowd, and dishes can get expensive. The restaurant features a French menu and French decor—the food is good, and the atmosphere pleasant. There's a downstairs section and two upstairs salons. Among the hotel restaurants in the area, the one at **Phu Gia** is recommended.

A Little Italian, 81 Tho Nhuom St., tel. 258167, is open for lunch and dinner. Unlike most Hanoi restaurants, it's open until 2300 during the week and midnight on Friday and Saturday. The restaurant serves pizza and pasta and features a cocktail bar. The restaurant's name refers to the owner's part-Italian ancestry. **Ho Guoi,** 17 Trang Tien, tel. 250625, is also a bar and restaurant, with an upstairs

252 Hang Bong, open 0700 to midnight. You can get an excellent breakfast here for under $2. The small café is family-run—Mr. Le Huu Chi and his sons and daughter make their own cheese, croissants, and cakes by hand. The house specialty is fresh-ground coffee with real milk, brought by bicycle from a dairy farm outside Hanoi every day. Excellent house cheese, fresh orange juice, fresh cream, chocolate cake, and éclairs. On the wall is a picture of a celebrity customer, Catherine Deneuve, after whom Mr. Chi named his yogurt. Down the street at 246 Hang Bong is **Bao Ngoc Café,** also popular.

In the Old Quarter, traveler cafés such as **Darling Café,** at 4 Hang Quat, and **Queen Café,** at 65 Hang Bac, serve banana pancakes, yogurt, fruit salad, fruit shakes, and noodles at low prices. Hang Than St., north on the perimeter of the Old Quarter, specializes in *banh com,* a kind of sticky rice filled with coconut and lotus seeds.

By the side of Hoan Kiem Lake is **Thuy Ta Café.** The food is boring, but the views of the lake and quiet ambience make up for it. Another place with views of the lake lies farther south. There is a second-floor deck in the building on the corner of Le Thai To and Hang Trong streets: the place houses **Cherry Blossom Inn,** a Japanese Restaurant, and **Five Royal Fish,** serving pizza, hamburgers, and Vietnamese food.

Trang Tien Hotel, at 35 Trang Tien St., features a ground-floor coffee shop that's good for breakfast. A tiny bakery here dispenses bread and cakes straight onto the street—great ice cream. The **Bodega Café,** on the ground floor of 57 Trang Tien, mimics a dimly lit Halong Bay grotto. This place is a student hangout—the spring rolls are good, the ice cream is okay, but the rest is fairly bland. French pastry addicts will be drawn to the Metropole Hotel's patisserie. The counter sells expensive goods that are delicious. The chefs make their own pastries, chocolate cake, pâté, and ice cream on the premises.

NIGHTLIFE

Cafés and bars are the nightlife in Hanoi. Hanoi dies after dark—the streets are deserted by 2300. The city is so bereft of nightlife that various embassies organize their own beery get-togethers, alternating each week. You need inside knowledge or an invitation to crash an embassy function. In the basement of the German Embassy at 29 Tran Phu is a small restaurant serving schnitzel, open weekends only.

Cultural Shows
Water puppetry is unique to Hanoi and the Red River Delta. There are several venues to see this fantastic art form in Hanoi (see the special topic "Water Puppetry"). The National Theater (Opera House) stages performances of traditional theater and music and offers concerts by visiting artists. Fare could include a Cuban flamenco guitarist, Hungarian folk dance troupe, or Shakespearean performance.

The Circus
Hanoi's Big Top is located in a circular concrete building in the northwest corner of Lenin Park. Performers seem to derive their inspiration from Groucho Marx rather than Karl. Acts are amateurish and often hilarious, with out-of-control monkeys, an uncooperative elephant, and flawless performing dogs. See also a variety of jugglers, contortionists, gymnasts, and acrobats. Tickets are cheap. Inquire through your hotel for performance times—the troupe could be on tour in other parts of the country.

Bars and Pubs
Nightspots in Hanoi are small; the venues are crosses between bars, cafés, bistros, and pubs. In the Old Quarter are several venues. **Tintin Pub,** 14 Hang Non, is run by Darling Café and serves all kinds of beer; the bar is decorated with Tintin T-shirts and is open 1900-0100, sometimes to 0200. **Art Café,** at 57 Hang Non, open 0900 to midnight, is a cocktail bar with a pleasant European atmosphere and tasteful music. The bar serves pizza, spaghetti, red wine, and beer; it's a family-run place—the owners have a couple of large dogs. **Apocalypse Now,** 46 Hang Vai, is open from 1700 and serves beer and snacks, but is not very lively. The bar is cousin to the infamous bar of the

same name in Saigon, trying to work the same formula, but not quite succeeding. Nearby are the two **Piano Bars**—the one at 50 Hang Vai is more of a restaurant, and the other, round the corner at 93 Phung Hung, is more a bar. Both offer live music in the evening, which is just as well since the food is mediocre and the service slow. Farther north, at 53 Hang Luoc St., is the **Emerald Bar,** an Irish pub serving Guinness and Scottish malts, as well as bangers and mash, hamburgers, and shepherd's pie in a Gaelic interior. You can play pool or darts; the bar is open till midnight.

In the Hoan Kiem District prices rise to $2 or $3 a drink and up, with food prices to match. The ritzy **Smiling Pub** is upstairs at 27 Trang Tien; around the corner is **Bar-Café Ruou.** At 59 Le Thai To is the upscale **Club Opera,** a businessperson's venue with drinks and a limited Western menu (croque sandwich, spaghetti, steak). Inside the Metropole Hotel is **Le Club,** where you can indulge in a fixed-price afternoon tea with pastries from 1500 to 1730; at night there's live music—traditional Vietnamese, classical, or jazz. The Metropole also features the poolside **Bamboo Bar** with exotic fruit cocktails and ice cream sundaes, and a barbecue in the evening. Over at 81 Tho Nhuom Street is **A Little Italian,** which is a restaurant but also a bar—you can sit in an open courtyard on $2 drinks. Much cheaper for a rendezvous is the

Starlight Bar, upstairs at the **Green Bamboo Café** at 42 Nha Chung—the bar is a combination pub and traveler café.

To the south of town is **Café de Paris,** 16 Nguyen Cong Tru, run by Vietnam Tourism, and featuring French decor. To the west side of town is the **Sunset Pub,** on the top floor of Dong Do Hotel on Giang Vo St., tel. 351382. It's open 1700-0100 or 0200 and serves drinks, pizza, and hamburgers.

Karaoke and Disco
Hanoi has little in the disco or karaoke line. Nightlife is more invested in *bia om,* or "beercuddle" bars, which are small places with hostesses. **Saigon Pull,** 217 Doi Can, is an entertainment complex with Chinese restaurant, bar, and top-floor disco; there's a $4 cover charge. The **VIP Club** next to the Boss Hotel is a multimedia entertainment center with disco, karaoke cubicles, and bar. Cover charge is $5—this is probably the closest to a Western-style disco in Hanoi. Downtown, near St. Joseph's Cathedral, is the **Palace,** a dance venue; **Kiku** Japanese restaurant is in the same complex. Otherwise, karaoke and disco venues occupy larger hotels. The **Dong Loi** and **Hanoi Heritage** Hotels feature karaoke lounges and dance floors. **Thang Loi Hotel** has regular *soirée dansante*— the big night is Sunday (2000 to midnight) when a live band plays.

SHOPPING

The souvenir trade is gearing up in Hanoi. To the south side of Hoan Kiem Lake, along Hang Khay and Trang Tien Streets, is a string of stores selling lacquerware, woodcarvings, silverware, antiques, and artwork; to the east side of Hoan Kiem are art galleries along Ngo Quyen Street; to the north side of Hoan Kiem are numerous small shops tucked into the Old Quarter.

Handicrafts and Antiques
The **Tourist and Handicraft Shop** at the corner of Ly Thuong Kiet and Hang Bai streets is run by Hanoi Tourism and features a large range of handcrafted goods at reasonable prices. Items include sculpture, silk paintings, water puppetry figures, and chess games. You can purchase mass-produced prints or silk paintings for $3-

12. A few antique stores are strung along Le Duan, south of the station, opposite Lenin Park. However, it's advisable to shop in government-run stores for antiques, as you'll receive an official receipt, which may be demanded upon exiting the country.

Original Art
Hanoi is the top place for buying original art in Vietnam, with over 60 galleries and many well-known painters. Artists concentrate on Hanoi street scenes, portraits of women, and abstract and surrealist themes. There are numerous galleries in the Hang Khay and Trang Tien areas. The government-run **Gallery 7** at 7 Hang Khay St. features several exhibitions, running concurrently.

HANOI HEADGEAR

Distinctive in the north is the green pith helmet worn during the Vietnam War. Originally copied from the French, the hat is called *mucoi* in Vietnamese because it is shaped like a mortar (as in mortar and pestle) when inverted. These helmets are often made from tree bark and covered with green canvas. The helmets are cheap, and useful to fight off the sun or rain, or deflect falling rocks when motorcycling along northern Vietnamese roads. It's odd that the helmet so closely associated with North Vietnam's Communist struggle should derive from the French. For nearly a hundred years, the white cork helmet was the symbol of French imperialism, just as the khaki pith helmet symbolized the British Empire. Derived from the French too are the ubiquitous berets, now mostly imported from Czechoslovakia, and French-style caps. Russian influence is obvious in earflap headwarmers—the wearers look like delegates to a Snoopy convention, except for the fact they're crouched over bamboo bongs, taking hits of tobacco. You'll sometimes see Hanoi men smoking a B-52 bong. The bamboo stem of the pipe features an ailing B-52, heading earthward;

attached to the smoking mouthpiece, the B-52 appears to be trailing smoke.

pith helmet

Spring Gallery, at 7 Trang Tien St., features works by young artists. **Mai Gallery,** located in a renovated colonial house at 3B Phan Huy Chu St. near the Fine Arts Museum, promotes established artists and famous old masters like Tu Nghiem and Bui Xuan Phai; **Salon Natasha,** at 30 Hang Bong St., promotes self-taught artists, operating outside the confines of the Ecole des Beaux Arts. Another good place is **Ecole de Hanoi Gallery,** at 14A Ngo Quyen Street. Prices vary $30-700 and up for signed works.

Clothing

Silk items—ready-made or custom-ordered—can be found on Hang Gai St. in the Old Quarter. You can purchase silk kimonos with brocade designs here. Embroidery shops, like the one at 109 Hang Gai, produce exquisite silk blouses and pajamas, as well as tablecloths and wall hangings. Designs feature majestic dragons, blue lotus flowers, or scenes of Vietnam. By leaving a picture behind, you can custom-order pieces; they may take time to produce. Around

the corner from Hong Gai, along Luong Van Can St., traditional *ao dai* dresses are made. Message T-shirts and hand-embroidered T-shirts are available on Ly Quoc Su Street. You can also have T-shirts custom-made.

Ho Chi Minh Souvenirs

The Vietnamese are not above making a few bucks off old Ho—with Ho T-shirts, Ho buttons, badges, stamps, and posters. The gift shops and sidewalk stalls outside the Ho Chi Minh Museum carry a large selection. Be aware that Ho Chi Minh kitsch may not go down well with Western war veterans.

Banners and Flags

Hang Quat Street in the old Quarter specializes in these items, which are usually intended for service awards or funerals. For an unusual but attractive wall hanging, purchase a scarlet banner with brightly embroidered gold or silver dragons and other symbols from one of the Hang Quat stores for $5-15. For a few dollars more, you can have your personal or business name and other information embroidered on the banner.

Markets

Dong Xuan Market, in the Old Quarter, is the largest market in Hanoi, stocking food, clothing, and other necessities. Smaller food markets are **Hang Da Market,** on the southwest side of the Old Quarter near the Protestant Church; and **19 December Market,** which runs between Ly Thuong Kiet and Hai Ba Trung Streets to the southwest of Hoan Kiem Lake. There are small street markets selling consumer goods in the Old Quarter. For army surplus, go to Le Duan Blvd. south of the railway station. Here you can find green pith helmets, fake-furry Russian hats, army surplus jackets, gloves, and so on—useful for travel in the cold north.

SERVICES AND INFORMATION

Traveler Cafés

There are a number of traveler cafés in Hanoi, but only a handful possess the necessary permits to deal with foreigners for tours, transport, and auto rentals. These cafés include Darling Café, Darling Café Hanoi, Green Bamboo Café, and Queen Café. Most traveler cafés handle paperwork, book tickets, and rent motorcycles and bicycles. The larger ones will also store luggage if you head upcountry—just make sure you attach a passport number to your baggage.

Like a guidebook, a meeting café should get you going and point you in the right direction—then you can find your own feet. Some travelers begin with a few day-trips from traveler cafés, then give up on the logistics of arranging trips themselves. They get lazy and rely totally on the cafés—they stay there, eat there, and take tours in minibuses. They spend all their time with other foreigners, a rather peculiar way of coming to grips with Vietnam.

Cafés are good for gathering information, but you should think twice about joining organized tours—they're not always satisfying. Check café traveler books and tour itineraries for ideas. Café bulletin boards are great for seeking other riders for shared jeep rides or minibuses for custom trips or travel to the northwest. Finally, several of the cafés offer low-budget accommodations and they do actually serve food, though it's generally bland. Sign of changing times—Darling Café Hanoi at 33 Hang Quat serves Israeli dishes. Traveler cafés are usually open all day, from 0800 to 2230 or 2300.

Old Quarter: The original traveler café is **Darling Café** at 4 Hang Quat, tel. 253038. This place is very popular, runs efficient tours, and can arrange jeeps for upcountry travel. Darling Café should not be confused with **Darling Café Hanoi,** the copycat counterpart down the street. One calls itself the "original" Darling Café, while the other claims to be the "real" Darling Café. The tale of the two Darlings is one the owners are glad to relate—the main benefit of this fierce rivalry is that they're constantly trying to outdo each other, which means good deals for you, the traveler. Darling Café Hanoi, at 33 Hang Quat, tel. 269386, offers trips, food, and accommodations. Around the corner is the **Tourist Café,** 6 To Tich, tel. 243051, with halfway decent coffee and hamburgers.

Queen Café, 65 Hang Bac, tel. 260860, is run by a remarkable family—extremely helpful with travel assistance, whether you use their services or not. The knowledgeable owner will assist with everything from transport rentals to custom trips. Hang Bac is an Old Quarter street with marble engravers and woodcarvers; the family who runs the Queen engaged in this trade before turning to tourism.

Traveler's Orchid Café (Thu Hien), 18 Hang Bac, tel. 261397, helps with hotel and ticket bookings, and can arrange bicycle and motorbike rentals. A bit difficult to find is the low-key **Rendezvous Café,** at 43 Ly Nam St., tel. 232830, on the other side of the railway tracks. The Rendezvous will assist with transport rentals.

Hoan Kiem District: The **Green Bamboo,** 42 Nha Chung St., tel./fax 264949, is located near St. Joseph's Cathedral. It's run by Darling Café and is a large place with café, bar, and four-room guesthouse. **Tourist Meeting Café,** 59A Ba Trieu, tel. 258813, rents motorcycles and bicycles and conducts tours out of town; it also arranges tickets for rail, air, bus, and water puppetry. **Sun Tourist Café,** 40 Quan Su St., tel. 250130, is useful for motorcycle rentals.

Tourist Information

Vietnam Tourism is located at 30A Ly Thuong Kiet near the Peace Hotel, tel. 264319, fax 257583—good for visa extensions, useless for anything else. **Hanoi Tourism,** 18 Ly Thuong Kiet, tel. 254074, and **Hanoi Tourism Service Company** (TOSERCO), at 94 Ly Thuong Kiet, tel. 255721, fax 267999, also handle visa extensions and official paperwork. TOSERCO is the travel and touring arm, with overpriced vehicle rentals and guided tours to many parts of the north. The Hanoi branch of **Saigon Tourist** is at 55B Phan Chu Trinh, tel. 250923.

Guides: Guides speaking English, French, German, and other languages are available from either official tourist organizations (expensive—$15 to $20 a day) or private agencies (better deal) or by inquiring through traveler cafés (the least expensive option).

Maps and Books

The best scale map of Hanoi is a joint-venture Canadian map produced by International Travel Maps (ITM) and Hanoi's Cartographic Mapping Institute. Check the date on maps—older touring maps may be of limited use. For business purposes, there's a fold-up laminated map produced by SCCI Hanoi pinpointing government and trading organizations, banks, foreign representative offices, and so on—buy it from the Metropole Hotel bookstore for $4. Barbara Cohen, a guidebook writer and longtime resident of Hanoi, has produced a laminated map of Hanoi as well as an annotated map of the Old Quarter.

Street vendors around the GPO and in the area along Trang Tien Street sell all kinds of maps. If you require high detail, vendors have topo maps tucked away—you might have to pre-order them. The **Cartographic Mapping Institute (CMI)**—the national mapmaking arm of Vietnam—is out in the Dong Da district, at 73 Lang Trung St. By the front gate is a small shop selling topo maps, atlases, giant wall maps of Vietnam, and thematic maps, all in a haphazard jumble of rolled sheafs.

Xunhasaba, the state corporation for import and export of books and periodicals, is at 32 Hai Ba Trung. Good for magazines on Vietnam. The **Foreign Language Publishing House** is at 46 Tran Hung Dao St.; this place publishes propaganda in English, French, Russian, and other languages. The **Foreign Language Bookstore,** at 61 Trang Tien, and the **State Bookshop,** at 40 Trang Tien, both stock books that are effusive in their praise of things Vietnamese. There is a concentration of bookstores along Trang Tien to the southeast of Hoan Kiem, and many bookstalls in passageways near the Bodega Guesthouse. These stalls stock books in English and French, with photocopied versions of everything from French guides of the 1930s to erudite botany manuals. Major hotels such as the Metropole feature kiosks with magazines and books.

Fax and Phone

The IDD/telecom center is next to the GPO on the southeast side of Hoan Kiem Lake; a branch at 66 Trang Tien also handles calls. Hotels can usually place IDD calls. Dial code for Hanoi is 84-4, followed by the number. Faxes are far cheaper than phoning, since they require only a minute to convey a page of information, and you don't have to worry about answering machines or time differences. Faxes are cheaper through the government telecom center—hotels tend to levy surcharges.

Help yourself to the information contained in the bilingual Hanoi Directory, an annual tome produced jointly by Hanoi Telephone Directory and Wordcorp Holdings of Singapore. The information section at the front provides full charts of IDD rates, postal services, express mail, parcel costs, and other telecommunications details. Emergency numbers: police, 13; fire, 14; ambulance, 15.

Satellite TV

Luxury hotels receive StarTV and other cable programs. These include the Metropole, Hanoi Heritage, Hanoi Hotel, Saigon Hotel, Army Hotel, and Tay Ho Hotel.

Post Office and Courier

The GPO is at 87 Dinh Tien Hoang St., on the southeast side of Hoan Kiem Lake. It handles poste restante, philatelic sales, and parcel mailing. Open daily 0700-2000. For postage and parcel rates, consult the Hanoi Directory. The GPO offers an express mail service (EMS), with a branch at 66 Trang Tien Street. Couriers in Hanoi include DHL, tel. 267020, and TNT, tel. 257615. Around the post office cluster map vendors (semi-legitimate), and moneychangers (illegitimate).

Photography and Film

A string of shops along Hang Khay Street on the south side of Hoan Kiem Lake sell imported slide and print film—not cheap. Print film developing is also possible here.

Banks

The **Bank for Foreign Trade of Vietnam,** at 47 Le Thai To St., is the major exchange point, open 0800-1130 and 1330-1530, closed Saturday afternoon, Sunday, and holidays. The bank offers commission-free conversions from traveler's checks to dong, but at a slightly lower rate. You can change traveler's checks to US cash for 1.2% commission. There's a branch of **Vietcombank** at 50 Trang Tien St., open 0900-1800, closed 1200-1300 for lunch.

The **ANZ bank,** at 14 Le Thai To, tel. 258190, is open 0830-1530 and Saturday 0830-1200—charges a $2 minimum commission to convert traveler's checks to dong and handles Visa cash advances with a four percent commission. An office at the Boss Hotel offers MasterCard advances with a 10% commission. Other foreign banks include **Banque Nationale de Paris,** 8 Tran Hung Dao; **Credit Lyonnais,** 8 Trang Thi; **Hongkong Bank,** 51 Le Thai To; **Deutsche Bank,** 25 Tran Binh Trong; and **Krung Thai Bank,** 34 Ba Trieu.

Street moneychangers lurk around the GPO—shortchangers would be a more accurate description of their profession. Changers often deliberately undercut on agreed amounts, and actually offer less than bank rates. The only advantages moneychangers offer are larger-denomination dong and the ability to change dong back to dollars when leaving Vietnam. Always be careful with street transactions.

Business Services

The Metropole Hotel has the best business center in town, with excellent secretarial and translation services. Other hotels with business centers include Boss Hotel, GMD/Army Hotel,

Saigon Hotel, Hanoi Hotel, Hanoi Heritage Hotel, and Tay Ho Hotel.

Health Care

The best place to seek medical advice in Hanoi is the **Swedish Clinic,** opposite the Swedish Embassy at #2, 358 St., off Kim Ma Road in the Van Phuc Quarter, tel. 252464. The clinic is open Monday and Friday 0900-1130 and 1330-1630, afternoons only on Tuesday, Wednesday, and Thursday.

Although the clinic was initially established for Swedish personnel, it's now open to all on a fee basis. Consultations are expensive, but when it comes to your health, it's not wise to cut corners. This foreign operation is an anomaly in Vietnam, allowed because of Swedish support for health care in Vietnam under the Swedish International Development Agency. In other parts of Vietnam, including Saigon, there is no comparable foreign clinic. Doctors come from Sweden on a one- to two-year contract and speak excellent English. Apart from the Swedish doctor and nurses, the attraction at the clinic is the medicine cabinet—over 200 drugs in stock, imported from the US Embassy Medical Unit in Bangkok or direct from Sweden. The clinic can arrange testing (blood, urine, stool), and uses disposable syringes. More advanced analysis and X-rays can be arranged in cooperation with nearby hospitals. The clinic also stocks vaccines for polio, rabies, measles, hepatitis, cholera, typhoid, and Japanese encephalitis. An inoculation costs $20 plus the cost of the vaccine.

You might like to contact your embassy for other medical or dental referrals; several embassies have their own doctors. French citizens can contact the French Embassy doctor. The **International Hospital,** on Phuong Mai, tel. 243728, deals with foreigners—the place is clean and uses disposable needles, but methods are not up-to-date, and aggressive treatment without proper testing can pose a problem.

Evacuation: International SOS Assistance can arrange evacuation—the office is located in the Boss Hotel, 60 Nguyen Du, Suite 208, tel. 226228, fax 269166. **AEA International** has an alarm center at 4 Tran Hung Dao, tel. 213555, fax 213523.

Rest and Recreation

Major hotels include fitness centers and gym facilities. Several hotels have swimming pools and tennis courts. The Metropole charges nonguests $5 to use the pool—one of the few pools in Vietnam that won't turn your hair green. Check the notice boards at the Metropole for news of Hanoi Hash House Harrier runs. Recreational boating opportunities can be found at the southeast corner of West Lake—sculling boats for rent here.

Buses leave the Metropole Hotel on Sunday morning for King's Island Golf and Country Club at Dong Mo, 45 km west of Hanoi. This is a $22-million resort with a luxury hotel and corporate villas; two 18-hole courses are under construction. In Hanoi, contact King's Valley Corporation, tel. 260342.

GETTING THERE

BY AIR

There are a dozen carriers flying into Hanoi's **Noi Bai Airport.** Noi Bai is a rough landing: the airport terminal is completely chaotic and offers little in the way of facilities. There are few signs to direct passengers, poor baggage handling facilities, and no luggage carts. If you find yourself stuck out this way, try the **Airport Hotel,** Noi Bai Airport, tel. 254745, with rooms for $40 double. An old French airfield at Gia Lam is being upgraded—some flights presently leave from there.

Entry Formalities

On arrival, you must fill in a document that looks like a visa application, with two photos required. Fill in the usual customs declaration form and entry-exit card—keep these with you, to be surrendered on departure. On the entry-exit card, look for the box specifying the place where you intend to stay: the best thing to write in here is "unknown." On the customs form, you must itemize cameras, video recorders, tape recorders, and other electronic equipment. You may have to declare currency above $3000.

Transfers into Hanoi

Noi Bai Airport lies about 40 km north of Hanoi. A taxi from the airport costs $15-25 for the one-hour ride to downtown Hanoi. The taxi mafia run the show, and will try and nail you for the highest price, so keep walking, keep talking. Prices may vary with the number of passengers and be prepared to pay in dollars. Noi Bai Airport minibuses—marked International Airport—that charge $4 on the way out suddenly want $10-15 for a seat coming back. In the reverse direction, from Hanoi to Noi Bai, traveler cafés charge $12-16 for a car. The Vietnam Airlines bus is $4 a passenger; buy your ticket from the Vietnam Airlines international booking office near Hoan Kiem lake preferably the day before departure. Check bus times; buses leave from the same place.

Airline Offices

The Vietnam Airlines international booking office is at 1 Quang Trung St., tel. 255229. This is the general agent for Lao Aviation, Cambodian Airlines, and Cathay Pacific. Vietnam Airlines operates direct flights from Hanoi to Bangkok, Vientiane, Phnom Penh, Guangzhou, Hong Kong, Seoul, Taipei, Beijing, Singapore, Dubai, Moscow, Paris, and Berlin. Other carriers also travel these routes.

If time is not a factor, consider indirect routes—they might work out cheaper, and are certainly an adventure. Instead of flying direct to Bangkok for $160 on Vietnam Airlines (or $180 on Thai Airways), take a plane to Vientiane for $90 on Vietnam Airlines or Lao Aviation (twice weekly service on Thursday and Sunday). Add $15 for a seven-day Lao transit visa, and $20 to cover the cost of a transfer into Nong Khai, and overnight sleeper to Bangkok, and your cost for a Lao layover is only $125.

Another spectacular route to consider is Hanoi to Kunming in stages by train, and a flight from Kunming to Bangkok. The Kunming-Bangkok flight is competitive in price with the Hanoi-Bangkok flight. Rail travel from Hanoi to Kunming is about $30 for sleepers; paperwork may cost another $50. Flying to Canton from Hanoi is much cheaper than direct flights into Hong Kong. If you add the Hanoi-Canton flight, Chinese visa, and Canton-Hong Kong boat, you can get to

Hong Kong for around $190, which is below the $270 tariff for a direct flight from Hanoi to Hong Kong. China Southern Airlines operates one-way flights from Hanoi to Canton for $125, Nanning for $80, and Beijing for $260.

BY LAND

There are two border crossings from China in the north—at Lao Cai in the northwest, approached from Kunming; and at Huu Nghi Quan (Friendship Gate) in the northeast near Lang Son, approached from Nanning. If entering this way, you need a valid Vietnamese visa stamped for entry at one of these points. You can arrange visas in Hong Kong, or possibly Beijing. For full particulars, see "Immigration and Customs" in the On the Road section of Vietnam. For exiting the north into China, you need a stamp for either Lao Cai or Huu Nghi Quan on your Vietnamese visa; you can pick up a Chinese visa in Hanoi.

GETTING AROUND

Metered Taxis

Hanoi Taxi, tel. 265252, runs a fleet of white Toyotas. These are radio-controlled and can be called to a restaurant or other location for pickup. There's a Hanoi Taxi rank outside the Saigon Hotel at 80 Ly Thuong Kiet Street near the railway station. Hanoi Taxi is run by Hanoi People's Committee, which also operates Red Taxi and PT Taxi. Another fleet, called V Taxi, is run by the Interior Ministry. Metered taxis are expensive: $1.50 to $2 for the first two km, and 45 cents to 70 cents for each subsequent km. Hanoi Taxi and Red Taxi charge the highest rates. Older, nonmetered taxis are also found around Hanoi—negotiate the fare before boarding.

Motos and Cyclos

Hanoi has few motos although you can find some around the railway station. Cyclos are everywhere, most with wooden seats. Prices depend on distance, but should be $1 or less. For stylish touring, the Metropole Hotel offers luxury white cyclos with padded seats for $1.20 an hour. Cyclos are not permitted on certain streets in Hanoi, particularly the road encircling Hoan Kiem Lake and along Trang Tien and Trang Thi Boulevards. This explains erratic maneuvering by cyclos in this area.

Two-Wheel Rentals

For **motorcycle rentals,** inquire through traveler cafés. Rental agents require a deposit for Japanese motorcycle rental—either a large sum of cash, or your departure card, paper visa, credit card, passport, or plane ticket. Avoid leaving a credit card or a passport. For a Russian motorcycle, a photocopy of your passport or an elaborate laundry bill will do. There's little in the way of

taking a break

insurance—inquire as to who's liable for the repair bill in the event of an accident or mechanical breakdown, and who pays if the bike is stolen. The Tourist Meeting Café charges $7/day for a 50cc Honda, $8/day for a 70cc, and $15 for a 100cc Japanese bike. For a Russian motorcycle, the charges are $5/day for 125cc or 175cc. Sun Tourist Café charges $7 for a Japanese bike, $5-7/day for a 175cc Czech motorcycle, and $5/day for a Russian 125cc.

A number of traveler cafés rent **bicycles**, and if they don't, there are bound to be private operators nearby that will. Bikes go for 60 cents to $1 a day, and you can negotiate keeping the bike overnight or for several days. If you do keep a bike overnight, park it in your hotel courtyard, off the street. Rentals are fairly relaxed, with little required in the way of deposits. Go for the black Chinese bicycles with encased chains—these are less liable to fall apart. Always check brakes and adjust saddle height. In the Old Quarter, the art gallery at 42 Hang Bac has lots of good Chinese bikes. Traveler's Orchid Café rents cycles, and so does the Darling Café at 33 Hang Quat. Another rental is next to Especen #4, at 16A Trung Yen. South of Hoan Kiem are several rental places along Trang Tien. Tourist Meeting Café and Sun Tourist Café both rent bicycles.

Your Own Wheels
You can buy used Russian motorcycles in Hanoi; inquire through traveler cafés. You can buy a used Minsk 175cc for around $250; a new one sells for $500. No papers are involved—you use the bike, then resell to locals or other travelers. You can purchase motorcycle parts and helmets along Hué Blvd. south of Nguyen Cong Tru St. east of Lenin Park, and also along Hang Bong St. in the Old Quarter.

Chinese-made black roadster bicycles are often smuggled in from the border. Vietnamese brands like Doan The (Corporate) or Huu Nghi (Friendship) are turned out at a French-built factory in Hanoi. These only cost around $30 each. Chinese bikes run $55 and up.

Boat Rentals
At the southeast corner of West Lake, near Tran Quoc Pagoda, you can rent rowboats and sculling

---

TOUR COMPANIES AND TRAVELER CAFE AGENTS

The reins of business have loosened in Hanoi, and small private entrepreneurs like Queen Café and Darling Café are keen for a piece of the new tourist trade. To get started, entrepreneurs need a government business license, and must pay taxes on profits. Those with the right connections can organize tours for foreigners; this system of paperwork and kickbacks means some cafés are more powerful than others. Shoestring tours are provided by traveler cafés, including Darling Café, 4 Hang Quat, tel. 243024; Darling Café Hanoi, 33 Hang Quat, tel. 269386; Queen Café, 65 Hang Bac, tel. 260860; and The Green Bamboo, 42 Nha Chung, tel. 264949. The Meeting Café and other small cafés also run day-trips.

Ann Tourist, Dong Do Hotel, 27 Tong Duy Tan, tel. 233275

Ecco, 50A Ba Trieu, tel. 254615—this agency has a poor reputation and is prone to overcharging and botching up arrangements

Especen Tourist Company, 79E Hang Trong St., tel. 266856, fax 269612—good agency for hotel bookings, car rentals

Hanoi Tourism Service Company (TOSERCO), 94 Ly Thuong Kiet, tel. 255721, fax 267999

National Oil Services Company (OSC), 38 Yet Kieu, tel. 264500, fax 259260—good for tours and vehicle rentals

Oscan Enterprises, 60 Nguyen Du (Boss Hotel), tel. 252690

Pacific Tours, 58B Tran Nhan Tong, tel. 267942

Vung Tau Intourco, 136 Hang Trong, near Phu Gia Hotel, tel. 252739

Vidotour, 51 Phan Chu Trinh, tel. 269875

Vietnam Veterans Tourism Service (VVTS), in the Army Museum, 28A Dien Bien Phu, tel. 232966, fax 232966

Vinatour, at 54 Nguyen Du, near the Boss Hotel, tel. 255963, fax 252707—splinter group from Vietnam Tourism; can arrange Land Cruisers

VEHICLE RENTAL

A car with driver is around $25-35 a day within the city.

Especen's price list for vehicles is as follows: Volga car, three passengers, $25 per 100 km; Toyota car $30/100 km; nine-seat Japanese minibus, no air-con, $30/100 km; same with air-con $35/100 km; 12-seat minibus $40/100 km; Land Cruiser, $45/100 km for four passengers. Sun Tourist Café charges $25 a day for a car and driver; Vinatour charges $33/100 km or for a one-day Hanoi tour.

boats for exercise, or, to go across the lake, speedboats or dragon boats. For dragon boat information and reservations at West Lake contact Olympic Café, 28 Thanh Nien, tel. 257105.

Vietnamese Visa Modifications

Extending a visa in Hanoi is sometimes straightforward, other times complicated. The Hanoi boys like to play games. Sometimes they find irregularities in the issuance of the visa (your visa was issued by a Haiphong agent; thus they have to contact them first). On several occasions, travelers applying for an extension have instead been handed an exit visa, meaning they have 72 hours to leave the country. That may mean a rush visit to the Lao visa office, and a fast flight out. Allow at least three working days, and preferably five, to extend your visa in Hanoi. If you want to exit to China via Lao Cai or Lang Son, you need that as the appropriate point for an exit stamp.

Visa Extensions: The Hanoi Boys at the Immigration Office will not deal direct—they will refer you to an agency like Vietnam Tourism. Agencies charge different fees—Vietnam Tourism, at 30A Ly Thuong Kiet, charges $15 for a one-week extension, $20 for a two-week, and $25 for three-to four-week extensions; requires three working days. Other outfits, like Boss Hotel, are cheaper. Saigon Tourist, at 55B Phan Chu Trinh, processes a three-week extension in two days for $16.

Border Crossing Stamps: Hanoi's Entry-Exit/Immigration Office at 40A Hang Bai St., tel. 255798, will refer you to a travel agent for Lao Cai or Huu Nghi Quan (Lang Son) border exit points. You must have a China visa stamp first. Vidotour charges $25 for a Lao Cai exit stamp; the Boss Hotel travel agency is half that price at $13. The actual stamp is worth $5. TOSERCO provides a two-week extension and exit point for $15, which saves time as well as money.

Re-entry Visa: It's possible to have your Vietnamese visa validated for re-entry to Vietnam after a visit to, say, Kunming in China's Yunnan Province. The re-entry stamp turns your existing visa into a double-entry visa. You'll need the border exit point stamped on the visa too.

GETTING AWAY

BY AIR

The Vietnam Airlines domestic booking office is in the Boss Hotel, 60 Nguyen Du St., tel. 255194. There are flights from Hanoi to Dien Bien Phu (twice a week), Hué (five times a week), Danang (daily), Nha Trang (twice a week), and Ho Chi Minh City (daily).

Vietnam Air Service Company (VASCO) operates several Aerospatiale Squirrel AS-350 helicopters with French pilots; available for custom flights. Contact VASCO at the Metropole Hotel, tel. 266919 (ext. 8015). Scheduled routes: Noi Bai Airport to Gia Lam Airfield, $150 one-way per person for the five-minute trip; Gia Lam Airfield to Haiphong, $250 one-way for a 25-minute trip. VASCO will arrange a two-day overflight of Halong Bay for $2000, for one to four passengers.

BY RAIL

The foreign booking office at Hanoi railway station is open 0730-1130 and 1330-1530. You can also make reservations by phone. Reunification Express trains run from Hanoi to Saigon. The following prices are for trains S7 and S9; other expresses, like S3, are more expensive. Hanoi to Hué is 688 km by rail (18 hours) and costs $20 for a hard seat, $23 for a soft seat,

AIRLINE OFFICES

Aeroflot, 4 Trang Thi, tel. 252376—flies to Moscow

Air France, 1 Ba Trieu, tel. 253484—direct flights to Paris several times weekly

Cathay Pacific, Binh Minh Hotel, 27B Le Thai To, Hoan Kiem, tel. 267298—flies to Hong Kong frequently

China Southern Airlines, Binh Minh Hotel, 27 Le Thai To, tel. 269233, flies to Guangzhou, Nanning, and Beijing

Czechoslovakia Airlines, 404 A2 Van Phuc Quarter, tel. 256512

Japan Airlines, 1 Ba Trieu, tel. 266693

Malaysian Airlines, in Metropole Hotel, 15 Ngo Quyen, tel. 268821

Pacific Airlines, 81 Tran Hung Dao, tel. 269333; second office in the Boss Hotel

Singapore Airlines, in Metropole Hotel, tel. 268888—flies to Singapore twice weekly

Thai Airways International, 25 Ly Thuong Kiet St. (opposite Hoa Binh Hotel), tel. 266893—frequent flights to Bangkok

$33-37-40 hard sleeper, and $44 soft sleeper. Hanoi to Saigon is 1,728 km (46 hours) and costs $48 hard seat, $56 soft seat, $82-91-99 hard sleeper, and $108 soft sleeper.

There are also rail spurs running from Hanoi to Haiphong (three hours, by fastest train), Lao Cai (11 to 12 hours, one day-train, one overnight-train), and Lang Son (eight hours, one day-train, one overnight-train).

BY ROAD

Vehicle Rental
You can rent minibuses, Russian Army jeeps, Land Cruisers, and Toyota cars for upcountry travel. For rough roads, you need a 4WD vehicle. Most tour agents can organize vehicle rental. Vinatour charges $44/100 km for a minibus; $66/100 km for a 25-seat bus and $90/100 km

for a 50-seat bus. TOSERCO charges $35/100 km for a 12-seat minibus, and $40/100 km for a 15-seat bus. Though most travel by train on the Hanoi-Hué leg, some traveler minibuses also ply the route. You can get a ride from Hanoi to Hué for around $20, taking 17 hours straight through (it's worth negotiating a two-day or longer trip so you can tour the DMZ from Dong Ha en route). Keep an eye on notice boards at traveler cafés, or put up your own note and assemble a group.

EMBASSIES

There are over 40 embassies in Hanoi, including the following. Van Phuc Quarter is an enclave to the west side of Hanoi; Trung Tu Quarter lies to the southwest of Hanoi. Embassies in Hanoi include:

Australia, 66 Ly Thuong Kiet, tel. 252763

Belgium, Room 105-108, D1 Van Phuc Quarter, tel. 252263

Burma (Myanmar), A3 Van Phuc Quarter, tel. 253369

Canada, 39 Nguyen Dinh Chieu, tel. 265840

Finland, B3 Giang Vo Quarter, tel. 256754

France, 49 Ba Trieu, tel. 252719

Germany, 29 Tran Phu, tel. 252836

India, 58 Tran Hung Dao, tel. 253409

Indonesia, 50 Ngo Quyen, tel. 253353

Italy, 9 Le Phung Hieu, tel. 256246

Japan, E3 Trung Tu Quarter, tel. 257902

Malaysia, A3 Van Phuc Quarter, tel. 253371

Mongolia, 39 Tran Phu, tel. 253009

Philippines, Room 305-308, E1 Trung Tu Quarter, tel. 257948

Russian Federation, 58 Tran Phu, tel. 254632

Sweden, 2-358 St., Van Phuc Quarter, tel. 254824

Switzerland, 77B Kim Ma, tel. 232019

Thailand, 63 Hoang Dieu, tel. 235092

United Kingdom, 16 Ly Thuong Kiet, tel. 252510

United States (liaison office), 7 Lang Ha, tel. 431500

Bus and Minibus Terminals

Northeast: Minibuses and buses to Halong Bay (Bai Chay) and Lang Son depart from Le Thanh Tong Street a short distance south of the Opera House, near the intersection of Dac Thai Than. Minibuses run to Lang Son between 2200 and 0100, taking five hours. On Dac Thai Than Street is a bus depot with departures to Hong Gai. On the east banks of the Red River is Gia Lam Ben Xe, with departures to Bai Chay 0630-1300, and buses to Haiphong and Lang Son.

Northwest: Kim Ma Bus Station, on the west side of Hanoi, handles departures to Hoa Binh, Moc Chau, Son La, and Tuan Giao daily, and Dien Bien Phu every two days. There are also departures to Tuyen Quang, Yen Bai, and Tuyen Quang.

South: Kim Lien Bus Station, at 100 Le Duan, and Giap Bat Bus Station, 15 km south central Hanoi, run departures in the direction of Thanh Hoa, Vinh, Hué, and points south.

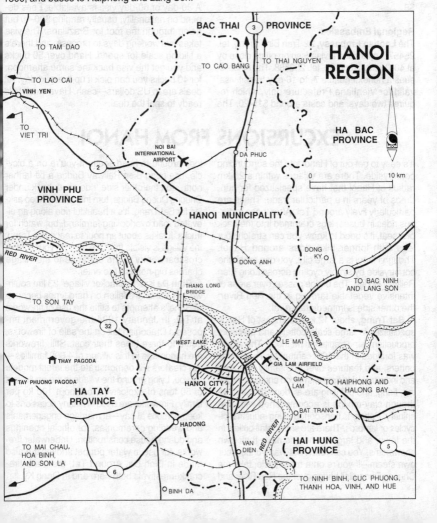

EXIT FORMALITIES

Although no one bothers checking the items on your customs form on exit, failure to produce the stupid piece of paper can result in incredible hassles. Get rid of all dong before exiting—the dong is not worth a damn outside the country. If you have a surplus of dong, you might have to change money on the streets in Hanoi to convert back to US dollars. International departure tax is $8.

Regional Embassies

The **Laotian Embassy,** 22 Tran Binh Trong, tel. 254576, maintains a visa-issuing office close by at 40 Quang Trung St., tel. 252588. The office issues a nonextendable 7- to 10-day transit visa, valid for Vientiane Prefecture only, which requires two days, and costs around $15-20. The **Embassy of Thailand,** 63 Hoang Dieu, tel. 235092, is open daily except Saturday, with visa-issuing hours 0830-1200; a regular 30-day visa takes one day to issue and costs $15. The **Cambodian Embassy,** at 71A Tran Hung Dao, tel. 253789, is open Mon.-Fri. 0830-1130. A visa costs $20 and takes several days to issue.

The **Chinese Embassy,** 46 Hoang Dieu, tel. 253737, staffs a visa-issuing office south of the main embassy, around the corner at 40A Tran Phu. Application hours are Mon.-Fri. 0830-1100. A 30-day or 60-day visa is available. Fees depend on nationality, usually ranging $20-40 but going through the roof for Brazilians. The visa takes five working days to process, and there's a sliding scale for speed. Hand over 50 bucks and you get the visa back the same afternoon; for 40 bucks you can pick it up the next day. All deals are in US dollars—cash. Have exact bills ready to seal the deal.

EXCURSIONS FROM HANOI

It's easy to get out of Hanoi into the surrounding countryside. There are villages within a 25-km radius of Hanoi that have specialized for hundreds of years in a particular trade. These are particularly lively around Tet. After those torturous rides in buses, legs crammed into the back of a seat, it's good to know you can stretch your legs with longer bike rides around Hanoi. Though Hanoi is a large city, you can reach the countryside by simply cycling across Long Bien Railway Bridge. The bridge passes over areas of intensive vegetable farming in the Red River; the other side is immediately rural.

Bat Trang, about 12 km southeast of Hanoi, specializes in large-scale pottery and porcelain production using traditional methods. The village was founded in the 16th century by Thanh Hoa potters, and features over 800 family-operated and industrial kilns fired with wood and coal. Molding, firing, and painting are all done by hand, although clay-mixing is accomplished with machinery. Pottery is transported using industrial bicycles or lambros. There are small retail outlets in the town, and larger concerns have their own showrooms. You can reach Bat Trang under your own steam—if you're on a motorcycle, take the Chuong Duong toll bridge over the Red River and loop around to head south. If you're on a bicycle, use Long Bien Railway Bridge a bit farther north—on the other side, ride south back under Chuong Duong Bridge, turn inland, and keep asking for Bat Trang. It's a beautiful ride along an elevated road overlooking farmland, but watch for trucks. It takes about an hour to reach Bat Trang; the village is visible from the road on your right. A crossbar sentry at the entrance to the village charges big-noses $1 to enter.

Binh Da is a "firecracker village" 23 km southwest of Hanoi. It's fallen on hard times because of Hanoi's attempts to stifle the use of fireworks at Tet. In January 1994 the government imposed a Draconian tax on the sale of fireworks, equal to three times their cost. Still, fireworks are handmade in this village of 4,000 families—the creators will demonstrate the latest models for you. Lying around the village is the equivalent of 50 tons of explosives, or about 100 kg per family. Fireworks are used on many occasions to keep demons at bay—at marriage engagements and wedding ceremonies, for official openings and during house construction. Underwater fireworks, for use in water puppet shows, are also made in Binh Da. Around Tet, there are firecracker festivals both here and in Dong Ky.

Dong Ky, 18 km northeast of Hanoi, specializes in antique Chinese-style wooden furniture, handmade and inlaid with mother-of-pearl or marble pieces. In the spring, a rocket festival features giant firecrackers eight meters long and two meters in diameter. Another village specializing in woodcarving is Van Ha, to the south of Hanoi. Skillful carvers produce fine furniture, religious icons, and small souvenir items. Among the most commonly produced items are wooden statues of Buddha and bodhisattvas, including complex versions with multiple heads and arms.

Van Phuc Village, 14 km southwest of Hanoi, is of interest to those who seek silk by the meter. Watch families with motor looms spin and wash silk here.

Villagers from **Le Mat,** eight km northeast of Hanoi, travel all over the north catching snakes. The serpents are kept in compounds around the house, in readiness for export to China, or for use in snake wine or traditional medicine. In Hanoi's Old Quarter a shop sells medicines made from Le Mat snakes. **Dong Ho** is a village along the Duong River in nearby Ha Bac Province that produces traditional woodblock prints. There is great activity here in December in readiness for the Tet celebrations of February. A Dong Ho print for the house is considered essential for welcoming the new year.

Pottery is all handmade in Bat Trang.

AROUND THE NORTH

Vietnam's greatest touring potential lies in the untapped north. The mountainous terrain, and the war, have isolated the area from travel since the 1940s. Now you can discover secrets like Sapa, a former French resort town up by the Chinese border, or Mai Chau, set in a beautiful valley near the Lao border. The north is intriguing because it is full of unknowns; it is less commercial than the south, and the people have an entirely different mentality. The north feels like a foreign place; central Vietnam seems nebulous; and in the south, everything looks a little too familiar.

The north has spectacular karst scenery—hills, deep gorges, and the kind of sugarloaf peaks found on islands in southern Thailand, in China's Yunnan Province, and on Palawan in the Philippines. At Halong Bay, bizarre limestone formations sprinkle the coastline, creating a dream-like landscape that inspires Vietnamese painters. Hundreds of grottoes are embedded in the karst islets. Karst formations also make for spectacular boat trips on rivers to the Perfume Pagoda and Tam Coc Caves to the southwest of Hanoi.

With scenery like this, trekking is only a step away. Several Hanoi tour operators now offer hiking itineraries. A jeep takes you to the trailhead, then you march three or four days, staying in villages along the route. Porters can carry supplies if needed. Ideal points for hiking include Mai Chau in the southwest, and Dien Bien Phu, Lai Chau, Phong Tho, and Sapa in the northwest. Mediocre national parks in the north offer limited hiking facilities; the best is Cuc Phuong National Park. Old French hill stations undergoing redevelopment are potential bases for independent treks with your own guide. Two stations, Sapa and Tam Dao, are operational; others such as Bavi will soon follow suit.

Many minority groups live in villages located in the northwestern mountains, especially toward the Chinese and Lao borders on the Son La-to-Sapa route. Not surprising, the French word for minorities is *montagnard,* meaning mountain people. You'll often notice minorities at markets, which are more animated on weekends, especially Sunday.

EXPLORING THE NORTH

In 1990, you couldn't beg, borrow, or rent a bicycle, much less a motorcycle, in Hanoi. Now you can rent—or buy—a Russian motorcycle and ride off into the hills all the way to the Chinese border. Travelers band together, rent a jeep or 4WD vehicle, and take off on wild 10-day journeys over dirt roads.

Because of a lack of bases in the north, trips tend to be roundtrip loops radiating out of Hanoi. Favored destinations include Tam Coc Caves and Bich Dong, and the Perfume Pagoda. Top overnight trips from Hanoi are Halong Bay and Mai Chau. Traveler cafés and tour agencies in Hanoi organize tours to these and other areas. Prices and services vary considerably. Some tours offer transport only; others include food, accommodations, and entry fees. Agencies like TOSERCO charge considerably more than the traveler cafés—they also use better hotels and transport and employ better guides.

For longer trips in the north, you should assemble a small group to split costs, and be prepared to negotiate. In Halong Bay you have to rent fishing boats; to get to Sapa via Dien Bien Phu, you must bargain for car, jeep, or Land Cruiser prices. Get as much finalized on paper as you can, as a kind of contract. If you paid half a jeep cost up front, for example, write the amount down and indicate the balance due at the end of the trip. Also sketch the route on paper to counter confusion and avoid possible misunderstandings. Make your trip flexible: negotiate a fee in advance if you decide to add an extra day. Negotiate what happens if your vehicle breaks down.

An alternative to loops from Hanoi is a one-way trip from Hanoi to China. Along the 1,600-km China-Vietnam border lie 25 major market points for cross-border trade. Two of them, Dong Dang near Lang Son, and Lao Cai, are open to foreigners at present. Others may open in the future. The Kunming-Bangkok flight costs the same as the Hanoi-Bangkok flight, so you might consider traveling by rail north to Lao Cai and on to Kunming in China. Paperwork and fares might run you an extra $80, but what a ride! For an unusual loop in the north, travel up

to Sapa, exit and carry on to Kunming, make your way back to Nanning, and re-enter Vietnam at Lang Son. For this exercise, you need a Chinese visa and a reentry stamp on your Vietnamese visa, as well as the appropriate border-point stamp.

Short Trips

Red River Delta: Excellent day-trips from Hanoi, or good stops if you're coming north from Thanh Hoa, include the Perfume Pagoda and Tam Coc Caves near Ninh Binh. Both involve boat trips through majestic scenery. Traveler cafés offer day-trips for $11 per person to Perfume Pagoda; $15 to Tam Coc and Bich Dong.

Southwest Loop: You'll need two days or longer for trips from Hanoi to this area. Good hikes here, with visits to ethnic villages in pretty Mai Chau Valley, and a glimpse of old growth forest in Cuc Phuong National Park. You can travel roundtrip to either Cuc Phuong or Mai Chau, or try the loop from Hanoi to Cuc Phuong to Mai Chau to Hoa Binh and back to Hanoi. For a longer trip, combine some destinations in the Red River Delta: Hanoi, Tam Coc Caves, Cuc Phuong, Mai Chau, Hoa Binh, Hanoi. In Hanoi the Darling Café at 4 Hang Quat offers a two-day trip to Mai Chau for $28 a person, and also organizes area hikes. Especen charges $35 a head for a two-day trip to Cuc Phuong, based on three passengers.

North by Northeast: A mixed bag, including Tam Dao hill resort, Ba Be Lakes Forest Reserve, and an exit to China via Lang Son. Minority groups live near the China border, in Cao Bang and Ha Giang. Hiking is possible at Ba Be Lakes. Darling Café at 4 Hang Quat offers a three-day trip to Ba Be, accommodations included, for $45-60 per person.

Gulf of Tonkin/Halong Bay: Visiting Halong Bay requires an overnight trip. Hire a fishing boat to tour the bay's wonders—waterscapes, grottoes, junks, marine activity. You'll find good accommodations and food at Bai Chay, the jumping-off point for Halong Bay. Traveler cafés in Hanoi offer two-day roundtrips for $18-30 per person, based on five to 20 passengers. The price includes minibus and boat transport, as well as accommodations and food. The best deal is a trip with an overnight boat. If you have more time, consider spending four to six days or longer on this route, proceeding from Hanoi to Haiphong to Bai Chay to Halong Bay to Cat Ba Island and back to Haiphong and Hanoi.

Tonkinese Alps/Northwest: Key destinations in this direction are Dien Bien Phu and Sapa. You can travel to Sapa directly in one day, or take a long loop via Dien Bien Phu in five days. Along the way you'll find spectacular mountain scenery, rough roads, and numerous minority groups. There is excellent hiking in Dien Bien Phu, Lai Chau, and Sapa. At Lao Cai, you can cross into China and take a train to Kunming. A minimum four-day trip to Sapa's weekend market is recommended from Hanoi; on the longer route, you need at least six days, and preferably eight.

Traveler cafés in Hanoi offer direct car and minibus rides to Sapa, departing Hanoi Friday and usually taking four days—two days of travel, two days in Sapa—for approximately $45-70 per person based on 4-14 passengers. Darling Café at 4 Hang Quat arranges two-day hikes in Sapa, and day-hikes in Lai Chau and Phong Tho.

You can organize your own jeep or Land Cruiser trips on the long route to Sapa via Dien Bien Phu. A jeep costs $300-400 for a six-day trip on the Hanoi-Son La-Dien Phu-Lai Chau-Sapa-Lao Cai-Hanoi route; split expenses between four passengers. Especen offers a Hanoi-Dien Bien Phu roundtrip in five days for $330 for a jeep, or $530 for a Land Cruiser, based on three passengers.

Accommodations

Tourism is new in the north, and there are few conventional hotels. Larger towns usually offer a UBND (People's Committee) guesthouse, where foreigners can secure a bed for $5 (local truckers pay 50 cents). These are basic places, but you usually get a warm quilt, mosquito net, and thermos of hot water—and that's the extent of the hot water. You can stay in a jungle lodge in Cuc Phuong National Park, on a fishing boat at Halong Bay, or in a village longhouse at Mai Chau. If worse comes to worst, seek out a noodlehouse or something similar and sleep on the floor. Food in the north is simple and monotonous, often a soup with beef, fried egg, rice, and cabbage, the national vegetable. At Halong Bay, however, you can get excellent seafood.

Gear

Some trips, such as those to Halong Bay, stay within range of civilization; other trips, especially to the northwest, verge on the expeditionary. If heading north to Sapa, or to Halong in winter, purchase warm clothing in Hanoi. You can buy a silk or wool scarf, a padded cotton jacket, or a Chinese-made parka to counter the cold and wind in the north. You'll find sweaters and gloves in Hanoi's Old Quarter. Silk provides excellent insulation as long as it doesn't get wet; you can find silk items along Hang Gai St. On Le Duan Blvd. south of the Hanoi railway station you can buy army surplus gear. A strong flashlight is necessary to compensate for lack of electricity and for stumbling through karst caves.

NEAR HANOI

RED RIVER DELTA

As the north's heartland and the cradle of northern Vietnamese culture, the Red River Delta has seen the rise and fall of emperors, dynasties, and a number of imperial capitals over the centuries. The Red River begins in China's Yunnan Province. After coursing though northern Vietnam, the river merges with two tributaries near Hanoi and forms a fan-like delta that empties into the Gulf of Tonkin. What the Mekong Delta is to southern Vietnam, the Red River Delta is to the north. This area of rich alluvial plains is intensively farmed and densely populated. It is the north's main rice-producing zone, but sometimes endures famines, when rice must be supplied from the south. Despite a system of canals and embankments, the Vietnamese have never been able to completely contain the Red River, particularly during monsoons.

The Red River Delta covers an area of 15,000 square km and extends over 200 km inland from the coast. It is roughly delineated by a triangle formed by Viet Tri (northwest of Hanoi),

Haiphong (east of Hanoi), and Ninh Binh (south of Hanoi). It covers the area bounded by Ha Tay, Hai Hung, Thai Binh, Nam Ha, and Ninh Binh provinces. You can make day-trips or overnight sorties into the delta, if you are based in Hanoi. If traveling north from Vinh or Thanh Hoa, you can overnight in Ninh Binh. The top day-trip from Hanoi is to either the Perfume Pagoda or Tam Coc Caves. Both offer similar karst scenery and boat rides, so you really should choose between them.

Perfume Pagoda

Perfume Pagoda (Chua Huong) is a cave-shrine 60 km southwest of Hanoi. The route features spectacular karst scenery, which really makes the trip worthwhile. Tens of thousands of visitors visit this site daily in peak pilgrimage season, usually March-April, during the spring festival. You can join an organized minibus tour from a traveler café in Hanoi or make your way out to the village of Ben Duc by hired car. At Ben Duc, two hours from Hanoi, hundreds of rowers clamor to transport you along the Swallow River to the Perfume Pagoda. The upstream boat trip takes one hour and is the only way to reach the pagoda. The open rowboats provide no shelter, so in summer take an umbrella and conical hat to avoid sunburn.

After the boat ride you face a one-hour hike on a rocky and sometimes slippery trail up the Mountain of Fragrant Traces, ending at a complex of Buddhist shrines thick with incense. The Perfume Pagoda itself is not impressive, consisting of a large cavern set into limestone cliffs. Inside, many of the stalactites and stalagmites are painted. Drops of water falling from stalactites are believed to possess healing powers. Legend has it that a Hindu bodhisattva transformed himself into Quan Am, Goddess of Compassion, in this cavern; an 18th-century statue of Quan Am carved from blue stone presides. Pilgrims burn paper offerings inside the pagoda to help their ancestors in the afterlife. They also consume lots of sodas—there's a big rubbish dump of empty cans inside the cavern.

The entry fee to the Perfume Pagoda is a whopping $6.50 for foreigners, $1.40 for locals. If you join a tour from Hanoi, the entry price is usually included. Traveler cafés run tours for $11 a head.

Thay and Tay Phuong Pagodas

While spectacular boat rides enhance the trips to the Perfume Pagoda and the temples at Bich Dong, the itinerary taking in Thay and Tay Phuong pagodas wears a bit thin. Traveler cafés organizing day-trips to this area throw in stops at Van Phuc, a silk-spinning village, and So, a noodle-making village. Thay Pagoda, 40 km west of Hanoi in Sai Son, was built during the 11th century, and includes a variety of enclosures with Buddhist figures. The pagoda is famed for a pavilion on stilts in a pond facing the pagoda. Water puppetry performances take place here at festival time, particularly in the third lunar month when pilgrims flock in. Eight km away is Tay Phuong Pagoda, sited on a hilltop above the village of Thac Xa. Parts of the pagoda date to the 8th century, but most of the structure was built in the 18th century. Inside are 75 jackwood figures modeled on monks once associated with the pagoda.

Ninh Binh

Ninh Binh is a small town 95 km south of Hanoi, reached by train (three hours), bus or car (2.5 hours). Ninh Binh itself offers little to see, and most travelers pass through en route to Tam Coc Caves, Bich Dong Temple, or other sites in the area. If you're coming from the south, Ninh Binh makes a great pit stop. If you're coming from the north, you can cover the area in a long day-trip. A popular day-trip route is Hanoi to Ninh Binh to Hoa Lu Temples to Tam Coc Caves to Bich Dong Temple and back to Hanoi. A similar itinerary might run thus: 0730 depart Hanoi; 1000 reach Van Lam village to visit Tam Coc Caves; 1330 lunch; 1400 Bich Dong Temple; 1600 drive back to Hanoi; 1830 reach Hanoi. Another longer routing would be a two- or three-day trip from Hanoi by rented vehicle: start in Hanoi, visit Tam Coc Caves and Bich Dong Temple, stay overnight in Ninh Binh, carry on to Cuc Phuong National Park and/or Mai Chau, then drive back to Hanoi.

If you want to tackle the routes yourself and base out of Ninh Binh, it's going to cost you. There's no public bus service from Ninh Binh to outlying areas, so you have to rent a car or motorcycle. A car costs $25-35 a day with driver, and a motorbike is $7-10. If you can lay your hands on a bicycle, it's only a five-km ride to Tam Coc Caves from Ninh Binh.

There are only a few hotels in Ninh Binh. Right in town off Highway 1 is the government-run **Ninh Binh Hotel,** with rooms for $8-15. But a better place to stay is the minihotel about 500 meters up the road from Ninh Binh Hotel and down a little alley to the left as you go north. This place offers five double rooms for $10 each, and the owner will gladly help arrange for cars and guides. On Highway 1 about one km north of town is **Hoa Lu Hotel** with rooms for $10-20.

Tam Coc Caves

Tam Coc is known as Halong Bay on Land. In fact, in the French movie *Indochine,* the drifting junk that carries the star-crossed lovers through Halong Bay comes to rest at Tam Coc. The movie director splices footage from both locations and makes them appear as one; the lovers rest up in Bich Dong Temple. Tam Coc's karst sugarloaf mountains resemble the topography at Halong Bay—the big difference is that Tam Coc

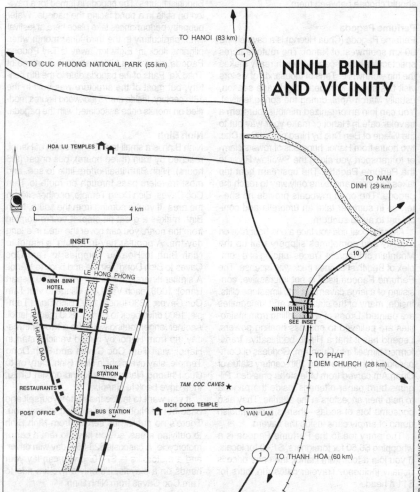

NINH BINH AND VICINITY

TO HANOI (83 km)

TO CUC PHUONG NATIONAL PARK (55 km)

HOA LU TEMPLES

TO NAM DINH (29 km)

0   4 km

TO THANH HOA (60 km)

INSET

LE HONG PHONG

NINH BINH HOTEL

MARKET

LE DAI HANH

TRAN HUNG DAO

TRAIN STATION

RESTAURANTS

POST OFFICE

BUS STATION

TAM COC CAVES

BICH DONG TEMPLE

VAN LAM

NINH BINH

SEE INSET

TO PHAT DIEM CHURCH (28 km)

has rice paddies. The area supports duck farmers, stray goats on the karst hillsides, and electric fishermen (that is, they fish with pitchforks electrified by car batteries). You can take a similar dreamy boat ride through karst landscape near Ninh Binh. At the village of Van Lam you rent a tar-coated open rowboat for a two- to three-hour trip. Your rower will negotiate the boat through shallow rice paddies and under three splendid long caves. The rice paddies are surreally framed by giant karst outcrops and grottoes.

After gliding through the caves, you get off the boat and walk to a Chinese-style shrine called **Thien**, set in a high cave with views of the area. From here you continue to **Den Thai Vy**, a small 13th-century temple, and jump into the boat again to return to Van Lam.

To get to Tam Coc Caves, go south along Highway 1 from Ninh Binh for 3.5 km. By the side of the road stands a sign for Ninh Binh Tourism—turn west there, cross a stone bridge, and drive along a dirt road for two km to Van Lam village. There's a $1 fee to enter the village. For a fixed price of $1.50 a person, you can hire a boat in Van Lam for a three-hour circuit through the caves and rice paddies. There are no accommodations in Van Lam; foodstalls provide a bit of nourishment. Traveler-café trips from Hanoi cost around $15 for the Tam Coc-Bich Dong trip, including entry fees and boat.

Bich Dong Temple

Three km beyond Van Lam village lies Bich Dong, known for its small temple. There's a $1 entry fee to the area. Local children will act as guides, and they expect a donation. Bich Dong Temple is set into the base of a limestone peak. The upper temple, located inside a cave, holds three blackened figures—a large stone Buddha in meditation posture, flanked by two protectors. From the upper temple you can climb to the top of a peak for splendid views over the entire area; watch out for the sharp limestone. There are two other small temples in the vicinity if you want to explore further: **Xuyen Thuy Dong,** reached by boat, and **Dong Tien,** a 500-meter walk from Bich Dong.

Near Ninh Binh

Hoa Lu: Site of an ancient royal capital, Hoa Lu is situated about 12 km northwest of Ninh Binh. Compared to Tam Coc or Bich Dong, there's not much to see. Guardians charge a $1.50 entry fee, which allows you to view a couple of crumbling temples. The main temple was dedicated to 10th-century Emperor Dinh Tien Hoang and rebuilt in the 17th century. Hoa Lu served as capital for 12 years under Hoang's reign and a further 29 years under the Le dynasty. There are half a dozen minor temples in the area. You can climb up Lang Ma mountain to visit the tomb of the Dinh emperors, and the peak provides a panoramic view. You can see similar vistas from Bich Dong.

Nam Dinh: A slew of (yawn) royal temples and pagodas pack the area around Nam Dinh, a filthy industrial town 28 km northeast of Ninh Binh. The temples and pagodas date from the

rice terraces near Mai Chau

12th-14th centuries, with later additions and renovations.

Phat Diem Cathedral: About 28 km southeast of Ninh Binh stands Phat Diem Cathedral, the center of Catholicism in north Vietnam. The stone structure is built in unique Sino-Vietnamese style with a pagoda-like belfry. The vaulted ceiling is supported by a series of massive wood columns; lining the nave are wooden carvings, and at the front is an altar sculpted from a single block of granite. The cathedral was founded in 1891 by a Vietnamese priest. Nearby is Thuan Dao Church, built in 1926 in an odd neo-Roman design, and a small seminary in Phuc Nac.

IN THE SOUTHWEST

Southwest of Hanoi you'll find several areas ideal for short hikes or longer treks—in the minority areas around Hoa Binh and Mai Chau, or the national park at Cuc Phuong. Visiting these places requires expeditionary planning—you need your own transportation, preferably a 4WD vehicle, and a guide. Although you can reach these places on day-trips from Hanoi, a trip two days or longer is preferable. Longer itineraries might include Hanoi to Hoa Binh to Mai Chau to Cuc Phuong to Hanoi, or Hanoi to Ninh Binh to Tam Coc Caves to Bich Dong to Cuc Phuong to Mai Chau to Hoa Binh and back to Hanoi. If you plan to travel to the Tonkinese Alps, you can arrange to spend extra time in Mai Chau en route.

Hoa Binh

Site of a huge Russian-built dam on the Black River (Song Da), Hoa Binh, 75 km southwest of Hanoi, is the largest hydroelectric plant in the country, with a capacity of 1,900 megawatts. Constructing the dam and reservoir involved flooding the valley and displacing an estimated 58,000 people, so the area has lost much of its attraction. However, Hoa Binh serves some tour companies as a base for jungle treks and visits to nearby Muong and Tai villages. The four-story **Khach San Song Da** hotel in Hoa Binh was built for Russian engineers. **Khach San Hoa Binh** displays more imagination, with Tai-style bungalows for $20.

Mai Chau

Mai Chau lies in a pretty valley with a patchwork quilt of rice paddies, farms, and longhouses. It's 60 km southwest of Hoa Binh, or about 135 km from Hanoi. In the spring, Mai Chau displays a riot of color with blooming flowers and peach blossoms. Using Mai Chau as a base, you can traipse through rice paddies to reach Black Tai and Hmong villages. The Black Tais live in raised wooden longhouses in the shape of tortoise shells, with sloping roofs made from palm or sugarcane leaves. Inside are polished bamboo-slat floors with woven mats, a fireplace for cooking, and a handloom; buffalo, chickens, and pigs live under the house. There are usually fishponds in the area.

Hmong villages are harder to locate. They're much poorer and composed of simple huts with earthen floors. The women wear elaborately patterned tops and skirts; the full outfit can take three years to embroider. The men smoke opium.

Opposite the bus station in Mai Chau is the central covered market, visited by minority groups in the area. The big day is Sunday. Moto drivers with Russian Minsks hang around outside the market and can take you to outlying villages.

About 1.5 km south of the market, the two-story **Mai Chau Guesthouse** offers nine comfortable rooms for $13 double with bath. You can also arrange to stay overnight in villages, though you need to bring a guide to do the talking. A longhouse "guesthouse" supplies simple fold-up mattresses, as well as mosquito nets. You can take in most sights on a three- to four-day trek in the Mai Chau area.

To reach Mai Chau, take a bus from Hanoi's Kim Ma bus station to Hoa Binh, then change for Mai Chau. A jeep or minibus takes four or five hours to get to Mai Chau from Hanoi. If coming by hired vehicle, you can stop at Man Duc, a town close to Mai Chau with great karst scenery. Traveler cafés in Hanoi typically charge $15-30 per person for a two-day minibus trip to Mai Chau with an overnight stay in a village. Darling Café, at 4 Hang Quat, organizes four-day hikes around Mai Chau. Especen organizes a two-day Hanoi-Mai Chau-Hoa Binh-Hanoi loop in a Russian car for $97, or $145 in a Land Cruiser.

CUC PHUONG NATIONAL PARK

Cuc Phuong is the best of a rum bunch of "national parks" in the north. The park, roughly 11 km wide and 25 km long, was created in 1962—the first area in Vietnam set aside as a national park. It covers an area of 25,000 hectares, but for the moment is a national park in name only. There are six Muong villages in the park: villagers farm and raise cattle on park lands, and hunt. Deforestation in the surrounding area steadily encroaches on parkland, and large amounts of brushwood disappear from the park daily. Rangers, poorly paid, turn a blind eye to poaching, or to weekend visitors carrying off orchids. Cuc Phuong is low-key: those expecting spectacular scenery with animals everywhere will be sorely disappointed.

However, Cuc Phuong contains plenty of attractions for botanists. The park supports a wide variety of flora species and patches of primeval forest, including 50-meter tall *Cinamomum, Parashorea,* and *Sandicorum* trees. You can find ancient trees with thick clusters of roots, and parasitic plants and ligneous creepers. Some tree species have been introduced from Burma, India, and Borneo. Clusters of orchards grow near cave entrances, where the moisture conditions and light are ideal. Varieties include coral, vanilla, snow-white, and butterfly orchids.

Larger mammals inhabit the park, including panthers and bears, but hunting has severely depleted their numbers. The park supports many

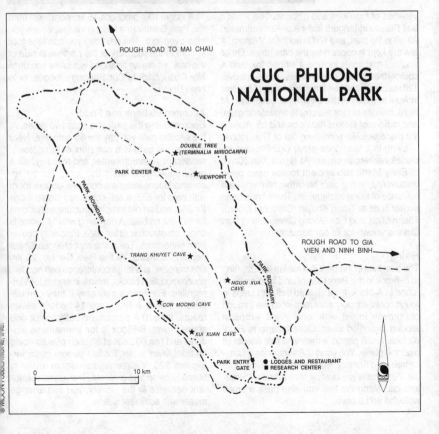

locals pilfering wood from the park

varieties of monkeys and gibbons. The world's last Delacourt langurs live here—an estimated 20 left in the park, and 100 in northern Vietnam. A few are kept in cages near the park gates. Other unusual mammals include a striped fox, and a squirrel that glides between trees. There are over 120 species of birds and many varieties of beetles; in April and May arrive swarms of butterflies. At night, millions of cicadas create a deafening din, and millions of fireflies flicker on and off, making the place look like something out of *The Hobbit*.

Lying in a limestone area, Cuc Phuong includes numerous caves. At Nguoi Xua (Cave of Early Man), two ancient tombs have been discovered, along with Neolithic remains and evidence of stone implements. There have been similar finds at Trang Khuyet (Crescent Moon), Thanh Minh, and Con Moong Caves. Hang Dan Cave is known for its bat population.

Hiking

The best hike in the park is a six-km trail, starting at B-Block in the Park Center and looping back round to A-block. It's a cleared trail with steps in rough spots, slippery after rain. You hike through old-growth forest with long vines wrapped around strangled trees. Quite bizarre is *Euta-da tonkinensis ganep,* a thick vine that shoots all over the place. You pass a *Parashorea assimi-ca* tree, and halfway round the trail a large, double *Terminalia miriocarpa* tree stands 45 meters tall. Along the trail you also pass a small waterfall and a cave.

A longer hike proceeds 15 km northwest from the Park Center to a Muong village, where you stay overnight. The next day you can hike four km out to the roadway at the northwest side of the park, where an arranged van takes you on to Mai Chau, back to Cuc Phuong's lodges, or to Ninh Binh.

Accommodations and Food

Upon entering the park you pass two gates. At the second gate you pay the $5 entry fee. Near the second gate is a complex of bungalows, restaurant, research center, and meeting hall; a hundred workers live in this area. Tourist accommodations include a concrete double room with bath for $35; a self-contained jungle lodge for $40, and an old temple structure with rooms for $10-20, no bath. A new wing with 17 rooms is under construction at the gate. Electricity comes from generators. The restaurant charges $2 per person for meals. At the Park Center, 20 km into the park, is a large conference hall and two accommodation blocks, mainly intended for Vietnamese. Foreigners may stay if they can negotiate a deal. A-Block has 14 beds in seven rooms, for $10 a person, no bathrooms, one shared toilet. B-Block is for Vietnamese students and has 60 beds at $3 each plus camping on front lawn; a tent for five people costs foreigners $20. Vietnamese students arrive in buses to camp and cook out. Though no restaurant operates in the vicinity, you can arrange meals with sufficient notice.

Getting There

The park lies 140 km from Hanoi, or 55 km from Ninh Binh. It sits astride the junction of Hoa Binh, Ninh Binh, and Thanh Hoa provinces. The only way to get to Cuc Phuong at present is by rented vehicle. The drive in from Ninh Binh via Gia Vien is along a rough dirt road and takes about two hours. You can base yourself in Ninh Binh for a day-trip to the park, or stay overnight at Cuc Phuong. Especen in Hanoi charges $95 for a car and driver to Cuc Phuong and back, the cost split between three passengers for the two-day trip. Queen Café charge $20-35 for a two-day tour, transportation only, based on 2-10 passengers. Park entry fee is $5 for each foreigner; the price includes a guide. Try to time your visit for the October to January dry winter season when there are no mosquitoes or leeches. The weather can be chilly at this time, as Cuc Phuong lies at 300 meters; it's generally a few degrees cooler than Hanoi. May to September is the rainy season, and June to August is very hot and humid, with leeches and mosquitoes.

NORTH BY NORTHEAST

Historically, the border zone to the far north and northeast has been contested by the Vietnamese and Chinese. The dense and hilly area is pierced by several alluvial plains—Cao Bang and Lang Son being two of them. In the 1940s the Vietminh ousted the French from Cao Bang and used the area as their base; Ho Chi Minh took refuge in a grotto here. Major battles were fought with the French in the early 1950s around Lang Son and Cao Bang. In 1979 the Chinese launched a 17-day war with the Vietnamese, destroying buildings in many border towns in the area. Since the normalization of relations in 1991, trade between China and Vietnam once more thrives, as does smuggling.

Close to the Chinese border reside minority groups, originally descended from China. A million Nung and Tay people live in the northeast, scattered in mountain valleys. Other groups include the Zao and the Hmong. Ethnic groups are found in larger concentrations around Cao Bang and Ha Giang.

The zone north by northeast of Hanoi hasn't sparked a lot of tourist interest yet, nor produced much in the way of hotels. It just doesn't seem to have the right kind of attractions or creature comforts to attract tourists.

Tam Dao Hill Resort

Tam Dao is a scruffy resort 75 km north of Hanoi. Set up in 1907 by the French as an escape from the heat of the Red River Delta, the resort lies at a 900-meter elevation and is 10 degrees cooler than the delta in the summer, and actually cold in the winter. The forest has reclaimed the ruins of summer homes the French torched in 1954 rather than hand them over to the advancing Vietminh.

Some Hanoi traveler cafés organize day-trips to the area, or you could get there via rented motorcycle. Local transportation falls short; there's a bus from Hanoi's Kim Ma bus station to Vinh Yen that takes 2.5 hours. Once you reach Vinh Yen, it's another 20 km to Tam Dao, so you have to hitch on whatever comes past, usually a motorcycle. At the bottom of the hill at a guard post a man will ask you for $3—that's $1 for entry and $2 for "insurance." Other motorcyclists have been charged a "motorcycle fee," so at least the rip-off is customized. You may wish to negotiate.

There's not much left of the old French hill station. Most of the old buildings have been replaced with concrete-block structures, including **Tam Dao Hotel** and several surrounding cabins. Rooms here go for $20 apiece; Tam Dao Tourism maintains an office at the hotel. What to do in Tam Dao? Well, you can swim in a refreshing outdoor pool, with mountain views. Or you can take a short walk to Silver Falls, nice if you can ignore the trash everywhere. Or you can hike around the forest. Close by is Tam Dao Forest Preserve, with an array of camellias, orchids, birds, and butterflies.

Ba Be Lakes

Ba Be Lakes (Ho Ba Be), 230 km north of Hanoi, was created as a forest reserve and tourist center in 1978. The name means "Three Seas," a reference to the three lakes within its confines. Two are minor lakes. The main lake, seven km long, and between 200 meters and one km wide, is surrounded by vertical rock walls to which many kinds of creepers cling, and a wild forest where many species of birds abound. From Ba

Be Town you can continue by land or boat along the Nang River for about three km to **Puong Cave,** Ba Be's major attraction. The cave opens into large chambers adorned with oddly shaped stalactites and stalagmites. You can reach **Dau Dang Falls** by foot or boat.

By hired car, it takes about eight hours to drive to Ba Be Lakes from Hanoi along Route 3 via Thai Nguyen and Bac Can. By bus you can go to Bac Can, transfer for another ride to Cho Ra, then take an 18-km moto ride into Ba Be Lakes. Ba Be Town is a conglomeration of shops, market, and dwellings. Construction of a guesthouse and restaurants is in progress on the shores of the lake. Several km from the lake is an inexpensive guesthouse.

Traveler cafés in Hanoi offer the Ba Be Lakes trip on an irregular basis. A three-day trip costs $45-60 based on 6-12 people and includes admission fee, guide, accommodations, and food.

Lang Son and the Chinese Border

Lang Son, 155 km northeast of Hanoi, is the closest town to the Chinese border crossing at Huu Nghi Quan (Friendship Gate). The town is uninspiring, much of it newly built after Chinese attacks in early 1979 inflicted considerable damage. At that time 85,000 Chinese troops streamed across 26 points along the border with Vietnam. Within 10 days, they'd taken every provincial capital except for Lang Son, which became the scene of intense house-to-house fighting. Chinese troops captured the town six days later, and several hours after announcing their success, withdrew to China.

For the next 10 years, nothing happened at the border apart from a few skirmishes. The residents of Lang Son lived in the ruins of their city under strips of canvas and plastic, without running water or other facilities. With the normalization of relations in 1991, the town faced a new invasion—an avalanche of cheap Chinese goods. An estimated 70% of the trade in Chinese goods involves smuggling.

Lang Son to Hong Kong: To cross the Chinese border at Lang Son you must have a Chinese visa and a Huu Nghi Quan exit stamp on your Vietnamese visa. Arrange the tedious paperwork in Hanoi, and allow a week to process it; anything faster will cost more. To reach Lang Son, take a minibus near Hanoi Opera House, or a bus from Hanoi's Gia Lam bus station (six hours). A day-trip is preferable so you can view the scenery. Several trains depart daily in the direction of Lang Son, taking six to eight hours for the journey.

From Lang Son, hire a jeep or moto for the 20-km ride to the border at Dong Dang, the terminus of Highway 1. Dong Dang features a bustling market with a sea of Chinese goods—cosmetics, toys, electric fans, Chinese beer. A blackmarket in money also flourishes, with exchanging in dong, dollars, and Chinese renminbi. There is about 600 meters of no man's land between border checkpoints. You cross on foot through the marble Huu Nghi Quan, or Friendship Gate (Youyi Guan in Chinese), to the Chinese side, where Vietnamese exports of coal, rubber, and coconut oil are stacked. For $5 you can take a share-taxi to Pingxiang, the first major town on the Chinese side, where you can catch a train or bus to Nanning (five hours). You'll find places to stay in both Pingxiang and Nanning. The journey from Nanning to Canton takes 24 hours by bus; from Canton, you can board an overnight boat to Hong Kong for about $25. The entire cost overland by rail, bus, and boat from Hanoi to Hong Kong should be under $50.

Hong Kong to Lang Son: Coming in the other direction, exiting China, you must have a valid Vietnamese visa with a Huu Nghi entry stamp on it. In Beijing you can obtain a Vietnamese visa in one week, valid for this crossing, though most travelers pick up a Vietnamese visa in Hong Kong. From Hong Kong you can travel overland via Nanning to the border crossing. If for some reason you can't get the border point stamped on the Vietnamese visa, you can fly from Nanning to Hanoi one-way for $80. Westerners coming from China with a valid Vietnamese visa but without Huu Nghi stamped on it have bribed their way through for $20.

GULF OF TONKIN

The Gulf of Tonkin was once the haunt of Vietnamese and Chinese pirates. At Halong Bay the romance of old Vietnam still lingers, with bizarre karst islets randomly scattered and the odd red-sailed junk clipping across the waters. This timeless waterscape seems a long way off in the dreary port of Haiphong, the key access point to the area by boat, but Halong Bay is only a short hop away. Halong Bay is accessed principally from the seaside resort town of Bai Chay, which you can reach by land from Hanoi via Haiphong, or by ferry from Haiphong. The Haiphong ferry lands at Hong Gai, a mining town and fishing port five km east of Bai Chay. Travelers consider Halong Bay one of the highlights of their trip in the north—seafaring in these waters is definitely an experience. You can laze about on deck, and opportunities abound for swimming, caving, and diving, not to mention enjoying fresh seafood.

HAIPHONG

Haiphong has the distinction of being the first place French warships landed in the Gulf of Tonkin in 1872, and the last place they left in May of 1955. In the late 1880s, after the harbor was widened, the port was developed by the French as the major conduit for extracting wealth from Tonkin, and Haiphong soon mushroomed into the second largest city in the north. Visiting in 1918, Reverend James Walsh wrote in his *Observations in the Orient* that Haiphong had "the appearance of a neat, prosperous, French city with wide streets, attractive public

HALONG BAY ROUTES

Plan a minimum two-day trip to Halong Bay. It's 105 km from Hanoi to Haiphong, another 60 km to Bai Chay, and a final five to Hong Gai. By sea, Cat Ba Island is 30 km east of Haiphong. Allow five days to cover the Haiphong-Bai Chay-Halong Bay-Cat Ba Island route. A week's itinerary might run: Hanoi-Bai Chay on the first day; spend two days in Bai Chay exploring Halong Bay; transfer by boat to Cat Ba; spend one or two days in Cat Ba; leave for Haiphong and transfer to Hanoi. Build in extra time for delays due to poor transport connections. You could cut a day by sightseeing across Halong Bay en route to Cat Ba Island. Or make it a two-day jaunt: sightsee in Halong, overnight on a boat in Halong, and continue to Cat Ba the next day. From mid-November to mid-March Halong Bay is colder and foggier, with increased rain and drizzle. Fog and rain can obscure visibility and defeat the purpose of the visit. At this time of year you need raingear, and blankets if sleeping overnight on boats.

Tour Options

Tour agencies and traveler cafés in Hanoi all offer one- to three-day tours of Halong Bay—typically $18-30 a person for a two-day trip, based on 5-20 people. This includes minibus and boat transport, one night's accommodations, and food. Queen Café organizes a two-day tour with an overnight on the boat, and occasionally arranges a Halong-Cat Ba combination tour. It's easy to band together with other travelers in Bai Chay to rent fishing boats. You could also put together your own small group and set off in a car or minibus. A Hanoi agency might charge $120 for a three-day package, not including a boat, which breaks down to $25-30 per 100 km of road travel, plus $15 for the driver, and $20 for a guide. TOSERCO charges $80-110 per person for a two-day trip to Halong, based on three to nine people. The agency books more expensive hotels, and you hope the boats are superior for that price.

For those with money to burn, Vietnam Air Service Company (VASCO) offers a two-day overflight of Halong Bay in a Squirrel helicopter with a French pilot. The flight begins from Hanoi's Gia Lam Airport, continues to Haiphong and Cat Ba, then wings over Halong Bay to Hong Gai. After a night in Hong Gai, return the next day to Gia Lam Airport. Cost is $2000 for one to four passengers. Contact VASCO at the Metropole Hotel, Hanoi, tel. 266919, ext. 8015.

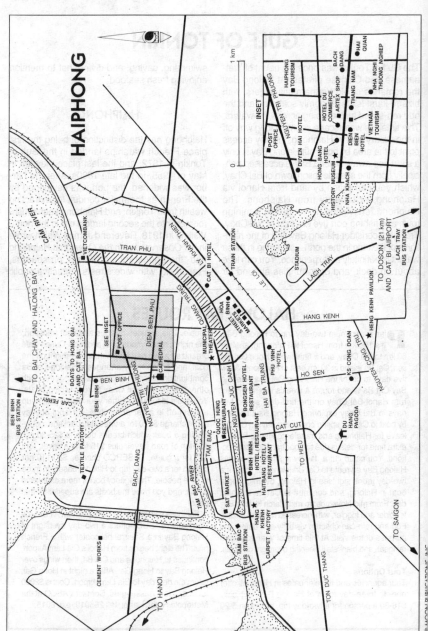

HAIPHONG

CAM RIVER

TO BAI CHAY AND HALONG BAY

VIETCOMBANK

TRAN PHU

LY KHANH THIEN

CAT BI HOTEL

TRAIN STATION

STADIUM

LACH TRAY

LE LOI

LACH TRAY BUS STATION

TO DOSON (21 km) AND CAT BI AIRPORT

HENG KENH PAVILION

HANG KENH

HO SEN

KS CONG DOAN

PHU VINH HOTEL

NGUYEN CONG TRU

DU HANG PAGODA

TO HIEU

CAT CUT

HAI BA TRUNG

BONGSEN HOTEL / RESTAURANT

QUOC HUNG RESTAURANT

NGUYEN DUC CANH

MUNICIPAL QUANG TRUNG

MARKETS / STREET

HOA BINH

THEATER

POST OFFICE

DIEN BIEN PHU

CATHEDRAL

SEE INSET

BOATS TO HONG GAI AND CAT BA

BEN BINH

CAR FERRY

NGUYEN TRI PHUONG

TEXTILE FACTORY

BACH DANG

TAM BAC RIVER

TAM BAC

BINH MINH HOTEL / RESTAURANT

HAITRANG HOTEL / RESTAURANT

SAT MARKET

HANG KENH CARPET FACTORY

TAM BAC BUS STATION

CEMENT WORKS

TON DUC THANG

TO HANOI

TO SAIGON

BEN BINH BUS STATION

INSET

1 km

0

POST OFFICE

NGUYEN TRI PHUONG

DUYEN HAI HOTEL

HONG BANG HOTEL

HISTORY MUSEUM

HAIPHONG TOURISM

HOTEL DU COMMERCE

ARTEX SHOP

THANG NAM

DIEN BIEN HOTEL

NHA KHACH

BACH DANG

HAI QUAN

NHA NGHI THUONG NGHIEP

VIETNAM TOURISM

TOURING HAIPHONG

Haiphong Tourism office displays pictures of Thailand's Pattaya Beach and Krabi under its glass tabletops, and if you ask about Haiphong, you'll receive a glowing report about the beach resort of Doson, 22 km away. There are only a few places to see in Haiphong. A couple of hours in a cyclo will get you round most of them, or simply walk. If you're going to take a cyclo, why not go in style? Several hotels—the Bach Dang in particular—have luxury cyclos with padded red seats, plush armrests, front suspension, fringed sunroofs, even headlights. All that's lacking is a karaoke machine up front. The imperialist-model cyclo will take two passengers, albeit slim ones, and costs about $1.20 an hour, not much more than the regular ratty cyclos with wooden boards for seats that bang you around from teakettle to breakfast time. The suspension-model super-cyclos, incidentally, are used for VIPs or for family members on marriage negotiation visits. Haiphong's streets are exceedingly quiet—the only things that seem to move along them regularly are cyclos. A suggested cyclo route starts on Dien Bien Phu Street to the History Museum and the Cathedral; then carry on to the Municipal Theater and Hang Kenh Carpet Factory, and visit Du Hang Pagoda. A good place to finish is the street market near Haiphong Railway Station.

buildings, comfortable-looking houses, well-equipped hotels, a large theater, and about every conceivable convenience for its French residents, of whom, in normal times there are 5,000." From Haiphong, rice, rubber, coal, and mineral resources were shipped back to France. The Japanese, arriving in 1940, used the same infrastructure to divert the flow of goods to Japan.

In 1946 in a dispute over who should collect customs duties, the French clashed with the Vietminh and bombarded Haiphong, leading to an outbreak of warfare that continued for the next eight years. Between 1966 and 1972, Haiphong was repeatedly attacked by US air and naval forces. In 1972 Haiphong harbor was mined in an attempt to reduce the flow of Russian military supplies, though the mines were cleared the following year as part of the Paris Accords. After 1975 Haiphong developed as an industrial town, with the establishment of brick, glass, cement, and textile plants, lime kilns and shipyards. Like Saigon and Hanoi, Haiphong functions as an independent municipality. The population of greater Haiphong, covering an area of 1,515 square km, is estimated at 1.5 million; the city proper consists of three districts and supports a population of around half a million.

Haiphong remains an industrial port town. Adjectives that spring to mind are dreary, gray, run-down, ugly, sleepy, and sluggish. Still, you don't have to fight over hotel rooms. Not many foreigners bother to look around Haiphong, so they receive better treatment here than in Hanoi.

Sights

Colonial Haiphong: Traces of Haiphong's colonial splendor remain along Dien Bien Phu Street, formerly known as Avenue Paul Bert and Avenue Marechal Joffre. Imposing here are the History Museum, the GPO, the Hotel du Commerce, and the cathedral. If your timing is right (Thursday, Saturday, and Sunday 1400-1600), the History Museum may be open. South of the cathedral stands the Municipal Theater, which has a bland exterior but a magnificent interior with opera galleries and solid wood fixtures and banisters. Another architectural relic is the railway station with its vintage freight trains, including a coal-fired Dutch engine from the 1930s, all stoked up and ready to go.

Du Hang Pagoda: Two km south of town, at 121 Hang Kenh St., this pagoda was built in the 17th century and renovated many times since. The pagoda, which houses half a dozen resident monks, is Vietnamese in style and contains brilliant woodwork, bronze statues, and a bonsai collection. An array of statues highlight a circular lotus pond in the peaceful gardens, an excellent place to reduce your blood pressure.

Hang Kenh Pavilion: This communal house at 53 Nguyen Cong Tru St. was once part of the village called Kenh; the village was long ago swallowed up by Haiphong. The small traditional house features intricate woodwork and sculpture and is dedicated to 10th-century national hero Ngo Quyen. You can safely skip this one if your time is short.

Municipal Theater

The Port: You'll no doubt see a good part of scummy Haiphong Harbour en route to Hong Gai or Cat Ba. But if you have some extra time, take a walk down by the docks, or hire a boat and cruise around. In the harbor chug old wooden fishing boats, barges, and heavy ships, while crane arms perch like giant praying mantises over container ships.

Accommodations

Most tourist services cluster along Dien Bien Phu Street, including half a dozen hotels and a few souvenir shops. Scattered around the train station and southwest side of Haiphong are a few other hotels and some private mini-hotels. Hotels do not fall into convenient price-range categories, since a top-end hotel may also offer cheaper rooms.

Near the Ferry: Ben Binh Hotel, also known as Nha Khach Thanh Pho Haiphong, 2 Ben Binh, tel. 42260, has nine cavernous rooms—$10-15 downstairs, and $25 upstairs. The place is favored by government officials and army personnel. Entry is via a café opposite Ben Binh ferry dock.

Around Dien Bien Phu St. (DBP): Nha Khach, 107 DBP, tel. 42292, is actually located on a side street south of DBP, near the History Museum. Rooms are $5, no bath. Also on a side street off DBP is **Nha Nghi Thuong Nghiep,** on Minh Khai St., tel. 42443, with 20 rooms for $5 double in two opposing wings.

Duyen Hai Hotel, at 5 Nguyen Tri Phuong

north of Dien Bien Phu St., tel. 42134, has 30 rooms in the $12-18-30 range, most of them $30. **Thang Nam Hotel,** 55 DBP, tel. 42820, fax 42674, offers 19 rooms for $12-20; you can bargain rates down in the off-season. **Dien Bien Hotel,** 67 DBP, tel. 42573, fax 42977, has 20 rooms—singles and doubles for $20, and some fancier models with fridge for $30.

Dien Bien Phu/Luxury: Hotel du Commerce, 62 DBP, tel. 42790, fax 42674, features 35 large rooms for $18-25-35. Singles cost $5 less than doubles. Great atmosphere, good restaurant; this French classic is run by Vietnam Tourism. Next door languishes a modern classic, a half-built 11-story wing now abandoned due to a falling-out between joint-venture partners. At last glimpse, the project remained surreally wrapped in tarpaulins. **Bach Dang,** 42 DBP, tel. 42444, has 21 rooms for $12-24-38 double. **Hong Bang Hotel,** 64 DBP, tel. 42352, fax 47510, has 28 rooms, mostly around $35, and some suites for $45. Rooms for drivers are $10-15.

Railway Station Area: KS Hoa Binh, 104 Ly Khanh Thien St., tel. 46907, is expanding to 75 rooms. The hotel caters to backpackers and charges approximately $8 d. **Cat Bi Hotel,** 30 Tran Phu, tel. 46306, manages a classier atmosphere with 17 rooms for $20-25-30. **Phu Vinh Hotel,** 27 Cat Dai, Hai Bai Trung St., tel. 48381, is a minihotel with 15 rooms for $15-25; the more expensive rooms include a shower and TV.

Tam Bac Area: Toward Sat Market you'll find some private minihotels. **Bongsen** (Lotus), 15 Nguyen Duc Canh St., tel. 46019, has doubles for $10 and its own restaurant. **Binh Minh Hotel,** 60 Nguyen Duc Canh St., tel. 45428, has six rooms for $10 double and a good restaurant, too. **KS Dulich Cong Doan** (Trade Union GH), 8 Ho Sen, tel. 46793, is a large government-run place with 30 rooms for $5-14, but beset with plumbing problems. **Haitrang Hotel,** 40-42 Cat Cut St., tel. 45467, fax 45016, has 15 rooms for $18 s, or $20 d.

Food

Street markets are good for snacks. Two lively areas are along the street in front of the train station and around Sat Market, with over a thousand shops housed in a huge concrete building. Side streets nearby hold soup places, stalls, and local restaurants.

The dining room at the Hotel du Commerce serves crab soup, steamed fish, steamed snails with ginger, and grilled eel for reasonable prices. A few private restaurants in the Tam Bac vicinity stand out, catering to Vietnamese wedding parties and to foreigners who can afford the bills. Asian and European food are served with a list of specialties. **Binh Minh Restaurant,** upstairs at 60 Nguyen Duc Canh St., tel. 45428, features an exotic menu with grilled pangolin, "brandy mixup pangolin's blood," grilled chopped snake, chicken stewed in Chinese herbs, and more conventional seafood dishes. **Quoc Hung,** at 50 Quang Trung, tel. 47639, near Binh Minh, is another private restaurant serving crayfish, squid, pigeon, eel, and beef. **Bongsen Hotel,** at 15 Nguyen Duc Canh St., tel. 46019, offers an extensive menu. **Haitrang Hotel,** 40 Cat Cut St., tel. 45016, has a fourth-floor rooftop restaurant.

Shopping

Artex Shop, on Dien Bien Phu St., run by Haiphong Art and Handicraft Export Company, sells a range of mother-of-pearl inlay furniture, rattanware, ceramics, woodcarvings, lacquerware, embroidery, and ready-made clothing. A bit farther east, at 48 Dien Bien Phu, **My Nghe Artshop** sells more of the same. Hotel lobby gift shops feature these items as well.

At 128 Nguyen Duc Canh St. is **Hang Kenh Carpet Factory** (Tapis Hang Kenh) with a showroom and retail store at the front. Raw New Zealand wool is spun, died, woven, and cut by hand in this factory, which employs 500 workers. Using vertical looms, a team of weavers can take three months to produce a larger carpet by hand. Carpets range 1-100 square meters in size and sell for $60-100 per square meter; lower prices for commercial quantities. Designs vary from traditional Chinese and Vietnamese to modern patterns; carpets can also be woven to order. There are four carpet factories in Haiphong, employing 2,000 workers total. The first factory was established in 1929 by the French, utilizing Chinese designs and mostly exporting to the French market. Today, Haiphong carpets are exported to Canada, France, Japan, Sweden, Australia, Italy, and Saudi Arabia.

Information and Services

Haiphong Tourism, at 15 Le Dai Hanh, tel. 42989, can arrange guides and car rentals. **Vietnam Tourism,** at 57 Dien Bien Phu, tel. 42432, fax 42674, arranges tours, cars, ticketing, and visa formalities. The Hotel du Commerce features a large map with old French street names painted on the wall, and sometimes sells the same in printed form with corresponding Vietnamese street names. Updated maps are unavailable. **Vietcombank,** 11 Hoang Dieu St., deals with foreign exchange, cash only; otherwise, try major hotels.

Getting There and Away

By Air: Cat Bi Airport lies several kilometers southeast from Haiphong, about a 10-minute drive from downtown. Flights from Haiphong to Saigon depart every Tuesday and Saturday, and other flights service Danang. Hanoi-based VASCO offers daily Squirrel Helicopter service between Hanoi's Gia Lam Airport and Haiphong's Cat Bi Airport. The helihop takes 25 minutes, costs $250 one-way per passenger. Maximum number of passengers is five. Inquire through VASCO's counter at the Metropole Hotel in Hanoi, tel. 266919, ext. 8015. VASCO can also arrange custom flights over Halong Bay.

By Train: Four trains leave daily from Hanoi to Haiphong—two crawlers, taking 4.5 hours one-way, and two expresses, requiring three hours one-way. The expresses are HP3, departing Hanoi around 0830, and HP1, departing

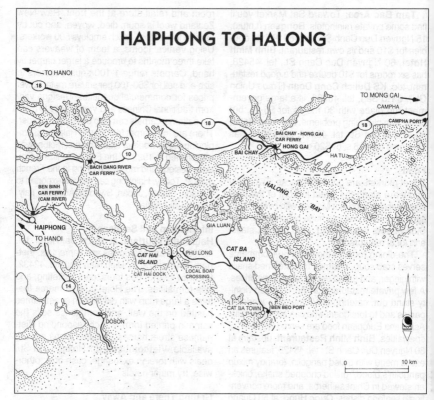

HAIPHONG TO HALONG

TO HANOI

18

TO HANOI

18

BACH DANG RIVER
CAR FERRY

BEN BINH
CAR FERRY
(CAM RIVER)

HAIPHONG
TO HANOI

10

BAI CHAY - HONG GAI
CAR FERRY
BAI CHAY   HONG GAI

HA TU

TO MONG CAI

CAMPHA

18   CAMPHA PORT

HALONG   BAY

GIA LUAN

CAT HAI
ISLAND

PHU LONG

CAT BA
ISLAND

CAT HAI DOCK   LOCAL BOAT
CROSSING

14

DOSON

CAT BA TOWN   BEN BEO PORT

0   10 km

Hanoi around 1430. In the reverse direction, expresses are HP2, departing around 0800, and HP4, departing around 1630. Express trains cost $4, foreigner price, for soft seat. Minibuses are cheaper but not necessarily faster—traffic jams routinely clog the Haiphong-Hanoi road. You also get more legroom on the train.

By Boat: Ben Binh Pier on the waterfront can be reached by cyclo for 50 cents from Haiphong railway station. The pier is divided into different sections. On the west end is a cross-river ferry, which cars and buses use for the route to Bai Chay. East of the ferry stretch two piers with boats to Cat Hai, Cat Ba, Hong Gai, Campha, Cua Ong, and Dan Tien (for Traco Beach). Travelers congregate at a café opposite the Cat Ba ferry to while away the time prior to departure.

Boats leave from Haiphong for Hong Gai at 0600, 1100, and 1600. The ride takes four hours and costs $3. The ferry, a nasty rusting hulk, is loaded to the gunwales with passengers, squawking chickens, bananas, and sacks of produce. You're best off sitting on the roof. The vessel passes heavy shipping in Haiphong Harbor before threading its way through the choppy waters of the northern reaches of Halong Bay, so on a clear day you get some limestone scenery into the bargain.

About 15 meters away from the Hong Gai ferry is the pier for ferries to Cat Hai and Cat Ba islands (Ben Beo Port), with departures usually at 0600 and 1300. There are two methods of getting to Cat Ba town. You can ferry from Haiphong to Cat Hai Island at 1300 for $2, arriving at 1530. Then you transfer to a small craft for a 15-minute run to Phu Long on Cat Ba Island, where you pick up a jeep to Cat Ba town—$2 for a one-hour ride. Total travel time from Haiphong is around four hours. Or you can stay on the boat from Haiphong: after docking in Cat Hai, it continues to Ben Beo Port, arriving at 1700. In Ben Beo, you disembark and walk three km to Cat Ba town. Total time for this route is 4.5 hours. The ferry from Haiphong to Ben Beo Port costs $5.

By Road: Minibuses usually take about 2.5 hours for the run from Hanoi to Haiphong. There is a minibus depot south of the Opera House in Hanoi; cost is around $3 for the run. Buses from Hanoi's Gia Lam Station on the east side of Long Bien Railway Bridge cost $2 to Haiphong.

In the other direction, Haiphong's Ben Xe Tam Bac (Tam Bac Bus Station), close to the Sat Market Building, dispatches buses and minibuses to Hanoi, Ninh Binh, Hadong, Thanh Hoa, Vinh, Ha Giang, Binh Minh, and other points. Check out the posted prices and expect to bargain: the minibus outfits will try and charge as much for the minibus as for the train. Ben Xe Ben Binh, on the north side of the Cam River, runs buses and minibuses to Bai Chay, Hong Gai, Campha, and Cai Rong. Ben Xe Lach Tray, to the southeast side of town, runs buses to Doson Beach.

Getting Around
There are a few Simson motos near the boat docks, but the most common form of transport is cyclos. Rent a cyclo for 90 cents an hour, or $1.10 per hour for a fancy one from Bach Dang Hotel. A rented bicycle would be the ideal way to get around Haiphong, but rentals are next to impossible to come by, though this may change—try asking hotel staff. Arrange car rentals through hotels for destinations like Doson or Bai Chay.

DOSON BEACH RESORT

Doson was established as an exclusive beach resort in 1886 by the French. The beach at Doson faces eastward, and half a dozen large hotels operated by Haiphong Tourism line the beachfront, north to south. Foreigner prices average $20-35 a room; hotels offer lower rates in the off-season (Nov. 15-March 15) when the cold weather prohibits swimming and the place is

deserted. Hotels include Hoa Phuong, Van Thong, Hang Doi, and Hai Au. The Van Thong is a well-equipped 60-room hotel with satellite TV, air-conditioning, and tennis court. At the southern tip of Doson is a French villa-hotel, the Van Hoa, with twin turrets. Built in 1938, it features commanding views and an above-average restaurant. Doson is also home to Vietnam's first and only casino, Hong Kong-invested and exclusively for foreigners—so you'll fit right in here.

Doson lies 22 km south of Haiphong. To get there, take one of the hourly buses leaving from the Lach Tray Bus Station in southeast Haiphong for 50 cents. Or hire a car and driver for $20 for the day and split expenses with others.

CAT BA ISLAND

Cat Ba Island is the largest island in the Cat Ba Archipelago, consisting of over 350 limestone outcrops adjacent to Halong Bay. Lying roughly midway between Haiphong and Hong Gai, the island falls under the administration of Haiphong City, while Halong Bay falls under the administration of Quang Ninh Province. With an area of 356 square km, Cat Ba encompasses forested zones, coastal mangrove and freshwater swamps, beaches, caves, and waterfalls. In 1986, the northeast side of the island was designated a national park, including a protected marine zone. Cat Ba Island supports a population of over 20,000, most of whom live off fishing or farming in the south, in and around Cat Ba Town. To confuse matters, "Cat Ba" may refer to Cat Ba Island (Dao Cat Ba), Cat Ba Town (Pho Cat Ba), Cat Ba Harbor, Cat Ba Port (Ben Beo or Cai Beo), or indeed any part of the island. To the west of Cat Ba Island is Cat Hai Dock on Cat Hai Island. Make sure you know where your boat is headed!

Cat Ba Town
Until the end of the 19th century, Cat Ba was home to Chinese and Vietnamese pirates, and the French maintained a customs station here. Both enterprises seem to linger—on landing or departure you may be hit with a 20-cent "port tax." Experiences on Cat Ba vary. Some travelers have found the islanders friendly; others have had rocks thrown at them, and midnight

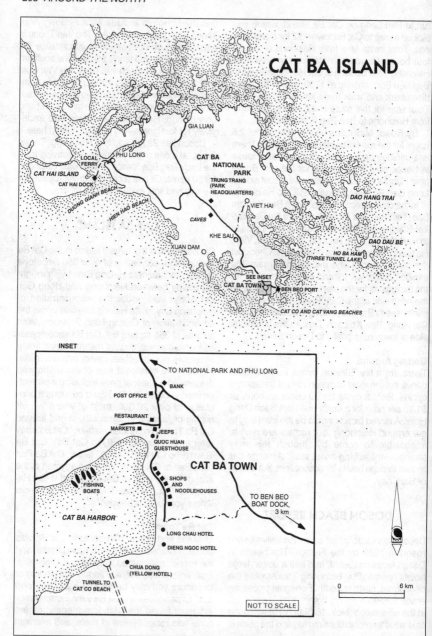

CAT BA ISLAND

GIA LUAN

CAT BA NATIONAL PARK

TRUNG TRANG (PARK HEADQUARTERS)

LOCAL FERRY

PHU LONG

CAT HAI ISLAND

CAT HAI DOCK

DUONG GIANH BEACH

HIEN HAO BEACH

CAVES

VIET HAI

KHE SAU

XUAN DAM

DAO HANG TRAI

DAO DAU BE

HO BA HAM (THREE TUNNEL LAKE)

SEE INSET

CAT BA TOWN

BEN BEO PORT

CAT CO AND CAT VANG BEACHES

0   6 km

INSET

TO NATIONAL PARK AND PHU LONG

BANK

POST OFFICE

RESTAURANT

MARKETS

JEEPS

QUOC HUAN GUESTHOUSE

SHOPS AND NOODLEHOUSES

FISHING BOATS

CAT BA HARBOR

CAT BA TOWN

TO BEN BEO BOAT DOCK, 3 km

LONG CHAU HOTEL

DIENG NGOC HOTEL

CHUA DONG (YELLOW HOTEL)

TUNNEL TO CAT CO BEACH

0   6 km

NOT TO SCALE

visits from police checking documents. Nevertheless, the town is small and ancient, easy to walk around, with clusters of fishing boats and inspiring sunsets across the harbor. A definite Chinese flavor remains to the town, particularly strong in the decrepit buildings on the northwest side. Chinese merchants and fisherfolk originally settled the town, but a mass exodus ensued in 1979 when hostilities broke out between the Vietnamese and Chinese.

The town curves around a crescent-shaped bay, with an esplanade following the foreshore. You can check out the catch of the day in the early morning, see cuttlefish dried over hot coals, or stroll around the old town. You can also pay a boatman for a few hours' harbor touring, or just rent a boat yourself and row around.

It's a short hike from Cat Ba Town through a tunnel to Cat Co Beach. Lurking in the tunnel, like a creature in a Greek myth, is a man who demands you pay $1. At times the ogre may be asleep, in which case you just tiptoe past. A set of steps leads to sandy Cat Co Beach; you can hike farther along to rockier Cat Vang Beach.

Farther Afield

A lack of available transport somewhat hampers exploring, though there's nothing to stop you walking out into villages, or even walking out to the small settlement of Trung Trang and the national park. Around the island you'll find other beaches and sandy coves, some accessible by boat. At the north end toward Phu Long are Duong Gianh and Hien Hao beaches.

You can club together with other travelers and rent a fishing boat from Cat Ba Harbor to view some of the beautiful karst islets in the direction of Halong Bay. Some islets offer fine sand beaches and sandy coves. Head for Ho Ba Ham (Three Tunnel Lake) on Dao Dau Be Island. Or charter a fishing boat from Cat Ba for an all-day ride north into Bai Chay, stopping at key points along the route. Suggested itinerary: Sail from Cat Ba Harbor to Ho Ba Ham, then on to the grottoes of Trinh Nu, Luon, Sung Sot, Bo Nau, and Dau Go before anchoring at Bai Chay.

Accommodations and Food

Cat Ba Town has only a few places to stay. Prices are negotiable, generally higher in summer and lower in winter. At the north end of town you'll find **Quoc Huan GH,** a small, family-run place charging $3 per head. The neighborhood is noisy, with market activity, barking dogs, and karaoke joints.

At the south end of the esplanade a fenced-off section holds three hotels run by Cat Ba Tourist, tel. 88010. For peace and quiet, try the **Long Chau Hotel** in the center. The 13 available rooms range from $9 for a triple room or $2-3 a bed. Nearby are the eight-room **Dieng Ngoc Hotel,** and four-room **Chua Dong,** a big yellow colonial building dubbed the Cat Ba Hilton by some travelers due to its strange, prison-mentality staff. Rooms here cost $6 double. Electricity is supplied for only a few hours a day in Cat Ba Town; when it runs out in the evening, private generators take over.

unloading the catch, Cat Ba Town

Small shops scattered along the esplanade sell processed cheese and bottled water. In the market at the southern end of town you can buy bread and fruit. Near the market is a yellow building, a small restaurant with an English menu. Jeeps and minibuses to Trung Trang and Phu Long leave from the market area. Up the hill, the **Agribank** handles foreign exchange, dealing only in cash.

Cat Ba National Park

Cat Ba National Park (Vuon Quoc Gia Cat Ba), near Trung Trang, lies about 16 km from Cat Ba Town, and 12 km from Phu Long. The park covers an area of about 200 square km, of which two-thirds is a forested zone and one-third a marine zone. Park headquarters are at the small settlement of Trung Trang.

The park consists mainly of inaccessible terrain; you have to fight your way through thickets and up steep gullies to get anywhere. Many side trails branch off main trails in the park— mostly new forest, not old growth. On longer hikes you may see birds, including kingfishers and warblers, and perhaps a tree-dwelling possum with a long bushy tail. The park is home to rare wild white-headed langurs, which live on steep coastal cliffs. Hanoi's Biological Institute has identified over 35 species of birds, 28 species of mammals (including wild boar, macaques, and deer), 20 reptile species, and over 600 plant species within the park. The marine reserve supports dolphins, seals, and hawksbill turtles.

The designation "national park" is a travesty when you consider that farming, logging, and fishing occur within park boundaries—as does poaching. When questioned about an animal trap close to a trail, a ranger responded that he had set it himself. The park brochure describes different marine species found within the park, and then goes on to say "most of them fetch high prices at market places." It seems that Vietnamese authorities just slap a national park label on stray bits of land to attract tourism.

Trung Trang Caves: Two km south of Trung Trang park headquarters a set of caves open into the side of a limestone cliff. The entrances to the caves are visible from the road, about 50 meters up the cliff. You need a flashlight to explore the limestone caves. They are over 300 meters long, and you can easily get lost without a guide—guides are available in Cat Ba Town.

There are a few rooms available at Trung Trang park headquarters for $4 a night; currently a hotel is under construction near the park. Otherwise, make a day-trip from Cat Ba Town. To reach the national park, set out early by jeep from Cat Ba Town to Phu Long, and get off in Trung Trang. It would be a good idea to hire a guide and to bring a flashlight. You can get off the jeep two km south of Trung Trang to visit Trung Trang limestone caves first. Securing a ride to Cat Ba Town in the afternoon after exploring the national park could present a problem. If you can't flag down a passing vehicle, the 18-km walk back takes about three hours. Or stay the night at the park and find transportation the next morning on a jeep returning from Phu Long.

Getting There and Away

Getting there and away is a conundrum that also involves getting around and across Cat Ba Island. Be aware that once you're on the island transportation is either meager or nonexistent. You can catch a moto, occasional jeep, or minibus—or walk. Approximate distances on the island are: Phu Long to Cat Ba Town, 28 km (two morning jeeps, one-hour ride, cost $2 a head); Phu Long to Trung Trang, 12 km; Trung Trang to Cat Ba Town, 16 km (jeep ride costs $1); Gia Luan to Trung Trang, six km (motos only). Ben Beo Port is five km from Cat Ba Town by road, or three km on a shortcut trail—a good half-hour walk.

Cat Ba to Haiphong Ferries: Cat Ba Island lies 30 km east of Haiphong. See "Getting There and Away" under "Haiphong," above, for information about ferries from Haiphong to Cat Ba. To get from Cat Ba back to Haiphong, you have two choices, both of which put you on the same ferry; cost works out about the same. You can rise at the crack of dawn and take a jeep for $2 from Cat Ba market at 0500, arriving in Phu Long at 0600. At 0630 you then make a 15-minute, small-boat crossing to Cat Hai for 20 cents to hook up with the Ben Beo ferry to Haiphong at 0815. Ferry cost is $2. Or you can rise at the crack of dawn, shoulder your luggage, and traipse three km to Ben Beo Port, catch the Ben Beo ferry at 0600, reaching Cat

Hai at 0815 and arriving in Haiphong around 1015. This ferry costs $5.

Bai Chay to Cat Ba Town: No direct ferry links Bai Chay or Hong Gai to Cat Ba Town; you have to go via Cat Hai. You could take a boat from Hong Gai to Cat Hai and then transfer to Phu Long and continue by jeep to Cat Ba Town. Or you could transfer at Cat Hai to another vessel heading to Ben Beo Port, which takes 2.5 hours and costs $3, and then walk from Ben Beo to Cat Ba Town.

It's possible to band together with other travelers and rent a fishing vessel for the trip. You need a larger vessel because the seas can get rough in the open waters toward Cat Ba Island. Arrange a boat in Bai Chay. Quotes range $40-100; a reasonable figure would be $60 split between 15 passengers. This also covers gas for the boat's return trip. Because the boat trip is not officially sanctioned, the captain may have to cover a $10 "fine" when docking at Ben Beo. Captains are reluctant to sail right into Cat Ba Harbor because of the extra distance and the police controls. They will most likely drop you at Ben Beo Port, which is a three-km hike from Cat Ba Town.

The boat trip from Bai Chay to Ben Beo Port takes about five hours one-way. If you start early from Bai Chay, you can combine touring Halong Bay with getting to Cat Ba, visiting grottoes and islands along the way and arriving at Ben Beo Port by nightfall. Or you can take two days, touring Halong the first day, spending a night on the water in the midsection of Halong Bay, and continuing on to Cat Ba the next day.

Negotiate carefully for a boat from Bai Chay. Captains would rather take a shortcut to the north end of Cat Ba Island and dump you at Gia Luan, where you'll be left to the mercy of stray moto drivers for a ride into Cat Ba Town. The boat drop from Bai Chay to Gia Luan should cost no more than $20 one-way. In the reverse direction, from Cat Ba Town to Bai Chay, you can find fishing boats that will take you, but negotiating a fair price for the trip will prove more difficult.

HALONG BAY

With 3,000 limestone and dolomite islets sprinkled over an area of 1,500 square km, Halong Bay offers a wonderland of karst topography.

Legend has it that when the Vietnamese were under attack long ago, a dragon came to their aid, splitting mountains to impede the progress of the enemy. The limestone topography was created by the lash of the dragon's tail as it thundered down from the mountains to the sea; consequently Vinh Halong, or "Halong Bay," means "Bay of the Descending Dragon." In geological terms, the mythical monster at work here is wind and water, weathering the porous limestone over a few million years. This process created the bizarre limestone cathedrals, colonized by stunted and twisted vegetation. The romantic setting of rugged island peaks and bays dotted with sailing junks has inspired a whole genre of Vietnamese painting.

Depending on which kind of beer you drink, the islets resemble animals or other shapes. Some have been christened Head of Buffalo, Neck of Horse, Fighting Cock Rock, Elephant, Crocodile Rock, or Duck Island, while others are called Black Cloud Island, Teapot Island, or Riceball Peak. You can indulge in the fine sport of naming the features yourself, as the French did in their time. The fisherfolk of Halong navigate by these landmarks and can reel off every nook and cranny by name—Hon Ga Choi (Fighting Cock Rock), Hon Con Coc (Toad Island), Hon Rong (Dragon), Hon Rua (Tortoise), Hon Dua (Buddha Praying Island). To follow Vietnamese names, *hon* means karst peak or islet, *dao* means larger island, and *hang* means grotto or karst cave.

Halong Bay allows you to see its geology from the inside—from grottoes with stalactites and stalagmites. This is a spelunkers paradise, with some very deep caves. Grottoes are prime places for shrines in Asia; Vietnamese and Asian visitors as well as locals pay their respects at Dau Go and Trinh Nu grottoes, among others. On a boat tour, you mainly view these karst grottoes. Otherwise, you relax on board, sunbaking, taking in the views, clipping off photos of the islands, eating seafood, or gazing at the sails of a junk heading off into the sunset. Sheltered sandy coves on the islands offer good swimming in summer. The beaches themselves are not the fine-sand variety, more often gravelled or pebbly, or with sharp shells. Halong Bay holds great potential for snorkeling, diving, and kayaking. Bring your own equipment; rental outlets

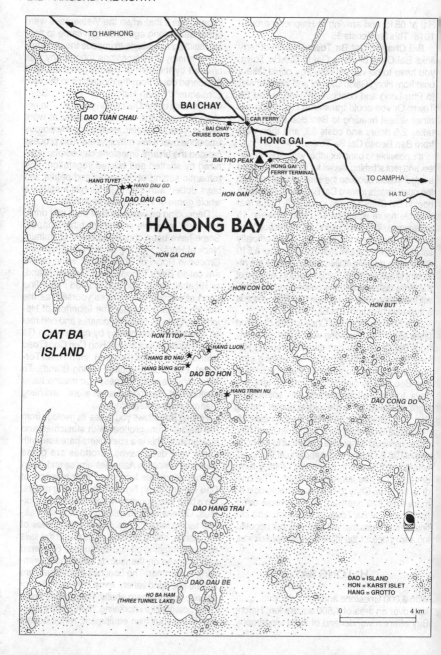

TO HAIPHONG

BAI CHAY

CAR FERRY

BAI CHAY
CRUISE BOATS

HONG GAI

DAO TUAN CHAU

BAI THO PEAK

HONG GAI
FERRY TERMINAL

TO CAMPHA

HANG TUYET   HANG DAU GO

DAO DAU GO

HON OAN

HA TU

HALONG BAY

HON GA CHOI

HON CON COC

HON BUT

CAT BA
ISLAND

HON TI TOP

CHANG LUON

HANG BO NAU

HANG SUNG SOT   DAO BO HON

HANG TRINH NU

DAO CONG DO

DAO HANG TRAI

N

DAO DAU BE

HO BA HAM
(THREE TUNNEL LAKE)

DAO = ISLAND
HON = KARST ISLET
HANG = GROTTO

0   4 km

have yet to take hold. Sea Canoe Thailand, which is based in Phuket, Thailand, has mounted some exploratory trips to Halong, using inflatable kayaks. Sea Canoe offers four- to 14-day journeys, including sea kayaking instruction. Tours are escorted by a wooden junk and most often occur in September and October. Mountain Travel Sobek in El Cerrito, California, USA, also conducts kayak tours in the Halong Bay area.

Chartering a Boat

You can hire cruise boats for exploring Halong Bay in the mainland towns of Bai Chay or Hong Gai. Or you can charter a fishing vessel from Cat Ba Harbor to tour the far south of Halong Bay, though fewer boats offer this service here.

Rental boats anchor around the pier near the post office in Bai Chay or near the car-ferry crossing at the eastern end of town. These boats will motor into Hong Gai if needed. You negotiate directly with the captain. Available boats vary from classy yachts and modified junks to simple fishing boats. The most common rental craft is a converted 11-meter diesel fishing boat, which can hold up to 30 passengers. These roomy vessels have a covered deck, so you can sit under cover, on the roof, or on the open back deck. There should be a small galley and toilet facility on board.

Some boats are fitted with sleeping cabins, which allows you to go for overnight trips—highly recommended as you get a sunset on the water, a canopy of stars at night, and a Halong Bay sunrise. The captain can navigate at night because fisherfolk are active then, and they use lights to attract fish. Sleeping onboard leaves the way open for private island-hopping: if you want to explore Halong for two or three days, this is the way to do it.

Junks can be hired, usually motor fishing boats with red canvas sails added. Junks are slower on the water, but more graceful and less noisy. These vessels are more expensive and harder to find. **Sea Travel Service,** with an office in Hong Gai, tel. 46365, has one junk available, and three motorized fishing boats. **Quang Ninh Tourism,** operating out of Halong Hotel in Bai Chay, can arrange for rental yachts.

If you can spare the time and money, spend two full days exploring Halong, with one night on a boat. Day-trips involve a full 10 hours on the water, starting at dawn. Charter cost depends on number of passengers, the season, the time, the distance, the route, position of the moon and stars, what the captain had for breakfast, and a few hundred other variables, but it usually all boils down to $3-5 an hour for the entire boat in winter, or $5-9 an hour in summer. Sailboats cost more—$10 an hour and up. A two-engine boat that can hold up to 20 people should cost about $60 a day for 10 hours. To sleep overnight, add $5 to the cost. So if you charter a boat for two full days and sleep onboard one night, you're paying for 20 hours and adding $5, which may total $65 in winter.

Food costs extra. Indicate whether you want the captain to arrange for meals. Find out if the boat has cooking facilities; most motorboats include rudimentary cooking facilities on board, and an ice chest for drinks. You can buy bread,

SETTING SAIL

Fishermen at Halong mount fan-shaped Chinese junk sails on their boats, the same sort of sails once deployed by pirates in these waters. Junks have been used for centuries by the Chinese, Japanese, and Javanese for fishing and transportation, and often as living quarters; a junk commonly includes a deck, high masts, and several cotton sails.

Halong is one of the last places where junk sails are still handmade by families of sailmakers. Coarse cotton panels are sewn together with silk thread, with every seam sewn by hand. To discourage rot and mildew, the completed sail is dipped in a liquid that comes from a beetroot-like plant of the yam family. The sail is dipped and dried three or four times, a process that gives the sail its dark red-tan color.

The sails are braced flat by bamboo strips or battens. The bamboo must be treated for a quite different problem—bamboo parasites can literally shred the wood while at sea. Bamboo may be treated with Japanese lilac leaves, pounded into a paste with lime and seawater. Lacquering can also render bamboo less susceptible to borers.

bananas, and other fresh food at the markets in Bai Chay before boarding. Take along bottled water. Bring along a bucket of seafood from the markets and ask the crew to cook it for you. You can also purchase fresh fish, crabs, and prawns off fisherfolk en route—prices are high—and have it cooked on board.

Supplies

Apart from food and bottled water, you should take along a swimsuit in summer, and sunglasses and hat to ward off the fierce midday sun. From November 15 to March 15, colder temperatures and drizzles predominate; you'll need raingear and blankets for sleeping on board. Take along garbage bags to pack your trash out; boat crew routinely heave bottles, cans, and plastic bags overboard. Help stop the practice before Halong Bay becomes a trash heap and the marine ecosystem breaks down permanently.

For grotto exploring you need a sturdy pair of hiking shoes, long pants, and a good flashlight. Bicycle gloves will protect your hands from sharp limestone as you clamber up karst formations. Be careful: Sudden slips and falls in grottoes can result in injury. Take along a small medical kit to share among travelers to deal with cuts and scratches from sharp shells, coral, or limestone.

Hazards

A number of Westerners—myself included—have underestimated the extent of the karst grottoes. They ended up panicking as sunset approached and they hadn't the foggiest idea how to get out of the labyrinth and back to the boat, or indeed in which direction they left the boat. Moral: Take along a Vietnamese guide if the cave looks deep.

In the water, sharks will not trouble you, but watch out for pirates. Pirates used to hide out in Halong Bay, and it seems a few still do. Travelers have reported thefts from boats, so be wary of sampan-dwellers who may board and take off with valuables, both at night and in broad daylight. These same boat people make a practice of ripping up what little coral remains around Halong Bay and selling it to tourists—don't encourage them by buying any. Other travelers have reported petty theft by crew members, though generally this is not a problem.

Getting Around

As a point of reference, it helps to have a map with islands identified in Vietnamese. Quang Ninh Tourism publishes a decent 1993 map of the whole coastline between Cat Ba and Campha. It also marks possible boat routes.

Don't let the captain control the itinerary; his idea of what's interesting may not match yours. To conserve gasoline, some captains will tell you a place takes two hours to get to and then motor very slowly, though the site may be only an hour away. A captain may dump you for hours at one site or spend hours eating lunch. Avoid Hang Dau Go cave, a favorite with captains because it's close to Bai Chay, and it can consume several hours of your time as there are two grottoes there. Head for the Bo Hon Island group first, and hit Dau Go when returning to Bai Chay. Get out your sextant, shoulder the parrot, hoist the mainsail—it's up to you to give some direction and keep the boat moving. If you've had enough of a cave, tell the captain to move on.

Approximate sailing times for an eight-hour trip might run thus: from Bai Chay about 60 to 90 minutes on the water to Bo Nau Grotto; from there 10 minutes to Sung Sot Grotto, and a further 20 minutes to Luon Grotto; 30 to 45 minutes to Trinh Nu Grotto; 60 minutes back north to Dau Go and Tuyet Grottos; and a final 40 minutes from there into Bai Chay. There are many variations for boat itineraries. You could skip Dau Go altogether, go straight out to Bo Hon Island, view that area, and then return to Bai Chay via the islands and port of Hong Gai.

Dau Go Island

On the north side of this island, about 40 minutes out from Bai Chay, are two deep grottoes—Hang Dau Go and Hang Tuyet. **Hang Tuyet** (Snow Cave), a fairly recent discovery, has thus far escaped the plague of graffiti and garbage. The large cave has a steep entryway. Be careful in here; you'll need a strong flashlight. Sparkling stalactites hang throughout the cave.

Nearby **Hang Dau Go** (Hiding the Timber Cave) is the largest grotto in the Halong area. The first French tourists who clambered ashore in the late 19th century christened it Grotte des Merveilles. Its three large chambers contain numerous stalactites and stalagmites in the shapes f birds and animals. One chamber holds a eshwater pool. The grotto especially appeals to hinese tourists, who love to take photos here nd engrave their names on the walls.

Halong Bay has been the setting for some famous naval battles. On three separate occasions in the maze of channels between Haiphong nd Halong the Vietnamese prevented the Chinese from landing. In 1288 Tran Hung Dao topped Mongol ships from sailing up the Bach ang River by placing steel-tipped bamboo takes at high tide. The ships ran against them at ow tide and sank. General Tran Hung Dao supposedly hid the bamboo stakes in Hang Dau Go when preparing to fight the Mongols.

Bo Hon Island

Bo Hon lies about 1.5 hours from Bai Chay (one our on a faster boat) and has four of the best rottoes in the Halong area within easy reach of ach other. The French called the place Ile de la Surprise. Allow at least six hours to get out to the rea, explore, and return to Bai Chay.

In a small islet off Bo Hon you'll find **Hang Bo Nau,** or Pelican Cave, apparently at one time requented by these birds. This grotto has a deepwater entrance, so tour boats can dock up close. Hang Bo Nau consists of a short cave with no xit. From inside the grotto you can take a classic hoto of the facing bay, framed by the mouth of he cave, with stalactites hanging down like giant eeth. Bo Nau is a prime touring destination, and shing families ply the area in sampans, letting pose obnoxious children who beg for money nd food in three languages, and try to sell shells nd coral pieces. The families also sell fresh fish nd shrimp at high prices to tourist boats.

Bo Hon Island faces Bo Nau, and a fiveminute cruise will put you into a wide semicircular bay. The area holds a sea-level shrine, nd two caves high up on cliffs. One cave is not accessible directly from the shore. A set of teps ascends 50 meters to the other, called **Hang Sung Sot.** Hang Sung Sot is very deep, with sparkling white stalactites. A one-hour hike will take you through it.

If you continue eastward by boat around Bo Hon Island for about 20 minutes, you'll reach **Hang Luon,** a perfectly circular pool accessible by a cave entrance by boat. If your boat is too all, transfer to one of the smaller fishing vessels

that wait at the entrance. You can dive off the boat here into the calm water.

Bizarre rock formations jut out of the sea to the north and east of Hang Luon. One resembles a tortoise, another a human head. Some guides call this a big-nosed Charles de Gaulle islet, but for American groups the name changes to George Washington. A nearby formation has limestone "bridges" suspended along its middle; east of the bridges lies a rock island that resembles a curved dragon's back rising out of the water.

Coming around the back of Bo Hon Island, a half-hour cruise will get you to a smaller island with a sea-level cave called **Hang Trinh Nu** (Virgin Grotto). You can scramble up to a back exit that opens onto two pretty coves at the back of the island. Watch out for sharp limestone when scrambling around here. Hang Trinh Nu is associated with a legend about a poor fishing family who rented a boat from a rich mandarin. When they could not pay what they owed him, the cruel mandarin demanded the hand of their exceptionally beautiful daughter. She refused to marry him, so he ordered his soldiers to seize her, but she escaped by boat and hid in Hang Trinh Nu. She ran out of food and died in the grotto—fishermen found her body and buried her here. One rock formation inside the grotto is said to resemble the woman; this has become a shrine, with offerings of incense, fruit, and money left for good luck.

Dau Be Island

One hour south of Hang Trinh Nu, or three to four hours out of Bai Chay, lies Dau Be Island, which has a small fishing settlement. To the western side of the island is **Ho Ba Ham** (Three Tunnel Lake), a deep grotto with three inland "lakes." You can access it only at low tide in a small rowboat; locals will offer to take you through. The tunnels flood at high tide and become very dangerous, so pay attention to the time and the turning tide. Dau Be Island features sandy coves excellent for swimming, also good diving spots with lots of coral. This island is worth visiting if you've chartered a fishing boat on the route from Bai Chay to Cat Ba Island.

Hong Gai Area

You can visit Hong Gai by boat, coming in close to the fishing trawlers that form their own kind of floating market in the morning. You can arrange to alight here to check out the onshore market in Hong Gai. Nearby, tucked away in an alley, is Long Tien Pagoda, named after the illustrious dragon; it's guarded by statues of mythical warriors in elaborate coats of armor. A short way out from Hong Gai is Hon Oan, the island portrayed in the film *Indochine* as L'ile du Dragon. In the movie, plantation owners from the south came up to the impoverished north to recruit workers. Hopeful workers were ferried out to L'ile du Dragon by night, examined by the plantation owners, and shipped off families split up in the process at this slave market. In real Hong Gai history, thousands of laborers were brought to the area to work in the coal mines. Intolerable conditions sparked an uprising against the French overseers.

East of Hong Gai

Adjacent to Halong Bay stretches **Bai Tu Long Bay,** accessed from Campha, another coal-mining area, or Hong Gai. You can get to Campha by taking a minibus parked near the Hong Gai side of the Bai Chay-Hong Gai car ferry or by taking a ferry from Haiphong.

Far from the crowds, Bai Tu Long Bay waits to be explored. A full day itinerary from Hong Gai eastwards might take in Hon Oan, Hon Dua (Buddha Praying Peak), Hon Reu (Monkey Island), and Cua Ong Pagoda. **Hon Reu,** a soil island about four hours from Hong Gai, supports up to 100 monkeys. You must pay a $5 landing fee here to locals living on the island; the fee includes rice for feeding the monkeys, which are raised for traditional Chinese medicinal purposes. Thirty km east of Hong Gai along the coast stands **Cua Ong Pagoda,** dedicated to Tran Hung Dao, who took on not only the Mongols but also rounded up pirates. He is thus a protector of fishermen, and many come to pay their respects. Dragon pillars adorn the richly decorated interior. The pagoda overlooks the coal-loading port of Cua Ong. From Cua Ong you can disembark and make your way back to Hong Gai by road.

Located between Ha Tu and Campha, **Hang Hanh,** is the spelunker's special—a tunnel of several kilometers accessible only on certain days of the month when the water level at the tunnel entrance is optimum. You'll need a small

LOST LAGOONS

Fishermen have explored every nook and cranny of Halong Bay. Or have they?

Karst islets may be hollowed out in parts of the interior. Some parts are accessible through grottoes, and some can be explored by small boat at low tide. This is the way to enter Ho Ba Ham (Three Tunnel Lake) on Dau Be Island, and Hang Hanh Grotto, between Ha Tu and Campha. But there are probably many more tidal caves waiting to be explored.

Enter John Gray, nicknamed "the Caveman" because of his insatiable craving for karst topography. In 1989 this Californian set up the company Sea Canoe in Phuket, Thailand, to pursue his twin interests of karst caving and kayaking. He astounded the Thai tourist world by announcing he had located hidden tunnels in karst islets around Phuket, accessible at low tide by kayak. These tidal caves lead to pristine inland lagoons, or *hongs* (Thai for rooms), totally enclosed by sheer cliffs. The *hongs* had been spotted from aerial surveys, but the walls were too sheer to climb. Only birds and bats visited these saltwater lagoons. Gray

was the first to launch a sea-level search for a way in.

Gray uses inflatable rubber kayaks of his own design. When the oarsman and passengers lie down in the boat, the overall height from the surface is negligible, thus enabling entry into a low tunnel. The *hongs* all differ—some are bare, some are full of mangrove trees and hanging vines, with lizards living in the vegetation.

Recently Gray turned his attention to other karst formations in Asian waters—Palawan in the Philippines, and Halong Bay. Preliminary exploration at Halong Bay has revealed the presence of expansive *hong* systems often interconnected by caves hundreds of meters long. Unfortunately, the cave systems at Halong Bay are deceptively dangerous—even slack tides create a difficult current. At new or full moons, a huge volume of water funnels through these caves, and the current may be impossible to swim or paddle against. Since the caves are carpeted with oysters, being cut to ribbons is a very real possibility. Gray has his work cut out for him at Halong Bay, so to speak.

boat to access the long grotto; also a strong flashlight to pick out the rock formations and stalactites within. Hang Hanh is unique among the caves of Halong Bay in the diversity and size of its stalactites and stalagmites.

Although fishing and coal-mining constitute the major industries around Hong Gai and Campha, other curious industries have prospered on the inhabited islands east of Campha. Silicate (glass) is made on Dao Quan Lan by a Chinese joint-venture concern. At the midsection of this island is the port of Van Don, which in the 12th to 14th centuries was a thriving exchange point for traders sailing junks from China, Japan, and Java. Trade with foreigners in gold, ivory, and precious wood was forbidden at the time, but smugglers abounded. Today, contraband is still trafficked in here, with beer, stereo systems, video players, and cigarettes brought in from China, Thailand, and Hong Kong.

Pearl prospecting thrives on Dao Co To. Off some islands lie rich abalone grounds—mother-of-pearl obtained from the shells is used in making Vietnam's lacquerware. On far-flung islets

daring climbers collect sea-swallow nests, highly prized for use in medicinal soup.

BAI CHAY

Bai Chay and Hong Gai serve as the twin jumping-off points for boat trips to Halong Bay, located 165 km by road from Hanoi and 60 km from Haiphong. They sit on facing slabs of land, connected by a car ferry that operates from 0500 to midnight. Should you stay in Bai Chay or Hong Gai? Most travelers choose Bai Chay, which is cleaner, offers a greater range of accommodations and facilities, features a strip of beach and—more to the point—offers the tour boats.

Hong Gai is an industrial coal-mining town, and boats must be summoned from Bai Chay for tours. Passenger ferries from Haiphong land in Hong Gai. To get to Bai Chay from Hong Gai, you go three km west to a car ferry, make the five-minute crossing, and travel another two km into Bai Chay. Land distance from Hong Gai dock to Bai Chay Post Office is about five km.

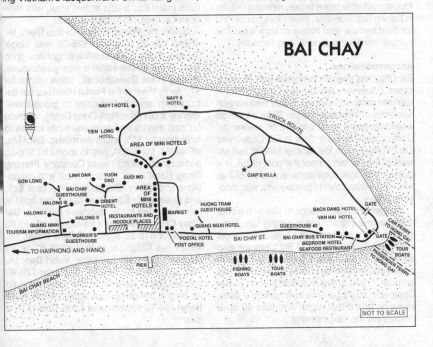

Bai Chay is undergoing development as a major seaside resort, with a flurry of hotel and guesthouse construction. In summer you can swim at Bai Chay Beach or take a boat out to the nearby island of Dao Tuan Chau, which has small beaches and decrepit French villas, including one that served as a vacation retreat for Ho Chi Minh. This island features a solitary hotel that charges a ridiculous $25 a night for poor accommodations; a French company is considering building a high-class hotel. You'll find sandy coves on several of the karst islets around Halong Bay, and you can also swim off your tour boat.

Climate
The weather influences tourism at Bai Chay, Hong Gai, and Halong Bay. In the July-August high season, visitors pack hotels and Bai Chay Beach. Crowds taper off during the shoulder seasons of April-June and September-November. During the November 15-March 15 low season, rates drop for hotels and cruise boats. At this time, however, the weather becomes colder, foggier, and more prone to rain, reducing visibility in Halong Bay. However, there's less competition for boat rentals, and hotels charge less. The coldest months are January and February.

Accommodations
Bai Chay has over 20 minihotels and 15 larger hotels. Rates vary with demand; a $10 room in summer costs $6 in winter. Rates also vary on weekends. A hotel that charges $8 for a room on weekdays might boost it to $12 on weekends. Demarcation lines are clear in Bai Chay: near the car ferry loom the fancier hotels; two km west of the car ferry, near the post office, is a cluster of budget minihotels; and west of that two cul-de-sacs cater to group tours, with moderate prices.

Budget: You can arrange to sleep on a boat during an overnight cruise in Halong Bay. Staying on board costs less than a hotel, and you get views, too. Boats docked in Bai Chay will also allow you to stay overnight for a few dollars even if you're not on a cruise, but security may be poor. If you arrive in the afternoon in Bai Chay, you might be able to negotiate a boat, sleep on board that night, and take off on a cruise early the next morning.

The street leading north from the Postal Hotel has a string of minihotels—usually two- or three-story structures with half a dozen rooms. Most are private. Stroll the strip, check out the rooms, and take the one that suits. Rooms cost $6-14 and up for singles, doubles, or triples; hot water often is available. Most places provide basic comforts like slippers, mosquito nets, and towels; some establishments have air-conditioned rooms. The more than 15 minihotels in the area include: Phuong Vi, tel. 46595; Thu Thuy, tel. 46295; Viet Hoa, tel. 46035; Peace (Hoa Binh), tel. 46009; Rose, tel. 46645; Hai Ha, tel. 46590; Huang Ha, tel. 46308; Viet Phuong, tel. 46493; Suoi May, tel. 46473; and Quoc Thanh, tel. 46004.

Farther up the hill is **Tien Long Hotel,** tel. 46042. This four-story hotel has 47 rooms for $8-10. Around the back of the hill are the **Navy I** (a.k.a. Hai Quan) and **Navy II** hotels for naval personnel. They'll also rent to foreigners if space permits, but rooms are on the derelict side. The Navy also runs two colonial mansions with sea views—three rooms in each house. General Giap maintains a villa in this area, with helicopter access. No tourists allowed.

Moderate: Postal Hotel (KS Buu Dien), tel. 46205, has 25 rooms for $25-30, with fridge, TV, and phone; the post office is right next door. East of the Postal Hotel a nice guesthouse, **Huong Tram Guesthouse,** offers rooms for $10 each. West of the Postal Hotel two cul-de-sacs with large hotels cater to group tours. **Worker's GH** (Nha Nghi Cong Doan), reserved for coal miners and workers, rents rooms to foreigners for $15, space permitting. **Suoi Mo,** tel. 46381, fax 46284, has 45 rooms for $26-55 and is run by Halong Tourist Company. **Phuong Dong Hotel** is an 18-room hotel with expansions under way. Standard rooms cost $25, and suites $45. Staff is pleasant; the hotel is recommended for its business facilities. **Bai Chay GH,** tel. 46440, is a six-story hotel with 80 rooms for $15-25 apiece. **Orient Hotel,** tel. 46323, has 100 rooms, going for $22-40; run by the Hong Gai Coal Company. **Vuon Dao,** tel. 46427, fax 46287, has 55 rooms for $28-40 apiece. There are two smaller places tucked up behind the group-tour hotels: **Minh Minh Hotel** ($6-10 rooms) and **Linh Dan** ($15 a room).

In the second cul-de-sac west of the Postal Hotel are three hotels run by Quang Ninh Tourist Company. **Halong I,** tel. 46321, fax 46318, includes 16 rooms and two suites for $50-80, all often booked. If this place has an institutional air, it's because it used to be a hospital. The hotel features walkways overlooking the beach. Catherine Deneuve stayed here during the filming of *Indochine.* **Halong II,** tel. 46445, offers 40 rooms in two wings—an old French wing and a more modern wing. Prices range $28-35 for a room with fridge, phone, and other creature comforts. **Halong III,** tel. 46316, a modern five-story structure, offers 56 rooms for $25-30. Farther up the hill are tennis courts. **Son Long,** tel. 46319, fax 46226, has 50 bungalow-style rooms for $10 s or $15 d.

Close to the Bai Chay-Hong Gai car-ferry dock stands **Van Hai Hotel,** tel. 46403, fax 46287, with 76 rooms for $22-35-44. Rooms include air-con, bath, phone, fridge, and TV. The hotel offers a full range of amenities including restaurant and souvenir shop, and is managed by Halong Tourist Company, which also runs nearby **Bach Dang Hotel** and **Bedroom Hotel.** Both charge roughly the same prices as the Van Hai. Another place down this way is **Guesthouse #2** (Nha Nghi So 2), tel. 46418, with three fan rooms for $7-10.

Food

There are times in Vietnam when you feel either you're not getting enough food, or it's too bland. Not so in Bai Chay with its great seafood, very reasonably priced. You should always, however, establish prices before dining, especially if the restaurant lacks a menu. Try grilled whole fish, squid, prawns—all fresh, all good. The food is often cooked at the table on charcoal braziers, and served with a garnish of lemon juice, salt, pepper, and spices. West of the post office try **Van Song Restaurant,** with excellent seafood and friendly owners, serving fried squid and fish with tomato sauce, as well as pancakes. In this area are **Minh Binh** and **Thanh Hung** restaurants. Opposite the markets on the minihotel strip you'll find Hoang Lan and Hong Minh restaurants. Noodlehouses crowd the corner of Bai Chay Street. Another excellent restaurant, located near Bai Chay bus station, serves fried squid cooked with pineapple, green onions, and garlic sauce.

Shopping

Souvenir stands line the seafront in Bai Chay, and are scattered around Hong Gai. Buying items made of coral will encourage the destruction of coral reefs. Coal, on the other hand, is a different matter. The shops sell intriguing coal sculptures made by local artisans, often fashioned in the shape of animals.

Information and Services

Restaurants in Bai Chay act as informal traveler cafés. The owners of Van Song Restaurant can arrange boats and answer questions. Good maps of Halong Bay *(ban do Vinh Ha Long)* are sold in hotel lobbies in Bai Chay; you can also buy them down by the docks in Bai Chay. Boat captains own detailed marine charts unavailable to the touring public, but you might talk them into showing you a few once you're on board. **Quang Ninh Tourism,** tel. 46312, located near Halong II Hotel, sells maps and offers pricey three- to eight-hour trips to the islands. The desk at Halong Hotel can change US cash; otherwise, the bank on Ben Doan, east of the market in Hong Gai, can change other currencies and traveler's checks.

Getting There

It's best to board a traveler minibuses from Hanoi to reach Bai Chay. You don't have to take a tour; just go as an extra passenger. The ride should cost about $4 one-way. Or you can take a one-way tour: board a minibus, cruise Halong Bay, then get off in Bai Chay. Negotiate a reduction for a one-way ride, say $21 instead of $25. You can hire cars or larger vehicles in Hanoi or Bai Chay; rates are calculated per 100 km.

The 165-km road trip from Hanoi to Halong Bay can be slow due to the poor condition of the road, and several ferry crossings with long lineups. Added to this are two one-way bridges to cross. There are train tracks in the middle, and bicycle lanes on either side. Only one lane of traffic can proceed at a time—the oncoming traffic waits its turn—and all traffic halts when a train comes through.

Buses from Hanoi's Gia Lam station, on the east side of Long Bien Railway Bridge, depart early in the morning and take five hours. The trip costs $1.50 one-way. Minibuses charging $3 depart from the area south of the Opera

House in Hanoi. Bai Chay's bus station, located near the car-ferry crossing to Hong Gai, offers five express departures daily to Hanoi (five hours) 0700-1400, and eight departures to Haiphong (two hours) 0700-1600. Minibuses are located nearby.

HONG GAI

Hong Gai lies in Vietnam's premier coal-producing area, with mines to the north of town and a setting straight out of the Industrial Revolution. For this reason, grimy Hong Gai does not attract much tourism. The coal mines once attracted the French, however: in 1882, Captain Henri Rivière and 600 men seized the mines for France. He was later ambushed and killed

near Hong Gai by Black Flag pirates, who carried his head from village to village as a symbol of France's defeat. The incident precipitated the decision of the French parliament to take over Tonkin and Annam as protectorates in 1883.

The town of Hong Gai wraps around a karst peak called Bai Tho, with sheer cliffs that plunge straight into the sea. Bai Tho means "Poem Mountain," so called because an emperor scrawled a poem high up on the cliffs. You can climb up here for a great view over the entire area of Halong Bay. Or walk around the seaside esplanade in front of the karst peak, approachable from the west side only. The markets on the east side of the karst peak are busy; if you arrive early, you can see the fish catch unloaded. Offshore, the fishing fleet creates its own floating market.

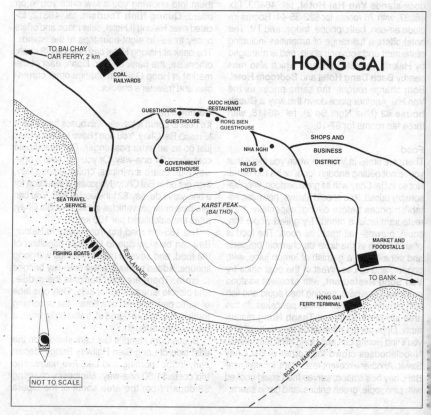

HONG GAI

TO BAI CHAY
CAR FERRY, 2 km

COAL
RAILYARDS

GUESTHOUSE
GUESTHOUSE

QUOC HUNG
RESTAURANT
RONG BIEN
GUESTHOUSE

SHOPS AND
BUSINESS
DISTRICT

NHA NGHI

GOVERNMENT
GUESTHOUSE

PALAS
HOTEL

SEA TRAVEL
SERVICE

KARST PEAK
(BAI THO)

FISHING BOATS

ESPLANADE

MARKET AND
FOODSTALLS

TO BANK

HONG GAI
FERRY TERMINAL

BOAT TO HAIPHONG

MOON

NOT TO SCALE

partial view of Hon Gai

Accommodations and Food

Over a dozen accommodations vie for your trade in Hong Gai. Most guesthouses are run by Hong Gai Tourism. You'll find budget and moderate accommodations in half a dozen guesthouses at the north side of the peak. Rooms in this zone cost roughly $7-20. The Government Guesthouse, up on a hill with views of the area, is sometimes reserved for official use. There are more small hotels and guesthouses in the market and business area closer to the main boat dock east of Bai Tho Peak. Typical of the guesthouses is **Rong Bien,** 36 Le Thanh Tong, tel. 25071, with seven rooms for $7 apiece, including bath and hot water. Three km to the west near the car-ferry crossing for Bai Chay is **Khach San Hong Ngoc,** 36 Le Thanh Tong, tel. 26330, with 18 air-con doubles for $25-30. Unusual is **Hong Gai Floating Hotel,** overlooking karst scenery. It's usually reserved for Vietnamese guests, but some foreigners have been accepted—rooms are $20-30.

Dining mostly takes place in hotel restaurants. Restaurants in town include **Quoc Hung,** serving seafood and Chinese dishes. Other small eateries cluster around Hong Gai market.

Getting There

Take the 0830 express train from Hanoi to Haiphong, a 50-cent cyclo ride across town to the boat terminal (Ben Binh), then board a boat to Hong Gai. In the reverse direction, three boats depart daily from Hong Gai to Haiphong, usually at 0600, 1100, and 1600; the trip costs $3 and takes about four hours.

No direct boats service the Cat Ba Town-Bai Chay/Hong Gai route; you have to hire a fishing vessel for the five-hour trip (see "Cat Ba Island" under "Gulf of Tonkin" for details). Or take a ferry from Hong Gai to Cat Hai Island and transfer to Phu Long at the north end of Cat Ba Island.

THE FAR EAST

Campha and Cua Ong

About 40 km east of Hong Gai lies the mining town of Campha, easily reached by minibus or ferry. Campha can serve as a base to explore islands off the coast; boat rentals are possible. Past Campha lie two other towns with guesthouses. Cua Ong is another mining town with a pagoda patronized by fishermen. On Cai Bau Island, a short ferry hop from Cua Ong, is the town of Cai Rong: offshore diving is good from this area.

You can reach Campha and Cua Ong directly by ferry from Haiphong, though some boats go via Hong Gai. Minibuses from a depot near the Bai Chay-Hong Gai car ferry, on the Hong Gai side, depart regularly for runs to Campha, Cua Ong, Cai Rong, Tien Yen, and Mong Cai.

Traco Beach

Right up by the Chinese border on the coast is Traco Beach, reputed to be one of the best in

Vietnam, and certainly one of the longest. Half a dozen large hotels and some guesthouses operate at Traco Beach, located on the island of Tra Binh. There are several ways of reaching Traco Beach. You can take the eight-hour ferry from Hong Gai, or another from Haiphong, running to Dan Tien. Or you can take a minibus from Hong Gai, a five-hour trip with five departures daily. From Mong Cai, a 15-km moto ride will get you to Traco Beach. There's a border crossing from Mong Cai into China for locals—it may open to foreigners in the future.

THE TONKINESE ALPS

Northwest of Hanoi toward the Chinese border lies the Hoang Lien Son Range, with Mount Fansipan, Vietnam's highest peak, elevation 3,143 meters. This range was christened the Tonkinese Alps by the French, who took a liking to the cool climate. Limestone largely comprises this northwest frontier where dramatic hills rise from the plains. From Hanoi to the northwest several routes will get you there, the most spectacular via Dien Bien Phu to Sapa. At Lao Cai, close by, you can cross into China and continue by rail to Kunming.

The northwest offers captivating mountain scenery; you can hike or trek into valleys around key towns. **Montagnards** inhabiting the valleys here include Tai, Hmong, Zao, and Muong groups. Some live in raised longhouses. Many still dress in traditional garb; intricate hand-embroidered clothing and silver jewelry are worn by the women. The best time to see minority people is on market day in the towns, when Montagnards hike in for days from surrounding areas. Thursday, Friday, Saturday, and Sunday offer the most animated markets; the big day is usually Sunday. To break the ice, you can buy something at a market—embroidery or clothing. If you want to take photos, you might have to hand over your precious lens for a few minutes to accustom them to it—let them look through the viewfinder.

Key destinations in the northwest include Dien Bien Phu and Sapa. Dien Bien Phu, toward the Lao border, is a small town that was the site of the Vietminh victory over the French in 1954. The village of Sapa remains the jewel of the northwest, a former French hill resort with splendid mountain scenery, a market thronged with people, and excellent hiking opportunities.

Route Notes

Most roads lead to Dien Bien Phu or Sapa, or both. You can travel roundtrip to Dien Bien Phu, or continue up to Sapa and loop back to Hanoi. Sapa can also be approached directly from Hanoi by train via Lao Cai, or by road via Yen Bai. By jeep, allow at least four days for a roundtrip to Dien Bien Phu. There is also a flight from Hanoi to Dien Bien Phu, which would be much faster. Allow at least six days for a loop from Hanoi via Dien Bien Phu to Sapa, or up to 10 days with longer stops; Sapa alone is worth two days. Or travel one-way to Sapa, cross the border at Lao Cai into China, and carry on to Kunming. Arrange your paperwork in Hanoi for this option. If coming in from China, it may be possible to join a tour going through Sapa back to Hanoi by jeep.

Hanoi-Lao Cai by rail is 295 km, an 11-hour trip, with a further 35 km by bus to Sapa, another two hours away. By road, from Hanoi to Viet Tri to Yen Bai to Pho Rang to Lao Cai to Sapa is 390 km, and takes 15-17 hours.

The circuitous route from Hanoi to Sapa via Dien Bien Phu is 750 km and requires three or four days one-way. From Hanoi it's 75 km to Hoa Binh, a further 125 km to Moc Chau, 120 km to Son La, 90 km to Tuan Giao, and 80 km into Dien Bien Phu. From Dien Bien Phu it's 105 km to Lai Chau, a further 80 km to Phong Tho, 86 km more to Sapa, and 35 km to Lao Cai at the Chinese border. From Lao Cai it's 355 km to Hanoi via Yen Bai. To save time, you can skip Dien Bien Phu and head directly from Tuan Giao to Lai Chau.

A jeep can do 45 kph on a sealed road but only 25 kph on dirt. The road is reasonably paved from Hanoi as far as Tuan Giao, then you hit dirt, with pavement resuming close to Sapa on the Lao Cai stretch. Paving is rough, with lots of potholes; blind corners are a hazard. Seasonal considerations are very important on this route—from May to October, the road beyond Son La often washes out or becomes im-

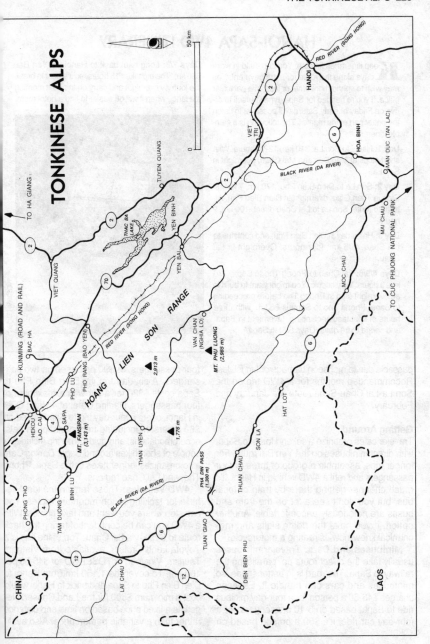

HANOI-SAPA 4WD ITINERARY

Keep itineraries flexible. You can build in extra days along the route for extra payment. You may wish to spend more time, or less, in a particular place. If you're headed for Sapa, time yourself to arrive on Friday or early Saturday if possible, to catch the better part of the market. The following is a sample itinerary.

Day 1: Hanoi to Son La, 310 km, 12-14 hours. With short stops at Man Duc and Mai Chau; overnight in Son La.

Day 2: Son La to Dien Bien Phu, 170 km, 7 hours. Stop in Tuan Giao; overnight in Dien Bien Phu. Alternate route: Son La to Lai Chau direct, 100 km, 9 hours.

Day 3: Half a day in Dien Bien Phu, and continue to Lai Chau, 105 km, four hours. Overnight in Lai Chau.

Days 4/5/6: Lai Chau to Phong Tho to Sapa, 170 km, 9 hours. Very scenic. You might want to build in an overnight stop at Phong Tho before proceeding to Sapa. Phong Tho to Sapa is 86 km, with three hours of spectacular climbing. Overnight in Sapa, and spend extra days (Days 5/6) in Sapa.

Days 7/8: Long haul back to Hanoi via Yen Bai, 390 km. The trip takes 15 hours, so it's best to break the journey overnight and carry on the next morning to Hanoi, when it will be easier to find a hotel room.

SCOTT HARRISON

passable due to monsoon damage or landslides. Recommended months for a 4WD trip on the Son La-Lai Chau-Sapa route are January and February.

Getting Around

Traveler cafés organize weekend tours to Sapa, with direct minibuses on the Yen Bai route. For longer trips, assemble a group of three or four passengers and rent a 4WD vehicle in Hanoi. It's much cheaper getting there by train or local bus, but you don't see a lot on the train and buses are notoriously uncomfortable. Another option, if you have the riding skills and mechanical know-how, is renting a motorcycle.

Minibuses and Cars: Traveler minibuses usually take the direct route up, paralleling the railway to Sapa. The road is in better shape, so minibuses and cars can handle it. Especen charges $46-50 a person for a four-day minibus ride to Sapa, based on 5-10 passengers; for a four-day car ride, it's $60 a person based on four passengers, or $90 pp based on two passengers. A six-day trip via Dien Bien Phu to Sapa costs $320 for a car with a maximum of four passengers. Darling Café, at 4 Hang Quat in Hanoi, offers a four-day trip to Sapa based on $60 a person, including transportation, meals, accommodations, and guide. The trip includes a couple of short hikes around Sapa. Darling Café also organizes longer hikes in the Sapa, Phong Tho, and Lai Chau regions.

4WD Vehicles: These remain the ideal vehicle for tackling rough mountain routes. You can stop where you want and take photos. With a 4WD you can be confident of taking the back route to Sapa, via Lai Chau. Top of the line is a Toyota Land Cruiser, available from Vietnam Tourism, Vinatour, or TOSERCO for $45-50 per 100 km. To cover the 1,150 km from Hanoi to Dien Bien Phu to Sapa and back to Hanoi would cost a minimum $500 for the Land Cruiser. Negotiate a fixed price based on time and distance rather than a variable per/km price. Also available are homegrown Mekong Land Cruisers, and the Land Cruiser II, a jeep version. A good sturdy vehicle is the Russian Gaz Army jeep, renting for $300 for five to six days, or around $30 per 100 km. This vehicle has two tanks, holding 40 liters of gasoline each, and two bucket seats up front with three gearshifts between them. In the back are three roomy seats and lots of luggage space at the rear. Especen charges $330 for a five-day roundtrip in a Russian jeep from Hanoi to Dien Bien Phu; for a Land Cruiser, the trip is $530.

Before setting off, have the driver write down a rough itinerary. Pay half up front, the other half on completion. Jeeps work out to $30 per 100 km, but it's better to negotiate the rate by the day—say, $50 a day. You should also negotiate how much extra to pay if you stay in a place longer, without driving; about $10 a day should suffice. Clarify other expenses also. You can cover the cost of the driver's lodging and food, which usually doesn't amount to much.

Motorcycle: You need a high-powered motorcycle for the hills and bad roads. A 125cc motorcycle can make it, but a 175cc Russian model is preferable. It's very tiring to motorcycle, bumping over rough roads for long distances. You must have tools and be able to improvise repairs—for example, when the headlight or muffler falls off due to vibration. You could ride a bike up to Sapa via Dien Bien Phu and then load it on the train back to Hanoi from Lao Cai. The bike costs $7, or roughly the cost of a hard seat.

Bus: Travel by bus in the northwest is slow, crowded, and uncomfortable. Usually only one bus a day travels in the direction you're headed, most likely leaving early, between 0500 and 0730. When it comes to viewing the landscape, bus travel is rather like riding in a submarine without a periscope, and you're so busy defending your turf you don't enjoy the trip. You do, however, meet lots of people, especially those who sit in your lap. Buses may not run daily, maybe every second day, or Tuesday, Thursday, Saturday, and Sunday. There is some jeep transport for short runs; another possibility is riding in postal vans.

Buses to the northwest leave from Hanoi's Kim Ma bus station. On the direct Sapa route you can take a bus to Yen Bai, stay the night there, then make your way north in stages to Lao Cai. For epic bus rides on the long route to Sapa, a bus departs from Hanoi for a two-day haul to Dien Bien Phu for $5, with an overnight stop in Son La. Hanoi to Son La takes 16 hours, if no breakdowns. From Dien Bien Phu, another three days of busing will put you in Sapa. Dien Bien Phu to Lai Chau is $3; Lai Chau to Sapa, $3, with an overnight stop in Phong Tho. Or skip Dien Bien Phu and head from Tuan Giao to Lai Chau. You could cover the entire route from Hanoi to Sapa for $12, but you might have to purchase several seats for legroom, say three seats bought for two people, which still makes the price less than $20.

Supplies

Take along a bag of nonperishable food in case the local fare of cabbage soup gets boring. You can buy fruit, biscuits, and small items along the way. Bring bottled water. Thermoses of hot water are supplied in truck-stop hotels; soak a thin towel with hot water—that's your shower. The hot water is purified; let it cool off and transfer it to a water bottle to drink the next day. Take cough and cold medicines along and water-purifying (iodine) tablets.

Do not underestimate the cold in the northwest, especially in winter. Sapa can hit freezing point. Although guesthouses supply quilts, rooms can still be clammy and cold; it's drafty and cold in jeeps and buses, especially when windows don't seal completely. Take a good sweater, Gore-Tex jacket, toque, gloves, and thermal underwear. You can outfit yourself in Hanoi; try the Old Quarter for wool and silk goods. You can also buy Chinese-made parkas and army surplus gear on Le Duan Boulevard. Cigarettes make good gifts for drivers and wayward officials.

HANOI TO DIEN BIEN PHU

Hanoi to Son La

By jeep, you can cover the 320 km from Hanoi to Son La in one full day, or about 10 hours of driving. Two hours out of Hanoi you reach Hoa Binh. An hour out of Hoa Binh you pass Man Duc (in Tan Lac district), a small town backed by karst peaks, with an interesting market. An hours' drive from here you can stop for spectacular views over Mai Chau valley to the south. The route continues for another hour past tea plantations and terraced rice paddies to reach Moc Chau. Near Moc Chau, you strike an area inhabited by Hmong and Black Tai. Moc Chau, five hours from Hanoi by jeep, has several hotels, including a UBND Guesthouse. A one-lane sealed mountain road leads to Son La and takes about four hours to drive, offering great views.

Son La to Dien Bien Phu

Not much to see in Son La, a truck stop. The prison built in 1908 by the French to incarcerate revolutionaries still stands in the middle of town. The main place to stay is the **UBND Guest-house** (People's Committee GH), tel. 52080, a large compound at the west end of town with a parking lot full of trucks and buses. The two-story hotel contains about 35 rooms. Rents run $20 for a double room, or $10 without bath. This government guesthouse typifies those along the route in larger towns. You get a bed with hard mattress, warm quilt, mosquito net, and Chinese thermos of hot water. Government guesthouses proliferate in the northwest, but foreigners may only be allowed to use the ones in the larger towns. Locals pay 40 cents and up for UBND guesthouses, whereas foreigners pay $5 and up. For food, go out of the hotel to the main road, and turn left—there are some small restaurants. Another place to stay is the **Trade Union Hotel** (Khach San Cong Duan), tel. 52244, costing $15 a room with two beds, $10 for three beds.

From Son La to Dien Bien Phu you'll see lots of minority villages—Black Tai, White Tai, Hmong, and Muong—some close to the road. You might also stray across a market. Black Tai (Tai Den) women wear black sarongs, and tight-fitting blouses with rows of silver or metal buttons down the front, attached tightly to the neck. The blouses are usually bright green, blue, or purple. A woman coils her hair in a topknot, covering it with a black turban embroidered with multicolored thread. After marriage, Black Tai women wear a silver hairpin. Some 800,000 Black Tai and White Tai live in the northwest.

After Thuan Chau, the road starts climbing to cross Pha Din Pass at 1,300 meters before reaching Tuan Giao. At Tuan Giao, you can turn west along the rough, dusty road to Dien Bien Phu, or skip that and carry straight on to Lai

Chau. White Tai villages lie along the route between Tuan Giao and Lai Chau. The White Tai (Tai Trang) women originally wore white skirts, but now wear more practical garb, even denim.

DIEN BIEN PHU

Dien Bien Phu (Chief Frontier Post) is an isolated market town 480 km northwest of Hanoi, famed as the site of the showdown between the forces of France and north Vietnam in 1954. It remains a pilgrimage site of sorts, for both Vietnamese and French, but a few things have changed since the big siege. The dirt track through the center of town has been paved, thatched roofs replaced with tiled roofs. Motorcycles and bicycles are now common. Karaoke bars pump out Boney M songs ("Ra Ra Rasputin, Russia's greatest sex machine"), video theaters do a brisk business, and market vendors sell Coca-Cola and Dien Bien

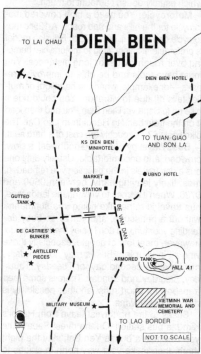

FRANCE LOSES AN EMPIRE

In 1954 the French made the fatal error of setting up a "fortress" to confront the Vietminh in the remote north at the valley of Dien Bien Phu. The base, supplied by aircraft, was picked by the French to guard Laos against Vietminh incursions and drive them back to the northern delta. Six battalions of French colonial troops were parachuted into Dien Bien Phu, along with airdrops of heavy equipment.

The Vietnamese chose Dien Bien Phu for a decisive engagement. In March 1954 Vietnamese General Vo Nguyen Giap assembled over 50,000 troops on the high ground surrounding 13,000 French troops in the valley. The French commander, Christian de Castries, created a series of heavily fortified strongholds, surrounded by barbed wire. He named the strongholds after women (said to be his mistresses): Claudine, Françoise, Anne-Marie, Dominique, Eliane, Beatrice, Gabrielle. The French colonial troops assembled included Vietnamese, Algerians, Moroccans, Senegalese, and Foreign Legionnaires. The French overestimated the strength of their air power, and underestimated the Vietminh, who laboriously dragged artillery onto the high ground overlooking the valley with the help of over 100,000 porters. Bad weather grounded French air power, and General Giap's howitzers and anti-aircraft guns were able to pound the airstrip. French aircraft were reduced to dropping supplies from great heights to avoid the artillery, and the parachutes could not be guided with the necessary precision. Consequently, much of the ammunition intended for the French went to the Vietminh. The Vietminh approached the perimeter of the French fortress in tunnels, and burrowed underneath the French defenses.

One by one the French strongholds fell; finally, the French pulled back to the area around the airstrip. On 7 May 1954 the French surrendered. They'd lost over 3,000 men; all the survivors were captured. The Vietminh losses were estimated at 20,000. An Asian guerrilla army had defeated professional French troops, including men from the Foreign Legion. It was a lesson the Americans did not heed; the same simple tactical tunneling used at Dien Bien Phu largely won the Vietnam War of the 1960s, too.

cigarettes. In 1993, sleepy Dien Bien Phu was designated the capital of Lai Chau Province because Lai Chau town, the old capital, will be partly submerged when a hydropower station on the Black River begins operating. Along with the new status comes a change of name—from Dien Bien to Muong Thanh, but it's dubious anyone will heed this change.

Dien Bien Phu consists of one main drag, Be Van Dan Street, lined with shacks and small restaurants lining both sides. As you come in from the north side, a minihotel stands on the right; 300 meters south of that is the main market, set back from the road, and the bus station. Another two km south is the Military Museum, also set back from the road on the right. Around the town lush fields of rice and corn flourish; rusted tanks and artillery pieces serve as playground equipment for local children.

Markets and Minorities

The central market at Dien Bien Phu is worth a browse. Ethnic groups shop here, among them colorful Hmong and Black Tai. Over a dozen ethnic groups live around Dien Bien Phu, the largest the Black Tai, with over 20,000 people. Other minorities include the Hmong, Nung, Cong, and Khomu groups. Some groups only number several hundred. You can organize day hikes to villages, such as the Hmong village of Noon Het to the south, or the Black Tai village of Na Nge to the east. The road leading to the Lao border to the southwest has a Xa minority village about 20 km from Dien Bien Phu; three km farther along the same road is a Lao village. Another 10 km farther on the road reaches the Lao border.

Battlefield Relics

Military Museum: The museum courtyard is filled with gutted French jeeps and tanks, and an eerie display of downed French planes. On the opposite side of the courtyard is well-preserved Vietnamese artillery. The contrast leaves no illusions about who won the battle. An obelisk marked 7.5.1954 commemorates fallen Vietnamese. Inside, the museum contains one large room with displays of photos, documents, battleground relics, and field telephones. The mu-

Stray artillery pieces still litter the fields around Dien Bien.

seum is open in theory 0800-1100 and 1400-1600 on Wednesday, Friday, and Saturday, but you might be able to coerce staff into opening on other days.

Souvenir shacks near the museum sell Dien Bien stamps, French maps of the area, commemoration stamps and badges, General Vo Giap's books on the battle, ethnic clothing and postcards, and some badly stuffed animals. There are photo cards of French President François Mitterrand, who helicoptered in for a visit in October 1993. Another illustrious visitor was General Vo Nguyen Giap, who returned in 1994 at the age of 83 for the 40th anniversary of the battle.

Cemetery: East of the museum is a large Vietminh war memorial and cemetery. It is not clear what happened to fallen French soldiers. Under the Geneva agreement, the dead from both sides were to be honored in a massive gravesite, but after a rift between north and south in 1955, the French were left where they'd fallen. In 1984 a stela commemorating the French dead was unveiled in Dien Bien Phu.

Military Hardware: To the north of the Vietminh cemetery is Hill A1, the former scene of fierce fighting. In this area you'll find an armored tank, bunker, war memorial, and tunnel complex. A few km west of town you can see abandoned French tanks, howitzers, and artillery pieces. You can visit the rebuilt command bunker of General Christian de Castries, preserved as it was on 7 May 1954, when the red flag of Vietnam was raised over it in victory. The French strongholds, surrounded with barbed wire, were scattered around the command bunker, especially to the north in the direction of the airfield. The French airfield was positioned roughly where the present airfield lies—there used to be an auxiliary airstrip to the south. General Giap's command headquarters, with a rebuilt bunker, is eight km away in Ban Muong Phan. You need a guide to visit.

Accommodations

Khach San Dien Bien, tel. 122, is a privately owned minihotel with 30 double rooms in the $10-20-40 range. The hotel has its own restaurant; sound effects courtesy of a karaoke bar next door. The cramped rooms allow only one person to maneuver in them at one time; however, this hotel is preferable to the nearby government-run **UBND Hotel.** Another possibility is **Dien Bien Hotel** on the road in.

Getting There and Away

Direct flights leave Hanoi for Dien Bien Phu on Tuesday and Friday for $130 roundtrip, but bad weather can delay flights. A chartered jeep from Hanoi is the best way to reach Dien Bien Phu; arrange for one through agencies in Hanoi. A five-day roundtrip in a Russian jeep might cost $330, based on 3-4 passengers; by Land Cruiser, probably more like $530. Buses wheeze into Dien Bien Phu from the direction of Son La or Lai Chau. An epic two-day run from Hanoi's

Kim Ma bus station costs $5 a seat, but you'll probably want to buy several seats for legroom.

DIEN BIEN PHU TO SAPA

Dien Bien Phu to Lai Chau

From Dien Bien Phu to Lai Chau you proceed along a French-built road. Hmong and Tai minority villages line the route. In Lai Chau you can stay at cozy **Lai Chau UBND.** A bed in a four-bed room costs $5; a double with bath and TV is $15; a room with a single and double bed is $20. The hotel is near the Lai Chau suspension bridge and up a hill. At the base of the same hill is a place with a papaya tree and a blue sign that simply says Restaurant—the place is family-run, with hearty fare. Like Dien Bien Phu, Lai Chau makes a good base for hiking into the surrounding area.

On the fringes of Lai Chau is the province's only drug rehabilitation center. Opium addiction represents a major problem among the Hmong

young Hmong women

in the mountainous regions of Lai Chau Province. Provincial cadres have tried to persuade the Hmong to grow peanuts instead of poppies, but to no avail. Lai Chau Province is home to over 12,000 addicts.

Lai Chau to Sapa

The region between Lai Chau and Sapa harbors a few Hmong villages. Coiffures become more elaborate among Red Hmong women, who pile hair in a massive topknot. But Big Hair doesn't keep the sun out, so a conical hat may rest over the topknot. Hmong men often wear green pith helmets. Toward Phong Tho you encounter Zao villages. The women here may wear patterned pants and elaborate black headdresses with rows of coins jingling off them.

The Lai Chau-Sapa route is really spectacular. Try and arrange a stop at **Phong Tho,** four km off the main road to Sapa on Route 4. Besides the primitive guesthouse here, Phong Tho offers fine opportunities for hiking, with Hmong and Zao hilltribes in the area. Phong Tho sits at the edge of the Hoang Lien Son Range, or the real Tonkinese Alps. From here the road snakes up to **Binh Lu,** another breathtaking location with a bowl of terraced rice paddies ringed by mountains. There is no guesthouse in Binh Lu, but it's an excellent place for hiking. From Binh Lu to Sapa more stunning scenery reels past during the three-hour jeep ride, with mountains and rolling hills winding up to Sapa. Take your time along here.

SAPA

Sapa is a magical combination of alpine landscapes, ethnic cultures, and bracing mountain air. This far-flung corner of Vietnam was "discovered" by a Jesuit missionary in 1918. In the 1920s the French—ever eager to duplicate parts of the Alps or the Pyrenees—decided to develop Sapa. They chased resident Hmong off the site and set up a cozy alpine resort serving a nearby mine. When the heat on the plains became unbearable, Sapa provided cool respite for French administrators. The town was dotted with French villa-estates with names like The French Roses and The Pearls—rambling orchards, gardens, and sloping lawns amid pine trees. The French constructed a small hydroelectric station, hotels, a church, tennis courts, even an aerodrome.

This tranquil existence was rudely interrupted by Vietminh incursions, which forced the French to abandon their villas. Further damage to the buildings was caused in 1979 when invading Chinese held the area for a short while before being driven out by the Vietnamese Army.

Today, the town supports a population of about 3,300; the entire Sapa district has a pop-

ulation of 32,000. The forest canopy in the area provides a source of medicinal herbs like ginseng and wild mushrooms, as well as wild honey. Orchards produce peaches, pears, and plums. The Hmong also grow opium in the surrounding hills. At 1,650 meters, Sapa enjoys bracing air—and bracing views overlooking the Muong Hoa River valley, with its luxuriant vegetation and rice terracing. Facing the village, across a deep valley, soars Vietnam's highest

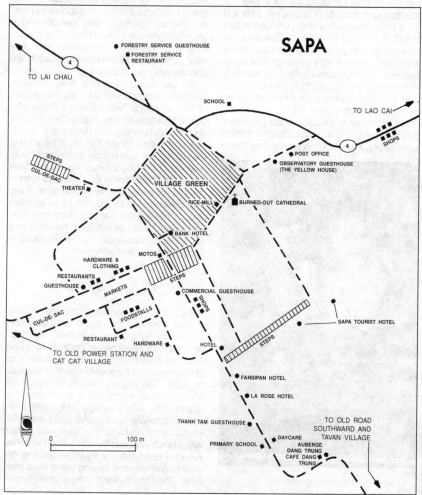

SAPA

TO LAI CHAU

TO LAO CAI

FORESTRY SERVICE GUESTHOUSE
FORESTRY SERVICE RESTAURANT

SCHOOL

SHOPS

STEPS
CUL-DE-SAC

THEATER

VILLAGE GREEN

RICE-MILL

POST OFFICE
OBSERVATORY GUESTHOUSE (THE YELLOW HOUSE)

BURNED-OUT CATHEDRAL

BANK HOTEL

MOTOS

HARDWARE & CLOTHING

RESTAURANTS
GUESTHOUSE

STEPS

MARKETS

COMMERCIAL GUESTHOUSE

SHOPS

CUL-DE-SAC

FOODSTALLS

SAPA TOURIST HOTEL

RESTAURANT

HARDWARE

HOTEL

STEPS

TO OLD POWER STATION AND CAT CAT VILLAGE

FANSIPAN HOTEL

LA ROSE HOTEL

THANH TAM GUESTHOUSE

PRIMARY SCHOOL

DAYCARE

AUBERGE DANG TRUNG
CAFE DANG TRUNG

TO OLD ROAD SOUTHWARD AND TAVAN VILLAGE

0   100 m

© MOON PUBLICATIONS, INC.

HOMO EKTACHROMO

Sapa has been open for tourism since 1993. At times in the weekend market, it seems that foreigners outnumber the locals. In this frail balance, it's hard to judge whether tourism benefits the local economy or erodes local lifestyles. Camera-toting travelers form a distinct ethnic tribe themselves—the *Homo ektachromo* group. When foreigners are confronted by aggressive Hmong women hawking embroidered items, it's debatable who appears stranger to whom. While the Hmong will actually pose for photos, Red Zao women and certain other hilltribers very much dislike having their photos taken, particularly close-ups. You should respect their customs and right to privacy. If you pay hilltribers in any fashion to pose for photos, this becomes a form of begging, which is definitely not to be encouraged.

---

peak, **Mt. Fansipan,** elevation 3,143 meters. Sapa is an excellent area for hiking through lush mountain valleys with minority villages.

Climate
It can get cold in Sapa. Every few years it even snows on the peaks nearby. Temperatures usually hover around 15-23° C, and up to 28° C in July, but can fall to zero in December. Sapa is gorgeous when the sun shines but mountain weather is fickle. The place could easily be socked in with low clouds and you might not see a thing for four or five days. Foggy days are common; it can grow damp and clammy. May to September is the rainy season, with heavy rain in July and August. At this time, trails and jeep tracks quickly turn to slush and are slippery and dangerous. The best time to tackle Mt. Fansipan is during the September-November dry season. The best time to admire the flora is in spring, April to May.

The Town
Downtown Sapa centers around the imposing burned-out cathedral overlooking the village green, now a kind of sunken soccer field where stray packhorses graze on weekends. The cathedral was apparently wrecked in 1952 by French artillery firing at a nearby building that housed Vietminh troops. There are plans to rebuild the 1920s French church; nearby is the abandoned French weather station. The main focus of the town is the market on the steps leading down from the church. The town retains charming stone-paved cul-de-sacs and French villas, many undergoing renovation and rebuilding as Sapa finds new life as a tourist resort.

Ethnic Groups
The Vietnamese actually represent a minority in the Sapa district, accounting for only 15% of the total population of 32,000. Vietnamese are highly visible, however, as they run most of Sapa's shops and stalls. Others are operated by Tay and Giay people. The Hmong and Red Zao live outside town in villages; there can be a lot of friction between shopkeepers who live in town and the hilltribers who drift in on weekends. Two minorities, the Hmong and Tay, interact well with foreigners. Others, like the Red Zao, remain extremely shy and avoid foreigners. Less often sighted are the Xapho and Tai people. Minority women are much easier to identify than men because the women more often wear traditional dress.

The minority groups in Sapa engage in subsistence farming, mainly rice cultivation. With only one crop a year, shortages often occur, and rice must be imported from the Mekong Delta to feed families. Livestock is reared to provide food during rice shortages or money to purchase necessities. Water buffalo, pot-bellied pigs, goats, chickens, and ducks are kept by local people. Other sources of income include foraging for wild mushrooms, ginger, and herbs in forests, hunting, and cultivating opium.

Minority peoples practice animism and ancestor worship, combining elements of Taoism, Confucianism, and Buddhism. They believe in the spirits of rice, the earth, wind, rivers, and mountains—altars to these spirits are often found at the bases of sacred trees. In spring, agricultural rites ensure a successful crop season.

Black Hmong: The biggest group in the area, the Black Hmong (Hmong Den), represent over 50% of Sapa's population. The Hmong, of Chinese origin, are thought to have immigrated to Vietnam at the end of the 18th century. Easily identified by their dark-blue or black clothing,

Hmong women wear large heavy earrings, bracelets, and necklaces. Traditional jewelry is often made of old French silver piastre coins, which also figure as part of the bride-price in marriage contracts. Hmong women wear their long hair rolled inside a headband, and go barefoot. Clothing is woven out of hemp and dyed with indigo. The Hmong engage mostly in farming; some cultivate opium poppies. Hmong interact more than other minority groups with foreigners and have taken full advantage of commercial opportunities, particularly selling hand-loomed clothing items.

Red Zao: With similar origins, and in the same linguistic family, the Red Zao (Dao Do) constitute 25% of the local population in the Sapa district, though they are less often seen in villages than the Hmong. Red Zao women wear black embroidered pants and loose tunic tops. They shave their eyebrows and a portion of the hairline, and wear spectacular red headdresses. They tie their hair in a topknot; a red turban is pinned to this, with braided or beaded sections, pom-poms, or coins dangling off it. They also wear silver neck pieces and carry shoulder-bags with red tassels. The reason that Red Zao dress stands out at Sapa's weekend market is partly due to matchmaking rituals. On market day, Red Zao men wear dark-blue jackets similar to the Hmong but with an embroidered rectangular patch on the back, and embroidered black turbans. Red Zao women put on their finest clothing—the more elaborate the head-

dress, the more pom-poms and bells and ornaments worn, the more marriageable the woman. Things build up to Saturday night, when Red Zao men and women check each other out with the aid of flashlights in darkened sections of the market. As Red Zao villages are scattered, the market serves as a gathering place where villagers can size up prospective spouses. Red Zao villages are quite small, perhaps only 30 to 300 people, whereas Hmong villages tend to be much larger.

Tay and Giay: Constituting less than 10% of the area's population, the Tay and Giay (pronounced Zai) minority groups have similar customs, clothing, and language due to their southern Chinese origins. Giay women from the Tavan Valley area wear black pants; solid-color cotton tunics, usually pink, green, or blue; and checked woollen headscarves in plaid patterns. The Chinese-style cotton tunic has a high neck collar and is secured with buttons at the waist and upper torso. Many Tay and Giay people have integrated into mainstream Vietnamese culture through intermarriage. They've adopted Vietnamese dress and may live in villages of mixed ethnic groups.

Sapa Market

There's a market every morning in Sapa, but the place swells on Saturday and Sunday when hilltribers converge on the town to buy and sell supplies and indulge in matchmaking rituals. Some walk for an entire day to get there; you

Red Zao men negotiate for a radio.

may see exotic groups in the market that you won't find even by hiking far into the surrounding terrain. Packhorses graze on the village green as villagers visit the wonders of the video shows at Sapa cinema.

The medieval-looking market is arrayed down a flight of stone-laid steps at the town center, with cobblestone alleys radiating off them. The market proceeds in ethnic waves. It starts around 0900 on Saturday and builds all day as Red Zao and Tay pour into town. The Saturday market is dominated by the Red Zao. Although it's particularly busy 0900-1200, the market continues all day, and eating and drinking go on well into the evening. On Sunday there's a changing of the guard; the Red Zao stream out of town, and the Hmong walk in with their wicker basketpacks. The market reaches a high point in the morning but continues till about 1400. The Sunday market sees mostly Hmong people who sell great embroidery. You can buy jackets for $15 and up, purses for a dollar, shawls, and ingenious infant-carry packs.

Accommodations

Because of an influx of ethnic visitors on weekends and amorous overnight stays, accommodations flourished around Sapa. Foreigners, however, seem to be confined to certain guesthouses. Those not intended for foreigners may be unmarked. More hotels and guesthouses are currently under construction to meet tourist needs, so expect additions to those listed here. Sapa generates electric lighting for only a few hours a night, and then hotel generators take over until 2200 hours. A new power hookup will eventually bring longer hours of electricity and more hot water.

Observatory Guesthouse, a.k.a. Meteo Guesthouse or The Yellow House, is family-run, with three rooms upstairs (four-bed dorm, three-bed dorm, five-bed dorm) and three other rooms for a total of 20 dorm-style beds for $2-3 each. The largest room upstairs includes a fireplace. Dinner costs $1 a head in the "garage" downstairs—you pre-order either vegetarian or meat from a fixed menu—good value.

The **Commercial GH** has 15 rooms with 43 beds, including some dorm-style four-bed rooms. Rooms cost $4 with bath, or $2 with shared bath. **La Rose Hotel** has 12 rooms with 30 beds for $5 a night. **Sapa Tourist Hotel,** (Nha Nghi Dulich Sapa), tel. 12, operates a total of 10 rooms in two wings for $5-6 d or t. The cavernous communal bathrooms feature vintage French plumbing—even bidets—which look great but don't function. Surly staff, when pressed, will fill a bathtub with cold water and supply a bucket. This hotel is set in what was obviously once a French orchard estate—you can make out the stone wall perimeter. The hotel occupies two wings of the original buildings.

Near the market stands the **Bank Hotel,** (Nha Khach Ngan Hang), tel. 10, a three-story building with another wing added for a total of 19 rooms, $5-7 d or t, with shared bathrooms. A wood-fired hot water system operates for a few hours daily. The guesthouse is popular with travelers; those on cheap tours from Hanoi often lodge here. An interior restaurant is run by the Agricultural Bank. **Auberge Dang Trung** has two dorm rooms downstairs with four beds each, $8 a bed, and three rooms upstairs for $15 d. Hot water is available. This hotel includes an excellent café. The owner, Mr. Trung, is very knowledgeable about the area and can arrange guides. His passion is orchid collecting; he maintains more than 200 specimens.

You'll find the most comfortable accommodations in Sapa at **Forestry Service GH,** (Nha Nghi Lam Nghiep Sapa), tel. 30, with 11 rooms for $12-15 d or t (off-season rates may be lower), baths and hot water available. Rooms are clean; some have fireplaces. The Forestry Service runs its own small restaurant down the hill from the guesthouse.

Food

Excellent vegetarian (anh chay) and other fare can be found in Sapa's market stalls. Shoot for the foodstalls at the southeast corner of the market. All have the same menu and offer good soups, spring rolls, tofu and peanut dishes, and delicious wild mushrooms. You can buy purified water here; Chinese beer is cheap due to Sapa's proximity to the border. For an extra buzz, try a hot lemon drink with honey produced by wild bees; the honey, said to be slightly toxic, is also available in bottles in Sapa market. On weekends dinner guests at the foodstalls are mostly visiting tribespeople. Apart from the foodstalls, several small restaurants near the market offer

English menus. Vegetarian food is the specialty at Café Dang Trung, which features a balcony overlooking the valley. The place seats 20 and can get crowded. The Forestry Service Restaurant near the Forestry Service Guesthouse serves good fare, but you must order in advance.

Services and Information

A booklet on Sapa, published in Hanoi by the Gioi in 1994, sells for a donation—recommended price $2. The book details area flora and fauna, especially birdlife, and describes hikes and walks. In Sapa, Café Dang Trung serves as the local hangout; this rooftop café will expand. Mr. Trung speaks English and French, and will assist with guides, and will change traveler's checks. You can change dollars to dong in the marketplace or at the Bank Hotel. The rate here is lower than in Hanoi.

Getting There

By Train: Two train routes from Hanoi will take you to Sapa. You can ride the rails overnight from Hanoi to Pho Lu (Bao Thang) and transfer to road transportation for the 75-km run to Sapa; or you can stay on the same train for another hour or so until it reaches the border town of Lao Cai, and make a 35-km road run to Sapa. Most travelers prefer the Lao Cai route, as more road transportation waits there.

Hanoi to Pho Lu is 262 km by rail. Catch an overnight train—departing Hanoi around 2030, arriving at Pho Lu 0600—then take a bus or jeep to reach Sapa at 1100. The bus takes about four hours. On arriving at Pho Lu station, walk 50 meters to the bus station. Buses run irregularly—Tuesday, Thursday, Saturday, and Sunday all see regular runs. If stranded in Pho Lu, you can stay at the rudimentary guesthouse next to the railway station for $4.

Hanoi to Lao Cai is 295 km by rail, and costs $7.50 for a hard seat, $10 soft seat, or $16 hard sleeper. Train LC1 takes 11 hours, departing Hanoi around 2030 and arriving at 0715; another train, LC3, departs Hanoi 0605 and reaches Lao Cai at 1800. Train schedules may fluctuate. From the rail station head west across a bridge to the left bank of Lao Cai to catch a bus to Sapa; you can make the four-km transfer to the bus station by moto for less than $1. In Lao Cai you can sometimes hire a jeep for the 35-km run to Sapa; costs average about $4 per head, or $20 for the jeep. Moto operators charge $6-8 for the long haul uphill from Lao Cai to Sapa. By bus the trip takes two hours and costs $1. The winding climb up into the hills of the Hoang Lien Son Range to Sapa is magnificent, with sheer drops by the side of the road. But the road remains in poor shape, with rocks, rubble, and landslide debris; buses are prone to breakdowns.

By Road: A variety of road routes lead to Sapa, most of them rough. A 4WD is recommended for these routes, although minibuses and wheezing local buses can handle the roads. Minibus tours from traveler cafés in Hanoi often opt for the direct 390-km ride to Sapa, via Yen Bai, Pho Lu, and Lao Cai, roughly paralleling the rail line. You can cover this route in one long day of travel by private car, about 12 hours; there's little in the way of scenic highlights. A four-day roundtrip jeep trip from Hanoi along this route costs $240; by Land Cruiser, as much as $400.

A direct bus to Sapa from Hanoi's Kim Ma station runs on Friday only, departing 0430 and arriving 2200 the same day; it returns to Hanoi on Monday. No news from any foreigner who has survived this epic journey—not recommended if you value your kidneys. You'd be better off tackling the bus route in stages. Take the first ride to Yen Bai and continue on from there.

Definitely more rewarding if you can spare the time is a longer trip of four days or more from Hanoi via Dien Bien Phu to Sapa, a wild ride of 750 km. Travel from Hanoi to Dien Bien Phu to Lai Chau to Phong Tho to Sapa, or the reverse. Excellent views and stops predominate along this route. A jeep or other 4WD vehicle is recommended, but you can also cover the ground in stages by bus.

Western motorcyclists have covered both road routes in two weeks, roundtrip—then sworn they'd never attempt the odyssey again. Their Russian motorcycles vibrated apart, and their nerves frayed from concentrating on potholes. Other motorcyclists have braved the Hanoi-Dien Bien Phu route to Sapa, then loaded their bikes onto the train from Lao Cai returning to Hanoi. For those who like rodeo broncos, an even more rugged road route runs from Hanoi to Van Chan to Than Uyen to Sapa. The scenery, though beautiful, may jump up and down a lot, and focusing on it may present a problem. Buses even run along these stretches—every second day, if you're lucky.

Getting Around
On foot, mostly. A dozen or so moto drivers hang around the market, ferrying heavy loads. Hire them if you want a head start on a longer hike; they also make runs to Lao Cai for hefty fees. Motos come equipped with sturdy racks and straps at sides and back, suitable for backpacks. Sapa provides ideal terrain for mountain biking, with the emphasis on "mountain." Some foreigners have negotiated some trails by bicycle.

Getting Away
A bus departs for Lao Cai from the steps of Sapa's burned-out cathedral most mornings around 0930 or 1000. The run is straight downhill, so it's fairly fast going—a bit over an hour if all's well with the engine. By moto, it's an hour. Train LC2 departs Lao Cai around 1700, and arrives in Hanoi at 0400; train LC4 departs Lao Cai around 0745, arriving in Hanoi at 1945.

For an alternate route, head to Pho Lu on one of the buses that departs from the crossroads to the northeast side of Sapa. The trip takes two hours. At Pho Lu, catch the Hanoi train. Other buses leave from the same crossroads northeast of Sapa on the long haul to Phong Tho and Lai Chau.

Hmong man toting a piglet in a bamboo cage

SCOTT HARRISON

HIKING IN THE SAPA REGION

You can embark on day hikes around Sapa by yourself. For overnight or longer hikes, where you face language problems and risk getting lost, you should consider hiring a guide/interpreter from a local guesthouse. Porters are also available. Locals along the trails will also act as impromptu guides, leading you through ricefields to the next village, with no payment expected. In theory you're not permitted to stay in villages without a guide, but some travelers have managed it. Villagers supply simple rice dishes; a small payment of one or two dollars is expected for lodging. Consider taking along gifts, but be discreet so as not to encourage begging. The best way to break the ice with the Hmong is to buy something—a purse for a dollar, whatever. Pack out all litter and bury organic waste at least 20 meters away from any water sources.

Trails around Sapa are often steep and can get slippery if wet. For longer hikes, consider a kick-start in the form of a moto driver; he can drop you at a trailhead or take you partway along your route. The roads are atrocious, so motos can be hard on the system—your suspension and the bike's.

Old Power Station
This walk requires about three to four hours. You hike to Cat Cat Village and the old power station, about three km from Sapa, or about 1.5 hours downhill. From Sapa, take the road down through the markets to the west, heading straight past a bombed-out French villa, an imposing castle-like ruin. On a clear day, there are good views of Mt. Fansipan from here. Following the trail to the power station is tricky—the old power lines and pylons lead there. A few hundred meters past the bombed-out villa you pass under power lines. Walk 100 meters and turn left down

a side trail. Follow this trail till it arcs back under the power lines again; keep following the power lines as best you can. Eventually, this small trail leads to the Hmong village of Cat Cat. Beyond the village you'll find some small cascades within a bamboo forest, and a few disused buildings that served as the French power station built in the 1920s. Several "grain robots" pound grain by means of an ingenious water-driven wooden contraption. You can hike farther west-

ward from the power station toward Mt. Fansipan through meadows, but paths are not clear and you may need a guide.

Sinchai Village

Start off as for the old power station hike—past the bombed-out French villa—but follow the main trail past the power lines to the northwest for about four km. This brings you to the large Hmong village of Sinchai, with a population of

TO SILVER FALLS,
BINH LU, PHONG THO
AND LAI CHAU

VILLAGES

TAPHIN VALLEY

MUONG HOA RIVER

4

DESTROYED SEMINARY

TO LAO CAI

SINCHAI

4

TO
MT. FANSIPAN

OLD POWER LINE

CAT
CAT

SAPA
BOMBED-OUT
FRENCH VILLA

OLD POWER STATION

DILINGHO

HIKING IN THE
SAPA REGION

MOON

LAO CHAI

MUONG HOA RIVER

0   5 km

= DIRT TRACK

= WALKING TRAIL

TAVAN RAY

© MOON PUBLICATIONS, INC.

*destroyed seminary
in Taphin Valley*

about a thousand. Along the way you witness the rhythms of rural life: villagers harvesting rice, or ploughing with water buffalo. You may also see snippets of Hmong life: someone dyeing clothing with indigo in huge vats, or playing a mouth organ (small piece in mouth, extension tube hanging below) made of brass and bamboo. Continue past the village, and when the path diverges, take a right fork to climb out of the valley. There are majestic views of the rice paddies below. Eventually you make it up to the main road, Route 4, where you can hitch a ride back to Sapa—or simply walk the distance.

Silver Falls Trail

Silver Falls (Thac Bac), about 12 km from Sapa on the Lai Chau route, is found near the road a few km south of Dinh Deo Pass, at 2,500 meters the highest point on the Sapa-Lai Chau route. There are stunning views over several valleys from Dinh Deo Pass; from there a short hiking trail leads to Quy Ho Lake, the source of Silver Falls.

Taphin Valley

Taphin Valley lies about 12 km northeast of Sapa. The trail into the valley is accessible by jeep, but few vehicles attempt it, so the valley mostly sees foot traffic. The hike goes through some pleasant terrain and passes several Hmong and Red Zao villages. The very shy Red Zao usually keep a low profile and are reluctant to let foreigners take photos.

To reach Taphin Valley, head along the Lao Cai route for about five km till you pass a kilometer stone that reads Pho Lu 69 km. Take the dirt turnoff that appears soon after this marker stone; the turnoff lies between the marker and a bridge. Hike in about three km on the Taphin Valley trail, past some Hmong villages, to the ruins of a large monastery. The seminary was destroyed by militant Vietnamese who suspected such a large place had a military connection. There is a small school and some Hmong houses in the vicinity. Take the road more or less straight ahead from here till you reach a fork, then take the right fork. You will pass a Zao village nearby. If you keep hiking past the end of the dirt road—about six or seven km in from the Lao Cai road—you'll come to a valley with several villages. Local kids can direct you to a karst grotto in this area.

Tavan Valley

In this direction (south of Sapa) a two-day hike is preferable, with an overnight stay in a village. You may need a guide; obtain one at a Sapa guesthouse like Auberge Dang Trung. To speed trailhead access, take a moto from the Sapa market down the dirt road south. Jeeps can run along here for about 15 km. Otherwise, traffic down this way is mostly on foot or with packhorses.

If on foot, head past Auberge Dang Trung downhill from Sapa for about 12 km, or about two to three hours. There are great views of mountain majesty and terraces laid out below in abstract patterns. Hike down to the Muong Hoa River on a trail and cross a bridge to the Hmong village of Lao Chai. If you pick your way over the rice paddies, you will reach the Giay village of Tavan Ray—look for a schoolhouse. In the vicinity you'll see ingenious bamboo plumbing and "grain robots," as well as bamboo bridges and small waterfalls. Farther down the valley is the Red Zao village of Tachai Man.

Mount Fansipan

At 3,143 meters, Mt. Fansipan is Vietnam's highest peak. Fansipan is not a distinct peak but a conglomerate. You'll need a guide from Sapa to make sure you've reached the right summit; a metal triangle marks the seat. Three routes lead to the top; the easiest ascent vaguely follows a riverbed from the foothills of Sapa. It's a minimum three days out to the summit and back; four to six days is preferable. You need a sleeping bag or blankets, tent, food, and good warm clothing. Some groups bring porters.

Along the way, when not cutting swaths through bamboo thickets, you might glimpse wild goats or monkeys. In this direction is Nui Hoang Lien Nature Reserve, an area of 30 square km that encompasses Mt. Fansipan. Some 12 square km of natural forest remains. Between 2,500 and 2,800 meters an elfin forest flourishes with gnarled trees covered in mosses, lichens, and flowering plants, particularly orchids. At higher elevations you'll come across dwarf rhododendron and bamboo. Over 150 species of birds have been spotted in the reserve. Some, such as the collared finchbill, the white-throated laughing-thrush, and the chestnut bulbul, are found only in the mountains of northwest Vietnam. On a clear day, views from the top of Fansipan are excellent.

LAO CAI TO KUNMING

Lao Cai sits right on the Chinese border, on the route from Hanoi to Kunming. It's also the junction for getting to the town of Sapa. The Red River enters Vietnam at Lao Cai, after covering 800 km from its source 2,000 meters up on China's Yunnan plateau, and tracing a section of the China-Vietnam border.

Much of Lao Cai was destroyed in 1979 by the Chinese. The place is mostly under reconstruction, rejuvenated by resumption of cross-border trade and smuggling. The rebuilding plan for Lao Cai calls for two zones on either side of the Red River. On the southern bank is Lao Cai town, with future plans for a market center, port, post office, market, hotels, and transshipment stores. Presently the town consists of one main drag lined with shops. On the northern bank is the Coc Leu area, with administrative offices and customs and immigration services. Linking the two areas is Coc Leu Bridge, begun in late 1992 at a cost of $1.5 million to replace an earlier bridge destroyed by bombs.

Most travelers do not stay in Lao Cai. However, there are some cheaper hotels in Lao Cai town on the southern side; right near Vietnam Immigration on the northern side is a hotel charging $10-15 a room. You can get around Lao Cai by moto—pick one up near Vietnam Immigration, outside the railway station, or near the bus station. An occasional jeep might wait near immigration too. It's about two km from Coc Leu Bridge to Vietnam Immigration, and about four km from Coc Leu Bridge to the railway station.

Transport

Hanoi to Lao Cai is 295 km by train (11 hours) and costs $7.50 hard seat, $10 soft seat, or $16 hard sleeper. There's an overnight train from Hanoi, LHC1, and a day train, LC3. You decide whether you want to see the scenery or get a night's sleep and be ready to carry on the next day. For the return leg, LC2 is the night train and LC4 the day train.

From Sapa to Lao Cai your choice is between a bus or a moto for the 35-km run; there may be the odd jeep available. A bus takes two hours for the run and costs $1. Motos charge about $6-8 to Sapa. They're well equipped with racks and straps at side and back to accommodate backpacks. The road runs straight uphill, with big cliff drops.

China Border Crossing

The Ho Kieu Railway Bridge links China and Vietnam. There's talk of restoring the French-built narrow-gauge rail link from Kunming to Hanoi and Haiphong, giving landlocked Yunnan Province access to a major seaport. But for the moment you pass over the narrow bridge—only walkers, bicyclists, and tractors are allowed across.

Exiting Lao Cai: It's hard enough crossing this border with perfect paperwork; don't give Immigration here any excuse for fundraising with incomplete or incorrect paperwork. Some travelers have negotiated $20-30 for a hand-written Lao Cai exit stamp. To exit at Lao Cai you go to Customs first, hand over your form, proceed to Immigration for a stamp out, walk across the bridge, check in at Chinese Immigration for a stamp in, go to Chinese Customs to fill out forms, and finally arrive at Chinese Quar-

antine to answer questions about cholera, plague, and yellow fever inoculations. It takes over an hour to finalize procedures between Vietnam and China if your papers are in order. There's a time difference of one hour between Lao Cai and Hekou, because Hekou runs on Beijing time. If the time is 0900 in Vietnam, it should be 1000 in Hekou.

Entering Lao Cai: The desperate who lack a Lao Cai entry stamp can try to bargain for one on the spot for $25. However, you may have the duration of your Vietnamese visa cut in half; check to see what the Immigration officials have freshly stamped on your visa. Even if your paper-

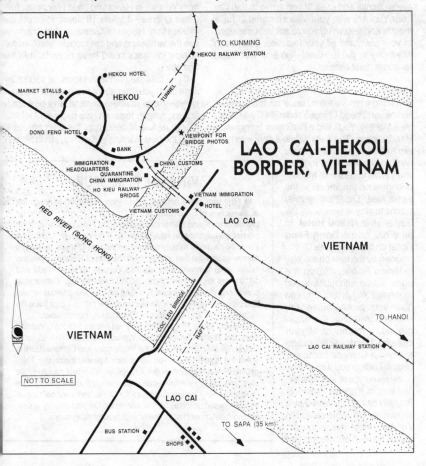

LAO CAI-HEKOU
BORDER, VIETNAM

CHINA

TO KUNMING

HEKOU RAILWAY STATION

HEKOU HOTEL

MARKET STALLS

HEKOU

TUNNEL

DONG FENG HOTEL

VIEWPOINT FOR
BRIDGE PHOTOS

BANK

IMMIGRATION
HEADQUARTERS
QUARANTINE
CHINA IMMIGRATION

CHINA CUSTOMS

HO KIEU RAILWAY
BRIDGE

VIETNAM IMMIGRATION

VIETNAM CUSTOMS

HOTEL

LAO CAI

RED RIVER (SONG HONG)

VIETNAM

VIETNAM

TO HANOI

COC LEU BRIDGE

RAFT

LAO CAI RAILWAY STATION

NOT TO SCALE

LAO CAI

BUS STATION

SHOPS

TO SAPA (35 km)

work is excellent, you can run into problems here. Some travelers report their one-month Vietnamese visa was reduced to seven days at Lao Cai. The Port of Entry official decides about registration on arrival and may choose to give you transit authority only. If this happens, you must head for Hanoi and get your visa extended.

Other travelers have reported irregularities with money declaration. One declared $3200, the officers insisted on counting it, found $3500, and fined the traveler $20 for the miscount. Another traveler came up $150 short at Customs after officers asked him to count out all his traveler's checks and cash. If you arrive in Lao Cai from Yunnan, with your visa stamped in for a month, and assuming you're still in possession of your cash and all your faculties, don't be in any hurry to get to Hanoi—go and visit Sapa for some quiet relaxation.

Hekou

If coming from Vietnam, once on the loose in Hekou you'll need Chinese *renminbi* (RMB, People's Money). You'll find a bank near Immigration Headquarters. The bank will deal only with traveler's checks or US cash. If you want to change dong to RMB you'll have to deal with money-changers on the streets in the same area. There are several places to stay in Hekou: try the Soviet-style **Hekou Hotel** up on a hill, or the **Dong Feng Hotel** on the main street.

Down by the river on the way to Hekou Railway Station is a photo set-up with multicolored umbrellas and props. You can have your picture taken with Ho Kieu Bridge in the background, a memento of your crossing. Hand over your camera and a Chinese photographer will oblige you with a shot.

In Hekou you're in a little-visited part of Yunnan Province. Roughly half of China's 50-plus minorities are represented in Yunnan; most live in border areas. You can explore this part of Yunnan by bus; the highway up to Kunming is in surprisingly good shape. Villages along the way hold Hmong; the women wear embroidered pastel dresses and leggings, the men Mao outfits.

Hekou-Kunming Train

The Hekou-Kunming train doesn't go anywhere of significance. Used by holiday-makers and smugglers, the red-and-yellow train runs on a narrow-gauge line, and the cars are narrower than standard Chinese trains. It has to be one of the cleanest trains in China. The French built the narrow-gauge line and engineered the numerous tunnels on this route to transport goods from Yunnan to Hanoi and on to Haiphong. Progress is slow—it takes 16 hours to cover the 470 km from Hekou to Kunming—but when you see the landscape and the tunnels, you'll marvel at how the track could have been built in the first place.

If you take the train from Hekou at 1300 (Chinese time) you'll get about five hours of fabulous views—deep ravines, banana and pineapple groves, jungle, terraced rice paddies. Unfortunately, darkness descends; the train arrives at 0600 the next morning at Kunming North Station.

VINTAGE RAIL SPUR

At the turn of the century, the French attempted to reach the riches of Southwest China through Vietnam via railway. Hekou, Simao, and Mengzi were opened to French trade, and the port of Kwangchowan was leased to the French in 1898. The French wrangled a railway concession through Chinese territory, a narrow-gauge line that snaked from the port of Haiphong through Hanoi up to Kunming in landlocked Yunnan. Between 1902 and 1910 more than a third of the 80,000 Chinese and Vietnamese construction workers perished building the line over perilous terrain. The project turned into a white elephant—the rail spur cost twice the initial estimate, and the riches of China barely materialized.

Until the 1950s this was the only rail line into China's Yunnan Province. The line fell into disrepair, and in 1979 the link was cut at Hekou due to fighting between the Vietnamese and Chinese. But the entire line is still in place: you just change trains at the border. Most of China's vast rail system is 1.435-gauge (standard gauge) while Vietnam's system is French-built meter-gauge (narrow gauge). The Hekou-Kunming line is vintage track for China, and a special narrow train is required on the route. The ride on the Chinese side must rank among Asia's finest rail journeys, with breathtaking views.

into the hills of Yunnan, bound for Kunming

In the reverse direction, the train leaves at 1530 from Kunming North Station, affording several hours of views; it arrives in Hekou at 0800 the next day. The train costs about $20 for a sleeper, half that for a seat. Hard sleeper in China means a comfortable mattress and blankets, the equivalent of Vietnam's soft sleeper. Alternatively, take a Hungarian-made bus from the station at the southern end of Beijing Road for an overnight ride to Hekou, costing about the same as a seat on the train, though not as comfortable.

KUNMING

Kunming, a boomtown with a fast-paced free-market economy, is rapidly becoming the powerhouse of China's southwest. With increasing international air connections from its new airport to Bangkok, Hong Kong, and Singapore, Kunming is assuming an important role in trade routes through China and Indochina. Kunming is the gateway to the fascinating minority areas of Dali (Bai people) and Lijiang (Naxi). With the border south of Jinghong now open into Laos, you could consider forging some trailblazer overland routes. However, visas aren't issued in Kunming, except to Laos and perhaps Burma. Vietnamese visas are issued in Hong Kong or Beijing.

At an elevation of 1,890 meters, Kunming has a mild climate, and a relaxing pace as Chinese cities go. Its wide boulevards are great for cycling. The main axis of Kunming is Beijing Road, a boulevard running almost five km between Kunming North Station and Kunming South Station; this is intersected by Dong Feng Road, the main east-west axis. At the intersection of Dong Feng and Beijing Roads sits the post office and Telecom building. The main commercial center of town is the quadrant north of Jinbi Lu and west of Beijing Lu. This part contains old streets, many retaining traditional green-and-red shuttered shop fronts now rarely found in China.

If coming from Hekou by train, you'll arrive at Kunming North Station. A ride in a three-wheeler from north to south stations costs less than a dollar; you can also hop on a 23 bus or take a metered taxi.

Accommodations

Backpackers head for **Kunhu Hotel,** at 44 Beijing Road, (toward Kunming South Station), tel. 313-3799. Rates run $5 a person in a three-bed room, or $21 for a double room. You can rent bicycles here. **Yunnan University Guesthouse,** a foreign student hostel at the northwest side of the city, charges $4 a person in four-bed rooms; some carpeted rooms with hot water and TV are available. **Camellia Hotel,** at 154 East Dong Feng, tel. 316-2918, offers rooms for $11-20 each. The hotel is huge, but many rooms are occupied by businesses.

There is no shortage of high-end accommodations in Kunming. **Holiday Inn Kunming,** at

25 Dong Feng East Rd., tel. 316-5888, fax 313-5189, is an 18-story building with 252 luxurious rooms for $80-115 and suites for $120-600. Aerial views from the nightclub on the top floor may prove worth the price. To the southern end of Beijing Road is a cluster of mammoth 200- and 300-room hotels charging $50-80 for rooms and $150 and up for suites. These include the 17-story **Golden Dragon,** at 575 Beijing Rd., tel. 313-3015; the 19-story **King World Hotel,** 28 Beijing Rd., tel. 313-8888; the 18-story **Tea Gardens Hotel,** Yongping Rd., tel. 313-9202; and the mega **Three Leaves Hotel,** 614 Beijing Rd., tel. 313-8644.

Food
Just north of Kunhu Hotel is a strip of small restaurants favored by backpackers, including **Happy Restaurant** and **Yuelai Café.** These serve Western food—pizza, fruit salad, fried goat cheese—and function as traveler cafés, with owners maintaining travel logs full of information updates. In Kunming's old town a string of restaurants sells steaming bowls of across-the-bridge noodles, the local specialty. You can find these restaurants by exploring the alleys immediately west of Zhengyi Lu and north of Jinbi Lu. Lots of street side eateries serve stir-fried food and clay steampots. For those who want to splurge, the Holiday Inn puts on a buffet breakfast and a buffet lunch.

Consulates
The **Lao PDR Consulate,** 23 Haigeng Rd., Room 501 (5th floor), tel. 414-4218, will issue a 7-day transit visa in one day for $28, but this most likely means you have to fly into Vientiane from Kunming. **Myanmar Consulate-General** (Burma) is on the 3rd floor of Building 3 at the Camellia Hotel, 154 East Dong Feng, tel. 317-6309. The consulate issues a two-week visa for around $35, obtainable in three days. You may have to fly into Rangoon, which will cost over $230 one-way on CAAC; there seems to be only a flight every couple of weeks.

International Flights
Kunming International Airport is eight km from the city. Departure tax on international flights is RMB60. Several carriers work the Kunming-Bangkok route. Yunnan Airlines operates several flights a week; China Southern Airlines schedules one flight a week. Both operate from the CAAC building opposite the Holiday Inn on Dong Feng East Road. Thai Airways International schedules five flights a week to Bangkok; $160 economy one-way, $225 business class, flight time two hours. The Thai Airways office is at 32 Chun Cheng Rd. in the Panlong District. Thai Airways also flies twice weekly to Chiang Mai; $140 economy class one-way. Singapore Airlines flies from Kunming to Singapore twice weekly for $402 one-way; the office is in the Holiday Inn, 25 Dong Feng East Rd., tel. 316-5888. Other connections from Kunming: daily flights to Hong Kong for around $195 one-way on China Southern Airlines or Dragonair (office in Golden Dragon Hotel); to Vientiane on Yunnan Airlines for around $150 one-way, flights once weekly. Royal Air Cambodge plans to fly from Kunming to Phnom Penh.

CENTRAL VIETNAM
HUÉ

Hué and Danang serve as twin gateways to central Vietnam. While Danang is the industrial, shipping, and air transport gateway, Hué is the cultural, religious, and educational heart. The landscape here—with its misty Perfume River and pagodas—is inspiration for poetry and painting. Hué has long been regarded as the "Third Capital" of Vietnam, after Hanoi and Saigon.

From 1802 to 1945, Hué served as Vietnam's political capital under the 13 emperors of the Nguyen dynasty. Emperor Gia Long, founder of the Nguyen dynasty, consolidated the country after several hundred years of civil war, and began building Hué Citadel. This was the first time in Vietnamese history a single court controlled Vietnam from north to south. The emperors built the Mandarin Road, now Highway 1. It was dotted with relay stations, and communication was further expedited by a system of couriers. The dynasty was headquartered in the Imperial City, off-limits to most mortals—only mandarins, princesses, and scholars resided here. In the finest Chinese tradition, the emper-

ors constructed elaborate tombs, scattered around Hué.

In 1883 the French invaded Hué. Tonkin and Annam became French protectorates, but the French found it expedient to maintain the illusion of imperial rule. A rapid succession of emperors marked the early days of French presence as rulers either fled or were replaced by the French.

Hué still represents a third political force in Vietnam. During the Vietnam War of the 1960s, educated Hué citizens backed neither the South nor the North. During the Tet offensive of 1968, Vietcong and NVA forces marched into Hué and held it for 24 days. The soldiers used the Citadel, with its 10-meter-thick ramparts, as their base. During the occupation VC and NVA forces went on a rampage. Suspected sympathizers of the Saigon government were rounded up, then shot, beheaded, or buried alive. It is estimated that 3,000 residents of Hué were killed during those 24 days. You can still see symbols over doorways, indicating where residents were killed. In fierce door-to-door fighting, the Americans eventually

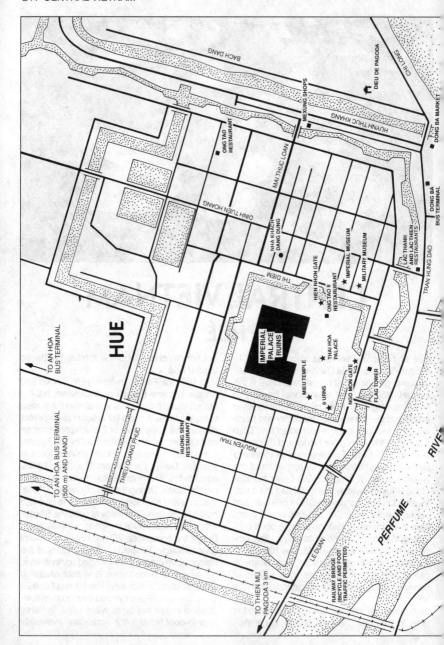

HUE

TO AN HOA BUS TERMINAL

TO AN HOA BUS TERMINAL (500 m) AND HANOI

TO THIEN MU PAGODA 3 km

BACH DANG

DIEU DE PAGODA

CHI LONG

MEKONG SHOPS

HUYNH THUC KHANG

DONG BA MARKET

ONG TAO RESTAURANT

MAI THUC LOAN

DINH TUEN HOANG

DONG BA BUS TERMINAL

NHA KHACH DANG DUNG

THI DIEM

IMPERIAL MUSEUM

MILITARY MUSEUM

LAC THANH AND LAC THIEN RESTAURANTS

HIEN NHON GATE

ONG TAO II RESTAURANT

TRAN HUNG DAO

IMPERIAL PALACE RUINS

MIEU TEMPLE

THAI HOA PALACE

9 URNS

NGO MON GATE

FLAG TOWER

THIEU QUANG PHUC

HUONG SEN RESTAURANT

NGUYEN TRAI

LE DUAN

PERFUME

RIVER

RAILWAY BRIDGE (BICYCLE AND FOOT TRAFFIC PERMITTED)

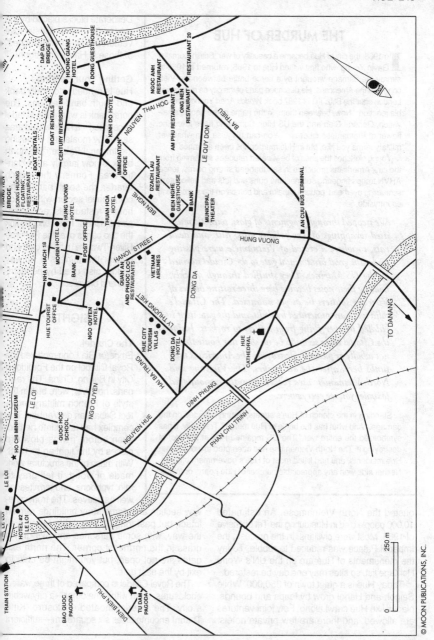

THE MURDER OF HUÉ

In 1968, the city of Hué became a casualty of war. British journalist Gavin Young, who first visited Hué in 1965, returned in 1968 to survey the damage wrought by a fierce battle between the Vietcong and the Americans. He described parts of the city as resembling London after the Blitz. In his 1987 book *Worlds Apart* Young sums up his reaction: "Now, between them, in the name of the people's salvation, General Giap and the US High Command have killed the flower of Vietnamese cities. . . . You can disguise it in whatever military terms you like, but in Hué murder has been arranged."

Young sketches the lines of bewildered refugees streaming from the city, Americans crouched in sandbagged strong points, tense ARVN troops fingering submachine guns and jets and helicopters screaming overhead, pouring napalm and bombs on the surrounding countryside.

We stepped through fragments of glass, pathetic muddied wrappings of Tet holiday gifts, filth and dead rats, to where a crowd of Vietnamese were passing under the great ornamental gate to the Citadel stormed by the US Marines. They shuffled through quickly, holding their noses because here three rotting bodies of Vietcong soldiers lie as yet unburied. The Citadel's solid walls are punctured by shells, and the gate itself is riddled by everything from bullets to rockets. Inside the Citadel there seems to be no shop nor house that is not wholly or partially destroyed. The Americans used tanks here, after the air strikes. The Vietcong and North Vietnamese used rockets from the camouflaged foxholes you see everywhere.

Standing in the stench of Hué's streets, Young reflected on the damage. "And what has the battle of Hué meant? Tragically, it has symbolized the entire war." The US regained Hué at the cost of destroying it. The North Vietnamese had attempted to indoctrinate Hué residents, and had killed most of Hué's government officials. Neither side won any appreciable number of Hué hearts or minds.

Deliberate blocks placed by the central government insist joint ventures in Hué be "branches" of those in Hanoi or Saigon.

Getting Your Bearings

Hué is divided into north bank and south bank sections. The north bank is where the Citadel once stood—a huge walled area sealed by moats and enclosing the Imperial Palace. The north bank is now largely a residential area. Formerly the French quarter, the south bank is the commercial sector, with banks, hotels, restaurants, and transport terminals. Three bridges link the two banks over the Perfume River. Two are used by cars and buses; the third is a railway bridge, also used by pedestrians and bicyclists.

SIGHTS

The Citadel

Emperor Gia Long modeled the Royal Citadel on the Forbidden City in Beijing, China. The ramparts, however, were built in the style of French military architect Sebastian de Vauban. The complex had fallen into neglect even before it was blown to pieces by the fighting of 1968. With much of the structural work made of wood, it fell prey to rain, typhoons, and termites, as well as thieves. The front gateway section and some stray buildings remain intact, but past that, it's vegetable farming all the way, with some nurseries and overgrown grass in the northeast corner. The north exit gates are not open, but you might be able to exit by the east gate.

The Royal Citadel is composed of three walled enclosures, each within the other—a city within a city. The exterior moated enclosure (Kinh Thanh) encompasses six square km—sufficient

ousted the North Vietnamese. An estimated 10,000 people died in Hué during the Tet offensive of 1968. Most were civilians. In the process, the Imperial Palace was reduced to rubble. Today the monuments of Hué are on the UN's World Heritage list, so sites may one day be restored.

Today Hué is a quiet town of 350,000. While Saigon and Hanoi grow by leaps and bounds, places like Hué crawl along. Few joint ventures are allowed, and there are few private hotels.

for housing the emperor, his family, administrators, bodyguards, and servants. Piercing the outer walls are 10 gates, each reached by a bridge across the moat. Toward the Perfume River is the Yellow Enclosure (Hoang Thanh), with six-meter-high walls about 2.5 km in length. Within this lies the innermost walled section—the former Imperial Palace, or Forbidden Purple City—of which very little now remains.

Most of what remains of the Citadel can be seen at the southern end, near the Perfume River. Approaching the Citadel you cross a moat by one of two gates, Nhon Gate or Quang Duc Gate. Inside the gates are two groups of cannons. The **Nine Cannons** were cast of brass in 1803. They're each five meters in length and are named after the four seasons and five elements. They've never been fired; their function is symbolic. Sandwiched between the two entry gates is the massive **Flag Tower.** The flag of the National Liberation Front flew here for 24 days in 1968.

Continuing north you come to **Ngo Mon,** or Royal Gate, where the ticket office is located. This massive gate was built in 1834 during the reign of Emperor Minh Mang. There are five entrances—in previous times, only the emperor was permitted to use the central one. Golden Water Bridge, directly beyond the gate, was also reserved exclusively for the emperor's use. Crossing that, you come to **Dien Thai Hoa,** the Palace of Supreme Peace, where the emperor, seated on a raised golden throne, held official receptions and supervised important ceremonies. On the steps of the palace are nine stone stelae, dividing the courtyard into areas of the nine mandarin ranks. Built in 1833, Thai Hoa Palace is one of the best-preserved buildings left in the complex and is undergoing further restoration. Behind Thai Hoa Palace are two huge bronze urns from the 17th century, decorated with birds, plants, and animals.

From here, walk to the west side of the complex: this easily overlooked section provides the Citadel's main visual interest. In front of elegant Hien Lam Cac Pavilion are the spectacular **Nine Dynastic Urns.** Cast in bronze between 1835 and 1837, they stand two meters tall and weigh between 1,500 and 2,500 kg each. Each is dedicated to a different Nguyen emperor—the central and largest one to Gia Long. The urns are engraved with various designs—landscapes, wild animals, birds, the sun, the moon, the stars—symbolizing the power of the Nguyen dynasty. The craftsmanship is superb. The bronze urns are a must-see within the Citadel. A short distance north of the urns is **Mieu Temple,** Temple of the Generations, built in 1821. It contains altars for worship of 10 Nguyen sovereigns.

Backtracking a bit, north of Thai Hoa Palace is the **Imperial Palace,** once reserved for the emperor, his concubines, and eunuch servants. Remaining buildings here are in very poor condition. The Hall of the Mandarins and the Royal Library have been partially restored. The government is investing several million dollars to restore Hué's monuments, so this phoenix may rise from the ashes yet. Financial and technical support has come from UNESCO; Vietnamese scholars traveled to the Oriental Museum in Paris to survey the original plans for construction of imperial buildings.

A good place to exit the Imperial City is by **Hien Nhon Gate,** on the east. Here you'll find Ong Tao II Restaurant, set in a charming courtyard—an ideal place for a drink. If you exit from Hien Nhon Gate, you can continue walking east to the Imperial Museum.

Imperial Museum

This museum, also known as the Hué Museum of Ancient Objects, is at 3 Le Truc street, just east of Hien Nhon Gate. Housed in a former royal palace, the museum's collection of antique furniture, bronzeware, screens, ceramics, musical instruments, and royal clothing give you a real feel for the mandarin period. Exhibits are unlabeled. Also down this way is the **Military Museum,** with a few stray tanks and other military hardware in the courtyard.

Thien Mu Pagoda

Thien Mu is about three km from downtown Hué, on the banks of the Perfume River. This Mahayana Buddhist temple is a peaceful place to spend time. It's the oldest monastery in Hué, dating back to the 17th century. Near the front stands seven-tiered Phuoc Nguyen Tower, long the symbol of Hué. It was built in 1844, each level containing an altar dedicated to a different Buddha. Near the tower are several smaller buildings; one holds the temple's massive bell. Cast in the early 18th century, the bell weighs

IMPERIAL TOMB TOUR

This tour takes in the imperial tombs, scattered in the countryside six to 12 km south of Hué. Actual cycling time is about two hours; be prepared for some uphill pushing. If you're in a tearing hurry, find a moto; if it's raining, adjust your route and switch to a boat. Start this tour on the south bank, where the old French quarter was once located. The tree-lined avenues around Le Loi Boulevard are great places to wander. Along the waterfront was prime French real estate—in the north, the Customs House; between the two bridges, the Cercle Sportif, official residences, and colonial villas; to the south, the French-constructed railroad bridge.

Make your way to **Ho Chi Minh Museum** at the west end of Le Loi. The museum is pure propaganda—skip it if you wish. Nearby **Quoc Hoc School,** established in 1896, was attended at different times by Ho Chi Minh, General Vo Nguyen Giap, and Ngo Dinh Diem; it would have been a pretty rowdy class if they'd all attended at once. Quoc Hoc is now a coed high school.

Follow Dien Bien Phu Street for a side trip to **Bao Quoc Pagoda**—an important center of study. There are an estimated 500 monks and nuns in Hué, and upwards of 100 small pagodas. Monks from different pagodas assemble here for instruction; Vietnamese students come to study in the tranquil gardens.

Nam Giao is not much to look at now, but it used to be the most sacred site in Hué. Built by Emperor Gia Long in 1802, Nam Giao was composed of three terraces—two square to represent the earth, and one circular representing the sky. As holder of the "mandate of heaven," the emperor would make sacrifices to the heavens here. The area was turned into a monument for fallen North Vietnamese after 1975—a controversial choice of statuary. From Nam Giao, it's downhill or flat to Khai Dinh Tomb, about 30 to 40 minutes by bike. You'll pass village life on quiet roads, forested zones, and farmed areas of sugarcane, rice, and vegetable plots. The countryside is the main reason for cycling through—you may find the imperial tombs disappointing.

It's hard to get excited about the mausoleums of Hué. The Hué emperors, believing they would be accorded as much splendor in their after lives as in their present ones spent their final days directing tomb construction. Some even threatened to exe-

cute artisans if their work was not up to standard. The tombs were copied from Chinese prototypes, but do not match the craftsmanship or ostentation of the originals. In fact, the imperial tombs of Hué are quite dull and gloomy, and exude a stagnant air.

Construction followed a formulaic design, although each emperor's deviated in details. The arrangement comprised five key elements: a brick courtyard with stone mandarin guards, horses, and elephants; a pavilion with marble tablets in praise of the emperor, inscribed by his son and heir; a temple for the worship of the emperor and empress; a lotus pond with a viewing pavilion; and, finally, a deep grave. During construction, the emperor used the viewing pavilion to direct operations; after his death, the temple at the site would be regularly visited by the emperor's widows. Although there were 13 emperors in the Nguyen dynasty (1802-1945), only seven reigned until their deaths, accounting for the low number of tombs in Hué.

Khai Dinh's Tomb, 10 km from Hué, was completed in 1931, and was 11 years in the making. After the grandiose entryway with dragon pillars, the mausoleum itself is an anticlimax. The architecture is an ugly mix of European and Asian, with grimy rows of mandarin guards in the courtyard. Inside the main hall are colorful glass mosaic frescoes; a life-size bronze statue of Khai Dinh, made in France in 1922, is positioned over the actual tomb.

At the village of Ban Lang, 12 km from Hué, you can leave your bicycle behind and take a small ferry (bargain hard) across the Perfume River to **Minh Mang Tomb.** Out on the water you'll see fishing boats, and sampans dredging for sand and rocks. Minh Mang is the finest of the imperial tombs. The attraction here is the harmonious garden with its frangipani and lotus blossoms. Minh Mang reigned from 1820 to 1840; the tomb was constructed after his death by his heir, Thieu Tri. The atmosphere is one of peace and tranquility.

Once back on the east bank, continue north. You could easily skip Thieu Tri and Dong Khanh Tombs—they're not much to look at. **Tu Duc Tomb,** enclosed by walls, features pine woods and a lakeside pavilion with lotus blossoms where the emperor once fished, listened to music, and wrote poetry—in between strenuous bouts of tomb building. Emperor Tu Duc went a bit overboard with the poetry, inscribing his own stones with praise of himself. Actually, he did this because he had no son to write the script, even though he had 104 wives and numerous courtesans. Tu Duc's tomb was more of a pleasure garden than a tomb: the emperor used it as a second residence, where he indulged in extravagant 50-course meals of incredible delicacies. Tu Duc reigned from 1847 to 1883; the mausoleum was constructed between 1864 and 1867 by a force of 3,000 laborers. More recently, the lakeside pavilion has been restored with the help of UNESCO.

From here, you can make your way north to downtown Hué. However, if you're still up for more touring, you could hop over to the north bank. If you take a left at the Perfume River, you'll find some tiny boats to carry you across to Thien Mu pagoda. You can put yourself and bike on the boat, visit Thien Mu, then return to Hué via the railway bridge.

NGUYEN DYNASTY EMPERORS

EMPEROR	DATE OF REIGN
Gia Long	1802-19
Minh Mang	1820-40
Thieu Tri	1841-47
Tu Duc	1847-83
Duc Duc	1883
Hiep Hoa	1883
Kien Phuc	1883-84
Ham Nghi	1884-85
Dong Khanh	1885-89
Thanh Thai	1889-1907
Duy Tan	1907-16
Khai Dinh	1916-25
Bao Dai	1925-45

several tons. In another pavilion is a marble turtle; stelae mounted on it chronicle the development of Buddhism in Hué.

Encased in glass at the front of the nearby temple is a brass statue of a Laughing Buddha, a figure with a fat, bare stomach reclining on a couch and laughing his bald head off. The Laughing Buddha is the nickname of 9th-century Chinese Zen master Poe-Tai Hoshang, who discovered the "Buddha within himself." This highly eccentric monk wandered blissfully through China without any worries. After his death he was worshipped throughout the Chinese world as a popular hero and a deity of good fortune. Three superb brass statues stand inside the temple: on the left the Buddha of the Past (Amitabha); in the center, the Buddha of the Present (Sakyamuni); on the right, the Buddha of the Future (Maitreya). There is also a smaller Laughing Buddha statue. The Laughing Buddha is sometimes associated with Maitreya.

At the back of the temple are gardens and nurseries where the dozen monks who live here cultivate vegetables and trees. They collect orchids from surrounding woods to plant at the monastery; you'll see bonsai trees on display. In this area is a shelter displaying the blue Austin in which Thich Quang Duc, a 66-year-old monk from Thien Mu, was driven to Saigon to immolate himself on a street corner on 11 June 1963 as a protest against repression under the Diem regime. Pictures of the scene gained international news coverage. The car is now revered as a sacred relic.

In May 1993, another immolation occurred outside Thien Mu Pagoda. The burnt Buddhist layman's name was not released, and no reason was provided for the suicide. When the abbot of Thien Mu, Thich Tri Tuu, tried to organize a Buddhist funeral for the man, local government

ENTRY FEES

Entry fees to museums and historic attractions are rarely quoted in this book because they're usually a pittance. Not so in Hué. Each tomb in Hué charges a stiff $5 entry fee—the highest in Vietnam. Permission to use a still or video camera will cost another $5. What's left of the Imperial Palace also costs $5 to enter. In 1992 the entry price was $1.20, so the price has tripled. The Imperial Museum is an extra $2. Only foreigners pay these fees; no Vietnamese could possibly afford such luxury. The locals just pay a few thousand dong. Visit five tombs and you hit $25, a lot of money in Vietnam. To be more selective, visit only Khai Dinh and Minh Mang tombs. Most of these are disappointing.

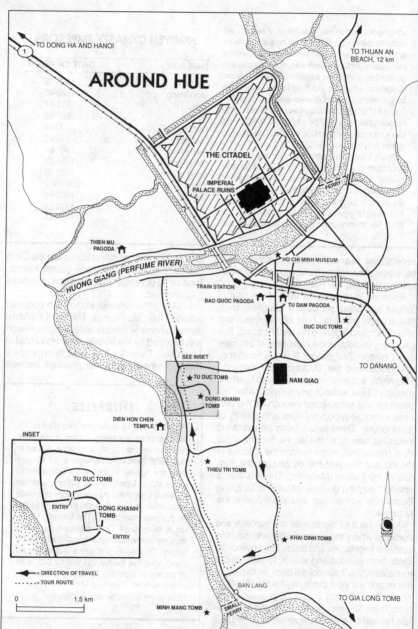

AROUND HUE

TO DONG HA AND HANOI

TO THUAN AN BEACH, 12 km

THE CITADEL

IMPERIAL PALACE RUINS

FERRY

THIEN MU PAGODA

HUONG GIANG (PERFUME RIVER)

HO CHI MINH MUSEUM

TRAIN STATION

BAO QUOC PAGODA

TU DAM PAGODA

DUC DUC TOMB

TO DANANG

SEE INSET

TU DUC TOMB

DONG KHANH TOMB

NAM GIAO

DIEN HON CHEN TEMPLE

THIEU TRI TOMB

KHAI DINH TOMB

INSET

TU DUC TOMB

ENTRY

DONG KHANH TOMB

ENTRY

BAN LANG

SMALL FERRY

TO GIA LONG TOMB

MINH MANG TOMB

= DIRECTION OF TRAVEL
...... = TOUR ROUTE

0   1.5 km

MOON

© MOON PUBLICATIONS, INC.

NORTH BANK TOUR

The sites mentioned here can be reached on foot, by bicycle, or by hired boat.

Start at Dong Ba Market, which can be reached by hired boat, by bicycle, or on foot directly over the Trang Tien Bridge. Or take a regular ferry from a landing to the east of the Century Riverside Inn, across Dap Da Bridge; you can load your bike onto the ferry. You can easily spend several hours at the market, with its profusion of women in conical hats engaging in just about every kind of food transaction known to Vietnam. Early in the morning country folk unload their produce at the market steps by the river, and fishermen from the coast bring in fresh seafood. The covered market features a large rice section.

From Dong Ba Market you can cycle or walk to the Citadel, park and visit, and then carry on to Thien Mu Pagoda several km to the west. If you backtrack from the pagoda about 100 meters, you'll find a small boat that will deliver you to the south bank again for about a dollar. You can also ride back along the north bank, using the railway bridge to cross the Perfume River.

In November, the abbot and three other monks from Thien Mu were arrested and subsequently sentenced to three- and four-year prison terms after a closed trial without lawyers or witnesses. This imprisonment may be part of a wider issue; the monks were known supporters of Thich Huyen Quang, a dissident Buddhist exiled to a small village due to his protests against government attempts to control Vietnamese Buddhism.

Hué Cathedral

To the south of downtown Hué on Nguyen Hué Street is Hué Cathedral, completed in 1962. The cathedral is a curious blend of Asian and Western architecture—a recognizable European cathedral, but with an Oriental octagonal steel spire and Chinese-style eaves. The altar is made from marble quarried at the Marble Mountains near Danang.

Thuan An Beach

About 13 km northeast of Hué, Thuan An beach stretches for several km and features a protected lagoon and South China Sea frontage. Foreigners pay a fee to enter the beach. Get there by bus from Dong Ba Market, or hire a

authorities intervened, claiming there was no proof he was a devout Buddhist. Several days later, Thich Tri Tuu was forced into a police car; six monks sat down in front of the vehicle in protest and a large crowd of supporters rallied around. The sit-down strike held up traffic for hours in what turned out to be the largest Vietnamese public protest since the Vietnam War. Eventually, the authorities and the abbot were forced out of the car. It was then overturned, and burst into flames.

Hué Cathedral

TOURING HUÉ

For touring Hué, it's a toss-up between biking and boating. You could load your bicycle onto a boat, head south, and visit temples and tombs, then cycle back. Vietnamese load bicycles onto boats all the time—it won't faze your boatman. Group tours often take a boat south on the Perfume River, and then return by car. You cannot use cyclos around Hué because of the hills. For the two tours mentioned here, mix and match destinations using boat, bicycle, or car transportation. Only a few tombs can be reached directly by boat; most are accessible by land. In any case, the ride's the thing—the tombs are fairly dull.

One factor influencing your transportation decisions is the weather. Hué is cool and foggy, with very high rainfall. Rain is heavy between August and October; the rainy season extends from May to December. That leaves a dry season from January to May.

Along the Perfume River

The Perfume River (Huong Giang) is named after a scented shrub that reportedly grows at its source. A languid half-day on the river is one of the pleasures of Hué. It's easy to rent a small craft and visit tombs and other sites around Hué. A number of boats dock on the south bank of Hué between Trang Tien and Dap Da Bridges. You could also try Dong Ba Market area. You can negotiate directly with boat owners, or arrange a vessel through a hotel or tourist agency. A whole boat for a five-hour trip is around $12-20, depending on the number of passengers

(0800-1300, maximum 10 people); a fancier dragon boat is $20-25 per hour. The Huong Giang Hotel and Century Riverside Inn have "folksinging boats," where you're serenaded as you drift along the Perfume River. Royal dishes are served on dragon boats as well—all for a price. Phoenix boats are even more expensive.

A sample itinerary follows this route: Trang Tien Bridge to Thien Mu Pagoda to Dien Hon Chen Temple to Tu Duc Tomb to Minh Mang Tomb to Trang Tien Bridge. Some tours skip Hon Chen Temple, and may cover Tu Duc Tomb on land. Tours from Century Riverside Inn cover a three- to four-hour journey by boat to Minh Mang Tomb, then to Ban Lang on the east bank where passengers transfer to a waiting car. Passengers then cover inland tombs by auto on the way back to Hué. A car for four to five people is $20; a minibus for seven people is $25. The tomb of Khai Dinh is two km from the Perfume River.

If you want longer on the river, ask to add Gia Long Tomb, farther south on the Perfume River. The tomb is not often visited and will cost extra—add $5 more for an ordinary boat. Gia Long Tomb is about 16 km from Hué. The tomb, built between 1814 and 1820, was damaged by bombing during the Vietnam War, and is today overgrown with bushes.

Another longer excursion by boat: Head east on the Perfume River to Thuan An Beach. At night on the river you can see people fishing with lanterns from sampans.

---

boat for a longer journey. There's a small hotel if you want to stay overnight.

BEING THERE

Accommodations

Hué is far enough north that hot water becomes a priority. It's often overcast or raining, and cold in winter. Hotels in Hué vary considerably—some, like the Morin, have lots of character; others, like the Dong Da, are impersonal concrete blockhouses.

Guesthouse/Budget: Hotel #2 Le Loi, tel. 22153, is the main backpacker hangout, a five-

minute walk from the train station. There are 150 rooms available in two buildings of five wings each: two-bed, three-bed, and four-bed rooms for $7 s or $10 d. Near Phu Xuan Bridge is **Nha Khach 18,** 18 Le Loi, tel. 23720. It offers one single for $5, four doubles for $10, and four doubles at $20 with bath.

Popular **Morin Hotel,** 30 Le Loi, tel. 23526, surrounds a courtyard. Lots of character—54 rooms go for $6-15 s, $8-20 d. Some rooms have more than their fair share of mildew and mosquitoes—go for the upper floors. Hot water available. You can rent bicycles here for $1 a day, motorcycles for $7 a day; cars can be arranged. Around the corner **Hung Vuong**

Hotel, 2 Hung Vuong, tel. 23797, offers 33 rooms for $8 d, $10 t with fan, $12 for a four-person room, and $15-22 d/t with air-conditioning.

Ben Nghe GH, at 4 Ben Nghe St., tel. 23687, is a concrete two-story hotel, $5 s or d, and $10 d with hot water. **Nha Khach 36,** at 36 Le Loi, tel. 22236, inside the Hué University of Teacher Education and Centre de Français de Hué, may rent rooms to travelers when not full of students. A double goes for $6 with bath but no hot water and $10 with air-con and hot water. About 13 rooms are available.

On the north bank of the Perfume River, close to the Citadel, is the 25-room **Nha Khach Dang Dung,** 3 Dang Dung, tel. 22478. The villa-style hotel charges $12 with bath.

Moderate: Hotel #5 Le Loi, tel. 22155, fax 24527, has 16 rooms in the $20-40-60 range. The hotel is located in an elegant yellow mansion with large gardens—lots of character, hot water on tap. **Ngo Quyen Hotel,** 11 Ngo Quyen, tel. 23278, has 26 rooms in A and B blocks for $12-17-20; a few rooms for $6.

Hué City Tourism Villas operated by Hué Tourism, tel. 23577, line Ly Thong Kiet Street; the villa number corresponds to the street number. They vary from older-style villas to new buildings. Villa 5, tel. 23945, offers nine rooms in a pleasant newer villa—five fan rooms for $10 (no bath), and four air-conditioned rooms at $30 with bath and balcony. **Minihotel 7,** next door, tel. 22167, offers four rooms for $15-20-25. **Villa 14** is a small house with three rooms, no phone; $15-20-30. **Villas 16 and 18,** tel. 23964, have gardens and 14 rooms—doubles and triples. Rooms available for $12-25-30; Villa 18 is more expensive.

In the Soviet concrete blockhouse class are the following three hotels. **Dong Da Hotel,** 15 Ly Thong Kiet, tel. 23071, offers 17 rooms for $10-15, one superior room for $35. **Thuan Hoa,** 7 Nguyen Tri Phuong, tel. 22553, fax 22470, is a blockhouse with a big extension at the back. The 65 rooms, mostly doubles and triples, cost $32-35, with a few singles at $20. **Kinh Do Hotel,** 1 Nguyen Thai Hoc, tel. 23566, has 39 rooms. Doubles are $25, with a few for $35; half a dozen cheaper rooms in the $10-18 range.

A Dong Guesthouse, 1 Chu Van An, tel. 24148, is a 10-room private hotel located in an alley opposite the Century Riverside Inn; rooms cost $20-25-30. Another private hotel, **Hoa Hong,** stands opposite the gates of the Century Riverside, at 46C Le Loi, tel. 24377. It features nine double rooms for $25-35-45.

Luxury: Century Riverside Inn, 49 Le Loi, tel. 23390, fax 23399, has 64 standard rooms for $45 s, $50 d; 22 superior garden-view rooms for $55-60; and 33 superior river-view rooms for $65-70. There are an additional 18 deluxe rooms for $75-80 and two suites for $140 each. Add 10% tax to all calculations. The hotel is five stories; the upper floors have views of the Perfume River. It features several restaurants and a disco. The Century is a joint-venture hotel, part of the Century International Hotels chain, and affiliated with Century Saigon Hotel in Ho Chi Minh City.

Huong Giang Hotel, 51 Le Loi, tel. 23958, fax 23424, is a large three-story hotel near the Century, with singles for $48-55, and river-view rooms for $55-60. "Royal bedrooms" are $90-110-140-160. The hotel provides full facilities, including a conference hall. Staff can arrange car rentals and tours; folk performances are held here, too.

Food

Hué is known for *banh khoai,* a crepe stuffed with bean sprouts, shrimp, and pork, eaten with salad, starfruit slices, and *nuoc tuong* (sesame and peanut sauce). A variation on this is *bun thit nuong,* which uses a noodle base. Wash it down with Huda, the local brew—a joint-venture Danish beer. For those with a sweet tooth, a sticky sesame-seed bar called *mexung* is hand-made on the premises at 135 and 137 Huynh Thuc Khang St., to the east side of the Citadel, along Dong Ba Canal. Hué residents debate which shop produces the superior version. The families have been making the stuff for the last 40-odd years. **Phuoc Hung,** at 41 Tran Hung Dao, also sells *mexung,* plus Chinese-type pastries. Streetstalls occasionally have croissants.

Strung along Hanoi Street are a number of noodlehouses with cheap and tasty fare. They serve fried rice noodle soup *(pho tai),* dry noodles *(pho kho),* and soft-fried noodles. **Trung Lam** at 7B Hanoi, serves good soups; on the opposite side is **Quan An** at number 6. Nearby, at number 8, is **Phuoc Loc** restaurant, offering *banh bao* Saigon (stuffed dumplings) as well as Chinese noodle soup. **Minh Y Restaurant,** at 10 Hanoi St., is a small Western-style restaurant great for breakfast. The menu features soup, omelettes, jam, bread, and cheese. At **Bun Bo Hué Restaurant,** 11 Ly Thong Kiet, you can find Hué-style soup.

North Bank Restaurants: Just off Tran Hung Dao Street is **Lac Thanh Restaurant,** at 6A Dinh Tien Hoang. This place is run by a deaf-mute family who communicate very well. They speak the language of food—lots of it, well prepared, on your plate. Try the crab soup and pancake. The family will assist with boat, motorcycle, and bicycle rentals. With similar dishes, and equally popular, is **Lac Thien,** next door at number 6.

The more upscale **Ong Tao,** at 134 Ngo Duc Ke, tel. 22037, features excellent food. There is a small upstairs section on an open roof. This small private restaurant serves seafood and Hué specialties; also good for breakfast. **Ong Tao II,** tel. 23031, is a branch of this restaurant inside Hien Nhon Gate east of the Imperial Palace—no entry fee required. Ong Tao II has a very pleasant setting—orchard, rattan chairs, old crumbled walls—but the food is below par, so perhaps stick to the drinks. Northwest of the Imperial Palace is **Huong Sen,** 42 Nguyen Trai, tel. 23201, with a pavilion jutting into a lake for outdoor dining. Food is mediocre and can be pricey here; the full menu includes frog, eel, fish, and some vegetarian dishes.

South Bank Restaurants: Song Huong Floating Restaurant, tel. 23738, is moored near Trang Tien Bridge. The restaurant has a terrace and indoor tables and features a full menu; pricey for seafood. **Dzach Lau,** 23 Ben Nghe St., tel. 22831, has moderately priced crab, shrimp, fish, chicken, and beef dishes.

On the southeast side of town is **Ong Nen Restaurant,** and almost opposite, **Restaurant 20;** both started out serving specialty soups—eel soup, shrimp soup—but now offer a full range of dishes. In the same area, on Nguyen Thai Hoc St., is **Am Phu Restaurant,** which is busy and cheap. Down the street at 29 Nguyen Thai Hoc is **Ngoc Anh Restaurant,** which is more expensive and cleaner. It has a pleasant covered courtyard; specialties include eel with lemongrass and chile, and frog legs stewed with garlic.

The top floor of the **Huong Giang Hotel** has a restaurant with a good reputation. Elaborate royal dinners are served at the Century Riverside Inn and Huong Giang Hotel—the bill often over $100 for a small group.

Shopping

Conical hats made from palm leaves and bamboo are a Hué specialty. Hold one of these *non bai tho* (poem hats) up to the light to reveal stenciled designs such as a pair of birds or a short poem, proverb, or song hidden between the layers of palm leaves. There is a string of silk and souvenir shops opposite the gates of the Century Riverside Inn. Artists also sell their work directly at major sites such as Thien Mu Pagoda and the imperial tombs.

Nightlife

Hué is quiet at night. Entertainment is mainly going to restaurants or cafés, though some hotels have dance floors. You might also want to look into a night cruise on the Perfume River—you can see locals night fishing with lanterns from sampans.

The Century Riverside Inn and Huong Giang Hotel stage formal, imperial dinners, and imperial song and dance ensembles for tourist groups. Two tourists dress as emperor and empress, and the rest of the party as mandarins. Ancient recipes of questionable authenticity are served. The complete package for three to five guests costs $100; for 6-10 it costs $160. Huong Giang Hotel has a curious price list: a royal dance performance is $200, and a round of folksongs $70 an hour for under 10 guests. If the round of folksongs is sung on a dragon boat, it's $20 an hour extra for the boat. For a phoenix boat, it's $35 an hour extra.

Services and Information

Café #3 Le Loi is the traveler hangout—it also serves good food. Backpackers frequent Hotel #2 Le Loi opposite. Café #3 rents bicycles for 75 cents a day and Hondas for $5 a day; the café will arrange a boat for $15 to cruise the Perfume River; it's $20 to tour pagodas and tombs by car. Café staff can organize cars or vans north to the DMZ, or south to China Beach and Hoi An. The family at Lac Thanh Restaurant, across the river, rents bicycles and motorcycles, and will assist with boats, guides, and good food.

It's very easy to find highly educated Hué residents who speak good French or English, or both. Try the Centre de Français de Hué at 36 Le Loi. People in Hué are friendly, and eager to practice their foreign-language skills.

You'll find **Hué Tourist Office** at 1 Truong Dinh St., tel. 23577. There are a couple of private tour outfits in Hué. **ATC Hué,** at 44 Le Loi (opposite the Century Riverside Inn), tel. 24500, arranges visa extensions, ticketing, accommodations, boat touring, royal dinners, and car rentals. A good tourist map of Hué, in English and French, issued by the State Department of Cartography, should be available in sheet form.

The **post office,** at 8 Hoang Hoa Tham, is open 0630-2030 and has a fax machine. The Hué area code is 84-54. The main bank for exchange is the **Bank of Industry** on Le Quy Don Street near the Municipal Theater. Another possibility is the **State Bank** at 6 Hoang Hoa Tham near the GPO.

Visa extensions are available at the **Entry/Exit Control Office,** 45 Ben Nghe St., tel. 22131, open 0700-1130 and 1300-1700.

Getting There and Away

By Air: From **Phu Bai Airport,** 14 km from town, there are scheduled flights to Hanoi, Ho Chi Minh City, and Dalat. The Vietnam Airlines office, 12 Hanoi St., tel. 3249, can arrange bus service to the airport for a dollar. A three-wheel shuttle operates from Dong Ba Bus Terminal to the airport.

By Train: Trains run to Hanoi and Ho Chi Minh City several times daily. Hué to Hanoi is 688 km. Foreign prices for Hué-Hanoi on Reunification Express trains are $20 hard seat, $23 soft seat, $33-37-40 hard sleeper, and $44

soft sleeper. These prices are 250% higher than local prices. Hué to Saigon is 1,038 km, and costs $29 hard seat, $35 soft seat, $50-55-60 hard sleeper, and $66 soft sleeper on a S7 train. On a CM5 train, prices are $40 soft seat, $55-60-66 hard sleeper, and $76 soft sleeper. A good compromise for price and comfort is soft seat. The reclining seat allows some latitude for sleeping. Like the bus trip, the train trip from Hué to Danang is spectacular. It takes four hours and costs $5. The Hué train station is located at the west end of Le Loi Street.

Private Car and Minibus: You can club together with other travelers and rent a car for the 108-km route from Hué to Danang for $25-40 one-way. Café #3 Le Loi arranges a $35 one-way trip by car or minibus for the route Hué to Lang Co Beach to Hai Van Pass to Danang (Cham Museum) to Marble Mountains to China Beach to Hoi An. Longer trips can also be arranged from Hué. A one-way trip from Hué to Saigon passing Hoi An, Qui Nhon, Nha Trang, and Dalat in eight days costs $400 for the minibus. A minibus to Hanoi costs $25 a person.

By Bus: An Cuu Bus Terminal, at the southern end of Hung Vuong St., handles destinations to the south, with departures at 0500 for Qui Nhon, Buon Ma Thuot, Pleiku, Nha Trang, Dalat, and Saigon. **An Hoa Bus Terminal,** northwest of the Citadel, handles connections to the north, departing at 0500 for Dong Ha, Vinh, Khe Sanh, and Hanoi. Local buses leave from Dong Ba Bus Terminal at the east end of Tran Hung Dao.

side canal, Hué

Getting Around

Cyclos lie in wait at the railway station, the bus stations, the market, and major hotels. There are also some motos for hire. Bicycles rent for about $1 a day—available from Café #3 Le Loi, Morin Hotel, and other hotels. The Morin Hotel rents motorbikes for $7 a day, and Café #3 Le Loi rents Hondas for $6 a day. Lac Thanh

Restaurant is another likely source of motorcycle and bicycle rentals. Cars can be rented here for around $20-30 a day from 0700-1700, with a maximum 100 km on the odometer; you can hire a minibus for $40 a day. Boat rentals cost $15 per half-day with four to six people in a regular boat, and $25 a half-day for a dragon boat with folk singing.

NORTH OF HUÉ

DONG HA

Largely destroyed in the 1970s, Dong Ha now supports a population of 60,000. It became the main town in the province by default. In 1972 NVA troops poured across the DMZ and laid seige to Quang Tri, once the provincial capital. American planes and South Vietnamese artillery reduced Quang Tri to rubble in four months of heavy fighting. After the war, all provincial government offices were moved to Dong Ha.

Dong Ha is basically a truck stop. At the junction of Route 9 and Highway 1 (called Le Duan here) there's a desultory collection of food shacks and small hotels, a market, bus station, gas station, post office, and Quang Tri Tourism Office. Ramshackle noodlehouses and bars with taxi girls complete the picture. Strung out along Highway 1 are half a dozen hotels, with rates varying $7-25 a night; there are other hotels deeper into Dong Ha.

Further into town, several km west along Route 9, you come to another center—a roundabout with railway tracks on one side, some discarded US tanks, a tank retriever, and a 105mm howitzer. The roundabout was once the site of a French defense bunker. Facing the tanks are the main post office and Party Headquarters building. Further west on Route 9 is Dong Ha's best hotel, the **Dong Truong Son Hotel;** in the $20-30 range, not well located. Good view of the DMZ area from the top-floor restaurant.

Quang Tri Tourism, tel. 52266, fax 52639, is on Le Duan Blvd. at the intersection of Highway 1 and Route 9. The company arranges cars for touring the DMZ for $45 a day and issues permits in a few minutes for $5 a person—quite a tidy sum of money, since the names of all in a group

are often entered on a single permit. The permit restrictions appear to be greater in the Khe Sanh area. You may be able to dodge permit requirements if you have a local guide with you.

Up to eight guides are available at Quang Tri Tourism. They speak several languages between them: Russian, English, French, Lao, and Thai. Guides are $10 for the day—they tell fascinating stories about the area. Sometimes the clients do the guiding—over 200 American veterans visited in 1993. One vet broke down and cried at a site close to the Lao border, where his camp was overrun by NVA infantry. A dozen of his friends were killed by fire from four Russian tanks. The vet left joss sticks in memory of his friends, offered prayers, and took photos.

THE DMZ

The 75-km stretch of road from Hué to Dong Ha was dubbed *La Rue Sans Joie* (Street Without Joy) by French Foreign Legionnaires. They took a beating along this narrow strip at the hands of the Vietminh, and only secured the road in 1953, a year before leaving Indochina. In July 1954, the Geneva Conference called for a line drawn at the 17th parallel, partitioning North Vietnam from South Vietnam. This area became known as the Demilitarized Zone (DMZ). In the 1960s, the Americans came up with the concept of building a "fence" to keep out the North. In 1967 the US erected the McNamara Wall at the 17th parallel—a zone of mines, fences, firebases, and hi-tech military gadgetry. The dividing line was the Ben Hai River, supposedly demilitarized for five km on either side. Invading North Vietnamese simply walked around the west end.

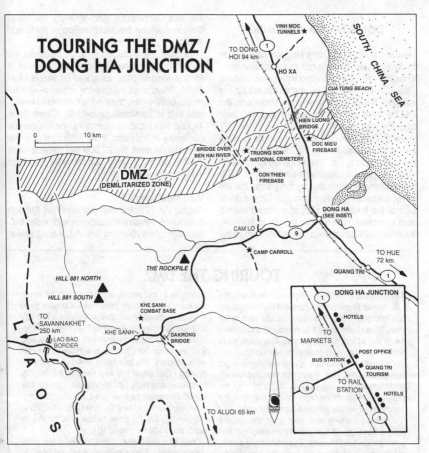

TOURING THE DMZ / DONG HA JUNCTION

VINH MOC TUNNELS ★

TO DONG HOI 94 km

HO XA

SOUTH CHINA SEA

CUA TUNG BEACH

HIEN LUONG BRIDGE

DOC MIEU FIREBASE

0   10 km

BRIDGE OVER BEN HAI RIVER

★ TRUONG SON NATIONAL CEMETERY

DMZ
(DEMILITARIZED ZONE)

CON THIEN FIREBASE

DONG HA (SEE INSET)

CAM LO

9

★ CAMP CARROLL

TO HUE 72 km

THE ROCKPILE

QUANG TRI

1

HILL 881 NORTH ▲

HILL 881 SOUTH ▲

KHE SANH COMBAT BASE

TO SAVANNAKHET 250 km

LAO BAO BORDER

KHE SANH

9

DAKRONG BRIDGE

L A O S

TO ALUOI 65 km

DONG HA JUNCTION

1

HOTELS

TO MARKETS

POST OFFICE

BUS STATION

QUANG TRI TOURISM

TO RAIL STATION

9

HOTELS

1

The incongruously named DMZ saw some of the war's most intense battles. The legacy: mountains of scrap metal, live ordnance, and chemically defoliated areas. Since the war, millions of pieces of live ordnance have been dug up throughout the zone, at a cost of over 5,000 limbless and dead. The zone from Dong Ha to Ben Hai River is only now beginning to be reused as farmland. Scrap-metal hunters abound in the DMZ; some use sophisticated metal detectors. The scrap goes to smelting factories in the north and south and is turned into reinforced rods, plates, and girders for use in structures like bridges. Other scrap is turned into ingots for export to Korea, Japan, and Taiwan. Top dong is paid for brass, followed by aluminum and steel. The larger DMZ leftovers—tanks, bulldozers, Armored Personnel Carriers—have now disappeared, leaving locals to forage deeper for shell casings and chunks of shrapnel. This is a risky business, as mines still infest the area. Impoverished families scavenge for scrap metal, including unexploded bombs, mortar rounds, and deadly white-phosphorous shells. Casualties often occur when farmers try to defuse live shells themselves instead of contacting military experts.

DONG HA TO VINH MOC

Heading north from Dong Ha, you stop at Doc Mieu firebase. There's not much to see here, except for red earth dented with bomb craters. Stick close to your guide, and watch out for live materiel. Never touch *anything* lying around the DMZ—there are lots of nasty things left over from the war.

From Doc Mieu, Highway 1 heads to Hien Luong Bridge, spanning the Ben Hai River 22 km north of Dong Ha. The bridge was bombed in 1967; the present bridge was completed in 1974. It was formerly controlled by the police, not the army, and mail still went through. On the north side of the bridge a statue of a soldier stands next to a pillar marked with the dates 20-7-54, the date that Vietnam was divided into two at the Geneva Conference, and 30-4-75, the fall of Saigon marking the reunification of north and south.

Not usually included in tours because the area is heavily mined is Con Thien firebase, a former Marine base attacked by the NVA in 1967. There's not much here anyway—the remains of trenches, bunkers, ammunition boxes, and bits of camouflage netting. Close by is Truong Son National Cemetery, the largest war cemetery in Vietnam. Row after row of white tombstones mark the 22,000 Vietnamese killed in DMZ battles. Truong Son Cemetery is 17 km west of Highway 1.

Vinh Moc Tunnels

Across the 17th Parallel you continue through surprisingly verdant ricepaddies, with water buffalo and cows roaming around. About seven

---

TOURING THE DMZ

The most popular day-trip out of Hué is to the former Demilitarized Zone (DMZ). Several hotels and guesthouses in Hué organize trips to the area. These tours cover a lot of ground, and are well worth the $15 or so per person. The countryside varies from bombed-scarred wasteland to luminous green rice paddies; along the way you get an earful of DMZ history and visit Vietcong tunnels and Montagnard villages. The DMZ visit is an experience—it gives you real insight into how the Vietnamese people suffered during the war.

For this excursion wear your worst clothes and take a flashlight. If you enter Vinh Moc Tunnels you'll get covered in muck. The following is a sample itinerary. Leave Hué around 0700, and take 90 minutes to drive to Dong Ha. After a stop in Dong Ha to obtain permits and pick up a local guide, the minibus heads north for the first leg of the tour, over the Hien Luong Bridge to Vinh Moc Tunnels. By around 1300 the minibus is back in Dong Ha for lunch, then departs for the second leg—west along Route 9 toward the Lao border, stopping at various sites, and finishing at Khe Sanh. By 1900, you should be back in Dong Ha, and in Hué by 2030.

Such an itinerary is available from Café #3, Hotel #2, or the Morin Hotel. Assuming a minibus is shared by six to 10 people, expenses work out to $55-60 for the minibus, $10-15 for DMZ guide, $5 a person for a DMZ permit, and a few bucks for extras like entry tickets. Sharing expenses, it breaks down to $12-15 a head. You can also arrange a two-day tour with an overnight stay in Dong Ha. This requires $85 for transportation, $20 for a guide, and $10 per person for a permit. In addition to the previous itinerary, this tour takes in Ashau Valley including Hamburger Hill and parts of the Ho Chi Minh Trail, and visits hilltribe villages. Other hotels in Hué also organize DMZ tours, but charge more. A full day tour from Dong Da Hotel is $60 for one to two people; $70 for three to four; $96 for five to eight; and $120 for nine to 10.

You can also take a bus to Dong Ha; stay overnight there. Find a moto driver to be your guide for about $10 a day. Two Western motorcyclists heading south from Hanoi toured the Dong Ha area, including the road to Lao Bao, by picking up a local guide. It's necessary to have a local guide to keep police at bay. In any case, it would be unwise to go by yourself in this area—there's still a lot of live ordnance around. If you're coming from Hanoi and don't want to backtrack from Hué, you can use Dong Ha as a base for touring the area. However, it will be difficult to put a group of travelers together in Dong Ha. You can wait at Quang Tri Tourism Office to join a minibus of Hué travelers coming through.

The tunnels dug in the red clay here are arrayed on 15-meter, 20-meter, and 25-meter levels. The water table is only a few meters below the deepest level. Apart from family dwellings, the tunnels previously contained a clinic, conference room, and warehouse; electric lighting was even installed in 1972. There are six exits to the sea, and seven to the air. You exit overlooking a surfing beach. Prepare to be hounded by enterprising youths selling soft drinks.

DONG HA TO LAO BAO

From Dong Ha, you now head west toward the Lao border along Route 9. Dong Ha to Khe Sanh is 57 km, about two hours with stops. Khe Sanh is only 18 km away from the Lao Bao border crossing into Laos. The road up to Lao Bao was built by the French and improved by the Americans and is in quite good shape. Here is a complete contrast in scenery from the Vinh Moc route; you'll see rolling hills on the way to Khe Sanh.

When American troops arrived here in 1965, they built camps, hospitals, command and logistics centers, and military firebases bearing names like Sharon and Ann. The firebases were an attempt to set up a string of strongholds along the DMZ. This area, just south of the 17th parallel, saw some of the bloodiest battles of the Vietnam War. Heavy fighting rocked Khe Sanh in 1968 and Hamburger Hill in 1969.

Today there's not a lot to see. Scrap-metal foragers have hauled off remaining pieces of military hardware. Camp Carroll was once the headquarters of US operations, but there's little to see except for some overgrown trenches. The camp is three km south of Route 9. The Rockpile—a huge mound of rocks—was a US lookout with an artillery base nearby.

South of Dong Ha

Dakrong Bridge, completed in 1976, is about 60 km from Dong Ha. Just before the bridge is a checkpoint where permits may be requested; police are looking for goods smuggled across the Lao border. West of the bridge are several Bru Van Kieu hilltribe villages with wooden and thatched housing. Cottage industries include traditional rattan collecting and, more recently, amassing scrap metal for resale. The Bru sort

guide at a Vinh Moc Tunnel entrance

km north of Ben Hai River you turn off Highway 1, and drive another 14 km along a dirt track to the fishing village of Vinh Moc.

After heavy bombardment of the area in the 1960s by US airplanes and offshore naval vessels, the 1,200 villagers of Vinh Moc went underground. They constructed three km of tunnels from 1966 to 1968, emerging only to work in the fields or fish. Later the tunnels were used by the Vietcong to keep supplies rolling to offshore Con Co Island. One guide claims one square meter of ground at Vinh Moc was subjected to 9.6 tons of American bombs from 1966 to 1972, although how such a precise figure was arrived at is not clear. Another statistic easier to grasp: 17 children were born in Vinh Moc Tunnels during the Vietnam War.

Upon arrival at Vinh Moc you're ushered into a small museum displaying photos, and models of the simple instruments used to dig the tunnels. There's a $1 entry fee for the museum, the tunnels, and the loan of a flashlight. The entrance to the tunnels is close to the museum; you exit above the nearby beach. Unlike Cu Chi Tunnels, the ones at Vinh Moc have only been slightly modified, with retimbered exits. This means you may have trouble getting around. If you suffer from claustophobia, do not venture into the tunnels. The tunnels can be quite slippery—your clothes may get covered in mud.

through artillery and cluster bomb casings, and load these onto trucks several times a month.

Farther to the south, across Dakrong Bridge, is a feeder of the **Ho Chi Minh Trail,** now overgrown with jungle. The famous trail is a dud as a sight. Scenery is quite ordinary, and the whole purpose of the trail was to be inconspicuous. Impeding the evolution of trekking routes are two factors: the huge amount of unexploded ordnance hidden along the trail, and uncertain security in the Central Highlands.

Minority villages are scattered along the route south, from Dakrong Bridge to **Aluoi**—once a US Special Forces base—and eventually on to Hué. Somewhere south of Aluoi in the Ashau Valley is Hamburger Hill; American forces fought a fierce battle with NVA troops here in May 1969, resulting in heavy losses for the Americans. Over 200 died in a single week. Hamburger Hill today is just a name. Even returning American vets cannot pinpoint the exact location, any more than Vietnamese can pinpoint the exact course of the Ho Chi Minh Trail. A better reason to venture farther down the Aluoi route is to visit minority villages. This part of the itinerary is not included in day-trips from Hué but is featured on the two-day trip. With a 4WD vehicle it's possible to travel the 65 km from Dakrong Bridge to Aluoi, and then continue another 60 km into Hué.

Khe Sanh

The rich, reddish soil around Khe Sanh is used for cultivating coffee, manioc, jackfruit, and pineapples. About 10,000 people live in the Khe Sanh area. Hilltribe women smoke long-stemmed pipes and wear embroidered skirts.

Khe Sanh is a strategic spot 75 km southwest of Dong Ha that once controlled Route 9 to Laos. In a hill area three km north of Khe Sanh town, the Americans maintained a large combat base, with an adjacent airstrip. A plaque inscribed in English and Vietnamese reads: "The Area Of Tacon Pont Base Built By US And Saigon Puppet." There's nothing left of the base except bits of barbed wire and scraps of metal, and holes dug by locals looking for scrap metal. To attract tourism, the government plans to rebuild the base, foxholes and all.

Khe Sanh is a famous battleground. Soon after it had been turned into a Marine stronghold in the mid-1960s, NVA infantry converged on it. The spectre of another Dien Bien Phu hung over Khe Sanh. To hold the combat base, American troops had to garrison the hills dominating the valley. In early 1967, a fierce exchange of fire occurred on Hill 861, Hill 881 South, and Hill 881 North—all areas held by the NVA. By late 1967, an estimated 20,000-40,000 NVA troops had converged on Khe Sanh and dug in.

The 77-day siege of Khe Sanh began in January 1968. Refusing to back off, US General William Westmoreland turned the siege into a showdown, with massive aerial and ground attacks on the surrounding area, and the build up of US and ARVN troops to over 6,000. In April 1968 US Army troops reopened Route 9 to the base, ending the seige. The cost was 248 American dead. Although they lost an estimated 10,000 troops, the North Vietnamese claimed the real objective of Khe Sanh was to distract American attention while the NVA launched the 1968 Tet offensive. The Americans, on the other hand, believed Tet was a diversion for Khe Sanh.

Khe Sanh was determined to be of no strategic importance, and the US quietly pulled out of the combat base in July 1968. Before withdrawal, American troops destroyed the base entirely to leave nothing for Vietnamese propaganda purposes.

Lao Bao Crossing

Khe Sanh is 20 km from the Lao Bao border crossing into Laos, which is slated to become a fast overland route for goods carried from Vietnam to Thailand. Trucks can cover the 350 km from Dong Ha to Savannakhet in Laos in a full 12-hour day of driving. The Lao Bao crossing has been open to foreigners since the beginning of 1994. Several have even bicycled the route from Thailand into Vietnam. You can pick up a Lao visa in Danang. More description of the route is given in the Laos chapter of this book.

THE NORTH COAST

There is little to recommend the thin strip of country north of Hué to Vinh and Thanh Hoa. Consider the facts: the Hué-Vinh strip, in places only a few hundred km wide, was subjected to saturation bombing during the Vietnam War, and remains one of the poorest parts of the

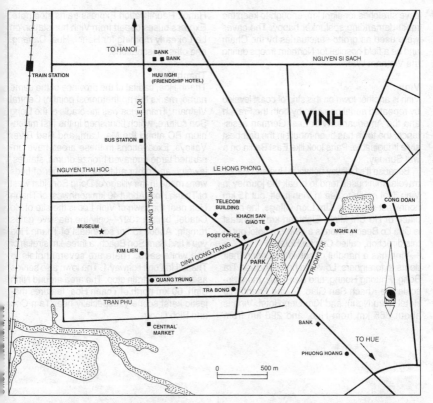

TO HANOI

BANK
BANK

NGUYEN SI SACH

TRAIN STATION

HUU NGHI
(FRIENDSHIP HOTEL)

LE LOI

VINH

BUS STATION

NGUYEN THAI HOC

LE HONG PHONG

QUANG TRUNG

TELECOM
BUILDING

CONG DOAN

KHACH SAN
GIAO TE

MUSEUM

POST OFFICE

NGHE AN

TRUONG THI

KIM LIEN

DINH CONG TRANG

PARK

QUANG TRUNG

TRA BONG

TRAN PHU

BANK

CENTRAL
MARKET

TO HUE

PHUONG HOANG

0   500 m

country. Highway 1 is in very bad condition here, sometimes disappearing into mud and potholes. To make matters worse, the area suffers some of the worst weather in Vietnam—typhoons, floods, hot dry spells. Most travelers speed through by train or plane. Traveling by a bus along this stretch is not recommended, but traveler minibuses can be arranged from Hué to Hanoi. It takes two days to drive the 660 km from Hué to Hanoi. Approximate distances on this route are: 75 km to Dong Ha, 95 km to Dong Hoi, 198 km to Vinh, 138 km to Thanh Hoa, 60 km to Ninh Binh, and 95 km to Hanoi.

Dong Hoi

Dong Hoi is a fishing port 170 km north of Hué. It was wiped off the map by US bombing during the Vietnam War, due to its position just north of the 17th parallel. Foreigners stay at **Hoa Binh Hotel,** with overpriced rooms. **Dong Hoi Tourist Office** is near the hotel.

Phong Nha Caves

A worthy stop north of Dong Hoi is Phong Nha Caves, ranked as a wonder on par with Halong Bay. A visit to the caves can be arranged by contacting Dong Hoi Tourist Office. The caves are 45 km northwest of Dong Hoi, about two hours by car. From Dong Hoi, drive north on Highway 1 to Bo Trach, then turn west on a dirt road to Son Trach village. In Son Trach you can hire boats that will take you on a great three-hour journey rowing and walking through the caves. You enter the caves via an underground river; a dry cave featuring stalactites and stalagmites extends several kilometers. The main cave stretches for eight km, enough to keep the most demanding spelunker happy. The caves were used as grotto-sanctuaries by the Cham and as a field hospital for Northern troops during the Vietnam War.

Vinh

Vinh is another town on this strip of coast leveled by repeated aerial bombing by both the French and the Americans. With East German assistance, the town has been rebuilt in the drabbest style imaginable. Parts look like East Berlin on a wet Sunday.

Because it's halfway between Hué and Hanoi, traveler minibuses tend to break the journey in Vinh. Not much to see in Vinh itself, but 15 km northwest of town is **Kim Lien village,** the birthplace of Ho Chi Minh. Eighteen km northeast is Cua Lo Beach. There's a 48-room hotel out in this direction, called Cua Lo Hotel.

Vinh has a handful of hotels that open their doors to foreigners. Low-end hotels include Tra Bong, Phuong Hoang, and Ben Thuy; more upscale are Khach San Giao Te, the Friendship Hotel (Huu Nghi), and Kim Lien Hotel. Vinh is about 365 km from Hué, and 290 km from Hanoi. Reunification Express trains stop here. Express buses depart from Vinh bus station on Le Loi early morning for Hanoi, Hué, Danang, and other destinations.

Thanh Hoa

Thanh Hoa, capital of the province of the same name, marks the northernmost point of Central Vietnam. Thanh Hoa was the cradle of the Dong Son culture, which flourished in the first millennium BC along the Ma, Lam, and Red River Valleys. Excavations in these areas have unearthed large engraved bronze drums, statues, jewelry, and other artifacts. A number of finds were made in the village of Dong Son, just west of Thanh Hoa. About 40 km northwest of Thanh Hoa near the town of Vinh Loc is the site of Ho Citadel, built in 1397—only the massive gates remain. About 15 km southeast of Thanh Hoa you'll find Sam Son Beach, a three-km stretch of fine white sand. There are several hotels in Thanh Hoa on Highway 1. The town also serves as an express train stop. The area around Ninh Binh, 60 km north of Thanh Hoa, features majestic karst scenery, especially near Tam Coc and Bich Dong.

DANANG

The road from Hue winds 108 km south to Danang, passing spectacular Lang Co Beach and Hai Van Pass. The latter marks the northern limit of the former Kingdom of Champa that once extended along the coast as far south as present-day Vung Tau. Danang served as center of the kingdom. Near Danang are the ruins of My Son; and in Danang itself is the excellent Cham Museum.

Danang succeeded Hoi An as the most important port in central Vietnam during the early 19th century. The French, seeking to open Vietnam to trade, mounted a naval attack on Danang in 1858, opening the way for almost a century of French domination. Under the French, Danang was known as Tourane. Vestiges of French presence appear in the colonial architecture of the cathedral and the former bank, town hall, and courthouse.

On 8 March 1965, another landing force hit Danang as the first American Marines waded ashore at Red Beach to secure an airfield. Danang developed into one of the biggest US military bases in Southeast Asia. Nearby China Beach, an R&R spot for US troops, has become well known in the West due to the American TV series of the same name.

Today, Danang is Vietnam's third largest city, with a population of around 800,000. An idle sailing ship waiting for a gust of wind, Danang is slated to become the major gateway to central Vietnam. Banking on the China Beach name, officials hope grandiose plans to develop Danang are realized. The Americans left behind a gigantic airbase near China Beach capable of receiving large commercial jets. And Danang's beaches are much closer to Hong Kong and Taiwan than the islands of Thailand or the Philippines. Cruise ships ply the coast, stopping at Saigon, Danang, and Haiphong, then continue to Hong Kong. Danang's deep-sea port can accommodate four 20,000-ton ships at a time. This port is of great interest to landlocked Laos. A land border opened in 1994 at Lao Bao has allowed container trucks to rumble up and down Highway 9 from Savannakhet in Laos through Lao Bao on to Dong Ha, and down Highway 1 from Dong Ha to Danang. Some independent travelers have used the same route. This shortcut is slated to link Thailand, Laos, and Vietnam for trade and tourism.

Joint ventures are being negotiated for resort hotels around China Beach. Under construction is **Indochina Beach Hotel,** a Hong Kong-Vietnamese venture for a 260-room hotel and villa complex. The American BBI group has signed a joint-venture deal to build a $250 million luxury resort and business center next to **Non Nuoc Resort Hotel.** The projected complex will feature a total of 1,200 rooms in four new hotels, a golf course, and a conference center. It's scheduled for completion in the year 2005. Another American firm, DeMatteis Construction, plans to build a resort with a five-star hotel, townhouses, offices, and a marina at Bac My An Beach outside Danang. Other joint-venture hotels in Danang are with a Hong Kong company (80-room hotel) and a Thai company (120-room hotel), making up for Danang's lack of international standard accommodations.

Danang is a port city. Unless you enjoy looking at container vessels and rusty hulks, consider using it simply as a base for trips to the Marble Mountains, China Beach, Hoi An, and My Son. In theory Danang is an international entry/exit point with the same powers as Saigon or Hanoi for customs and immigration. Although international cruise ships stop here, as yet no international flights head directly for Danang. Currently, planes out of Hong Kong fly straight past Danang to Saigon, passengers proceeding on to Danang on domestic flights. This situation may change when airport facilities are upgraded.

CHAM MUSEUM

This museum was set up by the French, who shipped off a number of exhibits to France; other pieces were stolen and sold to art collectors overseas. Nevertheless, the Cham Museum houses the world's largest collection of Cham sculpture, with over 300 sandstone pieces

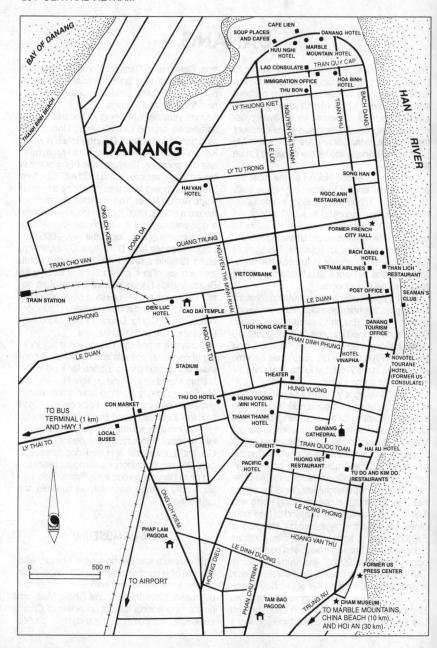

BAY OF DANANG

THANH BINH BEACH

HAN RIVER

DANANG

CAFE LIEN
SOUP PLACES AND CAFES
DANANG HOTEL
HUU NGHI HOTEL
MARBLE MOUNTAIN HOTEL
LAO CONSULATE
TRAN QUY CAP
IMMIGRATION OFFICE
HOA BINH HOTEL
THU BON

LY THUONG KIET
NGUYEN CHI THANH
TRAN PHU
BACH DANG
LE LOI

LY TU TRONG
SONG HAN

HAI VAN HOTEL

NGOC ANH RESTAURANT

ONG ICH KIEM
DONG DA

FORMER FRENCH CITY HALL ★
QUANG TRUNG
BACH DANG HOTEL
TRAN CHO VAN
VIETNAM AIRLINES
THAN LICH RESTAURANT
NGUYEN THI MINH KHAI
VIETCOMBANK
POST OFFICE
SEAMAN'S CLUB

TRAIN STATION
DIEN LUC HOTEL
CAO DAI TEMPLE
LE DUAN
DANANG TOURISM OFFICE

HAIPHONG
NGO GIA TU
TUOI HONG CAFE
PHAN DINH PHUNG
HOTEL VINAPHA
NOVOTEL TOURANE HOTEL (FORMER US CONSULATE) ★

LE DUAN
STADIUM
THEATER
HUNG VUONG

THU DO HOTEL
HUNG VUONG MINH HOTEL
CON MARKET

TO BUS TERMINAL (1 km) AND HWY 1
LOCAL BUSES
THANH THANH HOTEL
DANANG CATHEDRAL ✝
HAI AU HOTEL

LY THAI TO
ORIENT
TRAN QUOC TOAN

PACIFIC HOTEL
HUONG VIET RESTAURANT
TU DO AND KIM DO RESTAURANTS

ONG ICH KIEM
LE HONG PHONG

HOANG VAN THU

PHAP LAM PAGODA

HOANG DIEU
LE DINH DUONG

FORMER US PRESS CENTER ★

0   500 m

TO AIRPORT

PHAN CHU TRINH
TAM BAO PAGODA
TRUNG NU
CHAM MUSEUM ★
TO MARBLE MOUNTAINS, CHINA BEACH (10 km), AND HOI AN (30 km)

MOON

aspara *sculpted at a Tra Kieu base*

scenes, and the giant Dvaraparas and Dhamapala. There are friezes, lintels, altarpieces, and inscribed stones. Masterful sculptural skills are shown in the fluid forms of the celestial dancers, the *apsaras,* sculpted in stone in a piece in the Tra Kieu Room. Several pieces are associated with Cham fertility cults, including rows of breasts on the altar ornaments and pedestal bases in the Thap Mam Room. Also in the Thap Mam room are mythical animals, ranging from *garuda* (bird-man) to *makara* (aquatic monster) to *gaja-simha* (elephant-lion).

An art gallery at the back sells small-scale replicas in sandstone, marble, and terracotta. Outlets in the Marble Mountains and gift shops around town also sell replicas. There are some shops opposite the museum entrance. The museum is open daily 0700 to 1800; no closures for lunch, but it's been known to close earlier than posted if no tourists are clamoring for entry. Entry is $1; a still camera costs an additional 50 cents, video camera $2.

housed in a building constructed in 1915 by the Ecole Française d'Extrême-Orient, and expanded in 1935.

There is little English translation at the Cham Museum. You can buy some literature from a kiosk at the front gate, but it doesn't help much. The museum has four musty rooms named after the original sites where the displayed Cham sculptures were found—My Son, Tra Kieu, Dong Duong, and Thap Mam. These also denote sculptural styles of the following periods: My Son 8th-9th century, Tra Kieu 7th-10th century, Dong Duong 9th-10th century, and Thap Mam 12th-13th century. Since former Cham sites have been razed or extensively damaged during wars, the museum represents the last bastion of Cham culture.

Patrons to the museum encounter a culture at once alien and highly imaginative. The larger pieces here are stupendous—the Goddess Uma, the bust of Shiva, Vishnu backed by 13 *nagas,* the Tra Kieu altar with its Ramayana

ACCOMMODATIONS

Although Danang has over 40 hotels, it's estimated only a third meet international standards. A number of hotels are not accessible to foreigners. Most of the hotels open to big noses are listed below, but times change—suddenly a Vietnamese hotel comes of age, the plumbing is deemed up to scratch, and the doors are flung open to foreigners. Groups of hotels often fall under the same management: the Song Han and Hoa Binh hotels are run by Danang Shipchandler Company, while Danang Tourism runs the Hai Au, Phuong Dong, Hung Vuong, and Danang Hotels.

Budget
At the northern tip of Danang is a strip of backpacker hotels facing a traveler café. Previously called Danang 1, 2, and 3 buildings, these hotels used to house US troops, which might explain the dance bar, Hoang Gia, next door. This area is three km from the bus station or railway; you can reach the hotel strip by cyclo, or pay a bit more for a moto. Remember cyclos and motos receive a commission from the hotel for delivering you to the doorstep.

Marble Mountain Hotel, 5 Dong Da, tel. 23258, fax 21039, has 60 rooms, ranging from basic $5 rooms to $25 air-con rooms with hot water. In between, rooms differ by $2 and $3 increments, so you might get a room for $8, $18, or $22. The place is clean, quiet, and efficient, and will store luggage. **Danang Hotel,** 3 Dong Da St., tel. 21986, is mediocre. It features 103 rooms ranging from $5 to $20; facilities include a restaurant and bar. **Huu Nghi Hotel** (Dong Da Hotel), 7 Dong Da, translates to Friendship Hotel, but these kindly feelings do not extend to foreigners. Management will say all 68 rooms are taken without even looking at the register. If you can get in, the price range is $5-10.

Budget/Moderate

Hai Van Hotel, 2 Nguyen Thi Minh, tel. 21300, has 40 rooms ranging from $10 fan rooms to $15-20 rooms with air-con and hot water. **Hung Vuong Minihotel,** 95 Hung Vuong, tel. 23967, offers 10 rooms in a French-style building, $8 s and $12-15 d with air-con and hot water. Favored by backpackers, **Thu Do Hotel,** at 107 Hung Vuong, tel. 23863, features 35 rooms for $5 s and $6-12 d. **Thanh Thanh Hotel,** 54 Phan Chu Trinh, tel. 21230, has 44 rooms in the $5-12 range; seedy, with taxi girls about. The same management runs two other hotels nearby— the **Yen Minh Hotel,** at number 50, and **Yen Thanh Guesthouse** at number 42—but neither accept foreigners. **Hotel Vinapha,** 80 Tran Phu St., tel. 25072, has 16 rooms for $8 with fan, or $15-18 with hot water. There's a big hotel near the bus station called **Khach San Dien Bien.**

Moderate/Luxury

The following three hotels are on the waterfront, with views of the Han River. **Hai Au Hotel** (Seagull), 177 Tran Phu, tel. 22722, fax 24165, has 28 rooms for $32-55 s; $5 extra for doubles. The 90-room **Bach Dang Hotel,** 50 Bach Dang, tel. 23649, fax 21659, charges $20-44-64 s, $5 extra for doubles; the rooms have air-con, fridge, TV, phone, and other creature comforts. **Song Han,** 36 Bach Dang, tel. 22530, fax 21109, rents 49 rooms, $22-25-40 single or double.

At the north end of town is **Hoa Binh Hotel** (Peace Hotel), 3 Tran Quy Cap, tel. 23984, fax 23161, with 25 rooms in the $25-30-35-50 range, single or double; popular with group tours.

In Central Danang you'll find the following hotels. **Pacific Hotel,** 92 Phan Chu Trinh, tel. 22137, fax 22921, is an eight-story hotel with over 40 rooms for $15-26 s, $22-32 d, and $32 t. **Orient Hotel** (Phuong Dong), 93 Phan Chau Trinh, tel. 21266, fax 22854, is a six-story hotel popular with group tours; it features 36 rooms for $39-43 s, $49-53 d, or $65 t. **Dien Luc Hotel,** 37 Haiphong St., tel. 21864, fax 23263, offers 27 rooms in the $26-55 range; doubles run $28-60. **Marco Polo Hotel,** at 11C Quang Trung St., tel. 23295, fax 27279, is a luxury-class hotel with room prices starting at $95. The elegant rooms feature satellite TV, minibar, and safety deposit box; facilities include a VIP nightclub.

FOOD

Most eating in Danang takes place in hotels (expensive), or on the streets at noodlehouses (cheap). The Orient Hotel features a top-floor restaurant, and Bach Dang Hotel has a pleasant but pricey restaurant near the waterfront. Down the street is **Thanh Lich Restaurant,** at 42 Bach Dang Street, popular with foreign businesspeople—French and Vietnamese food. Some of Danang's best restaurants line Tran Phu Street—**Ngoc Anh,** at 30 Tran Phu, tel. 22778, expensive; **Tu Do,** at 172 Tran Phu, tel. 21869, moderate; and **Kim Do,** at 174 Tran Phu, tel. 21846. Near Phap Lam Pagoda on the south of town is a small vegetarian place, **Quan Chay.** It's located at 484 Ong Ich Khiem Street and closes around 1800.

In the café line, **Café Lien,** 4 Dong Da St., opposite Marble Mountain Hotel, has reasonable food and excellent gossip. There are many cheap noodlehouses farther west. A bit farther south, there's a string of soup shops on Ly Tu Trong, between Tran Phu and Nguyen Chi Thanh. **Tuoi Huong Café,** at 34 Phan Dinh Phung, is the place for a nightcap—popular with young Danang residents.

SERVICES AND INFORMATION

Traveler Cafés

Café Lien, at 4 Dong Da St., opposite Marble Mountain Hotel, is the prime foreign hangout in Danang. It's run by a good-humored family, and serves palatable food. Lien can fix you up with just about anything—Hondas or bicycles, cars to My Son, minibus rides down the coast. She'll even take care of baggage during your absence. Moto drivers hang around this area, offering guide services.

Tourist Information

Danang Tourism appears to go by many different names—Dana Tours, Quangnam Danang Tourist Service Company, Danang Tourist Company, Danang Travel Service—but operates out of one address at 68 Bach Dang, tel. 21423, fax 22854. The office displays an array of brochures about Monaco, Club Med in the Maldives, and Colorado—but nothing on Danang. Not that you can blame them. There are guides on hand that speak English, French, German, and Russian. The staff will arrange a car if you need one. Otherwise, Danang Tourism staff are deeply involved in the study of local newspapers; they only perk up when a cruise ship pulls into port and they smell big bucks.

Maps

A tourist map of Quang Nam Province and Danang City is issued by the State Department of Cartography. Destination information in Vietnamese and English makes this map useful for excursions out of Danang.

Communications

The **GPO** is at the corner of Bach Dang St. and Le Duan Blvd., with mail, telex, fax, and phone services. There's a foreign mail service counter at 62 Bach Dang Street. The Vietnam country code is 84 and the Danang area code is 51, so fax dial-in from outside Vietnam is 84-51 followed by the number. **TNT** courier service has an office in Danang, tel. 21685.

Banks

Vietcombank, on Le Loi, is open 0730-1100 and 1300-1530 Mon.-Fri.; 0700-1000 on Saturday. The bank charges a 1.2% fee for converting traveler's checks to US dollars, with a minimum $2 charge; if you change $200, you get $197.60.

Shopping

There are silk shops in the area of Pacific and Orient Hotels, and both hotels have souvenir shops. Try the **Cham Museum art gallery** for

---

LAO CONSULATE

Almost opposite the immigration office is the **Consulate General of Lao PDR,** tel. 21208. The consulate opened in 1993—look for a Lao flag draped from the building. The consulate handles four kinds of visas. A business visa requires an invitation letter stating the reason for your visit, and approval by the Ministry of Foreign Affairs in Laos. It's issued in two days and costs $10. Also requiring an invitation letter is a visa for visiting relatives; issued in five days for a cost of $10. If you have a confirmed Hanoi-to-Vientiane air ticket, you can obtain a seven-day transit visa, which takes two days to issue and costs $15. A tourist visa requires a guarantee letter from a Lao tourist company under the permission of the Ministry of Foreign Affairs in Laos. This visa requires up to five days to issue and costs $10. Lately, the consulate has been issuing travelers' visas valid for the Lao Bao crossing into Laos, although the Lao consulates in both Hanoi and Saigon insist such a visa is not possible and that you must join a tour. Hours for the consulate in Danang are 0800-1100 and 1400-1630.

---

figurines, paintings, and other souvenirs. There are some gift shops opposite the museum.

Immigration Services

Danang Provincial Public Security is near Hoa Binh Hotel, at 7 Tran Quy Cap, tel. 21078; open 0700-1100 and 1330-1630 daily except Sunday. The office handles emigration and immigration formalities, including visa extensions. Extensions come in 10-, 20- or 30-day versions, cost $15 and up, and are usually available the same day if you put the paperwork in early. This office has accommodated requests for exit stamps for the Lao Bao border into Laos, and may also provide Lao Cai or Lang Son borders into China for $15 apiece.

GETTING THERE AND AWAY

By Air
Danang International Airport is seven km from the city. A moto ride into town is around $1.50, by

taxi several times that price. There are connections from Danang to Ho Chi Minh City for $80, and to Hanoi for $85 daily, and twice-weekly flights to Qui Nhon, Nha Trang, Buon Ma Thuot, and Pleiku. Although Danang is supposed to be an international entry and exit point, flights are usually routed through Saigon or Hanoi from places like Frankfurt, Paris, Bangkok, or Sydney. Direct flights to Danang from Taipei, Tokyo, Seoul, and Hong Kong are expected within a few years. Vietnam Airlines booking office for domestic flights is at 35 Tran Phu St., tel. 21130.

By Rail

Danang is roughly the midway point between Hanoi and Saigon on the **Reunification Express** line. By express from Danang to Hanoi is 20 hours; to Saigon, about 22 hours. The ride to Hué from Danang costs $5 for a soft seat and is spectacular. The four-hour trip passes along the coastline. In the other direction, to Nha Trang, is an equally scenic four-hour trip.

By Bus

The Danang long-distance bus station is two km west of town, at 8 Dien Bien Phu St.—the western continuation of Le Thai To Street. Buses depart to Vinh, Hué, Haiphong, Hanoi, the Central Highlands, Nha Trang, and Ho Chi Minh City. Another express bus station operates out of 52 Phan Chu Trinh St., next to Thanh Thanh Hotel. Bus stations in Danang are bristling with vicious cyclo drivers who latch onto foreigners because they can make commissions by taking them to particular hotels. Keep walking when you first get out of a bus until the cyclos thin out. Then negotiate.

By Private Car and Minibus

A number of hotels can arrange cars. The run to Hué is worthwhile: get together with a few travelers and rent a car for the day, stopping at Hai Van Pass. You'll pass great viewpoints over Lang Co Beach, with a clear blue lagoon on one side and a strip of beach facing the South China Sea on the other. Lang Co is a fishing village—it's possible to stay overnight.

Café Lien in Danang rents cars for $35 per day roundtrip to Hué; a one-way run to Hué is $20. Café Lien will also coordinate lifts for traveler share-taxis or minibuses. Saigon-based

private minibus operators returning from the Saigon-to-Hué run drop in here to line up riders heading south. This early morning departure for Nha Trang costs $15 a person; other destinations are negotiable.

GETTING AROUND

Cyclo and moto transport is abundant and drivers will literally stalk you. It's cheaper to hire cyclo or moto operators by the hour—about 70 cents an hour for a moto driver, or $6 a day.

From Café Lien, opposite Marble Mountain Hotel, you can rent 50cc and 70cc bikes for $5 a day or $3 per half-day. Good bicycles cost $1 a day; 50 cents for an older model. Car rentals through Café Lien are $15 for the day around Danang including Hoi An, $25 roundtrip to My Son, and $30 roundtrip to My Lai. Danang Hotel rents bicycles. Car rentals are widely available through hotels in Danang or through Danang Tourism.

EXCURSIONS FROM DANANG

Due to its numerous hotels and transport rentals, Danang is the best base to explore the China Beach-Hoi An-My Son triangle of sites. Another possibility is to base yourself out of Hoi An, which has transport rentals, traveler cafés, and a far more pleasant atmosphere. However, Hoi An has few hotel rooms open to foreigners. Staying at China Beach is another option, though an expensive one.

Local transportation is exasperatingly slow and may drop you short of your destination. You can get rides from local pickups and three-wheelers to the Marble Mountains and China Beach from a depot a block west of Con Market in Danang. A better alternative is to hire your own car for half a day or a full day, splitting expenses with others. Or hire a moto, or rent a motorcycle or bicycle. Pack a picnic lunch, water bottle, and swimsuit, and a flashlight for the Marble Mountains. Some travelers stash their packs at a hotel in Danang, and spend several days on motorcycles exploring the area. If you don't want to ride your own motorcycle, you can hire a moto driver for about $6-7 per day to go to

Hoi An and Marble Mountains/China Beach. A one-way trip by moto to Hoi An with no stops is about $2. Motos charge around $8 to go to My Son Cham ruins.

Hoi An, 30 km from Danang, is a great town worth several days if you can find accommodations; the Marble Mountains and China Beach are worth up to a day; My Son, 70 km away, demands an entire day because of bad roads. If your time is short, you can set out early from Danang on a moto or motorcycle and get to the Marble Mountains in 20 minutes. You can see the Marble Mountains and China Beach in the morning, visit Hoi An during the afternoon, and be back in Danang by nightfall. If you have more time, consider staying in Hoi An a few days, and taking a boat from Hoi An to Danang.

My Khe Beach

The R&R beach featured in the *China Beach* TV series is actually My Khe Beach, about six km from Danang. However, in the interests of promotion, the beach further south has been called China Beach to draw people to the government hotel there. My Khe Beach is rarely visited by tourists.

Danang to the Marble Mountains

To get to the Marble Mountains, follow Tran Phu Street south past the Cham Museum till

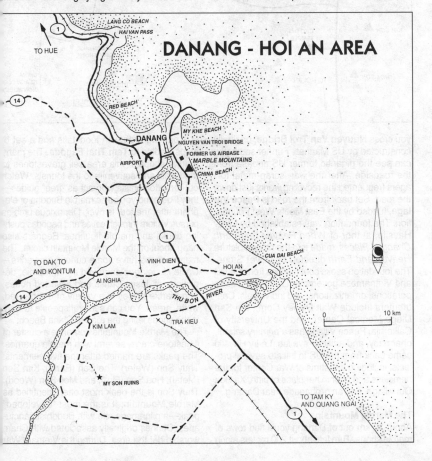

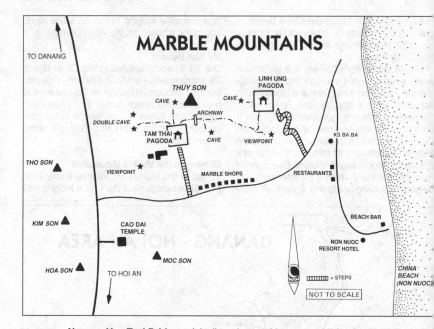

MARBLE MOUNTAINS

TO DANANG

THUY SON

LINH UNG PAGODA

CAVE

CAVE

ARCHWAY

DOUBLE CAVE

TAM THAI PAGODA

CAVE

VIEWPOINT

KS BA BA

THO SON

VIEWPOINT

MARBLE SHOPS

RESTAURANTS

BEACH BAR

KIM SON

CAO DAI TEMPLE

NON NUOC RESORT HOTEL

MOC SON

HOA SON

TO HOI AN

CHINA BEACH (NON NUOC)

⊞⊞⊞ = STEPS

NOT TO SCALE

you cross **Nguyen Van Troi Bridge,** originally constructed by US Marines. Further south you can see the gigantic former US airbase from the roadside. After the war, scrap-metal foragers frequented the recycling works just down the road. Set back from the road is **Peace Village,** funded by the East Meets West Foundation. The foundation was established by Le Ly Hayslip, author of *When Heaven and Earth Changed Places,* made into the motion picture *Heaven and Earth* directed by Oliver Stone. The foundation seeks contributions from the US and Vietnamese governments, as well as corporations, organizations, and individuals. Contributors include Walt Disney Corp., the San Diego Medical Center, and the University of California. Peace Village has a primary school, pharmacy, and artificial-eye lab. Le Ly Hayslip came back from the US to initiate several projects, including a Victims of War Center for the homeless and poor in her place of birth, Xa Hoa Qui village, and an orphanage near Danang.

The Marble Mountains

About 12 km out of Danang you'll find rows of marble shops. Turn left; about 200 meters along

is a parking area with foodstalls and a set of steps leading to **Tam Thai Pagoda.** The many marble shops in this area sell gravestones to the locals and souvenirs to the tourists. Watch out for extortionists who act as "free" guides—they'll demand you buy a marble Buddha or elephant after the tour is over. Obnoxious urchins pursue visitors through caves and pagodas pushing drinks and marble figurines. Beggars also hang about on the Marble Mountain circuit. The marble shops have some curious souvenirs—Uncle Ho images engraved in flat marble, depictions of Jesus Christ, and assorted nudes. The marble comes in a variety of colors—red, white, green. You can see craftspeople at work in the shops lining the road to China Beach.

The Marble Mountains comprise a cluster of limestone crags, several with marble quarries. The peaks are named after the five elements: Thuy Son (Water), Tho Son (Earth), Kim Son (Metal), Hoa Son (Fire), and Moc Son (Wood). Thuy Son is the peak most often identified as Marble Mountain. It is the most "developed" peak—a pilgrimage site with Buddhist sanctuaries. Shrines originally associated with Cham worship dot the area. During the Vietnam War the Vietcong used the area as a base for harrying troops at the nearby American airbase.

Your pilgrimage begins at one end with a steep set of marble steps, and finishes at the other down another steep set of steps. The two sets of steps are about 300 meters apart on the China Beach road. Marble shops are cunningly placed to entice you along the way. Park your transport at the west end of the road to China Beach; if you have a driver, arrange to meet at the east end steps, near Linh Ung Pagoda.

Climb the set of 120-odd steps toward Tam Thai Pagoda. Before you reach the small pagoda, turn to the left for a spectacular view over the entire valley. From here you can see other peaks, and marble quarries, and a Cao Dai temple at the base of Moc Son peak. Tam Thai Pagoda stands on the site of a former Cham temple; the present pagoda was first constructed in 1825 and rebuilt over the next century. Inside you'll find statues of Sakyamuni Buddha and the bodhisattva Quan Am. Around the back of the pagoda, on a trail westward, is an intriguing double cave, called **Hoa Nghiem Cave,** featuring a half-marble, half-cement statue of Quan Am at least two meters high. A side cave leads to a massive bell-shaped cave pierced by five crater-size holes at the top. The skylights were caused by US bombing in 1968, when the cave served as a VC field hospital. There's a large meditating Buddha halfway up the walls of the cave, plus a number of shrines and animal-shaped stalactites.

Off the path to the east of Tam Thai Pagoda you travel through an ancient archway pockmarked by bullets; nearby is a long, narrow cave called **Dong Van Thong** with a standing Buddha inside. Continue along the path to reach a viewpoint overlooking China Beach. The path eventually leads to **Linh Ung Pagoda.** The original pagoda was constructed on this site in 1825 but was destroyed by the Americans in 1968. The present Chinese-style structure went up in 1993-94. Linh Ung is an active temple with images of Sakyamuni and Quan Am inside. The statues guarding the main entrance represent Hell (on the left) and Heaven (on the right). The columns of entwined dragons and tree decorations on the side of the temple, as well as the rooftop dragons, are made of broken beer bottles and crockery. To one side of the pagoda is a huge stucco Buddha in meditation posture, shaded by a tree high on a rock. Round the statue nine panels show scenes from the life of Buddha, from birth to enlightenment to preaching to death.

China Beach

Non Nuoc (China Beach) lies about 15 km from Danang, only one kilometer or so from the Marble Mountains. You can get there by moto or rented car. By bicycle, it's a 1.5-hour trip one-way on pleasant roads—a full day-trip from Danang. There's also a local bus running from Danang. The beach is a glorious five-kilometer stretch of white sand—pristine for the moment, and great for walks. Swimming is a different story, marred by a wicked undertow. Red flags set up near Non Nuoc Resort Hotel warn swimmers—heed them. A hotel lifeguard is usually posted near the flags.

The surf at China Beach is entirely wind driven. The water may be glassy and flat, or feature one-meter waves. March to August is the main season for swimming, and the beach is crowded. It's very hot from May to July; the area is colder the rest of the year, and more prone to typhoons, but you'll have the beach to yourself. Because of wind conditions, surf is up around the typhoon season.

In October 1993 Vietnam's first surfing competition occurred at China Beach, with $50,000 in prizes drawing over 30 international surfing pros. The contest was the brainchild of David Garcia, a Californian who surfed in the area during his tour of duty before spending two years in captivity in Laos. "Surfer Dave" pitched the idea of a surfing contest to various sponsors and the Vietnamese government. It eventually gained the support of Prime Minister Vo Van Kiet; the surf complied with three-meter typhoon-driven waves. Day-glo-clad surfers amazed the locals with their nautical acrobatics; four young Vietnamese surfers also took part in the contest. The **Vietnam Surf Pro** may become a regular event.

China Beach Hotels: Set back from the beach is **Khach San Mini Ba Ba,** tel. 36219, with five rooms at $15 single or $25 double. It has a café-restaurant; there are several other restaurants close by. Right on the beach is **Non Nuoc Resort Hotel,** tel. 36217, fax 36335. This resort sprawls over a large compound and features a concrete main building with restaurants, foreign exchange office, souvenir shop, and conference hall, as well as several outlying buildings. It boasts around 100 rooms, with price tags of $29-42 single and $34-48 double. At present the hotel is on the dilapidated side, though an American company plans to renovate it. The hotel has tennis courts, and rents out umbrellas, beach chairs, inner tubes and swimsuits for beachgoers. There are three restaurants: some seafood is served at outdoor tables for $1-3 a dish. Down the way is the **Beach Bar,** a couple of thatched huts selling beer and beach souvenirs. Car and bicycle rentals available.

A few km along the beach is **Indochina Beach Hotel,** expected to feature 60 rooms of three-star quality; another 200 rooms in villas are under construction.

My Son Cham Ruins

The early Cham site of My Son is about 70 km southwest of Danang. Getting there is most of the adventure: the ruins themselves are humdrum, though set in lush rolling terrain. My Son is a group of brick edifices, thought to be where the remains of Cham kings were kept after cremation. The temples and towers that once stood here were dedicated to kings who had the status of deities. Stelae found at the site indicate the sanctuary was active between the 4th and 13th centuries. Methods of construction mystify experts. Some theorize the Cham structures were built using a firing process: dried bricks were laid, vegetable resin used as adhesive, and the

entire structure set afire from the outside for several days to seal the brickwork.

My Son may once have been an impressive sight: now there's little to see. After the French carefully began restoring the site, the Americans came along and blew it to bits. The Vietcong began using the ruins as a base; it was declared a free-fire zone by the Americans in the late 1960s, and masterpieces of Cham architecture were levelled by B-52s. The director of Guimet Museum in Paris, repository of many Cham and Angkor pieces, wrote a letter of protest to Richard Nixon, but the damage had been done.

The best pieces from My Son are in the Cham Museum in Danang. What remains at the site are some building shells with broken columns, decapitated Buddhas, and the odd sculpted lintel or bas-relief. One building has been turned into a barred storeroom containing sculpture. The rest of the place is damaged beyond recognition, or reclaimed by the jungle. Scattered around the site are a few lichen-covered lingas and rows of yoni bases. You can step over stones across a creek to reach a second site where very little remains except a yoni base. There are good views of the area from here. My Son makes a great picnic site in a romantic jungle location, but do not stray from the ruins as there may be mines and unexploded ordnance about.

Getting to My Son: Because of the rough trail, a rented car, jeep, high-powered moto, or rented motorcycle is the way to travel. No special permits are needed to visit the site. Take food

Cham ruins

(top left) moving banana tree trunks, Kontum; (top right) woman with blackened teeth, Buon Ma Thuot; (bottom) fish-sellers, Hué markets

(top left) monk, Phnom Penh; (top right) rural youngster wearing the *krama,* Siem Reap; (bottom left) classical dancer, Siem Reap; (bottom right) just married, Phnom Penh

and water along, as little is available along the way. By car or jeep it takes about three hours to reach My Son; a car rental should cost $25. You can organize a small group from either Danang or Hoi An for a car.

Overland head south along Highway 1, till you cross a bridge spanning the Thu Bon River. About two km past the bridge, turn right and proceed to the village of Tra Kieu. Tra Kieu, 40 km from Danang, marks the site of the first capital of Champa, but there's nothing left except traces of Cham Citadel ramparts. You can look out over the area from the Catholic Church (also called the Mountain Church), built over the foundations of a Cham tower.

From Tra Kieu, it's still about 28 km to My Son. Continue to the village of Kim Lam, and turn south. Along this part the road turns to dirt and, if it's been raining, mud. If there's any mud,

a car may not make it along the last bit. About three km short of the ruins is a river. A rock bridge has been built across it, and bulldozers are working on clearing the last few km so that My Son will become a drive-in ruin. Be aware: there may be mines in the area. Do not stray from proper paths, and use a local guide if the way is not clear.

A longer approach is by boat from either Hoi An or Danang. Smaller boats can get within eight km of My Son. From Hoi An, it takes about three to four hours to reach the area. Then you'll be looking at a two-hour walk to the ruins; however, if you bring a bicycle on the boat from Hoi An, you can ride in on the potholed route much faster. Sometimes local moto operators wait on the route, charging rip-off prices. Departing My Son you could take the boat back to Hoi An, or continue by boat to Danang—this would make a long day.

HOI AN

Hoi An is an ancient port town on the Thu Bon River no longer bustling with international trade, but certainly getting a new lease on life by attracting tourism. Hoi An Prefecture spreads over 60 square km, is home to 70,000 inhabitants, and consists of six mainland villages and Cham Island. The first inhabitants of the Hoi An area were the Champa, who occupied the area from the 2nd to 15th centuries. From the 15th to 19th centuries, under Vietnamese rule, Hoi An attracted foreign trade, with vessels coming to purchase silk, fabrics, tea, pepper, and Chinese medicines. Chinese traders would sail south in the spring, then stay in Hoi An for three or four months waiting for the wind to change direction and blow them back home in summer. Other ships came from Japan, Portugal, Spain, India, the Netherlands, France, and Britain.

On old marine maps Hoi An shows up as Faifo, Faiso, Haiso, or Cotham. It developed into one of the most important trading ports in Southeast Asia. By the early 19th century, Hoi An trade declined partly as a result of internal conflicts, mostly because the mouth of the Thu Bon River silted up, rendering the sea approach too shallow. The port of Danang gradually usurped Hoi An.

Hoi An is one of the rare places in Vietnam where you'll find genuine Vietnamese architecture. The Old Quarter, though heavily influenced by Chinese styles, has vestiges of native architecture. Much of the country was destroyed during wars but Hoi An survived, even the traumatic 1960s and 1970s.

SIGHTS

Along Hoi An's waterfront, from the Japanese Covered Bridge to the main market, lies its historic Old Quarter, featuring well-preserved old housing and pagodas. This section of town is protected against development and is slowly being restored with help from international experts.

Market to Museum
Hoi An market sells everything from larvae to lug wrenches. If you go early in the morning you can see the fresh seafood arrive at the dock. To relieve hunger pangs, try the string of open-air cafés along Nguyen Hue Street. Opposite the cafés is the entrance to **Hoi An Historical and Cultural Museum**. The museum occupies the site of former Quan Am Pagoda and features artifacts, old maps, photos, and information

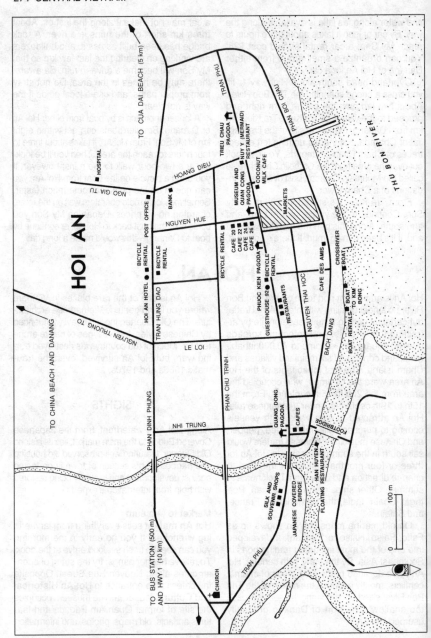

HOI AN

TO CUA DAI BEACH (5 km)

THU BON RIVER

TRAN PHU

PHAN BOI CHAU

TRIEU CHAU PAGODA

NUY (MERMAID) RESTAURANT

HOANG DIEU

NGO GIA TU

HOSPITAL

COCONUT MILK CAFE

MUSEUM AND QUAN CONG PAGODA

BANK

POST OFFICE

NGUYEN HUE

MARKETS

BICYCLE RENTAL

BICYCLE RENTAL

CAFE 20
CAFE 22
CAFE 24
CAFE 26

BICYCLE RENTAL

DOCK

CROSSRIVER BOAT

HOI AN HOTEL

TRAN HUNG DAO

NGUYEN TRUONG TO

PHUOC KIEN PAGODA

GUESTHOUSE 92

BICYCLE RENTAL

RESTAURANTS

CAFE DES AMIS

BOAT TO KIM BONG

BOAT RENTALS

TO CHINA BEACH AND DANANG

NGUYEN THAI HOC

LE LOI

BACH DANG

PHAN DINH PHUNG

PHAN CHU TRINH

NHI TRUNG

QUANG DONG PAGODA

CAFES

FOOTBRIDGE

100 m

SILK AND SOUVENIR SHOPS

JAPANESE COVERED BRIDGE

HAN HUYEN FLOATING RESTAURANT

TRAN PHU

TO BUS STATION (500 m) AND HWY 1 (10 km)

CHURCH

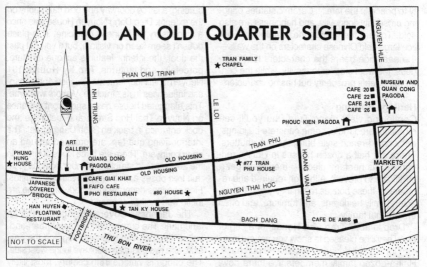

HOI AN OLD QUARTER SIGHTS

on history, culture, and architecture in Hoi An; English captions provided. Adjoining the museum is **Quan Cong Pagoda.** You enter from the museum through a small courtyard with goldfish in a rock pond. To the sides of the main altar in the pagoda are two full-scale horse statues, and two fierce guards. General Quan Cong is the seated figure with the red face and beard. He was a talented general of the 3rd century Three Kingdoms period in China. The Chinese-style exterior of this pagoda is photogenic, especially from the direction of Tran Phu Street.

Phuoc Kien Pagoda

The Chinese clans in old Hoi An established community halls to assist traders, depending on their origins—Fukien, Canton, Chaozhou, Hainan. These self-governing clans ran their own schools, hospitals, cemeteries, and temples. The temples were an eclectic mix of Buddhism, Taoism, Confucianism, and other imports from China. Phuoc Kien Pagoda, opposite 35 Tran Phu, is the former Fukien Community Hall. Phuoc Kien is the Vietnamese rendition of "Fukien." The temple dates to the late 17th century; it's been extended and renovated over the past 300 years.

This pagoda is dedicated to Thien Hau, goddess of the sea and patroness of sailors and fisherfolk; Thien Hau also retains elements of the Taoist Queen of Heaven. You enter the pagoda through a triple arch. To the right a large mural depicts a boat being tossed about on a stormy sea, with Thien Hau and an assistant with a lantern coming to the rescue. To the left is a battle scene showing a Fukien general.

Inside you'll find a series of altars. At the back sanctuary a glass case contains a statue of Thien Hau, made in Fukien. On either side of Thien Hau stand her helpers: on the left, a blue-skinned figure who can see great distances; on the right, a red-skinned emaciated being who can hear great distances. When either of these gentlemen sees or hears fisherfolk in distress, he tells Thien Hau. That was back in the 17th century—hopefully, the fisherfolk have radios by now. To the east side of the courtyard is a large scale model of a 17th-century Chinese war junk. The original vessel held about 100 people.

Behind the main altar, through a courtyard, is a set of wish-granting statues: the god of prosperity on the left, and on the right 12 midwives. Infertile women come here to pray for pregnancy. One of the central figures in this group, clothed in pink, apparently decides if a child will be born male or female. To ensure a successful visit, temple guardians sell small red plastic disks engraved with characters to promote all kinds of positive results—from auto, air, and boat safety to peace in the family. Ceramic statues bringing prosperity, longevity, and happiness are also sold. Toward the front of the temple you'll notice large gold Chinese characters on the walls—the east side bears the characters for happiness, the west side for longevity, while the center represents prosperity but has no characters.

Heritage Housing

Continuing west along Tran Phu you'll see moss-covered roofs, some concrete buildings, and some French-style buildings with shutters. There are half a dozen houses in Hoi An recognized as heritage pieces—they even get a certificate to prove it. Although repaired and remodeled, these houses retain their original character, family heirlooms, and furniture, and often the original family.

Drop in at **77 Tran Phu House** for a cup of tea. They'll be pleased to show you around in return for a small donation or souvenir purchase. Half-a-dozen family members live there now; on the wall hangs a portrait of the great-great-grandfather, a Chinese merchant and traditional medicine practitioner. The house is some 300 years old, but of course wood doesn't last that long—it's been replaced gradually. Wooden pillars are ingeniously mounted on marble bases to prevent rotting; ornate woodwork features dragons or unicorns on finials.

On Nguyen Thai Hoc, next door to number 80, you'll find another classic, **Diep Dong Nguyen House.** Diep Dong Nguyen is marked on the

building; a lattice doorway and bold calligraphy on the exterior. Diep Dong Nguyen House was once a dispensary for Chinese medicine. This place doesn't seem keen on visitors, but if you get past the door, the interior features antique furniture, porcelain, and lanterns. **Tan Ky House,** 101 Nguyen Thai Hoc, features Chinese and Japanese influences in its structure. Visitors welcome. This elongated house has a shop front entrance on Nguyen Thai Hoc Street, and a storage and dock entrance in back on Bach Dang Street. The interior living quarters are grouped around an open courtyard. There are three kinds of timber in the 200-year-old structure—timber from the jackfruit tree poses a problem as it attracts termites. Fine carvings decorate the woodwork; some are inlaid with mother-of-pearl.

The **Japanese Covered Bridge** is a Hoi An landmark. The curved bridge has a green-and-yellow tile roof, two guardian dogs on the east side, and two guardian monkeys to the west side. The bridge is vintage 16th century, most likely constructed by the Japanese community to link the Chinese quarter with the Japanese quarter. A small Japanese-style pagoda that protects sailors is built into the north side of the bridge.

Over the Japanese Covered Bridge is **Phung Hung House,** at 4 Nguyen Thi Minh Khai St., the mansion of the Phung Hung family for eight generations. The wooden structure has elements of Vietnamese, Chinese, and Japanese styles, contructed using 80 columns of ironwood with marble bases. The structure is held in place with

Hoi An's Old Quarter

arge wooden nails. The four-sided roof is made of Yin and Yang tiles, named after the way the tiles lock together. Another interesting feature of the house is a flood provision: a square opening on the ceiling allows hauling of belongings to the second floor. The last major flood hit Hoi An in 1964. The Phung Hung family welcome tourists, and sell souvenirs and T-shirts from a boutique at the front. In the same area, on both sides of the bridge but especially on the west side, other shops sell silk, art, souvenirs, and marble carvings. There's also an art gallery in a French two-story building near the bridge.

A short way east of the Japanese Covered Bridge is **Quang Dong Pagoda,** or the Assembly Hall for Maritime Commerce. This pagoda was open to all Chinese traders or seamen, and is dedicated to Thien Hau. It's a small Chinese-style temple, with a lintel-gate, a rockery courtyard, and lucky animals depicted in statuary—a lion and a phoenix mounted on turtles, and dragon-coiled columns inside. Strolling eastward along Tran Phu you'll come across some ancient buildings formerly used for cotton mills, weaving workshops, or furniture making, and now adapted for other uses.

Last stop for tea: the **Tran Family Chapel,** near the corner of Phan Chu Trinh, is entered from Le Loi Street. A small donation is expected. The ancestral chapel is maintained by eight members of the Tran family, who live in the house nearby. The Tran family is seeking funds for renovation of the chapel, which is 200 years old, and was last restored in the 1930s after a fire. With some houses occupied continuously for seven generations, ancestor worship is big in Hoi An. The altar holds wooden boxes containing the tablets of Tran family ancestors arranged in order from oldest to newest generations, with Chinese characters chiseled in the tablets to summarize their curricula vitae. The annual gathering of the Tran clan in December draws up to 100 relatives.

BOAT TRIPS

You can hire a boat for a few hours from the waterfront to explore the Thu Bon River and the area around Hoi An. Go to the boat dock near the market and bargain—$3 for a few hours is standard. A regular boat runs out to **Kim Bong Village** on **Cam Kim Island**—a 10-minute ride costing 10 cents. Kim Bong is a village of woodworking and boat-building families. Handcrafted boats range from simple fishing models to vessels the size of Noah's Ark. Families also carve statues and furniture, some incorporating marble from the Marble Mountains.

Long-distance boats travel to Cham Island and Danang. Cham Island lies about 20 km off the coast. A motorboat leaves the Hoi An Market docks early in the morning for the island, and returns in the afternoon. Cham Island has several fishing villages, and is famed as a source of swallows' nests, used in gourmet soups. Access to the island is restricted and requires a permit. From Hoi An, boats can sometimes make it out toward My Son and into Danang. This trip is not sanctioned by authorities, either (see "Getting There and Away" under "Being There").

Vicinity of Hoi An

If you have a place to stay, Hoi An is a great base to explore the Marble Mountains and China Beach by rented car, motorcycle, bicycle, or moto. Boat trips around Hoi An are pleasant. Hoi An Tourist Office has been known to organize trips for groups out to My Son Cham ruins; you need to assemble a small group.

Most sights in the vicinity of Hoi An can be approached by bicycle. A popular ride is to head for **Cua Dai Beach,** about five km east of Hoi An—a great beach for a swim or run. You can catch the sunrise if you're out there by 0500 or so—it's worth it because the water is cooler, and all the fishing boats come in to unload the night's catch. Alternatively, you can go when all the locals go, around 1600, to have a dip before dinner. There are shaded drink stands all along the beach, with tables and chairs; some also sell crabs. The only drawback is the children who pester you to buy coconuts or rice biscuits.

Other side trips reached easily by bike are to pagodas and sites around Hoi An. The oldest pagoda in the area is **Chua Phuc Thanh,** dating from the 15th century. The ride offers more to look at than the temple. To get there follow Nguyen Truong To Street north out of Hoi An, then turn left and follow a path for half a kilometer. At the opposite end of the spectrum is the brand-new **Chua Long Thuyen,** a Vietnamese pagoda, with main hall built in 1993 and a shrine still under construction. Take the first dirt track to the right after the bus station and gas station east of Hoi An, then continue for about 400 meters through rice paddies and loads of graveyards. Garish and fanciful, the pagoda features broken beer-bottle and porcelain decoration, and a multicolored lotus tower at the back. The low concrete wall around the pagoda is painted in the form of two dragons who come head to head to form a gate.

BEING THERE

Accommodations

Only a handful of hotels and guesthouses are open to foreigners, which means a chronic lack of rooms. In an effort to preserve the character of Hoi An, city hall will not entertain the idea of building new 10-story hotels—and you have to give them credit for that. **Hoi An Hotel,** at 6 Tran Hung Dao, tel. 61373, is a rambling compound with a total of 67 rooms and a planned extension of 30 more. Management is brusque, and will almost always tell you the cheap rooms are full, even if they aren't. In the main building are 30 rooms: $24 s, $30 d, $36 t, $42 for four-bed, with private bath, hot water, and air-con. Other rooms in outlying buildings run $15-20-27 with private bath and no air-con, $10-14-17 with toilet, and $8-12-16 with shared toilet. Often full by nightfall. The hotel will place international calls and rent cars and bicycles. Managed by Hoi An Tourist Service Company, it serves as a de facto tourist information headquarters.

Run by the same outfit is **92 Tran Phu Guesthouse,** at 92 Tran Phu St., tel. 61331, in the Old Quarter. It offers only six rooms, $4 a bed in a four-bed dorm, or $11 double rooms; all with common bath, but good location, small, and friendly. Three more minihotels are arrayed along Tran Phu Street. **Pho Hoi,** at 7/2 Tran Phu, tel. 61633, charges $12-16 a room; **Phu Thinh,** at 144 Tran Phu, tel. 61297, has rooms for $15-30; and **Vinh Hung Guesthouse,** at 143 Tran Phu, tel. 61621, charges $15-30 a room.

Food

Great news on the gastronomic front—Hoi An the place to satisfy your stomach, if not you soul. You can get Vietnamese, Western, and vegetarian fare. Restaurants are usually family-run, use fresh produce from the market, and offer a cozy atmosphere—better thought of as café-bistros. Hoi An has its own specialties. *Cao lau* is a bowl of thick noodles in a dark rich broth, topped with herbs, bean sprouts, slices of pork, and crunchy croutons, served with crispy rice pancake—delicious! A number of small eateries along Tran Phu Street serve *cao lau.* *Hoi An loanh thanh* is a special wonton soup. White Rose is fresh shrimp wrapped in rice paper with garlic, lemon, and chili sauce, fashioned to resemble a rose. For *Hoi An pancake,* you're supplied with all the spare parts—rice paper, egg, bean sprouts, slivers of raw banana, and lettuce. Assemble the pancake, then dip it in sauce, and add chili sauce.

Café-Bistros: In the market area is **Café 22,** at 22 Nguyen Hue, tel. 61603, run by the Ly family. This friendly café serves snacks and full meals. You can get vegetarian food, banana pancakes, fruit salad, hamburgers, and a great *cao lau* soup. Café 22 supplies tourist information, arranges car rentals, and will even do your tailoring. In the same area, offering good food with friendly service, are **Café 20, Café 24,** and **Café 26.** The latter can whip up a seafood extravaganza if you let them know ahead of time. For a very reasonable price you get clams, prawns, crab with roe sauce, ginger fish, squid, and spring rolls—all excellent.

Café des Amis, 52 Bach Dang, tel. 61360, near the market, is owned by Kim, who once cooked for French officers; this two-story restaurant is run by his family. Food is eclectic—French, Chinese, Vietnamese. There's no menu; you ask for, say, a vegetarian or seafood theme. Kim likes a challenge: one customer requested "something different, maybe escargot," and Kim came up with 10 courses, including three different types of escargot. A gastronomic experience! The ambience, the music, the flavors, and the textures are just right. Save some space for the excellent chocolate flan. Book ahead—meals are pricey, about $5 a person. Two other fine eateries along Bach Dang are **Café Can,** at

74 Bach Dung, run by a Chinese family and serving excellent seafood; and **Asia,** at 58 Bach Dang, with a selection of seafood, vegetarian, and Hoi An specialties.

Nuy Y (Mermaid) Restaurant, 2 Tran Phu, serves Hoi An pancake and special sauce, *mi quang* (noodle soup and seafood), prawn fritters, pizza laced with garlic, and pasta. The squid is especially good; this restaurant serves wonderful guacamole in season. Nearby is **Coconut Milk Café,** featuring coconut milk, beer, yogurt, and mineral water.

Along the midsection of Tran Phu, between Nguyen Hue and Le Loi streets, is a concentration of eating houses. **Number 42 Restaurant** specializes in *cao lau;* opposite, at number 31, is **Fukien Restaurant;** to the east is **Yellow River Family Restaurant;** further west is **Cao Lau** at 87 Tran Phu and **92 Tran Phu Guesthouse Restaurant;** and at 104 Tran Phu is **Faifoo Restaurant.** Phew!

Toward the Japanese Covered Bridge are three cafés with sidewalk tables. **Café Giai Khat** has a big drink list, *cao lau,* Vietnamese soup, breakfast, seafood, and banana pancakes. Next door is **Faifo Café,** for breakfast and vegetarian; omelettes and avocado sandwiches. There's a third unnamed café serving soup and *cao lau.* **Han Huyen** floating restaurant, tel. 61462, has a pleasant setting—the extensive menu includes deer, sea cucumber, and steamboat.

Shopping

Hoi An has a limited number of souvenir shops but the stock is high quality. In the vicinity of the Japanese Covered Bridge are shops selling silk paintings and sketches of Hoi An street scenes, pottery, marble carvings, and other handcrafted items.

Services

Traveler Cafés: Lots of hangouts. **Café 22** offers great food and will arrange car rentals and minibus rides; Kim at **Café des Amis** can arrange boat trips, and has traveler logbooks. **Hoi An Hotel** houses the Tourism Service Company, but staff there is not much help.

Moneychanging: You can change US cash only at the **bank** at 4 Hoang Dieu St., open Monday to Thursday 0700-1100 and 1300-1600, closed Thursday afternoon to Sunday. If the bank is closed, try changing US cash at Hoi An Hotel, or a jeweler's shop.

Getting There and Away

By Bus and Minibus: Several of the cafés will arrange long-distance minibus transport. Café 22 handles minibus connections to Nha Trang for $15 a person; Saigon $30. To Hué, a car can be arranged for $24 for two people, $26 for three, or $28 for four. A trip to Danang should cost $12-16.

Express buses do not pull into Hoi An. Take a moto to the Highway 1 junction for 30 cents and

The local ferry leaves when properly overloaded.

wait there to flag down an express bus for traveling along the coast to Hué, or down south to Quang Ngai. Try hitching too—sometimes it's faster than a bus. A moto costs $2 one-way to Danang.

Hoi An bus station mostly offers red-and-yellow Renaults on rice runs. The Renault van takes up to two hours to run the circuitous route from Hoi An to Danang, which involves unloading furniture and loading cases of drinks and tires. Another option is to take a jeep with an elongated back section.

By Boat: A boat trip from Hoi An to Danang takes about 4.5 hours. The trip is frowned upon by authorities in Danang, so the boat might drop you short of the city. Ask at Café des Amis about organizing a group for a boat. Prices operate on a sliding scale: $10 for two people, $15 for

four, and $20 for six. Only small vessels can make the trip—the boat goes along the Thu Bon River and turns up toward Ai Nghia.

Getting Around

Hoi An is easily covered on foot. A different perspective is from the water—rent a boat near the market; the boaters will approach you. Bicycle rentals run from 50 cents to $1 a day, with a small extra charge to keep the bike overnight. There are at least four rentals in town: the Hoi An Hotel, opposite the gates of the Hoi An, 92 Tran Phu Guesthouse, and a place just north of Café 20 on Nguyen Hue Street. Several places rent Honda 50cc and 70cc motorcycles—$5 for one person, or $6 for two people on the same bike. Café 22 will arrange car rentals around Hoi An: to China Beach $18-22 roundtrip, to My Son $24-28.

CENTRAL HIGHLANDS

The Central Highlands are located on the Cao Nguyen Plateau between the coast and the Annamite Mountain range. The plateau is sparsely populated by minority groups; economic activity centers around coffee, tea, cassava, and rubber tree plantations, the lumber industry, and cattle raising. Lush tropical forests are interspersed with farmed areas. The towns here have a frontier feeling to them—they're still under construction. Settlers come from overpopulated regions of Vietnam; the unemployed in the large cities are encouraged to move here and work on farms or forestry projects. The latter have not always been successful, and there has been friction between the settlers and minority ethnic groups, whom the Vietnamese discriminate against. Montagnard groups in the Central Highlands include the Ede (also Rhade or Raday), of Cham origin; the Jarai, Bahnar, Rongao, and Sedoun, also of Cham origins; and the Mnong, of Cambodian origin.

People here are becoming increasingly Vietnamized. They're losing the battle to maintain traditional life, language, and customs under increasing pressure from government authorities. These societies used to be matriarchal, but since 1975 that has changed.

Vietnamization means building new housing with tile or corrugated rather than thatched roofs, and wearing Vietnamese clothing instead of handwoven ethnic dress. Traditional wear is brought out for wedding parties, festivals, and ceremonies.

Resistance to Vietnamization started as armed warfare. After 1975, a band of Montagnards called Front Unifié de Lutte des Races Opprimées (FULRO) waged guerrilla war in the highlands. Though backed by France and the US, they were largely defeated by 1980. FULRO guerrillas based in Cambodia's Ratanakiri Province are still active, staging cross-border raids.

A major obstacle to Vietnamization is the suppression of religious practices. The Montagnards are mostly Christian but retain strong elements of animism. Harvest festivals may culminate in the sacrifice of a buffalo, chicken, or pig; to celebrate good harvests fermented rice wine is consumed from a common clay vat through long bamboo-stem straws. The Ede and Bahnar/Jarai stage tomb-leaving ceremonies at local burial vaults to honor the souls of the dead. In the interests of tourism, the powers that be organize ethnic ceremonies out of season, and advertise ethnic song and dance to order, phoning ahead to demand villagers appear arrayed in ethnic costume.

Tourism is new in the highlands. The area only opened in 1993, so it lacks infrastructure. Finding an English menu is tough, but most likely you can find an English-speaking local as a guide. Pleiku and Buon Ma Thuot were both US bases during the Vietnam War and many Montagnards learned their English during this period.

PLEIKU

Pleiku is a town of 40,000 people in an area inhabited by Jarai and Ede minority peoples. Pickings are slim in Pleiku. The market features a large basketry section; you might also check out the local museum. Out of town, within a 50-km radius, are Montagnard villages, as well as tea and rubber plantations, scenic spots, and former battlefields. **Gai Lai Tourism** organizes trips to all these destinations. Of greater interest are journeys to a Jarai burial vault at Plei Mrong Village, 37 km to the northwest of Pleiku and five km short of Yaly Falls; a Bahnar spirit house at Dektu Village, 35 km out; and an elephant ride at Nhon Hoa Village, 65 km to the south. If you make an appointment through Gia Lai Tourism, the Montagnards will no doubt don ethnic dress. Order an elephant in advance to avoid disappointment; a two-day notice may be required. Gai Lai Tourism organizes ethnic song and dance performances for outrageous sums of money. If you plan your own trips you won't see the song and dance, but you can save a lot of money. Find your own moto driver and head off from Pleiku.

Heading north on the road to Kontum, village visits can be combined with such scenic stops as **Bien Ho,** a lake eight km from Pleiku, and 40-meter-high Yaly Falls, 42 km from Pleiku west of

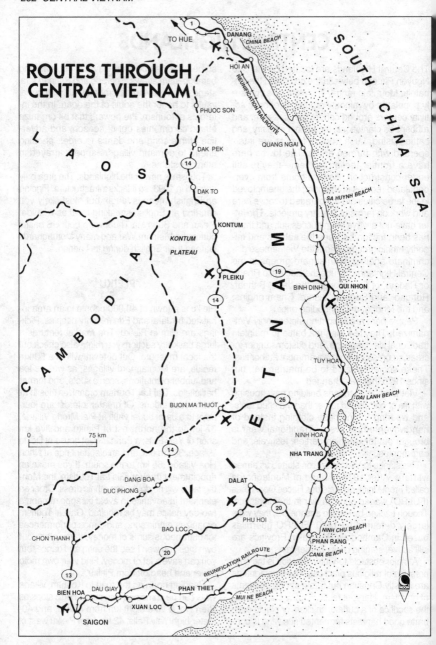

ROUTES THROUGH
CENTRAL VIETNAM

the main Pleiku-Kontum road. Police are sensitive about foreigners in the areas outside Pleiku and Kontum. You'll also hear rumors of tourists being robbed by tribespeople. Consult other travelers for the current wisdom. If in doubt, bring a local guide along to do the talking.

Accommodations and Food

Dining is largely confined to hotel restaurants and the market area. **Pleiku Hotel,** 124 Le Loi, tel. 24891, fax 24891, has 40 rooms—12 musty cubicles for $12 each, regular rooms for $17-27, rooms with air-con and fridge for $32-37. The hotel has a souvenir shop full of sad, stuffed creatures, including a tiger and a leopard. The Gia Lai Tourism Office is located here, along with a passable restaurant.

Khach San 86, at 86 Nguyen Van Troi, tel. 24674, has 20 rooms for $6; taxi girls, seedy. The 30-room **Khach San Vinh Hoi,** at 39 Tran Phu, tel. 24644, is right near the central market, and thus noisy. The **Movie Star Hotel** (Khach San Dien Anh), 6 Vo Thi Sau St., tel. 24626, has a good restaurant and car rentals. The hotel offers 20 rooms: six doubles for $10 each; a 4-bed room for $15; the remainder for $20-25 d with TV, $30 d with fridge.

Yaly Hotel, opposite the post office at 89 Hung Vuong, tel. 24843, has 54 good rooms in the $20-40 range, half with air-conditioning. Several guesthouses in Pleiku do not seem to accept foreigners—the two Nha Khaches on Quan Trung St., and one more north of Pleiku Hotel.

CENTRAL HIGHLANDS ROUTE NOTES

The most common road route is the highland bypass from Qui Nhon to Pleiku on Route 19, continuing on Route 14 to Buon Ma Thuot, then traveling along Route 26 to Nha Trang. To speed your passage, consider throwing in a plane ride—say from Hanoi or Danang to Pleiku, or from Buon Ma Thuot to Saigon. Weather could well be adverse, considerably affecting road conditions. Although this route is paved, parts may be impassable during heavy rains. In Buon Ma Thuot April-May and September-November are the months of light rain, June-August brings hard rain, and December-March is the dry season. The Central Highlands are actually not that high—the place is still humid and hot. Pleiku is at 780 meters, Kontum 525 meters, Buon Ma Thuot 450 meters.

To give an idea of distances on this route, from Danang it's 130 km to Quang Ngai, a further 154 km to Binh Dinh at the junction of Highway 1 and Route 19, 140 km from there to Pleiku, another 50 km to Kontum (backtrack to Pleiku), 197 km from Pleiku to Buon Ma Thuot, and a farther 160 km to Ninh Hoa at the junction of Route 26 and Highway 1. From there it's 33 km into Nha Trang.

Route 19 is a good sealed road, so the trip from Qui Nhon to Pleiku takes about four or five hours. The road climbs from rice paddies through scenic hill terrain. On hilly Route 14 from Pleiku to Buon Ma Thuot are coffee and gigantic rubber tree plantations, as well as peanut, pepper, and cassava farms. These crops are often dried along the road-

sides. A lot of development is in progress on this route, with new farms and housing. The area looks like a medieval Breughel canvas—strips of color, patches of farmland, laboring farmworkers. You should be able to cover the route in five hours, though a crawler bus might take seven. Buon Ma Thuot to Nha Trang on Route 26 is rough and hilly but scenic. The 190-km route can be covered by bus in about six hours.

A longer, rougher route proceeds from Saigon through Chon Thanh, Dang Boa, Buon Ma Thuot, Pleiku, Kontum, Dak Pek, Phuoc Son, and Hoi An. Although Buon Ma Thuot to Pleiku is plain sailing, the other two legs are formidable—sections may only be passable by motorcycle. At one time these routes were considered dangerous due to bandit activity, but this is apparently no longer the case. Route 14 South, from Saigon to Buon Ma Thuot via Dang Boa, can be accomplished in stages—it's possible to cadge rides in coffee trucks. The route is fair from Saigon as far as Dang Boa, and then in very poor condition from Dang Boa to Buon Ma Thuot. It takes an estimated 14 hours to cover this route—if you're lucky, and if there's no waiting time between rides. The route from Buon Ma Thuot to Dalat is currently inaccessible to motor vehicles. Kontum to Hoi An on Route 14 North is extremely rough, although attempts are being made to upgrade the road. From Kontum, it's 150 km to Dak Pek, a further 70 km to Phuoc Son, and a final 125 km to Hoi An.

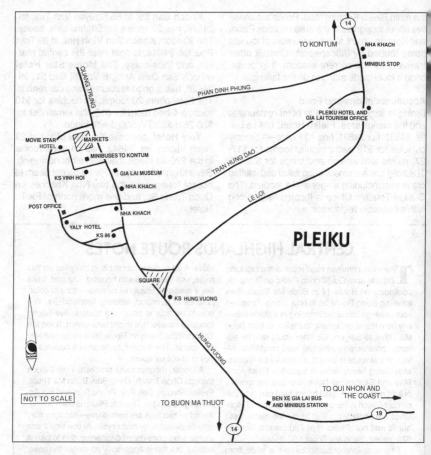

TO KONTUM

NHA KHACH

MINIBUS STOP

PHAN DINH PHUNG

QUANG TRUNG

PLEIKU HOTEL AND
GIA LAI TOURISM OFFICE

MOVIE STAR
HOTEL

MARKETS

MINIBUSES TO KONTUM

TRAN HUNG DAO

KS VINH HOI

GIA LAI MUSEUM

NHA KHACH

LE LOI

POST OFFICE

NHA KHACH

PLEIKU

YALY HOTEL

KS 86

SQUARE

KS HUNG VUONG

NOT TO SCALE

HUNG VUONG

TO QUI NHON AND
THE COAST

BEN XE GIA LAI BUS
AND MINIBUS STATION

19

TO BUON MA THUOT

14

14

Services and Information
Gia Lai Tourism Office, 124 Le Loi, in the Pleiku Hotel, tel. 24891, is, for a change, actually helpful. The staff run half-day (three-hour) and full-day (six- to eight-hour) tours to surrounding villages and scenic spots. If you're a small group of one or two people, they might set you up with motorcycle guides. The price is still expensive— $18 for a half-day trip, which breaks down to $6 for the motorcycle plus $12 for the guide and organizing fee. The tariff is $26 per day for one person with a motorcycle guide, $38 for two motorcycles and drivers. Organization fees vary from $20 to $40 depending on group size; guides are $12-18; a car for 100 km $30; elephant ride

$50; folk music performance $70; folk music and rice wine drinking hits the jackpot at $100.

Getting Around and Away
Vietnam Airlines staffs an office in the Yaly Hotel. The airport is 25 km from Pleiku, or 40 km from Kontum. Thrice-weekly flights leave Pleiku for Danang, Ho Chi Minh City, and Hanoi. The bus station, **Ben Xe Gia Lai,** schedules buses and minibuses to Buon Ma Thuot, to coastal destinations, and further afield to Hanoi or Saigon. Minibuses to Kontum run from the central market. For getting around Pleiku, rent a moto for around $6 a day, or hire a car through a larger hotel or Gia Lai Tourism.

KONTUM

Kontum, a frontier town of 35,000, lies about 65 km north of Pleiku. The old town of Kontum was destroyed in 1972 when hundreds of B-52s leveled the area during a major battle between North and South Vietnamese troops. A new town arose from the ashes—it's still under construction, with the paint barely dry, so expect changes. Bahnar, Sedoun, and Jarai minority groups inhabit the surrounding villages. The main pursuits around Kontum are of the farm and forest variety—the cultivation of coffee, tea, and cassava on a large scale. Cattle raising is also on the increase. The nearby forests provide lumber and medicinal plants like ginseng; furniture is fashioned from sandalwood and rattan.

Catholic Relics

Heard about missionaries with huge plantations in remote places like the Congo? Kontum conjures up that bygone era, with its large seminary on the east side of town. The French seminary dates from the 1850s, and must have been self-sufficient. It is an impressive three-story building with a chapel above a sweeping staircase, classrooms, and place to park vehicles below. Out front is a bust of Martial Jannin Phuoc, the seminary's first pastor. There were once as many as 30 priests and 35 nuns here. The last French citizen left in 1975, but by that time their work was completed—Kontum province is 80% Catholic.

To the east of the seminary stands a grotto with a shrine of Mary; directly south is a convent with maroon walls dating from the 1930s—a few Vietnamese nuns live here.

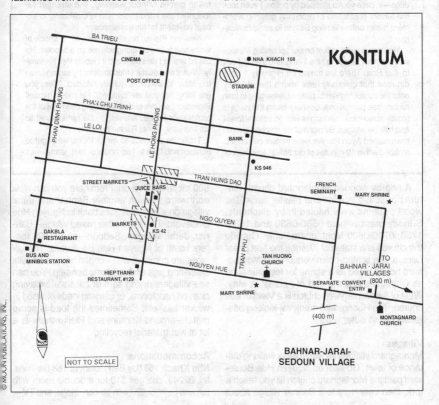

THE HIGHLANDS ON A MINSK
by Patrick Morris

With tanks full and fingers crossed, the three of us roared out of Saigon. We were riding Russian 125cc Minsk motorcycles, purchased with cash dollars in Saigon. On the map of the Central Highlands, thick red lines promised roads of some sort, and we decided to tackle them by motorcycle. Along for the ride were fellow American Alan and a young Londoner named Steve.

We chose the Minsks because they have sufficient power for mountain regions and are easily and cheaply repaired. None of us had licenses; supposedly you only need a license in Vietnam when riding a 150cc bike or higher. It is useful, however, to possess ownership papers—even forgeries—in case you're stopped by police. I even took the further precaution of procuring green government plates before leaving Saigon to avoid harassment.

Making an awful racket on our sputtering Minsks, we rode from Saigon to Nha Trang, and the next day to Tuy Hoa. There we turned off Highway 1 up a dirt road that gradually rises from a humid valley onto the cooler highlands plateau, emerging in lush rubber-tree plantations. Scenery along the route is mostly scrub mountain ranges with occasional forest and hilltribe villages. By nightfall we reached a small town named Ayun Pa. We were instant celebrities, mobbed within 10 minutes of our arrival. Iced lemonade was poured, and we were offered a shampoo at the beauty salon in front of the hotel. We were then led to $2 fan rooms with mosquito nets. We took bucket showers and retired exhausted to wood-slat beds that threatened to collapse with every movement.

From Ayun Pa to Route 14 the road becomes paved, passing through beautiful tree plantations. After a couple of hours Alan fell behind. We waited and waited, then finally turned around. We found Alan banged up on the side of the road, a man working on his bike. Alan showed us the scrapes he sustained when the handlebars fell off his bike. Like the former Soviet Union, a Minsk has been known to fall to pieces without warning. The stranger remounted the handlebars and left, refusing to accept payment for his assistance.

Nearing Pleiku, an older man with a shock of white hair pulled up alongside me on a scooter. He asked where I was from and if I would visit his family. Weary and dusty, I tried to defer by saying I was too filthy, to which he quickly retorted, "Yes, you are filthy, but you are civilized!" He called himself Professor Lee. We ended up staying overnight at the professor's house, listening to his rantings, while his son sang Lionel Ritchie numbers.

Traffic on all roads as far as Pleiku was light to nonexistent. One to two hours of rain, sometimes

---

A nearby wooden Montagnard church features a Gothic interior and plaster walls; the wood columns were hauled in by elephants. Sunday masses held 0530-0630 and 1630-1730; 0700-0800 Montagnards only. Outside the church is a statue of Kuenot, the first priest here, and a scaled-down version of a Montagnard house, used as a shrine for festivals such as Christmas and the end of harvest in May. West of the Montagnard church is a Vietnamese church, Tan Huong, with medieval-looking bas-reliefs on the outer walls.

Villages
Montagnard villages lie within easy walking distance of town. Go east on Nguyen Hue Boulevard past the Montagnard church till you reach a fork, then veer right to a Bahnar village about 600 meters further on. From here you can walk northward through another Bahnar and Jarai village on a path that goes back to Nguyen Hue Boulevard. There's another mixed village—Bahnar, Jarai, Rongao, Sedoun—about 400 meters south of Nguyen Hue Boulevard. The villages are primitive, with wooden houses on stilts sheltering pigs and chickens beneath. You can see villagers drying corn or cassava, weaving cloth on handlooms, or carrying loads of wood in wicker baskets. Sometimes the load is scrap metal—around Kontum and Pleiku there is a lot of war material recycling.

Accommodations
Nha Khach 168 (Uy Ban Hotel), at 168 Ba Trieu, tel. 62249, charges $10 for a double room with fan and bath, or $23 with air-con, fridge, and TV—

heavy, occurred almost daily in the afternoon. Confident now that we'd made it this far, in Pleiku we threw caution to the wind and rode to the old US base at Plei Mei, then caught a trail for the few kilometers toward the Cambodian border. But lots of attention from villagers spooked us, and we went back.

From Pleiku past Kontum to Dak To the road is paved, scenic, and rolling. Dak To to Dak Ngoi is dirt with rocks. The road from Dak Ngoi to Dak Pek winds through lush mountain passes. Dak Pek is a small town situated in a valley. Here we stayed in unnamed dormitories for $4. The hotel manager told me not to bother locking my Minsk, because "Dak Pek have no thief." The rural Vietnamese and Montagnards were very friendly—one Montagnard worked two hours fixing my friend's wheel and flatly refused to accept money. The children were shy, running away terrified when the motorcycles approached a hilltribe village.

We saw very little traffic along this section, mostly other motorcycles and the odd logging truck. We encountered no police problems in two weeks of motorcycling, stopped only once by frontier soldiers at an outpost on the way to Phuoc Son. The soldiers insisted we take a bath in a nearby stream, then harassed us with family photos, and foisted bitter tea and plates of food on us.

Dak Pek to Phuoc Son is incredible terrain. Two steep mountain passes make an all-rock road barely passable on a motorbike. One stream crossing was a meter deep. A van would never make it, and it would be totally impassable in the rainy season. We saw rainforest with waterfalls the entire 70 km. It took us a whole day to cover this section of the route over mountain passes strewn with loose rocks and dirt. In Phuoc Son the cinema provided our hard beds—$5 with fan. Meals were delivered by eager staff. Out of Phuoc Son we found 10 km of paved road, then a good dirt road mostly downhill or flat to Hoi An.

Apart from rough roads we had no problems and covered a lot of ground. I found the people along this route—especially the Montagnards—far friendlier and more hospitable than those along the more touristy Highway 1. The most important thing I've learned about traveling in Vietnam is to keep smiling. The Vietnamese are just becoming accustomed to foreigners, so it helps to be friendly and patient.

—*Patrick Morris is director of VeloAsia Cycling Adventures, an outfit based in Berkeley, California, that runs bicycle tours to Vietnam and other parts of Southeast Asia.*

an excellent value. The three-story building houses about 30 rooms. **Khach San 946,** 946 Tran Phu, tel. 62610, has 10 rooms for $15-25. The low end is a three-bed fan room; the high end a double room with air-con and TV. **Khach San 42,** at 42 Le Hong Phong, tel. 62461, offers doubles for $12 but no bath—a "short-time" place, with taxi girls.

Food
Hiep Thanh Restaurant,129 Nguyen Hue, tel. 25262, is one of the best in town—and the most expensive, charging around $5 a head for a good feed. In the market area is **Song Huong Restaurant.** A number of juice bars line Le Hong Phong Street. Depending on the season oranges, mangoes, jackfruit, pineapple, and bananas are available in the Kontum region. Near the bus station **Dakbla Restaurant** offers basic fare.

Getting There
Buses and minibuses run to Pleiku, Buon Ma Thuot, Binh Dinh, Qui Nhon, Quang Ngai, and even as far afield as Hué, Hanoi, Nha Trang, and Saigon, though not on a daily basis. Because the road north of Kontum is currently too rough, Kontum is a roundtrip from Pleiku. You might consider skipping Pleiku on the way in but stopping there on the way back.

Getting Around
Mostly on foot or by moto. You can get hold of a car or jeep through some of the hotels. Also inquire at **Kontum Tourist and Trade Company,** 218 Tran Hung Dao St., tel. 62222.

EXCURSIONS FROM KONTUM

Minority groups are not city folk—you have to get out of town to see them. You can organize a 60-km trip to the crossroads of Indochina, the meeting point of the Lao, Cambodian, and Vietnamese borders northwest of Kontum. A dirt road goes up Highway 14 through Dak Mot, and

loading a bus in Kontum

on toward the Lao border on Route 18 past a military base to the town of Ngoc Hoi (the entire district here is also called Ngoc Hoi). The border villages out of Kontum may require permits, but this is more likely a fundraising scam by the local constabulary. Hiring a jeep from Kontum will cost upwards of $40 for a full day of driving, plus $10 to rent a policeman, plus extra for a guide. Bargain hard for price and timing.

On the way to the border zone you pass scrap-metal dumps. The area around Dak To and Tan Canh was a battlefield, and some rusted tanks are still lying around. The Dak To area contains villages inhabited by Bahnar, Jarai, Sedoun, and Rongao. The farther west you go, the poorer the villagers, with grubby malnourished kids living on earthern floors. Jarai, Sedoun, and Bahnar villages feature a large, distinct structure with a towering thatched roof—the *rong,* or communal spirit house, where men gather to sing and drink. Another distinctive feature is a Bahnar-Jarai burial vault, a wooden structure with two long poles at either end— buffalo hooves and skulls hang from it.

BUON MA THUOT

Buon Ma Thuot, population around 65,000, is the largest town and unofficial capital of the highlands. The area specializes in coffee and lumber. Vietnam's finest coffee comes from this region, although the brewing process is not yet perfected in the local cafés. The French introduced coffee and rubber trees to the area in the 1930s, with large rubber plantations operated by Michelin. Sericulture was introduced in the 1990s, and there are plans for large-scale mulberry plantations in an effort to turn Buon Ma Thuot into one of the silk weaving centers of Vietnam.

The center of Buon Ma Thuot is a dusty traffic circle with a T-34 tank mounted on a block of concrete in the middle, one of the sacred vehicles that rolled in to liberate the area in 1975. In March of that year, NVA troops mounted an all-out attack on Buon Ma Thuot that turned into a rout of South Vietnamese forces, paving the way for the final assault on Saigon. Apart from the bizarre landmark tank, there's not a lot to see in Buon Ma Thuot. The surrounding countryside holds the real interest.

Minority Museum

This small museum focuses on the Ede, the dominant cultural group in the area. There are displays of musical instruments, wooden jewelry, costumes, weaving, baskets, models of Ede longhouses, and some moth-eaten stuffed animals. Pictures of the Liberation round out the tacky display. At the current rate of Vietnamization the entire Ede culture may end up in the museum. Open Tuesday, Thursday, and Saturday 0700-1100 and 1400-1700.

The Ede appear to have originated in Malaysia or Indonesia. They live in houses on stilts, with pigs and chickens scurrying around under the floor. Most have been converted to Catholicism or Protestantism, but retain traces of animist worship of spirits of the forest, streams, and hills. In festivals celebrating good crops, villagers drink wine from a large vat through bamboo-stem straws.

The stair leading to one Ede longhouse has a pair of wooden breasts at the top, symbolizing the power of women. The Ede are traditionally matriarchal, but since 1975 and Vietnamization, they're becoming less so. Another matriarchal group is the Mnong, with about 50,000 people living around Buon Ma Thuot. They speak a language similar to Khmer, have no written script, and live in houses flat to the ground. The Mnong are famed elephant catchers, using domesticated elephants to round up wild pachyderms. They practice elephant spirit worship.

Accommodations

Buon Ma Thuot has a rum bunch of hotels. **Hong Kong Hotel,** 30 Hai Ba Trung, tel. 52630, is a small budget joint with $7 rooms. **Khach San 43** at 41-43 Ly Thuong Kiet, tel. 52250, features 20 rooms at $7 each, no bath. **Khach San UBND** is a filthy guesthouse at 5-9 Hai Ba Trung; rooms are $6-12, no bath. The best hotel in town, **Tay Nguyen Hotel,** at 106 Ly Thuong Kiet, tel. 52250, features rooms for $15-20-35. The hotel is clean—a rare find in these parts. The upper-end rooms have air-con and hot water. The **Thang Loi** (Victory) at 1 Phan Chu Trinh, tel. 52322, is located near the tank in the center of town and has 36 rooms for $20 with fan and $32 air-con with bath.

Food

Next door to Hong Kong Hotel is **Bo Ne Restaurant,** which serves up a sizzling steak-and-egg breakfast for under a dollar. This place has a peculiar selection of animals marinating in jars of rice wine—a dollar a shot for wine with deer or monkey fetus. Other jars contain pickled birds,

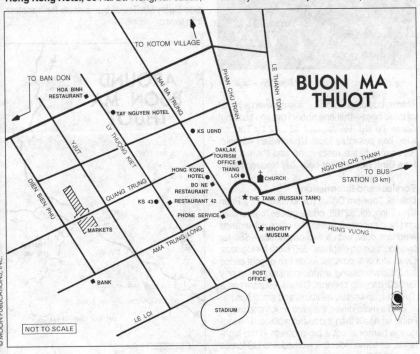

water buffalo and rider from Ban Don village

lizards, boa constrictors . . . there's even a jar full of dead bees—that one should get you buzzing! **Quan To Nu** (Restaurant 42), 42 Ly Thuong Kiet, has passable food; **Khach San 43** hotel (opposite) has a restaurant; and there's also **Hoa Binh Restaurant** near Tay Nguyen Hotel.

Services and Information
Daklak Tourism Office (Dulich Daklak), 3 Phan Chu Trinh, tel. 52108, offers guides, car rentals, and high-priced services. The office will arrange elephant rides with a two-day notice—$50 for two hours on an elephant, $90 extra for logistics. Other tour enticements: a ride in a dugout canoe for $30; witnessing a wine-drinking ceremony for $80, dancing optional. Daklak Tourism has a Toyota four-seater, minibus, and small bus.

Find a moto driver; they are much cheaper in lining up deals than the tourism office. The language barrier is not a big problem in the highlands, as some older folk worked with US forces before 1975.

Getting There
By Air: The daily flight from Saigon on a 34-seat light plane can be overbooked, so reserve well ahead. A one-way flight costs $45, a short flight avoids an 18-hour road trip—another reason for its popularity. There are also connections twice-weekly from Buon Ma Thuot to Danang and Hanoi. Buon Ma Thuot airport is 10 km out—take a moto to or from town for $2.

By Bus: Buon Ma Thuot bus station three km east of town has up to 25 departures daily; most leave in the early morning. The buses range from good Hungarian Icarus models to crawlers that seem incapable of making it over the next hill—let alone to Haiphong, Vung Tau, Hué, Saigon, or the other far-flung destinations advertised. Several buses a day travel to Pleiku and a number of points along the coast. Danang buses will stop in Pleiku. To Qui Nhon requires 11 hours by bus, to Nha Trang six hours, to Saigon 18 hours. Lambros lurk outside Buon Ma Thuot bus station for transfers into town.

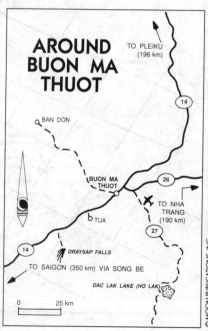

AROUND BUON MA THUOT

TO PLEIKU (196 km)

14

BAN DON

BUON MA THUOT

26

TO NHA TRANG (190 km)

TUA

27

14

DRAYSAP FALLS

TO SAIGON (350 km) VIA SONG BE

DAC LAK LAKE (HO LAK)

0   25 km

© MOON PUBLICATIONS, INC.

Getting Around
Use motos. Moto plus driver runs about $5 a day, or you can give the moto driver $5 and take it yourself. Lambros are available near the bus station.

EXCURSIONS FROM BUON MA THUOT

About two km north of Buon Ma Thuot is **Kotom,** a wealthy model village of immaculate longhouses with tiled roofs, hedgerows, electricity, and big motorcycles in the driveways. A paved road leading to Kotum provides easy access. The Catholic middle-class Ede residents of this ritzy strip appear to have received a large transfusion of money from official sources.

Tua, another Ede village on the tourist circuit (read: well-off model village) is 13 km southwest of town on the road to Saigon. To reach mediocre **Draysap Falls** continue down the same road and turn left at the 20-km marker. Follow a rough trail for seven more km—about 20 minutes on a motorcycle.

An excursion to **Ho Lak** (Dak Lak Lake) is recommended. This area lies about 60 km to the south. The route passes through pretty valleys and countryside. A few small ferry crossings can be found on this route. Ho Lak is ringed by mountains; on the lake you can see dugout canoes; in the villages you pass geese herders and basketmakers. A good viewpoint in the area is the burned-out Bao Dai villa. Boat and elephant races are staged here every spring; cranes and storks coat the place during migratory visits.

The village of **Ban Don** lies 55 km northwest of Buon Ma Thuot, or about two hours by moto. Local buses also make the trip. A rather ordinary town, it has been chosen as a model tourist site because elephants can be ordered into the

ELEPHANT HUNT

The poster on the wall of the Daklak Tourism Office caught my eye: it showed elephants at work. The man at the counter said there were 40 elephants in Ban Don, to the north of Buon Ma Thuot. To ride one required $50 for two hours for two people, he said, plus $50 for the car to Ban Don, $15 for a guide, $5 sightseeing fee, and $20 organization fee. Halfway through his litany, we knew the experience was well beyond budget, but still we wanted to see elephants at work. So we left the tourism office, flagged down some local moto drivers, negotiated $5 each for the day, and headed off for Ban Don.

Ban Don requires a permit charade to enter the village—the "permit" fee was settled on the spot at $2. To make the charade look good, an official from the People's Committee laboriously wrote down names, passport numbers and visa numbers at least three times. Finally, we entered the sacred precincts of Ban Don, the village of the elephants.

Only there weren't any elephants. When asked where the pachyderms were hiding, the moto guide said they were working in the jungle for the day. "Let's walk out there," I suggested. "No, no," he protested, "too far, can only get there on the river." "Right, we'll take a boat." "No, no—no boats today." "What if we returned at dusk, would the elephants be back then?" "No," said the guide, "they return late at night, and they leave early in the morning before sunrise." "Trees look pretty intact round here," said my travel companion, those elephants must be really well fed." We both looked at the ground. "How come there are no elephant droppings?" At this point, the guide flashed a guilty smile, developed a sudden case of amnesia, and nervously suggested we move on to the next village. Where, oddly enough, we did find some small elephants, recently captured, and chained to trees in appalling conditions.

Whither the elephants? During the Vietnam War, the pachyderms suffered major setbacks: domesticated elephants and water buffalo used by the Vietcong to move supplies were attacked and slaughtered by US pilots and ground troops. Wild elephants were adversely affected by the ecological warfare waged by the US. In 1980 there were an estimated 1,500 to 2,000 elephants in Vietnam, mainly living in the forests of the Central Highlands. By 1995 the number had dwindled to under 500, due to destruction of natural habitats and illegal hunting. The species is now endangered. Although protected under Vietnamese law, tuskers have come into increasing conflict with farmers encroaching on forest land. The only hope for the remaining population of wild elephants is the creation of a national park protection zone.

recently captured

village from nearby jungles on 48-hour notice. Authorities insist on a permit to visit Ban Don, but this is pure fundraising. Ban Don offers an eclectic mix in its small population of 300 people, including Ede, Jarai, Lao, Khmer, Bahnar, Thai, and Mnong peoples. The Mnong are famous elephant trainers; some practice their craft around Ban Don. None of the minority peoples wear traditional costume except at weddings or festivals. There are some Ede longhouses and Lao-style houses in the area.

Twenty or 30 km out of Buon Ma Thuot on the route to Ban Don you can visit perfectly good Ede villages engaged in the farming of peanuts, coffee, or pepper, and they don't require any permit nonsense.

QUANG NGAI TO NHA TRANG

QUANG NGAI

Quang Ngai, the capital of the province of the same name, is a dull town on Highway 1 about 130 km south of Danang. Twelve km to the east is the site of the My Lai massacre, now an on-site museum and memorial. If you keep going along the same road to the coast, there are fishing villages at fine-sand **Bien Khe Ky Beach.** It's simple to reach the **My Lai Memorial** site—you could spend a few hours there and carry on without stopping in Quang Ngai.

Accommodations
On the north side of town is **Song Tra Hotel,** 1 Quang Trung St., tel. 22664, run by Quang Ngai Tourism Company. The company also maintains offices here. The Song Tra is a vast, soulless concrete structure with a restaurant, dance floor, and souvenir counters; 38 rooms in the $10-25

range for a double. **Quang Ngai Hotel,** 62 Quang Trong, tel. 22757, offers 16 clean double rooms with bath for $20 each—it's also known as **Cong Doan** or **Trade Union Guesthouse.**

Closer to town on Phan Boi Chau is a cluster of hotels; if you don't get into one, walk over and try the next one. **Nha Khach UBND Quang Ngai,** 50 Phan Boi Chau, tel. 22873, a large compound opposite the church, features several wings, with a total of 45 rooms in the $8-22 range. Official guests lodge here so you might have trouble getting in; good tucker in the dining room. **Khach San Vietnam,** 41 Phan Boi Chau, tel. 23610, has 10 rooms at $8 each. **Khach San Kim Thanh** at 19 Phan Boi Chau, tel. 23471, is a private 20-room hotel; $6-12 single, $15-20 hot water and air-con. In the same area is **Hotel 502.**

Near the market a budget hotel, **Hotel #1** (Khach San So I) at 42 Nguyen Nghiem, tel. 3609, has 20 rooms at $5; friendly management. Try the central market for good foodstalls. Otherwise, most eating takes place in hotels—try the **UBND Quang Ngai** dining room.

Getting Around and Away

Buses run to destinations north and south on Highway 1, as well as to the Central Highlands, from **Lien Tinh Ben Xe** on the south side of Quang Ngai. Quang Ngai railway station is three km west of town; Reunification Express trains stop here. For car rentals in Quang Ngai, inquire at the hotels. Prices average $25 per day with driver. You can find motos near the market

THE COAST ROAD

Highway 1 was originally engineered by the Vietnamese imperial government over 200 years ago—it was then called the "Mandarin Route" and was about 1,150 km long, connecting Hanoi, Hué, Saigon, and Phnom Penh. Under the present government the road has been extended, stretching over 2,000 km from Lang Son on the Chinese border to Camau at the tip of the Mekong Delta. The World Bank recently announced plans to lend Vietnam $158 million to rebuild the most heavily traveled sections of Highway 1, so improvements may be on the way.

From Danang south to Phan Thiet is an 800-km coastal stretch sometimes within sight of the railway and Highway 1. The coastal plains support rice farmers, and fine harbors and beaches offer bases for fishing. Beach areas are undeveloped and unspoiled, with simple fishing villages reminiscent of those in Thailand in the 1960s. Unspoiled often also means inaccessible—a lot lie hidden off the main road. The most developed beach is Nha Trang, and even that is low-key.

Minibus drivers heading down the coast cover the trip in stages. From Danang it's 130 km to Quang Ngai, 175 km further to Qui Nhon, 188 km to Tuy Hoa, then 88 km to Ninh Hoa, 32 km to Nha Trang, another 105 km to Phan Rang, 150 km to Phan Thiet, and a final 198 km to Saigon. The railway largely parallels the road. Key junctions on the coast road are at Binh Dinh (17 km from Qui Nhon, marking the turnoff to Pleiku), Ninh Hoa (turnoff to Buon Ma Thuot), and Phan Rang (turnoff for the Dalat route to Saigon).

and at the bus terminal and other strategic sites, including the turnoff to My Lai.

MY LAI

The rural district of Son My was the site of the My Lai massacre in 1968. To get there, turn east from the bridge over the Tra Khuc River and proceed 12 km along a dirt road, passing through villages and rice paddies. On the same road, farther east past the My Lai site, is Bien Khe Ky

This plaque and wall mosaic commemorate villagers killed at My Lai.

Beach with a long stretch of sand. There are motos at the bridge over the Tra Khuc River; hiring a moto for two or three hours should cost under $4. A guide posted at the My Lai Memorial site will show you around; no permits or permissions needed, though a donation is expected.

The Massacre

On 16 March 1968 three companies of US infantry entered the Son My district by helicopter to search for Vietcong. The area was believed to be a Vietcong stronghold; several US soldiers had been killed by mines in the area a few weeks earlier. Under the orders of Lieutenant William C. Calley, the 1st platoon moved into the village of My Lai and shot and bayonetted unarmed civilians, killed livestock, blew up underground bomb shelters, and torched dwellings. Women were raped, dead animals tossed into wells to poison the water. Up to 150 villagers were herded into a ditch and cut down by machine gun fire. Calley's platoon accounted for some 350 deaths; over 500 Vietnamese were killed in the operation by the three infantry divisions combined, mostly in My Lai hamlet itself. At no point did US troops come under fire. The only US casualty that day was an American soldier who shot himself in the foot to escape involvement in the massacre. The remaining villagers were forced into camps.

It was not until eight months later that *New York Times* reporter Seymour Hersh managed to confirm the story and place it before the world. The resulting uproar had a demoralizing effect on the US military and was a turning point in the American public's perception of the war. The cover-ups reached every level of the US Army command. Military justice was a farce: of all those involved, only Lieutenant Calley endured court-martial and conviction. Found guilty of murdering 22 civilians, he was sentenced in 1971 to life imprisonment. He spent only three years under house arrest before being paroled.

The Memorial

My Lai has become a pilgrimage spot for both Americans and Vietnamese trying to heal the wounds of war, trying to come to grips with the atrocities of war. Visiting My Lai is a moving, humbling experience—a reminder of the insanity of war. Every year on March 16th, there is a special memorial gathering at the site.

The My Lai Memorial is built on the site of the former village, with gardens, reception halls, and a museum. At the far end lies an irrigation ditch bearing a plaque stating that GIs killed 170 villagers. Near the ditch is a model of a family bomb shelter, and coconut trees scarred with artillery holes. To one side, a large mosaic wall completed in 1988 by a group of Hanoi artists shows a Guernica-like mosaic of screaming figures, whirling helicopters, blazing guns, and dripping tears of blood.

Toward the reception halls is a statue group of Vietnamese villagers displaying sorrow and anger. The statue was sculpted by Ho Thu, husband of Vo Thi Lien, a massacre survivor. Vo Thi Lien was 11 years old at the time. She traveled in Europe in 1970, at age 13, to denounce the

United States. "I tell you this story," she said, "so peace may be restored in my country. So I can go to school and meet my friends and relatives again."

The on-site museum at My Lai is small but devastating—this place will leave a lump in your throat. Through photos and eyewitness testimonials, the museum recounts what took place that day. Some pictures have English captions; others are captioned in Vietnamese only. Ronald Haeberie, a US Army photographer present for the first hour of the carnage, had three cameras along—he turned over some official film and kept the rest. The photos appeared in a Japanese source, and later in *Life* magazine and *Newsweek*. The Vietnamese lifted the photos from these sources and enlarged them for the museum. His photographs show people before and after being shot. There are testimonials from half a dozen survivors and from two Vietnamese interpreters there for the first hour of the shooting. Paintings in the museum re-create the events. There's also a heart-wrenching display of some personal effects of villagers killed that day—teacup shards, a child's crayon, a Buddha statue from a destroyed family shrine.

In the reception hall at My Lai are several dozen thick guest books, filled with comments from Vietnamese and foreign visitors. Among the foreign entries, the most poignant come from Vietnam vets. One group came to My Lai in 1992 to build a US-funded health center, with vets contributing medicines and a solar power system on the roof. One vet wrote: "By coming back to Vietnam to build this clinic I have helped heal the deep psychological wounds that have plagued me for 21 years." In 1993, Hugh Thompson, one of the nine helicopter pilots at My Lai on 16 March, revisited the site: "On my first trip to My Lai, I was filled with pain and anger. On my second trip 25 years later, I am filled with sorrow and pain. I wish I could have prevented more death. Please forgive all former helicopter pilots. I hope all worlds can learn to live in peace."

SA HUYNH BEACH

Sixty km south of Quang Ngai is **Sa Huynh,** one of the few places along this coastal stretch with some facilities—seaside restaurants and a small hotel. If driving through, this is a pretty spot to break the journey. The beach is fringed with coconut palms and rice paddies; the town is known for its salt marshes and salt evaporation ponds.

QUI NHON

Qui Nhon, the capital of Binh Dinh Province, is a port town with a large fishing fleet. If traveling by car or minibus, it's a possible pit stop on the Saigon-to-Hué route; by public transportation, it's a disaster—you'll be dropped off way to the west of the town.

There's little to see in Qui Nhon. To make matters worse, the locals are rude, unfriendly, and ready to rip off the unwary. You can visit the museum **Bao Tang Binh Dinh;** three small salons offer ethnic and natural history through models of thatched housing, Cham artifacts, war memorabilia, and a few artillery pieces. Two Cham works stand out—an impressive Brahma statue from Thap Doi, and a garuda statue from Duong Long.

The two Cham towers in Qui Nhon are nothing to get excited about. The twin towers of Thap Doi are located at the northern edge of town, down an alley near 906 Tran Hung Dao St., three km from Qui Nhon center. Most of the tower statuary has been hauled off; one of the towers has been completely rebricked and reconstructed on a new stone and concrete base, so it's hardly a Cham ruin—wait till it grows some moss.

There are some other Cham towers around Qui Nhon, such as **Thap Duong Long,** about 30 km northwest and **Thap Banh It,** 20 km north, and the remains of **Cha Ban** and **Canh Tien,** 27 km north. None are as impressive as the ruins in Phan Rang or Nha Trang.

The beach at Qui Nhon looks pleasant enough—white sand, fishing boats—but it contains raw sewage and other pollutants. Close to the war memorial by the beach, stalls serve snacks. At the east end of the beach, past Qui Nhon Tourist Hotel, is a small enclosure with monkeys and sad black bears. It's free, which is what you wish you could say about the animals. In the center of Qui Nhon, **Long Kanh Pagoda** features a large standing Buddha in front, presiding over an industrial wasteland.

Accommodations

Budget Hotels: No shortage of accommodations in Qui Nhon. In town is a slew of hotels with similar prices, mostly under $15 a room. **Dong Phuong Hotel,** 39 Mai Xuan Thuong, tel. 2915, has fan rooms for $6 s, $8 d, and $12 t, and air-con rooms for $7-15—popular with backpackers. **Huu Nghi Hotel,** 210 Phan Boi Chau, tel. 22152, offers $6 rooms. **Binh Dinh Guesthouse,** 399 Tran Hung Dao, tel. 22012, is run by the Binh Dinh Investment Bank, and has 15 rooms: $5-6 no bath, $9 with toilet, $12 with air-con and hot water; $15 with TV.

The **Peace Hotel** (Hoa Binh), on Tran Hung Dao, tel. 22900, offers 62 rooms for $6 s and $9 d.

Right opposite is the **Nha Khach 264,** tel. 21611. Next door, on the corner of Dao Duy Tu and Tran Hung Dao, is **Saigon Hotel,** with 15 double rooms at $15 each. **Agribank Hotel,** at 202 Tran Hung Dao, tel. 22245, has 16 rooms for $9 s and $12-15 d. **Anh Thu Mini,** 54 Mai Xuan Thuong, tel. 21168, is a drive-in hotel with 10 rooms for $11-15 each. **Olympic Hotel,** near the stadium, tel. 22375, features 30 rooms in the $7-15 range.

Moderate Hotels: Vietincombank Hotel, 257 Le Hong Phong, tel. 22779, has 20 rooms in the $15-20-25 range. **Dien Anh Hotel** (Movie Star Hotel), 312 Phan Boi Chau, tel. 22876, offers 19 rooms for $18 each, with air-con and hot water; it's run by Binh Dinh Video Company.

Near Qui Nhon beach are two more expensive hotels. **Hai Ha Mini Hotel,** tel. 21295, charges $25 for each of its seven double rooms. **Qui Nhon Tourist Hotel,** 8 Nguyen Hue, tel. 22401, features more than 50 rooms in a large modern compound; $22-30 for doubles.

Food

There are no decent restaurants. **Ngoc Lien Restaurant,** at 268 Le Hong Phong, is reasonable; the area around it has lots of eateries. Otherwise, try foraging in hotel dining rooms. Qui Nhon is a fishing port so some seafood is served. About three km southwest of town is **Ganh Rang Restaurant** on the waterfront.

Services

Binh Dinh Tourism Office is in the same compound as the Qui Nhon Tourist Hotel. The Vietcombank is at 148 Le Loi Street.

Getting There and Away

Highway 1 is eight km west of Qui Nhon at Phutai; the railway is 10 km west at Dieu Tri; Phu Cat airport is 35 km north of Qui Nhon. Motos and lambros shuttle passengers from Qui Nhon back to road or rail junctions. A lambro is 50 cents to Dieu Tri, a moto $1. Both are available from the area in front of Qui Nhon bus station, **Ben Xe Binh Dinh,** on Tran Hung Dao Street.

Buses depart Qui Nhon at 0500 to Hanoi, Saigon, Nha Trang, Dalat, Danang, and Hué. If you don't want to get up at this unearthly hour, or if the bus station doesn't offer an express to the destination of your choice, consider heading out to Phutai on Highway 1 and flagging down a passing express bus. Although there's a rail spur into Qui Nhon, it's only used by local trains. Study Reunification Express time tables in a hotel in Qui Nhon before heading to Dieu Tri to catch a train. There are twice-weekly flights from Phu Cat airport to Danang and Ho Chi Minh City.

Getting Around

Try the hotels for rentals—otherwise, stick to cyclos or motos. Car and minibus rentals are available from the **Limited Responsible Tourist Car** company at 79 Le Hong Phong, tel. 23066. You can hire a car and driver for about $25 a day. Another place for rentals is **Central Vietnam Traveling,** at 176 Le Hong Phong, tel. 21199. This agency offers motorcycle rentals—Honda 50cc for $6 a day, 100cc for $8 a day. If you rent for a two-day period, you keep the motorcycle overnight. A Toyota Land Cruiser is about $30 per 100 km of driving, a 4-seat car is $28 for 100 km.

TUY HOA

There is no reason to visit Tuy Hoa except to sleep there. You can't miss the main hotel, the **Huong Sen,** which has doubles for $15 and suites for $25-35. The hotel includes a vast restaurant that is always empty but charges outrageous prices. A guesthouse in Tuy Hoa is also open to foreigners, charging $15 a night. A good restaurant is **Phong Lan,** at 156 Tran Hung Dao, with great noodle soup. Tuy Hoa is so boring the arrival of a plane is enough to cause hysteria. In 1955 after the Geneva Accords, the Vietminh withdrew north of the 17th parallel, so President Diem dropped into Tuy Hoa for a visit. Over 50,000 peasants turned up, mobbing the field when his small plane arrived, almost trampling Diem. The US Information Service photographed the frenzied welcome as proof the peasants and townspeople were overjoyed to be rid of oppressive communism.

DAI LANH BEACH

About 35 km south of Tuy Hoa is Dai Lanh, a picturesque fishing village with red-tile roofs. There's a high vantage point in the area known as Cap Varella, with sweeping views. Dai Lanh Beach extends along Highway 1; at the southern end it becomes a sand dune area that connects with the 30-km-long Hon Gom Peninsula, another scenic area. Sheltered in here is Vung Coo, one of the nicest beaches on the coast. The area around Hon Lon Island off the coast is good for diving, but there are no facilities as yet. Accommodations are scarce in these parts, but you can stay at Tuy Hoa, or just travel the extra 85 km from Dai Lanh to Nha Trang.

NHA TRANG

Established as a port town in the 1920s, Nha Trang now has a population of 250,000, and serves as capital of Khanh Hoa Province. Fishing is the major industry. Although Nha Trang is one of the most developed of all the beaches in Vietnam, beach "infrastructure" is largely confined to the rental of umbrellas, deck chairs, and inner tubes. In contrast to Thailand's coastal regions, there are no dive shops on the shore. Some prefer it this way—no jet skis or parasailing to disturb the tranquil setting. Nha Trang is pleasant for cycling, with wide boulevards and little traffic.

SIGHTS

Cham Towers

On the north side of Nha Trang, across Xom Bong Bridge, are the best-preserved Cham towers in central Vietnam, the sanctuary of Po Nagar. The towers were constructed between the 7th and 12th centuries. In the 9th century, warriors believed to hail from the Srivijaya kingdom of Sumatra ransacked the temple, plundering a linga of precious metal. Later, marauding Khmers removed a gold linga and other items. In the 16th century Nha Trang was the last stronghold of the Cham, before they were overrun by powerful Viet forces from the north. Today, only four of the sanctuary's original eight towers remain. The octagonal pillars that formed the original entrance have been completely rebricked. Though there is a lot of obvious new brick and concrete reconstruction on the north tower, the lichen-coated portions are clearly original masonry. The towers all face eastward. There are magnificent views of the surrounding area from the hill—a quiet and relaxing place.

A small on-site museum displays early plans of the site, as well as photos of French excavations. But the site itself is no museum: these smoke-stained towers are still used for spiritual purposes. Pilgrims make a circuit of the shrines, the main object of devotion the Uma statue in the north tower.

Three of the towers shelter lingas—phallic sculptures symbolic of Shiva and royalty, and popular objects of devotion in Cham art. A linga is usually coupled with a yoni, representing the female organs and symbolizing fertility. The linga

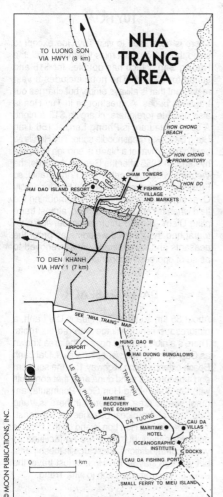

NHA TRANG AREA

TO LUONG SON
VIA HWY1 (8 km)

HON CHONG BEACH

HON CHONG PROMONTORY

CHAM TOWERS

HON DO

HAI DAO ISLAND RESORT

FISHING VILLAGE AND MARKETS

TO DIEN KHANH
VIA HWY 1 (7 km)

SEE "NHA TRANG" MAP

AIRPORT

HUNG DAO III

HAI DUONG BUNGALOWS

MARITIME RECOVERY DIVE EQUIPMENT

MARITIME HOTEL

DA TUONG

CAU DA VILLAS

OCEANOGRAPHIC INSTITUTE

DOCKS

CAU DA FISHING PORT

SMALL FERRY TO MIEU ISLAND

0   1 km

© MOON PUBLICATIONS, INC.

and yoni structure has spouts and drains for carrying water away in ceremonies. As you approach from the entrance gate you'll see the first tower, sheltering a small linga on a solid base. The tower is in bad condition. The next tower encases a meter-high stone linga on a lotus base. At the back, the northwest tower harbors a small but exquisite yoni and linga; two elaborate ceremonial fans stand behind the altar.

The main shrine is the north tower, which originally sheltered a gold linga. The precious linga was stolen by the Khmers; in its place, a statue of Uma was constructed in the 11th century. The 23-meter-high tower is a masterpiece of Cham art; its richly decorated roof remains relatively intact. At the entrance to the tower stand two huge sandstone pillars covered with inscriptions describing offerings to the goddess within; above the

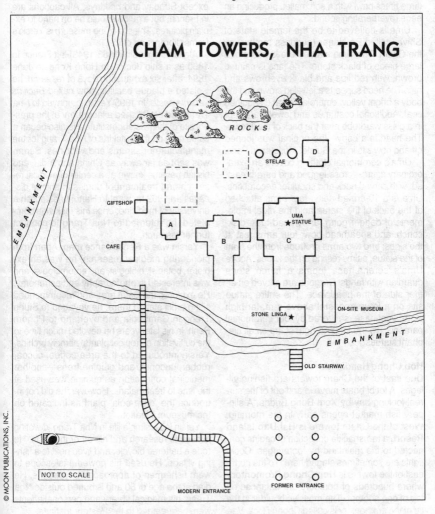

CHAM TOWERS, NHA TRANG

ROCKS

EMBANKMENT

STELAE

⬭ ⬭ ⬭ [D]

GIFTSHOP

A

UMA
★ STATUE

B

C

CAFE

STONE LINGA ★

ON-SITE MUSEUM

EMBANKMENT

OLD STAIRWAY

○ ○

FORMER ENTRANCE
○ ○

○ ○

○ ○

NOT TO SCALE

MODERN ENTRANCE

© MOON PUBLICATIONS, INC.

entrance doorway are three carved *apsaras* (celestial dancers). The Uma shrine is of the "wish granting" variety—patronized not only by Cham Hindus, but also by Chinese and Vietnamese Buddhists. The shrine is considered a source of miraculous cures and attracts its share of beggars. Visitors make offerings of fruit, flowers, incense, and candles; some prostrate themselves before the Uma statue, while an attendant hits a large brass bowl with a soft mallet, producing an eerie reverberating sound.

Uma is believed to be the female state of Shiva, called Po Nagar (goddess mother) by the Cham. The Uma statue here is made of a large piece of black stone. The face is painted brown, with red lips and black eyebrows and hair. The head supports a jeweled crown and the body a bright yellow embroidered and sequined coat. Additional costumes and jewelry are kept in a glass wardrobe near the back of the interior. The head is a copy—the original was lopped off and now sits in the Guimet Museum in Paris.

Uma's ceremonial clothing covers an extraordinary figure—cross-legged and bare-breasted, with carved neck and shoulder decorations. Uma is a 10-armed deity: four arms attached at the back of the statue hold the ritual implements of dagger-gong, arrowhead-tusk, diskconch, and spearhead-bow; four arms rest at the sides; and two arms protrude from the front of the statue, palms resting on the knees. Above Uma's serene face looms a fierce stone guardian with fangs. Dragons are carved on either side of the headpiece. The entire statue sits on a lotus pedestal above a meter-high stone yoni-base, sheltered by four ceremonial parasols. To the left and right stand small elephant statues.

Hon Chong Headland

Due east of the Cham towers are fishing villages. A lot of boats move in and out of the surreal-looking bay by Xom Bong Bridge. A slippery fish market opens early in the morning. West of the Cham towers is **Hai Dao Island Resort,** a ramshackle collection of cabins connected to the mainland by footbridges. Cockfights are sometimes staged here. To the northeast of the towers is **Hon Chong Promontory** where hundreds of boulders are balanced on top of one another. The massive boulder at the tip of the promontory is called Chong Rock. Various legends are associated with this boulder, which is said to bear the imprint of a large hand. There are shrimp farms in the vicinity and various lookouts, one with a refreshment stall.

Yersin Museum

At the north end of Tran Phu Boulevard behind Nha Trang's Pasteur Institute is a small but fascinating Yersin Museum, open 0730-1100 daily except Sunday and holidays. All captions are in French, but a guide should be on hand to explain pictures. The site of the museum is Yersin's former library and office.

Alexandre Yersin (1863-1943) left France in 1890 as a ship doctor. In Hong Kong, in June 1894, after six exhausting days of research, he isolated a plague bacillus, now called *Bacillus yersinia pestis*. In 1895 Yersin journeyed to Nha Trang and established a laboratory at the present site of the Pasteur Institute. He also began a cattle farm on the outskirts of Nha Trang for the manufacture of serums and vaccines. Serum was sent as far away as China and India, and his lab became known as a center of medical research and treatment of domestic animal diseases. In 1902 he went to Hanoi to establish a university of medicine; once this task was completed, he returned to Nha Trang to conduct further research.

Yersin was a Renaissance man. Apart from pioneering medical research, he was an explorer, botanist, biologist, and entomologist, and was interested in photography and astronomy. He explored the Dalat area and recommended siting a hill station there; he voyaged to Stung Treng in Cambodia and overland to Phnom Penh. In his later years he devoted much time to the cultivation of tropical plants, namely orchids. Yersin introduced to the area coffee, cocoa, rubber, coconut, and quinine trees—another medicinal connection as quinine was used at the time to treat malaria. However, he did not introduce the "coca-cola" plant as indicated on the museum's leaflet.

Yersin led a simple life in Nha Trang, devoting himself to research and his other interests. He rode a battered bicycle, and lived next to a fishing village. He used his powerful telescope to warn fishermen of approaching typhoons. He died at the age of 80 and is buried outside Nha Trang; his medical library and personal effects were bequeathed to the Pasteur Institute.

It was on Yersin's recommendations that his laboratory in Nha Trang and Dr. Albert Calmette's laboratory in Saigon were upgraded to the level of Indochina Pasteur Institutes, the first established outside Paris. Pasteur Institutes later appeared in Hanoi and Dalat, and microbiology labs opened in Hué, Vientiane, and Phnom Penh. The Pasteur Institutes in Vietnam continue producing vaccines and conducting research, but the budget is limited and the equipment old. Work continues now at Pasteur Institutes on a greater riddle—AIDS—though here it's probably limited to testing the Vietnamese for the presence of HIV infection.

Pagodas and Churches

On the northwest side of Nha Trang is **Long Son Pagoda,** an active temple featuring an unusual red brass Buddha on a wooden lotus pedestal. On top of a hill behind the pagoda is a massive white Buddha on a lotus throne. Embedded in the octagonal base are seven stucco likenesses of Buddhist martyrs, monks, and nuns who died protesting the repressive Diem regime. Several immolated themselves. The white Buddha was built in their memory in 1963.

On the other side of the tracks, east of the railway station, is **Nha Trang Cathedral,** complete with stained glass windows and French Gothic lines. It was built in the 1930s; daily masses are held early morning and late afternoon.

huge Buddha at Long Son Pagoda

RECREATION

Marine pursuits are the chief draw in Nha Trang—lazing around the beach soaking up the rays, taking a day-trip by boat to outlying islands. Assuming, of course, there are no typhoons. A smattering of other sights include the Cham towers to the north of Nha Trang. Skip the Oceanographic Institute to the south. It may once have been a center of marine study, but today offers only a motley collection of stuffed and pickled sealife, and a few live specimens. Displays are poorly presented, and half the tanks are empty. Did the creatures escape?

Nha Trang Beach

Nha Trang's palm-fringed beachfront stretches for five km. Hop on a bicycle, cruise along Tran Phu Boulevard, and pick your spot. Beachfront cafés provide shelter and drinks; a number of places rent beach umbrellas and deck chairs. The "civilized" end of the beach is from Vinagen Café northward; south of Vinagen the beach is more pristine. Roving vendors sell fruit and seafood; others offer beach massages. The water is slightly surfy in Nha Trang. Watch out for the rip tide—this is the Pacific Coast. The beach drops off very quickly, and soon you're out of your depth and in an undertow. Typhoons are a problem at Nha Trang, as elsewhere along the coast—those coconut trees can bend right over when there's a good wind in progress. The typhoon season is roughly October to mid-December. The high season at Nha Trang is in July and August when Vietnamese vacationers arrive in droves.

Islands Near Cau Da

Hon Tre (Bamboo Island) has beaches and sandy coves where fishing communities live—you can see people repairing nets. They use a basket boat *(thung chai)* to commute between the fishing boats anchored offshore and the beach. The *thung chai* is made of woven bamboo strips covered with tar; it's puzzling how these round coracles are steered.

Only one square kilometer in size, **Hon Mun** (Black Island) harbors some of the most pristine coral reefs and marine life in the area—

somehow it has managed to escape the dynamite fishing that has destroyed many nearby coral reefs. The World Wide Fund for Nature, based in Switzerland, is lobbying to establish Hon Mun as a marine park.

Vietnam is gifted with a 3,200-km coastline, harboring a diverse range of marine resources, but these habitats are under severe threat. Many coral reefs have been destroyed by dynamite fishing, coral mining, overfishing, pollution, and coastal development. The local government turns a blind eye to these practices; the Marine Resource Protection Department does not even have a patrol boat.

Outlying Islands

To the north of Nha Trang is **Hon Cu Lao,** an island off the coast with a monkey-rearing farm. The island has a very shallow approach with sharp, broken coral. There's a $2 landing fee; a bag of popcorn to feed the monkeys costs another $2. Some tour operators in Nha Trang will arrange car and boat transportation to reach the island, usually for $15 a head. Up to 100 monkeys live on the island, bred for export to Malaysia and Singapore and destined for use in traditional medicine.

Another traditional medicine ingredient highly sought after in Nha Trang is the swallow nest,

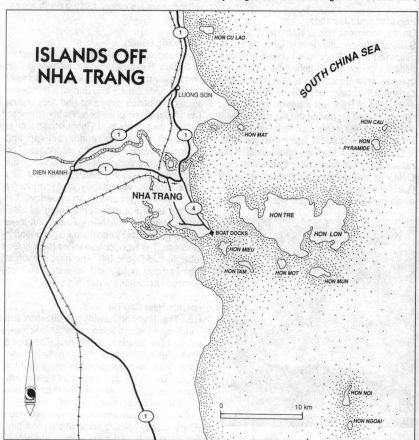

VISITING THE ISLANDS

Day-tripping to offshore islands by chartered fishing boat is popular in Nha Trang. You can swim and snorkel, dine on seafood aboard the boat, and visit a beach and fishing village. Weather permitting, chartered boats leave at 0900 from Cau Da Dock at the southern tip of Nha Trang. Deals vary: most itineraries include a full-day boat trip, taking in three to five islands—Hon Tre, Hon Mun, Hon Mot, Hon Tam, and Hon Mieu. Adapted fishing boats can carry 20-30 people; trips generally operate on a minimum of 10 people and maximum of 30. The full day-trip from 0900 to 1700 usually costs around $6 per person. Some operators will provide transport from Nha Trang to Cau Da Dock. If not, get there by cyclo or rented bicycle. There's regular lambro service from Dam Market to the dock, too.

You can also make your own trips to the islands from Cau Da. It's easy, for example, to take a small ferry from Cau Da Dock to Bai Mieu fishing village on Mieu Island. Most likely, you can also arrange your own small boat to reach some of the other islands from the Cau Da Dock area.

The choice for operators is a toss-up between Mama Hanh, Mama Linh, the Five Brothers, or Captain Cook. Who knows—by the time you get there, it might even be the Marx Brothers or the Magnificent Seven. They can be a rough bunch around Nha Trang, and competition for boat traffic is fierce, so once you've chosen do not switch allegiances. Operators offer attention-grabbing perks—some guarantee one kilo of seafood per person or will arrange vegetarian fare on request. Most boat operators will make some attempt to provide masks, snorkels, and even fins, but quality and size varies. Five Brothers provides free bicycles to Cau Da Port. Mama Hanh will arrange on-

board massage for $3 a person. **Mama Hanh** operates from Green Hat Café; **Mama Linh** is based out of the Hai Yen Café. The **Five Brothers** (actually one of them is a sister) operate from Vinagen Café, tel. 23591; and **Hoang Yen**, a.k.a. Captain Cook, is at 26 Tran Phu, tel. 22961. Captain Cook is somehow connected with Vietnam Tourism. The **Vien Dong Hotel** runs a shorter tour from 0830 to 1400, covering Mieu, Tam, and Mun Islands for $7 a head, with 7-16 passengers.

Try to direct the itinerary. Some operators are lazy and drop anchor in dull locations for long periods. On the way back to Cau Da, boats sometimes stop to visit an "aquarium" on Hon Mieu. This place is actually a fish-breeding tank and is deadly boring.

Cruising on a Junk

The French company **Voiles Vietnam** runs day cruises from May to September. Its Saigon office is at 17 Pham Ngoc Thach, tel. 296750. The company advertises through hotels in Nha Trang—check the Vien Dong Hotel notice board. Cruises are on a custom-built junk, the *Song Saigon,* with French skipper and Vietnamese crew. Overnight trips are possible: the maximum load is 10 adult passengers plus three children, sleeping in five cabins. Otherwise, for day-trips, the boat can carry up to 35 passengers. A minimum of five or six passengers may be required. Cruises are expensive: a full-day cruise is $60 a person; half-day cruise from 1100 to 1700 $48 a person; a minicruise 0800-1100 or 1400-1700 costs $25 a head. The company can arrange diving equipment. One-day itinerary: board the junk at Hon Tre; sail to the east coast to swim, eat, and visit a fishing village; and return to Nha Trang via the islands of Mun, Mot, Tam, and Mieu.

---

which, consumed in soup, is reputed to be therapeutic—some claim it's an aphrodisiac. Off the coast of Nha Trang are a number of small islands—**Hon Cau, Hon Pyramide, Hon Noi, Hon Ngoai**—where sea swallows (*salanganes*) make their nests. Both the male and female bird secrete a gel-like substance in their saliva that is used to build nests on a cliff crevice or in a cave. The bird chews, retches, and smears its spit to mold a small cup-shaped nest. The nests are usually white, though rarer varieties are orange

and red. When the nest is completed, the female lays two white-and-blue speckled eggs. The nests are collected only twice a year, in spring and fall.

Nest harvesting is a precarious venture. Harvesters rappel down rock faces to reach the nests, steering clear of the poisonous snakes that feed on swallow eggs. The motivation for risking life and limb is the high return on nests—they can fetch up to $2000 a kilogram on the open market.

Marine Sports

Nha Trang has little in the way of the sporting hardware associated with beach resorts in Thailand. Windsurfing equipment can be rented at the southern end of the beach, in the vicinity of the airport. You can also rent fishing tackle and boats through **Khanh Hoa Tourism.** Several diving organizations have tried to make a go in Nha Trang, but to little avail. French scuba diving equipment is available from **Nha Trang Maritime Recovery,** south of central Nha Trang at 44 Da Tuong St., tel. 22327 or 21492; all hotel referrals lead here. Maritime Recovery has equipment for 10 divers. The charge is $40 a day per person for equipment, including boat, two dives, and insurance. A guide is $10 a day; the Vietnamese dive master is navy trained. The coral around Nha Trang is often broken and unspectacular. Some of the better dive spots are the northeast side of Hon Tre, the area around Hon Mun, and the south side of Hon Lon.

ACCOMMODATIONS

Not all hotels in Nha Trang accept foreigners. Some cater to the rampant population of taxi girls in town; others employ guards who will wave you away with a gun, usually from exclusive villas for officials. You'll have to use your best judgment in considering the following listings: prices are often mixed, with a hotel offering $7 rooms in one wing and deluxe suites for $60 in another. Popular backpacker hotels include Thong Nhat, Vien Dong, Khach San 58, and Khach San 62. The classiest hotels are the Khatoco, Cau Dai Villas, and the Maritime Hotel.

In Town

Near the commercial district is the dull **Nha Trang #1 Hotel,** 129 Thong Nhat, tel. 22347, offering 50 rooms for $8-18-25. **Nha Trang #2 Hotel,** nearby at 21 Le Thanh Phuong, tel. 22956, has 30 rooms for $10-15-20. If you arrive late or want to depart early, try **Xuan Son Hotel,** opposite the bus station, 99A Duong 23/10, with 14 rooms for $3; cars for rent.

Beach, North End

Most of Nha Trang's hotels are arrayed down or within a few blocks of Tran Phu Boulevard.

The north end is closer to the business and commercial district of Nha Trang. The magnificent **Post Office Hotel** (Nha Khach Buu Dien) lies just a step away from the Post Office—very convenient for postcards. **Thang Loi,** 4 Pasteur St., tel. 22241, fax 21905, features 55 rooms, along with a 150-seat restaurant and 100-seat conference hall. Rooms range $20-30-38; some cheaper rooms available. **Thong Nhat,** 18 Tran Phu Blvd., tel. 22966, has 86 rooms—$10-12 d with fan, $17-25-30 d with air-con and hot water, $12-14 t with fan, $20 d with air-con and hot water, $27-30 with fridge and phone. Helpful staff can assist with visa extensions, and car, motorcycle, and bicycle rentals.

Beach, Midsection

The strip from Khach San 24 to Khach San 62 contains the greatest concentration of hotels. **Khach San 24,** at 24 Tran Phu, tel. 22671, is a Soviet-style blockhouse with rooms from $10 to $35. **Thuy Duong Hotel,** 36 Tran Phu, tel. 22534, has 11 rooms for $5 s, $10 d.

Vien Dong Hotel, 1 Tran Hung Dao, tel. 21606, fax 21912, has 84 rooms—24 in lower class for $10-18, 20 for $20-25-28, 20 superior rooms for $25-30-35, and another 20 deluxe rooms and suites for $40-60. Vast grounds contain a small pool, deck chairs, tennis courts, and billiard tables. The Vien Dong successfully appeals to a variety of travelers.

Hai Yen Hotel, 40 Tran Phu, tel. 22828, fax 21902, is a large place with good facilities. Fan rooms are $8-10-14, four-bed rooms with public bath $6-8, doubles with air-con and hot water $15-25, a few triples for $25-30, suites for $40-60 with TV, fridge, and phone. **Hung Dao,** at 3 Tran Hung Dao, tel. 22246, has 27 rooms for $6-8; this place is sleazy. Nearby is **Nha Trang #3,** 22 Tran Hung Dao, tel. 23933, a minihotel with two rooms for $20 each and three rooms for $10 each.

Hotel 44, 44 Tran Phu, tel. 22445, offers 54 rooms. Several cost $12-14, but most are $20-24-32. There's one suite the size of an apartment for $45. The more expensive rooms are in a classic old French structure that may have once been an office building; cheaper rooms in outlying wings.

Khach San 58 (Hai Quan), 58 Tran Phu, tel. 22997, is a characterless block with 35 rooms charging $6-7-8 s; $10 air-con; $12-15 air-con

(top) one of the enigmatic stone heads at the Bayon; (bottom left) South Gate, Angkor Thom; (bottom right) ruins of fountain at Neak Pean

(top left) painter at Fine Arts School; (top right) *apsara* bas-relief, Angkor Wat;
(bottom) National Museum, Phnom Penh

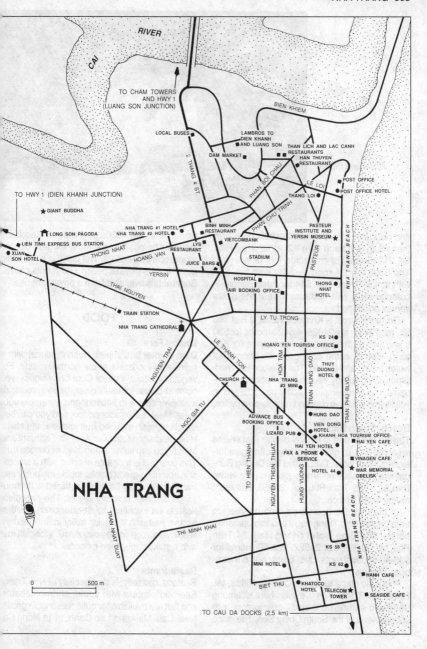

NHA TRANG

Nha Trang Beach

and hot water. You can rent bicycles here. Farther south is **Khach San 62,** at 62 Tran Phu, tel. 21395—lots of character, lots of taxi girls. The hotel has 31 rooms—$6 d with fan, $8 t with fan, $10 s air-con, $14 for three people. A colonial-style villa restaurant near the gates serves good food.

Down the street is **Khatoco Hotel,** 9 Biet Thu St., tel. 23724, fax 21925, with 22 rooms for $30 s and $40 d; there are also two suites for $60 each. Rooms come equipped with phone, hot water, fridge, and air-con. The Khatoco is a modern building run by Khanh Hoa Tobacco Company. The hotel employs spiffy receptionists in yellow and white *ao dais* and runs its own cyclos.

Beach, South End
Toward the airport is a hotel cluster that seems reserved for taxi girls. Desk staff often give foreigners blank looks. Dilapidated **Hai Duong Bungalows** accepts Vietnamese patrons only. **Hung Dao III,** at 96 Tran Phu, tel. 22350, has eight rooms for $6 apiece.

In the Cau Da dock area, about three km from central Nha Trang you'll find two upmarket hotels. **Maritime Hotel** (Hang Hai), 34 Tran Phu, tel. 21969, fax 21922, has 60 rooms for $25-40-60, and rents cars, bikes, and a motorboat. Disco on weekends.

A classic place to stay is **Cau Da Villas,** tel. 22449, fax 21906. The five villas here sit among trees and shrubs on a small promontory with superb views of the South China Sea. The place

was built in the 1920s as Emperor Bao Dai's summer home; 30 spacious, elegant double rooms cost $35 and up. The place is a short hop away from a private beach and tennis courts. Boat rentals available from a private marina.

FOOD

Market Fare
Dam Market has superb fresh produce, with a number of foodstalls at the northeast side. For vegetarian stalls, look for Com Chay signs—you point at dishes of cauliflower, bean sprouts, or whatever else is in season, and assemble your meal. Meat dishes abound too, and you can buy excellent fresh fruit and fruit juices at the stalls. Here be dragons and durians—in February and March you can savor *thanh long,* or dragon fruit. This oval fruit is magenta in color, with a smooth skin sprouting green petals. Inside the pulpy and translucent white flesh is scattered with thousands of black crunchy seeds. The succulent flesh is an excellent thirst-quencher. Another bizarre fruit with a similar milky interior texture is spiny soursop *(mang cau xiem),* a longish fruit with a spiky dark-green exterior.

Restaurants
Seafood, naturally, is the specialty of Nha Trang. Seafood platters with squid, shrimp, lobster, and fish are available for quite reasonable prices. Near Dam Market is **Lac Canh,** at 11 Hang Ca,

tel. 21391. It's always crowded, with lots of beggars hanging around the outdoor seating. Meat and seafood dishes served; you can cook at the table with charcoal braziers. **Thanh Lich,** around the corner at 8 Phan Boi Chau, tel. 21955, features similar fare and fewer beggars. **Hoan Hai,** at 6 Phan Chu Trinh, tel. 23133, serves delicious marinated beef, vegetarian dishes with tofu, and possibly the best spring rolls in Nha Trang. More upmarket and offering terrace dining is **Han Thuyen Restaurant,** on the corner of Phan Boi Chau and Dinh Phung Streets, tel. 22692. Also in the area is **Thuy Trang Seafood,** at 9A Le Loi, near Thang Loi Hotel. **Vietnam Restaurant,** 23 Hoang Van Thu, tel. 22933, is popular with travelers and serves a great hot and sour fish soup.

At 64 Hoang Van Thu St., **Binh Minh,** tel. 21861, serves good food at reasonable prices. Almost right opposite is **Lys,** 117A Hoang Van Thu, tel. 22006. If you fancy swallow saliva, you can order swallow-nest soup for $10 at Lys or Binh Minh. Across town at **Khatoco Hotel Restaurant** swallow-nest soup costs $25; another specialty served in this classy venue is braised sea cucumber.

Hotel restaurants are reasonable in Nha Trang. Try the courtyard-style restaurant at **Khach San 62** or the dining hall at the **Thong Nhat Hotel.**

Cafés

At the intersection of Yersin and Nguyen Trai Streets, several juice-bar cafés sell delicious concoctions of crushed fruit, ice, sugar, and condensed milk—called *sinh to* in Vietnamese. The cafés place red umbrellas out front and are numbered 58 and 60 but have no names. Among the exotic fruit offerings are jackfruit, sapodilla, star apple, custard apple, and dragon fruit. You can also sample durian or coconut ice cream, banana splits, and fresh yogurt. The cafés are great for snacks and breakfast, serving bread and cheese, good coffee, and Lipton tea.

Nha Trang also includes a sprinkling of seaside cafés. Opposite the Hai Yen Hotel is **Hai Yen Café.** Nearer the War Memorial obelisk is **Vinagen Café,** a large beachfront outfit serving seafood, snacks and beer. The beach umbrellas here feature Vinagen logos; Vinagen is a joint-venture Canadian beer. Farther south is

Hanh Café, a collection of odd tentlike structures. Cafés and restaurants fill the nightlife void in Nha Trang. The **Lizard Pub,** at 2 Hung Vuong, near the Vien Dong Hotel, has a beer garden, and nearby Thanh Lan Restaurant serves food.

SHOPPING

Down by the Cau Da Dock area lurk vendors of shell and coral items. These include shell jewelry and grotesque kitschy shell collages. There is a large souvenir shop on Tran Phu Blvd., almost opposite Nha Khach 24, selling lacquerware and pieces inlaid with mother-of-pearl. If you wish to encourage the destruction of coral reefs, there are pieces fashioned from coral. Numerous items made of shell are also found here. Some may be fashioned with shells washed up on the beach, but many more are likely harvested from the sea, the creatures inhabiting them destroyed in the process. All species of sea turtle are highly endangered.

SERVICES AND INFORMATION

Traveler Cafés

Vinagen Café is the major traveler interchange point. The Five Brothers group operates from here, acting as visa extension agents; renting bicycles, motorcycles and cars; arranging boat trips to islands; and organizing minibus trips to Saigon, Dalat, and Hué. Full moon parties are no doubt next on the horizon.

Hanh Café nearby provides similar services and serves great seafood. Hanh is a living example of what happens to entrepreneurs in Vietnam. She started by selling peanuts on the beach and soon attracted a lot of competitors. So she switched to selling crab, which again attracted imitators. Then she launched a boat trip service to the islands and opened a café. Seeing she was doing a good business, the local authorities boosted her café rent to astronomical proportions.

Tourist Information

Khanh Hoa Tourism, tel. 22753, fax 21912, is the provincial tourist authority; the office is on

Le Thanh Ton St. near the gates of Vien Dong Hotel. The organization runs a lot of hotels in Nha Trang, such as the Vien Dong, Hai Yen, Thong Nhat, and Thang Loi. Staff can arrange vehicle rentals—$25 a day for a car, $30 for a minibus. Guides cost $10 a day. The Hai Yen hotel sells sheet maps of Nha Trang, as do other hotels, but the maps are most likely out of date.

Hoang Yen Tourism, 26 Tran Phu, tel. 22961, offers boat trips, guides, transport, and long-distance minibuses for groups of 8-10 people. Like Saigon, Nha Trang has an official information line—dial 108 for info on rail and air travel, car rentals, and cultural and sporting events. Sounds too good to be true? The hotline will even arrange a wake-up call.

Services
Vietcombank, 17 Quang Trung St., will change major currencies, in cash or traveler's checks. The main **post office** is at the north end of Nha Trang at **2 Tran Phu Boulevard.** The **fax and phone center** is a few kilometers south at 50 Le Thanh Ton St., half a block from the beach. For **TNT Express** courier service, phone 21043.

Visa Extensions
Agents can handle visa extensions—$20 for a one-month extension through Thong Nhat Hotel, $25 for the same via Vinagen Café. A one-week extension costs $15. Extensions usually require a day to process.

GETTING THERE AND AWAY

By Air
There are six flights a week from Nha Trang to Ho Chi Minh City ($45), four flights a week to Hanoi ($130), and sometimes a flight to Danang ($55). Nha Trang airport is located right near the beach. **Vietnam Airlines** office in Nha Trang is at 86 Tran Phu St., tel. 21147. There's another airline booking office at 12B Hoa Tam, tel. 23797.

By Rail
Nha Trang to Saigon on CM6 or CM7 train is $17 soft seat, $23-27 hard sleeper, and $30 soft sleeper. Nha Trang to Hanoi on the same trains costs $50 soft seat, $70-80 hard sleeper, and $95 soft sleeper. The CM6 express has no

hard seats—it's the most expensive Reunification Express train; other trains are cheaper.

By Bus
Hai Yen Café and Vinagen Café maintain sign-up lists for traveler minibuses. Sign up at least a day before your intended departure. Vinagen Café can organize a six-day Central Highlands trip headed north for $350 for a minibus, 6-10 passengers. You can negotiate an extra two days for the run from Hué to Hanoi. If you want to move faster, the cafés can organize a one-day run from Nha Trang to Hoi An/Danang for $15 a head. The minibus takes 8-10 passengers, departs 0500, and arrives 1600 in Hoi An. Minibuses to Dalat are $7 a head, five hours; $10 a head to Saigon, 10-11 hours.

Lien Tinh Express Bus Station is on the west side of Nha Trang near Long Son Pagoda. Crack-of-dawn departures head north to Qui Nhon, Quang Ngai, Danang, Hué, Vinh, and Hanoi; to Central Highlands destinations Buon Ma Thuot, and Pleiku; and south to Dalat, Phan Rang, and Saigon. There's an advance bus booking office on Le Thanh Ton, near Vien Dong Hotel. You can also purchase advance tickets through a hotel travel agent. If you want to catch a bus later in the day, head out to Highway 1 and flag down a passing express bus. You can take a moto or lambro to Highway 1. Go to Dien Khanh, seven km to the west if headed for Dalat or Saigon; or Luong Son, eight km north of Nha Trang if traveling north. Three-wheel lambros operate as shuttles to these Highway 1 junctions, connecting to Dam Market. A bit north of Dam Market on 2 Thang 4 St. is a local bus station, with battered Renault vans that run to destinations mostly within 100 km of Nha Trang—about all a Renault engine can take without overheating.

GETTING AROUND

The easiest way of getting around Nha Trang is by rented bicycle. Motos and cyclos patrol the streets. Cyclo drivers can be on the aggressive side—their radar picks you up, they lock on, and relentlessly pursue you down the street.

Car Rentals: A number of places rent cars and minibuses—four-, eight-, 12-, or 24-seat vehicles for $25 and up. Hotels can arrange this transport too.

Motorcycle and Bicycle Rentals: A number of bicycle and motorcycle rental operators can be found around Hai Yen and Vien Dong Hotels, along Tran Phu, Le Thanh Ton, and Tran Hung Dao boulevards. Vinagen Café rents 20 bicycles for 50 cents a day each; motorcycles cost $5 for 50cc, $7 for 70cc, and $10 for 125cc models. Rent a car, motorcycle, or bicycle on

Tran Hung Dao near Hung Dao Hotel; around the corner next to the tourist office on Le Thanh Ton is a motorcycle and bicycle rental outlet; two more rental places are located in front of Vinagen Café and Hotel 44. The Vien Dong and Hai Yen Hotels also rent bicycles. Farther north on Tran Phu Boulevard, there's a bicycle and motorcycle rental place opposite Thuy Duong Hotel; Hoang Yen Tourism and Thong Nhat Hotel both rent bicycles for $1 a day.

SOUTH OF NHA TRANG

CAM RANH BAY

As recently as 1990, some 20 to 30 Russian warships, including submarines and an aircraft carrier, were based at Cam Ranh Bay. The two US-made runways were home to 40 naval and military aircraft, including Tu-95 naval reconaissance aircraft and a squadron of MiG-23 fighters. Some 7,000 Russian sailors and their dependents called Cam Ranh home, though it never developed the raucous atmosphere once associated with the American naval bases in the Philippines.

After the Americans pulled out of the Philippines, the Russians began to pack up and leave Cam Ranh Bay, and, in 1992, the Russian press reported the last major battleship had sailed back to Vladivostok. However, in 1993 a Russian guided missile cruiser was sighted in the South China Sea. The Russians admitted the cruiser was indeed stationed at Cam Ranh Bay, claiming it was required to protect Russian merchant ships from pirates. Vietnam probably wants Russian cruisers in the area to deflect Chinese claims of sovereignty to the Spratly Islands, and to ensure security for joint Russian-Vietnamese oil and gas explorations off the coast. There is a large signal intelligence station at Cam Ranh, capable of monitoring the movements of the Chinese South Sea Fleet. The Russian Cam Ranh agreement with Vietnam runs until the year 2000.

PHAN RANG

Phan Rang is hell on wheels—noisy, dirty, unpleasant. It's strung out along Highway 1, with trucks and buses barreling through day and

night, spraying everything with dust and diesel fumes as drivers hit their airhorns. In the midst of all this is a busy market, with a temple to one side. The 100-year-old temple has a pink exterior and bright red interior, and is dedicated to the deified Chinese general Quan Cong. A statue of black-bearded Quan Cong sits at the back of the temple; lining the way to the altar are Quan Cong's weapons, mounted on long poles. The main sight of Phan Rang, **Thap Cham Towers,** is six km to the northwest; an equal distance to the east is **Ninh Chu Beach.**

Accommodations
Hotels line Highway 1, most run by Ninh Thuan Tourism. Don't expect anything fancy; try and get rooms away from the highway. At the south end of town is **Huu Nghi Hotel,** 354 Thong Nhat, tel. 22606, a three-story hotel with 21 rooms, half of them $10 double, the rest $12-24. **Thong Nhat II,** at 194 Thong Nhat, tel. 22942, features seven rooms for $6 s or $8 d. **Thong Nhat I,** just up the street at 99 Thong Nhat, is a four-story building with rooms $15 and up. **Khach San Phan Rang,** 13 Thong Nhat, near the bus station, tel. 23057, has 17 rooms—$4 s or $9 d; triples available.

Food
Eateries are located along the main drag, Thong Nhat. There are a few others on Le Hong Phong, such as **Quan An** restaurant at number 18. The second floor dining room at **Huu Nghi Restaurant,** about 100 meters south of Huu Nghi Hotel on Thong Nhat, is the best in town, serving such delicacies as wild boar tongue, calf heart, grilled sparrow, and grilled mud fish. If those don't turn your crank, choose from regular fare like chicken

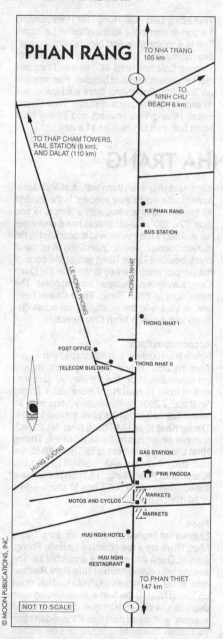

PHAN RANG

TO NHA TRANG
105 km

TO NINH CHU
BEACH 6 km

TO THAP CHAM TOWERS,
RAIL STATION (6 km),
AND DALAT (110 km)

KS PHAN RANG

BUS STATION

THONG NHAT

LE HONG PHONG

THONG NHAT I

POST OFFICE

TELECOM BUILDING

THONG NHAT II

HUNG VUONG

GAS STATION

PINK PAGODA

MARKETS

MOTOS AND CYCLOS

MARKETS

HUU NGHI HOTEL

HUU NGHI
RESTAURANT

TO PHAN THIET
147 km

NOT TO SCALE

© MOON PUBLICATIONS, INC.

and beef. A specialty on the menu is gecko
(dông)—eaten raw with vegetables, grilled, or
roasted with green mango. Gecko is a popular
specialty in Phan Rang restaurants. The lizards
are dipped in batter and pan-fried, or sliced into
slivers and served with a green mango salad.
Escher-like piles of squirming geckos are sold by
the kilo at Phan Rang's market.

Transportation

Highway 1 passes right through town. Phan Rang
bus station is at the north end of town. The train
station is six km out on the Dalat Road at Thap
Cham. You can find motos and cyclos around
Phan Rang bus station, and close to the market.

VICINITY OF PHAN RANG

Thap Cham Towers

Thap Cham Towers (Po Klong Garai) consists of
three towers and a brick platform from the 13th
century. The towers are a mix of old lichen-covered brick and brand-new graffiti-covered brick;
despite the rebricking and concrete ornaments,
the site is impressive. The two smaller towers
have nothing inside. The largest tower houses
bats and features a lintel supporting a dancing
six-armed Shiva, guardian deity of the site. The
door to this tower is locked—see the gatekeeper
for the keys. Inside is a small Nandin, or bull statue: on ceremonial occasions, Cham descendants offer herbs to this statue. Farther in you'll
find a mukha-linga altar (stylized phallus, symbol
of Shiva the Creator) under a conical parasol,
surrounded by a wooden frame. The face painted on the linga represents the head of Shiva;
the setting in a yoni base allows water to drain
away in ceremonies. Cham living in the Phan
Rang area and around the province hold an annual festival at these towers.

From the towers there are commanding views
over the entire valley. If you look past the entrance booth for the towers, you can see extensive railyards with hangar-like buildings. Thap
Cham was a strategic base for the French, and
heavily defended as the junction of the north-
south line and the line to Dalat. The railway from
Thap Cham to Dalat operated from 1930 to
1964, when it was shut down by Vietcong attacks. The French line used a *crémaillère*

Thap Cham Towers

17th century. Another group of decayed towers called **Hoa Lai** (Yan Bakran) lie 16 km north of Phan Rang, off the road to Nha Trang. Some Cham descendants live in the village of **Tuan Tu,** about five km south of Phan Rang. The men wear white turbans with red tassels hanging over the ears and a white costume; the women wear head-scarves. There are intermittent Cham festivals in the Phan Rang area, centering around Thap Cham Towers.

Ninh Chu Beach

The ride out to Ninh Chu Beach, about six km

pothook) system of switchbacks. Though the Dalat station still exists and the track is good for some 15 km out of Dalat, there are at present no plans to reinstate the service.

Thap Cham Towers are six km from Phan Rang, on the Dalat road, near Thap Cham rail station. You can visit Thap Cham en route to or from Dalat if you have your own transportation; otherwise, if leaving Phan Rang, get a moto to drop you at the towers, then flag down a vehicle heading to Dalat. If arriving by rail on the route to or from Saigon, you can exit at Thap Cham station, walk over to the ruins, then board another train. To reach Thap Cham Towers by road from Phan Rang, take the Dalat road until you cross the railway tracks; close by is a six-km marker stone. Turn right after the stone and you'll see the towers about 400 meters away on a cactus-covered hilltop.

Other Cham towers in the Phan Rang vicinity are in very poor condition. **Thap Po Rome** is about 15 km southwest of Phan Rang—named after the last king of Champa, who ruled in the

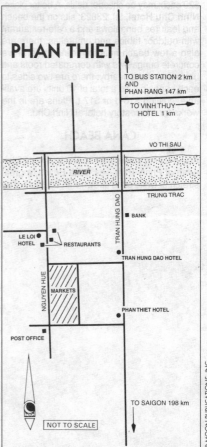

PHAN THIET

TO BUS STATION 2 km
AND
PHAN RANG 147 km

TO VINH THUY →
HOTEL 1 km

VO THI SAU

RIVER

TRUNG TRAC

■ BANK

LE LOI
HOTEL ●
■ ■ RESTAURANTS

TRAN HUNG DAO

TRAN HUNG DAO HOTEL

NGUYEN HUE

MARKETS

PHAN THIET HOTEL ●

POST OFFICE ●

TO SAIGON 198 km

NOT TO SCALE

MOON

© MOON PUBLICATIONS, INC.

from Phan Rang, is well worth it. On the way you'll see lots of rice paddies, grape trellises, cacti hedgerows, and salt pans. Set back from the beach is a hill with large rock formations and several small temples. The beach is fringed with coniferous trees, not palms, an indicator of the region's aridity. Ninh Chu features a long narrow white-sand beach and a fishing village with basket boats *(thung chai).*

There are two hotels in the area. The three-story **Huong Bien Hotel,** tel. 23216, is in the middle of nowhere, 1.5 km back from the beach on the road to Phan Rang. The 18 rooms run $20 each; may be cheaper deals. A better place, **Ninh Chu Hotel,** tel. 23823, sits on the beach and features bungalows and a café-restaurant with outdoor tables and umbrellas; there are also a few beach huts to recline under. Five concrete bungalows with corrugated roofs and balconies stand nearby; there are two sides to each bungalow, so a total of 10 units are available, costing $16 d or $17 t. Plans are in the works for a four-story hotel at Ninh Chu.

CANA BEACH

About 35 km south of Phan Rang, and 123 km north of Phan Thiet, lies Cana Beach, a great stretch of white sand strewn with boulders. The water is a beautiful turquoise; onshore, the area has been colonized by prickly pear cacti. **Haison Hotel,** tel. 64589, has doubles for $10; **Khach San Cana,** tel. 64554, is $10 d and $15 t; taxi girls hang around the hotel. Both hotels include bland but adequate restaurants.

PHAN THIET

Phan Thiet is an old Cham outpost of 75,000 people that supports a large fishing fleet and is famous for *nuoc mam,* or fish sauce. The unpleasant smell of fish and fish sauce permeates the downtown area, since the Phan Thiet River cutting through the center of town is packed with boats. Phan Thiet has a beachfront a few km to the east of town, but a bigger draw is the sand dunes at Mui Ne Beach, 22 km east of town. Local buses ply the route during the day from Phan Thiet bus station.

There are half a dozen places to stay in town, not all receptive to foreign faces. **Phan Thiet Hotel,** at 40 Tran Hung Dao, tel. 21694, costs $17-20 a room; no hot water. Toward the seashore is the more isolated **Vinh Thuy Hotel,** tel. 22394, with over 60 air-con rooms in the $26-36 range. Phan Thiet lies right off Highway 1, almost 200 km from Saigon. The nearest train station is at Muong Man, 12 km to the west.

DALAT

Dalat is an entire French town—railway station, cathedral, schools, shops, villas—plunked down in the Vietnamese highlands. With its pine forests, rolling hills, and tranquil lakes, the area could pass for any place in France—which explains its appeal to the French.

At 1,475 meters in elevation, Dalat provides a cool respite from the heat. In 1897 the first explorer of the area, Alexandre Yersin, recommended French settlement as a retreat for those suffering from the tropical climate of the lowlands. Governor Paul Doumer established a research center for agriculture and meteorology.

Within 15 years, the town was established; in 1933 it was linked by rail to the coast. Land grants were made to French, Chinese, and Vietnamese to develop the area. Tea, coffee, and rubber plantations flourished, along with intense vegetable cultivation. By the 1940s the hill station of Dalat was slated to become the administrative nerve center for the whole of French Indochina, and was called Le Petit Paris. Building in Dalat continued during WW II after Vichy-appointed Governor-general Jean Decoux concluded an agreement accepting the presence of Japanese troops in Vietnam. In March 1945

SAIGON–TO–NHA TRANG BIKE ROUTE

This roundtrip route, including rest days in Dalat and Nha Trang, takes about 15 days, with five days for each leg of the route. If you want to dawdle, take longer rest stops and allow 20 days for the route. On a motorcycle, the route can easily be accomplished in half the time.

Saigon-to-Dalat Leg

On this route, from Saigon it's 60 km to Dau Giay, a further 90 km to Suoi Thien, then 38 km to Bao Loc and a final 119 km to Dalat. To avoid heavy traffic out of Saigon and to avoid getting lost, try to have a travel agency or traveler café take you and your bicycle by minibus the 60 km to Dau Giay, the junction of Highway 1 and Route 20. From here, ride 90 km to **Suoi Thien,** where you can stay at **Suoi Tien Guesthouse,** run by Saigon Tourism, for $6 bungalow, $10 d, or $25 for a four-bed room. Suoi Tien to Bao Loc is only 38 km but mostly uphill with a steep grade. In **Bao Loc,** stay at **Seri Hotel,** $35 a room; or **Bao Loc Hotel,** $10 with fan. Bao Loc to Dalat is 119 km. Start early—it's a long ride with great views. The undulating terrain rises from Bao Loc at 850 meters to Di Linh at 1,010 meters; it's a little steeper from Di Linh to Dalat at 1,475 meters. The last 10 km or so is straight up. Rest in Dalat—there are some great bike rides in the vicinity.

Dalat-to-Nha Trang Leg

From Dalat it's 116 km to Phan Rang, and a further 110 km to Nha Trang. From there you can

backtrack to Phan Rang. From Dalat center, follow Hung Vuong Road out of town to the east. This road, actually Route 20, is not used by cars because it's potholed and in poor shape, but that's less of a problem for cyclists; the lack of motor traffic makes the ride pleasant. Dalat to Phan Rang is 116 km downhill, with spectacular scenery. Stay at **Ninh Chu Beach,** six km northeast of at Phan Rang, instead of Phan Rang. Phan Rang to Nha Trang is 110 km, with no stop permitted in Cam Ranh Bay. With a headwind, the ride takes maybe 10 hours, with a tailwind seven hours—you'll get one or the other depending on the season. After a rest in Nha Trang, take the same route back to Phan Rang. If short of time, cut Nha Trang out of the itinerary.

Phan Rang-to-Saigon Leg

From Phan Rang it's 42 km to Cana Beach, a further 123 km to Phan Thiet, then 120 km to Long Khan, and a final 78 km to Saigon. In Cana Beach, stay at **Khach San Cana,** $10 double, $15 for three; or **Haison Hotel,** $10 for two. In Phan Thiet, try **Phan Thiet Hotel,** $17-20, no hot water; or **Vinh Thuy Hotel,** $26-36. Cyclists will be pleased to know the coastal strip from Phan Rang to Phan Thiet is one of the most arid regions in Vietnam. The next leg is Phan Thiet to Long Khan, 120 km inland near Xuan Loc. Stay at **Hotel Hoa Binh,** $20 double. The last 78 km into Ho Chi Minh City is very busy with traffic; if it becomes a problem, flag down a passing bus and load your bike onto the roof.

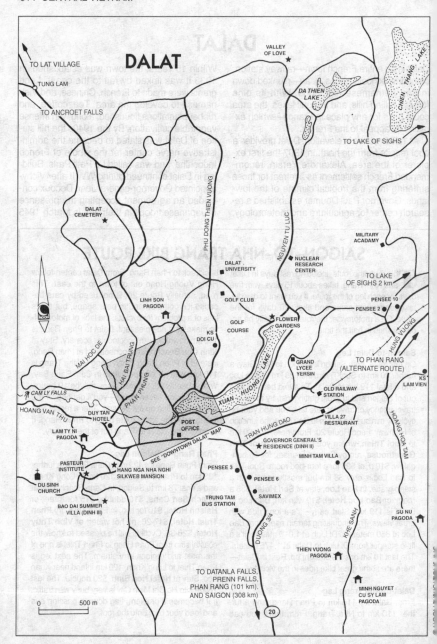

DALAT

TO LAT VILLAGE

TUNG LAM

TO ANCROET FALLS

VALLEY OF LOVE

DA THIEN LAKE

CHIEN THANG LAKE

TO LAKE OF SIGHS

DALAT CEMETERY

PHU DONG THIEN VUONG

MILITARY ACADAMY

NGUYEN TU LUC

NUCLEAR RESEARCH CENTER

TO LAKE OF SIGHS 2 km

DALAT UNIVERSITY

GOLF CLUB

GOLF COURSE

FLOWER GARDENS

PENSEE 10

PENSEE 2

HUNG VUONG

LINH SON PAGODA

MAI HOC DE

HAI BAI TRUNG

KS DOI CU

XUAN HUONG LAKE

GRAND LYCEE YERSIN

TO PHAN RANG (ALTERNATE ROUTE)

KS LAM VIEN

CAM LY FALLS

PHAN PHUNG

OLD RAILWAY STATION

HOANG VAN THU

DUY TAN HOTEL

POST OFFICE

SEE "DOWNTOWN DALAT" MAP

TRAN HUNG DAO

VILLA 27 RESTAURANT

HOANG HOA TAM

LAM TY NI PAGODA

GOVERNOR GENERAL'S RESIDENCE (DINH II)

MINH TAM VILLA

PASTEUR INSTITUTE

DU SINH CHURCH

HANG NGA NHA NGHI SILKWEB MANSION

PENSEE 3

PENSEE 6

SAVIMEX

SU NU PAGODA

BAO DAI SUMMER VILLA (DINH III)

TRUNG TAM BUS STATION

DUONG 3/4

KHE SANH

THIEN VUONG PAGODA

TO DATANLA FALLS, PRENN FALLS, PHAN RANG (101 km), AND SAIGON (308 km)

MINH NGUYET CU SY LAM PAGODA

0   500 m

20

the Japanese learned of Decoux's tardy plans to rebel and overthrew him, imprisoning his administrators and troops. At the conclusion of the war, Indochina fell into turmoil.

Dalat is now a resort town, a favorite with honeymooners and droves of tourists tramping through the former French villas. The Vietnamese wax poetic about Dalat and rave on in awestruck detail about every waterfall and valley, but in fact the scenery is nothing special. The deforestation around Dalat doesn't say much for wilderness conservation, and neither do the stuffed animals parked at various scenic spots. If you're looking for a place to exercise your lungs, however, the hills around Dalat are great for hiking, biking, or breathing in that pine-scented air. Or shoot a few rounds of golf. Dalat market has excellent and varied fresh produce, which means dining out in Dalat is great. A good spot to rest up for a few days and stretch those muscles atrophied from minibus rides.

Dalat is not known for clement weather. It's in the mountains, so rain could put a damper on your visit.

Getting Your Bearings

Dalat centers on Xuan Huong Lake, with the downtown area on the northwest side and exclusive villas on the south side. The heart of downtown Dalat is **Hoa Binh Square,** adjacent to the cinema; steps lead down from here to the Central Market. Motos, taxis, and lambros cluster round the top or bottom of the steps. With its narrow alleys and hilly streets, downtown Dalat is best negotiated on foot. However, if going around the south side of the lake, a bicycle or moto is desirable.

Dalat features some long-winded street names. There's Duong 3 Thang 4, or Duong 3/4, which runs south of Dalat and turns into Highway 20. The figure 3/4 refers to 3 April 1975, the date of the Liberation of Dalat by NVA forces. The cinema is called **Rap Chieu Bong 3/4.** Leading off the cinema is a street called Duong 3 Thang 2, referring to the February 3 anniversary of the 1930 founding of the Communist Party.

To really get into Dalat, you have to get out of it—get above it all into the pine forests, with great views and classic villas. The two tours outlined in the accompanying Special Topics

are best done by bicycle, motorcycle, or moto with some walking involved. You can complete both tours in one long day, back-to-back, but they're better attempted on separate days. Actual cycling and walking time for each tour is around 1.5 hours, so allow at least three hours with stops to complete each tour.

SIGHTS

The Last Emperor

Past the Pasteur Institute lies Dinh III, or **Bao Dai Summer Villa.** The 1930s villa is set in beautiful grounds, with gardens and views. The 25-room villa was the private residence of Bao Dai, the last emperor of Vietnam, who abdicated in 1945. Inside were rooms reserved for Empress Nam Phuong, Prince Bao Long, and Princess Phuong Mai. You can see photos of them on the walls, plus remaining pieces of family furniture. Upstairs, in the royal living quarters, decorated in bright yellow, is a large couch used by the emperor and empress for consultations with their three daughters and two sons.

Bao Dai was born in 1913, and was crowned in 1925 after the death of his father, Emperor Khai Dinh. Groomed by the French as the puppet emperor of Vietnam, Bao Dai was dispatched to Paris for an education, where he acquired a fondness for French women and tennis. Back in Vietnam in 1935, the playboy emperor spent his time in leisure pursuits—chiefly chasing women and hunting—oblivious to the intrigues of the Vietminh. His main palace was in Hué, but he kept villas in various parts of the country. He came to Dalat to hunt, play tennis, fish, and ride horses.

Bao Dai abdicated in 1945 at the request of the Vietminh, allowing Ho Chi Minh to be crowned new "emperor." In 1946, Bao Dai fled to Hong Kong. When the French attempted to regain control of Vietnam after the war, they required Bao Dai to resume his imperial duties, but he fled instead to Europe, shifting from city to city, hiding in cinemas by day and cabarets by night. Comically, Bao Dai was eventually found and returned to Vietnam in 1948, but he quickly slipped back to Europe, claiming he would not wear the crown until true unity and independence prevailed in Vietnam. In 1952 it was said Bao Dai received an official stipend of four million dollars a year, much of it squirrelled away in Swiss bank accounts as insurance against hard times ahead. By the time of the 1954 Geneva conference, Bao Dai lived in permanent exile in a luxurious Cannes chateau with his wife and five children. He kept a Vietnamese mistress in Paris and maintained a steady diet of French courtesans. Much of his time was spent at casinos in Monte Carlo, where he squandered extravagant sums of money. He has never returned to Vietnam.

After a lengthy rash of anti-Bao Dai propaganda, there's now a documentary video on sale in Dalat about the life of the emperor, titled *Riding You to the Palace*. It was produced by Saigon Films for Dalat's centennial. In the communist era, it's odd that this video should be subtitled: *A Sketch of an Unforgettable Epoch of our History.*

The villa is open 0700-1200 and 1330-1700; there's a token entry fee, and extra charge for camera or video. The villa has art deco features, but the interior is now quite modest considering the extravagant tastes of its former occupant. It's likely that many personal effects of the emperor have been removed.

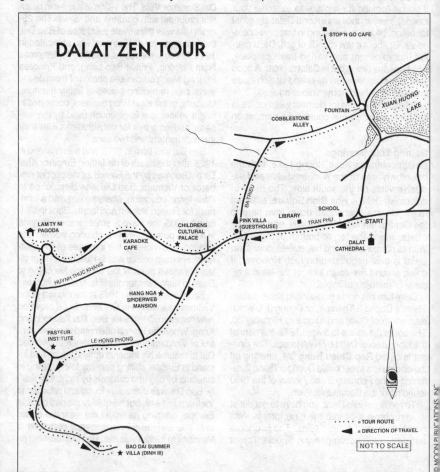

DALAT ZEN TOUR

STOP'N GO CAFE

XUAN HUONG LAKE

FOUNTAIN

COBBLESTONE ALLEY

BA TRIEU

PINK VILLA (GUESTHOUSE)

LIBRARY

SCHOOL

TRAN PHU

START

DALAT CATHEDRAL

CHILDRENS CULTURAL PALACE

LAM TY NI PAGODA

KARAOKE CAFE

HUYNH THUC KHANG

HANG NGA SPIDERWEB MANSION

PASTEUR INSTITUTE

LE HONG PHONG

BAO DAI SUMMER VILLA (DINH III)

····· = TOUR ROUTE

▶ = DIRECTION OF TRAVEL

NOT TO SCALE

MOON PUBLICATIONS, INC.

Other Sights

As a resort town, Dalat will in the future become a base for hikers and bicyclists, as well as rafting trips on the Da Nhim River. At present, sporting amenities are few. You can ride ponies at a few locations around town—the Valley of Love, Lake of Sighs—but they're mainly for photo purposes, with ponies led by a noose. Dalat Pine Lake Golf Course offers 18 holes on 55 acres, designed and landscaped by a Thai company; an international championship was held there in 1993. The original golf course on the site is Vietnam's oldest, established in the 1930s.

Off the northeast tip of the golf course you'll find **Dalat Flower Gardens**—with a modest showing of roses, camellias, lilies, and orchids. Dalat's temperate climate supports many species of flowers, including a large array of orchids. Buy cut flowers at the Central Market. For train buffs, there's a 1.5-hour run from Dalat Station to the village of **Trai Met,** about 10 km from Dalat; the journey winds through vegetable farms. A diesel engine hauls a small wagon with open seating twice daily for $2 per person roundtrip. Or you can hire the locomotive for $12 for a custom trip. Get out and explore Trai Met, where there's a Buddhist temple.

If you haven't had your fill of pagodas and churches in Vietnam by now, Dalat can provide healthy doses of both. **Linh Son Pagoda,** at 120 Nguyen Van Troi, is an active pagoda run by a dozen monks. Built in 1942, it's the center of Buddhism in Dalat. Vietnamese tourists flock to **Thien Vuong Pagoda,** about four km from town to the southeast. The pagoda, constructed in 1958, is pretty dull, but one building houses three massive standing Buddhas made of gilded sandalwood; the figure in the center is the historical Buddha, Sakyamuni. Reached by a path opposite is **Minh Nguyet Cu Sy Lam Pagoda,** dedicated to the bodhisattva Quan Am.

Churches are the landmarks of Dalat. On the south side of town is the towering spire of **Dalat Cathedral;** on the north side is the pink facade of **Domaine de Marie Convent.** In 1942, 300 nuns occupied the convent, and a handful of Vietnamese nuns still reside there. Up on a ridge above Mimosa Hotel is a **Protestant church** built in 1940. Near Cam Ly Falls stands a church with a twist—a small Montagnard church, constructed in 1968, that incorporates elements of animist worship. Another large former convent in this area—**Convent des Oiseaux,** southwest of Dalat—is now a school for ethnic minorities. Past Convent des Oiseaux, along Huyen Tran Cong Chua St., is **Du Sinh,** a small church built in 1955 in Sino-Vietnamese style.

ACCOMMODATIONS

Due to its abundance of colonial buildings, Dalat offers a great range of hotels, villas, minihotels, and guesthouses. However, few accept foreigners. Those that do must obtain "foreigner-dealing licences." At last count about 20 hotels were sanctioned for foreigners; by more than coincidence, 95% are operated by **Lam Dong Tourism.** Foreigners interested in renting villas also must go through Lam Dong Tourism; the few exceptions are those operated by large private companies. Keep an ear to the ground—places get declassified or reclassified, and released to foreign vermin to trample over; other hotels are being built or renovated.

Because of Dalat's high elevation nights can be cool, so hot water is an important consideration. Some hotels, like the budget Phu Hoa, supply hot water for several hours a day with wood-fired heaters. It's difficult to classify some Dalat hotels. A moderate hotel like the Duy Tan or the Haison may feature a main block with $25 rooms and another block with dormitory rooms for $7 a bed.

Budget

Backpackers congregate in half-a-dozen hotels around the center of Dalat. **Phu Hoa Hotel,** 16 Tang Bat Ho St., tel. 22194, has 38 rooms in the $5-10-15 range—the lower end has no bath; the upper end offers bath, bigger room, balcony, and bigger bed. Excellent value; irregular hot water supply. The derelict **Hoa Binh Hotel** at 67 Truong Cong Dinh St., tel. 22787, has run-down $5 s, or $9 d rooms.

The old backpacker standby, the 18-room **Cam Do** at 81 Phan Dinh Phung, tel. 22737, offers singles for $6-11 and doubles for $7-12-17. **Mimosa Hotel,** at 170 Phan Dinh Phung, tel. 22656, is often frequented by traveler minibus tours and offers 32 rooms. Singles are $6, doubles $10-12, some hot water on tap. Close to the Mimosa are

DALAT ZEN TOUR

Apart from a surfeit of French villas, the Vietnamese also inherited a taste for French bread—and poetry and art. As one Vietnamese source phrased it, "The Americans left us Coke, but the French left us poetry." Hanoi and Saigon dominate the art market in Vietnam, but it's towns like Dalat and Hué that are said to inspire the best poetry. So put on your beret, hop on your bike, tuck a baguette under your arm, and set off in search of inspiration.

Starting point for this tour is the traffic island near Dalat Cathedral; in the middle, find a statue of Jesus holding a lamb. If the door's open, it's worth looking inside **Dalat Cathedral** at the stained glass windows imported from Grenoble and woodcarvings of the crucifixion. The cathedral was completed in 1942. Services are held at 0530 and 1700 daily, and at 0530, 0700, and 1600 on Sunday.

This neck of the woods is Catholic Corner, what with the cathedral, Jesus statue, and the former St. Paul of Nazareth School. Dalat at one time was home to three churches, a seminary, two convents, and Catholic schools. An unusual educational facility was the Eau de Vie, a religious order of reformed French prostitutes who set out to reform other prostitutes around the world. Apart from the French influence, Catholicism was bolstered here by an influx of North Vietnamese Catholics after the 1954 partition.

Spiderweb Mansion

Continue past an elementary school and *thu vien* (library) housed in a yellow building. You pass a Bauhaus-like villa, and a three-story pink guesthouse villa, not for foreigners. Farther west is **Dalat Children Cultural Palace.** Catering to children from ages five to 15, it organizes movies, music performances, and camping trips. The Children's Palace was designed by Hang Nga, a Vietnamese architect and sculptor with a flair for the bizarre. Trained in Moscow, Hang Nga first came to Dalat in 1983, fell in love with the architecture and mountain air, and decided to settle here. She lives just up the hill from the palace at Spiderweb Mansion on Huynh Thuc Khang Street. It's easy to spot—look for a towering giraffe. Hang Nga has had trouble convincing the Vietnamese authorities to accept her ideas, and when you visit you can see why—this place actually displays imagination. The garden features wrought-iron spiderwebs, huge stone mushrooms, and a stack of futuristic-looking treehouses—go see this wild and wacky place.

The Last Emperor

Past the Pasteur Institute lies Dinh III, or **Bao Dai Summer Villa.** The 1930s villa is set in beautiful grounds, with gardens and views. The 25-room villa was the private residence of Bao Dai, the last emperor of Vietnam, who abdicated in 1945. For more information, see "Sights" under "Dalat" in the Central Vietnam section.

Poets and Eccentrics

Head downhill for the next stop—**Lam Ty Ni Pagoda.** The sole monk here, Thuc Vien, looks after the pagoda. When he joined the temple in 1968, there

---

dowdy **Thanh The I Hotel,** at 118 Phan Dinh Phung, tel. 22180, with 20 rooms in the $5-7-12 range; and **Thanh The II** at 90 Phan Dinh Phung, tel. 22780, with 14 rooms in the same range.

Near the Central Market, **Thanh Binh Hotel,** at 40 Nguyen Thi Minh Khai, tel. 22909, offers a total of 41 rooms for $7-10 s or $12-20-25 d. **Hoa An Hotel,** on the same street, has 12 rooms for similar prices. Nguyen Chi Thanh Street, leading south of Anh Dao Hotel, features a few small guesthouses. About a kilometer to the southwest of Dalat is **Lam Son Hotel,** at 5 Hai Thuong St., tel. 22362. The 12 rooms go for $10 apiece.

Moderate

In the Central Market area is nondescript **Haison Hotel,** 1 Nyugen Thi Minh Khai, tel. 22379. Block A, the better choice, features $25-35 s, $30-40 d, $40-45 t, and $45-50 for a four-person room. Block B has $10-30 s, $15-35 d, $25-40 t, $30-45 for four-person rooms, and $45 for a five-person room. **Thuy Tien Hotel,** at 7 Duong 3 Thang 2, tel. 22482, offers large doubles for $18-25—expensive for the facilities. **Ngoc Lan Hotel,** at 42 Nguyen Chi Thanh, tel. 22136, has 28 rooms and charges $15 and up per room.

West of central Dalat is **Duy Tan Hotel,** 83 Duong 3 Thang 2, tel. 22216, offering mediocre

were two other resident monks, but since 1975 Vien has lived alone, with a dog to keep him company. Not that he's short on visitors—he receives at least a dozen a day. The brown-robed monk welcomes you to visit his amazing **Divine Calmness Bamboo Garden** on the wonderful way toward drifting rosy clouds. He created the garden himself, and just about everything around it, as he will explain exuberantly. Thuc Vien has not only mastered half a dozen languages but also developed his own elliptical variations of them—he can run you round in circles in English, French, Vietnamese, Thai, or Khmer, with a good dose of surrealism and Zen mixed in. Thuc Vien is a published poet and an accomplished calligrapher of Vietnamese and Chinese script. A profusion of papers, painting, wood creations, and calligraphy fill his workspace. The monk will run you off a piece of calligraphy or art for a donation.

For a chance to see the interior of one of Dalat's fine villas visit the mansion converted into a karaoke café along Tran Phu Street. Continue eastward, past the Dalat Children's Cultural Palace, take a left, and go down the hill. Just after you cross a small bridge, take a narrow alley to the right; this cobblestone alley runs through a section of town that looks like it was lifted straight out of China. It ends near the main vegetable market, with some vegetarian foodstalls.

For a coffee, push up to the cinema in the downtown area, where you'll find **Stop'n Go Café.** The owner of Stop'n Go is Duy Viet, a leading Dalat poet and calligrapher, whose career has included stints as Dalat's town deputy and as a journalist in Saigon. Duy Viet looks like a bohemian—dressed in beret and scarf, chain-smoking. He welcomes travelers to the kitsch and clutter of his souvenir shop and café, overlooking the Central Market. He keeps log books for travelers, which are filled with poetry and calligraphy in 20 languages, plus sketches and photos of famous Vietnamese painters, singers, and poets who've passed through. You say stop and I say go, go, go—the name Stop'n Go Café derives from a haiku-like stanza written by Duy Viet:

> *The world is an inn*
> *The nature is mystical*
> *Human beings are travelers*
> *Stop'n Go*

rooms for $20-25-30 in one wing and $7-12-17 in another. To the southeast, on the outskirts of Dalat, is **Khach San Lam Vien,** at 20 Hung Vuong, tel. 22507. From a distance this place looks like a hospital—the blockhouse has 66 rooms in two wings, in the $20-25 range. You need some form of transportation to commute into town.

On the north side of Xuan Huong Lake is **Hotel Trixaco,** at 7 Nguyen Thai Hoc, tel. 22789. This 14-room mansion charges $35 for an upstairs room with air-con and hot water. In the same area, **Khach San Huong Tra** offers 25 rooms—six in a white building overlooking the lake for $30 each; the rest in another section for $15. The Huong Tra has its own restaurant building facing the lake.

Luxury
Anh Dao Hotel, at 50 Hoa Binh Square, tel. 22384, is one of Dalat's premier hotels. It has 27 clean and renovated rooms in the $30-55 range. On the south side of the lake is **Dalat Hotel,** at 7 Tran Phu, tel. 22363. This is a former colonial hotel from 1907, featuring 100 tourist-class rooms; it's under renovation by the US-HK joint-

venture company Dalat Resort Incorporated (DRI). Dalat's top-rated hotel is the **Hotel Sofitel Dalat Palace** at 12 Tran Phu St., tel. 25444, fax 25666. Sofitel is a trademark of the French group Accor, the world's biggest hotel group. The Palace offers 43 rooms $120-$160 d, and suites $200 and up; swimming pool, tennis courts, and garden café. There are sweeping views of Xuan Huong Lake from the landscaped grounds. The deluxe colonial hotel was originally built in the 1920s, and renovated in 1994.

Classic Hotels
Sleeping with History: Dinh II, the former Governor-general's Residence at 12 Tran Hung Dao, tel. 22092, has eight rooms upstairs—six for $35 each, and two for $45. The spacious rooms feature oversize bathrooms. Book through Lam Dong Tourism, 4 Tran Quoc Toan St., tel. 22125.

Southeast of Dinh II is **Minh Tam Villa,** at 20A Khe Sanh St., tel. 22447. Formerly the summer residence of notorious Madame Nhu (Tran Le Xuan), sister-in-law of President Diem, the villa was constructed in 1936. Larger-than-life

DALAT VILLA TOUR

In 1930 there were an estimated 400 villas in Dalat; by 1953 over a thousand. A favorite of rich French fleeing the stinking heat of Saigon summers. Dalat in 1944 had 5,600 French inhabitants out of a total population of 25,000. Dalat was spared the ravages of the Vietnam War—it was not bombed or mined, and the villas are largely intact, with the French plumbing still in place. The villas are scattered, with the most exclusive ones near the former Governor-general's Residence, on the south side of the lake.

Colonial Dalat can be explored by bicycle (some uphill walking required), moto, motorcycle, or car. If on a bicycle, allow at least three hours to cover the sights. A good place to start is a café perched right over the lake. You can still make out the old French name at the back—La Grenouillère (The Froggery). There's a diving platform out the back; drinks are served under umbrellas on the sundeck. Just down the way is the **Saosang** (Light Star) restaurant and bar, a favorite of Vietnamese wedding revelers. The restaurant features a menu of rabbit, chicken, crab, and shrimp. Under French ownership, the same building was the **Cercle Sportif** clubhouse, dating from 1931. The stadium, completed in 1942, is still there; the nearby buildings are used for gymnastics and karate training.

From here you have to push your bike all the way up to the **Governor-general's Residence,** at the top of a hill—look for the **Dinh II Hotel** sign. The residence was built between 1933 and 1937. Vichy-appointed Governor-general Jean Decoux used the residence as a summer workplace from May to October each year. The residence is open in theory all day, as it's also a hotel, but staff may disappear for lunch. If the building is closed you won't be missing much. The interior is uninspiring, with bland furniture, a Chinese lacquer screen, random souvenir cases, and a stuffed bear—presumably one bagged in a big game hunt around Dalat when the area was still home to big game. The residence has 25 rooms, but the upstairs section is a hotel and official guesthouse, so no touring is permitted. The gardens, with wattle trees, weeping willows, roses, cacti, and bougainvillea, are more interesting, and free. Dinh II offers excellent views over Dalat.

Exclusive Villas

Proceeding east from Dinh II, you wheel along through pine forests and on to a strip of Dalat's more exclusive villas—over a dozen of them. These 1940s villas were renovated in 1992 and are rented to tour groups from France and Hong Kong. French have even returned on nostalgic vacations to villas they once occupied. The area was developed by DRI, US-managed but fronted by a Hong Kong company; the staff received Swiss training. The restaurant in the area is Villa 27; you can stop by and look at the interior.

Farther along Hung Vuong Street, high on a hill, is **Nam Phuong White Villa,** a white three-story French villa with gray shutters and beautiful grounds with rose gardens and palms. You might be able to gain access to the grounds. Empress Nam Phuong, wife of Bao Dai, died in 1963. Farther east, past Khach San Lam Vien, is **Dinh I,** the former

Madame Nhu, nicknamed the "Dragon Lady" for her fiery rhetoric, took off for a conference in Europe in 1963. Shortly thereafter, Diem was killed, and Madame Nhu never came back. There are beautiful rose gardens on the grounds of the villa. Large crowds of visiting Vietnamese and Asian tourists descend daily in tour buses. Rooms go for $25-40; some bungalows are set back from the main hotel building.

Southwest of town, in a pine grove overlooking Dalat, is **Dinh III,** tel. 22449. This is the former summer villa of Bao Dai—live like an emperor for $35 a night. Bookings through Lam Dong Tourism.

Villas: The enticing villas around Dalat are mostly owned and operated by Lam Dong Tourism; foreigners make reservations through agents with advance bookings but walk-ins are possible. Try approaching Lam Dong Tourism, tel. 22496; with hard bargaining you might be able to secure a villa for under $15. However, you might need some form of transportation, as villas are not centrally located.

Near Dinh II are 10 classy French villas, renovated and upgraded by DRI; try the office at 25 Tran Hung Dao St., tel. 22203, fax 21241. Each villa is composed of four or five rooms, with bathroom facilities. There are about 35 rooms al-

workplace of Emperor Bao Dai. Tourist authorities are renovating it for a hotel.

Continue through villa land, go down Tran Quy Cap Street, and turn left onto Quang Trung Street to view more quaint villas, some converted for use by official bodies. Toward the railway station is a **double villa.** This double-turreted stone castle is reminiscent of a building style found in Provence, in the south of France. Painted Cambodian *apsaras* are emblazoned outside on the stone wall. At the time of my visit, the double villa housed half a dozen families—some involved in breeding pigs, others in the production of rice wine. It's close to Dalat's old railway station.

Ghost Station

Gare de Dalat (corrupted to "Ga Dalat" in Vietnamese) is a classic—a ghost station with a stopped clock out front. The russet-roofed station is an imaginative piece of French architecture completed in 1938. The Swedish-built crémaillère, or cog railway, ran from 1933 to 1964 down to Thap Cham junction outside Phan Rang. It was put out of commission by Vietcong attacks. A small part of the line has been revived for tourism, and a diesel locomotive runs 10 km out to the village of Trai Met a few times a day. Tea is served in a kiosk inside Dalat station, where the halls once echoed with departure announcements. A Swiss company is considering repair of the line.

Push on to the **Cartographic Institute.** The building with the distinctive sloping roof, was originally the French geographic institute established in the 1940s to produce maps for military purposes. The Cartographic Institute today produces maps of Vietnam, including some excellent topo maps (one of Dalat itself), but few of these top secret works seem to find their way onto the general market.

Past the Institute is **Grand Lycée Yersin**—named in honour of Alexandre Yersin, the French medical researcher who recommended Dalat be set up as a hill station. The curved brick building with the tower was completed in 1935. Formerly a French secondary school, today it's a Vietnamese school where the students are only too pleased to practice their foreign language skills.

From the lycée, make your way back down to **Xuan Huong Lake,** which is named after an 18th-century poetess whose works ridicule pompous officials and praise free love. The lake, created by the French in 1919 with the construction of a small dam at the west end, used to be called Grand Lac. You can stop for a drink at Thuy Ta Cafe, or continue riding around the lake to the north side to **Thanh Thuy Restaurant,** where you can sit outside. Thanh Thuy rents rowboats and swan-shaped pedalboats.

together, going for $20-30 s or $30-40 d. The villas are often assigned to group tours from France or Hong Kong, and can accommodate 50 people.

Volunteer Youth Company (VYC) is a private chain that manages the prestigious Omni Hotel in Saigon. VYC runs a total of 40 rooms sprinkled around Dalat, mostly in newer houses, but some in older villas. Toward the northeast fringe of town you'll find **Pensée 2,** on Lu Gia St., tel. 22933, with 20 rooms at $15 each. Close by, **Pensée 10,** at 10 Phan Chu Trinh, tel. 22937, offers six homey rooms for $15 each. In the direction of Dalat bus station is **Pensée 3,** at 3 Duong 3 Thang 4, tel. 22286. This is also the head office for VYC in Dalat. It's a two-story newer house with gardens, featuring seven doubles for $25 each. Rooms have bidets and garden and forest views; a bar is downstairs. Nearby **Pensée 6,** at 6 Duong 3 Thang 4, tel. 22378, has four double rooms for $20 each. South of that is **Savimex,** at 11B Duong 3/4, tel. 22640, with $25 rooms. It's a hotel for businesspeople, run by a rival Saigon agency.

Treehouses: Hang Nga Nha Nghi, a.k.a. Spiderweb Mansion, at 3 Huynh Thuc Khang, tel. 22070, is the wacky creation of architect Hang Nga. Hang Nga has constructed a series of treehouses around her original villa—there's not a straight line in the place. She offers five rooms in the pink mansion for $10-15 with shared bath. Rooms in the chalet are $30. The chalet has wild decor, lights set in a cave-type ceiling, a fireplace, and an upstairs den with mirror and bed. Hang Nga's latest venture is a four-story treehouse near the giraffe. The self-contained treehouse rooms go for $35-40 and feature round beds and zany windows. There's also a small "mountain" with a double room.

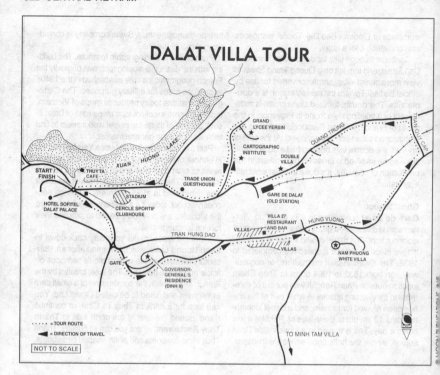

DALAT VILLA TOUR

XUAN HUONG LAKE

GRAND
LYCEE YERSIN

CARTOGRAPHIC
INSTITUTE

DOUBLE
VILLA

QUANG TRUNG

TRAN QUY CAP

START /
FINISH

THUY TA
CAFE

TRADE UNION
GUESTHOUSE

GARE DE DALAT
(OLD STATION)

HOTEL SOFITEL
DALAT PALACE

STADIUM

CERCLE SPORTIF
CLUBHOUSE

VILLA 27
RESTAURANT
AND BAR

VILLAS

HUNG VUONG

TRAN HUNG DAO

VILLAS

NAM PHUONG
WHITE VILLA

GATE

GOVERNOR-
GENERAL'S
RESIDENCE
(DINH II)

TO MINH TAM VILLA

······ = TOUR ROUTE
◄── = DIRECTION OF TRAVEL

NOT TO SCALE

FOOD

Street and Market Food

The **Central Market** (Cho Dalat) specializes in fruit and flowers, processed food, consumer goods, and clothing. There are a few juice bars down this way. A dazzling array of fruit grows in the temperate zone around Dalat, including strawberries, plums, cherries, apples, and avocadoes. Candied fruit and jam are made in Dalat. At night, on the steps leading down to the market, a constellation of kerosene lamps burn as women preside over cauldrons of hard-boiled quail eggs and snails, cooking for customers at narrow tables.

Dalat provides excellent fresh vegetables—the French introduced European varieties. At the produce market close to the bridge by the lake you'll find an abundance of vegetables—yams, squash, spinach, beans, peppers—as well as wholesale rice and grains. Half a dozen vegetarian stalls here; look for Com Chay signs. The vendors fashion tofu to resemble prawns or pork chops, though it's dubious whether this simulation appeals to a true vegetarian. For a change from the usual restaurant fare, try the delicious carrots in the produce market. Buy the carrots, take them over to a restaurant, and order them sautéed or however. Wash down your meal with a glass of Dalat mulberry wine; other liqueurs are also produced locally.

Noodlehouses

Tang Bat Ho, an alley that runs off the Phu Hoa Hotel, is hardly used by street traffic. At night, it's Soup Alley; inside and outside eateries serve Hué soup and other regional specialties.

Restaurants

Along Nguyen Thi Minh Khai Street, leading down from the Central Market to Xuan Huong

Lake, a string of small restaurants serve cheap, hearty fare. These include **Nhu Ngoc Restaurant,** opposite the Haison Hotel; farther south are **Mimosa Restaurant** and **Huynh Lien Restaurant.**

Up the top of the steps near the cinema is **Thanh Thanh Restaurant,** at 4 Tang Bat Ho St., tel. 21836, which has an elegant interior. It's small, cozy, clean, and offers good dining at reasonable prices. Particularly tasty are the soups: mustard vegetable, cauliflower, crab, and asparagus. Around the corner, the family-run **Long Hua Restaurant,** 6 Duy Tan, tel. 22934, does a brisk business and is popular with travelers. **Anh Vo,** 15 Truong Cong Dinh, tel. 23175, is a good restaurant in the center, with lots of vegetarian dishes; staff is fluent in French and passable in English. Other restaurants in this central area may disappoint—Shanghai is mediocre, Dong A has poor service, and Do Yen Restaurant is overpriced.

Phan Dinh Phung Street is the "Chinatown" of Dalat, with naturally more Chinese influence in the cooking. Coming from downtown, at the edge of Phan Dinh Phung is **Lys Restaurant,** at 98 Truong Cong Dinh, tel. 21120. Farther north is **Hoan Lan Resto** on the ground floor of the Thanh The I Hotel at 118 Phan Dinh Phung. Close by, **Caraven Restaurant,** 114 Phan Dinh Phung, tel. 21818, serves fish, eel, chicken, frog, and other specialties. Toward Mimosa Hotel is **Dieu Thao Restaurant,** a small, cheap vegetarian place next to 142 Phan Dinh Phung.

For French food in classic French surroundings, visit **Villa 27 Restaurant and Bar,** at 27 Tran Hung Dao Street, tel. 22743. It's on the south side of the lake, past the former Governor-general's Residence. At night there's a fireplace and a piano bar—drinks are $2. Villa 27 is also open for breakfast—you can get French bread, juice, tea, and two eggs for $3. Of course, it's the ambience you pay for, since the same fare would cost a lot less at the Central Market.

Cafés

Cafés have a lot of character in Dalat. They're the social hub of the town, functioning as rendezvous points, gossip and rumor mills, and nightclubs. To savor the taste of local tea and coffee, try **Le Ky Café,** at 249 Phan Dinh Phung, near the Mimosa Hotel; a small wholesale outlet with a few tables. For tea freaks, **Bao Loc tea,** produced close to Dalat, is considered one of the finest in Vietnam. Artichoke tea, made from the root of the plant, reputedly restores liver and diuretic functions. Just what you need after one of those long bus rides.

A daytime or sunset venue for drinks is **Thuy Ta Café** by the lakeside—an upscale joint with a relaxing sundeck run by Dalat Tourism. Even serves carrot juice. You can eat breakfast here; other meals should be ordered in advance by phoning 22288. On the north side of the lake is **Thanh Thuy Café,** which rents pedalboats to cruise the lake.

architect Hang Nga in one of her treehouse accommodations

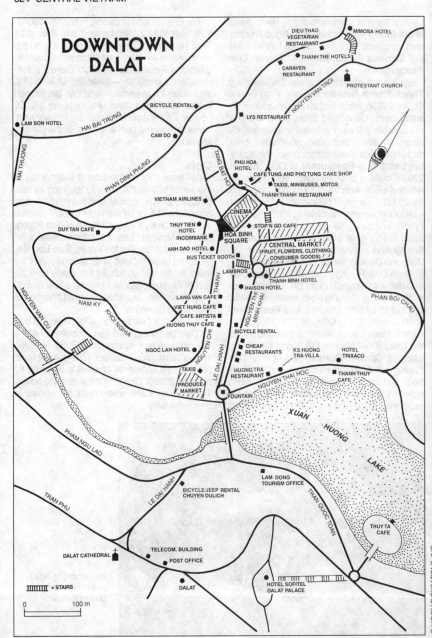

DOWNTOWN DALAT

- LAM SON HOTEL
- DIEU THAO VEGETARIAN RESTAURANT
- MIMOSA HOTEL
- THANH THE HOTELS
- CARAVEN RESTAURANT
- PROTESTANT CHURCH
- BICYCLE RENTAL
- HAI BAI TRUNG
- HAI THUONG
- CAM DO
- LYS RESTAURANT
- NGUYEN VAN TROI
- PHAN DINH PHUNG
- TANG BAT HO
- PHU HOA HOTEL
- CAFE TUNG AND PHO TUNG CAKE SHOP
- TAXIS, MINIBUSES, MOTOS
- THANH THANH RESTAURANT
- VIETNAM AIRLINES
- DUY TAN CAFE
- THUY TIEN HOTEL
- INCOMBANK
- ANH DAO HOTEL
- BUS TICKET BOOTH
- CINEMA
- STOP'N GO CAFE
- HOA BINH SQUARE
- CENTRAL MARKET (FRUIT, FLOWERS, CLOTHING, CONSUMER GOODS)
- LAMBROS
- HAISON HOTEL
- THANH BINH HOTEL
- NAM KY
- KHOI NGHIA
- NGUYEN VAN CU
- LANG VAN CAFE
- VIET HUNG CAFE
- CAFE ARTISTA
- HUONG THUY CAFE
- NGUYEN CHI THANH
- NGUYEN THI MINH KHAI
- PHAN BOI CHAU
- BICYCLE RENTAL
- NGOC LAN HOTEL
- CHEAP RESTAURANTS
- KS HUONG TRA VILLA
- HOTEL TRIXACO
- TAXIS
- LE DAI HANH
- PRODUCE MARKET
- HUONG TRA RESTAURANT
- NGUYEN THAI HOC
- THANH THUY CAFE
- FOUNTAIN
- PHAM NGU LAO
- XUAN HUONG LAKE
- TRAN PHU
- LE DAI HANH
- BICYCLE/JEEP RENTAL CHUYEN DULICH
- LAM DONG TOURISM OFFICE
- TRAN QUOC TOAN
- THUY TA CAFE
- DALAT CATHEDRAL
- TELECOM. BUILDING
- POST OFFICE
- DALAT
- HOTEL SOFITEL DALAT PALACE

IIIIIIII = STAIRS

0   100 m

In town, near the back of the cinema, is **Café Tung.** Old men gather here to shoot the breeze; the place was famed as a hangout for intellectuals in the 1950s. Café Tung serves only drinks, but if you need a snack, grab one at **Pho Tung Cakeshop,** at 1 Nguyen Van Troi. Pho Tung sells delicious coconut and marzipan cakes and other pastries; you'll find small sidewalk cake stalls a few blocks west on Truong Cong Dinh Street.

To bump into other travelers, head for the **Stop'n Go Café** overlooking the Central Market. Students from Dalat University sometimes visit to practice their English, and poets and painters sometimes drop by. This cozy place serves drinks, cakes, and full meals; there's an art gallery and souvenir shop attached.

Perched on a ridge along Nguyen Chi Thanh Street is a string of cafés with views—**Lang Van Café, Café Artista, Viet Hung Café,** and **Huong Thuy Café.** These places serve ice cream, iced coffee, and filter coffee and provide dark corners for Vietnamese couples to grope in. Even more romantic is **Duy Tan Café** on Nam Ky Khoi Nghia, featuring secluded open-air tables on several levels high above the street. Duy Tan is a karaoke café where tuneless patrons commit vocal atrocities on songs like "Country Roads." Fortunately, the karaoke is contained inside.

SERVICES AND INFORMATION

Traveler Cafés
The **Stop'n Go Café** at Khu Hoa Binh Square, tel. 21512, is a prime meeting spot. Owner Duy Viet is knowledgeable about the area; you can also peruse the traveler logbooks in the café.

Tourist Information
Lam Dong Tourism office, at 4 Tran Quoc Toan St., tel. 22125, is the provincial tourism authority. The office arranges transportation, guides, and permits for Lat Village. You can pick up maps of the Dalat area here. If you come across the bridge from downtown Dalat, Lam Dong Tourism occupies the second house on the hill to your left, overlooking the lake. The office advertises "tours to inner country including forbidden areas"—roughly translated, this means the people at Lam Dong Tourism made

the area forbidden so you'd have to visit them to get the permits.

There's a second office, **Chuyen Dulich,** at 9 Le Dai Hanh St., tel. 22479. As you come across the bridge the office lies to your right, not far along the road. This office provides transportation rental—bicycles go for $1.50 a day, a US jeep $25 a day, other vehicles also arranged. A guide is $15 a day.

Another agent in Dalat is **Phuong Nam Tourism,** 6 Ho Tung Mau, tel. 22781, conducting tours to the highlands and coast. Arranges trekking, climbing, camping, hunting, and visits to ethnic groups and old battlefields.

Post Office
The small GPO is at 14 Tran Phu, on the south side of the lake, with a telecommunications building nearby. Fax and IDD facilities available here.

Banks
Incombank (Ngan Hang Cong Thuong), 46-48 Khu Hoa Binh, next to Anh Dao Hotel, charges 1.2% commission for changing traveler's checks to dong, and two percent commission to convert traveler's checks to US cash.

GETTING THERE AND AWAY

By Air
There is intermittent air service from Dalat to Hué and Ho Chi Minh City. At present only light aircraft can land at **Lien Khang airstrip,** 30 km south of Dalat. Taxi transfer into Dalat should be under $10. **Cam Ly Airfield,** closer to Dalat, is slated to reopen. A **Vietnam Airlines** office is located at 5 Truong Cong Dinh St., tel. 2895, in the main square.

By Bus
The main bus station, **Ben Xe Trung Tam,** is four km south of Dalat; you can get there by moto or take a lambro from the foot of the Central Market steps. The bus station has minibuses, Peugeots, express buses, regular buses, and share-taxis to points north and south. The bus station is out of town, but you can still get bus pickup in town, an important consideration if the damn thing departs at 0500. A ticket booth is open 0600-2100 at the top of the main steps, north of Haison

THE DALAT ROUTE

From Nha Trang to Saigon there are two routes: following the coast via Phan Rang and Phan Thiet, or swinging west from Phan Rang and going via Dalat. The Dalat route is definitely more inspiring, climbing from the arid coast at Phan Rang to pine forests at 1,475 meters in Dalat. Dalat is 110 km from Phan Rang and 310 km from Saigon. From Dalat a forest zone extends some 20 km to the south, gradually giving way to fruit orchards and tea plantations.

The largest town on the route is Bao Loc, known for its silk industry. About 25 km from Saigon, at Bien Hoa, you can turn off to Vung Tau beach resort. Information on distances, road conditions and accommodations along the route can be gleaned from the special topic "Saigon-to-Nha Trang Bike Route."

Hotel; you buy a ticket in advance here, and on the appointed morning either wait at the booth or arrange for hotel pickup. Buses leave at very early hours. They circle the cinema area before 0600 (not legal after this), then head out. Some buses, like those to Nha Trang, depart 0500-0700 only. For Saigon there's hourly service from 0500 to 1500 by bus or minibus. The run takes about six or seven hours.

By Traveler Minibus

To avoid the rigors of local buses, travelers should keep an eye out for traveler minibuses plying the coast. If you're heading south, you might be able to find a seat on a minibus coming back from Hué. There are also minibuses running the Saigon-Dalat route. Inquire around Mimosa Hotel. To Nha Trang, it costs about $7 a person by traveler minibus. By comparison, a packed public minibus from the bus station to Nha Trang costs about $2.50.

GETTING AROUND

By Rental

You can arrange car and minibus rentals for getting around town through major hotels or through Lam Dong Tourism. The area at the top of the

steps above the Central Market has taxi rentals, old Peugeot 203s and 404s as well as small buses and lambros. At the bottom of the steps are lambros that run back to the bus station and to a few short-run destinations around Dalat.

By Moto

Motos cost $7 a day or $1 an hour. Lots of motos available near the top of the steps close to the Central Market. Dalat is hilly: a Honda 50cc carrying two people is going to crawl up a hill and will overheat easily, so try and get something with more power, like a 125cc or 175cc moto. If you want to drive yourself, offer a moto driver $5-7, commandeer the moto, and take off—agree on a meeting spot to return the bike. A deposit may be required.

By Bicycle

No cyclos traverse Dalat due to hills. But you can rent a bicycle from several places. In a parking lot near the Haison Hotel is a booth where you can rent a Chinese bike for $1.50 a day or 80 cents half-day. For a Vietnamese bike it's $1 a day or 50 cents half-day. At **Chuyen Dulich,** on the southeast side of town over the bridge, you'll find similar deals; perhaps half a dozen bikes for rent. Just north of Cam Do Hotel, next to 99 Phan Dinh Phung, is a tiny rental place with bikes going for $1 a day. The bikes have no gears, so expect to walk the bike at times. For really long climbs, put yourself and the bike on a minibus. This is the case when going to Prenn Falls—it's all downhill to get there, and all uphill on the way back.

EXCURSIONS FROM DALAT

Beauty Spots

If you've ever seen the Swiss Alps or the Rocky Mountains in North America, Dalat's much-vaunted scenic spots won't impress. These "beauty spots" become crowded with Vietnamese vacationers on weekends, making them even less attractive. **Cam Ly Falls,** two km west of central Dalat, is just a trickle, with ragged flower gardens and some poorly stuffed animals as photo props; more impressive is the **Montagnard church** nearby. **Datanla Falls,** five km south on the Saigon Road, is a minor cascade with a short forest hike down to the ravine where the falls are located. **Prenn Falls,** 15 km down the Saigon Road, is larger, but still another backdrop for honeymoon and family photos with all kinds of props, as well as restaurants large and small. If you want to see real waterfalls, go 50 km south to **Thac Pangour Falls** on the route to Saigon; the thundering falls are seven km in from the highway along a bad road.

Dalat is sprinkled with lakes, once surrounded by wilderness but now encompassed by thin woods. Still, the trees provide sufficient cover for Vietnamese couples intent on romance. You can bike the five km out to the **Valley of Love:** take Phu Dong Thien Vuong Street north past the golf course and Dalat University, then continue past vistas of farmland and a towering Quan Am statue. The Valley of Love is an area around Da Thien Lake with a tourist circus of souvenir stalls, paddleboat, canoe, and motorboat rentals, and pony rides.

From here you can cycle back straight south along Nguyen Tu Luc Street into Dalat via the **Flower Gardens,** or, if you're feeling energetic, take a longer loop out eastward, skirting the south end of Chien Thang Lake toward the **Lake of Sighs.** The unremarkable Lake of Sighs (Ho Than Tho) is about five km east of Dalat; Montagnard cowboys with plastic guns and Texas-style boots conduct pony tours on lakeside trails. The name of the lake is of uncertain origin—one theory is that it's named after the sighs of the women courted by the handsome young men from the nearby military academy.

Lat Village and Lang Bian Mountain

The original inhabitants of the Dalat area, the Lats, were pushed back to outlying villages. Lat Village is about 10 km outside Dalat, or half an hour by car. You can combine a visit to the area with a hike up Lang Bian Mountain. There are nine hamlets in the area, populated by Lat, Koho, and Ma tribes living in impoverished conditions in thatched-roof houses. The villagers grow rice, coffee, and potatoes, and produce charcoal. Lat Village has two small Christian churches.

Nearby Lang Bian Mountain has a series of peaks ranging from 2,100 to 2,400 meters. In three or four hours you can hike to viewpoints up the mountain—one place, used as a US base, has views of Ancroet Lakes. The dual Ancroet Lakes were created as part of a hydroelectric project. Also in the area is 15-meter-high **Ancroet Falls.** The Ancroet area, populated by Montagnards, lies about 15 km northwest from Dalat, and is reached by a separate route.

Getting There: Due to associations between the Americans and the Montagnards during the war, permits may be required for Lat Village—one of the last places to require a permit in Vietnam. The $5 permit takes 20 minutes to process from Lam Dong Tourism Office. Along with the permit comes a guide and transportation—a guide for a group of under 10 is $10, over 10 is

Lat villagers carrying firewood

$15. For one or two people it's $5 for a guide. The police station guide is "same price but different mind." To climb Lang Bian, it's $5 more for the guide. The tariff is $10-20 for a car for the day, or $30 for an air-con minibus; you can also hire a car from the back of the cinema. By bicycle, Lat Village is little more than an hour from Dalat, but be aware that foreigners attempting to visit Lat Village by themselves have been fined by police.

The Big Chicken

If you can't afford the Lat Village circus or don't want to deal with permits, then this is just the thing for you—the village of the big chicken, **Lang Ga.** Moto drivers will take you to a genuine Montagnard village 18 km south of Dalat on the Saigon route in about half an hour. Look for the 18-km marker stone; the village is about 500 meters off the highway. In Lang Ga villagers will walk around beating their breasts yelling "Montagnard," just to make sure you don't get them mixed up with the Vietnamese. The locals indeed look darker than Vietnamese, but their way of life is quite ordinary—subsistence farmers grow coffee and papayas, and they live in wooden housing with corrugated roofing. Women in the village use hand looms to create unusual weavings: there's a small thatched hut selling this garish stuff near the highway.

Towering over the village is a concrete rooster in a crowing stance, mounted on a rock base with an odd rockery waterway behind it. The symbolism of the three-meter-high bird is unclear: according to one version, the big chicken was presented to villagers by government officials after they succeeded in resettling the Montagnards here.

Although Lang Ga is 18 km out, it's easy to reach by bicycle. The first 12 km is straight downhill from Dalat, then it's flat highway. So getting there is quick, but going back you have to walk the bike. If you're too tired, wave down a bus or minibus and stick the bike on the roof.

SAIGON

. . . a French city flowering alone out of a tropical swamp

—OSBERT SITWELL ON SAIGON

Like Shanghai or Bangkok, Saigon comes imbued with its own myth—you have a vision in mind already. You've seen it on television, you've seen it in movies: the city of war, the city of sin, the city of changing fortunes. Saigon is busy and brash, the commercial hub of Vietnam, the industrial muscle of the nation. It's a city of economic contrasts, too. At temple festivals you'll see women in shimmering silk *ao dais* float by filthy ragged beggars.

Little is known of Saigon's early history, and the origins of the city's name are uncertain. In the 15th century Saigon was little more than swampland in a forest wilderness, an area under the Khmer sphere of influence. The Cambodians hunted in this area, then called Prei Nokor. Slowly it grew into a small market town; as forest was cleared and rice paddies were carved out, it became an outpost on the eastern flank of the Angkorian Empire.

As the Khmer and Cham empires shrank, the Vietnamese advanced from the north. In the early 17th century, on the condition they be allowed to settle the south, the Vietnamese agreed to help the Khmers fight the Thais. Fully in control by 1680, the Vietnamese allowed 3,000 refugee Chinese Ming soldiers to settle the area of Bien Hoa. A few years later the Chinese started a market at Cholon. Eventually, the Khmers were pushed back to the Mekong delta.

Saigon continued to grow as Vietnamese settlers arrived from the north, spreading out along the delta waterways and clearing forest. The settlement became the administrative center of the region, a trade base and tax-collecting center. Gia Dinh, a small fort housing the area governor and his administrators, was built. In the 17th century, factions of the Nguyen clan were crushed by a peasant revolt led by the Tay Son brothers, who captured Gia Dinh. In 1788 Nguyen Anh, with the help of the French Jesuit missionary Béhaine and an army of French mercenaries, recaptured Gia Dinh. In 1790 Nguyen Anh conscripted a force of 30,000 laborers and set about building a large Citadel in Gia Dinh, in the area

SAIGON (HO CHI MINH CITY)

TAY NINH BUS TERMINAL

TAN SON NHAT AIRPORT

TO CU CHI TUNNELS AND TAY NINH

CONG HUA

LE DAI HANH

HOANG VAN THU

MEKONG TRAVEL
HOTEL
DC
PHUON

CHAINS FIRST
HOTEL

LE VAN

HUONG LO 2

HUONG LO 14

TAN BINH DISTRICT

CACH MANG THANG TAM

AN VUONG

LAC LONG QUAN

GIAC LAM PAGODA

THUNG KIAT BLVD.

DISTRICT 10

NGUYEN TRI

GIAC VIEN
TU PAGODA

BINH THAI

RACETRACK

DISTRICT 11

BA HAM

3 THANG 2 BLVD.

DISTRICT 5

HUONG VUONG BLVD.

DISTRICT 6

LO HAU GIANG BLVD.

NGUYEN CHI THANH

HUONG VUONG BLVD.

TO MIEN TAY BUS
TERMINAL AND
MEKONG DELTA

BINH TIEN

CHOLON BUS
TERMINAL

DISTRICT 8

TO CAN GIUOC

SEE "CHOLON" MAP

BEN NGHE CHANNEL

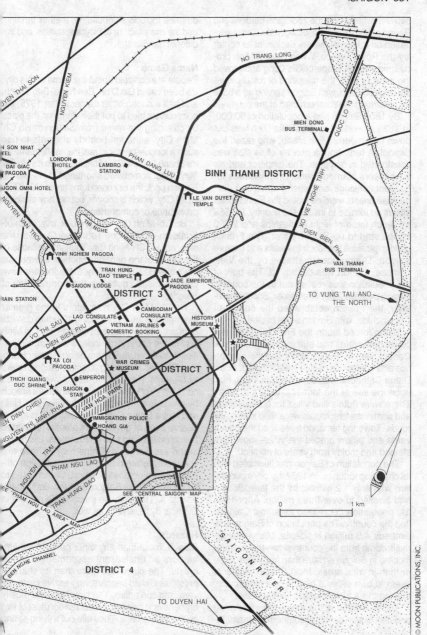

NO TRANG LONG

NGUYEN KIEM

NGUYEN THAI SON

QUOC LO 13

MIEN DONG
BUS TERMINAL

N SON NHAT
TEL

DAI GIAC
PAGODA

LONDON
HOTEL

LAMBRO
STATION

PHAN DANG LUU

BINH THANH DISTRICT

AIGON OMNI HOTEL

LE VAN DUYET
TEMPLE

XO VIET NGHE TINH

NGUYEN VAN TROI

THI NGHE CHANNEL

DIEN BIEN PHU

VINH NGHIEM PAGODA

VAN THANH
BUS TERMINAL

TRAN HUNG
DAO TEMPLE

JADE EMPEROR
PAGODA

SAIGON LODGE

DISTRICT 3

TO VUNG TAU AND
THE NORTH

RAIN STATION

LAO CONSULATE

CAMBODIAN
CONSULATE

VO THI SAU

VIETNAM AIRLINES
DOMESTIC BOOKING

HISTORY
MUSEUM

DIEN BIEN PHU

ZOO

XA LOI
PAGODA

WAR CRIMES
MUSEUM

DISTRICT 1

THICH QUANG
DUC SHRINE

EMPEROR

SAIGON
STAR

VAN HOA PARK

N DINH CHIEU

NGUYEN THI MINH KHAI

IMMIGRATION POLICE

HOANG GIA

NGUYEN TRAI

PHAM NGU LAO

EE "PHAM NGU LAO" AREA" MAP

PHAM NGU LAO

TRAN HUNG DAO

SEE "CENTRAL SAIGON" MAP

0   1 km

BER NGHE CHANNEL

DISTRICT 4

SAIGON RIVER

TO DUYEN HAI

© MOON PUBLICATIONS, INC.

between what is now the zoological gardens and Reunification Hall. The octagonal Citadel was based on a French military design; at its center lay the Royal Palace. When Nguyen Anh proclaimed himself Emperor Gia Long and moved the court to Hué, the trappings of royalty were transported north, with Saigon serving as a base for governing the southern third of the country.

By 1800 Saigon had a population of 50,000. In 1835 a peasant revolt at Gia Dinh was put down by Emperor Minh Mang, who razed the Citadel. A fort about a quarter of its size was constructed in its place. The emperor and his successors blamed French missionaries for peasant uprisings, and when French and Vietnamese priests were executed the French used this as an excuse to invade the country. In 1859 a French force of eight battleships and 2,000 troops started up Saigon River. The French used explosives to breach the walls and capture Saigon. During counterattacks by the Vietnamese, the fort was destroyed. The bulk of the population was moved out to the country, leaving perhaps 25,000 residents. Shortly thereafter, the French established the colony of Cochinchina, with Saigon as its capital.

Using forced labor, the French built a new city of boulevards and buildings in what is now Central Saigon. Public works like the post office and governor's palace were initiated. Notre Dame Cathedral was completed in 1883, built upon the site of the former Citadel's arsenal. There were hotels and villas for businessmen and administrators; canals were filled in to make roads. Towering tamarind trees lined the boulevards and palms graced the villas—now rain-stained and moldy from years of neglect.

The population of Saigon has fluctuated with its changing fortunes. In 1962 the city's population was only 1.2 million; by the late 1960s it had swelled to over three million. After 1975 the population decreased as ethnic Chinese fled the country. The population of Saigon now exceeds 4.5 million residents. Many new arrivals come from the countryside—the average income in Saigon is more than four times higher than in rural areas. Most Saigon residents seem to own either a bicycle or a motorcycle, making this a tricky place for pedestrians.

Today Saigon is the major manufacturing and distribution center of southern Vietnam. Industries include shipbuilding, leather tanning, and the manufacture of bicycles, textiles, and traditional handicrafts.

Name Game

People are schizoid about the name of this city. It's been called Gia Dinh, Ben Nghe, Ben Thanh, and half a dozen other names. After 1975, the communists tried to put their stamp on the place by changing the name from Saigon to Ho Chi Minh City, although nobody attempts to use such a tongue-twister in real life. In Vietnamese, it's Thanh Pho Ho Chi Minh; in French it's Ho Chi Minh Ville, sometimes shortened to Ho-ville. In English print, the city often turns up as HCMC, or HCM City, which is shorter, but not any easier to pronounce or comprehend.

Ho Chi Minh City hasn't stuck, even with officialdom—it's Saigon Tourist you'll see on the sign, not Ho Chi Minh City Tourism. Because of the failure of the general populace to embrace the name Ho Chi Minh City, the authorities compromised, dubbing the central district Saigon.

Ho Chi Minh City now refers to the greater metropolitan area, comprising 12 urban districts or *quan,* and six suburban districts. Ho Chi Minh City is one of the three independent municipalities in Vietnam, the others being Greater Hanoi and Greater Haiphong. Central Saigon refers to Districts 1 and 3, the downtown business core, with high-rise hotels and landmark French buildings like the old Hotel de Ville (City Hall) and Notre Dame Cathedral. District 3 is an exclusive zone of government offices, renovated French villas, and tree-lined streets. Districts 5 and 6 are Saigon's "Chinatown." These are commonly referred to as Cholon, although officially this name does not exist. Cholon used to be separated from Saigon, but grew until it melded into it. The Chinese presence is evident in Districts 8, 10, and 11 as well.

Hazards

Saigon, more than any other part of Vietnam, harbors an unpleasant assortment of rip-off artists. The place has more than its share of prostitutes, child beggars, aggressive cyclo drivers, and con artists. The street kids are mostly orphans or runaways, called *bui doi* (dust of life) by the Vietnamese. They eke out a living selling newspapers or lottery tickets. Many target tourists. Child beggars will lock on to your clothing or your leg, only releasing their grip upon payment in dong. You should discourage such ransom activity. Prostitutes have been known to lure customers off the streets, deliver a knockout, then take off with all valuables. Cyclo drivers occasionally attack and injure foreigners in arguments over prices. Be aware that some cyclo drivers may also be involved in drug dealing and other fringe activities. Merchants are fond of ripping off tourists—always carefully negotiate prices beforehand, and never pay for anything until the vendor has supplied the goods.

SIGHTS

COLONIAL SAIGON

Colonial Saigon can be explored by bicycle, motorcycle, taxi, or classic French automobile. Cyclos are a leisurely way of getting around—and you will go the long way round, because cyclos were banned from 50 streets in the city center in mid-1995 to ease traffic congestion. If on a bicycle or motorcycle, watch for one-way streets, and be wary of rush-hour traffic—the boulevards can be thronged, making it difficult to turn at major intersections.

Casting yourself back to 1930s and 1940s Saigon is easy. The grand colonial edifices still stand—dwarfed, it's true, by newer high-rises—but nonetheless providing sufficient illusion for the time traveler. In fact, Saigon functions as a large outdoor museum of French colonial architecture, most of it plain and ugly. The buildings also serve as navigation landmarks, particularly the cathedral and the Hotel de Ville.

Norman Lewis described 1950 Saigon in *A Dragon Apparent*:

A French town in a hot country . . . Its inspiration has been purely commercial and it is therefore without folly, fervour or much ostentation. There has been no audacity of architecture, no great harmonious conception of planning. Saigon is a pleasant, colourless and characterless French provincial city, squeezed onto a strip of delta-land in the South China Seas. From it exude strangely into the surrounding creeks and rivers 10 thousand sampans, harbouring an uncounted native population . . . The better part of the city contains many shops, cafés and cinemas, and one small, plain cathedral in red brick. Twenty thousand Europeans keep as much as possible to themselves in a few tamarind-shaded central streets and they are surrounded by about a million Vietnamese and Chinese.

Saigon has little in the way of native architecture, barring pagodas and Chinese-style shophouses. The city was largely built by the French. When the French captured Saigon in 1859, the area was swamp and marshland. They set about filling in canals, draining marshlands, and building roads, tree-lined boulevards, an opera house, court, arsenal, customs houses, cinemas, and schools. For entertainment, the French introduced exclusive sports clubs, glitzy casinos, and sleazy opium dens. Down by Saigon River lay the offices of the shipping and communications company Messageries Maritimes. At 74 Hai Ba Trung Street sat the state opium factory.

Saigon of the 1930s was cleaner and leafier than it is now—the French took great pride in their manicured lawns and botanical gardens—now the zoo area. They planted the tamarind trees that shade Saigon boulevards and break up the monotonous architecture. The French left behind their cars, too. In among the throng of cyclos and motorcycles plying the streets you might stray across a Citröen Traction, the 1930s classic French car with running boards. Traces of the French presence linger in the food as well. Sitting in a café you can crack open a BGI—a joint-venture French beer not far removed from the original beers of French Indochina—and indulge in a baguette with pâté.

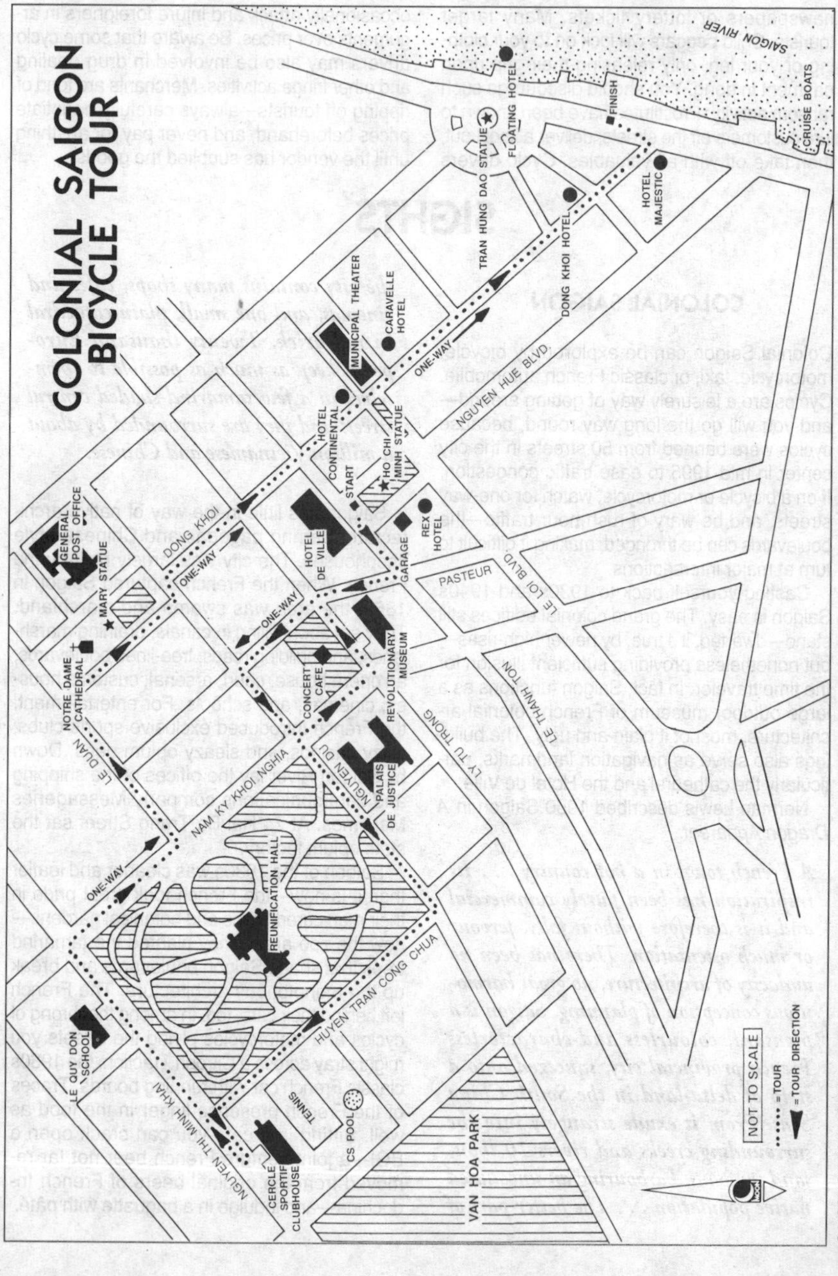

COLONIAL SAIGON BICYCLE TOUR

SAIGON RIVER

CRUISE BOATS

FINISH

HOTEL MAJESTIC

FLOATING HOTEL

TRAN HUNG DAO STATUE

DONG KHOI HOTEL

MUNICIPAL THEATER

CARAVELLE HOTEL

NGUYEN HUE BLVD.

HOTEL CONTINENTAL

HO CHI MINH STATUE

START

REX HOTEL

HOTEL DE VILLE

GARAGE

PASTEUR

LE LOI BLVD

GENERAL POST OFFICE

MARY STATUE

DONG KHOI

ONE-WAY

NOTRE DAME CATHEDRAL

ONE-WAY

CONCERT CAFE

REVOLUTIONARY MUSEUM

LE THANH TON

LY TU TRONG

PALAIS DE JUSTICE

NAM KY KHOI NGHIA

NGUYEN DU

LE DUAN

ONE-WAY

REUNIFICATION HALL

HUYEN TRAN CONG CHUA

LE QUY DON SCHOOL

NGUYEN THI MINH KHAI

CERCLE SPORTIF CLUBHOUSE

TENNIS

CS POOL

VAN HOA PARK

NOT TO SCALE

▰▰▰ = TOUR

▶ = TOUR DIRECTION

© MOON PUBLICATIONS, INC.

Hotel de Ville

The **Hotel de Ville,** at the northern end of Nguyen Hue Boulevard, still serves as Saigon's City Hall. With its ornate gingerbread facade, the Hotel de Ville looks like the town hall of a French town. Considerable debate raged over its design and location before it was finally completed in 1908. Today it's called the People's Committee Headquarters, but neither the people nor visitors are allowed to see the interior, where crystal chandeliers hang.

If you want to walk around this area, park your transport in the garage at number 155 near the Rex Hotel, used by taxis, tour buses, motorcycles, and bicycles. The original iron grill-work exterior is still intact and is possibly of German origin.

Big French stores like Les Grands Magasins Charner once lined Nguyen Hue Boulevard, then Boulevard Charner. Its motto: "We supply you with every requisite for colonial life, at the lowest prices . . ." Little has changed in this corner of Saigon, except for the addition of a large statue of Ho Chi Minh cradling a child, located on the strip of greenery facing the Hotel de Ville. A few red flags flutter from the building.

Neo-Classical Grandeur

The **Revolutionary Museum,** at 65 Ly Tu Trong, used to be the mansion of the French Governor of Cochinchina; under President Ngo Dinh Diem, it was known as Gia Long Palace. This is one building where you can see the interior. The neo-classical building itself and the grounds actually hold greater interest than the museum displays, which you'll see repeated in many military museums in Vietnam.

Downstairs are former ballrooms with high ceilings; a grand sweeping staircase leads to the upper salons. Downstairs you'll find random displays from the 1850s to 1940s including some pictures of old Saigon; memorabilia upstairs recalls the 1940s to 1960s and Vietnam's struggle against the French and Americans. Of interest here are displays of propaganda leaflets urging GIs to hurry home.

Outside, a parked Huey UH-1 helicopter overlooks landscaped lawns and gardens. Under the helicopter is a bunker with six meeting rooms and a tunnel leading to Le Thanh Ton Street and Reunification Hall. It was built in the 1960s under the Diem regime.

Also on the grounds are artillery pieces, two small planes, and a Russian tank used in the 1975 assault on Saigon. One of the planes, a US-built F-5E jet, was used that same year by defecting South Vietnamese pilot Nguyen Thanh Trung to attack the Presidential Palace; he then flew to Hanoi. The Revolutionary Museum is open 0800-1130 and 1330-1630, closed Monday. Free entry. Opposite the museum is a tranquil park and a café serving refreshments.

Due to the one-way streets here, you go against the grain to reach the museum. If on a bike, you can either get off and walk it to the museum, or loop around the block north of the museum, circling past the Palais de Justice.

escape helicopter on the grounds of the Revolutionary Museum

HONORED FRENCH

Not all the French were rubber-plantation slave drivers. A few are actually honored with street names. Duong Pasteur is a nod to Louis Pasteur, who established medical research institutes around the world to fight disease. Duong Pasteur features a Pasteur Institute (Vien Pasteur) at the north end. Two other Saigon streets with French names are also related to Pasteur—Rue Calmette and Rue Yersin, both named after protégés of Pasteur. Dr. Albert Calmette established a research lab in Saigon in 1890; Dr. Alexander Yersin set up a lab in Nha Trang in 1895. These were the first Pasteur Institutes established outside Paris. There's also a Rue Pasteur and Rue Yersin in Nha Trang. Another Pasteur protégée, Marie Curie, is also honored in Vietnam. Marie Curie School is little changed from its founding in 1918. The archway still bears her name, though Ecole Marie Curie has been changed to Truong Marie Curie. Located at 159 Nam Ky Khoi Nghia, the high school is attended by a thousand students studying English and French.

Cercle Sportif

From the museum, circle up Rue Pasteur, turn left on Nguyen Du, and loop around the back of Reunification Hall to Nguyen Thi Minh Khai Street. Step inside a north entrance, and you'll find ghostly traces of French presence in a dilapidated sports club, once the Cercle Sportif. The French set up a chain of Cercle Sportif clubs in Indochina; these clubs, of course, were exclusively French, with no Vietnamese allowed. Today the old Cercle Sportif building is part of a Vietnamese youth recreation club. You can still make out the Cercle Sportif logo, a C entwined with an S inside a circle, carved in wood at the former clubhouse entrance. The clubhouse overlooks some neglected tennis courts, and farther back is a vintage full-length swimming pool, surreally framed by Grecian columns. Trellised areas and plants shelter wicker chairs. There are two wading pools here, and a place still known as the Cercle Gym, housing the Cercle Cafeteria. Adjacent **Van Hoa Park** used to be Jardin de la Ville; it was turned over to the public by the French governor in 1869.

East of the Cercle Sportif is **Le Quy Don School,** formerly the French school Lycée Chasseloup-Laubat. The school was featured in the movie *The Lover.*

Notre Dame Cathedral

Notre Dame is a Gothic cathedral with twin brick towers tipped with iron spires and flying buttress-es, all faithfully reproduced in tropical Vietnam. All the parts were shipped from France. The cathedral was built between 1877 and 1883. It's a prominent Saigon landmark often featured on postcards. Services are held here six times on Sunday, and several times during the week. The cathedral overlooks a statue of the Virgin Mary in a small square once known as Place Pigneau de Béhaine, named after an 18th-century missionary who lobbied for French military intervention in Cochinchina.

Facing onto the same square to the east is the **General Post Office,** built in the 1880s. It looks pretty much the same today, apart from a red flag waving outside, a couple of big antennae sprouting on the rooftop, and, inside, a large Ho Chi Minh portrait presiding over the proceedings. Go inside to see the large glass dome and long vaulted ceiling.

Municipal Theater and the Hotel Continental

On Dong Khoi Street a few blocks southeast of Notre Dame Cathedral lies the Municipal Theater, also known as Saigon Concert Hall. Originally built at the turn of the century, it was renovated in the 1940s. After 1956, the building housed the lower division of the National Assembly. You'll notice an absence of the standard faded yellow pastel of the French era; it's here, but under more recent coats of white paint. Today the theater is used as a venue for traditional theater, gymnastics displays, and rock concerts. The interior is not as elaborate as the exterior suggests. Although there are plush red chairs and fancy wrought-iron banisters, there's hardly anything in the way of ceiling decoration. For bike or motorcycle parking, go to the back of the theater to the east side.

Almost facing the Municipal Theater is the Hotel Continental, a French hotel magnificently restored to its full colonial grandeur. The hotel was originally constructed in 1885 by the Societé des Grands Hotels Indochinois, part of a chain of elegant hotels also found in Hanoi, Hué, Vung Tau, and Phnom Penh. The sidewalk terrace outside the Continental was a popular rendezvous spot for highbrow French society. In the 1980s, the terrace bar was glassed in and transformed into an air-conditioned Italian restaurant. Graham Greene featured the terrace in his novel *The Quiet American.* Somerset Maugham described it in *The Gentleman in the Parlour* (1930):

> *Outside the hotel are terraces, and at the hour of the aperitif, they are crowded with bearded, gesticulating Frenchmen drinking the sweet and sickly beverages. . . . It is very agreeable to sit under the awning on the terrace of the Hotel Continental, and with an innocent drink before you, read in the local newspaper heated controversies upon the affairs of the colony.*

The "heated controversies" included how to treat domestics (should one hit a domestic?) and how many hours to spend in siesta (two or three?). Beyond domestic worries, the French tended to business affairs and the pursuit of leisure. After work a round of absinthe, a visit to a restaurant, the theater, and possibly a trip to a casino, brothel, or opium den. Their decadent lifestyle led to another big problem—large unpaid tabs.

Along Dong Khoi
Dong Khoi Street is a classy shopping thoroughfare with antiques, jewelry, Parisian fashions, and perfumes. During the French era this was Rue Catinat, an exclusive shopping area and haunt of spies, French police inspectors, and Annamese beauties. It was also the site of occasional terrorist café bombings. During the Vietnam War, the street became Tu Do (Freedom Street)—a redlight district—and was renamed Dong Khoi (General Uprising) Street after 1975.

Though it's seen better days, Dong Khoi Street still has an exclusive air about it, with art galleries, gift shops, laquerware shops, and a few cafés. On the east side of Dong Khoi art shops sell handpainted reproductions of famous canvases. For insight into this curious industry, go past the Dong Khoi Hotel and turn east on Ngo Duc Ke; here you'll find a whole workshop

of oil artists—some 20 of them—busy touching up their Monets, Gauguins, Van Goghs, and Picassos. Everything down to that Mona Lisa smile or Gauguin breast is copied from art books by graduates of the Fine Arts School of Ho Chi Minh City. A canvas that takes a week to copy starts out at $80-100, while a six-week effort may yield a hefty $600. Custom-made canvases can also be ordered.

The hotels along Dong Khoi are mostly operated by Saigon Tourist. The outfit makes select renovations, often in joint ventures. That means while the Continental has been brought up to international standards, the **Dong Khoi Hotel,** at 8 Dong Khoi, has been left pretty much to its old 1920s self, when it was called the Saigon Palace. Not much of a palace now, but check out the lobby, the original spiral marble staircase, and the vintage nonfunctioning French elevator. Musty rooms with cavernous bathrooms lie beyond. Pictures of the Dong Khoi in 1925 and 1995 show very little variation—instead of foot-powered rickshaws out the front, there are now bicycle-powered cyclos.

Down by the Saigon River the **Hotel Majestic** has seen extensive renovations. This old French hotel at 1 Dong Khoi is known in Vietnamese as the Cuu Long, or River of the Nine Dragons. Go to the 5th floor Sky Bar—it has the original marble floors, and affords great views of Saigon River.

WARTIME SAIGON

THE UNWILLING WORKING FOR THE UNABLE TO DO THE UNNECESSARY FOR THE UNGRATEFUL

—INSCRIPTION ON A US-ARMY ISSUE ZIPPO LIGHTER; SAIGON, 1970

Charles de Gaulle told John F. Kennedy Vietnam was "a bottomless military and political swamp." He forgot to mention the moral quagmire. American soldiers who fought in Vietnam paid a double price for a dumb and immoral foreign policy: they fought the war, then weathered the stigma of defeat and disfavor at home. Faced with these unpleasant truths, a number of Vietnam vets have returned to Vietnam as a healing process, to lay to

WARTIME SAIGON

NGUYEN BINH KHIEM

ZOOLOGICAL GARDENS

★ HISTORY MUSEUM

DIEN TIEN HOANG

MILITARY MUSEUM ★

MAC DINH CHI

HAI BA TRUNG

NGUYEN THI MINH KHAI

TON DUC THANG

FORMER US EMBASSY ★

★ FRENCH CONSULATE

FOUNTAIN ★

NAM KY KHOI NGHIA

NOT TO SCALE

LE DUAN

LE QUY DON

HAI BA TRUNG

ONE-WAY

PASTEUR

ONE-WAY

WAR CRIMES MUSEUM ★

VO VAN THAN

GATES OF REUNIFICATION HALL ★

VAN HOA PARK

© MOON PUBLICATIONS, INC.

rest the uneasiness that has plagued them since the war. The Vietnamese, for their part, had trouble understanding exactly why the Americans interfered in their affairs. Still, they treat returning US veterans the same as any other tourist—they bear no grudge. It's really the Vietnamese who should be bitter about the whole thing, but they're not. Life goes on.

War Crimes Museum

To take a shattering leap back to the wartime 1960s and 1970s, visit the War Crimes Museum, open daily 0800-1200 and 1300-1700 on Vo Van Tan near the intersection of Le Quy Don. To get there from downtown Saigon, take Pasteur Street north, and turn left on Vo Van Tan. The museum is on the grounds of a French villa that once housed the US Information Service. This small museum is by turns grisly, horrifying, sobering, and—ultimately—deeply disturbing. Few

English captions accompany the pictures on the walls, but they speak for themselves—the My Lai massacre, victims of antipersonnel weapons like napalm and Agent Orange, deformed babies. A series taken from the *Chicago Sun-Times* shows a Vietnamese POW being pushed from an American helicopter. This raises the ethical questions regarding war crimes: where does "normal" war end, and where do war crimes begin?

There is a photo parade of the guilty, from Lyndon Johnson to Richard Nixon, pictures of US antiwar demonstrations, a display of eight medals sent to the museum by American vets in 1990. There used to be a Chinese atrocity wing in this museum, related to the border wars of 1979. After Vietnam normalized relations with China, the display was discreetly removed. In the meantime, two Wartime Souvenir Shops popped up, selling Zippo lighters, war memorabilia, and other odd items.

Around the grounds you'll find an array of captured weaponry—M-41 tank, 175mm howitzer, M-113 flamethrower, A37B light bomber, U17A observation aircraft, a few Huey helicopters. There's also a French guillotine, brought to Vietnam at the turn of the century. As late as the 1950s it was hauled around the provinces to publicly decapitate Vietminh resistance fighters in the French colonial manner.

THE WARTIME SOUVENIR SHOP

In 1993 two shops opened on either side of the gates at the War Crimes Museum, each called Wartime Souvenir Shop. The proprietors sell a rather bizarre collection of souvenirs. How about a flower vase made from a 40mm cartridge, burnished to a bright gold? Or a pair of Ho Chi Minh tire-tread sandals? Perhaps a green NVA pith helmet, or NVA campaign and victory badges? Other items on sale include lighters made from M-16 cartridges, and small oil lamps the Vietcong recycled from M-79 cartridges and used to illuminate tunnels. There's even a set of Vietnam in Wartime postcards, one featuring a Vietcong woman in full combat gear, striking a heroic pose.

You can also buy US flashlights, watches, compasses, and field glasses. And there's a range of rusted US dog tags with name, religion, and blood type embossed on each one. Authentic? Probably not. Certainly morbid.

US army-issue Zippo lighters cost $5-20 depending on "quality" and whether or not they work. Many antique and souvenir shops in Saigon, as well as shops at Dan Sinh army surplus market, carry Zippos. Some feature a poignant, prayerful, military, romantic, or obscene slogan; others bear engravings such as nude women, Peanuts cartoon characters Snoopy and Lucy, or the bearded Zig Zag rolling-papers man.

During the Vietnam War, aluminum cans discarded by US soldiers were turned into hand grenades by the Vietcong. This came as a shock to American troops, who began to be more careful about what they threw away. The Vietnamese are still transforming those cans. At the Wartime Souvenir Shop and on the streets of Saigon, you can buy Huey helicopters, F-4 Phantom jets, F-111s, and Cessnas made of old Coke, Tiger, or Heineken cans. These origami-in-metal pieces sell for a dollar and feature painstaking detail—the helicopter doors are even detachable. You can almost conjure up the recycling scenario: scrap aluminum from downed US jets is gathered in Vietnam, exported to Japan and turned into beer cans, which then come back to Vietnam, and after use are discarded, picked up again, and remade into model Huey helicopters.

War materiel is recycled in the oddest places. Once, when I mentioned the war, my cyclo driver, a former ARVN soldier, pointed at his bicycle bell—a large brass cylinder struck with a small handlebar-operated device, like a gong. I took a closer look: the bell was made from a 105mm shell case, cut off at the bottom.

The shop offers many different souvenirs, some recycled from war materiel.

American Haunts

From the War Crimes Museum, head east until you reach an odd traffic circle. American civilians once occupied apartments around the circle, an exclusive residential zone. In the middle of the circle stands a shaft of concrete. At first glance this appears to be a piece of Socialist sculpture, but it doesn't look quite right. Then there's the surreal flight of stairs to one side—what is this? Yes, it's the core of an apartment building. The structure was demolished, leaving only the concrete center. Around the traffic circle are lots of open-air cafés where you can sit and contemplate the damage. Inside the derelict area a set of fountains have been installed, turned on for photo opportunities on special holidays.

Vietcong terrorists sometimes turned Saigon into a battlefield, bombing businesses patronized by Americans. Despite these attacks, Saigon was one of the safest places to be during the Vietnam War, and its legendary bars, restaurants, and hotels were the dreams of GIs in the field. Some of the places they frequented still thrive. The Rex Hotel was used by US officers, as was the Majestic; war correspondents gathered to watch the war on the roof of the Caravelle hotel; Maxim's nightclub was the same overpriced dive it is today.

The American Embassy

The ugly white building on Le Duan Boulevard with the concrete turret-style windows and a few sentry boxes on the corners is the US Embassy, designed with maximum security in mind. The Americans moved here in 1967 after the previous site was blown up by a 100-kg car bomb. But the new fortress-like building was not enough to stave off an attack: a plaque at the front of the embassy commemorates the attempt of a 17-man Vietcong commando unit to storm the embassy on 31 January 1968. The commandos, dressed as South Vietnamese soldiers, were killed, along with five American Marines and MPs.

The US Embassy closed on 30 April 1975 when the last of the staff boarded a helicopter from the roof as Saigon fell around their ears. The last chopper lifts were hectic. Thousands of Vietnamese who had worked for the Americans had been promised a lift out, but the US reneged and they were left behind. The furious Vietnamese sacked the embassy. In *All the Wrong Places,* English writer James Fenton recounts: "The place was packed, and in chaos. Papers, files, brochures, and reports were strewn around. . . . One man called me over to a wall safe and seemed to be asking if I knew the number of the combination. Another was hacking away at an air conditioner, another was dismantling a refrigerator." In their rush to get out, American embassy staff left behind files on those who worked for them, making it easy for the North to identify collaborators.

Presently the six-story embassy building remains closed, awaiting the return of Vietnam's best friends, the Americans? The US government has negotiated the return of the property for use as a trade center and site for an American consulate. The first floor of the building is used by the government oil company; staff use a side entrance to gain access.

Military Museum

The main target of Vietcong tanks rumbling through the capital was not the US Embassy but the gates of the Presidential Palace, two blocks to the west. Americans remember the last helicopter leaving the US Embassy, but for the Vietnamese the key image is that of tanks smashing down the palace gates. The tanks then rolled onto the lawn, formed a semicircle, and fired a salute.

The Vietnamese point of view on the war is presented at the Military Museum, just north of central Saigon (District 1). There's a big 1975 section on the fall of Saigon, complete with scale models, maps with lights indicating strategic campaign points, and data on the American imperialist aggressors and their southern puppets. The Vietcong infiltrated the capital well before the final attack, dressed in Saigon Army uniforms. They stayed in Cholon, where the Chinese—always shrewd businesspeople—were already manufacturing North Vietnamese flags. The real Saigon Army soldiers stripped off their uniforms and fled, leaving mounds of clothing, boots, and weapons on the streets. Others dressed in Vietcong-style black pajamas.

Apart from its centerpiece battle-plan model, the museum displays photos and small arms. Most signs are in Vietnamese, with scattered English captions. Although the museum covers some events from 1945 on, most cover the period from 1973 to 1975, including a garbled 15-minute video on campaigns of that era. Some pictures document the use of bicycles, which were very important to the military success of the North Vietnamese. They moved tons of supplies along the Ho Chi Minh Trail in caravans of modified and reinforced bicycles. These "steel horses" could each carry up to 200 kilos of supplies, even through deep mud. If the Americans bombed a bridge, NVA troops simply ferried their bicycles across and carried on.

In the museum's outer courtyard lie rusting leftover hardware—a jeep, 85mm guns, small planes. There's an incongruous bonsai nursery and an art gallery—regular art downstairs, revolutionary art upstairs. For $500 you can buy a canvas showing the Fall of Saigon; for $200, a Cu Chi Tunnels painting. The Military Museum is open 0830-1130 and 1330-1600, closed Monday; entry is free.

Puppets

When the American imperialists left, their South Vietnamese puppets were crushed—sent to re-education camps for the next six or seven years. But some puppets have never fallen out of favor with the North Vietnamese—water puppets. Right across the street from the Military Museum is the **History Museum.** Enter the grounds of the zoological gardens, 50 cents; go into the History Museum, $1; then find the **water puppet theater,** another $1 for entry. The 20-minute shows are intended to delight children—but will please all ages. Shows start when the puppeteers ascertain the audience has enough kids—usually once an hour. Small model water puppets are sold here, too. This is one of the few places you can see water puppets in Saigon. There are special performances for children at festivals in other temporary sites, but no fixed venue as in Hanoi.

The History Museum is open daily except Monday, 0700-1130 and 1300-1600. Interesting displays include the Cham sculpture section, with a superb standing bronze Buddha; the ethnography section, with displays of Central Highlands costumery and village models such as those from the Kontum-Pleiku area; a display of pieces from Funan, Oc-Eo, and Han Chinese periods; and the Buddha sculpture section, with

superb Buddha and Avalokitesvara statues from East Asia. Under the French this 1928 structure was known as Musée Blanchard de la Brosse, set in what were once the finest French botanical gardens in Southeast Asia. Saigon's motley zoo collection has since been added to the flora, making this a zoological gardens—a relaxing place to pass time and chat with the locals. It's best to stick to the flora side; the animals look rather forlorn. Despite the ravages of war, the gardens present a great variety of plant species.

CHOLON PAGODAS

In 1978 the government launched an assault on capitalist practices in Saigon, primarily targeting the wealthy Chinese business community in Cholon, the "Chinatown" of Saigon. The following year China engaged Vietnam in a vicious border war in the north, and a quarter of Vietnam's ethnic Chinese fled the country—the first of the "boat people." Most of the exodus was from Saigon and Cholon, where every shop and house was ransacked for valuables and gold and many

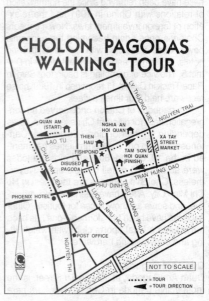

BIG MARKET

Cholon means "Big Market" and the area is certainly bustling. Especially in District 5, windows display luxury goods imported from China and Thailand, and the boulevards are jampacked with commuters on brand-new motorcycles and cyclos loaded with goods. Riverside warehouses are piled high with dried fish and sacks of rice; outdoor markets are thronged with customers. The largest market in Cholon is **Ben Tay Market** off Hau Giang Blvd. in District 6. A courtyard-type block contains open-air and covered stalls, mainly in wholesale trade. The market is vast and colorful, and sells everything from spices to silk; an ideal place to ramble for an hour or two.

An Duong Market opened in late 1991 near the intersection of An Duong Vuong Blvd. and Su Van Hanh St. in District 5. This market shows the confidence of the Chinese community in the new Cholon—it was built with a $5 million investment from almost a hundred Cholon businessmen. The five-story market complex has 24,000 square meters of commercial space. The top two floors comprise a Taiwanese hotel and office complex; the lower floors offer retail space, with the first floor for clothing. The basement houses many small restaurants—a good place to dine on a budget.

Chinese stripped of their wealth. In the 1980s Cholon was a ghost town. Cautiously, ethnic Chinese have been returning since the normalization of relations with China in 1991 and the relaxation of foreign investment laws. Now it appears Cholon is once again becoming the economic powerhouse of the city, with high rents, thriving hotels, nightclubs, and department stores in District 5. The vice of gambling is back, too: Saigon Race Track in District 11 reopened in 1989; horse races are held four times a week.

The pagodas of Cholon once served as congregation halls for different Chinese communities depending on their origins—Fukienese, Cantonese, and so on. The communities fragmented in the 1970s and '80s, and most pagodas were abandoned or fell into disrepair. Nevertheless, Cholon's pagodas are the finest in Ho Chi Minh City. A few have been restored, are active, and serve as showpieces for tourism. Other pagodas have been transformed—one has been turned into a local sports club, with weightlifting and bodybuilding hardware.

Quan Am Pagoda

Quan Am Pagoda, at 12 Lao Tu Street, is the most active pagoda in Cholon. Hawkers here sell incense sticks, paper offerings, and captive birds to a steady stream of devotees. About 25 nuns and monks are based at the temple, and several live on the premises. In front of the main altar is a white ceramic statue of Quan Am, known in Chinese as Guanyin, the Goddess of Mercy. There are also red wedding dresses and elaborate funeral chariots on display. The roof is richly decorated, with Chinese legends rendered in ceramic tiles.

Clear your lungs of incense, and walk south toward the Phoenix Hotel. In the distance you'll spot a yellow building; the post office. It bears a Buu Dien sign, but you can still make out the old French PTT sign. In the open area before the post office is a statue of Dinh Phung, a Vietnamese hero famed for fighting the French.

Pleasure City

At a disused pagoda on a corner, turn onto tiny Phu Dinh Street; halfway along, at number 7, is the house seen in the French movie *The Lover*. The Chinese shophouse looks rather bland and innocent now, difficult to imagine as a trysting place in a steamy affair between a Chinese man and a French schoolgirl. But remember the context: Cholon in the 1930s, '40s, and '50s was rife with opium dens, mahjong joints, and gambling joints like the Grand Monde Casino.

In 1957, French adventurer Gontran de Poncins wrote: "Cholon is the Chinese pleasure city. Cholon is the night city with electric signs in Chinese characters that gleam like rubies and taxi girls whose shapely bodies stir the customers . . . Cholon is the gambling city . . . the city of opium dives where, for a few piastres, you can have a flap-board bed, a nugget of opium, a boy to prepare your pipes and, if you so wish, a companion to lie beside you. Cholon is open to all desires!" Cholon had a reputation as a place for business and pleasure, often conducted in the same hotel. The City of Pleasure appears to be reviving, with seedy karaoke,

Huge incense coils hang from the roof of a Cholon pagoda.

nightclubs, and taxi dancers in major hotels catering to Asian businessmen.

Goddesses and Generals

Thien Hau Pagoda, at 710 Nguyen Trai, honors Thien Hau, the goddess of the sea, and protectress of sailors and fisherfolk. Thien Hau also retains elements of the Taoist Queen of Heaven, and is a popular deity in Hong Kong and Taiwan. The pagoda was constructed in the early 19th century and is one of the largest and busiest in the city. It was once the focus of the Cantonese community. Recently restored, it now serves as a showpiece for Saigon Tourism. Inside the front gate are two enormous incense urns; huge incense spirals burn for hours. The principal temple image is a gilded Thien Hau; a model boat lies nearby. More interesting visually are the intricate ceramic friezes on the temple roof, best viewed from a small courtyard. Opposite the temple is a run-down old fishpond, formerly connected with temple ceremonies. Although Thien Hau Pagoda is busy all day, there are special services on Sunday at 0600 and 1600.

One block to the east is **Nghia An Hoi Quan Pagoda,** at 678 Nguyen Trai. The temple was built by the Chaozhou Chinese congregation. After passing a carved wooden boat shading the entrance, you come to the larger-than-life red horse of Quan Cong, a revered Chinese general. The statue of Quan Cong is encased in glass and bears a red face, long beard, and green costume. He's flanked by two assistants, a general and a mandarin.

Continue to **Tam Son Hoi Quan Pagoda,** at 118 Trieu Quang Phuc Street, a Fukienese pagoda that has fallen into neglect. It's dedicated to Me Sanh, Goddess of Fertility—childless mothers patronize a statue at the back. The temple was built in the 19th century in Sino-Vietnamese style and is pleasantly uncluttered.

SAIGON PAGODAS

Saigon has upwards of 200 pagodas. Most are either run-down or humdrum; the best are found in Cholon. A pagoda is a community center of sorts and often a repository for small funerary jars, each containing the ashes of the deceased with a photo and nameplate. Newer pagodas, such as Xa Loi and Vinh Nghiem, are of more interest at festival time, when they're ablaze with incense and thronged with devotees and beggars. Some of the following pagodas are located on the fringes of Saigon.

At 338 Nguyen Cong Tru St., **Phung Son Tu Pagoda** lies south of Ben Thanh Market, close to the Army Surplus market in District 1. This Chinese-style pagoda was built by the Fujian community in the 1940s and is very similar in style to Cholon pagodas. Fierce warrior statues guard the entrance doors. The temple is dedicated to Ong Bon, guardian of happiness and virtue.

You'll find the small **Jade Emperor Pagoda** at 73 Mai Thi Luu St., off Dien Bien Phu Street. Built in 1900, it's home to a bizarre collection of carved wood deities—some Buddhist, some Taoist. Presiding at the main altar is Ngoc Hoang, the Taoist Emperor of Jade. The wooden panels in a side chapel, the Hall of the Ten Hells, show the thousand tortures awaiting evildoers. Near the main entrance, to one side of the temple, a chamber holds many small ceramic figures of mothers and children cloaked in red—a fertility shrine of sorts, visited by women.

Dai Giac Pagoda is located at 112 Nguyen Van Troi, near Saigon Omni Hotel. Dai Giac is cluttered with kitsch—more like a Chinese amusement park than a pagoda. Inside are Buddha and Quan Am statues in glass cases, a few lion statues, a magnificent brass gong, a huge black drum made of porcelain with mother-of-pearl inlay, and funerary urns bearing photos of the departed. In the courtyard is a huge Laughing Buddha made of wood, and a grotto with a Quan Am statue. To the north side of Dai Giac a six-level pagoda features an exterior coated in pieces of broken porcelain; linked to the pagoda are monks' quarters.

Vinh Nghiem Pagoda is also on Nguyen Van Troi, just south of Thi Nghe Channel. Here there are two buildings—the main temple and a seven-story pagoda. The latter contains funeral urns, and is open only on holidays and at festival time, when the place is packed. The temple was completed in the early 1970s with assistance from the Japan-Vietnam Friendship Association, which explains the Japanese architecture. The interior walls bear scrolls with scenes from the Jataka Tales. The temple's large bell was a gift from Japanese Buddhists, presented during the Vietnam War.

Xa Loi Pagoda, at 89 Ba Huyen Quan Thanh St. off Dien Bien Phu St. in District 3, is a large modern concrete structure, with a large newish Buddha backed by a neon halo. In the courtyard below is a stucco Quan Am. Xa Loi was the headquarters of militant Buddhists during their struggle to overthrow the Diem regime. In August 1963 thousands demonstrated to protest religious persecution; on 21 August special forces attacked the pagoda, and martial law was declared.

Thic Quang Duc Shrine is named for Thich Quang Duc, a 66-year-old monk from Hué, who immolated himself on 11 June 1963. A photograph of the monk in flames made front-page news around the world. Some 30 monks and nuns followed his example, protesting the Diem regime and US involvement in Vietnam. Diem's sister-in-law Madame Nhu made jokes about barbecued monks and said, "Let them burn—we shall clap our hands!" This shrine lies at the corner of Nguyen Dinh Chieu and Cach Mang Thang Tam Streets, a few blocks south of Xa Loi Pagoda. The car used to drive the monk to the immolation site is in Thien Mu Pagoda in Hué.

On the outskirts of Saigon in District 11, the Vietnamese-style **Giac Vien Tu Pagoda** is dedicated to Emperor Gia Long. The accumulation of 300 years of incense burning imbues this place with a striking atmosphere. There is a profusion of carvings—Buddhist, Taoist, and Confucian deities and mythical figures. The most significant is a large gilded statue of Amitabha, Buddha of the Past. After a body is cremated, the ashes are transported in a funeral carriage to the pagoda. Numerous funerary jars are on view in the first chamber. Twenty monks are attached to the temple, and half live on the premises. The temple is hard to find—it's about 200 meters off Lac Long Quan Street. Get there by moto or rental car.

Giac Lam Pagoda, at 118 Lac Long Quan St. in Tan Binh District, was built in 1744. It is believed to be the oldest pagoda still standing in Saigon. It's quite similar in architecture and atmosphere to Giac Vien Tu Pagoda. The two pagodas are a few kilometers apart; a visit to one or the other should suffice. Giac Lam is large and has darkened halls with carved jackwood statues. Senior monks wear yellow robes; novice monks wear brown robes.

OTHER SIGHTS

Additional Museums

The **Art Museum** (Bao Tang My Thuat), in a mansion at 97A Pho Duc Chinh St. in central Saigon, displays revolutionary art and sculpture, as well as artifacts from the Oc-Eo civilization.

The **Ho Chi Minh Museum** occupies the old French customs house, known as Dragon House Wharf, at the confluence of the Saigon River and Ben Nghe Channel. The French transport company Messageries Maritimes once had its headquarters here. The museum celebrates the exploits of Uncle Ho, who left Saigon at the age of 21 aboard a French freighter from this wharf. Signing on as a galley boy, he departed in 1911 on an extended journey through Europe, Africa, North America,

SAIGON RIVER BOAT TOURS

Since Saigon is a port, cruising the city gives you a different perspective. Look for boat rentals, costing roughly $5-10 an hour for up to 10 passengers, on the banks of the Saigon River, especially near the foot of Ham Nghi Boulevard. For a longer jaunt, head north through shipping to Thanh Da Island, a two-hour trip. Saigon Tourism arranges boats up that way with traditional food and dance, at a cost of $15 a head, or $5 for the show only. Boats depart three times weekly from the lobby of the Hotel Majestic. Three separate programs are performed on different nights. One is song and dance, the second traditional music, the third a traditional wedding ceremony. At night you can take dinner cruises on the Saigon River; see "Nightlife" later in this chapter for details.

Canals around Saigon are black and scummy. Ramshackle houses balance on stilts along the banks of tributaries, and you might get a glimpse of boats with leg-rowers. There are a few commuter boats along the canals, though foreigners rarely use them. You can reach Cholon from the Saigon River—take a regular boat from the pier at the foot of Ham Nghi Blvd. near the river. Or rent a boat and make it out to Cholon's Ben Tay Market in about three hours one-way. The boat goes along Ben Nghe Channel and drops you short of the market; then you walk up. Since you've already seen the scum, no need to take the boat back—use the bus or other transportation back to town.

The Hall was formerly the site of Norodom Palace, the residence of the French Governor-general of Indochina, built in 1868. The Governor-general spent little time there as his principal seat was in Hanoi. After the Geneva Conference in 1954 and the installation of President Ngo Dinh Diem, the place was renamed the Presidential Palace. In 1962, two South Vietnamese Air Force pilots turned their firepower on the palace in an attempt to assassinate Diem. The president and his family escaped to the cellar, but the palace was largely destroyed. The present structure was built in the late 1960s by Paris-trained architect Ngo Viet Thu. In early April 1975 another renegade pilot bombed the new palace, damaging part of it. On 30 April 1975, NVA tanks smashed down the front gates and took control of Saigon, arresting President General Duong Van Minh and his cabinet. A short career for General Minh—he'd become head of state only two days before. After a period of re-education, Minh was allowed to emigrate to France in 1983.

and Asia and did not return to Vietnam until 1941. A visit to the museum is compulsory for legions of Saigon schoolchildren, who have their photos taken with a statue of Uncle Ho in the background.

Museums in Ho Chi Minh City are usually open Tues.-Sun. 0800-1130 and 1400-1700.

Reunification Hall

Reunification Hall, or Thong Nhat Conference Hall, is one of those take-it-or-leave-it destinations. Some like it, some hate it—it will cost you $5 to find out. The entry price includes a brochure and some spotty postcards; there's also a crackly revolutionary film thrown in along the line. A cross between a museum and conference center, the rambling Reunification Hall exudes a sterile atmosphere. Sometimes the place is closed for state occasions; otherwise, it's open 0730-1030 and 1300-1530 daily. Foreigners must enter from a gate at 106 Nguyen Du Street on the south side of the grounds, and must take a guided tour. The English of the guides may be poor.

The hall has been preserved as it was on 30 April 1975. Various rooms are decorated with lacquered paintings and filled with 1960s furniture. More interesting are the basement and the rooftop. President Nguyen Van Thieu had a bombproof bunker built in the basement of the Hall; from here he conducted government affairs until April 1975, when he fled. You can view military maps, field radios, and other gizmos from the war. On the rooftop is a helipad with a helicopter parked on it. This makes a macabre photo-op—group tours are sometimes permitted to line up for pictures, pretending it's 1975 and they're scrambling for the last chopper out.

Hindu and Muslim Temples

Saigon's eclectic mix of temples includes a few mosques and Hindu temples. Like the ethnic Chinese, Hindus and Muslims were persecuted

North Vietnamese tanks arrive at the Presidential Palace.

PHOTO COURTESY OF UPI

by the revolutionary government and most, including the spiritual leaders, fled Vietnam. Still, there are a dozen mosques around Saigon. At 66 Dong Du St., off Dong Khoi, is **Saigon Central Mosque,** built by South Indian Muslims in 1935. The spotless blue and white structure features four minarets and is a tranquil retreat in the heart of the city.

Within a few blocks of Ben Thanh Market stand two Hindu temples. To the northwest of the market is **Mariamman Temple,** at 45 Truong Dinh Street. This century-old site is dedicated to the goddess Mariamman; it was taken over in 1975 and turned into a joss-stick factory. To the southeast of Ben Thanh Market is **Sri Then-**

day Litthapani, at 66 Ton That Thiep, a Hindu temple over a century old. It was disbanded after 1975, but in early 1993 the government returned the temple to Saigon's tiny Hindu community. Hindu adherents of several nationalities come to this sacred shrine. You enter through a colonnaded interior courtyard with a small shrine guarded by horse statues, and an ornate door with bells mounted on it. If the walls look bare, it's because a lot of the statuary went missing—the central statue has been replaced by a picture. Framed pictures of Indian deities and important figures grace the walls—Shiva, Vishnu, Ghandi, Nehru. On the roof are towers with detailed Hindu sculpture.

ACCOMMODATIONS

Saigon has the largest selection of hotels in Vietnam. Accommodations range from small homey guesthouses to luxurious suites. High-end hotels provide in-house movies, minibar, IDD, room safe, and individual air-conditioning control; facilities often include health club, business center, and restaurants. Major hotels charge 10% government tax and 5-10% service charge on top of listed prices; others include those charges in the tariff. Larger hotels will accept Visa, MasterCard, Diners Club, American Express, and JCB cards, but will surcharge up to four percent for using a credit card.

The two prime tourist accommodation zones are in District 1: Central Saigon appeals to business travelers, and Pham Ngu Lao is backpacker headquarters. However, the lines are becoming blurred as major hotels rise away from the downtown core. An upcoming area for business visitors is District 3. Asian businesspeople and tourists, particularly Taiwanese, stay in Cholon in District 5.

PHAM NGU LAO

Budget

Pham Ngu Lao is Saigon's version of Bangkok's Khao San Road—a rabbit warren of travel and transport agencies, cafés and bars, hotels and guesthouses, bicycle and motorcycle rentals, photo shops, souvenir shops, moneychangers, even railway ticketing offices. Add Western pop music and backpackers quaffing 333 beers under sidewalk umbrellas, and you've got the picture. There have been reports of thefts in some of the cheaper hotels—use your own padlock whenever possible.

Family-run guesthouses often hang out a sign that simply says Room for Rent, to avoid paying taxes. **Le Le Room for Rent,** 269 De Tham, opposite Kim Café, tel. 322110, has seven rooms for $8 s and $10 d. A few doors down at number 265 is another Room For Rent, tel. 331512, charging $15 triple.

Coco Loco Guesthouse, 351 Pham Ngu Lao, tel. 322186, is a family setup with super-clean rooms. This guesthouse is a great value and often full—the seven rooms go for $10-12 each. Next door at 349 is a place with no name, only a Room For Rent sign, tel. 395496. Opposite is **Rose Room for Rent** at 42 Pham Ngu Lao, tel. 322044. Rose offers 11 rooms for $12-15, with air-con and shower. Room For Rent signs are springing up in this area as fast as families can convert their houses into guesthouses—rooms go for $5-10, but fancier ones might cost $20. At 70 Bui Vien St. is **Guesthouse 70** (Phuong Lan), tel. 330569, featuring seven rooms with shared bath for $8-12, and one room with private bath for $14. Family lounge downstairs. Next door at number 72 is **Guesthouse 72** (Le Van Tam), tel. 330321, with five rooms for $7-10.

Budget/Moderate

Vien Dong Hotel (Far East), at 275A Pham Ngu Lao, tel. 393001, fax 332812, has 139 double and triple rooms. It attracts all kinds, from backpackers to businesspeople. There are 69 fan rooms for $12, 32 air-con rooms for $32, another 36 rooms for $50, and two suites for $70 each. Vien Dong is often booked. Hotel facilities include a restaurant, and ABC Karaoke Bar on the first floor. **Khach San Hoan Vu,** at 265 Pham Ngu Lao, tel. 396522, has singles, doubles, and triples for $10-12. The hotel has 160 rooms and the strangest elevator in all of Saigon. A bit run-down, but popular with backpackers. **Prince** (Hoang Tu), at 193 Pham Ngu Lao, tel. 322657, offers rooms for $6-12 including air-con in the upper range. The cheaper rooms are on the upper floors—no elevator.

Thai Binh Hotel, at 325 Pham Ngu Lao, tel. 399544, has 28 run-down rooms for $8 d, $9 t, $10 d air-con. Down the street is **Top Minihotel** (KS Thienh Dien), at 61 Do Quang Dau, tel. 353281, with 10 rooms for $40-50-60. **Le Canari** (Hoang Yen), 83A Bui Thi Xuan, tel. 391348, is an airy, clean minihotel featuring eight rooms for $18-25. At the back of Pham Ngu Lao, on Le Lai Street, are the following hotels. **Palace Saigon Minihotel,** 82 Le Lai, tel. 331353, has nine rooms, all with shower and TV, for $25 s or $35 d. **Le Suong,** 94-96 Le Lai, tel. 334137, is a six-story hotel with 20 rooms for $5 s, $7 d with fan, and $10-12 d air-con. **A Chau,** 92B Le Lai, tel. 331814, offers 10 rooms—$6 s or $7 d, with shower and fan.

Hotel Le Lai, at 76 Le Lai St., tel. 291246, fax 90282, is an eight-story building with 46 rooms for $23-47 s, $30-54 d, $36-61 t, and $69-94 for a suite. A bit farther to the north of Pham Ngu Lao is **Hoang Gia,** 12D Cach Mang Thang Tam St., tel. 294846, fax 225346, a nine-story hotel with 42 rooms from $30 to $50.

Luxury

There has been a flurry of joint-venture hotel building in this area. The **New World Saigon** at 76 Le Lai, tel. 228888, fax 230710, is Vietnam's largest hotel. This is a joint-venture project with Hong Kong's New World Development Company. There are 544 rooms in the 14-story building, with doubles from $185 and suites costing up to $500. The hotel boasts six restaurants, an Olympic-size pool, and even a golf driving range. The New World company plans to build a

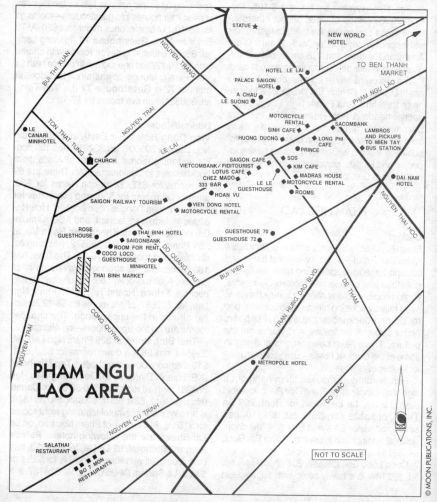

PHAM NGU LAO AREA

STATUE ★

NEW WORLD HOTEL

TO BEN THANH MARKET

HOTEL LE LAI
PALACE SAIGON HOTEL
A CHAU
LE SUONG

MOTORCYCLE RENTAL
SINH CAFE
HUONG DUONG
LONG PHI CAFE
PRINCE

SACOMBANK
LAMBROS AND PICKUPS TO MIEN TAY BUS STATION

LE CANARI MINIHOTEL

CHURCH

SAIGON CAFE
VIETCOMBANK / FIDITOURIST
LOTUS CAFE
CHEZ MADO
333 BAR
LE LE GUESTHOUSE
HOAN VU
VIEN DONG HOTEL
MOTORCYCLE RENTAL

SOS
KIM CAFE
MADRAS HOUSE
MOTORCYCLE RENTAL
ROOMS

DAI NAM HOTEL

SAIGON RAILWAY TOURISM

ROSE GUESTHOUSE
THAI BINH HOTEL
SAIGONBANK
ROOM FOR RENT
COCO LOCO GUESTHOUSE
TOP MINIHOTEL
THAI BINH MARKET

GUESTHOUSE 70
GUESTHOUSE 72

METROPOLE HOTEL

SALATHAI RESTAURANT
BO 7 MON RESTAURANTS

NOT TO SCALE

© MOON PUBLICATIONS, INC.

25-story office tower next to the hotel, and complete another hotel, the 32-story Ramada Riverside, by the Saigon River.

Hotel Mercure Saigon, 79 Tran Hung Dao, tel. 242525, fax 242533, is run by the French Accor group. This four-star hotel has 104 rooms with every conceivable creature comfort known to Vietnam, including electronic safe, minibar, and satellite TV—there's even a phone installed in the shower so you won't miss a call. Rooms range $80-100 for standard and superior singles, $12-140 for deluxe; for double occupancy add $30 to the single price. The hotel features a restaurant, nightclub, and business center.

The **Metropole Hotel** (Binh Minh), 148 Tran Hung Dao, tel. 322021, fax 322019, has 94 spacious rooms with air-con, minibar, IDD, room safe, and satellite TV. Costs range $86-95 standard, $109-120 deluxe, and $120-150 suite. It's run by Saigon Tourist, and facilities include a business center, swimming pool, and a sky bar on the 7th floor.

CENTRAL SAIGON

Most of the hotels around the downtown core in District 1 are owned and operated by Saigon Tourist, sometimes as a joint-venture. The Saigon Tourist hotels include the Rex, Caravelle, Majestic, Continental, Hnong Sen, and Bong Sen. You can spot the top hotels—look for satellite dishes on the roof. Special permission is needed for these satellite dishes, capable of receiving StarTV.

Budget/Moderate
Budget and moderate hotels are hard to find around central Saigon, and may not be great value, either. The following minihotels are tucked into the downtown area: **Viet Phuong,** at 105 Dong Khoi, tel. 295429; **Khach San 69,** 69 Hai Ba Trung, tel. 291513; and **Phong Cho Thue,** 26 Dong Du St., tel. 230164.

Van Canh Hotel, 184 Calmette, tel. 294963, has 13 rooms for $5-10-20 single, an additional $2 for doubles. The 40-room **Dong Khoi Hotel,** at 8 Dong Khoi, tel. 230163, offers single rooms for $10-18; add $2 for doubles. This old French hotel is run-down and musty, with huge rooms and cavernous bathrooms. **Hai Van Hotel,** 69

Huynh Thuc Khang St., tel. 291274, fax 291275, charges $22 s and $30 d. **Vinh Loi** (Champagne Hotel), at 129 Ham Nghi Blvd., tel. 292672, has 38 rooms for $20-30. **Orchid Hotel,** 29A Don Dat St., tel. 231809, fax 292245, has 32 rooms for $40-55.

The mock-Tudor **Dragon Inn,** 3 Hai Ba Trung, tel. 292190, fax 290784, has 10 rooms for $38 s and $48 d. If you're over 1.8 meters (six feet) tall, don't stay here—you'll bang your head on the door frames. **Ben Thanh Minihotel,** 14 Ho Huan Nghiep, tel. 230656, is close to Saigon Floating Hotel. The sliding rate scale works this way: $68 for a room on the first floor, $36 on the second floor, $32 on the third, and $25 on the fourth. There's no elevator, but the rooms have air-con and hot water.

Moderate/Luxury
Along Nguyen Hue and Dong Khoi Boulevards is a cluster of moderate and luxury hotels catering to businesspeople. Some are colonial structures newly renovated and upgraded. Renovation is an ongoing process, so be aware that price jumps can occur. The Kim Do Hotel, for example, on Nguyen Hue Blvd., was formerly a backpacker hangout with $5 rooms and bats and rats; now it's been converted to a sparkling four-star wonder called **Kim Do International,** at 133 Nguyen Hue Blvd., tel. 225914, fax 225913. The 135-room hotel features a host of facilities, with health club, business center, and top-floor bar. Rooms are $120 and up, with executive suites costing up to $480.

Saigon Concert Hotel, located right inside the back end of the Municipal Theater, at 7 Lam Son Square, tel. 291299, fax 295831, is as old as the venerable French theater. The 25 rooms cost $35-40 double. **Saigon Hotel,** 45 Dong Du St., tel. 299734, fax 291466, has 103 rooms for $25-50; $60-80 for a suite. **Huong Sen,** at 70 Dong Khoi, tel. 291415, fax 290916, charges $40-66, with 53 singles and doubles. Under the same management is **Bong Sen** (Lotus) at 117 Dong Khoi, tel. 291516, fax 299744, with 134 rooms for $45-65 and $65-140 suite.

Asian Hotel, 146 Dong Khoi St., tel. 296979, fax 297433, has 47 rooms for $55-80 s and $70-95 d. Facilities include a business center. The **Mondial,** 109 Dong Khoi, tel. 296291, fax 296324, charges $50-85 s and $65-100 d; 40

CENTRAL SAIGON

TON DUC THANG

CHU MAN TRINH

DON DAT

THI SAC

LE LOI

LE DUAN BLVD

NGUYEN DU

LY TU TRONG

LE THANH TON

HAI BA TRUNG

MAC DINH CHI

TO ZOO AND HISTORY MUSEUM

NGUYEN THI MINH KHAI

DONG KHOI

Municipal Theater
Caravelle Hotel

Asian Hotel

Saigon Tourist
Vietnam Airlines
International Bookings
Hotel Continental
Givral Restaurant

FORMER US EMBASSY
FRENCH CONSULATE

Stamp and Coin Market

Hotel de Ville

Norfolk Hotel

Buffalo Blues Bar
General Post Office

Saigon Connection Cafe

KEM Y PISA CAFE

THANH NIEN RESTAURANT

NOTRE DAME CATHEDRAL

Merlion Restaurant
IVY Restaurant
Tiger Tavern

Revolutionary Museum

HAI BA TRUNG

MADAME DAI'S RESTAURANT

NGUYEN VAN CHIEM

PASTEUR

NGUYEN DU

FOUNTAIN

NAPOLI CAFE

LE DUAN BLVD

HAN THUYEN

Embassy Hotel
EMBASSY STREET FOOD STREET

VISITOR'S ENTRANCE

TO AIRPORT

NAM KY KHOI NGHIA

VO VAN TAN

WAR CRIMES MUSEUM
LE MEKONG RESTAURANT
INTERNATIONAL HOTEL

REUNIFICATION HALL

VAN HOA PARK

TRANG CONG CHUA

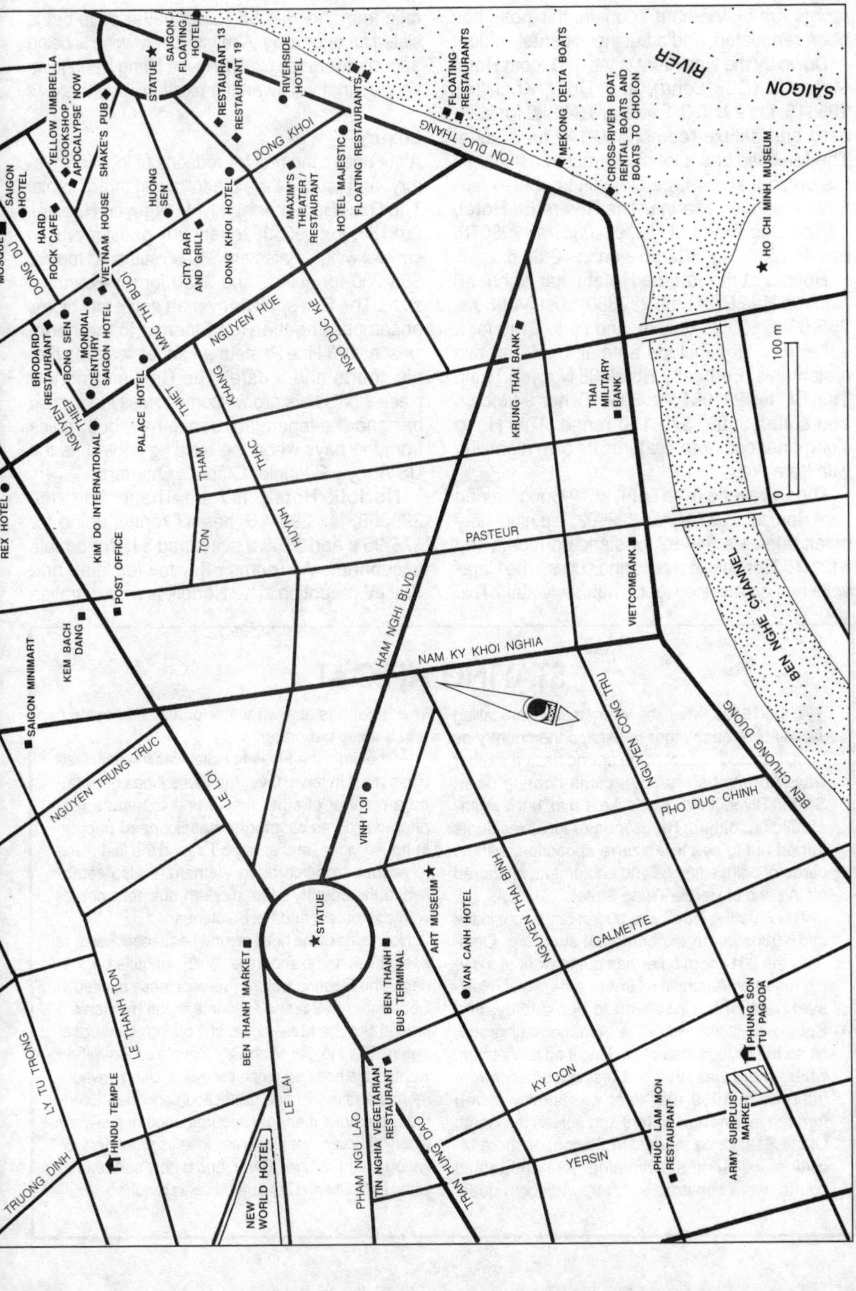
SAIGON RIVER
BEN NGHE CHANNEL
100 m
0
HO CHI MINH MUSEUM
CROSS-RIVER BOAT, RENTAL BOATS AND BOATS TO CHOLON
MEKONG DELTA BOATS
FLOATING RESTAURANTS
FLOATING RESTAURANTS
TON DUC THANG
SAIGON FLOATING HOTEL
STATUE
RESTAURANT 13
RESTAURANT 19
RIVERSIDE HOTEL
HOTEL MAJESTIC
MAXIM'S THEATER / RESTAURANT
DONG KHOI
DONG KHOI HOTEL
CITY BAR AND GRILL
HUONG SEN
SHAKE'S PUB
VIETNAM HOUSE
APOCALYPSE NOW
COOKSHOP
YELLOW UMBRELLA
SAIGON HOTEL
HARD ROCK CAFE
MOSQUE
DONG DU
MAC THI BUOI
BONG SEN
BRODARD RESTAURANT
MONDIAL
CENTURY SAIGON HOTEL
NGUYEN THIEP
PALACE HOTEL
NGUYEN HUE
NGO DUC KE
THAI MILITARY BANK
KRUNG THAI BANK
THAM
TON THAT THIEP
KHANG
HUYNH THUC
KIM DO INTERNATIONAL
REX HOTEL
POST OFFICE
PASTEUR
VIETCOMBANK
HAM NGHI BLVD.
KEM BACH DANG
SAIGON MINIMART
NAM KY KHOI NGHIA
NGUYEN CONG TRU
BEN CHUONG DUONG
PHO DUC CHINH
NGUYEN TRUNG TRUC
LE LOI
VINH LOI
NGUYEN THAI BINH
STATUE
ART MUSEUM
CALMETTE
VAN CANH HOTEL
BEN THANH BUS TERMINAL
BEN THANH MARKET
LE THANH TON
LY TU TRONG
TRUONG DINH
HINDU TEMPLE
NEW WORLD HOTEL
LE LAI
PHAM NGU LAO
TIN NGHIA VEGETARIAN RESTAURANT
TRAN HUNG DAO
KY CON
YERSIN
PHUC LAM MON RESTAURANT
ARMY SURPLUS MARKET
PHUNG SON TU PAGODA

rooms run by Vietnam Tourism, this hotel has been renovated, and a business center added.

Down by the waterfront is the 120-room **Hotel Majestic** (Cuu Long), at 1 Dong Khoi, tel. 295515, fax 291470. Rates are $45-80 for standard and deluxe rooms, $90-140 for a suite. The Majestic has a lot of character, as well as the original French marble fittings. It also features a pool and sauna. The **Riverside Hotel,** 19 Ton Duc Thang St., tel. 224038, fax 298070, has 45 rooms for $32-55 s and $42-66 d.

Rooms at the **Palace Hotel** (Huu Nghi), 56 Nguyen Hue Blvd., tel. 292860, cost $40-50 s, $55-60 d, $60-75 deluxe, and up to $140 for a suite. Facilities include a small pool and two restaurants. **Embassy Hotel,** 36 Nguyen Trung Truc St., tel. 231981, fax 295019, has 94 rooms and suites in the $70-120 range. This Hong Kong-financed hotel features its own nightclub with karaoke.

The **Caravelle** (Doc Lap), at 19 Cong Truong Lam Son, tel. 293704, fax 299902, is a nine-story hotel; rates are $46-92 for standard rooms and $121-150 for deluxe rooms and suites. The Caravelle has an art-deco lobby with surly staff. This relic from the '50s has seen better days but is slated for upgrading. A massive new wing is being added next to the Caravelle—a Hong Kong joint-venture that will dwarf the existing structure.

Luxury

A cut above the rest for reasons of location, history, and prestige are the following three hotels. The **Rex** (Ben Thanh), at 141 Nguyen Hue, tel. 292185, fax 296536, offers 207 guest rooms in several wings. Rates are $60-95 standard rooms, $85-200 for suites, and $450 for an executive suite. The Rex sprawls over an entire city block, encompassing the Rex Cinema; to the northwest at 146 Rue Pasteur an annex features tennis courts and a café. The Rex is a friendly place—outsiders are welcome to visit the rooftop bar and the legendary dance hall, both relics from the days when the building served as the US Army's Bachelor Officer's Quarters.

Norfolk Hotel, 117 Le Thanh Ton, tel. 295368, fax 293415, has 47 rooms going for $75-95 s and $150 a suite; add $15 for double occupancy. All rooms offer full facilities and StarTV reception. The Norfolk is an Australian

STAYING AFLOAT

In the 1980s, when the Vietnamese were falling all over each other to escape the country by boat, one odd vessel came sailing back the other way. An eight-story hotel came floating down Saigon River. It didn't look like a ship, but it wasn't a building, either. Thousands of local residents turned out to see this bizarre apparition, with its cargo of deluxe fittings and equipment, anchored off the end of Hai Ba Trung Street.

The **Floating Hotel** was built in Singapore in the mid-1980s as an experimental structure. Originally the 201-room hotel was put to work at a diving resort on Australia's Great Barrier Reef. However, lack of business led to bankruptcy, and Southern Pacific Hotels, a management group, hit on the brilliant idea of packing it off to Vietnam, where there was a lack of first-class accommodations. In 1989 the hotel was slowly towed through Indonesian waters and across the South China Sea. Once moored in Saigon, onshore facilities, including a swimming pool and tennis courts, were constructed on the adjacent quay. The hotel has its own water purification system and backup generator.

At the time, the Floating Hotel was the only first-class hotel in town. Over the years it has generated a number of other firsts—first to feature IDD phones, rooms catering to handicapped people, in-house video, and satellite TV, and the first place to accept credit cards in Vietnam. It also established the country's first modern business center with computers and fax machines.

Now parts of the hotel are the permanent home of executives and companies. Well, not quite permanent. The Floating Hotel's five-year lease expired in September 1994, and for some tense moments it looked like the hotel would sail off into the sunset again. The Ho Chi Minh City People's Committee wanted the hotel's license canceled, citing environmental and landscape protection concerns. Eventually the hotel manager secured another five-year lease, although the hotel may lose its prominent location on the Saigon River, and a new partnership with Ho Chi Minh City authorities is required.

Notre Dame Cathedral

eight-story island hotel provides 201 sanitized rooms—$130 for a panorama room, $195-230 premium room, $290-460 suite. Facilities include business center, health club, two restaurants, two bars, café, and disco. (For more about this hotel see the special topic "Staying Afloat.")

NORTH OF THE CATHEDRAL

An alternative to accommodations in the downtown core is District 3, north of Notre Dame Cathedral—still within reach of sights and amenities. This area was an exclusive residential zone under the French, and still maintains that aura.

Budget/Moderate
Emperor (KS Hoang De), 117 Nguyen Dinh Chien, tel. 231251, fax 230515. Rates for the 47 comfortable rooms are $28-60. **Liberty,** (Que Huong), 167 Hai Ba Trung, tel. 294227, fax 290919, has 60 rooms. Rooms cost $20-40 but are not the greatest value. **Dee's,** an eight-room minihotel at 223A Hai Ba Trung, tel. 231522, charges $20 s, $25 d, and has two rooms for $30 each.

Luxury
International Hotel, 19 Vo Van Tan, tel. 290009, fax 290066, has 50 rooms and a business center. This Hong Kong joint-venture hotel charges $80-110 for rooms, and $135-160 for a suite. **Saigon Star,** 204 Nguyen Thi Minh Khai, tel. 230260, fax 230255, is a Hong Kong joint-venture hotel overlooking Van Hoa Park; rooms run $99-120 and suites $150-180. Nearby is **Chancery Saigon,** 196 Nguyen Thi Minh Khai, tel. 299152, with 96 spacious rooms and full facilities, including eight business centers. **Saigon Lodge,** 215 Nam Ky Khoi Nghia, tel. 230112, fax 251070, offers 94 rooms for $77-99 standard and deluxe, $121-143 suite, and $330 penthouse.

Super Luxury
Farther north, toward the airport, is **Saigon Omni Hotel,** 251 Nguyen Van Troi St., tel. 449333, fax 449200, a vast hotel with prices to match. The 248-room hotel was completed in 1994 and features two wings. It lists the highest room rates in Saigon, varying from $140 for a standard room to $220 for a deluxe room. A junior suite is $300. On the 7th floor of the main

joint-venture hotel, with a 7th-floor business center, and conference and secretarial services. The hotel is adding 50 rooms.

Hotel Continental, 132-134 Dong Khoi, tel. 299201, fax 290936, is a classic French hotel, completely renovated in the 1980s at a cost of several million dollars. This hotel is prestigious due to its location and links with the past. Standard rooms cost $80-140, deluxe rooms $125-150, and suites $155-180. The Continental has excellent restaurants, and a courtyard garden café.

Super Luxury
Century Saigon Hotel, 68A Nguyen Hue Blvd., tel. 231818, fax 292732, is an 11-story hotel with 109 rooms, run by the Century International Hotel chain. Rates are $115-200 for standard and superior rooms, and $380-530 for a suite. Amenities include a health club, and a business center with multilingual staff.

Saigon Floating Hotel is moored at Hero Square, 1A Me Linh, tel. 90783, fax 90784. The

wing, an executive floor features rooms for $260-350. Prices go through the roof for the two Club Suites at $500 apiece, and the Continental Suite at $800 a night. There are 18 executive apartments listed for $200 a day for a minimum three-month stay. Omni facilities include a Vietnamese and a Thai restaurant, pool and sauna, business center, and three ballrooms.

CHOLON

West of Pham Ngu Lao, in Cholon (District 5), hotels cater mainly to Asian visitors, particularly Taiwanese. Some Westerners regard these accommodations as cheaper alternatives to downtown sites; some just like to get away from the tourist ghettos.

Phoenix Hotel (Phuong Hoang), 411 Tran Hung Dao, tel. 551888, fax 552228, has 70 rooms for $11 fan, or $22 s/d air-con. **Cholon Tourist Minihotel,** at 192 Su Van Hanh, tel. 257089, fax 255375, features rooms for $25-30. Nearby at number 174 is **Cholon Hotel,** with a similar price

range. **An Dong Hotel,** 9 An Duong Vuong, tel. 352001, has 25 rooms from $28 s to $38 d.

Rates at the 90-room **Tokyo Hotel** (Dong Kinh), 106 Tran Tuan Khai, tel. 355352, fax 352505, range from $15 to $25 to $40. The sixth floor features a dance hall and karaoke lounge. **Hanh Long Hotel,** 1027 Tran Hung Dao, tel. 350251, fax 350742, has 48 rooms with satellite TV and IDD. Saigon Tourist manages this nine-story hotel. **Arc En Ciel Hotel,** 52-56 Tan Da, tel. 552550, fax 550332, includes 91 rooms. Rates are $33-55 standard for singles or doubles, $38-60 superior, and $66-88 suite. The Arc En Ciel features Volvo nightclub and karaoke lounge on the second floor and a rooftop garden café. **Regent Hotel,** at 700 Tran Hung Dao, tel. 353548, fax 357094, offers 37 rooms for $40-75.

AIRPORT VICINITY

The Tan Binh District features some nondescript but functional hotels. A short distance from the airport is **Mekong Travel Hotel,** 243A

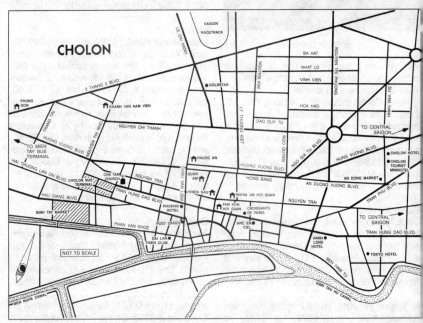

oang Van Thu, tel. 442986, fax 442981. It of-
ers 88 rooms equipped with IDD, satellite TV,
nd electronic safes. Rates are $55-85. Helpful
taff at the Mekong Hotel business center will
rrange visas, visa extensions, translation, and
ping. Confusingly, there's another place called
e Mekong Hotel nearby.

Down the street, and a number of notches
own in service and class, is **Dong Phuong I,**
11 Nguyen Van Troi, tel. 442088, fax 440895,
ith 31 rooms for $30-45. This place is run-down,
s is its sister hotel, **Dong Phuong II,** on Hoang
'an Thu Boulevard. At 200 Hoang Van Thu Blvd.,
an Son Nhat Hotel, tel. 241079, offers 25 dou-
les for $25-50. The place is in good shape; it
vas once a guesthouse for government officials.

Chains First Hotel occupies a quiet side
street at 18 Hoang Viet St., tel. 441199, fax
444282. It's a joint-venture hotel with two large
wings. There are 89 rooms in the new wing;
these run $65-85 for a standard room, and $100-
125 for a suite. The old wing, a brick blockhouse
across the street, provides 38 rooms for $35-
65. Chains First has sports facilities, several
restaurants, and a pool. Next door to Chains
First is **Starhill Hotel,** 14-16 Hoang Viet, tel.
443623, fax 444627, with 36 rooms for $25-40.

Farther east, in the Phu Nhuan District, is
London Hotel, 216 Phan Dang Luu, tel.
443344; its 23 rooms go for $20 s and $40-45 d.
Hotel l'Arc de Triomphe (Khach San Khai
Hoan Mon), is not far away at 135A Phan Dang
Luu, tel. 447941, fax 447940, with 20 rooms in
the same price range.

FOOD

ood in Saigon is mainly Vietnamese, Chinese,
nd Western, although the city offers the odd In-
lian, Thai, or Japanese restaurant. The best Chi-
lese food is found in Cholon; in central Saigon,
Vietnamese and Western food are the main fare.
Vietnamese food is cheap and the best value for
he money—Western food is expensive.

RESTAURANTS

Budget Dining

Bakeries: French bread is widely available, and
lest consumed fresh, in the early morning.
Sandwich assembly is easy—baguette vendors
vith mobile carts set up on many street corners. Large bakeries include **Givral's** bakery
at 169 Dong Khoi and **Brodard's** boulangerie at
11 Nguyen Thiep. Also try **Nhu Lan Bakery** at
66 Ham Nghi Boulevard. In Cholon, try **Croissants de Paris,** a bakery and tearoom at 274
Tran Hung Dao, west of Arc En Ciel Hotel.

Sidewalk Noodles: Amazing culinary impro-
visation artists appear daily along certain avenues, such as Ngo Duc Ke, on the side west of
Nguyen Hue Blvd, and the side streets off Pham
Ngu Lao. Pull up a sidewalk kindergarten stool
and dive into a heaping bowl of noodles or beef
soup. Areas close to produce markets are excellent places to find foodstalls—try the area west of
Ben Thanh Market. At **An Dong Market** in Cholon
is a basement section with small restaurants.

Street side foodstall perches make great vantage points for observing street life—you blend
in and watch everything flow past. You'll hear the
jangle of bicycle bells as schoolgirls in white *ao
dais* drift past, or the tock-tock of kids hitting
wooden bowls, patrolling the neighborhood taking soup orders. But the strangest sight may
be the slow motion monks of Saigon. These
saffron-robed monks make alms rounds in the
Pham Ngu Lao area with a slow-motion gait
that allows shopkeepers plenty of time to think
about whether to contribute.

Embassy Food Street: The food center, a
place where you can browse through a selection
of cheap eateries, is an idea that has worked
well in Bangkok, Hong Kong, and Singapore,
but is new to Saigon. Embassy Food Street, at
39 Nguyen Trung Truc St. near the corner of
Nguyen Du, tel. 231981, has stalls with Vietnamese, Taiwanese, and Singaporean fare. It
also features Malaysian barbecue and grilled
sate, Hong Kong-style seafood, Indian curries,
and Muslim food. The center is affiliated with
the nearby Embassy Hotel. The stalls are a
great value; you have a choice between common seating and mini air-conditioned rooms.

Roll Your Own: To the southwest of Pham
Ngu Lao, along Nguyen Cu Trinh Street, is a

string of inexpensive *bo bay mon* (beef seven kinds) restaurants—look for a laughing cow logo. For assembling your own meal, you're supplied with rice paper, lettuce, mint leaves, herbs, slivers of starfruit, pineapple, raw banana, bean sprouts, and cucumber. You order one of the seven beef dishes, which are cooked on a charcoal brazier at your table. When the beef is done, roll everything up, and dip in sauce. It's delicious! There are *bo bay mon* restaurants at 91, 93, 109, and 127 Nguyen Cu Trinh.

Vegetarian: It's difficult to find vegetarian food in Saigon. Most Vietnamese and Chinese restaurants, however, have a special vegetable section on the menu, with offerings like braised tofu, sautéed straw mushrooms, and stir-fried vegetables. Foodstalls, especially near markets, are another source of vegetarian fare. Near Ben Thanh Market, at 9 Tran Hung Dao Blvd., is **Tin Nghia Vegetarian Restaurant,** run by Vietnamese Buddhists. Staples here are tofu, mushrooms, and vegetables.

Central Saigon
The area near the south end of Dong Khoi offers a number of popular restaurants. On Ngo Duc Ke several restaurants serve Vietnamese food and seafood at very reasonable prices. Try **Restaurant 19** or **Restaurant 13.** Right at the east end of Dong Du and Thi Sach Streets on a corner is **Restaurant 333,** with similar food and prices. On Mac Thi Buoi Street you'll find the **Yellow Umbrella Cookshop,** and at number 62 is the **Yellow Dragon Restaurant** (Phuoc Thanh), tel. 296677. Both list moderate prices. **Lemongrass** at 63 Dong Khoi, tel. 298006, serves good Vietnamese food. Tucked in behind the mosque on Dong Du is a no-frills Indian halal restaurant serving curry fish, chicken, squid, goat, beef, and vegetarian fare. The family restaurant is busy at lunch; it is popularly known as "The Mosque."

Forgoing fancy decor but serving healthy portions at the right price are Givral Restaurant and Brodard Restaurant, two '60s-style eateries on Dong Khoi. **Givral,** at the corner of Dong Khoi and Le Loi, tel. 292747, has wonky tables—drop in for a coffee or a full feed. The fare includes spaghetti, steak, and seafood. **Brodard,** at 131 Dong Khoi, has a similar price range. Both places operate separate cake

shops: Givral's bakery is to one side of the restaurant, Brodard's is down the road from the restaurant at 11 Nguyen Thiep, between Nguyen Hue and Dhong Khoi.

Pizza has arrived in Saigon. **Napoli,** at 7 Nguyen Hue, tel. 225616, serves a full range of pizza and pasta, and offers home delivery. Down the road is **Pizza & Pizza,** at 103 Nguyen Hue with Italian and American food; home delivery.

A cluster of restaurants at the intersection of Nguyen Du Street and Nguyen Thi Minh Kha sell French food for midrange prices. Right on the corner is **Merlion,** at 172 Pasteur, tel. 231799; nearby is **Ami Jean Pierre** at 170 Pasteur, tel. 224015. Down a driveway at 164 Pasteur, you'll find **VY Restaurant,** tel. 296210. VY has fancy decor and a patio section where fresh fish and shrimp are grilled. The restaurant calling card claims you catch your own dishes.

Luxury: Vietnam House, 93 Dong Khoi at the corner of Mac Thi Buoi, tel. 291623, is a classy place serving fine Vietnamese food. On the menu are dishes as varied as grilled beef with lemongrass, and lotus roots with shrimp. A bar and small restaurant occupy the first floor; the main dining area is upstairs. Great decor in an old mansion, and great service. Nearby, **City Bar and Grill** at 63 Dong Khoi, tel. 298006, serves French nouvelle cuisine. Other recommended French restaurants are **Le P'tit Bistro** at 58 Le Thanh Ton, tel. 230219; **La Cigale** at 158 Nguyen Dinh Chinh, tel. 443930, with downstairs piano bar; and **L'Etoile,** at Hai Ba Trung tel. 297939, in a refurbished villa.

Chez Guido, on the ground floor of Hotel Continental, tel. 299252, serves excellent pasta, pizza, and seafood. For dessert, try Norman pancakes, mousse, or poached pears with amaretto ice cream.

Madame Dai's, a.k.a. La Bibliothèque, is in the vicinity of Notre Dame Cathedral at 84A Nguyen Du St., tel. 231438. The gate is unmarked, so pull the bell for attention. This is the residence of Madame Suzanne Dai, a Paris-trained lawyer and former opposition member of the South Vietnamese National Assembly. After 1975, when the practice of law fell away with the new order, she began to serve meals in the library of her law office. She speaks fluent French and good English. With advance booking, customers can eat in Madame Dai's study, surrounded by still-useless musty law volumes and antique ceramics she'll be glad to discuss. The area seats up to 20 or so. There's a set menu; the food is mediocre, but the atmosphere makes up for that. Madame Dai can arrange special performances of a mini cultural show featuring traditional instruments and dance.

North of the cathedral, **Thanh Nien Restaurant**, at 11 Nguyen Van Chiem, tel. 225909, is an excellent place for Vietnamese cuisine. The restaurant has a bamboo garden patio and offers nighttime piano entertainment in the bar. It's owned by the same manager as **Pisa Ice Cream** on Hai Ba Trung—you can walk through from one place to the other. **Le Mekong**, at 32 Vo Van Tan St., tel. 291277, is an elegant French joint-venture restaurant in a beautifully restored villa near the War Crimes Museum. Open for lunch and dinner.

South of Pham Ngu Lao is one of Saigon's top-rated Chinese restaurants, called **Phuc Lam Mon**, at 1A Tinh Van Can, tel. 223681. The restaurant specializes in wild game and seafood, and has an "advanced karaoke complex" with private rooms to help ease digestion. There's a branch of **VY Restaurant** nearby at 105 Yersin Street, serving French food.

CAFÉS

Pham Ngu Lao

Cheap and down-to-earth are Pham Ngu Lao sidewalk cafés. There are over a dozen small cafés where travelers congregate under sidewalk umbrellas to eat, drink, swap tales, play pool, or sign up for day-trips around Saigon or minibuses upcountry. Unlike those downtown, these cafés stay open late at night, so Westerners and Vietnamese alike patronize them in the evening.

The main concentration of cafés is around the intersection of Pham Ngu Lao and De Tham. On Pham Ngu Lao are Sinh Café, Long Phi Café, 333 Bar, Chez Mado, Lotus Café; on De Tham are Saigon Café, Kim Café, SOS Bar, and Madras House. Cafés offer full menus with mediocre western food, coffee, beer, juices, and fruit salad. The SOS in SOS Bar, next to Kim Café, apparently stands for Sound of Saigon, but some travelers have reported a different

meaning closer to the truth—Save Our Stomachs. Eat here and your intestines send out distress signals! Others have come up with interpretations that cannot be printed here.

Ice-Cream Cafés

You know a city has arrived when the ice-cream machines roll in from Rome, and pizza home delivery begins. Both are happening in Saigon, though you may have trouble recognizing the results.

Kem Y Pisa, at 133 Hai Ba Trung north of the cathedral, has installed Italian technology and serves snacks, ice cream, and drinks at Italian prices. Some items, however, would never appear on the menu in Italy: fruit ice cream with orange juice, orange and lemon floats, cocco bello (ice cream served in young coconut), and a dish called "coffee sunk"—one scoop of coffee ice cream sunk between two scoops of vanilla. In season, Pisa serves exotic items like custard apple *(mang cau)* ice cream. The owner insists the café only uses fresh milk and boiled water and that everything is safe.

A few blocks away is **Napoli Café**, at 5 Pham Quoc Thach St., with a menu similar to Pisa's. It's open early morning to late night and is good for breakfast as well as snacks. **Ciao Café** at 72 Nguyen Hue Blvd., tel. 251203, serves ice cream, pizza, and cake. **Saigon Connection Café**, at 114 Le Thanh Ton opposite the Norfolk Hotel, has the atmosphere of a US diner. The place is air-conditioned and clean; the music is '50s and '60s American. On the menu is a sundae served in a real pineapple base, and a dish called "fried ice cream"—a kind of fried sandwich with chocolate chip ice cream. Hamburgers and other food are available.

For cheaper ice cream try **Kem Bach Dang**, with two facing cafés at 26 and 28 Le Loi at the intersection of Rue Pasteur. Because of its proximity to a cinema, the place is packed with Vietnamese patrons.

Garden Cafés

Not great for food or drink but with good ambience, **Chi Lang Café** is located on Dong Khoi Street just north of the Municipal Theater, set back from the road in a small park. **Café Concert,** in the park opposite the Revolutionary Museum, offers a few plastic tables and rusted easy chairs and umbrellas arrayed around the roots of large trees. It's a low-key venue for a midcity breather. In the open-air courtyard of the Hotel Continental is **La Dolce Vita Café**—drinks can be expensive.

Rooftop Cafés

Major downtown hotels have rooftop bars or restaurants, and sometimes even a small pool. The craziest and coziest bar is **Rex Rooftop Café,** both a rooftop and garden café. It's a great place to relax at sunset, lounging around in wicker chairs high above the hubble and bubble of Saigon. You can order snacks or full meals; dining is outdoor on a terrace, and can be pricey. There is sometimes live entertainment on a podium under the revolving Rex

Crown, with traditional music combos. Otherwise, you'll hear twittering birds from the rooftop aviary. Bonsai trees, half-dead fish, plaster statues of elephants, and other high-kitsch artworks occupy the terrace. There's a small pool off to one side.

The **Caravelle** features a restaurant on the 9th floor. The food is mediocre; just drop in for a drink. This was the tallest building in Vietnam during the 1970s, when war correspondents used to gather on the roof to watch the fighting. There's no elevator to the very top; you must walk up one more flight of stairs from the restaurant. Other rooftop bars include the **Palace Hotel** with a 15th-floor bar and a small pool on the 16th floor; the rooftop bar and disco at the **Century Saigon Hotel;** and the Huong Sen and Bong Sen rooftop bar-restaurants.

NIGHTLIFE

Saigon nightlife is subdued, mainly revolving around restaurants and cafés. There's an unofficial curfew: bars close at 2300, though some hotels remain open until 0100 or 0200. Foreigners tend to end up in common areas when it comes to nightlife. In the Pham Ngu Lao area nightlife means sitting at cafés, which serve beer and stay open late; in central Saigon, entertainment revolves around a select number of venues. You can also indulge in the fine sport of cyclo racing to get from one part of town to another: cyclo drivers hurtle down one-way streets the wrong way without any lights, which certainly gets the adrenaline going.

Locals visit movie theaters, take in performances at the Municipal Theater, hang out at cafés, or croon over karaoke machines. On Saturday and Sunday nights thousands of young Vietnamese take to the streets. Dong Khoi and Nguyen Hue Boulevards come alive with Honda hordes, cruising the streets. If you stroll in the garden square in front of the Hotel de Ville, it's easy to meet people.

Traditional Music

Keep an eye out for traditional music and dance performers. Artists from the Saigon Conservatory of Music may appear at venues like the Rex Rooftop Café, Maxim's, or Madame Dai's.

Also check for scheduled performances at the **Conservatory of Music** at 112 Nguyen Du Street. The most intriguing of the music recitals is a performance on the *dan bau,* a single-stringe lute unique to Vietnam. The single steel string is manipulated to produce a haunting sound. Other wonders include the two-string vertical violin and the bamboo xylophone. Sometimes seen, too, are Vietnamese dance performances, including folk dances originating from rural traditions and sensuous Cham dances revived from centuries past.

Night Cruising

Saigon features some real floating restaurants, boats that go on short cruises along Saigon River, leaving the bright lights of Saigon behind. The boats usually depart between 1900 and 2000 for a one- or two-hour trip; you dine onboard. There's only a minimal charge for the cruise, but food and drinks are expensive. The best part is the cruise; the food is mediocre. Some boats have live bands onboard, and several decks crowded with diners; others are commandeered by private Vietnamese groups for wedding banquets or birthday parties.

Four of the floating restaurant cruise-boats are strung along the Saigon River between Dong Khoi Street and Ham Nghi Boulevard. These include **Siren Floating Restaurant; Ben Nghe Tourism Boat,** cruise 1900-2130 with additional departure 1630-1830 on Sundays and holidays; **My Canh Floating Restaurant,** cruise departs at 2000; and **Tau Saigon Floating Restaurant,** cruise 2000-2115. **Saigon Tourist** operates a longer cruise/dinner/cultural show combination, from 1730 to 2130 on Tuesday, Thursday, and Sunday for $15. Another departure runs 1900-2000, costs $5, and features the cultural show alone.

Life in the Fast Lane

On Saturday and Sunday nights there's an exuberant parade of scooters and motorcycles in a clockwise circuit of Dong Khoi and Nguyen Hue Boulevards. Hundreds of young Vietnamese tour the boulevards in an Asian version of *Saturday Night Fever*. Young women are decked out in tight jeans and T-shirts or silk *ao dais*; young men show off shiny new Hondas. In the squares near the Hotel de Ville, riders congregate for a rest or to chat up the opposite sex. This marriage of youth and motorbikes is known as *chay long rong* (living fast).

Central Saigon

Under the Americans, Rue Catinat, or Dong Khoi Street, became Tu Do, or Freedom Street. Bars, nightclubs, and strip joints crowded the south end, and names like Bluebird and Papillon flashed in neon. The same area now appeals to young Vietnamese and foreigners, and still has its share of sleaze, with beggars, pickpockets, and assorted pushers on patrol. In 1992 a string of bars along Dong Du Street—Good Morning Vietnam, Cyclo Bar, Apocalypse Now—recalled Tu Do Street in the days of the Vietnam War. The authorities became concerned about the proliferation of taxi girls and drug-dealing cyclo drivers; one day in 1993 the bright yellow police jeeps arrived to confiscate all the stereos and close down the bars. In the 1993 mop up police closed 45 nightclubs around Saigon.

Maxim's theater-restaurant is a Saigon institution surviving from the US era, its plush red decor intact. The theater is located at 15 Dong Khoi St., tel. 225554. Maxim's is open 1100-2300; the floor show starts around 1900. In the 1960s Maxim's was reserved for American officers—the loose women within were said to be untouchable for less than a month's pay. Banking on nostalgia, Maxim's still charges outrageous prices for drinks. Watch your wallet in this place; surcharges are common. Theater acts seem stuck in the '60s. Some performances are so bad they'll have you rolling in the aisles. Crooners do lip-sync numbers, artists play traditional Vietnamese instruments, others perform sundry song and dance routines. The food—Vietnamese, Chinese, and European—is touted as the best in Saigon, but is in fact mediocre and pricey. The chef relies on the fact that the lights are low and your taste buds will be numbed by sound effects.

The famous, or infamous, **Apocalypse Now** is located on Mac Thi Buoi, halfway between Dong Khoi and Hai Ba Trung. It's not hard to find—cyclo drivers cluster round the bar, drawn like moths to a flame. Directly opposite is the popular **Hard Rock Café.** On the wall at Apocalypse Now is a large poster from the movie of the same name, autographed by Martin Sheen. The bar does a brisk trade in Apocalypse Now T-shirts at $5 apiece. The patrons are mostly Westerners; the place is smoky (and not just from cigarettes), and when the staff cranks up mesmerizing lyrics by the Doors, Saigon of the '60s is not too far away. If you're feeling blue, ask for a shot glass of Apocalypse Whiskey, a medicinal Chinese concoction—the pickled cobra sits coiled in a glass jar of rice wine behind the counter. Cobra wine is surprisingly smooth and mellow.

Hotel Bars and Discos: Major hotels operate nightclubs, bars, and discos. The dance halls at the Rex and the Palace are popular with visitors. Upscale discos are the **Starlight,** on the 11th floor of Century Saigon Hotel; the **Down Under Disco** at the Floating Hotel; and **Venus Disco** at Saigon Star Hotel.

Upscale Bars: The following places charge $2 and up for a beer, or $5 and up for a glass of wine. **Q-Bar,** located in the south side of the Municipal Theater, is run by an American-Vietnamese couple from Los Angeles. The Q in the name is a pun on "Viet Kieu," meaning overseas Vietnamese. It's constructed along a narrow space—at one end is the bar, and farther back are some alcoves with café tables. Huge Caravaggio murals grace the walls; offbeat lighting adds to the atmosphere. Q-Bar serves hamburgers, French fries, salsa and chips, and spaghetti; drinks are expensive. On the other side of the theater in the basement is **Saigon Headlines,** with a Spanish-type decor and live music; the pub sells beer and wine.

A low-key place for a quiet drink is **Tiger Tavern** at 227 Dong Khoi, south of the GPO. A noisy place for a drink is the **Buffalo Blues Bar,** east of the GPO at 72A Nguyen Du—look for neon lights. This place features a live blues band, and is usually packed with Westerners and well-heeled Vietnamese. Open till midnight. Toward the Saigon River, **Shakes' Pub,** at 16-32 Phan Van Dat St., has good food and great views. In the same area on the sixth floor of Dragon Inn is the **Terrace Bar,** also with sweeping views.

Karaoke Clubs

Karaoke has taken Saigon by storm. Karaoke lounges are intended primarily for Asian visitors or rich Vietnamese, and can be sleazy, with private rooms ostensibly for karaoke singing but including a "karaoke hostess." Drinks can be very expensive. There are several nightclub complexes in Saigon. Vien Dong Hotel on Pham Ngu Lao hosts the **ABC Karaoke Bar. Queen Bee,** near the Hotel de Ville at 106 Nguyen Hue, features dancing, karaoke, and a restaurant. The **VIP Club** at 2 Pham Ngoc Thach St. in District 1 has a bar, disco, karaoke rooms, video games, and snooker tables. On the fringes of town in District 11 is the **Shangri-La Complex** at 1196 3/2 St., with Pink Cadillac disco, karaoke rooms, business center, and health club. Near the airport at 431 Hoang Van Thu St. you'll find a large venue called **Superstar Disco,** with imported light and sound systems and a karaoke lounge.

Cholon Clubs: Cholon nightlife targets Asians, especially Taiwanese. Karaoke is the keyword here. Activity revolves around hotels with karaoke, discos, and massage parlors. The Arc En Ciel Hotel operates **Volvo Nightclub** on the second floor; Hotel Tokyo has a dance hall on the sixth floor; and **Dai La Tien Nightclub** features a dance floor and karaoke rooms.

SHOPPING

he main area for antiques, paintings, and hand-crafts is Dong Khoi Street and Nguyen Hue Boulevard, as well as side streets running off nese. You can wander along and comparison hop.

ntiques

he market for antiques is dwindling. Items are ften faked to look older, or are honestly sold as opies. This includes old porcelain, clocks, and ems of silver, jade, or ivory. If the product in uestion was a genuine antique, you might have ouble getting it out of the country without a overnment permit. Vestiges of the colonial past

are part of the antique trade: vendors sell over-priced banknotes, coins, and stamps from French Indochina.

Painting

Art galleries along Dong Khoi Street and Nguyen Hue Boulevard display original works by Viet-namese artists. The selection includes fine wa-tercolors, oil paintings, gauche, and paintings on silk, often depicting Vietnamese rural scenes, landscapes, cityscapes, portraits, and abstract themes. The Military Museum art gallery has some interesting "revolutionary" painting. Fine Arts students make excellent copies of West-

THE CYCLO ART GALLERY

At 64 Dong Du St., off Dong Khoi, is one of Saigon's more unusual art galleries. The owner, Hoang Van Cuong, is a former UPI photo-journalist whose pictures of wartorn Vietnam ran in newspapers around the world. After the fall of Saigon, Hoang worked as a farmer in the Mekong Delta for nine years. He was then arrested and forced to serve six years in re-education camps. While in detention, he kept his negatives hidden and now continues to print again and sell photos to tourists.

In 1990 Hoang opened the **Cyclo Art Gallery and Gift shop;** he lives above the store. His family has been in the antique business for generations, and he's keeping the tradition alive. The Cyclo Art Gallery sells antiques and enlarged news photos from the Vietnam War era for $20, or pocket-size prints for $1. Featured in a lot of Western media, in-cluding the BBC, Hoang has achieved untouchable status. He says he's lived through so many close calls he's no longer afraid of consequences.

Hoang Van Cuong displays one of his histori-cal photos.

ern art in oil, working from art books. These can be custom-ordered—just bring the artwork in print form and they'll copy it. Galleries to check include: **Espace NK,** at 218A Pasteur, exhibiting contemporary art; **Art Gallery Particulier,** at 43 Dong Khoi, with private collections of famous Vietnamese artists.

Handicrafts

In the Dong Khoi Street and Nguyen Hue Boulevard. area are a number of shops packed to the ceiling with handmade goods. Major hotels also include gift shops selling local crafts. You can buy handpainted silk pictures and greeting cards, embroidered clothing articles, woodcarvings, lacquerware items, ceramics, statuettes, jewelry boxes, seals, and *non la* (conical hats). Larger items for sale, if you can figure out a way to transport them, include bamboo and rattanware, carved wood furniture, and ceramic elephants. Be aware that wood and lacquerware can crack when removed to cold, dry climates. At the History Museum, in the back of the water-puppet theater, you can buy handmade wooden puppets. If you're attracted to a particular handicraft, you can go straight to the source. There are several lacquerware factories around Saigon, for example, where you can learn about the intricate production process.

Ao Dais

Unique to Vietnam are silk *ao dais,* the graceful billowing dresses worn by Saigon women. You can buy one of these ready-made, or custom order it at a tailor's. Like dresses, *ao dais* come in a great variety of forms, from bright solid colors to flamboyant hand-embroidered patterns. Tailors who specialize in *ao dais* and *cheong sams* include **Thanh Chau,** at 244 Dinh Tien Hoang St., Q1, tel. 231031, and **Tram Huong,** 212A Tran Quoc Thao, Q3, tel. 443934.

Message T-shirts

From street vendors you can buy message T-shirts reading Miss Saigon, Tintin in Vietnam, or Ho Chi Minh for a few dollars. Direct from the relevant bars you can buy Apocalypse Now or Hard Rock Café Saigon T-shirts for $5. T-shirts vary in quality; some are made of flimsy material that will disintegrate after a few washes. Look for hand-embroidered T-shirts. These cost around $3—a great value.

MARKETS

The largest food market in Saigon is **Ben Thanh.** The landmark building was constructed by the French in 1914, and looks little changed. Under the cupola is a vast array of food, hardware, electronics, and fabric stalls embracing 11,000 square meters. It's well worth strolling in the area around the market. The side streets are bustling with activity too, presenting great photo opportunities, particularly around Tet when everybody is buying miniature trees. Out in Cholon is **Binh Tay Market,** a huge food and consumer goods center; and **An Dong Market,** a large clothing and retail venue. You can purchase *ao dais* here.

Dan Sinh Army Surplus market is located at 104 Nguyen Cong Tru St., near Phung Son Tu Pagoda, south of Ben Thanh Market. Clothing, housewares, and new and used army goods are sold here. Some of the vendors sell US Army-issue goods: everything from fungicidal foot powder to dog tags and field glasses. Some are real, most cleverly copied. Zippo lighters—probably not originals—sell for $10-20 if working, $5 if not. Other army-surplus items are Chinese or Russian, and include gas masks and stretchers. On a more practical note, the market sells compasses, and webbing and lacing (good for fixing a backpack). Small hammocks go for $4, and mosquito nets for $3-7, depending on size and quality. Other items of interest are gloves, socks, and jackets, useful if traveling to the Central Highlands or the mountainous north. A flak jacket might be a wise investment if heading to Cambodia.

The **Thieves Market** runs along Huynh Thu Khang and Ton That Dan Streets—it used to be the place stolen US Army goods were sold, then became a blackmarket for electronic goods, but the trading is now quite open. The market sells a great range of consumer and luxury goods, some still smuggled in by Vietnamese sailors and visiting overseas Vietnamese.

SERVICES AND INFORMATION

Traveler Cafés

Your finest source of information in Saigon is any one of the traveler cafés strung along Pham Ngu Lao. Just sit down at one of these sidewalk cafés and find someone who's come from the direction you're headed; maybe offer to buy a cold beer. The cafés serve decent food and are usually open 0800-2200. The café owners run tours and may have traveler logbooks recounting recent voyages in Vietnam.

Pham Ngu Lao Street in District 1 features a string of traveler cafés—combination restaurants, cafés, travel agents, meeting points, amusement halls, and pubs. These cafés handle visa extensions, day-trips, bicycle and motorcycle rentals, guides, and traveler minibuses to Hué. For day-trips and longer, the big cafés are Sinh Café, Kim Café, and 333 Bar. Saigon Café and Lotus Café also dabble in tours. These cafés do a roaring trade—in the morning outside Sinh Café there might be half a dozen minibuses about to take off for various day-trips, with an organizer standing outside with a mobile phone directing traffic.

The two original cafés are **Sinh Café,** 6 Pham Ngu Lao, tel. 251842, fax 222347; and **Kim Café,** 270 De Tham, tel. 398177, fax 298540. Kim Café has its own travel agency next door, with a knowledgeable English-speaking staff.

Newer agents on Pham Ngu Lao include **Long Phi Café,** at 171 Pham Ngu Lao, tel. 323124; and **333 Bar,** at 217 Pham Ngu Lao, tel. 331231, fax 251550. **Fiditourist** has a branch at 199 Pham Ngu Lao, tel. 322324. **Saigon Railway Tourist Company,** 6 Pham Ngu Lao, tel. 783644, handles visas, flights, bicycle and motorcycle rentals, and even rents a few guesthouse rooms. Up the road is **Saigon Railway Tourism Centre,** at 14 Pham Ngu Lao, tel. 223747, fax 291275.

Tourist Information

Saigon Tourist Travel Service, 49 Le Thanh Ton (corner of Dong Khoi), tel. 295834, fax 224987, is the official arm, but not a friendly one. This outfit is money hungry—if the staff smells money, information is forthcoming; if not, you'll get a pair of glazed eyeballs that will quickly disappear behind a newspaper. Saigon Tourist runs more than 50 hotels and 45 restaurants. **Vietnam Tourism,** at 234 Nam Ky Khoi Nghia, tel. 290760, fax 290775, is not much better, though the brochures are glossier. Both agencies sell overpriced tours. Saigon Tourist, for example, charges a whopping $30 a person for a Cu Chi Tunnels tour, and $60 a head for a day-trip to Vung Tau. Out in Cholon is **Cholon Tourist,** the official agency catering to ethnic Chinese tourists.

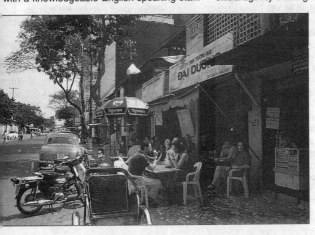

café on Pham Ngu Lao Street

Unofficial private operators offer services identical to state-run Saigon Tourist at a fraction of the price. Through travel agents, guides are about $10 a day. Freelancers operate from street corners. Moto and cyclo drivers know the city well and can arrange for half-day or full-day tours. Some cyclo and moto operators are former soldiers or translators who worked with the Americans—they speak good English, and now, after years in re-education camps, find conditions changing in their favor. They're conversant with American idioms and slang. Hiring a guide with a motorcycle is a good way to see Saigon.

Maps and Books

Shoddy and outdated sheetmaps of Saigon are available in numerous places, particularly from the street vendors around Dong Khoi Street and Nguyen Hue Boulevard. If you intend to use one of these maps, buy a magnifying glass as well—there's a lot of detail squished into a tiny space. Check out the upcountry destination maps from the sidewalk vendors; there's a good selection, and who knows when you'll see these maps again. The Cartographic Mapping Institute of Hanoi publishes a superior scale map of Saigon with the Canadian company International Travel Maps.

Saigon offers few English-language books, the result of government import bans on foreign material. You'll do better at the bookstore in the Bangkok Airport than in the entire city of Saigon. You might try the bookstore at 187 Dong Khoi, across from the Hotel Continental. At 201 Dong Khoi is **Le Anh Bookshop,** with secondhand English and French books. A charming bookstore with dusty tomes lining the shelves is located off 26 Dong Khoi Street at 20 Ho Huan Nghiep. It's just called "bookstore" and sells Vietnamese, French, and English books. It also doubles as a café.

Most reading material is sold by street vendors in the Dong Khoi and Nguyen Hue area, who peddle outrageously expensive photocopied booklets. From the street vendors, and in major hotel lobbies, you can get a range of Western magazines and newspapers—*International Herald Tribune, Bangkok Post, Paris Match, Le Figaro, L'Express, Le Monde, Sydney Morning Herald, Time,* and *Newsweek.* Some

are simply left behind by hotel guests and recycled. Check dates.

Fax and Phone

For IDD information, consult the Ho Chi Minh City Telephone Directory. It gives country codes for direct dialing, time differences, and full details on rates in US dollars. The Saigon area code is 848. By looking at the column for the first minute of an overseas call, you can figure out approximate fax rates. Hotels may add a surcharge when sending faxes. A fax is about $5 a page to the West (Australia, North America, Europe). Most hotels can place IDD calls, as can the GPO. Overseas calls from Vietnam are expensive—a fax is cheaper.

Some useful numbers: Police, 13; Fire, 14; Ambulance, 15. For telephone inquiries, dial 16. **Ho Chi Minh City Post and Telecom** has an information service—dial 108 for rundowns on air and rail tickets and schedules, hotels, restaurants, law consultation, tourist information, and even storytelling for children, or so the phone book claims.

Help yourself to addresses in the **Ho Chi Minh City Telephone Directory**—white pages and yellow pages in one fat volume. This tome is produced annually as a joint-venture between Ho Chi Minh City Post and Telecommunications and Worldcorp Holdings Singapore. Most major hotels possess a copy. Since the Vietnamese language uses a Roman alphabet you can dig out most of the information yourself. It takes a while to steer through the listings—the thin residential section, for example, lists people by *first name,* followed by family name in alphabetical order. The limited number of Vietnamese first names is the reason for this anomaly. This section is followed by a white page business directory, given first in Vietnamese, then in English. Some fax numbers are also provided with company listings. At the back is a yellow pages classified index.

Satellite TV

Permits are needed for satellite dishes in Saigon, and few places seem to have the paperwork together. Norfolk Hotel, Saigon Omni, and Dainam Hotel have satellite dishes that can pick up StarTV (BBC) as well as Chinese and Malaysian TV, a total of around 10 channels.

st Office and Courier

e GPO, facing Notre Dame Cathedral, has ste restante, plus EMS, DHL courier counter, d IDD phones. Down the street, at the corner Nguyen Du and Hai Ba Trung, is the parcel pping section. Be aware that sending parcels uires a lot of form-filling, soul-searching, and ds inspection. **TNT Vietrans Express** has office at 406 Nguyen Tat Thanh St., Q4, tel. 5520.

otography and Film

sks selling film are found along Nguyen Hue levard. Since the lifting of the trade embar- Kodak has returned to Vietnam, now com- ting with Fuji. Print film can be processed ckly at labs in the Nguyen Hue area; prints ke great gifts for Vietnamese friends.

nks

anging money in Saigon is easy, unlike other ts of the country. Hotels usually offer ex- ange counters, and there are a number of k branches that will convert traveler's checks dong. Several of these branches are found und Pham Ngu Lao; others are located in tral Saigon.

he main banking area in central Saigon lies the south near Ben Nghe Channel. In this a you can witness the wonders of economic gress—people in suits unloading dirty sacks dong from sparkling new cars. Banks either ploy a staff of hundreds to count the dong, or dong-counting machines. Banks charge 1- commission for converting traveler's checks dong. Some charge no commission, but offer wer rate of exchange; yet others charge a imum $1 fee. Conversion rates are slightly ver for cash US dollars than for traveler's cks; rates depend on the size of the notes of- ed—higher for larger bills. You can convert -dollar traveler's checks to US cash for 1- commission. Insist on clean bills with no s or tears, as older wrinkled bills may be re- ted by hotel staff. Visa, MasterCard, JCB, ers Club, and American Express are now ning into use in Saigon. You can get Visa h advances, but expect a 4% commission nimum $5 charge) on transactions.

Banks are usually open 0800-1130 and 1300- 0 Monday to Saturday, although they usually only open in the morning on Saturday. The main foreign exchange bank is **Vietcombank,** at 29 Ben Chuong Duong Street. Here you can ex- change dollars to dong commission-free, and convert US-dollar traveler's checks to US cash for a 1.2% commission. **Thai Military Bank,** down the street at 11 Ben Chuong Duong St., has a one percent commission for dollars to dong, with a minimum $1 charge. **Vietnam Agri- bank,** 7 Ben Chuong Duong, charges one per- cent for converting US traveler's checks to cash.

Foreign banks with branches in Saigon in- clude **Banque National de Paris** and **Credit Lyonnais;** rep offices include **Deutsche Bank, Hong Kong Bank, Britain's Standard Char- tered Bank,** and **Internationale Nederlanden Bank.** More foreign banks, including American ones, are standing in line, waiting for licenses. A number of Thai banks have opened, including **Bangkok Bank,** at 117 Nguyen Hue Blvd., and **Krung Thai Bank,** at 33 Ham Nghi Boulevard.

Business Services

Major hotels in Saigon offer their own business centers with fax and IDD facilities, work stations, computers, photocopiers, equipment rental, and secretarial and translation services. There are also some independent operators such as **Lotus Business Centre,** 71 Hai Ba Trung, Q1, tel. 223053, fax 298348; and **Saigon Business Centre,** 49 Dong Du St., tel. 298777, fax 298155. The latter offers telecommunications services, desktop publishing, short-term office and work- station rental, mailing address and mail for- warding, and even mobile phone rental.

Health Care

Health facilities are poor. Contact your embassy for the latest recommendations. The Emergency Center at 125 Le Loi, tel. 292071, has a 24- hour casualty section with English- and French- speaking doctors and a well-stocked pharmacy. In Cholon, Cho Ray Hospital, at 201 Nguyen Chi Thanh Blvd., tel. 554137, has a 10th-floor section with English-speaking doctors for for- eigners. It's $25 per night in the foreign ward. Bring a donor if you're likely to need blood, as certain blood types are in short supply. Evacu- ation from Vietnam can be arranged by **SOS International,** at 151 Vo Thi Sau, Q3, tel. 294386 or 242866; this organization employs a French-speaking doctor in Saigon. Another agency to contact is **AEA/OSCAT**, at 65 Nguyen Du St., Q1, tel. 298520. This clinic provides consultation, pharmacy, and dental services, and emergency evacuation.

Rest and Recreation

Major hotels have fitness centers and health clubs, with gym and sauna. Some feature tennis courts and swimming pools. Outsiders can use the pool at Saigon Floating Hotel for $5—said to be the best (cleanest?) in town. The Rex and the Palace also allow nonguests to use the swimming pool for a fee. The finest tennis courts in town are those at Saigon Floating Hotel and the Rex annex.

Saigon Hash House Harriers stage runs on Sunday and sometimes Saturday. Up to 50 runners take part—a great way to meet expats and locals. Get information at Apocalypse Now, Q-Bar, Tiger Tavern, the Floating Hotel Business Centre, or the Norfolk Hotel.

Accompanying the headlong rush into capitalism are some decadent bourgeois pastimes.

Billiards is very popular, with many parlors Saigon. A round of golf at the country club? Th can be arranged at **Song Be Golf Resort,** abc 20 km north of Saigon. The last word on ca talist enterprise, this resort is a multinational d velopment with Olympic-size pool, tennis cour jacuzzi, and bowling alley. Membership fe start at $25,000. There's another course abc 20 km east of Saigon—contact Saigon Tou for details. **Saigon Race Track** (Phu Tho) dat back to 1932. As the South Vietnamese gc ernment began to crumble in the mid-1970s t track's owners closed it down, and the new gc ernment left it shuttered as part of its crac down on gambling. In 1989 Vietnamese-C nese businessman Philip Chau proposed to open the track, with taxes collected on tra earnings. It was soon up and running. On good day at Phu Tho up to 10,000 enthusias show up. The maximum wager is $2, and t wagerer must pick both first and second pla horses. The track is north of Cholon in Distr 11; races are staged on Saturday and Sund afternoons.

GETTING THERE

BY AIR

Tan Son Nhat Airport is 12 km from downtown Saigon. The large, modern airport features adequate facilities—gift and duty-free shops, café, tiny post office, and IDD calling booths.

Entry Formalities

If entering Saigon on an international flight, the authorities sometimes ignore the visa you already have and force you to fill out paperwork for another visa. There's no charge for this visa, but it costs $2 for passport photos. If you don't happen to have any handy, a photographer waits in the wings. Then the authorities keep the new paperwork. Mysterious, huh?

On arrival you fill in the usual customs declaration form and entry/exit card, which you keep with you, to be surrendered on departure. Confusion reigns over how much money to declare. Only currency above $3000 must be declared,

and nobody's going to check the form when y depart anyway. Officials are also in the habit handing out a small cardboard folder that hote are supposed to stamp. Since there's no spec prize or punishment for this effort, the best thi to do is lose it.

Transfers into Saigon

The airport is 12 km from the Hotel de Ville. drive downtown takes 15 to 30 minutes by c depending on traffic. Cab fare should be abc $5-7, but drivers will probably ask for mo Keep walking, keep talking—you can bring t price down. Major hotels charge $10-15 for a port transfer. A moto costs $3 to or from the a port.

Airline Offices

Airline offices in Saigon are mostly cluster around the Hotel de Ville and on the boulevar radiating off it—Dong Khoi, Le Thanh Ton, Loi, and Nguyen Hue. Right in front of the H de Ville is **Vietnam Airlines** international book.

SAIGON AIRLINE OFFICES

The following is a listing of airline offices in Saigon. Frequency of flights may vary with season and demand.

Aeroflot, 4G Le Loi at the corner of Nguyen Hue, tel. 290076; flies to Moscow once a week

Air France, 127 Tran Quoc Thao, tel. 290985; ticket confirmation in the Caravelle Hotel at 130 Dong Khoi; flies to Paris three times weekly

Asiana Airlines, 141 Ham Nghi Blvd., tel. 222663; flies to Seoul twice a week

Cathay Pacific, 49 Le Thanh Ton, tel. 223308; flies to Hong Kong daily

China Airlines, 132 Dong Khoi St., tel. 251387; office in the Hotel Continental; flies to Taipei four times a week

China Southern Airlines, 52B Pham Hong Thai St., tel. 291172; flies to Guangzhou twice weekly

Eva Air, 127 Dong Khoi, tel. 224488, flies to Seoul

Garuda, 106 Nguyen Hue Blvd., tel. 293644, fax 293688; flies to Jakarta and Singapore several times a week

KLM, 244 Pasteur St., tel. 231990; flies to Amsterdam

Lufthansa, 132 Dong Khoi, tel. 298529; office in the Hotel Continental; flies to Frankfurt twice weekly

Malaysia Airlines, 116 Nguyen Hue Blvd., above Vietnam Airlines, tel. 292118; flies to Kuala Lumpur daily

Philippine Airlines, 4A Le Loi, tel. 292113; flies to Manila

Singapore Airlines, 6 Le Loi Blvd. (in the mall attached to Rex Hotel), tel. 231583; frequent flights to Singapore

Thai International, 65 Nguyen Du St., tel. 223365; in the Officetel Building near the GPO; flies to Bangkok daily

at 76 Le Thanh Ton. Qantas Airlines has a rep office at 24 Ly Tu Trong, tel. 394720. Japan Airlines flies from Osaka to Ho Chi Minh City twice weekly. Pacific Airlines has a connection from Ho Chi Minh City to Kaohsiung, Taiwan. US airlines negotiating for services include United, Northwest, Delta, and Continental. Canadian Airlines International is working on a route from Toronto via Paris to Ho Chi Minh City. Fares on some of these direct routes are expensive, so shop around. Asiana Airlines, for example, quotes a one-way fare of $400 from Ho Chi Minh City to Seoul, or $700 roundtrip, while Singapore Airlines offers a one-way flight from Ho Chi Minh City to Singapore for $237. If you can't find any direct flights at the right price, your best bet is to fly to Hong Kong or Bangkok and proceed from there.

BY LAND

You can travel by road from Saigon to Phnom Penh, but if you're conscious of time and safety you should fly. One-way flights take 30 minutes and cost $50; you can pick up a Cambodian visa on arrival. For cheaper travel, try the $5 bus ride that takes an entire day to cover the 248-km route. Your paperwork needs to be in order for the crossing; otherwise, you may be turned back. The Moc Bai land border is open 0630-1800. The road on the Cambodian side is paved and has few military checkpoints; it's considered one of the safest in the country. To smooth your passage however, carry packs of cigarettes—either Marlboro or 555 brand.

Phnom Penh to Saigon
You must possess a valid Vietnamese visa with a Moc Bai border entry stamp. Vietnamese visas

office, 116 Nguyen Hue, tel. 292118; for flight information dial 443179. Vietnam Airlines flies on a number of international routes and is boosting its safety reputation by phasing out old Russian aircraft and using Western models. Vietnam Airlines is the agent for **Lao Aviation,** offering flights to Vientiane, and **Royal Air Cambodge,** for flights to Phnom Penh. Vietnam Airlines handles the Hong Kong-Saigon and Bangkok-Saigon legs of flights in a joint service with airlines like Qantas and Cathay Pacific.

More carriers than the ones listed below are waiting to offer flights into Saigon. Korean Airlines has a rep office next door to Pacific Airlines

take two to five working days to obtain in Phnom Penh—best arranged through an agent. If you already obtained a Vietnamese visa elsewhere you can get a Moc Bai entry stamp added the same day for a small fee. It's advisable to carry small US dollar bills for transportation and other expenses. There are several junctions along the way where moneychangers will approach you; at a ferry crossing over the Mekong you can trade dollars or riels for Vietnamese dong.

By Taxi: You can charter a taxi from Phnom Penh to the border, or all the way to Saigon. Assemble your own group and negotiate with a driver. An alternative is to join Cambodian passengers in a share-taxi to Bavet on the Cambodian side of the border, walk across to Moc Bai on the Vietnamese side, then take a Vietnamese share-taxi to Saigon. A share-taxi to Bavet costs $5-10 a person, with six or more passengers jammed into the car. The main departure point for share-taxis to Bavet is a depot just over the east side of Monivong Bridge, at Street 369, in the Chbampao Market area. Taxis leave from 0600 to 1300. You can reach Monivong Bridge by moto. Make sure your share-taxi takes you all

the way to the border—some stop a few kilo meters shy. Once on the Vietnamese side, th share-taxi to Saigon costs under $10 per head There are also motos waiting on the Vietnames side; a moto ride into Saigon should be under $ By car, it takes about three hours to the borde half an hour for paperwork, and another tw hours to Saigon.

By Bus: A bus leaves at 0530 daily excep Sunday from Phnom Penh. The ticket office i near the intersection of Street 182 and Stree 211, close to Nehru Blvd.; open 0500-1000 an 1400-1700. A sign here simply says Ticket O fice. Buy tickets one day in advance. It cost $5 for a regular Cambodian bus, or $12 for a air-con Vietnamese bus. The buses alternate so that only one leaves each day. If all goe well, the bus should arrive in Saigon by 150C However, greedy Vietnamese police are prone to disassembly of the bus in search of contra band, and major delays can be caused by ne gotiating "taxes" on smuggled goods. One wa to avoid this circus is to get off the bus at th Vietnamese border and change to a share-tax for the final leg.

GETTING AROUND

Before the mid-1980s, traffic in Saigon was almost exclusively bicycles. Now the motorcycle rules. There were only a few thousand motorcycles in the early 1980s; by 1994 the figure eclipsed one million. No license is required for motorcycles under 150cc. You'll see 10-year-olds as well as grandmothers riding Hondas, and hooligans on high-powered bikes. Hardly anyone bothers with the dismal bus system.

Metered Taxis
Vinataxi, tel. 222990, runs a fleet of 180 yellow metered Toyotas. The meter runs in dollars, and payment is accepted in dong or dollars, or both. It's $2 for the first kilometer, and 25 cents for 300 meters after that, for a total of around $3 for three km, which is expensive. **Airport Taxi,** tel. 446666, is a rival outfit with 200 white Japanese and Korean cars, including limousines. This company regards Tan Son Nhat Airport as its turf and will menace any yellow cabs out this way. Expected to join the fray is Saigon Taxicabs.

Motos and Cyclos
You can hire a moto for only a little more than the cost of a cyclo, and moto drivers don't snap back at you. Moto drivers are not always easy to find, however. A moto will get you across town for 50 cents; by the hour, motos cost a dolla or so. Few moto drivers wear helmets—and neither do passengers.

In mid-1995 authorities in Ho Chi Minh City banned cyclos from 50 streets in the city cente to reduce traffic congestion. An estimated 40,000 cyclos operate in the city. Another pos sible reason for keeping cyclos out of the city center is that they are extremely aggressive to ward tourists.

You can put yourself and the bicycle on a cyclo—that's how you get the bike home after an accident. Even a motorcycle can be loaded onto a cyclo. Cyclo drivers will sometimes try to man handle you into their carriages. Bargain with cyclo drivers but in a friendly manner—don' push them too far, or they might turn nasty. One

SAIGON TOUR COMPANIES AND AGENTS

Numerous agencies in Saigon will handle visas, paperwork, ticketing, transportation rentals, tours, guides, hotel reservations, day-trip packages, and upcountry travel. Some of the agencies in Central Saigon (District 1) are listed here.

Ann Tourist, 58 Ton That Tung, Q1, tel. 332564, fax 225626 (efficient, reliable agency with good guides)

Atlas Travel, 41 Nam Ky Khoi Nghia, tel./fax 298604

Cam On Tour, 62 Hai Ba Trung, Q1, tel. 222166, fax 298540

Eden Tourist, 106 Nguyen Hue Blvd., tel. 293651, fax 230783

Exotissimo Travel, 7 Mac Thi Buoi, tel. 251723, fax 251684

Fiditourist/Sunimex, 71 Dong Khoi, tel. 296406, fax 222941 (guides, interpreters, motorbike rentals, visa extensions)

Oil Services Co. (OSC), World Travel & Tour Service, 65 Nam Ky Khoi Nghia, tel. 296658, fax 290195

Peace Tours, 60 Vo Van Tan, tel./fax 294416

Saigon Tours, 95 Hai Ba Trung, tel. 294253, fax 297215 (visas, land packages, service for business travelers)

Vidotour (VTS), 58 Ngo Duc Ke, tel. 291438, fax 231278 (comprehensive services, upscale market)

Voiles Vietnam, 17 Pham Ngoc Thach, Q3, tel. 296750, fax 231591 (French-run outfit offering cruises on a junk and diving on the coast)

Volunteer Youth Company (VYC), 178 Nguyen Chu Trinh St., tel. 399428, fax 330399 (runs Saigon Omni Hotel and several private hotels in Dalat)

course). The best way to avoid this kind of argument is to pay up front in dong. With whole dollars there's no change, with dong you can bargain smaller increments. Cyclos can be hired for about $3.50 for a full day, or around $1 per hour. A trip across town costs 30 to 50 cents, which is still an inflated foreigner price. To get an idea of prices, the luxury Norfolk Hotel sets rates of $1.30 per hour per person, and $4 for half a day. Keep in mind this is for plush white cyclos with sunroofs.

Two-Wheel Rentals
Motorcycle Rental: A number of places in the Pham Ngu Lao area rent motorcycles. **Saigon Railway Tourist Office,** next to Sinh Café, rents bikes; there's also a rental outlet next to Vien Dong Hotel, and another on De Tham opposite Kim Café. Rates are around $5 a day. At 101 Dong Khoi is a motorcycle rental outfit with 50cc, 70cc, and 90cc bikes for $6 a day each; nearby **Fiditourist,** at 71 Dong Khoi, also rents bikes. Use designated motorcycle parking in Saigon to ensure your motorcycle is not stolen. If renting overnight, put the machine right inside your hotel gates or compound. It's a double whammy for motorcycles—if it's stolen, you may have to pay for it; if it's in an accident, you may have to pay for the damage. Clarify liabilities before renting.

Bicycle Rental: Many bicycle rental agencies operate in the Pham Ngu Lao area. Bike rentals cost 50 cents to $1 a day, depending on bike quality and other factors. Chinese-made Forever and Phoenix brands are solid and sturdy. There are other rentals around the Dong Khoi area. **Saigon Tourism** rents bikes, but they're expensive at $3 a day. Some places want your passport as a deposit, but avoid leaving such a valuable document. Some just want a $10 deposit and charge $40 if the bike is

traveler related how he paid an inflated price for a one-way cyclo journey, and then refused to hire the same cyclo for the return journey. When he started walking away, the cyclo driver attacked him with a metal bar. Many cyclo drivers carry a weapon of some kind, usually a knife or crowbar, under the seat.

Always negotiate the destination and full price before setting out on a cyclo. Make sure the driver knows where he is taking you. Saigon cyclo drivers are notorious for taking their customers "for a ride," charging foreigners 15 to 20 times the local rate. Make sure you're negotiating in dong rather than dollars. Cyclo drivers are quick to capitalize on misunderstandings. If you hold up two fingers indicating 2000 dong, the driver may choose to interpret it as $2 (after you arrive, of

stolen. Sinh Café requires a passport or $50 deposit for rental of a Chinese bike.

Vehicle Rental

Numerous agencies around Dong Khoi or Pham Ngu Lao can arrange a car and driver, or 15-seat minibus and driver, or something even larger. Rental depends on condition of the car (Russian or older models are cheaper), the kilometers racked up on the odometer, the number of proposed passengers, and whether the vehicle has air-conditioning. Some agencies quote a flat rate to save the half hour on the calculator. **Kim Café,** for example, offers custom car trips for a flat $30 for four passengers, including driver and gas. Daily rental is usually based on an eight-hour day; if you exceed that, overtime rates apply. Make bookings at least one day in advance. Some agents have accident damage insurance, but no theft protection. They require you to leave a passport or cash for a deposit.

The following rates are taken from Saigon Railway Tourism at 14 Pham Ngu Lao. A non air-conditioned four-seat Volga or Peugot is $25 a day and 12 cents/km; overtime $2/hour; overnight an extra $5.50 to cover the driver's expenses. An air-con four-seat Toyota for one day is $35 plus 13 cents/km; overtime $3/hour; if the vehicle is out overnight, it's an extra $7. An air-con Toyota 12-15 seat minibus starts at $37 a day, plus 18 cents/km; a 50-seat bus runs $55 a day.

Classic Wheels

Saigon Tourist and several of the major hotels rent chauffeur-driven Citroëns. A 1938 Citroën Traction 15 is the ideal luxury touring vehicle, with lots of legroom in the back. This is the gangster model, with running boards, dashmounted gearstick, and a windshield that can be winched open for ventilation. Via **Sunimex** and **Hoang Minh** shop at 103 Dong Khoi St. you can hire a 1960s Chevrolet Nova 400—open top, white exterior, red interior—for $20 an hour with driver and guide. A few vintage cars along Pham Ngu Lao are available to rent. The owner of 333 Bar collects cars. He rents a gray Mercedes for $40 a day, and a VW convertible and black Citroën $30 a day each. Many of Saigon's nonmetered taxis are classic autos too—1950s-vintage Peugot 203s, Peugot 305s, old Renault Dauphins. There is another class of taxi referred to as "wedding taxis"—used by married couples on their wedding day. These include spacious Dodges, Ford Falcons, even US Army jeeps. However, most couples now prefer newer Japanese cars for their wedding day.

Your Own Wheels

If you're buying your own motorcycle to head up-country, try the vicinity of New World Hotel, along Ly Tu Trong Street, with scores of motorcycle shops. These mostly sell brand-new Hondas imported from Japan or Thailand, but also showcase a few Russian motorcycles. The model fa-

Saigon traffic

SAIGON CLASSICS
by Hans Kemp

Imagine a society where cars have been frozen in time, where private car ownership was suddenly banned, where the country isolated itself from the rest of the world, and prevented aging autos from being snapped up as collectors' items. This is exactly what happened in Saigon. In the 1950s, this city was the jewel in the crown of the French Asian empire—money flowed, and both expatriates and locals spent heavily on cars—first on French models, then on other European cars such as Mercedes, Volkswagen, Fiat, and MG.

During the American occupation the money continued to pour in, bringing a generation of Fords and Dodges onto the streets. Then came 1975. With Saigon overrun by the North Vietnamese, ownership of a car became a capitalist sin. Owners either "sold" them to the state or stashed them in some remote barn. Private cars disappeared from the streets for a decade.

When the Hanoi leadership committed itself to a market-oriented economy in the mid-1980s, Saigon's automotive classics were dusted off and cautiously brought out of hiding. Unfortunately, plunderers also began scouring the country looking for classic treasures, intent on shipping them abroad for huge profits.

Some Saigon classics have been put to work as taxis, including a number of Peugeot 203s from the 1950s. Some of the drivers date to the 1950s too—Mr. Ngoc has been driving his 1952 Renault 4 since he bought it over 40 years ago. Among the taxis operating out of a bus station on the outskirts of Ho Chi Minh City is another French classic, a 1930s Citroën Traction Familiair. Looks are less important here than capacity, and the already long chassis of the vintage Citroën has been chopped and extended to accommodate 12 passengers. Other Citroëns are parked within the bus station compound, alongside custom-enlarged American cars—their bigger wheels and truck suspensions bumping up the profits.

Other vintage automobiles are maintained by collectors for private use. "People say I'm crazy to buy old cars," says Mr. Dong. "If I have the money I buy a car and not a house, whereas nowadays a house would be a better investment." Mr. Dong's collecting began in 1988 when he stumbled across a Volkswagen Kharman Ghia convertible on a visit to a local hospital. "I found it in a shed, along with discarded towels, blood, mice, and ants." A French doctor gave it to the hospital in 1975, but the hospital director thought it beneath his dignity to be driven around in a car with only two doors. The battery was dead, so the VW was shoved into a corner of the hospital grounds and used as a rubbish dump. "There is only one like this in the whole of Vietnam," Dong smiles. "I bought it for only $60, though many times more has been spent on repair and maintenance."

Mr. Dong couldn't have found a better car. Foreign visitors adore it, and by renting it out Dong was able to earn enough to buy a mid-1950s Mercedes 190. Later he bought a six-cylinder Citroën Traction 15 from an old woman who'd inherited it from her father. "I used to be brought to school in a car like this," says Dong, whose father was the chief accountant for IBM in the days before 1975.

Another avid collector is Mr. Huynh Van Mui, who runs a tailoring shop opposite the Hotel de Ville. He has been in business for over 40 years. "I had three cars before '75," says the white-haired tailor, "one for business, one for the family, and one for myself. Now the Rolls and the Mercedes are gone, but I could never part with my MGA." He bought the car in 1961 from a catalog in Hong Kong with 30 ounces of gold, and although times are tough, no way will Mr. Huynh sell his pride and joy.

Mr. Pham loves American cars. The drawers of his desk are filled with old brochures and magazine ads of every model available in the 1960s. "Plymouth is out to win you over," extols an ad clipped from an old *Playboy*. Under the photographic gaze of Uncle Ho, Mr. Pham's desk is soon covered with his paper collection. The only real car he owns is parked outside his office—a 1957 Dodge badly in need of work. Pham dreams of having enough money to restore it to its original state.

Pristine American models are sometimes sighted cruising the streets of Saigon. A young couple may hire a spacious American car for a wedding day cruise around town, although today these "wedding taxis" are increasingly Japanese models. Other US cars sighted include shiny Mustangs and a Chevrolet Nova 400. It's not hard to imagine this 1965 classic with GIs crammed into the red seats, cruising the bars of downtown Saigon.

HANS KEMP

Peugeot 203 taxi

vored by the Vietnamese, the Honda Dream II, sells new for up to $2800. A Russian Minsk 125cc costs $500. Opposite the New World Hotel is a string of stalls selling motorcycle helmets and accessories. You might also try to buy a motorcycle from a fellow traveler—check the notices posted at Kim and Sinh Cafés. Officially you need some sort of license if operating a motorcycle over 70cc but the police don't seem to care.

If you're staying longer in Saigon, or want to ride around the Delta or the countryside, consider buying a bicycle. For around town, a bike with a wire basket up front; for longer touring, a model with racks and a water-bottle cage. On Le Thanh Ton near the New World Hotel two small shops

sell 10-speeds, and two other shops sell mountain bikes. Low-end prices range from under $60 for a Thai bike or a Peugot made in Vietnam to $70 for a gearless Chinese-made Forever. High-end prices for Taiwan-made 10-speeds or pseudo–mountain bikes range from $130 to $230 depending on quality. Even higher end are bikes fitted with real Shimano components.

Boat Rentals
You can hire a boat to cruise up and down the Saigon River and its tributaries for around $5-10 an hour from the docks near the Floating Hotel.

Vietnamese Visa Modifications
The following stamp additions to your Vietnamese visa are handled by either **Ho Chi Minh Department of Immigration and Foreigners Affairs,** 161 Nguyen Du St., tel. 297107, or the **Immigration Department,** 254 Nguyen Trai St., tel. 391701. Travelers usually have the paperwork handled by an agent to expedite delivery, but you can try it yourself if you don't mind a bit of aggravation.

Visa Extension: There's a sliding fee scale for extensions depending on whether a week, two week, or longer extension is requested. Extensions are best handled through agents; the average cost is around $15.

Border-Crossing Stamp: If you intend to travel from Saigon to Phnom Penh by road, you will need a Moc Bai border exit stamp on your Vietnamese visa. The cost varies from $5 to $25—officially, the fee is $5. The Cambodian Consulate may be able to arrange the Moc Bai stamp while issuing a Cambodian visa. In any case, you'll need to obtain a Cambodian visa before proceeding with the Moc Bai stamp.

Re-entry Visa: If you wish to re-enter Vietnam after visiting Cambodia, you need a Vietnamese re-entry stamp, in effect turning your Vietnamese visa into a double-entry visa. This costs about $25.

GETTING AWAY

BY AIR

The **Vietnam Airlines** domestic office is at 15 Dinh Tien Hoang, tel. 299980. Here you can book flights directly, or via travel agents such as **ATC,** 63 Ly Tu Trong St., tel. 230234. Tan Son Nhat Airport is the busiest in the country, with scheduled domestic departures to the Central Highlands towns of Dalat, Buon Ma Thuot, Pleiku; Nha Trang and Qui Nhon on the coast; and points north like Hué, Danang, Haiphong, and Hanoi. There's also a flight to Phu Quoc Island in the southwest. Sample fares from Saigon: to Dalat, $25; Nha Trang, $45; Danang, $85; Hué, $90; Hanoi, $160; Haiphong, $150. Foreigner prices all. Be sure to reconfirm your ticket. Flights are continually overbooked and schedules altered. The booking system, allegedly computerized, doesn't seem to work very well, as passengers often fail to materialize. So if the plane you want is overbooked, go to the airport on standby and chances are you'll still be able to board.

The only alternatives in domestic carriers are Pacific Airlines and Vietnam Air Service Company (VASCO). VASCO operates light planes and helicopters on a charter basis, with regular flights to Con Dao Islands and Cantho. Contact VASCO at 27B Nguyen Dinh Chieu St., or use Vietnam Airlines as the booking agent. Pacific Airlines flies from Saigon to Hanoi and Haiphong; the outfit has an office in the same building as Vietnam Airlines domestic (Dinh Tien Hoang, tel. 299980) and another office downtown at 76D Le Thanh Ton, tel. 231285, near the Hotel de Ville. See "On the Road" earlier in this chapter for more details on internal flights.

BY RAIL

Saigon Railway Station is about six km from the Hotel de Ville, about a 15-minute drive. You can get advance tickets from travel agencies, such as **Saigon Railway Tourism Company,** at 14 Pham Ngu Lao. Most hotels have rail schedules; you can also get the information by phone by calling 108. Foreigners pay premium prices on trains, much more than locals.

Saigon is the end of the line; from here you can go only north along the coast to Hué and Hanoi. For more information about Reunification Express trains on the 45-hour Saigon to Hanoi run, refer to "On the Road" earlier in this chapter. Sample fares from Saigon to Hué, a distance of 1,038 km, on an S7 train: $29 hard seat, $35 soft seat, $50-55-60 hard sleeper, and $66 soft sleeper. From Saigon to Hué on a CM5 train, prices are $40 soft seat, $55-60-66 hard sleeper, and $76 soft sleeper; no hard seats. Train travel is more comfortable and more expensive than bus travel, but not much faster.

BY ROAD

Traveler Minibuses

A number of Saigon outfits can arrange up-country tours by car or minibus. You can arrange a custom trip with your own small group, or join other travelers. If accompanying others, you don't have to complete the trip; just bail out wherever you want. Traveler cars and minibuses are more comfortable than Vietnamese bus or minibus transport, and the logistics will be simpler. Weighed against this is the higher price, and the fact that you're traveling with other Westerners who'll all take out their cameras at every stop. There are sign-up boards for traveler vans heading up the coast at cafés on Pham Ngu Lao. Usually up to 10 passengers per minibus are required; for cars, four passengers.

Express Minibus: Pham Ngu Lao cafés offer transport only on minibuses (no tours). Direct to Dalat costs $7 a person (six hours), and express to Nha Trang runs $12-15 (nine hours). Sometimes the rider is put in with a touring group. Vietnamese agencies offer the same service to popular destinations. Addresses keep changing, so inquire at your hotel desk about possibilities. A minibus office at 39 Nguyen Hue Blvd. arranges rides to Dalat, Vung Tau, Nha Trang, and the coast. Vietnamese minibuses

CONSULATES IN SAIGON

Most embassies and consulates are located in Hanoi. However, because of frequent land/air connections or other reasons of expediency, some are based in Saigon. A few consulates of note are: **China,** 261 Hoang Van Tu St., tel. 441-024; **France,** 102 Hai Ba Trung, tel. 297231; **Germany,** 126 Nguyen Dinh Chieu, tel. 291967; **India,** 49 Tran Quoc Thao, tel. 294498; **Russia,** 40 Ba Huyen Thanh Quan, tel. 392937; and **United Kingdom,** 261 Dien Bien Phu, tel. 298433. The Australian government and the US government are also establishing consulates in Saigon.

Regional Consulates
The **Cambodian Consulate,** at 41 Phung Khac Khoan, Q1, tel. 292751, issues a seven-day visa; it requires four photos and costs $20. A 14-day visa is $30. Visa issue is possible same day or next day, but if you pay an extra $30 it only takes 20 minutes. If you fly into Phnom Penh you can get a one-month visa at the airport for $20; if crossing by land from Vietnam, you must get your Cambodian visa in Saigon, and you need a Moc Bai exit stamp on your Vietnamese visa.

The **Lao Consulate,** 181 Hai Ba Trung St., tel. 299272, issues a five- to seven-day transit visa for $20; it takes three working days to process. There are also Lao consulates in Danang and Hanoi.

Singapore Consulate, 5 Phung Khac Khoan, Q1, tel. 225173, fax 251600, is open Mon.-Fri. 0830-1230 and 1330-1700. The Consulate-General of Thailand is just up from the Rex II annex at 77 Tran Quoc Thao St., Q3. Visa issue takes two working days, and costs $15.

are packed to the maximum, and you won't see much along the way.

Bus Terminals
The two main bus terminals are Mien Tay, with buses to the south, and Mien Dong, with departures to the north. Try to purchase express bus tickets a day in advance by having your hotel desk or an agent phone ahead. Bus stations are all located on the fringes of Saigon, so allow time to get out to these places if you anticipate a 0500 departure. Some stations are up to 10 km out of town. Arrange a taxi to get to the station, or find a regular lambro shuttle for a few thousand dong. The lambro is slower because of frequent stops. There are also some regular buses connecting the outlying terminals with Ben Thanh Bus Terminal near Ben Thanh Market in Central Saigon. Ben Thanh Bus Terminal also runs buses to Cu Chi.

Some of the bus terminals on the fringes of Saigon are huge and serve as bases for other transportation such as minibuses, old Citroën share-taxis, Renault vans, and other mobile wonders. Bus travel is cheap: you can make it all the way from Saigon to Hanoi in under 50 hours for $20, although your kidneys will never be the same. You may be a few inches shorter by the time you arrive too—buses and minibuses crowd those passengers in. Although presumably there's no foreign markup, the ticket sellers routinely gouge big noses, especially on the minibus runs.

Mien Tay Bus Terminal: Located 10 km southwest of central Saigon on Huong Vuong Blvd., this sprawling terminal handles departures to the Mekong Delta and points south. There are buses to Vinh Long, Cantho, Phung Hiep, Camau, Long Xuyen, Chau Doc, and Rach Gia. Timing depends on ferry crossings along the route: three hours to Cantho, 12 hours to Camau. Buses go to Mien Tay from the Ben Thanh Market area; you can also hop on a lambro from the east side of Pham Ngu Lao.

Cholon Bus Terminal: No express buses run to Mytho from Mien Tay Terminal, just regular buses. It's more convenient to take a Mytho bus from Cholon Bus Terminal (Ben Xe Khach Cholon) in District 5, a lot closer to central Saigon. Other departures from this terminal go to My Thuan, Caibe, and Long An.

Mien Dong Bus Terminal: This station is located on Quoc Lo 13, about six km northeast of central Saigon; follow Xo Viet Nghe Tinh Street all the way out. You can take a bus from the Ben Thanh Market area, or a moto. The station handles most departures to the north, to Vung Tau, Dalat, Buon Ma Thuot, Hué, Danang, and the coast road to Hanoi. Express buses leave around 0500.

Other Bus Stations: Tay Ninh Bus Terminal in Tan Binh District west of the airport has departures to Tay Ninh, Cu Chi, and other points northwest of Saigon. **Van Thanh Bus Terminal,** on Dien Bien Phu Street in Binh Thanh District to the northeast of town, handles short-range trips out of Saigon, with some smaller vehicles running to Vung Tau and Long Hai Beach.

Saigon to Phnom Penh

To enter Cambodia by road you need to obtain a Cambodian visa in Saigon and a Moc Bai exit stamp on your Vietnamese visa. If you plan to cross into Cambodia and then return to Saigon, you'll need a re-entry stamp for your Vietnamese visa.

Taxi to Phnom Penh: A share-taxi is $30 to the Moc Bai border, only $7.50 when split between four people. Try Saigon's **Mien Tay Bus Station** on the western outskirts of town, or negotiate with a downtown taxi driver if you have your own small group. Once over the border you can arrange another share-taxi for about $5-10 a person—just crowd in with the locals. Depending on immigration holdups, the full trip from Saigon to Phnom Penh should take seven to eight hours.

Bus to Phnom Penh: Cambodian buses (non air-con) cost $5, and leave Thursday, Friday, and Saturday from an old Mercedes-Benz dealership at 145 Nguyen Du, around the corner from Hoang Gia Hotel. The Vietnamese air-con bus leaves from the same area on Monday, Tuesday, and Wednesday, and costs $12. You can purchase tickets for both buses at the garage next to the Rex Hotel, 155 Nguyen Hue Boulevard, tel. 230754; one-day advance purchase recommended. The seller must see your Cambodian visa before issuing the ticket. No buses on Sunday or holidays, which means no buses for three to four days around Tet. The trip takes about nine to 10 hours. Buses leave at 0530 and arrive around 1500 or 1600 in Phnom Penh. However, if there are delays due to contraband spot checks, the trip could take 12 hours or longer.

BY BOAT

For those who like leisurely boat travel, wooden boats depart from Saigon to Mytho, Camau, and other points in the Mekong Delta from a dock at the foot of Ham Nghi Boulevard. See "Mekong Delta" under "Around the South" for details.

EXIT FORMALITIES

On exit you surrender your customs form, though nobody seems to check it. If you have a paper visa, you surrender this too. International departure tax is $8; no domestic departure tax. When boarding a domestic or international flight, you have to pass through two sets of Heimann scanners, the same kind used at Bangkok Airport. They say "Film Safe" but it's still advisable to divert film around them.

AROUND THE SOUTH

Most travelers use Saigon as a base for roundtrip explorations of the south. Popular sites outside Saigon include Mytho, a riverine town 70 km southwest; the beach resort of Vung Tau 115 km southeast; and Cu Chi Tunnels and Cao Dai Great Temple to the northwest. Numerous Saigon tour agencies package these destinations as day-trips or overnight journeys. You can also ride tourist vans one-way to these destinations, then take off on your own.

A number of traveler cafés on Pham Ngu Lao in Saigon organize cheap day-trips by minibus, usually venturing out 0900-1800. The day-trip to Cu Chi and Cao Dai Great Temple is $6 a head; a Mytho day-trip costs $7. The 333 Bar runs a tour to Vung Tau and Long Hai Beach, two days, $8-12 not including accommodations. Long Phi Café offers a day-trip to the lacquerware village of Songbe, complete with a visit to porcelain factories and boat trips through fruit orchards, for $5-6 per person.

NORTHWEST OF SAIGON

Saigon's most popular day-trip is to Cu Chi Tunnels and the Cao Dai Great Temple at Tay Ninh. Although you can reach these areas by public transportation, the logistics are complicated. For $5, a minibus from a traveler café will take care of all the driving and directions. Tours generally leave Saigon at 0900, reach Tay Ninh for the 1200 Cao Dai service, then leave at 1300 for

Cu Chi Tunnels. You're usually back in Saigon around 1800 or 1900. The Cao Dai Great Temple stop is short—if you'd like to spend more time at Tay Ninh, for a small extra fee the tour bus will drop you at the Cao Dai Temple, then pick you up the next day. In the interim you can spend more time at the temple and visit Black Lady Mountain, overnighting in Tay Ninh.

CU CHI TUNNELS

Cu Chi Tunnels are located near the village of Ben Suc, about 75 km northwest of Saigon, and some 40 km from the town of Cu Chi. The tunnels were part of an underground network that zigzagged from the southern tip of the Ho Chi Minh Trail near the Cambodian border to the Saigon River. Most Vietcong tunnels in the Cu Chi area have been sealed, but a few passageways were doubled in width and height to accommodate Western tourist bodies.

There are actually two tunnel locations, both in the direction of Ben Suc village. Backpackers usually go to Ben Dinh, where the entry price is $1.50. They're shown a short video, given a garbled spiel about the tunnels, and allowed to crawl through a 50-meter passage. Swanker tourists head for Ben Duoc, about five km away, where a $3-4 entry price pays for a more articulate translator, a superior Saigon Tourist video, and wider tunnels. Insecticide is sprayed daily and the tunnels are cleared of any crawlies such as snakes or scorpions (tiny bats like the tunnels too).

The Vietcong used to crawl on their bellies through the dark, dank tunnels, but visitors can walk around hunched over. After scrambling through the tunnels for a claustrophobic sweaty 15 minutes you wonder how anybody could last a day in the tunnels, let alone a year. The Vietcong carried on much longer than that—people got married and women gave birth underground. Below ground was a complete system of

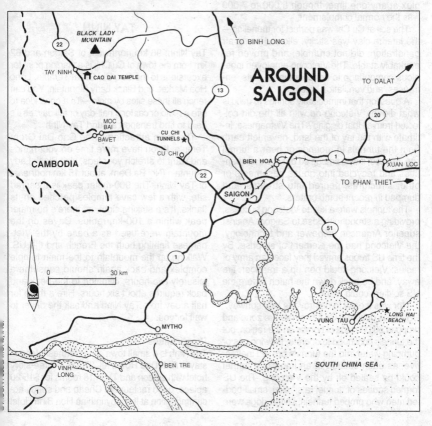

AROUND SAIGON

kitchens, rudimentary clinics and operating rooms, meeting rooms, and sleeping chambers with bamboo beds. The network also incorporated storage chambers for weapons and rice, drinking wells, ventilation shafts, false tunnels, and booby-trapped passages.

The Vietnamese spent decades digging in the reddish-brown laterite clay in this area—the tunnels were all built with simple hand tools. Up to 50 km in tunnels were constructed by the Vietminh fighting the French between 1948 and 1954. Between 1960 and 1965 their successors, the Vietcong, added an astonishing three-level network four times as big, bringing the total up to over 200 km. The deepest layer of tunnels lay eight to 10 meters underground. Up to 16,000 guerrillas could live in the tunnel complex at any one time, though 5,000 to 7,000 was the normal complement.

The soil at Cu Chi was perfect for tunneling—the laterite clay was sticky, allowed some air penetration, did not crumble, and proved remarkably stable. The Vietcong employed ingenious camouflage to conceal tunnel exits, entrances, and ventilation holes.

A question that immediately springs to mind is what did the Vietcong do with all the dirt collected from all that digging? The Vietnamese, intimate with the lay of the land, never left earth from the tunnels in mounds or near a tunnel site. Instead, it was smuggled out in small quantities and recycled into house basements or other structures, poured into streams, and dumped in recent bomb craters.

The tunnels were a key to Vietcong success, providing a stronghold close to Saigon. Against superior American firepower and technology, the Vietcong had the element of surprise. By the time US troops arrived they faced an army of moles: Vietcong could pop up a trapdoor, fire away, and be back down the hatch before the US soldiers could react.

Nor was it easy to destroy the VC "subway." US forces declared Cu Chi a free-fire zone and dropped 50,000 tons of bombs on the region, but the tunnels continued to operate. Blowing gas or pumping water into the tunnels proved ineffective, as each section of an important tunnel could be sealed off by the Vietcong. The US formed squads of "tunnel rats," slim, small-bodied men who probed tunnels; sniffer dogs were also used. These rat squads only partially uncovered the mysteries of the underground labyrinth. Among the visitors to Cu Chi are US veterans who come back to see this incredible network with their own eyes.

The Cu Chi Tunnels area is the most accessible and commercial yet, dubbed "Cong World" by a visiting Western reporter. After crawling around in the tunnels, you can move over to a nearby firing range, where you can empty an AK-47 or M-16 rifle at targets of paper tigers or water buffalo for an American dollar a shot. Souvenir shops sell war-related paraphernalia—you can buy a genuine pair of rubber sandals once worn on the Ho Chi Minh Trail. Attendants at the shops wear black pajamas and rubber sandals, just as the Vietcong did.

TAY NINH

Tay Ninh, 96 km northwest of Saigon and 62 km from the town of Cu Chi, is a staging point for excursions to the Cao Dai Great Temple, Long Hoa Market, and Black Lady Mountain. You can reach all these sites by moto—it's a good idea to hire a moto or car for a half-day or full day, as it's hard to find transport around Tay Ninh.

The main attraction is the Cao Dai Great Temple. If you have more time on your hands and want to stretch your legs, visit Black Lady Mountain (Noi Ba Den), about 15 km northeast of Tay Ninh. The 900-meter peak is a sacred site, with a few cave temples perched on its flanks. It's a striking sight, as there's no major peak within a 100-km radius. Caves on the mountain were used as a base by the Vietnamese fighting both the French and the US. Walking up the mountain to the main temple complex and back again should consume a leisurely two hours; climbing to the peak and back requires about six hours. Hire a moto for half a day from Tay Ninh and ask the driver to wait for you.

Practicalities

Tay Ninh is a small town. The cleanest place to stay is **Anh Dao Hotel,** tel. 27306, a three-story hotel with air-con and TV in 18 rooms for $15-20 apiece; good restaurant. Cheap and seedy accommodation at the labyrinthine Hoa Binh Hotel runs $5 for fan rooms and $10 for air-con. This run-down socialist palace is a short-time hotel, with rooms rented hourly, and taxi girls and cockroaches hanging about. There are a few other hotels around town in the $10-20 per room range. Foodstalls and small restaurants are strung out along the main drag of Tay Ninh. Buses leave Tay Ninh hourly from 0600 to 1300 for Saigon—the trip takes three hours, with frequent stops. Buses to Tay Ninh depart Saigon from Tay Ninh Bus Terminal on the northwest fringe of the city.

CAO DAI GREAT TEMPLE

The Temple

From the outside, the Cao Dai Great Temple is already bizarre, combining the lines of a French baroque church with pagoda-like steeples. Inside you enter a realm described by Graham Greene as "a Walt Disney fantasia of the East, dragons and snakes in technicolour." Greene himself took the faith very seriously and at one point considered conversion to Cao Daism.

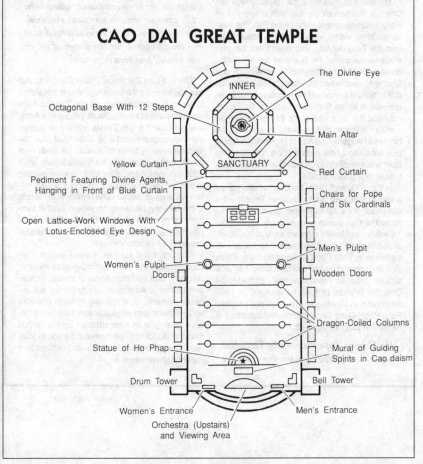

CAO DAI GREAT TEMPLE

- INNER
- The Divine Eye
- Octagonal Base With 12 Steps
- Main Altar
- Yellow Curtain
- SANCTUARY
- Red Curtain
- Pediment Featuring Divine Agents, Hanging in Front of Blue Curtain
- Chairs for Pope and Six Cardinals
- Open Lattice-Work Windows With Lotus-Enclosed Eye Design
- Men's Pulpit
- Women's Pulpit
- Doors
- Wooden Doors
- Dragon-Coiled Columns
- Statue of Ho Phap
- Mural of Guiding Spirits in Cao daism
- Drum Tower
- Bell Tower
- Women's Entrance
- Men's Entrance
- Orchestra (Upstairs) and Viewing Area

CAO DAISM

What do Winston Churchill, Joan of Arc, Jesus Christ, Confucius, Moses, St. John the Baptist, Charlie Chaplin, and Louis Pasteur have in common? They are divine agents, of course, adopted as patron saints by the Cao Dai sect. This oddball faith is a synthesis of Buddhist, Confucian, Taoist, and Christian beliefs, with a dash of Islam thrown in. Cao Daism copies its organization from the Roman Catholic Church, with cardinals, bishops, archbishops, and a pope, though there is no pope at present.

The sect was founded in the 1920s by Ngo Van Chieu, a civil servant blessed with a series of visions, including several of the Divine Eye. The messenger in the visions was Ly Tai Pe, a literary figure from the Tang dynasty, who maintained that previous revelations of the Supreme Spirit—Confucianism, Buddhism, Christianity—took place at a time when people had little contact with each other due to deficient means of transportation. As a representative of the Supreme Spirit, Ly Tai Pe announced the time had come to reorganize the world's disparate religious elements and form the Universal Religion of the Age of Improved Transport, thus achieving a harmonious whole. The Supreme Spirit was henceforth to be known as Cao Dai, symbolized by a giant eyeball.

In the 1930s and 1940s the Cao Dai sect gained a steady following, and the Great Temple—the equivalent of the Vatican—was constructed at Tay Ninh. The Cao Daists were estimated to number 1.5 million, and fielded a private army of 20,000 tolerated by the French because the sect was anti-Vietminh. In 1943 Cao Dai Pope Ngo Van Chieu died and was succeeded by Pham Cong Tac, who suffered under the French and was deported to the Comoros Islands. In 1946 he returned. In 1950 writer Norman Lewis visited Tay Ninh and glimpsed Pope Pham Cong Tac, an encounter described in his book *A Dragon Apparent:*

His Holiness, Pope Pham-Cong-Tac, whose name means "the Sun shining from the South," awaited us, beneath the golden parasol, attired in his uniform of Grand-Marshal of the Celestial Empire. He was carrying his Marshal's baton, at the sight of which, according to Cao-Daist literature, all evil spirits flee in terror.

Physically, the Pope looked hardly able to support the weight of his dignity. He was a tiny, insignificant figure of a man, with an air of irremediable melancholy. His presence was, in any case, overshadowed by the startling architectural details of the cathedral, for the design of which he himself had been responsible.

The last Cao Dai Pope, Pham Cong Tac suffered again under the Diem regime and was forced to flee to Cambodia. Because the Cao Dai Army was incorporated into the South Vietnamese Army, and because the Cao Daists refused to support the Vietcong, the sect was disbanded after the 1975 takeover by the north. All Cao Dai lands were confiscated and the sect's leadership broken up. In 1985, however, many of the temples were returned to the Cao Daists. The sect today has several million followers in Vietnam and is particularly strong in the Mekong Delta region, where smaller temples are modeled after the Cao Dai Great Temple. There are an estimated 1,000 Cao Dai temples throughout southern Vietnam.

Although it first appears a weird religion, Cao Daism follows the same basic precepts as other religions, with common goals of peace, justice, and harmony. Among its key practices are ancestor-worship, spirit contact through séances and mediums, and vegetarianism; Cao Daists believe in a cycle of reincarnation similar to that found in Buddhism. Like other religions in Vietnam, Cao Daism is restricted in its practices by a watchful government.

*the eye of Cao Dai
in the main temple*

After removing their hats and shoes, visitors pass a mural of the guiding spirits of Cao Daism. The figure holding the inkstone is Sun Yatsen; writing in French is Victor Hugo; at the right is 15th-century Vietnamese poet Nguyen Binh Khiem, famous for his prophecies. On the other side of this wall are three statues mounted on lotus buds and raised on a three-step dais. The central figure is Ho Phap, a symbol of Justice, flanked by statues of cardinals. Draped around Ho Phap is a seven-headed serpent: the top three heads symbolize Love, Joy, and Bliss; the lower heads symbolize Jealousy, Anger, Hatred, and Uncontrollable Desire.

The dragon, symbolizing the force of intellect, is a dominant temple feature. Down the nave are two rows of dragon-coiled pillars supporting a lofty vaulted ceiling, dotted with clouds and inlaid with flying dragons. The lotus, symbolizing purity, is another prominent motif. Piercing the walls are open lattice-work windows composed of a striking lotus design. Each lattice window encloses a Cao Dai eye set in a triangle, just like the one on the US dollar bill.

While Cao Dai worshippers wear white, Cao Dai priests wear red, blue, or yellow robes—red symbolizes Confucianism, blue Taoism, and yellow Buddhism. Separating the inner sanctuary from the main temple are three curtains, one each in red, blue, and yellow. Suspended from the ceiling is a pediment featuring divine agents. There are eight small figures here—at top left is Lao Tzu, the founder of Taoism; below him

the Bodhisattva Quan Am. In the middle, from top to bottom, are Sakyamuni Buddha, Ly Thai Bach (Ly Tai Pe, the spiritual Pope), Jesus Christ, and Cuong Thai Cong (a mythological figure). To the right, at the top is Confucius; below is Quan Cong, a deified Chinese general. Among the Western patron saints in the eclectic Cao Dai pantheon are Joan of Arc, Vladimir Lenin, William Shakespeare, Aristide Briand, La Fontaine, and René Descartes—all spirits the Cao Daists have contacted through mediums.

Smooth tiled flooring leads up nine broad steps to the main altar. The inner sanctuary sits on an octagonal base with 12 steps, enclosed by eight dragon pillars, with a flying dragon embedded in the ceiling. In Taoism the octagon symbolizes creation and the celestial regions. An octagonal table supports a huge globe, on which is painted the all-seeing all-knowing Divine Eye, symbol of Cao Dai or the Supreme Spirit. Only high priests are allowed to approach the octagonal table during the emotionally moving service. Offerings of fruit, flowers, incense, candles, tea, and wine are made to the Divine Eye.

The Compound

The Cao Dai Great Temple is set in a large compound of residences, administrative buildings, schools, and gardens. There are a few places where you can sit down for a quiet cup of tea. A short walk south of the main temple is the Temple of the Divine Mother, smaller in scale than the Cao Dai Great Temple. It is here that important figures are given last rites. Three km south of the Cao Dai Great Temple is Long Hoa Market, with mostly food and poultry on sale, and lively trading in progress.

Conduct

Scanty attire upsets the Cao Daists. Cover your arms and legs—perhaps bring some loose pants and a jacket to slip on before going into the temple. Remove shoes and hats before entering; men enter to the right, women to the left. You may walk around the temple before the service—women are supposed to walk clockwise around the temple, men counterclockwise. During the service you're restricted to the back top gallery, near the orchestra. Photography from this point is permitted—the popping of flash-bulbs seems an accepted part of the ceremony and doesn't faze anyone.

Getting There

The Cao Dai Great Temple lies 100 km from Saigon, four km east of Tay Ninh at the village of Long Hoa. Services are held daily at 0600, 1200, 1800, and midnight, and last about 45 minutes. The best plan is to arrive 30 minutes before the noon service so you can tour the entire temple and take in the service as well. Most tours permit only about an hour at the temple. If you wish to stay longer, take one tour in, stay overnight in Tay Ninh (you can reach the temple from Tay Ninh by moto), and hop back on the tour bus the following day. For full control of your itinerary, hire a car from Saigon for about $40 a day, which works out to $10 each for four passengers.

SOUTHEAST OF SAIGON

VUNG TAU

Vung Tau is an old port town 115 km southeast of Saigon, developed under the French as a seaside resort called Cap Saint Jacques. It served as a rest center for French officers, and later for Australian and American troops on R&R during the Vietnam War. Next came the Russians—they're still here, drilling for gas and oil at rigs 60 km off the coast. The Russians have lots of company these days; BP, BHP, Petrofina, Total, and the Japan-Vietnam Petrol Association (JVPC) are also exploring these waters.

Apart from oil, gas, and fishing, the main industry in Vung Tau appears to be prostitution. There are large numbers of bamboo brothel shacks around, mainly catering to groups of men from Taiwan, Hong Kong, and China who tour the minibrothels chaperoned by a state tour guide in the air-conditioned comfort of a government-owned bus. Then the town is plastered with AIDS-awareness posters.

Vung Tau is a town of about 100,000. The population swells in July and August when Vietnamese vacationers arrive in droves. The commercial end of Vung Tau is at Front Beach, or Bai Truoc, where you'll find banks, businesses, high-end hotels, nightlife, and shopping. Foreign oil workers and businessmen base themselves here; tour groups lodge here because of better hotels. As a beach, however, Front Beach is a joke—thin, short, crowded, hemmed in at the north end by an embankment, and at the south by fishing boats and freighters. A few kilometers south of Front Beach is a rocky cove with a few umbrellas sticking out of it—this "beach" is called Bai Tam Huong Phong. There are several guesthouses in the area. About three km north of Front Beach is Bai Dau, a paltry strip of sand hard to reach because of poor roads. Some budget accommodations are out here.

The best place for swimming is Back Beach, or Bai Sau, with a six-kilometer stretch of sand; the beach offers budget and moderate-priced hotels and run-down cafés and is a magnet for backpackers and budget travelers. The French called the place Au Vents Beach—it can get extremely windy, causing a bad rip tide.

The White Villa

The White Villa, or Bach Dinh, located to the north of Front Beach, was built in the 19th century as a summer palace for Indochina Governor-general Paul Doumer. It was later used by other luminaries, including South Vietnamese Presidents Ngo Dinh Diem and Nguyen Van Thieu. The villa is perched on a hillside amid tranquil

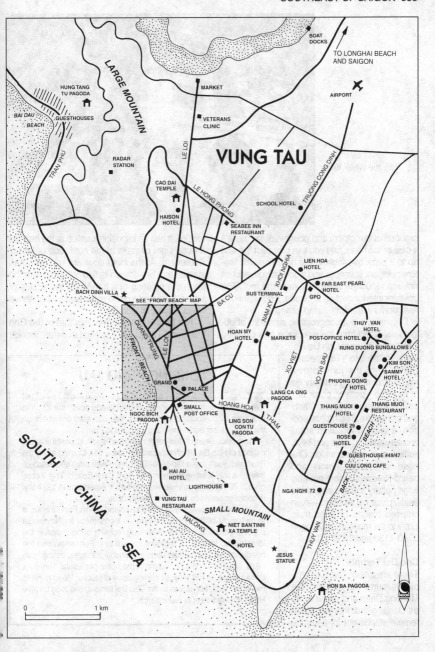

LARGE MOUNTAIN

BOAT DOCKS

TO LONGHAI BEACH AND SAIGON

HUNG TANG TU PAGODA

MARKET

AIRPORT

BAI DAU BEACH

GUESTHOUSES

VETERANS CLINIC

TRAN PHU

RADAR STATION

VUNG TAU

LE LOI

CAO DAI TEMPLE

LE HONG PHONG

SCHOOL HOTEL

TRUONG CONG DINH

HAISON HOTEL

SEABEE INN RESTAURANT

LIEN HOA HOTEL

BACH DINH VILLA

SEE "FRONT BEACH" MAP

KHOI NGHIA

BUS TERMINAL

FAR EAST PEARL HOTEL

GPO

BA CU

NAM KY

THUY VAN HOTEL

FRONT BEACH

QUANG TRUNG

HOAN MY HOTEL

MARKETS

POST-OFFICE HOTEL

XO VIET

RUNG DUONG BUNGALOWS

KIM SON

VO THI SAU

SAMMY HOTEL

LE LOI

PHUONG DONG HOTEL

GRAND

PALACE

HOANG HOA

LANG CA ONG PAGODA

THANG MUOI HOTEL

THANG MUOI RESTAURANT

NGOC BICH PAGODA

SMALL POST OFFICE

LING SON CON TU PAGODA

THAM

GUESTHOUSE 29

ROSE HOTEL

BACK BEACH

GUESTHOUSE #49/47

CUU LONG CAFE

SOUTH CHINA SEA

HAI AU HOTEL

LIGHTHOUSE

NGA NGHI 72

VUNG TAU RESTAURANT

SMALL MOUNTAIN

HALONG

NIET BAN TINH XA TEMPLE

THUY VAN

HOTEL

JESUS STATUE

HON BA PAGODA

0   1 km

MOON

the White Villa

grounds of frangipani and bougainvillea; there's a café at the base, and you can hike past the villa up to a peak overlooking the bay. The villa features elegant stairwells and wood fittings, and art nouveau touches outside up near the roof. The upstairs interior section is closed; it consists of a few rooms with moth-eaten furniture.

Downstairs is an engrossing museum of objects salvaged from the wreckage of a Chinese junk that sank near Con Dau Islands in the late 17th century. Relics from the junk form a microcosm of Qing dynasty life at the time—pottery, porcelain, earthenware, bronze artifacts and stoneware. The bronze section is fascinating, with small bronze cannons, locks and keys, kettles, nails, sundial watch, Chinese coins, small mirrors, and beard-tweezers. There are also large pottery storage jars, stone seals, pieces of sail cord—even charred pieces of dried fruit. Entry to the museum is $1; open 0700-1130 and 1330-1700.

Cao Dai Temple

There are lots of Cao Dai temples around Saigon and the Mekong Delta and as far north as Danang, but the Vung Tau temple stands out for its architecture. It has an imposing location at the head of a huge flight of stairs at the north end of Le Loi Boulevard. At the front door are two guardian statues and two dragon-coiled columns; over the door is a painting of a hand with the scales of justice, held over a globe of the world, while above floats the eye of Cao Dai.

The temple interior matches that of the Cao Dai Great Temple at Tay Ninh in detail, though

TOURING VUNG TAU

Vung Tau has a motley bunch of sights—you might as well get a moto, rented motorcycle, or bicycle and polish the lot off in one long loop around the headland. You can start anywhere on the circuit described—the Vung Tau Grand Prix.

From Back Beach, head south round the headland, past the island pagoda of Hon Ba, which is accessible at low tide. Coming round the headland, you'll see a Rio-style Giant Jesus with arms outstretched; there's a trail leading to the statue from Back Beach. This incongruous 30-meter statue was erected by the Americans in 1971 and is complemented by a smaller Mary statue.

On a hill to the west side of the headland is Niet Ban Tinh Xa, a large temple built in 1971. Niet Ban is Vietnamese for Nirvana, a concept embodied in a 12-meter-long reclining Buddha statue; the temple also features a massive bronze bell. Farther around the headland is a trail leading up to a French lighthouse, dating from 1910, which affords a panorama of the entire peninsula. There's a military base up this way, so photography is touchy. Head north to the White Villa, cut across to the Cao Dai temple, and then take Le Hong Phong Street to Back Beach.

not in size. There are several rows of dragon-coiled columns, and flying dragons are embedded in the ceiling. Up front is a beautiful altar with the eye of Cao Dai mounted on a board. If you can find someone with a key, you may be allowed to view the interior—try the residence at the back. There is a small turnout for services at 0600, 1200, 1800, and midnight.

Whale Pagoda

Closer to Back Beach is Lang Ca Ong Pagoda (Dinh Than Thang-Tam), a small temple built in 1911 with a maritime theme—pictures of boats, and a couple of real wooden longboats. The main altar is enclosed by six dragon columns, the two up front topped by phoenix with popping lights for eyeballs. Behind the altar is a glass case with whale vertebrae and bones. This temple is dedicated to the whale, a deity of Vung Tau fisherfolk. Whale worship derives from ancient Cham customs, in which the whale is considered a friend and benefactor.

Con Dao Islands

About 180 km off the coast of Vung Tau is the Con Dao archipelago, a group of 14 islets with unspoiled beaches, coconut groves, coral, and crystal-clear water. The largest island, at about 20 square km, is Con Son, which is partially forested with teak and pine trees. Sea turtles lumber ashore here to lay eggs from February to July. Under the French, Con Son was a top security prison known as Poulo Condore, where opponents of French colonialism were held in appalling conditions. Part of the prison system has been turned into a museum. Though few travelers make it this far, there are accommodations on Con Son. Local authorities want to turn the island into a resort spot with the development of a national park, marine reserve, bird sanctuary, and beaches. The island is served by intermittent boat service (about 13 hours from Vung Tau); flights may also be possible. Inquire at the Vietnam Airlines booking office at 27 Quang Trung, Front Beach, in Vung Tau. Vietnam Air Service Company (VASCO) operates flights between Saigon and Con Dao aboard Jetstream aircraft, carrying 19 passengers.

Front Beach Practicalities

A lot of the hotels at Front Beach are run by the National Oil Services Company of Vietnam (OSC), with offices at 2 Le Loi, tel. 59863, fax 52834. In addition, OSC maintains a dozen expensive villas for rent or lease in the Front Beach area; some are used by foreign businesses. The OSC issues its own map of Vung Tau and area, but it's hard to find.

Budget: The north end of Front Beach has some rooms in the $10-20 range, formerly favored by visiting Russians. Don't expect wonders in the plumbing department. In this category are **Rang Dong Hotel,** at 5 Duy Tan, tel. 52133; next door is **Song Hau Hotel,** tel. 52601; along Truong Vinh Ky St. are **Song Hong Hotel,** tel. 52137; and **Song Huong Hotel,** tel. 52491. **Halong Hotel,** at 45 Thong Nhat St., tel. 52175, near the church, has lower-priced accommodations.

Moderate: The following hotels are in the $20-45 price range. **Pacific Hotel,** 4 Le Loi, tel. 52391, fax 52239, 32 rooms. **Grand Hotel,** 26 Quang

---

VETERANS CLINIC

Completed in 1989, the Veterans Clinic on Le Loi Boulevard was the first building constructed by Americans in Vietnam since the end of the war in 1975. Although the clinic is dedicated to general medicine and obstetrics, sick travelers are welcome here, providing they have hard currency.

The 14-room primary health care facility, known as the Friendship Clinic, was the first project of the Veterans Vietnam Restoration Project (VVRP). The VVRP sends over teams of American vets on humanitarian aid projects. Veterans have helped thousands of Vietnamese, and in the process have themselves experienced significant healing.

Since the Vung Tau project, VVRP has completed six additional projects in Vietnam, building medical clinics, adding wings to hospitals, supplying medical and alternative energy technology, and delivering much-needed medical equipment and supplies. In 1994 VVRP helped set up a facility near Saigon to house Vietnamese amputees being fitted for artificial limbs. The limbs are provided free by another American NGO, Vietnam Assistance for the Handicapped.

Trung St., tel. 52469, fax 52088, has 70 rooms, tennis courts, fitness center, and several restaurants; cheaper rooms are available. **Hai Yen Hotel,** 8 Le Loi, tel. 52571, has 24 doubles. **Rex Hotel,** 1 Duy Tan St., tel./fax 59862, features 84 rooms, several restaurants and bars, tennis courts, and business facilities. **Diamond Hotel,** 8 Tran Nguyen Han, tel. 59236, fax 59237, has about 50 rooms for $40 apiece, as well as a disco-karaoke setup. **Future Star KTV Hotel,** on Tran Hung Dao, is a Taiwan joint-venture—foreigners are waved away.

Luxury: A notch up, in the $35-60 price range, are the following hotels. **Seabreeze Hotel,** 11 Nguyen Trai St., tel. 52392, fax 59856, is an Aus-

tralian joint-venture hotel with a pool and full facilities. **Palace Hotel,** opposite Seabreeze Hotel, tel. 52265, fax 59878, is owned by OSC; it has 105 air-con rooms, including eight suites and three apartments, and conference halls. **Canadian Hotel,** 48 Quang Trung St., tel. 59852, fax 59851, has 52 rooms. Single prices are standard $36, ocean view $58, suite $64, sea-view suite $68; for doubles add $10. The hotel features in-house video, restaurants, and a business center—popular with foreign businesspeople. **Petro House Hotel,** 93 Tran Hung Dao, tel. 52014, fax 52015, is the classiest place in Vung Tau, a beautifully renovated older building with 59 rooms for $42-48 standard, $78-168 suite.

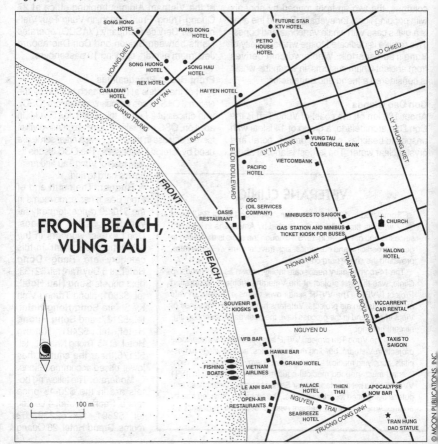

FRONT BEACH, VUNG TAU

© MOON PUBLICATIONS, INC.

South of Front Beach: Hai Au Hotel, 100 Halong St., tel. 52178, fax 59868, is a six-story waterfront hotel with full facilities. It has 52 rooms, ranging from $25 to 35 for standard rooms; 10 deluxe rooms $40 each; eight suites $55-100. The hotel features a business center and disco. It's jointly run by the OSC and Vietcombank, so currency exchange won't be a problem here. About a kilometer south of Hai Au Hotel is a strip of guesthouses at Bai Tam Huong Phung.

Restaurants and Bars: There are half-a-dozen seafront seafood places opposite the Grand Hotel featuring al fresco dining—a magnet for Front Beach diners. For breakfast, try the upstairs section of L.A. Café. The Oasis Restaurant, at 1 Le Loi, has sharp decor and serves Western food at reasonable prices, including seafood pizza, Italian food, steak sandwiches, and Western breakfast. For high-class dining there's a French restaurant, Ma Maison, at Petro House Hotel, 93 Tran Hung Dao, tel. 52248. In a building jutting into the South China Sea south of Hai Au Hotel is another classy place—Vung Tau Restaurant.

There is a small strip of rowdy bars along the Front Beach waterfront. These include Le Anh Bar, VFB Bar, and Hawaii Bar—patrons here are beseiged by beggars and bargirls. Hotels like the Rex and the Hai Au have their own discos, and karaoke cafés proliferate in the area. Expats and oil workers frequent the Apocalypse Now Bar, at 438 Truong Cong Dinh, east of the Seabreeze Hotel. There's a bar with pool tables and a bulletin board for Hash House Harriers. The bar features an upside-down helicopter painted on the ceiling, with the swishing ceiling fan serving as the chopper's blades.

Bai Dau Beach Practicalities
Bai Dau Beach, to the north of Front Beach, is a logistical nightmare because the road leading to it is in such bad shape. The beach is not recommended—small and thin, with a few run-down pagodas and a motley bunch of eateries. There's plenty of accommodations in guesthouses occupying former villas—a dozen are strung along Tran Phu Street, catering mainly to Vietnamese. Some are basic, with shared bath costing $4-8; others have private baths, and even air-conditioning, for up to $15. The places are so low-key they often have no name. They just use the street number, so you'll see Nha

Nghi 19, Nha Nghi 78, and Nha Nghi 66. Some villas, Nha Nghi Mytho at 47 Tran Phu, offer ocean views. Fronting the main beach are several larger concrete structures. These include Savimex, at 180 Tran Phu, tel. 58553; Nha Nghi DK 142, almost next door; and Khach San Haideng, at 194 Tran Phu, tel. 58536, near the giant Quan Am statue.

Le Hong Phong Practicalities
Without a beach in sight is Le Hong Phong Street, which stretches across the north end of Vung Tau. Hotels here range from budget to moderate. Haison Hotel, 27 Le Loi, tel. 52955, contains 30 rooms going for $8-10-15 in a white concrete building with zero character. School Hotel (Khach San Truong), at 156 Truong Cong Dinh, tel. 59964, has 15 rooms from $8-25. Lien Hoa Hotel, 50 Le Hong Phong St., tel. 59604, fax 52225, has 21 rooms for $25-30-35 d air-con. Far East Pearl Hotel, at 28 Le Hong Phong, tel. 58871, fax 59838, offers 30 rooms in the $30-35 range, as well as a fancy restaurant. Hoan My Hotel, at 30A Nam Ky Khoi Nghia, tel. 58118, is a karaoke dive with 16 rooms in the $15-22 range. Post Office Hotel (Nga Nghi Buu Dien), at 1 Le Hong Phong, tel. 59793, has 45 rooms from $25-30 for a double air-con, with "private communication facilities available"—meaning a private phone. This hotel is brought to you by Ho Chi Minh Post and Telecommunications, and is close to Back Beach.

Food: The western end of Le Hong Phong features cafés with signs in Cyrillic script catering to Russians who live in concrete high-rises in the area. For a restaurant, try Seabee Inn (Ong Bien Quan), at 283 Le Hong Phong, with French, Chinese, and Vietnamese food, and a small garden out back.

Back Beach Practicalities
Back Beach features budget and moderate hotels, and is a growth area, with new hotels like Kim Son and Sammy Hotel going up.

Budget: There are a few family-run guesthouses in the midsection of Back Beach. Guesthouse 29, at 29 Thuy Van, is a café-restaurant-motel right on the beach with nine rooms at $5-8-10. Guesthouse 49 and Guesthouse 47 have about half-a-dozen rooms each for $5-6. Rose Hotel (Khach San Mini Rose), at 39 Thuy Van, rents 14 rooms for $10-12 each. Thang

Muoi Hotel, 6 Thuy Van St., tel. 52665, features roomy doubles and triples for $10, billiard tables, small pool, and a Thai massage parlor. **Nha Nghi 72,** at 72 Thuy Van St., tel. 59472, is a secure, comfortable place—61 rooms with a tariff of $10-20-35. Gardens and bicycle rental.

Moderate: Thuy Van Hotel, tel. 59518, fax 59519, has 100 rooms going for $20 s and $30 d, plus 10 bungalows at $5 each. **Phuong Dong Hotel,** 2 Thuy Van, tel. 52158, includes 54 rooms in the main building, three villas, and 10 beach bungalows. Rooms are mostly $30, with four rooms priced at $45. There are four rooms in each of the villas, with a tariff of $30 per room; negotiable monthly rate for an entire villa. Tennis courts, small pool (why do they always look so big in brochures?), and karaoke lounge. Caters mainly to Asian visitors.

Food: Apart from hotel bars, there is a string of small cafés along the middle of the beachfront. The tiny **Cuu Long Café,** at 55 Thuy Van, serves simple fare, seafood, and drinks, and functions as a kind of traveler café. Rents bicycles for $1 a day; will also arrange motorbikes and guides. The largest venue along Back Beach is **Thang Muoi Restaurant,** opposite the hotel of the same name.

Services
The General Post Office, on the corner of Le Hong Phong and Xo Viet Nghe Tinh, has fax and EMS service counters. The Vung Tau area code is 64. Vietcombank at 27 Tran Hung Dao, in Front Beach, is open 0700-1130 and 1330-1700; closed Thursday afternoon and Sunday; traveler's checks accepted. Vung Tau Commercial Bank (Ngan Hang Thuong Mai), at 59 Tran Hung Dao, has similar hours but only accepts cash. AEA/OSCAT clinic at 1 Duong Than Thai, Vung Tau, tel. 58776, handles foreigners. Vietnam Airlines maintains a booking office at 27 Quang Trung, Front Beach, tel. 59099.

Getting There and Away
Saigon to Vung Tau is 115 km. Taxis and minibuses take under two hours, whereas buses can take three or more hours. The bus terminal in Vung Tau is located at 52 Nam Ky Khoi Nghia Street. Other transport leaves from the church area on Tran Hung Dao Street in Front Beach. A kiosk in a gas station near the church handles minibus tickets to Saigon, with departures every

half hour. Taxis leave one block south, closer to the Tran Hung Dao statue. From Saigon you can catch a bus to Vung Tau from Van Thanh or Mien Dong bus terminals, or hook up with a traveler minibus.

Getting Around
There are plenty of cyclos around, useful for shorter trips. There are also some motos. Many find a rented bicycle or motorcycle preferable for getting around. You can rent a bicycle at Back Beach through some hotels like Nha Nghi 72; for motorcycle rentals try Thang Muoi Hotel or Cuu Long Café. For shuttling between Front Beach and Back Beach, take Hoang Hoa Tham Street—it's only a few kilometers. You can rent cars through major hotels, or through a touring company like Viccarrent at Front Beach.

LONGHAI BEACH AND VICINITY

Superior to the beaches at Vung Tau are those at Longhai, about 40 km east or an hour by moto. The road out of Vung Tau is the same as the Saigon route—about 20 km out, you veer off on a right fork leading to Longhai Beach. There is no direct bus from Vung Tau to Longhai, but there is a Saigon-Longhai direct connection. You can easily reach the beach from Vung Tau as a daytrip, or spend a few days in the area. Longhai echoes the shape of Vung Tau, sited at the tip of a peninsula. The main activity in Longhai is fishing; there are also salt pans in the area.

Longhai Beach
Longhai town is strung along Longhai Beach (Huong Bien) to the west. Located here are cafés, juice bars, and the offices of Longhai Tourist Corporation, which runs several of the hotels in town. Longhai Tourism (tel. 8401) deals in guides, accommodations, transportation, and information. To the north end of Longhai Beach is a fishing village with shanty housing. The beach is poor because of scummy garbage and smelly fishing detritus. Fishermen here catch sea snakes, which sets you wondering. The south end of Longhai Beach is much cleaner, palm-fringed, and better suited to swimming.

Though Longhai Beach has half-a-dozen hotels, they can be crowded on weekends or holidays, especially around Tet. Several kilometers

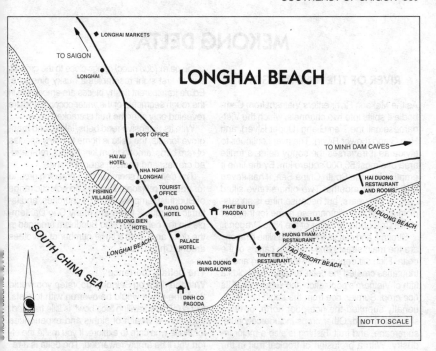

LONGHAI BEACH

LONGHAI MARKETS

TO SAIGON

LONGHAI

POST OFFICE

HAI AU HOTEL

NHA NGHI LONGHAI

TOURIST OFFICE

FISHING VILLAGE

RANG DONG HOTEL

HUONG BIEN HOTEL

PHAT BUU TU PAGODA

TO MINH DAM CAVES

HAI DUONG RESTAURANT AND ROOMS

HAI DUONG BEACH

TAO VILLAS

HUONG THAM RESTAURANT

PALACE HOTEL

LONGHAI BEACH

THUY TIEN RESTAURANT

TAO RESORT BEACH

HANG DUONG BUNGALOWS

SOUTH CHINA SEA

DINH CO PAGODA

NOT TO SCALE

north of town near the central market is **Longhai Hotel,** with 18 rooms in the $15-20 range and one air-con suite for $30.

Closer in, **Hai Au Hotel** has a seedy and derelict air to it—massage and steam bath, 15 fan rooms for $8, and two rooms (no bath) for $6. **Nha Nghi Longhai,** tel. 8312, has 40 rooms, most of them $10 fan rooms, and 10 doubles at $15 each. **Rang Dong Hotel,** tel. 8356, has 20 rooms, $20-22 d and $25 t. **Huong Bien Hotel,** tel. 8430, rents 10 rooms and five bungalows for $15 d.

Outclassing the rest is the **Palace Hotel,** tel. 8364. The Palace features terraced areas with gorgeous frangipani trees. On the top floor is a dome with a small dance floor; great views from the open rooftop. The hotel features vintage Chinese furniture and wall decorations of unicorn, dragon, and tortoise designs. There's a restaurant, and across the street are tennis courts. A total of 18 rooms at $20-25 d air-con, with fridge, TV, and bath; some rooms have sea views.

Other Beaches
Proceeding round the headland to the east, beaches become cleaner and more secluded. Close to town is a beach with a set of bungalows facing it—**Hang Duong Bungalows,** a large compound with its own restaurant and 20 wooden bungalows. The bungalows contain only a bed, but the price is right—$4 single, $5 with two beds. There are two dozen kiosks on the way in, selling souvenirs and drinks; you can also rent deck chairs. Farther east, Tao Resort Beach has sand dunes and is rocky in parts. **Tao Villas**—two of them—have three rooms each for $20, no phone. Hai Duong Beach, about six km from the Palace Hotel, includes a restaurant, a few thatched huts, and a few cheap rooms for rent. There's a new hotel under construction. A few kilometers east are mountain caves once used by Vietcong Generals Minh and Dam. The caves are dull, but the mountain hike is good. Farther east, along a dirt road, are more beaches and fishing villages.

MEKONG DELTA

RIVER OF THE NINE DRAGONS

As the Mekong River enters Vietnam from Cambodia it splits into two channels, which the Vietnamese call the Tien Giang (Upper River), and Hau Giang (Lower River). The river continues to divide as it traverses the soggy delta, a fertile area of almost 50,000 square km. By the time it empties into the South China Sea, it has seven branches, or mouths. Two others have silted up over the years, but because nine is an auspicious digit, the Vietnamese name for the river is still Cuu Long, or River of the Nine Dragons.

Streams and canals linked to the Nine Dragons are the main streets and irrigation canals of the delta. Rich silt deposited by the Mekong and its tributaries created the delta, an area that holds a fifth of Vietnam's population and supplies half its rice crop. Surplus rice from the south has traditionally supplied the rice-poor north, or been shipped abroad. Other crops include coconuts, sugarcane, and fruit. Fishing is also a major industry. With a profusion of tropical fruit in the delta, there are bound to be some exotic varieties. A unique species of vegetation lining the delta's canals is the water coconut palm. The fruit of the palm *(dua nuoc)* hangs close to the ground, and at first sight resembles a husky pinecone. Edible transparent fleshy pieces are embedded in the rough segments of the water coconut and are revealed only after the fruit is cracked open.

With its extensive reed beds, lakes, and mangrove forests, the delta is home to many species of rare birds, among them kingfishers, red-headed cranes, and eastern saurus cranes.

The delta also seems to be a breeding ground for oddball religions. Besides an eclectic range of Buddhist temples, Catholic churches, and Islamic mosques, there are many Cao Dai temples in the delta. Hoa Hao Buddhism emerged in the delta area, with a large number of devotees around Chau Doc.

The Delta Experience

With the delta on Saigon's doorstep you would think the place would be overrun with tourists. Not so. This sprawling "rice bowl" is little traveled, yet offers a wealth of sights and experiences for those who care to explore. If you make the effort you'll be amply rewarded. The delta is a region of extraordinary energy and market commerce, with burgeoning markets, floating markets, fruit orchards, and more coconuts than you'd want to contemplate. The delta is a relaxing place, with good food (seafood!), pleasant river trips, cheap boats, and friendly people.

You're never far from water in the delta, and boats in some districts are the main mode of transportation. Intriguing in the backwaters are the floating markets, which have disappeared in other parts of Asia.

Getting Around the Delta
By Bus: Mien Tay Bus Station in Cholon, seven km to the west of Saigon, serves most delta destinations. You can reach Mien Tay from central Saigon by moto for $1.50; cheaper by

---

"All around the ferry is the river, it's brimfull, its moving waters sweep through, never mixing with, the stagnant waters of the rice fields. The river has picked up all it's met with since Tonle Sap and the Cambodian forest. It carries everything along, straw huts, forests, burned-out fires, dead birds, dead dogs, drowned tigers and buffalos, drowned men, bait, islands of water hyacinths all stuck together. Everything flows towards the Pacific, no time for anything to sink, all is swept along by the deep and headlong storm of the inner current, suspended on the surface of the river's strength."

—Marguerite Duras describing the swirling waters of the Mekong in her novella, *The Lover,* set during the 1920s. Her hometown was Sadec.

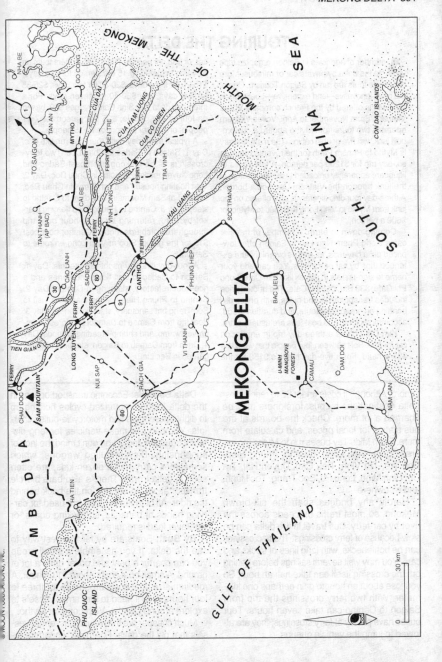

TOURING THE DELTA

A number of agencies in Saigon organize trips to the delta by private car or minibus. More expensive tours are run by Saigon Tourism. One of the most innovative—and expensive—boat tours in the delta is offered by the French company Voiles Vietnam. From November to April, Voiles Vietnam operates two tours from Mytho aboard a custom-built junk with five double cabins. The main itinerary is Mytho to Phnom Penh (or the reverse route), a six-day trip for $1200 per person. A few cases of liquor are apparently unloaded to assist passage of the junk through the Vietnam-Cambodia border. A three-day roundtrip itinerary is also offered on the junk from Mytho to Vinh Long to Sadec to Mytho for $600 a person.

Coming down to earth, a number of traveler cafés along Pham Ngu Lao in Saigon offer low-priced delta day-trips, as well as overnight and extended trips by car or minibus. You can add your name to sign-up lists in places like Kim Café, Long Phi Café, 333 Bar, or Sinh Café. The quoted price includes transportation and guide, with prices depending on group size, route, and duration. Food, accommodations, and boat fees are usually extra.

Kim Café offers a three-day trip in an air-con car for $90. Split between four people that would be $23 a head. For a five-day trip, it's $150 for the

car, or $38 per person. The 333 Bar offers tours on a sliding scale—$10-15 per person for two days, $15-20 for three days, $20-30 for four days, $25-35 for five days, and $30-40 for seven days. For a three-day delta tour Sinh Café charges $30, based on four to five people; $25 per person for 7-11 people; or $20 per person for 12-15 people.

A typical three-day delta tour may run like this. Day 1: Saigon to Sadec to Chau Doc. Two ferry-crossings of the Mekong, then past Sadec and Long Xuyen market, sleeping in Chau Doc. Day 2: Visit floating houses and fish farms in Chau Doc, temples at Sam Mountain, and drive to Cantho to sleep. Day 3: Cantho to Phung Hiep floating market by road, returning by three-hour boat trip through fruit orchards around Cantho; boat cost $15 for the group. Stop at Vinh Long en route to Saigon.

A four-day itinerary might run like this. Day 1: Saigon to Sadec to visit flower nurseries and a rice-noodle factory, sleeping in Cantho. Day 2: Cantho to Phung Hiep floating market, a visit to Soc Trang bat sanctuary, sleep in Camau. Day 3: Boat trip from Camau to Damdoi bird forest, mangrove swamp, and shrimp-breeding grounds. Day 4: Drive from Camau to Saigon, stopping at a bird garden in Bac Lieu.

---

lambro. Although it costs under $2 to reach most delta destinations by bus, foreigners may be charged a lot more. Check the boards at the bus station for local prices, and calculate from there. From Mien Tay buses run to Mytho (no express bus), Vinh Long, Cantho, Phung Hiep, Ben Tre, Tra Vinh, Tieu Can, Duyen Hai, Tra Cu, Binh Minh, Long Pu, Soc Trang, Toc Hanh, and elsewhere.

Hardly any bridges span the silt-brown Mekong, so most traffic proceeds across the river by car-ferry. Bus travel in the delta can be slow because of ferry crossings. These crossings can be bottlenecks, with long lines of trucks and cars. You may wait several sailings before getting on; the crossing itself can take half an hour. So you lose about an hour to gain perhaps one kilometer. With two ferry crossings the trip from Saigon to Cantho can take seven hours. Tour buses have priority at ferry crossings; they are allowed to jump the vehicle queues.

Delta Specials: Eccentric transport options in the delta include motorized cyclos holding up to eight passengers and motorcycle-pulled chariots. You can use these vehicles for long distance transport, too, if you don't mind the lack of suspension. Bicycle-pulled wagons, which sometimes carry half a dozen kids, are often seen in delta towns. There's also bare bicycle transportation—locals hop on the back behind the rider. All of these vehicles are used for carrying hands of bananas, squawking ducks, or whatever load is required.

By Boat: Boats are by far the best way to see the delta. If you assemble a small group you can charter a boat and cover quite a lot of ground. A small boat costs about $1 an hour. A medium-size boat costs around $5 for three to four hours. You'll need to hire small vessels to explore around Cantho, Vinh Long, or Mytho.

Much cheaper are the regular passenger vessels that ply the delta. For these, departure in-

MEKONG DELTA ROUTE NOTES

I t's easy to tour the delta by yourself. Still, a small group of two to three travelers is recommended to avoid the discomfort of curious stares in the remote regions of the delta, and for splitting expenses on hired boats and hotel rooms.

You can make a day-trip to Mytho, or you can cover the major delta towns of Mytho, Vinh Long, and Cantho in three to five days. A week-long loop through the delta might run like this: from Saigon, cover the 70 km to Mytho and continue another 69 km to Vinh Long; from there it's 32 km to Cantho and a further 61 km to Long Xuyen, where you can cover the final 55 km to Chau Doc. You could take a boat from Saigon to Mytho on the outbound journey and/or Chau Doc to Mytho on the return trip. Another itinerary might include Saigon to Vinh Long to Cantho to Tra Vinh to Ben Tre to Mytho to Saigon, with a possible boat trip from Tra Vinh to Ben Tre along canals.

Delving deeper into the delta might require seven to 10 days. Not many venture to the further reaches of the delta, so expect to be treated like a Martian in places like Ha Tien. You can't continue to anywhere

from the delta, so you might as well base yourself in Saigon—lock your bags in hotel storage, and head off. Take a water bottle, lots of dong, and a small pack.

Some travelers make motorcycle tours of the delta. This doesn't mean you have to keep to roads: a boat captain won't bat an eyelid if you load a motorcyle onto the roof of a riverboat. A local did, however, bat an eyelid when an Australian couple moored alongside his sampan in kayaks. The couple flew the kayaks into Saigon and paddled along the Mekong for a few weeks. They packed the folding kayaks onto a local ferry for the run back to Saigon.

For some reason, travelers seem to give up on travel in the delta by themselves, and opt for group tours in minibuses. That's fine, but what if you discover a really interesting place and you've only got two hours on your fixed tour itinerary? If your time is limited, minibus tours are good—you can travel faster, and get priority at ferry crossings. But if you're looking for interaction and want to mix with the locals, tackle it yourself.

---

formation may be elusive—the authorities do not like foreigners traveling by public boat. A larger wooden boat, called a *dò*, can carry about 60 passengers and freight, with the emphasis on freight. Freight covers the floor and the top deck of the boat. Some loads look dangerous, as if this is Noah's Ark, or the last boat out. There's very little in the way of safety equipment: only a few life buoys are provided. More to the point might be firefighting equipment, since passengers sometimes cook onboard with charcoal braziers.

The *dò* is an enclosed boat with the captain up front, engine at the back, and passenger section in the middle. Wooden benches run the length of the boat on either side, and there are wooden slide up window slots. There's a rudimentary cooking area and toilet near the engine. There may be a small upper deck, used for sleeping, on top at the back of the boat; overnight passengers sleep on mats on the floor in the main section of the boat, or string up hammocks. At night the captain uses searchlights to warn approaching vessels, and lights a front shrine with incense and candles. Nice and cool out there at night.

Although goods—bananas, bicycles, dried coconut, live ducks, baskets—are scattered all over the roof of the boat, you're not supposed to sit up there. However, once the vessel leaves port and you're past police checkpoints you can ride on the roof—which is very pleasant, with panoramic views. Destination and intermediary points for the boat are painted on a chalkboard at the departure point. The approximate departure time may be posted, but usually the boat leaves when full.

Departures from Saigon: Covered wooden boats for Mytho leave from the pier at the foot of Ham Nghi Boulevard where it faces the Saigon River. Daily departures at 1000 and 1500; the seven- to eight-hour trip costs $1 for locals, $5 foreigners. There's a boat to Tra Vinh twice a week, normally Tuesday and Sunday for $5; the trip takes 14 hours. There are also departures to Cantho (24 hours), and a boat once a week to Camau (36 hours, usually freight only).

Delta Hubs: A chalkboard at a delta boat terminal lists destinations and departure times. For these boats there appears to be no exact depar-

Wooden ferries are typical Delta transport.

ture time or advance tickets—boats leave when full. Keep asking, and asking, and asking about departures, as the story changes from hour to hour. Tickets are dirt-cheap—a day-trip by boat is about $1, overnight $2. Cantho is a major boat junction because of its central location; other boat hubs are Ben Tre and Chau Doc. Journeys vary from a great five-hour trip through canals from Tra Vinh to Ben Tre to an epic 18-hour trip from Chau Doc to Mytho. Trips flow faster downstream.

MYTHO

Mytho, 70 km southwest of Saigon, is a market town of about 100,000 on the banks of the Tien Giang, or upper Mekong. The town was under Khmer domination till the 17th century, when advancing Vietnamese forces took over. The French gained control of the area in 1862.

In Town
Both sides of Bao Dinh Canal are active market areas. On the east side, toward the Mekong, are fish markets and warehouses. The west side is a honeycomb of food vendors and foodstalls, with a dizzying array of flowers and fruit. The outer sections toward the water sell mainly food, fish, and produce; further inland are stalls selling hardware and household goods; at the north end is a section with ceramics and basketry.

Temple pickings are slim around Mytho—to the east is Vinh Trang Pagoda, with 30 monks

and 20 nuns. Go across a bridge to the north; at the first fork across the bridge take the left and ask—the pagoda is about a kilometer from here. There's a small Cao Dai temple to the west of Mytho.

To the Islands
There are excursions from Mytho around the four small islands in the center of the Mekong—Tan Long, Phung, Quy, and Thoi Son. The islands are inhabited, with walkways and waterways between fruit orchards. Tan Long, known for its longan orchards, can easily be reached by a five-minute boat ride from the dock at the southern tip of Le Loi Boulevard in Mytho, near Cuu Long Restaurant.

It's a good idea to rent a boat for a longer period; smaller boats can access orchards via channels that crisscross the islands. Some of the tighter canals are lined with water coconut palms; kingfishers and other bird species live in the groves. A full day's excursion of five to seven hours by boat is recommended, taking in fruit orchards and the Temple of the Coconut Monk (see below).

A trip to three islands for five hours should cost around $20 for the boat, but the rental is made trickier by the fact that Tien Giang Tourism seems to have a monopoly on the trade. There's a police box down by the junction of the Tien Giang River and Bao Dinh Canal, where officials scan the water searching for local fishermen taking foreigners out for a spin. You may have to smuggle yourself out; our crew took us north on

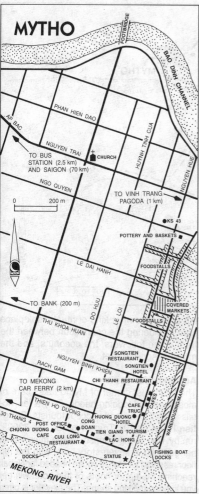

MYTHO

PHAN HIEN DAO

BAO DINH CHANNEL

FOOTBRIDGE

HUYNH TINH CUA

NGUYEN HUE

AP BAC

NGUYEN TRAI

CHURCH

TO BUS
STATION (2.5 km)
AND SAIGON (70 km)

NGO QUYEN

TO VINH TRANG
PAGODA (1 km)

KS 43

POTTERY AND BASKETS

0   200 m

LE DAI HANH

FOODSTALLS

TO BANK (200 m)

DO HUU

LE LOI

COVERED
MARKETS

THU KHOA HUAN

FOODSTALLS

NGUYEN BINH KHIEN

SONGTIEN
RESTAURANT

RACH GAM

SONGTIEN
HOTEL

CHI THANH RESTAURANT

TO MEKONG
CAR FERRY (2 km)

THIEN HO DUONG

CAFE
TRUC

CAFES

30 THANG 4

POST OFFICE

CONG
DOAN

HUONG DUONG

WAREHOUSING MARKETS

CHUONG DUONG

TIEN GIANG TOURISM

CAFE

CUU LONG
RESTAURANT

LAC HONG

DOCKS

STATUE

FISHING BOAT
DOCKS

MEKONG RIVER

straight across to Phung Island to reach the Temple of the Coconut Monk, instead they take the long way round down the coast and cut through a river on Thoi Son Island

Dong Tam Snake Farm

Dong Tam Snake Farm is about 10 km west of Mytho. You can bicycle there in an hour. Small boats can get within several km of the farm; the boatman can drop you off and wait while you walk to the farm. Entry fee is $1. The place is no big deal as a sight, with concrete enclosures harboring various venomous snakes. Antivenin serum is made on the premises. There are also monkeys and other small animals that look suspiciously ready for illegal traffic. A shop on-site sells snake wine (snake pickled in rice wine), as well as other snake pills and potions—including bottles of Cobratonic "for insomnia, rheumatism and neurasthemia," and Cobratox, an ointment made from dried cobra-venom, menthol, and eucalyptus "for rheumatism, arthritis, myositis and neuralgia."

Temple of the Coconut Monk

The Mekong Delta is a breeding ground for weird religions, among them Cao Daism and Hoa Hao Buddhism. Even weirder is the congregation surrounding the coconut monk of Phung (Phoenix) Island. The cross-river ferry acting as a bridge over the Mekong near Mytho passes by the temple, but it's worth actually visiting the site for a closer look. Rent a boat in Mytho for the trip; if you go directly it takes about 30 minutes from Mytho, if you skirt around other islands it can take 1.5 hours. You might also be able to arrange boat transportation from the Ben Tre Province side.

The coconut cult was initiated by Nguyen Thanh Nam (1909-90) who studied in France for seven years, then returned to Vietnam to marry. In 1945 he left his wife and daughter to lead the life of a monk, and is said to have meditated at Sam Mountain for a lengthy period. Thereafter he created the temple at Phung Island—between 1969 and 1975, worship was in full swing, with up to 3,000 devotees. The coconut monk was periodically imprisoned by the South Vietnamese and, after the 1975 takeover, by the communists. After 1975, the temple was closed, and its followers dispersed. The coconut monk died in obscurity in Ben Tre Province in 1990.

foot, where we crossed a bridge to the east bank, walked another 10 minutes, transferred to a boat, and were then told to lie flat until we reached open water. The boatman dropped us on Tan Long Island and told us to follow the guide to the south side of the island where the boat would pick us up again—a strategy necessary because of a police box on the northeast side of the island. Other complications include crossing over to Ben Tre Province. Fishing boats will not go

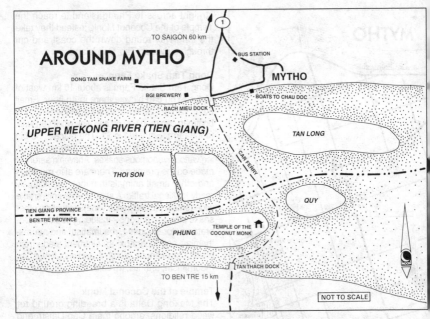

AROUND MYTHO

TO SAIGON 60 km

BUS STATION

MYTHO

DONG TAM SNAKE FARM

BGI BREWERY

BOATS TO CHAU DOC

RACH MIEU DOCK

UPPER MEKONG RIVER (TIEN GIANG)

TAN LONG

CAR FERRY

THOI SON

QUY

TIEN GIANG PROVINCE
BEN TRE PROVINCE

PHUNG

TEMPLE OF THE
COCONUT MONK

TAN THACH DOCK

TO BEN TRE 15 km

NOT TO SCALE

The front of the Phung Island temple is constructed in the shape of a grotto for meditation, with a throne for the coconut monk. Above is a tower with a metal map showing Hanoi and a small bridge linking it to Saigon—the monk advocated peaceful reunification of north and south, which did not go down too well with the South Vietnamese government at the time. Nearby is another tower, with an Apollo rocket that can be hoisted up and down. Facing the throne is a dais with nine dragon-coiled pillars raised over lily ponds. The dais is large enough to seat several thousand followers.

The coconut cult appears to have been a mix of Buddhism, Cao Daism, and Catholicism, with a healthy dose of coconuts. The role of the coconuts is not clear, but the monk is said to have lived on a diet of vegetables and coconuts during meditation. According to some sources, the monk at one point ate only coconuts, but this seems hard to believe. Certainly there is no shortage of coconuts in Ben Tre Province, which grows more coconut palms than any other province in Vietnam. Since none of the pictures on display show the coconut cult in action, you're

left to wonder what kind of rituals took place here, pondering the connection between the throne, the followers, the coconuts, and the movable Apollo rocket.

Accommodations

The southeast corner of Mytho takes care of most food and lodging needs. Only a few hotels in Mytho currently accept tourists. **Songtien Hotel,** at 101 Trung Trac St., tel. 72009, run by Tien Giang Tourism, is the main tourist hangout. It's a seven-story hotel with the top floor reserved for staff. If you're headed for Nepal, reaching the upper floors of this hotel will get you in good trekking shape. The elevator is often out of commission; practice with backpack loads. There are 38 rooms in the $6-20 range; the high end includes air-con, hot water, and TV.

Huong Duong Hotel, 33 Trung Trac, tel. 72011, offers 30 rooms for $8-14 and "gracious receptionists." The following low-priced hotels are reluctant to accept foreigners, and will probably make the screwing-in-the-lightbulb gesture (don't know, don't care, go away) if you ask about rooms: **Thanh Binh** (dilapidated, only a few rooms), **Khach San 43, Lac Hong** (no bath, no water), and **Cong Doan.**

Food

A block to the west of Songtien Hotel is **Songtien Restaurant,** with garden gazebos—ritzy for Mytho. A classy garden restaurant is **Trung Luong,** reached by boat up the Bao Dinh Canal. About three km north, on the route to Saigon, this is the place to order bat, rat, or grilled snake if you are so inclined. At number 56 Trung Trac St. is **Chi Thanh.** There's also a string of cafés along here, and the back alleys hold lots of soup places. Next door to Chi Thanh is the **Duyen Tham** ice-cream shop at number 54, with coconut cakes and coconut croissants.

On the south side of town are the more expensive Cuu Long Restaurant and Chuong Duong Café.

Services and Information

Mytho is fairly well set up for tourism because it's the closest delta destination to Saigon. Tien Giang Tourism at 65 April 30 St., tel. 73184, fax 72154, offers guides at $7 a day, as well as boat and car rentals. The staff are willing to answer questions. For an inexpensive local guide, pay a boatman—he knows where to go. Café Truc, on Trang Truc Street, will assist with informal guides and bicycle rentals, acting as a kind of traveler café. Ngan Hang Cong Thuong bank, on the west side of town, handles most transactions.

Getting There and Away

Buses from Saigon can take up to two hours to cover the 70 km to Mytho due to traffic holdups and waits at ferry crossings. Tourist minibuses have priority at ferry crossings. The Mytho bus station is about three km from the town center, on the Saigon road. There are connections here to Vinh Long, Cantho, Chau Doc, and other delta destinations; also buses to Tay Ninh and Vung Tau.

A regular boat from Saigon, leaving from the foot of Ham Nghi Boulevard, takes seven to eight hours to reach Mytho and costs $5. There is also a boat from Mytho to Chau Doc. For exiting Mytho, you might try a hired boat on the route to Saigon. Go north upriver to Trung Luong Restaurant, then continue toward Highway 1, get off the boat, and flag down a bus.

Getting Around

Tien Giang Tourism offers car and boat rentals. Cyclos are easy to find. You can rent bicycles from cafés on Trang Truc Street, also from Cuu Long Restaurant and Chuong Duong Café on the south side.

VINH LONG

Vinh Long faces the Co Chien River (a Mekong tributary) to the north side; rivers and canals on the other three sides make it virtually an island. Most of the tourist action takes place at the northeast promontory.

Vinh Long has been one of the key points for the spread of Christianity in the Mekong Delta, which explains the Catholic church and seminary in town, the church on nearby Bin Hoa Phuoc Island, and the spectacularly sited church at Caibe.

In Town

The market in Vinh Long is very active. It covers about one square kilometer, and features a wide range of fruit and vegetables, some from the fruit orchards on the opposite banks. The market also offers a curious trade in animals, hopping with fish, snakes, turtles, eels, and frogs. There are bins filled with live eels, large frogs tied together, fish unloaded at the docks at the crack of dawn, and bicycle runners delivering live geese and chickens for killing, cleaning, and cooking.

Down by the Co Chien River to the west of Cuu Long B Hotel is a small military museum with a phantom fighter, Huey helicopter, and tanks.

To the Islands

Take a half-day or longer trip out to the town of Caibe, and come back through the islands north of Vinh Long. You need about four to five hours to cover the distance; allow time for stops. The trip is best accomplished in the early morning when you can catch a floating market at Caibe. It takes about 1.5 hours to reach Caibe by boat, with the floating market operating roughly 0600-1100. If you miss the market, try the fixed market near the bridge in Caibe. There's a Catholic church with a spectacular location at the head of the river. The church is open on Sundays.

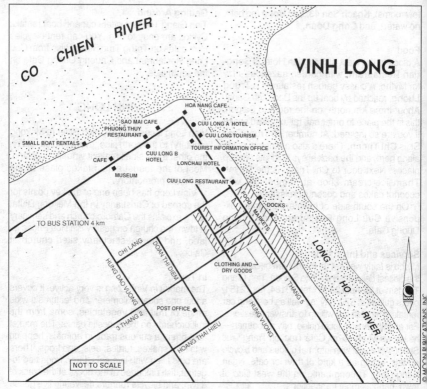

On the return route you can stop at various rambutan and longan orchards on Binh Hoa Phuoc and An Binh Islands north of Vinh Long. Some orchards are open to boat tourists—reach these via waterways and footpaths. Tea is provided at the orchard manor, and some kind of donation may be expected. In Binh Thuan hamlet is a bonsai nursery and longan orchard. Binh Hoa Phuoc Island features a settlement midway along the large channel cutting through it; you can see a church and school here.

Small boat rentals for these trips are available near Phuong Thuy Restaurant in Vinh Long. The going rate is $2 an hour or less for a small craft. Covered boats are preferable unless you want to get roasted in the sun. You'll get a better deal on a half-day or full-day rental—say $5 for half a day (about four hours). Make up a rough schedule of places you want to visit. Cuu

Long Tourism arranges larger boats for $25 for three hours, or $35 for four hours. Bigger is not necessarily better, as some canals are very shallow and can only be negotiated by smaller craft.

Accommodations

The **Cuu Long Hotel** chain monopolizes the Vinh Long waterfront, with three hotels of 20 to 25 rooms each arrayed along First of May Street. **Cuu Long A,** tel. 22494, has 21 rooms for $10-20-30, with some rooms overlooking the river. Nearby is **Longchau Hotel,** tel. 23611, with rooms for $6 each; either a double bed or two singles. **Cuu Long B,** a.k.a. Vinh Tra, tel. 23656, has 25 air-con doubles for $25-35 and a quiet garden set back from the Mekong; the hotel has tennis courts. To round out the Cuu Long monopoly, there's Cuu Long Restaurant and Cuu Long Tourism. Cuu Long Tourism runs a set of villas, known as Truong An Tourist Villas, about four km from Vinh Long town.

Food

There's a pleasant bunch of cafés along the waterfront promenade, including **Hoa Nang** and **Sao Mai. Phuong Thuy** floating restaurant, serving European and Asian food, is popular with travelers. The Cuu Long hotels include dining rooms. Foodstalls in the market.

Services and Information

This town has not one but *two* tourist information offices—**Cuu Long Tourism** and, almost opposite, a place called **Tourist Information Office**. They're both after your business for guides, but will also answer questions. They even have a few maps on the walls. The Tourist Information Office has two bikes for rent at $2 a day each; Cuu Long Tourism, tel. 23616, can arrange cars, minibuses, and boats.

Getting There and Around

Vinh Long bus station is four km southwest of town, with links to Tra Vinh, Cantho, and other delta towns. A smaller station closer to town operates buses to Sadec. Use cyclos for getting around town. Near Phuong Thuy Restaurant you can hire a boat to visit the islands around Vinh Long.

CANTHO

Cantho, population 200,000, is the largest town in the delta by virtue of its central position, and its location near the Hau Giang, or lower Mekong. Cantho is a major transport center at the junction of numerous canals and roads; it also has an airport. The town has a university and a teacher training college.

Sights

The market along the banks of the Cantho River is bustling with fresh produce and poultry, and

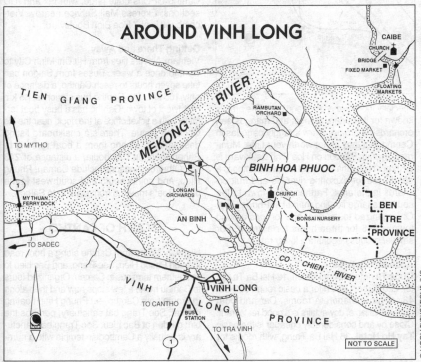

AROUND VINH LONG

TIEN GIANG PROVINCE

MEKONG RIVER

TO MYTHO

MY THUAN FERRY DOCK

TO SADEC

RAMBUTAN ORCHARD

BINH HOA PHUOC

LONGAN ORCHARDS

AN BINH

CHURCH

BONSAI NURSERY

CAIBE
CHURCH

BRIDGE

FIXED MARKET

FLOATING MARKETS

BEN TRE PROVINCE

CO. CHIEN RIVER

VINH LONG

VINH LONG
BUS STATION

TO CANTHO

TO TRA VINH

PROVINCE

NOT TO SCALE

© MOON PUBLICATIONS, INC.

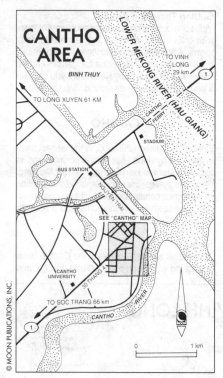

CANTHO
AREA

BINH THUY

TO VINH
LONG
29 km

TO LONG XUYEN 61 KM

LOWER MEKONG RIVER (HAU GIANG)

CANTHO
FERRY

STADIUM

BUS STATION

NGUYEN TRAI

SEE "CANTHO" MAP

CANTHO
UNIVERSITY

30 THANG 4

TO SOC TRANG 66 km

CANTHO

RIVER

0   1 km

© MOON PUBLICATIONS, INC.

specialty foods like snakes and eels. The area is known for its durian, orange, and mangosteen orchards. There are a few straggly pagodas in Cantho, but they're not worth your time. Muni-rang Syaram Pagoda on Hoa Binh Boulevard is a Khmer Hinayana Buddhist temple. Cantho is a good base for exploring river life and fruit orchards in the area. Farther out of town to the south is a large floating market at Phung Hiep. On organized tours, boat hire for trips around town is $15 for three hours for a group. For smaller groups negotiate a lower rate.

Accommodations
Quoc Te (International Hotel), 12 Hai Ba Trung, tel. 22079, cost $10 d for a basic room, $23-36-43 for more elaborate rooms. Car and boat rentals available; downstairs is a good restaurant. Close by and considerably cheaper is the basic **Tay Ho Hotel,** 36 Hai Ba Trung, with rooms for

$5-6. **Hau Giang Hotel,** 34 Nam Ky Khoi Nghia, tel. 21806, includes 35 air-con rooms. **Hoa Binh Hotel,** at 5 Hoa Binh Boulevard, tel. 20536, has 22 fan and air-con rooms. There are three hotels on Chau Van Liem Boulevard—**Khai Hoan, Phong Nha,** and **Tay Do** hotels.

Food
The market contains many foodstalls. **Vinh Loi Restaurant,** near the boat dock, serves cheap and hearty fare. A bit pricier is the ground floor restaurant at the Quoc Te Hotel, with a regular menu, and exotica like snake sausage, stewed tortoise, and tossed eel. Cantho's waterfront cafés are good, using fresh produce from the market. **Café Congvien Ninh Kieu** is a good vantage point; there are also open-air cafés north of the GPO.

Services
The government-run Cantho Tourism Company is located at 27 Chau Van Liem, tel. 21804. Cantho GPO is quite large, with fax and IDD sections; Express Mail Service nearby. Vietcombank is at 7 Hoa Binh Boulevard.

Getting There and Away
Vietnam Airlines flies from Ho Chi Minh City to Cantho once a week. Buses from Saigon can take seven hours to reach Cantho, a distance of only 165 km. The Cantho bus station is 1.5 km northwest of town. Cantho has a busy boat terminal with a ticket office at the dock, near the Ho Chi Minh statue. There's a chalkboard listing destinations, among them a boat running to Phnom Penh in Cambodia, a distance of 243 km. Other destinations include Camau, Phung Hiep, and points south and southwest in the delta. Boats may run from Cantho to Saigon.

SOUTH OF CANTHO

Highway 1 runs from Cantho along a poor road through Phung Hiep, Soc Trang, and Bac Lieu to its southern terminus in Camau. Organized tours to Camau make a few stops now and then along the route from Cantho—at Phung Hiep floating market, Soc Trang bat sanctuary, perhaps the bird garden at Bac Lieu. Soc Trang bat sanctuary is actually a Cambodian temple with a num-

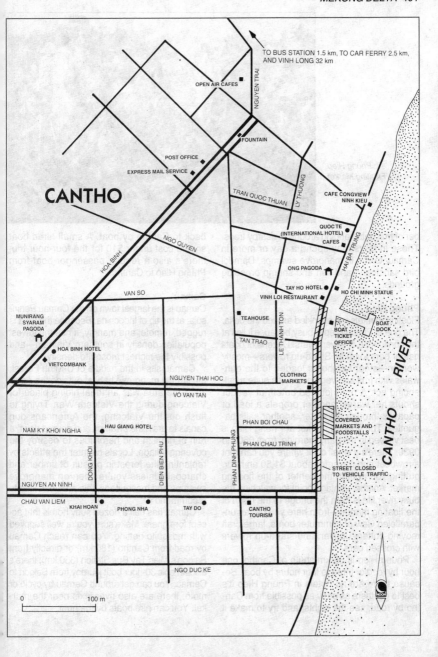

TO BUS STATION 1.5 km, TO CAR FERRY 2.5 km,
AND VINH LONG 32 km

OPEN AIR CAFES

NGUYEN TRAI

FOUNTAIN

POST OFFICE

EXPRESS MAIL SERVICE

CANTHO

TRAN QUOC THUAN

LY THUONG

CAFE CONGVIEW
NINH KIEU

HOA BINH

NGO QUYEN

QUOC TE
(INTERNATIONAL HOTEL)

CAFES

HAI BA TRUNG

VAN SO

ONG PAGODA

TAY HO HOTEL

HO CHI MINH STATUE

VINH LOI RESTAURANT

MUNIRANG
SYARAM
PAGODA

TEAHOUSE

BOAT
DOCK

HOA BINH HOTEL

TAN TRAO

LE THANH TON

BOAT TICKET
OFFICE

VIETCOMBANK

NGUYEN THAI HOC

CLOTHING
MARKETS

VO VAN TAN

CANTHO
RIVER

PHAN BOI CHAU

COVERED
MARKETS AND
FOODSTALLS

NAM KY KHOI NGHIA

HAU GIANG HOTEL

DONG KHOI

DIEN BIEN PHU

PHAN CHAU TRINH

PHAN DINH PHUNG

STREET CLOSED
TO VEHICLE TRAFFIC

NGUYEN AN NINH

CHAU VAN LIEM

KHAI HOAN

PHONG NHA

TAY DO

CANTHO
TOURISM

NGO DUC KE

0   100 m

MOON

Phung Hiep
Floating Market

ber of fruit bats hanging around in nearby trees. Those in tours may spend a day or more in Camau, taking in mangrove swamps, Damdoi bird sanctuary, and fish and shrimp breeding grounds.

Phung Hiep

Floating markets are sprinkled around the delta. The one at Phung Hiep is busy because it lies at the confluence of seven rivers. Dozens of boats gather here to trade. Stand-up rowers—mostly women—steer longboats loaded to the gunwales with fruit and vegetables. It's quite a balancing act. A red-mouthed betel-nut vendor shouts her wares, another propels a load of papayas through the water, another sells baguettes. The floating market at Phung Hiep is best viewed in the early morning, from 0600 to 0930. There's a small dock where you can rent a rowboat and rower for about $1.50 an hour, putting you right in the center of the floating market. Another vantage point for watching the busy river life is from the bridge to the north of the floating market—from here you get an unparalleled view of commuter boats, large craft moving pottery upriver, and stand-up rowers with crossed oars.

Phung Hiep is 35 km south of Cantho, one hour by road or three to four hours by boat. Because there are no hotels in Phung Hiep it's best to get there as early as possible from Cantho by road, see the sights, and try to make it

back to Cantho by boat. A small hired boat should cost under $10 for the four-hour trip; there's also a regular passenger boat from Phung Hiep to Cantho.

Camau

Camau is the largest town on the Camau Peninsula, at the tip of Indochina. Because the area is rugged, remote, and marshy, it has the lowest population density in southern Vietnam—and possibly the highest mosquito density.

Camau sits in the middle of U-Minh Forest, the largest mangrove habitat outside the Amazon. The area was an ideal hiding place for Vietcong during the Vietnam War. Trying to flush out the Vietcong, the Americans dug canals to drain the swamps and poured down a rain of napalm and herbicides to destroy the covering foliage. Locals counter the effects by replanting the forest in pursuit of timber and charcoal. Unless you're keen on mangrove swamps and mosquitoes, this area has little to recommend it.

Camau has half a dozen surly hotels that accept foreigners. Make sure you're well supplied with mosquito netting. You can reach Camau by road from Cantho (180 km) or directly from Saigon's Mien Tay Bus Station (350 km); there's also an epic 30-hour boat journey from Saigon to Camau. You can get around Camau by cyclo or moto; there are also river-taxis near the market. You can hire boats by the hour.

EAST OF CANTHO

Tra Vinh

Tra Vinh is a small town with little to see, but the locals will certainly enjoy looking at you—you may end up the main attraction. There are a few pagodas in the vicinity; Ong Met Pagoda, in town, is home to about 30 monks and a Khmer school. Five km to the southwest of town is a rice-paper factory; two km north is a coconut garden.

Tra Vinh has a handful of hotels. **Khach San Cuu Long** at 999 Nguyen Thi Minh Khai St., tel. 62625, offers 17 rooms for $6 s, $12-22 d. Closer to Long Binh Bridge are **Huong Tra Hotel** at 67 Ly Thuong Kiet ($5 a room), and **Khach San Thanh Tra.** One of the better restaurants in town is the **Viet Hoa.**

An interesting boat route runs from Tra Vinh to Bai Xan to Mocay to Ben Tre, taking five hours, for $1. The journey moves off the wide rivers and cuts through narrower sections with extensive coconut groves. The daytime boat trip, leaves from Long Binh Bridge, 1.5 km from Tra Vinh. There are occasional boats to Saigon from Tra Vinh, taking 14 hours.

Ben Tre

Ben Tre is small. There's a dock area with a riverside market; farther back is Truc Giang Lake with the main hotel facing it. Out of town are a sugarcane factory, whiskey factory, sawmill, and brickyards.

Dong Khoi Hotel, near the lake at 16 Hai Ba Trung, tel. 22240, offers 25 rooms. A basic fan room is $6; air-con rooms are $16-30-33 for singles, a few extra dollars for doubles. The Dong Khoi also features a large restaurant. There are two other hotels in Ben Tre, including the **Hung Vuong Hotel,** by the river.

Ben Tre Tourist Company, 65 Dong Khoi St., tel. 29618, lies about 400 meters west of Dong Khoi Hotel. It charges $50 a day for a car and $10 a day for a guide. The tourist company arranges trips to floating markets, fruit orchards, and a stork farm.

There are boats from Ben Tre to Tra Vinh, Thuoi Thuan, Camau, Song Doc, and other southern destinations.

NORTHWEST OF CANTHO

Sadec

On the outskirts of Sadec over 150 families operate private nurseries: flowers, shrubs, and young trees are grown here in large quantities. These are shipped all over Vietnam, especially around Tet in February. The nurseries are located about four km from the center of the city; just wander through the gardens, and someone will show you around. Best time to view the blooms is December. By the river are numerous home-factories where young men churn out noodles using flour, water, rice, and sunshine.

Khach San Sadec, at 108 Hung Vuong St., tel. 61430, has $7-10-15 fan rooms and $20-25 air-con rooms. It's run by Dong Thap Tourism, which is based in the hotel. Nearby is a good restaurant, **Cay Sung,** tel. 61749, at 4 Hung Vuong Street.

fish for sale

Long Xuyen

Long Xuyen, population 100,000, is the uncharming capital of An Giang Province, and was formerly a stronghold of the Hoa Hao sect. The faith began in 1939 in the village of Hoa Hao in Chau Doc province. A breakaway Buddhist sect, it emphasizes simplicity, discouraging temple building and ritual worship. Until the mid-1950s the Hoa Hao constituted a major force in the region, maintaining its own army; even today there are believed to be 1.5 million adherents in the delta.

Since the Hoa Hao are not keen on temple building, you'll have to settle for Long Xuyen Catholic Church on Hung Vuong Street. The cathedral, completed in the 1970s, is one of the largest in the delta. Along Le Minh Nguy On Street are two pagodas, Dinh Than and Quan Thanh. Organized tours passing through Long Xuyen usually focus on the market. You might also want to visit Tong Duc Thang Museum, with artifacts from the Oc-Eo civilization.

Long Xuyen features half-a-dozen smaller hotels. The cheapest among them include the **Binh Dan, Thien Huong,** and **Phat Thanh** hotels, all on Nguyen An Ninh Street, with rooms for under $5. Not much more expensive are **Kim Tinh Hotel,** tel. 53137, and **Song Hau Hotel,** tel. 52979. **An Giang Hotel,** at 40 Hai Ba Trung, tel. 52297, has 16 rooms for under

LONG XUYEN

LOWER MEKONG RIVER (HAU GIANG)

FERRY TERMINALS

LE THI NGIEN

FERRY

MAIN MARKET

TO CHAU DOC 55 km

PHAM HONG THAI

POST OFFICE

AN GIANG HOTEL

DINH THAN PAGODA

LE MINH NGUY ON

NGO GIA TU

MEKONG HOTEL

LONG XUYEN

NGUYEN VAN CUNG

NGUYEN HUE

QUAN THANH PAGODA

TRAN HUNG DAO

DRY GOODS MARKET

NGUYEN AN NINH

THIEN HUONG

PHAT THANH

BINH DAN

HAI BA TRUNG

CATHOLIC CHURCH

SONG HAU HOTEL

LY TU TRONG

KIM TINH HOTEL

NGUYEN THI MINH KHAI

LUONG VAN CU

TO BUS STATION 1.5 km AND CANTHO 60 km

XUAN PHONG

NGUYEN TRAI

HUNG VUONG

NOT TO SCALE

$15. **Long Xuyen,** at 17 Nguyen Van Cung St., tel. 52927, offers almost 40 rooms for under $20 each. The 24-room **Mekong Hotel** (Cuu Long), at 21 Nguyen Van Cung, tel. 52365, has doubles for $20 and up.

Long Xuyen bus station lies several kilometers to the south of the town. From Long Xuyen there are connections to Saigon, Vinh Long, Cantho, Chau Doc, Camau, Ha Tien, and Rach Gia. You might consider private minibuses for some of these runs—minibuses stop near the Catholic church on Hung Vuong Street. Boat transport is available to Chau Doc and Rach Gia.

Chau Doc

Chau Doc is an attractive town of 80,000 on the banks of the Hau Giang, by the Cambodian border. Until the mid-18th century, Chau Doc was part of Cambodia. Today it supports the largest Khmer population in the delta—the ranks of the Khmer were swelled by refugees escaping persecution under the Pol Pot regime. Chau Doc also has the largest Cham contingent in the delta, and a sizable Chinese community. The Chau Doc area is additionally the seat of the Hoa Hao religion, with a concentration of devotees.

You can hire a local boat to visit Chau Doc's floating houses. These are houseboats built on empty metal drums, with suspended metal nets beneath them. A family lives on the floating house and fattens up the fish by throwing handfuls of cooked mush through a trapdoor; when they're fat enough, the fish are "harvested."

Chau Doc features a large market along the river, offering produce and Thai blackmarket goods smuggled in through Cambodia. About one kilometer to the southeast of town is a ferry crossing that takes you to Chau Giang Mosque, which serves the Muslim Cham community. From here you can hop on a Honda and ride a further 15 km to Tan Chau district, famed for its silk industry; the market offers imported Thai goods.

About five km southwest of Chau Doc is Nui Sam, or Sam Mountain—so named because it resembles a king crab, or *sam*. The site draws pilgrims and tourists who visit several pagodas at the foot of the mountain. Although the pagodas date to the 19th century, they've been extended and rebuilt this century. Tay An Pagoda contains a display of over 200 statues; nearby Chua Xu Temple has a revered statue of Lady Xu, en-

shrined in a new multitiered pagoda. Close by is the tomb of Thoai Ngoc Hau (1761-1829), a former local mandarin, buried here with his two wives. Thoai Ngoc Hau is revered as the person responsible for building the Chau Doc Canal.

The short hike to the top of the mountain rewards you with panoramic views of the delta. En route you pass Chua Phuc Dien Tu, a pagoda that backs onto a cave and contains a shrine dedicated to Quan Am.

Chau Doc Hotel, at 17 Doc Phu Thu St., tel. 66484, is popular with backpackers; rooms $5-10. The **Tan Tai** and **Thai Binh** hotels are substandard dumps. Two budget possibilities

are **Nha Khach 44,** and **Hotel 777.** South of Thai Binh Hotel is **My Loc Hotel,** 51 Nguyen Van Thoai, tel. 66455, with rooms for $8-12. About a kilometer south of town, near Chau Giang ferry terminal on Le Loi Street, is **Hang Chau Hotel,** tel. 66196, with air-con rooms for $20 and up—this place has a noisy nightclub.

Chau Doc bus station is two km from town, along Le Loi St.; connections to Long Xuyen, Cantho, and Vinh Long. There is no direct road to Ha Tien, but you might try a boat route along canals to get there. Other boats from Chau Doc run to Rach Gia, and via Vinh Long to Mytho.

GULF OF THAILAND

Rach Gia

Rach Gia, the capital of Ken Giang Province, is a deep-water fishing port on the Gulf of Thailand with a population of 125,000. Major industries include fishing, fish-sauce production, and smuggling from Thailand. The population includes a number of ethnic Chinese and Khmers. The center of town is an island at the mouth of the Cailon River. Rach Gia is a rather ramshackle place with widespread prostitution—many hotels serve as brothels.

There are a number of pagodas in and around Rach Gia. On the mainland north of town off Quang Trung Street is Phat Lon Pagoda. This airy Khmer Hinayana Buddhist pagoda features Cambodian and Thai-style sculptures and is home to 30 monks. Closer to the Cailon River on Nguyen Cong Tru Street is a temple dedicated to Nguyen Trung Truc, who led resistance against the newly arrived French in the 1860s. One raid resulted in the burning of the French warship *Esperance*. Nguyen Trung Truc turned himself in after the French took his mother and a number of civilians hostage and threatened to kill them. The resistance fighter was executed in Rach Gia's marketplace in 1868. A statue of Nguyen Trung Truc stands at the center of town.

Not far from this is the Chinese-style Ong Bac De Pagoda on Nguyen Du Street; to the south of town is Tam Bao Pagoda, which features trees pruned in the shape of dragons and other animals. Rach Gia has two markets: a luxury-goods market along Hoang Hoa Tham Street, and a main market area on the northeast side of the island, running along Bach Dang Street.

About 12 km north of Rach Gia (and 30 km southwest of Long Xuyen) lie the ruins of Oc-Eo, a powerful trading port from the 1st to 6th centuries AD. Oc-Eo was part of the Funan Empire, trading with India and China, and possibly even with Persia and the Roman Empire. The site was unearthed in the 1940s. There is little to see here now—just a pile of stones and potsherds. The site is presently reached via the town of Tan Hoi, where you hire a boat for a one-hour journey to Oc-Eo. You can see artifacts from the area at Saigon's History Museum and Art Museum, Hanoi's Art Museum, and Long Xuyen's Tong Duc Thang Museum.

Most hotels are located on the island. Fan rooms in Rach Gia's budget hotels go for $5, while air-con rooms are $10-15. In this price range are **Thanh Binh** and **1 Thang 5** hotels. Some budget hotels do not accept foreigners, or do not want to deal with them. **To Chau Hotel** on Le Loi St., tel. 63718, has superior air-con rooms for $15 and up. Rach Gia is famed for its seafood, served laced with *nuoc mam* and black pepper. There are a dozen restaurants on the island serving good Vietnamese and Chinese dishes; on the western end of the island is **Hoa Bien Restaurant,** which has views.

Express buses to Rach Gia leave Saigon's Mien Tay station, taking about eight hours for the trip. Rach Gia bus station is several kilometers south of town, with connections to Cantho, Long Xuyen, and Ha Tien. On the north side of Rach Gia is another express bus office at number 33 on 30 Thang 4 St., with departures to Ho Chi Minh City, Ha Tien, and Cantho. Regular boats run from Rach Gia's Mui Voi ferry terminal to Chau Doc, Long Xuyen, and Tan Chau.

Rach Gia to Ha Tien

The road from Rach Gia to Ha Tien is rough but scenic. It passes many duck farms, and affords glimpses into canal life. The scenic coastline between Rach Gia and Ha Tien comprises a number of fine beaches and caves to explore. On a promontory 30 km from Ha Tien is Chua Hang Grotto, with an entrance behind the altar of a pagoda set against the base of the hill. Next to the grotto is Duong Beach, with fine sand and crystal-clear water. Offshore is Father-and-Son Island. A bit farther along the coast, 25 km from Ha Tien, is Hang Tien Grotto, accessible only by boat. Another 10 km toward Ha Tien is Mo So Grotto, with tunnels that can be accessed on foot during the dry season, and by boat during the rainy season.

Ha Tien

Ha Tien faces the Gulf of Thailand, lying only seven km from the Cambodian border. During the Pol Pot era the town was subjected to harassment by the Khmer Rouge and tens of thousands of people fled. The Khmer Rouge massacres of Vietnamese in places like Ha Tien eventually contributed to Vietnam's 1978 invasion of Cambodia.

Today Ha Tien is a town of 100,000, thriving on fishing, and items made from tortoiseshell. Around the town are limestone crags and caves, making this an area quite unlike other parts of the delta. There are a few pagodas in town, but more interesting are the cave temples outside town. About three km from town is Thach Dong, or The Grotto that Swallows the Clouds, which shelters a Buddhist sanctuary.

Four km west of Ha Tien are beaches at Mui Nai. About 15 km off the coast of Ha Tien are the secluded beaches of Hon Giang Island, which you can reach by boat. The inhabitants make a

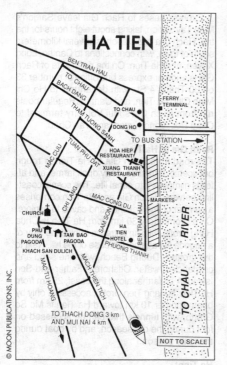

HA TIEN

BEN TRAN HAU
TO CHAU
BACH DANG
THAM TUONG SANH
TO CHAU
DONG HO
TUAN PHU DAT
MAC CUU
HOA HIEP RESTAURANT
XUANG THANH RESTAURANT
CHI LANG
MAC CONG DU
CHURCH
PHU DUNG PAGODA
TAM BAO PAGODA
SAM SON
HA TIEN HOTEL
PHUONG THANH
KHACH SAN DULICH
MAC TU HOANG
MACH THIEN TICH
TO THACH DONG 3 km AND MUI NAI 4 km

FERRY TERMINAL
TO BUS STATION
BEN TRAN HAU
MARKETS

TO CHAU RIVER

NOT TO SCALE

© MOON PUBLICATIONS, INC.

living by harvesting sea-swallow nests, a delicacy prized for medicinal soup.

You enter the fair city of Ha Tien via a floating toll bridge. Across the bridge are two hotels—**To**

Chau** (cheap and nasty), and **Dong Ho** (reasonable). **Khach San Dulich,** farther south, has more expensive rooms with bath. For dining, try **Xuang Thanh** and **Hoa Hiep** restaurants, as well as the nearby market area. Buses to Ha Tien leave from Cholon's Mien Tay terminal and take about 10 hours for the trip. There are departures from Ha Tien to Rach Gia, Cantho, and other delta destinations. There's also a regular boat from Ha Tien to Chau Doc, departing in the early morning from the terminal near the floating bridge.

Phu Quoc

The 16-island archipelago of Phu Quoc lies about 40 km west of Ha Tien in the Gulf of Thailand. It is governed from Ha Tien as a district of Ken Giang Province. The major island—Phu Quoc—is 48 km long, and covers an area of 1320 square km. Lying only 15 km off the Cambodian coast, the island is disputed territory, also claimed by the Cambodians. Phu Quoc Island boasts lush tropical forest and mountain zones. The main activities are fishing and *nuoc mam* production; about 18,000 inhabitants live mainly in the town of Duong Dong, on the west side of the island. Phu Quoc Island holds great potential for tourism, with unspoiled beaches, especially in the south. The area is great for swimming, snorkelling, and fishing. At present, the island is not easy to reach. There are direct flights several times a week from Saigon to Duong Dong on Phu Quoc for $65 one-way. There may also be a boat service to Duong Dong from Rach Gia.

CAMBODIA

"Beneath a carefree surface there slumber savage forces and disconcerting cruelties which may blaze up in outbreaks of passionate brutality. . . ."

—FRENCH ARCHAEOLOGIST
BERNARD-PHILIPPE GROSLIER
ON CAMBODIA

INTRODUCTION

The Four Horsemen of the Apocalypse—Conquest, War, Famine, and Death—have ridden roughshod over Cambodia. During the 1970s Cambodia suffered from the twin horrors of war and famine—the invading Vietnamese called it "a land of blood and tears, hell on earth."

Cambodia is hardly the place to go for a relaxing holiday. Visiting the country is a humbling experience—you wonder how people can possibly manage to even crack a smile after what they've been through. And yet they have the widest smiles and must be the friendliest people in Indochina. Their willingness to start anew speaks volumes for the resilience of the human spirit. Here's a country starting from scratch, rebuilding its traditions, culture, laws, government, and economy. The gruesome past is still around. Every month more than 400 people are maimed by landmines; Cambodia has the highest number of amputees per capita of any country in the world.

Cambodia flies the world's only flag with a building on it—the triple towers visible from the causeway at Angkor Wat. All political factions of all inclinations, including the Khmer Rouge, have depicted Angkor Wat on their version of the Cambodian flag. The Angkor Wat towers are the national logo, also found on Cambodian money, the national beer label, as a backdrop to TV newsreaders, and the official seal on the Cambodian visa.

Angkor is also the brand name of a number of products and services, though the Cambodians draw the line at foreigners using the logo. The Cambodian coalition government filed an official complaint against a Thai company for using "Angkor Wat" as a brand name for its fish sauce, citing this use by a non-Cambodian company as an "illegal and unfriendly act." The Foreign Affairs ministry argued that Angkor Wat is the symbol of Khmer national identity. And so it is: Angkor is the cornerstone of Khmer culture, symbol of national pride and past greatness, and inspiration for painting, sculpture, and woodcarving.

Angkor is also a symbol for hope, because it is Angkor that draws tourists, and foreign exchange generated from tourism can help rebuild the economy. Angkor casts its spell over all who visit. Despite the risks of travel, or perhaps because of them, Cambodia is an extraordinary adventure.

THE LAND

Covering 181,035 square km, Cambodia is roughly the size of England and Wales combined. Over the last few centuries its borders have shrunk due to encroachment by Thailand and Vietnam. The Khmer Rouge control border zones to the north and northwest.

To the southeast side of the country lie the central plains, a vast, flat agricultural area. Cambodia has three densely forested mountain ranges—the Dangrek Range on the northern border, the Cardamom Mountains to the west, and the Elephant Mountains, southwest of Phnom Penh. Phnom Aoral, elevation 1,813 meters, is the country's highest peak, located in the Cardamom Mountains. In the southwest, 340 km of coastline along the Gulf of Thailand gives Cambodia access to the ocean.

The Mekong River courses 500 km across the country. It enters Cambodia from Laos over a crashing set of cataracts at Khong Phapheng; there are also rapids around Stung Treng and Kratie. At Phnom Penh the Mekong joins two tributaries, the Bassac and Tonle Sap. The Tonle Sap River, coursing for 100 km, links the Mekong to Lake Tonle Sap, the largest freshwater lake in Southeast Asia. An annual phenomenon is the enlarging of Lake Tonle Sap from 2,600 square km to 10,400 square km at the height of the June-October rainy season. In June, swollen by monsoon rains, the Tonle Sap River reverses direction and proceeds northward to Lake Tonle Sap. The lake acts as an overflow reservoir for the Mekong. In November, after the rains subside, the river

CAMBODIA IN BRIEF

The Land: Cambodia occupies an area of 181,035 square km and borders Laos, Thailand, and Vietnam. The country is divided into 20 provinces. To the north is the Dangrek Range; to the west, the Cardamom Mountains; to the southwest, the Elephant Mountains. The Mekong courses 500 km through Cambodia. The country's second longest river is Tonle Sap River, which connects the Mekong to Lake Tonle Sap.

Climate: Tropical monsoon climate, with high humidity. March to May is very hot with occasional rain; June to October is the monsoon season; November to March is the cooler dry season.

People: Cambodia's population is estimated at 10.4 million. The Khmers constitute 90% of the population. The remainder is composed of hilltribe groups, Cham, Vietnamese, Chinese, and Thais. The breakdown is 88% rural and 12% urban. The largest city is Phnom Penh, with one million people.

Language: Khmer, the official language, is a nontonal language of the Mon-Khmer family, enriched by Pali and Sanskrit. French is the second major language, closely followed by English. Russian, Vietnamese, and Chinese are also spoken in Cambodia. Literacy rate is a low 40%, a legacy of the Pol Pot years.

Religion: Theravada Buddhism was almost annihilated under the 1975-79 reign of terror of the Khmer Rouge, but it has since been reinstated as the national religion of Cambodia. Minority groups adhere to other religions such as Catholicism (mainly Vietnamese), Taoism and Confucianism (Chinese), and Sunni Muslim (Cham).

Government: UN-supervised elections in 1993 resulted in a coalition government composed of FUNCINPEC (United Front for an Independent, Neutral, Peaceful, and Cooperative Cambodia) and CPP (Cambodian People's Party) ministers. There are two prime ministers. King Sihanouk has a symbolic role as constitutional monarch.

National Flag: After the 1993 elections, the flag reverted to that of the Sihanouk era—three white Angkor towers set on a red background, edged with blue trim.

Economy: Agriculture employs about 75% of the workforce. Top exports are timber, rubber, cane furniture, and garments. The shadow economy in Cambodia is impossible to track but is clearly quite large. The Khmer Rouge mine and log near the Thai border, and a lot of smuggled goods pass through central Cambodia. Per capita income is $200. The unit of currency is the riel; US$1=2400 riel.

Festivals: The biggest festival is Cambodian New Year in mid-April, similar to Lao and Thai celebrations. In November there are boat races to celebrate the reversing current of the Tonle Sap River.

CLIMATE CHART

All temperatures in degrees Celsius. Rainfall measured in millimeters.

PHNOM PENH

	JAN.	FEB.	MAR.	APRIL	MAY	JUNE	JULY	AUG.	SEPT.	OCT.	NOV.	DEC.
Maximum Temperature												
	31	32	34	35	34	33	32	32	31	30	30	30
Minimum Temperature												
	21	22	23	24	24	24	24	25	25	24	23	22
Rain												
	7	10	40	77	134	155	171	160	224	257	127	45

changes course again and flows once more—together with the Bassac and Mekong rivers—to the sea. It maintains this course for the November-May season, and then the cycle starts anew.

Cambodia has suffered terrible ecological damage. Deforestation has had drastic effects: waterways are beginning to clog up, and fish are dying from siltation in the Tonle Sap River. Before 1970, over 70% of Cambodia was forested; the cover is now down to 40% or less. Although the government placed a ban on the export of logs or sawn wood, it offered forest concessions to investors allowing the export of processed timber such as veneer furniture. The government awarded a 30-year renewable lease to Samling Corporation on a 800,000 hectare concession—Sarawak-based Samling is one of the world's logging giants. There are two areas of virgin rainforest in Cambodia: to the west, bordering Thailand, and to the northeast, bordering Vietnam. In the west, forest areas under Khmer Rouge control are being ravaged for teak and mahogany logs, which are sold to Thailand. One of the great ironies of Cambodia is that the best deterrent to further deforestation is the presence of landmines.

Gem mining in Khmer Rouge-controlled zones has created a lunar landscape. Trucks operating 24 hours a day remove earth and take it across the Thai border, where it is panned and valuable gemstones removed. The Khmer Rouge levy a 45% tax on all gems removed.

To the southwest, under government control, intensive shrimp farming has ravaged mangrove forests on Koh Kong.

Climate

Cambodia has a tropical monsoon climate with two periods of rainfall. The sequence of seasons is hot, bloody hot, light rain, and heavy rain. There is high humidity throughout, sometimes up to 90%. Overall, Cambodia is a sweaty place.

Hot Season: The northeast monsoon blowing in from China brings the "mango rains" in March, the first showers of the season. March, April, and May are deadly hot, with April the cruelest month. Humidity reaches 90%, and the thermometer can hit 35° C. Higher elevations and coastal regions afford the only respite from high heat and humidity.

Rainy Season: From early June to early October the southwest monsoon arises over the Indian Ocean and brings heavy rains and high humidity. The streets of Phnom Penh flood at this time. Rainstorms occur in the afternoons; the wettest months are August and September. The southwest monsoon accounts for roughly 75% of total annual rainfall. Rainfall varies considerably from area to area.

Cool Dry Season: November to March is "cool" and dry, and obviously the best time to visit, though it's somewhat dusty. December to February sees milder temperatures; January is the "coolest" month.

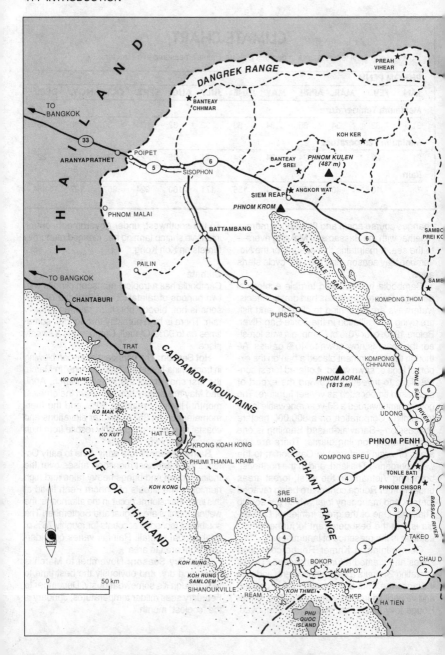

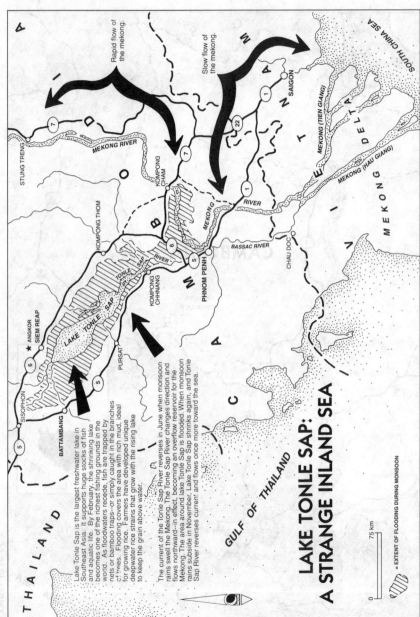

LAKE TONLE SAP: A STRANGE INLAND SEA

Lake Tonle Sap is the largest freshwater lake in Southeast Asia. It supports huge stocks of fish and aquatic life. By February, the shrinking lake becomes one of the richest fishing grounds in the world. As floodwaters recede, fish are trapped by nets or bamboo traps—or simply caught in the branches of trees. Flooding covers the area with rich mud, ideal for growing rice. Farmers have developed unique deepwater rice strains that grow with the rising lake to keep the grain above water.

The current of the Tonle Sap River reverses in June when monsoon rains swell the Mekong. The Tonle Sap River changes direction and flows northward—in effect, becoming an overflow reservoir for the Mekong. The area around lake Tonle Sap is flooded. When monsoon rains subside in November, Lake Tonle Sap shrinks again, and Tonle Sap River reverses current and flows once more toward the sea.

0   75 km

= EXTENT OF FLOODING DURING MONSOON

FLORA AND FAUNA

The flat central plains of Cambodia are primarily agricultural, used for growing rice and other crops. The transitional plains are mostly covered with savannah grasses. Cambodia's coastal strip supports evergreen and mangrove forests. In the southwest, primary-growth forest in the Cardamom and Elephant ranges contains hardwood trees such as teak, with pine forests at higher elevations. Forested areas harbor a profusion of lianas and orchids. In the northern mountains, trees soar above an undergrowth of vines, palm trees, bamboo thickets,

and ground plants. Palm trees and bamboo are the main source of village building materials; the sugar palm tree is also used to make wine, vinegar, and medicine.

Cambodia has extensive mammal, reptile, bird, and insect life. Among the larger mammals are elephants, Malaysian sun bears, tigers, clouded leopards, barking deer, pangolins, and monkeys. The rarest mammal is the *kouprey* ("jungle cow"), first identified in 1939. It was declared Cambodia's national animal in 1963 and has not been seen since. The *kouprey* is a

TIGER BONES

At the dawn of the 20th century, after a millennium of tiger-hunting, perhaps 100,000 tigers remained in the wild, ranging from the Caspian Sea in the west to Sumatra in the east to Siberia in the north. Trophy hunting and habitat destruction eliminated the Balinese tiger more than 40 years ago; the Caspian and Java cats disappeared in the 1970s and 1980s. The Indochinese tiger may well be next. Wildlife experts believe that fewer than 5,000 tigers are left today, and that the majestic cat is headed for extinction by the year 2010.

The two largest tiger species remaining today are the Bengal tiger (estimated population 2,000), and the Indochinese tiger (500 to 1,000). The Indochinese tiger ranges over the Indochinese peninsula from Burma to Malaya. Cambodia has 100 to 300 Indochinese tigers; there may be 300 left in Vietnam; the number remaining in southern Laos is not known. Tigers are more likely to be found in remote border areas; in Cambodia these areas often fall under Khmer Rouge control. Tigers were a casualty of the Vietnam War—during the 1970s hundreds of tigers were killed by Vietnamese troops forced into remote areas. In both Vietnam and Cambodia environmental degradation and poaching continue to take their toll.

Despite laws protecting tigers, poaching is rampant. Tiger products—including skin, bones, kidneys, lungs, and penis—are on sale in wildlife markets along the borders of Cambodia, Vietnam, and Laos, and are dealt openly in Phnom Penh and Poipet. The sale of a tiger skeleton can net the

equivalent of 10 years' income for a Cambodian farmer.

Despite a ban on tiger hunting as a sport by most of the tiger-range nations by 1970, and despite the outlawing of the trade in tiger skins, tigers are killed in alarming numbers. The parts once discarded—bones, blood, and body parts—are now the most valued. Behind the booming trade in tiger parts is the market for ancient Chinese medicines and potions. The Chinese exhausted their own tiger-bone stockpiles in the late 1980s, which is when conservationists began to notice an increase in tiger poaching.

The insatiable appetite of the Chinese for animal parts used in aphrodisiacs and traditional medicines remains the greatest threat to many endangered species in Asia. There is heavy traffic in snakes, frogs, lizards, turtles, geckos, and monkeys. In Hong Kong, Korea, China, Taiwan, and Chinatowns across the globe apothecaries do a steady trade in tiger wines, balms, and pills. These are valued by the Chinese and other Asian peoples who believe tiger-bone potions cure rheumatism, whiskers provide strength, and tiger-penis soup boosts a flagging libido. Tiger parts are also used in the treatment of typhoid and dysentery. By the time tiger bones, claws, eyes, penis, and whiskers reach Taiwan, the value can increase exponentially. A study by the monitoring arm of the World Wildlife Fund revealed that a tiger penis can sell for $1700 in Taiwan, and powdered tiger bone for $135-500 a gram. A single tiger can yield as much as 10 kilograms of bones.

palm trees in Kep

bovine with large lyre-shaped horns and a long dewlap drooping from the neck. The *kouprey* is now thought to be close to extinction, its numbers depleted by mines and guerrillas hunting for meat. It was once found along the Dangrek Range on the northwestern Cambodian border, and it may also inhabit Khmer Rouge territory in Mondulkiri. The most remote part of Cambodia, and hence the area with the most abundant wildlife, is to the northeast, in Ratanakiri and Mondulkiri provinces.

There are numerous reptile species in Cambodia, including crocodiles and several species of poisonous snake (kraits and cobras). Among the birdlife of Cambodia are herons, cranes, storks, wild duck, pelicans, cormorants, pheasants, and egrets. Cambodia's rivers and lakes teem with fish. Some are unusual: the elephant fish, in Lake Tonle Sap, is a species that flops overland to deeper pools as floodwaters recede. In the Mekong waters at the Lao-Cambodian border in the northeast lives the endangered freshwater Irrawaddy dolphin, threatened by indiscriminate use of explosives for fishing. Marine-life abounds around Cambodia's offshore islands on the Gulf of Thailand.

There is little protection of wildlife in Cambodia—stuffed wild animals are on sale at markets around the country. In early 1995 the country's first national parks were established. Preah Sihanouk National Park, at Ream about 20 km east of Sihanoukville, covers 21,000 hectares abutting the coast, and includes a marine zone with two islands and a coral reef. Kirirom National Park, straddling Kompong Speu and Koh Kong provinces, covers 35,000 hectares in a pine forest zone. In other parts of the country, the government plans to establish seven national parks, 10 wildlife sanctuaries, and three multiple-use zones. However, a number of the proposed parks lie in Khmer Rouge territory and may well be riddled with mines.

HISTORY

The forerunners of Khmer culture were the civilizations of Chenla, centered near Kompong Thom, and Funan, based in the Mekong Delta. Funan and Chenla are Chinese names for what may have originally been Khmer states. The Indianized Funan culture ruled from the 1st to 6th centuries AD, its wealth based on maritime trade through the key port of Oc-Eo. The people of Funan were described by Chinese travelers as dark-skinned and crinkly-haired, possibly of Melanesian origin. There is scant historical knowledge about the Funan and Chenla empires, but it appears the land-based Funan territories were absorbed by the Chenla Empire in the 7th century AD, while coastal portions were taken over by the Srivijaya Empire of Indonesia. The Chenla Empire rose between the 3rd and 7th centuries in the hills of northern Cambodia. In the early 8th century it split into two kingdoms—one based to the north of Lake Tonle Sap, the other east of the lake. Toward the end of the 8th century, the Mekong Delta region became a vassal state of Java's powerful Sailendra dynasty, and members of Chenla's ruling family were taken to the Sailendra court.

The Rule of Angkor

The Khmers remained under Sailendra suzerainty until a Khmer prince returned to the land of his ancestors and proclaimed independence. At Phnom Kulen, 45 km northeast of Angkor Wat, Jayavarman II arranged his coronation by a Brahman priest in 802 AD. He declared himself a *devaraja,* or divine king. At this time the Hindu deities Shiva and Vishnu were worshipped as a single entity, called Harihara; early Khmer kings adopted the Hindu trinity of Shiva, Brahma, and Vishnu, each becoming the basis for cult worship. The history of this period has been reconstructed from depictions in bas-relief and over 900 inscriptions in stone within the boundaries of the former Khmer Empire. Still, knowledge of Khmer history is vague and highly speculative.

The 200-square-kilometer plains of Angkor, situated between Phnom Kulen and Lake Tonle Sap, are comparable in size to Egypt's Nile Valley. They were inhabited first by Jayavarman II, and then by successive kings for over 500 years. The kings established the powerful Angkorian culture, known for its brilliant achievements in architecture and sculpture. Angkor developed into one of the world's greatest urban centers, and held dominion over large swaths of present-day Thailand and Vietnam.

The Khmer king's spirit was said to reside in a linga (sacred phallus, symbol of Shiva) housed in a temple-pyramid. People believed the king communicated with the gods at the summit of this structure. The all-powerful king ensured the prosperity of his kingdom. Subsequent kings transferred the *devaraja* cult to other temple-pyramids. The Khmer Empire continued to expand, vying with neighboring kingdoms—the Cham, Vietnamese, and Burmese.

Although Jayavarman II is credited with establishing the Khmer kingdom, it was 10th-century king Yasovarman I who founded the first capital city on the site now known as Angkor. Yasovarman I built a temple-pyramid at Phnom Bakheng, near the site of Angkor Wat, ushering in a Khmer golden age. He governed an empire that stretched from the south of Laos to the Gulf of Siam. Each new king added temples, monuments, palaces, and residences to the Angkor area; surrounding these urban complexes were vast ricefields with an intricate system of canals and irrigation networks. The Angkor region borders Lake Tonle Sap, which floods annually; as the waters recede, fish are caught in abundance—this is one of the world's richest fishing grounds. An economic surplus derived from agriculture, fishing, and a royal monopoly on foreign trade enabled Angkorian kings to embark on grandiose architectural projects symbolizing their prestige and authority.

The relationship between the royal center at Angkor and the provincial frontiers was highly unstable. More or less autonomous provinces were satellites of the central court; authority extended from Angkor through an arrangement of alliances with petty rulers. The fluctuating peripheries of the empire were of secondary concern to the kings, who were preoccupied with the splendor of the royal center at Angkor.

The zenith of the Khmer Empire was achieved under Suryavarman II, who reigned from roughly 1112 to 1152. He undertook the building of Angkor Wat and a number of other temples; under his rule, the Khmer Empire expanded into present-day Malaya, Thailand, Burma, and Vietnam. He deposed the King of Champa in coastal Vietnam in 1145; however, the Cham regained their independence a few years later. Toward the end of his rule, Suryavarman II mounted a disastrous foray into north Vietnam to attack the Cham again. A large number of his troops perished from fever on jungle marches.

Angkor Under Attack

Upon the death of Suryavarman II, the nation was weak and divided, prey to Cham revenge. The Cham devised a cunning method for attacking Angkor—they came across Lake Tonle Sap in war canoes from the south, guided by a Chinese pilot. They sacked Angkor in 1177 and drove out its people.

Angkor had never before been attacked. The sacking by the Cham cast a shadow over the infallibility of both Angkor's kings and the Hindu deities that were supposed to render them infallible. A new contender to the throne routed the Cham in 1181, pushing them back to Annam. Crowned Jayavarman VII, this king inaugurated Mahayana Buddhism as the nation's faith. Temples were dedicated to Lokesvara, the bodhisattva of compassion. Jayavarman VII undertook

a frenzied building and social works program, constructing the city of Angkor Thom with a royal palace and temples. Angkor Thom was a thriving metropolis with a large system of reservoirs and irrigation canals. Jayavarman VII extended the boundaries of the empire from the vicinity of Pagan in Burma to the Vietnam coast, and from Vientiane in Laos to the Malay Peninsula.

Fall of the Khmer Empire

After Jayavarman VII's death in 1218, the Khmer Empire declined. His sons and heirs reverted to Shivaism, and Indian Brahmans gained great influence at the court. For unknown reasons a malaise gripped the core of the Khmer Empire in the 13th and 14th centuries. Theories abound as to why Angkor declined: climate change, shift of trade from land- to sea-based empires, exhaustion of resources in warfare and on building projects, or a change of religion to Theravada Buddhism, undermining the royal and priestly hierarchy. In any case, the elaborate irrigation system, no longer properly tended, fell into disrepair and silted up. Canals became clogged, ricefields reverted to swampland, food production dwindled. Stagnant water probably led to an increase in the number of malaria-carrying mosquitoes.

To the west, Thai chieftains shook off Khmer rule and established the first Thai kingdom of Sukothai. Another Thai kingdom from the south,

Khmers battle the Cham.

in Ayuthaya, expanded quickly and became a major threat to the Khmers. In the 14th century there were repeated attacks by the Siamese and counterattacks by the Khmers, with skirmishes in 1353, 1394, 1401, and 1421. When the Siamese invaded Angkor in 1431 they went on a rampage, killing, destroying, and looting. They stripped Angkor of its wealth and destroyed its infrastructure.

Khmer Dark Ages

After its magnificent beginnings, the kingdom of Cambodia fell on hard times, becoming a vassal state of the Thai kingdom of Sukothai. For the next 400 years a weak Cambodia became a political football, kicked back and forth by its powerful neighbors, Siam and Vietnam. Worse still, there were dynastic squabbles among the Khmers. In this lackluster period of Khmer history, the court—what remained of it—moved continuously. In 1434 it located to Phnom Penh. A short-lived attempt to rekindle the capital at Angkor was stymied when the Siamese sacked the capital again in 1473. There were further attempts by the court to return to Angkor in the 16th and 17th centuries, but nothing came of them. In the 16th century, Khmer King Ang Chan built a fortified capital at Lovek north of Phnom Penh. Taking advantage of the Thai preoccupation with fighting the Burmese, Ang Chan started taking back lost Cambodian territory. However, after recovering from Burmese assaults, the Thais captured Angkor, Battambang, and Pursat. An attack on Lovek in 1593 caused the Khmer royal family to flee to Laos.

In 1603 the Thais released a captured prince to rule over the vassal state of Cambodia. In 1618 the Khmers tried to shake themselves loose from Siamese suzerainty, driving out the Siamese garrison. The king asked the Vietnamese for help: however, this meant the Khmer court was obliged to pay tribute to Vietnam. Successive kings would seek Siamese assistance against the domination of Vietnam.

In the early 1700s the kingdom of Cambodia was centered in Udong, to the northwest of Phnom Penh. By 1750 the Khmer royal family had split into pro-Vietnamese and pro-Siamese factions. Only the Thai wars with the Burmese and internal squabbles in Vietnam prevented these two nations from taking over Cambodia

entirely. The Khmers lost control of the Mekong Delta to the Vietnamese in the late 18th century, blocking the nation's access to the sea. In 1793 the Siamese gained the western Cambodian provinces of Siem Reap and Battambang. In the 1840s Thai and Vietnamese armies fought on Cambodian territory. Cambodian King Norodom was under the control of the Siamese Resident in the capital and paid tribute to the Vietnamese.

Enter the French

French designs on Cambodia were apparent soon after they gained a foothold in neighboring Cochinchina (southern Vietnam). The French sought a buffer between Cochinchina and Siam, where the British had established trading interests. The French were also keen on exploring the Mekong as a trading route from China, and wanted to secure the upper reaches of the Mekong. In 1861 Admiral Charner, the French commander in Saigon, sailed up the Mekong and on to the Cambodian capital of Udong to tell King Norodom the French would help Cambodia maintain its freedom by providing military assistance.

Under French pressure, Norodom signed a treaty in 1864 whereby Cambodia became a French protectorate. This was merely a switch of masters—the French Resident, Captain Doudart de Lagrée, replaced the Siamese Resident. In 1867, in return for Siamese renunciation of sovereignty over Cambodia, the French ceded the provinces of Battambang and Siem Reap to the Siamese. King Norodom protested, to no effect; the two provinces were later returned to Cambodia under a 1907 treaty.

In 1884 the French tried to gain full control of Cambodia by forcing King Norodom to sign an agreement handing over all power to the French Resident. This sparked an insurrection, mainly in the eastern part of the country, most likely supported by the disgruntled king. The French eventually conceded and withdrew some of their demands. However, to diminish the power of the king, they paid attention to a rival branch of the royal family, the Sisowaths, who were considered more malleable. When King Norodom died in 1904, the French discounted his heir and arranged for his half-brother, Prince Sisowath, to succeed him.

The French were not greatly interested in developing Cambodia. Tax revenues were used to build rail lines and roads; in the 1920s, private-sector investors planted rubber estates in Kompong Cham in eastern Cambodia, as well as tea, coffee, pepper, and cotton plantations.

Shaking Off the French

In the late 1930s nationalism began to stir in Cambodia as intellectuals educated in France returned to their homeland. A key figure in disseminating anticolonial ideas was Son Ngoc Thanh, an ethnic Khmer from Vietnam's Mekong Delta. In 1937 he founded *Nagaravatta (Angkor Wat)*, the first Cambodian-language newspaper. Son Ngoc Thanh rallied a group of Buddhist monks, rich Khmers, and Cambodian intellectuals to his cause.

To counter nationalism, in 1941 the French decided to switch royal families once again. When Sisowath's son Monivong died in 1941, they reverted to the Norodoms. Nineteen-year-old Prince Norodom Sihanouk was crowned king. The French hold on Cambodia was weakened during WW II when Indochina was occupied by the Japanese. In 1945 the Japanese took full control of Cambodia from the Vichy French, and ordered Sihanouk to declare independence. Under Japanese pressure, Sihanouk appointed Son Ngoc Thanh as prime minister.

When Japan surrendered, Thanh attempted to declare a republic but was arrested by the French and sent into exile. Thanh believed only armed struggle against France and an end to the monarchy could liberate Cambodia. He conducted a guerrilla campaign from the forests of Thailand and the south of Vietnam, forming the Khmer Serei (Free Khmers). In 1946 the French secured their hold on Battambang and Siem Reap provinces. In 1949 Sihanouk negotiated partial freedom from the French; in 1953 came full independence. Sihanouk had proved himself an astute negotiator.

In 1954 the Geneva Peace Conference agreed to a temporary division of Vietnam into north and south. It also recognized Cambodia's neutrality and called on the country to hold elections based on universal suffrage. It became clear the Democratic Party, republican-minded followers of Son Ngoc Thanh, would win. There appeared to be little sympathy for the monarchy,

so Sihanouk decided to wade into the elections himself. In 1955 he abdicated the throne in favor of his father and formed a movement, the Sangkum, a loose coalition of royalist and Buddhist forces. Sihanouk was victorious at the polls and became prime minister.

Calm Before the Storm

From 1955 to 1965, Cambodia was miraculously insulated from the brutality that engulfed the rest of Indochina. Protected by the deft neutrality of Sihanouk, the country drifted along almost oblivious to the bloodshed in Vietnam and Laos. Phnom Penh offered the charm of a provincial French town. Food was stacked high in the central marketplace, and there was little evidence of the sort of slums that plagued Bangkok or Saigon. In the countryside rural folk lived around their pagodas, worked the rice-fields, and fished the streams. North Vietnamese troops moved through the mountains of northeast Cambodia; deep in the forest was a ragtag band of Cambodian guerrillas. But all this seemed remote to the bulk of the population.

THE RAVAGES OF WAR

Sideshow

In 1965, suspicious of CIA involvement in plots against him, Sihanouk broke off diplomatic relations with the US and aligned himself with China. At the same time he continued to crack down on domestic dissent. Primary targets included French-educated radicals who had returned from Paris to teach or take civil service jobs in Phnom Penh. These men and women were disillusioned by the rampant corruption in the city. Among them were Leng Sary, Son Sen, Khieu Samphan, and Saloth Sar (later known as Pol Pot). In 1963 a number of them headed for the jungles and mountains. In 1967 there was an anticorruption insurrection in Battambang Province. Sihanouk savagely put down the peasant revolt by liquidating the rioters. The uprising was blamed on leftists—remaining Phnom Penh radicals fled to join their comrades in the jungle. Sihanouk dubbed the Cambodian Communists Khmer Rouge (Cambodian Reds).

Meanwhile the US sought ways of preventing the North Vietnamese Army and the Vietcong from escaping to sanctuaries in neighboring Laos and Cambodia along the Ho Chi Minh Trail. Secret raids by US and South Vietnamese operatives in the late 1960s preceded the B-52 bombings of Cambodia in March 1969. These actions were referred to by the Nixon White House as "a sideshow to Vietnam." Flight crews assumed they were bombing Vietnam when in fact their targets lay inside Cambodia. President Richard Nixon and Secretary of State Henry Kissinger maintained the areas were unpopulated by all save North Vietnamese troops, but in fact many places were populated by Cambodians. More than 3,600 B-52 sorties were flown against suspected Communist bases in Cambodia over the next 14 months. William Shawcross provided an overview in his book *Sideshow:*

> *By the beginning of 1969, Vietnam and Laos were torn apart by war, their people driven into camps, their societies already irrevocably destroyed. Thailand had endured no fighting, but it too had been corrupted by the commerce of war and now, under a repressive military dictatorship, served as a "land-based aircraft carrier" for the B-52 bombers that daily pounded the grounds of its Indochinese neighbors. Only Cambodia was unassailed. Her neutralism was vulnerable and abused by all parties to the conflict.*

Lon Nol Regime
In March 1970 Sihanouk was deposed in a US-backed coup led by General Lon Nol. The new regime abolished the monarchy and declared a republic; Sihanouk, in Moscow at the time, subsequently moved to Beijing where he passed his time in exile in luxury. Lon Nol got off to a bad start. To compensate for lack of peasant support, he tried to exploit the traditional Khmer fear of the Vietnamese by launching a murderous campaign against Vietnamese civilians in the south. Lon Nol's regime soon became even more dictatorial and corrupt than Sihanouk's. In April 1970 Nixon announced that American and ARVN troops had crossed into Cambodia to attack an alleged Vietcong headquarters. The base was never found and the troops withdrew a few months later.

In early 1971, Lon Nol suffered a stroke that left him with slurred speech and a tenuous grasp on reality. Yet he remained in power for four more years, bolstered by the White House. Cambodia became heavily dependent on American aid in political, economic, and military affairs. Lon Nol's troops were poorly disciplined; the government controlled only the areas around Phnom Penh and the provincial capitals. In the countryside the Communists ruled, and each year they captured more territory. By 1974 only Phnom Penh remained in government hands. In April 1975, Lon Nol fled to Hawaii.

Rise of the Khmer Rouge
The obscure Khmer Rouge were thought to number only 5,000 in the 1960s. By the early 1970s the Khmer Rouge army had grown to perhaps 50,000 men, and could hold its own against Lon Nol with some support from the North Vietnamese.

The dramatic change was due to several factors. When Sihanouk went into exile, he was piqued by the Lon Nol coup. He abandoned neutrality and allied himself with his former enemies, the Khmer Rouge and the North Vietnamese, against Lon Nol, South Vietnam, and the US. The Khmer Rouge thus gained national appeal. Many Cambodians switched allegiance because the Khmer Rouge represented opposition to the corruption of the Lon Nol regime. By 1973, US B-52 raids had killed at least 100,000 Cambodian civilians. Pol Pot used the bombing as both recruitment propaganda and an excuse to purge moderate socialists. Although Pol Pot was deeply resentful of foreign influence, he was forced to accept North Vietnamese help in the early 1970s. As soon as his forces were strong enough, Pol Pot appealed to Khmer nationalism—and any cadres who'd been trained by the Vietnamese were marked men.

The Year Zero
On 17 April 1975, 13 days before the fall of Saigon, the Khmer Rouge rolled into Phnom Penh. Having methodically secured the city, they ordered everyone out, including the dying in hospitals. More than two million people were sent to the countryside in the next 48 hours with

BROTHER NUMBER ONE

Behind the Khmer Rouge bloodbath was Pol Pot, a psychopathic mass murderer. Born Saloth Sar in Kompong Thom in 1928, he was one of seven children in a rural family. The family had royal connections—his cousin had grown up a palace dancer, becoming one of King Monivong's principal wives; his eldest sister was chosen as a royal consort. In 1928 his eldest brother, Loth Suong, began a career in palace protocol, and Saloth Sar joined him six years later. After a year in a royal monastery, he spent six years in a strict Catholic school.

After attending technical college in Phnom Penh, Saloth Sar received a scholarship to study radio electronics in Paris in 1948. Study at a French university was the ultimate goal of ambitious Cambodians, who avidly sought scholarships. Saloth Sar failed his examinations in Paris three times—he preferred to spend his time at Marxist revolutionary meetings. He kept company with Khieu Ponnary, eight years his senior, and the first Khmer woman to receive a French degree. They were married in 1956. Among their circle of student friends were Khieu Samphan, Ieng Sary, and Son Sen.

Upon returning to newly independent Cambodia in 1953, Saloth Sar taught history and geography at a private school in Phnom Penh and worked as a left-wing journalist. By 1962 he had risen to the rank of Deputy General Secretary in the underground Cambodian Communist Party. Members had code names like "Free Khmer" or "Khmer Worker." Saloth Sar's *nom de guerre* was Pol Pot, meaning "Original Cambodian."

In 1963 he fled Phnom Penh in the wake of a crackdown by Sihanouk. Pol Pot was trained in guerrilla warfare and became leader of the Khmer Rouge forces, advocating armed resistance. When the Khmer Rouge took Phnom Penh in 1975, Pol Pot—alias Brother Number One—ruled as virtual dictator, with Khieu Samphan as head of state. Few Cambodians had ever heard of him when he came to power; he had always kept a low profile. Loth Suong didn't find out who was responsible for the genocide in Cambodia until he saw a portrait of Pol Pot on a wall in Kompong Thom in 1978—and recognized his younger brother. Pol Pot's wife, Khieu Ponnary, reputedly went mad.

Occasionally, Pol Pot was heard over the radio. His early training in radio electronics proved useful in this regard—radio was one of the few technologies retained by the Khmer Rouge. In September 1977 he gave a five-hour speech over Radio Phnom Penh, laced with Maoist rhetoric. He calmly recited the new national anthem of Democratic Kampuchea, which roughly translates as: "Bright red blood which covers the towns and plains of Kampuchea, our motherland, sublime blood of workers and peasants, sublime blood of revolutionary men and women fighters!"

Pol Pot still lives in the Cardamom Mountains, where he still issues orders to the Khmer Rouge under the code name "87."

---

neither food nor possessions. They were informed that American planes would bomb them and that there was no need to take anything because they could return in a few days. Later, they were told a different story. This was the Year Zero in Democratic Kampuchea, and *Angka Loeu,* Pol Pot's administrative arm, would provide for a new future. *Angka Loeu* (the Organization on High) was run by a handful of people—all French-educated and related by revolutionary experience and/or marriage. Together they launched a bloodbath.

The Killing Fields
From 1975 to 1979 the Khmer Rouge strove to realize Pol Pot's vision of a peasant nation of self-reliant agricultural work brigades, modeled on the Khmer Empire. This was to be accomplished without machinery—everything would be done with bare hands. "We will burn the old grass and new will grow," went one slogan. A practical side of this strategy was that the Khmer Rouge could split up and isolate any possible opposition. The Khmer Rouge enforced a revolution that probably went farther and faster in destroying a society than any other in history. They made no attempt to re-educate the urban population—they simply set about killing "traitors." Cities were emptied, imported technology (including medical equipment) was destroyed, temples dynamited, schools and hospitals closed, books burned, all in an attempt to turn

the nation into a rural paradise. There were no medical facilities, no education, no transport. Money, telephones, and newspapers were outlawed. Books, holidays, and music were banned. Buddhism was forbidden.

Khmer Rouge methods of killing were particularly brutal. Refugees who escaped to Thailand reported that pregnant women were disemboweled, babies torn apart limb from limb, men buried up to their necks in sand and left to die, others suffocated with plastic bags over their heads. Within months of the takeover, the entire administrative order of the old regime was gone—all executed. Those evacuated from the cities were placed in rural communes and made to work as slave labor on often pointless projects. Khmer Rouge irrigation-cum-drainage systems were poorly engineered and resulted in serious environmental damage.

In communes the people were separated into three groups—those from the city, those from market towns, and rural people. The rural contingent was put in charge. Each citizen was required to submit a verbal autobiography to the commune and its cadres. Those who revealed they had been technicians, teachers, monks, or doctors were executed. Those who spoke French, English, or Vietnamese, or who had studied abroad, were likewise liquidated. Simply having fair skin or wearing glasses was cause for execution.

Ethnic Cleansing

Pol Pot envisioned a pure Cambodian race. National impurities were to be expunged, territory lost to Vietnam and Thailand regained. The minorities in Cambodia—Chinese, Vietnamese, Cham, and hilltribe groups—were decimated. The Muslim Cham numbered 250,000 in 1975. The Khmer Rouge emptied all 113 Cham villages in Cambodia and massacred 90,000 Cham. Islamic schools and religion and the Cham language were banned. Only half the estimated 500,000 ethnic Chinese survived the Pol Pot era, one of the worst disasters ever to befall the Chinese in Southeast Asia. China passed over the slaughter of Cambodia's Chinese because the Khmer Rouge were killing Vietnamese, and China resented Vietnam's alignment with the Soviet Union at the time. The 450,000-strong Vietnamese community had

mostly been expelled under the Lon Nol regime; those who remained in 1975 were driven out by Pol Pot or murdered.

The bloodiest period of Khmer Rouge reign was in 1978, when Pol Pot's troops crushed an uprising in eastern Cambodia. Pol Pot's radio broadcast a call not only for the extermination of the Vietnamese but also for purification in the Cambodian masses. Estimates of the number killed in the 1975-79 period range from 300,000 to three million (out of a total population of around seven million in 1975). Research based on extensive interviews with survivors by two independent Western researchers puts the figure at 1.5 million dead, from execution, starvation, or disease.

Barring the Chinese, the Communist nations refused to recognize Democratic Kampuchea, but did little else. Western nations, intent on improved relations with China, remained silent. As essayist George Steiner put it: "In previous times, we were not bombarded with the graphic demonstration of our own impotence or indifference. [In Cambodia] we knew, day by day, that 100,000 people were being buried alive, and we did nothing."

Vietnamese Occupation

In several years of border fighting with the Khmer Rouge the Vietnamese suffered the deaths of perhaps 30,000 troops and an equivalent number of civilians. In a move censured by the West, the Vietnamese invaded Cambodia in December 1978. Within two weeks the Vietnamese Army had pushed its former ally back to the Thai border. Over half a million people became refugees in Thailand, assisted by an international humanitarian effort. The Vietnamese installed a client regime in Phnom Penh, the **People's Republic of Kampuchea** (PRK), headed by Heng Samrin, once a member of a pro-Vietnamese group within the Khmer Rouge. He defected from the Khmer Rouge in 1977 and fled to Vietnam. Others in the PRK, like Hun Sen, were also Khmer Rouge defectors.

Vietnam's invasion was seen as part of a wider plan to combine the countries of Indochina into a single political and economic bloc—Ho Chi Minh's dream. Suddenly, the genocidal Khmer Rouge were given military support by outsiders. According to the Vietnam Veterans of

America Foundation, the British and American governments provided $88 million in assistance to Pol Pot and the Khmer Rouge between 1980 and 1986. The UN called on Vietnam to withdraw from Cambodia, and seated the Khmer Rouge (as part of a coalition government) in the security council in New York. The Chinese invaded North Vietnam as a punitive measure—this backfired and the Chinese were forced to withdraw after heavy losses.

Following the Vietnamese invasion, three Cambodian factions banded together in an uneasy alliance. Apparently under pressure from the US, the alliance was forced to include the Khmer Rouge as part of a broader plan to legitimize its operations.

The **Party of Democratic Kampuchea** (PDK), more commonly known as the Khmer Rouge, fielded an army of 40,000 troops. Their force was called the **National Army of Democratic Kampuchea** (NADK), and was mostly based in the Cardamom Mountains. The **United Front for an Independent, Neutral, Peaceful, and Cooperative Cambodia** (FUNCINPEC, a French acronym), was formed in 1981 by Sihanouk, then living in exile in China. This group fielded the 12,000-strong **National Army of Independent Kampuchea** (ANKI), otherwise known as the Armée Nationale Sihanoukiste. The **Khmer People's National Liberation Front** (KPNLF) was an anticommunist group headed by former prime minister Son Sann. It worked in cooperation with the **Buddhist Liberal Democratic Party** (BLDP), and commanded the 8,000-member Khmer People's National Liberation Armed Forces (KPNLAF).

These three forces made up the **Coalition Government of Democratic Kampuchea** (CGDK), under the nominal leadership of Sihanouk. Thailand protected Pol Pot and his followers, helping rebuild the Khmer Rouge into a potent guerrilla force.

The CGDK was arrayed against the 70,000 troops loyal to the Vietnamese-installed government of President Heng Samrin and Prime Minister Hun Sen. Their army was called the **Cambodian People's Armed Forces** (CPAF). In 1989 the government was renamed the **Party of the State of Cambodia** (SOC), with a new flag and national anthem. In a shuffle, Hun Sen rose to leadership. Under increasing economic pressure, and eager to reduce its international isolation, the Vietnamese withdrew from Cambodia in September 1989.

A FRAGILE PEACE

Paris Peace Accords

Since 1986 there had been negotiations between key players to try and resolve the crisis in Cambodia. Throughout 1991 these efforts intensified. The four warring factions—SOC, FUNCINPEC, KPNLF, and the Khmer Rouge—were repeatedly brought to the negotiating table to hammer out a peace deal. Argument erupted

a UN armored personnel carrier

over the use of the word "genocide"—the Hun Sen government insisted any agreement should condemn the Khmer Rouge's genocidal acts, while the Khmer Rouge refused to accept any such language.

Under the auspices of the UN in Paris, the four factions signed a political agreement ending civil war in Cambodia on 23 October 1991. The agreement called for a 70% reduction of all armed forces, and for the remaining troops to be placed under the temporary jurisdiction of the **United Nations Transitional Authority in Cambodia** (UNTAC) pending multiparty democratic elections in 1993. Sihanouk returned to Cambodia several months later to head the **Supreme National Council** (SNC), a 12-member unit representing all four factions. The SOC transformed itself into the **Cambodian People's Party** (CPP), still headed by Hun Sen. At this point, Cambodia had three different governmental units—the Hun Sen government, the SNC, and UNTAC.

The Khmer Rouge were invited to participate in the electoral process. This anomaly was made possible by the Cambodians' hatred of the Vietnamese. In 1989 Sihanouk said, "The Khmer Rouge are tigers. But I would rather be eaten by a Khmer Rouge tiger than a Vietnamese crocodile, because the Khmer Rouge are true patriots. Oh, they are vicious, they are cruel; they are murderers. But they are not traitors like Hun Sen." In the end, the Khmer Rouge did not honor the Paris treaty, claiming some Vietnamese forces still occupied Cambodia. The Khmer Rouge remained in their guerrilla strongholds, refused to disarm, and declined to take part in UN-supervised elections.

The Blue Berets

Cambodia was placed under the jurisdiction of UNTAC in July 1992 for a period of 18 months. Monitoring elections were 22,000 UN personnel, including 16,000 blue beret peacekeepers from over 30 nations, 2,500 civilian personnel, and 3,600 civilian police monitors. At the time it was the largest operation in UN history and cost over two billion dollars. Cambodia was awash with white UN vehicles—white jeeps, white tanks, white helicopters, white planes.

Apart from guiding the country through "democratic elections," the UNTAC mandate in Cambodia included demobilization of soldiers and repatriation of Cambodian refugees. Another key aspect was assistance in repairing an infrastructure severely damaged in 13 years of civil warfare—mine clearing and building of roads, transport, communications, schools, hospitals. At a cost of $800 million, **United Nations High Commission for Refugees** (UNHCR) resettled 350,000 Cambodian refugees from six Thai border camps. This enormous task took over a year, with 10,000 refugees settled each week.

Other parts of the Paris Peace Accords were not implemented. Demobilization and disarmament did not occur. The Khmer Rouge refused to allow UNTAC troops to patrol areas under their control, and fired at UN helicopters that flew over their zones. They insisted Vietnamese residents in Cambodia not be allowed to vote, and attempted to disrupt the electoral process.

Not all the UN's work was positive: highly paid UN workers contributed to massive inflation in 1992-93. There was wide-scale prostitution in Phnom Penh and elsewhere in Cambodia catering to the highly paid foreign troops and personnel, causing a spread of AIDS. Personnel from some nations were unused to driving and caused accidents. A large amount of UN property disappeared—and not all of it could be attributed to theft.

The Elections

Despite setbacks in fulfilling the Paris Peace Accords, UNTAC pushed ahead with preparations for 1993 elections, launching a massive campaign to register voters. There were widespread attempts to intimidate voters; some 20 FUNCINPEC organizers and candidates were assassinated before the elections. Hun Sen's CPP was implicated in these attacks, and was also accused of restricting access of other parties to territories under government control. Both the CPP and FUNCINPEC accused each other of assassination attempts. The Khmer Rouge killed Vietnamese civilians in Siem Reap Province, prompting an exodus of 30,000 Vietnamese. The Khmer Rouge threatened to resort to violence to disrupt polling, and polling stations in more remote areas were shelled.

The elections finally took place in May 1993, with a huge voter turnout. Over 20 parties were represented, but the two most popular were the CPP and FUNCINPEC. The royalist FUNCIPEC -

THE TROUBLE WITH CAMBODIA

Cambodia has so many problems it's hard to know where to begin. Until the problems of banditry, Khmer Rouge guerrilla activity, and corrupt army soldiers are solved, travel will remain risky. In the event the country does settle down, there's still the reality of millions of landmines strewn throughout the nation.

Human Rights

Repression is the order of the day in Cambodia. On the heels of the UN peacekeeping mission, the United Nations Center for Human Rights (UNCHR) set up a base in Phnom Penh in October 1993 to assist the government in meeting its human rights obligations. This was something of a precedent in Asia. China and Indonesia swiftly announced opposition to the center, while Malaysian officials asked the UN to close it. In 1995 the co-premiers of Cambodia also requested the office be banished— the present government sees UNCHR activities as opposition lobbying. The UNCHR has investigated secret prisons in Battambang, the murder of newspaper editors, threats against members of parliament, ill treatment of ethnic minorities, draft, immigration, and press laws, and the corrupt conduct of military personnel.

The Cambodian judicial system is in its infancy. Many prisoners are held without trial; the majority of judges will bring a case to trial only when they receive money. Freedom of speech has come under government attack. In September 1994 a newspaper editor who had published accounts of official corruption was gunned down in Phnom Penh, the third journalist killed in Cambodia that year. In January 1995 the government filed defamation suits against two Cambodian newspapers for criticizing the co-premiers. An editor arrested for running a cartoon of the co-premiers received a one-year jail sentence and a fine of $2000. The government also threatened to restrict circulation of some Western magazines, barred two French reporters, and launched a defamation suit against two French newspapers in Paris. The papers reported on abuses by the Cambodian military that were first reported by the UNCHR in Phnom Penh.

In mid-1995 the Cambodian parliament passed a tough new law stating, "The press shall not publish or reproduce information which affects national security and political stability." Violations are punishable by jail terms and fines of up to $6000. Another section restricts "rude" language and pornographic pictures.

Corruption

Corruption is rampant in Cambodia. Underpaid civil servants, police, and soldiers frequently resort to other means of fundraising, turning to extortion or bribes. Border battalions are heavily involved in smuggling. Military officials often collect pay for phantom soldiers. The coalition government says it has taken some steps toward cutting corruption. In 1995, it reduced the number of army generals from almost 2,000 to just 200.

Banditry

Demobilized or unemployed soldiers and police have been known to turn to banditry. Bandits have staged armed robberies on the highways and byways of Cambodia, attempting to steal 4WD vehicles or motorcycles, sometimes killing the owners to do so. NGO cars are a favorite target. An hour after a car is stolen, it could be transformed and on its way to the Vietnamese border for resale. Lawlessness prevails in Phnom Penh, especially at night. Shootouts between security forces and bandits have revealed that some bandits are in fact local police or security forces in civilian clothing. To counter gangsterism, embassies and hotels in Phnom Penh have posted round-the-clock armed guards.

Mines

One reason government troops can't get at the Khmer Rouge is mines. This is called "the war of the mines" because the Khmer Rouge are reluctant to engage RCAF troops in firefights. Mines are the weapon of choice for guerrilla forces—they're cheap, easy to deploy, and extremely effective in immobilizing enemy forces and disrupting social and economic life. Antipersonnel mines are designed to maim, not kill, creating an economic burden for the government, and terrorizing civilians. There are estimated to be three to seven million mines in Cambodia scattered throughout rice paddies and forests. The UN described the carnage left by mines in Cambodia as "one of the worst modern manmade disasters of the century." Angola, Afghanistan, and Cambodia rank as the countries most afflicted by mines.

The **Cambodian Mine Action Center** (CMAC) was set up in July 1992 under UNTAC auspices to educate people about mines, map and mark mined areas, and start mine clearing. Producing a countrywide map of mined areas is a large part of CMAC's work. About 2,000 Cambodians were trained in de-mining before UNTAC pulled out. Clearing mines is a slow and tedious process. Although the de-miners have suffered few casualties, 11 de-miners were injured by bullets during a train ambush near the Thai border. Under UNTAC's auspices less than 15 square km were cleared of mines. De-miners pulled 40,000 mines from that bit of ground, so with possibly 300 square km of mined areas remaining, there are probably some three million more mines left to go. And the Khmer Rouge continue to lay fresh mines.

Cambodia has more amputees per capita than any other country. One in every 300 Cambodians is missing a limb. Amputees are outcasts—many rely on friends and family for care. They are doomed to spend lives with shattered dreams. There is an entrenched prejudice in Cambodia against physical deformity: to lose part of your physical being is to lose part of your soul. Every month, 300 to 600 Cambodians are killed or injured in land-mine accidents. Ironically, one of the few fields of employment open to an amputee is mine clearing.

Although mines have been laid by different factions, the main culprits are the Khmer Rouge, who were trained by British SAS troops at camps in Thailand and Malaysia in the 1980s. Mines laid include the Chinese Type 72 antitank mine and the Italian Valsella VS-50 all-plastic antipersonnel mine. Mines are cheap—under $10. Finding them is expensive. It is calculated it costs $1000 to find a mine in Cambodia. One expert calculates that to rid itself of the mine scourge Cambodia would have to spend $7 billion—a figure equivalent to its gross domestic product for five to seven years.

Mines are not the only obstacle laid by the Khmer Rouge. Trip-wired booby traps are fashioned from unexploded ordnance and laid in ricefields and farms in Battambang Province. There's a lot of unexploded ordnance lying around—hand grenades, 60mm and 80mm mortars, air-to-ground rockets, antipersonnel bomblets, even 250 kg bombs dropped from B-52s. Under UNTAC, de-mining teams destroyed 170,000 pieces of unexploded ordnance.

---

party, led by Prince Norodom Ranariddh, gained 58 seats, but failed to attract sufficient support to rule outright. The CPP picked up 51 seats. CPP leader Hun Sen agreed to accept the results and persuaded members of his party to form a coalition government with FUNCINPEC. With the passage of the first constitution in September 1993, the role of UNTAC expired. Solders who previously served in ANKI, KPNLAF, and CPAF were issued uniforms in the newly unified **Royal Cambodian Armed Forces** (RCAF).

Prince Chakrapong, a son of Sihanouk and bitter rival of Ranariddh, refused to accept the election results and led an unsuccessful secession movement in the eastern provinces. In July 1994 Chakrapong and renegade general Sin Song staged an unsuccessful coup. Chakrapong was allowed to fly to France in exile, and Sin Song remained under house arrest.

Kingdom of Cambodia
A surprise outcome of the UN elections was the reinstatement of Sihanouk as reigning monarch in August 1993. Sihanouk is a maverick with semidivine status who commands widespread respect. Though his role is largely symbolic, the king has since given Phnom Penh a shot of 1960s nostalgia, returning old names to the major boulevards, setting up Royal Air Cambodge, and reintroducing the pre-1975 flag. RCAF soldiers wear a small lapel badge with a portrait of Sihanouk, and the new Cambodian currency features the king. A number of Cambodian ceremonies and festivals involving the king have been revived.

Outlawing the Khmer Rouge
After the election of the coalition government, war with the Khmer Rouge escalated. In November 1993 the last contingent of UN peacekeepers left. Long overdue but finally passed in July 1994 was a law outlawing the Khmer Rouge. Thirty-year prison terms are decreed for acts of secession and incitement to take up arms. When the Khmer Rouge office in Phnom Penh was shut down, Khmer Rouge Radio responded, "The move to close the office was a dictatorial and fascist measure by the police and troops of the

THE KHMER ROUGE TODAY

This insidious group was given its name by Prince Sihanouk, who derisively dubbed them "Cambodian Reds." When the Khmer Rouge were ousted in January 1979 after a four-year reign of terror, the leaders fled to Beijing. With Chinese support they formed an uneasy alliance with Sihanouk's forces and waged civil war against the Vietnamese-installed Heng Samrin regime. Even after the withdrawal of Vietnamese troops in 1989, and the Paris Peace Accords of 1991, the Khmer Rouge remained intransigent. They refused to surrender their arms to the UN, boycotted the UN-sponsored elections, and attempted to disrupt the voting process.

Membership figures for the Khmer Rouge are unknown, but it is guestimated there are perhaps 5,000 regular troops and 5,000 auxiliary troops left. Arrayed against them is an RCAF army of 130,000—on paper, anyway. As long as the leadership remains intact, the Khmer Rouge survives.

In July 1994 the elected government passed a bill outlawing the Khmer Rouge. This bill included a six-month amnesty program whereby defectors could be accepted into the RCAF. The government claims the amnesty program was a big success, with thousands of defections weakening Khmer Rouge strength. China has withdrawn its support for the Khmer Rouge; it's probable the Thai military still supports them.

The remarkable thing is that the Khmer Rouge are still around in the first place. Khmer Rouge policies do not appear to be any different today than they were during the days of the killing fields. The slaughter of innocent civilians continues. They have targeted ethnic Vietnamese—more than 100 Vietnamese were killed in racist attacks prior to the 1993 elections, which prompted 30,000 other Vietnamese to flee Cambodia. The Khmer Rouge have even attacked their trading partners, the Thais. In November 1994 the Khmer Rouge killed 17 loggers at a camp on the Thai border. The Khmer Rouge continue to blame foreign nations for Cambodia's problems—the US, Australia, France, and Vietnam.

Rebels Without a Cause

In 1994, for the first time since they were ousted from power by the Vietnamese, the Khmer Rouge targeted Khmer peasants, effectively abandoning their "hearts and minds" strategy and their traditional base of support. In the northwest they burned entire villages, in some cases massacring all the villagers. Some of these villages were populated by families of Khmer Rouge cadres, which caused defections to the government side. A number of military experts believe the Khmer Rouge are doomed because they have lost their ideological base. Their cause is hopeless, and without clear objectives. All they have now is an army, which has turned against the people. Others, however, point out that except for their four-year reign of terror in the 1970s, the Khmer Rouge have lived underground in difficult jungle conditions since the 1960s, waging war with governments more formidable than the present regime.

Hard-line Khmer Rouge leaders are now in their sixties. Pol Pot, Brother Number One, is thought to live in the Cardamom Mountains in western Cambodia; the other leaders, like Noun Chea (Brother Number Two), Ieng Sary, Son Sen, and Khieu Samphan, are believed to be in Phnom Malai in northwest Battambang Province near the Thai border. Khmer Rouge Radio operates from Phnom Malai. Controlling the sector on the northern border of Cambodia is the notorious one-legged general Ta Mok.

In 1979 Pol Pot and Ieng Sary were tried in absentia and convicted of genocide, though the verdict has not been recognized internationally. There are few historic precedents for the crime beyond the Tokyo and Nuremburg war trials. There has been no attempt to prosecute those involved under the Geneva convention's three violation headings— War Crimes, Crimes Against Humanity, and Genocide—and legal action in the World Court under the Genocide Convention has always faced Chinese and US opposition. In 1994, however, the US State Department established an Office of Cambodian Genocide Investigation, which is rather hypocritical considering the US caused the deaths of at least 50,000 Cambodians in bombing runs from 1969 to 1975, and backed the Khmer Rouge during the 1980s. In January 1995 the US State Department granted $700,000 to the Cambodian Genocide Project to document the Pol Pot era and drum up evidence for legal proceedings. Herein lies a problem: a number of the present leaders of Cambodia, including Second Prime Minister Hun Sen, are former members of the Khmer Rouge. And should former US Secretary of State Henry

Kissinger and his principal aide Winston Lord, who were primarily responsible for the secret bombing of Cambodia, be investigated also?

Today the Khmer Rouge control possibly 10-20% of Cambodia. Battambang is their last stronghold; they've held the area since 1965. In this zone the Khmer Rouge live in wooden houses equipped with electricity and television. They have their own farming equipment and operate their own sawmills and gem-mining operations. Both the Cambodian government and the UN Peacekeeping mission have accused the Thai military of collaborating with the Khmer Rouge, shipping arms to the guerrillas and buying or smuggling gems and timber. The Khmer Rouge are still a force to be reckoned with, as government troops learned when they attacked the unofficial Khmer Rouge capital of Pailin in early 1994. They held the base for several weeks and then suffered a humiliating defeat when the Khmer Rouge took it back and captured their tanks.

Corruption is an obstacle—Khmer Rouge troops managed to buy supplies directly from government officials during the campaign against Pailin.

Other Khmer Rouge bases in the north, such as Phnom Kulen, were captured with the help of Khmer Rouge defectors. These areas are now administered by former Khmer Rouge commanders. The government has received assistance from other nations in its fight. Training assistance is provided by Australia, France, and the US; in 1994 the government received a shipment of Czech tanks and Soviet Mi-17 helicopters. Increasingly, the government is coming round to the view that the best way to defeat the Khmer Rouge is not with guns but with economic and social development—building roads, electrifying villages, suppressing corruption, and raising living conditions. Anti-Vietnamese propaganda spread about by the Khmer Rouge may not work anymore: what people want are schools, medical care, and housing.

communist Vietnamese puppets." The Khmer Rouge made a declaration of a new provisional government with Khieu Samphan as leader. During a six-month amnesty period for defectors, thousands reportedly left the Khmer Rouge.

GOVERNMENT

On paper, Cambodia is a constitutional monarchy, run by a coalition in which ministerial portfolios are divided equally between Norodom Ranariddh (FUNCINPEC) and Hun Sen (CPP). First Prime Minister Ranariddh, son of the king, and Second Prime Minister Hun Sen, of the previous Vietnam-backed government, jockey for supreme authority. The bureaucracy is choked with FUNCINPEC and CPP duplicates for almost every important post. The coalition controls 109 of the national assembly's 120 seats, which makes the idea of opposition almost irrelevant. The BLDP holds a meager 10 seats.

Although the coalition was elected democratically, the behavior of those in power can hardly be called democratic. One of the assembly's few accomplishments was to vote its members a pay increase to $650 a month, in a country where the standard civil wage is around

$30 a month. They're also allowed to import cars without payment of duties; some members promptly sold their duty-exempt rights to third parties. The two prime ministers enjoy significant powers, approving major foreign investment deals and government contracts without parliamentary scrutiny. In 1994 they granted contracts worth $1.4 billion to five Malaysian companies, including management of Royal Air Cambodge, a logging concession for five percent of the country's land mass, and a casino in Sihanoukville. All revenue from logging was granted to the Ministry of Defense, bypassing the central treasury.

Administration: There are 20 provinces—most named after the provincial capital. Thus Battambang is the capital of Battambang Province, and Siem Reap the capital of Siem Reap Province.

THE MERCURIAL SIHANOUK

Nine-meter-high posters of the king graced the front of the Royal Palace and other key spots around Phnom Penh for the November 1993 celebration of 40 years of independence from the French. The portraits showed the handsome Sihanouk of the 1960s, with black hair and ruby-red lips. Sihanouk, with his love of pomp and pageantry, was in his element for the celebration. Today he is in his seventies, white-haired, and in frail health. He suffers from cancer and ailments of the arteries, and frequently flies to Beijing for treatment. Sihanouk bounced back into Phnom Penh in 1991 after 10 years in exile—he's good at reappearing.

Sihanouk once said it would take a Shakespeare to do literary justice to his early reign. An apt title might be: *The Man Who Would Be King—Again.* In a country buffeted by big powers, ruled by revolutionary lunatics, wracked by civil war, and bombed to bits by B-52s, Sihanouk is the ultimate survivor.

portrait of a young Sihanouk

Considered malleable by the French, Sihanouk was installed as king in 1941 when he was 19. He managed to negotiate independence from the French with a campaign employing threats, arrogance, charm, persuasion, and ultimatums. These became his trademark tactics. He abdicated in favor of his father in 1955 to become prime minister. Head of state again in 1960, when his father died, he presided over an autocratic regime that repressed or killed opponents, rigged elections, and pilfered funds. But he is popular among the peasants, who revere him as a god-king. During the 1950s and 1960s he promoted a national consciousness and unity of purpose that brought modest but solid prosperity to Cambodia. In 1970, while visiting Moscow, Sihanouk was deposed by the US-backed General Lon Nol. Sihanouk joined the radical Khmer Rouge in a guerrilla war against Lon Nol, but after the Khmer Rouge took power in 1975 they held Sihanouk and his family virtual prisoners in the Royal Palace.

In 1979, with the approach of the Vietnamese, royal family members flew by Chinese aircraft to Beijing, where they spent the 1980s in exile. Sihanouk still occupies a large government-donated compound near Tiananmen Square in Beijing, and a 60-room lakeside palace north of Pyongyang in North Korea. He receives a hefty stipend from the Chinese government, travels in a North Korean jetliner, and is shadowed by a retinue of North Korean bodyguards. His entourage includes a bevy of chefs who specialize in different cuisines, and a person who tests his food for poison. Sihanouk played a significant part in the Cambodian peace talks of 1991: without his involvement, they would not have been successful. After the Paris Peace Accords were signed, Sihanouk returned in triumph to Phnom Penh to head the Supreme National Council, paving the way for free elections. After the 1993 UN-sponsored elections ushered in a coalition government, Sihanouk was once again crowned king of Cambodia.

Although he has symbolic power only, Sihanouk has dabbled—some say meddled—in coalition policy and politics, influencing the outcome of proceedings. He is prone to ambiguous statements and rapid turnarounds of opinion. After a coalition decree outlawed the Khmer Rouge, Sihanouk argued to include them as a political force; a few

(previous page) doorway detail from Wat Xieng Thong, Luang Prabang;
(top) monks celebrating abbot's birthday at Wat Siene, Luang Prabang;
(bottom) niches inlaid with tiny Buddhas at Wat Sisaket, Vientiane

months later, he said that Pol Pot deserved to "go to the deepest hell."

Sihanouk presides over a personal household apparently riven with rivalries and intrigue. During the 1940s and 1950s Sihanouk took six wives or consorts and fathered 14 children. Two liaisons were with his aunts, both princesses; he also married a cousin. Prince Norodom Ranariddh, his eldest son and currently first prime minister, is one of two children Sihanouk fathered by a star of Cambodia's royal dance troupe. Prince Norodom Chakrapong, exiled after an attempted coup in 1994, was one of seven children born to the late Princess Pongsaomoni. Five other siblings died, some during the Khmer Rouge holocaust.

Sihanouk's current wife, Princess Monique Monineath, is the daughter of a Cambodian woman and an Italian diplomat—she caught Sihanouk's eye as a beauty queen in the early 1950s. She has become Sihanouk's principal adviser, and wields considerable influence.

Princess Monique and Prince Norodom Ranariddh are known to detest one another. Before his deportation Chakrapong swore to kill his stepbrother Ranariddh. In April 1994 Ranariddh fired the Foreign Minister, Prince Norodom Sirivudh, who is King Sihanouk's stepbrother. Although Prince Norodom Ranariddh is in line for the throne, there is at least one other contender: Prince Norodom Sihamoni, son of the king and Princess Monique. He lives in Paris, where he teaches classical western ballet; he's also the Cambodian ambassador to UNESCO. Sihamoni shares his father's interests in film, dance, and culture.

King Sihanouk is a saxophone player and a one-man Cambodian movie industry. In 1941 the prince made his first 16mm film; in 1966 he began directing color 35mm films in Khmer with French and English subtitles. Among his works are *Apsara* (1966), *The Enchanted Forest* (1967), *The Little Prince of the People* (1967), and *Rose of Bokor* (1969). These movies recall the halcyon days of the 1960s when the king and queen rode around in an open American sports car—the plot is invariably a melodramatic love story with opulent settings and automobiles. Sihanouk claims to have spent much of his 1980s exile in Pyongyang watching countless movies with fellow film fanatic Kim Il Sung. Sihanouk's favorite filming location is the Angkor region, to which he returned to make *I Shall Never See You Again, Oh My Beloved Kampuchea* (1991), *To See Angkor Again and Die* (1994), and *Peasants in Distress* (1994). The films are processed at a lab in Pyongyang, North Korea.

Introducing Khmer exhibits shipped for a special showing in Australia in 1992, King Norodom Sihanouk said, "They [the Khmer exhibits] represent the great cultural achievement of our people; they not merely celebrate the power and affluence of our great kings who built Angkor Wat in our golden age, but also the skills and artistic brilliance of the Cambodian people. As we embark on our reconstruction . . . we remain inspired by our Angkor heritage, and are confident we will once again achieve the greatness which was once ours." In later interviews, Sihanouk conceded his countrymen "can't match the glory of the Angkor period," but he reckoned they could at least rebuild the nation in the image of the socialist state he led in the 1950s and 1960s. Since then, the king has given himself to erratic emotional outbursts of dark despair over Cambodia's future.

ECONOMY

In the 1960s Cambodia supported itself from its own natural resources. Until 1970 it exported rice, sugarcane, coffee, cotton, rubber, spices, and fish. Civil war turned Cambodia into the beggar of Asia: in 1994 there were shortfalls of around 100,000 tons of rice due to drought, floods, and civil unrest. During the Pol Pot years Cambodia's economy was destroyed. The country lost its entire educated elite—engineers, architects, doctors, lawyers. The Hun Sen government that followed faced a trade and aid embargo from the West and was the only Third World country denied UN development aid. In the mid-1980s the State of Cambodia began a transition to a more liberal market economy, paralleling changes in Vietnam. However, the cessation of Soviet subsidies and the withdrawal of Vietnamese troops in 1989 forced the government to spend more on arms to defend itself. Cambodia's ailing economy was then given a tremendous boost in the 1992-93 UNTAC era by the presence of highly paid UN personnel. Their arrival sparked a boom that eased the country's transition to a market-driven economy, although at first causing high inflation. Today Cambodia's economy is heavily supported by foreign aid and investment.

Cambodia's government is desperate to jumpstart an economy ravaged by civil war and Vietnamese occupation. The hopes of the government lie with foreign investors and joint ventures. Increased stability has made Cambodia more attractive; the largest foreign investors are the Thais, Japanese, and French. The biggest investment is concentrated in the service sector, with hotels, restaurants, and bars. The markets are flooded with goods from Thailand, Vietnam, and Singapore.

Cambodia's economy revolves around agriculture, forestry, and marine resources. About 75% of the workforce is employed in agriculture, producing rubber, rice, maize, cassava, fruit, and timber. Boosting agricultural production is a major government priority, a task severely hampered by the presence of landmines. Rice production shortfalls caused by drought, floods, and civil unrest were recorded in the early 1990s. Despite a ban on logging imposed in 1992, operations continue on a large scale, with most exports going to Thailand and Japan. The Khmer Rouge oversee huge logging and gemmining operations, selling to the Thais with the apparent involvement of the Thai military. The cut is thought to be 50% for Thai contractors, five percent for the Thai military, and 45% for the Khmer Rouge. There are Thai villages close to Khmer Rouge zones where the main occupation is furniture making—all the wood used is Cambodian, as Thailand is virtually logged out.

Cambodia's tiny industrial base consists of a handful of factories making textiles and garments, furniture, farm implements, tires and rubber products, and agricultural processing. Cambodia's economy is hard to track because of the wide extent of blackmarketing, smuggling, corruption and graft. The government has little central control of the economy, and cannot police border zones.

THE PEOPLE

The Khmers

The Khmers account for roughly 90% of Cambodia's 10.4 million people. They are a mixed race of Austro-Indonesian origin with Melanesian features, and belong to the Mon-Khmer peoples, who most likely migrated from China some 4,000 years ago. The Indianized culture of the Khmers was influenced by contact with the civilizations of Java and India; over the centuries the Khmers mixed with other groups including the Thais, Vietnamese, and Chinese. The Khmers look physically different from Laotians, Thais, or Vietnamese. Their skin is noticeably darker, and they have thick black wavy hair. This might be the result of intermixing with Indian immigrants, who came into Cambodia from the 3rd century BC onwards.

A common Khmer garment is the *krama,* a checkered scarf (usually blue and white or red

Magical tattoos are believed to protect the body from bullets and knives.

and white). Apart from a headdress for both men and women, it can be used as a shawl, towel, belt, sunshade, or to carry goods or babies. Women like to wear brightly patterned sarongs and tops—the more eye-blinding the colors and patterns the better. This is a legacy of the Pol Pot years, when everyone was forced to wear black. The *sampot* is a Cambodian garment consisting of a rectangular piece of cloth worn around the hips and tied in front, with the gathered cloth then inserted between the legs and passed through the back of the belt.

The majority of ethnic Khmers live in small agricultural settlements. Up to three-quarters of the population occupies fertile regions between Lake Tonle Sap in the northwest and the area south of Phnom Penh. Most live in houses raised on stilts, safe from the damp, thieves, snakes, and feral animals. Structures are open on all sides to the air to allow breezes to pass through. Rural communities work on a cooperative basis, with little competition between individuals—perhaps attributable to the effect of centuries of Buddhist faith. This might also account for the people's cheerful, open disposition and friendly nature.

Minority Groups

Minority groups in Cambodia were decimated in the 1975-79 Pol Pot era. Many were killed or starved to death; others fled across the borders into Vietnam or Thailand. The result is that less than 10% of the current population consists of non-Khmers.

Hilltribe Groups: A number of tribal groups inhabit the forested mountain zones of Cambodia, and may number over 200,000 people. In the Elephant Mountains to the southwest are the Saoch, in the Cardamom Mountains the Peur, in the northwest the Kuy. The largest hilltribe groups live in the northeast in Ratanakiri and Mondulkiri provinces. Over 80% of Ratanakiri's population of 72,000 is classified as hilltribe people, mainly Jarai, Krung, Brou, and Tampuan. The 12 ethnic minority groups of the northeast are collectively called Khmer Loeu (highlanders). Some of these groups are found across the border in Vietnam's Central Highlands or southern Laos.

Because these areas are remote and the infrastructure is weak, highlanders have little access to education or health care. Most are animist and live by hunting and slash-and-burn agriculture. They farm rice and grow vegetables and raise water buffalo and cows. Although most hilltribers conform to Khmer dress, others retain their customs. Krung tribeswomen wear sarongs, go bare-breasted, and smoke long-stemmed pipes. Brou tribeswomen have large pierced earlobes and wear earrings sculpted from chunky ivory tusks. Their faces are tattooed, and they wear bead necklaces and brass anklets.

Cham: The historic enemy of the Angkor kings, the Cham originally came from the Vietnamese coastal kingdom of Champa. In the 15th century, the Cham were attacked by the Viet from the north and pushed south into the Mekong Delta and Cambodia, where they settled along rivers and lakes to pursue fishing. The Cham originally adhered to Hindu and Brahman beliefs, but, influenced by the Malays, they converted to Islam—most are Sunni Muslim. There are about 165,000 Cham in Cambodia. Their schools, mosques, and other buildings were all destroyed by Pol Pot's forces. Some 20 mosques have been rebuilt in the 1990s. The Cham live in riverside towns north of Phnom Penh, such as Kompong Chhnang and Kompong Cham, and engage in fishing, cattle trading, and silk weaving. They wear batik sarongs, similar to those found in Malaysia. Because of the laws of the Koran, intermarriage is rare with the Khmers.

Chinese: The Chinese in Cambodia number perhaps 175,000, and are found mainly in Phnom Penh and larger towns. Seafaring Chinese traders found their way to Cambodia as early as the 12th century. In the 18th and 19th centuries, large numbers of Chinese immigrated to Southeast Asia. In the French era, the Chinese were employed as middlemen and plantation workers. As in neighboring Thailand, the Chinese integrated with the community through intermarriage and controlled a significant amount of banking, transport, and trade. After their numbers were decimated during the Khmer Rouge years, the Chinese appear to be resuming their old role, at least in Phnom Penh.

Vietnamese: The Vietnamese, numbering perhaps 150,000, usually live in separate communities in Cambodia, and are called "youn" by the Khmers—a derogatory term that means "savage from the north." The Vietnamese have always been at odds with the Khmers; the once-great Khmer Empire shrank when attacked by the Vietnamese and Thais. Khmer lands in the Mekong Delta were taken by the Vietnamese, and offshore islands are still subject to dispute. The Vietnamese settled in Cambodia as rice farmers, plantation workers, and fisherfolk. In Phnom Penh, the Vietnamese are mostly artisans or shopkeepers.

Under the Lon Nol regime, and again under Pol Pot, many Vietnamese were killed or expelled. In the 1979-89 period the Vietnamese returned—with the Vietnamese army. Following Khmer Rouge attacks in 1993, about 20,000 Vietnamese fishing people fled Lake Tonle Sap to Chrey Thom on the border of Cambodia and Vietnam. The government has drafted a new immigration law that calls into question the status of those Vietnamese who immigrated in the 1990s. The UN has protested the tenor of the bill.

Thai: The latest traders to arrive in significant numbers are the Thais. They're involved in border trading with the Khmer Rouge, and are also numerous in Phnom Penh where they work in joint-venture businesses.

Khmer Krom: These ethnic Cambodians do not live in Camodia, rather the south of Vietnam, mostly in the Mekong Delta. Estimates of their numbers range from one to six million. Their ancestry dates back to the 17th century, when the area was governed by Cambodia. The Cambodians call this region Kampuchea Krom: the Khmer Krom dress as Vietnamese and carry Vietnamese national identification cards, but remain staunchly Khmer in their beliefs and customs. They are discriminated against by both the Cambodians and the Vietnamese.

RELIGION

THERAVADA BUDDHISM

Early Cambodia was largely Hindu, although this was always tempered with a large measure of animism and Brahmanism. Mahayana Buddhism was favored by 12th-century King Jayavarman VII, but his successors reverted to Shivaism, with court ceremonies influenced by Indian Brahmans. Eventually it was the Theravada strain of Buddhism that took hold in Cambodia. Theravada Buddhism was imported from Sri Lanka via Burma and Thailand in the late 13th century. In the 19th century, Cambodian monastic orders modeled themselves on the Thammayut (royalist) and Mahanikai sects of Theravada Buddhism in Thailand. The Thammayut sect is a stricter order than Mahanikai and operates under royal patronage. Both sects have recently been revived in Cambodia.

Before civil war erupted in Cambodia in the late 1960s, the temple, or *wat,* was the focal point of most Cambodian communities. Monks played an active role in Cambodian nationalist movements of the 1930s and 1940s and assumed an even larger role in mass education and the elimination of illiteracy. When the Khmer Rouge came to power Theravada Buddhism was not merely prohibited—it was physically expunged. Temples were turned into storehouses, factories, slaughterhouses, and prison centers; others were closed down or demolished. The monkhood was disbanded. Monks were ordered to work in the fields or face execution. Nuns were likewise forced to abandon their faith. Buddhism was linked by the Khmer Rouge with the monarchy and thus represented an obstacle to revolutionary change. Khmer Rouge Education Minister Yun Yat observed in 1978: "Under the old regime peasants believed in Buddhism, which the ruling class utilized as a propaganda instrument. With the development of revolutionary consciousness, the people stopped believing and the monks left the temples. The problem gradually becomes extinguished. Hence there is no problem."

Before 1975 Cambodia supported an estimated 64,000 monks; by the time of the Vietnamese takeover in 1979 fewer than 2,000 remained, mostly in Thai refugee camps. The rest had died from execution, starvation, or disease. Most of the country's 3,000 temples and monasteries were destroyed. Buddhism in Cambodia has not yet recovered.

In 1989 Theravada Buddhism was again sanctioned as the national religion, and novices were again accepted into monasteries. Buddhist leaders are once more highly respected leaders of

temple offerings

the local community. The Supreme Patriarch, Preah Maha Ghosananda, was nominated for the 1994 Nobel Peace Prize for his efforts in promoting peace and reconciliation. Ghosananda led several peace marches across Cambodia in the early 1990s, and has been active in preserving the environment. Cambodian monks have set about teaching and rebuilding what the Khmer Rouge destroyed.

Karmic Carryover

Buddhism is based on the ethical philosophy of Siddhartha Gautama, born around 560 BC in North India. After six years of meditation Gautama became the Buddha, or "the enlightened one"; he spent the latter half of his life traveling and preaching. It was only later the Buddha came to be worshipped as a divine figure, along with an ever-increasing pantheon of other deities. A number of Buddhist schools developed—the two largest are Theravada, which spread to southern Asia, and Mahayana, dominant in northern Asia. The more austere Theravadans believe in a personal quest for enlightenment, while Mahayana Buddhists work toward the enlightenment and salvation from suffering of all beings. Theravadans claim to adhere to the original teachings of Buddha; Mahayana Buddhists believe in both Buddha and a vast array of bodhisattvas, or enlightened beings.

Buddhist beliefs focus on the causes and eradication of suffering. The ultimate goal is cessation of suffering, or attainment of the state of nirvana (enlightenment, ultimate truth, gaining of wisdom). Buddha taught that the answers to life's mysteries could be found within oneself, and that a person leading a worthy life (avoiding extremes, doing right actions) could carry over karmic energy into a later existence.

Classical Buddhism interprets the goal of nirvana as breaking a long cycle of birth, death, and rebirth; contemporary Buddhism also sees nirvana as enlightenment attainable during one's own lifetime. In any case, only a

Khmer-style Buddha seated on naga Mucilinda

BOB RACE

select few who renounce worldly pursuits and devote their lives to study and meditation can expect to attain nirvana. For most adherents, a more humble pursuit involves redressing the balance of karma. Karma is cause and effect. A tree drops a seed that becomes a tree—but this tree is not the same as the original one. Theravadans believe that energy from one life can be attached to a new person in the next life; higher monks, it is believed, can direct karmic energy and channel it into specific rebirth. Theravadans also believe that they may have inherited some bad karma from previous existences— a situation that must be corrected by doing good deeds in the present life.

Buddhist practices in Cambodia hinge on accruing merit—making donations to temples or giving food to monks, for example. By becoming a monk for a short period of time, a young man can accrue merit not only for himself but also for his entire family. To release captive birds at a temple is considered meritorious, even though the birds are captured and sold for this express purpose. Common temple offerings consist of incense sticks, flowers, candles, and sometimes food.

Iconography

Buddhist statuary and art features a system derived from Pali texts of 32 special physical features of the Buddha. There are several poses, called *asanas,* and a variety of hand gestures, called *mudras,* which illustrate key events in the Enlightened One's life. Think of this as a kind of sign language—each gesture conveys a meaning to the onlooker. The seated position indicates meditation; the standing position denotes preaching; the reclining position represents Buddha's entrance into nirvana at the moment of his physical death. In Khmer art, Buddha is mostly represented in the seated meditation pose.

A popular depiction of Buddha in Khmer sculpture is the *naga*-protection pose. It shows a meditating Buddha under the shelter of a hood formed by a multiple-headed *naga.* According to Buddhist legend, on the day of Buddha's enlightenment a torrential downpour began, but Buddha was in such deep meditation he was unaware of the rain. The serpent Mucilinda coiled his body to form a throne, lifting Buddha off the ground; the serpent's cobra-like multiple heads formed a large hood to shelter Buddha from the rain.

OTHER FAITHS

Because the Khmers are the overwhelming majority in Cambodia, there are few other religious groups in evidence. The Chinese community practices Taoism and Confucianism; the Vietnamese community includes Catholics and some followers of quasi-Buddhist Mekong Delta cults; the Cham are Sunni Muslim.

To the northeast, hilltribe groups practice animism and ancestor worship. So, to some degree, do most rural Cambodians. Animism, or spirit worship, coexists with Buddhism, which has always been tolerant of it. Sacrifices are offered to the spirits of wind, water, and earth, upon which harvests depend. Spirits in all material things—trees, rivers, mountains, stones—exert a profound influence on daily life. Animist practices are evident at harvest festivals, and also surface in ceremonies such as weddings and funerals. Departed ancestors become guardian spirits, who must be honored to ensure the well-being of the family.

MYTHOLOGY AND THE ARTS

Cambodia's cultural traditions were virtually destroyed under four years of Khmer Rouge domination and are only just beginning to recover. The return of Sihanouk has bolstered the arts—he is, for instance, a keen patron of Cambodian dance.

Most early Khmer literature has been lost or destroyed through conquest. Only stone inscriptions survive, etched in either ancient Khmer, Sanskrit, or Pali. Modern Cambodian script derives from southern India with overlays of Sanskrit: it is written from left to right with no separation between words.

Cambodian artforms derive from Hindu and Buddhist legends—the Indian epics of the Ramayana and the Mahabharata, and the Jataka Tales. Another Khmer epic is the poem of Angkor Wat. The Mahabharata is a partly narrative and partly didactic epic, describing the struggle between two family clans—the heroic Pandavas and the evil Kauravas—for possession of northern India. After 18 days of frenzied battle the Pandavas emerge victorious, and the eldest Pandava is crowned king. The Jataka Tales—fables detailing the previous lives of Buddha—are well known in Cambodia, in several modern adaptations. The Jataka Tales detail the lives of Buddha. They often take the form of parables, rather like Aesop's fables, with dramatic adventures resolved by nonviolent means. The most important lives of Buddha are the last 10, during which a particular virtue was perfected.

Modern Cambodian writing is mostly the work of exiles living abroad, and is heavily influenced by French literature.

Ramayana

The Reamker is the Khmer adaptation of the Sanskrit epic poem the Ramayana; the full version of the Reamker takes about 50 hours to recite. The Ramayana, first written by Valmiki over 2,000 years ago, is the most important myth in Southeast Asia, with varying forms extant in India, Thailand, Laos, Burma, and Indonesia.

The Ramayana tells the story of Prince Rama, an incarnation of the Hindu god Vishnu, who sets out in quest of his princess, Sita, and to destroy Ravana, a powerful demon intent on world domination. The epic portrays the struggle between good and evil with many subplots and doses of sex, drugs, violence, adventure, and magic. Subplots are embroidered with local myth and folklore. In the Cambodian version, beautiful Sita is abducted by the 10-headed, 20-armed, wicked King Tosakan, who imprisons her in his palace on the island of Lanka (Sri Lanka). Prince Rama sets off to rescue Sita; in this endeavor he is assisted by his brother Lakshman and a simian army under the mischie-

(continues on page 443)

DANCE IN CAMBODIA

by Toni Shapiro

Dance, music, and drama have always been prominent in Cambodian life, indispensable as rites of passage and religious and national ceremonies. Traditionally, each temple in Cambodia had its own *pin peat* orchestra, an ensemble accompanying religious ceremonies, classical dance, and shadow puppet plays. It consists of xylophones, string and wind instruments, and three types of drums. Throughout the centuries, dance troupes have performed episodes from epic tales and legends for the people in temple compounds around the country.

Cambodians trace the unique stylized movements of their dances back hundreds of years to bas-relief sculptures of celestial dancers *(apsaras)* at the grand 12th-century temple of Angkor. As far back as the 7th century, inscriptions tell of dancers associated with temples. In many of the ancient Hinduized states of Southeast Asia, thousands of magnificent carvings of celestial and earthly dancers adorn temple walls. Dancers also had a place within the confines of the palace as they formed part of the king's regalia, used in the maintenance and symbolic display of royal prowess.

The Angkor Court

Along the east gallery of Angkor Wat is a panel of bas-reliefs featuring a huge stone *naga* (sacred serpent) that twists and pulls, while the mythic Sea of Milk churns in turbulence. From this movement, hundreds of flying *apsaras* are born. *Apsaras,* thought to embody purity of spirit and eternal beauty, dance to entertain the gods. They symbolize the well-being of the Cambodian people.

For centuries, royalty communicated through the medium of dance with the divine world, seeking to guarantee fertility of the land and prosperity for the people. At least once a year a sacred ceremony known as *buong suong* was installed under royal patronage. In *buong suong* divine beings are asked for blessings in exchange for offerings of elaborately presented fruits, meats, incense, flowers, and, most importantly, sacred music and dance. Swathed in velvet and brocade, wearing golden tiaras or fearsome masks and delicate flowers, the dancers enact sacred stories.

New Year Ritual Dance

As part of a sequence of dances in the *buong suong* ritual, dancers would recreate the battle between the legendary figures of Moni Mekhala and Ream Eyso. The female deity Moni Mekhala is protectress of the waters, the giant Ream Eyso controller of storms. Legend has it that long ago these two were students of a wise and powerful hermit. One day the hermit offered them a challenge. Each was to collect the morning dew; the first to present a glassful of nature's gift would be the winner, and receive a magic ball. Early next morning Ream Eyso gathered as many leaves as he could, letting the droplets of dew slide from each leaf into his glass. Moni Mekhala spread a handkerchief on the grass and left it overnight; by morning, the cloth was damp. Squeezing it, she filled her glass. She arrived at the hermit's abode with a full cup of dew before the giant did.

As a reward for her ingenuity, the hermit fashioned a magic glittering ball of dew and bestowed it on her. Ream Eyso received a magic ax as a consolation prize. But the small ball of Moni Mekhala was much more powerful than Ream Eyso's ax; he *had* to have that ball. Ream Eyso stalked Moni Mekhala and threatened her; she teased and scolded him in return. In desperation and fury, Ream Eyso flung his spangled ax, barely missing the goddess. Moni Mekhala tossed her ball into the air, creating a bolt of lightning that blinded the giant. He collapsed, and Moni Mekhala glided away. But the giant did not die; seconds later, sight regained, he realized what had happened. In frustration and anger, he disappeared into the clouds.

Through this tale Cambodians trace the origin of thunder and lightning. Ream Eyso's ax crashes through the air, and Moni Mekhala's sparkling ball lights up the heavens. Together they bring rain—the symbol of renewed life, imparting fertility to Cambodia's farmlands. The confrontation between Ream Eyso and Moni Mekhala recurs every year, around the time of the Cambodian New Year in mid-April. This is the height of the hot season, just before monsoon rains wash away the dust and bring nourishment to the fields. When Cambodians see dark clouds forming in the sky, they know Ream Eyso and Moni Mekhala will soon engage in their eternal battle, flooding the ricefields. The giant will be vanquished, but only temporarily. Sooner or later he will return.

Sihanouk's Patronage

Over the centuries, Cambodian royal dancers remained, for the most part, cloistered within the palace compound. They danced for the public, as well as for deities, at the annual Water Festival in Phnom Penh, and at various sites during ritual ceremonies. Provincial troupes, some headed by retired court dancers, were found throughout the country.

After Norodom Sihanouk ascended to the throne in 1941, circumstances changed. Though they still performed at sacred and royal functions, dancers lived on their own for the first time, outside the palace walls, free to marry and raise children.

Since the middle of this century, Cambodian dance has combined spirituality with a growing emphasis on secular performances held on a proscenium stage in front of an audience. Queen Kossamak, Sihanouk's mother, was particularly influential in elevating dancers to the role of international symbols of Cambodia. Besides providing domestic entertainment for foreign dignitaries in Cambodia, the Royal Dance Troupe often accompanied Sihanouk on his official visits abroad. The association between the dancers and Cambodia grew so strong that in the 1960s a French observer noted: "Rare are the countries who by their name evoke the image of a dancer. This is the privilege of Cambodia, from where the vision of the refined dancer rises."

In the 1960s the University of Fine Arts was founded. The school offered professional training in several forms of Cambodian theater, shadow puppetry, music, and folk dance. In 1970, after a coup sent the royal family into exile, the court dancers were no longer messengers between the sovereign and the deities. Yet they continued practicing in the Royal Palace compound, performing and touring abroad.

The Khmer Rouge Years

Under the Khmer Rouge regime all dance and music, as the Cambodians knew them, were forbidden. Along with the entire urban population, dancers were sent into the countryside in 1975. Fearful the Khmer Rouge would kill them if they knew of their previous connections to the palace, many dancers tried to hide their identities, telling cadres they'd been vegetable sellers, pedicab drivers, or seamstresses.

There were some dance performances during the years of Khmer Rouge rule, but the style of dancing was unrecognizable to those who had practiced or watched this art before. "Sometimes they marched us and forced us to watch their dances," remembers one royal dancer. "They wore only black and danced in place, glorifying manual labor. But I must admit part of me could sit back and recall the beautiful memories of my past, when I was practicing or performing, guided by my teachers. And I could imagine what it would be like to be dancing again."

(continues on next page)

Classical dancers practice under the watchful eye of their instructor.

DANCE IN CAMBODIA

(continued)

Contemporary Dance

After the Vietnamese ousted Pol Pot in 1979, surviving dancers regrouped. They discovered that close to 90% of their professional colleagues—dancers, musicians, actors, playwrights, poets—had perished. Almost all the delicately carved instruments and intricately embroidered costumes and accoutrements had been lost or destroyed. In one instance, artists found a priceless *roneat* (xylophone) base in use as a pig trough. The artists immediately set about reclaiming their rich cultural heritage by performing and teaching. They hoped to instill a sense of pride in their students and in their shattered communities. The school of dance, a division of the University of Fine Arts, reopened in Phnom Penh in 1980. Many of the students were children of artists who'd died. Now those children are teachers and performers, and new classes open each year.

Dance retained a high profile throughout the 1980s and continues to do so today. During the 1980s dancers toured the countryside, performed on television at New Year celebrations, and were the highlight of many national ceremonies. Dance and music were also priorities in the chaotic and dangerous refugee camps on the Thai-Cambodian border. Since the return of royalty and renewal of open expression of religious faith, dancers have again become official messengers to the deities, asking for spiritual blessings in ceremonies staged at the Royal Palace and the temple of Angkor. Princess Bopha Devi, King Sihanouk's daughter, was a star dancer of the 1960s; she returned to Cambodia with her father and now helps oversee dance training and performances.

Dancers are invited to perform at temple festivals and for tourist groups, photojournalists, and filmmakers. The National Department of Arts sponsors performing arts festivals every year or two. Troupes and individual artists from all over the country participate. Dancers also perform at the government's request to honor visiting dignitaries and on national holidays. Dancers from two prestigious troupes—the University of Fine Arts Troupe and the Royal Dance Troupe of the National Department of Arts—are often busy touring abroad.

Dance was previously performed for tourists in Phnom Penh's Bassac Theater, but in February 1994 this historical site was severely damaged by fire. Check with a hotel receptionist or the Ministry of Culture and Fine Arts for the location of cultural performances. The Hotel Sofitel Cambodiana stages regular performances.

Training

Annual auditions for the dance school in Phnom Penh attract more than a hundred applicants. In the past, children began dancing at five or six years of age when their bones and muscles were considered supple enough to be trained and molded properly. Today youngsters audition at age eight or nine, after a few years of public schooling. This is necessary, school officials insist, to raise the general educational level following the devastation of the Khmer Rouge years.

Mastering Cambodian dance requires many years of discipline and dedication. Students work on technique every morning and attend academic classes in the afternoon. At the dance school, a division of the University of Fine Arts in Phnom Penh, dancers specialize in classical (court) dance, folk dance, or *lakhon khol*. Court dancers perform episodes from the Reamker, or Cambodian Ramayana.

The dancers were traditionally all female, until Sihanouk's time, when men began to dance the roles of monkeys and the hermit. *Lakhon khol* is an all-male form of masked dance-drama. This kind of troupe was attached to temples or performed at provincial governors' palaces; there is still a *lakhon khol* troupe in Kandal province. Many folk dances were created in the 1960s and '70s by teachers and students at the University of Fine Arts. They based these works on rituals, music, daily activities, movement patterns, or the dances of people in the provinces.

The first phase of dance school studies emphasizes training in rhythm and memorization of the basic positions and movements. The second phase begins after the sixth year of study and continues for another three: in this phase, students are taught to analyze the movements, emotions, and symbolism of the dance. Throughout the dancer's career, a special exercise routine is practiced; designed to encourage the hyperextension of the elbows, the deep arch of the spine, and the extreme flexibility of the fingers—all essential to the Cambodian dance aesthetic.

The first months of study are undertaken without musical accompaniment. A teacher beats out the rhythm on the floor with a wooden stick; as they move, the children sing the rhythm of the *sampho*, the drum that carries the beat in the *pin peat* ensemble. This allows the younger dancers to master both the rhythm and the basic postures and movements of Cambodian dance without being distracted by the complexity of the music. With a live orchestra, advanced students practice an expanded version of the same series of thousands of core gestures and steps. Elaborate dances and dance-dramas are constructed from combinations of these movements and postures. Individual dancers also work on perfecting movements particular to a character role in Cambodian dance or dance-drama. The role could be the graceful and gentle female (a princess or female deity), the brave and noble male (a prince or male deity), the forceful and fearsome giant, or the sprightly monkey. The monkey is a role danced only by men.

Before each performance, dancers light incense and offer prayers of thanks to their teachers and to the spirits of the dance, asking for guidance and blessings to ensure a successful performance. The dancers add an extra prayer these days—one for lasting peace in Cambodia.

Repertoire

In a stage performance, you're likely to see a combination of classical and folk dances, with perhaps a *lakhon khol* excerpt. Some of the dances are briefly described here.

Classical Dance: Apsara was choreographed in the 1950s, with costuming based on the bas-relief carvings of celestial dancers at Angkor Wat and danced by five or seven women wearing distinctive multispired crowns. The chorus sings of the delight of being surrounded by beautiful flowers in a garden. **Hanuman and Sovann Macha** is an excerpt from the Reamker dance-drama. Monkey-general Hanuman pursues and flirts with the golden mermaid Sovann Macha. **Moni Mekhala and Ream Eyso** is performed as part of the sacred New Year ceremony; the duet is also danced as a theatrical piece. **Tep Monorom** is a large group dance where the women appear as celestial beings moving in and out of formation, around and across the stage, while the chorus sings of their heavenly bliss.

Folk Dances: Beh Korvanh (Cardamom Picking) is derived from the Peur people of western Cambodia, who collect spices in the Cardamom Mountains. This dance portrays aspects of Peur lifestyle and clothing. **Nesat** (Fishing) uses different kinds of real fish traps as the dancers present a comic and romantic outing in the countryside. **Tbal Kadeung** (Rice Threshing) depicts adventures in the countryside, when women become angry at the men for abandoning their tasks at the first sight of the palm juice seller. **Kangaok Pailin** (Peacock of Pailin) comes from the Pailin region and features a story of a princess who dreams of a peacock presenting a Buddhist sermon. Shortly thereafter, the princess falls ill; nobody can cure her. The king's hunter takes a female peacock into the forest and has her dance to attract a male peacock, who can speak. The hunter catches the male peacock; asked to recite sermons for the princess, the captured peacock said he'd be delighted to if only she'll set him free. She does so, and he promises to return every Buddhist holy day. Two elaborately adorned "peacocks" enact this dance of attraction, with onlookers clapping and beating drums.

vous monkey-god Hanuman. Overcoming impossible obstacles, the rescuers build a causeway to Lanka. After a pitched battle between the monkey army of Hanuman and the demons and giants of Tosakan, Tosakan is killed by an arrow from the magic bow of Rama, and Sita is rescued. Rama suspects her of unfaithfulness, so she throws herself on a burning pyre to prove her purity. Agni, the god of fire, takes her from the flames, and reunites the couple.

The Ramayana is the basis for classical dance in Cambodia, which has transcended mere culture and become fused with the Cambodian national identity. Classical dancers are Cambodia's true diplomats abroad. The Ramayana is also the basis for folk plays and shadow plays. Shadow-play characters are cut out of leather and painted. Peripatetic shadow puppeteers usually perform at local festivals.

ARCHITECTURE AND SCULPTURE

From the 10th to 13th centuries, the kings of the powerful Khmer Empire erected scores of temples and military outposts. Apart from those found in present-day Cambodia, Khmer temples are also scattered across northeast Thailand, particularly at Phimai, and at Wat Phu in Laos.

KHMER SCULPTURAL MOTIFS

Motifs in early Cambodian sculpture, bas-reliefs, and lintel carvings were heavily influenced by Brahmanism and Hinduism. In Hinduism are three important gods: Brahma, the Creator of the Universe; Shiva the Destroyer and Reproducer; and Vishnu the Preserver. Each inspired a cult of worship at Angkor, and each is depicted with special objects, clothing, and mount. Four-faced Brahma rides a sacred goose called Hamsa. Four-armed Vishnu rides a half-man, half-bird creature known as Garuda; Vishnu's consort is Lakshmi, goddess of beauty. Shiva carries a trident and rides Nandi, a bull; his consort is Uma. The son of Shiva and Uma is Ganesh, who has a corpulent human body and the head of an elephant. Other common figures are Indra, god of the sky, who rides a white three-headed elephant; eight-armed Yama, the judge of the dead; and two-headed Agni, god of fire, who rides a rhinoceros. Kama, the god of love, carries a bow and a case of floral arrows made of lotus, jasmine, and lily.

Linga: One of the most important motifs in Khmer sculpture is the linga, a stylized erect phallus, symbolic of Shiva and his powers of reproduction. It rests upright on a yoni base, symbolizing the female organ. The linga on a yoni base was adopted by Khmer kings as a symbol of their divine power: each king built a new temple to shelter his special linga. Lingas were usually made of stone, but some were made of quartz and others were reputed to have been made of solid gold.

Naga: The snake or aquatic serpent figures prominently in Hindu mythology as part of fertility cults. The Khmers claim their descent from the mythical union of Indian Brahman Kaundinya and Soma, the daughter of the *naga* king. *Nagas* proliferate through Khmer temples—found in the form of stylized cobras on balustrades, finials, and bas-reliefs. The *naga* may feature five, seven, or nine fan-shaped heads. Ananta was the name of a large serpent that Vishnu reclined on during a cosmic sleep. Vasuki is a serpent that served as a rope in Churning the Sea of Milk (a Hindu creation myth) to release the essence of life. The *naga* crossed over into Buddhism where it is considered the deity of rain, and also the protector of Buddha's law.

Garuda: Half-bird, half-man, this creature is the mount of Vishnu, and the enemy of the *naga*. Garuda is usually portrayed with the torso of a human, and the beak, wings, legs, and claws of an eagle. Garuda appears on lower temple walls, appearing to help support the structure, with arms stretched above his head grasping the tails of serpents.

Apsara: The celestial dancer is a Khmer innovation. Born of the action of Churning the Sea of Milk, the beautiful *apsaras* live in the heavens. These dancing angels are the epitome of female beauty at the court of Angkor, and indulge the sexual pleasures of ultimate Khmer male incarnations. Placement of the legs in arched position with bent knees is associated with flying.

Lotus: In Buddhism, the lotus is symbolic of purity and divine birth. Like the Buddha born into an impure world, the lotus originates in impure mud and rises above the murky water to blossom high above it. The lotus may be sculpted at the base or crown of statuary. At Angkor's Neak Pean, a tower island set in an artificial lake is decorated with lotus petals at the base, and capped with lotus blossoms. *Apsara* dancers are sometimes shown in bas-reliefs dancing on a bed of lotuses.

Lokesvara: In Mahayana Buddhism, the bodhisattva of compassion is Lokesvara (Avalokitesvara in Sanskrit). It is thought the four-headed entry gates and massive stone Bayon heads at Angkor are renditions of Lokesvara, combined with features of King Jayavarman VII. The serene heads, with downcast eyes and faint smiles, are the icons of Angkor.

Guardians: Serving as guardian statues at numerous temples are Khmer-style lions, or **singhas.** These often line temple entrances and steps. Because the lion is not native to Cambodia, features are crude and stylized. A guardian appearing over temple doorways is **Kala,** a jawless monster with bulging eyes, grinning face, horns, claws, and pointed ears. Kala had a voracious appetite, and asked Shiva for a victim to satisfy its hunger. Angered by the request, Shiva commanded Kala to devour its own body. Kala swallowed its body, but not its head. Shiva ordered the head placed over temple doors as a reminder of his powers. A similar-looking bodyless creature is the demon **Rahu,** with hands but no claws. Rahu may hold the moon in its mouth: according to legend, the moon is the source of the elixir of immortality. Rahu sometimes swallows the moon, causing an eclipse—the moon reappears shortly, popping out of Rahu's throat.

Early Khmer temples were made of brick and laterite. After about AD 950 sandstone was reserved for sacred temples, while brick was used for secondary structures and laterite for foundations. Wooden buildings have not survived centuries of warfare and decay.

Khmer temples were built according to symbolic criteria. The central tower, or *prasat,* was built on a pyramidal base representing sacred Mount Meru, navel of the world in Hindu cosmology. An enclosing wall represented the earth, a moat beyond was viewed as the cosmic ocean. The spirit of the devaraja (divine king) was enshrined in a linga (stylized phallus, symbol of Shiva) at the center of the temple complex. People believed their king communicated directly with the gods. The central tower sanctuaries housed images of the Hindu—and later Buddhist—deities to whom the temples were dedicated. After death, the king, members of the royal family, and high priests may have been cremated, their ashes kept at the temple. A subsequent king would dedicate a new temple to shelter his special linga.

Although sandstone Khmer temples followed formulaic structural codes, there was great latitude for innovation. Most structures are oriented from east to west, with the main entrance at the east. Many structures were crudely erected, relying on gravity and a good fit between stones to hold the structure in place, although bronze clamps were sometimes employed. The arch or vault was unknown to Angkorian architects—they employed a false vault, known as the corbel arch.

The most distinctive feature of Khmer architecture is the sanctuary tower in the shape of a budding flower, a refinement that dominates Angkor Wat. Philip Rawson describes Angkor Wat's towers in *The Art of Southeast Asia:* "The tower spires have eight stories and a crown, and are square, with a series of multiple recessed profiles and center projections that makes them look octagonal. They show the full-fledged curved outline of a sprouting bud, which gives the impression that each story is rising out of the one beneath. This impression, combined with the facade motifs of all the gable-ends—which have upturned corners and rise well beyond the ridges of their roofs—is responsible for the extraordinary dynamic, rising effect of the structures."

In the 12th century, King Jayavarman VII added a new dimension to Hindu inspiration, layering on a design that derived from Mahayana Buddhism. This led to the stunning innovation of the Buddhist temple-mountain of the Bayon and the gates of Angkor Thom.

There was no great emphasis on temple interiors in Khmer architecture—the structures were not built for the people, but for the king and high priests. Thus the interiors tend to be windowless, and many have false doors. In this sense, the buildings could be considered gigantic sculptures—ornately carved walls and

heads of Lokesvara at the Bayon

lintels festoon the exterior, while the interiors are bare. The soft sandstone used at Angkor lent itself to relief sculpting: niche and bas-relief carving in sandstone in the Angkor region is especially elaborate. In some places, such as at Banteay Srei, no exterior surface is left unadorned. Galleries at Angkor Wat and the Bayon bear huge bas-reliefs of Hindu and Khmer historical themes.

Free-standing sculpture appeared in the 9th century, in the role of temple guardians. Khmer lions lined stairways, five-headed *nagas* formed balustrades, garudas appeared at foundation corners. Lintels bearing monsters guarded temple entrances. Temple interiors bristled with bronze and stone sculpture. Toward the end of the 12th century the development of portraiture in stone was one of the most remarkable achievements of Khmer art. A sophisticated

level of bronze-casting technology was achieved at Angkor, revealed in a massive bronze reclining Vishnu torso unearthed in 1936 at Angkor. A number of smaller bronze items, such as oil lamps and incense burners, survive. Wooden sculpture most likely existed at Angkor too, but none has survived. Carved wood pieces from the 18th century display the considerable skills of Khmer craftsmen.

Modern Khmer sculpture and mural painting is fostered at the School of Fine Arts in Phnom Penh, where students fashion copies of Angkor statuary in wood, marble, bronze, and cement. The traditional Cambodian art of wood carving is particularly fine, with decorative panels, portrait heads, and other items produced at the School of Fine Arts. Other traditional crafts, such as Khmer silk weaving and silversmithing, are also being revived.

CUSTOMS AND CONDUCT

Temple Manners

In a predominantly Buddhist country, temples are sacred places. Dress properly when entering a temple, remove your shoes and hats when approaching the central sanctuary, and regard all Buddha images with respect. Angkor Wat, though a ruin, is also a pilgrimage site for Buddhists and Hindus.

Body Language

The head is considered pure and sacred in Buddhism; do not touch anyone, including children, on the head. The feet, which come into contact with dust on the street, are lowly; do not point your feet at anyone, or at any Buddhist image. If sitting in a temple, either squat or sit with the legs tucked to the side so the soles of the feet point backward.

Likewise, do not point at a Buddha image with a forefinger or hand. When beckoning someone toward you, gesture with palm down and four fingers cupped together. As in Thailand and Laos, a commonly used greeting is the *wai* (called *sompeah* in Khmer), a prayerlike gesture with palms placed together. Cambodians doing business with foreigners are also familiar with the handshake. Expect a frosty reception if you shout or otherwise display anger: Buddhists greatly admire the "cool heart."

Taboo Shots

You are free to photograph most things in Cambodia. Be careful, however, when dealing with armed subjects. Troops manning checkpoints are extremely touchy about photographs because the checkpoint may not be legal—set up simply for personal fundraising. In one case, a foreigner photographed a checkpoint from a passing boat—whereupon several shots were fired across the bow. You can take pictures of soldiers—some tourists even pose with borrowed guns—but always ask first. A few cigarettes come in handy here.

ON THE ROAD

At the turn of the century Europeans were afflicted with Angkormania. Colonial exhibitions in France featuring Khmer statuary and models of Angkor structures were very popular. In 1906 a Khmer dance troupe wowed audiences all over Europe. There were near-riots when people demanded entrance to the performances of sacred and sensual dance. Sculptor Auguste Rodin compared the dancers to Greek nymphs. In 1907 the Siamese ceded the Angkor region to the French, and in 1908 the first car forged through to Angkor from Saigon. In 1922 the Marseilles Colonial Exhibition featured a recreation of the central towers of Angkor Wat; the same exhibition appeared in Paris in 1931. In the 1920s travel agencies led trips to Angkor, and motor traffic was so busy that laws were enforced for parking and speed limits. For added thrills, globetrotters and colonial visitors could roam around ruins on elephant-back.

Cambodia was extremely popular with tourists between the two world wars, when it could be reached from both Bangkok and Saigon. Through the 1960s about 60,000 tourists a year visited Cambodia; in the early 1970s civil war made the country inaccessible. The tourist flow did not resume again until 22,000 UNTAC personnel arrived in 1992. In 1994 about 178,000 tourists passed through Pochentong Airport in Phnom Penh.

The situation in Cambodia is highly unstable: it's hard to guess what will happen. The information given in these pages comes freighted with lots of ifs and buts; the situation could change overnight. Areas upcountry are insecure: keep an eye on the newspapers, and consult your embassy. After a spate of highly publicized kidnappings of foreigners, in 1995 the British Embassy advised their nationals not to visit Cambodia. The Australian Embassy advised its citizens to exercise due care in Phnom Penh, and to avoid nonessential travel outside the city. The US embassy did not rule out visits to Angkor, but discouraged travel by boat to Siem Reap, and advised embassy personnel not to travel by train.

CAMBODIA HIGHLIGHTS

Travelers to Cambodia who visit despite the risks will find the Cambodians amazingly hospitable. The violence and mines have kept the tourist hordes from trampling over Angkor Wat, a plus from the conservationist's point of view. There are no Holiday Inns or Pizza Huts or Mc-Donalds in Cambodia, and upcountry you'll most likely be the only foreigner around. If you like adventure and don't mind people waving guns in your face, this is the place to be.

Cambodia is a war zone. Apart from Khmer Rouge guerrillas, risks include bandits, soldiers seeking handouts, mines, and unexploded ordnance. The country's tourism minister claims the zones of Phnom Penh, Angkor Wat, and Sihanoukville are safe for tourists, as long as they're approached by air. The Interior Ministry says units of special tourist police will be established at Phnom Penh, Siem Reap, and other parts of the country in a setup similar to a successful tourist protection program in Thailand. In another move in early 1995 the Cambodian government created a new province in the northwest of the country from three districts formerly contained in Siem Reap province. The creation of the new province of Oddar Meanchey was widely seen as a way of dissociating Siem Reap, home of Angkor, from the fighting in the north.

Phnom Penh: Traces of the city's former splendor are visible at the Royal Palace, en-

THE KILLING GOES ON

The Khmer Rouge will do anything that burdens or embarrasses the government. In 1993 the Khmer Rouge massacred dozens of Vietnamese fishing families on Lake Tonle Sap. In 1994 the Khmer Rouge claimed responsibility for the killing of at least 20 Thais. That same year 70 villagers collecting wood in Battambang Province were captured by Khmer Rouge, and 50 massacred. The Khmer Rouge then began burning down entire villages in Battambang Province to create large numbers of internally displaced people.

In the early 1990s a few foreigners experienced close calls with the Khmer Rouge; some were detained and released minus their possessions. A handful of peacekeepers were killed by the Khmer Rouge in the 1992-93 UNTAC era. In 1994 the Khmer Rouge started kidnapping foreign travelers for the first time—and killing them. It is believed foreigners may be targeted because of military training offered by the governments of Australia, France, and the US to the government. On 26 July 1994 a force of 60 Khmer Rouge soldiers stopped the Phnom Penh-Kampot train by detonating mines on the tracks. The guerrillas then opened fire on the train, killing 13 passengers and overcoming government soldiers. The Khmer Rouge looted the train, making off with three larger vehicles, 50 motorcycles, pigs, chickens, and rice. They took over a dozen hostages, including three Westerners.

Australian David Wilson, Briton Mark Slater, and Jean-Michel Barguet from France were all backpackers in their twenties. On 31 July the Khmer Rouge demanded a ransom of $150,000 in gold. On 11 August government troops surrounded the kidnappers' position on Vine Mountain, deep in Kampot Province. Five days later the Khmer Rouge demanded that Britain, France, and Australia end military aid to Cambodia by the end of the month; later they demanded the Khmer Rouge be made legal again. On 20 August the government agreed to pay a ransom, but negotiations stalled on other issues.

A key Khmer Rouge negotiating condition was that government troops would not shell their guerrilla base. In September government troops stepped up their assault on the base, and on 25 October overran it. The Khmer Rouge had already fled. The bodies of the three Westerners were found in a shallow grave. As many as 100 RCAF troops were killed or wounded in the assault. The British and French criticized the government's handling of the crisis. Defectors say the Khmer Rouge is now offering the equivalent of $8000 to kidnap Australians and Americans.

Another 10 foreigners are thought to have been caught up in the Khmer Rouge net in 1994 and 1995. An NGO worker was kidnapped and later released. On 11 April 1994 Australian Kellie Wilkinson and Britons Tina Dominy and Dominic Campbell were pulled from a taxi along Route 4 on the way to Phnom Penh and killed by suspected Khmer Rouge. Along the Thai-Cambodian border near the Preah Vihear temple ruins (occupied by the Khmer Rouge), a Briton and a Thai female disappeared in January 1994. Two Belgians—Michael Baran and Nathalie Roobaert—disappeared in the same area three months later. In December 1994 German Mathias Wulf disappeared while motorcycling in Thailand close to the Cambodian border. In early 1995 American Susan Hadden was killed in an ambush only 15 km from Angkor. A dozen other tourists in the five-car convoy survived the attack, which was linked to ex-Khmer Rouge soldiers.

DANGER!! MINES!!

At the time of writing, only a handful of places in Cambodia were considered reasonably safe for tourists. Problems include the Khmer Rouge, bandits, and corrupt government troops. An even greater limitation to travel in Cambodia is landmines. Even areas once cleared may be re-mined by the Khmer Rouge. The only known cases of foreigners falling victim to Cambodian mines have been UNTAC staff who ventured into known mined areas or handled unknown explosive devices. Remaining a biped is easy if you're alert to potential dangers. The following advice is adapted from a supplement published in the *Phnom Penh Post*.

Be sensible: Bright red skull-and-crossbones signs in Khmer and English mark suspect areas. Heed the signs. Stay alert. Do not become complacent and think that because you've not seen any mines the area is safe. Realize where you are and understand the consequences of a wrong action. Don't be foolhardy and "brave" in front of your companions; you might put them into danger as well.

Use a guide: If you must travel outside the villages, make sure you stay with a guide who knows the area and will lead the way. Do not enter any region outside a known safe area without first asking local people if there are mines about ("Mian min teh?"). Don't travel outside the towns after 1600 or before 0800: mines may be laid during the night for protection, and, in theory, retrieved in the morning.

Stay on the path: Stick to well-trodden trails at all times. Do not go off a known safe path for any reason, and do not take a shortcut, even if it looks safe. You must do all your business (which includes the toilet) on the safe path, no matter what the circumstances. Don't go off the safe path to explore ruins or derelict military equipment. Do not walk in long grass; snakes could be a problem here as well.

Do not touch: Never approach or touch any mines or unexploded ordnance. The Khmer Rouge rig up live ordnance as booby traps, often with trip wires. It's not uncommon for someone to want to show you their collection of mines, or even pass one to you for inspection. If this happens, make excuses to leave.

Driving: Make sure your driver knows where he's going. Ask the locals, or take along a local guide. If you need to stop in a potentially mined area, make sure the car is away from the edge of the road so you don't have to venture off the road when you get out. Mines are commonly laid on the edges of roads and paths. If your car breaks down in a mined area, you must climb out onto the roof of the car, make your way to the back of the vehicle, and then walk in the tire tracks.

In a mined area: If you find yourself in a mined area, warn everyone else around you to stop walking. If you can see your footsteps, you must stand completely within them and retrace all the way back to the known safe area. If you cannot see your footsteps you must not move. Call for help and wait until someone comes to rescue you. This may take a long time, but it is better to wait one day in a minefield than to be an amputee for life. If the worst happens, and someone is injured, do not rush into the mined area to rescue them. Many people have been killed or injured doing this. It's better to wait and find someone who knows how to safely enter a mined area. The safest way to enter a minefield is by prodding, which is an exact technique that must be learned thoroughly before being used in the field.

skull and crossbones warn travelers

closing the Silver Pagoda. The National Museum houses the world's finest collection of Khmer artifacts. The proud achievements of the Khmer culture are offset by the horrors of the Tuol Sleng Holocaust Museum.

Siem Reap: The small gateway town to Angkor Wat is a good place for rest and relaxation, with good food. Around town are quiet rural areas and forested zones; within reach is Lake Tonle Sap, with fishing activity and floating houses.

Angkor: Angkor is fabulous! The Angkor region casts its spell over all who visit—the stuff of dreams. This is the top archeological site in Southeast Asia, and worth three to 10 days or more. It was declared a World Heritage Site in 1992. The romantic ruins are a wonder of the eastern world, with 70 sites sprawled over an area of 200 square km. Giant tree roots drape down over sandstone Buddha faces, banyan trees sprout over cloister roofs, and lines of celestial nymphs appear on 100-meter friezes. Angkor Wat and Angkor Thom are the star sites. Transportation options here include bicycling, motorcycling, and driving.

Sihanoukville: A port and resort town on the Gulf of Thailand, with several sandy beaches and good seafood. Earmarked for major development, with an offshore island casino resort.

River Trips: A key attraction in Cambodia is its wild jungle terrain and forests. Most is inaccessible because of mines or the Khmer Rouge. You can view some terrain from boats, although this kind of travel may be risky. A fast boat runs from Phnom Penh up the Tonle Sap River and across Lake Tonle Sap to a dock near Siem Reap. You can take river trips of several days up the Mekong northeast to Stung Treng. Ratanakiri, in the northeast, is a hilltribe area; it's possible to ride elephants here.

Festivals: In mid-April is Cambodian New Year, with three days of celebration at the peak of the hot season. At full moon in October or November is a festival celebrating the reversal of the current of the Tonle Sap River, with boat racing, processions, and games. The biggest venue for the celebration is Phnom Penh.

HAZARDS

Drugs

Marijuana is openly available at marketplaces around Cambodia, usually in the spice or tobacco sections. Cambodians use marijuana as food flavoring in noodle soups, while foreigners seem to be the biggest consumers of the smokable variety. The herb is grown in regions along the Mekong River. While it is not illegal in Cambodia, possession of marijuana is a serious criminal offense in neighboring Thailand.

Beggars

Phnom Penh has a roving population of amputee beggars and street kids. As a fat wealthy foreigner, you will be an obvious target. In isolated cases it's okay to give some small riel bills to a beggar, but if there are others in sight, you risk being mobbed—which can lead to pickpocketing and other unfortunate consequences. Beggars and homeless children also abound at the major ruins of Angkor. They can be very persistent and aggressive. Kids often demand pens, sweets, or dollar bills.

Theft

Petty theft is a problem in urban areas. Armed robberies of tourists have been reported at night in Phnom Penh; if out at night, avoid walking by yourself. Use a motorcycle-taxi or cyclo instead. Phnom Penh is prone to blackouts, making theft easier. Never travel after dark in the countryside.

Women Travelers

In Buddhist countries harassment of Western women is usually not a problem. In Cambodia, however, there have been cases of intimidation reported by Westerners concerning Cambodian government soldiers. They will try and intimidate anyone, but have also made approaches with sexual overtones to females in the Angkor area. A German woman was asked for a kiss— possibly a joke, but frightening when demanded by seven soldiers with guns.

FESTIVALS AND HOLIDAYS

National Holidays

Jan. 7: National Day—celebrates the 1979 fall of the Khmer Rouge.

March 8: Women's Day—parades with floats in the main towns.

April 17: Independence Day, celebrating the fall of the Lon Nol regime in 1975. There's a parade in Phnom Penh. In mid-April is Cambodian New Year.

May 1: Labor Day.

May 9: Genocide Day, commemorating the victims of Khmer Rouge rule. The main ceremony is at Choeung Ek, near Phnom Penh.

June: Two parades in Phnom Penh, on **June 19** celebration of the 1951 founding of the Armed Forces, and a **June 28** commemoration of the 1951 founding of the People's Revolutionary Party of Cambodia.

Oct. 31: King Sihanouk's birthday.

Lunar Calendar Festivals

Festivals were banished under the Khmer Rouge because of links to Buddhism and royalty, and were downplayed by the Hun Sen government. They've been revived with the return of Sihanouk, who is very fond of pomp and ceremony. Lunar festivals are moveable and usually coincide with the full moon. The Royal Plowing Ceremony, held in May, was revived in 1994 after a 25-year hiatus; the Water Festival was revived in 1990.

January/February: Tet, or Chinese Lunar New Year, is celebrated by the Vietnamese and Chinese communities. Shops may be closed.

April: In mid-April is Chaul Chhnam or Cambodian New Year—three days of festive celebration, similar to Pimai in Laos and Songkran in Thailand. It marks the beginning of the year on the traditional Khmer calendar, and is celebrated with feasting, games, and offerings of food, flowers, candles, and incense to welcome the Songkran Goddess, believed to descend to Earth for three days at this time. Water-splashing, originally related to washing Buddha statues, prevails only in certain parts of the country, such as Siem Reap and Battambang. In April/May is Visak Bauchea, the commemoration of the birth and enlightenment of Buddha.

May: The Royal Plowing Ceremony is an ancient Brahman ritual, celebrating the start of the rice-planting season. In Phnom Penh the ceremony is presided over by the king. Court officials are charged with appraising the taste buds of eight royal oxen; results are used to predict the outcome of rice, corn, and bean harvests for the year that follows.

July: Start of Buddhist Lent and the rainy season proper, a time when novices join monasteries.

FESTIVAL OF THE REVERSING CURRENT

This boat-race Water Festival dates back to the 12th century, when Angkor king Jayavarman VII defeated the Cham in a naval battle. Linked to royalty, the three-day festival was revived in 1990 after a 20-year hiatus. In 1994 boat races were held at Siem Reap in the spectacular location of Angkor Wat moat.

A month before the festival starts, ceremonial longboats are hauled out of monastery sheds around the country, and crews begin training. The crew consists of 40 or more oarsmen. Although boat races are held in October or November in different parts of Cambodia, the biggest venue is Phnom Penh, where up to 200 longboats compete in the rowing regatta. Thousands converge on the riverbanks opposite the Royal Palace to see the arrival of the boats and oarsmen, followed by small orchestras of gongs and drums, and accompanied by monks or village dignitaries. Boat races take place in the afternoon. The oarsmen, spurred on by rhythmic singing and drumbeats, compete on a short stretch of the river. At night, dragon boats cruise up and down and fireworks soar skyward. At the climax of the festival, the king commands the Tonle Sap to reverse direction and flow to the sea—which it duly does within a few days.

September: End of Buddhist Lent, sometimes celebrated with boat races. Another festival at this time is Prachum Ben when offerings are made to ancestors.

October/November: Bon Om Tuk, the Water Festival or Festival of the Reversing Current, is held at the full moon at the end of October or beginning of November. When monsoon rains subside, the flow on the Tonle Sap River reverses, and is celebrated with three days of boat races, processions, music, and games.

ACCOMMODATIONS

Only Phnom Penh offers a full range of accommodations, from budget to first class hotels. The number of hotels and guesthouses mushroomed both in Phnom Penh and upcountry with the 1992-93 UNTAC operation. Guesthouse and midrange hotels can be found in Siem Reap and Sihanoukville, the two main tourist centers upcountry, with fan rooms ranging $5-25, and rooms with air-conditioning and hot water for $25-45. Facilities in hotels can be basic—the public supply of electricity and water is intermittent. Malaria is a problem upcountry in Cambodia; make sure your room is equipped with a good mosquito net.

Guesthouses are a great way to mingle with a Cambodian family—in Siem Reap there are dozens of them. You get a simple fan room for perhaps $5-10: guests lodge in a handful of rooms upstairs, and the family lives downstairs. Showering is with cold water, a bucket, and a dipper. At the other end of the scale, in Phnom Penh, the 300-room Hotel Sofitel Cambodiana offers a pool, satellite TV, business center, five restaurants; prices range from $150 to 200, double that for suites. Luxury hotels charge an extra 10% government tax and 10% service charge. Hotels offer discounts for groups and longer stays; prices also drop in the monsoon season.

FOOD

Food in Cambodia tends to be bland. Staples are rice, fish, and bread. A typical Cambodian meal consists of fried or steamed rice mixed with pieces of salted, dried, or cooked fish, seasoned with chiles or garlic. Soup accompanies the meal. Popular dishes include *an sam chruk,* a roll of sticky rice filled with soybean cake and chopped pork, and *khao phoun,* a noodle dish with a coconut sauce. Freshwater fish comes from Lake Tonle Sap; seafood is also found in

sidewalk café in Phnom Penh

the Gulf of Thailand at Sihanoukville. Fish comes grilled (*trey aing*), steamed whole (*trey chorm hoy*), or fried with vegetables (*trey chean neung spey*). *Somla machou banle* is sour fish soup; *somla machou bangkang* is spicy prawn soup.

Cheaper selections of food are mainly found in and around the central market in each town. Foodstalls abound in these areas, selling fresh fruit and other fare. Upcountry there's not much in the way of restaurants, although the selection in Siem Reap and Sihanoukville is reasonable. In Phnom Penh a large number of restaurants sprang up to cater to the UN trade. The restaurant variety includes French, Thai, Vietnamese, Chinese, and Western. Fresh baguettes

are sold in Phnom Penh, a legacy from colonial days and a habit not even the Khmer Rouge could eradicate.

Food generally costs $2-3 for a simple meal and $5-10 per person for a restaurant meal. Larger hotels in Phnom Penh charge upscale prices. For drinks, stick to tea or coffee, beer, and imported soft drinks. Angkor Beer is the national brew. Bottled water is widely available in Phnom Penh and Siem Reap.

Restaurants and hotel bars often offer nightlife, particularly in small towns. There is a group of bars patronized by foreigners in Phnom Penh, but the city is not safe by night, and armed holdups have been reported.

SHOPPING

Due to the association between crafts like silk weaving and silversmithing with Cambodian royalty, craftsmen were targeted in the Khmer Rouge era. The skills of the few survivors are now being passed on, and Sihanouk and his entourage are again patronizing these crafts. Under the Khmer Rouge, master silk weavers were ordered to weave plain cloth or work in the fields; today Khmer silk is back in favor with the royal family, and the textile trade has resumed. The craft of silversmithing is also being

revived, with small-scale handcrafting of silver boxes and jewelry. Modern Khmer sculpture and mural painting is fostered at the School of Fine Arts in Phnom Penh, where students fashion copies of Angkor statuary in wood, marble, bronze, and cement. The traditional Cambodian art of woodcarving is particularly fine, with decorative panels, portrait heads, and other items produced at the School of Fine Arts. Handcrafted goods are on sale at a number of outlets and markets in Phnom Penh and Siem Reap.

IMMIGRATION AND CUSTOMS

VISAS AND PAPERWORK

Visa on Arrival
Because there are so few Cambodian embassies and consulates, visas are issued on arrival at Pochentong Airport. You fill in a form on the spot, supply three passport photos, add a $20 bill, and the visa is stamped. It's valid for one to four weeks, depending on how the authorities take to you, and what the prevailing policy is at the time. There has been talk of implementing a free 14-day visa on arrival, similar to Thailand's entry visa.

Paperwork within Cambodia
Unlike Vietnam or Laos, paperwork is straight-

forward in Cambodia—you pay, you get what you need. The travel permit system was scrapped in 1992 under pressure from UNTAC. No permits are required for travel anywhere in Cambodia.

CAMBODIAN EMBASSIES AND CONSULATES

Since the formation of the coalition government in 1993, Cambodia has designated ambassadors to Thailand, Malaysia, Singapore, Indonesia, Japan, Laos, North Korea, the European Union, France, Germany, the US, and the UN. Relations with some of these countries were severed from 1973 to 1993. Cambodian embassies open at the time of writing are in

Bangkok, Saigon, Hanoi, Vientiane, Dehli, Paris, Berlin, Prague, Moscow, Washington, and Havana; others are planned for Australia, New Zealand, and China.

Within Asia

Thailand: The Cambodian Embassy opened for business in Bangkok in 1994 after a closure of 20 years. It's located on Rajadamri Rd., just north of Lumpini Park; phone 294-3528. A Cambodian visa takes about five working days, and is valid for up to three months. It's also available through travel agents for $40.

Vietnam: In Hanoi, the Cambodian Embassy at 71A Tran Hung Dao, tel. 253789 or 265225, issues a visa for $20. It may only be valid for a week or two, and takes three days or longer to obtain. In Saigon, the Cambodian Consulate at 41 Phung Khac Khoan, Q1, tel. 292751, issues a seven-day visa for $20, or a 14-day visa for $30. The visa is issued same day or next day.

Laos: In Vientiane, the Cambodian Embassy in the Saphathong Nua area, tel. 314952, is-

sues a one-month visa for $20 in one day. You need three photos.

TOURING CAMBODIA

Because of limited access due to mines and guerrilla activity, most travelers visit only Phnom Penh and Angkor. You could do a roundtrip from Bangkok to Phnom Penh to Angkor and back to Phnom Penh for Bangkok, or fly Bangkok to Phnom Penh, take a side trip to Angkor, and exit by road or air to Saigon. Some travelers also go to Sihanoukville from Phnom Penh.

Numerous travel agencies in Bangkok arrange fully escorted tours to Cambodia. Escorted tours solve logistical problems and provide the security of numbers, but often do not allow enough time to fully explore Angkor. As long as you keep to Phnom Penh, Angkor, and Sihanoukville, security should not be a problem for an individual traveler. You can usually find someone to team up with in Bangkok or in Phnom Penh to go to Angkor.

MONEY, MEASUREMENTS, AND COMMUNICATIONS

MONEY

The unit of currency in Cambodia is the riel, with exchange rates hovering at around 2400 riels to the US dollar. To promote use of the riel over the dollar, in 1995 the National Bank issued new notes and coins minted and printed by the French. The notes are in denominations of 1000, 2000, 5000, 10,000, 50,000, and 100,000 riel, with stainless steel coins of 50, 100, 200, and 500 riel. The new notes bear both a watermark and a metallic strip; all but two feature King Norodom Sihanouk. The 100,000 note shows both the king and queen, and is worth about $40. Previously, the only bills in circulation were 100, 200, and 500 riel notes. Since the latter was worth only 20 cents, huge bundles of cash were needed to pay for anything.

Restaurant menus in Phnom Penh often quote three prices—dollars, riels, and Thai baht. There are no US coins circulating, so if a dish is priced at $1.30 or $1.70, and you pay in dollars, you'll receive change in riels. If you pay in baht, change will come in baht or riels.

Banking

There are lots of banks in Phnom Penh, but few anywhere else. However, you can usually use US cash upcountry, or find locals who'll change dollars into riel. Jewelers in markets upcountry will change money. Credit cards are of limited use in Cambodia, though the larger hotels in Phnom Penh will accept Visa and MasterCard. Cash advances mean high commissions.

Counterfeit Bills

Beware of fake high-denomination US bills. Some are obviously of poor quality, but others are hard to distinguish from the real thing. In March 1995 two Thais and two Cambodians were arrested in Poipet for illegally importing $1.5 million in fake US$100 bills. Two months earlier Thai police in Aranyaprathet arrested two Thais with $390,000

in fake US$100 bills. Although police confiscate the fake bills, banks in Phnom Penh may hand bad bills back, which means they remain in circulation. In early 1995 police confiscated almost 30,000 fake US$100 bills peddled by Phnom Penh moneychangers. A further 100,000 fake Thai baht bills were also confiscated.

MEASUREMENTS AND COMMUNICATIONS

Telecommunications

Back in the 1970s Cambodia only had a few international phone lines to Moscow; today, Cambodia has the world's lowest density of telecom facilities. There are very few phone connections upcountry in Cambodia. For the 1993 elections a UN satellite network, including a cellular phone system, was installed by Australian company OTC/Telstra at a cost of $50 million. It was handed over to Cambodia when the UN left and provided communication among all of Cambodia's provinces, though it quickly fell into disrepair due to theft, vandalism, and lack of maintenance. The network is being refurbished by Indonesia's Indosat company; other phone systems will be installed by the Thai company Shinawatra and Malaysia's Tricelcam.

The Thai company Samart offers a satellite phone system, and handles IDD and mobile phone calls in Phnom Penh, Siem Reap, Sihanoukville, Battambang, and Kompong Cham. Embassies and major hotels use Samart satellite dishes for IDD and fax contact. Major hotels in Phnom Penh and elsewhere use the Samart system for IDD calling.

IDD calls from Cambodia are expensive. From Phnom Penh Post Office calls are $5.30 a minute to Europe, $4.50 to other parts of Asia and the US, $4 to Thailand, and $3.80 to Australia. The Phnom Penh IDD code is 855-23; Siem Reap is 855-15. Phnom Penh is seven hours ahead of Greenwich mean time.

Post from Cambodia is slow, expensive, and unreliable. Post offices are signposted PTT (Poste Télégraphe Téléphone). Parcel weights are accepted up to two kilograms, and everything is shipped airmail rate. One kilogram costs $26 to ship to Canada, or $10 to Bangkok. It's cheaper and more reliable to send mail from a point like Hong Kong or Bangkok—if flying to these points, hold onto your mail. Courier offices in Phnom Penh include DHL, UPS, and TNT.

Metric and Electric
Cambodia uses the metric system. Electricity, when available, is 220V, 50 cycles. Electricity is a scarce commodity in Cambodia—even in Phnom Penh many hotels and businesses must rely on inhouse generators during blackouts or when the public power is turned off.

SERVICES AND INFORMATION

Traveler Network
The dangers of travel in Cambodia have created a great sense of camaraderie on the trail. Most travelers find the Cambodian people among the friendliest in Asia and end up staying longer than planned. Tourist information from official sources is almost nonexistent, and where it does exist, is not likely to discuss mines or bandits.

Maps and Books
A timely, accurate map of Cambodia is important. An excellent map is the Periplus Travel Map of Cambodia, including submaps of Phnom Penh and Angkor. The maps are handsomely produced, with annotated material, and take into account such recent changes as new street names for Phnom Penh and checkpoints on the roads to Angkor Wat. Another detailed map of Cambodia is produced by International Travel Maps from Canada. This map is good for geographical features, upcountry locations, and the road network. Stock up on maps and books on Cambodia in Bangkok or Hong Kong—there's precious little in Cambodia itself, apart from photocopied ver-

THE LANGUAGE WAR

A battle rages in Phnom Penh over the use of French or English as the country's second language. The older generation was schooled in French; the younger generation wants to study English. Makeshift English schools proliferate in Phnom Penh temples, alleyways, and roadside shacks. While Laos and Vietnam accepted the reality of English as the language of business, pro-French King Sihanouk opted for French. First Prime Minister Ranariddh was schooled in France, as were a number of prominent members of parliament.

Cambodia is France's last bastion in Asia. France has mounted a major campaign to bring French back to Cambodia's intellectual, business, and cultural life. The French Embassy has signed deals that allow France to exclusively train and equip Cambodian government organizations—the military, legal and health professions, and the civil service. French advisers are urging that hundred-year-old colonial laws serve as new civil and legal codes.

Cambodia's education system is mainly dependent on foreign donors; the country is the world's largest recipient of French aid on a per capita basis. France makes its multimillion-dollar contributions—programs, training, books, equipment—conditional on the use of the French language. In 1993 a thousand students at Phnom Penh's Institute of Technology staged street demonstrations against a requirement that they study French. The students wanted to study courses in English. Institute courses were taught in Russian from the mid-1980s to 1992; the curriculum switched to French after France agreed to renovate laboratories—on the condition courses be taught in French. The protesting students claimed learning French as a second language would hamper Cambodia's development and international relations.

Elsewhere in Asia, Anglo-American is the language of business and law. The Cambodian Finance Ministry declared the French accounting system the only one acceptable to the new government for foreign business transactions. Critics say this will deter foreign investment. All ASEAN states use an international accounting system incompatible with the French model.

sions falling apart at the seams. Also take along some background and cultural material on Angkor. A good companion is Dawn Rooney's *Guide to Angkor,* with excellent site descriptions and background material. Also useful is the May 1982 issue of *National Geographic,* which contains two illustrated articles on Angkor.

Media

Cambodia has more than 30 Khmer publications, two French-language newspapers, and three English journals. The *Phnom Penh Post* is an excellent publication issued twice a month. Since its creation in 1992, it has won accolades from journalists worldwide as an essential tool for understanding events in Cambodia. The *Post* is owned by an American couple, printed in Bangkok, and maintains offices in Phnom Penh. The centerfold contains a map of Phnom Penh featuring paid advertisers; useful as a base map nonetheless. A second English-language newspaper is *The Cambodia Times,* published by a Malaysian public relations firm based in Kuala Lumpur. The paper is pro-government, which does not make for inspiring copy. There's also *Cambodia Daily,* in a smaller format with international news summaries. In French, *Cambodge Soir* is published three times a week, while *Le*

VIDEO STARS

In the late 1980s, expatriate Cambodian visitors left behind a few VHS camcorders for their poorer cousins. Local entrepreneurs, struck by the appeal of third-rate Indian, Vietnamese, and Soviet-bloc films, set about making two-hour dramas. In 1990, when the government organized the first Cambodian Film and Video Festival, there were over 150 companies registered with the Ministry of Culture's Film Department. The industry has made instant celebrities of a handful of Cambodian actors and actresses. Huge brightly painted billboards announce the current attractions.

The videos play to packed movie houses around Phnom Penh. After that, they make the rounds of noodlehouse VCRs to generate extra revenue. Some videos find an audience overseas in cities with Cambodian expats like Long Beach, California.

Plots are melodramatic and little is preplanned. The crew of 15 shoots with just a camera, monitor, and some reflector boards. Actors mouth whatever the director tells them to say—it doesn't really matter because the scenes are dubbed with sound later anyway. The budget is $2000 to $3000. Actors come from the University of Fine Arts Theater School, although talented neighbors and friends are considered. Shooting takes a month, and post-production perhaps another two weeks. Video is edited at the Film Department's facilities, then dubbed by a special team of a dozen people who provide all the voices. One person might take on the dialogue of two or three characters in a single movie. Soundtracks can be pirated from any source since there is a lack of copyright laws.

After Hollywood on the Mekong has done its job, the effort hits the big screen, where voices shake due to distortion and echo effects. Like any other moviegoers, Cambodians want escapist entertainment. This is provided with rags-to-riches stories, and melodramatic and sentimental romances. Male characters drip gold jewelry, wear leather boots, drive cars, and use cellular phones; actresses wear miniskirts, use lots of makeup, and provocatively sway their hips, in contrast to the modest apparel and movements of the average Cambodian woman.

Fame and fortune come to those acting in the video dramas. They can enjoy new Honda Dream motorcycles, and watch their portraits sell out in local photo shops. However, there are drawbacks. Actors and actresses known for playing angry heroes or vixens are not necessarily welcomed in person by Cambodian society, with its Buddhist ethics. As one young screen idol put it, "After I graduate from university, I will stop acting, because no Cambodian family will let their daughter marry an actor."

The country's best-known celluloid creator is King Sihanouk, who wrote, directed, and even starred in his own movies during the 1950s and 1960s. In a country with a ruined infrastructure, it's remarkable that celluloid production has started up again. Using equipment thrown away by Vietnamese and Czech film crews, some filmmakers are now producing work in 8mm and 16mm formats. Students at Phnom Penh's National Cinema Center are instructed by Rithy Panh, who wrangled a scholarship to study film in France in the 1980s. Panh has been hailed internationally for his feature, *The People of the Ricefields,* filmed in 1993.

*Phnom Penh
newspaper dealer*

Mékong is published monthly. The latter is available in Hong Kong, Bangkok, and Saigon.

There is one state-owned television station and one private one. Thai telecom giant Shinawatra operates a TV channel with a 100 square kilometer radius around Phnom Penh. Satellite dishes can pick up Hong Kong's StarTV (BBC World Service Television), Australia's ATVI, and CFI, a French channel, retransmitted over Phnom Penh by the French Cultural Center. On radio, you can pick up Radio France Internationale (RFI), the BBC, VOA, and Radio Australia.

Services

Business centers can be found in Phnom Penh at major hotels and a few independent locations. They operate computing, translating, and secretarial services, as well as telecommunication and photocopy facilities. There are film labs in downtown Phnom Penh that sell brand-name film, but you'd be better off purchasing it in Bangkok or Hong Kong to ensure freshness. In

Phnom Penh most offices are open from 0700 to 1100 or 1130, followed by a lunch siesta, reopening from 1400 to 1700 or 1730. Most are closed Sundays. Some businesses, especially joint-venture concerns, keep Western office hours of 0900-1700. Embassies are usually open mornings only.

Health Care

The standard is very poor. Most of Cambodia's doctors were killed or sent into exile during the Pol Pot era, which means a severe shortage of skilled medical staff. Foreign aid groups like the Red Cross fill the vacuum. In serious cases, evacuation to Bangkok, Hong Kong or Singapore is advised. A few foreign doctors and dentists operate privately in Phnom Penh—ask your embassy for recommendations. In association with SOS International is IMC Clinic, at 83 Issarak Blvd., Phnom Penh, mobile tel. 015-912765, with international standards—it's a primary and emergency health care facility.

GETTING THERE

BY AIR

The only international entry point is Phnom Penh, with frequent connections to Bangkok and Saigon. Phnom Penh's Pochentong Airport terminal underwent a major face-lift in 1994, and a new national airline—Royal Air Cambodge (RAC)—made its maiden flight in January 1995. RAC is the reincarnated national airline from Sihanouk's reign in the 1960s, and presently the fleet consists of Boeing 737s, ATR-72 turboprops, and some Russian aircraft. RAC is a joint venture between government-owned Kampuchea Airlines and Malaysia Airlines. RAC flies to Bangkok, Kuala Lumpur, Singapore, Hong Kong, and Saigon. RAC also flies direct into Kunming and Guangzhou from Phnom Penh. The airline plans to establish direct links to Paris soon. The RAC Bangkok-Phnom Penh flight is $125 one-way.

Carriers flying into Phnom Penh include Thai International, daily flights to Bangkok, $140 one-way, roundtrip possible $200; Malaysia Airlines to Kuala Lumpur, three flights a week, $260 roundtrip; SilkAir, frequent flights to Singapore, $300 roundtrip; Dragonair, flights to Hong Kong, $360 roundtrip; Vietnam Airlines, flights to Saigon daily, $50 one-way, and to Hanoi, once or twice a week, $155 one-way; Lao Aviation, to Vientiane, once a week, $150 one-way; Transasia Airways to Taipei, twice weekly; Singapore Airlines, frequent flights between Phnom Penh and Rangoon; Aeroflot, several flights a month to Moscow via Dubai. For many years business interests in Bangkok have pushed for direct Bangkok-Siem Reap flights. Bangkok Air and Thai Airways International are currently competing for rights on this route; most likely they'd use 140-seat aircraft.

Customs

Customs on entry is simple. You declare any video, radio, TV, or audiocassette equipment, as well as amounts of money exceeding $10,000. None of this is checked on exit. You can import 200 cigarettes, one bottle of spirits, and a bottle of perfume for personal use. Export of antiques or Khmer artifacts is forbidden, a policy enforced by the National Heritage Protection Authority of Cambodia. Foreigners are liable to searches when exiting Phnom Phen or Siem Reap. International departure tax is $10.

BY SEA

The best chance of a legitimate entry is from Thailand to Cambodia. Some travelers have entered Cambodia on a day-trip from Thailand, visiting offshore islands and returning the same day. Others have visited Cambodia for a week or so, then returned to Thailand by the same sea route with the Thai visa still valid—it's better, however, to possess a paper Cambodian visa for this trip. A third option is to enter Cambodia from Thailand, then carry on to Vietnam later. This assumes no intention of returning to Thailand—if you did, officials would question your lack of an exit stamp on the original Thai visa.

No Thai exit or entry stamp is given at this sea crossing, but you can obtain a Cambodian entry or exit stamp at the town of Krong Koah Kong. There are half a dozen places that answer to the name of Koah Kong—the province of Koah Kong, Kong Island (Koh Kong), and the port town of Krong Koah Kong. Piracy is a problem on the high seas in the Gulf of Thailand—a major smuggling route.

From the Thai side take a bus to Trat and on to Ban Hat Lek. From there ride a 10-person longtail through mangroves for about an hour to get to the area around Phumi Thnal Krabi, which is close to the Cambodian seaport of Krong Koah Kong. Here you get yourself stamped into Cambodia, then find out what boats are available for onward travel. There are a variety of routes from the Krong Koah Kong area to Peam Kay and Sre Ambel daily, or to Peam Kay and Sihanoukville every few days. A large fishing boat with 100 passengers should take about 12 hours for the run from Krong Koah Kong to Sihanoukville—most likely an overnight trip (passengers string up hammocks to sleep).

Once you reach either Sre Ambel or Sihanouk-ville, you can stay in a hotel and look around, then go by road to Phnom Penh. An alternative is to fly from Koh Kong direct to Phnom Penh. Air service here is irregular.

In the reverse direction, Cambodian officials will stamp you out of Cambodia at Krong Koah Kong, but there is no Thai entry stamp. You would have to grovel before immigration authorities in Bangkok—and present a good story.

BY LAND

Some travelers enter the country at Bavet. Buses with padded seats travel the 248-km Phnom Penh-Saigon route. The bus is not recommended because of hassles from soldiers and Vietnamese police along the way—it's a notorious smuggling run. A share-taxi on both sides is preferable, or at the very least for the Vietnamese portion of the trip.

A second unofficial crossing point is in the northwest, at Poipet. This route is closed to foreigners for the moment—you cannot be stamped in or out. This border was porous during the UNTAC era and some travelers managed to slip through, returning by the same route. The road route from Bangkok to Siem Reap is actually a lot faster than the road from Phnom Penh to Siem Reap. Khmer Rouge activity in the area makes the border zone perilous.

GETTING AROUND

BY AIR

Only travel by air is considered safe; a second option is fast boats upriver to Siem Reap or Kratie. Domestic flights operate daily to Siem Reap, Koh Kong, and four times a week to Sihanoukville. Less frequent flights head for Kratie, Stung Treng, Kampot, and Battambang. Domestic service is on old Russian crates—Tupolevs (TU-134) and Antonovs (AN-24). RAC flies a few French ATR turboprops on the Siem Reap run. Schedules are prone to rapid change and planes may be cancelled. One-way flights from Phnom Penh include Siem Reap, $50, up to three flights a day; Battambang, $45, three times a week; Sihanoukville, $40, several flights a week; Kampot, several per week; Koh Kong, $50, four flights weekly; Stung Treng, $48, twice weekly. Roundtrip tickets double. Domestic departure tax is $4.

BY BOAT

With such dismal and dangerous roads, travel by fast boat is preferable. There is a fast boat service to Siem Reap ($28) and to Kompong Cham and Kratie ($25). It's better to take a fast boat because the slow cargo boats may be stopped at marine checkpoints. Soldiers have, on occa-sion, fired a few shots across the bow of a boat to indicate it should come ashore to pay "taxes." Stung Treng is only accessible by slow boat when the waters run high, in the postmonsoon season, around September to January. In seasons where the waters are low, boat trips take longer because the captain has to navigate the shoals, exposed rock, and other obstacles. On overnight boat trips you need to bring a hammock and mosquito net, and your own food and water. A small library of books would be a good idea in case you run aground upriver.

BY TRAIN

Cambodia has two French-built rail lines: south from Phnom Penh to Kampot and Sihanoukville; and north from Phnom Penh to Pursat, Battambang, and Sisophon. Service depends on whether the track or engines have been blown up.

There are 600 km of track. Service is a far cry from the heyday of the 1960s, when 30 trains carried a total of two million passengers a year. The railway company has 10 French locomotives dating from the 1960s, four Czech engines purchased a few years ago, and five shunting locomotives. All but two are marred by war damage. The French are funding a project to restore old trains and tracks in Cambodia, but the task is daunting. The rail system is a favorite target of the

the train to Battambang

ification to the 1960s French locomotive on the Kampot run is a steel plate across the cabin with two visors cut for visibility—this to reduce the chance of the engineer being taken out by a bullet. There are often two flatbed cars out front on a Cambodian train—if the train hits a mine, the flatbeds will be blown up, not the precious engine. Passengers can ride the flatbeds for a reduced fare. Women ride inside the front cars on the train, while men sit on the roofs of the cars, which can get very hot in the midday sun.

Fares on trains are negligible, and so is the Khmer Rouge's regard for life in these parts. There have been numerous train ambushes. Although trains carry their own militia with AK-47s, they've been unsuccessful in beating off attacks. The Sihanoukville-Phnom Penh train, loaded with port goods, was attacked by Khmer Rouge forces four times in 1993, and at least that many times in 1994. Some trains have been assaulted with rockets, and a few have been held up by bandits. An attack usually starts by exploding mines on the track to stop the train. In early 1995 a force of 20 Khmer Rouge stopped a train this way 50 km north of Phnom Penh. After the train came to a halt, the Khmer Rouge ran toward the cars, firing AK-47s and grenade launchers. Eight passengers were killed and another 30 injured. The guerrillas robbed the passengers of valuables and looted sacks of rice from the train. Government soldiers arrived about six hours later.

Khmer Rouge, who vow to "cut the railway into pieces." In the first half of 1995 a total of 327 pieces of railway track were blown up, along with 12 bridges.

Trains remain the most dangerous form of transport in Cambodia and are only used by the poor. The worst route is the Phnom Penh to Battambang line. Trains are supposed to run daily here, but in the course of six months only two or three trains typically complete the journey. The line may only run as far as Pursat if track on the Pursat-Battambang section has been blown up or bridges are down. RCAF soldiers assigned to guard the line sometimes stand on the tracks with rifles and grenade launchers to stop trains and ask for money, batteries, shoes, radios, or just a free ride. A dozen illegal checkpoints operate along the route.

In better times, the Battambang line actually ran all the way to Bangkok. The section from Battambang to Sisophon was used to repatriate refugees from Thailand.

Rail is essentially for moving freight in Cambodia—passengers are an afterthought. Trains move at crawl speed, around 15 kph on the Battambang run, taking 16 hours to cover the distance. Phnom Penh to Kampot requires seven hours. Cars are probably old Indian stock, with wooden seats and metal shutters—most are crammed with goods, with a few up front reserved for female passengers. An unusual mod-

BY SHARE-TAXI

Very few foreigners use the vintage Dodge buses with wooden seats that provide bone-jarring rides over Cambodia's rough roads. These are packed to the gills with produce, and progress is painfully slow. A packed—but smoother and faster ride—is provided by share-taxis, sometimes referred to as "death-taxis." These collective taxis operate on set routes. They usually depart from the town marketplace; in Phnom Penh they leave from half-a-dozen market depots partway up the line. Share-taxis keep piling people in, leaving when critical mass is achieved. They may drop off and pick up passengers along the fixed route. A ride is $5 a head, or you can commandeer the whole taxi for $20 a day.

Start early in the day—off by 0730—and try and complete the journey by 1400 hours. By late afternoon checkpoint soldiers are drunker and more aggressive. Travel toward nightfall is dangerous. Main routes have tollbooths with soldiers—and they're hungry. Like waiters, the soldiers depend on "tips" and "taxes" for their real income. Donations are expected in the form of foreign-brand cigarettes or small riel-bills tossed from the taxi. In the early days of Cambodia travel, a western photographer's driver used to throw out entire packs as he approached checkpoints—the soldiers would be so busy scrambling for them, they wouldn't think to stop the car. Avoid stopping at any checkpoints or at bridges guarded by soldiers—it's best to simply reduce speed, and toss money out of the car.

The Battambang route is especially dangerous. In one case, a group of foreigners was held at gunpoint, soldiers demanding and getting $30 from each passenger as the driver was told to lie face down on the ground.

Another hazard on this route is freshly laid mines. A share-taxi nearing Battambang ran over an antitank mine, most likely laid by the Khmer Rouge. The explosion killed all eight occupants.

AROUND TOWN

Cyclos are the most common method of getting around town. You can also flag down a private motorcycle just about anywhere for a pillion ride. Upcountry use moto drivers as tour guides. Taxis are operated by major hotels, and can be hired by the day. Renting a bicycle is a good way to get around Phnom Penh.

The figure of kala *is a common protection motif at Banteay Srei.*

PHNOM PENH

Phnom Penh: uncontrolled intersections, open sewers, stagnant pools, scum and garbage strewn down side streets and vacant lots, amputee-beggars, squatters, prostitutes, lawlessness, blackouts. Welcome to Cambodia. In the rainy season, the muck floats as the monsoon rains deluge the streets, while foreigners from aid groups show off their 4WDs and cellular phones.

Phnom Penh is a mess. Sanitary conditions are poor because of destroyed water and sewage facilities. Up to 20% of all households do not have toilets. When the first rains hit, the streets are flooded: the sewer system doesn't function, and there's no money to repair water pumping machinery. Drains and sewers are clogged with garbage. There is a chronic lack of education facilities and teachers.

Forty-five percent of Phnom Penh's population is under the age of 15, and there are roving bands of street kids, many from the provinces.

Phnom Penh does exude an eccentric charm. Seen from the river, palm trees and the pagoda-like spires of Khmer royal buildings rise over French-era shophouses and villas. In the 1950s and 1960s this was one of the finest cities in Southeast Asia. The riverine city's yellow-ocher buildings, squares and cafés, and frangipani-lined boulevards give it the atmosphere of a French provincial town. The city is located at what the French called les Quatre Bras (the Four Arms), where two arms of the Mekong meet the Bassac and Tonle Sap tributaries. The city's original name, Chaktomuk, means Four Rivers.

Phnom Penh has witnessed rapid—and bizarre—changes of fortune. After Angkor fell to the Siamese in the 15th century, Cambodian King Ponhea Yat founded a new capital at Chaktomuk. This city was soon abandoned as well, and from the mid-17th to mid-19th centuries the Cambodian capital was in Udong, 40 km northwest of Phnom Penh. King Norodom moved the capital to Phnom Penh in 1866. The city is largely a French creation—even the Khmer-style buildings and temples were built under French supervision. Wide boulevards and stately mansions were constructed in the French colonial era, and Phnom Penh quickly became an important commercial center. The city was—and still is—the only major port on the Mekong above the delta; it is

GETTING YOUR BEARINGS

Direction finding in Phnom Penh is completely chaotic, the map's full of streets known only by numbers. An address may be rendered 112 Rue 106, 112 Street 106, 112 106 Street, or No. 112 St. 106. To avoid confusion, the French-ordered system of 112 Street 106 has been adopted for this guide. Reference is also made to landmarks—for example, "north of Wat Phnom" or "east of Central Market." Sometimes Phnom Penh addresses cover all bases—providing street number, street junction, and local landmark. An example is La Paillote Hotel, Marché Central-No.234, Rue 130-53. The hotel address translates as 234 Street 130 at the corner of Street 53, near the Central Market.

Even-numbered streets generally run east-west, with low numbers starting from the north; odd-numbered roads run north-south, with low numbers starting from the east. Thus you'd expect to find Street 19 running north-south at the east side of Phnom Penh. Easy, huh? The only snag is that half the streets are dead ends, anarchically numbered in semisequential fashion. Boulevards are named, but on these long wide roads you need to know the junction of two streets to get your bearings, or else you could be a kilometer or two off. Phnom Penh stretches some seven km from north to south, and five km from east to west. The designation "Eo" in an address stands for *étage zéro*, French for ground floor. Thus 4 Eo Street 118 means the ground floor at number 4 on Street 118.

In the 1970s and 1980s the Lon Nol regime, the Khmer Rouge, and the Vietnamese wiped King Sihanouk's royalist names off the map. After the triumphant return of Sihanouk in 1991 and his crowning in 1993, boulevard names began to revert from the revolutionary and Communist heroes imposed by the Vietnamese to the royalist names of the 1960s. This process is ongoing and can be very confusing. Some businesses use the old boulevard names, not having the time, money, or inclination to change signs or business cards.

It's best to navigate by landmarks, as even locals are hazy about the location of certain streets. Key landmarks include Wat Phnom, Chruoy Changvar Bridge, Central Market building, the Royal Palace, National Museum, Hotel Sofitel Cambodiana, and Independence Monument.

Here are some name changes for boulevards:

NAME FROM 1980s	POST-1993 NAME
Achar Mean Blvd.	Monivong Blvd.
Quay Karl Marx	Sisowath Quay
Lenin Blvd.	Samdech Sothearos Blvd.
Sivutha Blvd.	Preah Sihanouk Blvd.
Tousamouth Blvd.	Norodom Blvd.
Achar Hemcheay Blvd.	Charles de Gaulle Blvd.
Kampuchea Vietnam Blvd.	Kampuchea Krom Blvd.
USSR Blvd.	Pochentong Blvd.
Keo Mony Blvd.	Issarak Blvd.
Pokambor Blvd.	Monireth Blvd.

navigable by ships of up to 7,000 tons. From Phnom Penh, smaller vessels can navigate upriver to Siem Reap or Kratie.

In the late 1960s prosperous Phnom Penh had a population of perhaps 600,000. Almost two-thirds of the population consisted of Vietnamese and Chinese merchants and workers. The Chinese, Vietnamese, and Khmer ethnic groups occupied their own distinct neighborhoods. Business and trade congregated in streets of their own, with sections devoted to basket making or silversmithing. By 1975, swollen with refugees from civil war, the city had a population of over two million.

On 17 April 1975, Phnom Penh became a ghost town, emptied out by the Khmer Rouge within 48 hours. During the 1975-79 reign of terror, the city's inhabitants were mostly soldiers and prisoners. By 1978 there were only 15,000-30,000 people in the city. The Khmer Rouge painted over all signs in Phnom Penh—traffic signs, advertising signs, markers of any kind. Wrecked cars lay where they were abandoned in 1975. All shops and hotels were closed. A number of buildings were blown up or demolished, including the Catholic Cathedral and the National Bank. Up to two-thirds of the city's houses were damaged. The plumbing system was destroyed.

(top left) lower temple at Wat Phu, near Pakse; (top right) bomb shells recycled into planters, Luang Prabang; (bottom) on the Plain of Jars

(top) cruising the Mekong, out of Luang Prabang;
(bottom) wall locked in the embrace of a strangler fig, Ta Prohm

People started streaming back to the city shortly after the Vietnamese takeover in January 1979; over 100,000 returned in that year alone. The current population is close to a million.

Phnom Penh was the main base of operation for UNTAC in 1992-93—the place was swamped with UN personnel. Thousands of white UNTAC Land Cruisers, jeeps, and trucks created traffic jams on Phnom Penh's boulevards. After UNTAC came a rush of business-people—Thai bankers and Japanese businessmen—to make deals in the fragile peace under the new coalition government. The Japanese funded a major renovation of the Phnom Penh port.

Phnom Penh, like the rest of Cambodia, is in a boom-or-bust situation. If peace reigns, tourists and businesspeople come in and the economy does well. If the Khmer Rouge attack, everybody backs off and hotels stand half empty.

SIGHTS

The city's most exclusive real estate is toward the Tonle Sap River, with French villas and institutions in the north, and the Royal Palace, Silver Pagoda, and other traces of the former royal city to the south. Options for touring include walking, bicycling, hiring a cyclo or motorcycle. If bicycling, watch out at uncontrolled intersections—traffic is chaotic in peak hours.

THE ROYAL PALACE

Since the return of King Norodom Sihanouk in November 1991, the palace has been closed to public viewing. The gates are thrown open for three consecutive days in early November, when the compound becomes a kind of fairground. The rest of the year the palace is off-limits, although it is possible to peek at the palace from various side gates. It occupies a huge block between Streets 184 and 240, facing Samdech Sothearos Boulevard.

The Royal Palace was built in stages in the early 20th century over the site of Banteay Kev, a 19th-century citadel. A number of the present buildings were built in concrete under French supervision, emulating previous Khmer-style wooden structures. Between 1970 and 1979 the palace was looted and sustained considerable damage. The most accessible feature of the Royal Palace is Chan Chaya Pavilion (Pavilion of Dancers), which fronts Samdech Sothearos Boulevard. Built in 1913, it served as a public events podium, a venue for music and dance performances on special occasions, and for speeches by the king. King Sihanouk put the podium to royal use again for the celebration of the 40th anniversary of independence in 1993. Above the pavilion is a large portrait of King Sihanouk; under the pavilion is the main entrance gate to the palace, which is closely guarded.

Depending on the mood of the guards, you might be able to peek through the gates. Buildings at the palace include the Royal Residence (Khemarin Palace), built in 1930; an Officers' Club, built in 1958 for officers of the royal guard; and Phochani Hall, built in 1913 for performances of royal dance. The Throne Hall, topped by a four-headed tower (inspired by Angkor's Bayon Temple), was completed in 1917 under King Sisowath. The glazed tiles on the layered roof were added in 1993 during a German-funded renovation project.

The hall, once used for coronations, is now employed for traditional ceremonies and official receptions. In the center are thrones for the king and queen, and seats for court officials. The walls are decorated with Ramayana murals. The king and queen were once ferried around for royal processions in sedan chairs or gilded wooden chariots, and sometimes by elephant. An elephant-mounting pavilion is located just north of the Throne Hall; elephants were previously stabled within the grounds.

From the barred gate along the alley entryway to the Silver Pagoda you can see an ornate gray French pavilion. This was originally presented by Emperor Napoleon III to Empress Eugenie during the Suez Canal opening celebrations in 1869. The prefabricated summerhouse was then dismantled and packed off to Cambodia as a gift to King Norodom. Erected at the Royal Palace in 1876, the structure was renovated by a group of French volunteers in

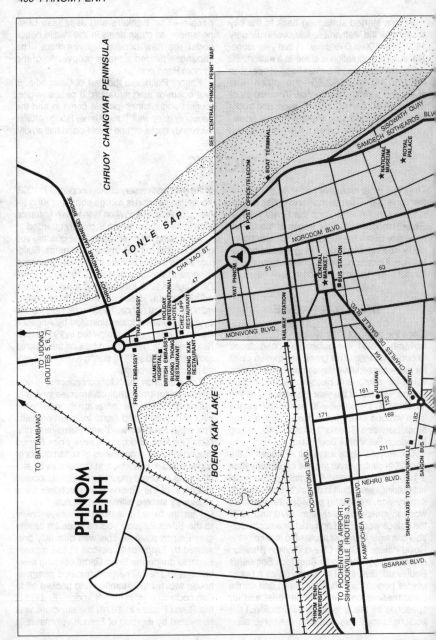

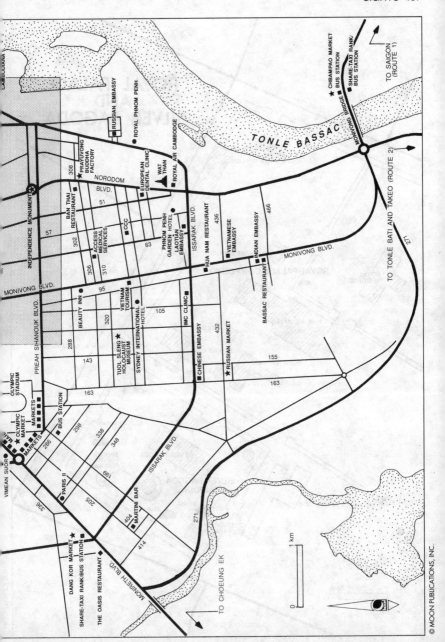

TONLE BASSAC

TO SAIGON
(ROUTE 1)

CHBAMPAO MARKET ★
BUS STATION ■
SHARE-TAXI RANK/ ■
BUS STATION

MONIVONG BRIDGE

RUSSIAN EMBASSY ■
● ROYAL PHNOM PENH

PRAYUVONG ★
BUDDHA
FACTORY

308

NORODOM

BLVD.

51

BAN THAI
RESTAURANT ●

57

302

ACCESS
MEDICAL
SERVICES

306 310

CCC

63

EUROPEAN ■
DENTAL CLINIC

WAT
THAN ▲ ● ROYAL AIR CAMBODGE

PHNOM PENH
GARDEN HOTEL ■
LAOTIAN ■
EMBASSY

ISSARAK BLVD.

436

HUA NAM RESTAURANT ■

VIETNAMESE ■
EMBASSY

INDIAN EMBASSY ■

466

MONIVONG BLVD.

BASSAC RESTAURANT ■

TO TONLE BATI AND TAKEO (ROUTE 2)

271

INDEPENDENCE MONUMENT

MONIVONG BLVD.

● SHINTA SIHANOUK BLVD.

PREAH SIHANOUK BLVD.

BEAUTY INN ●

95

320

VIETNAM ●
TOURISM

105

IMC CLINIC ■

288

TUOL SLENG ★
HOLOCAUST
MUSEUM

SYDNEY INTERNATIONAL
HOTEL

143

CHINESE EMBASSY ■

432

RUSSIAN MARKET ★

155

163

163

OLYMPIC
STADIUM

MARKETS ■■

OLYMPIC ★
MARKET

BUS STATION ■

MARKETS ■■

286 298

338

348

ISSARAK BLVD.

271

VIMEAN SUOR ●

PARIS II ●

199

205

MARTINI BAR ■

404

414

DANG KOR MARKET ★

SHARE-TAXI RANK/BUS STATION ■

THE OASIS RESTAURANT ●

596

336

MONIREETH BLVD.

TO CHOEUNG EK

1 km

0

© MOON PUBLICATIONS, INC.

ROYAL PALACE AND SILVER PAGODA

STREET 13

STREET 184

SAMDECH SOTHEAROS BLVD.

STREET 216

PUBLIC EVENTS PODIUM AND GATE (CHAN CHAYA PAVILION)

GATE

ELEPHANT PAVILION

ROYAL PALACE COMPOUND

ROYAL RESIDENCE

THRONE HALL

TREASURY

BANQUET HALL

ROYAL OFFICES

PAVILION OF NAPOLEON III

ENTRY TO SILVER PAGODA

STUPA

LIBRARY

EQUESTRIAN STATUE

STUPA

BELL TOWER

SILVER PAGODA

BUDDHA FOOTPRINT PAVILIONS

SILVER PAGODA COMPOUND

SAMDECH SOTHEAROS BLVD.

STUPA

STUPA

CELEBRATION PAVILION

STREET 240

STREET 7

0   50 m

MOON

© MOON PUBLICATIONS, INC.

1990. The Royal Offices stand just behind this building, built in 1948 and used as a residence by the Regent. Beyond you can see the outlines of the Throne Hall.

SILVER PAGODA

The Silver Pagoda is the royal chapel, located within the Royal Palace grounds but walled off in a separate enclosure. The pagoda was built in 1962, replacing an earlier 1892 version. After suffering damage and neglect in the Pol Pot era, it is cracked and peeling. The temple is intermittently closed due to restoration work, ongoing since 1993. The Silver Pagoda takes its name from the estimated 5,000 silver tiles covering the floor of the main temple. Each tile is made from a kilogram of silver. Although plundered by the Khmer Rouge, the Silver Pagoda contains some superb Buddha statuary; a few artifacts from the royal collection are displayed in glass cases.

Near the central dais in the main temple is a standing Buddha, made of solid gold and weighing in at 75 kg. The Buddha is not only life-size, it conforms to the vital statistics of King Norodom. The image was made in 1907 in the royal workshops, inlaid with over 9,000 precious stones, including diamonds studded on the forehead and palms. Companion statues include a silver and a bronze Buddha.

On the central dais sits a crystal Buddha image, copied from Pra Keo, the Emerald Buddha, at Bangkok's Grand Palace. The Emerald Buddha is regarded throughout Southeast Asia as a powerful talisman, imbued with miraculous powers. The inspiration for the Silver Pagoda is believed to be Bangkok's Wat Pra Keo. In Khmer, the Silver Pagoda is known as Preah Vihear Keo Morakot because it houses the Emerald Buddha knockoff.

At the rear of the dais is a standing Buddha made of Italian marble. Right at the back of the pagoda is a large marble Buddha in the Earth Witness pose, a gift from Burma. Beside it is a litter used for coronations—it was carried by a dozen men. More coronation regalia and dozens of smaller statues are displayed here.

In the courtyard of the Silver Pagoda compound are four large stupas (shrines) built by the Norodom family. The original temple arose during the reign of King Norodom—the stupa to the northeast is dedicated to him, and there's an equestrian statue of the king nearby. Actually, it's a statue of Napoleon III with Norodom's head. Three other stupas in the compound are dedicated to Norodom royal family members; the stupa to the southwest commemorates Sihanouk's favorite daughter, who died of leukemia in 1953. The others honor Sihanouk's father, King Norodom Suramarit, and the 19th-century king Ang Duong. Also in the courtyard is a bell tower, a library that once contained manuscripts on palm leaves, and a pavilion used for celebrations by the royal family. There are two Buddha footprint pavilions—one footprint is made of bronze, and comes from Sri Lanka.

Running the length of the walls enclosing the compound are 600 meters of covered galleries. Starting at the east gate and proceeding in a clockwise direction, the galleries depict episodes from the Reamker. The murals are in bad condition due to water damage and neglect—a Polish government group is restoring them.

The Silver Pagoda used to be under the control of the Ministry of Culture, but is now under the aegis of the palace. Entry fees and opening times chop and change—you have to negotiate with guards at the eastern entry gate. Due to restoration work, entry is not guaranteed—you might have to try several times before you get in. Guards may charge $3 to enter the grounds and a further $1 to enter the actual pagoda. It should be open daily except Monday, from 0700-1100 and 1400-1700. Remove your shoes when entering the Silver Pagoda; an attendant may require you to deposit your camera at the entrance.

NATIONAL MUSEUM

The National Museum is housed in a magnificent russet pavilion on Street 13 between Streets 178 and 184. It was designed by French archaeologist and painter George Groslier, and constructed in traditional style by Cambodian craftsmen in 1917-18 as an annex to the Ecole des Beaux Arts. The museum first opened in 1920. It's small, but harbors an astonishing wealth of Khmer stone, bronze, and wooden sculpture. The imposing wooden doors to the

TOURING THE ROYAL CITY

The southern sector of Phnom Penh close to the Tonle Sap River exudes a strong royal Khmer presence, with a wealth of Cambodian traditional architecture. The city was once rich in temples—many were destroyed under the Khmer Rouge, but some are being reconstructed. This tour starts at Wat Ounalom, opposite the Phnom Penh Tourism office.

Wat Ounalom is a Mahanikai Buddhist temple and highly respected institute of learning, with 50 monks in residence; before 1975 there were 500 monks here. This is the residence of the Supreme Patriarch of the Mahanikai sect. The temple was founded in the 15th century; a large number of its buildings were destroyed under Pol Pot, including the library. The temple has since been partially restored. The compound contains two residences, and a three-floor building which functions as a temple; the interiors are stark and bare. On the ground floor is a marble Buddha from Burma—smashed by the Khmer Rouge, but pieced together again in 1979. On the second floor is a brass statue of the patriarch of Cambodian Buddhism, Somdech Huot Tat, who was murdered by the Khmer Rouge. The statue, made in 1971, was flung into the river, but retrieved in 1979. On the third floor the walls depict scenes from the Jataka Tales.

From Wat Ounalom you can skirt round past the **National Museum.** The museum is notable not only for its outstanding exhibits but also for its superb traditional-style architecture. To do justice to the place, you really need to spend several hours. In this area is the Ecole des Beaux Arts (School of Fine Arts) where students often work on reproductions of famous Khmer artifacts. The souvenir and gift shops in the surrounding blocks are especially good for paintings, wood sculptures, and crafts. The School of Fine Arts has its own retail outlet.

Back on Samdech Sotheraos Boulevard you can cruise past **Chan Chaya Pavilion,** which doubles as a front gate to the Royal Palace and a public events podium. Above the pavilion is a huge portrait of King Sihanouk. The Royal Palace is closed to the public—what you glimpse through the gates is about it, unless you arrive in November when the palace is thrown open for three days. At the southern end of the palace grounds, you can drop in and visit the **Silver Pagoda.** Skirt the walls of the palace and head south to Wat Botum.

Buddhas and Bayon Heads

Wat Botum is known as the "Temple of the Lotus Blossoms"—the original site was a small island surrounded by a lotus-filled pond. This temple is the center of the Thammayut (royalist) sect of Buddhism in Cambodia. The royalist sect has been revived since the return of Sihanouk; about 85 monks now reside at Wat Botum. In July 1992, more than 150 bonzes (monks) were ordained here. At the front of the temple is an unusual cluster of stupas with Bayon-style four-headed tops; the ceremonial stupas hold the ashes of members of the royal family.

Opposite Wat Botum in a park is the **Liberation Monument,** carved from Angkor marble by the staff of the School of Fine Arts in 1989 to commemorate the 1979 liberation of Phnom Penh by Vietnamese troops. Proceed south and turn onto Preah Sihanouk Boulevard to see some of the best-preserved colonial mansions and manicured gardens in Phnom Penh. Over the boulevard to the west is the **Independence Monument,** looming like a kind of Cambodian Arc de Triomphe. Also called the Victory Monument, this Khmer-style *prasat* (tower) was built in 1958 to commemorate independence from France, but has since assumed the role of a war memorial. Wreath-laying ceremonies honor the dead. Like the towers of Angkor Wat and the four-headed spires of the Bayon, the monument is a national logo.

From the Independence Monument you can detour about 300 meters south to the **Prayuvong Buddha factory.** In the grounds of Wat Prayuvong, a neighborhood of workshops produces statuary and "spare parts" used in repairing temples smashed by the Khmer Rouge. The workshops turn out stupas and Buddhist artifacts, including gaudy cement Buddhas, Bayon heads, *nagas,* and mythological figures. You can walk around the various workshops and watch the artisans at work.

High Tea

Back on Preah Sihanouk Boulevard, head east past the *naga* fountain and along Samdech Sotheraos Boulevard to the **Hotel Sofitel Cambodiana.** The Cambodiana is a peculiar structure: it looks like the architect decided at the last minute to cap a European building with a pseudo-Khmer tile roof. Drop into the foyer to see the huge wooden model of the Bayon. A small gift shop sells books on Cambodia. High tea at the Cambodiana is held between 1400 and 1700—stuff yourself with sandwiches, pastries, fruit, and drinks for around $5; live classical music will ease your digestion. A plunge into the swimming pool will set you back $5. Khmer-style roofing also caps the nearby Ministry of Foreign Affairs, which looks like a converted wat, and Chaktomuk Theater.

Waterfront Pavilion

Locals turn out for a stroll at the end of the day past the tiny slope-roofed pavilion fronting the Tonle Sap River, opposite the Royal Palace Gates. At sunset impromptu picnickers frequent the place; police pursue food vendors up and down Sisowath Quay. Cyclo drivers arrive for river baths, and roving pho-

(continues on next page)

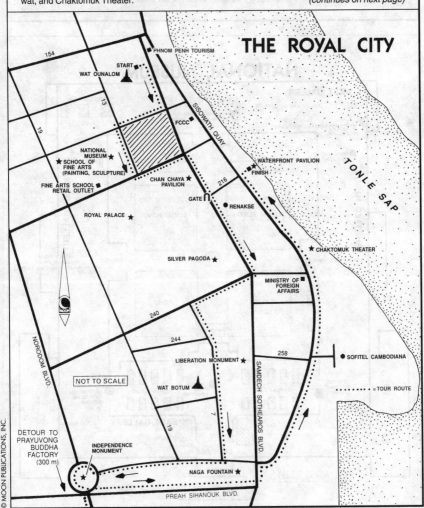

THE ROYAL CITY

TOURING THE ROYAL CITY
(continued)

tographers work the crowds. This is an excellent place to mingle. There are two shrines for offerings of garlands of jasmine and coconuts spiked with incense sticks and lotus buds. North of the pavilion are many sidewalk vendors. For drinks, try a beer stall on the banks of the Tonle Sap. For a more refined drink, the Foreign Correspondents Club of Cambodia (FCCC) top-floor bar is a colonial-era throwback, with swishing fans and elegant furnishings. The bar affords great views over the river.

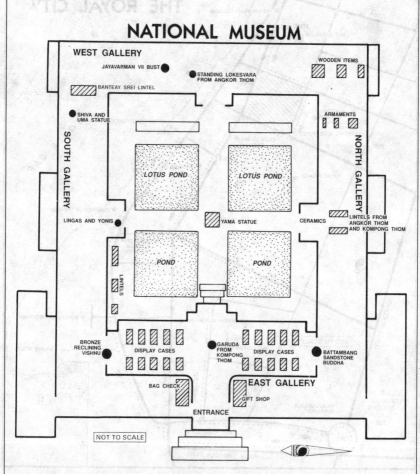

NATIONAL MUSEUM

WEST GALLERY

JAYAVARMAN VII BUST

STANDING LOKESVARA FROM ANGKOR THOM

WOODEN ITEMS

BANTEAY SREI LINTEL

SHIVA AND UMA STATUE

ARMAMENTS

SOUTH GALLERY

NORTH GALLERY

LOTUS POND

LOTUS POND

LINGAS AND YONIS

YAMA STATUE

CERAMICS

LINTELS FROM ANGKOR THOM AND KOMPONG THOM

POND

POND

LINTELS

BRONZE RECLINING VISHNU

DISPLAY CASES

GARUDA FROM KOMPONG THOM

DISPLAY CASES

BATTAMBANG SANDSTONE BUDDHA

EAST GALLERY

BAG CHECK

GIFT SHOP

ENTRANCE

NOT TO SCALE

© MOON PUBLICATIONS, INC.

VISIONS OF VISHNU

On your far left as you enter the National Museum is a fragment of a huge bronze head of Vishnu. Undoubtedly one of the greatest bronzes in Southeast Asia, it was cast using the lost-wax method—an achievement on par with the casting skills of the ancient Greeks or Romans. The original statue is estimated to have been six meters long; it presumably showed the four-armed Vishnu reclining on the serpent Ananta, pondering the future of the new world about to be born. The facial features were once inlaid with precious metal and gems.

Chinese chronicler Zhou Daguan, who visited Angkor in the 13th century as envoy to Timur Khan, left the only description of the original Vishnu, which functioned as a fountain: "At the center of the Eastern Lake stands a stone tower, with dozens of stone chambers. In it lies a recumbent bronze Buddha, from whose navel flows a steady stream of water." Zhou Daguan mistook the type of statue (it's not a Buddha) and the location (not the eastern lake but the western)—which is probably just as well since it foiled treasure hunters for years.

Incredibly, the location of the fabled statue was finally divined in a dream. Following the advice of a Siem Reap resident who had a vision of Vishnu in a dream, French archaeologists excavated an island-temple in the Western Baray reservoir, reaching the head of Vishnu in 1936.

museum, which weigh over a ton, were made by teachers and students from the Ecole des Beaux Arts. Passing through these doors you can witness the passage of a great civilization—as great as that of ancient Egypt, Greece, or China. A set of galleries arrayed around four lotus ponds, the National Museum is a tranquil and relaxing place.

The museum is open daily except Mondays and public holidays, from 0800-1030 and 1430-1630. Lunch hours tend to be flexible if you push your case. Entry fee is $2, plus $2 for a still camera, $5 for video camera. Photography of the courtyard only. An English- or French-speaking guide costs $2 for a one-hour tour, $10 for groups. There are brief labels in Khmer and French and sometimes in English: if you want more details, hire a guide. An excellent—and expensive, at $20—glossy catalogue titled *The Age of Angkor* was created for a 1992 exhibition of National Museum pieces in Australia. It may be available at the front. Scaled-down copies of well-known Khmer pieces are on sale at the museum gift shop, the pieces most likely creat-

ed by students at the adjacent School of Fine Arts. A number of handicraft shops in the area also sell these artifacts.

The museum's collection will undoubtedly change as renovation proceeds. There are currently more than 400 works in the collection, including massive stone heads from Angkor brought to the museum as late as 1994 for protection from theft. A conservator from the Australian National Gallery, who decided to tackle a flooding problem in the basement, came across 120 unopened crates in the dusty light. Boxes of rare artifacts were rushed by road from ancient temple sites around the country by the Ecole Française d'Extrême Orient for safekeeping as civil war escalated in 1970, and were never unpacked. As the museum's collection is documented and photographic and computer records compiled, more of Cambodia's treasures may surface. In 1992 a special exhibition of 35 stone and bronze pieces was arranged in Australia, which led to pledges by the Australian government for assistance at the National Museum.

Of special interest at the National Museum are pieces from the Angkor region, moved to this location for safekeeping. If you're going to Angkor, a visit to the museum before (and after) will bring the place to life. Angkor has hardly a single Buddha head left in place, as most have been looted. Small objects are likewise nowhere on display at Angkor, but in the east gallery of the National Museum you'll find display cases filled with exquisite smaller pieces. These include delicate bronze oil lamps and incense holders, some shaped like lotuses, as well as jewelry, silver spittoons, bronze spoons, fine bronze Buddhas, heads, hands, fragments, and such rarities as a small quartz linga from Angkor Thom. The National Museum itself is not immune from headhunters—during the confusion of the 1970s, several pieces were stolen.

TOURING THE FRENCH QUARTER

Might as well go straight to the heart of Phnom Penh: step right up and meet Madame Penh herself. She's the revered figure encased in a tiny shrine on the top of **Wat Phnom,** the temple on the hill overlooking the city from the north end of Norodom Boulevard.

Wat Phnom is the oldest temple in town. Legend has it that in the 14th century a wealthy widow, Madame Penh, discovered four statues of Buddha in a tree trunk that washed up on the riverbank. It turned out that these Buddhas originally came from Laos and were miraculously carried downstream by a flood. With the help of villagers, Madame Penh built a small pagoda to house the images. Phnom means "hill," so this is the hill of Madame Penh. The name was later transferred to the settlement that grew up around the hill.

Madame Penh looks very Buddha-like herself—big eyebrows, big earlobes, and earrings. The residents of Phnom Penh make offerings of fruit, flowers, incense, and money at this small shrine. They come to this and other small temples on the hill to pray for protection on journeys, success in exams or the lottery, or healing from sickness.

The eastern stairway is the most dramatic approach to this sacred area. There are two huge five-headed *nagas* sliding down the stairs here, beggars and bird sellers line the steps; the purchased birds are released for luck or meritmaking, and are quickly recaptured. At the top of the steps is the main temple; out back is the tiny Madame Penh shrine, and to the south side a massive stupa. The stupa is said to contain the ashes of Ponhea Yat, the post-Angkorian king who made Phnom Penh his capital.

Eventually Madame Penh's pagoda was replaced by larger temples, built in 1806, 1894, and 1926. The main temple houses a resplendent seated Buddha. The exterior features painted Angkor *apsaras* in relief; a series of frescoes on the life of Buddha cover interior walls. Worshippers make their rounds, leaving incense at various shrines or offering food for blessing before it's taken home to the family table. The Chinese and Vietnamese residents of Phnom Penh have constructed a shrine off to the side. Raw meat is sometimes placed in the mouths of two lion statues here, near a burner for Chinese-style paper money.

On the north slope of Wat Phnom once stood a mini-zoo with elephant rides. Now there's a white elephant in the form of an enormous *chedi* (stupa) scuttled halfway through construction when it was discovered the foundations were only 10 meters deep, instead of 25. Amid charges of fraud, corruption, and graft, plans for a 50-meter-high *chedi* were abandoned after a million dollars had been spent on the project, intended to house a sacred bone of the Buddha. There are plans to turn the site into a museum for Buddhist scriptures. On the south slope is a plaque inscribed "Traite Franco-Siamois 1907 Battambang-Siem Reap-Sisopon, Consul de France 1903," commemorating the French-orchestrated return of Siem Reap and Battambang provinces to Cambodia; the French had ceded these same territories to the Thais in 1867. Opposite Wat Phnom to the northeast is a building that served as UNTAC Headquarters from 1992 to 1993. Opposite is the site of the former Cercle Sportif, the French sports club. The tennis courts are still in operation.

French Villas

Proceeding from Wat Phnom north on Street 47 you encounter a string of villas—the old French residential area, with structures under renovation for use by companies like TNT and Castrol. Some villas here are in great condition, others decayed and crumbling. Turn right on Street 80 toward the Tonle Sap River and follow the banks up to the bridge.

Chruoy Changvar Bridge was built in 1965 and destroyed 10 years later. Until 1993 the initial spans jutted out from both sides of the Tonle Sap. Enterprising stall vendors set up impromptu restaurants at the very edge of the Phnom Penh side of the blown-up bridge, and motorcyclists would run out for an afternoon snack. The bridge was reconstructed with Japanese aid and reopened in 1994 as the Cambodian-Japanese Friendship Bridge. It leads to fishing villages and farmland on the Chruoy Changvar Peninsula.

West of the bridge, along Street 72, is the **French Embassy** compound where foreigners took refuge after the Khmer Rouge takeover of Phnom Penh on 17 April 1975. Some 800 foreigners and 600 Cambodians crowded onto the grounds; meanwhile, Phnom Penh's entire population was forced into the countryside. The French vice-consul was informed that if he did not expel all the Cambodians within 48 hours, the foreigners would forfeit their lives: the Khmer Rouge recog-

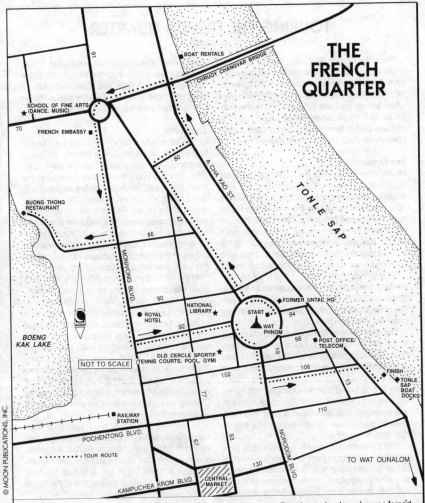

nized no diplomatic privilege. Only Cambodian women married to foreigners could remain, and a number of marriages were hastily arranged to safeguard some of the Cambodian women. The Cambodians left the embassy quietly—very few survived. Within two weeks, the foreigners were driven in trucks to the Thai border and released. Among those released was a Cambodian child born on the embassy grounds—the child's mother gave

him to a young French couple when she was forced to leave the compound. After terms as an orphanage, ammunition dump, and a place for squatters, the embassy compound was returned to the French in 1991, when diplomatic relations were restored. The building was completely gutted and restored, with the addition of landscaped gardens, and the embassy reopened with a champagne toast to Bastille Day in 1995.

(continues on next page)

TOURING THE FRENCH QUARTER

(continued)

From the French Embassy, head south. You might want to detour to Boeng Kak Lake, accessed from Street 86. There are several floating restaurants fronting the lake. Buong Thong Restaurant offers breezy pavilions jutting onto the lake, with pricey Thai and seafood dishes and drinks. The northern part of Boeng Kak Lake contains a large shantytown district with taxi girls called Tuol Kork.

The Royal

Moving south, you'll reach the Royal Hotel on Street 92. The Royal was originally constructed as part of a chain of flashy hotels by the Societé des Grands Hôtels Indochinois. It was the best-known tourist hotel in Phnom Penh in the 1920s and 1930s—well-heeled travelers motoring up to Angkor or en route to Bangkok or Saigon would stay here. In the 1970s it was the preferred residence of journalists covering the war. In the early 1990s the hotel served as an elaborate brothel, with a bar full of Vietnamese taxi girls. Today the Royal has a derelict air about it: Singapore's DBS Land group, which owns the Raffles Hotel, recently signed a $25-million deal to renovate the 200-room hotel.

The **Bibliothèque Nationale** (National Library), built in 1924, is not much to look at and has very few books. What is remarkable is that it has any books at all. When the Khmer Rouge moved into Phnom Penh they intended to wipe out recorded history. They tore up books to make cigarettes and hurled volumes into the street. Some 20% of the collection was destroyed. Pigs were raised at the front of the library to supply meat to Chinese experts staying next door at the Royal.

After the Khmer Rouge were ousted in 1979, people returning to Phnom Penh took cartloads of books to their homes—some to read, some to sell, some to use as wrapping paper. The library reopened in 1980 with bare shelves. It had to rely on foreign donations in the form of books, equipment, and training. Today, there are fewer than 200,000 titles—139,000 in Khmer, 23,000 in French, and 17,500 in English. Library staff hope to access works written in Khmer by importing microfilms of French collections.

The Docks

On the other side of Street 92, to the west side of Wat Phnom, is the old Cercle Sportif—the swimming pool, gym, and tennis courts are still in operation. Skirting Wat Phnom, take the road to the south of the wat, which passes between two children's parks, and turn left on Street 106. This district is part of the former French administrative area, with huge grassy strips in the middle of wide boulevards. The architecture is a study in contrasts—finely refurbished colonial mansions with satellite dishes on the rooftops juxtaposed with colonial edifices now blackened by charcoal and smoke.

At the far east end of Street 106 is a busy dock area, with porters loading (or is it overloading?) boats on the Tonle Sap River. Goods are transported by cyclo or motorized three-wheeler, then carried to boats on the backs of porters—sacks of rice, crates of beer, bags of coconuts, giant pots, sacks of charcoal. Slow cargo boats proceed from here upriver to Siem Reap or Kompong Cham. There are a lot of warehouses for rice and other products in the strip along the waterfront. Many of these commercial enterprises were previously run by Chinese and Vietnamese—their presence is still apparent in the area.

To see more port activity, hire a sampan or other vessel. Boat rentals are available at the docks, and also north of Chruoy Changvar Bridge. A covered boat is a good idea to keep you and your camera sheltered from the harsh sun. A one- or two-hour boat trip offers a unique perspective of the Royal Palace and other waterfront landmarks.

In the courtyard at the center of four ponds is a seated statue, originally from the Terrace of the Leper King at Angkor Thom. French archaeologist Groslier noticed saw marks on the head of the statue and had it removed to Phnom Penh. A concrete copy was left at Angkor Thom, but even that was subsequently decapitated. The sandstone statue in the National Museum is one of the most celebrated images in Khmer art. While some identify the statue as Yama (Judge of the Dead in Hindu legend) or a naked ascetic (possibly an incarnation of Shiva), others speculate it's a likeness of Yasovarman I, the Angkor king who reigned 889-910 and reputedly died of leprosy.

Large sculptures in the courtyard galleries are arranged haphazardly. The south gallery contains pre-Angkor pieces, including a rare 6th-century eight-armed Vishnu from Takeo, and a few colossal lingas on yoni bases. The west gallery features sculpture and lintels from the 9th-13th century Angkor period and 13th-14th century Bayon period. In the north gallery are wooden pieces from the 15th to 19th centuries, some 16th-century armaments, and a display of ceramics.

Some Angkor-related pieces to look for include the following.

Banteay Srei Pediment

In the southwest corner of the museum is one of the finest examples of Khmer narrative sculpture prior to Angkor Wat. It is a 10th-century pediment—a large sandstone triangular decoration above a doorway—from Banteay Srei. Only six such pediments are known to have survived: four are at Banteay Srei, northeast of Angkor; the fifth is here; the sixth was removed by the French and sits in the Musée Guimet in Paris. The National Museum piece shows a scene from the great Hindu epic the Mahabharata, with Bhima battling Duryodhana.

Shiva and Uma

Close to the Banteay Srei pediment is a small sandstone image of Shiva with his consort Uma, believed to have been sculpted in the 10th century. The statue once presided over the south sanctuary of Banteay Srei temple; a French army officer removed the image to Phnom Penh in 1914. Uma's head was lopped off and stolen from the National Museum during the 1970s. Earlier photographs of the complete piece reveal the missing head resembles Shiva's, but on a smaller scale.

Jayavarman VII

Near the center of the west gallery is a magnificent sandstone bust of Jayavarman VII, the great Angkor king who ruled from 1181 to 1218. The statue comes from Siem Reap, and is sculpted in 12th-13th century Bayon style. Jayavarman's eyes are downcast; the arms are missing, but presumably the king is sitting in a meditative pose. Portraiture was one of the great achievements of the Khmers. In the same area

Shiva and Uma statue: Uma's head was stolen in the 1970s.

is a portrait head of a younger-looking Jayavarman VII, found in 1958 at Kompong Svay, 105 km east of Angkor. Another huge piece in this part of the museum is a two-meter-high standing Lokesvara from the Gate of the Dead at Angkor Thom, dating from the 12th to 13th centuries.

Woodcarving

Most elaborate woodwork from Angkor has completely disappeared, including the wooden structures of the royal palace. At the northwest corner of the museum is a small section with wood (particularly teak) items from the 15th to 19th centuries. These give an idea of the considerable skills of Khmer woodcarvers. Items on display include a royal boat, wooden temple ornaments, and weaving looms. Also in the north gallery is a display of armaments, and ethnology and ceramics sections.

Angkor Thom Lintel

At the center of the north gallery are two sandstone lintels, decorative elements used above doorways. One is an 11th-century piece from Kompong Thom, depicting a battle between Krishna and the *naga* serpent-king Kaliya. The

BATMAN AND THE SECOND CEILING

In the early 1990s the Australian government, the Australian National Gallery, and Australian corporate sponsors worked to document the National Museum collection, train staff, introduce modern management and marketing techniques, and fund roof repairs. The Khmer-style roof had a number of missing and broken tiles, which allowed seeping water to damage exhibits. Timber supporting the roof rotted, and was also attacked by white ants and termites. Restoration work involved cleaning, painting, and repairing the roof, towers, and decorative panels.

But those problems were minor compared with the bats, whose smelly guano is responsible for the museum's odor, presented unique challenges. Bat guano is highly acidic—it can eat into stone.

The bat problem apparently intensified during the Pol Pot era, when most Phnom Penh buildings were left derelict. Research revealed upward of two million twittering bats living in the ceiling of the museum—perhaps the largest bat colony in any artificial construction. The National Museum is the only structure in the capital capable of harboring the bats in such large numbers. Because of their sheer number, and the amount of insects they consume

and the guano they deposit, the bats can't be removed without causing a serious ecological problem.

Enter Batman—an Australian bat expert. Batman's reconnaissance work identified three species of bats at the museum; one tiny critter is apparently an agent for pollinating durians. The majority of the museum's bats belong to a hitherto unknown species dubbed the Cambodian Freetail.

The Australian solution was to build a secondary ceiling below the roof, preventing bat guano (and lice) from falling on museum visitors and exhibits. This would allow easy inspection and cleaning of the roof. Work on the roof was completed in 1995 at a cost of over half-a-million dollars. Today three truckloads (about 1,000 kg) of bat guano are removed every month and sold as fertilizer, raising about $250. Proceeds from the droppings are used to cover museum expenses, providing flashlight batteries for museum guards and brooms for cleaning. Sometimes people come into the museum to try and catch bats. According to Cambodian folklore, the blood of a bat can cure a child's cough. And the flavor of bat meat is said to be tasty when the flesh is boiled with rice. A permanent solution to the bat problem is being explored to protect both the local ecosystem and the museum's exhibits.

---

second lintel, from Angkor Thom, also depicts a scene from Hindu mythology. Both lintels reflect the perfection of sculptural techniques and fluid florid forms in sandstone that prompted several early Western theorists to conjecture the Khmers had borrowed elements from Italian Renaissance sculpture—in fact, they predated it.

TUOL SLENG HOLOCAUST MUSEUM

This chilling place has been dubbed "Auschwitz on the Mekong." Tuol Sleng and Auschwitz are indeed remarkably similar and remarkably sickening. Genocidal purges targeting those with racial, religious, or other differences are no different today—witness the "ethnic cleansing" in Bosnia, Tibet, and Rwanda. What stands out in Cambodia is the sheer scale of the operation. Over 1.5 million people were slaughtered under Pol Pot's genocidal regime. Twenty years on, Pol Pot and

his cohorts remain at large—and the Khmer Rouge are still active—and still killing people.

Tuol Sleng, also known as Security Prison 21 (S-21), is a former high school transformed into a detention and interrogation center. Cambodians and their families accused of being "traitors" were brought to S-21. An estimated 14,000-20,000 inmates passed through Tuol Sleng, tortured to death or killed by summary execution, either here or at Choeung Ek. Mass graves are located in the school grounds. This insane program of extermination extended to former Khmer Rouge cadres and functionaries—and to the executioners themselves. Incoming prisoners were numbered and photographed on arrival. They were violently coerced into writing elaborate confessions of life-long allegiance to the CIA, KGB, Vietnamese, or all three. The Tuol Sleng manual revealed the sole purpose of torture was to extract these absurd confessions of foreign allegiance. With meticulous efficiency,

Photos of victims line the walls at the Tuol Sleng Holocaust Museum.

the confessions were carefully filed away with the black-and-white snapshots of the victims. Then the "traitors" were put to death at Tuol Sleng, or taken to Choeung Ek and executed.

Into the Compound

When the invading Vietnamese entered Phnom Penh in 1979, they captured Tuol Sleng, the instruments of torture, and the archive in a fairly intact state. With assistance from East German experts, the Vietnamese turned the building into a holocaust museum.

The compound consists of four buildings of similar size. Signs are posted in English, including a translation of the stark S-21 Security Regulations. Building A consists of three stories with 20 cells. Ten cells were used for interrogation of high officials, who were chained to beds. Nearby are the graves of the last 14 victims, found tortured to death when the Vietnamese took the building in 1979. Another seven prisoners were found alive—they had survived because they had mechanical skills useful to their captors. Some had worked turning out busts of Pol Pot.

Building B contains rooms and rooms of black-and-white photos of those arrested and tortured, from the record-keeping archives of the Khmer Rouge. Thousands of stark snapshots overlook the same rooms where the victims were most likely tortured. The Khmer Rouge often took pictures both before and after torture, with gruesome results. The most shocking pictures are not displayed on the walls, as

two Western photographers restoring the negatives found out. From 6,000 negatives of S-21 inmates, the Photo Archive Group selected 100 to make high-quality prints to be housed in archives in Cambodia and abroad.

On the ground floor of Building C former classrooms were divided by brick partitions into single cells. The second floor was for mass detention. Barbed wire was installed on the third floor to prevent inmates from jumping off to commit suicide. In Building D are artists' renditions of tortures carried out at Tuol Sleng— mostly captioned in Khmer, and occasionally in French. Paintings show mass detention in Building C, single-cell inmates, use of the courtyard for water torture, and Khmer Rouge soldiers bayoneting babies and dashing them against coconut trees. A few photos depict the expulsion of the population from major urban centers. Some material is clearly Vietnamese propaganda to justify its invasion of Cambodia—a map details some 6,000 acts of aggression by Pol Pot and company against Vietnam from 1975 to 1978.

Building D contains a huge map of Cambodia fashioned out of human skulls and bones, with rivers painted blood-red. This macabre skullmap is of questionable taste, showing a lack of respect for the dead. The intention is to show physical evidence of Khmer Rouge atrocities. The skulls were assembled in the shape of a map of Cambodia by the Vietnamese for their own propaganda purposes. In 1994, King Siha-

RELIVING THE HORROR

In April 1975 New York Times correspondent Sydney Schanberg and several other journalists were held at gunpoint on Chruoy Changvar Bridge by the Khmer Rouge. Only the pleading of Schanberg's Cambodian aide and friend Dith Pran saved them from summary execution; later they managed to gain the sanctuary of the nearby French Embassy. But Schanberg could not in turn save Dith Pran, who was forced to walk out of the embassy gates into the hands of the Khmer Rouge. Pran was one of the very few Cambodians who left the embassy and survived.

After four years of hellish experiences with the Khmer Rouge, he escaped to a refugee camp in Thailand, where eventually Schanberg located him. His haunting real-life story is portrayed in the 1984 movie *The Killing Fields,* directed by Roland Joffé and based on a series of articles by Schanberg in the *New York Times Magazine.* The movie was filmed mostly in Thailand, with the Hua Hin Railway Hotel standing in for Phnom Penh's Royal Hotel.

The Killing Fields featured a stunning debut by Dr. Haing Ngor, who received an Academy Award for his portrayal of Dith Pran. He was not exactly acting—it was closer to reenacting. Dr. Ngor was performing an emergency operation in Phnom Penh when the Khmer Rouge broke into the hospital, demanding to know the identities of the doctors. Haing Ngor suddenly switched professions to taxicab driver. He survived Khmer Rouge atrocities and eventually reached the safety of a Thai refugee camp.

Ngor saw the film as a way of bringing his nation's ordeal to light. "If I die now from now on, OK," Ngor said. "The film will go on for 100 years." *The Killing Fields* is a powerful tool to keep the memory of Khmer Rouge atrocities alive. On the eve of the May 1993 elections the film, dubbed in Khmer, was aired by state television.

nouk proposed the bones and skulls of Khmer Rouge victims in the museum be cremated. Buddhists believe cremation is necessary to liberate the soul. Sihanouk contributed money for the cremation ceremony, and to build a stupa for the ashes. However, he abandoned the idea after pleas from the Cambodian People's Party, which claimed most Cambodians wished to retain the bones as evidence of Khmer Rouge crimes. The deputy director of Tuol Sleng Museum said, "If we keep the display of bones it goes against our Buddhist belief, but if we cremate them we lose the evidence of Khmer Rouge crimes."

Tuol Sleng Museum is located on the southern side of Phnom Penh off Street 350; the entrance is on the western side of the compound. The museum is open daily 0700-1130 and 1400-1700; a contribution is expected upon entry. Visitor books are kept by the museum custodians—you might want to read the comments, and add your own. A follow-up to Tuol Sleng is a trip to the Killing Fields at Choeung Ek, 15 km southwest of Phnom Penh.

MILITARY MUSEUM

This small museum is of specialized interest, and offers little English labeling. It's located on Norodom Boulevard near the corner of Street 172. A $2 entry fee includes a guide who escorts you round the exhibits. There are several salons inside the main building. One shows the fight against the French in 1951, with US, French, and Chinese military hardware displayed. Another section concerns the Vietnamese fight against the Khmer Rouge in 1979. There are three sculptures from Angkor Wat, intercepted from smugglers on the Thai border. A large painting depicts the construction of Angkor.

The Khmer Rouge received the bulk of their supplies from the Chinese. In the courtyard are captured Chinese and Russian equipment: a MiG-19 seized at Pochentong, half a dozen Russian T-58 and Chinese T-59 tanks, a dozen artillery pieces, a Chinese truck, and an army boat used on the Tonle Sap.

STARTING OVER

In the southern section of Phnom Penh on Norodom Boulevard is Wat Than, an unusual temple compound. In one corner lies a temple, with residences for several dozen monks; the rest of the grounds are used as a national rehabilitation center for the disabled. Here several NGOs work with amputees, usually mine victims, in a program established in 1982. Up to 100 amputees may occupy the premises at one time. Handicap International initially treats amputees, AFSC works with prosthetics, and Maryknoll provides six months of skills training for amputees. A small shop sells wooden items, tailored clothing, and handicraft items made by those disabled by mines; you're welcome to visit the shop and browse.

At Wat Than everything is located on the grounds—medical facilities, artificial-limb making, schoolrooms and workshops for teaching tailoring, furniture making, and secretarial skills. Wheelchairs are improvised from wooden chairs with mounted bicycle wheels. Those with amputations below the knee are fitted for prostheses and wait two weeks for limbs. Those with amputations above the knee must wait a month for a fitting. Artificial arms are also available.

Since rice growing is a major activity in Cambodia, a prosthetic limb must withstand long periods of submersion in water. The Jaipur limb is a fully mobile prosthesis made from locally available materials. It was designed by an Indian doctor for agricultural work. The Vietnam Veterans of America Foundation (VVAF) has established a clinic to produce the prostheses and train Cambodians as skilled technicians in the Jaipur limb system. There's no shortage of customers: Cambodia has over 40,000 amputees, more per capita than any other country in the world.

There are four facilities for amputees in Phnom Penh, and 15 or so other centers around Cambodia. Half a dozen foreign aid groups in Cambodia are involved in manufacturing prosthetics and wheelchairs. Eventually, Cambodia aims to be self-reliant in the production and fitting of limbs. Cambodia Trust established a national school of prosthetics and orthotics at Phnom Penh's Calmette Hospital in 1994 to train Cambodians to fit artificial limbs.

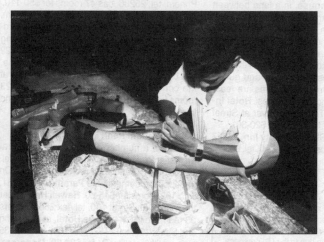

crafting prosthetic limbs at Wat Than

ACCOMMODATIONS

GUESTHOUSE/BUDGET

The main backpacker hotel is the **Capitol,** on Street 182 at the corner of Street 107. On the ground level is a restaurant and café; above are several floors of rooms for $5 s no bath or $8-10 d with bath. The Capitol Restaurant is the place to meet other travelers, and to arrange cheap taxis or visa extensions. Also run by the owners of the Capitol is the low-priced and seedy **Happy Guesthouse,** next door with paper-thin walls. Around the corner on Street 111 is family-run **Guesthouse 20,** with a few rooms available for $5 each. The **Naga Guesthouse,** at 48 Street 111 near the corner of Street 232, offers double rooms in the $15-40 range.

On the north side of Phnom Penh is **Lotus Guesthouse,** at 121 Samdech Sothearos Blvd., close to Street 104; 10 rooms with fan and shower. **Sok Sin Guesthouse,** in a lane between Calmette Hospital and the French Embassy, features a dozen fan rooms for $5 each. Near the mosque at Boeng Kak Lake is **Number 9 Guesthouse** with fan rooms for $6.

In the area close to the Tonle Sap River are some sleazy Chinese-run hotels and guesthouses—some of the smaller ones are massage parlors and short-time places. **Hotel Indochine,** near the Tonle Sap River at Street 144, tel. 27292, has 10 rooms for $20-30.

South of Issarak Blvd. is **Beauty Inn,** at 537 Monivong Blvd. (opposite Street 294), tel. 64505.

EXTRA VOLATILE

The information contained here can change instantly—street names revised, phone numbers altered, new money introduced. Many recent upheavals are due to the UN presence and its aftermath. With 20,000 foreign soldiers and UN workers coming in, businesses mushroomed—and many hotels and restaurants folded when they left.

This minihotel offers 17 rooms with all mod cons for $12 s or $15-23 d.

MODERATE

Midrange hotels are concentrated along or near Monivong Blvd. in the section near the Central Market. Most were built or renovated for the UN trade and offer creature comforts like air-conditioning, hot water, satellite TV, phone, minibar, and so on. Rooms in midrange hotels generally cost between $25 and $50. You can often negotiate 20-30% discounts in the following hotels, particularly for longer stays. Rates may not include government tax and service charges.

North of Pochentong Boulevard: The **Royal Hotel,** near Wat Phnom, is undergoing renovation. It may offer cheaper rooms for about $35 apiece. **Wat Phnom Hotel,** just east of Wat Phnom, tel. 26286, has 47 rooms for $50-110. The **Riverside,** by the river east of Wat Phnom, charges $70-90 a room. A few Chinese-run hotels are found near the river including **Mekong Thmey Hotel,** 35 Street 108, tel. 60087, with 29 double rooms for $30-40 with fridge, phone, and bath; and **Cathay Hotel,** 123 Street 110, at the corner of Street 19, tel. 22471, with 23 rooms for $25-40 d with air-con, hot water, and fridge.

Central Phnom Penh

There are a number of hotels in the Central Market area. The **Pailin** on Monivong Blvd., tel. 22475, has 81 renovated rooms for $33-66. On the opposite corner is the **Paradis,** tel. 22951, with 102 rooms for $45-60. **Hawaii Hotel,** near the market on Street 130, tel./fax 26652, offers 33 rooms for $30-40. **Asie Hotel,** at Monivong and Street 136, tel. 27825, fax 26334, rents 135 rooms with satellite TV for $25-60. **Monorom,** 89 Monivong, tel. 26149, fax 26073, is an older hotel with 63 rooms; singles $35-45 (no TV), doubles for $55 with fridge and TV. **Singapore Hotel,** 62 Monivong, tel. 25552, fax 26570, has 25 rooms for $25 s or $40 d with all mod cons.

To the east side of the Central Market is **La Paillote,** on 130 Street at the corner of Street 53, tel. 22151, fax 26513—an old building with 24 rooms for $30-80. **Regent Hotel,** 7 Street 109, tel. 27651, fax 27649, has 21 rooms for $35 s or $40 d. In the same area are Neakpean and Mittapheap Hotels, catering to the karaoke crowd.

Renakse Hotel, 40 Samdech Sothearos Blvd., tel. 22457, fax 26100, is right opposite the Royal Palace. It's run-down, but the location and price are right, and it has a big garden. There are 30 rooms in this building, used as a government building in the 1950s. Prices are $25 s and $30 d, with air-con and hot water but no TV or phone. **Hotel Pasteur,** at 60 Street 51 near the corner of Street 174, tel. 24746, fax 26727, has 16 quiet rooms for $35-55. Nearby, with slightly higher prices, is **International House,** at 35 Street 178, tel. 62159. **China-town Hotel,** 46 Street 214, tel. 23445, fax 27641, offers 20 rooms for $30 s or $40-65 d with air-con, TV, fridge, and phone. More on the fringes, southwest along Charles de Gaulle Blvd., is a string of hotels—Oriental, Sangkar, Borei Thmei and Vimean Suor.

South of Preah Sihanouk Boulevard
A short way south of the Independence Monument is the **Green Hotel** at 145 Norodom Blvd., tel. 26055, with 35 rooms going for $65-75. Nearby is **Rama Inn,** at 10 Street 282, with 28 rooms for $35-45; terrace and bar. **Sydney In-ternational Hotel,** on Street 360, tel. 27907, features a lobby decor of Fosters cans and a model of the Sydney Opera House; it offers 45 rooms with full facilities for $21-50. Near the corner of Streets 57 and 398 is **Phnom Penh Garden Hotel,** tel. 27264, fax 27345, with 22 rooms for $60 s and $80-120 d.

LUXURY

Allson Star on Monivong at Street 128, tel. 62008, fax 62018, offers 67 rooms for $80 and up. The Singapore-managed hotel has room safes, satellite TV, IDD, and minibar. **Holiday In-ternational Hotel,** on Street 84 near Calmette Hospital, tel. 27400, fax 27401, has 60 rooms for $70-90 apiece; small pool. **Diamond Hotel,** 184 Monivong, tel. 27221, fax 26637, has 86 rooms for $70-90 s and $120 d.

The Thai-managed **Royal Phnom Penh** is located at the south end of Samdech Sothearos Blvd., tel./fax 60036. The hotel features 40 rooms at present, for $120-150 single or double; there are plans to add another 300 rooms with a high-rise wing and a pool, making this a resort. The hotel has a good restaurant—the Bassac—and a nightclub.

The latest luxury addition is the **Landmark Boulevard Hotel,** 63 Norodom Blvd., tel. 26943, fax 28506. **Hotel Sofitel Cambodiana,** 313 Sisowath Quay, tel. 26288, fax 26392, is Phnom

the Hotel Cambodiana

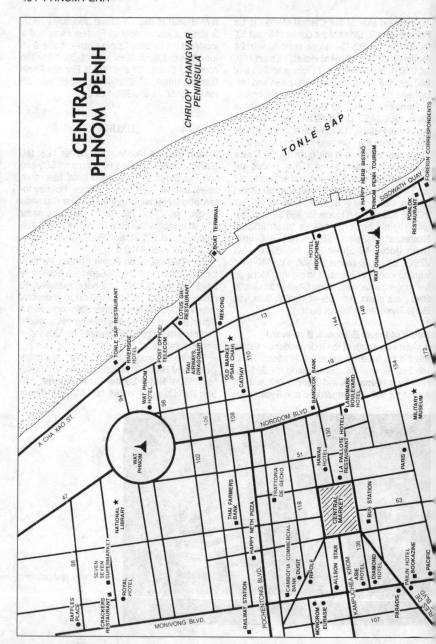

CENTRAL PHNOM PENH

CHRUOY CHANGVAR PENINSULA

TONLE SAP

SISOWATH QUAY

FOREIGN CORRESPONDENTS

HAPPY HERB BISTRO

PHNOM PENH TOURISM

PONLOK RESTAURANT

WAT OUNALOM

HOTEL INDOCHINE

BOAT TERMINAL

TONLE SAP RESTAURANT

RIVERSIDE HOTEL

POST OFFICE/ TELECOM

LOTUS GH RESTAURANT

MEKONG

THAI AIRWAYS, DRAGONAIR

OLD MARKET (PSAR CHAH)

CATHAY

BANGKOK BANK

LANDMARK BOULEVARD HOTEL

A CHA XAO ST.

WAT PHNOM HOTEL

WAT PHNOM

NORODOM BLVD.

MILITARY MUSEUM

NATIONAL LIBRARY

THAI FARMERS BANK

HAPPY NETH PIZZA

TRATTORIA DE GECKO

HAWAII HOTEL

LA PAILLOTE HOTEL/ RESTAURANT

PARIS

SEVEN SEVEN SUPERMARKET

CENTRAL MARKET

BUS STATION

RAFFLES PLACE

CRACKERS RESTAURANT

ROYAL HOTEL

RAILWAY STATION

CAMBODIA COMMERCIAL BANK

DUSIT

RIPOLE

ALLSON STAR

HAPPY NETH PIZZA

POCHENTONG BLVD.

KAMPUCHEA KROM

ASIE HOTEL

DIAMOND HOTEL

PAILIN HOTEL

BOOKAZINE

PACIFIC

MONOROM

EURASIE

PARADIS

MONIVONG BLVD.

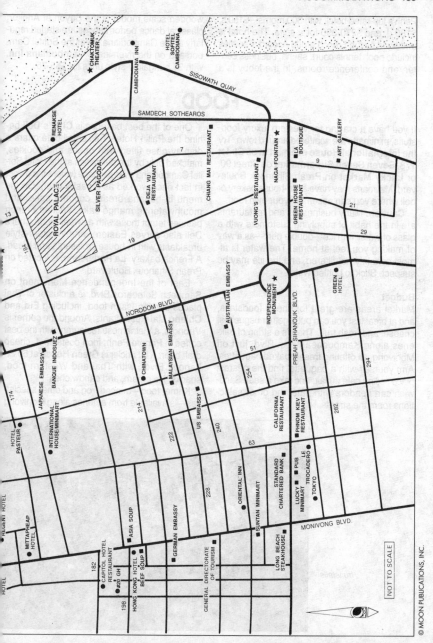

Map labels (reading across the map):

CHAKTOMUK THEATER ★
HOTEL SOFITEL CAMBODIANA
CAMBODIANA INN
SISOWATH QUAY
RENAKSE HOTEL
SAMDECH SOTHEAROS
LA BOUTIQUE
ART GALLERY
9
7
CHIANG MAI RESTAURANT
DEJA VU RESTAURANT
GREEN HOUSE RESTAURANT
21
ROYAL PALACE
SILVER PAGODA
13
VUONG'S RESTAURANT
NAGA FOUNTAIN ★
29
184
19
INDEPENDENCE MONUMENT ★
GREEN HOTEL
NORODOM BLVD.
AUSTRALIAN EMBASSY
PREAH SIHANOUK BLVD.
JAPANESE EMBASSY
HOTEL PASTEUR
INTERNATIONAL HOUSE/MINIMART
CHINATOWN
MALAYSIAN EMBASSY
BANQUE INDOSUEZ
51
254
294
174
214
222
US EMBASSY
240
CALIFORNIA RESTAURANT
PHNOM KIEV RESTAURANT
282
REGENT HOTEL
MITAPHEAP HOTEL
ASIA SOUP
GERMAN EMBASSY
ORIENTAL INN
228
SUNTAN MINIMART
63
STANDARD CHARTERED BANK
LUCKY MINIMART
PUB
LE TROCADERO
TOKYO
HOTEL
182
198
CAPITOL HOTEL RESTAURANT
#20 GH
HONG KONG HOTEL
BEEF SOUP
GENERAL DIRECTORATE OF TOURISM
LONG BEACH STEAKHOUSE
MONIVONG BLVD.

NOT TO SCALE

© MOON PUBLICATIONS, INC.

Penh's top-rated hotel, with 300 rooms—$150 s, $180 d, and $270-390 for a suite. The hotel is managed by the French group Accord. Facilities include pool, tennis court, sauna, business center, and conference rooms. In the lobby is a wooden scale model of the Bayon at Angkor; classical dance performances are staged regularly at the Cambodiana. Near the Sofitel Cambodiana on the riverside is **Cambodiana Inn,** with 21 bungalow-style units for $55-75.

FOOD

If you have a craving for Western luxury foodstuffs, minimarts are scattered around town. Try the **International House** minimart at 35 Street 178, **Seven Seven Supermarket** on Street 90, or **Lucky Market** on Preah Sihanouk Boulevard. Minimarts may have an in-house bakery or deli where you can assemble your own food.

Caution: Many businesses and restaurants are in the habit of supplying customers with a glass of water with ice—double peril—as a way of making you feel at home. The water is almost certainly not filtered, and the ice may be suspect. Stick to bottled water.

Budget

Market areas are great for cheap foodstalls, and at breakfast you can put together baguettes, cheese, and fresh fruit. There's a string of bakeries along Kampuchea Krom Blvd. just off Monivong, all offering freshly baked baguettes. Arm yourself with a baguette, find the nearest place selling café au lait, and take a seat. Sandwich cart vendors with pâté and other selections roam the streets.

One of the best bakeries is **Chef's Deli** behind the Pailin Hotel. This small café offers a display case filled with cakes and cookies, matched only by the delicacies at the Hotel Sofitel Cambodiana's *boulangerie* (where the owner in fact once worked as a pastry chef). On the menu is banana bread, coconut cake, and mouthwatering mango cake. Wicked French pastries tempt those with a sweet tooth. Chef's Deli also serves Eastern- and Western-style breakfasts with in-house croissants and bread. A French bakery, **La Parisienne,** is located on Preah Sihanouk Boulevard.

East of the Independence Monument on Samdech Sothearos Blvd. is a cluster of Thai places serving Issan food, including **Eid** and **Chiang Mai** Restaurants. Around the corner is **Vuong's,** a Vietnamese restaurant with the best coffee in Phnom Penh; food costs $2-4, cheap draft beer. A bit pricier is **Green House** at 50 Sihanouk Blvd., with Thai and Western food, snacks, ice cream, and sandwiches.

Khmer food—minced frog and other specialties—is available from eateries along Monivong

fruitstalls

Blvd. south of Red Cross Street, not far from the Capitol Hotel. Here you'll find **Asia Soup, Beef Soup,** and **Paris Pizza** (Italo-Franco-Khmer food). **Lotus Restaurant,** at 121 Samdech Sothearos Blvd. north of Street 106, serves Indian curry and Muslim halal vegetarian and nonvegetarian dishes—a great vegetable and cheese pizza for $2.

Moderate

To the east side of the Central Market is **La Paillote,** with great French food and excellent desserts. Almost next door is **City Lotus Restaurant,** serving Indian, Malaysian, and Singaporean spicy dishes—vegetarian and nonvegetarian, plus some Western selections. The **Green Room** at the Pailin Hotel and **Great Wall Restaurant** at Hotel Paradis both offer buffet lunches for about $6. **Chao Phraya Restaurant,** on Norodom Blvd. at Street 172, serves Thai buffet lunch for $6; the dinner buffet, at $12, features an assortment of barbecued crab, shrimp, lobster, chicken, duck, sushi, and Thai salads. The restaurant is located in a stylish 1930s building that served as the Health Service Office in French days.

Battling it out for top pizza honors are Happy Herb Bistro and Happy Neth Pizza, one a renegade offshoot of the other. **Happy Neth Pizza,** 295 Pochentong Blvd., tel. 60443, serves pasta and three sizes of pizza. **Happy Herb Bistro,** near Phnom Penh Tourism on Sisowath Quay, tel. 62349, dishes up 17 varieties, including a double-happy Happy Herb pizza. Both parlors offer free delivery. Not far from Happy Herb's is **Ponlok Restaurant,** serving Asian food. Ponlok can be pricey, especially for seafood.

Along Preah Sihanouk Blvd. near Street 63 are **Phnom Kiev** (Khmer and French) and **Mont-Rouge. Cordon Bleu,** at 97 Preah Si-

hanouk Blvd., offers French food with steak tartar; quality varies. **California Restaurant** serves hamburgers, tacos, Tex-Mex, and ice cream. Serving similar fare is **Long Beach Steakhouse** at 477 Monivong; dishes are $4-8. Further west at 139 Monireth Blvd. is **The Oasis,** small and cozy with European home cooking. Dishes are in the $7-12 range.

North of Wat Phnom: At Boeng Kak Lake there's breezy lakeside dining at a handful of restaurants, including **Buong Thong,** with Thai dishes and seafood. Buong Thong consists of five wooden open-sided buildings on jetties over the water. Dishes are around $5-7 each; evening buffet. On Monivong Blvd. a bit farther south are two reasonably priced restaurants. **Chez Lipp** serves Khmer-French cuisine, including frog legs, pepper steak, and soufflé. **Calmette Restaurant,** next to the hospital, is popular with Cambodian customers for soups. **Crackers,** an upscale place on Street 90 off Monivong, serves a buffet lunch for $5-8.

Upscale

Deja Vu, at 22 Street 240, is a French mansion with tasteful art deco—Mediterranean food, French panache, French prices ($8-15 a dish). The restaurant is open for lunch and dinner; the weekly set lunch menu is lower-priced. **La Mousson,** on the top floor of Café No Problem at 55 Street 178, tel. 27250, is an exclusive restaurant serving nouvelle French cuisine; open for lunch and dinner, catering to the diplomatic and corporate jet set. **Hotel Sofitel Cambodiana** boasts five restaurants with Asian and Western specialties including L'Amboise, a French restaurant with cellar, and Dragon Court, serving Chinese food. There are lunch buffets for $9-15 in several of the restaurants, and afternoon tea with French pastries from the hotel's own boulangerie.

NIGHTLIFE

A curfew and siege mentality permeates nights in Phnom Penh—foreigners tend to gather at a handful of exclusive bars and cafés that originally sprang up to serve the UN trade. The setup smacks of French imperialism—segregated nightlife with foreigners frequenting exclusive clubs, and locals congregating at disco and karaoke places or the local movie house. Otherwise, all quiet on the Phnom Penh front. Most, deprived of electricity, are soundly snoring in readiness for an 0500 wakeup.

Because guests are reluctant to venture out at night, the management in upper-end hotels attempts to provide nightlife with an in-house bar or disco. The **Cyclo Bar** at the Hotel Sofitel Cambodiana sometimes stages revues. A rare treat, if you can find out where performances are being held, is classical Khmer dancing. Sometimes the Hotel Sofitel Cambodiana stages dance perfomances.

Muggers are abroad at night. If you're out after 2000, travel in a group, and carry enough cash for the evening's expenses but no more. Avoid walking; use a moto or cyclo. Make sure you're aware of the route back to your hotel—cyclos can easily get lost. Cyclos do not have lights and can be dangerous when creeping down the wrong side of the road, with you up front facing oncoming traffic.

The presence of highly paid UN staff resulted in rampant prostitution in Cambodia—some say UNTAC stood for UN Transmission of Aids in Cambodia. In Phnom Penh the prostitutes are often Vietnamese. Around Phnom Penh are scores of places with taxi dancers and karaoke booths, like the Pacific Nightclub and B Boss KTV, both on Monivong Boulevard.

Phnom Penh by night can be dangerous—armed bandits are on the loose. Several foreigners and diplomats have been pinned down in crossfires when robbers armed with machine guns tried to hijack an expensive vehicle at night, and a security guard fired back. Travelers have also been known to be stopped by police demanding money.

Heart of Darkness is a hole-in-the-wall bar—blackened walls, red ceiling—near the corner of Street 172 and Street 51 about six blocks from the Capitol Hotel. This student hangout is favored by backpackers, and has a pool table out the back. It's run by the owners of Saigon's Apocalypse Now bar. **Ettamoogah Pub,** at 154 Sihanouk Blvd. near Lucky Market, is run by Australians—it serves hamburgers and fish-and-chips between pints. The **Irish Rover,** at 78 Sihanouk Blvd., is an Irish pub that serves salads and sandwiches; look for a shamrock sign. The **Trattoria de Gecko,** at the corner of Streets 114 and 61, serves snacks, meals, and drinks.

An excellent venue for a drink, snack, meal, game of billiards—even a movie—is the **Foreign Correspondents Club of Cambodia** (FCCC), at 363 Sisowath Quay, tel. 27757. The FCCC is an accredited organization but you don't have to be a member—anyone can use the facilities. The top-floor bar serves dinks, and a small restaurant section offers spaghetti, steak, and other dishes for $5-10 each. There are special photography exhibits; in the past, these have included showings by Tim Page and Roland Neveu. Foreign movies are regularly screened at the FCCC and special topics panels are arranged. The FCCC is a cozy place with great views across the Tonle Sap River.

The **Center Culturel Français,** at Street 184 off Monivong Blvd., screens French films several times a week. **Café No Problem,** at 55 Street 178, is an upscale venue run by a Parisian. Downstairs is a bar and billiard table room; upstairs is an expensive French restaurant. The building was formerly a colonial mansion, at one time used by Cambodian royalty. Interior decoration was imported from Thailand; the wicker furniture is from Vietnam.

In the Olympic Stadium area is a disco called **Fantazia,** where you can while the night away to a pulsating beat. The infamous **Martini Bar** is a hostess disco on the southern fringe of Phnom Penh, near the junction of Issarak and Monireth Boulevards in the Olympic Stadium area. It stays open until 0200 or later.

Casino

Moored off the Hotel Sofitel Cambodiana is a 12,000-ton floating vessel with five floors of casinos and dozens of blackjack, baccarat, and roulette tables. The entertainment complex is run by Ariston, a Malaysian company that made a multimillion-dollar secret deal with the government. In the hold of the ship is a pirate theme park where those weary of the roulette tables can experience the thrill of buccaneers roaming the seven seas in search of buried treasure. The floating casino can accommodate up to 1,000 customers at a time.

SHOPPING

Clothing

Khmer multipurpose *kramas* (checked scarves) made of silk or cotton are a good purchase. Souvenir T-shirts bear such designs as Angkor Wat, Bayon faces, and Holiday in Cambodia. Also watch for clothing made from Khmer silk—elegant fashion reflects French and Khmer inspired designs. **La Boutique,** at 36 Sihanouk Blvd. next to Paris-Glaces, sells locally made clothing in Western designs, and handicrafts of cotton and silk.

Handicrafts

Handicrafts can be found at the Russian Market on the south side of the city, and at a number of shops in the National Museum vicinity, especially along Street 178. For handicrafts available through NGOs, try **Khemara Handicrafts,** at the Cooperation Committee of Cambodia on the first floor of 25 Street 360, selling silk bags and clothes; and **Wat Than Handicrafts,** south end of Norodom Blvd., selling tailored clothing and wooden items made by mine victims.

Silver boxes and jewelry are often alloys, sold by weight. Shops sell silver opposite the Hotel Sofitel Cambodiana, and along Monivong near the Diamond Hotel. Silver boxes were originally made to hold ingredients for betel-nut chewing; often they bear animal designs.

Angkoriana

In 1993 the government approved stiff penalties for trafficking in antiquities. Do not buy stolen Khmer artifacts, sculpture, or bronzes. Quality reproductions are widely available in Phnom Penh, especially in the block around the National Museum. The National Museum gift shop sells heavy cement copies of famous Khmer sculptures. Wooden, cement, bronze, and marble copies of Buddhas, *apsaras,* and Angkor statuary are made at the School of Fine Arts—they're sold in nearby shops and at a Fine Arts retail outlet south of the National Museum. Khmer painting mostly depicts *apsara* dancers at Angkor Wat. For a touch more class, an art gallery at 20 Street 9, close to Green House Restaurant, mounts exhibitions of contemporary Khmer paintings and drawings.

the Central Market

GECKO WINE, TOAD WINE

At markets around Phnom Penh vendors of traditional medicines and herbs sell bags of ganja, and all kinds of dried and skinned life forms, including geckos. The lizard is being hunted to extinction in rural Cambodia to feed the insatiable appetite in China and Vietnam for gecko wine and other potions.

Gecko wine is made by preserving a gecko in a liter of white wine for six months. In China and Vietnam, gecko wine is sought as a curative for asthma, coughs, and breathing ailments, and for improving muscle tone.

The word gecko comes from the Malay gekok, in imitation of its cry. In some villages in Takeo province, the cry of the gecko is hardly heard any more, nor kids repeating it. A Vietnamese businessman came to catch geckos in the province in the 1980s, recruiting young boys to roam around with bamboo sticks and cages to hunt and seize the reptiles. The dried geckos were brought back to Vietnam by boat. In Battambang during the 1970s the Khmer Rouge ordered people to catch geckos for export to China. Geckos are now found only in remote parts of Cambodia, in the far north and northeastern provinces. Lizard traders must move further afield to capture them.

Unlike gecko wine, which is believed to have originated in China and Vietnam, another variant, toad wine, is an ancient Khmer recipe. Toads are dried, fried, crushed, and mixed in white wine, along with herbs and black sugarcane. Toad wine is believed to cure sexually transmitted diseases such as syphilis, and promote good appetite and sound sleep. The stout-like toad wine is much cheaper than beer or whiskey. Buckets of live toads can be seen at Phnom Penh markets.

You have to wonder about the effect on the environment if toads and geckos disappear from Cambodia—they spend a good deal of time catching harmful insects that destroy crops. Their disappearance will not help in the fight against malaria either—live geckos consume prodigious amounts of mosquitoes.

Markets

Most of the markets around Phnom Penh are of interest to locals, and deal in electronic goods, housewares, or food. The most popular are the Central Market, Russian Market, and Olympic Market.

The **Central Market,** also called the New Market, or Psah Thmay, was constructed by the French in 1937. You can't miss it—a huge yellow art deco building between Norodom and Monivong Boulevards. Four arms radiate off the domed hall. The central area is dominated by gold, silver, and jewelry merchants, who also trade in currency. A large portion of the market features food and household goods. You can buy supplies for upcountry travel here, such as hammocks and mosquito netting. There is armysurplus gear for sale, too. The main area of interest for foreign shoppers is on the east side of the market, toward Street 53. Here you'll find stalls selling T-shirts, kramas, garments, fabrics, paintings, and handicrafts, and kiosks selling maps, phrasebooks, temple rubbings, and postcards. Bargain hard.

The **Russian Market,** also known as Psah Tuol Tom Pong, is located south of Issarak Blvd. off Street 155. The Russian Market is the place to go for tailor-made clothing, sarongs, fake and genuine antiques, handicrafts, jewelry, and souvenirs. Nearby is a furniture market.

SERVICES AND INFORMATION

Traveler Cafés

The café under the Capitol Hotel is backpacker headquarters, a good source of information on who's been where and when. The food is terrible but the information is fresh. Staff at the Capitol will also arrange visa extensions, rent bicycles, and provide taxis for trips to Choeung Ek, Tonle Bati, and Udong. The Foreign Correspondents Club of Cambodia (FCCC) bar at 363 Sisowath is the meeting spot for journalists, photographers, businessmen, and expats. The FCCC sponsors Wednesday evening "talks"—a good venue for reporters and others interested in what's happening in Cambodia.

Tourist Information

The people at Phnom Penh Tourism, 313 Sisowath Quay, tel. 24059, are pretty useless unless they smell money. The place is set up for group tours, not individual assistance. The office organizes day-trips around Phnom Penh, often advertised through the Hotel Sofitel Cambodiana. You might inquire about performances of classical dance. The General Directorate of Tourism, also known as Cambodia Tourism, on Monivong Blvd. at the corner of Street 232, tel. 25607, organizes tours and arranges vehicle rental.

Maps and Books

The bi-weekly *Phnom Penh Post* prints an up-to-date map in the center of the newspaper with recent street names. However, the entries on the map are mostly paid advertising, so many details are missing. Phnom Penh Tourism provides outdated, overpriced, and unwieldy maps of the capital; these are also sold at the Central Market. English-Khmer and French-Khmer phrasebooks are available at stalls on the east side of the Central Market. The booklets and dictionaries are sold mainly to Cambodians learning English or French, but they're useful for foreigners too.

At 228 Monivong Blvd. is **Bookazine,** Cambodia's largest bookshop, stocking books and magazines from around the world. Extensive title selection on Indochina and Southeast Asia. For second-hand English novels and paperbacks, try **Bert's Books,** at 63 Street 178, near Café No Problem. Supermarkets and minimarts stock some magazines and books—try International House Minimart. The Hotel Sofitel Cambodiana has a small bookstore and gift shop.

Media

It's extremely important in Cambodia to keep tabs on what's happening. The best source of information is the *Phnom Penh Post,* published every two weeks, and *Le Mékong,* a French paper issued monthly. Other publications include the *Cambodia Daily, Cambodia Times* (English), and *Cambodge Soir* (French). You can buy Bangkok English newspapers and international magazines at supermarket stands and gift shops. There's satellite TV reception in Phnom Penh—hotels can pick up Hong Kong-based StarTV (BBC World Service) and Australian ATVI. Canal France International (CFI) TV is retransmitted from the French Cultural Center. The Thai company Shinawatra operates Channel 5 in Phnom Penh, and there are two channels on Khmer TV. On radio, you can pick up Radio France Internationale (RFI), the BBC, VOA, and Radio Australia.

Fax and Phone

The main post office offers a 24-hour section with IDD phones and fax machines. Fax and IDD calls are expensive—around $7 a minute, paid in quarter, half, or three-quarter minute billings.

You can place IDD calls through hotels, though these tend to surcharge. At the main post office, calls are $5.30 a minute to Europe, $4.50 to other parts of Asia and the US, $4 to Thailand, and $3.80 to Australia. A Thai company, Cambodia Samart Communications, at 33 Samdech Sothearos Blvd., charges $6-7 a minute for IDD calls to Canada, Thailand, or Europe, plus a $2 service charge. Cambodia Samart specializes in satellite dishes and mobile phones. A number of embassies and businesses use Samart's service—the cost is $2800 to install a dish, $1600 for a mobile phone, and a monthly fee of $17.

Because regular phone lines are intermittently down in Phnom Penh, cellular or mobile phones are useful—but only to contact other mobile phone users. Businesses in Phnom Penh specify up to five different phone numbers on their calling cards—local phone, IDD phone, fax number, maybe a mobile phone number. Mobile phones have nine-digit numbers, while regular Phnom Penh numbers are five-digit. The Cambodia country code for phone/fax is 855. Phnom Penh's area code is 23, Siem Reap's 215; there are only mobile phones in Sihanoukville at present.

Post Office and Courier
The main post office is on Street 102 at the corner of Street 13 near Wat Phnom. The post office is open 0700-1800 seven days a week; the fax and phone section is open 24 hours. Mail is expensive from Cambodia—it all goes airmail, even packages of several kilos. You might be better off sending mail to a drop-off point in Hong Kong or Bangkok, and posting it from there later. For example, a 1.5 kg package to Canada costs $45 airmail; to Bangkok, the same

package would be $17. Courier services in Phnom Penh include **DHL,** 28 Monivong Blvd., tel. 27726; **UPS,** 8 Street 134, tel. 66323; and **TNT/Continental Indochine,** 139 Monireth Blvd., mobile tel. 018-810767.

Photography and Film
There are photo shops on Monivong Blvd. in the area near the Central Market. Although brand-name film—Agfa, Kodak, Konica, Fuji—can be purchased in Phnom Penh, check the expiration date and storage conditions. Film may have water streaks from exposure to humidity and high temperatures. Print film can be processed quickly; snapshots make fine gifts for Cambodian friends.

Banks
Banks charge two to five percent to convert US traveler's checks to US cash. Banks are clustered around the central core, near the Central Market. The most active Cambodian bank is the **Cambodia Commercial Bank** at the corner of Monivong and Pochentong Boulevards. Foreign banks in Phnom Penh include Siam City

KHMER ROUGE CURRENCY

Part of Pol Pot's mad vision was a society without money. The country reverted to the barter system—the only country to do so in recent history. To emphasize the point, the Khmer Rouge blew up the National Bank in Phnom Penh—it was rebuilt on the same site on Norodom Blvd. in the late 1980s.

At first the Khmer Rouge wavered on the question of money; in 1975 they printed a batch of bills, apparently in China. The bills show Khmer Rouge mortar and machine-gun crews, factory workshops, rice harvesters, the towers of Angkor Wat, and Bayon-style sculpture. They were never circulated. However, invading Vietnamese troops arriving in 1979 looted thousands of sets of these banknotes from the treasury of Cambodia. The bills then found their way back to Vietnam for sale to collectors.

The Khmer Rouge bills were not the only useless notes floating around. Currency issued under Lon Nol in the early 1970s and the money printed by the Vietnamese-backed Heng Samrin regime is now used for other functions—a kind of historic wallpaper. During these unstable times, Cambodi-

ans reverted to hoarding wealth and trading in small bars of gold.

In 1993, the Khmer Rouge proclaimed their new-found admiration for the "market" by coming up with a brand-new idea: money. In their section of "liberated Cambodia" the Khmer Rouge issued banknotes of 5, 10, 50, and 100 riels bearing the signature of Khmer Rouge leader Khieu Samphan. Pol Pot envisions setting up a monetary economy in the "liberated areas," using agricultural banks to hold the surplus earning of farmers.

In early 1995, French-educated economist Sar Kim Lemouth—said to have been responsible for Khmer Rouge finances—defected to the government. He claimed ignorance of the rebel finances, reputed to include accounts in Beijing, Hong Kong, Switzerland, and Bangkok. The Khmer Rouge bankroll their military campaigns through the sale of millions of dollars' worth of gems and timber to Thailand. Western governments have never been able to discover where Khmer Rouge money is stashed.

NGOs

There are over 100 foreign and 50 Cambodian nongovernmental organizations (NGOs) in Phnom Penh. These aid agencies cover a wide range of educational, medical, archaeological, and other fields. NGOs will be delighted if you volunteer—Cambodia needs your skills. Working for an NGO, you'll see a totally different side of Cambodia. For more information, approach the relevant NGOs directly, or visit the Cooperation Committee for Cambodia (CCC), which acts as a liaison between organizations. It's located at 25 Street 360, tel./fax 26009. The CCC stocks reports and publications on NGOs in the capital and upcountry.

Bank, Bangkok Bank, Thai Farmers Bank, Standard Chartered, Banque Indosuez, and Singapore Banking Corporation. Diamond Hotel has a moneychanging office. You can change cash US dollars into riel with the gold and jewelry merchants inside the Central Market. Be aware that lots of fake US dollars circulate in Cambodia. When paying for hotels or restaurants in Phnom Penh, you can use US dollars, Thai baht, or Cambodian riel.

Credit Cards: The Commercial Bank of Cambodia wants $30 up front to start proceedings on cash advances for Visa credit cards. You might have better luck with the Thai banks—try Bangkok Bank. Thai Farmers Bank wants $10 to process Visa cash advances; it will advance up to $800 a day.

Business Services
The FCCC at 363 Sisowath Quay, tel. 27757, fax 27758, has a business center, open 0730-2300, with secretarial services, Khmer typing, and computer equipment rentals. For faxes, the FCCC charges $7 per minute to the US or Europe plus a $7 service fee; $5.50 a minute to Australia plus $5.50 service charge; to Vietnam $4 a minute plus $4 service charge. Incoming fax is $1 a page plus a $3 service fee. Major hotels have business facilities, and there's a 24-hour business center on Monivong Blvd. near the Eurasie Hotel with fax machines, IDD phones, and photocopiers. Global Business Center, at 378 Sihanouk Blvd., offers equipment rentals and secretarial services.

Health Care
In association with SOS International is **IMC Clinic,** at 83 Issarak Blvd., mobile tel. 015-912765—a primary and emergency health care facility with international standards. There's also a **European Dental Clinic** at 195A Norodom Blvd., tel. 62656.

Rest and Recreation
The Hotel Sofitel Cambodiana pool costs $5 for nonguests. The price includes towel and drink; you're not permitted to bring your own drinks. Poolside showers; you can leave your bag with an attendant.

The International Youth Club, at the western side of Wat Phnom, has a pool, gym, and tennis court. The entry fee works out to about $5. For runners, Phnom Penh offers a chapter of the Hash House Harriers.

*Khmer Rouge
10-riel note*

GETTING THERE

BY AIR

Phnom Penh's Pochentong Airport is at present the only international arrival and departure point in Cambodia. The terminal received a major face-lift in 1994 and boasts a duty free shop. Royal Air Cambodge (RAC), the flag carrier of the sixties, was revived in January 1995 in a joint deal with Malaysia Airlines. Domestic carrier Kampuchea Air came under the wing of Royal Air Cambodge. RAC flies to Bangkok, Kuala Lumpur, Hong Kong, Singapore, and Saigon. The daily RAC flight to Bangkok is $125; Thai Airways International flies to Bangkok daily for $140 one-way. SilkAir to Singapore is $300 roundtrip, five times weekly; Dragonair to Hong Kong, twice weekly, $350 roundtrip; Lao Aviation to Vientiane, $150 one-way, once a week; Vietnam Airways to Saigon daily for $50 one-way, to Hanoi once a week, $155 one-way; Malaysia Airlines to Kuala Lumpur, $260 roundtrip, three times a week. There are also flights to Taipei on Transasia Airways, and Aeroflot has a few flights a month to Moscow via Dubai.

Entry and Exit Formalities

Customs and immigration are relaxed on arrival and departure. Export of Khmer artifacts is forbidden. International departure tax is $10; domestic departure tax $4.

Transfers into Phnom Penh

Pochentong Airport lies eight km southwest of Phnom Penh. An entire taxi should cost $5-8, depending on the number of passengers. You can also jump onto a moto for a cheap ride. In the reverse direction, a taxi from the Capitol Hotel costs $3.

Airline Offices

Royal Air Cambodge is at 206A Norodom Blvd., mobile tel. 017-20230. Thai Airways International is at 16 Street 106, tel. 22236, near the river. SilkAir is in the Pailin Hotel on Monivong Blvd., tel. 24852; Dragonair is at the same address at Transpeed Travel, tel. 27665. Lao Aviation is located at 58 Sihanouk Blvd., tel. 26563. Malaysia Airlines is in the Diamond Hotel, Air France in the Hotel Sofitel Cambodiana, tel. 26426. Vietnam Airlines has a branch office in the Beauty Inn minihotel, 537 Monivong, tel. 27426. You'll find Aeroflot in the Allson Hotel.

BY LAND

The only viable road route at present is Route 1 from Phnom Penh to Saigon, a distance of 248 km. Your paperwork must be in order to cross: this means valid visas, with a Moc Bai entry or exit stamp on your Vietnamese visa.

By Bus: There are two species of bus on the Phnom Penh-Saigon route. The non-air-con Cambodian crawler costs $5; the air-con Vietnamese bus is $12. Buses leave Phnom Penh on alternate days at 0530 except Sunday and holidays, departing from a ticket office near the intersection of Street 182 and Street 211, close to Nehru Boulevard. The office is open 0500-1000 and 1400-1700; buy tickets one day in advance. In Saigon, purchase tickets at the garage next to the Rex Hotel at 155 Nguyen Hue Boulevard. Buses heading east from Cambodia are frequently stopped for contraband checks on the Vietnamese side, turning what should be a nine-hour trip into a 14-hour odyssey. Grandmothers tuck cigarettes under their belts, young women hide goods in overhead racks, the driver and crew hoard goods in the roof and under the floor panels. Vietnamese police try to take a cut of this booty or confiscate the lot—a great introduction to avarice, greed, bad tempers, and another day in Vietnam. Sometimes they take the whole bus apart. It would be prudent to cover the Vietnamese sector by share-taxi: if heading east from Phnom Penh, get off the bus at Moc Bai and continue by taxi.

By Share-taxi: Share-taxis run as far as the border from each side; a through taxi costs a lot more. A share-taxi from Phnom Penh to Bavet runs $5-10 a person, with six or more passengers jammed into the car. The main departure point for share-taxis to Bavet is a depot east of Monivong Bridge at Street 369 in the Chbampao Market area. Taxis leave from 0600-1300. On the Vietnamese side, you pick up a share-taxi to Saigon for under $10 per head, or $30 for the whole taxi. Motos also wait on the Vietnamese side; a ride into Saigon should be about $5. By car, it is about a three-hour trip to

the border, half an hour for paperwork, and another two hours to Saigon. From the Saigon end, a share-taxi is $30 to the Moc Bai border. Try Mien Tay Bus Station on the western outskirts of town or negotiate with a downtown taxi driver if part of a ready-made group. On the Cambodian side in Bavet, you can arrange another share-taxi for $5-10 a person.

GETTING AROUND

Although Phnom Penh features some green city buses donated by a Parisian council, most people get around the city on foot, cyclo, bicycle, or motorcycle. Foreigners and dignitaries sometimes use taxis. At night it's not advisable to walk; hire a moto to get around from point to point.

By Boat
You can rent a sampan for a few hours and travel along the Tonle Sap and Bassac Rivers to small villages. A longer trip will take you out to Ko Dach, a weaving village north of Phnom Penh. The Hotel Sofitel Cambodiana operates larger wooden cruise boats for half-day excursions and sunset viewing of the Royal Palace.

By Taxi
Major hotels and travel agents can arrange taxis for about $20-30 a day. It's also possible to hire minibuses. Numerous taxis wait near the gates of Hotel Sofitel Cambodiana. Taxis not attached

to hotels are usually operated by private citizens who own a car and want to make extra money. Some of the lower-priced hotels can arrange deals—the Capitol can get a taxi for $20 a day. Share-taxis, which lurk at various depots around Phnom Penh, are also available for private hire at similar rates.

By Cyclo
Cyclos are the most common method of getting around; most destinations around town run 50 cents to a dollar. You can hire them by the hour, half-day, or the day. Cyclo drivers don't speak much English. It may be your responsibility to follow maps and supply directions. You're up front—just provide the appropriate left or right turn hand signals to direct the driver.

By Moto
Motos are not much more expensive than cyclos; a ride across town is a dollar or less. Prices may rise slightly at night because of the dan-

locals crammed onto a ferry

ger factor and the fact you can't bargain as hard since you have no other transportation choice. By the hour a moto is maybe $1. Motos are mostly offered by private owners making an extra buck. Just stand on a street corner and wave a hand, and someone will pull over. The only credentials a moto operator needs, it seems, are a baseball cap, a frayed collar, broken tail and signal lights, an ability to knock down customers to get their attention, and a poor sense of direction. A moto driver who speaks a fair amount English or French is great for touring and upcountry destinations. One big caveat with motos—occasionally bandits shoot moto drivers to get their motorcycles. If you happen to be in the way . . . not a pleasant thought. Stealing vehicles is big business in Phnom Penh, the cause of a lot of shoot-outs.

By Two-Wheel Rentals

A bicycle or motorcycle is a good way of getting around, but very few places rent them. The Capitol Hotel peddles ratty rental bicycles, and nearby Street 107 sells new bicycles. Try hotel staff at other budget hotels in this area too. If riding a motorcycle or bicycle, be wary at intersections and roundabouts—turns can be difficult in chaotic peak hours.

Motorcycle rentals in Phnom Penh are not recommended because the risk of theft is too high. Even in broad daylight, robbers will shoot a Cambodian off a motorcycle to steal it. Around the corner from the Capitol are two motorcycle rental places at number 413 and 417 Monivong, near the Hong Kong Hotel. Motorcycle rentals are $15 a day for a Honda 250cc at 417 Monivong; at 413 Monivong a Honda Dream 100cc is $8 a day, a 250cc Honda Rebel $15 a day. If your bike is stolen, you have to pay the cost of a new one: the Honda 250cc is worth $2000, the 100cc Dream $1200. If there's an accident, you pay for the repairs. Your passport is required as a deposit. It might be preferable to get a moto driver for the day, or ask a moto driver if you can use his bike.

Gasoline is sold by roadside entrepreneurs in old soft drink bottles. Sometimes they sell cigarettes and lighters too. Cambodian drivers drop by to light up a cigarette and refill the gas tank. Makes sense, doesn't it?

Tour Companies

There are more than 25 travel agencies around Phnom Penh. They can arrange tours around town or upcountry, provide air tickets, arrange taxis and minivans, and assist with visas and other paperwork. Some maintain good contacts in Vietnam or Laos, and can arrange tours and visas for those countries. Travel agents include:

Apsara Tours, 29 Street 150, tel./fax 25408

Angkor Voyages, Champs Elysées Hotel, 183 Street 63, tel. 27268, fax 27268

Bopha Angkor Tourism, 797B Monivong Blvd., tel. 27933

Diethelm Travel, 8 Samdech Sothearos Blvd., tel. 26648, fax 26676

East-West Group, 170 Street 114, tel. 26648, fax 26189

Eurasie Travel, 97 Monivong, near Monorom Hotel, tel./fax 23620

Khemara, 134 Preah Sihanouk Blvd., tel. 27434, fax 27434

Naga Travel, Renakse Hotel, Samdech Sothearos Blvd., tel. 26288

Orient Express Tours, 19 Street 106, tel. 26248, fax 26313

Peace Travel, 246 Monivong Blvd., tel. 24640, fax 26533

Skylink, 124 Norodom Blvd., tel. 27010

Thai Indochina Supply, 4 Street 118, tel./fax 27143

Transindo (Transair), 16 Monivong, near the French Embassy, tel. 26298, fax 27119

Cambodian Visa Extensions

Extensions cost $30-35 for one month, $50 for two months, and $60 for three months. Go through a travel agent or hotel staffer.

GETTING AWAY

By Air

Domestic flights leave daily for Siem Reap and Koh Kong, and four times a week to Sihanoukville. Less frequent flights depart for Kratie, Stung Treng, Kampot, and Battambang. Flights cost around $40-55 one-way. Domestic schedules are erratic, and flights may be suspended. Domestic departure tax is $4.

Fast Boat: There's fast boat service to Siem Reap ($28 one-way) in the northwest, and Kompong Cham ($10) and Kratie ($25) in the northeast. The service is operated by Golden Sea, using 76-seat riverboats from Malaysia, with onboard video. Slow cargo boats are not recommended due to checkpoint dangers; they run to Siem Reap and to Stung Treng.

By Rail

Trains run to Battambang in the north and Kampot and Sihanoukville in the south. These are freight trains, and passengers are a secondary consideration. Passengers are sitting ducks for Khmer Rouge ambushes or mines.

By Land

Collective taxis operate on set routes, packing in passengers and departing when full. The fare is around $5 a person for a day's run. The record seems to be nine passengers—four in the front (plus driver) and five in the back. Not comfortable, but better than a wooden bench on a bus, and faster too. Bus and share-taxi depots are usually situated near a market partway in the direction of travel. There are several depots near the Central Market: northwest of the market you'll find share-taxis to Battambang; southwest of the market is a minibus station to Udong, Kompong Speu, and Battambang, plus share-taxis to Kompong Cham. West of the Capitol Hotel is a depot with share-taxis to Kampot and Sihanoukville. At Dang Kor Market, to the southwest of town, share-taxis run to Takeo. At Chbam Market, southeast of town across Monivong Bridge, share-taxis run to Koki Beach, and to Bavet at the Vietnamese border.

Visa Shopping

Vietnamese Embassy: The embassy does not deal with people directly, except for business visas. Approach through an agent. At the Capitol Hotel it requires two to five days to obtain a one-month visa for $55; other agents ask for $75. Two photos required. There's a Vietnam Tourism Office at 657 Monivong, opposite Street 362.

Lao PDR Embassy: The embassy is open Mon.-Fri. 0800-1130 and 1400-1700, and Saturday 0800-1130. A seven-day transit visa direct from the Lao Embassy takes one working day. A 14-day tourist visa requires three days and costs $25, which is much cheaper than in Bangkok. For this visa you need to submit your original passport and three photos. If these visas are not available through the embassy, try an agent—who will also try and talk you into a travel package. Visas via agents run $25-80 and take two to four days.

Thai Consulate: The Royal Thai Consulate is open Mon.-Fri. 0830-1200. You can receive a 30-day tourist visa for $10 in three working days; a 60-day visa runs $15.

PHNOM PENH EMBASSIES AND CONSULATES

Phnom Penh has over 20 embassies and consulates. These include:

Australia, 11 Street 254, tel. 26254

China, Issarak Blvd. at Street 163, tel. 26271

France, north end of Monivong Blvd., tel. 26278

Germany, 76 Street 214, tel. 26381

India, 777 Monivong Blvd., tel. 25981

Japan, 75 Norodom Blvd., tel. 27161

Laos, 15 Issarak Blvd., tel. 26441

Malaysia, 161 Street 51, tel. 26167

North Korea, 39 Street 268, tel. 27224

Russia, Samdech Sothearos Blvd. at Street 312, tel. 22081

Thailand, 4 Monivong Blvd., tel. 26182

UK, 29 Street 75, tel. 27124

US, 27 Street 240, tel. 26804

Vietnam, Monivong Blvd. at Street 436, tel. 25481

EXCURSIONS FROM PHNOM PENH

Around Phnom Penh are a number of destinations within day-trip range—nothing special, but a chance to get into the countryside and receive a blast of oxygen after the fetid air of Phnom Penh. With the exception of Choeung Ek, the sites described here are picnicking destinations, popular with the weekend escape crowd. Travel agents offer packages to sites, leaving early in the morning. You can also arrange your own taxi or moto.

Choeung Ek

There are killing fields all over Cambodia, skull-and-bone cairns that stand as stark memorials to Khmer Rouge atrocities. At Choeung Ek, 15 km to the southwest of Phnom Penh, an estimated 17,000 people were killed, most clubbed to death to save ammunition. Many were taken from the interrogation center at Tuol Sleng. There are over 120 mass graves in the area; half have been disinterred. A stupa-like tower of glass panels was erected in 1988 to house the grisly remains, with shelf after shelf of skulls—an unnerving sight. Be sure to read the moving visitor book here. Moto drivers charge $5 for a roundtrip to Choeung Ek; a taxi should cost about $10, which can be split between several passengers.

Koki Beach

Koki Beach, about 12 km east of Phnom Penh on the Saigon route, is a popular weekend and public holiday destination. Residents of Phnom Penh decamp to the river and rent huts raised on stilts for a day of picnicking, talking, or romance. Cafés here sell grilled fish and chicken. Don't expect much in the way of a beach, though there is a strip of sand and it is possible to swim. Most visitors rent a stilt hut to take a nap, ward off the heat, or counter the floodwaters of the monsoon season. You can hire a boat to tour the lake; waterborne vendors come alongside to sell food. Crowded on weekends, with lots of food vendors, but nothing much happening during the week. Share-taxis run to Koki Beach from a stand near Chbam Pao Market on the east side of Monivong Bridge; you could also take a moto.

Mekong Trips

Phnom Penh Tourism and the Hotel Sofitel Cambodiana organize trips to a tourist trap called **Mekong Island,** which is actually Okn-hatey Island, about an hour by boat from Phnom Penh. The island is a theme park with ersatz Cambodian culture packaged for the tourist masses—a model village, handicraft produc-

skulls from Choeung Ek

tion, zoo, traditional dance and music ensembles, and restaurant. The trip costs around $25 and includes lunch and show. Another, longer trip organized by Phnom Penh Tourism is to **Koh Dach,** a silk weaving village northeast of Phnom Penh. A boat ride up the Mekong to Ko Dach takes three hours roundtrip. You can also visit fishing villages and see river life along the way. Hire your own vessel, or join a group through a travel agent.

Udong

Udong, 40 km northwest of the capital along Route 5, is the site of an ancient capital, with a cluster of kings' tombs. This is another popular picnic site, affording great views of the surrounding area. Udong was the seat of Cambodian kings from 1618 to 1866. Almost all the buildings of the former royal city were razed when Lon Nol launched air strikes against Khmer Rouge hideouts in the 1970s; other sites were later blown up by the Khmer Rouge. A Khmer Rouge prison was located here. A memorial to the victims was erected in 1982, with torture devices and bones from mass graves on display, as well as murals depicting Khmer Rouge atrocities. To reach Udong, hire a taxi for $20, or take a motorcycle.

Tonle Bati

About 33 km south of Phnom Penh on Route 2 is a turnoff that leads several km to Tonle Bati. This is a popular picnic spot, with a lake and two temples, Ta Prohm and Yeay Peau. A taxi from the Capitol Hotel should cost around $15. On weekends the place is full of foodstalls and picnic paraphernalia. Soldiers and amputee beggars demanding money sometimes try to stop cars coming into the area.

Twelfth-century **Ta Prohm Temple** looks similar to a minor Angkor temple. Some attribute the handiwork to King Jayavarman VII, who ruled in Angkor from 1181. According to legend, the temples were built by Ta Prohm. While traveling through Tonle Bati, an Angkor king fell in love with Yeay Peau, the beautiful daughter of a fisherman. The king passed three months with her and she became pregnant. Upon leaving, the king gave her a ring with instructions to send the child she bore to Angkor. When her son, Prohm, duly presented the ring at Angkor, he was welcomed at his father's palace and given an education. The king later sent him back to govern Takeo province. Prohm built a temple similar to those he'd seen at Angkor, and named it after himself. For his mother, he built Yeay Peau temple.

Phnom Chisor

Some 20 km south of Tonle Bati is a hilltop ruin dating from the Angkor period. The turnoff to Phnom Chisor is 55 km south of Phnom Penh; the temple is about four km from Route 2. The main sanctuary—what's left of it—is an 11th-century structure dedicated to Brahma. This spot is isolated, so do not go alone. Bring a guide. The temple is reached by a staircase on the northern side of the hill. From the top are expansive views over the countryside—you can see two other temple ruins to the east. Leave the hilltop by the southern staircase.

Takeo

The town of Takeo is 75 km south of Phnom Penh on Route 2. It can also be reached by Route 3—the trip is 87 km from Phnom Penh, but the road is in better shape. This is stretching the limits of a day-trip from the capital because travel time alone is six hours roundtrip by taxi. About 20 km east of Takeo is the modern village of Angkor Borei, which is thought to have been the site of Vyadhapura, the last capital of the Funan Kingdom. South of town is a hill called **Phnom Da.** Statues discovered in caves at Phnom Da by French archaeologists are displayed at Phnom Penh's National Museum. The Phnom Da style was identified as the first stage of pre-Angkorian art. On top of Phnom Da is a small building made from heavy basalt blocks.

ANGKOR

With a retinue of bearers, eccentric French naturalist Henri Mouhot hacked his way through the Cambodian jungle in January 1860, in search of beetles and butterflies. Though his interest lay more in insects than antiquities, he spent three weeks exploring the ruins of Angkor. He arrived by way of Lake Tonle Sap, where, he noted, fish were so abundant they impeded the progress of his boat. As a collector, Mouhot was entranced by butterflies the size of soup plates lazing on the stones. He was also intrigued by the stones themselves. In his diaries he claimed Angkor's ruins were grander than those of ancient Greece or Rome. He raved about a monument equal to the temple of Solomon, erected by some ancient Michelangelo. The sight of the ruins, he wrote in his diary, made the traveler "forget all the fatigues of the journey, filling him with admiration and delight, such as would be experienced in finding a verdant oasis in the sandy desert. Suddenly, and as if by enchantment, he seems to be transported from barbarism to civilization, from profound darkness into light."

Mouhot was not the first European to visit Angkor. A long line of traders, missionaries, and travelers had passed this way before him in the 17th, 18th, and 19th centuries. In fact, Mouhot's visit was inspired by the travels of French missionary Charles-Emile Bouillevaux, who visited in 1854. For some reason, the reports of others had gone unnoticed by the West. Mouhot, traveling under the auspices of England's Royal Geographical Society, was the most publicity-conscious of the visitors. He died in Laos in 1861 from a malarial fever; his diaries and travel correspondence were published posthumously in 1863 in a magazine called *Le Tour du Monde,* triggering European interest. More writings, focusing as much on natural wonders as on archaeology, appeared in a book *Voyage in Siam* in 1868. Englishman John Thompson took the first photographs of Angkor in 1866, and the ruins exercised a powerful hold on the 19th-century European imagination. The image of ruined temples emerging from thick jungle vegetation became part of colonial romanticism—the lost city rediscovered.

It was not until after World War II, when archaeologist Bernard Groslier made aerial surveys of the area, that the full extent of Angkor was realized. Angkor comprises 70 monuments scattered over an area of 200 square km. The complex of tombs, temples, palaces, moats, reservoirs, and causeways was built over a period of 400 years; only Egypt's Nile Valley can compare to this array of monuments.

There is nothing like Angkor in Southeast Asia. Only two monument complexes come close: 9th-century Borobodur in Indonesia, and 11th-century Pagan in Burma. The French could not imagine the Khmer kings were responsible for such monumental work. Theories as to who constructed Angkor's monuments ranged from the ancient Romans to Alexander the Great. Indeed, the structures echo styles from other monumental ruins. Angkor Wat is built in classical Indian style, with elements of the Java ziggurat of Borobodur, and yet the numerous bas-reliefs have a strangely Egyptian character. The columns and arches at Preah Khan Temple evoke those of the Greeks and Romans, while the pyramid of Phimeanakas resembles those of the Maya at Tikal, Guatemala.

The inspiration for Angkor architecture comes from a unique mix of Hinduism and Buddhism. The early rulers of Angkor promoted various Hindu sects, mainly dedicated to Shiva and Vishnu. Shiva was initially the most favored deity, but by the 12th century, Vishnu had replaced him. At the same time the kings encouraged Buddhist scholarship; Jayavarman VII introduced Mahayana Buddhism as the court religion by the end of the 12th century. Layered onto these concepts was the tradition of deification of kings in sculptural form. This mix resulted in Angkorian structures that have no parallel, such as the fantastic South Gate of Angkor Thom and the bizarre Bayon.

Angkorian Architecture

How were these colossal works constructed? The caste system of the Khmers was similar to the hierarchy extant in ancient Egypt and Mexico when the Pharoahs and Maya erected their pyramids. There was a line of kings, a class of priests and merchants, and a cast of thousands of slaves (captives of war), laborers, masons, sculptors, and decorators. Artisans, including architects, belonged to the lower echelons of society. They remain anonymous—nothing is

known of the stone masons and sculptors who worked for the Angkorian kings.

Wooden buildings in the Angkor area have not survived. The use of brick or stone was reserved for sacred temples and monuments. Architects must have worked with priests on the design of such buildings: a number are temple-mountains representing the paradise of Mount Meru, center of the universe in Hindu-Buddhist cosmology. Rigidly geometric and symmetric patterns radiating in concentric circles compose the ground plans of a number of Angkor buildings. The effect is similar to a mandala, or sacred diagram of the cosmos, with Mount Meru at the center. To translate these concepts into three-dimensional form, Angkor's architects probably worked from wax models.

Early Angkor buildings were made of large bricks, with a mortar of vegetable-based adhesive. From the 10th century on, sandstone foundations were laid, and laterite was used in walls. Laterite is a red, porous material that is actually a kind of iron-bearing soil. It is easily quarried; cut into large blocks, then left to harden upon exposure to the air. Angkor Wat and Angkor Thom rest on laterite foundations; the temples were mostly fashioned from sandstone quarried at Phnom Kulen, 45 km northeast of Angkor. The sandstone exhibits a wide range of coloration, from gray to pinkish, yellowish buff to greenish. The sandstone was floated down the Siem Reap River and dragged to the building site using ropes, rollers, and winches. A bas-relief in the west inner gallery of the Bayon depicts the hauling and polishing of sandstone. The roughly dressed blocks were perfectly fitted, smoothed off, and the surfaces decorated with bas-reliefs. Some stones were held in place with bronze clamps, others relied entirely on gravity.

Signature in Stone

At the time of construction, temples at Angkor most likely bore the names of the kings who built them and the gods to whom they were dedicated. The name "Angkor" surfaced in the 16th century—the place was called Anjog, Onco, Anckoor, Ongcor, Angcor, and Vat Nokor by Western explorers. Angkor is believed to be a corruption of the Khmer *nokor* (*nakhon* in Thai, and *nagara* in Sanskrit), meaning the royal city of the Khmer Empire. Wat was added because of

a Siamese monastery established on the grounds by Buddhist monks in the early 19th century, when the area fell under the Kingdom of Siam. Angkor Thom means "Great City."

The designation "Angkor" has several layers of meaning. Geographically, it refers to the 200-square-km plain between Lake Tonle Sap and Phnom Kulen, the abode of the *devarajas* (divine kings). It also refers to the Khmer capital city, as well as to the 802-1431 period when the Angkor kings reigned. In addition, to art historians, Angkor denotes an art style prevalent from 802 to 1175; work from roughly 500 to 800 is considered pre-Angkorian art, while art from 1177 to 1230 is classified as post-Angkorian or Bayon art. Angkor art is further subdivided into nine styles; the 1100-1175 period is called the Angkor Wat style.

Because no palm-leaf or parchment books survive from the Angkor period, inscribed stones are the primary source of information. Most of these stelae have now been deciphered. They bear lines in Pali, Sanskrit, or ancient Khmer script praising the king. Sometimes they provide inventory information; some offer insight into daily Angkor life. A Sanskrit inscription at Preah Khan lists property belonging to the temple—a set of gold dishes weighing over 500 kg; 35 diamonds; 40,620 pearls; 4,540 precious stones; 876 Chinese veils; 512 silk beds; 523 parasols.

In the 19th century, the French asked the locals what the names of Angkor's temples were. The old temple with the big mango tree? That was Prasat Svay, the mango-tree temple. The old temple in the forest? Banteay Prei, the Forest Temple. The one with fine bas-reliefs, and niches inset with statues of beautiful women? Banteay Srei, the Citadel of Women. The one with the stone lion statue? Prasat Sing, the Temple of the Lion. Unfortunately for archaeologists, there were lots of forests, fine bas-reliefs of women, and stone lions. Another EFEO (Ecole Française d'Estrême Orient) expedition numbered the monuments, but talking about a magnificent temple as Monument 497 did not win many hearts. Some of Angkor's lesser ruins are still identified by number.

Eyewitness at Angkor

Angkor, the capital of the Khmer Empire, was undoubtedly as splendid as any European city. It

was built between the 9th and 14th centuries as the administrative and religious center of the powerful Khmer Empire. Bas-reliefs like those at the Bayon and Angkor Wat provide clues about life at Angkor, but the only detailed eyewitness account comes from Zhou Daguan, an envoy from China. Daguan reached Cambodia by boat and land and stayed a year, from 1296 to 1297. At this time, Indravarman III had just ascended the throne. The Khmer Empire was past its zenith but still powerful. Zhou Daguan was the Chinese envoy from the Mongol court of Timur Khan, his mission to induce the Khmer court to pay homage to the court of the Khans (a tribute exacted from sovereigns all over Asia). There is no mention in his writings of whether he was successful.

On his return to China, Daguan jotted down some impressions. Fragments from his *Notes on the Customs of Cambodia* date from the early 14th century. The manuscript is short, with occasional apologies for forgetting place names and other details. Surviving fragments were partially translated by Jesuit missionaries in Peking and published in Paris in 1789. A more complete French version was published in 1819; French scholar Paul Pelliot issued the best-known translation in 1902.

Brief as they are, the notes nevertheless bring Angkor to life. Zhou Daguan describes a glittering city of palaces and pagodas, palanquins and elephants, concubines, celestial dancers, and slaves. Life revolved around the Royal Palace and the temples of Angkor. Villagers were pressed into service for temple construction or maintenance tasks. The king's family held all the important posts of state, but if a commoner were chosen for office, the king offered his daughter as a royal concubine. A hierarchy of ministers, generals, astronomers, and other functionaries could be identified by their insignia. Daguan was not admitted to the grounds of the Royal Palace, where, by his estimation, the king lived with five wives and some 3,000 concubines.

Daguan exposed some darker sides of life at Angkor. Slaves were treated badly, chained at the neck. Serious criminal offenders could be punished by burial alive; for lesser offenses, the accused lost their hands, feet, or nose. Still, for this visitor, Angkor seemed like paradise on earth. "Chinese sailors coming to the country

DEVARAJAS

The Angkor period is generally designated as the 630-year stretch from 802 to 1431. In 802, Jayavarman II ascended to the throne and established a line of *devaraja*s (divine kings); in 1431 the Siamese overran Angkor. Except for a brief period in the 10th century, kings continuously occupied the plains of Angkor.

The Khmer kings adopted the Hindu trinity of Shiva, Brahma, and Vishnu, and each became the focus of cult worship. In Shiva cults, the spirit of the king was embodied in the statue of a giant sacred phallus, sheltered in a temple built by the king for that purpose.

Angkorian rulers frequently changed names during their reign. Names were adopted from gods, or denoted a king's special quality. Thus Indravarman means "He Who Enjoys the Protection of the God Indra," Jayavarman is "Protected by Victory," and Udayadityavarman denotes "Protected by the Rising Sun." Relying on site inscriptions, French scholars developed a chronology of Khmer art and Khmer kings using each king's most common name. Recurring names were sequenced I, II, III, and so on. Precise chronology of rulers is, at best, guesswork, and archaeologists contradict each other. Thirty-odd kings ruled between 802 and 1431; a dozen of the most significant are mentioned here. Some kings reigned only briefly—succession was often contested, and foul play occasionally befell monarchs.

Shivaite Jayavarman II, 802-850, built a temple at Phnom Kulen, 45 km northeast of Angkor Wat. Indravarman I, 887-889, also a Shivaite, was a usurper who established his capital at Roluos, to the east of Angkor Wat. Yasovarman I, 889-900, built his capital of Yasodhapura at Phnom Bakheng, near Angkor Wat, and constructed the East Baray and the brick temple of Lolei at Roluos. The empire of Yasovarman I stretched from the south of Laos to the Gulf of Siam. Jayavarman IV, 928-942, was a usurper who moved the capital to Koh Ker, 70 km northeast of Angkor.

Rajendravarman II, 944-968, built East Mebon and Pre Rup temples. Although he was Hindu and employed Brahman advisers, he also relied on Buddhist ministers. His chief Brahman adviser, Yajnavaraha, oversaw construction of the beautiful sandstone temple of Banteay Srei. After about 950, important structures were built of sandstone, while brick was reserved for secondary sites. Jayavarman V, 968-1001, built the sandstone temple-mountains of Takeo and Phimeanakas, which became classic models.

Suryavarman I, 1002-1050, extended Cambodian rule into Siam. He is credited with the building of far-flung Preah Vihear sanctuary on today's Cambodian-Thai border and Phimai sanctuary in northeast Thailand, both as part of a royal highway that stretched from the Angkor region to the borders of Burma. He also acquired the region of Louvo (Lopburi) in Siam. Udayadityavarman II, 1050-1066, ordered the construction of the West Baray and the great temple of Baphuon.

Suryavarman II, 1112-1152, was one of the greatest Angkor kings. He was a Vishnuite responsible for the building of Angkor Wat, Chau Say Tevoda, and Thommanon, and probably also undertook Wat Phu in southern Laos. Under his rule the Khmer Empire expanded into present-day Malaysia, Thailand, Burma, and Vietnam. In a disastrous attempt to conquer north Vietnam, his armies were decimated by fever on a march through jungles and mountains.

Jayavarman VII, 1181-1218, embarked on a grand building binge, constructing Angkor Thom (the Bayon, walls and gates, Royal Palace), Neak Pean, Ta Som, Ta Prohm, Preah Khan, and Banteay Kdei among other works. Jayavarman VII designated Mahayana Buddhism as the kingdom's main faith; some temples were possibly dedicated to Lokesvara, the bodhisattva of compassion. During his reign the boundaries of the empire extended from Pagan in Burma to the Vietnam coast, and from the vicinity of Vientiane in Laos to the Malay Peninsula.

After Jayavarman VII the Khmer empire declined, and no stone building of any significance was constructed. His sons and heirs reverted to Shivaism, and Indian Brahmans gained great influence at the court. Inscriptions give the names of five kings who reigned after Jayavarman VII. All were unable to prevent the rise of the Thai kingdom of Sukothai; increasingly violent attacks by the Siamese led to the collapse of Angkor in the 15th century.

note with pleasure that it is not necessary to wear clothes, and, since rice is easily had, women easily persuaded, houses easily run, furniture easily come by, and trade easily carried on, a great many sailors desert to take up permanent residence," wrote Zhou Daguan.

It could not last. Weakened by huge construction projects and vast territorial gains that needed governing, Angkor went into decline. Its intricate irrigation system fell into disrepair, and crops failed. The Cham sacked Angkor in 1177. Siamese armies ravaged the area with attacks in 1353, 1393, and 1431. Finally, Angkor was abandoned. Well, not entirely—parts were occasionally used by subsequent Khmer kings, including a 50-year stretch in the mid-16th century.

Much is missing today. No wooden buildings have survived, and all the residential compounds have disappeared. In 1431 the conquering Siamese killed, looted, and destroyed, carrying off thousands of slaves, stripping the palaces and temples of their statuary and ornaments encrusted with precious stones, and removing the gold coatings from towers and rooftops. Gone are the wooden palaces and dwellings with their terracotta roof tiles; gone are the sumptuous carpets and furnishings, Chinese pottery and ceramics, bronze weapons and cult objects, jewelry and utensils, silk beds and parasols. What remains are the huge sandstone blocks that could not be carted away. Some artifacts—statuary, jewelry, ritual objects—are on display at the National Museum in Phnom Penh. The rest—the vast kingdom peopled by priests, celestial dancers, astronomers, ministers, and generals, and the court of Angkor with its banquets, music, dancing, rich tapestries and paintings, merchants coming and going—is left for you to conjure. In the haunting contrast between past grandeur and present decay lies the perverse pleasure of ruins.

The Plumbing Puzzle

Contrary to the design of most great cities, which grow on the banks of substantial bodies of water, Angkor lies inland some distance from a major river or port. Why was this site chosen for a capital? And how did the city sustain itself? The answer may lie in the city's proximity to Lake Tonle Sap. The Khmer Empire depended on the annual flooding of the Great Lake for rice harvests and an abundant supply of fish; Lake Tonle Sap is one of the world's richest fishing grounds.

Initially, researchers believed the Khmers established a sophisticated system of reservoirs and canals for irrigation at Angkor, enabling them to grow three or four rice crops a year. The reservoirs, the theory went, filled in the monsoon season, and were used for irrigation during the dry season. The reservoirs could hold millions of gallons of water, making Angkor a hydraulic society par excellence.

However, this view is now being challenged. Water is never once mentioned on stone inscriptions at Angkor sites. Zhou Daguan, a 13th-century visitor, did not describe Angkor's plumbing except to mention bathing. Bathing was undoubtedly popular—the Chinese delegation took great pleasure in observing women bathing nude several times a day, "covering their sex with their left hand." Some geographers argue the barays and canals were only for urban use—for bathing, ritual ceremonies, drinking, transport, beautifying the landscape, and perhaps for supplying fresh fish.

Using remote sensing equipment and satellite images to study land formations, engineers have found little evidence of extensive irrigation. Researchers calculate the combined storage capacity of all Angkor reservoirs is sufficient to irrigate only a paltry 400 hectares of ricefields—hardly enough to support a population estimated at up to a million. The large moats around Angkor's monuments could not have been used for irrigation because there were no outlets into the fields. The annual flooding of Lake Tonle Sap is instead credited as the major water supply for rice growing. If Angkor's plumbing was instead for urban use, it was also an easy target for enemy saboteurs. A recent theory is that after Angkor's elaborate reservoirs and canals fell into disrepair, the pools became stagnant breeding grounds for mosquitoes, causing an outbreak of malaria.

Several Western experts have lobbied to restore the canals and reservoirs of Angkor, or at least raise the water table, to stabilize the monuments by hydraulic pressure and thus prevent further collapse.

Saving Angkor

Since 1989 UNESCO has coordinated international efforts to restore the monuments of

ANGKOR HIGHLIGHTS

You could spend an entire week in Angkor, sunup to sundown, and still not see it all. Siem Reap itself is slow-paced and relaxing, with reasonable restaurants and lots of countryside. It's a good place to sit on the front porch, swap tales with other travelers, and watch the geckos climb the walls.

Angkor and Siem Reap are the kind of places you have to tear yourself away from. If your time is short, concentrate on the two main complexes, Angkor Wat and Angkor Thom. Opinions vary on the rest; everybody seems to have a personal favorite.

The soundest advice on touring Angkor is, in a word, *variety*. Avoid concentrations on a series of temples in the same style, as you may become blasé and won't be able to remember one from the other later. Angkor Wat is very different in style from Angkor Thom, and the jungle-locked ruins of Ta Prohm and Preah Khan are worlds away again. For a different perspective, hike up to a viewpoint, or visit an artificial lake like Neak Pean. With more time you can spend a day at the ruins, then take a day to visit the rural areas around Siem Reap.

Following are the star sites:

Angkor Wat: Large and classical, this awesome site is the world's largest temple, with the world's longest bas-relief panels. On the second terrace are friezes of celestial dancers. Expect to spend at least half a day here, or make several visits.

Angkor Thom: This cluster of sites is another must-see, and will again easily consume at least half a day. The spectacular South Gate is the best-preserved entry to Angkor Thom. The central temple, the Bayon, is small in scale, but bizarre, mysterious, and imaginative—the favorite of many visitors. North of the Bayon are fine friezes at the Leper King Terrace.

Aerial Views: A hike up Phnom Bakheng affords fine sunset views of Angkor Wat. North of the Bayon is a hike to a hilltop behind Baphuon temple. Both hilltops give you a sense of jungle and forest vegetation.

Jungle-locked Ruins: Preah Khan and Ta Prohm are romantic and spooky sites, covered by centuries of vegetation. The French left Ta Prohm untouched to give an impression of how Angkor looked in the 19th century, with tree roots and foliage winding through the stonework.

Artificial Lakes: To get an idea of the waterworks in the Angkor region, visit the ceremonial bathing sites of Neak Pean and Sra Srang or journey to the West Baray for boating or swimming.

Rural Living: Take a road in any direction from Siem Reap and you're in the countryside. Best excursions are 13 km east to Roluos, where you can view village life, or 15 km south to Lake Tonle Sap to see floating houses sitting over fish-holding pens.

Angkor, with half a dozen international agencies providing financial and technical aid. Looking forward to a more stable political situation, in December 1992 UNESCO adopted Angkor as a World Heritage Site, simultaneously placing Angkor on the World Heritage in Danger list. In October 1993, at a Tokyo conference hosted by Japan and France, funds were pledged to preserve the ruins and promote Angkor as a special tourist destination. A Japanese survey identified as a key priority supporting the foundations of Angkor Wat, the Bayon, Baphuon, and Preah Khan.

From 1870 to 1970, Angkor survey and restoration work was conducted exclusively by the French. Louis Delaporte participated in the French expedition to survey the Mekong in 1866-68, with an initial stop at Angkor in 1866. He returned to Angkor in 1871 to compile extensive maps and sketches. Delaporte removed over a hundred of Angkor's finest statues to Paris, where they are now housed in the Guimet Museum. His published survey results appeared in *Voyage au Cambodge: l'architecture khmère* in 1880, and he returned to Cambodia again in 1882-83. In Paris he organized colonial exhibitions of Khmer art and architecture, featuring three-dimensional building replicas taken from moldings of smaller sites.

In 1898 the EFEO began clearing jungle, mapping sites, and making inventory lists, as a prelude to restoration. Such prominent French archaeologists as Henri Marchal, Henri Parmentier, George Coedes, and Bernard Groslier made major commitments to preserving Angkor. Using local work teams, the French cleared vegetation, installed hidden drains to prevent water damage, and reconstructed a number of temples with anastylosis—the process of disassembling a structure, then reassembling it using the original methods and materials on top of a new cement foundation. French restoration work ceased when they were driven out in 1970 by the Khmer Rouge.

Miraculously, Angkor survived the Pol Pot era largely intact. The Khmer Rouge lit fires in the galleries, used Angkor Wat as an ammunition dump, fired at bas-reliefs for target practice, and hacked off heads of statues to sell on the international market to help finance their war efforts. With a few exceptions they did not dynamite entire structures, as they did with wats in other parts of the country. Buddha images were singled out for destruction—a large Buddha next to the Bayon was dynamited. But mostly Angkor was left alone, because as a cornerstone of Khmer culture, it served as inspiration for the Khmer Rouge too. Pol Pot extolled the independent greatness of Angkor as a model to be emulated, and the Khmer Rouge flag featured the triple towers of Angkor.

Western experts are sharply critical of the Indian-led efforts to restore Angkor's monuments in 1986, under the Vietnamese-installed regime. Archaeologists maintain the chemicals used to clean monuments of mold and lichen actually damaged the stonework by stripping the protective patina. Indian teams also used concrete with great abandon to reinforce structures, in some cases replacing original stone pillars with crude concrete replicas, even though the originals could have been restored. Concrete ages at a different rate than sandstone, creating a jarring two-tone effect over time.

A highly contentious issue is exactly how to restore Angkor's monuments. Debate has raged since Mouhot rediscovered Angkor in 1860. Some advocate complete restoration, rebuilding buildings to their original design; others are from the "do no harm school" and believe the ruins should be left as ruins—the only goal to prevent further decay. Water damage occurs during the annual monsoon when the reddish laterite foundation stone turns soft and spongy. The stone is further ravaged by lichen, algae, mold, acidic bat droppings, insect nests, thick jungle growth, and fumes from logging trucks.

Tourism could save Angkor by providing funds for repair and maintenance. In the past, Angkor

Tourism restricted access to high-paying group tours; in 1992, UNTAC personnel visited in large numbers, paving the way for independent travelers. However, too much tourism could create the same problem that has plagued the Acropolis in Greece—large numbers of people trampling through can damage the buildings.

Conservation efforts at Angkor are coordinated through the UNESCO international campaign to safeguard Angkor. The EFEO has returned to Cambodia, offering technical advice and restoring the Elephant Terrace. An eight-year $5.6 million EFEO project will rebuild and restore 11th-century Baphuon, using advanced computer technology to graphically visualize the reconstruction. The EFEO dismantled, labeled, and stockpiled the stones of the Baphuon before departing in the 1970s. Now, it must reassemble them. Other restoration groups include the United Nations Development Programme (UNDP), restoring Angkor Wat moat; World Monuments Fund, working on Preah Khan restoration; and Waseda University of Poland, engaged in restoring the Bayon. The Archeological Survey of India and Japan's Sophia University are also involved in restoration projects.

Art Heists

After centuries of plunder, Angkor has been stripped to its stone structures and heavy stone sculptures. Now these are under threat, too, from a new breed of treasure hunters. Since 1970, there has been a phenomenal incidence of statuary theft from Angkor sites. The Cambodian government does not have the people and resources to prevent theft, and corrupt officials may in fact be involved in the trade. Even well-guarded sites are subject to looting. In early 1993 thieves armed with machine guns launched an attack on the Angkor Conservancy in Siem Reap. They shot one of the guards, fired a rocket-propelled grenade at a storeroom door, and made off with 11 valuable pieces worth up to half a million dollars on the open market. Down the road, at Sihanouk's villa, a 100-kg statue as tall as a human was stolen from the courtyard. The rare 9th-century piece, a female divinity who'd lost her head to previous plunderers, had stood in the courtyard only a few months. The same week, five stone heads were reported stolen from the northern gate of

beheaded half-human, half-animal guardian statue

Angkor Thom, worth three to four thousand dollars in Thailand.

Local officials say these pieces, like most Khmer sculptures, were smuggled into Thailand. Moving a 100-kg statue across the border requires considerable logistics and a sophisticated level of organization. In early 1995 a truck loaded with rice was intercepted at Aranyaprathet on the Thai border; five Khmer artifacts were hidden under the grain, including a

Shiva linga, a Buddha image, and a stone *garuda* carving. Other pieces have been seized on the Thai-Cambodian border. There is little doubt the Khmer Rouge are involved in the lucrative trade; a 1994 attack on a Khmer Rouge base in Anlong Veng in northern Cambodia revealed a huge stone piece stolen from Angkor Wat.

In the mid-1970s Khmer sculpture began to appear at leading auction houses and in private art collections in the West. Thailand is not a signatory to the UN's 1970 convention against antiquities trafficking; Cambodia is. Although Thailand stringently protects its own cultural heritage, it allows Bangkok dealers to trade in Burmese and Cambodian pieces. Unethical Western buyers have even been able to place orders for pieces of their choice through black-market dealers in Bangkok or Singapore.

Few pieces seized in Bangkok find their way back to Cambodia—a major source of friction between the two countries. The Cambodian Ministry of Culture is still trying to recover 13 artifacts seized from a Bangkok antique dealer in 1990 and held in storage at Bangkok's National Museum. The French government is more obliging. In 1994 a 10th-century four-headed statue of Brahma was smuggled into Thailand, then cut into four pieces, each with one face. When a Thai dealer offered one piece for auction in France, the French National Museum became suspicious, seized it, and returned the piece to Cambodia.

Under UNESCO guidance Cambodian authorities are now training special forces to police Angkor's ruins and document missing pieces for identification. The National Heritage Protection Authority of Cambodia was set up to prevent trafficking in statuary.

SIEM REAP

Siem Reap is the small gateway town to the ruins of Angkor, located 250 km northwest of Phnom Penh and 15 km north of Lake Tonle Sap. The town has a relaxing frontier air to it: there are few phones, and the electricity and water supply is erratic. Running through the center of town is the polluted Siem Reap River. Traces of the French presence have survived in a small quarter of colonial buildings to the southwest side—the rest of Siem Reap was badly damaged by bombing and civil war. In the early 1970s, during the Pol Pot era, people were fed to the crocodiles in Siem Reap. There is a "killing fields" memorial to victims of the Khmer Rouge to the northwest of town. In 1979 the province was the scene of heavy fighting between the Khmer Rouge and the Vietnamese Army. Since 1990 the Khmer Rouge have staged sporadic attacks on the civilian population and Cambodian government troops around Siem Reap. In 1993 they massacred Vietnamese fishing families at Lake Tonle Sap, precipitating an exodus of Vietnamese to the Mekong Delta. To safeguard Angkor, the government has stationed 900 troops, ringing the entire zone of ruins.

It's an uneasy peace in Siem Reap, but there is normal life around Angkor: farmers transporting goods in oxcarts, village women clad in sarongs cycling to market, Buddhist monks in flowing orange robes out for morning strolls, kids lolling about on the backs of water buffalo in green fields. For tourists, this is a chance to see rural life. For locals, tourism itself, however small in scale, is seen as a return to normalcy after years of savage war and upheaval. A number of new hotels, guesthouses, and restaurants have appeared in Siem Reap in the 1990s, catering first to visiting UNTAC troops and later to the Angkor-bound tourists who arrived in their wake.

Angkor Conservancy

Anything moveable at Angkor has disappeared. Even the heads of the larger stone statues have been hacked off by treasure hunters. To guard against art theft, virtually all smaller Angkor statuary, wood items, and artifacts have been removed to museums, particularly to the National Museum in Phnom Penh. Thousands of pieces rest at the Angkor Conservancy, located several km to the north of Siem Reap. You need special permission from the Ministry of Culture in Phnom Penh to visit. The Angkor Conservancy was established by the French in 1907 when Siem Reap Province was restored to Cambodia by the Thais. From 1953 to 1970 the Angkor Conservancy was jointly operated by the French and Cambodian governments. With the exception of a period during WW II, the French at Angkor worked steadily, at times directing more than a thousand employees. In 1972 the civil war forced the French to leave.

Angkor Conservancy is a warehouse for some 7,000 sculpture fragments and artifacts from the Angkor region. Fresh concrete heads are stocked here, destined to replace ones removed from the Angkor area by bandits or Khmer Rouge. Museum staff also remove heads before bandits can get to them. There are two floors of statuary at Angkor Conservancy. On the ground floor are the larger Buddhas, Vishnus, and lintels; the upper floor houses smaller Buddhas, hand fragments, stone animals, and large wooden Buddhas. Unfortunately, the pieces are not safe even here—the place has been broken into several times.

ACCOMMODATIONS

Guesthouses

Siem Reap boasts more than 20 guesthouses, charging $5-30 a room. There are half a dozen on downtown Achar Hem Chiev, five or so toward the market, and another eight on the airport road. These last are classier. Prices fluctuate with seasonal demand. Fan rooms in guesthouses are generally under $10, while air-con rooms go for $15-20. Guesthouses are often two-story abodes run by families, originally converted for UNTAC visitors. Usually guests lodge upstairs, and the family lives downstairs. There are basic rooms with mosquito nets and fans, and shared bathroom facilities downstairs. The owners can arrange moto rentals, bicycles, and guides.

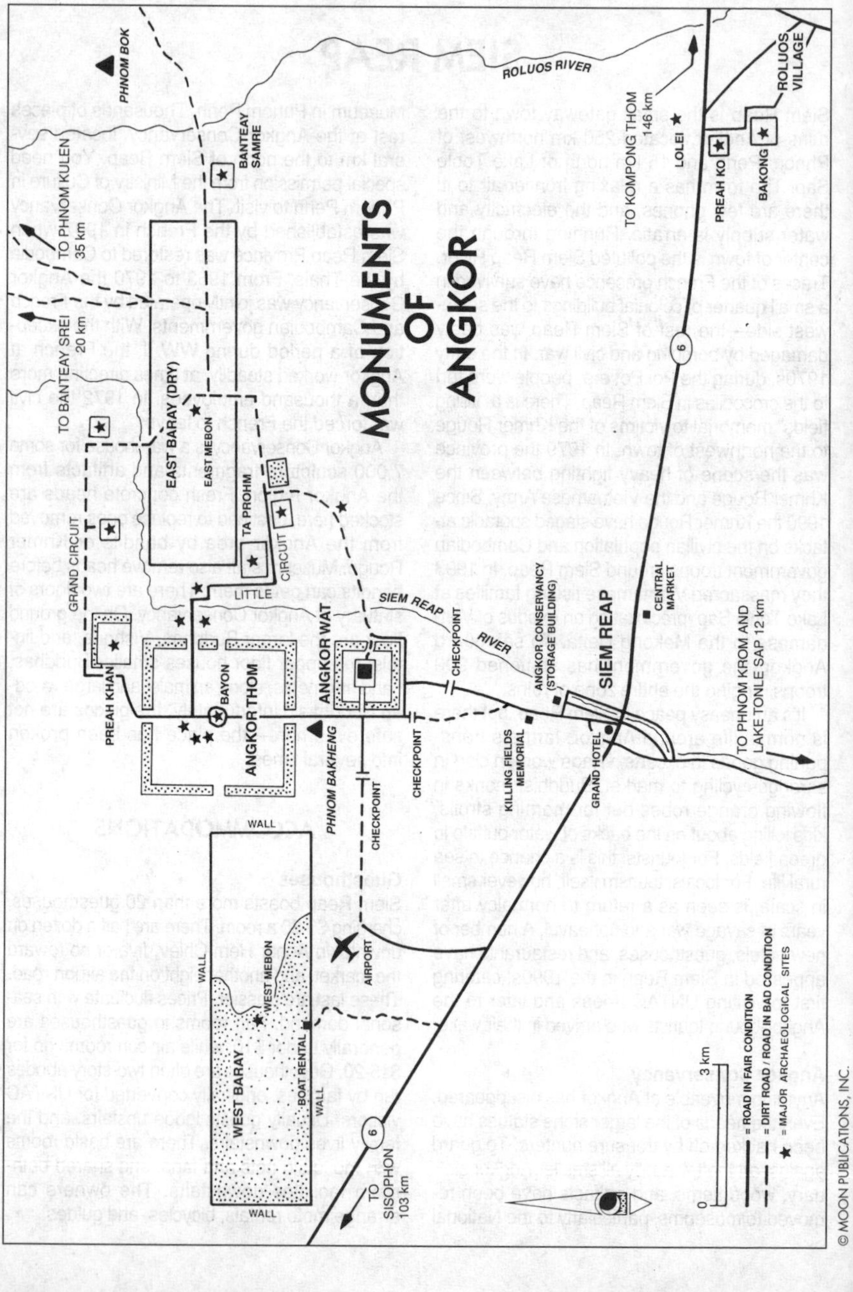

MONUMENTS
OF
ANGKOR

TO PHNOM KULEN
35 km

TO BANTEAY SREI
20 km

PHNOM BOK

ROLUOS RIVER

BANTEAY
SAMRE

ROLUOS
VILLAGE

LOLEI

PREAH KO

BAKONG

TO KOMPONG THOM
146 km

6

EAST BARAY (DRY)

EAST MEBON

TA PROHM

LITTLE
CIRCUIT

GRAND CIRCUIT

PREAH KHAN

BAYON

ANGKOR THOM

ANGKOR WAT

PHNOM BAKHENG

SIEM REAP
RIVER

CHECKPOINT

CHECKPOINT

CHECKPOINT

KILLING FIELDS
MEMORIAL

CHECKPOINT

GRAND HOTEL

SIEM REAP

CENTRAL
MARKET

ANGKOR
CONSERVANCY
(STORAGE BUILDING)

TO PHNOM KROM AND
LAKE TONLE SAP 12 km

WALL

WALL

WEST MEBON

WEST BARAY

BOAT RENTAL

WALL

WALL

AIRPORT

6

TO SISOPHON
103 km

© MOON PUBLICATIONS, INC.

= ROAD IN FAIR CONDITION

= DIRT ROAD / ROAD IN BAD CONDITION

★ = MAJOR ARCHAEOLOGICAL SITES

0   3 km

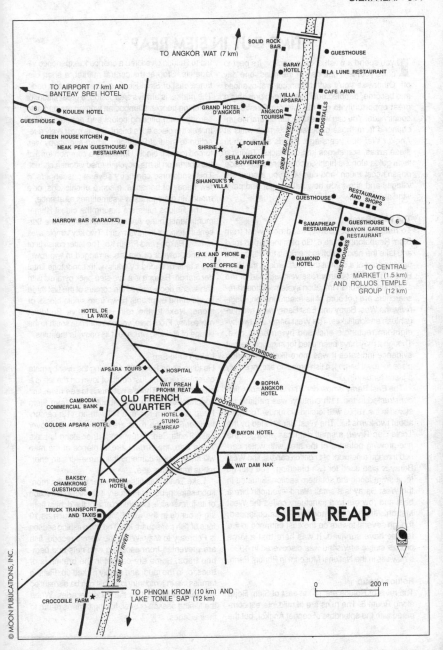

TO ANGKOR WAT (7 km)

SOLID ROCK BAR

GUESTHOUSE

BARAY HOTEL

LA LUNE RESTAURANT

CAFE ARUN

VILLA APSARA

TO AIRPORT (7 km) AND BANTEAY SREI HOTEL

6

KOULEN HOTEL

GUESTHOUSE

GREEN HOUSE KITCHEN

NEAK PEAN GUESTHOUSE/RESTAURANT

GRAND HOTEL D'ANGKOR

ANGKOR TOURISM

SHRINE

FOUNTAIN

SEILA ANGKOR SOUVENIRS

SIHANOUK'S VILLA

FOODSTALLS

SIEM REAP RIVER

GUESTHOUSE

RESTAURANTS AND SHOPS

6

NARROW BAR (KARAOKE)

SAMAPHEAP RESTAURANT

GUESTHOUSE BAYON GARDEN RESTAURANT

GUESTHOUSES

FAX AND PHONE

POST OFFICE

DIAMOND HOTEL

TO CENTRAL MARKET (1.5 km) AND ROLUOS TEMPLE GROUP (12 km)

HOTEL DE LA PAIX

FOOTBRIDGE

APSARA TOURS

HOSPITAL

WAT PREAH PROHM REAT

BOPHA ANGKOR HOTEL

CAMBODIA COMMERCIAL BANK

OLD FRENCH QUARTER

FOOTBRIDGE

GOLDEN APSARA HOTEL

HOTEL STUNG SIEMREAP

BAYON HOTEL

BAKSEY CHAMKRONG GUESTHOUSE

TA PROHM HOTEL

WAT DAM NAK

TRUCK TRANSPORT AND TAXIS

SIEM REAP

MOON

SIEM REAP RIVER

0   200 m

TO PHNOM KROM (10 km) AND LAKE TONLE SAP (12 km)

CROCODILE FARM

© MOON PUBLICATIONS, INC.

TIME OUT IN SIEM REAP

If you spend a week or so in Angkor, it's best to pace yourself: one day at the ruins, one day off. Otherwise you'll suffer from cultural overload and become "templed out." Siem Reap presents a great opportunity to get out into the Cambodian countryside. You can witness facets of rural life unchanged from those depicted on temple walls at Angkor Wat 800 years ago. Roads are rough in these areas, sometimes just dirt tracks. Taking a local guide along is highly recommended. A guide doesn't cost much, and can take you around the villages and show you how palm sugar and palm wine are brewed.

The West Baray

To reach the West Baray, head northwest from Siem Reapalong Route 6. Go past the airport road and take the next turnoff to the right: this leads to a parking area at a dam at the south side of the West Baray. The West Baray reservoir was part of the elaborate Angkorian irrigation system, although researchers are not sure of its exact function. Originally, the West Baray and East Baray were two gargantuan artificial lakes. The West Baray is a two-by-eight-km rectangle enclosed by an earth dike. Though it may have been used for irrigation, recent evidence indicates it was more likely a mooring place for royal barges, a fish-breeding site, or simply a place for bathing.

The East Baray is now dry. The West Baray, first constructed in the 11th century, was partially restored in the 1950s with foreign-aid funds. Today it's about two-thirds full. The West Baray is fed by the Tonle Sap River; a small dam has enlarged the rice-growing potential of the area with water carried through a network of irrigation canals. The West Baray is also used for fish breeding. You can go for a swim along the southern section. Situated in the West Baray is a small island—you can hire a boat and row out to a sanctuary called the West Mebon. Much of the stonework has collapsed, though several towers on the east entrance to the temple have survived. It was here that a large bronze statue of Vishnu was discovered in 1936. It now sits in the National Museum in Phnom Penh.

Roluos Group

The ruins of Roluos are 13 km east of Siem Reap along Route 6. The ruins are of mild interest compared with the splendors of central Angkor, but the trip to Roluos gives you a chance to experience village life. Stop at the central market, a short distance east of Siem Reap, on the way out or back. The market is always engrossing, a great place for watching people. Cambodian women are partial to sarongs with blinding colors and patterns, which makes the place quite bright. This is most likely a reaction to the Pol Pot years, when everybody was forced to wear black. Upcountry a common form of transportation is the bicycle-hauled wooden chariot. This workhorse can carry several passengers, a few hands of bananas, a score of chickens, or a mountain of vegetables—sometimes all at once.

The Roluos ruins are among the oldest Khmer monuments in the Angkor area, dating to the 9th-century reign of Indravarman I. Two key temple sites remain, Bakong and Preah Ko. The latter consists of six brick towers or *prasats*, arranged in two rows; the site is bounded by walls, with sandstone lintel decoration. Bakong is a five-step brick pyramid with sandstone doorways. At the corners of the first three levels stand elephants hewn from single blocks of stone. Next to the ruin is an active Buddhist monastery. From here, you can continue south to the village of Roluos, which lent its name to the ruins.

Lake Tonle Sap

Head south on Route 29, following the river by moto or rented bicycle. Just south of town on the left is a crocodile farm. There's not much to see here, just concrete and crocodiles. About 12 km from Siem Reap is Phnom Krom, a hill with an 11th-century temple. From the ruins are expansive views over Lake Tonle Sap. A few km further along is Lake Tonle Sap, the Great Lake. A glance at the map will show how it came by this name—it's an enormous freshwater sea.

Lake Tonle Sap fills with water during the monsoon season, but by February it shrinks to a fraction of its former size, becoming one of the richest fishing grounds in the world, yielding as much as 10 tons of fish per square km. The main fishing season is February to May. When the waters recede, fish are prevented from escaping with nets and bamboo traps. Some are caught in the branches of trees, or in the mud, and simply picked up. Fishing families live in temporary huts that can be dismantled and moved forward as the water recedes. When the fishing season is over, fishing families return to their villages.

The flooding of the Tonle Sap covers the area with a rich mud ideal for growing rice. Farmers have developed unique deepwater rice strains that grow with the rising lake to keep the grain above the water. Under Pol Pot, large parts of the flooded forest around Tonle Sap were sacrificed to expand the area for ricefields. During the war much of the rice seed stock was lost, and deepwater rice cultivation declined.

Coming from Siem Reap you reach a boat dock on the shores of Lake Tonle Sap. It's a scummy area, with boats loading and unloading goods, fish drying in the sun, and assorted video cafés. The lake itself is peaceful and uneventful, but hidden dramas abound. If you hire a boat for an hour, or row out yourself, you can reach floating houses suspended over huge bamboo fish-holding pens. Families here fatten up the fish in the pens; some houses are rigged with trapdoors that open so feed can be dropped. A fish pen may be three meters deep, and hold thousands of fish. You don't realize how many fish there are until feeding time when you see them thrashing around in the water. This kind of "fish farming" is also practiced in Vietnam's Mekong Delta.

Because the lake keeps shrinking and expanding, a species of fish has evolved here that can survive several hours out of water, flopping overland in search of deeper pools. This species, known as *hock yue,* or elephant fish, is considered a delicacy in Asia. Another highly prized delicacy is the sand goby, or *soon hock,* a greenish-gray trout-like specimen. One company ships the fish live to Phnom Penh, where they're held in tanks. For transportation to restaurants in Singapore and Kuala Lumpur, the fish are placed in tanks filled with ice and a mild sedative. In a semi-inert state they're air-freighted in plastic bags pumped with oxygen. They must reach their destination within 16 hours. In a Singapore restaurant, a single sand goby, cooked with ginger, chili, tomato, and mushrooms, is worth $40-60, depending on its size.

Rooms are $6 on Achar Hem Chiev. In a row here are **Moms, Sunrise, Kim Hong, Mahogeny** and a place just called **Guesthouse.** Each rent six to 10 rooms. On the opposite side of the street is **Kim Phan,** run by the family of a retired doctor—there's a small pharmacy at the front of the house. **GH 594** also occupies this side.

Along Route 6, the airport road, signs simply read Guesthouse or bear a number—GH 108, GH 361, GH 394, GH 018, GH 260, GH 279. There are about a dozen places on the airport road. **Neak Pean** has a dozen rooms for rent for $10-15. Toward the central market on Route 6 is **Ban Thai,** with air-con rooms for $15 and a restaurant serving Thai and Western food. To the south edge of Siem Reap, **Baksey Chamkrong** offers seven air-con rooms for $20 with bath, and three fan rooms for $10 each. A cluster of guesthouses are found around this area on the west side—**Star** and **Vimean Thmey** among them. Rooms go for $5-15.

Moderate

Because of a lack of telecom facilities in Siem Reap, rooms can be booked through agents in Phnom Penh or Bangkok. Some Siem Reap accommodations are affiliated with hotels in Phnom Penh. To the west of Siem Reap, **Koulen Hotel** offers 12 double rooms with air-con, fridge, and bath, for $30. With a bar and dancing this place is noisy. To the north of town, the **Baray Hotel** has 12 air-con rooms for $40. In the center, the Thai-managed **Diamond Hotel,** tel. 913130, fax 910020, has 27 bungalow-style doubles for $35.

On the southern edge of town **Hotel Stung Siemreap,** tel. 912379, has 33 rooms in the $35-45 range with satellite TV and air-con. The hotel is a renovated French mansion, located in the old French quarter. **Golden Apsara Hotel** rents 16 air-con rooms for $20-30. **Hotel de La Paix,** tel. 912322, has 40 rooms for $20-35—this colonial-era hotel is slated for renovation. The motel-like **Bopha Angkor Hotel,** tel. 911710, has 21 air-con rooms with satellite TV—singles for $45-50, doubles for $60. The **Bayon Hotel,** tel. 911769, features 44 rooms for $30-35 single and $35-40 double. Rooms include air-con, private bath, fridge, and minibar.

Luxury

Several four-star and five-star hotels are under construction around Siem Reap in joint ventures with Hong Kong and Malaysian companies. A recent classy addition is **Bantei Srei Hotel,** on Route 6 toward the airport, tel. 913839, with 55 rooms for $55 and up. By the Siem Reap River is **Ta Prohm Hotel,** tel./fax

911783, with 58 luxury rooms for $70-90 and several suites for $100-120. Rooms include all mod cons—fridge, minibar, satellite TV.

Built in the 1920s for the French tourist trade is **Grand Hotel d'Angkor,** tel. 911292, fax 911291. At present the Grand has 65 rooms, plus an additional 20 rooms at **Villa Apsara** across the way. Standard rooms are $35-60; 10 deluxe suites go for $70-90. Prices decline when there are few tourists around. The hotel offers satellite TV, swimming pool, air-conditioned restaurant, and a tea lounge with pastry counter. There's also a business center with IDD phones and fax, photocopy, and computer facilities. The French empire lives on in a derelict fashion at the Grand Hotel—pending renovations, cheaper rooms do not have hot water, and the old French cage elevator doesn't function. The salient features for the casual visitor are the bar, with overpriced drinks, and the gift shop, with overpriced film, books, and novels and newspapers left behind by guests. The Grand is being renovated under a $30-million agreement with Singapore's DS Land, which owns the Raffles Hotel in Singapore. The plan is to expand the Grand into a five-star 300-room hotel.

FOOD AND DRINK

The variety and quality of food in Siem Reap is impressive. It's close to Lake Tonle Sap, so there's a lot of fish on the menu. In cheaper restaurants, a meal runs $1-3; in more expensive restaurants expect to pay perhaps $2-8. The Central Market, five km east of town, is scummy, but displays lots of fresh food. Out this way on Route 6 is **Ban Thai** restaurant, just west of the Central Market; Thai dishes are about $2.

In town, there's cheap eating at foodstalls along the Siem Reap River. Small restaurants here include **La Lune,** serving Khmer food, and **Café Arun,** with big portions of Chinese, Khmer, and continental food. North of Villa Apsara is **Samaki,** with low-priced Khmer and Western food. The popular **Samapheap Restaurant** serves a good selection of Cambodian and Western dishes at reasonable prices. The Samapheap offers good *loclac,* a plate of sliced beef spiced with lemon and black pepper.

The **Bayon Garden Restaurant,** on Achar Hem Chiev, is pricier—go to the garden in the rear courtyard. There's some good Thai food on the menu, including curry served in young coconut. On the west side of town is **Green House Kitchen,** with excellent Khmer and Thai food; nearby is a backpacker hangout, **Neak Pean Guesthouse Restaurant.**

The hotels around Siem Reap have their own restaurants, all on the expensive side. Hotel Stung Siemreap and the Baray Hotel offer good selections, and the Grand Hotel d'Angkor features elegant dining with a bar.

Nightlife: Yes, karaoke comes to Angkor. On the outskirts of town are taxi-dancing venues, with signs like Motel-Bar-Dancing or Solid Rock.

bamboo fish farm at Lake Tonle Sap

To the west side of town is **Narrow Bar** disco, and a dance-drink spot called **Sky Palace.** Guesthouse gates are often locked for security reasons at 2000. Larger hotels like the Grand Hotel d'Angkor offer satellite TV. The Grand may stage *apsara* dancing at night—there's been an attempt to establish a dance school in Siem Reap.

SHOPPING

There's a cottage souvenir industry at Siem Reap, with stalls near the ruins and in town. Most of the items are also on sale in Phnom Penh.

Angkoriana: Ta Prohm Hotel and Grand Hotel d'Angkor include gift shops selling Angkor kitsch, as well as postcards, books, and newspapers. In the center of town near the Siem Reap River is Seila Angkor souvenir shop—a kiosk where you can ponder your purchases over an Angkor Beer. Rice-paper prints made from charcoal rubbings of bas-reliefs of Angkor temples are inexpensive, and come close to the original artwork.

Film: You can buy E6 and print film in Siem Reap, but supply is limited and film may be of dubious quality. Hotel gift shops also sell film. There are some one-hour photo places in Siem Reap that develop print film.

SERVICES AND INFORMATION

Banking

Bring cash from Phnom Penh—you can easily deal in US dollars in Siem Reap. Credit card use is very limited. There is a branch of Cambodia Commercial Bank on the southwest side of town.

Telecom Services

Don't expect wonders from the post office, located on the west side of Siem Reap River. If you prod them, they might shell out a few stamps—a postcard from Angkor, if it makes it back home, will certainly have tremendous snob-appeal value. Next door, Cambodia Samart Communications has a satellite dish and a mobile IDD phone. You can phone home from here, though it's expensive. The office is open 0800-1800. Samart has installed dishes in several hotels around Siem Reap, which links them to Phnom Penh, and sometimes provides fax and IDD capabilities. The Cambodia country code is 855, and the Siem Reap area code is 15. Satellite TV, also operating off dishes, can pick up StarTV and BBC. Ta Prohm Hotel and Grand Hotel d'Angkor have both installed the Samart system.

GETTING THERE

By Air

Royal Air Cambodge runs daily flights—sometimes several a day—with Antonovs, Tupolevs, and some ATRs. These planes hold about 70 passengers. During the peak December-to-March season, up to eight flights a day leave for Siem Reap. The cost is $50 one-way. Talks continue on a direct Bangkok-Siem Reap airlink. Bangkok Air has plans to use 140-seat 734-400s to fly the Bangkok-Siem Reap route; Thai Airways International is also keen to fly here.

The airport at Siem Reap lies eight km northwest of town. The larger hotels maintain airport representatives who will arrange taxis. If arriving on your own, you can transfer to town for $2 by car, or take a moto. You may be offered free rides to a guesthouse (where they get a commission); then they'll try to line you up for moto tours of Angkor. Choose wisely! On departure from Siem Reap airport, passengers' bags and personal effects may be searched for Angkor statues and artifacts.

By Boat

Westerners can take the boats from Phnom Penh up the Tonle Sap River and across Lake Tonle Sap, arriving at a dock 15 km south of Siem Reap (transfer to moto for the land leg). Fast boats do not slow down at checkpoints manned by government soldiers in search of handouts, especially in the region on both sides of Kompong Chhnang, where the river narrows. Timing depends on the direction of the Tonle Sap River. There are several fast boats; from Phnom Penh it costs $28 to Siem Reap, and the journey takes five to seven hours. The boat is seasonal and runs when waters are high, from November to February. The fast boat usually leaves from a point one km north of Chruoy Changvar Bridge in Phnom Penh. The Capitol Hotel runs its own fast boat service for $17 a head, with a truck to Kompong Chhnang and a fast boat leaving from there to Siem Reap. This boat has a poor performance record—it has sunk several times and run aground on sandbars.

There are two or three boats a week, a double-deck cargo boat takes anywhere from 18 to 26 hours. One traveler reported a journey of 36 hours, though the first 12 hours were spent in Phnom Penh with propeller troubles. The cost is $5-8. Inquire at the docks at the eastern extremity of Street 108 in Phnom Penh about de-

ANGKOR ROUTE STRATEGIES

Angkor Archaeological Park consists of 70 ruins in an area of 200 square km, although the key ruins are clustered in a zone of some 60 square km. The French engineered routes of hard-packed earth around the Angkor area in the 1920s to facilitate visits by car. Several roads were later paved, and dubbed *le Petit Circuit* (the Little Circuit) and *le Grand Circuit* (the Grand Circuit), but there are really no set patterns. You can mix and match, or come up with your own routes.

Start early. The heat of the day can get to you even by 0900. Fortunately there are well-shaded sections, especially around the Bayon, and if you move along by bicycle or motorcycle you get some breeze. It's a good idea to take a siesta in a cool spot: find a foodstall selling noodles (the biggest collection of foodstalls is opposite the main gates to Angkor) from 1100-1400, or just go back to town and rest. Dawn and dusk add special magic to Angkor. Angkor Wat at the break of dawn is awesome. A little later, at the Bayon, it's misty and mysterious, with the sun filtering through the forest canopy, illuminating enigmatic smiling faces; the chirping of birds breaks the silence. The last glows of the setting sun over Angkor Wat are dramatic, viewed from either the causeway or the viewpoint of Phnom Bakheng. Then sound the frogs and cicadas, the birds and the bats.

Angkor Wat is overwhelming. The mind cannot take it in at one visit. Neither will your camera—attempts to fit Angkor into a standard lens viewfinder are frustrating. Angkor can monopolize your time, consuming half a day or more. You're better off making several visits to Angkor Wat. Drop in and walk down the causeway to get acquainted, then take off to smaller ruins up north like the Bayon, and maybe return to Angkor Wat in the late afternoon to take in a bit more.

Limiting factors on routes are available time, hot spells, transportation, and road conditions. The best road conditions are found going north from Angkor Wat to Preah Khan on the northern axis, and east

from Baphuon to Ta Prohm on an eastern axis. Other roads are in bad shape and potholed, slowing progress. Some ideas for routes follow, but you can chop, change, or add destinations to suit.

In a car or by motorcycle you can cover the Little Circuit in an hour of actual travel time; by bicycle, you'll need 2.5 hours for the same route. From the Grand Hotel to the west entrance of Angkor Wat is seven km. For the following routes, the start and finish point in Siem Reap is the Grand Hotel.

Northern Axis: Siem Reap (Grand Hotel), Angkor Thom (South Gate, Bayon, Baphuon, Leper King Terrace), Preah Khan, back south to Angkor Wat west entrance, Phnom Bakheng (sunset), Siem Reap. Distance: 29 km.

Little Circuit: Siem Reap, Angkor Wat west gate, Bayon, Victory Gate, Takeo, Ta Prohm, Sra Srang, Angkor Wat east entrance, Siem Reap. Distance: 30 km.

North and East Axes: Siem Reap, Angkor Wat west entrance, Bayon, Preah Khan, back to Leper King Terrace, Victory Gate, Chau Say Tevoda, Takeo, Ta Prohm, retrace route to Elephant Terrace, Angkor Wat again, Siem Reap. This erratic route is designed to take advantage of the best road conditions, especially if cycling. Distance: 38 km; if Preah Khan is eliminated, 32 km.

Grand Circuit: Siem Reap, Angkor Wat, Angkor Thom (South Gate, Bayon, Baphuon, Leper King Terrace), Preah Khan, Neak Pean, Sra Srang, Angkor Wat east entrance, Siem Reap. Distance: 40 km.

Combination Circuit: Siem Reap, Angkor Thom (South Gate, Bayon, Leper King Terrace), Preah Khan, Neak Pean, Sra Srang, Ta Prohm, Victory Gate, Elephant Terrace, Angkor Wat west entrance, Siem Reap. Distance: 45 km.

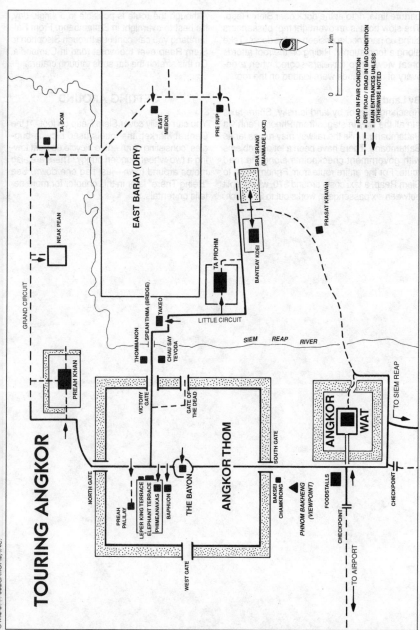

TOURING ANGKOR

GRAND CIRCUIT

LITTLE CIRCUIT

TA SOM

NEAK PEAN

EAST BARAY (DRY)

EAST MEBON

PRE RUP

SRA SRANG (MANMADE LAKE)

PRASAT KRAVAN

BANTEAY KDEI

TA PROHM

TAKEO

SPEAN THMA (BRIDGE)

THOMMANON

CHAU SAY TEVODA

SIEM REAP RIVER

VICTORY GATE

GATE OF THE DEAD

PREAH KHAN

NORTH GATE

PREAH PALILAY

LEPER KING TERRACE

ELEPHANT TERRACE

PHIMEANAKAS

BAPHUON

THE BAYON

ANGKOR THOM

SOUTH GATE

WEST GATE

BAKSEI CHAMKRONG

PHNOM BAKHENG (VIEWPOINT)

FOODSTALLS

ANGKOR WAT

TO SIEM REAP

CHECKPOINT

CHECKPOINT

CHECKPOINT

TO AIRPORT

= ROAD IN FAIR CONDITION
= ROAD / ROAD IN BAD CONDITION
= DIRT ROAD / ROAD IN BAD CONDITION
= MAIN ENTRANCES UNLESS OTHERWISE NOTED

1 km

0

parture time; ditto at the dock near Siem Reap. The slow boat is an overnight trip; passengers string up hammocks or sleep on the decks. Take along a food supply. Riding on the roof affords great views; two travelers scored when a delivery of mattresses were loaded on the roof.

By Land

Reaching Angkor by land is risky. Share-taxis run all the way in stages from Phnom Penh via Battambang, while the railway may run as far as Battambang. There have been a lot of problems with government checkpoints along the road route. For the entire route from Phnom Penh to Siem Reap, a taxi costs around $70, which, split between six passengers, works out to $12 each.

Although the route is possible in a single day, it's best to overnight in Battambang. From Battambang you can continue through Sisophon to Siem Reap over the worst road in Cambodia. On this stretch the car surfs through craters.

GETTING AROUND

You can easily cover Siem Reap on foot. At the Central Market, the locals used bicycle-buggies, consisting of an entire bicycle up front towing a two-wheel wooden buggy. There are also motos around town—just flag one down. See "Being There" later in this chapter for more details on rentals.

ANGKOR WAT

"Angkor is not orchestral; it is monumental. It is an epic poem which makes its effect, like the Odyssey *and like* Paradise Lost, *by the grandeur of its structure as well as by the beauty of the details. Angkor is an epic in rectangular forms imposed upon the Cambodian jungle."*

—ARNOLD TOYNBEE, *EAST TO WEST*

Occupying an entire square kilometer, Angkor Wat is the world's largest temple and the best-preserved of all Angkorian temples. This masterpiece of Khmer design is contemporary with the major Gothic cathedrals of Europe. Angkor Wat's central tower soars 65 meters, equivalent in height to Notre Dame Cathedral in Paris. Angkor Wat is estimated to contain the same cubic volume of stone blocks as Egypt's pyramid of Cheops. And every stone surface at Angkor is carefully dressed, carved, and decorated.

Angkor Wat is a three-tier pyramidal structure symbolizing Mount Meru. In Hindu cosmology, Mount Meru is a holy mountain composed of seven terraces, upon which 33 gods are enthroned, all surrounded by an ocean. Hindu epics describe Mount Meru as the navel of the world—a vast peak with flanks of gold, crystal, ruby, and lapis lazuli.

The building of Angkor Wat began around 1120 under King Suryavarman II—the king actually lived to see the work completed some 30 years later. Suryavarman II dedicated Angkor Wat to the Hindu deity Vishnu, with whom he identified as divine king. As part of the Vishnu cult, sacred lingas and Vishnu statues were sheltered in sanctuaries at the temple; a large Vishnu statue remains near the front entrance. Suryavarman II was one of Angkor's greatest kings, extending the Khmer Empire into present-day Malaya and Thailand, invading Burma and parts of Vietnam, and sending emissaries to the imperial court of the Khans in Peking. Under Suryavarman, Angkor reached its zenith. Toward the end of his reign, Suryavarman's forces suffered a major defeat in north Vietnam, and the king lost a number of his territories.

Because it faces westward, Angkor Wat is thought to have served as a funerary temple for the king. Site inscriptions support this theory, and the first terrace bas-reliefs are meant to be viewed in a counterclockwise direction, which indicates a mausoleum—clockwise circumambulation is the norm for temples. Otherwise, archaeologists are in the dark. We do not possess the keys to Angkor's grandeur—we stumble along blindly through the colossus, not sure how it functions, how it all fits together.

Entrances

There are two ways into or out of Angkor Wat—the west or front entrance, and the east or back entrance. It's seven km from the Grand Hotel north to the front entrance of Angkor Wat, where there's a parking lot for cars and tour buses, and a foodstall area. You can access Angkor's gallery of bas-reliefs quickly from the back entrance by a rough dirt road, not always passable in the rainy season.

The Causeway

The western approach to Angkor Wat is guarded by Khmer-style lions and seven-headed cobras (called *nagas*) with hoods outspread. A majestic 220-meter causeway, paved with large stone slabs and lined with colossal *naga* balustrades, leads across a moat to the temple. The *naga* balustrades not only line the causeway, they encircle the entire temple. The temple complex is bounded by a laterite wall, representing the earth; this is enclosed by a square moat over five km long, symbolizing the oceans. The moat is 1.3 km long from north to south, 1.5 km from east to west, and 200 meters wide. The few meters of water in the plant-choked moat teem with frogs, and are also home to lolling water buffalo and herons, who use it as a wading pool. The moat serves as a cooling off spot for local kids, too. Boat racing in the moat has been revived for the November Water Festival, a celebration of victory in a naval battle against the Cham dating back to the 12th century.

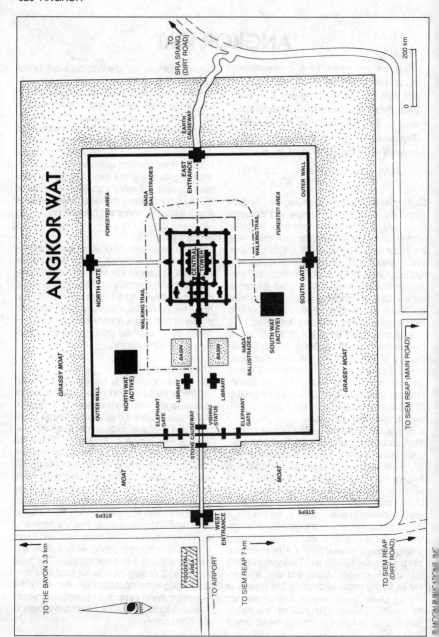

ANGKOR WAT GROUND PLAN

NAGA BALUSTRADES

NW CORNER PAVILION

LIBRARY

SECOND TERRACE

FRONT TOWER

QUINCUNX TERRACE

CENTRAL TOWER

TERRACE OF HONOR

EAST ENTRANCE

GALLERY OF A THOUSAND BUDDHAS

FIRST TERRACE

FRONT TOWER

BROKEN TOWER

LIBRARY

SW CORNER PAVILION

NAGA BALUSTRADES

BASIN

BASIN

0   50 m

Farther along you reach a second entrance, a triple-tower entryway. This leads to a second section of the causeway about 350 meters long. The regal approach here is breathtaking. On the spot, and in three dimensions, the perspective is grander than anything words or photos can convey. Closer to the temple, to the left and right of the causeway, are two small isolated buildings, thought to have been libraries housing sacred scriptures on palm leaves. On the left is a pool that reflects Angkor's towers at sunset. Ahead loom the triple towers of Angkor Wat; two more are hidden out of view at the back.

A cruciform terrace stands in front of the principal entrance to Angkor Wat. The terrace prob-ably served as a review stand for the king; ritual dances may have been performed here. Called the Terrace of Honor, this area features steps flanked by Khmer lions. There may have once been some 300 stone lions guarding stair-cases and entryways at Angkor Wat.

First Terrace

There are three rectangular terraces at Angkor, each rising above the other in pyramid fashion. The first terrace, measuring 200 meters by 180 meters, is four meters from ground level; the second, 115 meters by 100 meters, rises six meters above that; and the third, 60 meters by 60 meters, is a further 13 meters up. Thus on

---

ON PILGRIMAGE AT ANGKOR

Even after it was abandoned in the 15th century, Angkor continued to operate as a pilgrimage site. Under the Siamese, Buddhist monks later occupied part of the site, which explains why Angkor Wat is the best-preserved temple in the entire region—the monks cleared away encroaching jungle. Angkor is on the pilgrimage circuit not only for Cambodians and Buddhists from neighboring countries but also for visiting Indians, since the temple is consecrated to Hindu deities. There are two small monasteries on the grounds of Angkor Wat, the North Wat and South Wat; at dawn, orange-robed monks stroll about the ruins.

Since a lot of Angkor's free-standing statuary has been looted or removed for safekeeping, there are only a few areas of interest for pilgrims. The first is the huge eight-armed Vishnu statue located to the south side of the second causeway entrance tower. Joss sticks and other offerings are left here. Cambodians often come to consecrate food, which is then presumably taken off and eaten. Another popular site is the top sanctuary, where pilgrims *sompeah* the statues and the courtyard is smoky from burning joss sticks.

---

to offer. The figures face straight ahead with feet in profile. Framed by elaborate floral decoration and arranged in coquettish groups of two or three, they link arms and strike seductive poses, rather like models on a catwalk.

These bare-breasted angels were most likely modeled on the king's entourage of dancers, and are the height of Khmer chic. The king of Angkor maintained a bevy of dancers as part of his royal harem. Hindus considered dancing a sacred act, and female dancers devoted their lives to performing to please the gods. At Angkor dance was both sacred and sensual: through the medium of dance the women communicated with the divine world, guaranteeing fertility for the land and well-being for the people. While the men were out hunting, women at the court of Angkor evidently spent long hours grooming, styling their hair, preening, and adjusting their jewelry and girdles. The bas-reliefs display the elaborate coiffures—hair knotted on the crown and braided or bejeweled—and the fantastic fashions at the court of Angkor, with jeweled crowns, skirts, hip girdles, and upper-arm bracelets. The king's dancers were often spoils of war—when the Siamese invaded, they took Khmer dancers back to the Thai court.

In the 1950s under Sihanouk's patronage an *apsara* dance was created, with costumes and jeweled headpieces based on these bas-relief carvings—though with more modest apparel. The *apsara* is danced by five or seven women (odd numbers are auspicious) wearing multispired crowns and garlands of frangipani. The chorus sings of the delight of being surrounded by beautiful flowers in a garden. In the 1950s and 1960s tourists were treated to performances of *apsara* dancing at Angkor Wat itself. In November 1994, for the first time in decades, *apsara* dancers performed again at Angkor Wat under the full moon during the Water Festival. Light was provided by 600 youths bearing torches.

---

the third terrace you are 23 meters above ground level.

The main feature of the first terrace is the massive gallery of bas-reliefs. Viewing the gallery is time-consuming and distracts from the main fare—the uppermost sanctuary. It's best to view the first terrace gallery after you've climbed to the top of Angkor and come back to earth. Walking the entire length of the gallery traverses 750 meters.

Consolidating the grand entry to Angkor Wat is a series of cruciform courtyards. One of these is the Gallery of a Thousand Buddhas, which contained many images from the period when Angkor was Buddhist. Scarce few remain today, though there's a large standing Buddha with open palms. This section may have once been used for the ritual ablutions of priests.

Second Terrace

A flight of steps takes you to the second terrace, where galleries and staircases are adorned with baluster windows with seven twisted stone columns. The interior walls and niches of the second terrace gallery are decorated with the ethereal forms of over 1,700 stone *apsaras* (celestial dancers) and *devatas* (goddesses). Sculptors evidently spent long hours crafting these bas-reliefs—they're the finest Angkor has

GALLERY OF BAS-RELIEFS

Girdling the walls of Angkor Wat's first terrace are eight panels of bas-reliefs displaying scenes from Khmer historical events and the Hindu epics Ramayana and Mahabharata. The two-meter-high panels cover 1,200 square meters of sandstone carving—the longest continuous bas-relief in the world. This mind-boggling work of art must have been undertaken by innumerable sculptors working in teams. Bas-relief sculpting varies considerably in quality; panels were sculpted in various eras by different craftsmen. Some sections have been damaged; others have acquired a glossy sheen—the result of either lacquer coating or centuries of pilgrims rubbing their hands over the figures. Some panels may originally have been painted or gilded.

The panels essentially depict the battle between good and evil—keeping these forces in balance produces harmony. A prominent figure is four-armed Vishnu, shown quite large (the larger the figure on the bas-reliefs, the more important). Vishnu the Preserver was summoned whenever troubles arose in heaven or on earth. He is credited with at least 10 incarnations, among them Krishna and Rama. The righteous Rama was specifically incarnated to destroy evil demons.

The galleries at Angkor Wat are meant to be read in a counterclockwise direction, a circumambulation signifying a mausoleum. If you don't have the time or inclination to walk around the entire building, the most striking section is panel 4, Churning the Sea of Milk.

In the **West gallery, panel 1** depicts the civil war that is the main subject of the Hindu epic the Mahabharata. An army of Kauravas, advancing from the left, meets Pandavas with pointed headdresses attacking from the right. In the upper part of the panel lies Bhima, the leader of the Kauravas, struck down by arrows. In the center is Arjuna, leader of the Pandavas, in his war chariot. The **southwest corner pavilion** shows scenes from the Ramayana and the life of Krishna.

South gallery, panel 2 features two images of Suryavarman II, the builder of Angkor Wat. He is first shown on an upper tier, seated on a low throne, giving his court instructions. Further along he appears with sword in hand, shaded by 15 ceremonial umbrellas, riding an elephant in a triumphal procession and readying his troops for battle. Other commanders also appear on elephants. Bringing up the rear are musicians and Brahman priests carrying holy fire. The figures with raffish headgear are probably Siamese mercenaries.

The left tiers of the **South gallery, panel 3** show people proceeding toward 18-armed Yama, the Hindu Judge of the Dead here riding a buffalo, with his two assistants. On the upper tier the good advance to the leisurely pursuits of the 37 heavens, in celestial palaces filled with angelic *apsaras*. On the lower tier the wicked are cast into the realm of the 32 hells, where they are starved, bludgeoned, sawn in half, shackled, savaged by wild animals, or spiked with nails, among other tortures.

East gallery, panel 4 is a famous 50-meter-long panel depicting the Hindu legend, Churning the Sea of Milk. The east entrance to Angkor Wat is located between panels 4 and 5.

East gallery, panel 5 depicts war between demons and gods for possession of the ambrosia *amrita*, the essence of life. Four-armed Vishnu is victorious over the demons. This panel is poorly executed and was left unfinished.

In the **North gallery, panel 6** shows Krishna advancing to attack the demon-king Bana. A wall of fire blocks his progress but is extinguished by Garuda, the mount of Vishnu. Bana (multiple arms, mounted on rhinoceros) is captured, but upon the intervention of Shiva, Krishna spares his life. On the far right, thousand-headed Krishna kneels in front of Shiva.

North gallery, panel 7 displays another battle between gods and demons, with a procession of 21 deities in the Brahman pantheon riding their traditional mounts. This panel is poorly executed, but if you continue to the **northwest corner pavilion** there are some finely wrought bas-reliefs of Ramayana scenes.

In the **West gallery, panel 8** depicts the Battle of Lanka from the Ramayana. Evil is personified by the demon-king Ravana (10 heads, 20 arms) who has abducted the beautiful Sita, consort of Prince Rama, and taken her to Sri Lanka. Assisted by the monkey army of Hanuman, Rama launches an attack on Lanka to rescue Sita. Ravana and Rama fight near the center of the panel: Rama stands on the shoulders of the monkey king Sugriva, while Ravana rides in a chariot drawn by mythical lions; monkey warriors fight giant demons nearby.

Quincunx Terrace

Dizzying steps lead from inner courtyards to the third terrace. It is believed only the king and high priests ascended to this terrace. The temples at Angkor were not designed to accommodate devotees—pilgrims were restricted to open ground-level courtyards. Steps to the third terrace are steep, and best tackled sideways in a zigzag pattern; the south stairway has concrete steps and a handrail.

The third terrace is in the shape of a quincunx—a square platform supporting five towers, one in each corner and one in the center. The central tower soars to a height of 65 meters. Here you get a closer look at the flower-shaped towers, an innovation in Khmer architecture at the time. The tower spires feature eight stories and a crown, and are actually square, although multiple projections make them look octagonal. They display the curved outline of a sprouting bud. Four more partly-destroyed towers sprout from the corners of the second terrace.

Originally, the central or uppermost sanctuary probably held a great image of Vishnu, which has long since disappeared. Now the central sanctuary features standing Buddhas set into niches, some seated, some free-standing, and one reclining Buddha. These images are in poor condition, added by Buddhist monks who once lived in the area. A passageway behind the free-standing Buddha in the south section leads to the hollow core of the central tower, currently occuped by bats. This entrance was walled up after the sacking of Angkor by the Siamese in the 15th century. Inside the central core French archaeologists discovered a 30-meter vertical shaft with a cache of gold objects at the base.

You can walk all around the top terrace for great views of Angkor and the surrounding terrain. On the western perimeter is a seated stone Buddha, sheltered by a *naga*. The statue gazes over the causeway—lone sentinel to the theft and destruction of statuary at Angkor Wat.

Angkor's Back Door

You can approach Angkor Wat from the east side along a dirt road through the forest, passing by a slab of Angkor's old wall. The east entrance leads directly to the bas-relief panel Churning the Sea of Milk. This back door route to Angkor Wat was probably used for delivering building materials and supplies to the temple. It

CHURNING THE SEA OF MILK

Every culture has its legends of the origin of the species. The Hindu creation myth Churning the Sea of Milk is shown in the bas-relief panel at the East gallery, panel 4 of Angkor Wat. In Hindu mythology, 13 precious things including the elixir of immortality were lost in the churning of the cosmic sea. Finding them again required a joint dredging operation between gods and demons. Assisting in this endeavor was the giant serpent Vasuki, who offered himself as a rope to enable twirling of a "churning stick." The serpent was yanked back and forth in a giant tug-of-war that lasted for a thousand years.

In the bas-relief panel, the front end of the serpent is being pulled by a long line of surly-looking *asuras* (demons), anchored by the 21-headed demon king Ravana; on the right are almond-eyed *devas* (gods) pulling on the tail, anchored by monkey-god Hanuman. The central pivot, or churning stick, is a complicated piece of imagery. Vasuki has wrapped himself around Mount Mandara, represented by a tower.

At one point Mount Mandara started to sink, and had to be propped up by a giant tortoise, an incarnation of Vishnu. The Sea of Milk, or the Ocean of Immortality, is represented by innumerable fish and aquatic creatures, torn to shreds as they swim close to powerful air currents near the churning stick.

Directing operations at the center is the large four-armed figure of Vishnu, closely associated with Angkor Wat's builder Suryavarman II. The smaller figure above Vishnu is Indra, god of the sky. The actions of the gods and demons cause Vasuki to rotate the tower-mountain and churn the sea into foam, like a giant cosmic blender. This releases a seminal fluid that creates a divine ambrosia, *amrita,* the essence of life and immortality. Many other treasures are also flung up. Born of this action are *apsaras,* or celestial dancers, a purely Khmer innovation. The seductive *apsaras* promise a joyful existence for those who attain the ultimate incarnation; it is assumed that higher incarnations will be male in form.

upper steps of Angkor Wat main towers

appears to have also been the elephant docking bay; in the center of the back gallery is a stairless section probably used by Khmer royalty for mounting and dismounting elephants. Making allowances for elephant arrival and departure is a curious feature of Khmer architecture found elsewhere at Angkor Wat and Angkor Thom. Elephants draped in ceremonial colors transported royalty; the pachyderms were valuable as "tanks" in pitched battle, too.

Phnom Bakheng

An aerial view of the Angkor region is the attraction at Phnom Bakheng, 1.3 km north of Angkor Wat. The ideal time to visit is toward sunset, when lighting is dramatic; dawn is also good. Although Phnom Bakheng is a temple-mountain, the emphasis today is more on the mountain than the temple. You hike to the summit of the 65-meter peak up steep steps once lined with guardian lions; a few remain near the top. At the summit are half-demolished ruins of a pyramid dedicated to Shiva: Phnom Bakheng was the 9th-century center of King Yasovarman's city, Yasodharapura. Numerous small towers that once stood in the area have vanished.

Due to its strategic position, the hill has often served as a camp for troops, including the Khmer Rouge, and after them the Vietnamese. There may be mines planted around the hill—watch for danger signs. Government troops occupy the hill, and may demand money or cigarettes from passing travelers. On a clear day, from the top you can see the West Baray, Phnom Krom (to the southwest), and parts of Angkor Wat. To gain elevation, you can shimmy up a radio mast and onto a platform with direct views over Angkor Wat—from this position, you'd need a long lens and a tripod to take effective pictures.

ANGKOR THOM

Angkor Thom (Great City) encloses an area of nine square km, and may have held a population of over 100,000 at its height, living in tiled or thatched houses. The building of the citadel dates to around the year 1200. Angkor Thom enclosed the Royal Palace (now vanished) and a handful of major temples; the complex was bounded by walls and a moat (now mostly dry) and pierced by five gates. The city was surrounded with ricefields, which provided food; these were irrigated with reservoirs, which also supplied drinking water.

While Angkor Wat is Hindu in inspiration, Angkor Thom resonates with sculpted images expressing the Mahayana Buddhist ideal of Lokesvara (compassion), Prajnaparamita (wisdom), and the Buddha (enlightenment). Although still incorporating Hindu elements, Angkor Thom is a three-dimensional representation of Buddhist cosmology. Temple ground plans reveal a mandala-like base, with radiating symmetrical forms.

Numerology played a part in the design. The Khmer consider odd numbers auspicious, so a *naga* is likely to be five-headed, seven-headed, or nine-headed. Angkor Thom features five gates; the king of Angkor had five wives at the time of Zhou Daguan's visit in 1296. One wife lived at each of the cardinal points of Angkor

Thom, with a fifth in the central palace. A sacred number in Mahayana Buddhism is 108. Rosary beads used in counting meditation are 108 in number—the devout were supposed to recite the name of Buddha 100 times; the extra eight beads were provided in case the user became forgetful or lost some. The gods and demons at each gate of Angkor Thom number 108. At the Bayon it's no accident there were once 54 towers with four heads each, for a total of 216 heads—double 108.

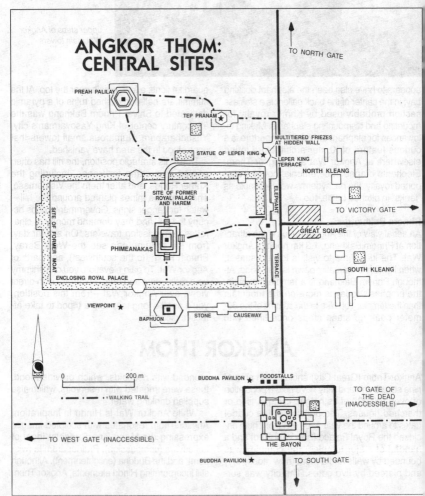

ANGKOR THOM:
CENTRAL SITES

PREAH PALILAY
TEP PRANAM
MULTITIERED FRIEZES AT HIDDEN WALL
STATUE OF LEPER KING
LEPER KING TERRACE
NORTH KLEANG
SITE OF FORMER MOAT
SITE OF FORMER ROYAL PALACE AND HAREM
ELEPHANT TERRACE
TO NORTH GATE
TO VICTORY GATE
GREAT SQUARE
PHIMEANAKAS
ENCLOSING ROYAL PALACE
SOUTH KLEANG
VIEWPOINT
BAPHUON
STONE CAUSEWAY
0   200 m
MOAT
WALKING TRAIL
BUDDHA PAVILION   FOODSTALLS
TO WEST GATE (INACCESSIBLE)
THE BAYON
TO GATE OF THE DEAD (INACCESSIBLE)
BUDDHA PAVILION
TO SOUTH GATE

A stone motif that runs through Angkor Thom is a four-headed deity, most likely derived from Mahayana Buddhism. It's found at the gates to Angkor Thom, and at entrances to a handful of major temples like Preah Khan and Ta Prohm. At the Bayon the four-headed motif comes into its own in a stunning and bizarre design. The motif is the one most often featured in Angkoriana—in statuary, paintings, and on banknotes.

The four-headed motif is the trademark of Jayavarman VII, regarded as the last great king of the Khmer Empire. After Cham legions sacked Angkor in 1177, Jayavarman VII not only set about rebuilding Angkor Wat, he also built Angkor Thom, incorporating previously built works like Baphuon and the pyramid of Phimeanakas. He embarked on a frenzy of slapdash building, throwing up the outer wall and five monumental gates of Angkor Thom, constructing roads and stone bridges and hundreds of hospitals, monasteries, and pilgrim resthouses throughout the empire. For these enterprises he received support from his favorite wife Jayadevi, who taught Buddhism in the monasteries.

Capping all these achievements he created the masterpiece of the Bayon, the last great temple constructed at Angkor. In the process, Jayavarman VII used up an enormous amount of sandstone. The building frenzy virtually exhausted the quarries of Phnom Kulen, which may explain why no more large temples were built of sandstone after his reign. Jayavarman VII quite likely exhausted his country and its population, too. After him the empire declined, ravaged by internal conflict and by war with the Siamese.

Jayavarman VII was a complex figure. It seems he was a humble monk who was twice denied the throne, then became the greatest of all Angkor kings. When Suryavarman II died, Jayavarman VII was off fighting a campaign in Champa and his half-brother took the throne. Jayavarman VII then withdrew to Preah Khan temple in Kompong Svay, about 105 km to the east of Angkor. A rebellion broke out in 1166 and his half-brother was killed by a usurper who subsequently seized the throne, denying Jayavarman VII a second chance at rule. In 1177 this Khmer king died in battle when the Cham fleet came up the Mekong and across Lake Tonle Sap. Jayavarman VII took up the fight against the Cham, destroyed their fleet, and forced them to retreat. He then ascended to the throne in 1181, in his late fifties.

Stelae and temple inscriptions praise Jayavarman's deeds, and Bayon bas-reliefs depict the entire story of the battle against the Cham. From these sources, we know more about Jayavarman VII and his reign than about any other Khmer king. He fought against the Dai Viet, wreaked vengeance on the Cham Empire, advanced into Laos, and reached the borders of Burma. Yet other parts of his life remain obscure. His date of birth and death are uncertain—the latter is variously given as 1201 or 1218—and it is not known how he viewed Mahayana Buddhism. Surviving portrait heads of Jayavarman VII show him in a meditative pose with a facial expression that is at once humble, pious, scholarly, and ponderous. His hair is slicked back into a small chignon on top of his head. Jayavarman VII left some of his own thoughts, chiseled in stone: "He suffered more from his subjects' infirmities than from his own, for it is the people's pain that makes the pain of kings and not their own."

SOUTH GATE

There were originally five gates to Angkor Thom—only three are now accessible. The South Gate, several kilometers north of Angkor Wat's west entrance, is the best preserved. The south approach over the moat to Angkor Thom is a causeway of the giants, guarded by two magnificent balustrades of mythical figures and a four-headed portal. On the left balustrade are 54 celestial *devas* involved in a tug-of-war with a nine-headed *naga;* on the right are 54 underworld *asuras* engaged in a similar struggle. Together they total the sacred number of 108. The demons grimace and pull faces; the sterner-looking gods wear conical headdresses. The dual balustrades of gods, demons, and *nagas* are most likely a three-dimensional representation of the Hindu creation myth, Churning the Sea of Milk, which is depicted in more detail in a bas-relief at the back of Angkor Wat.

Some heads in the balustrade lineups are copies—you can tell by the lack of lichen growth on the pale concrete substitutes. This configuration of 108 statues is repeated at two other gates—the North Gate and the Victory Gate. If you look at the balustrade from the side, you'll see that it forms part of a stone causeway or bridge over the grassy moat of Angkor Thom. The moat was probably once stocked with crocodiles to discourage enemy advances.

The South Gate's stone portal is 23 meters high. The inner section is large enough to admit with ease a fully caparisoned royal elephant. On either side of the archway are sentry-box niches, once lined with wood. The imposing tower-gate is crowned with four heads facing the cardinal points; 13th-century Chinese chronicler Zhou Daguan mentions a fifth head on the portal, made of gold, in the central position. At the lower half of the gate on each side is a sculpted three-headed elephant, the mount of the Hindu deity Indra. Indra appears at the center of the elephant holding a thunderbolt, framed by an *apsara* on each side. The three elephant trunks, which appear as pillars, pluck lotuses.

Tall trees line the avenues to the Bayon. Among the 80-odd species of trees found in the Angkor region are a number that have died out in other parts of Cambodia.

THE BAYON

"At whatever hour one walks around the Bayon, and particularly by moonlight on a clear evening, one feels as if one were visiting a temple in another world, built by an alien people, whose conceptions are entirely unfamiliar."

—HENRI MARCHAL,
GUIDE ARCHÉOLOGIQUE
AUX TEMPLES D'ANGKOR

If Angkor Wat is classic and grand, the Bayon is wild and erratic. Who could've conjured this fantastic structure, and then—even more incredible—fashioned it from stone? Like Stonehenge or the Pyramids, the bizarre Bayon baffles with its design, its mysterious structure, its aura. The structure is simply amazing. What at first appears to be a random pile of masonry actually consists of massive stones shaped into fluid sculptures, without apparent use of cement or mortar.

The Bayon was once even more elaborate, the central tower apparently covered in gold leaf. Zhou Daguan described it in the 13th century: "At the center of the Kingdom rises a Golden Tower flanked by more than twenty lesser towers and several hundred stone chambers. On the eastern side is a golden bridge guarded by two lions of gold, one on each side, with eight golden Buddhas spaced along the stone chambers." Oddly enough, Zhou Daguan failed to mention the massive heads on the Bayon towers.

The importance of the Bayon was not realized until early this century, when French archaeologists cleared 10 square km of land at Angkor Thom. This made it possible to sketch accurate maps for the first time, and it was discovered that the Bayon lay at the exact center of Angkor Thom. French archaeologists surmised the Bayon was built over the foundations of an earlier structure, resulting in dark galleries, deep courtyards, and towers crowded next to one another. Some parts were walled over, the original sculptures left intact within. Hidden below the upper terrace, Henri Parmentier in 1924 discovered a fine pediment of Lokesvara, the bodhisattva of compassion. This indicated the Bayon was Buddhist, and not, as previously thought, Hindu. The discovery of a large Buddha statue within the central sanctuary of the Bayon confirmed this.

Disorder in the construction of the Bayon is reflected in the numerous architectural changes. It seems that after the Cham sacked Angkor in 1177, Jayavarman VII decided the Hindu deities had failed, so he switched allegiance to Mahayana Buddhism. However, he made no attempt to alter existing Hindu elements. The Bayon was caught in the middle—the foundations are Hindu, but the superstructure is Buddhist. It is estimated that the Bayon took 20 years to build. Jayavarman VII's son and grandson reverted the use of the temple to Hindu (Shivaist) worship, with Brahmans from India gaining great influence over the Angkor court. Heads and faces on statues were destroyed and replaced with Hindu gods.

Entrances

The square outer gallery of the Bayon serves as its walls. You can approach it from four entrances; inside is an inner enclosure, another gallery of bas-reliefs. The original main entrance

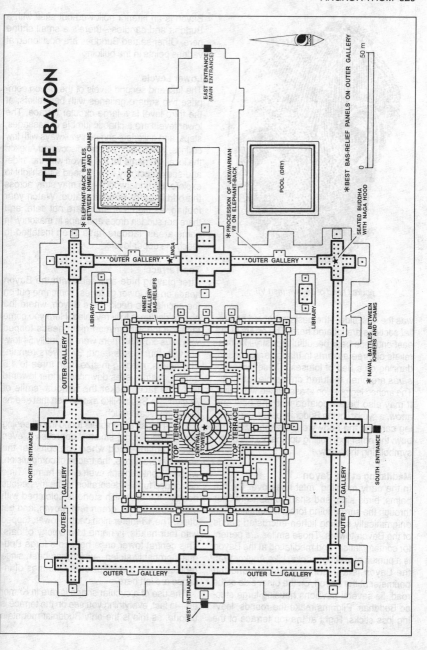

THE BAYON

EAST ENTRANCE
(MAIN ENTRANCE)

POOL

POOL (DRY)

* ELEPHANT-BACK BATTLES BETWEEN KHMERS AND CHAMS

* PROCESSION OF JAYAVARMAN VII ON ELEPHANT-BACK

Seated Buddha
WITH NAGA HOOD

* BEST BAS-RELIEF PANELS ON OUTER GALLERY

0   50 m

OUTER GALLERY

OUTER GALLERY

LINGA

INNER GALLERY BAS-RELIEFS

LIBRARY

LIBRARY

* NAVAL BATTLES BETWEEN KHMERS AND CHAMS

OUTER GALLERY

OUTER GALLERY

TOP TERRACE

TOP TERRACE

CENTRAL TOWER

NORTH ENTRANCE

SOUTH ENTRANCE

OUTER GALLERY

OUTER GALLERY

OUTER GALLERY

OUTER GALLERY

WEST ENTRANCE

BOB RACE

portrait head of Jayavarman VII

was the east side—the best-preserved bas-relief sections are located here. The pillars at the east entrance bear beautiful tapestry-like bas-reliefs of three *apsaras* in triangular formation, dancing on a bed of lotuses. These flying *apsaras* are often featured on temple rubbings. The arched leg position is associated with flying. It may also be associated with the bow and arrow, a symbol of the Buddhist path—the flexed leg carrying the body weight symbolizing the bow; the other leg, pulling up against the body, symbolizing the arrow.

Meditating at the Bayon

In the early morning, mist rises over the fan palms, birds sing, and shafts of sunlight filter through the surrounding forest to illuminate the enigmatically smiling lichen-encrusted heads of the Bayon towers. Those smiles are perfect for contemplation, and meditating at the Bayon is a pursuit of visiting monks. Like Angkor Wat, the Bayon is a pilgrimage site. Around the perimeter of the Bayon, on the other side of the road, lie several pavilions housing large stucco Buddhas. Pilgrims make the rounds, leaving joss sticks. Right at the top terrace of the

Bayon is an interior hollowed-out shell with a Buddha and candles—there's a small shrine here. Other seated Buddhas are positioned at various points in the building.

Lower Levels

The first and second levels of the Bayon comprise two square galleries with bas-reliefs; at the third level is a large circular terrace. The lower levels are a chaotic jumble of passages, steps, and galleries, and dim walkways with low ceilings. When Henri Mouhot discovered Angkor, the local nickname for the Bayon was the "hide-and-seek sanctuary." You'll need a flashlight to explore this underworld—you may stray across the odd linga or Buddha statue. Watch your footing, as flights of stairs are not safe, and there are sudden drops and gaps in masonry. In some areas, ladders have been installed to reach the upper levels.

Top Terrace

After playing hide-and-seek with the Bayon heads on the lower galleries, you come out on the circular top deck of the Bayon, where the bizarre design is fully revealed. Here you come face-to-face with myriad giant heads topped with lotus crowns. There were originally 54 towers with four heads each; 37 towers remain. The heads, ranging in size from three to 4.5 meters, feature eyes downcast under lowered lids. The faces flicker the famous "smile of Angkor"—a Sphinx-like expression that seems to communicate much.

Early French adventurers found the all-seeing heads threatening, sinister, oppressive, even blood-curdling—odd when you consider the serene expressions, the traces of compassion, wisdom, contentment, even divine humor. Time has added further decoration to the mysterious heads—the brownish stone is splotched with moss, gray lichen, green fern growth, and bat dung. The 43-meter-high central tower, topped with four heads, is home to a colony of bats. This central tower once housed a large Buddha—probably stolen—which has been since replaced with a smaller one. Offerings of incense are left here.

The use of a circular shape is rare in Khmer art—in fact, everything you see on the terrace is unique, as this is the only Buddhist mountain

BAYON GALLERIES

Bas-reliefs at the Bayon are less refined but livelier than those at Angkor Wat. They depict historical events and mythical stories, and offer rare glimpses into daily life at Angkor. There are two series of bas-reliefs, one at the outer gallery and one at the inner gallery. The galleries are meant to be read in a clockwise direction, starting from the east entrance.

Outer Gallery

The magnificent outer gallery depicts land and sea battles between Cham and Khmer. The best parts are on the east and south sides with two- and three-tier panels. If your time is short, you could just cover the section from the east entrance to the south entrance, then enter the Bayon from the south side. While the east and south sections are in good condition, others have either collapsed, suffered water damage, disappeared beneath moss or lichen, or are too dark to make out. Some panels were never completed.

The east gallery depicts battles between the Khmer and their historic enemy, the Cham. The Cham are easily identified by distinctive headgear, which looks like an inverted lotus. Troop commanders, including Jayavarman VII (identified by umbrellas with insignias), are mounted on elephants. Musicians accompany cavalry and foot soldiers; oxcarts bringing up the rear carry military provisions.

Turning the corner at the south gallery, two- and three-tier bas-reliefs show naval battles between Cham (with headdress) and Khmer (no headgear); one boat makes a 90-degree turn in stone at the corner. In 1177 the Cham sailed across Lake Tonle Sap to sack Angkor; warriors are armed with javelins, bows, and shields. Corpses are thrown overboard, sometimes to the crocodiles. The lower panels record everyday life—a woman removing lice from another's hair, a patient in a hospital, an archer hunting, fishermen on Lake Tonle Sap. Palace scenes depict wrestlers, chess players, sword fighters, and princesses partying with their suitors. Further along the south gallery, the battle between Cham and Khmer resumes—this time, in 1181, the Khmer are victorious, and Jayavarman VII sits in the palace surrounded by celebrating subjects. The military chronicle continues around the outer gallery, though bas-relief quality deteriorates and the north gallery is mostly destroyed.

Inner Gallery

These sections are punctuated by jutting cells and other obstacles. If you persist you can follow the panels, again proceeding in a clockwise direction from the east entrance. Some panels are eroded and hard to make out; the better preserved sections are to the east side. The bas-reliefs are mostly drawn from Hindu legends, but these Khmer picture books in stone also offer accurate detail of the common people of the time, with vignettes showing a fisherman casting his net, a man climbing a coconut tree, and scenes of temple construction.

beyond the outer Gallery of the Bayon

temple in Cambodia. Archaeologists are unsure if the heads are meant to represent Buddha, Brahma, Shiva, Lokesvara, or Jayavarman VII. Brahma is often depicted as a deity with four heads, representing deliverance, compassion, tolerance, and piety. Several French archaeologists concluded the Bayon heads are a combination: Jayavarman VII deified in the pose of Buddha or Lokesvara. Lokesvara is the bodhisattva of compassion in Mahayana Buddhism. Some manifestations of Lokesvara bear multiple heads—between three and 11—and a forest of arms. In one form, he boasts 11 heads—said to have burst from the original head as a result of contemplating the suffering of human beings. Portrait heads of Jayavarman VII today found in museums in Phnom Penh, Bangkok, and Paris bear an uncanny resemblance to the Bayon heads, with broad forehead, long earlobes, downcast eyes, wide nostrils, and thick, slightly curled lips.

The development of the personality cult—depicting real individuals in the form of a Hindu deity in sculpture—was common with the earlier kings of Angkor. Jayavarman VII may have raised the *devaraja* cult to new heights, transferring the cult to Buddhism and considering himself as an embodiment of a bodhisattva. Through such sculpture, the king could be connected to the power and compassion of the deity. The real story behind the heads may never be known—and perhaps this piece of sorcery is better left that way. As Rose Macaulay says of the Bayon towers in her book *Pleasure of Ruins,* "All is now desolate, fantastic, and ambushed with ghosts; the erroneous opinions of archaeologists twitter among them like bats."

NORTH OF THE BAYON

Baphuon

A few hundred meters north of the Bayon is Baphuon, worth a visit for its viewpoint. The entryway to Baphuon is unusual—a sandstone causeway supported by short columns. This leads to a shell of a sanctuary, originally constructed by Udayadityavarman II in the mid-11th century. Baphuon was once one of the grandest of Angkor's temples, now fallen on hard times. A hike up the hill behind Baphuon will reveal stun-

ning views over the dense jungle canopy, with the pyramid of Phimeanakas visible to the north. In 1995 the EFEO returned to Cambodia to continue the reconstruction of Baphuon begun in the 1960s. The eight-year $5.6-million project will rebuild and restore Baphuon; advanced computer technology will be used to graphically visualize the reconstruction, including the return of innumerable stones to their original location.

Phimeanakas

Phimeanakas (Celestial Palace) is a three-terrace pyramid of rough-hewn sandstone blocks. It has little decoration, but Khmer lions stand guard at the corners of the terraces and the entrance stairs. Though Phimeanakas lies within the former Royal Palace walls, it was built in the late 10th and early 11th centuries before the palace was constructed. The pyramid was developed by several Khmer kings. At the top of the pyramid is a destroyed temple.

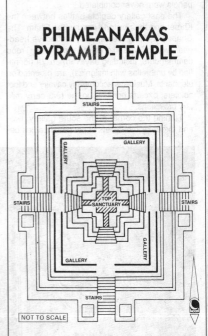

PHIMEANAKAS PYRAMID-TEMPLE

STAIRS

GALLERY

GALLERY

STAIRS   TOP SANCTUARY   STAIRS

GALLERY

GALLERY

STAIRS

NOT TO SCALE

THE SOVEREIGN COMES FORTH

Adjoining the pyramid of Phimeanakas was the Royal Palace, which, having been constructed of wood, has not survived. The palace, it is believed, was once arrayed in five great courtyards, with separate areas for the king's wives and concubines. The only description of this structure extant is in the manuscript of Chinese envoy Zhou Daguan. No stranger to opulent palaces, Zhou Daguan was nevertheless astonished by the splendors of Angkor. Although he was not permitted to enter the grounds of the tightly guarded palace, he described the exterior as it appeared in the year 1296:

> The Royal Palace, as well as official buildings and homes of the nobles, all face the east. The Royal Palace stands to the north of the Golden Tower [the Bayon] and the Bridge of Gold; starting from the gate its circumference is nearly one and a half miles. The tiles of the central dwelling are of lead; other parts of the palace are covered with pottery tiles, yellow in color. Lintels and columns, all decorated with carved or painted Buddhas, are immense. The roofs, too, are impressive. Long colonnades and open corridors stretch away, interlaced in harmonious relation. In the chamber where the sovereign attends to affairs of state, there is a golden window, with mirrors disposed on square columns to the right and left of the window-trim, forty or so in number. Below the window is a frieze of elephants.

During his stay at Angkor, Zhou witnessed the Khmer sovereign Indravarman III venture forth from his palace several times, along with an entourage from the palace harem. With an Arthurian touch, Indravarman III bore the sacred golden sword of office, which he'd wrested from his brother-in-law to claim the throne. Here is Zhou's description:

> When the Sovereign leaves his palace, the procession is headed by the soldiery; then come the flags, the banners, the music. Girls of the palace, three or five hundred in number, gaily dressed, with flowers in their hair and tapers in their hands, are massed together in a separate column. The tapers are lighted even in broad daylight. Then came other girls carrying gold and silver vessels from the palace and a whole galaxy of ornaments, of very special design, the uses of which were strange to me. Then came still more girls, the bodyguard of the palace, holding shields and lances. These, too, were separately aligned. Following them came chariots drawn by goats and horses, all adorned with gold; ministers and princes, mounted on elephants, were preceded by bearers of scarlet parasols, without number. Close behind came the royal wives and concubines, in palanquins and chariots, or mounted on horses or elephants, to whom were assigned at least a hundred parasols mottled with gold. Finally the Sovereign appeared, standing erect on an elephant and holding in his hand the sacred sword. This elephant, his tusks sheathed in gold, was accompanied by bearers of twenty white parasols with golden shafts. All around was a bodyguard of elephants, drawn close together, and still more soldiers for complete protection, marching in close order.
>
> The Sovereign was proceeding to a nearby destination where golden palanquins, borne by the girls of the palace, were waiting to receive him. For the most part, his objective was a little golden pagoda in front of which stood a golden statue of the Buddha. Those who caught a glimpse of the King were expected to kneel and touch the earth with their brows. Failing to perform this obeisance . . . they were seized by the masters of ceremonies, who under no circumstances let them escape.

Viewed from Baphuon, Phimeanakas looks eerily like the jungle-locked pyramids of the Maya at Tikal, Guatemala—a lost world suddenly revealed. Odd rituals were performed at the temple on top of the pyramid. Phimeanakas is legendary as the site where the Khmer king had nightly union with the serpent goddess in the shape of a beautiful woman. Chronicler Zhou Daguan recounts: "Every night this *naga*-spirit appears in the shape of a woman, with whom the sovereign couples. Not even the wives of the King may enter here. At the second watch the King comes forth and is then free to sleep with his wives and concubines. Should the *naga*-spirit fail to appear for a single night, it is a sign that the King's death is at hand. If, on the other hand, the King should fail to keep his tryst, disaster for the kingdom is sure to follow."

Elephant Terrace

The Royal Palace was not bounded by a wall but by the raised Elephant Terrace. From this vantage point, according to chronicler Zhou Daguan, royal family members could watch parades, games, and processions on the Great Square. The venue was apparently also used to dispense justice and oversee audiences for affairs of state. The Elephant Terrace may date from the 11th-century reign of Suryavarman I, with later renovations by Jayavarman VII. The terrace takes its name from a frieze featuring life-size elephants and an elephant hunt. There are a few three-dimensional elephant trunks at the bases of stairs. Interspersed along the massive frieze are *garudas* and lions, a mythical five-headed horse, and demons and dancers. Much of this area has been cleared and restored by the EFEO, which is also restoring Baphuon. Opposite the Elephant Terrace is a vast open area—the Great Square. Pavilions for dancers who entertained the king probably once stood here. Further back are the ruins of the north and south *kleangs,* thought to have been either storehouses or centers for visiting envoys to the capital.

Leper King Terrace

The terrace to the north, attributed to Jayavarman VII, is known as the Leper King Terrace. High-tech anastylosis restorations in 1993 at a half-hidden inner wall have resulted in an assembly of multi-tiered friezes, with row upon row of seated figures. Kings, sword in hand, are surrounded by courtiers and dancers; the lower tiers feature five- and nine-headed *nagas.* The friezes are stunning works of art, on par with those at the Bayon.

Some archaeologists believe Khmer aristocracy were cremated on the Leper King Terrace. The place derives its current name from a kneeling statue atop the terrace. This may or may not be a representation of Yasovarman I, the founder of Angkor, who may or may not have died of leprosy. In any case, the statue is a copy. Archaeologist George Coedes noticed some saw-marks on the head of the original

restoring friezes at the Leper King Terrace

and had the statue removed to Phnom Penh's National Museum for safekeeping. The substitute at Angkor is made of concrete, but was still convincing enough to fool a bandit who lopped its head off. Behind the Leper King Terrace is a path leading to a small temple, Tep Pranam, with a 4.5-meter-high statue of Buddha. The temple is attributed to Yasovarman I; monks and nuns live in the area. Farther back is another ruin, Preah Palilay, built by Jayavarman VII.

North Gate

The North Gate of Angkor Thom features a monumental causeway with four-headed portal and 108 mythical figures, like the South Gate, but facing northward. A few of the heads are made of concrete, replacing those either stolen or considered in danger of theft. Beyond the North Gate lies the great temple of Preah Khan on the Grand Circuit.

Victory Gate

The Victory Gate lies to the east, with a four-headed portal and 108 mythical figures facing eastward. However, the Victory Gate is not true east from the Bayon. At true east is a gate that is no longer used—the Gate of the Dead. This gate lies 500 meters south of the Victory Gate, and is reached by a narrow forest trail. It's a crumbling four-headed gate with no other statuary. To the far west of Angkor Thom is the West Gate, in a similar overgrown state. Beyond Victory Gate to the east is the jungle-locked temple of Ta Prohm.

OUTER TEMPLES AND SITES

LITTLE CIRCUIT

The route comprising the sites of Victory Gate, Thommanon, Chau Say Tevoda, Spean Thma, Takeo, Ta Prohm, Banteay Kdei and Prasat Kravan was called *le petit circuit* by the French. About 1.5 km east of Angkor Thom's Elephant Terrace, along a drive with tall trees, you come to **Victory Gate** or the east gate of Angkor Thom. About 500 meters beyond are two small facing temples called **Thommanon** and **Chau Say Tevoda.** The temples are similar in plan and style, and are believed to be the early 12th-century work of Suryavarman II. Thommanon is in better condition, with some fine decoration on exterior walls, particularly carvings of female divinities.

About 200 meters east of Thommanon you cross a bridge over the Siem Reap River. The bridge is made of wood and steel, but closer examination reveals the supports are sandstone. **Spean Thma,** an early Khmer bridge, is more clearly viewed from a path to the side of the road, where you'll see other sandstone arch supports and Khmer masonry. Soldiers on guard here may become agitated if you appear to be reconnoitering in detail—the Khmer Rouge blow up bridges with abandon. Continuing east you'll come to **Takeo,** a five-tiered pyramid dating from the late 10th century. Entry to the temple is from the south side. Takeo was the first temple built of sandstone in the central Angkor region. Each of its five towers was laid out in a cruciform pattern, but they were never finished. The temple is dedicated to the Hindu deity Shiva, and is devoid of decorative reliefs or sculptures.

Ta Prohm

The great temple of Ta Prohm was constructed by Jayavarman VII in 1186 to house an image of his mother in the likeness of the goddess Prajnaparamita. In Mahayana Buddhism, Prajnaparamita is the personification of wisdom, and mother of all Buddhas. She is depicted in Khmer statuary with 11 heads and myriad arms. A 12th-century Sanskrit inscription from Ta Prohm tells of Jayavarman's victories over the Cham, and provides other curious details. The place functioned as a vast monastery, with 39 sanctuaries, 566 stone dwellings, and 288 brick dwellings. Housed in these dwellings were 18 abbots, 2,740 monks, and 2,817 other residents, including 615 dancers. Some 70,000 men and women from surrounding villages were pressed into service at Ta Prohm.

The main entry to Ta Prohm is at the west side, with a fine four-headed tower similar to those at the gates of Angkor Thom. The central temple is approached by a forest path of 400 meters. To the side, remains of stone mythical

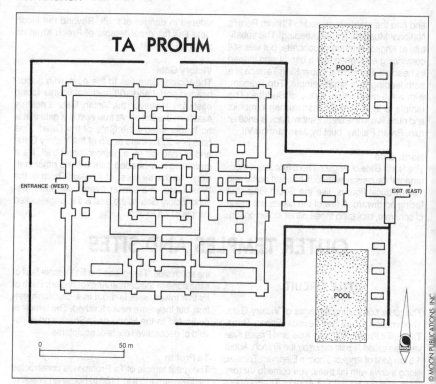

TA PROHM

ENTRANCE (WEST)

EXIT (EAST)

POOL

POOL

0   50 m

© MOON PUBLICATIONS, INC.

creatures lie scattered about. Passing through an entrance pavilion you reach the central shrine, surrounded by dense jungle. Light filtering through the branches of tall trees provides an ambience similar to that of a Gothic novel.

French archaeologists left Ta Prohm to the elements, to the giant fig, kapok, and banyan trees, with their fantastic roots wrapped around walls and towers. The flora adds an element of mystery to the ruins. Guy de Pourtalès describes the haunting phenomenon in 1931: "The tree roots flow over the roofs, tumbling in all directions like a flow of lava, sometimes breaking the stones apart, sometimes holding them together. Here and there, the jungle respects a façade, frames a row of columns without destroying it. And, in places, it even cements together with its powerful creepers a porch that was on the point of collapsing, props up a crumbled archway and grasps pillars or an emblature

in its strong arms . . ." Some of the trees may eventually have to be felled to prevent destruction of stonework; other trees actually hold masonry in place.

The inner temple is a series of galleries, halls, and passages, with some entrances blocked off. If you keep to worn paths you can work out where to go, discovering a frieze, bas-relief, or the odd statue set in a niche. To exit, move through Ta Prohm's east gate (turn right and head to the roadway), or retrace your steps back to the west entrance.

Other Sites

On the route back to Siem Reap you can make a few more stops if time permits. First check out the temple of **Banteay Kdei,** accessed from its east gate, which lies opposite **Sra Srang.** Further south is **Prasat Kravan** (Cardamom Sanctuary), which is unusual for its row of five brick towers, built in the 10th century, and brick bas-reliefs depicting scenes from the myth of Vishnu. From here you pass a back entrance to Angkor Wat—it's possible to take a side trail for a few hundred meters to view the colossus from the back. The main road skirts the mighty moat of Angkor Wat and heads south back to Siem Reap.

GRAND CIRCUIT

The grand circuit contains a number of sites in 12th-century Bayon art style, including Preah Khan, Neak Pean, Ta Som, East Mebon, Pre Rup, Banteay Samre, Banteay Kdei, and Sra Srang. The bold hand of Jayavarman VII is at

work here—the inspiration for construction is Buddhist, or a mix of Hindu and Buddhist. You can view Angkorian plumbing features at Neak Pean and Sra Srang. There's a fair bit of ground to cover on this route; by motorcycle this isn't a problem, but by bicycle the going can be slow, especially since the road is in bad shape in parts. From the Bayon it's about 10 km to Neak Pean, and from there it's another 12 km to Sra Srang—quite a haul on a bicycle without gears, along potholed roads. Because some of these temples lie farther out, they're targets for art thieves. Preah Khan carries a sign that says the temple is protected with explosives against looting and theft between dusk (1800) and dawn (0600).

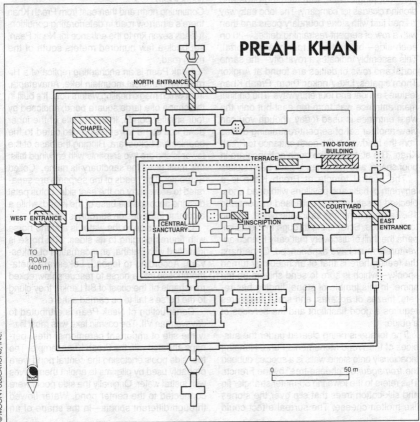

PREAH KHAN

NORTH ENTRANCE

CHAPEL

TWO-STORY BUILDING

TERRACE

COURTYARD

WEST ENTRANCE

CENTRAL SANCTUARY

INSCRIPTION

EAST ENTRANCE

TO ROAD (400 m)

0   50 m

N

Preah Khan

Preah Khan (Sacred Sword) was designated the temporary Khmer capital by Jayavarman VII after the sacking of Angkor in 1177 by the Cham and before the completion of Angkor Thom. A stela discovered at the site glorifies Jayavarman VII; it also enumerates the staff at Preah Khan. Temple maintenance required the services of 98,840 men and women from neighboring villages, as well as 444 chefs, 4,606 footmen, and 2,298 servants. The Buddhist temple itself housed upward of 15,000 monks, dancers, and members of the Khmer hierarchy.

Preah Khan lies 3.3 km north of the Bayon. You need to walk in almost 400 meters from the roadway to reach the main temple: it's a pleasant jungle walk, with chirping birds and droning cicadas for company. The long entryway is lined first with stone boundary posts and then with a row of serpent-restraining deities—20 on each side—backed by a four-headed portal. This assembly indicates a royal city—the same portal and rows of deities are found at Angkor Thom's gates. Like Angkor Thom, Preah Khan features a moat and four entryways. The original main entrance was from the east but only the west entrance is used today, though you can view another set of serpent-restraining deities from the roadway at the north entrance to Preah Khan. The statues at the north entrance are in poor shape, and many heads have been stolen.

The central temple at Preah Khan is a labyrinth of halls and pavilions with dead ends, blocked passages, and collapsed masonry. In 1989 a freak hurricane struck the place, adding to the chaos. Scrambling through the ruins imparts the thrill of discovery that early French adventurers must have experienced. Or perhaps the feeling here is that of archaeology turned spooky—which is sure to send shivers up the spine. In this jumble of stone, finding bas-reliefs, friezes of *apsaras,* and small sculptures requires a good flashlight and the services of a guide.

The foliage is being cleared under the auspices of the World Monuments Fund. Hanging tenaciously onto stone walls is a species dubbed the *fromageur* or "cheese-tree" by the French. This refers to the towering 50-meter strangler fig and silk-cotton trees that slip over the stones like molten cheese. The surreal effect could come straight from a Salvador Dali painting with melting clocks, a metaphor for the persistence of memory.

Out back is the shell of a unique two-story building, with supporting rounded columns that look positively Grecian. This is the only known example of two-story Khmer architecture. The function of the building is obscure—it may have been a library, or it may have housed the sacred sword for which the temple was named. Jayavarman II left his successor a sacred sword, passed on to future kings. Since Preah Khan was built to shelter a statue of Jayavarman VII's father, it was a logical place to keep the king's sword.

Neak Pean

Continuing north and then east from Preah Khan there's a narrow road in deteriorating condition. It leads seven km to the entrance for Neak Pean, set back a few hundred meters south of the main road.

Neak Pean is an enchanting replica of a Himalayan paradisal mountain lake, Anavatapta, from which magic healing waters flow. It's built in the shape of a large square pond, enclosed by four smaller ponds. In the middle of the inner pond is a stone tower-island dedicated to the bodhisattva Lokesvara. Ringing the base of the tower-island are two serpents with entwined tails: this motif gives the sanctuary its name, "Coiled Serpents". The heads of the serpents are separated to allow entry on the east side. Lotus petal designs decorate the base of the island, while a blooming lotus design surrounds the top.

Off to the side in the water is a stone horse with figures clinging to its sides. The horse is identified with Balaha, an incarnation of Lokesvara. According to legend, Lokesvara metamorphosed into a horse to rescue shipwrecked merchants off the coast of Sri Lanka; they clung to the horse's tail to be carried ashore.

Construction of Neak Pean is attributed to Jayavarman VII. The cosmic lake was most likely the site of important ceremonial rites, perhaps affiliated with the Preah Khan temple. The four side pools enclosing the central pond were probably used by pilgrims to anoint themselves with lustral water. Originally the side pools were connected to the center pond. Water flowed through different spouts—in the shape of an

NEAK PEAN

TO ROAD

BASIN

ELEPHANT-HEAD
SPOUT

COSMIC LAKE

HORSE
STATUE
(BALAHA)

BASIN

HORSE-HEAD
SPOUT

BASIN (DRY)

HUMAN-HEAD
SPOUT

CENTRAL SANCTUARY

LION SPOUT

BASIN

0   30 m

© MOON PUBLICATIONS, INC.

elephant (north), human head (east), lion (south), and horse (west). Trees and plants have invaded the site, and bas-reliefs are hard to make out, but Neak Pean still retains its aura. The side pools are now mostly dry, only filling at the end of the rainy season. Monks occasionally come to Neak Pean to bathe.

Other Sites

A few kilometers farther along the road is **Ta Som,** a small unrestored temple built by Jayavarman VII; the temple has some fine sculpture on lintels and doorways. The **East Mebon** and **Pre Rup** were both built in the latter half of the 10th century by Rajendravarman II, and are almost identical in style. The East Mebon sits at the center of what was once the East Baray, a large reservoir, now dry and planted with rice. The East Mebon is a weathered pile of rubble with stone elephants at the corners. Pre Rup is a brick ruin, believed to have once been the focus of cremation ceremonies. From a turnoff between the East Mebon and Pre Rup a 400-meter detour to the east leads to **Banteay Samre,** a

12th-century temple painstakingly restored by the French. The main shrine is well preserved, with bas-reliefs depicting scenes from Vishnu and Krishna legends.

Heading south back on the Grand Circuit, you can stop at Banteay Kdei and Sra Srang, at the junction of the Little Circuit. **Banteay Kdei** (Citadel of the Cells), a small unrestored temple, features a four-headed entryway at the east side; visible in the temple is a Buddha statue in meditation posture. Fallen blocks of stone lie scattered about. Across the road from the Banteay Kdei's east entrance is **Sra Srang,** a large artificial lake with a landing terrace. The lake is surrounded by greenery and provides an illusion of calm, majesty, and immensity. On the landing terrace are *naga* balustrades flanked by Khmer-style lions. A building used to sit in the middle of the lake, but is now just a heap of stones. Sra Srang (the name means "Royal Bath") is a serene spot, especially when bathed in soft sunset light.

NORTH OF ANGKOR

Banteay Srei

Banteay Srei is a bewitching miniature temple 25 km northeast of Angkor Wat, reached by a rough dirt road running past rural villages. Because of its remote location, the temple poses a major security problem. The area is mined and close to Khmer Rouge activity, and the temple is a target for bandits involved in theft of statuary. In January 1995 an American woman and her Cambodian guide were killed by gunfire in the area. They were in a five-car convoy heading to Banteay Srei temple; gunmen fired automatic rifles and rocket-propelled grenades at the group. Another tourist was seriously injured. A dozen other tourists escaped, and several armed police in the convoy fled. Eleven suspects, identified as bandits with Khmer Rouge backgrounds, were later arrested. Subsequently, tourist authorities placed Banteay

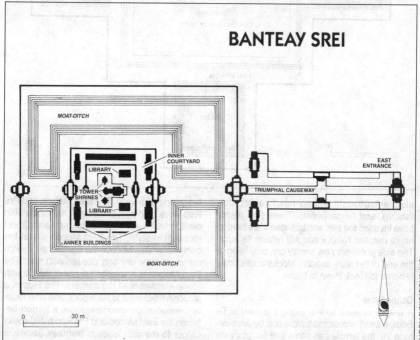

BANTEAY SREI

MOAT-DITCH

INNER COURTYARD

LIBRARY

TOWER SHRINES

LIBRARY

ANNEX BUILDINGS

MOAT-DITCH

TRIUMPHAL CAUSEWAY

EAST ENTRANCE

0   30 m

Srei off limits. Inquire if the temple is currently accessible.

Banteay Srei was discovered by the French in 1914, but the site was not cleared until 10 years later. The temple was restored in the 1930s by archaeologist Henri Marchal. This was the first temple in the Angkor region to be restored by the process of anastylosis—removing and repositioning each block—a method developed by the Dutch at Borobodur in Java. Banteay Srei is small, but the bas-reliefs, pediments, lintels, and statues are the finest in the Angkor region. This jewel of Khmer art is remarkably well preserved. The temple is unusual in that its building was not sponsored by royalty but by the king's chief Brahman adviser, Yajnavaraha. The temple was founded by two Brahman brothers at the royal court in 967 AD, according to an inscription at the site. Banteay Srei decoration is virtually intact, with a wealth of symbolism. For archaeologists it's a rich source of detail on how Angkorian temples were constructed.

A triumphal causeway with stone boundary posts leads to the inner sanctuary, enclosed by

Banteay Srei temple pediment

a moat-ditch and triple walls. The sanctuary consists of a courtyard with three sandstone *prasats,* or tower shrines, on a single raised plinth. The tallest *prasat* is 10 meters high. A combination of red sandstone, gray lichen, green moss, and fern growth give the towers peculiar coloration. Guarding the entrance stairs are sculpted kneeling figures of human torsos, originally bearing monkey or lion heads. Most of the heads have been hacked off by treasure hunters. Some figures are copies; the originals are in the Phnom Penh National Museum. The inner sanctuary is dedicated to Shiva and a Shiva linga was the main image of worship in the central *prasat.* A statue of Shiva and Uma presided over the southern *prasat;* this statue was taken to Phnom Penh in 1914 by a French army officer and now rests in the National Museum. Set in niches on the central towers are harmonious sculptures of male and female divinities.

To either side of the tower-shrines are two small library buildings featuring beautiful triangular pediments with scenes from the Hindu epics of Indian literature, the Mahabharata and the Ramayana. Projecting from the lower corners of each pediment are five-headed *nagas,* held by the jaws of lion-headed figures. Enclosing the assembly of central towers and libraries is a brick wall; between this and an outer wall are six long annex buildings, which may have been resthouses for meditation, or part of a monastery. Think of Banteay Srei as a large piece of sculpture: almost every surface of red sandstone at Banteay Srei is carved with floral garlands, geometric patterns, demons, coiled *nagas,* or mythical figures. The mask-like head of Kala—a demon that devoured its own body—is a common motif over doorways, where it serves as a temple protector. The carvings are amazingly fluid—at first it's hard to believe they're fashioned in stone. Right at the back of Bantei Srei is an entry tower with another fine carved lintel. Beyond that, mine-infested jungle.

River of a Thousand Lingas

About 45 km northeast of Siem Reap is Phnom Kulen, a holy mountain that is the mythical birthplace of Cambodia. The mountain lies deep in Khmer Rouge territory and was taken by government troops in 1995. Phnom Kulen is where sandstone was quarried for the building of the monuments of Angkor, the stone floated down the Siem

THE MALRAUX HEIST

The most contentious heist of Khmer statuary took place at Banteay Srei in 1923. A French couple in their early twenties, André and Clara Malraux, scandalized Clara's relatives—first by marrying, and then by squandering her inheritance. After a visit to Guimet Museum of Oriental Art in Paris, the Malraux hatched a hare-brained scheme to find an unclassified Khmer temple and make a fortune selling Khmer relics to American museums. André came across an article by Henri Parmentier on a 1916 visit to Banteay Srei, and decided this was the temple—Malraux even lined up buyers in New York.

Joined by a friend, Louis Chevasson, André and Clara Malraux set sail for Cambodia aboard the SS *Angkor* in 1923. In the Angkor area they hired several local guides (one of whom later turned out to be a police informer), a dozen coolies, horses, and four ox-carts of equipment. After several days of hacking through jungle, they reached Banteay Srei. André Malraux later wrote in *The Royal Way*, "Something inhuman brooded over all these ruins and the voracious plants which now seemed petrified with apprehension: a presence of supernatural awe guarded with its dead hand these ancient figures holding their lonely court among the centipedes and vermin of the forest." The place was enclosed by dense overgrowth; snakes slithered over the surfaces, monkeys chattered in nearby treetops. Working feverishly, the trio managed to hack off four large blocks of sandstone comprising a beautiful bas-relief. These pieces were slung into the oxcarts.

Back in Siem Reap, they loaded their treasure, an estimated 400 kg of it, onto a river steamer in boxes labeled Chemical Products, and headed for Saigon. In Phnom Penh they were arrested. Clara fell seriously ill and was allowed to return to France, smug-

gling with her the head of a Khmer *apsara* in a hat-box. Chevasson was sentenced to 18 months imprisonment; Malraux received three years in jail. French literary luminaries rallied to Andre's defense. His lawyer argued that if two young men were to be imprisoned for taking stone from Banteay Srei, should not the same penalty be meted out to various governors, high commissioners, and administrators who'd done the same thing? Banteay Srei was not classified as a historical site, and no court had ruled on this issue before. The judge reduced André's conviction to a one-year suspended sentence, and gave Louis an eight-month suspended sentence. The bas-reliefs, meanwhile, were sequestered at the museum in Phnom Penh, later returned to the temple walls of Banteay Srei.

André became an eloquent spokesman for the commoner in Indochina. He returned to France, picked up Clara, and went back to Saigon in 1925 to start up *L'Indochine,* a newspaper that dared to criticize the colonial administration. The French powers responded by intimidating any printer who handled the newspaper, effectively shutting it down after two months of operation. Undaunted, the Malraux sailed to Hong Kong to purchase ancient wooden type from Jesuit missionaries. With this type they printed a bi-weekly broadsheet, *L'Indochine Enchaînée* (Indochina in Chains). In 1926, the Malraux decided they could agitate more forcefully by returning to France. André wrote a trilogy of Asian novels—*The Conquerors (Les Conquérants), The Royal Way (La Voie Royale),* and *Man's Fate (La Condition Humaine).* The latter earned him the prestigious Prix Goncourt in 1933. *The Royal Way* was a fictionalized, heroic retelling of the Banteay Srei expedition and Phnom Penh trial.

Reap River on rafts. The mountain summit boasts a 900-year-old reclining Buddha—the largest in Cambodia—and the slopes offer fragments of 9th-century Khmer temples. Before 1975 Phnom Kulen was a popular pilgrimage site.

The most astonishing feature of Phnom Kulen is the River of a Thousand Lingas. This sacred river is named after the series of lingas carved into riverbed rock, lying about 15 cm below crystal-clear water. The lingas are about 25 cm square and 10 cm deep, arranged in a perfect grid pattern. Between the lingas are some well-

preserved statues of *apsaras* and Vishnus carved in underwater sandstone. One of the largest lingas is carved just before a 15-meter waterfall. At one point on the river, the rock rises above the water to form a natural bridge, Kbal Spean, which is covered with sculpture—bulls, frogs, Vishnu lying on a *naga,* innumerable lingas. The lingas were possibly carved to sanctify the waters irrigating the Angkor plain. Past kings are said to have performed mystical rites at Phnom Kulen. Because of land mines, the only present access to the area is by helicopter.

BEING THERE

You need three full days at Angkor. It's not difficult to organize a trip—you can hire motorcycle guides to visit the ruins, or head off on rented bicycles. With a small group of three or four you can rent a vehicle and guide for the day from Angkor Tourism in Siem Reap—cheaper than a package tour and allows greater flexibility.

Escorted tours to Angkor are organized by a host of agents in Phnom Penh and Bangkok. Tours originating from Bangkok entail more logistics and middlemen, so prices escalate. From Phnom Penh an Angkor tour of two days and one night is about $220 a person, including flights, hotel, food, guide, and local transportation. Such a short tour will probably prove unsatisfactory; between flights you'll only spend one full day at the ruins.

When to Visit
November to March is the peak touring season, with dry conditions. April to July is sizzling hot; August to October is the rainy season. Some like to see the ruins in the mist and rain—romantic, if somewhat slippery. The reservoirs around Angkor are fuller, and the lush vegetation offsets the reddish sandstone. At this time Angkor is also devoid of crowds.

Travel Agents
Located near the Grand Hotel, government-run Angkor Tourism handles guides and transportation in cars and minibuses for organized groups. Staff are not interested in assisting individual travelers unless guides and rentals are requested. Branches of Phnom Penh agents stationed in Siem Reap include Apsara Tours and Diethelm Travel.

Guides
Angkor Tourism has about 40 guides on tap, the majority speak English or French, although some also speak Japanese, Thai, Chinese, and Khmer. Angkor Tourism guides are expensive at $15 a day, and will expect to be shuttled around in the comfort of a car. Hired on your own, a motorcycle guide is $2-3 a day. If he rides a separate motorcycle the fee may go up. A moto guide is a bonus for a number of reasons: backup in the event of mechanical failure or a flat tire, another eye on the bike to prevent theft, reduced likelihood of problems if stray soldiers are encountered. And finally, some guides speak quite reasonable English and can point out features you may not notice. Assess the guide's level of English and the vehicle's condition before departing.

motorcycle guide at Takeo Temple

Guidebooks

French archaeological specialists like George Coedes and Henri Parmentier have published detailed guides to Angkor. Photocopied versions of their works are peddled in gift shops in Phnom Penh and around Siem Reap. These guides may be well out of date, the author describing statuary long ago stolen, beheaded, or removed to a museum. Highly recommended is a more recent comprehensive guide, Dawn Rooney's *A Visitor's Guide to Angkor* (the Guidebook Company, Hong Kong, 1994), with in-depth cultural background material and excellent site descriptions. The May 1982 issue of *National Geographic* with two articles on Angkor features good maps and pictures useful for site identification. In French there's the admirable book of Bruno Dagens, *Angkor: Heart of an Asian Empire* (Gallimard, 1989).

Even detailed guidebooks appear inadequate when confronted with the sheer majesty of the buildings, and a lot of questions go unanswered. Of course some prefer mysteries to remain mysteries, allowing the imagination to run riot. It is possible to take perverse pleasure in the shattered grandeur, the crumbled dreams, the tree roots run amok, the jumble of towers and walls.

Photography

At Angkor it's best to bring five times more film along than you think you'll need. A sturdy tripod is invaluable for sunrise and sunset shots, and for close-ups of bas-reliefs. Angkor Wat is extremely difficult to photograph because of the sheer scale of the place, and results can be very disappointing. You'll have more success at the Bayon, where the stonework at least fits into the viewfinder. The Bayon's gallery bas-reliefs are also easier to photograph because they're not covered by a projecting or overhanging roof—those at Angkor Wat are, and so require a flash. Wide-angle lenses are also very useful at Angkor.

The most photographed sections of Angkor are the gateways to Angkor Thom, which benefit from wide-angle lenses. Avoid the harsh midday sun, which results in washed-out pictures. The best light is in early morning, since most temples face eastward. Angkor Wat, on the other hand, faces west, so the best light is in the late afternoon. Angkor monuments look very different depending on blue or gray skies, dusk or dawn, new or full moon. Patience is required for dramatic lighting conditions, which can make or break a photograph. It's wise to scout locations for the best angles and vantage points.

Conduct

Angkor is a series of sacred temples, so appropriate behavior should be observed. Khmer visitors may be on pilgrimage and may resent having their photos taken. Similarly, do not disturb monks by hounding them for photographs. Under no circumstances remove debris or artifacts from temple sites, or places where restoration is in progress. Travelers' bags are checked on exit at Siem Reap airport to prevent theft of statuary and artifacts.

Safety

Although the following section may sound daunting, life in Siem Reap and Angkor is quite simple, and if you exercise common sense your trip will be smooth—and very special. Just avoid visiting the ruins alone, especially those farther out.

Tourist Police: A special tourist police force has been established at Angkor; for the moment its primary mission is to guard Angkor itself and prevent theft of statuary. Sometimes soldiers with AK-47s appear in and around the ruins, especially at the Bayon or Angkor Wat. More soldiers materialize when a visiting dignitary tours the ruins—you can tell how important the visitor is by the number of escorts. Occasionally bored policemen put on a special security show for a VIP, all in the interests of fundraising.

Military Activity: The perimeter of the Angkor region is guarded by hundreds of government troops. Some soldiers are assigned to guard bridges, a favorite Khmer Rouge target. Government soldiers can be a problem—depending on when they were last paid, and if they've been drinking. On Phnom Bakheng, the hill overlooking Angkor Wat, soldiers have been known to ask for money or cigarettes. Some travelers contribute, some don't. Handing around a few cigarettes wouldn't hurt, but dispensing dollar bills is bad form.

You can sometimes hear the sound of distant gunfire around Angkor. An American woman overheard at Angkor Wat: "That's not thunder. Do you think they're bombing the airport?" Her com-

armed guard at Bayon

panion turned and listened intently. "No honey, I think they're bombing where we were yesterday." At night, sporadic gunfire is explained by guesthouse owners as "people hunting birds." Nocturnal hunting would not account for the bullet that grazed the head of a Portuguese tourist sitting in his room at the Grand Hotel. In January 1995 an American tourist was killed 15 km from Angkor when gunmen opened fire on a tourist van heading to Banteay Srei.

Mines: The Siem Reap area is heavily mined. According to Cofras, a French mine-clearing firm, over 1,000 landmines and 7,000 unexploded shells were removed from the fields and forests around the temples of Angkor in 1994. In the first three months of 1995 over 800 mines were discovered. Although the main tourist areas are believed to be mine-free, this is not the case at more remote temples and in outlying village areas. Be careful. Use a guide, keep to the major ruins, stick to well-trodden paths, and do not venture into areas with long grass. There have been no reports of death or injury to tourists resulting from landmines or unexploded ordnance, but as one traveler put it, "Who's going to tell you that

last week they blew up a Parisian?" Mine signs of a very different kind are sometimes posted at outlying temples, which are prone to theft of statuary. Enigmatic signs here warn that the site is actually *protected* with explosives from dusk to dawn. This may be bluff, but it may also mean trip wires rigged to explosives.

Loose Rubble: Ruins are unstable. There may be sharp drop-offs, steep stairs, loose or broken masonry, crumbling galleries, or piles of rubble. It's rather like a giant construction zone. Tread carefully, and don't venture into dark areas without a flashlight.

Other Hazards: Poisonous snakes exist— some cobras, and the small emerald-green tree snake. This variety, called *hanuman* by locals, drops down on its victims from above, and can be deadly. Avoid long grass, which may also harbor mines. Malaria is a hazard—Lariam, also known as mefloquine, is the best drug for the Siem Reap area. To prevent bites use a repellent, cover exposed flesh at sundown, and sleep under a mosquito net.

Checkpoints and Entry Fees

There are checkpoints on the three roads leading to Angkor Wat. The major checkpoint used by visitors is the one 4.5 km north of the Grand Hotel on a paved road. You can obtain entry tickets at the checkpoints, at Siem Reap airport, or from Angkor Tourism in Siem Reap. In mid-1994 the Ministry of Tourism took over ticket collecting, charging a flat $20 a day to visit the temples. Three-day passes are $40, seven-day passes $60. Once past the checkpoints you can go anywhere you want. Previously travelers had to negotiate with soldiers at these checkpoints, haggling over the price of individual ruins. The money often went into the soldiers' deep pockets. The *Phnom Penh Post* reported that in the months prior to the Ministry of Tourism takeover, monthly revenues from entrance fees suddenly leapt from $20,000 to $70,000, despite no increase in the number of tourists.

Gearing Up for Tourism

Mass tourism has yet to arrive at Angkor, though the potential is certainly there. There are no entry signs, billboards, ticket booths, or restaurants. Just the odd DANGER!! MINES!! skull-and-crossbones sign. There's not even a museum or visitor information center. It's all very casual. In the heady 1920s and 1930s hordes of foreign tourists arrived by boat from Saigon, or motored in from Bangkok.

One of the sad realities of life in Cambodia today is that the infrastructure was better in 1930. In 1930, you could catch a hydroplane from Saigon or Bangkok and land right in the moat of Angkor Wat, then tour the area by car, horse, or elephant. Visitors could stay in the Hotel des Ruines, opposite Angkor Wat's main entrance. According to a French guidebook of 1930, "just before sunset one can see from the Hotel clouds of bats that leave the towers of Angkor Wat by millions in the cool of the evening, circling around them and finally dispersing in all directions in search of food and water."

In 1968 more than 70,000 visitors toured Angkor, mostly French and American. Two luxurious hotels were constructed opposite the main causeway to Angkor Wat. Evening performances by traditional Cambodian dancers on the causeway were commonplace—afterwards, hotel guests could stroll around by moonlight. The hotels were destroyed by the Khmer Rouge. From the early 1970s until the early 1990s there was hardly any tourism. Then, spurred by UNTAC, visitors began come back again. An estimated 90,000 people visited in 1994. According to UNESCO, the maximum yearly capacity for the site is around 500,000 to 700,000 tourists.

Along with a new influx of tourists, cottage industries have appeared around the ruins. Enterprising food and drink vendors set up stalls every morning outside Angkor Wat, the Bayon, and other key sites. Beggars occupy strategic gateways at Angkor Wat, hawkers sell souvenirs at roadside stalls, and tribes of obnoxious urchins push Angkor Wat and Bayon T-shirts, rubbings of Angkor bas-reliefs, wooden cowbells, crossbows, joss sticks, rolls of film, musical instruments, and other paraphernalia. But mostly they sell cold drinks. The cold drink brigade can be very persistent. "Cold drink, mister?" "You buy cold drink, madam?" At some sites, these kids will not leave you in peace until you hold a cold drink in your hands. In any case, you won't suffer from dehydration at Angkor. Many kids try to earn pocket money by acting as guides. Touts are becoming more numerous, soliciting for guesthouses and motorcycle tours.

Getting Around

By Car: Angkor Tourism handles taxi and minibus transportation for organized groups. A car runs $35-45 a day with driver, plus an extra $15 for a guide. A minibus seating 10 costs $65 a day including driver, plus $15 for the guide. Travel agents can also arrange cars in Siem Reap, and there are privately owned vehicles obtainable through guesthouses—ask around.

By Motorcycle: Independent travelers can visit Angkor on hired scooters, with or without a local guide. Obtain Honda 70cc and 90cc scooters for $5 a day through guesthouses. Check the motorcycle thoroughly for mechanical problems, or your grand tour of Angkor might end up being a short circuit. Good motorcycle handling skills are required, especially if taking on a pillion passenger. If unsure of your motorcycling skills, hire a "chauffeur" for an extra $2 a day. Road hazards include occasional sand or water patches, stray cows and water buffalo, plus craters and potholes, especially on the more isolated northern route where roads are gouged by monsoon rains. Motorcycle theft is a problem; park where someone can keep an eye on your vehicle. If that means buying a drink at a nearby foodstall, do so.

By Bicycle: Bicycles cost $2 a day from guesthouses. Bicycles are gearless, possibly three-speeds if you're lucky. Cycling is a great way to see the ruins as long as you avoid the midday sun. Some sections around the Bayon are sheltered by forest—with serene cycling through the woods. Park your bike near a foodstall and perhaps tip someone to watch it while you're gone. Count on progress of 10 to 12 kph on a bicycle. The roads are usually flat, sometimes with a slight grade, but may be unpaved.

It's about 11 km from the Grand Hotel to the Bayon, requiring an hour of pedaling. You should start early if you want to cover a bit of ground. Allow 2.5 hours actual cycling time to cover the Little Circuit; taking in stops and a midday siesta means a full day of biking. Looping around the Grand Circuit is possible by bicycle, but you have to move quickly to cover the ground, and road conditions are poor. It's a long way between temples on the Grand Circuit, and you may spend more time in the saddle than at the sites. Getting up to Preah Khan Temple on the Grand Circuit is 30-minute roundtrip from the Bayon on a good road.

AROUND CAMBODIA

Towns in Cambodia are small. Due to recent upheavals, population figures are hard to come by, but towns range in size from 15,000 (Kampot) to 80,000 (Battambang). The French-built towns of Battambang, Kratie, Sihanoukville, Kampot, and Kep are infrequently visited, for the very good reason that travel upcountry is dangerous. You take your chances even in Phnom Penh and the Angkor region—other parts of the country present a much higher risk. The Tourism Ministry claims the zones of Phnom Penh, Angkor, and Sihanoukville are well protected, but three foreigners were killed traveling by road to Sihanoukville in 1994, and a tourist died in a rocket attack 15 km from Angkor in early 1995. Khmer Rouge activity intensifies to the western side of Cambodia, toward the Thai border. Mines are sometimes laid on the roads in the northwest, and guerrillas regularly blow up bridges, making roads impassable by car.

During the 1992-93 UNTAC era battalions of foreign soldiers were stationed in most Cambodian towns, and travel to these places was more secure because of the armed UN presence. Since the UN withdrawal the situation has deteriorated. Although travelers have reached some of the following destinations, they might well be off limits due to fighting or other dangers. Always check on the current situation before embarking on any overland journey.

Obviously the best way to get upcountry is to fly. There are several daily flights to Siem Reap; less frequent flights to Sihanoukville, Kampot, Koh Kong, Battambang, Kratie, and Stung Treng. The next best course is to take a fast boat upcountry to Siem Reap or Kratie. These boats do not slow down for government checkpoints, whereas the slower boats do. Driving along Route 1 from Phnom Penh to Saigon is reasonably safe, with few government checkpoints on the Cambodian side, and no Khmer Rouge activity reported.

SOUTHERN CAMBODIA

Accessible areas south of Phnom Penh include the beach resort of Sihanoukville and Route 1 to Saigon. During the colonial era the area along the Gulf of Thailand was renowned for its seaside resorts and mountain spas. These resorts were largely destroyed during the civil war, when they were first occupied and then blown up by the Khmer Rouge. Roads are dangerous due to Khmer Rouge activity, government checkpoints, and bandits, and road travel cannot be recommended. Sihanoukville and Kampot can, however, be reached by plane from Phnom Penh.

KAMPOT

Kampot is a small town on the Tuk Chhou River, five km inland from the sea. Fishing and farming are the main activities; durians and melons grow in abundance. To the south end of town is a large dusty traffic circle with three hotels arrayed around it—**Phnom Kieu, Phnom Kamchay,** and **Tuk Chhou.** Each has its own restaurant; Tuk Chhou offers a seedy nightclub. Also on the circle is **Prachummith Restaurant,** close by is **Amar Restaurant.** To the south near the river is the GPO and telecommunications building. At the north end of town, about 1.5 km away, is the Central Market, with foodstalls. All Kampot

transportation is concentrated within range of the market—cyclos, motos, taxis, trucks, and buses. The railway station lies farther north. There's zero of interest in Kampot except to walk around town and look at crumbling French-built blue-shuttered shop fronts. Previously Kampot was a stepping-stone to Bokor and Kep.

You can reach Kampot by irregular plane service from Phnom Penh. It's also possible—but not advisable—to get there by share-taxi. It takes about five hours to cover the 150 km from Phnom Penh to Kampot. From Sihanoukville it's 105 km to Kampot by a very dangerous and treacherous dirt road. The train from Phnom Penh to Kampot, when it runs, takes seven hours. The train is a frequent target of the Khmer Rouge—in a 1994 ambush, three foreigners were captured and later murdered.

Vicinity of Kampot
Kep, 25 km southeast of Kampot, is easily reached by moto on a day-trip. The resort was founded in 1908; in colonial days, Kep-sur-Mer was a favorite vacation spot for French administrators and Cambodian aristocrats. Sihanouk maintained a private offshore island to entertain guests. The French constructed villas, residences, hotels, and a handful of public buildings. In the 1970s the Khmer Rouge methodically

village near Kampot

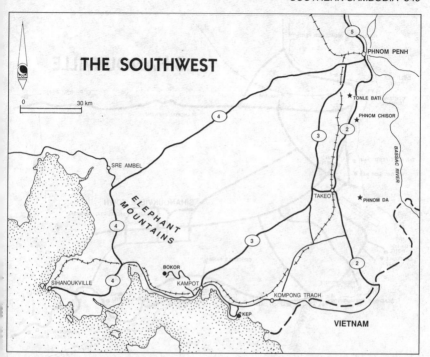

dynamited every single one. This is an eerie place to visit—Cambodian fishermen huddle in the shells of palatial French villas, cooking over open fires. The beaches at Kep are hardly suited to swimming—most are pebbly or hard-sand strips with coconut palms. The tiny main beach is deserted during the week, but since Kep is closer to Phnom Penh than Sihanoukville it's deluged on weekends. A restaurant and food-stalls near the beach sell fresh crab. Facilities are limited, with only a few guesthouses in operation. You could stay with locals.

About 40 km west of Kampot, reached by a rough winding road, is the former French hill station of **Bokor.** Sitting at 1,080 meters in the Elephant Mountains, the resort was known for its mild climate, forest, gurgling streams, waterfalls, and panoramas of the Gulf of Thailand. The resort now lies in ruins, and the area has been off limits for some time due to Khmer Rouge activity. Popokvil Falls are close to the access road to Bokor.

The Khmer Rouge razed all the buildings at the hill resort of **Kirirom** in the Elephant Mountains. At 700 meters in elevation, Kirirom once provided a cool respite from summer heat for the Phnom Penh elite. With forests of rare pine trees, and a rich stock of wildlife and fauna, Kirirom was selected in 1995 as the centerpiece of a 35,000-hectare national park straddling Kompong Speu and Koh Kong provinces. Kirirom lies about 115 km southwest of Phnom Penh off Route 4, on the way to Sihanoukville.

SIHANOUKVILLE

Because the Mekong was long Cambodia's major thoroughfare, the coastal region never developed as a trade center. With the Vietnam War, however, Cambodia was forced to look for alternate routes. A road was built from Phnom Penh to the coast with American aid in the 1960s. Sihanoukville was founded in 1964

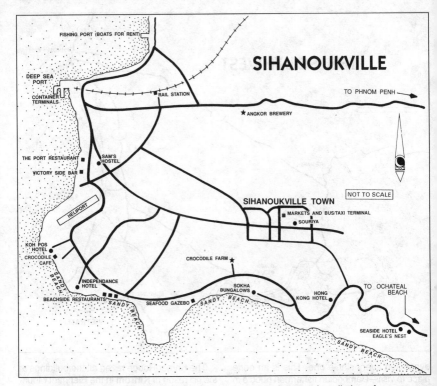

FISHING PORT (BOATS FOR RENT)

SIHANOUKVILLE

DEEP SEA PORT

TO PHNOM PENH

CONTAINER TERMINALS

RAIL STATION

★ ANGKOR BREWERY

THE PORT RESTAURANT

SAM'S HOSTEL

VICTORY SIDE BAR

HELIPORT

NOT TO SCALE

SIHANOUKVILLE TOWN

MARKETS AND BUS/TAXI TERMINAL

SOURIYA

KOH POS HOTEL

CROCODILE CAFE

CROCODILE FARM ★

SANDY BEACH

INDEPENDANCE HOTEL

SOKHA BUNGALOWS

TO OCHATEAL BEACH

BEACHSIDE RESTAURANTS

SEAFOOD GAZEBO

SANDY BEACH

HONG KONG HOTEL

SEASIDE HOTEL

EAGLE'S NEST

SANDY BEACH

by its namesake, underwent a name change under the Khmer Rouge to Kompong Som, and reverted to its original name upon the return of the king in 1991.

Sihanoukville is two entities, port and resort. This deep-water port in the Gulf of Thailand was developed with Soviet aid to circumvent the need to pass through Vietnam's Mekong Delta. Fishing is a major activity in Sihanoukville, with a cannery north of the main port. The national beermaker, Angkor Brewery, operates from Sihanoukville. There are plans to build an oil refinery, and international companies are exploring along the Gulf of Thailand for offshore oil and gas.

The port is undergoing a $5-million face-lift thanks to a dramatic rise in shipping activity. Renovations include the construction of a new container terminal, repairs to 1950s-era water-front warehouses, installation of new cranes and cargo-handling equipment, and the purchase of new tugboats. With the new facilities, Sihanoukville could become an important transit stop for inter-Asia cargo. The town is receiving a massive transfusion of foreign investment funds, and has been earmarked for major tourist development. Sihanoukville is slated to become Casino City. There are plans for a $400-million casino resort on Naga Island off the coast, complete with an international airport. The Tourism Ministry says casinos will be restricted to foreign passport holders, and that strict controls will be implemented to prevent criminal activities. The government plans to levy a one-percent gaming tax for distribution to worthy cultural and welfare organizations and causes. In the 1950s and 1960s several casinos operated in Cambodia.

Being There

Sihanoukville is scattered over a wide area. There is a downtown section with shops, and all local transport piles up near the Central Market. The town maintains some links with the outside world: Cambodia Samart telecommunications group has an office in Sihanoukville with mobile phones and satellite hookup.

Beaches

As a beach resort, Sihanoukville has it all over Kep. There are several long stretches of white sand with palm trees, and coves of white sand with scattered fishing villages. Beaches are christened after the nearest hotel. Sokha Beach is home to Sokha Bungalows: the wide stretch of white sand runs 1.5 km here, and is fringed by fir trees. Fishing boats make this area picturesque. The area in front of the Independence Hotel is the main local beach, with a stretch of wide, white sand. Farther west, Koh Pos Hotel offers its own small sandy cove; the beaches are rockier toward Victory Side Bar. Right to the east is Ochateal Beach, with a thin strip of sand and no tree cover.

At the fishing port to the north of Sihanoukville you can rent a vessel from fishermen to reach offshore islands, which offer possibilities for snorkeling and diving.

Accommodations and Food

Accommodations are widely scattered in Sihanoukville; restaurants are either attached to hotels or owned by hoteliers. In Sihanoukville town are a few hotels **Victory, Soriya**—generally in the $20-40 range, but these are far from the beaches. Proceeding down the coastline from the north side you'll find the following accommodations.

Sam's Hostel, on a hill overlooking the last beach before the port, is run by a former UN volunteer. Rooms are $4. Sam is a Cambodian cook; her fish dishes are excellent. Up this way is the **Kamsab Hotel** with eight rooms for $33. Along the coast are two pricey restaurants, **The Port** and **Victory Side Bar.** The latter offers dancing.

The family-run **Koh Pos Hotel,** with $25-35 doubles, has its own private cove of sand nearby. The Koh Pos runs a wooden seafront restaurant called the **Crocodile Café,** which serves

up superb food—shrimp, grilled fish, and bean-sprout pancakes. The seedy **Independence Hotel** was the pre-1975 Hilton; now it's a derelict flophouse with Vietnamese taxi dancers at night. There are 24 rooms for $15 each. At the beach near the Independence Hotel is the **Seaview Hotel,** with doubles for $10. The next beach east, Sokha Beach, offers **Sokha Bungalows** for $20-40 for a cabin, and the **Hong Kong Hotel,** with similar prices for rooms. **Sokha Seafood** gazebo to the west end of the beach serves delicious sautéed prawn dishes and stuffed crab.

At Ochateal Beach is the **Seaside Hotel,** with rooms for $20-40, with hot shower and satellite TV, and a sunset terrace. Next door is **Eagle's Nest,** a restaurant and hotel, with air-con rooms with satellite TV for $25.

Getting There

By Air: Royal Air Cambodge flies an Antonov several times weekly to Sihanoukville for $40 one-way.

By Road: Sihanoukville is 230 km from Phnom Penh on Route 4. This highway, constructed by USAID in the 1950s, is being rebuilt by the US and is in reasonable shape. There are numerous checkpoints along the way. A taxi costs $20 from Phnom Penh's Dang Kor Market, and takes about three hours one-way. Although Route 4 seems to be safe from Khmer Rouge attacks, bandits and government troops are a force to be reckoned with. Bandits are unemployed soldiers; irregular checkpoints are set up by RCAF soldiers to fleece travelers. There have been up to 50 checkpoints on this road in the past. If you must travel this route, depart at dawn. It could be very dangerous by the afternoon, when soldiers at checkpoints get drunker. In April 1994 three foreigners were abducted on Route 4 by suspected Khmer Rouge in the vicinity of Sre Ambel and killed.

By Rail: The slow goods train from Phnom Penh via Kampot takes at least 12 hours to reach Sihanoukville and may come under fire from the Khmer Rouge. For these reasons, it is not a practical or sensible option.

By Sea: Boats from Krong Koah Kong near the Thai border commute to Sihanoukville, but this route is dangerous due to piracy. On occasion cruise ships have docked in Sihanoukville.

Much upcountry travel is done by ferry or cargo boat.

Getting Around

Local transportation is clustered round the market downtown. Motos are the best way to get around Sihanoukville. It's possible to rent motorcycles or bicycles through hotels. You can rent small boats from the fishing docks to the northwest to visit offshore islands.

Vicinity of Sihanoukville

The country's first national park, Preah Sihanouk National Park, was established in 1995 at Ream, 20 km east of Sihanoukville. The park covers 21,000 hectares of forest and beaches and embraces a marine zone. There's a visitor center at the park. Ream is a port with a naval base.

THAI MARINE BORDER CROSSING

Some travelers have been able to enter Cambodia by sea from Trat Province. Cambodia recognizes the crossing as legitimate, and will stamp you in; the Thais let you in and out, but do not recognize legitimate entry from the Cambodian side. Thais themselves seem to cross over without problems.

This boat crossing is part of a busy smuggling route, with kickbacks to all involved. There's air service to Koah Kong Province from Phnom Penh. Some travelers have taken daytrips from the Thai side to islands in Cambodia for $40-50. It's possible—but hazardous—to take a speedboat from Ban Hat Lek at the tip of

Thailand to the Cambodian side and carry on. From Ban Hat Lek, 10-person longtail boats run for an hour through mangroves to reach the area of Phumi Thnal Krabi. Boats are available for onward travel from Phumi Thnal Krabi and the seaport of Krong Koah Kong to Koh Kong, Peam Kay, Sre Ambel, and Sihanoukville. Frequency varies from daily to every few days. Most of the boats pass by Koh Kong, a smuggler-infested hangout. A large fishing boat should take about 12 hours for the run from Krong Koah Kong to Sihanoukville. For overnight trips passengers string up hammocks.

SOUTHEAST TO SAIGON

The only reason to travel along Route 1 is to get to Saigon: the landscape is dull. Route 1 from Phnom Penh to Saigon is in excellent shape, sealed for rapid troop movement when Vietnam occupied Cambodia from 1979 to 1989. The route is safe to travel—there are few government checkpoints, and no Khmer Rouge activity has been reported.

The border crossing point is at Bavet on the Cambodian side and Moc Bai on the Vietnamese side. Your paperwork needs to be in order for the land crossing. To exit Cambodia you need a valid Vietnamese visa with a Moc Bai border entry stamp; this stamp, added to an existing visa, costs $20 at the Vietnamese Embassy Consular Section on Monivong Blvd.

near Issarak Boulevard in Phnom Penh. In the reverse direction, you need a Moc Bai exit stamp for your Vietnamese visa and a valid Cambodian visa—both documents can be obtained via travel agents in Saigon. If you plan to cross into Cambodia and then come back to Saigon, you'll need a re-entry stamp for your Vietnamese visa. Moneychangers offer poor rates at the border, so you're better off carrying small US bills to pay for any transportation or other expenses. Less documentation is required to fly; rates are $50 for the half-hour trip.

The Bavet-Moc Bai border is in theory open 0630-1800 daily, which means you need to leave Phnom Penh early. At Phumi Banam, 60 km from Phnom Penh, you must catch a ferry across the Mekong; traders will change dollars into Vietnamese dong at reasonable rates here. Once in the border town of Bavet you can walk through to Vietnamese customs and immigration. Clearing both sides takes about half an hour. Phnom Penh to Saigon by taxi requires six to seven hours. A bus ride can consume eight to 14 hours depending on police checks on the Vietnamese side. More information on this route is located in the Phnom Penh and Saigon sections of this book.

Boats ply the Mekong from Phnom Penh to Saigon, but for the present traffic is restricted to locals. The Saigon-based French group Voiles Vietnam runs a reconditioned junk that crosses from the Mekong Delta to Phnom Penh. Gifts of whiskey and other luxury items help smooth the passage.

NORTHERN CAMBODIA

Apart from the Angkor region, travel north of Phnom Penh cannot be recommended due to Khmer Rouge activity, mines, poor roads, or a combination thereof.

BATTAMBANG AND THE NORTHWEST

Battambang Province is a very dangerous, heavily mined Khmer Rouge stronghold. On the Thai border is Pailin, a Khmer Rouge-operated gem-mining and logging center. Sales to Thailand of resources pulled from this area finance Khmer Rouge military activity. Give the northwest a miss until better times—fly over it.

Along Route 5 north, **Kompong Chhnang** is a port and fishing town on the Tonle Sap River accessible by road or boat. The area around the town is known for its pottery. The next town of any size on Route 5 north is **Pursat,** which is on the rail line. The area is famed for its pink marble. About 30 km south of Pursat, around the town of Leach, elephants are trained to work in teak forests.

Battambang

Battambang is the second largest city in Cambodia, with a population of perhaps 80,000. Due to its position near the Thai border the town has profited from large-scale blackmarket trading.

Fishing is secondary. Dengue fever is a big problem in the area and theft is rampant—motorcycles, cars, generators, and medical supplies all go missing. Facilities are primitive, electricity and water limited. Some areas enjoy electricity only a few hours a day. The town is close to Khmer Rouge bases and is sometimes threatened by them: in mid-1994 heavy fighting forced 40,000 civilians, mostly aid workers, to leave.

There are eight or nine hotels in Battambang, a legacy of UNTAC. Prices range from $5-10 a room at the **Samakai Hotel** to $10-25 a room at the **Paris Hotel.** Two hotels by the river offer $12-20 rooms, the **Victory** and **Angkor.** Near the Victory is a large swimming pool. **Sarika's Restaurant** serves good Thai food, steak, and pizza.

Getting There: There are three flights a week from Phnom Penh for $45 one-way. Westerners have been allowed to ride the train from Phnom Penh to Battambang and sometimes even further up to Sisophon. If the track is blown up, the train runs only as far as Pursat. Riders may have to sit on the roof of a carriage for this 12- to 17-hour trip because the train interior is packed with goods; female passengers ride inside. It can get pretty hot on the roof. And not just from the sun—sometimes the Khmer Rouge fire on the train. The train leaves Phnom Penh at 0630 every few days and in theory arrives at Battambang at sunset. By share-taxi the kamikaze run from Phnom Penh to

Battambang takes five to seven hours and costs $5 per person, based on six passengers. One group of travelers experienced 10 "holdups" on the Phnom Penh-Siem Reap route. Most were soldier checkpoints, but one was definitely a bandit—with a hook instead of an arm, and a gun pointed into the taxi.

Thai Border Crossing

The border at Poipet on the Cambodian side and Aranyaprathet on the Thai side is an open zone with day-trips allowed. There is no customs or immigration setup on the Thai side. From Cambodia you can visit Aranyaprathet without documentation, but cannot venture further into Thailand without special permission. The penalty for visiting Thailand without a valid visa can be a week in jail. In the UNTAC era travelers found ways to get through this border. One method was to cross from Thailand into Cambodia, proceed to Angkor, then cross back into Thailand on the original Thai visa.

If visiting Aranyaprathet, be aware you're passing close to a Khmer Rouge zone. Do not

MINEFIELDS AND MINDGAMES

by Gary McFarlane

"**Y**ou've got to trust the de-miners. If you don't trust their work you might as well quit before you start because the stress'll kill you."

I was talking with Commander Roar Holm, Chief Engineer, Norwegian People's Aid (NPA), about the attitude needed to enter a minefield. Faith, I suppose, would also help.

Last week I was in Saigon eating ice cream. Now I'm standing in a Cambodian minefield and my legs won't work. How do I get myself into these things? While riding through Sisophon on a mountain-bike tour, I'd been distracted by the sight of a Norwegian flag topping an official looking building, then lured in by thoughts of pasta, newspapers, and a shower. At dawn the next morning I found myself accompanying the Norwegian De-mining Team into a minefield outside Poipet.

The minefield layout was simple: mines could be anywhere. Mine variety is impressive: the undetectable Vietnamese homemade N0M Z2B, packed with grease oil and chicken bones to promote infection; the German-made POMZ; Chinese 72As; and the Valmara 69 jumping mine, infamously known as a Bouncing Betty, which, when triggered, devastates a 20-meter kill zone.

As we entered the minefield thoughts of becoming a statistic dogged every step I took. Where Roar stepped, I stepped. Exactly. I didn't see much of the area, staring at my feet the whole time. At one point, after stopping to take a photo, I looked up to see Roar 20 meters away, with no obvious trail between us. I knew he'd walked through, I'd been assured the area was clean, but still I hesitated badly. I was sweating. The first steps were the worst. Frightened into silence, I continued. A piggyback would've been nice.

Coming to the live area all work stopped, resuming only after I'd cleared the vicinity. Red-and-white striped poles designated between regions "clean" and "live." Red skull-and-crossbones signs (DANGER!! MINES!!) emphasized the areas to avoid. The safe areas were meter-wide paths marked by orange tape crossing from one section to another. Excessively careful to step directly in the middle of the path, nervously forgoing the cleared edges, brave enough to no longer follow exact footsteps, I tiptoed along this checkerboard pattern of safety.

Stopping beside a tree jutting into the path, Roar pointed at three stakes in the ground at the tree's base. "That's where we found mines, placed where people are most likely to take cover. On the other side there," he pointed to the far side of the tree where uncut brush accentuated the orange tape, "we'll find at least three more."

Walking away from the tree a stray branch knocked my hat off. I froze while it settled in the dirt behind me. On the path. Realistically, a falling hat doesn't carry the force needed to set off a landmine. Try telling that to a tight sphincter.

Time for lunch. Two of the de-miners took me in their vehicle to the Thai border town, Aranyaprathet, for a meal—an illicit crossing for me. Our chosen restaurant out of cheesecake, I settled for Thai fried rice. Crossing back into Cambodia a border guard offered to sell me his Colt revolver. Cool souvenir but not a good idea. I spent the afternoon watching the detonation of live mines, safely tucked in behind a hillock outside the 100-meter "safe zone." Funny, I didn't feel all that safe.

leave Poipet after 1400—there are bandits on the route. Between Sisophon and the border the road is in good condition, used by NGOs and UNTAC as a supply route in 1993. There are at least four blockade-checkpoints with guard towers along this section.

Banteay Chhmar
About 70 km north of Sisophon near the Thai border is the temple of Banteay Chhmar, built by Jayavarman VII as a memorial to his son and four generals killed in the war against Cham invaders in 1177. The story of the battle is engraved on stone walls surrounding Banteay Chhmar, in a style similar to that of Angkor's Bayon temple. The forest-covered temple is in a remote zone controlled by Khmer Rouge and bandits. Statuary has evidently been looted by military groups and transported to Thailand.

DUE NORTH OF PHNOM PENH

The zone directly north of Phnom Penh, embracing Kompong Thom and Preah Vihear provinces, falls under the Khmer Rouge sphere of influence. The town of **Kompong Thom,** 165 km northwest of Phnom Penh on Route 6, was previously the launching point for trips to ruins in the north, but neither the town nor the ruins are presently accessible. About 35 km northeast of Kompong Thom is **Sambor Prei Kok,** the 7th-century capital of the Chenla Empire. The temples have been vandalized, but some brick terraces with sandstone ornamentation remain. **Preah Khan,** 104 km due north of Kompong Thom, is a large sandstone temple dating from the 11th and 12th centuries. **Koh Ker,** even further north, was the capital of Jayavarman IV in the 10th century. A great brick temple here has been severely damaged.

The Angkor-period temple complex of **Preah Vihear** lies in disputed territory on the Thai-Cambodian border in the Dangrek Range. Built in the early 11th century during the reign of Suryavarman I, the mountaintop complex was constructed on four different levels, each connected by stairways. Walls and doorways are decorated with a profusion of carvings. The best structures are those at the summit.

In 1962 the International Court of Justice awarded the area to Cambodia. However, the temple complex is perched on top of a 700-meter cliff accessible only from Thailand. In the early 1990s travelers could cross from Thailand for the day into Cambodian territory to visit the temple, then return to Thailand. In July 1993 the temple fell into Khmer Rouge hands; in 1994 government troops laid siege to the temple from the cliff base.

THE NORTHEAST

Accessible by air or boat is the Kompong Cham-Kratie-Stung Treng route. The Khmer Rouge are around, and malaria is a high risk in this area. You should carry your own mosquito netting and repellent, and if traveling by boat you'll need a hammock too. To reach the far northeast the best option is to fly into Stung Treng. You can also take a fast boat to Kompong Cham and Kratie; the fast boat carries 50 passengers inside and another 20 on the roof, and costs around $25 one-way for foreigners to Kratie. From Kratie there should be a slow boat to Stung Treng when the water is high, in the September-January season. The boat takes 1.5 days to travel from Kratie to Stung Treng, navigating water obstacles; the entire slow boat trip from Phnom Penh to Stung Treng requires 3.5 days.

Kompong Cham is a river port on the west bank of the Mekong, 145 km from Phnom Penh. Typical of Cambodian riverine towns, it has its complement of French shophouse architecture. You can stay at **Hotel Mekong,** by the river. It's possible to reach Kompong Cham by fast boat in under five hours. By road, a share-taxi on Route 7 requires about three hours and costs $25, or $5 per person. Kompong Cham lies in a zone of rubber plantations with rich, red earth. There are a few shrines and temples in the vicinity, including Wat Nokor and Prey Nokor. The town of Kompong Cham and the surrounding province of the same name were a former base of the Cham people, renowned as skilled fishing folk. They settled riverbanks east and north of Phnom Penh and along the shores of the Tonle Sap. During the Pol Pot era the Cham were persecuted because of their Sunni Muslim religion and their unique language and customs; only a third of the Cham in Cambodia survived. They're gradually regaining their confidence,

CHARTING THE MEKONG

In the mid-19th century, the British and the French competed for the new China trade. Europeans saw China—rich in silk, tea, and textiles—as a kind of El Dorado. The British were expanding along the Yangzi from Shanghai on China's east coast; the French thrust into China came through Indochina. By this shortcut the French hoped to beat the competition to Yunnan province.

Very rough terrain lay between China's southwest and the seaports on the coast of French-dominated Vietnam. Could the Mekong serve as a trade route between the port of Saigon and landlocked Yunnan province? The French organized an expedition to find out. Leading the expedition were Captain Ernest Doudart de Lagrée and his deputy, Lieutenant Francis Garnier. Doudart de Lagrée was the first French Resident in Cambodia; Garnier was a 27-year-old naval lieutenant. In the grand tradition of the time the Frenchmen set off in 1866 on what was to be a two-year journey. The 10-member expedition was imperially motivated and semiscientific in nature, with a botanist, geologist, two doctors, a cartographer/artist, and several naval officers.

The explorers and their native bearers left Saigon in June 1866, detouring via Lake Tonle Sap to Angkor Wat, rediscovered by Henri Mouhot in 1860. The expedition mapped the ruins of Angkor and returned to the Mekong. They then proceeded upstream to Laos, apparently consuming large amounts of alcohol to counter the effects of mosquitoes, disease, and the inhospitable climate and terrain. They traveled up past the Kratie rapids to the Lao-Cambodian border, where sandbars impeded their progress. They then encountered Khong Phapheng Falls, which posed a major obstacle to boat transport. Garnier stumbled across the ruins of Wat Phu, an Angkor-era temple complex in southern Laos. The expedition finally reached Vientiane in April 1867, a year after setting out.

At this point the expedition had established that the Mekong was not a viable trade route, but, obsessed by a maniacal drive, Garnier persuaded the group to forge on. Two weeks later they were in Luang Prabang, the royal capital of Laos. Then they pushed north into China, where Doudart de Lagrée collapsed and died in Yunnan from fever and fatigue. Garnier led the group down the Yangzi River to Shanghai, and back to Saigon. Of the 9,960 km covered on the expedition, over 5,000 km represented uncharted territory. The explorers had discovered abandoned Khmer ruins, encountered remote hilltribe groups, and forged through virgin jungle.

The report of the expedition is a landmark work on Indochina, and one of the finest of its genre. Garnier's two-volume *Voyage d'Exploration en Indochine* was published in Paris in 1873. A lavishly illustrated collection of details, it was very popular at the time, unfolding the mysteries of the Mekong.

---

re-establishing themselves in their old neighborhoods, and rebuilding mosques.

Farther north on the Mekong is **Kratie,** a fishing and logging town. The Mekong is navigable year round from Phnom Penh to Kratie. Boat trips are faster when the river runs high, from September to January; in other seasons the captain has to navigate around obstacles, and the going is slower. There may be air service to Kratie. Some 30 km north of Kratie is the site of the ancient capital of Sombor, which lies close to the Mekong. Crocodiles are said to inhabit the river in this area.

Stung Treng

Stung Treng is the capital of the province of the same name. The town lies 485 km north of Phnom Penh and 210 km south of Pakse in Laos, it's only 40 km from the Lao border. The town is perched on the banks of the Sekong River, not far from the Mekong. Sights around town are few—a couple of rapids and waterfalls. You can rent a boat for trips along the Mekong. Stung Treng's market is brimming with goods that come in by road, river, or plane, down from Laos, across from Vietnam, or up from Phnom Penh. Thai, Chinese, and Vietnamese goods all find their way here.

You can reach Stung Treng by boat from Phnom Penh from September to January. To save time and "river taxes" at government troop checkpoints, take a fast boat to Kratie and change to a slow boat from Kratie to Stung Treng. There's also a rough truck route from Kratie to Stung Treng; share-taxis cost $4 per person for the six-hour run. There are two flights

The first volume describes the voyage and is illustrated with engravings; the second volume comprises technical appendices, with observations on history, geography, meteorology, archaeology, anthropology, and language. There were also two magnificent folios: an atlas with extensive maps and plans of areas previously unseen by European eyes, and a pictorial record of peoples, landscapes, and ruins provided by expedition cartographer and artist Louis Delaporte.

In his grand opus Garnier expounded the theory that France should not wait to fulfill its imperial destiny, but should act immediately. Debate raged at the time in France on the ethics of expansionism in foreign places, viewed by some as a waste of funds.

Garnier then took matters into his own hands. He'd given up on the Mekong as a navigable route, focusing instead on the Red River as a route from China to ports on the Gulf of Tonkin. Enter Jean Dupuis, a gunrunner who'd met Garnier along the Yangzi. Dupuis sold weapons to a warlord in Yunnan, and needed an alternative route to the Yangzi. After a successful experiment on the Red River, the governor of Cochinchina, Admiral Dupré, deployed French warships near Haiphong as a gesture of support for Dupuis.

Dupuis transported weapons to Yunnan in March 1873 and returned two months later to Hanoi with a cargo of tin and copper. When mandarins who controlled the salt monopoly in Hanoi blocked the departure of Dupuis with a cargo of salt, Garnier joined forces with Dupuis, stormed Hanoi Citadel, and declared the Red River open to trade. Within a month their forces had conquered the entire region between Hanoi and the sea, including Haiphong. On 21 December 1873, under attack outside Hanoi by Black Flag mercenaries fighting for the Vietnamese, Garnier led a charge and was cut down by a hail of bullets. He was 35 years old. His exploits came to symbolize the glories of imperialism.

The French withdrew from Tonkin, but, concerned that colonial powers like Britain or Germany might seize the coal mines at Hong Gai, Captain Henri Rivière followed in Garnier's footsteps. He was killed near Hong Gai by Black Flag forces who paraded his head from village to village. In 1883 the French set out to take Tonkin a third time, and by the end of the year had over 20,000 men in Tonkin. Not content with the Red River trade route, the French built a railway concession between Hanoi and Kunming, completed in 1910. The line cost a fortune, and the fabled riches of China barely materialized.

The source of the Mekong was one of the world's last great geographical mysteries. In April 1995 a Franco-British expedition led by Michel Peissel announced the discovery of the source in the mountains of northwest China's Qinghai Province, at the 4,975-meter head of Rupsa Pass, the watershed between the Yangzi and Mekong river systems. The discovery was reported in *Geographic Magazine,* linked to Britain's Royal Geographic Society.

---

a week from Phnom Penh to Stung Treng; roundtrip $95. A decayed government guesthouse in Stung Treng offers accommodations at very reasonable prices.

Ratanakiri

Bordering Vietnam's Central Highlands are the remote provinces of Ratanakiri and Mondulkiri, both with thickly forested hilly terrain, hilltribe people, and abundant wildlife. Commercial enterprises in the region include logging, gem mining, and rubber plantations. A fertile basalt plateau with red dusty soil lies between the Se San and Srepok rivers. Mondulkiri is virtually cut off, roads impassable. The provincial capital of Sen Monorom is best reached from Vietnam; Ratanakiri is accessible by air from Phnom Penh.

Over 80% of Ratanakiri's population of 72,000 is classified as hilltribe people, mainly Jarai, Krung, Brou, and Tampuan. The 12 ethnic minority groups are collectively called Khmer Loeu (highlanders), a name coined by Sihanouk in the 1940s. Some of these groups are found across the borders in Vietnam's Central Highlands or in southern Laos.

The recent history of Ratanakiri is not a happy one. During the Vietnam War the province of Ratanakiri was devastated by American carpet bombing because it formed part of the Ho Chi Minh Trail. The Khmer Rouge used Ratanakiri as their main base of operations in the early 1970s; when they came to power in 1975, the Khmer Rouge wiped out at least half the tribal population. Because the area is so remote and infrastructure so weak, the highlanders today have little access to education or health care. Deaths result from malaria, diarrhea, and childbirth complications. There is a high incidence of malaria in both Ratanakiri and Mondulkiri provinces.

Most highlanders in Ratanakiri are animist and practice slash-and-burn agriculture. They farm rice and grow vegetables, and raise water buffalo and cows. They also hunt, using crossbows with poison-tipped bamboo arrows. Sacrifice to the numerous animal spirits of the forest is common, and regularly performed for any special event such as marriage, the construction of a new thatch-roofed hut, or a move to a new village location. At these events a feast is held, a pig sacrificed, and large quantities of rice wine consumed. At these gatherings the spirits are believed to take possession of certain individuals, who in a trance lose their own personality and take on that of the spirit, acting out a particular animist trait. Priestesses regarded as spiritual healers contact ancestral spirits and relay dreams.

Highland women enjoy as much freedom as men. They're free to divorce a husband who is cruel, and decisions on childbirth are the exclusive domain of women. If an unmarried woman finds herself pregnant, she is not disgraced—the man responsible, if not willing to marry, must reimburse the woman's family. The going rate is four buffalo, some pigs, a few chickens, and rice wine. Abortions are common after four or five children, with herbal potions used to end an unwanted pregnancy.

Although some hilltribers don Khmer dress, others retain traditional wear. Krung tribeswomen wear sarongs, go bare-breasted, and smoke long-stemmed pipes. Brou tribeswomen have large pierced earlobes and wear earrings sculpted from chunky ivory tusks. Their faces are tattooed and they wear bead necklaces and brass anklets.

Ban Lung, population 10,000, is the principal town in Ratanakiri Province, and lies 155 km east of Stung Treng. There may be direct flights into Ban Lung. The hotel in Ban Lung charges $5 a room; the town has a post office and bank. You can get to Ban Lung for about $5 on a truck from Stung Treng. The trip takes five to seven hours, but the road may be washed out in the May-November monsoon season. In parts of Ratanakiri, the only vehicles that move during the rainy season are oxcarts and elephants.

LAOS

The Vietnamese plant the rice, the Cambodians watch it grow, and the Laotians listen to it grow.

—saying attributed to French colonists describing the inhabitants of their Indochinese territories

INTRODUCTION

To many Westerners Laos is so obscure that without a detailed map of Asia, most couldn't say where it is, much less anything else about it.

Laos dropped out of the news after the Pathet Lao takeover in 1975. And therein lies its charm. The country's isolation, for reasons of war and politics, has preserved an older, slower, and more traditional way of life. Old Asia, Asia without the crowds. This is the perfect antidote to the frenzied pace of Bangkok—or New York or London, for that matter.

Laos is one of the poorest countries in the world. Yet people do not go hungry here, and you rarely see beggars when traveling around the country—a tribute to the fact that the Lao social fabric has its own social welfare system woven in. This is a culture where relatives and neighbors provide support for each other. Laos is very sparsely populated—mostly rural, with a patchwork of hilltribes, especially in the wild northern provinces. Health care in the provinces is mostly of the herbal kind, augmented by rare visits from health officials. Buddhist practices form a significant part of the Lao social fabric.

These practices are ingrained in Lao life: at the crack of dawn in Vientiane, Luang Prabang, and other towns, barefoot orange-robed monks file out of the monasteries to collect food donations from the locals. The Lao Buddhist calendar is studded with festivals, often lasting four or five days, with lively temple fairs.

As Laos moves ahead with modernization and foreign investment, its fragile social fabric is at risk. There is considerable controversy in Vientiane over how to handle increased exposure to Western influence. Laos favors controlled tourism: although the authorities have announced relaxation of travel restrictions, Laos caters primarily to high-priced escorted tours. These tourists have little impact on the local culture, and are taught about Lao customs and culture prior to arranged encounters with locals. Laos is in a unique situation when it comes to tourism because of its unspoiled natural environment and unexposed ethnic cultures. Here customs and ceremonies are meaningful, and rural hospitality is genuine. By carefully regulating tourism, Laos hopes to keep it that way.

THE LAND

Laos stretches a thousand km from China to Cambodia, with the Mekong forming its westerly border with Thailand and Burma and the Annamite Range dividing it from Vietnam. From east to west, the country ranges from 150 to 500 km in width; total land area is 236,800 square km. Laos is about half the size of Thailand, or two-thirds the size of Vietnam, and is 30% larger than Cambodia. The principal geographical features are mountains and the Mekong: tributaries of the river rise in the mountains and flow through deep valleys. Over 75% of the country is rugged and mountainous.

In the north, heavily forested mountain ranges and plateaus are intersected by deep valleys. The nation's highest mountain, Mount Phu Bia (2,850 meters), lies at the edge of the Xieng Khuang Plateau, which includes the Plain of Jars. Running along the eastern border of Laos is the rugged Annamite Range, with peaks ranging 1,600 to 2,700 meters in elevation. In the center of the range is the Khammuan Plateau, with sparsely forested limestone terraces, gorges, and grottoes. Farther south is the basalt-covered 10,000-square-km Bolovens Plateau, rising over 1,200 meters. In this area

LAOS IN BRIEF

The Land: Laos has an area of 236,800 square km. It is landlocked, sharing borders with Thailand, Cambodia, Vietnam, Myanmar (Burma), and China. The Mekong meanders some 1,800 km through Laos, forming the major part of its borders with Burma and Thailand; to the east, the Annamite Range separates Laos from Vietnam. Laos is mostly mountainous, especially to the north and east, with villagers living in isolated valleys.

Climate: Hot and humid, tropical and temperate, with monsoon activity from May to October and a cooler dry season from November to February—the best time to visit. February to May is the hot dry season, with occasional rain.

People: With 4.8 million inhabitants living in an area the size of Britain, Laos is the most sparsely populated country in Asia, with a scant 17 people per square km. About 80% of the population is rural—mostly hilltribe groups and riverine farmers. Vientiane, the capital, has a population of only 150,000. Population estimates for other towns are hard to come by because of refugee exoduses and returns. Three "urban" centers are Luang Prabang, Savannakhet, and Pakse—each with no more than 50,000 people.

Language: Lao is a tonal language of the Thai language family. The Vientiane dialect is the standard. Because of exposure to Thai media, many Laotians can understand Thai, but the reverse may not be true. Other languages spoken in Laos include French, English, Chinese, Vietnamese, and Russian. The literacy rate is estimated at only 50%.

Religion: Theravada Buddhism suffered severe setbacks under the Pathet Lao but is now making a comeback as the country's main faith. The hilltribe groups follow shamanist practices and animist beliefs. A small number of Laotians are Protestant or Catholic, perhaps 80,000, mainly living in the towns. No figures are available for those professing no religion.

Government: The Lao People's Revolutionary Party is directed by the Party Congress, which meets every four or five years to elect party leaders and discuss policy.

National Flag: A white circle centered on a blue stripe, sandwiched between two horizontal red stripes.

Economy: Major industry includes timber, garments and textiles, beer, detergent powder, and agriculture, with rice, maize, tobacco, sugarcane, coffee, and cotton the major crops. Opium production is a major source of foreign exchange. Major exports are garments and textiles, timber, and electricity. There is tremendous potential in energy production, as the Mekong has yet to be fully tapped. Per capita income is around $230. The currency unit is the kip; 720 kip=US$1.

Festivals: Laos is home to an unwieldy number of holidays and festivals. The biggest festival is Pimai or Lao New Year in April—with three official days of holidays. This is followed in May by the Rocket Festival. The Water Festival, with longboat racing, marks the end of the rainy season in October.

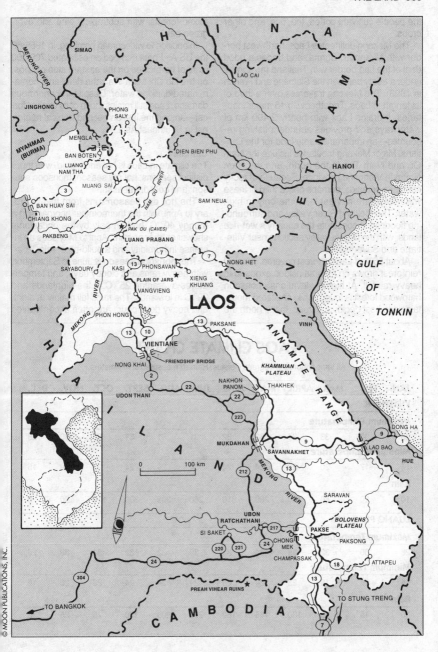

the people cultivate coffee, tea, rice, and other crops.

The Mekong delineates Laos' northwest border with Myanmar (Burma) and traces a good deal of the Lao border with Thailand (as agreed under a treaty between the Siamese and French in 1893). The Mekong traverses over a third of its length in Laos. Together with 15 major tributaries, it drains Laos with nearly 2,400 km of waterways and provides abundant fishing resources—an important staple food for the Laotians. Major Mekong tributaries include the Nam Ou and Nam Tha in the north, and the Nam Ngum in Vientiane Province. Because of rocky stretches or rapids, perhaps only a third of these waterways are navigable, some only in high water. The Mekong River Valley and surrounding floodplains constitute the country's wet-rice lands, with the largest valley sections near Vientiane and Savannakhet.

About 55% of Laos is forest covered. Tropical rainforest grows on mountainsides exposed to heavy rainfall. At higher elevations, monsoon hardwood forest is found, while sheltered mountainsides host deciduous trees. In the north are mixed forests, with subtropical pine and evergreen oak.

In addition to widespread bombing, in 1965-66 the US Air Force dumped an estimated 700,000 liters of herbicides on the eastern side of Laos, on the Ho Chi Minh Trail; the defoliants contaminated drinking water. Despite the enormous damage, Laos still retains much of its original forest—among the last untouched tropical rainforest in Southeast Asia.

Climate

The climate in Laos is hot and humid, with three distinct seasons: hot dry season, monsoon season, and cool dry season.

The **hot dry season** runs from mid-February to April, with the thermometer approaching a muggy 40° C, broken only by the occasional shower or "mango rain." April to May sees an increase in humidity and a build-up of rain.

The **monsoon season** is June to September, with heavy rains and cloudy days, and temperatures averaging 25° C in the highlands and 29° C in lowlands. The rains fall mainly at night, and heavy downpours are often accompanied

LAOS CLIMATE CHART

All temperatures in degrees Celsius. Rainfall measured in millimeters.

JAN.	FEB.	MAR.	APRIL	MAY	JUNE	JULY	AUG.	SEPT.	OCT.	NOV.	DEC.
VIENTIANE											
Maximum Temperature											
28	30	33	34	33	32	31	31	31	30	30	28
Minimum Temperature											
14	17	20	23	24	24	24	24	24	22	19	15
Rain											
10	20	40	100	260	310	260	305	300	110	20	5
LUANG PRABANG											
Maximum Temperature											
28	30	32	39	34	34	32	32	32	31	30	29
Minimum Temperature											
14	16	19	23	24	25	24	24	24	23	20	16
Rain											
10	15	25	100	165	150	235	300	170	75	25	10

by storms. Laos experiences an average of three storms per week in May and June and two per week from July through September. Humidity is high in this season. Rivers run high, roads turn to mud, and there's often flooding. By mid-October the rain eases off. Rainfall in Laos varies with location and elevation: Vientiane and Savannakhet get 1,500-2,000 mm of rainfall a year, while Luang Prabang and Xieng Khuang see 1,000-1,500 mm a year. The mountains of the southeast, bordering Vietnam, may receive over 3,000 mm.

November to February, the **cool dry season,** is the best time to visit. In November there's reduced humidity; temperatures may dip as low as 15° C in December and January, and down to freezing in mountain areas like the Xieng Khuang Plateau or the Bolovens Plateau.

FLORA AND FAUNA

Vegetation in Laos is a rich mix of tropical and subtropical, with an abundance of flowering species such as orchids. Monsoon forests consist of several layers: towering up to 30 meters are hardwoods such as teak or Asian rosewood; below is grass and bamboo undergrowth, especially along riverbanks. A great variety of fruit trees and tropical palms are found in Laos; on plateau areas, grassy savannah is the main feature.

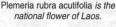

Plemeria rubra acutifolia is the national flower of Laos.

With such copious forest cover and a sparse human population, Laos has plentiful wildlife. There are both resident and migrating birds, thought to number up to 500 species, including pheasants, partridges, ducks, songbirds, and hawks. The reptile population includes king cobras, banded kraits, vipers, lizards, and crocodiles. Larger mammals include wildcats, bears, leopards, tigers, wild cattle, macaques, gibbons, and flying squirrels. Exotic Laotian species include the pangolin, a kind of scaly creature that feeds on ants and termites; several species of civet, a nocturnal possumlike creature; pygmy slow loris, a nocturnal primate with large eyes and thickly furred body; lesser panda; snub-nosed langur; and raccoon dog.

For centuries, wild Asiatic elephants have been caught and domesticated for use in warfare, carrying freight, and hauling logs. For many years Lao hunters and even forestry officials have used antlers taken from the Vu Quang ox and the giant muntjac as hatracks or parts of ceremonial altars—oblivious to the fact these trophies represented species unknown to science. It was only in 1992 that British and Laotian field-workers under contract to New York's Wildlife Conservation Society managed to take blood samples from a live specimen of a giant muntjac in a menagerie owned by a Lao military group; it is said to be double the weight of the previously known species of muntjac.

Another giant found in Laos is an aquatic one—the *pla buk,* or giant catfish. This monster of the Mekong grows up to three meters long, can weigh up to 300 kg, and takes between six and 12 years to attain full

---

WILDLIFE TRAFFIC

The brisk trade in rare species from Laos continues, with most animals going to Thailand, China, and South Korea—countries where there's a high demand for certain species for the cookpot and for use in traditional medicine.

Laos is not a signatory to the UN Convention on International Trade in Endangered Species (CITES). The exact size of the trade in rare and endangered species in Laos is hard to gauge, but in Saravan in the nation's center is a large wildlife market with monitor lizards, pythons, mynah birds, red leaf monkeys, and other species from the Bolovens Plateau. Some species are on the CITES endangered list. Saravan is a great staging point on the smuggling route to Bangkok.

size. The world's biggest scaleless freshwater fish is found only in the Mekong River. Little is known about its life cycle. The females are said to live in Cambodia's great lake, Tonle Sap, swimming north to meet male fish in Dali Lake in China's Yunnan Province. The flesh is considered a delicacy in Laos and Thailand; fishermen trap the catfish in Bokeo Province from April to June as it heads for spawning grounds in China. Dam construction in southwest China and blasting of rapids to clear the way for commercial navigation, combined with overfishing, have reduced the number of giant catfish to the endangered level. Another rare river species is the freshwater Irrawaddy dolphin, found in the southern Mekong bordering Cambodia. The dolphin is not captured for food or sport as it is considered a reincarnated human; however, the species is threatened by gillneting in Laos and explosives fishing in Cambodia. The Mekong is a biological gold mine— many species of Mekong fauna are still unknown to science.

HISTORY

For much of its history, Laos has been under the thumb of its neighbors—at various times the Cambodians, Burmese, Vietnamese, Chinese, and Siamese (Thais). The result is that Laos has experienced great difficulty in establishing a national identity.

The earliest inhabitants of Laos were migrants from southern China. From the 11th century onward, parts of Laos fell under the Khmer Empire, and later under Siamese influence from the Sukhothai dynasty. With the fall of Sukhothai in 1345, the first kingdom of Laos emerged under Fa Ngum, a Lao prince brought up in the court of Angkor Wat. As the Khmer Empire crumbled, Fa Ngum welded together a new empire, which he modestly christened "Lan Xang"—the Land of a Million Elephants. Lan Xang covered the whole of present-day Laos plus most of Issan (northeast Thailand). Fa Ngum declared himself king of the realm in 1353. Fa Ngum was unable to subdue the unruly highlanders of the northeast regions; these remained independent of Lan Xang rule.

Upon Fa Ngum's marriage to a Cambodian princess, the Khmer court gave the Lao king a sacred gold Buddha called Pra Bang. Fa Ngum made Buddhism the state religion, and Pra Bang became the protector of the Lao kingdom. Nobility pledged allegiance to the king before the statue. Named after Pra Bang was the city of Luang Prabang, the cradle of Lao culture and the center of the Lao state for the next 200 years.

Monarchs of Lan Xang

Fa Ngum's son Samsenthai who reigned 1373-1416, consolidated the royal administration, developing Luang Prabang as a trading and religious center. His death was followed by unrest under a swift succession of lackluster monarchs. Luang Prabang came under increasing threat from incursions by the Vietnamese and later the Burmese. In 1563, King Settathirat declared Vientiane the capital of Lan Xang, and built Wat Pra Keo to house the Emerald Buddha, a gift from the king of Ceylon, as a new talisman for the kingdom. Settathirat is revered as one of the great Lao kings because he protected the nation from foreign subjugation. When he disappeared in 1574 on a military campaign, the kingdom rapidly declined and was subject to Burmese invasion. There was a quick and lackluster succession of kings after Settathirat. King Souligna Vongsa, who ruled 1633-94, brought stability and peace back to the kingdom—a period regarded as Lan Xang's golden age.

Siamese Satellite

When Souligna Vongsa died in 1694 without an heir, the leadership of Lan Xang was contested, and the nation split into three kingdoms. The area around Vientiane was taken over by Souligna's nephew, supported by the Annamites from north Vietnam; Souligna's grandson controlled the area around Luang Prabang, while another prince controlled the southern kingdom of Champassak, with Thai backing. China, Burma, and Vietnam briefly held sway over these kingdoms; bands of Chinese marauders terrorized the north of the country.

The power of Lan Xang waned; gradually, the Thais extended their influence over most of Laos until it became a Siamese satellite state. In the 1820s Vientiane's King Anou rebelled against

Siamese interference and attacked the Thais. The Thai response was to sack Vientiane in 1827, razing most of the city.

Land of the Lotus-Eaters

In the late 19th century the king of Siam, seeking to keep Thailand free of foreign domination, ceded a large tract of territory—equivalent of what is now Laos and Cambodia combined—to the French. A series of treaties released more Lao territories to the French between 1893 and 1907. Former Lao territories were thus united again, although the three kingdoms founded in the late 17th century remained in existence, and tribal princes were able to increase their power by collaborating with the French. The French gave the new protectorate the name Laos, from *les Laos,* the plural term for the people of Laos.

Laos was a low-key French protectorate, known as the land of the lotus-eaters, where an indolent lifestyle prevailed. It was too mountainous for plantations, there was little in the way of mining, and the Mekong was not suitable for commercial navigation. The French built very few roads—the main colonial route constructed was from Luang Prabang through Vientiane to Savannakhet and the Cambodian frontier. The French built no higher-education facilities; some half-hearted attempts were made to cultivate rubber and coffee, but the main export under the French was opium. Only a few hundred French resided in Laos. They adopted a dissolute lifestyle with Lao or Annamite consorts, and left the running of the place to Vietnamese civil servants. The king was allowed to remain in Luang Prabang, trade was left to resident Vietnamese and Chinese, and the Lao carried on farming as they had for hundreds of years.

During the colonial period, administration, health care, and education hardly made any impact or progress at all. The only significant change for ordinary folk was the presence of obnoxious tax collectors, a frequent cause of uprisings. In the lowlands, revolts were quickly put down, but in the highlands of Xieng Khuang and the Bolovens Plateau the French had trouble deploying their heavy weaponry. Sometimes a remission of taxes led to pacification.

The 50-year French sojourn in Laos came to an abrupt end in March 1945, when the Japanese took control of the government and interned the Vichy French. With the surrender of Japan in August that year, the Lao Issara (Free Laos) movement declared liberation from the French in September and set about establishing an alternative government. The Lao Issara leader was Prince Phetsarath, a nephew of the king. Other key players in the Lao Issara were his half-brothers, Prince Souvanna Phouma and Prince Souphanouvong.

King Sisavang Vong sided with the French, and the movement for Lao independence was crushed, causing Prince Phetsarath and Prince Souvanna Phouma to flee to Thailand. King Sisavang Vong was crowned constitutional monarch of all Laos in 1946. Meanwhile, the Lao Issara dissolved, and a splinter group called the Pathet Lao formed a new resistance group based in northeast Laos. The Pathet Lao were led by Prince Souphanouvong and backed by the Vietminh of North Vietnam. Prince Souvanna Phouma returned to Vientiane and joined the newly formed Royal Lao Government.

The French granted full sovereignty to Laos in 1953, but the Pathet Lao regarded the royalist government as Western-dominated. When in 1954 the French made a last stand at Dien Bien Phu it ended badly, with a stunning defeat. The weary French started a withdrawal from Indochina; at this point, the US started supplying the Royal Lao Government with arms.

Civil War Skirmishes

The US-backed Royal Lao Government ruled over a divided country from 1951 to 1954. The Geneva Conference of July 1954 granted full independence to Laos but did not settle the issue of who would rule. Prince Souvanna Phouma, a neutralist, operated from Vientiane; in the south, the right-wing pro-US Prince Boun Oum of Champassak dominated the Pakse area. In the far north Prince Souphanouvong led the leftist resistance movement the Pathet Lao, drawing support from North Vietnam.

In 1959 the Lao king died and was succeeded by his son, Sisavang Vatthana. Over the next few years there were a number of unsuccessful attempts to set up a coalition government to bring royalists and communists together. Souvanna Phouma became Prime Minister in 1956 and tried to integrate his half-brother's Pathet Lao forces into a coalition government. That government was toppled in 1958. Fighting broke out between the Royal Lao Army and the Pathet Lao in 1960; in 1961, a neutral independent government was set up under Prince Souvanna Phouma, based in Vientiane. A second attempt at a coalition government floundered in 1962 due to the widening war in Vietnam. The neutralists later joined forces with the Pathet Lao to oppose forces backed by the US and Thailand.

The Dirty War

For the next decade, Laos was plagued by civil war, coups, countercoups, and chaos, and was dragged headlong into the Vietnam War. Laos became a pawn of the superpowers, with Hmong tribesmen trained by CIA agents, Thai mercenaries fighting for the Royal Lao government, and the Pathet Lao receiving help from the Chinese, the Russians, and the Vietminh.

During the Vietnam War, Laos was effectively partitioned into four spheres of influence: the Chinese in the north, the Vietnamese along the Ho Chi Minh Trail in the east, the Thais in western areas controlled by the US-backed Royal Lao Government, and the Khmer Rouge operating from parts of the south. Because of the Ho Chi Minh Trail, Laos was subjected to saturation bombing by aerial raids launched from Thailand and from within Laos. In this undeclared dirty war, the tonnage of bombs dropped by US bombers on the northern Lao provinces of Xieng Khuang, Hua Pham, and Phong Saly between 1964 and 1973 exceeded the entire tonnage dropped over Europe by all sides during WW II. It is estimated that US forces flew almost 600,000 sorties—the equivalent of one bombing run every eight minutes around the clock for nine years. This air assault was shrouded in secrecy, since under the terms of the Geneva Accord of 1962 no foreign personnel were supposed to operate on Laotian territory. The Vietminh and the Chinese also violated Laos' neutrality with infantry divisions deployed in the north. In the early days of the bombing, American pilots dressed in civilian clothing flew old planes with Royal Lao markings; Thai and Hmong pilots were also trained to fly missions.

So confusing did the number of Laotian coups become that the Americans were unsure which Phoumi, Phuouma, Phoui, Souvanna, or Souvanou was in power at any given time. American

journalist Malcolm Browne described this bewildering era thus:

Laos was as improbable as the Looking Glass world ruled by the Red Queen, the White Queen and Alice. Its towns and trackless jungles swarmed with guerrillas, communist agents, Special Forces troopers, armed tribesmen, opium growers, an international corps of mercenaries and sundry camp followers. Vientiane was awash with the dollars pouring in with the foreigners. The Chinese-owned gold shops along Samsentai Street did a booming business in twenty-four-karat gold bracelets, each weighing five ounces or more. Customers included pilots of the CIA's Air America, French military advisers, Belgian mercenaries, spooks, assassins and journalists. Foreigners bought gold bracelets on the theory that if they were shot down or wounded, they could pay for help from tribesmen with gold, the only currency universally respected in Laos.

Pathet Lao Victory

In 1973, as the US began a strategic withdrawal from Vietnam, the Pathet Lao gained the upper hand, controlling most of the country's provinces. In 1975, with the fall of Saigon and Phnom Penh, opposition to the Pathet Lao crumbled. The Pathet Lao took Pakse, Champassak, Savannakhet, and finally Vientiane without opposition, establishing the Lao People's Democratic Republic (Lao PDR).

Refugees and Re-education

As Vientiane fell to the Pathet Lao, the country's political and professional elite fled across the Mekong into Thailand, knowing that 30 years of struggle by the Pathet Lao would not end without retribution. Tempered by 30 years of harsh existence in the remote limestone caves of the north, the new Laotian leadership brought a revolutionary puritanism that was unparalleled. Traditional religious festivals were frowned upon, Buddhist practices were discouraged, freedom of movement was curtailed, personal dress and lifestyle were monitored, and all signs of decadent bourgeois culture—rock music, dancing, Western fashion—were roundly condemned.

A combination of witch-hunts and harsh economic conditions resulted in an exodus of refugees. Getting out of Laos is simply a matter of crossing the Mekong—large numbers of Lao refugees drifted into northeast Thailand, and over 350,000 Laotians settled abroad. In the Lao PDR, an estimated 30,000 people were imprisoned for "political crimes," and a further 40,000 were sent to "re-education camps," in-

cluding the last king of Laos. The Lao PDR was closed to Westerners, and it established relations with Russia and Vietnam; some 50,000 Vietnamese troops were stationed in the country.

With the 1988 departure of the Vietnamese, Laotian policy changed course: the Lao PDR has closed its re-education camps, released surviving political prisoners, opened again to the West, and invited compatriots who fled across the Mekong to return.The year 1991 ushered in a period of "new thinking" *(chitanakan mai)*. Regulations eased, though state-controlled radio and television still rail against Thai rock music and decadent Western fashion.

GOVERNMENT

Since 1975, the Lao People's Revolutionary Party (LPRP) has been the sole party in power. Until his death in 1992, the most influential party figure was President Kaysone Phomvihan, a Pathet Lao leader who held several key LPRP posts. After his death, leadership passed to President Nouhak Phoumsavan and Prime Minister Khamtay Siphandone.

Phomvihan was a comrade of Ho Chi Minh, and the LPRP government is similar in structure to that of the Socialist Republic of Vietnam—although the Marxist-Leninist base of the LPRP has undergone some curious revisions in the 1990s. Every four or five years, the LPRP convenes a congress to dictate the party's path. At the March 1991 Fifth Congress the hammer and sickle were removed from the state emblem, and the state motto was changed from "Peace, Independence, Unity and Socialism" to "Peace, Independence, Democracy, Unity and Prosperity." For "Prosperity" read "Capitalism"—free enterprise through market reforms is where the country is heading. So far "Democracy" refers only to elections within a one-party system, as when Lao citizens elect members of the Supreme People's Assembly. Advocates of multiparty democracy are dealt with harshly in Laos, drawing stiff prison sentences—the LPRP brooks no criticism.

The first official Laotian constitution was adopted in 1991, and it is only in the last few years that the government has drafted and adopted codes for common law, penal law, and foreign investment law.

THE RED PRINCE

Prince Souphanouvong was born in Luang Prabang as the 20th son of Prince Boun Khong, viceroy of the French protectorate, and a commoner concubine. Among his half-brothers were Prince Boun Oum and Prince Souvanna Phouma. Souphanouvong attended the exclusive Lycée Albert Serraut in Hanoi, obtaining a civil engineering degree from the Sorbonne in Paris in 1937. He returned to Laos and in 1945 joined the Lao Issara (Free Laos) movement against the French. In 1949 he was expelled from Laos because of his ties to Ho Chi Minh, and he helped form the Pathet Lao in 1950. Pathet Lao means "Land of the Lao." The Pathet Lao are a mysterious lot, their story cloaked in myth rather than hard facts.

When Laos gained independence in 1954, Souphanouvong joined the first coalition government as the Pathet Lao leader; in 1958 that government was toppled, and he was imprisoned for 15 months. Upon his release he rallied the Marxist Pathet Lao to fight US-backed royalist forces. Souphanouvong was known as "the Red Prince"; the guerrilla group was known for its extreme brutality. After the Pathet Lao takeover in 1975, Souphanouvong was named to the largely ceremonial post of president, which he held until 1986. He died in January 1995, at the age of 86—the last of the communist old guard.

Administration

Laos is divided into 16 provinces, plus the independent prefecture of Vientiane. The provinces are divided into regions *(muang)*, districts *(tas-seng)*, and villages *(ban)*. Provinces, towns, and villages are administered by People's Revolutionary Committees that receive orders from the Central Committee of the LPRP.

ECONOMY

Eighty percent of Laotians are subsistence farmers, toiling away on soil that rarely produces more than one crop a year. And not always a successful crop—Laos periodically experiences rice shortages.

To its credit, Laos was the first of the three Indochinese nations to experiment with market reforms, which were remarkably successful in curbing runaway inflation and restoring stability in the 1980s. After the complete withdrawal of Soviet aid in the 1990s, the Laotion economy has been propped up by foreign aid—particularly from Japan. The full gamut of NGOs and UN agencies is in evidence in Vientiane. The 1991 constitution promotes the development of a free-market economy. Laos is opening up, forging new links with its powerful neighbors. Thawed relations with Thailand and China have led to a significant trade boost. The Lao government is committed to a policy of attracting investors, even as it's adept at strangling them in red tape.

Thailand is easily the largest foreign investor in Laos, followed by France, Australia, the US, Taiwan, Hong Kong, China, and Vietnam. Laos is especially vulnerable to its richer neighbors. Having shaken off the Vietnamese, who stationed troops in the country until 1988, Laos is not keen on becoming a Thai province either, and thus is courting investment and economic help from elsewhere—particularly China. Vietnam is uneasy about the prospect of Chinese trade in Laos, since these trade links also involve military agreements. The Chinese have established several signal-intelligence stations near Champassak in southern Laos capable of listening in on Vietnamese Army units. And in

---

LIFE AFTER THE BRIDGE

The most pressing problem in Laos is weak infrastructure. In April 1994 the Friendship Bridge, spanning the Mekong near Vientiane, linked Thailand and Laos for the first time. The $28-million bridge was funded by the Australian government: the opening ceremony brought together the King of Thailand, Thai Prime Minister Chuan Leekpai, Australian Prime Minister Paul Keating, and Lao Prime Minister Khamtay Siphandone. Keating presented the span to Thailand and Laos, and King Bhumibol became the first Thai monarch to stroll across the Mekong.

The 1.2-km bridge will greatly impact the economy and society of Laos in trade and tourism. Laos hopes the impact will be positive, though critics say the bridge could lead to Thai exploitation of the nation's natural resources, as well as increased smuggling and pollution. Says one Lao diplomat, "My gut feeling is that Laos is shaking hands with the big bad wolf." Or at least a hungry tiger. Laos finds itself caught in a buffer zone between its powerful neighbors.

With the normalization of relations between Thailand, Laos, Vietnam, and China, the Friendship Bridge paves the way for a Pan-Asian highway from Singapore to Beijing. There is a place on the span for a railway, so Singapore could eventually be linked by rail through Thailand and Laos to Vietnam and China, and ultimately, Europe. For the moment, the bridge promotes truck trade between Thailand, Laos, and China's Yunnan Province.

Road transport in Laos is abysmal: much of the terrain is mountainous, and the rainy season, which prevails from May to September, swiftly turns the dirt roads into muck—a great hindrance to communications in a country the size of Britain.

The Friendship Bridge provides Laos with access to the port of Bangkok, though Laos is looking towards coastal Vietnam as well. In 1994 a land crossing opened from southern Laos into Vietnam. From the border it's a day's drive into Danang, central Vietnam's major seaport.

THE OPIUM TRADE

Laos is the world's third largest producer of opium. The Golden Triangle, which Laos shares with Burma and Thailand, provides 60% of the world's heroin supply. Opium growing is associated with the hilltribes that descended from southern China, particularly the Hmong and Mien. The opium poppy is grown all over northern Laos, on steep slopes (1,000 to 2,000 meters) in poor soil, and cash returns are high. Some hilltribes use opium in traditional medicine. There is significant opium addiction in Phong Saly, Hua Phan, Luang Prabang, and Xieng Khuang Provinces. Most opium in Laos is smoked—nearly all refined opium is earmarked for export.

The opium poppy, *Papaver somniferum,* is one of more than 250 species of poppy. When the petals fall, the seed pod is sliced to release a milk-white juice that dries to a brown fudge that can be stored for years without loss of potency. The brown substance can be refined into heroin for easier transport—there are thought to be hidden labs in the north of Laos that handle this process. Opium is grown in 10 Laotian provinces; marijuana is planted in provinces along the Mekong River. The annual opium yield in Laos is upwards of 200 tons. Some is used locally by hilltribe addicts; the rest is smuggled through to Thailand or China. Opium and heroin are used for bartering in Thai consumer goods. In 1994, Laos seized 53 kg of heroin, 292 kg of opium, and 9,402 kg of marijuana, according to an official report by the National Commission for Drug Control.

Most of the heroin was intercepted at Vientiane's Wattay Airport, the cannabis in Savannakhet Province. Laotian output is still small compared to that of Burma, where annual opium production is estimated at over 2,200 tons.

The opium trade was once legal in Laos. The practice of growing opium was forced upon the Hmong by the French government of Indochina, which secretly sold opium to Marseilles gangsters to finance the war against the Vietminh. Later the CIA became involved in the trade, using the profits to finance US operations in Indochina.

Opium dens were permitted until the Pathet Lao takeover in 1975. These were small places, similar to a country pub, where patrons would drop by for a few pipes. In 1975, Vientiane featured 60 licensed dens, and a lot more unlicensed houses. There is some evidence that even after 1975, Lao Army elements and provincial officials continued a clandestine role in opium and heroin production to ameliorate the disastrous financial situation of the late 1970s and 1980s.

In 1990, Laos agreed to cooperate with the US and UN in narcotics control. The main thrust of the program is to substitute cash crops like coffee or mulberry trees for opium poppies. There have been arrests of drug traffickers, but in the unruly Golden Triangle enforcement is difficult. The Counter-Narcotics Unit, Laos' enforcement agency, was set up in 1992. It employs only 26 officials, and relies heavily on foreign support.

1993 China delivered several thousand tons of military hardware to Laos.

With a shared language and culture, the Laotians find it easy to do business with the Thais. Thailand, which logged its own teak forests out of existence, is now eyeing the tropical hardwood stands of Laos. Laotian forests contain teak, mahogany, and rosewood trees. Concerned about overcutting, the Lao government imposed a strict quota system, but this seems to have had little effect, and forest products still form a major portion of Lao exports. Few Laotian resources have been tapped. Gold, bauxite, and lignite deposits lure foreign investors; geological surveys indicate reserves of lead, zinc, coal, iron ore, and precious stones. Western companies are prospecting for oil and gas.

Tapping the Mekong

One of Laos' main exports could soon be energy generated by the mighty Mekong. So far Laos has tapped only 200 megawatts from hydroelectric projects—over 70% is sold to Thailand, accounting for 25% of the country's foreign exchange earnings. Thailand plans to buy at least half the hydropower from future projects, including a large plant at Thakhek. It is estimated the Mekong and its tributaries possess a hydropower potential of 18,000 megawatts in Laos alone.

When it runs high in the monsoon season, the murky Mekong is Laos' lifeline for the transportation of goods and passengers. In the north, small cargo boats ply the Mekong between Jinghong in southern China and the Laotian town of

Ban Huay Sai. Goods are then shipped to Thailand, or sent down the Mekong through Laos to Luang Prabang, Vientiane, and Savannakhet. Further south, rapids render stretches of the Mekong unnavigable.

When French adventurers Doudart de Lagrée and Francis Garnier tried to sail upriver from Cambodia into Laos on their 1866-68 Mekong Expedition, they came up against the crashing chain of cataracts known as Khone Falls. This discovery dashed the dreams of the French to use the Mekong as a trade route from Yunnan in China down to Saigon. A century later, however, the very obstacle that stymied the French may provide Laos with its greatest trade—the power of the river itself.

Most of the Mekong's enormous hydroelectric potential, it is calculated, lies within Laos. Power exports could well be Laos' salvation, as the country has virtually nothing else to generate foreign income. Laos finds it difficult to export timber or agricultural products, but would find it easy to export electricity to power-hungry Thailand. The Laotians could also export power to Burma, China, Cambodia, and Vietnam—Laos has already been dubbed the "battery" of Southeast Asia.

The source of the Mekong is the 5,000-meter Tibetan Plateau in China's Qinghai Province. For half of its 4,350-km length, the river runs through remote reaches of western China, then crosses into Laos. After China, Laos is the country that sees the most of the Mekong—Nam Khong (Mother of Waters), as the Mekong is known in Laos, courses some 1,800 km through the country, forming most of its border with Burma and Thailand. Leaving Laos, the Mekong moves through Cambodia before emptying into the sea in Vietnam. The Mekong is pretty much untamed: for its entire length, there is hardly any industrial build-up, and the river only passes one major city—Phnom Penh. The Mekong is presently only dammed at Manwan, north of Jinghong in China. Manwan Dam generates 1,500 megawatts of power for industry near Kunming; the Chinese plan to build eight more dams along the most turbulent sections of the river in Yunnan Province.

The Mekong Committee, a UN-sponsored development agency headquartered in Bangkok, was resurrected in the 1990s to monitor the Mekong. Current committee members are Laos, Thailand, Cambodia, and Vietnam, with China and Burma participating in some sessions. The committee is currently reviewing plans for four giant hydroelectric dams on the lower river. The first under consideration is the $2.8 billion project at Pa Mong, about 20 km upstream from Vientiane. The project is controversial; critics argue the dam would disrupt fish migration and displace some 50,000 villagers as its reservoir floods 600 square km of land. Half a dozen Laotian sites along the Mekong and its tributaries are being considered for hydroelectric plants; there are also plans to dynamite rapids in the Mekong to enable year-round navigation.

Altering the course of nature comes with a price. Dams will undoubtedly disrupt fauna migration patterns, thereby threatening the livelihood of people who live by fishing. Fish catches are already down in southern Laos due to dynamite fishing on the Cambodian side of the Mekong. Very little is known about life in the Mekong—it has only recently been discovered that the Mekong contains an astonishing migratory fauna, featuring, in some places, a complete change in fish species between the dry season and the wet.

THE PEOPLE

Laos is largely a nation of hilltribes. The Lao—the dominant ethnic group—form only half the population; the rest is a mosaic of over 60 hilltribe groups. Add to this ethnic stew a sprinkling of other Asians—resident Chinese, Vietnamese, Thais, and Khmers. The Chinese and Vietnamese live mainly in the towns, running restaurants or hotels, or retail and wholesale shops. The Vietnamese originally arrived with the French to serve in administrative posts. There are Indian and Khmer shopkeepers in the south of Laos.

The Lao

Also called the Lao Loum, or Low Lao, the Lao live in the Mekong River valley and its tributaries. These rice cultivators descended from southern China in the 6th and 7th centuries and are closely related to the Thais of northeastern Thailand. A large proportion—perhaps one-fifth—live in towns. Most follow Theravada Buddhism, but many also practice animism. The Lao are racially mixed; many have round, full faces with flat noses, but you also see narrow faces with long noses. Men wear long pants and open shirts. Women mostly wear a wrap-around skirt called a *sinh,* fastened with a silver belt, and blouses of cotton or silk. The traditional hairstyle for women is a bun on top of the head, decorated with flowers and jewelry.

Hilltribe Groups

Hilltribes make up a large part of the population and in certain areas outnumber the Lao. Hilltribes in Laos are usually identified

according to language, cultural practices, and favored geographic terrain. They fall into three broad groups—Lao Tai, Lao Theung, and Lao Sung—although there is overlapping.

Lao Tai: This group is closely associated with the ethnic Lao—in fact, in government statistics, the Lao Tai are included with the Lao Loum. The difference is that Lao Tai are more tribal and have retained animist beliefs. Subgroups are "color coded" and readily identifiable by their dress—White Tai, Black Tai, Red Tai.

Lao Theung: With 45 subgroups, the Lao Theung constitute the largest hilltribe contingent. They're also the poorest. The semi-nomadic Lao Theung are of Mon-Khmer origin and favor mountain slopes in northern and southern Laos, where they practice slash-and-burn agriculture. In the north are the Khamu; on the Bolovens Plateau dwell the Alak and Akha groups, while the Htin live in Sayaboury.

Lao Sung: The Lao Sung, or High Lao, favor the high mountains of the north. They migrated from southern China, Tibet, and Burma. Main groups are the animist Hmong (Meo) and Yao (Mien). They belong to the Austro-Asiatic language family, through some linguists place them in the Sino-Tibetan family. The Hmong are divided into Black, Red, White, and Striped, distinguished by their clothing. Most practice shifting cultivation, although some are settled and grow mountain rice, sugarcane, maize, tapioca, and yams. Their main cash crop is opium. The Lao Sung are animists who worship their ancestors.

BOB RACE

THE HARRIED HMONG

The word "Hmong" was coined in the mid-1970s by a French-educated Hmong tribesman. It means "mankind" in the Hmong language. Prior to this, the tribal group was known as the "Meo," which derives from Man Meo (Wild Cat), a name the French used to describe the agility of these high-mountain people. To the Hmong, however, this term has come to mean "savage" and is considered derogatory.

The Chinese developed an intense disliking for this warrior tribe and drove them out of southwest China in the 19th century, forcing them into Laos. The Hmong practice slash-and-burn agriculture, growing rice and maize; they raise animals and hunt and forage to supplement their diet. Their main cash crop is opium. Refined opium is transported on horseback to markets in Thailand. Hmong embroidery is also exported to Thai markets for sale to tourists.

The French recruited the Hmong to help fight the Vietnamese communists. Under General Vang Pao, some 30,000 Hmong mercenaries were recruited and paid by the CIA to fight the Pathet Lao. Illiterate Hmong villagers were even trained to fly US T-28 fighter bombers. It is said locals in remote villages would carefully examine the undercarriages of these contraptions to determine their sex.

Up to 100,000 Hmong perished during the Laotian civil wars, and even after 1975 the Pathet Lao government occasionally conducted mop-up operations to flush out the Hmong. The new government vigorously attempted to reduce slash-and-burn agriculture and resettle the unruly Hmong at lower elevations. The Hmong resented this infringement, as well as their backward status—they had, and have, little access to adequate educational and medical services.

In 1975, when it became clear the Pathet Lao would win the war, Hmong General Vang Pao and 3,000 of his closest supporters were airlifted to Thailand and eventually resettled in the US. After two years on a ranch in Montana, Vang Pao moved to California's Central Valley, which has the largest concentration of expatriate Hmong in the world. Some 200,000 Hmong now live in the US and other Western countries. Many have not adapted well to life in the West. The Hmong seem to fare better in Thailand, although the Thais want to close the refugee camps and repatriate Hmong refugees to Laos under UN auspices.

Hmong refugees in camps along the Thai border have been a headache for the Lao government; the camps have been used as bases for mounting rebel attacks on Lao territory. General Vang Pao, who fled to the US, is said to fund and direct Hmong insurgent efforts. Confusion abounds on the size of the rebel forces on the border, with estimates varying from 800 to 8,000 troops. A myriad of organizations claim to represent the resistance, including the Free Democratic Lao National Salvation Force, the Free Lao National Liberation Movement, the Lao United Independent Front, the Chao Fa (Soldiers of the Clouds), and the Movement for Democracy in Laos.

Though the resistance is thought to be weak, there are pockets where Hmong rebels are active. One such area is a mountainous zone straddling the provinces of Vientiane, Luang Prabang, and Xieng Khuang. In 1993, in a pitched battle in Xieng Khuang Province, more than 100 rebels and 50 government soldiers were killed.

RELIGION

THERAVADA BUDDHISM

The precepts of Buddhism were devised by Siddhartha Gautama, born around 560 BC in north India. After six years of meditation, Gautama became the Buddha, or "the enlightened one"; he spent the latter half of his life traveling and preaching.

The main school of Buddhism in Laos is Theravada Buddhism, a faith shared with Buddhists in Thailand, Burma, and Cambodia. Although Theravada Buddhism was probably introduced to Laos more than 600 years ago, it wasn't until the 17th century that Buddhism was taught in Lao schools.

Prior to 1975, Buddhism in Laos was divided into two sects, Mahanikai and Thammayut. The Thammayut sect, associated with Thai royalty, was banned after the 1975 Pathet Lao takeover, together with all Buddhist literature written in Thai. Buddhism was banned as a primary school subject. Since 1989 things have eased up for Buddhists in Laos, and the number of monks has increased. There is now only one official sect, the Lao Sangha (Song Lao). But the curriculum is somewhat different—Marxist doctrine is part of monastic training under the Department of Religious Affairs.

The ultimate goal of Buddhism is the attainment of nirvana, or the cessation of suffering. The Lao believe that on the path to nirvana are successive rebirths or reincarnations. Many Buddhist practices in Laos hinge on accruing merit, or doing good deeds—by following the right path in this life, it is believed a person will be able to carry over karma into the next life. Karma is cause and effect—good deeds have good effects, bad deeds have bad effects. Making donations to temples is a common way of accruing merit. Women accrue merit by giving food to monks who go around with alms bowls in the morning. By becoming a monk—for a week, a month, three months—young men can accrue merit for not only themselves, but also their families. Monks renounce worldly pursuits, leading simple lives devoted to study and meditation.

Iconography

Creating artwork for temples, or funding it, is considered meritorious. Although Buddha declined to countenance images of himself during his lifetime, Buddha statues now abound in temples. Laypeople demanded some sort of physical presence for worship, something to focus on. In Lao sculpture and art, Buddha is usually painted or sculpted to conform with a Pali system of physical features, such as a beaklike nose, long earlobes, and tightly curled hair.

There are specific poses for Buddhas and a variety of hand gestures, known as *mudras*, that illustrate key events in Buddha's life. A seated Buddha, for example, indicates a meditation pose, while a reclining Buddha represents Buddha's entrance into nirvana at the moment of his physical death. Two distinctive Lao *mudras*

Buddha statue in the attitude of Calling for Rain

are the Calling for Rain posture (a standing Buddha with long arms hanging straight down, palms inward), and the Contemplating the Bodhi Tree attitude (standing with arms crossed in front of the body), a reference to the large tree under which Buddha meditated before attaining enlightenment.

SHAMANISM

The Lao tend to mix Buddhist, animist, and Brahman practices. Hilltribes in Laos are primarily animist. Officially, under the communist government, animism is banned, but in practice, worship of *phi,* or spirits, continues. The main image worshipped at Vientiane's Wat Simuang is the city pillar—the guardian spirit of the city. Animist worship has found its way into a number of Lao ceremonies. A common one is the *baci,* where strings representing the guardian spirits of body organs are tied round the wrists of guests of honor. For a description, see "Festivals and Holidays" in the On the Road chapter.

Hilltribes believe that everything—from mountains to opium poppies—has a spirit or *phi.* Some spirits are bad, some are good. To counter sickness and catastrophe, the *phi* must be placated. The village shaman plays an important role, capable of exorcising bad *phi* from his patients. Animal sacrifices to appease *phi* are common among hilltribe groups.

CUSTOMS AND CONDUCT

Temple Manners

In a predominantly Buddhist society, Buddhist monks and statues are treated with great respect. Entering a temple requires appropriate dress (cover arms and legs, wear clean clothes) and removal of shoes and hats. Monks are not supposed to touch a woman—if a woman must hand something to a monk, she should place it on a table for the monk to pick up, or hand it over via a male. Women should not attempt to shake hands with a monk, or sit beside him.

Body Language

The head is high; the feet are low. The head is considered sacred in Laos: do not touch a Lao on the head. The feet are considered lowly—do not point your feet at a Lao person or a temple altar. If sitting on the temple floor, do not cross your legs. Either kneel, or tuck your legs under yourself. Do not pass food overhead, stand over a Lao person, or step over people seated on the floor to get past them. When entering a family house, remove your shoes; do not pat children on the head, and do not point your feet at anyone. Pointing or beckoning with the index finger is considered rude. It is considered extremely bad form to lose your cool in Laos. Buddhists greatly admire the "cool heart," restraining strong emotions and practicing moderation in all things.

Although Lao businesspeople shake hands, the traditional form of greeting is the *wai,* a prayer-like gesture with a slight bow of the head. There are various degrees of *wai,* and foreigners are not expected to know all the nuances—a smile and a nod are acceptable. The Lao commonly use the first name, not the family name, when addressing each other.

Prostitution is a serious offense in Laos; women are usually treated with great respect. Lao women dress modestly, covering the shoulders and thighs. Foreign women should likewise to avoid giving offense.

Taboo Shots

Ask permission before photographing anyone within temple grounds. Avoid photographing or videotaping official functions. Some areas, such as Nam Ngum Dam, are of military importance, and no photos are permitted.

ON THE ROAD

From 1975 to 1989, Laos was largely closed to tourism. In 1994 an estimated 150,000 tourists visited Laos, a 50% increase over the year before. Almost half the arrivals were international visitors, the rest mostly Thais and Chinese. Laos is not prepared for any great expansion in tourism—there are few hotels and little infrastructure for travelers in the way of service personnel, guides, and so on. The 1994 liberalization of travel regulations has made the country more accessible to individual travelers.

Laos has a stable political situation, and there are no gun-waving guards or militia about the place. There are, however, residual insurgency problems, and certain roads are not considered safe because of bandits and Hmong rebel groups. In May 1994, a convoy of Ministry of Agriculture trucks carrying diesel fuel to Xieng Khuang Province was ambushed: six people were killed, including an Australian. The attack was the first involving the death of a foreigner since 1981. In December 1994, four Laotian staff from the UN Drug Control Program were killed when assailants opened fire on their car with machine guns and rocket-propelled grenades near the town of Kasi.

Tourism is a Pandora's box for Laos—it can generate desperately needed foreign exchange, but can devastate the fragile Lao culture. Laos looks nervously at what happened in neighboring Thailand, where rampant tourist development created severe social problems and pollution. Luang Prabang, with a population of only 25,000, could easily be inundated by tourists. The town may find itself in a situation similar to Thailand's Chiang Mai, not far across the Mekong. While Chiang Mai farmers increased their income by selling food and handicrafts to tourists, selling food soon led to selling drugs and the quality of handicrafts began to deteriorate. Dance events were performed purely for tourists, out of sync with the Buddhist calendar and therefore meaningless. Competition for tourist dollars diminished rural trust and turned a self-reliant society into a begging culture. Farmers became lazy—they didn't want to return to the fields to plant rice. Some gave up farming and migrated to the cities, accelerating problems there.

Besides the social problems that come with tourism, protecting the environment and historic sites are key concerns. Thus, the Lao national tourism authority prefers working with tour operators and tour groups rather than individual travelers. Tourism in Laos is presently directed towards group tours that have the least impact on locals—they stay for only a short period and spend a lot of money. With controlled tourism, Laos hopes to promote cultural awareness—cultural interaction where tourists come to look at weaving and traditional culture but not look down on it.

LAOS HIGHLIGHTS

Devoid of beaches or outstanding historical attractions, Laos' main draw is its laid-back lifestyle and *bo pein nhang* (never mind, take it easy) attitude. As J.B. Priestley puts it, "a good holiday is one spent among people whose notions of time are vaguer than yours." Laos offers great natural beauty, with as yet unspoiled mountain, plateau, and river regions.

Vientiane: There's little to see in the capital apart from a handful of temples—Wat Prakeo Museum, Wat Sisaket, and That Luang. Vientiane, however, is a great place to bicycle and walk around, with wide boulevards and little traffic. The top day-trip from Vientiane is to Nam Ngum Lake, where underwater logging takes place.

Luang Prabang: The old capital offers the major cultural attractions of the Palace Museum and Wat Xieng Thong. Luang Prabang is considered one of the best-preserved traditional cities in Southeast Asia, with a number of 16th-century temples, as well as colonial and traditional timber houses. There is an excellent day-trip to Pak Ou Caves on the Mekong. Luang Prabang is a laid-back town with little traffic, eminently walkable, with lots to see. Worth at least three days.

Other Sites: To the northeast is the over-rated Plain of Jars. Unless you want to see the surrounding countryside, the trip is not worth the expense. Pakse, in southern Laos, is a departure point for Wat Phu, an abandoned Khmer temple worth a day's excursion. Wat Phu is not as impressive as the Khmer ruins in Thailand, and it's not even remotely comparable to the ruins of Angkor Wat.

River Trips: Laos' real attraction for future tourism could well be its primeval forests and pristine environment. There is great potential for rafting trips, complete with a whitewater experience. Stretches of the Mekong are lined with stands of giant bamboo and primary-growth forest, particularly between Ban Huay Sai and Luang Prabang; on the lower section of the Mekong near the Cambodian border are thundering rapids. Mekong tributaries such as the Nam Ou near Luang Prabang offer spectacular limestone gorges.

Trekking: Visitors can jungle-trek and elephant-ride in the Bolovens Plateau area. Trekking is still in its early stages in Laos, and expenses can run high. There are numerous hilltribe groups in the mountain areas of northern Laos—mostly inaccessible for the present.

Festivals: Laos has preserved traditions that have long disappeared from other parts of Asia. This is most obvious in its festivals, of which there are a large number. The biggest celebrations are Pimai, or Lao New Year, in April, and the Water Festival at the end of the rainy season in October. Some tours to Laos are specifically timed to take in special festivities.

HAZARDS

Unexploded ordnance is a major problem in Laos, particularly in Xieng Khuang and Savannakhet Provinces. Antipersonnel devices left over from the 1960s and 1970s injure hundreds of people each year. Use of a guide in such areas is recommended. There is banditry in some parts of Laos, related to opium growing and hilltribe antigovernment insurgency. Road travel may be risky, especially on the Vientiane-Luang Prabang, Vientiane-Paksane, and Luang Nam Tha-Ban Huay Sai roads. The alternative is to fly over all this in an aging Russian turbo-prop, which also has its hazardous side. In opium-growing areas of northern Laos, especially toward the Burmese border, foreigners may be mistaken for drug traffickers or, even worse, drug enforcement agents.

MYTHOLOGY AND THE ARTS

There are two streams for the arts in Laos—classical and folk. Classical arts are strongly associated with Hindu mythology, Buddhism, and former Lao royalty, while folk arts are connected with animist Lao hilltribes. The stronger and more vibrant stream is the folk arts.

Mythology

There is very little in the way of Lao literature, ancient or modern. Older Lao manuscripts were engraved on palm leaves, bundled together, threaded, and wrapped in cloth. Many Lao sacred texts were looted by the Thais in the 19th century.

Laotian mythology is heavily dependent on the Sanskrit epic the Ramayana, written by the Indian poet Valmiki over 2,000 years ago. The Ramayana pits lovers Rama and Sita against the wicked demon Ravana. The story parallels Western myths from the *Iliad* to *Star Wars* in focusing on the struggle between good and evil. There are good doses of sex, violence, magic, adventure, and intrigue in the Ramayana. The Lao version of the myth, called *Phra Lak Pralam,* parallels the original story but adds new episodes. These were later a source of inspiration for the Thai version.

The Jataka Tales, stories about the lives of Buddha, are also well-known in Laos. The stories suggest Aesop's fables and present dramatic adventures resolved by nonviolent means. Although the Jataka Tales recount hundreds of Buddha's lives, the most important are the last 10, during each of which a particular virtue was perfected.

Classical Arts

As in Thailand and Cambodia, the main patron of the performing arts was royalty. When royalty and Buddhism fell out of favor under Communism, the arts suffered. One casualty is classical dance based on Ramayana themes, once performed for the royal court. Classical Lao music is now heard only during Ramayana performances. A standard ensemble consists of a xylophone with bamboo crosspieces *(ranyat),* a set of bronze cymbals hung from a wooden frame *(khong wong),* bamboo flute *(khui),* and Lao-style clarinet *(pii).*

There are three main styles of temple architecture in Laos: Vientiane, Luang Prabang, and Xieng Khuang. Since Xieng Khuang Province was heavily bombed during the Vietnam War, hardly any examples of this form remain. Of the other two styles, only a few significant structures have survived repeated ransacking over the centuries. None are uniquely Lao, sharing features borrowed from northern Thailand. Temples in Vientiane have high-peaked roofs with three, five, or seven layers, while Luang Prabang style temples feature dramatic low-sweeping roofs.

Sculpture, carving, and mural design are strongly associated with temple architecture. Temple frescoes and bas-reliefs draw inspiration from the Jataka Tales—the fables can be retold by following the mural sequence. Depicting scenes from the Ramayana are beautifully carved wooden doors and shutters—and entire facades—at temples in Vientiane and Luang Prabang. Lao sculpture consists mainly of images of Buddha, with the best pieces from the 16th to 18th century.

Folk Arts

Hilltribe lore and customs provide Laos with its cultural identity; folk song and dance are closely related to festivals. Lao folk dances have survived for many centuries, telling of the joys of life and work. The national dance is the *lam wong,* a slow revolving circle dance with men on the inside and women on the outside. Partners move their hands in graceful, expressive gestures. Music for the *lam wong* is provided by the *khen,* a handheld bamboo reed instrument related to South American pan pipes. The *khen* is difficult to play—performers must produce a continuous melody by exhaling and inhaling without catching their breath. Other instruments include the *khong wong,* hand drums, bamboo flute *(khui),* and a bowed string instrument, the *saw.*

Performed at festivals and temple fairs is *maw lam,* Lao folk theater. *Maw lam* is a combination of talking, singing, and costume drama.

It's bawdy, witty, and profane, embracing topics like sex and politics, and appears to be impervious to official censure. *Maw lam* is also heard on the radio.

Handicrafts

Weaving has a long tradition in Laos. It's mostly done by hand in villages, on simple wooden looms; skilled weavers are held in high regard. The most common type of weaving in cotton or silk is for the *sinh,* a long wraparound skirt worn by most Lao women. Exquisite pieces are also produced for ceremonial purposes, such as the shawl women wear over their shoulders at important events like weddings or festivals. Textile-making techniques and patterns vary widely according to the hilltribe group and geographic location. Luang Prabang patterns, for example, feature gold and silver brocade, while Khmer-influenced patterns are found in the south. Motifs are often based on folktales, legendary crea-

tures, nature, or geometric patterns. Designs from the northeast are highly prized—they have achieved "antique" status because the hilltribe weaving tradition in that zone was severely disrupted by decades of war; attempts have been made to revive lost patterns. Recipes for mixing natural textile dyes are closely guarded secrets; the dyes derive from tamarind, turmeric, and indigo, among other sources.

A quite different form of weaving involves the making of mats and baskets, the hilltribe method of packaging. These are woven from straw or reed. Silversmithing is important to the Hmong and Mien not only for display purposes but also as a kind of portable wealth, carried in the form of silver jewelry, ornaments, belts, and other pieces. In Luang Prabang, silversmithing was once a royal craft. Several of the smiths who made silverware for the royal palace before 1975 still work around the old capital, producing finely crafted pieces.

FESTIVALS AND HOLIDAYS

The Lao are addicted to festivals. They kick off the year with three different celebrations—Western New Year, Chinese New Year, and Lao New Year. Authorities despair that farmers would rather spend money on festivals than save funds in the bank.

Buddhist celebrations are based on the moveable lunar calendar: the full moon figures prominently in these calculations. Many traditional villages still use the lunar calendar to follow the passage of the seasons. Festivities are often centered around local wats, which are transformed into country fairgrounds with games, foodstalls, live music, dancing, and other entertainment.

In addition to the Gregorian calendar, the Lao follow the Buddhist Era calendar, which in Laos starts 638 years before the Christian era. Add 638 to the Western year to get the corresponding B.E. year: thus 1997 corresponds to 2635 B.E.

Celebrating any auspicious occasion—wedding, birth, new year, recovery from illness, a welcome or a farewell—is the uniquely Lao *baci* ceremony. Of animist origins, the *baci* centers around an elaborate "tree" made from banana leaves

and flowers, surrounded by rice wine, cakes, and other symbolic food. A village elder lights candles and delivers a monologue in Pali and Lao, after which villagers tie white cotton strings round participants' wrists as blessings are spoken. If you're a visitor, the blessing may be that no calamity befall you in Laos. The several dozen strings correspond to internal organs and represent good health and prosperity. After the string tying, rice wine and refreshments are served, followed by *lam wong* dancing. It is considered unlucky to take the strings off until three days pass; the strings should then be untied rather than cut.

The following list of festivals and holidays is by no means exhaustive—ethnic minorities march to a different drummer and have a great variety of festivities. *"Boun"* is Lao for "festival."

National Holidays

Jan. 1: New Year's Day, celebrated with *baci* ceremonies

Mid-April: Lao New Year (Pimai)—three days of festivity

May 1: International Labor Day, with parades in Vientiane

Longboat racing marks the end of Buddhist Lent.

Dec. 2: National Day, celebrating 1975 victory by the Pathet Lao with parades and speeches

Lunar Calendar Festivals

January: The story of Prince Vessanthara's reincarnation as Buddha is celebrated with Boun Pha Vet, featuring temple recitals and theater and dance performances. This is a popular time for ordination of monks.

February: Maha Puja is an important Buddhist holy day celebrating an occasion of impromptu preaching by Buddha. Meritmaking ceremonies take place during the day at temples throughout the country; at dusk there are candlelit processions around principal wats as the full moon rises. The festival is celebrated chiefly in the capital, Vientiane, and at Wat Phu in southern Laos. Chinese New Year (Vietnamese Tet) in late January or early February is marked by deafening fireworks and visits to Chinese and Vietnamese temples. Many Chinese and Vietnamese businesses close for three days.

March: The Harvest Festival, or Boun Khoun Khao, is celebrated in wats upcountry after rice has been harvested.

April: Pimai, the Lao or Buddhist New Year, occurs in the fifth lunar month, usually mid-April. There are three official days of holidays, and a few more unofficial. The entire country closes down for festivities, which are quite elaborate in Luang Prabang. People clean their houses, put on new clothes, and assemble for ceremonial washing of Buddha images in the temples. April

is the hottest month, and Pimai is a good excuse to throw buckets of water over all and sundry on the streets—and that includes visitors.

May: Visakha Puja is a full-moon festival marking the birth, death, and enlightenment of Buddha. It is celebrated in local wats, with candlelit processions at night. The Rocket Festival, or Boun Bang Fai, takes place around the same time. This rainmaking festival is staged before the start of rice planting; rockets are burnt as a sacrifice to Phagna Thene, the god of rain. Large bamboo rockets are carried in procession by monks, and then fired heavenward to loosen up the skies and bring down rain. The higher the rocket, the more propitious the omen. Designers of failed rockets are thrown in the mud. In some places male participants blacken their bodies with lamp soot, while women wear sunglasses and carry carved wooden phalluses. The Rocket Festival is one of the wildest festivals in the country, with plenty of music and dance—especially irreverent *maw lam* performances.

June: Khao Pansa marks the beginning of the rains retreat, when Buddhist monks are expected to stay at one monastery. This is the traditional time for young men to enter the monkhood for short periods.

August/September: Boun Kao Padabdin is the Festival of the Dead. Many cremations take place at this time, and gifts are presented to monks who chant on behalf of the deceased.

October: Boun Ok Pansa marks the end of the three-month rains retreat; monks are allowed to travel, and are presented with robes, bowls, food, and other offerings. In conjunction with this is Bun Nam, the Water Festival, with longboat racing in such major towns as Vientiane, Savannakhet, Pakse, and Luang Prabang. Longboats with crews of 50 or more, accompanied by drummers, participate in regattas.

November: In Vientiane the That Luang Festival takes place on the full moon of the 12th lunar month, usually mid-November. The festival lasts three days, with offerings to assembled monks, a week-long fair, a parade through town, fireworks, and a candlelit procession around the sacred stupa of That Luang.

ACCOMMODATIONS

There is a chronic lack of hotel rooms in Laos. There are very few cheap guesthouses compared to Thailand, and very little in the way of luxury-standard hotels—only a handful in Vientiane and Luang Prabang would qualify. Most rooms fall in the $15-40 range—double the cost of similar accommodation in Thailand. Hotel rooms usually feature a fan and attached bathroom; air-conditioning and hot water are available only in better hotels.

Mosquito nets are generally provided in areas with malaria—Vientiane is not considered a risk. Facilities can be basic—erratic electricity and blackouts—so bring a flashlight. Upcountry, hotels may be located in renovated (you hope) French villas or chalets. If you really get off the track and there aren't any hotels in town, you might be allowed to stay in a government guesthouse.

Vientiane has the largest selection of hotels in the country. High-end hotels like the Lane Xang, Royal, Riverview, and Belvedere offer a range of creature comforts, with business centers, nightclubs, restaurants, and health and sports facilities. Rooms range $40-60; suites or apartments cost $80 and up. The Singapore-managed Belvedere hotel charges $120 for a double room and over $150 for a suite.

FOOD

Lao food shares a lot in common with Thai food, and selections verge on the hot and spicy. Lao people also eat a lot of less spicy Chinese food. Vietnamese food is found in Vientiane and a few other cities. In the larger towns, French cuisine is widely available, with fresh baguettes, Lao-style pâté, croissants, and Lao coffee available at streetstalls and small cafés. Restaurants serve pricey dishes including steak and filet mignon. Cheaper selections of food are mainly found in and around the central market in each town; foodstalls abound in these areas. More formal restaurants are small affairs, often a family-run shop front. In larger places like Vientiane or Luang Prabang, hotel restaurants serve tasty fare.

For Lao cuisine, rice is the staple—either glutinous sticky rice, served in small lidded baskets and eaten with the hand, or plain white rice, eaten with a spoon. Sticky rice is often rolled into a ball and dipped into the various dishes. When eating Lao food it's common to share dishes—each party orders one dish, so portions are usually large. Lao dishes are cooked with fresh ingredients, using vegetables, freshwater fish, duck, beef, pork, and chicken. Spicing is tangy, using lemongrass, chiles, ginger, tamarind, coriander, lemon juice, and aromatic herbs like marijuana. Beware of dishes with raw or undercooked freshwater fish or derivatives, as these may promote liver flukes. Particularly avoid *paddek,* made of chunks of fermented freshwater fish, and *nam paddek,* a sauce from fermented fish. The risk is higher in rural areas.

Dessert dishes include grilled bananas and sticky rice with coconut milk and black beans.

A common Lao dish is *larp,* made of minced meat, chicken, fish, or vegetables tossed with garlic, chiles, green onions, and lime juice. It's served with rice on a plate of lettuce, mint, and steamed mango leaves, and eaten by wrapping a little *larp* in the lettuce. The dish is served cold, but watch out for the hidden heat in the spicing.

spices on sale at the Morning Market, Vientiane

Tam som is a green papaya salad, made by pounding shredded green papaya and adding lime juice, chiles, garlic, and other ingredients in a mortar. At a street side stall, the preparation involves customer participation. One of the great beauties of *tam som* is that it tastes fine without any chiles at all, so specify this as the salad is pounded in front of you at a market. **Pho** is a Lao version of Chinese noodle soup, often served with a garnish of lettuce, mint, bean sprouts, lime, and basil. Ingredients are added to the soup as desired.

Bottled water is widely available in Laos. Coffee grown on the Bolovens Plateau provides an excellent brew; it is usually served with sweetened condensed milk unless you specify otherwise. Imported soft drinks and beer are widely available. The Lao Brewery Company in Vientiane produces Bia Lao (labeled Bière Larue), which is a good value; draft beer from plastic pitchers is also available in Vientiane. The local firewater is *lao lao,* a rice whiskey made from fermented sticky rice. It's usually served on ice, with lime and soda or Coke.

IMMIGRATION AND CUSTOMS

VISAS

Be careful when applying for visas; specify exactly what you want to do in Laos. Some travelers are disappointed to find themselves restricted to Vientiane Prefecture on a transit visa; businesspeople have been issued one-month visas valid only for this zone. Others have found their visa is valid only for entry at Vientiane, sometimes only by air, and were not able to enter another land border from Thailand. Lao visas and other documents are issued mostly in Lao script, which means you have to double-check what you're getting. Let the travel agent know your travel plans and which border you'd like to cross. Any Roman alphabet entries on the visa will be in French, not English.

Transit Visa: Generally valid for five to 10 days, transit visas are nonextendable, and in theory valid for Vientiane Prefecture only. These visas are available in Saigon, Danang, or Hanoi and cost around $15-20. They're used by travelers seeking a cheap way back from Vietnam to Thailand, with a short stopover in Vientiane. Some travelers have been able to travel along Route 9 from Vietnam, crossing the Lao Bao border, on a transit visa. This crossing is not guaranteed, as the policy seems to change.

Tourist Visa: Valid for 15 days, a tourist visa costs $100 in Bangkok and takes up to five working days to obtain. You can go upcountry, but technically you're part of some tour. In theory, you must have a guarantee letter from a Lao tourist company under permission of the Ministry of Foreign Affairs in Laos, but a travel agency in Bangkok can act as your sponsor, in conjunction with a tour agent in Vientiane. The name of the Vientiane sponsor tour agency is written on your visa in Lao script, and you're supposed to be their charge while in Laos. A tourist visa is technically nonextendable, but this rule may bend if your tour is booked for the projected extra period of time. Some travelers have been able to obtain a 30-day visa direct from the Lao Embassy for only $12, but this requires repeated visits.

Business Visa: Valid for 30 days, business visas are renewable in Vientiane for 30, 90, 180, and 365 days depending on circumstances. Businesspeople are the advance guard of tourism—investing in Laos and opening it up for trade—and are therefore allowed certain liberties. There are fewer upcountry travel restrictions on this visa, but you're still expected to tour with an escort. You're permitted multiple entry-exit during the life of the visa.

For this visa, you need a letter of invitation stating the reason for your visit, approved by the Ministry of Foreign Affairs in Laos. A business visa costs $12 in Bangkok for an application made directly to the embassy; through a tour agent, the cost can run 10 times that. Allow several working days to process the visa. Some tour agents in Vientiane and Bangkok can arrange the necessary invitation and paperwork—allow up to a month for processing if applying from abroad. No tour agency is stamped on the visa, which gives the business visa holder a choice of agents upon arrival. Business visas do not pay government tax on travel arrangements, so travel paperwork may be cheaper.

Other Visas: Letters of invitation are required for those visiting relatives, or for diplomatic visas. It's very difficult for photographers and writers to obtain official permission to visit.

Visa Issue

Vientiane: If you have a prior fax-link with a travel agent in Vientiane, it's possible to have a tourist or business visa issued on arrival in Laos. This is applicable to arrivals at Wattay Airport by air, or at Tha Deua by land. Expect to pay at least $60—an immigration fee of $30, plus an agent fee of $30-50. Since Laos does not have many embassies abroad, a visa on arrival is an alternate method of processing.

Cambodia: A Lao tourist visa valid for 15 days is issued in Phnom Penh for $20. It can be obtained in three working days.

Thailand: Bangkok is the most common place to obtain a Lao tourist visa. Although the visa itself costs only $12, you normally go through a travel agent, and the visa costs around $60-100, including a first night in a Vientiane hotel. Since the hotel is worth only $20, there is an unexplained $70 agent fee, which you can be very sure involves kickbacks all the way along the line. Smaller Bangkok agents operate through bigger agents. The Lao embassy deals with the following travel agents in Bangkok for tourist visas: MK Ways, tel. 254-4765; Chansiam, tel. 287-4798; Diethelm, tel. 255-9150; Exotissimo, tel. 253-5240; Tritee, tel. 233-6896; Transindo, tel. 249-1117; JP Travel, tel. 255-2233; Precha, tel. 233-5316; Siamwing, tel. 235-4757; Prestige, tel. 314-5498; Spangle Tours, tel. 212-1583; Scenic World, tel. 513-5314; Thai-Indochina Supply Co., tel. 233-5369; and Vista Travel, tel. 281-0786. More agents are listed in the front of this book. These agencies chop and change, so phone ahead to initiate contact.

You can fax ahead to Bangkok agents so the paperwork is completed by the time you arrive. Fax a photocopy of your front passport pages and the agent will fax back a visa application. You need to transfer the fee for the visa. On arrival in Bangkok, the agent will need the actual passport for 24 hours, to take it to the Lao embassy for visa-stamping.

Some guesthouses in Nong Khai (such as the Meeting Place) operate as travel agents and send paperwork to either Vientiane or Bangkok. Initial charges are $12 for a Bangkok visa, or $30 for a Tha Deua border-issued visa, with additional fees charged by the agent. A tourist visa costs around $60-100 and takes one to five days to obtain. In Nong Khai a 30-day business visa can take up to 10 days.

Vietnam: In Hanoi, you can acquire a five- to seven-day (sometimes 10-day) Lao transit visa. It requires two days and costs $15-25, and you may be asked for a confirmed Hanoi-Vientiane air ticket. An extra $10 under the table will speed up proceedings. The Lao Consulate in Saigon issues a five- to seven-day transit visa in three working days at a cost of $20. You may be able to obtain a Lao tourist visa in either Saigon or Hanoi—if not directly through the Lao consulate, then perhaps through a travel agent. Danang Lao Consulate General offers business visas in two days for $10; seven-day transit visas for

$15, processed in two days; and tourist visas for $10. The tourist visa may require up to five days. Lao visas are also available from Rangoon, but are more difficult to obtain.

PAPERWORK WITHIN LAOS

Arrival and Departure
You need to complete the standard arrival/departure card and Customs declaration form. The arrival/departure card should be treasured, as it functions as a kind of pass to be stamped upcountry. You can bring 500 cigarettes, two bottles of wine, and one bottle of liquor. The Customs declaration form asks you to itemize cameras and valuables. Export of antiques and Buddha images from Laos is forbidden.

If entering or exiting a land border in Laos, be aware that greedy border officials on both sides may cause delays by finding "irregularities" in your paperwork. A few cartons of cigarettes will work wonders here.

Extensions
Visa extensions are processed in Vientiane at the Immigration Department. The process is best handled by a travel agent, preferably the sponsoring agent indicated on your visa (if issued in Bangkok). You may have problems with extensions if no sponsor is indicated on your original visa. Visa extensions can take three days to process. Extensions cost roughly $3 for each day you intend to stay. An alternative is to simply overstay your visa—you can then negotiate a $5 per day "fine" (some have negotiated $3 a day), which you pay upon exiting. In Thailand, overstaying a Thai visa is a fixed $4 a day, so Laotian officials probably follow this parameter. It seems that visa extensions are stamped only in Vientiane, as is the case with other major paperwork.

Internal Travel Permits
In 1994 the Lao government abolished requirements for travel permits outside Vientiane Province; opened a few new borders to Thailand, Vietnam, and China; and permitted foreigners to travel on some land and river routes. However, your progress is still closely monitored at checkpoints, and what is said in Vientiane is not necessarily communicated properly to authorities upcountry, who have the last say in local matters. In addition, some areas are still off-limits due to their sensitivity—these may require special permission.

Previously, to exit or enter by an obscure land border, you needed a travel permit specifying the particular point. This seems to have been liberalized, but policy can change. It's best to ask in Vientiane about current regulations. If no travel permits are required, try to get a letter in Lao from an official source that says so—this you can show to provincial authorities. The same goes for border crossings. Don't rely on hearsay, but try to obtain a piece of paper that says it's okay to cross that particular border.

Prior to 1994, the travel permit required for upcountry travel, visits to sensitive areas, or exits by a land border came in the form of a *laissez-passer,* a permit for one Lao province. This document cost $10-60 through a travel agent. The *laissez-passer* was a photocopied piece of paper specifying destination and province, exact dates of travel, the agency responsible, date of issue, and other particulars (age, country, passport number). The document was stamped numerous times when the traveler passed through airports and land checkpoints, and was also demanded for certain modes of transport and when exiting a land border.

In late 1994, the travel permit system was scrapped, but this does not mean authorities do not check your progress. The *laissez-passer* has been replaced in part by the arrival/departure card, which is stamped on the back when traveling by air or boat within the country, although by truck or bus no one seems to bother.

LAO EMBASSIES AND CONSULATES

The success rate in dealing direct with Lao embassies and consulates is low—in most places, you must go through a travel agent or passport handling agency. However, there's no harm in trying the direct option. Several travelers have managed to squeeze a 30-day visa out of the embassy in Paris. Staff at the Lao embassy said they would only deal with group tours, but travelers have received visas anyway. Try a passport-handling agency on home ground.

LAO EMBASSIES AND CONSULATES

WITHIN ASIA

Burma (Myanmar); NA1 Diplomatic Quarters, Fraser Rd., Rangoon

Cambodia; 15-17 Issarak Blvd., Phnom Penh, tel. 26441

China; N23 Haigeng Road, Room 501, Kunming (consulate), fax 414396; 11 Sanlitun Dongsijie, Beijing (embassy), tel. 5321224

Indonesia; Jalan Kintamani Rajac, 15 N.33 Keningantimur, Jakarta, tel. 5202673

Japan; 3-3-22 Nishi-Azabu Minato-Ku, Tokyo, tel. 541-12291

Thailand; 520, 502/1-3 Soi Ramkhamhaeng 39, Bangkapi, Bangkok, tel. 539-6667

Vietnam; 22 Tran Binh Trong, Hanoi, tel. 252271 (embassy); 181 Hai Ba Trung, Saigon, tel. 299272 (consulate); Tran Quy Cap, Danang, tel. 21208 (consulate)

OUTSIDE ASIA

Australia; 1 Dalman Crescent, O'Malley, Canberra, Australian Capital Territory

Cuba; Sta. Avenida No.2808 ESQ A30 Playa, Miramar, Havana

France; 74 Ave. Raymond Poincare, 75116 Paris

Germany; AmLessing 6, 53639 Koenigwinter, Bonn

India; E53 Panchsheel Park, New Delhi

Mongolia; 27 Stalin Ave., 2F, Apartment 10, Ulan Bator

Poland; Ul. Rejtana 15/26, 02-516, Warsaw

Russia; Ul. Katchalova 18, Moscow

U.S.A.; 2222 S. St. NW, Washington, DC 20008, tel. (202) 332-6416; Lao PDR UN office, 317 East 51st St., New York, NY 10022

TOURISM AGENTS

Agents in Vientiane can assist with visa issue, permits and paperwork, immigration problems, transport rentals, hotel reservations, guides, and so on. Although you can approach the Immigration Office (off Lane Xang Blvd., near Bangkok Bank) yourself for paperwork, dealing with the staff can be tedious. Agents can speed up the process—for a price.

The large agencies have links upcountry, with branch offices. Larger agencies are all linked to agents in Bangkok—Raja Tours, for instance, has links with MK Ways and half a dozen other agents in Bangkok, while Lane Xang deals with Chansiam Travel, and Sodetour with Transindo. The name of the Lao agent may be stamped right on your Lao visa—as your "sponsor." Although you can deal directly with Lao agents, faxes to Laos can be slow and trying. It might be easier to deal with a Bangkok agent. For a list, see "Via Bangkok" under "Getting There" in the Indochina chapter, earlier in this book.

Business Travel

Following are agents who deal with business travelers. **Lao Investment Promotion Corporation (LIPCO)** handles business-type travelers, helping with visa issue, agents and brokers, permits and registration for companies, car rentals and guides, typing, translation, and legal work. Located in Building 1, Luang Prabang Rd., Vientiane, P.O. Box 795, tel. 169645 or 169945, fax 9646. **Laovilay,** 100 Tha Deua Rd., P.O. Box 843, Vientiane, tel./fax 314350, handles investment documents, business license extensions, visas, car rentals, and travel arrangements.

Travel Agents

Diethelm, Namphu Square, Settathirat Blvd., tel. 215920, fax 217151, is a Bangkok-based company that is both upscale and high-priced. It has a branch in Luang Prabang. Diethelm is the American Express agent in Vientiane.

Inter-Lao Tourisme, on the corner of Settathirat and Pangkham, tel. 214232, fax 216306, maintains links to Luang Prabang and Savannakhet. **Lane Xang Travel,** Pangkham Rd., tel. 212469, fax 215777, has branches in Luang Prabang, Xieng Khuang, and Pakse; offers lower-priced tours. **Raja Tour,** Anou Hotel, 2nd Floor, 3 Heng Boun St., tel. 213633, fax 215797, offers good links with Luang Prabang.

Sodetour (Societé de la Developpement Touristique), 16 Fa Ngum, tel. 216314, fax 216313, is run by a long-time French resident; good links to Pakse and the southeast. **Vieng Champa Tours,** Tha Deua Rd. KM3, in the Vientiane Club complex, tel./fax 314412, handles Thai tourism. **On-Time Travel Service,** near Inter-Lao Tourisme at 35 Settathirat, books train and bus tickets in Thailand.

MONEY, MEASUREMENTS, AND COMMUNICATIONS

MONEY

The unit of currency in Laos is the kip, with four bills—50, 100, 500, and 1000. Smaller denomination bills—1, 5, 10, and 20 kip—are being withdrawn from circulation. The conversion rate in 1995 was 720 kip to the dollar. Although the kip is a stable currency it's useless once out of Laos, and because the biggest bill is little more than a dollar, it's very impractical to carry around large amounts of kip—your pockets will overflow with the stuff. Use kip for small transactions, but pay for larger purchases in dollars or Thai baht.

Thai baht is accepted in most parts of Laos and is preferable to dollars because you can receive change in baht, whereas you're unlikely to get change from $1. There are 1-baht (4 cents, or 30 kip) and 5-baht (20 cents) coins circulating in Vientiane.

Laos has a largely cash economy. In remote areas, not even cash is used; trading is based on barter. Credit cards are rarely used in Vientiane—some hotels, restaurants, and shops in the capital accept them, and you can buy tickets on Lao Aviation with a Visa card. The agent for Visa in Vientiane is Banque pour le Commerce Extérieur. Cash advances for Visa and MasterCard are available in baht through Thai banks in Vientiane. The agent for American Express is Diethelm Travel in Vientiane.

Costs

Because of the high cost of visa, paperwork, domestic flights, and jeep rentals, you can rack up over $100 a day if going upcountry—and that's in a country where one dollar is a *lot* of money (the minimum monthly wage is around $35). If you can keep transport expenses down by traveling overland by boat or bus, your costs will be considerably lower. Part of the problem here, however, is time. By restricting your visa to two weeks, the Lao government applies the time-money twist. If you have less time, you have to travel faster, and you end up paying more.

MEASUREMENTS AND COMMUNICATIONS

Until 1990 Laos maintained only a single phone line to the outside world, bar lines to the Soviet Union and Thailand. The situation has improved since then, but most of the links are to Vientiane—few other parts of the country are connected by phone. Where phones exist, IDD calls and faxes are expensive. A one-page fax to Europe costs $15 from Vientiane; to Bangkok a page costs $6. Vientiane is seven hours ahead of Greenwich mean time. The country code for Laos is 856.

There are post offices (PTT) in the larger towns—Vientiane, Luang Prabang, Pakse, and Savannakhet. Service may be unreliable. Courier services operating from Vientiane include DHL, TNT, and UPS.

Under the French, Laos issued beautiful postage stamps with traditional themes—temples, Buddhist art, legends, flora and fauna—all printed in Paris. Some of the modern stamps still feature these themes. Today's stamp subjects also include dinosaurs, the American Bicentennial, the 100th anniversary of Ho Chi Minh's birth, Barcelona 92 Olympics, and The War

Against Drugs Campaign. The stamps will cover half a postcard—best to apply them first, then add the text.

Metric and Electric
Laos uses the metric system. Electricity is mostly 220 volts, 50 cycles, using two-pin sockets, both flat and round plugs. If you're bringing 110-volt devices you'll need a converter. A computer surge protector is a good idea.

SERVICES AND INFORMATION

Tourist Information
The Lao National Tourism Authority (NTSA) was established in 1991, and as yet assists only group tours. None of the NTSA offices in Laos are useful to individuals. You're better off asking travel agents for information.

Traveler Network
Because there are so few hotels in the country, it's easy to meet other travelers. In Vientiane are a few watering holes where travelers hang out, like the Mixai Café by the Mekong.

Maps and Books
Any kind of printed material on Laos is hard to come by—scrounge where you can. International Travel Maps publishes a useful Laos Travel Reference Map. You can obtain topo maps of most parts of Laos from the State Geographic Service in Vientiane. Good maps of Vientiane itself are available, but the rest of the place is a blank. The only bookstore of any note in the entire country is Raintree Bookstore in Vientiane.

Information Highway
The "information highway" is coming to Vientiane. Around 1992, the Lao government for the first time permitted foreign newspapers, international direct dialing, private fax machines, and satellite dishes. While these changes mean little to the average farmer, they herald a major shift in attitude. In 1994, the Lao Information and Culture Ministry started a weekly newspaper, The Vientiane Times—the country's first English-language newspaper since 1975. Laotians, however, worry about the spread of Thai pop culture with this new media onslaught—

most of the television, pop songs, and magazines in Laos are Thai.

Media
Lao National Radio broadcasts news in English twice a day, but most expats in Vientiane prefer the shortwave version on BBC, VOA, or Radio Australia. The national television station on Channel 8 broadcasts in Lao for about five hours a night. Most prefer watching Thai television, received from across the Mekong, and broadcasting a mix of Thai and English programming. Satellite dishes are starting to sprout up around Vientiane; a regular dish can pick up StarTV, which includes BBC World Service, while a large dish will receive CNN. Satellite dishes are provided to the Lao market by Samart Group, the largest dishmaker in Thailand. The Thai group Shinawatra signed a number of telecom and broadcasting deals with the Lao government in 1993. Among them was the opportunity to set up a nongovernment television station—Vientiane's Channel 3—run by International Broadcasting Company (IBC). It will provide mostly Laotian programs.

Services
The Laotians are not big on services. The major hotels in Vientiane and Luang Prabang handle business services and recreational efforts like the odd swimming pool. Computers are used (sparingly) in Vientiane: Lao- and Thai-style fonts can be imported into English programs through Windows. Vientiane also offers photocopy services and film labs. You're best advised to bring film with you—buy it in Bangkok or Hong Kong. Outside of Vientiane and Luang

Prabang, don't count on even the most basic of services. Business hours for shops and offices in Vientiane are roughly 0800-1200 and 1400-1700, Saturday 0800-1200, closed Sunday.

Health Care

By Western standards, medical care in Laos is poor to nonexistent. Carry good medical supplies with you, and if the situation warrants it, travel to Thailand for proper medical care. Equipment considered obsolete in the US is state of the art in Laos. Western doctors visiting southern Laos have witnessed the use of blunt razor blades for eye "surgery," and a hand-pumped ambu-bag fashioned from the inside of a football for resuscitation. Lao health services are severely lacking in supplies, equipment, and training.

The situation is better in Vientiane, where the Australian and Swedish embassies maintain their own clinics. In worst case scenarios, evacuation is available by Westcoast Helicopter from Vientiane to Udon Thani in Thailand. Lao Westcoast Helicopter (tel. 512023) charges about $850 for the run to Udon, 50 km south of Nong Khai.

GETTING THERE

BY AIR

The only air arrival point is Vientiane's Wattay Airport. Approximate one-way fares for direct flights are: Bangkok, $100; Hanoi, $90; Phnom Penh, $150; Saigon, $170; Kunming, $120; Guangzhou, $280; Beijing, $338. Some are stopover destinations: there's a Vientiane-Kunming-Guangzhou flight, and a Vientiane-Saigon-Phnom Penh flight. There are twice-weekly flights from Vientiane to Rangoon. Lao Aviation flies to Chiang Mai-Vientiane twice weekly on 50-seat ATRs; some group tours have managed to fly direct from Chiang Mai in Thailand into Luang Prabang. Singapore Airlines offers twice-weekly service between Vientiane and Singapore. New routes may open from Vientiane to Kuala Lumpur, Rangoon, and Hong Kong. Lao Aviation, in a joint venture with China's Yunnan Airlines, is planning to expand services to connect Laos with Yunnan Province, with direct flights into Xishuangbanna, and more frequent connections to Kunming. Lao Aviation uses its best planes on the international routes, including Boeing 737s and French ATRs.

Most international connections to Vientiane pass through Bangkok first. Bangkok serves as the hub for international flights to Vientiane; Air France, for example, routes passengers through Bangkok, where they transfer to a Lao Aviation B-737 flight to Vientiane. Bangkok to Vientiane takes an hour; ticketing is jointly operated by Lao Aviation (mostly weekday flights) and Thai Airways International (weekends). Pricing is $100 one-way, but you can sometimes obtain special fares. Lao Aviation in Bangkok is located at 491/17 Ground Floor, Silom Rd., tel. 236-9822; Thai Airways is at 485 Silom Rd., tel. 233-3810.

If you're bumped from a Bangkok-Vientiane flight, an alternative is to fly north to Udon Thani. From Udon Thani airport there's a Thai Airways express bus to the office in Nong Khai, 53 km north. From here, you can cross by land into Vientiane.

Customs

Airport arrival formalities are relaxed. There's no limit on the amount of foreign currency brought in—the most useful currency to carry is Thai baht. Since Thai baht is commonly accepted in Vientiane, you can eliminate the need for airport moneychanging by arriving with baht. You can bring in 500 cigarettes, two bottles of wine, and one bottle of liquor. The Customs declaration form will ask you to itemize camera equipment and valuables.

BY LAND

In early 1994, the Lao National Tourism Authority officially announced a number of new border checkpoints open to group tours and possibly individuals. Some may work as back doors for leaving Laos, but not always as front doors. Your paperwork must be in order to exit or enter at all land borders other than the Friendship Bridge—that is, you may need the entry point stamped on your Lao visa. More border points are expected to open in the future.

To Thailand: The Thailand-Laos border is 1,750 km long, with 650 km on land and the rest along the Mekong. Thai border crossings account for the majority of entries into Laos. The major crossing is at Nong Khai-Tha Deua over the Friendship Bridge. Thai transport is allowed as far as the Lao side of the bridge; then you must transfer to Lao transport. From Nong Khai to the bridge by minibus is around $1, then you take a cheap bus or a $4 taxi for the last 20 km into Vientiane.

There are four other points where foreigners can cross the Mekong: at Ban Huay Sai, northwest Laos, opposite the Thai town of Chiang Khong; at Thakhek, opposite the Thai town of Nakhon Phanom; at Savannakhet, opposite the Thai town of Mukdahan; and at Chong Mek, southern Laos, about 40 km west of Pakse (you cross at Chong Mek, and proceed to Ubon Ratchathani in Thailand). Crossing at Thai border points without a Thai visa is not a problem— you're given a 15-day stamp, which is nonextendable unless you have excellent reasons.

To Vietnam: From Savannakhet you can take Route 9 east and cross at the Lao Bao border, exiting to central Vietnam toward Dong Ha in the former DMZ (Demilitarized Zone). You'll probably need the Lao Bao border point stamped on your Vietnamese visa; this can be arranged at the Vietnamese Consulate in Savannakhet. Some travelers use this route to bypass Cambodia. In the reverse direction, there's a Lao Consulate in Danang to assist with paperwork; the Vietnamese immigration office in Danang can arrange a Lao Bao stamp for your Vietnamese visa.

To China: There's an exit through the town of Ban Boten in Luang Nam Tha Province to Mengla in China's landlocked Yunnan Province. This border crossing leads to fascinating minority areas of China like Jinghong, home to the Dai people. From Jinghong you can carry on to Kunming. Chinese visas are easy to obtain in Bangkok.

GETTING AROUND

Around Town

In Vientiane and the smaller towns, you can use cyclos (also called *samlors*) for shorter distances; you might also be able to rent a bicycle. Motorized transport consists of three-wheelers carrying up to four passengers, similar to *tuk-tuks;* or jumbos, a larger version seating up to eight passengers. There are no motos, but you can hire motorcycle sidecar-taxis in places like Luang Prabang or Pakse. These vehicles seat two, and are a blast for open-air touring. In Vientiane, Luang Prabang, and Savannakhet are a few rental cars of Russian ancestry for hire by visiting businesspeople or tourists—these are often attached to hotels. Metered taxis from Thailand made their debut in Vientiane with the opening of the Friendship Bridge.

BY AIR

The Lao domestic air fleet consists of a handful of serviceable planes, and getting a ticket can be difficult. With a reduction in trade with Russia, Laos has found it difficult to stock parts for its aging Russian crates, which include 50-seater Antonov-24s. Smaller planes include Chinese-made Yun-7s and Yun-12s. As for in-flight service: there isn't any. Lao Aviation has been known to send the occasional trolley down the aisle on a domestic flight—a flat Coke is about all you can expect. Stewardesses are clad in *sinhs,* the national dress. Purchase domestic tickets at Lao Aviation in Vientiane, or obtain them through a tour agent.

Domestic route airfares will continue to increase. One-way fares (foreigner price) from Vientiane: Muang Sai, $49; Luang Nam Tha, $57, with four flights a week; Phonsavan (Plain of Jars), $32, daily; Luang Prabang, $40, daily; Ban Huay Sai, $64, three times a week; Thakhek, $49; Savannakhet, $54, four flights a week; Saravan, $86, once a week; Pakse, $95, four flights a week. Return fares are double the one-way price.

Flights to other locations, such as Viengxay and Sayaboury, may be available. In the north, Luang Prabang is emerging as an air hub, with connections on Yun-12 aircraft to Ban Huay Sai, Xieng Khuang, Phong Saly, and possible flights to Chiang Mai in Thailand. In the south, there are connections on light aircraft from

Yun-12
Chinese aircraft

Pakse to Saravan, Savannakhet, Attapeu, and Moung Khong.

Be aware that flights can be heavily booked, particularly if the plane is the only way in, as is the case with Luang Nam Tha, poorly served by road. Weight limit for domestic flights is 20 kg; domestic departure tax is 50 cents. Flights leave in the morning, and usually return the same day.

Helicopter: For those with money to burn, Lao Westcoast Helicopter, tel. 512023, offers charter operations throughout Laos on AS350B Squirrel helicopters. The New Zealand-backed company operates from a hangar near Wattay Airport and is involved in seismic and aerial surveys, resource exploration, and medical evacuation.

BY BOAT

Stretches of the Mekong are navigable in high water. Decrepit wooden cargo boats ply these routes: fares are dirt cheap and the boats are basic, if not primitive. From Vientiane, boats to Savannakhet leave from the Southern Boat Terminal at Tha Deua KM4—the two-day trip costs under $10. The Mekong is navigable year-round from Luang Prabang to Savannakhet, but larger boats (50 tons) can ply the river only in the rainy season. Boats are quite basic—some are two-deck with sleeping areas, others single deck.

Cargo boats ply the upper Mekong from Ban Huay Sai to Luang Prabang, and from Luang Prabang to Vientiane. They take about two to three days to cover 300 to 400 km. Downstream from Luang Prabang to Vientiane takes three days, and costs $15. There are several checkpoints along the route. From Ban Huay Sai to Luang Prabang there's a longtail speedboat service, cutting the route from two days to a mere six hours. This part of the Mekong is especially scenic.

BY ROAD

Road travel is still a pioneering experience. The main highway is Route 13, which on paper snakes from Luang Prabang through Vientiane and south past Muang Paksane to Savannakhet, Pakse, and the Cambodian border. Only parts of the road are paved. Certain roads are considered unsafe because of bandits and opium warlords—there have been attacks on buses on the Vientiane-Luang Prabang, Vientiane-Paksane, and Luang Nam Tha-Ban Huay Sai roads, with deaths resulting from shoot-outs. Laos is not the easiest place to get around by land. Infrastructure is weak—there is no railroad, and the roads are mostly dirt. Roughly half the road bridges in Laos need to be replaced. Cratered and potholed roads are dust bowls in the dry season and rivers of muck in the wet season—bridges may be down during this time, and rivers

TRANSPORT RESTRICTIONS

Although foreigners are expected to fly up-country, some boat and road travel is permitted. Travel by boat may be slow, but Mekong scenery is an added bonus. Authorities are edgy about foreigners traveling anywhere outside Vientiane without an escort, because they're nervous about bandits and unexploded ordnance. It's debatable which is more dangerous: a roadtrip through bandit territory, or venturing aloft in a Soviet hand-me-down turboprop.

On the ground, foreigners are expected to travel by jeep with driver and guide. Use of local transport outside of Vientiane is frowned upon. In several places, such as Luang Prabang and Pakse, travelers have been told not to use motorcycle sidecar-taxis. At the Plain of Jars, travelers have been instructed not to use local buses. Despite restrictions, some travelers manage to break through. Against all odds, a Frenchman managed to cycle from Vientiane to Luang Prabang on a mountain bike, and a Canadian cycled from Savannakhet through Lao Bao into Vietnam. However, being in the wrong place without permission may result in a fine of up to $200, deportation, even a brief stay in a Lao jail.

too deep to drive through. In the rainy season, the water level is sufficient that the Mekong is navigable for much of its length. Boats and buses work in tandem: in the dry season, river water is low, so passengers take buses; in the wet season, roads may be washed out and rivers run high, so people take boats.

Jeep Rentals
Upcountry, foreigners are expected to use rented transport, such as a jeep with driver and guide. You can rent minibuses and cars, but due to the nature of the terrain, your best bet is a 4WD vehicle like a jeep. If you're not in a group tour when you arrive, you may be by the time you're done with Laos—to share costs for jeeps, hotels, guides and so on. A jeep runs $20-50 a day upcountry, and three to four trav-

elers can defray expenses; a guide costs $5 a day and up for one group. Vehicles for rent are mostly of the rugged 4WD type—jeeps, Land Rovers, or converted pickup trucks. The price includes cost of gasoline.

Rental agencies are usually open 0800-1700. Pay by time rather than distance—some drivers want to restrict driving distances to save on gasoline and may exaggerate the time needed to reach a destination. It's best to retain control over the itinerary; also, indicate clearly if you wish to stop frequently to take photos or visit villages. Misunderstandings can arise—halfway through a tour, the guide will suddenly bring up a new fee. Get your agreement written down at the outset with cost breakdown as a guarantee against such abrupt changes of mind.

Local Transport
The locals get around by small bus, *songtao* (a converted pickup truck with two rows of seats in the back), or truck. Trucks feature two rows of seats in the back to carry passengers over longer distances, such as sections of the Vientiane to Luang Prabang route. They are not known for their suspension.

TOURS

Group Tours
Group tours can reach sites that may otherwise be off-limits; paperwork headaches are also reduced on a group tour. Weighed against this is the expense: group tours are not cheap. You can join a larger tour abroad (see "On the Road" in the Vietnam chapter), or book through a Bangkok travel agency. You can customize a group tour—Bangkok agencies will assist a group of four, three, two, or even one. A typical package running five days, four nights from Bangkok to Vientiane to Luang Prabang runs about $900 per person including flights and hotels. Another possibility is linking up with a travel agent in Vientiane, making arrangements on the spot. A list of agents is provided in this book's Vientiane section. Here you can oscillate between group tour and individual travel, and control your schedule more. It's a good idea to build in free time to wander around on your own.

LAOS ROUTE STRATEGIES

Nothing is certain in Laos. You can chart a route through the country, but you might be stymied by red tape, or transport mode restrictions, or poor transport, or bad weather. Or you simply might run out of time—15 days is not very long. Coming up with an ideal route is a matter of juggling the variables of land border crossings, transport restrictions, and the complications of obtaining appropriate visas. You can base yourself in Thailand and make a loop through Laos, or attempt overland routes like Thailand-Laos-Vietnam-China. You might be able to enter Laos from Thailand near Pakse, then exit north into China and continue to Kunming. The following route ideas are Bangkok-based; many other plans are possible.

Bangkok Loop: Start in Bangkok, take a train to Nong Khai, and cross to Vientiane. Make a roundtrip to Luang Prabang. From Vientiane travel by land or air to Pakse, exit to Thailand at Chong Mek, and take a train back to Bangkok from Ubon Ratchathani. Obtain a Thai multiple-entry visa if planning long stays in Thailand. Because flights to the southern tip of Laos are expensive, a one-way flight to Pakse and traveling overland from Pakse back to Thailand makes sense. Another viable route, in-

volving more plane hops, is to start in Bangkok, travel to Vientiane and Luang Prabang, fly from Vientiane to Phnom Penh, explore Cambodia, then fly from Phnom Penh back to Bangkok.

Bangkok-Hanoi-Kunming: Start in Bangkok, head north, enter Laos through Ban Huay Sai, take a boat along the Mekong to Luang Prabang, then continue by boat (if possible) to Vientiane. Travel south by road or boat to Savannakhet and exit Lao Bao into Vietnam, arriving at Dong Ha. From Dong Ha either go north to Hanoi or south to Saigon.

A variation on this route involves crossing from Thailand into Laos by land at one of several border points, proceeding to Savannakhet, crossing into Vietnam at Lao Bao, traveling to Dong Ha, then heading north to Hanoi, and proceeding across the Lao Cai border to Kunming in China. From Kunming you can fly to Bangkok for little more than the cost of the Hanoi-Bangkok flight. Or you can carry on through China to the end of the Eurasian continent.

Transiting Vientiane: Fly from Hanoi into Vientiane. Make your way from there to Luang Prabang, then take a boat upstream on the Mekong to Ban Huay Sai, exiting into Thailand.

Individual Travel

Solo travel in Laos is in constant flux. Sometimes the doors are flung wide open, and travelers pour in. Then a tourist is caught stealing a Buddha image from a temple, and the doors are slammed shut again. At the time of writing, regulations had eased, and no travel permits were necessary.

Officially, there is no individual travel in Laos. Individuals are regarded as an aberration; Laos is not yet set up for individual travelers. Even if a "group" consists of only one or two people, it's still sponsored by some tour agency and requires a guide. If you don't start off in a group,

you may well join one for economic reasons—get together with fellow travelers, for example, if going upcountry to defray the costs of hired jeeps or boats. With three to four travelers in a jeep safari pool the cost of a guide remains the same, and you can share a hotel room, and transport and paperwork costs.

There are two constraints on your movements in Laos—internal travel permits and mode of transport. The first has seemingly been abandoned since 1994; the second is becoming less of a problem. However, do not underestimate red tape in Laos—it's the greatest obstacle to travel in the region.

VIENTIANE

Vientiane's Revolutionary Museum, housed in an old French palatial building, has a sign posted with entry hours, but the doors rarely open. That's because the Revolution is no longer what it used to be. Marxist ideology has been firmly sidelined—these days, young Laotians pursue rampant capitalism. Vientiane is as cosmopolitan as Laos gets. You can catch glimpses of new Japanese cars and motorcycles, satellite dishes, minimarts, and even discos—signs of things to come. Young Laotians, at least in Vientiane, are copying the carefree lifestyles of swinging Thailand, promoted by Thai television and magazines. The new revolution here is led by Toyota, Honda, and Mitsubishi: with the opening of the Friendship Bridge, hundreds of Japanese cars, pickups, and motorcycles are crossing over from Thailand. This influx has led to the deployment of traffic police at main intersections in Vientiane during "rush hour," and the introduction of a road-safety campaign to combat a jump in the number of traffic accidents.

Vientiane means either "Citadel of the Moon" of "Citadel of Fragrant Trees." It became the capital of Laos under King Settathirat in 1563.

The king constructed a palace and two wats—That Luang and Wat Pra Keo—and fortified the riverine town. Vientiane steadily expanded and prospered, until it was abandoned after the Siamese sacked it in 1827. In 1866 the French found the ruins of Vientiane overgrown by jungle, with little more than a fishing village remaining. Because of its position on the Mekong, favorable for shipping, the French initiated building of large colonial structures and wide boulevards at the turn of the century. Until the late 1930s there were no cars in Vientiane.

Today Vientiane is a laid-back town of 150,000 strung along the lazy Mekong. Architecture is a mix of Buddhist temples, French colonial buildings, Chinese shophouses, and Russian blockhouses. The French left in 1953, and in some quarters there appears to have been no repair since then: dilapidated French villas once occupied by a single family are now shared by half-a-dozen Lao families. The Russians left too—in some places you'll see hammer-and-sickle neon lights which no longer function. Office buildings sorely in need of a coat of paint preside over traffic circles swirling with dust. The winds of change are blowing, however—French villas are undergoing renovation for use as businesses and small hotels, mainly catering to investors and visitors from Thailand.

Orientation

Vientiane actually refers to three entities. Vientiane City has a population of 150,000, there are 180,000 people in Vientiane Prefecture, and Vientiane Province contains 300,000 inhabitants.

Vientiane is a city of villas and boulevards. Street signs are mostly in Lao script—or occasionally French—but getting around is easy. Points of reference are more often landmark statues, monuments, or prominent wats rather than streets.

Nam Phu Square, arrayed around a fountain, is the center of town. A bit farther north is That Dam, a large stupa stranded in a traffic circle. Legend has it a seven-headed dragon lurks beneath the Black Stupa, ready to rise up to protect the city in time of dire need. Vientiane's answer to the Arc de Triomphe is Pratuxai Monument, at the northeast end of Lane Xang Boulevard. If you continue along the axis from the Presidential Palace past Pratuxai, you reach That Luang. This huge stupa is the most sacred site in Vientiane and often appears in illustrations as an icon for the city.

Two other landmarks are the statue of King Sisavang Vong, in a traffic circle near Wat Simuang, and the Three Elephants Statue, on Luang Prabang Road. Erawan, the three-headed elephant, comes from Hindu mythology. In Laos, it was a former royal symbol, adopted by Lao kings in keeping with the Kingdom of Lan Xang, or Land of a Million Elephants.

Out in embassy land, along Tha Deua Road, addresses are based on kilometers from the Presidential Palace. Thus Tha Deua KM4 is four km down Tha Deua Road from the palace, Tha Deua KM5 is five km, and so on. Tha Deua Road stretches some 20 km to the Tha Deua foot-passenger crossing opposite Nong Khai.

SIGHTS

Vientiane does not possess the wealth of traditional sites common in other Asian capitals; Vientiane's original wats and sacred sites were mostly destroyed by the Thais in 1827. Modern touches like the Revolutionary Museum are little more than crude propaganda—the museum features photo displays chronicling the revolutionary struggle, plus military hardware. If you're in Vientiane during a festival, there will be lots of action on the streets; otherwise, Vientiane is not the place for temples or nightlife—Bangkok is the place for that. Visitors come to Vientiane to slow down. Get yourself a fresh coconut or beer, kick back, chill out, and watch the sun go down over the Mekong.

Wat Sisaket

Wat Sisaket is the oldest surviving temple in Vientiane, and easily the most impressive. It was built in 1818 by King Chao Anou and survived the Thai incursions of 10 years later. The temple is active, with some 20 monks attached who live in *kutis* to one side.

Wat Sisaket has an intriguing design—a central temple with a Thai-style five-tiered roof, enclosed by a square cloister, a courtyard with covered passageways facing the temple. The cloister galleries contain over 300 seated and standing Buddhas; set in niches behind them are several thousand smaller silver and ceramic Buddha images. The count of Buddhas large and small at Wat Sisaket is estimated to exceed 6,000. During Lao New Year, the Buddhas are ritually cleansed—water is poured over them. At the end of Buddhist Lent, the larger Buddha statues in the courtyard are "fed"—Laotians make a circuit of the temple, placing sticky rice in the hands of each of the larger statues.

On the walls of the galleries are Jataka murals depicting stories from the life of Buddha. Most are damaged, and restoration work is being funded by UNESCO. To one side of the compound is a raised library building with a Burmese-style roof; the scriptures were spirited off to Bangkok. Wat Sisaket is open to the public Tues.-Sun. 0800-1130 and 1400-1630, closed Monday and public holidays.

Wat Pra Keo Museum

Down the road is Wat Pra Keo Museum. This wat was originally constructed as a royal temple in the 16th century, built by King Settathirat to house the Emerald Buddha, Pra Keo. The Thais carted off the Emerald Buddha in 1778—it now

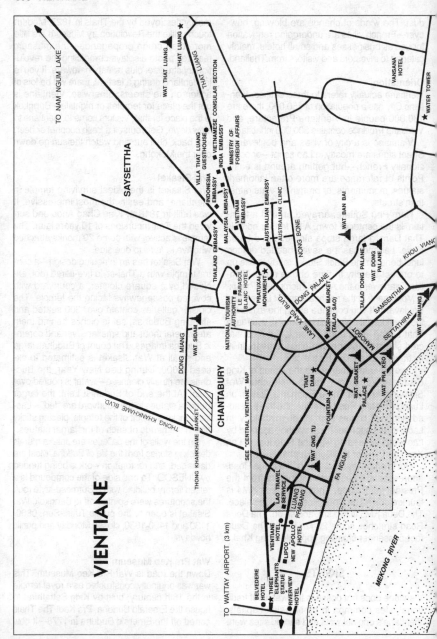

VIENTIANE

TO NAM NGUM LAKE

TO WATTAY AIRPORT (3 km)

SAYSETTHA

CHANTABURY

WAT THAT LUANG

THAT LUANG

VANSANA HOTEL

WATER TOWER

Villa That Luang Guesthouse

Vietnamese Consular Section

India Embassy

Ministry of Foreign Affairs

Indonesia Embassy

Malaysia Embassy

Thailand Embassy

Vietnam Embassy

Australian Embassy

Australian Clinic

WAT BAN BAI

NONG BONE

DONG MIANG

DONG PALANE

Le Parasol
Blanc Hotel

National Tourism Authority

Patuxai Monument

TALAD DONG PALANE

WAT DONG PALANE

KHOU VIANG

WAT SIDAM

MORNING MARKET (TALAD SAO)

LANE XANG BLVD

MAHOSOT

SAMSENTHAI

WAT SIMUANG

SETTATHIRAT

THONG KHANKHAME BLVD

THONG KHANKHAME MARKET

SEE "CENTRAL VIENTIANE" MAP

THAT DAM

FOUNTAIN

WAT ONG TU

WAT SISAKET

PALACE

WAT PRA KEO

FA NGUM

BELVEDERE HOTEL

THREE ELEPHANTS STATUE

RIVERVIEW HOTEL

VIENTIANE HOTEL

LPCO

LUANG PRABANG

NEW APOLLO HOTEL

LAO TRAVEL SERVICE

MEKONG RIVER

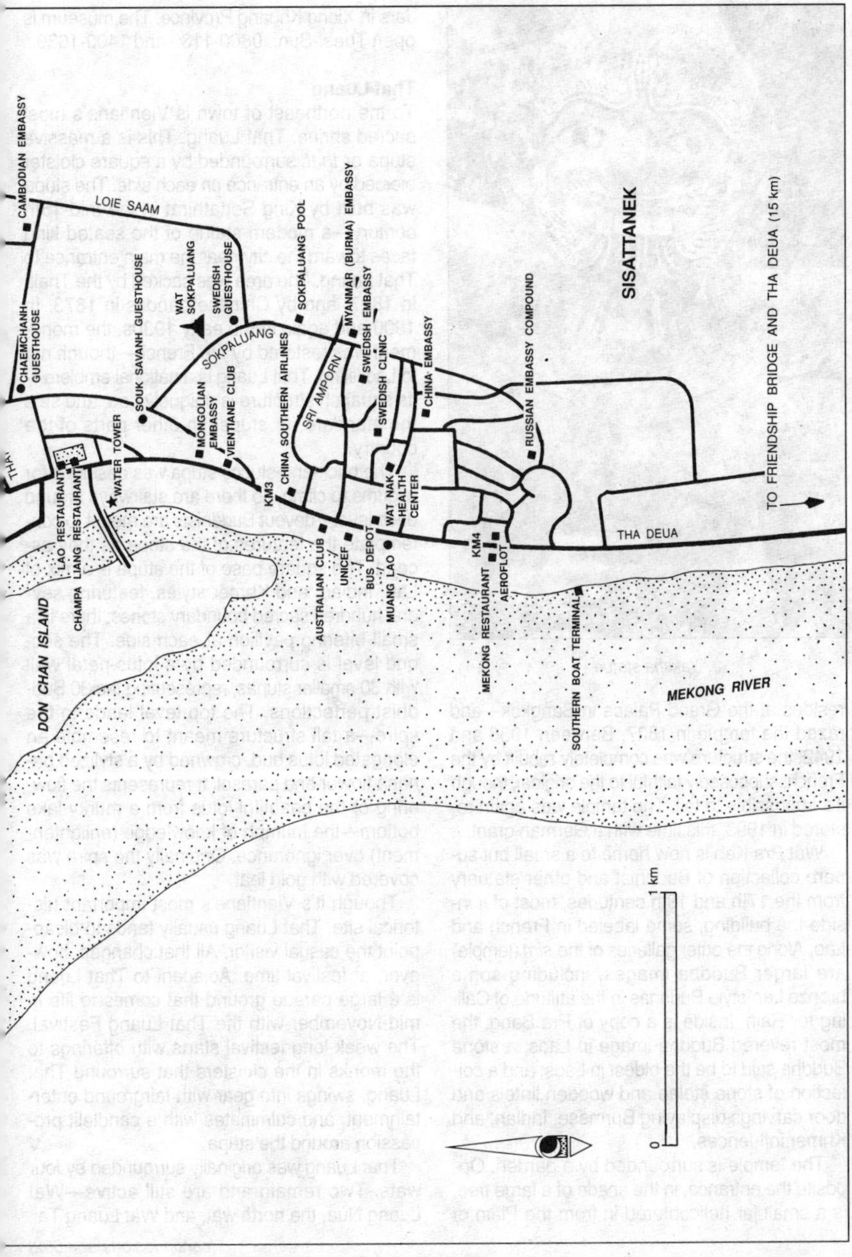

CAMBODIAN EMBASSY

LOIE SAAM

CHAEMCHANH GUESTHOUSE

SOUK SAVANH GUESTHOUSE

WAT SOKPALUANG

SWEDISH GUESTHOUSE

SOKPALUANG POOL

MYANMAR (BURMA) EMBASSY

SWEDISH EMBASSY

SWEDISH CLINIC

CHINA EMBASSY

MONGOLIAN EMBASSY

VIENTIANE CLUB

SOKPALUANG

SRI AMPORN

CHINA SOUTHERN AIRLINES

RUSSIAN EMBASSY COMPOUND

SISATTANEK

THAI

WATER TOWER

KM3

LAO RESTAURANT

CHAMPA LIANG RESTAURANT

DON CHAN ISLAND

WAT NAK HEALTH CENTER

AUSTRALIAN CLUB

UNICEF

BUS DEPOT

MUANG LAO

KM4

AEROFLOT

THA DEUA

TO FRIENDSHIP BRIDGE AND THA DEUA (15 km)

MEKONG RESTAURANT

SOUTHERN BOAT TERMINAL

MEKONG RIVER

1 km

0

© MOON PUBLICATIONS, INC.

Yaksha statue

resides at the Grand Palace in Bangkok—and razed the temple in 1827. Between 1936 and 1942, the structure was completely rebuilt by the French, supposedly faithful to the original, though it's impossible to tell. The temple was again restored in 1993, this time with a German grant.

Wat Pra Keo is now home to a small but superb collection of Buddhist and other statuary from the 17th and 18th centuries, most of it inside the building, some labeled in French and Lao. Along the outer galleries of the *sim* (temple) are larger Buddha images, including some bronze Lao-style Buddhas in the attitude of Calling for Rain. Inside is a copy of Pra Bang, the most revered Buddha image in Laos; a stone Buddha said to be the oldest in Laos; and a collection of stone stelae and wooden lintels and door carvings displaying Burmese, Indian, and Khmer influences.

The temple is surrounded by a garden. Opposite the entrance, in the shade of a large tree, is a small jar helicoptered in from the Plain of

Jars in Xieng Khuang Province. The museum is open Tues.-Sun., 0800-1130 and 1400-1630.

That Luang

To the northeast of town is Vientiane's most sacred shrine, That Luang. This is a massive stupa or *that,* surrounded by a square cloister pierced by an entrance on each side. The stupa was built by King Settathirat in the mid-16th century—a modern statue of the seated king faces toward the city near the main entrance to That Luang. The area was sacked by the Thais in 1827, and by Chinese bandits in 1873. In 1900 and again in the early 1930s, the monument was restored by the French—though not to Lao liking. That Luang is a national emblem—its squarish structure is uniquely Lao, and sets the standard for stupas in other parts of the country.

The brick-and-stucco stupa was designed for pilgrims to climb, so there are stairways around each level—devout Buddhists are meant to contemplate the features of the stupa as they ascend. The square base of the stupa is a mix of Lao, Indian, and Khmer styles, featuring several hundred sacred boundary stones; there is a small offering pavilion at each side. The second level is surrounded by a lotus-petal wall with 30 smaller stupas, representing the 30 Buddhist perfections. The top level leads to the spire—a tall structure meant to resemble an elongated lotus bud, crowned by a stylized banana flower and parasol. It represents the flowering of the beautiful lotus from a murky lake bottom—the triumph of knowledge (enlightenment) over ignorance. Originally the spire was covered with gold leaf.

Though it's Vientiane's most important historical site, That Luang usually tends to disappoint the casual visitor. All that changes, however, at festival time. Adjacent to That Luang is a large parade ground that comes to life in mid-November with the That Luang Festival. The week-long festival starts with offerings to the monks in the cloisters that surround That Luang, swings into gear with fairground entertainment, and culminates with a candlelit procession around the stupa.

That Luang was originally surrounded by four wats. Two remain and are still active—Wat Luang Nua, the north wat, and Wat Luang Tai,

(continues on page 602)

BIKING VIENTIANE

The following tours can be accomplished by bicycle, cyclo, motorcycle, or even on foot. The tours are intended as a rough guide only—if you see something interesting along the way, take a tangent! Use designated bike-parking areas in places like markets; impromptu bike-repair stands around Vientiane are marked by a hanging inner tube or tire. Avoid the killer midday sun: both tours are best attempted in the morning, when it's cooler and there's more activity.

TOUR 1

Vientiane is a great place for bicycling, with spacious boulevards and none of the frantic-paced traffic of Thailand. Not yet, anyway. This is one of the last Southeast Asian capitals where pedestrians and bicyclists still rule the roads.

For breakfast, or to stock up on picnic supplies, head for the south side of the markets, opposite the GPO. There are lots of French bread vendors, and you can buy processed cheese, Spam-pâté, mandarins, fried bananas in batter, and soup. Or frequent a minimart like Phimphone and buy real cheese; eat with the market bread. It's a good idea to carry a bottle of purified water when cycling in Vientiane—stores don't always carry water, and the sickly soft drinks they do stock will only increase your thirst.

Vientiane is a cluster of distinct neighborhoods—this tour takes in a few of them. Start outside the gates of the **Presidential Palace,** the most exclusive turf in town, located on a power axis facing Vientiane's version of the Champs Elysées. Kilometer-counting for areas around Vientiane starts from here. You won't be allowed into the palace—you won't be allowed to even photograph the palace—but at least you can peer through the gates at this stucco belle epoque mansion with its French garden. Formerly the site of the Royal Palace, the building is now used for official state receptions and as a guesthouse for VIPs. The area around the Palace features some of the classiest villas in Vientiane—the palace was the focus of the traditional administrative area, and later the center of French colonial life. Former French villas in this zone vary—some (west of the palace) have been superbly renovated for use by government ministries or foreign investors; some are run-down and occupied by half-a-dozen families; others are slated to be torn down to make way for Thai banks, hotels, and other developments.

First stop: Wat Sisaket and Wat Pra Keo. The more interesting of the two, architecturally, is **Wat Sisaket**—drop in for a quick look. Nearby the French tricolor flies over the **French Embassy** compound: this huge enclosure is a French ministate with French school, French club, and so on. On a building facade to the east of the embassy you can still make out "École de Médecine." Diagonally opposite the rear of the French Embassy is a Catholic church, with masses every morning at 0630 in Lao, and services at 0700, 0830, and 1600 on Sunday.

City Pillar

The main offering at **Wat Simuang** along tree-lined Settathirat Boulevard is young coconuts, followed by bananas, incense, flowers, and candles—which explains the stock of roadside vendors here. Wat Simuang functions as a wish-granting shrine—coconuts and bananas are offered if a wish has been fulfilled. The city foundation pillar, a sacred stone wrapped in cloth and festooned with popping lights, forms the centerpiece of the altar inside the main temple. The stone—probably of Khmer origin—was positioned here in the 16th century, when King Settathirat established Vientiane as his capital. In front of the altar is a small Buddha imbued with magical powers, frequently consulted by Lao people to answer troublesome questions. Wat Simuang is one of the "powerhouses" of Vientiane—packed at festival time, with coconuts strewn all over the floor and the smell of incense thick in the air.

Past Wat Simuang, on a traffic-island park, is a statue of King Sisavang Vong, who died in 1959. Curiously, this Russian-made statue survived the Pathet Lao takeover. Farther along the road, you come to some lakeside restaurants, breezy places for a pit stop. You can make a quick side trip here—take the trail behind the **water tower,** which leads to a narrow bridge to Don Chan Island. From the bridge you can see extensive fruit and vegetable farming on the island, supplying Vientiane's markets.

Back on dusty Tha Deua Road you'll find some exclusive real estate—ambassadorial residences, clubs, private guesthouses for visiting VIPs. Past Vientiane Club and the Prince's Palace, where official government guests are hosted, you come to a Lao gas station. Turn left just past the station, pulling into a more rustic neighborhood featuring basket weaving and coconut grating.

(continues on page 601)

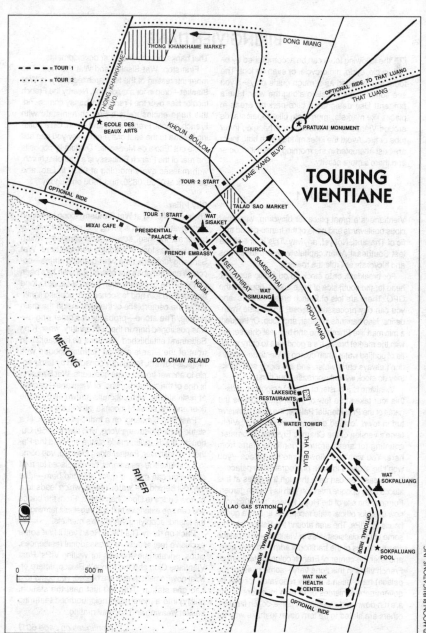

DONG MIANG

THONG KHANKHAME MARKET

- - - = TOUR 1
··········· = TOUR 2

OPTIONAL RIDE TO THAT LUANG

THAT LUANG

THONG KHANKHAME BLVD.

KHOUN BOULOM

★ ECOLE DES BEAUX ARTS

LANE XANG BLVD.

● PRATUXAI MONUMENT

TOURING VIENTIANE

OPTIONAL RIDE

TOUR 2 START

TALAD SAO MARKET

TOUR 1 START

WAT SISAKET ▲

■ MIXAI CAFE

PRESIDENTIAL PALACE ★

FRENCH EMBASSY ■

† CHURCH

SETTATHIRAT

SAMSENTHAI

FA NGUM

WAT SIMUANG ▲

KHOU VIANG

MEKONG

DON CHAN ISLAND

LAKESIDE RESTAURANTS ■■

★ WATER TOWER

RIVER

THA DEUA

WAT SOKPALUANG ▲

OPTIONAL RIDE

0   500 m

LAO GAS STATION ■

OPTIONAL RIDE

OPTIONAL RIDE

★ SOKPALUANG POOL

WAT NAK HEALTH CENTER

OPTIONAL RIDE

© MOON PUBLICATIONS, INC.

BIKING VIENTIANE

(continued)

Forest Wat

Follow the road up to a fork and turn right. A short way along the road is a yellow-and-white triple archway, the entrance to the forest temple **Wat Sokpaluang.** Set in the leafy grounds are three *sims;* about 25 monks and 10 nuns live in residences scattered through the forest and gardens. The peaceful location is ideal for meditation; the abbot conducts courses in *vipassana* meditation. Tucked into a corner of the wat is a primitive but effective herbal sauna—a tiny six-seater box on a second level of a hut, with a 10-gallon drum under burning wood. The sauna is run by nuns and is open all day; a few of the monks and nuns speak English and French. Payment is by donation; there's a teahouse attached.

Some like it cool—down the road is Sokpaluang swimming pool. Open 1300-1900 Tues.-Fri., and 1000-1900 Saturday and Sunday; entry $1. The pool has changing rooms, umbrella shelters, drinks—even swimsuit rentals. Outside and around the corner is a small "traditional medicine sauna" offered by one of the locals. An optional ride (see map) involves going farther south, to the Swedish part of town (Swedish school, Swedish guesthouse, Swedish Embassy), where you're bound to find more in the way of saunas—and yes, there's a largish operation at Wat Nak Health Center, with Finnish sauna 1630-2130 and Lao traditional sauna 1430-2130.

After visiting the Sokpaluang district, you can retrace your route back to Khou Viang street, or loop right around and back to the same street. Khou Viang is very pleasant—a narrow road lined with tamarind trees. These trees have bean pods that the locals like to chew on, but which will make you pucker up like you've never done before. Khou Viang is elevated—it was once part of the old city wall, an earthen fortification with moats on either side. Remnants of the moat are used for growing crops like watercress.

Khou Viang leads right to **Talad Sao,** the Morning Market, with four cavernous two-story buildings—more like a department store. Talad Sao offers mostly consumer goods and hardware, but there's a section in the building to the north selling weavings, Lao cotton, basketware, wood and ceramics, and souvenirs. Oddities include old Soviet cameras, Lao music tapes, jars of herbal medicines—and marijuana, which is sold in the tobacco section. You can call it a day here—there's always tomorrow—or head off on the next tour.

TOUR 2

Start this ride on Lane Xang Boulevard, Vientiane's answer to the Champs Elysées. There at the end looms—can it be?—the Arc de Triomphe. Well, not quite—but they tried. Pratuxai (Victory Gate) Monument was built in the 1960s to honor those who fell in civil wars. Set in a star of radiating boulevards—fashioned after l'Étoile in Paris—the monument is nicknamed "the vertical runway." During construction, the project ran out of cement, so hundreds of tons of the stuff were diverted from a US aid package, meant for an extension for B-52 bombers at Vientiane's Wattay Airport.

Pratuxai is a mix of French and Lao design elements, with Byzantine-like spires cast in US-aid concrete; the interior is popular with local graffiti artists. You can clamber up the concrete steps for a bird's-eye view of the town from the top battlements. There's a small café at the base of the monument, and bike parking for a token fee. The monument is open 0800-1700.

This tour is short—to get your quota of exercise, ride a few km out to That Luang, the great stupa. Then ride back to Pratuxai Monument, and on to Talad Thong Khankhame—the largest produce market in Vientiane, and much cleaner than Talad Sao. Poking around produce markets always reveals some weird variety of flora or fauna. The market is more active in the morning, although it's open all day. Foodstalls serve up cheap Lao food as well as exotic offerings like bat kebabs, or frog or deer meat. Some consumer goods are sold here; lining the road opposite the markets are basketry shops, with ingenious variations on packaging. Use the market's designated bike parking.

A fitting end to a day's hard touring is a cold drink by the Mekong. Unfortunately, there aren't many places where this is possible. One popular spot is Mixai Café, which serves draft Lao beer in plastic tumblers—or bottled beer or other drinks if you prefer. Spicy Lao food is available too. For a quieter place, head in the other direction, past the Riverview Hotel, where you'll find small waterfront huts serving young coconuts, juice, bottled Lao beer, and maybe green papaya salad or barbecued chicken. A mortar and pestle is used to grind up green papaya or green banana, which is then mixed with chiles, garlic, lime, and other condiments. Spicing is done to order—if you're not keen on chiles, order a dish without them. The stalls are great vantage points to catch those last rays over the Mekong.

the south wat. Wat Luang Nua is the more important of the two, with a glittering gold facade. To the east lies That Luang markets; to the north is the National Assembly Building and the Unknown Pathet Lao War Memorial; to the northwest is a Pathet Lao museum (open only to VIPs) with a few tanks, trucks, guns, and aircraft visible within the compound.

You can easily bicycle out to That Luang: it's three km from central Vientiane, or about two km from Pratuxai Monument. That Luang is open 0800-1130 and 1400-1630; closed Monday and public holidays.

Other Sights

Vientiane is a 40-wat city. Most, though they date from the 16th century, were destroyed by the Thais and then rebuilt in the 19th and 20th centuries. The wats are not so interesting for their architecture—more for the fact they're active and the center of festivals. Apart from Wat Sisaket and Wat Simuang, the most important is Wat Ong Tu, which was once connected with Lao nobility. It sits on an axis with four other wats radiating from it—Wat Inpeng to the west, Wat Hay Sok to the north, Wat Chan to the south, and Wat Mixai to the east. With such a tight cluster of wats, there is a lot of dawn activity along Settathirat Boulevard as monks file out to collect alms. Buddhist practices do not permit women to stand higher than monks: women kneel when offering food to the monks, whereas men stand. Both men and women offering food often dress in traditional sash.

Wat Ong Tu is an important center of learning, with a Buddhist Institute that attracts monks from all over Laos. The main temple here has exquisite carved wooden doors and windows depicting scenes from the Ramayana; inside is a huge bronze Buddha from the 16th century. Some other features of note: Wat Chan houses a large seated bronze Buddha from the original site, with panels of sculpted wood; Wat Inpeng offers an elaborate wood and mosaic facade; at Wat Mixai there are some goofy-looking *yaksha* statues—Bangkok-style temple guards—near the front gates.

If you're in town during a festival, you'll find the grounds of key wats become fairgrounds, filled with shooting galleries, food and drink vendors, and such carnival games as trying to throw a hoop over the neck of a live duck among a group of penned ducks. Elaborate presentations of food and gifts to the monks take place at key wats at festival time.

ACCOMMODATIONS

Guesthouses

State Culture GH is the Guesthouse of the Ministry of Culture—a grandiose title for a fleabag hotel, but at least it's downtown. It's located on Manthaturat Road. Rooms are $5, $6, and $10—three beds in a room usually, for as low as $2 a bed. The building has 24 rooms; none appear to have been cleaned since the place opened. The upper floors have no water pressure. North on the same street is a place simply called **Guesthouse** with rooms for $6-8 a person. **Hua Guo GH,** 359 Samsenthai Rd., tel. 8633, is Chinese-run and a bit weird, but the price is right—$8-18 for a room, with hot showers available.

Down by the Mekong are **Inter Hotel** (formerly La Chaleune), 24-25 Fa Ngum Rd., tel. 2408, with 15 rooms for $10 s and $10-15 d; and **Mixai Guesthouse** at 30/1 Fa Ngum Rd., tel. 216213, with eight basic rooms for $8 fan or $12 air-con. The **Phornthip Guesthouse,** at 72 Inpeng Road, is small and clean; it charges $8 a person.

Near the stadium is **Santisouk Guesthouse,** at 77 Nokeo Khoumane St., tel. 215303, with 15 rooms upstairs; downstairs is Santisouk Restaurant. The rooms cost $10-12 s and $15 d, with huge bathrooms, sometimes shared between several rooms. In the same area is **Syri GH,** Chao Anou Quarter, near the stadium, tel. 2394, nice and homey, family-run, with 14 rooms $15-17 s without bath, and $20-25 d with bath. **Lani Guesthouse 2,** 286 Saylom St., tel. 213022, offers seven rooms that go for around $15 apiece.

Vientiane Hotel, opposite the New Apollo on the west side of town, tel. 6250, has 45 uninspiring rooms; $10 fan, $15 air-con, $20-22 with fridge. To the south side of town near a small lake is **Souk Savanh GH,** tel. 4850, with 22 rooms $3-6 a bed—run-down, but popular with visiting Indians and Pakistanis.

Moderate

Hotel rates are subject to government tax of 10-11% plus a service charge of 10%. You can bargain discounts of 10-25% for longer stays. Extra beds added to the room run $7-10. Some hotels include breakfast in the tariff.

Asian Pavilion, 379 Samsenthai, tel. 21430, fax 21432, used to be the Hotel Constellation, which was the pre-1975 roosting place for foreign gunrunners, opium dealers, gold smugglers, spies, mercenaries, and journalists. In the 1960s it was run by Maurice, a gentleman of Corsican, Vietnamese, Chinese, and Lao extraction. Renovated under a Thai joint venture, the hotel still retains some of its old atmosphere. Today the Pavilion offers 43 rooms, ranging from $26 standard and $45 superior to $60 for a suite; an extra bed is $10. **Ekalath Metropole,** on Samsenthai Rd. near That Dam, tel. 2881, fax 4163, has 32 rooms; $10 fan, $20-22 s and $28 d air-con. Inside the hotel is Melody Club disco. **Phimmasenh GH,** at 100 Samsenthai, tel. 8934, features 18 rooms in the $25-40 range—mostly singles.

Lani Guesthouse 1, 281 Settathirat Blvd., Hay Sok, tel. 215639, fax 216103, is down an alley near Wat Haysok—great location, with a beautiful garden. The guesthouse includes 11 rooms in the $25-30 price range. **Anou Hotel,** 3 Heng Boun St., tel. 3324, fax 9378, has 48 rooms, costing $18 and up. It's possible to rent some single rooms for under $18; double rooms run $16-25; suites are $28-35. The hotel has a restaurant and a disco—Anou Cabaret—that is one of the most popular in town. **Saysana Hotel,** Chao Anou St., tel. 213581, features 34 rooms for $20-25 each. **Samsenthai Hotel,** on Manthaturat St., tel. 216287, fax 212116, most likely has midrange prices.

Near Pratuxai Monument is **Le Parasol Blanc,** on Sidamdouan Rd., tel. 216091, fax 214108. The hotel has a lounge and restaurant in a restored colonial mansion; accommodation is in bungalows set in pleasant gardens with a small pool; the restaurant serves European food. There are 34 rooms—$30 s or d; the hotel also rents bikes and cars. Farther east along That Luang Boulevard is the family-run **Villa That Luang,** 307 That Luang Rd., tel. 3617, with 11 rooms in the $20-30 range.

On the west side of town are several new hotels that are most likely moderately priced: the **New Apollo Hotel,** at 69 Luang Prabang, and **Senesouk GH,** at 100 Luang Prabang Rd. KM2, tel. 215567.

On the eastern fringe of Vientiane, and somewhat isolated, is **Vansana,** 9 Phonethan Rd., tel. 413171, fax 413171—a multistory hotel with satellite TV, swimming pool, and lush gardens. It offers 45 rooms for $25 s or $35 d.

To the southern end of town are several moderate places: **Chaemchanh GH** at 78 Khou Viang, tel. 3002, with five rooms for $11 fan/share toilet; $15 s air-con, private toilet; $22 d; also has five $33 apartments with kitchen. The guesthouse has a nice garden. **Oudomphone GH,** 22/241 Dongpalane Rd., tel. 2589, has eight rooms in the $20-25 range. **Thienthong GH,** off Sokpaluang near Wat Nak, rents rooms for $15-20. **Muong Lao (China Hotel),** at Tha Deua KM3, tel. 216287, is parked near the Mekong, and charges $20 for rooms or $40 and up for suites. It has a Thai-Lao restaurant. The **Swedish Guesthouse,** at 34 Sokpaluang, features singles for $30 and doubles for $40-45 with sports facilities—Swedish nationals are given preference.

Luxury

Lane Xang Hotel, Fa Ngum Rd., tel. 214102, fax 214108, is right near the Mekong; centrally located, with a good pool, sauna, tennis court, restaurant, and disco. Decor leaves a lot to be desired—but you can't expect too much from Russian architecture. This dowdy place used to be government-run, but was privatized in 1992. The hotel has 40 rooms for $42 s or $54 d; an additional 20 apartments go for $70-80 apiece.

The Royal (Dokmaideng) Hotel, Lane Xang Ave., tel. 214455, fax 214454, is located just south of Pratuxai Monument. It has air-con rooms and suites, satellite TV, business center, swimming pool, and a nightclub with karaoke lounge—obviously angled for Chinese visitors.

Riverview Hotel, Fa Ngum Rd., tel. 9123, fax 9127, is sited on the western edge of town, close to the Mekong, with 32 rooms—$35-44 s, $44-48 d, $56 t, and $80 for a suite.

The Belvedere, Thanon Luang Prabang KM2, in the direction of Wattay Airport, tel. 213574, fax 213572, is Vientiane's top hotel. It attempts French-style architecture, but the Singapore architect didn't quite bring it off. The Sin-

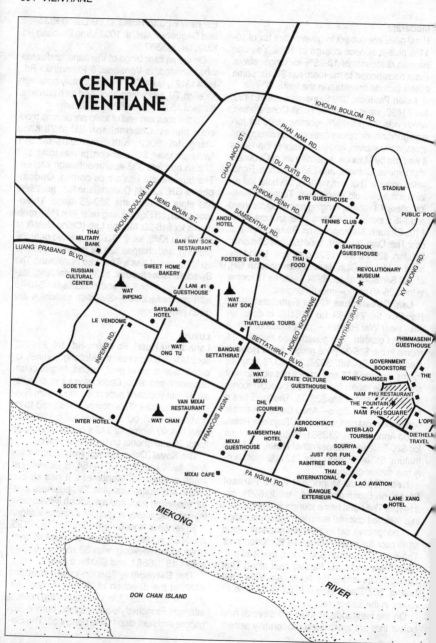

CENTRAL VIENTIANE

KHOUN BOULOM RD.

PHAI NAM RD.

CHAO ANOU ST.

DU PUITS RD.

PHNOM PENH RD.

SYRI GUESTHOUSE

STADIUM

PUBLIC POOL

SAMSENTHAI RD.

HENG BOUN ST.

TENNIS CLUB

ANOU HOTEL

KHOUN BOULOM RD.

THAI MILITARY BANK

BAN HAY SOK RESTAURANT

SANTISOUK GUESTHOUSE

LUANG PRABANG BLVD.

FOSTER'S PUB

THAI FOOD

KY HUONG RD.

SWEET HOME BAKERY

RUSSIAN CULTURAL CENTER

WAT INPENG

REVOLUTIONARY MUSEUM

LANI #1 GUESTHOUSE

WAT HAY SOK

SAYSANA HOTEL

LE VENDOME

THATLUANG TOURS

PHIMMASENH GUESTHOUSE

INPENG RD.

WAT ONG TU

BANQUE SETTATHIRAT

SETTATHIRAT BLVD.

NOKEO KHOUMANE RD.

MANTHATURAT RD.

GOVERNMENT BOOKSTORE

MONEY-CHANGER

THE

SODE TOUR

WAT MIXAI

STATE CULTURE GUESTHOUSE

NAM PHU RESTAURANT

THE FOUNTAIN

NAM PHU SQUARE

VAN MIXAI RESTAURANT

FRANCOIS NGIM

DHL (COURIER)

INTER HOTEL

WAT CHAN

AEROCONTACT ASIA

L'OPE

MIXAI GUESTHOUSE

SAMSENTHAI HOTEL

INTER-LAO TOURISM

DIETHELM TRAVEL

SOURIYA

JUST FOR FUN

RAINTREE BOOKS

FA NGUM RD.

MIXAI CAFE

THAI INTERNATIONAL

LAO AVIATION

LANE XANG HOTEL

BANQUE EXTERIEUR

MEKONG

DON CHAN ISLAND

RIVER

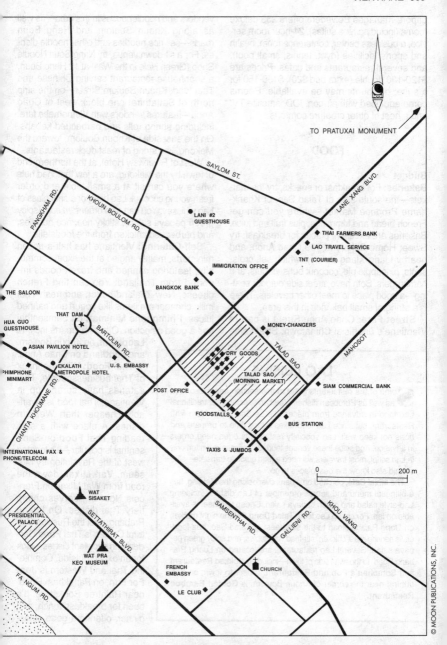

TO PRATUXAI MONUMENT

SAYLOM ST.

LANE XANG BLVD.

PANGKHAM RD.

KHOUN BOULOM RD.

LANI #2
GUESTHOUSE

THAI FARMERS BANK

LAO TRAVEL SERVICE

TNT (COURIER)

IMMIGRATION OFFICE

BANGKOK BANK

THE SALOON

THAT DAM

HUA GUO
GUESTHOUSE

BARTOLINI RD.

MONEY-CHANGERS

ASIAN PAVILION HOTEL

EKALATH
METROPOLE HOTEL

U.S. EMBASSY

PHIMPHONE
MINIMART

CHANTA KHOUMANE RD.

DRY GOODS

TALAD SAO
(MORNING MARKET)

TALAD SAO

MAHOSOT

SIAM COMMERCIAL BANK

POST OFFICE

FOODSTALLS

INTERNATIONAL FAX &
PHONE/TELECOM

BUS STATION

TAXIS & JUMBOS

0   200 m

SAMSENTHAI RD.

KHOU VIANG

WAT
SISAKET

SETTATHIRAT BLVD.

GALLIENI RD.

PRESIDENTIAL
PALACE

WAT PRA
KEO MUSEUM

FRENCH
EMBASSY

CHURCH

LE CLUB

FA NGUM RD.

gapore-managed Belvedere offers 233 deluxe rooms (including nine suites), 24-hour room service, a business center, conference room, health and sports facilities (gym, tennis, small pool), and several restaurants and cafés. Prices are $120-130 double (extra bed $20); $150-160 for a suite; discounts may be available. Rooms come equipped with air-con, IDD, satellite TV, and a host of other creature comforts.

FOOD

Budget
Bakeries: For breakfast or snacks, try the markets—the south side of Talad Sao, or Khankhame Produce Market—where you can get French bread and trimmings, plus fruit and juice. Bakeries are excellent places for breakfast; try Sweet Home Bakery at 109 Chao Anou, and nearby Liang Xiang Bakery, which sell croissants, pineapple pie, coconut buns, donuts, and hamburgers. Both have street side outdoor seating—a good place to meet other travelers. There is a string of small bakeries in this area.

Street Fare: Chao Anou Street is part of Vientiane's unofficial Chinatown. Street side vendors and noodlehouses in this area—as well as along Khoun Boulom and Heng Boun roads—sell rice noodles and other noodle dishes. For a sit-down venue, try Nang Souri Noodle Shop (Green Hole in the Wall) at 12 Heng Boun, a shophouse restaurant serving Chinese and Thai food. Khoun Boulom Street—on the strip north of Settathirat one block west of Chao Anou—features vendors with Vietnamese fare, including spring rolls and barbecued kebabs. On the east side of Khoun Boulom, toward the Mekong, is a string of roast duck restaurants.

West of Riverview Hotel, at the northern end of town by the Mekong, are a few thatched huts where you can sit at a small table and order fresh young coconut, Lao beer, or a shot glass of Lao whiskey. You can also order *tam som* (spicy green papaya salad), sticky rice, rice noodles, and barbecued chicken from the foodstalls.

Self-Catering: Vientiane has half-a-dozen minimarts, mainly angled at the expat community, featuring canned and frozen goods imported from Thailand. You can find French cheese, New Zealand butter, and fresh Thai milk; cheaper are items like yogurt and canned juices. **Phimphone Minimart** on Samsenthai has a good selection. Other minimarts include **Laophanit,** on Khoun Boulom, and **Foodland** on Chao Anou.

Thai Food: With the influx of Thai businesspeople, Thai eateries have sprung up in Vientiane. Thai food is invariably cheaper than Western dishes. A place with a sign reading **Thai Food** on Samsenthai is popular—it's located west of the Revolutionary Museum. **Van Mixai,** down the road from Wat Mixay on Francois Ngin St., serves cheap fiery Thai dishes. On Luang Prabang, past the Russian Cultural Center, is **Thai Food Garden** with excellent dishes—look for an oxcart outside. Combining Thai and Western is **Just For Fun,** on Pangkham Road, near Raintree Bookstore. It's open for breakfast, lunch, and dinner, offering a good selec-

---

LAO CUISINE

Some of the restaurants listed in this section serve Lao food as well as European dishes. You can special order traditional Lao food in advance from places like Le Souriya or Nam Phu Restaurant, but since Lao food takes a long time to prepare and does not keep well, Lao specialty restaurants often need orders in advance. And since these venues tend to offer menus written only in Lao script, most travelers will need a food guide to translate—s/he should also know the best places to go.

The **Mixai Café,** perched on a bank overlooking the Mekong, has a bilingual menu and serves a number of Lao dishes, including Lao-style salad and green papaya salad. Cheap Lao beer is available on tap. For cheap Lao food, **Talad Dong Palane** night market, on Dong Palane Road to the southeast of Talad Sao, has foodstalls serving roast chicken, stir-fried vegetables, and spicy green papaya salad. Several Lao restaurants are located on Luang Prabang Road, to the west side of town—including **Nokkeo Restaurant** and **Somchan's Pub and Restaurant.** Closer to town, on Settathirat near the corner of Khoun Boulom, is **Golden Bamboo Restaurant.**

festival offerings

tion of dishes. Among the vegetarian offerings are fried bean curd with sweet peanut sauce, and lemongrass fried with spicy vegetables. The restaurant also sells cookies, cakes, brownies, a full range of herbal teas, and 10 kinds of coffee—French roast, Lao, Viennese. Just For Fun is a fundraiser for a weaving cooperative.

Other: Pricier—but still affordable—are some places on the west side of town. **Noorjhan,** at 366 Samsenthai, serves up good Indian food—curries, samosas, chapattis, masala dosa—at fair prices. **Ban Hay Sok Restaurant,** across from Anou Hotel, offers Chinese food. On the ground floor of the Inter Hotel is a place that serves up sizzling platters of steak and fries—honest portions at reasonable prices.

Upscale

Nam Phu Square: This area is known for its upscale restaurants. Right next to the fountain is **L'Opera,** tel. 215099, a branch of a Bangkok restaurant. L'Opera has Italian pizza and wines, Italian chef and management, and, of course, Italian opera. The restaurant boasts the only Italian ice-cream machine in Laos—stop by for a gelato takeaway. Also facing the fountain is **Nam Phu Restaurant,** tel. 216248, a long-established venue with an interior of white-washed walls and dark timber, and tables of smoked glass with varnished rattan. This low-key place has a selection of fine French dishes including frog's legs Provençale and steak au poivre vert. The French-speaking proprietor

waits on the tables herself. You can special order Lao dishes in advance. Around the corner is **the Taj,** tel. 212890, with an extensive menu of north Indian and halal cuisine.

French Cuisine: One of the premier venues for French food is **Le Souriya,** at 31/2 Pangkham Road, tel. 215887. The menu features some imaginative items: courgette veloute with cheese, stuffed green peppers, green asparagus souffle, and duck in pineapple, along with fine wines. You can order in advance for traditional Lao food. The atmosphere is identifiably French colonial, with an interior decorated with Parisian posters. The restaurant is owned by a Hmong princess. The **Arawan Restaurant,** at 474 Samsenthai, offers a range of French dishes—coq au vin, lobster thermidore, crab farcie, and filet mignon, as well as appetizers, soups, salads, cheeses, and wines. Next door, owned by the same family, is a charcuterie selling delicacies imported from France—wines, cheeses, and pâtès. **Le Vendôme,** near Saysana Hotel, has French ambience, French food, French management, and French prices. Located in an old mansion, it has a range of pizzas from a wood-fired oven. The interior is decorated with Lao and Thai antiques; there are breezy tables on a shaded verandah. Near the Revolutionary Museum is the **Saloon,** with Thai and European food served in a Wild West decor saloon.

Garden Restaurants: A good place for breakfast is the garden of **Le Parasol Blanc;** the interior dining room, in a beautiful old mansion, is known for its European cuisine. **Lani Guesthouse 1** also has tables in a garden setting—great for breakfast.

Water Views: To the south end of town are three lakeside pavilions—a breeze wafting off the lake here breaks the heat. Visit these places for a meal or drinks, or both. **Champa Liang Restaurant** serves seafood and can be pricey—eat either outside on a terrace or inside in air-conditioned comfort. The restaurant nearby serves Lao food, including a hotpot dish cooked at the table; no English menu. **Sala Icecream**, the third pavilion, serves cheaper Thai dishes.

Farther south, fronting the Mekong, is the pricey **Mekong Restaurant** at Tha Deua KM4, tel. 312480—a vast venue serving international and Asian food, and catering to large groups. This air-conditioned place is popular with expats and upper-income Lao people.

NIGHTLIFE

In the early 1970s, before the Pathet Lao took over Vientiane, the city had a high-flying nightlife that catered to CIA agents, Air America pilots, French advisers, and hippies on the overland trail. Exotic bars like the White Rose, the Purple Porpoise, the Green Latrine, and le Rendezvous des Amis sprang up. Paul Theroux summed up the nightlife in his 1975 work *The Great Railway Bazaar*, "The brothels are cleaner than the hotels, the marijuana is cheaper than pipe tobacco, and opium easier to find than a glass of cold beer." Marijuana is still cheaper than tobacco (it's used as a cooking spice for soup by the locals), but the brothels have been turned into guesthouses—the women exiled to an island in Nam Ngum Lake for re-education—and the opium dens are gone.

Vientiane is quiet at night. The era of complete austerity under the Pathet Lao has been loosened—Stalin is dead and has been replaced by Madonna, at least with the younger set. You can join them at the **Anou Cabaret**—the hottest disco in town, attached to the Anou Hotel—or at the **Vienglaty,** on Lane Xang Boulevard, near Talad Sao, featuring live bands. There are half a dozen other dance venues around Vientiane, mixing Western disco and Lao *lam wong* dance music. The older set indulges in ballroom danc-

AT THE MOVIES

The Lao PDR has no film industry to speak of: a black-and-white movie called *Red Lotus* was shot in 1988 by the State Cinematographic Company, but since then, only propaganda efforts have appeared. Therefore only imports are viewed in Vientiane. There are two snags: strict government censorship, and a stipulation that all dialogue must be rendered in Lao. Since dubbing and subtitling in Lao is prohibitively expensive, exhibitors must provide translations of the screen dialogue for readers to speak *live* over the PA system during projection. At the Odeon Rama cinema on Talad Leng Road in the Chanthabouly district, four readers sit hunched in a little booth next to vintage Russian projectors. As the film is projected, the original dialogue must be switched off when a character speaks, with Lao dialogue simultaneously substituted. Although popcorn is sold in the lobby, Laotian filmgoers prefer munching on black watermelon seeds. Film offerings are largely limited to recent Thai and Chinese films. No Westerns are allowed—government censors apparently don't like gunfights.

ing at the **Blue Star** out on the airport road past the Belvedere Hotel. Otherwise, entertainment mostly focuses on major hotels (which usually have a bar or disco) and a few popular watering holes. Hotel soirées may feature traditional music—one venue is the Saysana Hotel restaurant, 1800-2100; the Saysana also has a disco. Salongxay Restaurant at the Lane Xang Hotel has similar digestion-easing music; the hotel also features a nightclub. The downstairs bar and lounge at Le Parasol Blanc hotel often features live piano music.

Embassy staff have created their own nightlife—movies, video rentals, in-house bars, and so on. The French have Le Club, the Aussies the Australian Club. These places are usually for members only, but if you have the right passport, you may be able to get in.

Expats congregate at the open-air bar around Nam Phu, the fountain at the center of town. The fountain was out of action for many years, but was restored to working order in 1991 courtesy of a Swedish joint venture, and lights up in full gushing majesty for an hour or so at 2100. Drinks are pricey—beers cost double the regular tariff. If you want cheap draft beer, go to **Mixai Café** on the Mekong. After hours, **Fosters' Modern House Pub** is open 2200-0200.

SHOPPING

An excellent map for finding shops is enclosed in the back flap of *The Vientiane Guide,* issued in Vientiane; you might be able to obtain the map separately. The map is annotated with fine detail on which section of town sells what. Textile, clothing, and handicraft shops are mainly located along Samsenthai, Pangkham, and Settathirat roads. Some shops specialize, others carry a full range of Lao handmade products. The northernmost building of the Morning Market (Talad Sao) stocks cotton goods, modern weavings, basketry, silverware, and handicrafts. There's an excellent range of textiles, and a great array of silverware, including betel nut trays, opium pipes, and silver bowls. Inquire what percentage silver is used. Visitors should note that exporting antiques and Buddha images is strictly banned in Laos.

Textiles

Vientiane sells a wide range of silk and cotton fabrics in attractive designs and colors. These are mostly handmade by loom—items are fashioned into scarves, shawls, *sinhs,* small bags, pillowcases, slipcovers, and wall hangings. Pure silk is expensive, so weavings often consist of cotton, or a blend of silk and polyester. Hilltribe embroidery is usually sold at the textile shops. You might also find some antique textiles—family heirlooms of hilltribe origin, up to 150 years old. There are also re-creations of ancient designs.

Lao Textiles, at 84 Nokeo Khoumane, housed in an old French villa, designs handwoven silks for major couturiers in Europe and North America. The shop sells fabrics, accessories, and museum-quality wall hangings—prices are high. Lao Textiles was founded in 1990 by textile designer Carol Cassidy, who uses a Macintosh computer to interpret traditional colors and designs; her master weavers then use handlooms to transform these designs into fabrics for fashion and decor.

The UNICEF-supported **Art of Silk,** on Manthaturat St. opposite Samsenthai Hotel, offers a variety of textiles, clothing and accessories, and antique weavings. Operated by the Lao Women's Union, the Art of Silk preserves old textiles and trains weavers in traditional techniques. Upstairs is a small museum of old textiles.

To the west side of town, north of Luang Prabang Road and near Wat Oupmoung, is the factory and salesroom of **Lao Cotton,** supported by the UN to preserve weaving skills and develop contemporary products. Lao Cotton has a wide range of cotton fabrics and readymade articles, including bed linen, table linen, and upholstery items. There is a small Lao Cotton shop on Settathirat Blvd. near the fountain, and another branch on Sokpaluang Road, opposite the Swedish Guesthouse.

Clothing

There are many Vietnamese tailors north of Nam Phu Square, on Pangkham and Samsenthai Roads. You can hand over a piece of clothing and have it copied; all material purchased from Talad Sao should be preshrunk before dressmaking. Lao Vilai Fashions, at 24 Samsenthai, has designer-created fashions for women, using Lao cotton—it exports to Europe.

Handcrafted Goods

Talad Sao is a good place to look for handmade goods. Opposite Talad Thong Khankhame, the market to the northwest of town, is a large basketware section. Along Pangkham Road are a number of shops selling woodcarvings, silver ornaments, and cotton and silk goods. Two of these are **Kanchana Boutique,** near That Dam; and **Lao Phattan Art and Handicraft,** opposite Lao Aviation. At 18-20 Settathirat is **Somsri Handicrafts,** with a selection of crafts and antiques upstairs. **Nang Xuan,** at 385 Samsenthai, features a selection of old opium pipes and hilltribe jewelry. **Phonethip,** at 55 Saylom St., offers handicrafts and ceramics. Furniture items made of rattan, bamboo, and teak can be found in Vientiane, or you can custom order them from workshops on the fringes of town.

SERVICES AND INFORMATION

Communications services are poor in Laos, but changes are coming rapidly to Vientiane. In 1992, the Lao government permitted foreign newspapers, IDD, private fax machines, and satellite dishes for the first time. In 1993, the government signed a telecom and broadcasting deal with Thai giant Shinawatra; in 1994, the Lao Information and Culture Ministry issued a small-circulation weekly newspaper, the *Vientiane Times*—the country's first English newspaper since 1975.

Tourist Information

Don't bother with Lao National Tourism Authority—its only function, it seems, is to attend to the issuing of documents, or research ways of boosting tourism. There's a dearth of information about current conditions in Laos. Aerocontact Asia is a tourism promotion and development company at 23 Manthaturat Road, tel. 217294, which issues a magazine called *Discover Laos,* published every few months—a good source of current news and events, with up-to-date hotel listings. Lao Aviation publishes its own in-flight magazine, *Dok Champa,* which sometimes features illuminating articles, and carries a good map of Vientiane. You might bag one at the Lao Aviation office.

Maps

The Lao National Tourism Authority distributes a large detailed map of Vientiane, printed in China and most likely difficult to find. It might be available from Raintree Bookstore or the Lane Xang Hotel shop. Map street names are given in both English and Lao script; the reverse side carries a bilingual map of Vientiane Prefecture. In the back flap of *The Vientiane Guide,* available at Raintree Bookstore, is an oversize sketchmap of Vientiane, issued by the Women's International Group. This map has excellent annotations for those interested in shopping; you might be able to purchase it separately from *The Vientiane Guide.*

The State Geographic Service, located on a side street to the west of Pratuxai Monument, has topo maps of a number of regions in Laos. They're plastered all over the walls, so you just point to the relevant map and the clerk will trot off and attempt to find it.

Books

Raintree Bookstore, at 25 Pangkham Road, tel./fax 212031, caters to English and French speakers, stocking Thai newspapers and some travel books. Since it's the only decent bookstore in Laos, it's the sole source of information on travel conditions—check the notice board. Raintree sells *The Vientiane Guide,* an annual tome written in Vientiane by the Women's International Group, and a booklet called *Guide to the Wats of Vientiane.* It also sells some Lao-English dictionaries and phrasebooks, as well as artifacts.

The Lane Xang Hotel has a small book counter. You might try the gift shops of other major hotels in Vientiane, such as the Belvedere Hotel. On the north side of the fountain is the government bookstore—more for Laotians learning English—stocking some posters, maps, folk tapes, and children's books.

Satellite TV

Satellite dishes are starting to sprout up around Vientiane—a regular dish can pick up StarTV, which includes BBC World Service; a large dish picks up CNN. Satellite dishes are provided to the Lao market by Samart Group, the largest dishmaker in Thailand.

Fax and Phone

International phone, fax, and telex service is available on Settathirat, near Nam Phu Square, in a set of restored villas. The telecom section is open 0800-2200 daily. Fax is expensive—$15 a page to Switzerland, $6 a page to Bangkok. The phone system has been greatly expanded since 1990, and is chaotic: various aid projects have resulted in many kinds of phone lines, so the numbers keep changing as the streets are dug up and new systems laid by the Australians, Japanese, Germans, and French. Starting in 1994, phone numbers were being replaced citywide to configure them to IDD. In this mixing and matching, phone numbers are notoriously unreliable. Cellular phones are now making an appearance, prompted by Thai businessmen. The city code for Vientiane is wildly variable—21 is the most common code, but 31, 41, 16, 17,

VIENTIANE EMBASSIES

Foreign embassies in Vientiane are roughly grouped in two areas—to the east of Pratuxai Monument, around That Luang Boulevard; and to the south end of town, around the Sokpaluang area. There are over 20 foreign embassies in Vientiane. These include:

Australia, Nehru St., Wat Phon Xay area, tel. 413610

Cambodia, Saphathong Nua area, tel. 314952

China, Wat Nak St., Sisattahanak area, tel. 315103

France, Settathirat Blvd., tel. 215258

Germany, 26 Sokpaluang, tel. 312111

India, That Luang Rd., tel. 413802

Indonesia, Phon Kheng Rd., tel. 413910

Japan, Sisangvone Rd., tel. 212623

Malaysia, That Luang Rd., tel. 414205

Mongolia, Tha Deua KM2, tel. 315220

Myanmar (Burma), Sokpaluang Rd., tel. 312439

Russia, Thaphalanxay area, tel. 312219

Sweden, Wat Nak, Sokpaluang area, tel. 315018

Thailand, Phon Kheng Rd., tel. 214582

U.S.A., Bartolini, That Dam area, tel. 212580

Vietnam, That Luang Rd., tel. 413400

and 101 also appear. For the international operator, dial 16.

Post Office and Courier

The General Post Office (PTT) is on the corner of Lane Xang Blvd. and Khou Viang. It's open 0730-1130 and 1400-1700 daily, 0800-1000 Sunday, and handles mail, poste restante, and local phone calls. The post office stocks huge stamps with flora and fauna and other eye-catching designs—worth a visit if you're a collector. Wondrous though the huge Lao postage stamps are, make sure you see them cancelled in front of you on an envelope, or they might be recycled. Contents of packages must be inspected before they are sealed. The post office offers Express Mail Service (EMS).

Commercial courier service in Vientiane is handled by DHL at 52 Nokeo Khoumane Rd., tel. 216830; and by TNT on Lane Xang Boulevard, tel. 214361. A UPS office also operates in Vientiane.

Banks

The Thai baht has become the coin of the realm in Vientiane, partly because it's easy to shift funds back and forth over the Mekong in baht. There has been a frenzy of Thai bank building in Vientiane, with half-a-dozen banks now installed—Bangkok Bank, Siam Commercial, Thai Military, Thai Farmers, Krung Thai, Bank of Ayudhya. Thai banks give a slightly better rate than Lao banks for US cash to kip, but slightly worse rate for traveler's checks to kip.

The **Banque pour le Commerce Extérieur Lao,** at 1 Pangkham Rd., charges no commission on traveler's checks to kip. It charges 1.4% for converting US traveler's checks to US cash, so a $100 traveler's check nets $98.60 cash; Thai banks charge two percent for the same conversion. The Banque Extérieur is the agent for Visa in Vientiane, but charges four to six percent commission on Visa withdrawals. Try the Thai banks if you need a cash advance on a credit card. **Diethelm Travel,** near Nam Phu Square, is the American Express agent in Vientiane.

For fast changing, or if changing when banks are closed, try the private moneychangers who deal in cash—one near Nam Phu, two more to the north side of Talad Sao market. Higher-denomination US bills fetch a slightly higher rate.

Business Services

Computers are creeping in, with specialist shops near the intersection of Chao Anou and Settathirat Roads. Typing and word processing are available at the **Russian Information Center,** tel. 3228, which also has audiovisual equipment for rent. Photocopy shops are easy to find downtown; one-hour film processing is on its way, with Kodak setting up shop. Business hours for shops and offices in Vientiane are roughly 0800-1200 and 1400-1700; Saturday 0800-1200; closed Sunday.

Health Care

The Australian and Swedish embassies both operate their own clinics for embassy staff, but may be consulted by other foreigners on a paying basis. The Australian clinic is located in the Australian Embassy Compound, tel. 413603; on weekends or after hours, call 312343. The Swedish clinic is near the Swedish Embassy, tel. 315015. Both clinics are normally open mornings only; on weekends or after hours, call 312343 or 217010. There's also the International Clinic, Mahosat Hospital Compound, Settathirat Blvd., tel. 3113 or 214018.

Rest and Recreation

Swimming Pools: Lane Xang Hotel pool is $1 0800-1800—approach it from Settathirat Blvd.; there's a bar nearby in the garden. Near the stadium is a public pool charging 50 cents; Tues.-Fri. 0730-1100 and 1300-1600, Saturday and Sunday 0600-1700. To the southeast is **Sokpaluang Swimming Pool,** open Tues.-Fri. 1300-1900, and Saturday and Sunday 1000-1900; it has changing rooms, umbrella shelters, drinks, and swimsuit rental.

Saunas: In the Sokpaluang area are a number of saunas—some attached to wats, some private. Herbal saunas are provided at Wat Sokpaluang and Wat Sri Amphorn; Wat Nak Health Center offers a Finnish sauna. Some hotels, like the Royal, also offer saunas.

Other: Vientiane Golf Club has a six-hole course at KM6. There is a small pro shop with golf supply rentals and sales, and a clubhouse. Vientiane Hash House Harriers organize a run every Monday at 1700, open to all. The Hash venue is posted each week at the Australian Embassy Recreation Club and a few other locations.

GETTING THERE

By Air

International and domestic arrivals and departures are from Vientiane's **Wattay Airport,** three km west of town. As Laos opens up, there may be more direct flights into the country. For the moment, Bangkok serves as the main staging point for international flights to Vientiane. Air France, for example, routes passengers through Bangkok, where they transfer to a Lao Aviation B-737 flight to Vientiane. Bangkok to Vientiane takes an hour; ticketing is jointly operated by Lao Aviation (mostly weekday flights) and Thai Airways International (weekends). The price is $100 one-way, but you can sometimes get special fares. Lao Aviation in Bangkok is at 491/17 Ground Floor, Silom Rd., tel. 236-9822; Thai Airways is at 485 Silom Rd., tel. 233-3810.

If you're bumped from a Bangkok-Vientiane flight, an alternative is to fly north to Udon Thani. From Udon Thani airport there's a Thai Airways express bus to the office in Nong Khai, 53 km north. From here, you can cross by land into Vientiane. There are also twice-weekly flights from Chiang Mai to Vientiane.

Flight information for Laos is unreliable. Services fluctuate depending on traffic volume and the air-worthiness of Russian turboprops used on some runs. There are two return flights a week from Hanoi to Vientiane—one on Tuesday on Lao Aviation, and the other on Thursday on Vietnam Airlines. The tariff is $90 one-way on both airlines. In Hanoi, Vietnam Airlines is agent for both airlines; in Vientiane, Lao Aviation serves as agent for both. There are also connections to Saigon/Ho Chi Minh City on Lao Aviation for $170 one-way.

Lao Aviation flies Vientiane to Phnom Penh once or twice a week for around $150 one-way—flights may go to Saigon first. Royal Air Cambodge flies Phnom Penh to Vientiane once a week. From China, there's a flight from Guangzhou via Kunming on China Southern Airlines once a week, which costs $280 one-way from Guangzhou and about $120 one-way from Kunming. The Kunming-Vientiane fare seems to change often, but since it's only one hour by air, you shouldn't pay too much. There's also a five-hour flight from Vientiane to Beijing; $338 one-way, $475 return on Saturday. Lao Aviation plans to open new routes to Rangoon, Singapore, and Hong Kong.

Transfers into Vientiane: Bargain hard—it's not far from Wattay Airport into town. Metered taxis charge $2, and a jumbo should cost under $2 for the 10-minute ride. Drivers often try to charge $7. In the reverse direction, fares are lower.

Airline Offices: Lao Aviation, 2 Pangkham St., tel. 212051/4, fax 212056, handles most international and domestic bookings, including arrangements for other carriers such as Air France, which does not fly out of Vientiane though you can make Bangkok bookings through Vientiane. Almost opposite Lao Aviation is the office of Thai Airways International, tel. 216143. Lao Air Bookings, at 43/1 Settathirat Blvd., tel. 216761, is a Lao Aviation and Vietnam Airlines agent handling international tickets. China Southern Airlines has an office at Tha Deua KM3; the Aeroflot office is at Tha Deua KM4.

By Land

From Thailand, the access town to Laos is Nong Khai, a relaxed town along the Mekong with pleasant riverfront guesthouses and restaurants. Nong Khai offers a full range of accommodations, from the budget Mekong Guesthouse to the upscale Mekong Royal Holiday Inn. There are a few guesthouses in Nong Khai that handle Lao visas—some are couriered back to Bangkok, others go over the Mekong to Vientiane for approval. The process can take from a day to two weeks. To reach Nong Khai from Bangkok takes 12 hours by overnight train and costs $14 for a regular sleeper. You can also get there by air-conditioned bus, or travel by air to Udon Thani and then take a bus. Thai bus companies run direct air-con luxury buses from Bangkok into Vientiane over the Friendship Bridge for around $20.

Roughly 60% of arrivals in Laos come overland at Nong Khai. Previously, the main crossing from Nong Khai was by foot-passenger ferry to Tha Deua, or by car ferry two km upstream. These operations have been eclipsed by the 1994 opening of the Friendship (Mittaphab) Bridge, with a link to Tha Naleng, about five km from Nong Khai. From the Thai side, you can reach the bridge for $1 by *tuk-tuk;* then you take a minibus across the bridge. At the Lao side of the bridge, you must change transport; there's direct bus and taxi service from the Lao side into Vientiane, a distance of about 20 km. The cost is about 30 cents by local bus, or $4 in an old taxi—double that in a newer metered taxi. A fleet of new Korean metered taxis sits at the Lao immigration side of the bridge waiting for customers for the Vientiane run. Traffic moves on the left in Thailand, on the right in Laos. This must have posed an interesting design prob-

lem for the bridge engineers. The resolution: bridge traffic moves on the left.

Thai Immigration and Customs is located at the south end of the bridge; Lao Immigration and Customs is at the north end, at Tha Naleng. Immigration checkpoints are open every day 0800-1730, with a small "overtime" service fee charged between 1200 and 1400, and on Saturday afternoon and Sunday. Immigration formalities are very simple—you get a Thai exit stamp, a Lao entry stamp, and a Customs declaration form. Coming off the north end of the Friendship Bridge there's a crossover where left-handed traffic moves to the right-hand side of the road. Right-hand traffic from Laos approaching the bridge moves to the left-hand side.

GETTING AROUND

There are no motorcycle-taxis in Vientiane—use **jumbos** for longer distances (either shared with Laotians on fixed runs, or hired individually), or **cyclos** for short distances. Vientiane is small—you can cover the ground by bicycle or on foot.

A fleet of sleek Daewoo cabs from South Korea made their appearance after the opening of the Friendship Bridge. A total of 80 **metered taxis** will be introduced to gradually replace older nonmetered taxis. Fare is 250 kip or 10 baht a kilometer, with a charge of $8 to the Friendship Bridge. Taxi hire is $60 for an entire day. Older nonmetered taxis with no air-conditioning are much cheaper.

For **car rentals** inquire through hotels. A car and driver from Le Parasol Blanc hotel is $40 a day in town (0800-1900) and $50 a day out of town.

Nissan Motors on Settathirat, near the Fountain, has 80cc Yamaha **scooters** for $8 a day (0800-1700). Le Parasol Blanc rents **motorcycles** for $10 a day.

Bicycle rentals cost around $2 a day, though some hotels charge higher. Costing $2 a day are rentals from Phimphone minimart, near Nam Phu; Kanchana Boutique, the handicraft shop opposite Ekalath Metropole Hotel; Inter Hotel; and Syri GH, renting to guests only. Le Parasol Blanc charges $4 a day. Chinese bikes, if you can get them, are sturdier.

traffic near Pratuxai Monument

If interested in **buying a bike,** Chinese and Taiwanese pseudo–mountain bikes are for sale near the central markets—they come complete with derailleurs and back rack for $150. An increasing number of Laotians are using them around Vientiane.

GETTING AWAY

Foreigners are expected to take domestic flights to upcountry destinations. There are flights from Vientiane to Muang Sai for $49 (one-way); Luang Nam Tha, $57; Phonsavan (Plain of Jars), $32; Luang Prabang, $40; Ban Huay Sai, $64; Thakhek, $49; Savannakhet, $54; Saravan, $86; and Pakse, $95. Frequency varies from daily to weekly. Flights to other locations may be available—check with Lao Aviation. Return fares are double one-way fares.

Restrictions have relaxed on other modes of transport. The bus terminal near the Morning Market (Talad Sao) runs a frequent service south to Tha Deua and points in and around Vientiane Prefecture; north to Thalat (Nam Ngum Dam), Vangvieng, and Kasi; and to Thakhek. Another bus station located out by That Luang Market has some buses running to the far south, including departure to Savannakhet (takes 12-14 hours, departs 0530, costs $11), and Pakse (20 hours, overnight trip, costs $14). There are boats to Savannakhet from the Southern Boat Terminal. You can also take a cargo boat from Vientiane to Luang Prabang, but from this direction the journey is upstream and therefore takes longer. It's best to travel from Luang Prabang to Vientiane in the downstream direction. There may be a longtail fast boat service from Vientiane to Luang Prabang; the eight-person boats can cover the distance in eight hours.

Leaving Laos

For information on flight arrivals and departures, call 212066. International departure tax is $5. Get rid of all Laotian kip notes before leaving—the currency is useless outside Laos. Use Thai baht for last-minute money needs. Export of antiques and Buddha images from Laos is strictly forbidden.

Visa Shopping

A **Vietnamese** visa is obtainable only through agents unless you're applying with an invitation; it requires three working days. Costs range $110-150, depending on which agent you deal with. Telex to Vietnam is said to be expensive, but that doesn't account for the $100 markup over the cost of the same visa in Bangkok. If you're applying directly for an invitation visa, the visa section is in a building east of the embassy along That Luang Boulevard.

If flying into Cambodia, you don't need a visa—you can get one on arrival at the airport. If you want to play safe, the embassy in Vientiane issues a one-month **Cambodian** visa for $20 in one day. You need three photos. The embassy is open 0730-1130 and 1400-1700, plus Saturday 0730-1130.

A **Thai** visa runs 400 baht or $16 for a 60-day tourist visa; 500 baht or $20 for a 90-day non-immigrant visa. A visa for **Myanmar** costs $20; you apply yourself. A 30-day **Chinese** visa costs $20 and gives you two months' leeway to get there; issued in four working days. It's worth mentioning that **Mongolian** visas are readily dispensed in Laos, though they may start running immediately.

EXCURSIONS FROM VIENTIANE

If you're on a seven-day transit visa to Laos, you'll probably run out of things to see and do around Vientiane in a matter of several days, so it's wise to look further afield. On a transit visa, you're not supposed to venture out of Vientiane. Check a map of Laos for what this means and you'll find three areas called "Vientiane." There's Vientiane City, Vientiane Prefecture, and Vientiane Province. This confusion can work in your favor. The transit restriction apparently refers to Vientiane Prefecture, which extends for a 20-60 km radius around Vientiane. However, it seems you don't need special permission to visit certain sites in Vientiane Province, which is the much larger area north of Vientiane Prefecture.

East of Vientiane

About 25 km to the east, a few km past the Tha Deua ferry crossing, on the banks of the Mekong, is Buddha Park, also known as Wat Xieng Khuan. Here you'll find bizarre reinforced concrete statues of Buddhist and Hindu deities. The park was built in the 1950s by eccentric monk Bunleua Surirat, who had a large following in Laos and northeast Thailand. When the Pathet Lao moved into Vientiane in 1975, the monk repaired across the Mekong, where—with the help of donations—he built a bigger, even wilder version of concrete kitsch at Wat Khaek in Nong Khai, Thailand. Since the monk had abandoned the original site, the Lao authorities opened it as a public park. You can get there by jumbo from Vientiane.

North of Vientiane

There appears to be no special permission required to visit Nam Ngum Reservoir, about 90 km north of Vientiane. You can make a roundtrip or overnight trip up Route 13 north to Phon Hong, turning right to Nam Ngum Reservoir, then coming back along Route 10 to Vientiane. Route 10 is more scenic, but could be slower going due to a ferry crossing. Options include renting your own motorcycle, hiring a car and driver, or taking local buses. Taxis charge about $30 roundtrip to the lake. A regular bus departs early from Vientiane's Morning Market Station direct to Nam Ngum Dam; otherwise there are five buses a day running to Ban Thalat, from where you can take a pickup to the dam.

If you have your own transport, there are a few picnic stops along the way to Nam Ngum on Route 13. Past KM16 there's a turnoff leading to Khu Kana Falls, about 10 km along a gravel road. Two other picnic spots are Tat Son, with a turnoff at about KM22 and a 15-km journey down a dirt road, and Nam Suang rapids and waterfall off KM40. The falls are only impressive during the rainy season. North of that, at KM52, is a market where Hmong people are sometimes seen. At about 70 km from Vientiane is Phon Hong; turn right at Phon Hong, and there's another market at Ban Thalat, selling forest animals such as deer, rodents, and spiny anteaters (pangolins). Past this lies Nam Ngum Reservoir.

South of Nam Ngum Reservoir, about three km past Ban Keun on Route 10, is a small deer park, with a salt factory nearby. Continuing farther south there's a car ferry across the Nam Ngum River. About five km before the junction of Route 10 and Route 13 there's a turnoff to Houei Nhang Forest Reserve, open daily from 0800 to 1700, with a nature trail leading in from the parking lot. The trail is a leisurely two-hour loop, with points of interest—mainly plant and insect life—explained by a guide.

Nam Ngum Reservoir

East of Ban Thalat you cross a narrow bridge and roll in to Nam Ngum Dam, which dams the Ngum River. The dam is the pride of the nation—the 150-megawatt hydroelectric plant provides much of the electricity for the Vientiane Valley, and power exported to Thailand is an important source of foreign exchange. Thailand buys power via high-voltage lines stretching as far across the Mekong as Udon Thani.

Nam Ngum Reservoir is home to the strangest loggers in the world. They log *underwater*. The forested hillsides here were intentionally flooded to create a lake. It was not until much later that Laotians realized the value of the drowned hardwood trees. It was then determined that submergence underwater had no harmful effect on the quality of the timber. So a Thai-Lao joint venture figured out a system for retrieving the wood. Barges scout the lake's surface, divers locate the lumber, then a subaqua chainsaw is lowered. The diver cuts the tree, and the log is delivered to the surface. Slow and painstaking, but in Laos there's no particular rush.

Countless small islands dot the reservoir. You can arrange a scenic cruise, but you'll have to bargain hard with the boatmen. Fishing, swimming, and picnicking are the major Nam Ngum pursuits. Among the islands are Done Nang (Island of the Men) and Done Nang (Island of the Women), where re-education camps were once located. In 1975 the Pathet Lao rounded up

prostitutes in Vientiane and banished them to a 15-year re-education stint on Done Nang.

For accommodations at Nam Ngum there's a floating hotel—actually a converted barge—with $20 rooms, close to the logging operations. Next door is a floating restaurant with fresh fish below deck. Toward the dam is a set of bungalows for around $15 each per night.

Vangvieng

On the road to Luang Prabang is Vangvieng, a picturesque area with karst formations, caves, and waterfalls. About 160 km north of Vientiane, the Vangvieng area is inhabited by Hmong and Yao tribespeople. A number of caves line the river several km from the town. Ask local boatmen to show you the way—they'll act as guides for a small fee. You need a powerful flashlight to explore; the locals use burning bundles of brush to illuminate the caves. There are half a dozen buses running daily to Vangvieng from Vientiane's Morning Market; the trip takes five hours. An alternative is to hire a car. Another (slow) approach to Vangvieng is to hire a boat at Nam Ngum Dam

and then cross to the northern tip of the reservoir, where you can transfer to road transport. There are a few basic guesthouses in Vangvieng near the market and bus station.

Warning: There is sporadic banditry along Route 13, particularly around Vangvieng and Kasi—which is one reason why the authorities do not like foreigners visiting. It's unclear if this is Hmong insurgency or Hmong banditry—probably the latter. It seems there are opium shootouts between dealers and others in the vicinity, and Hmong with small-caliber weapons sometimes shoot up whole truckloads of passengers for their valuables. On average, a dozen people a year die this way.

Here's a cheery thought: apparently the road is safer during the rice-harvesting season, as potential gunners are then too busy with their crops. In the off season, farmers in the hills are idle and bored and hungry, and their thoughts turn to other cash crops. In 1993 a Western traveler was held up on the road to Vangvieng. The bandits allowed him to take pictures of the hold-up squad, gave him the film, and then took the camera.

LUANG PRABANG

Luang Prabang is the splendid old capital of Laos, featuring a cluster of shimmering royal temples, remnants of the faded grandeur of the Lao monarchy. The town is sited on a tongue of land at a strategic junction of the Mekong and Khan Rivers—originally, ramparts to the south and west sealed off the land approaches. The town is encircled by peaks, and camouflaged by palm trees and dense tropical foliage. Only golden-spired stupas can be seen from a distance.

Luang Prabang has long been the site of local kingdoms; in the 14th century, the first kingdom of Laos, Lan Xang, was established here by King Fa Ngum. The kingdom lasted two hundred years before the royal seat was transferred to Vientiane. When the kingdom of Lan Xang split up on the death of King Souligna Vongsa in 1694, Luang Prabang was one of three independent kingdoms created. The city-state has seen its share of invasions—the place has been sacked and rebuilt, and many older wooden structures have disappeared without trace. Under French rule, a commissariat was established in Luang Prabang, which led to a spate of French residential building. The Lao monarchy endured in Luang Prabang, surviving right up until 1975.

The present population of Luang Prabang is only 25,000—even less in the downtown area. Luang Prabang works its charm on visitors: it has the aura of a place caught in a time warp, with orange-robed monks making their rounds, market and Mekong commerce, women cycling along with parasols to ward off the midday sun. The days of Luang Prabang's isolation, however, are numbered. The town has been ominously earmarked for "development," with plans for a major airport enlargement and a paved road snaking in from Vientiane. When the new airport is fully functional, direct flights to Chiang Mai or Kunming may be possible, leading to a substantial boost in tourism. On the drawing board is a road linking Luang Prabang all the way north to the Chinese border.

Festivals

Usually two to five days should suffice to see Luang Prabang, but if it's festival time, plan to stay longer—if you can find a hotel room. Because of its previous links with royalty, Luang Prabang festivals are elaborate, sometimes lasting a week or longer. The place is packed around festival times, especially at Pimai (Lao New Year) and for the annual boat racing in August. For Pimai, people from all over the province make a

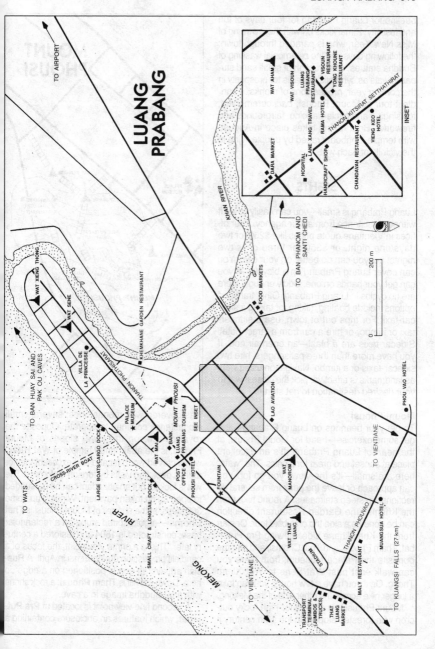

LUANG PRABANG

INSET

Wat Aham
Wat Visoun
Luang Prabang Restaurant
Visoun Restaurant
Yong Khoune Restaurant
Rama Hotel
Lane Xang Travel
Hospital
Handicraft Shop
Dara Market
Vieng Keo Hotel
Chandavan Restaurant
Thanon Kitsirat Setthathirat

Khan River

To Ban Phanom and Santi Chedi

Food Markets

200 m

To Airport

To Ban Huay Sai and Pak Ou Caves

Wat Xieng Thong
Wat Sene
Khemkhane Garden Restaurant

To Wats

Mekong River

Cross-River Boat

Large Boats/Cargo Dock

Small Craft & Longtail Dock

Villa de la Princesse

Palace Museum

Bank
Luang Prabang Tourism
Post Office
Phousi Hotel
Wat Mai
Fountain

Thanon Phothisarat

Mount Phousi

See Inset

Lao Aviation

Phou Vao Hotel

Wat Manorom

Thanon Phouvao

Wat That Luang

Storm

Muangsua Hotel

Maly Restaurant

Transport Terminal (Trucks)

That Luang Market

To Vientiane

To Kuangsi Falls (27 km)

beeline for Luang Prabang for four days of fun and festivity. Pimai kicks off with the crowning of Miss New Year, who is paraded through town; the following days see the ceremonial washing of Buddha statues, construction of small sand stupas in wats as symbolic requests for prosperity in the coming year, processions of monks, a candlelit tour of Mount Phousi, *baci* ceremonies, folksinging and circle-dancing, fairgrounds and fireworks. Boat racing takes place in August, with temple longboats raced by people living in the vicinity of each wat.

SIGHTS

Luang Prabang is small—you can easily cover it without assistance from a tour agency. Tour offices in Vientiane quote prices like $250 for two days/one night, or $350 for three days/two nights, but you can do better on your own. You can cover Luang Prabang on a bicycle—if you can get your hands on one. Oddly enough, there are no cyclos in Luang Prabang. Other transport options include boating, hiking, or taking a sidecar-taxi. For trips out of town, use a sidecar-taxi or jumbo, or hire a car from a larger hotel. Sidecar-taxis are a blast—an open-air ride. If you have more than three passengers, hire two sidecar-taxis or a jumbo. Navigation using wats as landmarks is effective; pick the closest wat to your desired destination to get started.

Mount Phousi

To get your bearings on Luang Prabang—and get some exercise—head for Mount Phousi, at the heart of Luang Prabang. It's an excellent place at sunset and great for picnics. The "wats" here are small—it's the views you go for. You can approach or leave the peak from several directions, up steep staircases. A round hike from the Khemkhane Garden Restaurant direction can be done as a side trip on a bike tour. Or start from the Khemkhane side, viewing Pra Puttabat, Tham Phousi, and That Chomsi, and emerge opposite the Palace Museum; from there you can walk east past Wat Sene to Wat Xieng Thong. Or, if you have a few hours, you can take a longer hike across the other side of the Mekong.

Mount Phousi is a 150-meter-high rocky outcrop with forested slopes. In the 18th century it

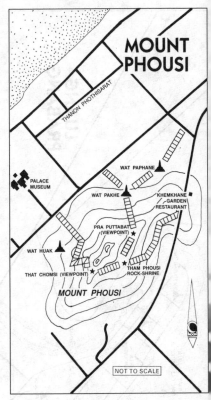

was covered with monasteries; several small monasteries continue to operate. Opposite the royal palace, on the lower slopes of Mount Phousi, is the abandoned temple of **Wat Huak,** with a carved wood facade and excellent interior murals depicting visits by foreign diplomats. The wat is locked, but an attendant can be persuaded to open up on token payment. Winding up some 300 steps, at the summit of Mount Phousi is **That Chomsi**—a gold-spired stupa on a rectangular base, constructed in 1804 and restored a century later. This is a prime viewpoint, the focus of a candlelit procession during Pimai in April. A Russian antiaircraft gun is positioned on a ridge up here. Down the hill is **Tham Phousi,** a rock shrine with a fat Buddha image in a cave.

A second fine viewpoint is located at **Pra Puttabat,** which features an enclosure containing a giant Buddha footprint. You have to locate one of the monks in the vicinity to open the sanctuary. The original wooden temple on this site dates back to the 17th century, with the present structure erected in 1959. Back down at the base of Mount Phousi on the northeast side are two wats; **Wat Paphane** has a classic carved and painted facade.

Palace Museum

The Palace Museum is open for viewing by appointment only. Apparently you need a guide to take you through because officials are paranoid about theft. Arrange your appointment through a tour company or the tourism office in Luang Prabang. A guided tour is $3. If when you drop by there's a group tour going through, you may be allowed to join. Hours are erratic: best bet is weekdays 0830-1630.

The Royal Palace was built 1904-09, with later extensions and renovations. It's surrounded by a high fence and extensive gardens. Although occupied by Lao King Sisavang Vong, the building was commissioned by the French colonial administration, which explains the mix of French and Lao architecture. This effect was intentional—meant to cement the relationship. At the front entrance, high up on the front of the building, is Erawan, the three-headed elephant symbolizing the three kingdoms of Laos. The pillars below bear French fleur-de-lys emblems; you sweep up steps made of Italian marble. Inside are French mirrors and Czech chandeliers alongside traditional Lao lacquered and gilded furniture.

Oil portraits of the last king, Sisavang Vatthana, and the queen and crown prince, painted by a Russian artist in 1967, gaze down from the walls of the former queen's reception room. In the same room is a hodgepodge of diplomatic gifts from foreign heads of state, including items from Mao Zedong, Norodom Sihanouk, Leonid Brezhnev, and Lyndon Johnson. Among the gifts on display is a piece of moon rock collected by Apollo 13, donated by President Richard Nixon in December 1972 "to the people of Laos"—a rather absurd gesture after almost 10 years of carpet bombing by US aircraft. Behind the palace, if you get that far, is the king's favorite car, a white Ford Edsel donated by the US government.

THE KING WHO DISAPPEARED

When King Sisavang Vong died in 1959, he was succeeded by his son Sisavang Vatthana, who set about modernizing the palace—and that's where the trail abruptly ends. Given the sorry history of Laos, and the fact that the Pathet Lao spent years battling Royal Lao forces, the Palace Museum is very odd indeed. A museum brochure claims the last king offered the palace to the Pathet Lao shortly after 1975, and that "the palace was then converted into a national museum, the main aims of which are to preserve the palace and the royal collection and inform the public of the history of the former monarchy."

Official guides are either unable or unwilling to inform the touring public about the palace's last resident, the last king of Laos, Sisavang Vatthana. Ask your guide what happened to the king and you'll draw a blank. First there's the question of whether he was ever even a real king, as the official version has it he was never crowned. Then you have to try and establish if he's alive or dead—some seem to think he's still alive somewhere.

The disappearance of the king is a taboo topic in Laos—the Laotians have never been publicly informed of his fate. After the Pathet Lao takeover in 1975, the king remained in the palace for several years as an "adviser." But with simmering insurgency in the jungles close to Luang Prabang, the monarchy became a symbol of the resistance, so in 1977 the king, queen, and crown prince were shuffled off to the far north, where the Pathet Lao once convened in hidden caves. Locals say the king went to a seminar "to study Marxism"—a polite way of saying he was dispatched to a Pathet Lao re-education camp. When pressed for details by Paris-based journalists in 1989, Communist Party Chief Kaysone Phomvihan said the king had died of natural causes. "It happens to all of us," explained Kaysone, who would not divulge any further details. Queen Kham Phuoy apparently also died in the north—no word was ever given on the fate of Crown Prince Vongsavang, though he is presumably dead too.

The palace was meant to dazzle, and the king's former audience room, used for receiving foreign envoys, certainly does that. The room is located to the right of the entry hall, and the walls are covered with paintings of traditional festivals and daily life in Luang Prabang, rendered in the 1930s by French artist Alex de Fautereau. In the same room are two gilded and lacquered screens depicting scenes from the Ramayana, created by Lao master craftsman Thit Tanh, and three French-made busts of Lao monarchs. In the former Throne Room magnificent glass-mosaic murals on reddish walls depict Lao legends and festivals. The mosaic decoration was commissioned by Sisavang Vatthana, the glass imported from Japan. By contrast, the royal residential area is surprisingly modest—even spartan. It has been preserved as it was the day the royal family was sent into exile.

The Palace Museum includes a small but impressive collection of Lao artifacts and Buddha statues, many brought in for safekeeping by monks from wats or stupas abandoned or destroyed. Even the palace was not the safest place to stash priceless Buddhas. In 1910 the French government sent a specialist to Laos to select articles from the royal collection for the Louvre Museum. A treasure of gold and bronze Buddha statues, works in silver, and other decorative objects was loaded onto a boat that subsequently sank without trace in the Mekong River.

The most sacred image at the Palace Museum is Pra Bang, the standing Buddha image that gives Luang Prabang its name (City of the Great Buddha). The image has both hands held palm out in the attitude of Dispelling Fear, stands 83 cm tall, weighs around 50 kg, and is reckoned to be 90% pure gold. You're most likely looking at a copy, as the original is rumored to rest in a bank vault in Vientiane. The image is reputedly from the first century AD, made in India, presented to the King of Ceylon, then to the King of Cambodia, and eventually finding its way into the hands of Lao King Fa Ngum, founder of the kingdom based in Luang Prabang. In 1778, the Thais invaded Laos and carted the image back to Bangkok. It was then determined, however, that Pra Bang and the Emerald Buddha—taken from Vientiane at the same time—did not see eye to eye; legend has it that if both occupy the

same city, misfortune will befall the place. So the Thais kept the Emerald Buddha, and some 60 years later packed Pra Bang back to Luang Prabang, where it remains a source of spiritual protection for Laos.

Wat Xieng Thong

Every so often, Laos serves up a spectacular feast for the eyes and soul—this is definitely one of them. Wat Xieng Thong has richly decorated chapels and a magical aura about it—the stuff of Oriental fairy tales. The temple was easily reached by boat from the royal palace, as both sites enjoyed Mekong access. At the temple Lao kings were crowned and cremated, and royal ceremonies held. Some ceremonies endure: a temple longboat is housed in a shed to the north side, for use at Lao New Year in April and the annual boat racing festival in August.

Wat Xieng Thong was built by King Settathirat in 1560 and remained under royal patronage for four centuries. The temple survived raids by intruders and has been kept in immaculate condition. Present upkeep is the responsibility of monks—the temple is active, with monks' residences scattered throughout the compound.

Wat Xieng Thong takes its name from a bodhi tree, or *thong,* standing on the site. The rear of the main temple is encrusted with colored glass pieces in a red background, depicting the bodhi tree. The *sim* is pure Luang Prabang style, with low-sweeping roofs; inside, gold-stenciled wooden pillars support a ceiling decorated with dharma wheels. The walls bear rich frescoes. Behind the *sim* are two small chapels. To the north is the Library Chapel, built in 1828, which houses the Tripitaka, or Theravada Buddhist sacred texts. This chapel is normally locked. To the south is the Red Chapel, containing a rare bronze Reclining Buddha with graceful lines that dates from the construction of the temple. A red exterior with glass-inlay mosaic depicting village life was added in the late 1950s.

A similar style of mosaic is found in the interior of the Chapel of the Funeral Chariot—the mosaic here was never completed. It's hard to believe that anything so dazzling—and with such sensuous carvings—could be a garage for a funeral chariot, but that's what this chapel is. Inside is a 12-meter-high gilded wooden hearse enclosing a 12-sided royal funerary urn of the king; up front is a seven-headed *naga* prow, and the entire assembly is mounted on the chassis of a six-wheel truck. The golden hearse was fashioned by Lao master sculptor Thit Tanh to transport the urn of King Sisavang Vong to the stadium next to Wat That Luang for cremation in 1959—the last elaborate funeral rites enacted for a Lao king. The sumptuous exterior chapel panels are sculpted in wood with gold-leaf overlay and show episodes from the Ramayana with erotic overtones. In the late afternoon, if the sun is out, the chapel is bathed in a gorgeous light that really brings the sculpted figures to life.

Near the west gate is a 1990s addition: a small pavilion set in a rose garden houses a seated Buddha in the Earth Witness pose. At the south or city gate are hitching posts for royal elephants; at the north side, outside the temple, a pair of large white cat statues guard the steps down to the Mekong River.

Wat Mai

Next to the palace is Wat Mai, a temple inaugurated in the 18th century. It took more than 70 years to build, and was once home to the Supreme Patriarch of Lao Buddhism. The wooden *sim* is built in classic Luang Prabang style, with a magnificent five-tiered roof and pillars with gold patterns stenciled on black. The dazzling exterior wall bears gold stucco bas-reliefs recounting the legend of Pravet, the last incarnation of the historic Buddha, amid a profusion of village scenes; the top band depicts scenes from the Ramayana.

On the grounds of the wat are some "elephant pillars"—posts painted in red. At Lao New Year, several royal elephants—draped in ceremonial blankets—were tethered at this site; an ear of each elephant was lifted up and a sermon was whispered into it before the elephants took part in a procession. The ceremony continued until the

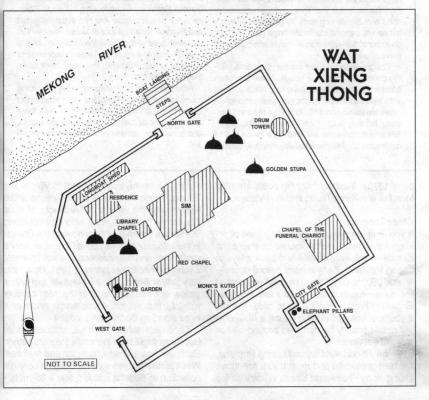

MARKET AND MEKONG BIKE TOUR

Visitors to Luang Prabang tend to focus on the temples, glossing over the town's other charms, like Mekong bustle and market life. Touring by bicycle or with a sidecar-taxi is the easiest way to get a glimpse of local activity. If on a bicycle, park in designated areas when visiting markets.

Start this tour at the foot of Thanon Kitsirat Settathirat, where a flight of stairs leads down to a small-craft loading area. It's very busy here in the early morning, with boats coming in from outlying areas, boats headed upstream for Phong Saly, and longtail boats getting ready to take off for Ban Huay Sai.

Cycle southwest to That Luang market, the largest food market in Luang Prabang, packed with a wealth of produce. Photo opportunities always abound at markets like these—not inside, since the markets are covered and you need a flash, but outside where huge loads are stacked onto motorcycle sidecars. Past the stadium is Wat That Luang, where the nation's penultimate king rests. King Sisavang Vong's ashes are interred inside the large gold stupa at one end of the compound—locals often come to leave offerings.

Straight ahead is Dara market, the prime trading center for consumer goods. Hmong women sometimes shop here, wearing long black dresses with blue sashes and pompom hats. Hmong villages are found about 15-30 km out of Luang Prabang, but they're up in the hills and hard to get to. Silk and cotton sinhs are sold here for $4 to $15 depending on design and quality; textiles, embroidery, and bags are on sale too. Silver is sold by weight, though quality craftsmanship is a factor. Luang Prabang is closer to Kunming than Bangkok, and in the markets Thai consumer goods are starting to give way to Chinese goods. You can find Chinese soap, bicycles, Mao caps, thermoses, and American baseball caps made in China.

From Dara Market, head southward on Thanon Kitsirat Settathirat and turn left toward the Khan River: a small food market is located here at a crossroads. There's a school south of the crossroads; the intersection fills with bicycles when school lets out. From this direction you're treated to a striking view of Mount Phousi, with the gold spire of That Chomsi rising high above. Riding toward Mount Phousi, to the left is Wat Aham, with two banyan trees in the grounds—an important spirit shrine. A pleasant place to take a breather is Khemkhane Garden Restaurant, overlooking the Khan River. An option here is to leave your bike at the restaurant and head off for a foot tour of Mount Phousi. You can climb a set of stairs near the restaurant, hike to That Chomsi, and return via Tham Phousi and Pra Puttabat to Wat Paphane, then walk back along the road to the restaurant.

From Khemkhane Restaurant, carry on cycling round to Wat Xieng Thong, the most stunning of Luang Prabang's many wats. Along the river there are a few open-air places serving drinks and snacks, and sometimes serving up a Mekong sunset as well.

---

early 1970s; elephant hitching posts are also found at Wat Xieng Thong and Wat Visoun.

Other Temples

If you're up early, you'll catch long lines of orange-robed and barefoot monks on their alms rounds on the main streets and back alleys of Luang Prabang. Early means before dawn—around 0500 to 0600. You'll be most welcome at the wats—many of the monks are studying English or French, so it's easy to make friends. If you're in Luang Prabang during a festival, it will most certainly be centered around one or more of the wats.

Of the 40-odd wats around Luang Prabang, the best-preserved and most lavish are those strung along Phothisarat Street, in line with the Palace Museum, from Wat Mai to Wat Xieng Thong. These wats were formerly associated with royalty; the villas and residences of royal Lao family members were also located along this strip, as were the residences of the French in the colonial days. Villa de la Princesse, now a small hotel, was the residence of a real princess; it was returned to her family in 1991. Down this way is **Wat Sene,** with a Thai-style sim with a yellow-and-red roof, built in the 18th century with later restorations. A side temple encloses a large standing Buddha and a drum.

Those interested in Lao art, architecture, or Buddhism might want to explore the wats further. Each wat has its own character and features. **Wat Visoun** features a sim with a high ceiling, a collection of Buddha statues, and a 35-meter-

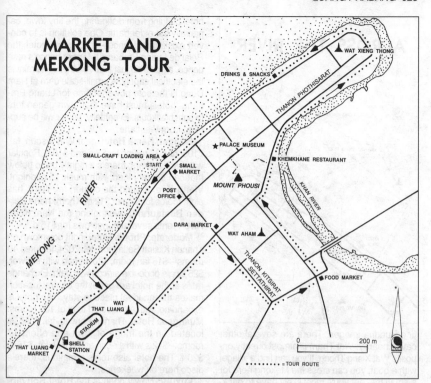

MARKET AND MEKONG TOUR

WAT XIENG THONG

DRINKS & SNACKS

THANON PHOTHISARAT

★ PALACE MUSEUM

SMALL-CRAFT LOADING AREA
START

SMALL MARKET

◆ KHEMKHANE RESTAURANT

MOUNT PHOUSI

KHAN RIVER

POST OFFICE ◆

DARA MARKET

▲ WAT AHAM

MEKONG RIVER

THANON KITSIRAT SETTATHIRAT

◆ FOOD MARKET

WAT THAT LUANG ▲

STADIUM

SHELL STATION

THAT LUANG MARKET

0   200 m

N (MOON)

•••••• = TOUR ROUTE

high Lotus Stupa, called the "melon stupa" because of its shape. **Wat Manorom** is noted for its large armless bronze Buddha, reckoned to weigh several tons and reputedly cast in the 14th century.

Hiking across the River

There are good views of Luang Prabang from the other side of the Mekong—you can ramble along the foreshores here for two to five hours through villages and derelict wats. This side of the river is ideal for hiking because there's hardly any motor transport—even motorcycles disappear. Cross the Mekong by small craft at the landing at the back of the Palace Museum. There's no regular service—the boatman waits till there are half a dozen passengers and then goes. The locals pay about 30 cents; for you the price is double or triple. You can hire the entire boat for $2 for the crossing.

Once across the river, walk to the right to Wat Xieng Mene, in a village of the same name—the wat has an elaborate gilt door. Two km from the village in the forest is the royal cemetery with sculptures of royal family members who could not be cremated—victims of contagious diseases, or children who died as infants. It's hard to persuade local guides to visit this place as they're terrified of ghosts. From Wat Xieng Mene, you can walk up to destroyed Wat Chom Phet, a peaceful spot with expansive views. The walking trail continues to Wat Long Khoun, with a nicely sculpted door and some fading interior murals—there are monks in residence here.

From this point there's a forest trail to Wat Tham, an abandoned wat in a deep limestone cave, with stairs cut out of stone—you need a flashlight to explore. The cave-temple was a storage depot for statuary from destroyed wats around Luang Prabang, and is stacked with rot-

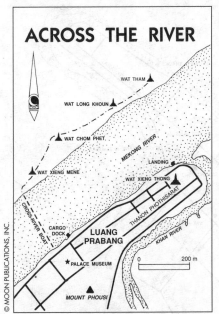

ACROSS THE RIVER

WAT THAM

WAT LONG KHOUN

WAT CHOM PHET

MEKONG RIVER

LANDING

WAT XIENG MENE

WAT XIENG THONG

THANON PHOTHISARAT

CARGO DOCK

CROSS-RIVER BOAT

LUANG PRABANG

KHAN RIVER

★ PALACE MUSEUM

0   200 m

MOUNT PHOUSI

© MOON PUBLICATIONS, INC.

ting Buddha images. There are several other caves nearby. Wat Tham is almost directly opposite Wat Xieng Thong. If you can find a villager with a boat, you can cross the Mekong here for a small fee, but you'll most likely have to backtrack to the Wat Long Khoun area to find a boat.

Boat Touring

The royal way to see Luang Prabang is to cruise the river—see the waterfront docks, visit Wat Xieng Thong, tour the opposite bank of the Mekong, and explore the Khan River. Boats cost around $5 to $10 an hour, and can be hired from docks along the Mekong. Most travelers save their shekels for the boat ride along the Mekong to Pak Ou Grottoes, described under "Excursions from Luang Prabang."

PRACTICALITIES

Accommodations

Luang Prabang has an acute shortage of accommodations. New hotels are being built, but they will not be able to keep pace with the projected tourist influx. The problem is how to keep

hotel building from disfiguring the tiny town, especially the older parts. One solution is to convert existing residences—a 25-room hotel, the Relai de Luang Prabang, a former prince's residence, aims to do just that. Another constraint is the electrical supply. A small-scale dam at Nam Dong is the sole power source for Luang Prabang: hotels must have their own generators to fight blackouts. Eventually, power will be supplied from Vientiane.

Budget: Rama Hotel, near Wat Visoun, tel. 7105, has 33 rooms for $8 s and $10 d. Popular with backpackers; there's a nightly disco below that can be very loud, with music till midnight. **Vieng Keo,** around the corner, tel. 7048, has eight rooms for $7 s or $12 d. **Khemkhane Garden Restaurant,** overlooking the Nam Khan River, rents several bungalows for $15 d.

Moderate: Phousi Hotel, right downtown on Thanon Kitsirat Settathirat, tel. 7024, features 40 rooms—$15 fan room, $20 air-con with shower, $25 single or double air-con with bath. Exchange rates at the hotel are good; the central location makes this an ideal place to stay. The hotel is expanding, with a projected total of 100 rooms. **Muangsua Hotel,** Thanon Phuvao, tel. 7056, is located on the fringe of town and offers 17 rooms—$12 s with air-con and hot water, $15 d, $20 t. The hotel also rents a minibus; there's disco here on weekends.

Luxury: Newly open is the **Hotel Souvannaphoum,** on Thanon Phothisarat, tel. 212200. This converted mansion includes 20 balcony rooms, two grand suites, and three junior suites. It's run by Inter-Lao Tourisme and contains a garden restaurant featuring classical Lao cuisine. The French-managed **Phou Vao Hotel** (formerly Mittaphab), at the southern edge of town, tel./fax 212194, is a modern hotel with 52 rooms—$38 d with air-con, hot water, and minibar; 15 new rooms are being added. The Phou Vao has the only swimming pool in Luang Prabang—not counting the Mekong, of course.

Villa de la Princesse, on Thanon Phothisarat, tel. 7041, has 10 air-con doubles and one single—all $40 each—in a beautifully restored colonial villa with a small garden. Lao antiques provide interior decor for the 120-year-old mansion. The boutique hotel is run by Princess Kampha, daughter of the Crown Prince, who disappeared along with the king in 1977. Royal property was confiscated in the 1970s, but in 1991 the government returned the villa to the princess. She renovated it with her husband, the manager of Lane Xang Travel. They plan to launch a second 14-room hotel in Luang Prabang. Villa de la Princesse stages Lao folk dances and *baci* (welcoming) ceremonies for group tours, and serves excellent Lao food. There are half a dozen bicycles for rent at $2-4 a day.

Food
Luang Prabang has a number of culinary specialties. Watercress grows around waterfalls and is used in salads; a river moss from the Khan River is mixed with sesame; soups are flavored with spicy or bitter-hot herbs. At market stalls, you can find excellent *tam som* (green papaya salad), ground as you watch; locals also make tamarind jam and pineapple jam, and their own moonshine liquor, *lao lao.*

Markets are a great source of fresh and tasty food, and good places to hunt for breakfast. Markets are humming from 0800 to 0900; here you can find French bread and spam-pâté, and sometimes crude croissants. At the south side of Dara Market you can get good soups and French bread, as well as fresh mandarin juice and coffee. Look for small pineapples and finger bananas to supplement your breakfast rations.

There's a cluster of family-run restaurants in the vicinity of the Rama Hotel, with meals for about $3-5 a head (not including beer). **Yong Khoune Restaurant** and **Visoun Restaurant** have selections of Chinese and Lao dishes; **Luang Prabang Restaurant** serves European and Lao. Cheaper is **Chandavan Restaurant** near Vieng Keo Hotel, with Lao food.

For real atmosphere, **Khemkhane Garden Restaurant** has thatched cottages perched over the Nam Khan (Khan River), a tributary of the Mekong. The tariff is roughly $4 a head for a meal, or just have drinks—very pleasant. Overlooking the Mekong, on the strip between the Palace Museum and Wat Xieng Thong, are a few thatched and wooden structures that serve drinks and snacks. Just cruise along and you'll find a place.

The classiest place to sample Lao food is **Villa de la Princesse,** where a Lao fixed evening meal costs $8 a head—best to book ahead. The hotel also has a bar—ask about

local concoctions. Other hotels in town have mediocre dining rooms; the Phousi Hotel has a bar in the garden. On the west side of Luang Prabang is **Maly Restaurant,** quite a few notches down from the Princesse in decor, but no loss at all in the food department—and considerably cheaper. Maly serves a good range of Lao dishes, including spicy eggplant soup, chicken salad with lemongrass, and curried fish dishes.

Shopping
Dara Market is the place to go for silver items and textiles. Silk and cotton *sinhs* are available; silver jewelry and other items are sold by weight and often purchased by Hmong hilltribes as portable wealth. Larger hotels—the Phou Vao, Phousi, and Princesse—have higher-priced gift shops. There are a few specialty shops—between Dara Market and the Vieng Keo Hotel is a shop that sells high-quality textiles and handicrafts; down by the Mekong, near Villa de la Princesse, is a silversmithing shop, with items made on the premises. Opposite Wat Mai is a woodcarving place.

Services
The Tourist Trade: Luang Prabang Tourism Office, on Thanon Phothisarat near the Phousi Hotel, arranges permission to visit the Palace Museum. You can also go through a travel agent—there are several in town. Lane Xang Travel is located near Dara Market, and Diethelm Travel is opposite Wat Sene. Inter-Lao Tourisme can be contacted through Hotel Souvannaphoum. Also setting up shop in Luang Prabang are Southern Lao Travel and Lao Travel Service. Travel agents can arrange tours, cars, and guides, and can arrange extended trekking trips or boat trips upcountry. Guides cost $5-9 a day (negotiable). There's a decent Lao-French map of Luang Prabang issued in 1990 by the State Geographic Service.

Bank: Lane Xang Bank is right near Luang Prabang Tourism: rates are higher for cash than for traveler's checks, and not as good as rates in Vientiane for traveler's checks, but comparable for cash. The bank is open 0830-1530. Hotels like the Phousi offer much the same rates for US cash as the bank.

GETTING THERE AND AWAY

By Air

Roundtrip fare from Vientiane is $90; one-way is $45. There are usually at least three flights a day on this route—sometimes extra charters are added. The flight takes 40 minutes; the aircraft is a 50-seater Antonov-24—a turbo that drones on, with authentic dry-ice effects in the cabin. En route, if you crane your head out a porthole, you'll see Nam Ngum Reservoir, dotted with lots of islands. Luang Prabang airstrip has no radar, so in the rainy season morning departures are often delayed due to lack of visibility. Luang Prabang is emerging as an air hub with connections by light aircraft to Ban Huay Sai, Xieng Khuang, and Phong Saly. With Thai assistance, the airport at Luang Prabang is undergoing a major face-lift that will enable it to service larger planes such as Boeing 737s. Already, some group tours are flying directly from Luang Prabang to Thailand's Chiang Mai airport, a 1.5-hour flight.

Luang Prabang airport is three km from the town by car—transfers take 10 minutes. In a jumbo it's 75 cents for locals and double that for foreigners. There's a Lao Aviation office in Luang Prabang—be sure to confirm reservations. Domestic departure tax is 50 cents.

By Boat

Upstream on the Mekong from Vientiane to Luang Prabang on a wooden cargo boat takes four days—passengers deploy hammocks to rest, or sleep on deck. The trip costs about $15; you must bring your own food and drink. From Luang Prabang to Vientiane, a distance of over 400 km downstream, a boat takes three days (two nights). There are no time tables for these boats—you hang around the landings and keep asking where the boat is going and when. Prior to departure, you need to go to the police and immigration desk (behind a foodstall at Dock B) and get a departure stamp on your departure card. There is a fast boat service by eight-person longtails from Luang Prabang to Vientiane; the trip takes about eight hours. For the Luang Prabang-Vientiane boats, you must also check in with police and immigration at the Vientiane arrival point.

Dock A, at the back of the Palace Museum, is for large cargo boats to Vientiane or Ban Huay Sai. There's a concrete driveway for heavy cargo loading, and cars can be driven directly onto the boat. There are frequent departures during the rainy season, when the Mekong runs high; the boats take passengers for extra income.

Dock B, down from the post office and accessed by a steep set of steps, is for small craft only—covered wooden longboats going to Pak Ou Grottoes, longtails (speedboats) to Ban Huay Sai, and wooden craft to Ban Hat Sa in Phong Saly. You can rent boats here too.

Out of character for Laos, six-person longtail boats imported from Bangkok cover the 320-km route to Ban Huay Sai in a mere six hours, versus the regular slow boat timing of two to three days. The midway point is Muang Pak-

longtail boats

SLOWLY DOWN THE MEKONG

There are no longer any passenger boats on the Luang Prabang-to-Vientiane run; only wooden cargo boats are used. These offer very basic facilities. American traveler Phil Schlesinger reports, "good scenery, but very noisy, very hot, very tiring, very unsanitary. The crew is friendly, but often drunk on *lao lao*. We tied up at small villages at night, and bought live chickens which were cooked on board and eaten with sticky rice. The trip is a lot more fun if you bring food and earplugs! Passengers sleep on the floor of the engine room."

British traveler Martin Saunders writes:

Our cargo boat was full of Chinese apples and pears, so we figured we wouldn't starve if we ran aground on a sandbank. It was a beautiful trip—three days, two nights. Our impromptu group of five Westerners slept in the settlements where we stopped. One traveler spoke some Lao, so we took over someone's house for the night. I had to admire the captain. The Mekong can be a treacherous river, with rapids and rocks all over the place, and he knew the river well. Even in the middle of nowhere officialdom reared its ugly head. Three to four hours short of Vientiane we were pulled over to the bank. We walked to a small brick building, where a policeman fetched an old exercise book, tore one sheet out, ripped it into five sections, stamped the back of each, and charged us 500 kip for the pleasure. It seems the captain has to declare his cargo and any big-noses aboard. All this took several hours, and we had to go through the same exercise when we reached Vientiane.

---

beng. Passports and papers are checked at Ban Don, 10 km from Luang Prabang, and at Muang Pakbeng. For a hefty fee you can charter a speedboat to Ban Huay Sai, or try to join assembled passengers for the run. The advantage of chartering the boat is that you can tell the captain to stop along the route—pulling in at Pak Ou Grottoes, Muang Pakbeng, and so on. Ever since a Thai passenger died when a boat crashed in 1992, passengers have been required to wear crash helmets and life jackets. Actually the the crash-helmet visor serves to protect the faces of passengers from the sting of spray churned up at 70 kph.

The slow boat to Ban Huay Sai takes at least two days, with an overnight stop in Muang Pakbeng, and costs around $10. If you want to soak in Mekong scenery, the slow boat will give you ample time—maybe too much time. The slow boat is windowless and stuffy, and facilities are basic.

In high-water season only, small craft run to Phong Saly: the first day the boat navigates the Nam Ou past Muang Ngoy and overnights at Muang Khoua; the second day the boat carries on to Ban Hat Sa, with passengers transferring by bus to Phong Saly, the capital.

By Road

A new paved road linking Luang Prabang with Vientiane is scheduled for completion in 1996. A good 4WD vehicle like a Land Cruiser can make the trip in one long 12-hour driving day—it's around 420 km. On a series of local "buses," the trip takes between three and five days, depending on waiting time between connections. Vientiane to Vangvieng takes a day by bus; Vangvieng to Kasi consumes another day; and you can probably get from Kasi to Luang Prabang by truck on the third day. The "buses" are converted Isuzu trucks with seating in the back. In Luang Prabang, these vehicles, along with jumbos, are found next to That Luang Market. Occasionally there are direct buses from Vientiane to Luang Prabang, taking roughly 20 hours depending on rest stops. Foreigners are discouraged from using local transport due to sporadic banditry along Route 13, particularly around Vangvieng and Kasi. Local truckers travel in convoys at these points and are armed in case of attack.

GETTING AROUND

There are no cyclos in Luang Prabang. Options include touring on foot, by boat, by bicycle, sidecar-taxi, or jumbo. Some hotels rent cars. Villa de la Princesse rents bicycles for $2-4 a day; across from Rama Hotel is a restaurant that rents bikes for $4 a day. More rentals may surface, but a special permit is needed to operate the rentals. Ask staff at your hotel if they can arrange a bike.

Motorcycles with sidecars are the most common way of getting around. Sidecar-taxis cost 30 cents for most destinations round town, or 75 cents for longer hauls; you can hire one by the hour for $1.50. You can also hire jumbos or three-wheelers for around $2 an hour. These vehicles congregate near markets and boat docks—there's a large transport depot near That Luang Market.

A variety of small boats, including speedboats, can be rented from docks along the Mekong.

EXCURSIONS FROM LUANG PRABANG

Pak Ou Grottoes

The top trip from Luang Prabang is a full day's excursion by boat along the Mekong to Pak Ou Grottoes, at the confluence of the Nam Ou River, about 25 km upstream from Luang Prabang. On the way you can stop in the village of Ban Sang Hae, where moonshine whiskey is made. Just as interesting as the destination is the trip along the Mekong—the river runs wide, cutting a swath through jungle-clad banks and limestone gorges. There are times, on a slow boat headed down the river, when you are completely alone—not even a village in sight.

Boats for hire from the small-craft dock north of Luang Prabang Tourism office include open longtails (speedboats), open longboats (slow boats), and covered wooden longboats. It's a long trip in the harsh sun, so unless you have an umbrella, a covered boat is preferable. Longtails are twice as fast, but the Mekong scenery whips by you. Covered boats take two hours to get to Pak Ou Grottoes and 1.5 hours back

(downstream), so you need to hire a boat for at least six hours. Assemble a group to split expenses—the boats can easily hold 10 or more passengers. Boats are expensive—$20 for an open longboat, $25 for a longtail, $30 on a larger covered boat. Negotiate timing and itinerary.

About 20 km—or 90 minutes—out of Luang Prabang along the Mekong is **Ban Sang Hae,** a village engaged in the production of rice whiskey. In the rainy season, the villagers grow glutinous rice, which is fermented in water and yeast in the dry season—a process that takes 10 to 15 days for each batch. This under-the-table whiskey, or *lao lao,* sells for 75 cents a liter or $1 a bottle in Luang Prabang. This firewater is best drunk over ice, with a dash of lime and soda—or Coke if you prefer.

Pak Ou Grottoes are sacred caves tucked into limestone cliffs, filled with hundreds of gilded and wooden Buddha statues. Many of the images are in the distinctive Lao stance of Calling for Rain. Cave temples have been of religious significance throughout Asia from the earliest days of Buddhism, creating unique places for Buddhist monks and hermits to dwell and worship; the Pak Ou Grottoes were once occupied. Now candles and filtered light illuminate the caves, pervading them with an aura of holiness. The lower cave, Tham Ting, is reached by a series of steps from the Mekong. From here, you climb to the upper cave, Tham Phum, which is deeper and darker and requires a flashlight to explore. There are picnic shelters for lunch between the lower and upper caves. The caves are thought to be the home of guardian spirits, and the site was once inhabited by monks. The king of Laos used to visit here once a year; today, at Lao New Year, hundreds of pilgrims wend their way out from Luang Prabang.

"Pak Ou" means mouth of the Ou River. After stopping at the grottoes, you can detour up the **Nam Ou** tributary—a great ride, as the banks here are much closer than on the Mekong. This route is used by small craft heading to Phong Saly province.

Longer Mekong Trips

The most spectacular section of the Mekong in Laos is the upper section, westward from Luang Prabang. Routing ideas include taking a slow boat or longtail speedboat from Luang Prabang to Ban Huay Sai, or following the reverse route. From Ban Huay Sai, you can fly to Vientiane or cross over to Thailand. For more details, see "Ban Huay Sai" under "The Golden Quadrangle" in "Northern Laos" in the Around Laos chapter.

For a longer excursion on the Mekong from Luang Prabang, a group can arrange a tour up-country by boat and van if river conditions are favorable (a nonstarter in the dry season). A two-day roundtrip itinerary from Luang Prabang proceeds thusly: take a slow boat along the Mekong past Pak Ou to the town of Muang Pakbeng, a full day's trip. After a night in Pakbeng, transfer to hired van or local truck for an overland drive north to Muang Sai (140 km), then drive east along Route 1 to Nambak (another 100 km) or Muang Ngoi. From there, take a speedboat south down the Nam Ou River back to Luang Prabang. The land portions of this trip are dull, but on both rivers the scenery is spectacular. Individual travelers have also managed to cover this route—it may turn into a four-or-five day trip.

Santi Chedi

About three km east of Luang Prabang is a forest wat, Pra Phon Phao, famed as the abode of meditation master Saisamut, who died in 1992. The gold-spired Santi Chedi, or Peace Pagoda, was constructed in the 1970s and 1980s and completed in 1988. The octagonal yellow stupa has three floors and a view terrace at the top. The exterior features beautifully carved wooden shutters and doors; inside, on the ground floor, are hellish comic-strip frescoes showing the fate awaiting adulterers, murderers, and thieves—scenes that appear to spring straight out of Dante's *Inferno*. (In the Buddhist system of reincarnation, there are half a dozen realms for rebirth—among them the realm of the Hungry Ghosts, and the realm of the Hells. Since Buddhism predates Christianity, Christian representations of Hell may well have been copied from Buddhist versions.)

The upper floors contain frescoes with peaceful episodes from the life of Buddha. Make your way through to the top cupola for views of Luang Prabang. Santi Chedi is open daily 0800-1000 and 1300-1630. You can bicycle out there or take a sidecar-taxi. A little way out of Luang Prabang to the southeast you come to a fork in the road—the left fork goes to Santi Chedi, the right fork to Ban Phanom.

Village Visits

Head out of Luang Prabang in any direction and you'll strike villages. Some travel outfits can arrange long treks through village areas: Lane Xang Travel arranges a three-day trek through Hmong, Lao Theung, and Khamu villages.

You can combine visits to scenic sites with village visits en route. The best picnic and waterfall spot around town is **Kuangsi Falls,** 30 km to the south of town. The pretty falls are multitiered and accessed by forest trails. In a nearby village are water-driven rice mills, and about 10 km short of the falls are several villages engaged in

Santi Chedi

the spinning of raw cotton. There's a jumbo running out in this direction from the transport depot next to That Luang Market.

Closer to town, the villages of higher interest are those specializing in a particular craft. You can reach these places by local transport, bicycle, or sidecar-taxi (not good on the hills). **Ban Phanom,** three km southeast of town, is an ancient weaving village—people working hand-looms under the houses turn out cotton and silk shawls and *sinhs*. Visitors are led to the village tourist trap, a circular area where the village women practically leap into the air with hard-sell tactics.

Four km west of Luang Prabang is the village of **Ban Chan,** which produces ceramic storage jars and pots. The village can be reached by boat along the Mekong, or by road and a short boat hop. Right near the airport is the village of **Hat Hien,** whose inhabitants use simple implements to make knives and metalware. Take a dirt track just before reaching the main terminal building—the village is 500 meters down this road. This is not a quiet place. The air is filled with the din of sledgehammers striking metal, supplemented by the odd plane overhead and intense heat from bellows-operated foundries.

AROUND LAOS

Beyond Vientiane and Luang Prabang, Laos remains barely explored. It offers a handful of archaeological riddles—the mysterious Plain of Jars, and the abandoned temples of Wat Phu—and high ethnic interest with numerous hilltribe groups in the northern mountain valleys and the plateaus to the east. Then there are natural wonders—the mystique of the Mekong, from its majestic passage through northern Laos to its foaming and frothing departure at Khone Falls near the Cambodian border.

Laos is opening up, but it's a slow process. Described in the following pages are sites accessible to the independent traveler at the time of writing. Other places may become accessible, so keep an ear to the ground.

LOGISTICS

Outside of Vientiane is group tour territory—as an individual, your movements, choices, and modes of transport may be restricted. In Vientiane you can rent a motorcycle or bicycle and run around; not so in other parts of the

country, where they'll even question your use of sidecar-taxis. Luang Prabang is fairly lax—you can do mostly everything yourself—but other parts of the country are tricky. Authorities may question you if you're outside a town on public transport—you're supposed to be in a jeep with a guide. While you can get away with more during daylight hours, watch out at night—if you sleep in weird places, you'll attract a lot of police attention. It's often worth hiring a guide for $5 a day to keep authorities at bay. Check in Vientiane to determine if you need an exit permit to depart Laos from a particular land border. Once you're out of Vientiane, communication becomes difficult—the phone system is primitive. Tie up all loose ends in the capital before leaving.

Tours: If thinking of booking a tour through one of the agencies in Vientiane, make sure you know exactly what's included and what isn't. Usually the airfares, ground transport, and guide are included. For the Plain of Jars, a few Vientiane agencies quote a two-day one-night itinerary for around $170, hotels and food not included, or $250 per person for an all-inclusive two-person trip; with extra passengers, a marginal difference in pricing. For a trip to the Bolovens Plateau—Vientiane, Savannakhet, Pakse, Vientiane—Diethelm charges $600 each for two people, and $550 each for three people for a three-day two-night itinerary. Another option is to arrange a tour once you're on the spot in, say, Pakse or Savannakhet. Jeep rentals range from $25 to $50 a day, including driver; guides are $5-10 a day.

NORTHERN LAOS

THE GOLDEN QUADRANGLE

The most difficult part of Laos to reach—and the least explored—is the far north, leading to the Chinese border. This zone is known for its opium cultivation—part of the notorious Golden Triangle at the intersection of Burma, Laos, and Thailand. In a new twist—adding China to the equation—there are plans to develop the region as a trade route known as the "Golden Growth Quadrangle," with emphasis on economic growth that is not poppy-dependent. While the far north holds nothing in the way of historic sights, it is certainly the most intriguing in terms of ethnic groups. The provinces of Phong Saly (22 ethnic groups), Udomxai (23 ethnic groups), and Luang Nam Tha (39 groups) have the country's greatest diversity of hilltribes. The best place to see these people is at the markets.

At present, travel to this region is difficult and slow; most locals rely on boat transport. Road travel is rough, and can be dangerous, although the road from Pakbeng to Muang Sai is drivable. There is intermittent air service from Vientiane to Luang Nam Tha, $57; Muang Sai, $49; and Ban Huay Sai, $64. There are also air connections from Luang Prabang to Ban Huay Sai.

Ban Huay Sai

The easiest route to tackle in the north is the Ban Huay Sai to Luang Prabang boat trip. You can enter or exit Thailand at Ban Huay Sai; the Thai town across the Mekong is Chiang Khong. If you're entering, your Lao visa may have to be endorsed for Ban Huay Sai. The ride from Luang Prabang west to Ban Huay Sai takes at least two days by cargo boat—the boats stop along the river at night because of the danger of rocks and reefs. Boat service may be infrequent, and the boats themselves are windowless and stuffy, with very basic facilities. You might persuade the captain to let you sit on the roof once you're out of sight of officialdom.

A more expensive alternative is a longtail boat, which takes a mere six hours to cover the distance. The scenery is majestic, with limestone cliffs, monsoon forest, stands of giant bamboo, and fishing villages. You get to see the many moods of the Mekong—running the gamut from serene to surging currents. The midway point is Pakbeng, a collection of wooden housing with a few wats and guesthouses. It takes a skilled boatman to navigate the Mekong: at times limestone outcrops and rocky reefs emerge above the water, and low tide exposes huge sandbanks. When the river narrows—sandwiched between limestone cliffs—the currents are especially tricky, and sometimes whirlpools form as different currents collide.

The town of Ban Huay Sai sees a brisk trade in Chinese goods—it's an important commercial center along the Mekong, as is its counterpart in Thailand, the town of Chiang Khong. Barges come all the way downstream from Yunnan in China. Ban Huay Sai has a checkered past as part of the opium and heroin route to Chiang Mai in Thailand; the area is known for its poppy fields. Sapphires are mined in the area, and timber is exported through the town to Thailand. You can hike up a set of stairs lined with *naga* balustrades to the top of Wat Chom Khao Manirat for a superb view of the town.

From Ban Huay Sai, you can take a ferry to Chiang Khong in Thailand. Chiang Khong is 137 km from Chiang Rai, one of Thailand's largest trekking centers; from Chiang Rai, it's 197 km to Chiang Mai, with excellent connections to other parts of Thailand.

China Border Crossing

There are plans to link Thailand, Laos, China, and Burma with a ring road, as part of a Golden Growth Quadrangle. The new ring road—still some years away because of "opium armies" and unruly minorities—would connect Chiang Rai in Thailand with Jinghong, China for the purposes of trade and tourism. The road through Laos is in very bad shape: the projected route goes from the Thai town of Chiang Rai to Chiang Khong, across the Mekong at Ban Huay Sai, along Route 3 to Luang Nam Tha, then crosses via Ban Boten to the Chinese town of Mengla and runs to Jinghong. Completing the ring road, from Jinghong the road arcs south to Kengtung in Burma, then to Tachilek, crossing the Thai border to reach Mae Sai and Chiang Rai.

On 2 February 1996 China and Laos officially opened a second border point for motor traffic. The crossing, called Mohan, northwest of Luang Nam Tha, provides a link to China's Yunnan Province.

Even without proper roads, the Lao border point of Ban Boten sees a brisk trade in luxury automobiles, delivered from Thailand to China. Hundreds of luxury cars, shipped into Thailand from Bahrain and the Gulf states or the US, are driven to Chiang Khong, ferried across the Mekong to Ban Huay Sai, and driven to Ban Boten. Traders spend about $1000 on "handling charges" to get the cars through Thailand. On the Chinese side, taxes can exceed 200% of the value of the car, though less costly arrangements can be negotiated with border officials.

Roads on the Chinese side are in good condition. Already, Chinese tourists from Kunming take trips by road through the area, crossing south of Mengla—Phong Saly Province is in fact more accessible from Mengla than from Luang Prabang. If trade flourishes at the Lao-China border, and if road transport is upgraded, this area may develop as a crossing point into China's Yunnan Province.

Boat routes are also being developed. Small cargo boats now ply the Mekong between Jinghong and Ban Huay Sai (Chiang Khong); passenger boats also make the run. Phong Saly can also be reached by boat from Luang Prabang along the Nam Ou River, though the two-day route is only deep enough in the June-October rainy season. If you have transport lined up, and if river conditions are right, you can make a roundtrip by boat from Luang Prabang into the north. Take a boat along the Mekong to

Pakbeng, go by road to Muang Sai and Nambak or Muang Ngoy, and take another boat down the Nam Ou back to Luang Prabang.

THE PLAIN OF JARS

The Plain of Jars is a plain with a lot of big jars on it—worth a few hours of your time to figure out what the heck all those jars are doing there. How did they get there? Who made them? Why? Nobody knows.

Is it worth flying up from Vientiane to look at a stack of old jars? Here you have to weigh several factors—the expense involved, the fact that the jars are overrated, and the fact that this is a remote and little-visited area. If you like to get right off the track and into the surrounding countryside, then the area holds interest; the jars alone do not.

The tiny gateway town to the Plain of Jars is Phonsavan, population 6,000—the capital of Xieng Khuang Province, to the northeast of Vientiane. Flying into Phonsavan you can see the bomb-scarred terrain of Xieng Khuang plateau: this province was heavily bombed during the Vietnam War era and was off-limits for tourism until quite recently. Teams of American MIA searchers were allowed to scour the zone starting in 1993—what's remarkable is that they're allowed in at all after all the destruction wreaked by US bombing.

During the Vietnam War, the Xieng Khuang plateau became a strategic battleground. On one side were US-backed royalist forces, and Hmong fighters under General Vang Pao; on the other side were the Pathet Lao, supported by the North Vietnamese Army. For the Vietnamese, the plateau was the rear flank to Hanoi; by 1972 the NVA had seven divisions in Laos supporting the Pathet Lao. American B-52 bombing of the plateau had a devastating effect on villages in the area; in addition to direct bombing, B-52s returning from raids on Hanoi jettisoned bomb loads over Laos en route to the US air base at Udon Thani in Thailand.

Villages around Phonsavan use scrap metal from bomb casings and downed US planes for building materials. Scrap metal is taken to small warehouses in Phonsavan and later melted down as a source of cheap metal.

Logistics

Take a few supplies from Vientiane—they're limited in Phonsavan. That's why you'll see passengers loading up on French bread at the airport in Vientiane—baguettes are not made in Xieng Khuang, and they make nice gifts for local hosts. Plain of Jars Mineral Water, however, is available. Bring lots of cash—the bank in Phonsavan gives a similar exchange rate to those in Vientiane, but deals only in cash. Bring a jacket if you're visiting from December to February, as temperatures can fall to zero overnight in Xieng Khuang Province at that time of year. Xieng Khuang plateau sits at an elevation of 1,000 meters, which means the weather is mild.

Transport is a headache in Phonsavan; you'll more than likely be held for ransom by local tour companies as there aren't many options for local transport. Roads—even in the dry season—require 4WD vehicles in some areas, and buses are prone to breakdowns. In the rainy season the roads are often impassable. It would be wise to hook up with a guide in Phonsavan—guides cost about $5 a day, regardless of the size of the group. Regulations are strict here—the place is still back in the communist era, more remote, with fewer visitors. If you're wandering around by yourself, you must be a spy. Authorities are also sensitive about exploding foreigners—there's a lot of leftover ordnance lying around. A guide should be aware of danger areas.

Another reason for the heightened security lies just west of the Plain of Jars: a huge new airbase, destined to be the headquarters of the Lao Air Force. Vientiane is considered too close to Thailand for a strategic base.

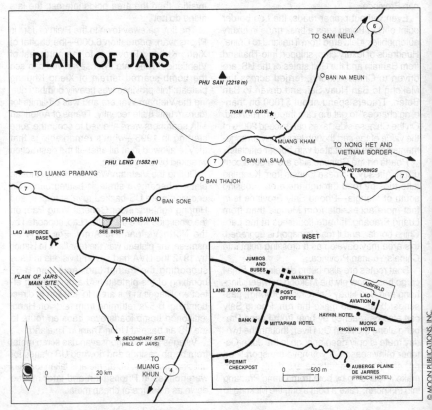

Authorities are vigilant about paperwork in Phonsavan. Your papers may be checked at Phonsavan airfield and at the checkpoint on the road to the Plain of Jars.

Phonsavan Market

Phonsavan is the base for exploring the area. There's little to see in the town except for the market. Besides the foodstalls, fresh vegetables, and rice, the market sells dry goods—mainly household goods from the Vietnamese border like thermoses and blankets. Look closely, and you'll find spoons of aluminum recycled from US planes. On sale too are *sinhs,* Hmong necklaces, and opium in the form of a black fudge, sold by Hmong tribespeople.

The Plain of Jars

There are eight sites with jars in the area around Phonsavan, with a total of perhaps 200 or 300 intact jars. Most are concentrated at two sites. The main site is about 12 km from town on a gravel road—it takes about 20 minutes by jeep or maybe half an hour by jumbo from the markets. The site is fenced off, with a pavilion at the entrance charging a $1.40 entry fee, extra for a still or video camera. Unfortunately, the jars have recently been numbered in white lettering, in order of size starting with 001 for the really big one down to fragments numbered at around 290. Look for round lids to the rimmed jars too—there are several lying around.

The jars stand one to 2.5 meters high, with diameters ranging from half a meter to two meters. Some weigh in at the size of cars—600 kg to six tons. Some archaeologists speculate masons in ancient Laos found a way to produce a cement that looks exactly like stone, like the fabled medieval alchemists who turned lead to gold. The material looks like gray sandstone, covered with lichens. Some jars appear to have been chiseled from granite or limestone. Other theories run the gamut from extraterrestrial activity to the Land of the Giants; similar urns have been found in Central Sulawesi, Indonesia, and are also of unknown origin. The jars may be connected with the Dongson culture of the Bronze Age, which flourished in the Thanh Hoa area of Vietnam's Red River Delta.

As to the function of the jars—theories vary from funerary urns to rice storage to wine fermentation vessels. Some jars required lids, which suggests there was a reason to open and close them. The most plausible theory is that the larger jars were used as sarcophagi for aristocracy, and the smaller jars for those of lesser rank. The fact that human bones have been found in some of the smaller jars adds weight to this theory. The cave at the site could have been where cremations took place, or where the jars were fired. There are no stone quarries in the vicinity, so how the jars were transported is a puzzle. Some kind of civilized society was responsible for the jars, but this culture disappeared without a trace.

An even greater mystery is just how all these jars survived saturation bombing by the US Air Force. According to the guides, only a few were shattered by bombs. Considering the Pathet Lao maintained their headquarters in the cave next to the site, it seems odd the area survived unscathed.

The Hill of Jars

A secondary jar site about 20 km south from the Plain of Jars is reached over a rough dirt road. It takes about 50 minutes to get there by jeep, which will give you some idea of road conditions. This one is a Hill of Jars, sited on a nice slope overlooking valleys. There are over 50 pieces here—several jars are longer than two meters, with larger pieces resting on the ground rather than upright. This area is more remote; follow your guide.

Accommodations and Food

Just around the corner from the airstrip is the main drag. Phonsavan is still under construction, with most of the hotels built in the 1990s. Right near the airfield are two hotels: **Muong Phouan** with rooms going for $7-11, and **Hayhin,** with basic rooms for $5. To the west of this are the post office and the markets. About two km from the airfield is **Mittaphab (Friendship) Hotel,** Vietnamese-run and charging $10-15 for a room with outside bathroom. The classiest place in town, requiring taxi service, is the **Auberge Plaine de Jarres,** also known as the French Hotel—$30-50 a cabin, with hot water, fireplaces, and a generator till 2100. This chalet resort is about five km from the airfield, out of town on Mount Pupadeng. It has great views and its own dining hall. For food in Phonsavan, try the hotel dining rooms—the Muong Phouan is good—or the foodstalls in the markets.

Getting There

The plane is a Yun-12 Chinese light turboprop which has yet to receive international certification—a comforting thought. The plane seats 17 passengers, but three seats are taken up by passenger baggage, so that means 14 passengers. The flight consists of 40 minutes of aerial terror—the terror factor depending on weather, visibility, and thermals. Concentrating on the scenery is a good idea—the plane passes over mountain terrain, including the highest peak in Laos, Mount Phu Bia, at 2,850 meters. The locals seem to take it all casually—at the other end, in Phonsavan, you walk off the plane to find water buffalo eating grass near the runway. Return airfare from Vientiane is $65. A second airfield accommodating larger aircraft—Yun-7s and ATRs—opened in early 1995. There is now a twice-weekly flight from Xieng Khuang to Luang Prabang, making it possible to loop by air from Vientiane to Xieng Khuang to Luang Prabang and back to Vientiane.

Getting Around

Several tour outfits in town handle travelers. **Xieng Khuang Travel** operates a regular taxi on good roads—the charge is $48 roundtrip to Nam Het, the trading town on the Vietnamese border. **Lane Xang Travel,** with an office near the markets, maintains a Land Rover and jeep. The Land Rover is $25-40 a day, including driver; a guide is $5 a day extra. Set schedules: $33 roundtrip south to Muang Khun; $30 east to Tham Piu Cave and the hot springs. Negotiate your itinerary carefully—once you've agreed on the route, the driver is very reluctant to change plans. Hidden extras include food for the crew, site entry fees, and permit paperwork if necessary.

There's a transport depot near the markets, with jumbos for rent. Although small buses run to local towns, the authorities may decide you're not allowed to use them—regulations can change, however. Reaching the main site of the Plain of Jars is not a problem. A local jumbo will take you there, but there's a checkpoint en route; they may balk if you don't have a guide with you, so take one. No bicycle or motorcycle rentals available.

Touring

Whichever way you look at it, visiting the Plain of Jars is an expensive proposition—you've got the plane fare, jeep escort around Phonsavan, and so on. You can easily clock up $100 a day per person. If your time is short in Phonsavan, establish a liaison with a travel agent in Vientiane and line up transport. Assemble your own small group to defray expenses on a rented jeep—the ideal number of passengers is three to four.

Typical package prices from Vientiane for two days and one night include touring and airfare, but not accommodations or food, and run $186 for one person, $167 each for two people, $159 for three to four people, and $155 for five to six.

AROUND PHONSAVAN

Route 4 South

The old capital, formerly known as Xieng Khuang and now called **Muang Khun,** is 35 km south from Phonsavan on Route 4. The village was completely destroyed by US bombing, its temples reduced to rubble. A forlorn-looking Buddha statue presides over the rubble. There are plans to rebuild the temples, as well as a 30-meter stupa that overlooks the town. The town has been rebuilt since 1975, and population is now around 10,000. You can secure accommodations in Muang Khun—ask a guide to arrange it. The town is a dead end of sorts as the road south of Muang Khun is in very bad shape. There are four buses a day to Muang Khun from Phonsavan, but authorities may block your use of local transport—you're expected to go by jeep. You may also be asked to flash a permit for visiting Muang Khun.

Along Route 4 south are lots of villages. Villagers are poor and there is evidence of malnutrition, with cases of goiter; malaria is also a problem. The people live in thatched huts on stilts, some supported by bomb casings; casings are also used for fences and pig troughs. No mystery here—the bombs were dropped by American warplanes during saturation bombing raids in the 1960s and 1970s. Most of the Lao in Xieng Khuang Province fled; an estimated 8,000 civilians were killed by US bombs, and entire towns were razed.

village bus,
Muang Khun

The bomb casing used to support a hut is half a CBU, or cluster bomb unit. This is composed of a "mother bomb" with a pea-pod casing containing 150 tennis-ball sized bomblets. At a predetermined altitude, the CBU casing splits open, releasing the bomblets. Each antipersonnel bomblet contains several hundred steel pellets—some detonate upon hitting the ground; others, insidiously, fall to earth to detonate only when something or someone comes in contact with them. Up to a dozen people a month are killed or injured by bomblets.

Route 7 East

Route 7 east leads 115 km to the town of Nong Het, close to the Vietnamese border. The road out this way is sealed and in good shape, which means you can cover a lot of ground quickly. The major junction along the way is Muang Kham, at the intersection of Route 6 and Route 7. From Phonsavan, it's 53 km to Muang Kham, and then 62 km on to Nong het, which is 25 km short of the Vietnamese border. Buses travel out to Muang Kham and Nong Het, but authorities usually do not permit foreigners to use them. The trip from Phonsavan to Nong Het takes about eight hours by local bus, three hours by taxi, or 4.5 hours by jeep one-way, so it's a very full day-trip to reach Nong Het, with a suggested stop at Tham Piu Cave near Muang Kham. The route features lush bamboo, banana, fir, and

spruce trees, and villages of Hmong (Meo) and Thai Dam (Black Thai) people. Heading out of Phonsavan on Route 7 you pass the villages of Ban Sone, 12 km out; Ban Thajoh, 30 km; and Ban Na Sala, about 45 km. Sunday could be market day in one of the villages.

You can stop at the villages and wander around—villagers sometimes approach tourists to sell embroidery, bugs, or fighting beetles. There are foodstalls at **Muang Kham,** a bit over an hour from Phonsavan by car. From Muang Kham, your transport can drop you a little way north on route 6, to the trailhead for **Tham Piu Cave.** A half-hour hike—take a guide—gets you to the cave. On 8 March 1968, two US T-28 fighter-bombers swooped in from Thailand and fired rockets into Tham Piu Cave, which served as an air-raid shelter. Over 300 villagers were killed in the rocket attack; the interior of the cave is littered with rubble, a stark war memorial.

About 18 km east of Muang Kham are some hot springs off Route 7. The springs are quite ordinary, with hot water piped 200 meters from the springs into a miniresort enclosure with four standard bathtubs. You can take a bath for 60 cents, but entry to the area is a rip-off $3.50. The compound was built as a retreat for high-ranking officials; huts rent for $5-20.

Nong Het is a trading town, with lots of commerce as Vietnamese goods flow across the border. It's 25 km shy of the actual border crossing.

SOUTHERN LAOS

THAKHEK

Thakhek was founded in 1911 as a French outpost—its old name is Khammoun. There's not a lot to see around Thakhek. Seven km south of town is Wat Sikhotaboun, built on the banks of the Mekong by King Chao Anou in the 19th century. It was restored in 1956, and a large wall was thrown up around it in 1970 by King Sisavang Vatthana. About 50 km to the east of Thakhek on Route 12, near the town of Mahaxai, are striking limestone formations, accessible by boat. Mahaxai lies en route to the Khammoun Plateau, which the Thais would like to develop as an access point to Vietnam. There's been talk of building a bridge over the Mekong from Nakhon Phanom to Thakhek, then improving the road to connect Thakhek to Vinh in Vietnam. Thakhek is only 240 km from Vinh along Route 8, compared with the 540-km journey from Savannakhet to Danang along Route 9. The port of Cua Lo near Vinh, however, can only carry ships of 3,000-5,000 tons, while shipping at Danang can take 15,000-20,000 tons. Also on the drawing board is a hydroelectric plant at Thakhek to tap the Mekong.

There are several guesthouses in Thakhek, and more under renovation in anticipation of increasing trade. Ferries across the Mekong to the Thai town of Nakhon Phanom operate frequently during the day. You can reach Thakhek by road from Vientiane in nine to 11 hours, but it's a few hours faster by boat along the Mekong—foreigners may have trouble obtaining permission for such trips. There are occasional flights from Vientiane to Thakhek.

SAVANNAKHET

Savannakhet is a trading town of 45,000. There is very little to see here—most visit the place because it happens to be on the way, or gets in the way. Recently, Savannakhet has found itself in the way quite a lot, as it's a key town on a fast new overland route from Thailand through Laos to the Lao Bao border crossing into Vietnam—a route travelers are just beginning to explore. Chinese- and Vietnamese-made goods stream across the Mekong to Thailand from Savannakhet; trucks loaded with lumber from Khammoun Province bank up for kilometers on the outskirts of town—from Savannakhet, the lumber moves to Thailand or Vietnam. More activity can be seen at the well-stocked central market in the northeast part of town.

Trading in Laos in the French colonial era was largely in the hands of resident Chinese and Vietnamese, which explains the yellow Catholic Church and the Chinese temple in town. These communities were disrupted in 1975, when many residents fled across the Mekong—since then, a number have returned. There are now large Chinese and Vietnamese trading communities, and ornate Chinese-

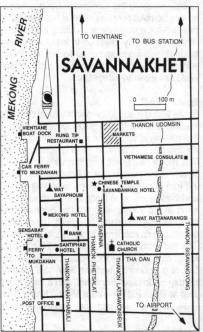

financed hotels; the Chinese school is said to be the best in town.

North of Savannakhet is the top sacred site of the area—That Ing Hang. The 16th-century Lao-style stupa is nine meters high, and was most likely built at around the same time as Vientiane's That Luang. Some resident monks live in temple buildings nearby. To get there, go along Route 13 north for 12 km, then turn east for three km.

There's a Jurassic-period site about 120 km east of Savannakhet where a French-Lao team is digging for dinosaur bones. The results of these excavations may show up in a museum in Savannakhet.

Accommodations and Food
Savannakhet is well-supplied compared to other provincial capitals. It has 24-hour electricity, cable TV, and foreign newspapers in hotel lobbies. There are a dozen hotels in and around the town, including the 47-room Chinese-run Nanhai Hotel. Toward the river are three cheaper hotels: the **Sensabay, Santiphab,** and **Mekong,** with rooms for $4 fan and $7 air-con. Near the post office is the **Phome Vilay Guesthouse** with rooms for $4. In town is the **Savanbanhao Hotel,** which houses the head office for Savannakhet Tourism, and charges $7-14. To the northeast of town is **Phone Praseuth Hotel,** with rooms for $20, complete with all creature comforts; across the street is a full-size swimming pool, charging a $1 entry fee. Apart from hotel restaurants and local noodlehouses, the eating options are slim. The one restaurant of note is **Rung Tip,** serving Lao and Thai dishes— the restaurant has a disco too.

Transportation
By road there are connections during the dry season from Vientiane to Savannakhet (14 hours), and from there to Pakse (six to eight hours). An overnight boat plies the route from Vientiane to Savannakhet every few days in the rainy season only (June to November). Permits for buses and boats are hard to get—try Savannakhet Tourism for a boat permit to travel north.

Group tours generally fly into Savannakhet, go overland to Pakse, and fly back to Vientiane from Pakse—or the reverse. There are daily one-hour flights from Vientiane to Savannakhet

on Yun-7 turboprops, costing $54 one-way. On Sunday, the same flight continues to Saravan. Three days a week, the flight goes to Pakse first, stopping at Savannakhet on the route back to Vientiane.

Thai Border Crossing
You might want to consider flying to Savannakhet, exploring the south, and exiting to Thailand from either Savannakhet or Pakse. Or exit to Vietnam from Savannakhet via the Lao Bao border to Dong Ha. For entry or exit here, your paperwork must be in order. Some group tours approach Savannaket directly from Thailand.

You don't need a Thai visa if you cross into Thailand and stay less than 15 days. However, you may need a Lao entry permit endorsed for Savannakhet to cross the Mekong. There is frequent ferry service between Savannakhet and Mukdahan on weekdays, and half-day on Saturday.

SAVANNAKHET TO LAO BAO

East of Savannakhet along Route 9 is a road exit to Vietnam via the Lao Bao border. The Vietnamese Consulate in Savannakhet may issue visas valid for this crossing; once you have a Vietnamese visa, you must also fix up Lao paperwork to travel this route and exit at Lao Bao— try Savannakhet Tourism for the stamps. From the reverse direction, on the Vietnam side, Lao visas valid for Lao Bao entry are issued at the Lao Consulate in Danang. At the time of writing, such visas were only available in Danang, not from the Lao visa offices in Hanoi or Saigon. Route 9 is a rough road, and it may be difficult to traverse during the June-October rainy season. Travelers have reported some trouble with Lao and Vietnamese border officials at Lao Bao, including demands for large US bills. Presumably the border guards are used to making deals, as this is a smuggling point for rare animals, lumber, and motorcycles from Laos to Vietnam.

Savannakhet to Dong Ha is 350 km. Savannakhet to Dong Ha is 350 kilometers. It's 170 km from Savannakhet to Xepon, and a further 80 km to Lao Bao; from there, it's 100 km to Dong Ha. If you have transport lined up on the Vietnamese side, you can cover the route in 12 hours of driving. A chartered vehicle from Savannakhet to Lao Bao costs a minimum $150. You can take a local bus as far as Xepon, but transport after that is uncertain. On the Vietnamese side, from Dong Ha, it's 75 km—or 1.5 hours of driving—to Hué. On both the Lao and Vietnamese sides of Route 9 are remnants of the Vietnam War, due to the proximity to the former DMZ. From the town of Xepon, 170 km to the east of Savannakhet, you can arrange visits to parts of the Ho Chi Minh Trail, if you like looking at scrap metal and downed planes. In the Xepon district is a village on the roadside with the skeleton of a US Army helicopter; next to it is large stone statue of Vietnamese and Pathet Lao soldiers advancing with AK-47s. Many of the houses in the area are partly built of scrap metal; bomb shells and spent fuel canisters still litter the landscape.

Another 80 km from Xepon brings you to the border at Lao Bao; from there it's about 100 km east to Dong Ha. About 20 km east of the Lao Bao border is the former battlefield of Khe Sanh, which technically requires a Vietnamese permit to visit. Tours in the DMZ can be arranged in Dong Ha through Quang Tri Tourism—see "Dong Ha" under "North of Hué" in the Central Vietnam chapter.

THE BOLOVENS PLATEAU

The scenic Bolovens Plateau sits astride the border of Saravan and Champassak Provinces; the main towns are Paksong and Saravan. The plateau is home to such obscure southern Laos ethnic groups as the Alak, Katu, Suay, Tahoy, Ngai, and Suk. Its climate and red volcanic soil are ideal for the growing of cardamom, arabica coffee, and tea—crops first introduced by the French in the 1920s and 1930s. Durian and other fruit trees also fare well here. You can reach the plateau by road from the towns of Saravan or Pakse, or by driving between the two. You can travel overland from Savannakhet to Saravan, then make your way to Paksong and eventually Pakse. With stops, this takes several days. Although Savannakhet to Pakse on the direct road is only 250 km, roads in the region are atrocious—full of broken bitumen and potholes. A 4WD vehicle is therefore preferable. Saravan to Paksong is about four to five hours; from there it's two to three hours to Pakse.

Saravan

Like a number of towns on the Bolovens Plateau, Saravan was leveled during the Vietnam War, and the only reminder of French colonial influence is the post office. Since the town is being reconstructed, guesthouses are hard to come by. The lowlight of Saravan is its daily market, which is stocked with wildlife to be smuggled across the border into Thailand—destined for the cooking pot or Chinese medicine store, or sold to animal collectors and foreign zoos. Thailand turns a blind eye to this profitable and illicit trade in endangered species. Fauna on sale in Saravan includes pythons, wild pigs, mynah birds, and monkeys; less offensive is a great variety of jungle fruit and vegetables. At Lake Bua, 14 km east of town, is a crocodile-breeding area. There's an airfield at Saravan, with weekly flights from Vientiane via Savannakhet on Sunday. One-way fare to Saravan from Vientiane is $86, from Savannakhet $32.

Tha Teng

On the road between Saravan and Paksong you can visit several Alak and Katu villages. At roughly the midway point on this route lies the village of Tha Teng, with several Alak villages close by. The Alak live in thatched huts; under rice storage huts they store wooden coffins for each member of the household. Both Alak and Tahoy shamans in this area perform buffalo sacrifices on special occasions.

Paksong

Paksong is a small market town about 60 km northeast of Pakse, originally a French hill resort, and favored for its mild climate. The area is known for its fruit and vegetables. It takes two to three hours to get there from Pakse, depending on the type of vehicle, so day-tripping from Pakse is possible. Another way of reaching Paksong is to take a share-taxi from KM2 outside Pakse, costing about $4 one-way. On this route you gain elevation on a dirt road, driving past fruit orchards, tea and coffee plantations, stands of teak, and numerous species of flowers. At higher elevations on the Bolovens Plateau you'll see grazing cattle.

A few kilometers west of Paksong are Tadphan Falls, with a 130-meter drop, and Tat Lo Falls, with a 10-meter cascade. Right near Tat Lo

Falls is accommodation at **Tat Lo Resort** in chalets and bungalows, plus an open-air dining room and sitting area. About 15 rooms are available, costing $15-20 a night, with a few at $30 overlooking the falls. The resort is operated by Sodetour; you can book through the office in Pakse. Swimming in the deep pool at the base of Tat Lo Falls is safe. The resort lodge arranges elephant rides, usually an hour's worth, but a longer ride can be arranged to a local Alak village.

PAKSE

Pakse, on the banks of the Mekong, is the main town of southern Laos and the capital of Champassak Province. The area had strong links with the Khmer Empire over the centuries. The town was established by the French as an administrative post in 1905, and is still a small place, with a population of around 50,000. More refugees fled Champassak during the post-1975 era than from other Lao provinces, as it developed a reputation for repressive and Stalinist policies. Even viewing Thai television was banned. Today Pakse welcomes joint ventures and foreign tourists—though few reach southern Laos—and Lao refugees are welcomed back to their former homes.

One of the major activities around Pakse appears to be the transport of timber across the border to Ubon Ratchathani in Thailand. Although the Lao government sets a strict quota on logging, it seems Khmer logging companies take logs from Laos, haul them back to Cambodia, and sell them to Lao middlemen, who then sell them to Thai companies. Lacking sufficient manpower, the authorities in Pakse are said to be powerless in cracking down on this laundering of logs.

Pakse Market

Pakse's market is the hub of local interaction, with hawking and bargaining in full swing. Markets are the best places to people-watch, although it's more likely *you* will be the center of at-

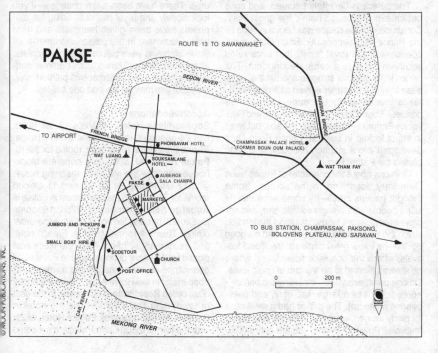

tention. While you're poking around, do some shopping yourself—you'll need supplies if heading off to Wat Phu or out of Pakse for a day-trip.

Champassak Province is famed for its handwoven silks and cottons. Eleven km northwest of Pakse (take the Russian bridge up Route 13) is **Saphay,** with a weaving marketplace. Saphay sits right on the Mekong, so it's a pleasant spot. Take a jumbo or sidecar-taxi, or find a local with a motorcycle.

Boun Oum Palace

The rambling palace that dominates Pakse is sited on a prime piece of land overlooking the Sedon River. The building was confiscated in 1975; the authorities couldn't decide whether to turn the place into a socialist cultural center or a tourist hotel. In the end the tourists won. The 60-room hotel has function rooms to handle 150 people, as well as a fitness center, sauna, and disco with karaoke. The interior has echoes of its original opulence, with teak fittings and tile floors, and a parquet-tiled ballroom.

The palace is definitely haunted, and cries out for explanation, so here's the ghost story. Construction of the palace was begun in 1968 by the Prince of Champassak, Boun Oum, a descendant of the royal family that once ruled southern Laos as a separate kingdom. The prince led a guerrilla struggle against the Japanese in WW II and later served as Prime Minister in Vientiane. By the early 1960s, three princes—Boun Oum, Souphanouvong, and Souvanna Phouma—ruled jointly in Laos, but were in effect locked in combat. Prince Boun Oum developed into a staunch anticommunist who battled the Pathet Lao.

Opinions about the character of Prince Boun Oum vary according to the source. Some thought he was cruel—by some accounts he killed people who disagreed with him, and appropriated peasant lands, including the land on which the palace was built. But he had his good points—he threw great parties at traditional festivals, where the rice wine flowed, and where he allowed himself to be the butt of ribald jokes. On one point, everyone—including the prince—agreed: he was a large, fat, ugly, and overbearing aristocrat. The prince had a weakness for pretty women, whom he invited to sing during festivals. "Powerful Prince, you are enormously

fat, you are ugly, you are old, and yet you ask me to speak to you of love," they would sing. And the prince would laugh loudly, and sing back through an intermediary: "You are right to say that, pretty maid. It's true that I am old and fat and ugly. But I am like a tough old elephant who will leave you ivory when it dies."

In 1975, with the Pathet Lao about to take over, the prince fled Pakse with the "ivory" in tow: he departed in style for Thailand with five elephants and a cavalcade of trucks reputed to contain priceless artifacts. He left behind only the unfinished palace. The prince died in Paris in 1984 at the age of 72. Under the relaxing of restrictions in Laos, his surviving sons and daughters have been invited back to visit.

Renovating the palace has given local authorities a few headaches. At the top of the central building, on the fifth level, is a small dome that commands a great view of town; it used to be a casino. The small concave ceiling of the dome bears elaborate frescoes of tigers, elephants hauling teak logs, and Ramayana figures. There have been a few changes—if you look closely, the royal mahouts riding the elephants have been given hammers and hard hats. Elsewhere in the palace, hammer-and-sickle emblems were painted over royal crests; after Laos dropped Marxism, the hammer-and-sickle emblems were themselves painted over, though there may be the odd one still left.

Accommodations

Souksamlane Hotel, on Route 13, tel. 8002, has 24 adequate rooms in the $10-18 range. **Phonsavan Hotel** rents basic rooms for $6-10. **Pakse Hotel,** tel. 8065, is a concrete blockhouse opposite the markets, meaning noisy, with 17 fan rooms for $6-12, and 11 air-con rooms for $12-16. On the main street in Pakse is **Auberge Sala Champa,** tel. 8254; 15 rooms for $20-25, bar and terrace, and advance-order dining. This is a former colonial French hotel and exudes an air of old Asia: the place was closed for 10 years during hard-line Pathet Lao dominance as the manager is a former paratroop major in the Royal Army. There's a pricey hotel called **Residence du Champa** to the east of town, near the stadium. The top hotel in Pakse is the **Champassak Palace Hotel,** which was the former Boun Oum Palace. It's located

*Champasak
Palace Hotel*

on the banks of the Sedon River, with 60 well-appointed rooms and suites, all featuring air-con, private bath, TV, and minibar.

Food

The markets have foodstalls; near the markets, on the same street as Pakse Hotel, are a few small restaurants serving Chinese, Thai or Vietnamese food. The **Auberge du Champa,** inside the Auberge Sala Champa, has advance-order dining in a fine setting with French, Lao, and other dishes. The Champassak Palace Hotel's in-house restaurant serves Lao, Thai, Vietnamese, and European cuisine. **Sengta-van Cabaret,** near Sodetour, serves Lao and Thai cuisine, with taxi dancers in the evening.

Getting There

Pakse airport is a convenient two km from town, over the old French metal bridge to the west. A ride into town in a jumbo should cost $2-3. A one-way Vientiane-Pakse ticket is $95—an expensive proposition if you double that for a roundtrip. If you plan an exit from Pakse through Chong Mek to Thailand, you can save on the return airfare. There are intermittent flights on light aircraft from Pakse to Saravan, Savannakhet, Attapeu, and Muoang Khong.

Chong Mek Border Crossing: If your paperwork is in order, you can exit or enter Thailand from Pakse via Chong Mek. Pakse is far easier to reach by land from Thailand's Ubon Ratchathani than from Vientiane. You may need to have your Lao visa endorsed for a Chong Mek entry or exit. If entering Thailand without a visa, you'll get 15-30 days stamped into your passport.

To exit Pakse to Thailand, first take a five-minute car ferry across the Mekong. On the other side you may have to walk several km to find jumbos or *songtaos,* which park across a narrow bridge. If you don't want to walk, take a jumbo on the car ferry to cover the gap. Jumbo and *song-tao* drivers ask for high prices to Chong Mek, so bargain hard. Chong Mek is about an hour's drive in a *songtao,* 40 km west of the Mekong on a good road. The Lao side of the Chong Mek crossing is open 0730-1130 and 1330-1630; you can change kip to baht at an informal bank.

Once on the Thai side, you switch from driving on the right side to the left side of the road. It's 75 km through Pibun to Ubon Ratchathani, about two hours by *songtao.* In contrast to Laos, Thailand has an excellent travel infrastructure—good roads, fast air-con buses, express trains with sleepers—and roving vendors in smart uniforms dispensing beer and seafood. From Ubon you can travel to other parts of Laos by bus; the train line runs westward to Korat and Bangkok.

If your timing is right, you can catch an overnight train from Ubon to Bangkok. There are three rapid trains in the late afternoon, taking 11 hours to cover the ground, and an afternoon plane from Ubon to Bangkok. You can make it all the way from Pakse to Bangkok overland in under 24 hours for less than $20—including $14 for a sleeper from Ubon.

Getting Around

You can easily cover Pakse on foot. Jumbos, pickups, and three-wheelers congregate near the banks of the Sedon River, close to the Mekong. In this zone you can also rent small boats for Champassak (Wat Phu) and Khong Islands. Around the markets are sidecar-taxis: the maximum load is three passengers—two in the sidecar, and one sitting behind the driver on the motorcycle. A sidecar-taxi will get you to Saphay weaving village. For car rental, try **Lane Xang Travel,** tel. 8262, with an office in the Souksamlane Hotel; or **Sodetour,** tel. 8056, near the Mekong car ferry.

VICINITY OF PAKSE

The bus terminal is out of town to the east; at KM2 are share-taxis to Paksong and Saravan. Local transport to Paksong and Saravan can be slow, and accommodations in either place are limited or nonexistent. The other land option is rented transport: Sodetour and Lane Xang Travel rent jeeps, fat-tired pickups, and minibuses at exorbitant prices—to the tune of 50 cents per km. You can use Pakse as a base for visiting the market town of Paksong (see "The Bolovens Plateau," above) or sites to the south, such as Wat Phu. In this direction, boat transport can be hired to go part way.

Um Muang Ruins

The Khmer ruins of Um Muang are located 44 km south of Pakse. There are two sanctuaries here, built at roughly the same time as Wat Phu, plus an assortment of sandstone *nagas* and *lingas.* This minor site is dilapidated and moss-covered, and not as impressive as Wat Phu, but it depends how you like your ruins—Um Muang gives you the thrill of discovery because the site has not been cleared of encroaching jungle. The ruins are approached from Ban Nakham Noi— you can get there by road from Pakse by turning at Ban Thang Beng, but the more interesting approach is to travel to Ban Nakham Noi by boat, and hike in half an hour to the ruins. Local kids will act as guides on the jungle trail. You can either hire a boat from Pakse or pick up a local boat for about $14 roundtrip from Ban Muang, the riverside village to the north. It might

AROUND PAKSE

be possible to squeeze in a trip to both Wat Phu and Um Muang ruins if you line up your transport the right way—both Um Muang and Champassak can be reached by boat.

About 27 km east of Route 13 on the road to Attapeu is the village of Ban Phapho, where young elephants are trained for hauling hardwoods and rice, and other hard labor. There are up to 90 pachyderms in the elephant school.

CHAMPASSAK AND WAT PHU

Located 42 km south of Pakse are the ruins of Wat Phu, reached via the village of Champassak. Wat Phu, an outpost of the Khmer Empire, is not as impressive as Angkor Wat in Cambodia or Khmer sites in Thailand. However, it makes for a great hour-long boat trip down the Mekong—which runs very wide here—and there's a good hike up a mountain to view the top sanctuary. Allow a full day for the excursion and a minimum of three hours at the site. It will take at least an hour to hike to the top and back.

Champassak

Champassak is an agricultural village strung for several kilometers along the banks of the Mekong. Prince Boun Oum began building another of his rambling mansions at the edge of town—it's unfinished, and considerably more modest than the one in Pakse. In town are a couple of French-style houses, formerly owned by the Prince's brothers. There's a small hotel and restaurant in Champassak near the boat pier.

Wat Phu

Wat Phu's history is sketchy. Apparently an outpost of the far-flung Khmer kingdom based in Angkor Wat, this "lost city" lay abandoned in the jungle until French explorer Francis Garnier stumbled across it in 1866. Unlike Angkor Wat, however, Wat Phu was never really "abandoned"—it continued as a place of worship over the centuries. Little is known about the history of the temple—locals told Garnier the temple had been built by "another race." Inscriptions found by archaeologists suggest the mountain was already an important place of worship in the 6th century when the Cham ruled the area. The temple complex appears to have been built in the 12th century—the handiwork of Khmer King Suryavarman II, who also initiated work on Angkor Wat. At some point, possibly in the late 13th century, the temple switched from Hindu to Buddhist; in the 14th century the Lao conquered the area.

The temple is the focus of thousands of Buddhist and Hindu pilgrims from Laos and northeast Thailand who converge here for a full moon festival in February every year. Pilgrims leave offerings and participate in football, boat racing, and boxing competitions, as well as singing and dancing. Water buffalo are sacrificed during the three-day festival; another buffalo sacrifice takes place in June to appease the earth spirit of Champassak.

At present the temple complex is in bad shape—with collapsed walls and mossy blocks of stone scattered around. Encroaching vege-

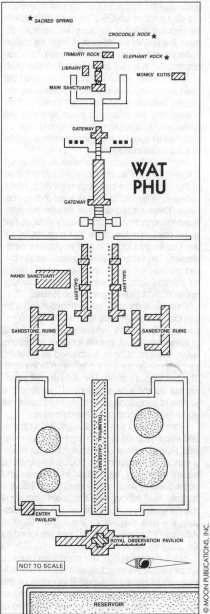

WAT PHU

- ★ SACRED SPRING
- CROCODILE ROCK ★
- TRIMURTI ROCK
- ELEPHANT ROCK ★
- LIBRARY
- MONKS' KUTIS
- MAIN SANCTUARY
- GATEWAY
- GATEWAY
- NANDI SANCTUARY
- GALLERY
- GALLERY
- SANDSTONE RUINS
- SANDSTONE RUINS
- TRIUMPHAL CAUSEWAY
- ENTRY PAVILION
- ROYAL OBSERVATION PAVILION
- NOT TO SCALE
- RESERVOIR

© MOON PUBLICATIONS, INC.

tation and the ravages of unchecked monsoons are also evident. UNESCO is involved in possible reconstruction of the complex: experts estimate the project would cost at least six million dollars and take six years. The method of reconstruction is known as anastylosis—also used at Angkor Wat—which involves taking apart the main sanctuary and staircase, numbering the pieces, building a new concrete base, and reassembling the structures piece by piece. An underground drainage system would also be installed to counter the considerable damage of the annual monsoon.

The Wat Phu temple complex is strewn up 1,400-meter-high sacred Mount Phu. At the base of the mountain are two large reservoirs, which collected rainwater to irrigate surrounding ricefields. There are two decayed wooden pavilions down this end, both of 20th-century vintage. The larger pavilion in the center was constructed for the Lao king to lodge in and to observe ceremonies. The second pavilion is now used to collect minimal entry fees (there are extra charges for still and video cameras); the site is officially open 0800-1630 but there are no fences.

Past the entry gate, you proceed along a triumphal causeway, once lined with *nagas,* lions, and other guardians—virtually nothing remains of these. Up ahead, there's a pair of sandstone ruins, thought to have functioned as housing for pilgrims—women to the left; men to the right. The buildings are shells. The walls are still standing but the roofs have collapsed, resulting in a jumble of sandstone blocks. You can make out some lintel decoration on the doorways.

From this point you start to climb a long stone-laid slope, passing through a gateway with several *Plumeria* trees. *Plumeria rubra acutifolia,* a species of frangipani, is a tropical flower with a heavy fragrance, also found in Vietnam and other parts of Asia, and sometimes called the "temple tree." Although the frangipani blossom is the national flower of Laos (called *dok champa*), the tree originally comes from Central America; *Plumeria acutifolia* trees are found as far afield as Tahiti and Brazil.

Up the mountain is the main sanctuary, a small sandstone structure with the ruins of a library and a gallery attached. Bas-reliefs on the temple's columns and lintels depict major themes of Hindu mythology—the Churning of the Sea of Milk, scenes from the Ramayana, and the cosmic sleep of Vishnu. Behind the sanctuary, carved into a large boulder, is a Trimurti consisting of Brahma (at left), Shiva (standing at center), and Vishnu (kneeling at right). Other less elaborate rock carvings in the area—those of a *naga,* elephant, and crocodile—may once have been associated with human sacrifice.

Behind the temple is a mountain cliff. A spring at the base of the cliff was channeled by a system of stone pipes to the inner sanctuary to anoint a sacred Shiva linga, or stone phallus. The sanctuary is now linga-less: the sculpted piece disappeared long ago. Water from the spring is considered sacred—or, at the very least, good luck—so Laotians sprinkle it on themselves. The top sanctuary affords serene views over the valley, which the few resident monks up this way have plenty of time to contemplate.

With a guide, it's possible to hike farther up Mount Phu, itself perceived as a linga by the Khmers. Hiking to the top may require camping out overnight.

Getting There

There are several ways of reaching Wat Phu. The intermediate point to aim for is the village of Champassak, 34 km south of Pakse; from there it's another eight km to the ruins. Pakse to Champassak is downstream, so tour groups generally take a rented boat on the outbound journey—1.25 hours downstream, half an hour longer upstream. At Champassak, tours rendezvous with a jeep that covers the last eight km to the ruins. On the return trip, the jeep crosses the Mekong by small ferry at the village of Ban Phaphin, five km north of Champassak, to the village of Ban Muang Kao; then you drive back to Pakse. Take picnic supplies—bananas, bread, bottled water—as there's very little in Champassak.

On your own, you have a few options. The easiest is to hire a jumbo or pickup from the dock area of Pakse, or even a sidecar-taxi from the markets, and ride all the way out to the ruins, crossing the Mekong by car ferry. Roads can be rough; by jumbo, the one-way trip can take 2.5 hours. A more scenic option is to rent your own boat from the docks for $20—the boatman will take you to Champassak and wait for your return. Unfortunately, at Champassak you're still eight km short of the ruins—so the return trip would be 16 km, which is a fair walk when you consider the hiking on site at Wat Phu. A solution is to somehow get your hands on a bicycle in Pakse, put that on the boat, and cycle in from Champassak. You could also try to track down a vehicle for hire in Champassak (difficult) or hitch-hike on a passing truck or other vehicle (rare).

There's an irregular ferry service to Champassak. In theory, longboats leave the Sedon River in Pakse at 0800, 0900, and 1000; 75 cents for locals and maybe $3 for you. If you take the ferry, you come up against the problem of how to walk the distance from Champassak to Wat Phu. Bringing a bicycle would solve that problem, but if you stay too long you might still have to spend the night in Champassak and catch another boat back to Pakse next morning.

MEKONG ISLANDS

At the southern tip of Laos, about 150 km south of Pakse, the Mekong reaches a breadth of 14 km—the greatest width of the river in its entire 4,200-km course from Tibet to Vietnam. Swollen by tributaries, the Mekong here splits to create a maze of channels; the area is known as the 4,000 Islands, or "Si Phan Don." This optimistic figure takes into count sandbars that appear during the dry season—the number of islets varies with water level.

Don Khong, the largest of the islands at 16 km long and eight km wide, is inhabited year-round and is used as a base for exploring the region—to visit nearby waterfalls and rapids, or go fishing. Swimming in the area cannot be recommended as there is a slight chance of picking up schistosomiasis, which is caused by tiny flatworms that burrow through the skin and enter the bloodstream. If that one sounds nasty, consider the fact that opisthorchiasis (liver flukes) may also be contracted from swimming in contaminated waters around Don Khong or from eating raw fish.

The main village on Don Khong is **Muang Khong,** a former French settlement, about 130 km from Pakse. It is reached by car ferry from Hat Xai Khun. Muang Khong has a market, a few cafés, and wats; near the pier are several guest-houses. Accommodations at Auberge Don Khong

can be booked through Sodetour in Pakse or Vientiane. The zone is a budding tour resort, as yet still difficult to reach.

The major attraction of the Mekong Islands is the spectacular set of cascades towards the Cambodian border. A 10-km chain of cascades and rapids south of Don Khong is loosely referred to as Khone Falls. There are in fact two impressive falls in the area. Off Don Khone Island are **Khong Phapheng Falls,** among the largest in Southeast Asia. The falls are about 22 km south of Muang Khong, along Route 13. The falls can be viewed from several perilous vantage points just below Ban Thakho; watch local fishermen perform daring stunts on the rocks near the falls. Located to the west of Don Khone Island is **Li Phi Falls,** another roaring torrent. The best way to get there is to hire a small boat from Ban Nakasang for a one-hour roundtrip costing $6 or so. The boat goes through fast-flowing channels and requires a skilled boatman; islands in this area are renowned for the cultivation of coconut, bamboo, kapok, and hardwoods. Another approach is on foot on Don Khone Island—walk westward past Wat Khone Tai.

Seething Mekong activity in this vicinity will explain the presence of an old **French rail line,** built across Don Khone and Don Det Islands. The five-km line—the only section of railway track in Laos—was built to bypass the treacherous rapids and facilitate transport of French cargo boats between Pakse and Phnom Penh around the turn of the century. The line has concrete piers at either end; an old customs house sits next to a railway bridge at the main town of Ban Khone, with a rusted locomotive and boiler. There's a thicket surrounding the locomotive—stay well clear as it bears a toxic fruit that can cause a rash if it brushes the skin. You can hike along the railway track, passing through ricefields, forest, and small villages. Start at the north side and make your way south.

Rare freshwater **Irrawaddy dolphins** come upriver to spawn between January and March; they're unable to pass the rapids, so the only place you might catch a glimpse of these rare mammals is at the southern end of Don Khone Island. You can hire a boat here to reach offshore islands; viewing is best in the late afternoon. Don't get your hopes up, though: there are estimated to be less than 50 of this endangered species left. The main habitat of the dolphin is the area above Stung Treng in Cambodia. The dolphin is threatened by indiscriminate use of explosives for fishing in Cambodia, as well as the use of gillnets in Laos. Dolphins are considered reincarnate beings, with many stories about dolphins coming to the rescue of fishermen and saving them from drowning or crocodile attacks. Thus Lao fishermen do not intentionally trap dolphins for food or

sport, but if a dolphin becomes entangled in a net, the fisherman may be reluctant to cut it free because of the $20 cost of replacing the net. The net traps the dolphin underwater and it drowns. On the Cambodian side, where lawlessness prevails, fishermen use explosives, which are strictly banned in Laos. In an effort to halt this deplorable practice, the Lao government banned the import of fish from Cambodia in 1993.

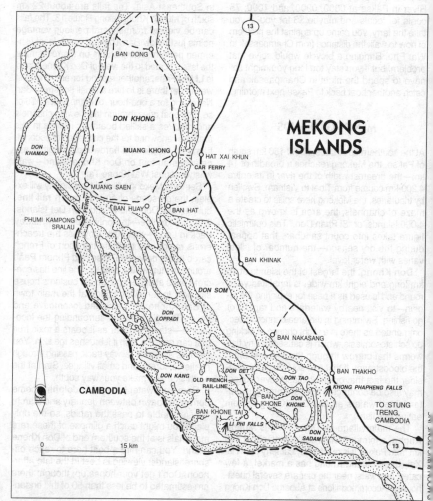

MEKONG ISLANDS

At the same time, the Lao government approved a plan for Thai development of a $360-million resort on the banks of the Mekong near Khong Phapheng Falls. The project includes three riverside hotels, campgrounds and bungalows, three golf courses, and a casino and conference facilities. The resort would provide a total of 2,000 rooms for tourists. The agreement also allows for construction of a 20-megawatt hydroelectric power station, a water and waste treatment plant, a local airport, and internal roads. Relocation of 10,000 Laotians will be necessary—apparently, a new town of Khon Phapheng will be built for them. Citing negative impact on the environment and fisheries, the Laos Forestry Department in 1992 recommended the area not be developed; however, this was overruled by highly placed members of the central government.

Getting There

Hiring a jeep to reach the area from Pakse is a very expensive proposition. The 150-km run to Khong Phapheng Falls takes about five hours one-way. An alternative is to try to commandeer a boat from Pakse. The larger boats can run as far south as Mounlapamok; you may then need to transfer to a smaller boat or hit Highway 13. From Pakse, allow a full day for boat transport to the Mekong Islands vicinity. There are several buses a day from Pakse to Hat Xai Khun, where you transfer to a primitive car ferry to Muang Khong. Passenger trucks also run from Ban Muang, opposite Champassak, to Ban Khinak, south of Hat Xai Khun. Vehicle transport is in short supply in this area, and so are roads. You should consider boat transport for getting around the Mekong Island area. There's a ferry service from Muang Khong to Ban Khinak on the route south, for example, or you can hire a boat to cover the same route.

If you want to travel in style, Sodetour runs a 34-meter-long steel hull barge, converted into a wooden floating hotel with 10 separate air-conditioned staterooms, each with two beds and private bath. The vessel, the *Vat Phou,* is self-contained, with its own restaurant and sundeck. Passengers board the *Vat Phou* in Pakse and take two- to four-day cruises to Don Khong Island, stopping at sites like Champassak en route. From Don Khong Island, passengers head for Khong Phapheng Falls by car. The cost is prohibitive, around $650 a person for a three-day tour. Some passengers are recruited from Vientiane and fly into Pakse; others cross from Thailand at Chong Mek to join the boat tour.

The Mekong Islands sit right on the Cambodian border. A ferry covers a short hop from Muang Saen on the west side of Don Khong Island to the Cambodian town of Phumi Kampong Sralau. The crossing is used by locals but is unlikely to be open to foreigners, since the area falls within the Khmer Rouge sphere of influence. There's another land border on Route 13 south, leading to Stung Treng.

Relations are testy between the Cambodians and the Lao at this border zone. There are rumors of anti-Lao resistance groups operating in the area, along with Khmer Rouge log dealers; reports have also reached Vientiane of Khmer bandits crossing over into Laos to rob buses and cars. In early 1994, Cambodian police opened fire on a boat with officials from Thailand after they refused to pull over when the police accused them of violating Cambodian territory.

---

*G*oing up that river was like travelling back to the earliest beginnings of the world, when vegetation rioted on the earth and the big trees were kings. An empty stream, a great silence, an impenetrable forest . . . The broadening waters flowed through a mob of wooded islands; you lost your way on that river as you would in a desert, and butted all day long against shoals, trying to find the channel, till you thought yourself bewitched and cut off for ever from everything you had known once—somewhere—far away—in another existence perhaps, . . . I got used to it afterwards.

—JOSEPH CONRAD, *HEART OF DARKNESS*

COMMUNICATING

The more you can communicate and interact with locals while on the road, the more you'll get out of your trip. The language sections that follow are starter kits for Vietnamese, Khmer, and Lao. You're advised to brush up on any French you know, as it's useful in all three countries. If you speak some Thai, you can take advantage of the fact that Laotian and Cambodian vocabularies draw from the same word base as Thai. English is a kind of lingua franca in Asia, and many Asians are keen to practice. You can conduct a lot of transactions, particularly in large cities, in English.

Attempt to get at the basics of the native language, even if it is only simple vocabulary. Languages may appear daunting to tackle, but the actual number of words you need to handle basic situations is minimal.

Vietnamese and Lao are tonal languages. Basic phrases in tonal languages are sometimes identical to insults, give or take a tone. In Lao, the word for "friend" (moo, spoken with a mid-tone) is a few tones away from the word for "pig." Cambodian is non-tonal. You can't learn exact tones from phrasebooks, you can only really grasp them from imitating a native speaker or repeatedly listening to a tape. Before you travel, it's worth getting your hands on an audiotape. Hearing the foreign phrase spoken twice, followed by the phrase in English, will attune your ear to the nuances of pronunciation. Think of it this way: can you really get an idea of what a symphony sounds like from just looking at sheet music? Some travelers carry a minicassette recorder to record locals.

Strategies

Carry a pocket-size phrasebook—they're inexpensive and light. If you're interested in attaining the pidgin plateau of communication, concentrate on verbs, nouns, pronouns, and adjectives. Once you've mastered a few of those, skip any pretense at making whole sentences or observing grammar rules, rather combine gestures with basic vocabulary to get your message across. Take along small blank cards that can fit in your wallet. Write down frequently used constructions in local script and transliteration. Or add them directly to your phrasebook.

Flattery: A positive attitude will take you a long way. Go at it with gusto: enthusiasm works wonders for improving communication, and flattery will get you everywhere. The most important words to grasp in the new language are "good," "very good," "delicious," and "beautiful." These can be accompanied by a thumbs-up gesture. Once you've learned the right words, try these on your host or hostess (point at things or areas if you don't know the word): "Your house is beautiful!" "The wine is terrific!" "I love this country!" Enjoy the language of food: sit back and allow your host to force-feed you, uttering grunts of appreciation. Avoid negatives, but learn the word for "okay." This can have a negative connotation by inference—for example, "okay" meaning "that's enough food, thank you" with an accompanying hand gesture.

Pictures and Numbers: Pictures communicate fast. Take along photos of your family, your dog, your city. Examination of pictorial subjects—theirs and yours—can lead to long dialogue. Written Arabic numerals are universal, so use them to exchange statistical information such as: How many years married? How many children do you have? How many ducks? How many water buffalo? Prices can be negotiated by holding up fingers for digits. In Vietnam each finger represents one thousand dong, so three fingers means 3000 dong. Beware, however: some foreigners have been unpleasantly surprised when the bill comes to $3!

Gestures: Use mime, facial expressions, and hand gestures to ham it up and cut through the language barrier. However, some Western gestures are considered rude, such as beckoning using the forefinger. This is used for animals in Asia. To beckon people, use the full hand, palm down, and motion with all fingers wriggling together. In a restaurant, to ask the waiter for the bill, write up an imaginary bill in the air. To indicate to a taxi driver you want the airport, slap the right hand off a horizontal, stationary left palm in imitation of a plane taking off.

Brain Teasers: In Vietnam, thanks to Jesuit missionaries, you're semi-literate. In Laos and Cambodia, you may well consider yourself a total illiterate. But are you really? If you're any good at puzzle patterns, you can start decoding those script squiggles. Try it with destinations by matching symbols on a road sign to those on a bilingual map, for example. Phrasebooks can aid your use of script and attempts to decode it. Phrasebooks also make excellent gifts upon departure—your hosts may use them for figuring out English.

VIETNAMESE LANGUAGE

Vietnamese is a tonal language, possibly derived from Austro-Asiatic or Sino-Tibetan languages; Chinese has been a major influence on Vietnamese literature. There are three main dialects in Vietnam—northern, central, and southern—although the language is mutually intelligible.

Good Morning, Vietnam: The minute you open your mouth in Vietnam you put your foot in it because the first thing you need to say is "hello." Unfortunately, "hello" is quite complicated in Vietnamese. There is no way round "hello," as the Vietnamese rarely use "good morning" or "good evening." A straight "hello" is rude—you need to address the person as well. You can wing it, and get away with *chào, bạn,* (hello, my friend) if talking to a younger person or *chào, các bạn* (hello, my friends). But this won't work with older folk. If you're looking for a catch-all "friends, Romans, countrymen," there isn't one. You have to take into account the person's sex, age, and level of familiarity (formal or informal). Vastly underestimating or overestimating a woman's age can be a big faux pas!

The correct forms of address are as follows: *chào ông*—when addressing an old man; *chào anh*—to a young man; *chào bà*—to an old woman; *chào cô*—to a young woman; *chào chị*—to an older woman; *chào em*—to younger people; *chào cháu*—to a young child; *chào các bạn*—hello friends, if addressing a younger audience. If you know the given name, add that. So now it's *chào cô Lan*—hello young woman Lan. The conversation may then lead to "How old are you?" or "Where are you going?" or "What are you doing?" Some Vietnamese like this gambit with foreigners: "How much money do you make?" With some perseverance, you can build up a stock of simple phrases such as *đẹp lắm* or *rất đẹp,* both mean beautiful or very pretty. These will get you through a variety of situations.

Tones: The sound of Vietnamese has been likened to the twittering of birds. Mastering the sing-song warble-like tones is essential to conveying correct meaning. The same word can mean six different things, depending on the tone— "ma" for instance, can mean ghost, mother, but, tomb, horse, or rice seedling.

As satirist P.J. O'Rourke puts it: ô *Cờm* (cooked rice), *không* (no), *cam* (orange), *cấm* (not allowed) and *kem* (ice cream) are all pronounced, to the American ear, "kum." Thus you can ask someone for an ice cream and wind up in the market with a forbidden orange dog.

The six tones are rendered (with "o" as an example only): midtone, no marker; ó high rising, starts high and rises sharply; ò low falling, starts low and falls to lowest level of voice range; ỏ low rising, starts low, dips, and rises to high point; õ high broken, starts above midtone, dips slightly, rises abruptly; and ọ low broken, starts below normal range, falls abruptly and immediately to a lower level and gets cut off. In addition to these markers the vowels a, e, i, o, and u carry special marks such as a hat or a little hook for sounds that have no approximations to English sounds. Go over the Vietnamese phrases that follow with a Vietnamese speaker to get the sounds correct. Or record the speaker on a cassette, listen repeatedly, and mimic.

Negatives and Questions: Vietnamese sentences follow this word order: subject, verb, object. To make a negative, simply add the word *không* between subject and verb. Question words are usually placed at the end of the sentence. Take the affirmative statement without the answer and add the question word. For example, "This book is how much?" For yes/no questions, the word *có* (yes) is added before the verb, and the word *không* (no) is added at the end of the sentence to make the question. The word order is thus: subject, *có,* verb, object, *không*? The trickiest question in Vietnamese is a negative one. "You haven't gone to the market yet, have you?" is answered in the positive "Yes," meaning "Yes, I haven't."

Reading: After being completely illiterate in Thailand, China, Laos, and Cambodia, it comes as quite a shock to suddenly find that in Vietnam you can actually recognize the letters on signs, street names, museum labels, and even the odd newspaper headline. For this you can thank Alexandre de Rhodes, the 17th-century French Jesuit who devised *qu ôc ngữ* script—basically to convert the Bible into Vietnamese, and the people into Catholics. Alexandre de Rhodes also came up with the system of tone markers above and below the letters. This replaced a system with Chinese-based ideographs. *Qu ôc ngữ* set Vietnam apart from the rest of continental Asia.

If you have trouble getting your message across with tonal pronunciation, try writing it down, adding the tone markers if you can. Without the appropriate tone markers, the Roman alphabet can still be understood, although the Vietnamese person would have to guess at the meaning. Expect the odd transliteration methods, which derived from French. *Gion-Xón* is Johnson; *xàlách* is salad. Signs like *Cóm Chay* (vegetarian) or *Cảnh Sát* (police) are handy to recognize.

Phrasebooks and Tapes: Many dirt-cheap phrasebooks and dictionaries are sold in Saigon and Hanoi for English-Vietnamese or French-Vietnamese. If your pronunciation doesn't work, you can at least count on pointing to phrasebook or dictionary entries. Vietnam boasts an exceptional 88% literacy rate. Ho Chi Minh personally promoted this cause, proclaiming, "an ignorant nation is a weak nation." Because of the unusual sounds in Vietnamese, you can go only so far in learning the language from a phrasebook. It is preferable to listen to a tape to attune your ear at least to recognizing the sounds. **The Language 30** series, produced by Educational Services Corporation, consists of a booklet and two cassettes, with one hour of recording. Phrasebooks are also issued by Lonely Planet and by Editions Duang Kamol (Bangkok). A Viet-Anh and Anh-Viet dictionary makes sense, but unfortunately those on the market abroad are hefty and expensive tomes, impractical to lug around.

Vietnamese transliteration varies from English pronunciation, and sounds vary slightly from north (N) to south (S). Some variants include:

c—"k"

ch—at the beginning of a word is pronounced "ch" as in "cheek"; at the end of a word it's "ck" as in "lick"

đ—"z" (N) and "y" (S); for example, the national dress *áo dài* is pronounced *áo zài* (N) or *áo yài* (S)

Đ—"d" as in "dog"

gì—"z" (N) and "y" (S)

kh—"ch" as in the German "Bach"

nh—in the beginning or middle of a word, pronounced ñ as in the Spanish "mañana"; at the end of a word it's "ng" as in "running away"

ph—"f"

r—"z" (N) and "r" (S)

th—"t" as in "tea," but strongly aspirated

tr—"ch"(N) and "tr" (S)

s—"s" (N) and "sh" (S)

x—"s"

VIETNAMESE PHRASES

TONES

The following tones appear on the phrases below. The letter "o" is used as an example.

midtone	no mark
high rising	(ó) starts high, rises sharply
low falling	(ò) starts low, falls to lowest voice range
low rising	(ỏ) starts low, dips, and rises to high point
high broken	(õ) starts above midtone, dips slightly, rises abruptly
low broken	(ọ) starts low, falls abruptly, and gets cut off

OPENERS

Hello (my friend)	Chào bạn. (bạn tôi)
Goodbye	Tạm biệt nhé
Pleased to meet you	Hân hạnh được gặp bạn
How are you?	Bạn có khỏe không?
Very well, thank you	Cám ơn bạn, tôi khỏe
Where are you going?	Bạn đi đâu đấy?
What's your name?	Tên bạn là gì?
My name is . . .	Tên tôi là…
I only speak a little Vietnamese	Tôi chỉ nói một ít setiếng Việt
I don't understand	Tôi không hiểu
Do you understand?	Bạn có hiểu không?

GETTING PERSONAL

Where are you from?	Bạn từ đâu đến?
Canadian/ Australian/British	Canada/Úc/Anh
American/ French/Russian	Mỹ/Pháp/Nga
Vietnamese/Lao/Thai	Việt Nam/Lào/Thái
Cambodian/Chinese	Cam-pu-chia/Trung Hoa
My job is . . .	Việc làm của tôi là…
How old are you?	Bạn bao nhiêu tuổi?
married/single	có gia đình/độc thân
husband/wife	chồng/vợ
mother/father	mẹ/cha
children/son/daughter	con cái/con trai/ con gái
older brother/sister	anh/chị
younger brother/sister	em trai/em gái

FLATTERY

good/very good	tốt/tốt lắm
The food is great!	Món ăn ngon lắm!
terrific food!	ngon tuyệt!
Cheers!	Chúc mừng!
To your health!	Chúc sức khỏe!
I love this town!	Tôi thích thành phố này!
very beautiful	rất đẹp
very interesting	rất thích!
I had a great time!	Tôi có một thời gian tuyệt vời
Good luck!	Chúc bạn may mắn!

NEGATIVES, QUESTIONS, REQUESTS

yes/no	vâng(N), có(S)/không
okay/no problem	được/không sao
not okay/no good	không được/không tốt
please/thank you	làm ơn/cám ơn bạn
enough, thank you	đủ rồi, cám ơn
I want/need	Tôi muốn/cần
don't want/don't like	tôi không muốn/ không thích
sorry, excuse me	xin lỗi
don't know	không biết
Can I take a photo?	Tôi có thể chụp hình nhé?
What's this called in Vietnamese?	Cái này tiếng Việt gọi là gì?
What does that mean?	Cái nghĩa đó là gì?
Can you write it down for me?	Bạn có thể viết ra đây không?
where/where is?	đâu?/ở đâu?
when?/who?/ why?/how?	khi nào?/ai?/ tại sao?/thế nào?
how much/many?	bao nhiêu?
how long?/how far?	bao lâu?/bao xa?

RED TAPE

passport	giấy thông hành
tourist/ business person	du khách/ thươnggia
visa/Thai visa	chiếu khán/chiếu khán của Thái
I want to extend my visa	Tôi muốn gia hạn chiếu khán
travel permit	giấy phép du lịch
I need a translator	Tôi cần thông dịch viên
What is the problem?	Có vấn đề gì đấy?

MEDICAL

sick	ốm đau (N)/bệnh (S)
diarrhea/ headache/fever	tiêu chảy/ nhức đầu/sốt
cold/sore throat	cảm/đau họng
please help!	giúp tôi với!
need a doctor/dentist	cần một bác sĩ/ nha sĩ
emergency	khẩn cấp
hospital	bệnh viện
drugstore	nhà thuốc tây

ASKING/GIVING DIRECTIONS

I want to go to . . .	tôi muốn đi đến...
I want to see . . .	tôi muốn gặp...
how many kilometers to...?	bao nhiêu ki lô mét đến...?
how long will it take to get to...?	Đi bao lâu thì tới...?
turn right/turn left	quẹo phải/quẹo trái
straight ahead	đi thẳng
fast/slow	nhanh/chậm
slow down/ take it easy!	chậm lại/ cứtừ từ!
Stop here!	Dừng lại!
Wait here	Đợi ở đây
Let's go!	Chúng ta hãy đi!
north/south	bắc/nam
east/west	đông/tây
map	bản đồ
Where can I get a map?	Tôi có thể mua bản đồ ở đâu?

TRANSPORT

timetable	lịch trình
Please write down the timetable.	Xin viết lịch trình ra.

TRANSPORT (continued)

ticket	vé
Can you buy a ticket for me?	Bạn có thể mua hộ tôi cái vé?
Where can I leave my luggage?	Tôi có thể để hành lý ở đâu?
plane/helicoptor	máy bay/máy bay lên thẳng(N), trực thăng(S)
bus/minibus	xe buýt/xe ô-tô con
express bus	xe buýt tốc hành
bus station/ minibus station	bến xe buýt/ bến xe con
Where is the bus station?	Bến xe buýt ở đâu?
How many buses a day are there?	Một ngày có bao nhiêu chuyến xe buýt?
What time is the first bus?	Mấy giờ bắt đầu có chuyến xe thứ nhất?
What time is the last bus?	Mấy giờ bắt đầu có chuyến xe cuối?
When does the next bus leave?	Chuyến xe tới xuất hành vào giờ nào?
When does the bus arrive?	Khi nào xe buýt tới?
railway station	ga xe lửa
express train	tàu tốc hành
hard seat/soft seat	ghế ngồi cứng (ghế gỗ)/ghế ngồi mềm (ghế mềm)
hard sleeper/ soft sleeper	giường nằm cứng (giường gỗ)/ giường nằm mềm (giường nệm)
What time is the next train?	Chuyến tàu tới chạy vào lúc mấy giờ?

taxi/taxi station	tắc xi/bến xe tắc xi
motorcycle-taxi	xe mô-tô ôm
cyclo(trishaw)	xe xích lô
truck/4WD vehicle	xe vận tải/xe díp
boat/boat dock	tàu thủy/bến tàu
ferry/ferry dock	phà/bến phà

RENTALS

motorcycle	xe mô-tô
bicycle	xe đạp
Where can I rent a bicycle?	Tôi có thể thuê xe đạp ở đâu?
How much per hour?	Bao nhiêu tiền một giờ?
How much for one day?/half a day?	Bao ýnhiêu tiền một ngày?/nửa ngày?
Where can I rent a motorcycle	Tôi có thể thuê mô-tô ở đâu?
driver/guide	tài xế/người hướng dẫn
Where can I hire a car and driver?	Tôi có thể thuê ô-tô con và tài xế ở đâu?
Where can I hire a minibus?	Tôi có thể thuê xe buýt nhỏ ở đâu?
Where can I hire a boat?	Tôi có thể thuê tàu thủy ở đâu?

PLACES

airport	phi trường
airline office	phòng bán vé máy bay
embassy	tòa đại sứ
post office	bưu điện
bank (foreign exchange)	ngân hàng (đổi tiền ngoại)
tourism bureau	văn phòng du lịch
bookshop	cửa hàng sách

gas station	trạm xăng
police station	đồn công an
market	chợ
temple/pagoda/church	đền/chùa/nhà thờ
museum/theatre	bảo tàng/rạp hát

DINING OUT

restaurant/cafe	nhà hàng ăn uống/quán nước
Let's eat!	chúng ta hãy ăn/mời bạn!
Please bring the menu	Làm ơn cho xem thực đơn
not hot (spicy) please	xin đừng làm cay
May I have...?	Tôi có thể có...?
fried rice/ steamed rice	cơm rang/ cơm nóng
sticky rice	xôi
croissant/ French bread	bánh sừng bò/ bánh mì Pháp
sandwich/ noodle soup	bánh mì kẹp/ tô mì sợi
chicken/ pork/beef	thịt gà/ thịt lợn/thịt bò
fish/shrimp	cá/tôm
vegetables/fruit	rau/quả
vegetarian food	món ăn chay
hot/cold	nóng/lạnh
salad	sà lách
I'll have the same thing	Cho tôi cùng món đó
water/cold water	nước/nước lạnh
boiled mineral water	nước suối đóng chai
boiled water	nước sôi
No ice, thanks	Không đá, cám ơn
hot tea/hot coffee	trà nóng/ cà phê nóng
lemon/sugar	chanh/đường
beer/soft drink	bia/nước ngọt
fruit juice	nước qủa(N)/nước trái cây(S)
young coconut	nước dừa tươi
Two beers please	Xin cho hai chai bia
The bill please	Làm ơn tính tiền

HOTEL

a good hotel	một khách sạn tốt
budget hotel	khách sạn bình dân
(family-run) guesthouse	nhà khách(gia đình làm)
air-conditioned	có điều hòa không khí
fan	quạt
telephone	điện thoại
room with bath	phòng có buồng tắm
single room (one bed)	phòng một giường
double room (two beds)	phòng hai giường
triple room	phòng ba
dormitory	nhà ngủ
toilet	nhà vệ sinh
toilet paper	giấy đi cầu
men's toilet/ women's toilet	nhà vệ sinh nam/ nhà vệ sinh nữ
shower/hot shower	vòi tắm hương sen/vòi tắm hương sen có nước nóng
sheets/towel	khăn trải giường/ khăn tắm
blanket	chăn đắp(N)/mền đắp(S)
thermos of hot water	bình thủy nước nóng
mosquito net	màn ngủ(N)/ mùng(S)
May I see the room, please?	Tôi có thể xem phong được không ?

Can you give me a discount?	Bạn có thể bớt cho tôi được không?

BARGAINING

How much is this?	Cái này bao nhiêu?
Do you have . . . ?	Bạn có…?
big/small	lớn/nhỏ
old/new	cũ/mới
expensive	đắt(N)/mắc(S)
Do you have anything cheaper?	Bạn có cái nào rẻ hơn không?
Can you give me a better price?	Bạn có thể cho tôi một giá thấp hơn không?
I will come back.	Tôi sẽ trở lại

TIME AND NUMBERS

today/now	hôm nay/bây giờ
tonight	đêm nay
yesterday/tomorrow	hôm qua/ngày mai
morning/ afternoon/evening	sáng/ chiều/tối
year/month/ day/hour	năm/tháng/ ngày/giờ
Monday	Thứ Hai
Tuesday	Thứ Ba
Wednesday	Thứ Tư
Thursday	Thứ Năm
Friday	Thứ Sáu
Saturday	Thứ Bảy
Sunday	Chủ Nhật
zero	không
one	một
two	hai
three	ba
four	bốn
five	năm
six	sáu
seven	bảy
eight	tám
nine	chín

ten	mười
twenty	hai mươi
thirty	ba mươi
fourty	bốn mươi
fifty	năm mươi
sixty	sáu mươi
seventy	bảy mươi
eighty	tám mươi
ninety	chín mươi
one hundred	một trăm
five hundred	năm trăm
one thousand	một nghìn
two thousand	hai nghìn
five thousand	năm nghìn
ten thousand	mười nghìn
twenty thousand	hai mươi nghìn
fifty thousand	năm mươi nghìn
one hundred thousand	một trăm nghìn
one million	một triệu

PLACE-NAMES AND GEOGRAPHICAL TERMS

District	Quận
forest	rừng
jungle	rừng nhiệt đới
mountain	núi
river	sông
beach	bãi tắm
bay	vịnh
island	đảo
lake	hồ
waterfall	thác
cave	hang động
valley	thung lũng
highway	xa lộ
bridge	cầu
City	Thành phố
boulevard	đại lộ
street	phố (N)/đường (S)
town square	bùng binh
gardens/ park	vườn/ vườn hoa (công viên)

KHMER LANGUAGE

The Cambodian language belongs to the Mon-Khmer family. Khmer is spoken throughout the Kingdom of Cambodia and by several million people in southwest Vietnam and northeast Thailand. Due to the influence of Buddhism and Brahmanism in Cambodia, many Sanskrit and Pali words entered the Khmer language. A large proportion of words in Cambodian share the same base as the Thai language, though the linguistic association is not immediately recognizable in the spoken language because Thai is tonal, and Khmer is nontonal.

Although Khmer is nontonal, pronunciation can be difficult. There are consonants that sound between d and t, between ch and j, or between b and p. There is no standard system of transcribing Cambodian script into Roman letters to suit an English speaker. Many sounds in Cambodian do not have precise English equivalents. The following phrase list attempts only an approximation of the correct sounds. You should go over the phrases with a native speaker to attune your ear.

Polite Forms: When addressing someone, it's polite to take into account the person's sex, age, and social standing. There are a variety of polite forms of "you," depending on whether you're addressing a man, a woman, a boy, a girl, or a person older than 60. In general, address a man of high standing *lohk* (mister) and a woman of high standing *lohk srei* (madam); for addressing someone the same age or of equal standing, use *neak* (my friend) or use the person's name. Certain Khmer forms are spoken only by women (*jah,* meaning "yes," for example) or by men (*baat,* meaning "yes").

Useful Phrases: Opening conversation gàmbits in the UNTAC era: "Thank you for showing me your wonderful gun." "I am delighted to accept your invitation to lie down on the ground." "Please accept my watch and this quantity of US dollars as a small sign of the high regard in which I hold you." Jokes aside, one of the most useful phrases to know in Cambodian is: *mian min teh?* (any mines around here?). The word for mine is easy—it's *min.* Another useful term to understand is *kmei grahawm,* meaning Khmer Rouge. Any of them around here?

Negatives and Questions: Questions are indicated by adding the question-words *reu teh* or just *teh* to the end of a sentence, spoken with an upward inflexion. Since Cambodian is nontonal, you can make a question by using an upward inflexion to a statement alone, as in English. Question words such as where, what, when, and why are placed at the end of a sentence, as in, *this coconut is how much?* Negatives are formed by inserting *meun,* (meaning "no") before the verb.

Reading: Khmer has a mammoth 74-letter alphabet with 33 consonants and a remarkable number of vowels and diphthongs. Some letters have no current usage. The alphabet derives from southern India. Examination of early Cambodian stelae inscriptions reveals that two different kinds of writing were in use simultaneously: one was based directly on Hindu; the other developed and adapted to Cambodian. The latter became the established medium, and has changed only slightly over the centuries. The writing system is extremely complicated to the Western eye. Vowels and dipthongs may be above, below, before, and after consonants. Consonants may be written below text as subscript.

Phrasebooks and Tapes: Crude photocopied language materials can be bought cheaply at the Central Market in Phnom Penh. These are more often intended for Cambodians learning English, so they might have important omissions, such as transliteration of Cambodian sounds. It's helpful to have the transliteration and the Cambodian script side-by-side. Useful is a palmsize version of Seam and Blake's *English-Khmer Dictionary,* originally printed in Bangkok, which uses its own phonetic system with exclamation marks. For serious attempts at the language, try *Colloquial Cambodian* by David Smyth, with a book and two tapes for $50.

The following phrases are transcribed as if addressing a man—the particle is *lohk*; to address a woman, substitute *lohk srei*; to address someone of equal standing, substitute *neak.* The word *sohm* (as rhyming with "home") denotes politeness.

OPENERS

hello	joom reap soo-uh (suisdei)
goodbye	leah sun hi
Pleased to meet you . . .	Knyom reek reuh na toybon chewuhk lohk . . .
How are you?	Sohm lohk sok sabei chea teh?
Very well, thank you.	Baat sok sabei, awkun. (spoken by men)/Jah sok sabei, awkun. (spoken by women)
Where are you going?	Sohm lohk, dtiw nah?
What's your name?	Sohm lohk, chmou ei?
My name is . . .	Knyom chmou . . .
I only speak a little Khmer.	Knyom nee-yeay pee-uh-saw Kmei bantec, bantuec.
I don't understand.	Knyom meun yul teh.
Do you understand?	Sohm lohk, yul reu teh?

GETTING PERSONAL

Where are you from?	Lohk mohk pee sroknah?
Canadian/ Australian/British	Kanada/ Ostralee/Anglae
American/ French/ Russian	Amerikang/ Barang/Rossey
Vietnamese/Lao/ Thai	Vietnam/Layo/Tai
Cambodian/Chinese	Kmei/Jhen
My job is . . .	Knyom tve kah . . .
How old are you?	Sohm lohk, ayut bpon mahn?
married/single	riapkah/kom law
husband/wife	pdei/prawpun
mother/father	madei/owpuhk
children/son/daughter	kon/kon bproh/ kon srey

older brother/sister	bong bproh/ bong srey
younger brother/sister	puh-own bproh/ puh-own srei

FLATTERY

good/very good	lu-awh/lu-awh nah
The food is great!	Mahop chngainh!
terrific food	mahop nee ochar nah
I love this town!	Knyom sraalanh khoom nee!
very beautiful	suh-awt nah
very interesting	coor chat aram nah
I had a great time!	Pbehl vilea nee u-awh nah!
good luck	somnang lu-awh

NEGATIVES, QUESTIONS, REQUESTS

yes/no	baat (spoken by men), jah (by women)/baat teh (men), jah teh (women)
okay/no problem	ban/meun ei teh
not okay/no good	meun ban/ meun lu-awh
please/thank you	sohm/awkun
enough, thank you	krup kroen hai, awkun
I want/need	knyom jong/knyom treu kah
don't want/don't like	knyom meun jong bahn/meun jol jet
sorry, excuse me	sohm toe/ot-toe
don't know	meun dong
Can I take a photo?	Dta knyom at tot rub bahn teh?
What's this called in Khmer?	Nee kay how tah avei?
What does that mean?	Dta peak nee mienei jong meitch?
Can you write it down for me?	Dta lohk at sohsei, bahn teh?

where? where is? — ai nah?/ti nah?

when? who?
why? how? — ongkal?/neak-na?/
hat-ei?/jong
meitch?

how much/many? — tlai bpon mahn?

how far? — chngei bpon mahn?

RED TAPE

passport — lee keut chlong-
daehn

tourist/businessperson — taih suhcha/neak
choom new-one

visa — visa

extend a visa — visa bpun-jia bpehl

I need a translator. — Knyom treu kah
neak bop bpraeh.

What is the problem? — Mien panyaha ei?

MEDICAL

sick/very sick — chue/chue klong

diarrhea/ headache/
fever/
stomach ache — riak/chue kbal/
run kdow/
chue phuah

cold/sore throat — padasay/johk
bombpoung ko

please help — sohm jewy bong

need a doctor/dentist — treu kah krew bpet/
bpet tahmenh

emergency — bon toen

hospital — moonty bpet

drugstore — hong luek tnam

ASKING/GIVING DIRECTIONS

I want to go to . . . — Knyom jong dtiw . . .

I want to see . . . — Knyom jong kheun. . .

How many
kilometers to . . .? — Bpon mahn
kilo dtiw . . .?

turn right/turn left — bot dtiw sdam/
bot dtiw chwaingh

straight ahead — dtiw dtrong

fast/slow — loeun or chop chop/
djuet or muey
muey

slow down/
take it easy — sohm dtiw
muey muey

Stop here — chop tee nee

Wait here. — Jaam tee nee.

Let's go! — Dtiw kah dtiw!

north/south — jeung/tbohng

east/west — kaet/lehj

map — paehn-tee

TRANSPORT

time table — dah rahng bpehl

ticket — somboht

Can you buy a
ticket for me? — Sohm lohk,
atting somboht
owee knyom
baan teh?

Where can I
leave my luggage? — Dta kon lai na
bao knyom at
took vallee robah
knyom?

plane/helicopter — joo-uhn haw/
helikopter

bus/minibus — lawn kroang

bus station — chamnot lawn
kroang

Where is the
bus station? — Chamnot
lawn kroang niw
kon lei na?

What time
is the first bus? — Lawn kroang
tee muey chain
maowng bpon
mahn?

When does
the bus arrive? — Dta lawn
kroang mohk dal
niw maowng
bpon mahn?

railway station — sattani rot pleung

train — rot pleung

taxi/taxi station — tak-si/sattani tak-si

motorcycle-taxi — moto dop

cyclo (trishaw) — cyclo

three-wheeler — lambretta

truck — lahn truck tome

TRANSPORT (continued)

small boat	dtuk
medium-size boat	kanoht
big boat	kobpal
ferry	salang
boat dock	kompong tei

RENTALS

motorcycle	moto
bicycle	kong
Where can I rent a bicycle?	Kon lei na knyom joul kong chee?
How much per hour?	Muey maowng tlei bpon manh?
half a day	kanlah tngei
Where can I rent a motorcycle?	Kon lei na knyom al joul moto?
driver	neak bowk lawn (car) neak bowk moto (moto) neak bowk taksi (taxi) neak bowk cyclo (cyclo)
guide	neak nai noum

PLACES

I want to go to . . .	Knyom jong dtiw tee . . .
airport	jomnot joo-uhn haw
airline office	krohmhun ahkasjo
embassy	stahn-doot
post office	praisinee
bank	tanee-akeea
tourism bureau	kariyalei samrap puok taih suhcha
bookshop	hong luek see-uh-piw
gas station	satani preng
police station	bot polis
market	psah

temple	wat
museum/theatre	sahrah-munti/ rohng kohn

DINING OUT

restaurant/café	poachania tahn/hong cafe
Let's eat!	Dta, onjeunh tiw nyam!
Please bring the menu.	Sohm owee see-uh-piw menu.
not hot (spicy) please	ot heul teh
May I have . . .	Knyom jong . . .
fried rice/steamed rice	mae cha/mae saw
sticky rice	mae donap
French bread	Nom pong
sandwich/ noodle soup	noum sandwit/ guay tiao
chicken/ pork/beef	sik moan/ sik chrouk/sik ko
fish/shrimp	sik trey/sik mongeya
vegetables/fruit	bunlae/plei cheu
hot/cold	kdow/trocheat
salad	salat
I'll have the same thing	knyom jong man doich knia
water/ cold water	teuk/teuk trocheat
bottled water	teuk suh-awt
boiled water	teuk bpu
no ice, thanks	min dak teuk-awh teh, awkun
tea/coffee	teuk tai/kahfay
lemon/sugar	kroj mah/skaw saw
young coconut	dong kchei
two beers, please	sohm owee knyom beer pi
the bill, please	sohm owee kut loy

HOTEL

a good hotel	sonta kia lu-awh
(family-run) guesthouse	pteah pneu
air-conditioned	machine trocheat

fan	kong ha
telephone	tourosap
room with bath	bantuop mien bon dtoop teuk
single room (one bed)	bantuop mien tei krey muey
double room (two beds)	bantuop mien tei krey pee
triple room	bantuop tom mein krey buey
toilet/paper	bong kuen barah/bong kuen setrei
men's toilet/ women's toilet	mun koun bproh/mun koun setrey
shower/hot shower	nguet teuk/nguet teuk kadow
sheets/towel	kome raht took/ kone saeng choot kluen
thermos of hot water	boam toam teuk kadow
blanket	pouy
mosquito net	mung
can I see the room?	jong dtiw meul bantuop sen, bahn teh?

BARGAINING

How much is this?	Nee talei bpon manh?
Do you have . . .?	Sohm lohk, mien . . .?
big/small	tom/toic
old/new	ja/tmei
expensive	tlei
Do you have anything cheaper?	Sohm lohk, mien evei towk cheang nee?
Can you give me a better price?	Sohm lohk, choe talei bantec?
discount	bahn-choe domlay
I will come back.	Knyom bon troe op mohk vanh.

TIME AND NUMBERS

today	tngay nee
now	aylao nee
tonight	yoop nee
yesterday/tomorrow	msel minh/suh-eik
morning/ afternoon/evening	preuk/ reuseal/langeat
year/month/ day/hour	chnam/kei/ tngei/mowng
Monday	Tngay chan
Tuesday	Tngay awng keah
Wednesday	Tngay bput
Thursday	Tngay prohoea
Friday	Tngay sok
Saturday	Tngay saow
Sunday	Tngay atut
zero	sohn
one	muoy
two	pi
three	buey
four	buon
five	pram
six	pram muoy
seven	pram pi
eight	pram buey
nine	pram buon
ten	dop
eleven	dop muoy
twelve	dop pi
thirteen	dop buey
fourteen	dop buon
fifteen	dop pram
twenty	mapuey
thirty	sam sup
forty	sae sup
fifty	ha sup
sixty	hok sup
seventy	jet sup
eighty	bpad sup
ninety	kaow sup

one hundred	muoy roy	river	tonle (stung)
five hundred	pram roy	beach	chne samot
one thousand	muoy poan	bay	choe samot
two thousand	pi poan	island	koh
five thousand	pram poan	lake	boeng
ten thousand	muoy meun	waterfall	teuk tliak
twenty thousand	pi meun	cave	rung phnom
fifty thousand	pram meun	highway	ploechit
one hundred thousand	muoy saen	bridge	spean
one million	muoy lee-uhn	city	krong
		river town	kompong
GEOGRAPHICAL TERMS		boulevard	moha vithei
district	songkhat	street	pleu
forest	prey cheu	market	psah
jungle	prey	gardens/park	soun chbah
mountain/hill	phnom	temple	wat

LAO LANGUAGE
by Alison Norman

The Lao spoken and written in Vientiane sets the standard for language in Laos. The Vientiane version of Lao is one of the many dialects of the Thai language family, which also encompasses Thailand and Laos, extends to northern Vietnam, northern Burma, southern China, and even parts of Bangladesh. Within Laos there are different dialects as you move from north to south, and even 60 kilometers from Vientiane, at Phon Hong, the tones of standard Lao begin to change.

Any effort the foreign traveler makes to learn and use standard Lao will be greeted with delight by the locals. If you have spent any time in Thailand prior to visiting Laos, you can use any Thai that you have acquired, as most Laotians understand Thai. Laotians are bombarded by Thai media—radio, TV, newspapers, magazines, textbooks. Therefore, they have picked up both spoken and written Thai. The reverse, however, does not apply—very few Thais can understand Lao. With the exception of Issan people in the northeast, Thais usually cannot understand spoken Lao, and only a few elderly Issan folk can read Lao script.

Tones: Lao is a tonal language with six distinct tones, which are placed on syllables. Hence a monosyllabic word only carries one tone, but a polysyllabic word may have several. Tones affect meaning, and therefore cannot be left out of speech. Tones are somewhat easier to produce than to hear. To help convey your meaning, you can mimic the tone patterns by tilting your head up or down to match the particular tone by nodding, or by moving your chin from side to side as you speak. You may look a bit odd but if the words you produce are understood, it's worth it! In Lao dictionaries, the six tones in Lao are: (with "o" as an example only) low tone, no marker; ō midtone, normal voice pitch; ò high falling; ŏ low rising; ó high pitch; and ô low falling. An example of the variation in tones follows: the Lao word for "almost rotten" is mòo; the word for "pig" is mŏo; while the word for "friend" is mo-o. Just think what you could accidentally say: "You're a real pig!"

Lao has 20 consonant sounds and 28 vowel/diphthong sounds. Most of the consonants are similar to English with the exception of the initial "ng," and the hard "p," "t," and "g," which are not aspirated. The vowels are more difficult, as quite a few are not found in English. The best way to learn them is to listen to a Lao speaker on tape or in person.

Negatives and Questions: While pronunciation is complex, Lao grammar is simple. To make a negative, just put the word "bor" in front of an adjective or verb—for example, "bor dii" (not good); "bor mak" (don't like). To make a question, put the word "bor" at the end—for example, "dii bor" (is it good?); "mak bor" (do you like it?). Be careful to keep the tone on "bor" low in a question; don't make it a rising intonation as in English. Verb tenses are easy to deal with in Lao. To render a past tense, you simply add "layo" after the verb—for example "gin layo" (ate, or have eaten), "maa layo" (came, or has come). To form a future tense, you just put "si" in front of the verb—for example, "si gin" (will eat). It doesn't matter who the subject of the verb is—I, you, she, he, they—the subject has no effect on the verb at all, and is not usually stated if it is obvious to whom the speaker is referring.

Script: Lao script is modeled on early Thai script, written from left to right with no spacing between words. Reading and writing this script presents a real challenge. Unless you are planning a long stay in Laos, or have an intense academic interest, it is unlikely you will want to tackle the written word. However, if you have already mastered Thai script, you will find Lao easy to read and much easier to spell than Thai. Lao script has 32 consonant symbols, 28 vowel/diphthong symbols, three classes of consonants, and tone markers. The Lao disagree on the spelling of many words, especially those derived from Sanskrit.

The traveler will not fare much better with transliteration of Lao into the Roman alphabet. Transliteration of Lao is extremely confusing because standardization does not exist, and while the French provided spelling for Lao words, the British transliterated Thai. Hence the Thai name "Sunthorn" is spelled "Sounthone" in Laos, even though the pronunciation and derivation is identical. The French often use "x" for an "s" sound (as in the province of Xieng Khuang), and rarely have a "w" sound; the French wrote "v" in transliteration even though this sound does not exist in Lao. Vientiane is actually pronounced "Wiang Jun."

Phrasebooks: Not much has been produced to help learners of Lao. Your best bet is to scour bookstores in Bangkok. Check places like **Asia Books.** The Lao, Cambodian, and Vietnamese material is usually grouped together and is easy to find. In Vientiane you can try **Raintree Books,** the sole bookstore that caters to foreigners. The bookstore stocks Russell Marcus's *English-Lao dictionary; Lao for Beginners,* by Russell Marcus and Tatsuo Hoshino, as well as Klaus Werner's *Learning Lao.* Using your own cassette player to record Lao sounds would be extremely useful.

LAO PHRASES

TONES

The following tones appear on the phrases below. The letter "o" is used as an example.

low tone	(o) no marker
midtone	(ō) normal voice pitch
high falling	(ò)
low rising	(ǒ)
high pitch	(ó)
low falling	(ô)

OPENERS

hello	sábai dee
goodbye	laá gǒn der
Pleased to meet you.	Nyiňdee teá hòo júk jaò.
How are you?	Sábai dee bǒr?
Very well, thank you	Sábai dee, kop jai.
Where are you going?	Jaò jà pai sǎi?
What's your name?	Jào sēr nyǎng?
My name is . . .	Kôy sēr . . .
I only speak a little Lao.	Kôy wòw láo dài nòy nŷng.
I don't understand.	Kôy bǒr kao jai.
Do you understand?	Jaò kâo jai bǒr?

GETTING PERSONAL

Where are you from?	Jào maa tēh sǎi?

Canadian/ Australian/British	kanada/ australie/angkìt
American/ French/Russian	amerika/ farangsêt/sowiet
Vietnamese/Lao/Thai	vietnam/laó/tai
Cambodian/Chinese	káměn/jeen
My job is . . .	Kôy hed wiǎk . . .
How old are you?	Jaò anŷu taōdai?
married/single	tǎng ngárn/sôat
husband/wife	pǔa/mǐa
mother/father	měh/pōr
children/son/daughter	lùke/lùke sái/ lùke sǎo
older brother/ older sister	ài/èay
younger brother/ younger sister	nong sái/ nong sǎo

FLATTERY

good/very good	dee/dee lǎi
The food is great!	Ahǎrn sàp lǎi!
terrific food	sàp ēe lěe
Cheers! To your health!	Nyōke nyōke! Peǎy soukhaphap!
I love this town!	Kôy hǔk meuǎng nèe!
very beautiful	ngarm laǎy
very interesting	son jaī laǎy
I had a great time.	Mūan lǎi.
Good luck!	Sowk dee!

NEGATIVES, QUESTIONS, REQUESTS

yes/no	měn/bŏr-měn
okay/no problem!	tóke lóng/ bŏr meě punhăa!
not okay/no good	bŏr toké long/ bŏr dee
please/thank you	kalouna/kop jai
enough, thank you	pór làyo, kop jai
I want/need	koŷ yârk dai/ tong garn
don't want/don't like	bŏr yârk dai/ bŏr mŭk
sorry/excuse me	kŏr toàt/kŏr ápái
don't know	bŏr hoò
Can I take a photo?	Kôy kŏr tāi hòop dài bŏr?
What's this called?	An neè ern wăa nyăng?
What does that mean?	An neè măi kwárm wăa nyăngdai?
Can you write it down for me?	Jaò kiăn bòk hâi kôy dài bŏr?
where? where is?	yoŭ săi? theè neè yoŭ săi?
when? who? why? how?	meŭadai? měn păi? pen yăng? yă ngdai?
how much/how many?	taŏdai/laăy tăodai?
how long? (time)	doan parndai?
how far?(distance)	kài parndai?

RED TAPE

passport	but părn dan
tourist/businessperson	nuk tong tiăo/ pŏr káa
visa/Thai visa	wisa/ wisa meŭang tai
I want to extend my visa.	Kôy tongkarn kŏr tŏr wisa.
travel permit	but ánŏonỳart tong tiăo
I need a translator.	Kôy tonggarn kon pleh pasăa.

What is the problem?	Meě punhaă yang?

MEDICAL

sick	bŏr sábai
diarrhea/ headache/fever	pănyàrt lóng tong/jép hŭa/kai
cold/sore throat	pen wát/jép kór
Please help.	Suăy něh.
need a doctor/dentist	tonggarn haă mŏr/mŏr kâyo
emergency	gá tún hŭn
hospital/clinic	hóng păn ỳabarn/ hóng mŏr
drugstore	bŏn kăi yaa

ASKING/GIVING DIRECTIONS

I want to go to . . .	Kôy tonggarn pai . . .
I want to see . . .	Kôy yârk bŷng . . .
How many kilometers to . . .?	Júk gilómět pai . . .?
How long will it take to get to . . .?	pai thŷng . . . sài wéláa tăodai?
turn right/turn left	loŭay kwăa/ loŭay sàai
straight ahead	pai sěr sěr
fast/slow	wái/sàa
slow down/take it easy	saà lóng/jai yen yen
Stop here!	Yóot těe nèe!
Wait here.	Tâa yŏu nèe.
Let's go!	Pai gun tŏr!
north/south	tarng něua/tarng tài
east/west	tawún ôk/tawán tóke
Where can I get a map?	Kôy já aw phan tee yŏu săi?

TRANSPORT

time table	táláng wéláa
Please write down the time table.	Garuna kiăn táláng wéláa sai but.
ticket	but
Can you buy a ticket for me?	Garuna sèr but hâi kôy dài bŏr?

TRANSPORT (continued)

Where can I leave my luggage?	Kôy já páa hêep wài săi?
plane/helicopter	hǎ̆ya bin/helikopter
bus/minibus	rôte may pájum tarng/rôte may sŏng tǎyo
bus station	sátaĭnee rôte may
Where is the bus station?	Sátaĭnee rôte may yôu săi?
How many buses a day are there?	Rôte may mǎee júk tiǎo tôr mèr?
What time is the first bus?	Wélǎa júk móng rô te may tiǎo tée nǎng?
What time is the last bus?	Wélǎa júk móng rô te may tiǎo soótài?
When does the next bus leave?	Rôte may tiǎo tôr pai já ôk júk móng?
When does the bus arrive?	Wélǎa tôrdai rôte may já maa hot?
taxi/taxi station	taxi/sátǎrnee taxi
motorcycle sidecar-taxi	saǎm lòr rôte júk
cyclo (trishaw)	saǎm lòr
truck/4WD vehicle	rôte bantŭk/ rôte gabah
boat/boat dock	hǎ̆ya/tǎr hǎ̆ya
ferry/ferry dock	hǎ̆ya bák/tǎr hǎ̆ya bák

RENTALS

motorcycle	rôte júk
bicycle	rôte teĕp
Where can I rent a bicycle?	Kôy já sǎo rôte teĕp yôu săi?
How much per hour?	Sūamóng nyǎng lákáa tǎodai?
How much for one day? Half a day?	Mèr nyǎng tǎodai? Kyǎng mèr tǎodai?
Where can I rent a motorcycle?	Kôy já sǎo rôtejúk yôu săi?
driver/guide	kón kup rôte/ pôu nĕ núm

Where can I hire a car and driver?	Kôy já sǎo rôte léh cháng kón kuprôt yôu săi?
Where can I rent a minibus?	Kôy já sǎo rôte sŏng tǎyo yôu săi?
Where can I rent a boat?	Kôy já sǎo hǎ̆ya jarng yôu săi?

PLACES

airport	sanaǎm bin
airline office	hónggarn kǎi peè yón
embassy	sátǎrn toòt
post office	hónggarn pai sáneĕ
bank (foreign exchange)	tǎ ná kárn
tourism bureau	gom tŏng tiǎo
bookshop	harn kǎi pěrm
gas station	bôn kǎi naàm mán
police station	hông garn tumruat
market	tálârt
temple	wǎt
church	bôat
museum	hǒr pěe pit tá pun
movie theater	hông sinay

DINING OUT

restaurant/café	harn ahǎrn/gafe
Let's eat!	Serñ gin!
Please bring the menu	Garuna ao láigarn ahǎrn hâi nĕh.
not hot (spicy) please	garuna yǎa hêt pét laǎy
May I have . . .	Kŏr . . . dài bôr
fried rice/steamed rice	kûa kâo/kâo là là
sticky rice	kâo niǎo
French bread/sandwich	kâo jĕe/kâo jĕe patay
Chinese noodle soup/ Vietnamese soup	phǒ chin/ phǒ viet
chicken/pork/beef	gǎi/mǒo/sèen
fish/shrimp	paa/gung
vegetables/fruit	púck/mârk mài

vegetarian food	ahärn púck	expensive	páng
hot/cold	hòn/yen	Do you have anything cheaper?	Mêe naýo tŷk gwaa nèe bõr?
water/cold water	naàm/naàm yen	Can you give me a better price?	Lot lákáa dài bõr?
mineral water/ boiled water	naàm gan/ naàm tom		
no ice, thanks	bõr ao naàm gòn	I will come back.	Kôy já maa eêk.
hot tea/coffee	sa hòn/gafé		
lemon/sugar	mârknao/numtarn	**TIME AND NUMBERS**	
beer	bia	today/now	mèr nèe/diao nèe
fruit juice	naàm mârk mài	tonight	mèr láng
the bill, please	kõr bai gép ngern	yesterday/tomorrow	mèr wárn nèe/ mèr ĕrn

HOTEL

		morning/ afternoon/evening	ton sào/ bãi/láng
a good hotel	hónghém sãn dee	year/month/day	pee/deuan/mèr
budget hotel	hónghém tŷk tŷk	Monday	wan jun
air-conditioned	hông ai yen	Tuesday	wan angkárn
room with bath	hông thée mĕe hông naàm	Wednesday	wan põot
		Thursday	wan pãhárt
single room (one bed)	hông poû diao (tiang diao)	Friday	wan sõok
		Saturday	wan saõ
double room (two beds)	hông sõng kón (sõng tiang)	Sunday	wa aatit
		one	nyŋg
triple room	hông saãm kón	two	sõng
dormitory	hõr pũck	three	saãm
toilet	hông naàm (in rural areas: wēet)	four	sēe
		five	haâ
men's toilet/ women's toilet	hông naàm pôu sái/hông naàm pôu nyïng	six	hóke
		seven	jét
		eight	bât
shower	bõn arp naàm	nine	gao
sheets/towel	pâ pu tiang/ pâ sĕt tua	ten	síp
		twenty	sáo
mosquito net	mung	thirty	saãm síp
May I see the room, please?	Kôy kõr bŷng hông dài bõr?	forty	sēe síp
		fifty	haâ síp
Can you give me a discount?	Jào lot lá káa dài bõr?	sixty	hóke síp
		seventy	jét síp
BARGAINING		eighty	bât síp
		ninety	gao síp
How much is this?	Nèe rákáa tõrdai?	one hundred	hòy
Do you have . . . ?	Mêe . . . bõr?	five hundred	haâ hòy
big/small	nyãi/nòy	one thousand	pún
old/new	gão/mãi	two thousand	sõng pún

TIME AND NUMBERS (continued)

five thousand	haâ pún
ten thousand	síp pún
twenty thousand	sáo pún
fifty thousand	haâ síp pún
one hundred thousand	hòy pún
one million	larn nÿng

MAP FEATURES

district	kâte
forest	paã
jungle	paã dong
mountain	poú
river	hûay-nãm
beach	hârt-sai
island	don
lake	thapay
waterfall	naàm tóke
cave	tûm
valley	hôm poú
highway	tãrng luâng
bridge	kõo-ah
city	meuãng
boulevard	tánõn nyãi
street	tanõn
gardens/park	suãn/suãn sãtárãnã

GLOSSARY

VIETNAM

Annam—former French protectorate of central Vietnam

ao dai—Vietnamese traditional dress, originally worn by both sexes, but now worn by women

ben xe—bus station

bonze—monk

Cao Daism—a mix of Catholic, Buddhist, Confucian, and Taoist beliefs, originating in the Mekong Delta in the 1920s

Cham—people who inhabited the central coast of Vietnam. They rose to prominence in the 10th and 11th centuries AD and were eclipsed by the Viet in the late 15th century.

Champa—the former coastal kingdom of the Cham people, with its capital at Vijaya, near present-day Qui Nhon

chua—active temple or pagoda

Cochinchina—former French colony of southern Vietnam

Confucianism—Chinese code of ethics based on the teachings of the philosopher Confucius (from the 5th century BC)

doi moi—"renovation" or new political thinking, a policy announced in 1986

Hoa Hao—breakaway Buddhist faith from the Mekong Delta, emphasizing simplicity of worship and abandonment of ritual

Ho Chi Minh Trail—a network of jungle trails that served as a conduit for supplies and soldiers from North Vietnam through border areas of Laos and Cambodia into South Vietnam during the 1959-75 period

Huey—American helicopter, derived from model names UH-1A, UH-1B, and UH-1D

khach san—hotel

lien xo—Russian, also applied to all foreigners who look like Russians. The term is derogatory since Vietnamese have a poor opinion of Russians.

Maitreya—the Buddha of the Future

Montagnards—minorities of Vietnam, from the French word for mountain people

nha khach—hotel or guesthouse

nuoc mam—fish sauce, flavoring many Vietnamese dishes

overseas Vietnamese—see Viet-Kieu

pagoda—eight-sided tower; also commonly denotes a temple

Quan Am—bodhisattva of compassion, a female deity usually sculpted as a standing all-white figure holding a vase of holy water, sometimes with a willow branch to sprinkle the water

Quan Cong—a deified Chinese general from the Three Kingdoms period (3rd century AD); a guardian depicted in statuary as red-faced with a long beard, sometimes on a red horse

quoc ngu—Romanized Vietnamese script

R&R—Rest and Recreation, or vacation leave for American soldiers during the Vietnam War days

song—river

Taoism—belief system based on the teachings of Chinese philosopher Lao Tzu from the 6th century BC. Taoism emphasizes the pursuit of harmony.

Tet—Vietnamese Lunar New Year

Thien Hau—goddess of the sea, and patroness of sailors and fisherfolk; a figure seen in some pagodas of Chinese origin

Tonkin—former French protectorate of northern Vietnam

Vietcong—short for Vietnamese communist; at first a derogatory name coined to describe all the South Vietnamese groups opposed to President Diem in the 1960s. Other terms used for the Vietcong were VC and Charlie (short for Victor Charlie). These terms no longer carry a derogatory meaning.

Viet-Kieu—overseas Vietnamese, who are often resented by locals when they return because of their wealth and arrogance

Vietminh—nationalist and communist group led by Ho Chi Minh in the fight against the Japanese and the French in the 1940s and 1950s

CAMBODIA

anastylosis—taking apart the main sanctuary of a crumbling site, numbering the pieces, building a new concrete base, and re-assembling the structure piece by piece

apsara—celestial dancer or angelic nymph. The seductive *apsaras* promise a joyful existence for those who attain the ultimate incarnation.

asura—mythical demon

Avalokitesvara—see Lokesvara

banteay—Khmer citadel

baray—artificial lake or spillway reservoir

bas-relief—sculptural relief in which the projection from the surrounding surface is slight

bodhisattva—an enlightened being who delays achieving nirvana in order to help others attain this ultimate goal on the Buddhist path

Brahma—four-headed Hindu deity of Creation

deva—male god or celestial power

devaraja—divine king. As part of a cult instituted by Jayavarman II, the Khmer king was an emanation of a deity and would be reunited with that deity upon death.

devata—goddess

Ganesh—elephant-headed Hindu deity worshipped as the remover of obstacles

Garuda—mythical figure having the beak and talons of an eagle and the torso of a man; the mount of Vishnu

Hanuman—mischievous white monkey of the Ramayana; chief of the monkey army

Indra—Vedic god of war and thunder

kala—mythical monster sculpted in stone with wide face, bulging eyes, claws, and pointed ears

Khmer Krom—ethnic Cambodians living in the south of Vietnam, mainly in the Mekong Delta region

Khmer Rouge—quasi-Marxist military group that rose to power in Cambodia in 1975 and launched a bloodbath until ousted in 1979. The Khmer Rouge still wage guerrilla warfare in the countryside.

koh—island

kompong—port or river town

krama—checkered Khmer all-purpose scarf

linga—phallic sculpture, symbolic of Shiva

lintel—stone or wood crossbeam resting on two upright posts. On a Khmer temple, it is above a door or window opening, and supports the pediment.

Lokesvara—bodhisattva of compassion

Meru—mythical golden mountain at the center of the Hindu universe

naga—snake or serpent deity, usually a cobra with multiple heads

Mahabharata—Hindu epic narrating the struggle between two warring families for control of northern India

pediment—triangular upper portion above a temple doorway

phnom—mountain or hill; can also refer to temple or sacred site

pilaster—column used on the side of an open doorway

prasat—main tower of a temple

preah—holy, sacred; used as honorific title for important Buddhist images or abbots

Ramayana—Indian cycle of legends, known all over Asia, portraying the trials of lovers Rama and Sita

Ravana—demon king who abducts Sita in the Ramayana legend

Reamker—Cambodian name for the Ramayana

Shiva—Hindu deity, the Destroyer and Reproducer

singha—mythical lion

stela—stone panel inscribed with historical data

stung—river

Tonle Sap—"sweet water"; name of the inland sea in northwest Cambodia, and of the river linking it to the Mekong

varman—suffix denoting "protected by," often incorporated into the title of Khmer kings

Vishnu—Hindu deity, the Preserver

wat—Thai word for temple with monks in residence, also spelled vat

LAOS

asana—hand gesture of the Buddha in statuary

baci—traditional Lao welcoming ceremony

ban—village

boun—Lao festival

Hmong—ethnic group whose people favor mountainous terrain

Jataka Tales—series of mythological life stories of the Buddha

jumbo—three- or four-wheel vehicle that can take six to eight passengers

kuti—monks' residence

lam wong—traditional slow-moving circle dance

mudra—pose of the Buddha in statuary

naga—snake or serpent deity, usually a cobra with multiple heads

Pathet Lao—military arm of the communist party, based in northeast Laos until it came to power in 1975

phi—spirits believed by animists to reside in trees, forests, and mountains

Phra Lak Pralam—Lao version of the Ramayana

Pimai—Lao Lunar New Year, taking place in mid-April

pra—holy, sacred; used as honorific title for important Buddhist images or abbots

Ramayana—Indian cycle of legends, known all over Asia, portraying the trials of lovers Rama and Sita

sangha—the Buddhist brotherhood or community

sim—main temple

sinh—sarong or strip of woven cloth worn by Lao women

songtao—pickup truck converted to carry passengers

talad—market

tham—cave

thanon—street or road

that—(pronounced "tat") bell-shaped monument similar to a stupa, and containing sacred relics or ashes of important person

Trimurti—Hindu trinity, comprised of Brahma, Vishnu, and Shiva

viharn—secondary prayer hall or sermon hall

yaksha—fierce temple guardian; may be good or evil

SUGGESTED READING

Books on Vietnam, Cambodia, and Laos fall into the feast-or-famine category. There are probably more books written about the Vietnam War than any other conflict in modern history, yet when it comes to the extension of the same conflict in Laos, only a handful of books can be found. Even more gaping holes exist in coverage of contemporary Indochina. Among the following books, some are either hard to locate or out of print. These are marked with an asterisk (*). Your best chances of finding these books are in Hong Kong, Bangkok, or Singapore, although you might also find them in a library collection. The Gioi Publishers in Hanoi prints glossy booklets on such subjects as water puppetry, traditional painting, folk sculpture, and traditional medicine—these are available in Vietnam.

INDOCHINA

Evans, Grant, and Kelvin Rowley. *Red Brotherhood at War.* New York: Routledge, Chapman & Hall, 1990. Good coverage of politics and history in Vietnam, Cambodia, and Laos since 1975.

Lewis, Norman. *A Dragon Apparent.* London: Eland Books, 1991. Well-written and lucid account of travels in 1949, right before the fall of the French empire in Indochina. This classic by Englishman Norman Lewis was first published in 1951.

The Mekong
The Mekong courses through Laos, Cambodia, and Vietnam. A broad overview of the people and places on the river is provided by these two large-format coffee-table books.

Hoskin, John, and Allen Hopkins. *The Mekong: A River and Its People.* Bangkok: Post Publishing, 1991. Takes in life along the murky river from its source in China to the South China Sea. A CD-ROM title, *Beyond the Nine Dragons* produced by Black Box, Inc., of Hong Kong, is based on this book. The CD-ROM offers the added dimension of sound and video.

Yamashita, Michael. *Mekong: A Journey on the Mother of Waters.* New York: Takarajima Books, 1995. Grand voyage along the Mekong by a National Geographic photographer.

VIETNAM

History
Taylor, Keith. *The Birth of Vietnam.* Berkeley: University of California Press, 1991. Covers early history.

Wintle, Justin. *The Vietnam Wars—Wars of the Modern Era.* London: Weidenfeld and Nicholson, 1991. Good summary not only of the Vietnam-American War but of all the conflicts in Vietnamese history.

The French in Vietnam
Fall, Bernard. *Street Without Joy.* Pennsylvania: Stackpole Books, 1994. Covers the 1946-54 period. Another tome by French scholar Fall is *Hell Is a Very Small Place* (New York: Da Capo Press, 1985), about the siege of Dien Bien Phu.

The Americans in Vietnam
Fitzgerald, Frances. *Fire in the Lake.* New York: Random House, 1989. First published at the height of the conflict in 1972, this Pulitzer-prize winner presents some interesting Vietnamese perspectives on the war.

Herr, Michael. *Dispatches.* New York: Avon Books, 1978. This work offers a first-hand account of events in Vietnam told by a war correspondent.

Karnow, Stanley. *Vietnam: A History.* New York: Viking Penguin, 1983. Authoritative and detailed history of Vietnam, concentrating on the American War era—well researched and easy to follow. This classic was written to accompany the PBS documentary series *Vietnam: A Television History.*

MacPherson, Myra. *Long Time Passing: Vietnam & the Haunted Generation.* New York: Doubleday, 1993. Includes more than 500 interviews with men and women involved in the war.

Mangold, Tom, and John Penycate. *The Tunnels of Cu Chi.* London: Pan Books, 1986. Intriguing reconstruction of tunnel warfare at Cu Chi by two BBC journalists, based on interviews with Vietnamese and American survivors.

McNamara, Robert. *In Retrospect: The Tragedy and Lessons of Vietnam.* New York: Random House, 1995. The former US Secretary of Defense delivers his confessional—some 25 years after the fact.

Prochnau, William. *Once Upon a Distant War.* New York: Times Books, 1995. Relates the adventures of five war correspondents covering the conflict.

Sheehan, Neil. *A Bright Shining Lie.* New York: Vintage Books, 1989. Vietnam War history woven around a biography of American commander John Paul Vann. Sheehan followed up this fat tome with a slim volume, *After the War Was Over* (New York: Vintage, 1991), about a postwar visit to Hanoi and Saigon.

Vietnamese Writers on the War

Hayslip, Le Ly. *When Heaven and Earth Changed Places.* London and New York: Penguin, 1989. This autobiographical account formed the basis for the Oliver Stone movie, *Between Heaven and Earth.* Hayslip's books have yet to be published in Vietnam due to Culture Ministry objections to the way the North Vietnamese are portrayed.

Huong, Duong Thu. *Novel Without a Name.* New York: William Morrow, 1993. Tells the story of a 28-year-old captain in the NVA during the war. Huong is one of Vietnam's very few outspoken dissidents. Her 1988 novel, *Paradise of the Blind* (New York: Viking Penguin, reprinted 1994), portrays the communist system as exploitative and corrupt.

Ninh, Bao. *The Sorrow of War.* London: Secker and Warburg, 1993, and Pantheon Books in the US. The voice of a Vietnamese soldier who recalls his war experience and postwar trauma. Bao Ninh overturns the official version of soldiers returning from the glorious front lines healthy in body and spirit.

*Tang, Truong Nhu. *A Vietcong Memoir.* New York: Random House, 1986. This memoir covers the 1961-75 period; written by a young revolutionary who became disillusioned after 1975 and left Vietnam.

Modern Vietnam

Kamm, Henry. *Spirit of the Mountains, Spirit of the Waters: Vietnam Today.* New York: Arcade Publishing, 1996. By senior foreign correspondent and bureau chief of the *New York Times,* this book goes behind the scenes to interview Vietnamese military, writers, and dissidents, as well as ordinary people.

Illustrated Accounts

Bakaert, Jacques, and Tim Hall. *Vietnam: A Portrait.* Hong Kong: Elsworth Books, 1993. A pictorial guide to the country.

Népote, Jacques, and Xavier Guillaume. *Illustrated Guide to Vietnam.* Hong Kong: Odyssey Guides, 1992. Strong cultural background material.

West, Helen, ed. *Vietnam.* Singapore: Insight Guides, 1994. This officially sanctioned guide is good for reading before you go, but not something you'd want to pack in a suitcase or backpack.

Smolan, Rick, and Jennifer Erwitt. *Passage to Vietnam.* Against All Odds Productions, 1994. For this book, 70 photojournalists were allowed a seven-day period to photograph Vietnam. They shot over 200,000 photos and 100 hours of video. The best 200 photo frames are featured in this book, which was assembled, start to finish, in 12 weeks in 1994. A separate *Passage to Vietnam CD-ROM* includes the book's text and photos, plus video interviews and six interactive "passages" covering such subjects as river life, street life, history and the war, and a host of "side trips" exploring aspects of Vietnamese culture and commerce.

Culture and Customs

Ellis, Claire. *Culture Shock! Vietnam.* Singapore: Times Editions, 1995. A guide to the customs of Vietnam—from how to eat with gusto to taboos when making business deals. Particularly useful for the business traveler and the resident foreigner.

Travel Narratives

Downie, Sue. *Down Highway One.* Sydney: Allen & Unwin, 1993. From a 1988 road trip by an Australian journalist who spent over a decade reporting from Indochina.

Fenton, James. *All the Wrong Places.* New York: Atlantic Monthly Press, 1988. Covers a handful of destinations in Asia, with a longish section on southern Vietnam. British poet Fenton finds poetry in the sacking of the American embassy as Saigon falls.

Page, Tim. *Derailed in Uncle Ho's Victory Garden.* London: Simon & Schuster, 1995. One of the most celebrated photographers of the Vietnam War returns 20 years later to visit old haunts.

Visser, Carolijn. *Voices & Visions: A Journey Through Vietnam Today.* London: Paladin, 1994. Translated from the Dutch original, this book includes travels from Saigon to Hanoi and encounters with dissident writers and a surviving princess.

Wintle, Justin. *Romancing Vietnam.* London: Penguin, 1991. Goes beyond the Rambo curtain and the Hanoi gloss on this extensive 1989 trip—at times self-centered and trivial, but other times bang on.

Fiction

Butler, Robert Olen. *A Good Scent from a Strange Mountain.* New York: Viking Penguin, 1993. A selection of well-written stories that provide insight into the Vietnamese way of thinking.

Duras, Marguerite. *The Lover.* London: Flamingo, 1986. A lyrical novella set in Saigon and southern Vietnam in the 1930s; it portrays a love affair between a French schoolgirl and a man from a wealthy Chinese family.

Greene, Graham. *The Quiet American.* London: Penguin, 1973. This novella, first published in 1955, relates a love triangle between a British correspondent, his Vietnamese mistress, and a young American obsessed with channeling economic aid. Uncannily prophetic on what was about to pass in Indochina.

Grey, Anthony. *Saigon.* London: Pan Books, 1983. Novel of intrigue set in Saigon.

Koch, Christopher. *Highways to a War.* New York: Viking Penguin, 1995. Set in South Vietnam and Cambodia, this novel relates the story of an Australian combat photographer who travels a long road through the Vietnam War, then strays into Khmer Rouge territory and disappears. The characters are fictional; the background events portrayed are very real.

CAMBODIA

Current print material on Cambodia is hard to track down, with many books now out of print.

History and Politics

Chanda, Nayan. *Brother Enemy.* New York: Collier Books, 1988. Covers Cambodia in the context of Indochina from 1975 to 1985.

Chandler, David. *A History of Cambodia.* Colorado: Westview Press, 1992. Revised second edition of this well-written history.

Chandler, David. *Brother Number One: A Political Biography of Pol Pot.* Colorado: Westview Press, 1992.

Kiernan, Ben. *How Pol Pot Came to Power.* New York: Routledge, Chapman & Hall, 1985. A history of communism in Cambodia from

1930 to 1975 by one of the world's leading Khmer-speaking scholars.

Osborne, Milton. *Sihanouk: Prince of Light, Prince of Darkness.* Sydney: Allen & Unwin, 1994. By an Australian specialist on Cambodia, who, however, made no attempt to interview the king.

Ponchaud, François. *Cambodia: Year Zero.* London: Penguin, 1977. An account of Cambodia under the Khmer Rouge.

Shawcross, William. *Cambodia's New Deal: A Report.* New York: Carnegie Endowment for International Peace, 1994. This 110-page book analyzes the impact of the UN in Cambodia, from 1991 to 1993. It's the most recent offering from a reporter who has closely followed the situation in Cambodia. His earlier books are now out of print. *Sideshow: Kissinger, Nixon and the Destruction of Cambodia* (New York: Simon & Schuster, 1979) covers the events of 1969 to 1978. *Quality of Mercy: Cambodia, Holocaust and Modern Conscience* (New York: Simon & Schuster, 1984) covers the 1978-83 period.

Personal Accounts

Gray, Spalding. *Swimming to Cambodia.* New York: Theatre Communications Group, 1985. Spalding Gray's irreverent account of his role as an extra in the movie *The Killing Fields.* Gray turned his thoughts into a performance theater monologue.

Hall, Kari, and Dith Pran. *Beyond the Killing Fields.* New York: Aperture Foundation, 1992. Documentary photography, with an introduction by Dith Pran, who survived the Khmer Rouge years.

*Ngor, Haing. *Surviving the Killing Fields.* London: Chatto & Windus, 1985. Haing Ngor was the principal actor in the movie *The Killing Fields.* The book relives his own experience as a survivor of the Khmer Rouge pogrom.

*Szymusiak, Molyda. *The Stones Cry Out.* New York: Hill and Wang, 1986. Subtitled: a Cambodian childhood 1975-80. Szymusiak was

a teenager at the time of the Khmer Rouge takeover; she escaped to Thailand and migrated to France.

Angkor

Angkor has an entire genre to itself, with many books, ranging from scholarly works to coffee-table photobooks.

Angkor: The Serenity of Buddhism. London: Thames & Hudson, 1993. Large-format book featuring moody black-and-white photos by French master lensman Marc Riboud, with text by Jean Lacouture and Jean Boisselier.

*Brand, Michael. *The Age of Angkor: Treasures from the National Museum.* Canberra: The Australian National Gallery, 1992. A glossy catalog, in book form, of Khmer artworks that toured Australia in 1992.

*Coedes, George. *Angkor: An Introduction.* London: Oxford University Press, 1986. A lucid account from prominent Angkorologist George Coedes, but no new material has been added since 1961 when the book was first published in French.

Dagens, Bruno. *Angkor: Heart of an Asian Empire.* New York: Harry Abrams, Inc., 1995. Excellent background material on restoration at Angkor by former member of the EFEO, with numerous illustrations.

Freeman, Michael, and Roger Warner. *Angkor: The Hidden Glories.* Boston: Houghton Mifflin, 1990. Coffee-table photobook.

Giteau, Madeleine. *Khmer Sculpture and the Angkor Civilization.* New York: Harry Abrams, Inc., 1965.

McDonald, Malcolm. *Angkor & the Khmer.* Singapore: Oxford University Press, 1987. Reprint of original from 1958.

Rooney, Dawn. *Angkor: Introduction to the Temples.* Hong Kong: The Guidebook Company, 1994. Most up-to-date detailed guide to Angkor available, with good illustrations.

Standen, Mark, and John Hoskin. *Passage Through Angkor.* Bangkok: Indochina News Corp., 1995. Stunning images by English photographer Mark Standen.

*Ta-kuan, Chou (Zhou Daguan). *The Customs of Cambodia.* Bangkok: The Siam Society, 1992. The original manuscript is around 700 years old—the only eyewitness account, albeit a brief one, of the glories of the Angkor court.

LAOS

Current print material on Laos is extemely difficult to come by—the best source is Bangkok, where you might find books on Lao textiles and handicrafts. You're more likely to stray across material on Laos tucked into books on the Indochina region.

The Secret War

*Castle, Timothy. *At War in the Shadow of Vietnam.* New York: Columbia University Press, 1993. Details covert US activity and military aid to the royal Lao government from 1955 to 1975. The book is based on declassified materials as well as on interviews with dozens of American and Laotian participants.

Hamilton-Merritt, Jane. *Tragic Mountains.* Bloomington: University of Indiana Press, 1993. The subtitle is: The Hmong, the Americans, and the Secret Wars for Laos, 1942-92.

Robbins, Christopher. *The Ravens.* New York: Bantam Press, 1988. Ravens was the code name for the US pilots who fought in the secret war on Laos. This book, by a British journalist, was the first to reveal many details hidden from the US public.

Modern Laos

Sesser, Stan. *The Lands of Charm and Cruelty.* New York: Knopf, 1993. The 50-page essay, "Laos—the Forgotten Land," included in this book, is one of five essays on Asia published in the *New Yorker* in the early 1990s.

Stuart-Fox, Martin. *Laos: Politics, Economics & Society.* New York: Pinter Publishers, 1983. Some detail on post-1979 reform.

ON-LINE ACCESS

Staying up-to-date on new information is essential for Indochina. The last word can be obtained from the following web sites and newsgroups.

For health concerns, the **Centers for Disease Control and Prevention** in Atlanta, Georgia, maintains a web site *(http://www.cdc.gov/cdc.html)* with the latest information on prevention guidelines and strategies. At the **Moon Publications web site** *(http://www.moon.com),* you can access the text for *Staying Healthy in Asia, Africa, and Latin America.*

For general travel tips, brainstorming, and entertaining travel angles, try **GNN Travelers' Center** *(http://nearnet.gnn.com/meta/travel/index.html).* Some down-to-earth travel advice is dispensed at an Australian site called **NSITT** *(http://www.magna.com.au/~travdude/).*

For current travel advisories, contact the **US State Department** *(http://www.stolaf.edu/network/travel-advisories.html)* or the **British Foreign Office Warnings** *(http://www.fco.gov.uk/).* For current statistics on Vietnam, Cambodia, and Laos, consult the **CIA World Factbook** *(http://www.odci.gov/cia/publications/95fact/index.html).*

Two online magazines from Hong Kong offer snippets of current news and features, plus back-issue archives. At the *Asia Inc Magazine* site *(http://www.asia-inc.com),* you can use the search function to bring up news items related to Vietnam, Cambodia, or Laos. You can search easily from a newsmap on the *Asiaweek Magazine* site *(http://pathfinder.com/Asiaweek).*

Vietnam Links *(http://www.public.iastate.edu/~sogiti/links.html)* is an excellent round-up web reference for sites related to Vietnam. **Journey to Vietnam** *(http://maingate.net:80/vn/)* is a travel and commercial information site with some news briefings. **Vietgate** *(http://www.saigon.com)* provides a variety of Vietnamese community links in the US, Australia, and Canada. **Global Directions Incorporated** *(http://www.well.com/ user/ gdist/)* divulges snippets from *Destination Vietnam,* a travel magazine. The **Cambodian Information Center** *(http://www.cambodia.org/)* offers many links for Cambodia, including news archives, photos, and other resources. **Lao Links in the Net** *(http://minyos.xx.rmit.edu.au/~s914382/*

hmong/lao.htm) is a site operated by Hmongs living in Australia.

For discussion and posting of questions, try these newsgroups:

news:alt.politics.vietnamese
news:soc.culture.vietnamese
news:soc.culture.cambodia
news:soc.culture.laos

INDEX

Page numbers in **boldface** indicate the primary reference to a given topic. *Italicized* page numbers refer to information in charts, illustrations, maps, photos, or special topics.

ABOUT THE AUTHOR

Born in England and raised in Australia, Michael Buckley now calls Canada home. A self-taught writer and photographer, he spends part of each year on the road. He has traveled extensively throughout Asia and trekked and mountain-biked in the Himalayan and Karakoram ranges.

In addition to *Vietnam, Cambodia & Laos Handbook,* Buckley is author of *Bangkok Handbook,* co-author of a guidebook to China and a guidebook to Tibet, and author of *Cycling to Xian,* a travelogue about bicycling across China and Tibet. He has contributed stories to *Travelers' Tales Thailand* and *Travelers' Tales India.*

Buckley gains his knowledge from direct experience—he puts his big feet in

everywhere. To cover the ground for *Vietnam, Cambodia & Laos Handbook,* he visited Indochina three times, logging thousands of kilometers by train, bus, jeep, boat, moto, bicycle, and on foot. The hardest part of researching the book was the cartography. Buckley had to assemble some maps from scratch, reconnoitering from the back of a moto or from the saddle of a bicycle. The greatest thrill was exploring the remote regions of Indochina and meeting the people, who are disarmingly friendly after what they've been through.

Buckley believes that travel is transformation. "Travel cuts across barriers of time and space. It gives you a special sense of being wide awake—everything is new and different and magical, and there's so much to be discovered, so much to learn. Real travel means encountering people whose way of life is very different from your own and learning from them. And there is much to learn in Indochina—it's been closed for so long that a whole different world awaits discovery."

MOON TRAVEL HANDBOOKS
THE IDEAL TRAVELING COMPANIONS

Moon Travel Handbooks provide focused, comprehensive coverage of distinct destinations all over the world. Our goal is to give travelers all the background and practical information they'll need for an extraordinary travel experience.

Every Handbook begins with an in-depth essay about the land, the people, their history, art, politics, and social concerns—an entire bookcase of cultural insight and introductory information in one portable volume. We also provide accurate, up-to-date coverage of all the practicalities: language, currency, transportation, accommodations, food, and entertainment. And Moon's maps are legendary, covering not only cities and highways, but parks and trails that are often difficult to find in other sources.

Below are highlights of Moon's Asia and Pacific Travel Handbook series. Our complete list of Handbooks covering North America and Hawaii, Mexico, Central America and the Caribbean, and Asia and the Pacific, are listed on the order form on the accompanying pages. To purchase Moon Travel Handbooks, please check your local bookstore or order by phone: (800) 345-5473 Monday-Friday 8 a.m.-5 p.m. PST.

MOON OVER ASIA
THE ASIA AND THE PACIFIC TRAVEL HANDBOOK SERIES

"Moon guides are wittily written and warmly personal; what's more, they present a vivid, often raw vision of Asia without promotional overtones. They also touch on such topics as official corruption and racism, none of which rate a mention in the bone-dry, air-brushed, dry-cleaned version of Asia written up in the big U.S. guidebooks."
—*Far Eastern Economic Review*

BALI HANDBOOK
by Bill Dalton, 428 pages, **$12.95**
"This book is for the in-depth traveler, interested in history and art, willing to experiment with language and food and become immersed in the culture of Bali."

—*Great Expeditions*

BANGKOK HANDBOOK
by Michael Buckley, 221 pages, **$13.95**
"Helps make sense of this beguiling paradox of a city . . . very entertaining reading."

—*The Vancouver Sun*

FIJI ISLANDS HANDBOOK
by David Stanley, 275 pages, **$13.95**
"If you want to encounter Fiji and not just ride through it, this book is for you."

—Great Expeditions

HONG KONG HANDBOOK
by Kerry Moran, 347 pages, **$15.95**
"One of the most honest glimpses into Hong Kong the Peoples Republic of China would like never to have seen."

—TravelNews Asia

INDONESIA HANDBOOK
by Bill Dalton, 1,351 pages, **$25.00**
"Looking for a fax machine in Palembang, a steak dinner on Ambon or the best place to photograph Bugis prahus in Sulawesi? Then buy this brick of a book, which contains a full kilogram of detailed directions and advice."

—Asia, Inc. Magazine

"The classic guidebook to the archipelago."

—Condé Nast Traveler

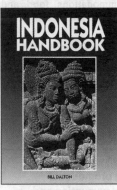

JAPAN HANDBOOK
by J.D. Bisignani, 952 pages, **$22.50**
Winner: Lowell Thomas Gold Award, Society of American Travel Writers
"The scope of this guide book is staggering, ranging from an introduction to Japanese history and culture through to the best spots for shopping for pottery in Mashie or silk pongee in Kagoshima."

—Golden Wing

"More travel information on Japan than any other guidebook."

—The Japan Times

MICRONESIA HANDBOOK
by David Stanley, 342 pages, **$11.95**
"Remarkably informative, fair-minded, sensible, and readable . . . Stanley's comments on the United States' 40-year administration are especially pungent and thought-provoking."

—The Journal of the Polynesian Society

NEPAL HANDBOOK
by Kerry Moran, 466 pages, **$18.95**
Winner: Lowell Thomas Gold Award, Society of American Travel Writers
"This is an excellent guidebook, exploring every aspect of the country the visitor is likely to want to know about with both wit and authority."

—South China Morning Post

NEW ZEALAND HANDBOOK
by Jane King, 544 pages, **$19.95**
"Far and away the best guide to New Zealand."

—*The Atlantic*

OUTBACK AUSTRALIA HANDBOOK
by Marael Johnson, 432 pages, **$18.95**
Winner: Lowell Thomas Silver Award, Society of American
Travel Writers
"Well designed, easy to read, and funny"

—*Buzzworm*

PAKISTAN HANDBOOK
by Isobel Shaw, 660 pages, **$22.50**
Pakistan Handbook guides travelers from the heights of the
Karakorams to the bazaars of Karachi, from sacred mosques in
Sind to the ceasefire line of Azad Kashmir. Includes a detailed
trekking guide with several itineraries for long and short treks
across the Hindu Kush, Karakorams, and Himalayas.

PHILIPPINES HANDBOOK
by Peter Harper and Laurie Fullerton, 638 pages, **$17.95**
"The most comprehensive travel guide done on the Philippines.
Excellent work."

—*Pacific Stars & Stripes*

SOUTHEAST ASIA HANDBOOK
by Carl Parkes, 1,103 pages, **$21.95**
Winner: Lowell Thomas Bronze Award, Society of American
Travel Writers
"Plenty of information on sights and entertainment, also provides
a political, environment and cultural context that will allow visitors
to begin to interpret what they see."

—*London Sunday Times*

SOUTH KOREA HANDBOOK
by Robert Nilsen, 590 pages, **$14.95**
"One of a small number of guidebooks that inform without being
pedantic, and are enthusiastic yet maintain a critical edge . . . the
maps are without parallel."

—*Far Eastern Economic Review*

SOUTH PACIFIC HANDBOOK
by David Stanley, 832 pages, **$22.95**
"Moon's tribute to the South Pacific, by David Stanley, is next to
none."

—*Ubique*

TAHITI-POLYNESIA HANDBOOK
by David Stanley, 243 pages, **$13.95**

"If you can't find it in this book, it is something you don't need to know."

—*Rapa Nui Journal*

THAILAND HANDBOOK
by Carl Parkes, 800 pages, **$19.95**

"Carl Parkes is the savviest of all tourists to Southeast Asia."

—Arthur Frommer

TIBET HANDBOOK
by Victor Chan, 1,103 pages, **$30.00**

"Not since the original three volume Murray's Handbook to India, published over a century ago, has such a memorial to the hot, and perhaps uncontrollable passions of travel been published. . . . This is the most impressive travel handbook published in the 20th century."

—*Small Press Magazine*

"Shimmers with a fine madness."

—*Escape Magazine*

VIETNAM, CAMBODIA & LAOS HANDBOOK
by Michael Buckley, 650 pages, **$18.95**

The new definitive guide to Indochina from a travel writer who knows Asia like the back of his hand. Michael Buckley combines the most current practical travel information—much of it previously unavailable—with the perspective of a seasoned adventure traveler. Includes 75 maps.

STAYING HEALTHY IN ASIA, AFRICA, AND LATIN AMERICA
by Dirk G. Schroeder, ScD, MPH, 197 pages, **$11.95**

"Read this book if you want to stay healthy on any journeys or stays in Asia, Africa, and Latin America."

—*American Journal of Health Promotion*

MOONBELT

A new concept in money-belts. Made of heavy-duty Cordura nylon, the Moon-belt offers maximum protection for your money and important papers. This pouch, designed for all-weather comfort, slips under your shirt or waistband, rendering it virtually unde-tectable and inaccessible to pickpockets. It features a one-inch high-test quick-release buckle so there's no more fumbling around for the strap or repeated adjustments. This handy plastic buckle opens and closes with a touch, but won't come undone until you want it to. Moonbelts accommodate trav-eler's checks, passports, cash, photos, etc. Size 5 x 9 inches. Available in black only. **$8.95**

PERIPLUS TRAVEL MAPS

Periplus Travel Maps are a necessity for traveling in Southeast Asia. Each map is designed for maximum clarity and utility, combining several views and insets of the area. Transportation information, street indexes, and descriptions of major sites are included in each map. The result is a single map with all the vital information needed to get where you're going. No other maps come close to providing the detail or comprehensive coverage of Asian travel destinations. All maps are updated yearly and produced with digital technology using the latest survey information. **$7.95**

Periplus Travel Maps are available
to the following areas:

Bali
Bandung/W. Java
Bangkok/C. Thailand
Batam/Bintan
Cambodia
Chiangmai/N. Thailand
Hong Kong
Indonesia
Jakarta
Java
Kuala Lumpur

Ko Samui/S. Thailand
Lombok
Penang
Phuket/S. Thailand
Sabah
Sarawak
Singapore
Vietnam
Yogyakarta/C. Java

MOON TRAVEL HANDBOOKS

NORTH AMERICA AND HAWAII

Alaska-Yukon Handbook (0161)	$14.95
Alberta and the Northwest Territories Handbook (0676)	$17.95
Arizona Traveler's Handbook (0536)	$16.95
Atlantic Canada Handbook (0072)	$17.95
Big Island of Hawaii Handbook (0064)	$13.95
British Columbia Handbook (0145)	$15.95
Colorado Handbook (0447)	$18.95
Georgia Handbook (0390)	$17.95
Hawaii Handbook (0005)	$19.95
Honolulu-Waikiki Handbook (0587)	$14.95
Idaho Handbook (0617)	$14.95
Kauai Handbook (0013)	$13.95
Maui Handbook (0579)	$14.95
Montana Handbook (0498)	$17.95
Nevada Handbook (0641)	$16.95
New Mexico Handbook (0153)	$14.95
Northern California Handbook (3840)	$19.95
Oregon Handbook (0102)	$16.95
Road Trip USA (0366)	$22.50
Texas Handbook (0633)	$17.95
Utah Handbook (0684)	$16.95
Washington Handbook (0455)	$18.95
Wyoming Handbook (3980)	$14.95

ASIA AND THE PACIFIC

Bali Handbook (3379)	$12.95
Bangkok Handbook (0595)	$13.95
Fiji Islands Handbook (0382)	$13.95
Hong Kong Handbook (0560)	$15.95
Indonesia Handbook (0625)	$25.00
Japan Handbook (3700)	$22.50
Micronesia Handbook (3808)	$11.95
Nepal Handbook (0412)	$18.95
New Zealand Handbook (0331)	$19.95
Outback Australia Handbook (0471)	$18.95
Pakistan Handbook (0692)	$22.50
Philippines Handbook (0048)	$17.95

Southeast Asia Handbook (0021) $21.95
South Korea Handbook (3204). $14.95
South Pacific Handbook (0404) $22.95
Tahiti-Polynesia Handbook (0374) $13.95
Thailand Handbook (0420) $19.95
Tibet Handbook (3905) $30.00
Vietnam, Cambodia & Laos Handbook (0293) $18.95

MEXICO

Baja Handbook (0528). $15.95
Cabo Handbook (0285) $14.95
Cancún Handbook (0501). $13.95
Central Mexico Handbook (0234) $15.95
Mexico Handbook (0315) $21.95
Northern Mexico Handbook (0226) $16.95
Pacific Mexico Handbook (0323) $16.95
Puerto Vallarta Handbook (0250) $14.95
Yucatán Peninsula Handbook (0242). $15.95

CENTRAL AMERICA AND THE CARIBBEAN

Belize Handbook (0307). $15.95
Caribbean Handbook (0277) $16.95
Costa Rica Handbook (0358). $19.95
Jamaica Handbook (0129) $14.95

INTERNATIONAL

Egypt Handbook (3891). $18.95
Moon Handbook (0668) $10.00
Moscow-St. Petersburg Handbook (3913) $13.95
Staying Healthy in Asia, Africa, and Latin America (0269) . . $11.95

PERIPLUS TRAVEL MAPS
All maps $7.95 each

Bali	Indonesia	Phuket/S. Thailand
Bandung/W. Java	Jakarta	Sabah
Bangkok/C. Thailand	Java	Sarawak
Batam/Bintan	Kuala Lumpur	Singapore
Cambodia	Ko Samui/S. Thailand	Vietnam
Chiangmai/N. Thailand	Lombok	Yogyakarta/C. Java
Hong Kong	Penang	

WHERE TO BUY MOON TRAVEL HANDBOOKS

BOOKSTORES AND LIBRARIES: Moon Travel Handbooks are sold worldwide. Please contact our sales manager for a list of wholesalers and distributors in your area.

TRAVELERS: We would like to have Moon Travel Handbooks available throughout the world. Please ask your bookstore to write or call us for ordering information. If your bookstore will not order our guides for you, please contact us for a free title listing.

> Moon Publications, Inc.
> P.O. Box 3040
> Chico, CA 95927-3040 U.S.A.
> tel.: (800) 345-5473
> fax: (916) 345-6751
> e-mail: travel@moon.com
> website: http://www.moon.com

IMPORTANT ORDERING INFORMATION

PRICES: All prices are subject to change. We always ship the most current edition. We will let you know if there is a price increase on the book you order.

SHIPPING AND HANDLING OPTIONS: Domestic UPS or USPS first class (allow 10 working days for delivery): $3.50 for the first item, 50 cents for each additional item.

EXCEPTIONS: *Tibet Handbook* and *Indonesia Handbook* shipping $4.50; $1.00 for each additional *Tibet Handbook* or *Indonesia Handbook.*

Moonbelt shipping is $1.50 for one, 50 cents for each additional belt.

Add $2.00 for same-day handling.

UPS 2nd Day Air or Printed Airmail requires a special quote.

International Surface Bookrate 8-12 weeks delivery: $3.00 for the first item, $1.00 for each additional item. Note: Moon Publications cannot guarantee international surface bookrate shipping. Moon recommends sending international orders via air mail, which requires a special quote.

FOREIGN ORDERS: Orders that originate outside the U.S.A. must be paid for with either an international money order or a check in U.S. currency drawn on a major U.S. bank based in the U.S.A.

TELEPHONE ORDERS: We accept Visa or MasterCard payments. Minimum order is US$15.00. Call in your order: (800) 345-5473, 8 a.m.-5 p.m. Pacific standard time.

ORDER FORM

Prices are subject to change without notice. Be sure to call (800) 345-5473 for current prices and editions or for the name of the bookstore nearest you that carries Moon Travel Handbooks • 8 a.m.–5 p.m. PST. (See important ordering information on preceding page.)

Name: _____ Date: _____

Street: _____

City: _____ Daytime Phone: _____

State or Country: _____ Zip Code: _____

QUANTITY	TITLE	PRICE

Taxable Total_____

Sales Tax (7.25%) for California Residents_____

Shipping & Handling_____

TOTAL_____

Ship: ☐ UPS (no P.O. Boxes) ☐ 1st class ☐ International surface mail

Ship to: ☐ address above ☐ other _____

_____

Make checks payable to: **MOON PUBLICATIONS, INC.**, P.O. Box 3040, Chico, CA 95927-3040 U.S.A. We accept Visa and MasterCard. **To Order**: Call in your Visa or MasterCard number, or send a written order with your Visa or MasterCard number and expiration date clearly written.

Card Number: ☐ **Visa**   ☐ **MasterCard**

☐☐☐☐ ☐☐☐☐ ☐☐☐☐ ☐☐☐☐

Exact Name on Card: _____

Expiration date: _____

Signature: _____

THE METRIC SYSTEM

1 inch = 2.54 centimeters (cm)
1 foot = .304 meters (m)
1 mile = 1.6093 kilometers (km)
1 km = .6124 miles
1 fathom = 1.8288 m
1 chain = 20.1168 m
1 furlong = 201.168 m
1 acre = .4047 hectares
1 sq km = 100 hectares
1 sq mile = 2.59 square km
1 ounce = 28.35 grams
1 pound = .4536 kilograms
1 short ton = .90718 metric ton
1 short ton = 2000 pounds
1 long ton = 1.016 metric tons
1 long ton = 2240 pounds
1 metric ton = 1000 kilograms
1 quart = .94635 liters
1 US gallon = 3.7854 liters
1 Imperial gallon = 4.5459 liters
1 nautical mile = 1.852 km

To compute celsius temperatures, subtract 32 from Fahrenheit and divide by 1.8. To go the other way, multiply celsius by 1.8 and add 32.

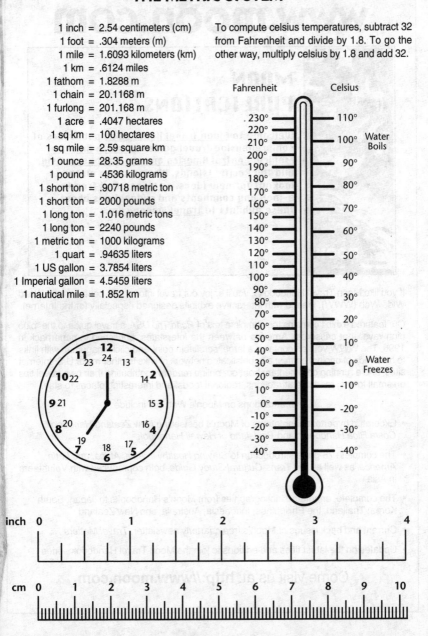

www.moon.com

VIETNAM
CAMBODIA AND LAOS
HANDBOOK